The Almanac of

Edythe Draper, EDITOR
Helen Gorges, RESEARCH EDITOR
Kenneth Petersen, PROJECT EDITOR

Tyndale House Publishers, Inc.
Wheaton, Illinois

The Almanac year runs from July 1, 1989, to June 3, 1990.

Editorial offices for the Almanac are located at 203 East Farnham Lane, Wheaton, IL 60187.

The purpose of *The Almanac of the Christian World* is to provide the Christian public with a yearly resource book that covers all facets of the Christian world. It presents historical and contemporary information, products, and services of interest to evangelical Christians. The purpose of the Almanac is to inform, not to endorse.

ISSN 1052-2670
ISBN 0-8423-0396-0

Printed in the United States of America

96 95 94 93 92 91 90
8 7 6 5 4 3 2 1

Some of us have been given special ability as apostles; to others he has given the gift of being able to preach well; some have special ability in winning people to Christ, helping them to trust him as their Savior; still others have a gift for caring for God's people as a shepherd does his sheep, leading and teaching them in the ways of God.

Why is it that he gives us these special abilities to do certain things best? It is that God's people will be equipped to do better work for him, building up the church, the body of Christ, to a position of strength and maturity; until finally we all believe alike about our salvation and about our Savior, God's Son, and all become full-grown in the Lord—yes, to the point of being filled full with Christ. . . .

We will lovingly follow the truth at all times—speaking truly, dealing truly, living truly—and so become more and more in every way like Christ who is the Head of his body, the Church. Under his direction, the whole body is fitted together perfectly, and each part in its own special way helps the other parts, so that the whole body is healthy and growing and full of love.

Ephesians 4:11-13, 15-16
The Living Bible

Contents

The Year in Review

THE YEAR IN REVIEW: JULY 1, 1989 TO JUNE 30, 1990

JULY 1989

➤NATIONAL

U.S. Supreme Court decisions—The U.S. Supreme Court concludes 1988-89 sessions with decisions on many issues of interest to the Christian community.

- The Court upholds a Missouri law limiting abortion. It also upholds language in the Missouri law which states that life begins at conception.
- The landmark California Supreme Court decision protecting church counselors stands. Churches have no legal duty to refer counselees to other professionals. Church counselors are now free to continue to help people who seek advice.
- The Court upholds the right of public hospitals to employ chaplains. This allows hospitals to continue to offer a holistic treatment approach to patient care. It also permits accommodation of a patient's religious rights.
- States can't deny unemployment benefits to an individual who refuses to work on his Sabbath day, even if he isn't a member of an organized religion.
- Prosecutors can't use testimonials about the character of murder victims to persuade juries to give a harsher/easier sentence. The 5–4 decision in *South Carolina v. Gathers* holds that a prosecutor acted wrongly by telling a jury that a murder victim was a churchgoing man.
- Congress may ban obscene dial-a-porn services but it must permit telephone sex messages that are merely indecent. Difficulties in proving that material crosses the line between indecent and obscene may render useless Congressional efforts to restrict "phone sex" companies.
- Racketeering laws allow for prosecution for sale of obscene materials, but limits the seizure of certain obscene materials before trial.
- Strikes down a nativity scene display at the Allegheny County Courthouse in Pittsburgh as unconstitutional while saying the display of a Hanukkah menorah on Pittsburgh city hall is acceptable. The Court rules the menorah display is acceptable because the menorah is accompanied by secular symbols, including a Christmas tree. The decision implies that government can tolerate a religious symbol only if it is stripped of any religious significance. Government may celebrate Christmas in some manner and form, but not in a way that endorses Christian doctrine.

Adultery a crime in New Hampshire—New Hampshire's senate votes to keep a 200-year-old law on the books that makes adultery a crime punishable by up to one year in jail. Senate leaders explain that it is not an attempt to bring about enforcement of the law (which hasn't been enforced in decades) but to show that the state still cherishes some traditional values.

Mennen and Clorox boycott—Christian Leaders for Responsible Television (CLEAR-TV) announce a one-year boycott of the Mennen Company and Clorox Corporation because of their sponsorship of television programs that contain sex, violence, and profanity.

Boycott organizers say a deep indignation at offensive TV shows will dry up sales of sponsors' products. "The people are ready," says Billy Melvin, chairman of

THE YEAR IN REVIEW: JULY 1, 1989 TO JUNE 30, 1990 cont.

CLEAR-TV and executive director of the National Association of Evangelicals. "All we need to do is tell them where to boycott."

CLEAR-TV objects to Mennen's advertising on ABC's "A Man Called Hawk"; CBS's "The Equalizer" and "Tour of Duty"; and NBC's "Dream Street," "Miami Vice," and "Midnight Caller."

CLEAR-TV, in existence since 1986, includes 1600 Christian leaders, including 70 denominational heads from Protestant, Catholic, and Orthodox groups. Donald Wildmon of the Tupelo-based American Family Association serves as executive director.

Mystical experiences increase—The proportion of adults who say they have been in touch with the dead is now 42 percent compared to 27 percent eleven years ago. Close to 20 million Americans report mystical experiences.

United Methodist Church moves into the ghettos—Demographics showing the United Methodist Church has become a white, moderately well-to-do denomination represents a serious problem to its leadership.

"To a significant degree, John Wesley's fear of the Methodist societies becoming prosperous and spiritually cool has been realized," says Rev. George Morris, director of an outreach effort among poorer communities.

The goal of a new program at Atlanta's Candler School of Theology is to bring more poor people into the 9.5 million-member church, the second largest Protestant group in the U.S. To accomplish its task, the School for New Congregational Development at Candler will train lay students to spread the gospel in the ghettos, barrios, and poor rural areas, hoping the result will be new churches supported and run by the poor.

Biblical equality of women and men—Christians for Biblical Equality, meeting for their first national conference July 20–23 at Bethel College and Seminary in Arden Hills, MN, insist the Bible upholds equality of women and men.

The preparation of a statement of equality represents the first major project of the 500-member Minnesota-based organization, which is less than two years old.

The statement "points people to the Bible rather than to human viewpoints or denominational positions and certainly not to personalities. The multiplicity of Scripture references encourages interested persons to search God's Word for themselves," says Gretchen Gaebelein Hull, a New York City ordained Presbyterian elder and author of a book, *Equal to Serve,* published by Fleming Revell.

Christian foundation for Amerasian children—As thousands of Vietnamese children of U.S. servicemen resettle in this country through programs set up by the U.S. government, World Vision, a California-based humanitarian aid organization, is creating resettlement transition camps to prepare them for U.S. culture. World Vision officials point out the camps provide an opportunity to "lay a Christian foundation."

➤INTERNATIONAL

Lausanne II—A torch lit in April 1988 is carried through some 50 countries around the world by Christian runners to highlight the opening ceremony of Lausanne II. Close to 4,000 evangelical leaders from 186 countries meet in Manila from July 11–20 to rekindle the flame and prepare for the evangelization of our world in the final years of this century.

Delegates attend a choice of 425 workshops on various topics of social concern such as poverty, the role of the laity and the use of media. Plenary presentations cover 31 topics, sometimes with two speakers on the same topic. The theme: "Proclaim Christ Until He Comes," with a sub-theme of "Calling the Whole Church to Take the Whole Gospel to the Whole World."

Educator Peter Wagner describes the forty individuals who came to Manila at their own expense to pray specifically for the conference in around-the-clock six-hour shifts as "a spiritual nuclear power plant."

Delegates approve *The Manila Manifesto* which seeks to address the needs of a changing world. The manifesto pays special attention to the uniqueness of Christ, the primary need for evangelism, the importance of social concern, the role of women and laity in the ministry, and the need for personal integrity in light of some of the recent religious scandals.

The manifesto supplements the Lausanne Covenant, a document issued by the first Lausanne congress, held in Lausanne, Switzerland in 1974.

"Where the Lausanne Covenant is a timeless document, the manifesto is more timely," says Leighton Ford, chairman of Lausanne II. "It is almost an agenda for the future, raising a number of issues that press upon us right now."

The Lausanne movement will continue under Tom Houston, former president of World Vision, who is the new international director. The entire text of *The Lausanne Covenant* and *The Manila Manifesto* appears on pages 49 and 55.

Colombia ELN releases missionary in captivity for 9 months—The July 19 release of Bruce Olson, age 47, a 28-year missionary among the Indians of northeastern Colombia, ends a 9-month captivity. Olson was captured October 24, 1988, by two dozen armed guerrillas of the Communist Union of the National Liberation Army (known as the ELN).

Olson believes God answered his prayers, "not for liberation but to be effective where God had me placed," sustaining him through primitive jungle conditions, life-threatening illness, psychological pressure, and a mock execution.

"I'd say about 60 percent of the 200 guerrillas I had Bible studies with came into a definite understanding of Jesus Christ and a Christian commitment. A guerrilla is just as much a hostage as I was, because once they're taken into the organization, they can't leave it. They realize that death can be just one tree away, so they think often of death and the purpose of life," Olson says.

Upon Olson's release a national leader of the ELN tells him, "We will never forget you. You are the first person in our camp we have captured that has been a friend and understood us."

Billy Graham in Budapest— A crowd of 90,000 flock to People's Stadium in Budapest on July 20 to hear evangelist Billy Graham, the largest group to attend any event in the 75,000-seat, two-tiered oval stadium. After Graham concludes a message on the cross and its meaning for today, more than 25,000 people walk onto the playing field in response to his call to "come to Christ" or recommit their lives to him.

Millions more listen to the service live on Hungarian state radio. The following weekend, Hungarian television airs a 90-minute program which includes almost all of Graham's message. The daily press, including new independent national newspapers, also provide major coverage.

"This is the first time an evangelistic effort has penetrated the entire country on such a scale," Methodist superintendent Frederick Hecker says.

Radio station encourages pro-democracy Chinese demonstrators—High Adventure Broadcasting Network (HABN), which operates Voice of Hope World Network, is launching a project to broadcast news and Christian encouragement to Chinese pastors, church members, and students in the pro-democracy movement.

"Wherever there are people living under oppression, we must do all we can to give them hope," says George Otis, president.

During the June revolt in Beijing's Tienanmen Square the media cameras did not show Christian students openly witnessing to their faith and the large white banner with the sign of the cross and Chinese characters proclaiming "God Loves the World!" according to a U.S. journalist. Nor did they show one church leader leading his congregation into Tienanmen Square carrying a 10-foot cross, singing hymns of praise and explaining to the demonstrators that

THE YEAR IN REVIEW: JULY 1, 1989 TO JUNE 30, 1990 cont.

Christianity is the only foundation for true democracy.

On another front, in a statement with a June 27 date made public nearly a month later, Chinese church leaders from the China Christian Council and the Chinese Christian Three-Self Patriotic Movement Committee, the state-approved church, resolutely endorses the government's massacre of protesting students. The statement contradicts a May statement giving strong support for the students' demands and petitioning the government to enter into dialogue with the students.

Soviet publisher promotes Christian book—Soviet authorities plan to print 500,000 copies of *How to Really Love Your Child* by psychiatrist Ross Campbell in the Russian language, selling them in Soviet bookstores and health centers throughout the nation. It is the first Christian book contracted by a state-run Soviet publisher. Victor Books is the U.S. publisher.

AUGUST 1989

➤NATIONAL

Church membership trends—The Roman Catholic Church and conservative denominations continue to experience membership increases while many mainline Protestant denominations continue to lose members, reports the *Yearbook of American and Canadian Church 1989*.

According to 1987 membership figures, the last year for which data is available, membership gains are slightly above the one percent growth in the U.S. population.

Reports from 219 religious bodies in the U.S. indicate that 143,830,806 Americans belong to a church, synagogue or religious congregation. This represents 58.6 percent of the U.S. population.

Denominations reporting significant membership increases include Christian and Missionary Alliance, up 2.33 percent to 244,296; Church of God—Anderson, Indiana, up 5.24 percent to 198,552; Church of the Nazarene, up 2.42 percent to 543,762; Free Methodist Church of North America, up 2.15 percent to 73,225; International Church of the Foursquare Gospel, up 3.28 percent to 192,327.

Assemblies of God, up 1.2 percent to 2,160,667; Mennonite Church, up 1.9 percent to 92,902; Presbyterian Church in America, up 1.53 percent to 190,960; Roman Catholic Church, up 1.14 percent to 53,496,862 and Southern Baptist Convention, up 0.74 percent to 14,722,617, also report gains.

Among denominations showing membership losses, the Christian Church/Disciples of Christ is down 1.81 percent to 1,086,668; Episcopal Church, down 1.69 percent to 2,462,300; Presbyterian Church USA, down 1.31 percent to 2,967,781, United Church of Christ, down 0.81 percent to 1,662,568 and United Methodist Church, down 0.74 percent to 9,124,575.

The yearbook also reports a 98 percent increase in the number of ordained women during the 1980s from 10,470 to 20,730. The Assemblies of God has the largest number—3,718 women clergy.

Religious giving increases—The American Association of Fund Raising Counsel indicates religious giving is up 8.2 percent to $48.2 billion. Total philanthropic giving increases 6.7 percent to $104.3 billion.

Much of the money classified under religious giving benefits schools, hospitals, food pantries and facilities for the homeless. A 1988 study by the Independent Sector and the Gallup Organization finds 54 percent of money given to religion goes to maintain church activities, while 46 percent goes to social programs.

Aramaic dying out—Aramaic, the language Jesus spoke, is slowly but perceptibly dying out, say experts. Aramaic was once the common language in the Middle East—a language that in ancient times was used by travellers because most people, regardless of their particular national background, understood it. The words that Christ spoke on the cross, "Eli, Eli, lama sabachthani?" were

Aramaic. Today speakers of Aramaic number less than 25,000 and they do not read or write the 22-character alphabet. Part of the reason for its fading use is that it has no words to describe modern ideas such as electricity and television.

Religious investment scams—While national attention focuses on the financial affairs of television evangelists and other charities, the North American Securities Administrators Association and the Council of better Business Bureaus report more than 15,000 people have lost over $450 million in the past five years to religious investment scams.

Securities experts say religiously oriented scams are on the rise. Self-proclaimed "born-again" financial planners, con artists claiming endorsement by local and national church officials and givers of divinely inspired investment advice about coins, precious metals, real estate and oil and gas well programs prey on the faithful.

NASAA president John Baldwin says that religiously oriented swindles have become the "fraud du jour" of the investment world.

Confronting divorce—In 1986, Jim Talley, assistant pastor of singles at First Baptist Church in Modesto, CA, presented a "Community Marriage Policy" to Modesto's pastors, priests and rabbi to require couples to participate in a premarriage program before being married. The first draft was signed by 95 religious leaders.

Today, Talley points with some satisfaction to a new set of statistics in his city. In 1987, Modesto had a population of 138,823 with 1,923 divorces. In 1988, the population jumped to 144,682 but the number of divorces dipped to 1,812. The city also had a slight drop in the number of marriages.

"Most divorces are not bad marriages, just poorly prepared marriages," says Talley.

Rock music lyrics—A study reports teenagers watch an average of two hours of music videos each day; 75 percent of concept music videos (those involving a theme in contrast to a concert performance) contain sexually suggestive material; 56 percent of music videos contain violence. A special committee of the American Medical Association urges doctors to be alert to the listening habits of young people saying musical preferences may be an indicator of emotional health. The committee concludes that music is a greater influence in teenagers' lives than television. TV viewing is often supervised and censored by parents, while music is largely uncensored.

Conversely, Bob Beeman, founder and pastor of Sanctuary, a West Coast-based network of churches with a ministry to hard rock fans, says his ministry receives about 4,000 calls each month on its 800 lines from teenagers who have become Christians through Christian heavy metal music.

Black Pride—The 8 million-member National Baptist Convention USA, America's largest black denomination, dedicates its new $10 million world headquarters in Nashville, TN, and announces plans for a cable-TV show highlighting the achievements of blacks.

President T. J. Jemison says the TV show, "Black World Today," will feature positive stories of black people to instill in them a sense of pride and accomplishment. The program will be the good news regarding the black community, to offset reports of drugs, crime, and violence on the nightly news.

United Methodists fight drugs—The United Methodist Church invokes for the first time a little-known provision of the denomination's *Book of Discipline* that allows a bishop to be assigned for one year to an issue "deemed of sufficient importance to the welfare of the total church."

In doing so, the leadership appoints Bishop Felton E. May, administrator of the Harrisburg, PA, area to launch guerilla warfare against drugs and violence in Washington, DC. May begins his new assignment January 1, 1990.

He is the first high-ranking religious leader assigned full-time to the war on drugs. Yet he does not want to be known as the "drug czar" of U.S. churches.

"What we're dealing with is a spiritual

THE YEAR IN REVIEW: JULY 1, 1989 TO JUNE 30, 1990 cont.

crisis. Our society is in the throes of moral deterioration, and the drug and alcohol crisis is only one manifestation of that deterioration," May asserts.

Assemblies of God celebrates diamond anniversary—At the 43rd biennial general council of the Assemblies of God August 8–13, Assemblies of God leaders from 85 nations are on hand to celebrate the denomination's diamond anniversary. Assemblies of God youth carry a torch 800 miles from Hot Springs, AR, where the church was started in 1914, to the Indianapolis Hoosier Dome, where the final runner presents it to general superintendent G. Raymond Carlson.

The convention launches "Decade of Harvest," an evangelistic program with four goals: to enlist one million prayer partners to pray for the church daily throughout the next decade, to win 5 million people in the U.S. to Christ, to launch 5,000 churches nationally, and to train 20,000 new ministers in this country.

Divorce gains acceptance—Delegates to the International Pentecostal Holiness Church overturn a position the church has held for most of its history by approving a recommendation allowing divorced and remarried persons to be eligible for ministerial ordination and for service as elders and deacons.

What's in a name?—The 420,000-member Wisconsin Evangelical Lutheran Synod decide to keep "Wisconsin" in its name even though the church, which began in Wisconsin 139 years ago, now has congregations in all 50 states and three Canadian provinces.

ELCA becomes NCC member—The 5.2 million-member Evangelical Lutheran Church in America (ELCA) votes August 25 to become the second largest denomination in the National Council of Churches. The ELCA's ability to talk with both Roman Catholics and evangelical conservatives makes it a key player in the formation of inter-denominational cooperation on social issues.

A seminary for the Chinese—Gordon-Conwell Theological Seminary of South Hamilton establishes a new seminary to train pastors, missionaries, and evangelists for work among Chinese people in North America, Asia and other parts of the world.

The Great Commission Theological Seminary will locate in the greater Los Angeles area. In its initial stages, it will function as an associate school of Gordon-Conwell, but plans to be fully independent and accredited by the turn of the century.

➤INTERNATIONAL

Religious freedom—Religious liberty is now being granted in the Marxist nation of Mozambique. New churches are being built, confiscated property is being returned, and church groups—including Western religious groups—are being allowed to do social and relief work, the result of the Mozambique Congress declaring an end to Marxist Leninism last year.

In 1975 Mozambique became a Marxist-Leninist state and during the ensuing years suffered economic setbacks, famine, and war. The United Nations lists Mozambique as one of the poorest countries in the world.

Chinese persecution—Chinese Christians experience fines, arrests, and the confiscation of radios for listening to Far East Broadcasting Company broadcasts.

The persecution follows a June 9 warning by the Beijing government which bans all foreign radio broadcasts, an attempt to monitor information about the counterrevolutionary movement.

Poland opens up—The Polish branch of the international student mission IFES, the Christian Student Union, receives state approval to work at universities in Poland. This approval represents the first time an evangelical student mission has officially been allowed to establish itself in an Eastern European country.

Read-a-Long Bible program—Because Burmese Buddhists consider it offensive and improper to read the sacred books of another religion unless invited to do so, Far Eastern Broadcasting Company's Burmese director offers listeners a copy of a Bible portion and invites them to read along with the radio program. The response, almost all from Buddhists, averages more than 3,000 letters a month.

Ethiopia church growth—The Ethiopian Evangelical Church with 20,000 members in 1951 reports membership has grown to 776,000 in 1988. More than 350 churches closed by the government have reopened.

OM leaves Nepal—Twenty-five Operation Mobilization workers leave Nepal because of unlivable conditions that include extreme repression of Christianity by the government. The decision to withdraw stems from an incident late last year in which two OM workers were imprisoned for distributing Christian literature and Bibles during a five-week trek through the country.

The Nepali Supreme Court hands down from three to six year sentences to several Christian leaders for preaching the gospel, making a total of 100 Christians currently in Nepalese prisons for their faith. Since 1970 close to 100 incidents of persecution have been documented. Yet the church is growing. There were no Christians in Nepal 35 years ago; today there are approximately 50,000.

Irian Jaya earthquake—Early August 1, entire villages collapse or disappear in landslides and rockfalls as an earthquake shatters the countryside. At least 115 die. Most fatalities occur where Regions Beyond Missionary Union works. More than 25 die in the Tangma and Pasema areas where the Christian and Missionary Alliance works.

SEPTEMBER 1989

➤NATIONAL

Something's Happening USA—Labor Day weekend, more than 1,000 high school student leaders attend a Student Venture, high school ministry of Campus Crusade for Christ, conference in St. Paul, MN, to pray for and plan a way to make a spiritual impact in their schools.

Rhode Island considers witch coven a religious group—Rhode Island tax administrator R. Gary Clark rules that a coven of witches deserves tax-exempt status as a legitimate religious group. The coven has 30 to 40 members and meets about three times a month. The state allows the coven to officiate over marriages and burials.

Members pay homage to a deity with male and female attributes whose psychic energy they believe can be tapped. While the power can be used for good or ill, the witches claim they do not use it for destructive purposes.

Miss America, 1990—Debbye Turner, Miss Missouri and a marimba-playing veterinary student, begins her reign as Miss America 1990 September 13. Turner, the third black woman to hold the title, gives God the glory for her success in the pageant.

At her first press conference, she tells reporters who ask about her great poise that her daily quiet time for personal devotions is responsible.

A notch for prolife—Concluding that human life begins at conception, Judge W. Dale Young of Tennessee grants custody of seven embryo "children" to their mother. Young further rules that if any of the embryos survive through pregnancy to live birth, he will at that time decide further questions of custody and child support.

National Right to Life president John Wilke says the decision will have enormous implications for abortion litigation. "Once society recognizes that human life begins at conception, killing human beings at will through abortion is clearly unacceptable," Wilke says.

Episcopal Church compromises on women clergy—Bishops of the 2.4 million-member Episcopal Church reach a compromise they say should avert a split by dissenting traditionalists who reject women clergy. The bishops unanimously adopt a compromise statement during their bicentennial meeting in Philadelphia, September 28.

Though Bishop Barbara Harris of Boston becomes the first woman bishop in the 70

THE YEAR IN REVIEW: JULY 1, 1989 TO JUNE 30, 1990 cont.

million-member worldwide Anglican communion, opponents of women priests and bishops receive acceptance of their views. Six of about 100 U.S. Episcopal dioceses refuse to ordain women priests.

The carefully worded compromise statement declares: "We joyfully affirm ordained women—indeed all women—in the ministries which they exercise in and through the church. . . . We acknowledge within Anglicanism those who believe that women should not be ordained hold an accepted theological position. . . . We affirm them as loyal members of the family. . . . There is a need as well to be pastorally sensitive to those who do not accept the ordination of women."

➤INTERNATIONAL

Church growth in Thailand—New Life Training Centers, a program of Campus Crusade for Christ's New Life 2000, is responsible for more than 2,300 new churches in six denominations in northeast Thailand during the past five years. More than 150,000 people participate in 16,600 home Bible study fellowships, reports Roy Rosedale, a Fuller Seminary student.

New Life Training Centers are mobile schools to prepare students for ministry in evangelism, discipleship, and spiritual multiplication. Students attend 60 hours of class instruction and 75 to 100 hours of field ministry work while in the program.

HCJB among the world's most popular short wave radio stations—Research confirms that Heralding Christ Jesus' Blessings (HCJB) in Quito, Ecuador, is one of the top ten short wave radio stations.

Voice of America reports HCJB eighth among most-listened-to stations in a 1989 survey. An earlier survey by British Broadcasting Corporation in January 1988 ranks HCJB tenth among the most-listened-to stations.

Adopt-a-Church—ASSIST International (Aid to Special Saints in Strategic Times) links U.S. churches with congregations in Communist countries. The sister-church relationship gets off to a running start with a relationship between a church in Havana, Cuba and Calvary Chapel in Costa Mesa, CA.

Founder Dan Wooding, a British journalist and author, reports fifty Cuban churches and fifty Nicaraguan churches are waiting to be adopted by American churches. His vision is to arrange sister-church relationships throughout the world. What the Western churches can do to help is dictated by the suffering church's unique circumstances, including the government system it is under as well as economic, societal, and other forces.

Moscow International Book Fair—The thirty U.S. Christian book publishing companies in Moscow September 12–18 for the seventh annual Moscow International Book Fair report unprecedented desire for Bible commentaries, doctrinal and theological books, and Bible study aids.

Peter Deyneka, Jr., president of the Slavic Gospel Association, reports that two hours after the start of the fair all books at his exhibit, including those just for display, were gone.

Doug Ross, executive director of Evangelical Christian Publishers Association, says the 1989 Moscow Book Fair is unique among international book fairs because of the interest in Christian literature. "At other fairs, it is primarily a business interaction which takes place, but in Moscow the spiritual hunger of the Soviet people is phenomenal," he says.

Soviet leader encourages Bible distribution—During an unprecedented meeting September 22 between high-level Soviet officials and representatives from Slavic Gospel Association, Yuri Khristoradnov, chairman of the Soviet Council for Religious Affairs, tells Peter Deyneka, Jr., president of SGA, that the Soviet government will not try to stop the flow of Bibles into the USSR but will encourage it. The Russian Orthodox Church is calling on the west to provide 20 million Bibles. Today there are about 4 million Bibles for the Soviet Union's 60 to 100 million Christians.

The Soviets authorize a study of the Ten Commandments in a search for a new value system to substitute for the failed god of Marxism.

Amity Press, China, prints one millionth Bible—The one millionth Chinese Bible rolls off the press September 28 at Amity Printing Press in Nanjing. In some areas of China the law of supply and demand hike the cost of a Bible up to thirteen times the asking price.

The printing of the one millionth Bible follows closely on the heels of another landmark this year: the release, on Easter Sunday, of the Chinese Bible in simplified script.

The Amity Printing Company is a joint venture between the United Bible Societies (UBS) and the Amity Foundation, a social service organization initiated by Chinese Christians. Operations began in December 1987 after years of negotiation and a successful fundraising effort from Christians around the globe.

OCTOBER 1989

➤NATIONAL

New England stirs—Some New Englanders note an increasingly visible surge of evangelical piety in a region known for its reserve and some say that another awakening may be in the offering.

Signs of resurgence take several forms, say evangelical church leaders. Perhaps the most noticeable are the growing number of churches. Assemblies of God congregations have almost doubled in the last twenty years with church membership climbing from less than 8,000 in 1968 to approximately 25,000 in 1988, according to Sherri Doty Coussens, statistician at the denomination's international headquarters.

While the Southern Baptist Convention claimed only 31 congregations in New England two decades ago, the figure now stands at 175. Some are small and without church buildings, but Larry Martin of the Greater Boston Baptist Association says many are thriving. "God seems to be opening doors faster than we can keep up with," he says.

Christians respond to earthquake needs—Christian agencies respond with material relief and spiritual counseling in the aftermath of the devastating earthquake that kills 63 and leaves 14,000 homeless in San Francisco, CA, on October 17.

Minutes after the earthquake, the Salvation Army despatches staff, vehicles and equipment to areas throughout the city. The Salvation Army's thirty facilities become relief centers, providing shelter, food, clothing and counseling to victims. During the first week Salvation Army volunteers provide nearly 7,000 hours of labor.

Evangelist Billy Graham tours relief sites, praying with victims and encouraging volunteers working around the clock. While visiting, Graham donates $100,000 to the Salvation Army, totally depleting his organization's disaster relief fund.

World Vision conducts meetings with pastors to help coordinate church response. Pastors arrange 24-hour counseling services for victims and emergency workers facing grisly rescue operations.

Southern Baptist workers and a $60,000 donation arrive less than 24 hours after the earthquake.

Church World Service and Presbyterian Church in America are also on the scene to help with relief efforts.

Church home concept changing—The concept of a single church which people call their church home is changing, according to a study from the Barna Research Group.

"Recognizing that they have a breadth of needs, and recognizing that most churches are incapable of satisfying that range of needs, adults will attend several churches, visiting each on a rotating or as needed basis," reports George Barna, president.

Barna indicates that this trend is especially evident among single adults. Yet, multiple church behavior can be seen among married adults as well, particularly members of the baby boom generation.

THE YEAR IN REVIEW: JULY 1, 1989 TO JUNE 30, 1990 cont.

UCC/Disciples move toward unity—A joint panel of the United Church of Christ and Christian Church (Disciples of Christ) recommends that the two mainline denominations strengthen their ecumenical partnership by doing "nothing separately that could be done together." The 1.6 million-member United Church of Christ and million-member Disciples of Christ endorsed shared Communion and interchangeable ministries this summer.

The joint panel votes to prepare the two churches for a simultaneous gathering of their highest deliberative bodies in St. Louis in 1993.

Revised English Bible (REB)—Oxford University Press releases The Revised English Bible, an update of The New English Bible published in 1970. The publishers also announce the REB Charity program. For every Bible purchased, fifty cents will be donated to one of six charities: Prison Fellowship, Habitat for Humanity, the AIDS National Interfaith Network, Reading Is Fundamental, Save the Children, or Food for the Hungry, Inc.

Minnesota fines landlord for religious convictions—October 27, Layle French, of Marshall, MN, pays a $1,048 fine for his refusal to rent property to an unmarried couple, using dollar bills given to him by hundreds of people who support his convictions.

When an administrative law judge found French in violation of Minnesota's antidiscrimination law, French contended that renting property to an unmarried couple violated his religious convictions. The fine is under appeal.

➤INTERNATIONAL

Fourth Temple?—Israel's Ministry of Religious Affairs convenes a first ever Conference of Temple Research to discuss whether contemporary Jews should rebuild the Temple. Several small organizations in Jerusalem are making preparations for the new Temple despite doctrinal obstacles and the certainty of provoking Muslim fury.

Police cancel a planned ceremony on the Temple Mount when Arab students begin to riot. "Muslims believe this is a plot to take over their holy place," says Jerusalem Mayor Teddy Kollek. The Temple Mount Faithful, a group of Jewish activists, brings a three-ton stone to Jerusalem on October 16—a cornerstone for the fourth Temple.

Terrorists attack churches— "Shining Path," a terrorist group in Peru, South America, singles out evangelicals as victims of their brutal killings. An entire church congregation in the high jungle of Ayacucho watches as the group murders all male members. The group destroys Bibles and musical instruments and breaks pews to pieces.

Hong Kong exodus—Surveys reveal that one-third of Hong Kong's 5.6 million population would leave the British Colony if possible before China takes possession in 1997. In 1989, more than 45,000 emigrated. Since the standoff in Beijing's Tienanmen Square requests for exit visas have jumped 200 percent .

Many of Hong Kong's senior pastors have been siphoned off by rapidly growing new Chinese churches in North America.

"In Toronto, there are more than 100 Chinese churches, all of them packed. Many are looking for senior pastors, and they are shopping in Hong Kong," says Philemon Choi, general secretary of Breakthrough, a multimedia ministry to Hong Kong youth.

Their exodus leaves Hong Kong churches with young, inexperienced leaders to face a daunting future. Perhaps as many as half of Hong Kong's pastors are less than thirty years old. Those who qualify for emigration are generally mature, financially established people. So Christian laypeople who leave are often pillars of their churches—experienced members who have served as elders, deacons and teachers.

NOVEMBER 1989

➤NATIONAL

SC hurricane victims persevere—Evangelist Billy Graham and his son, Franklin, head of Samaritan's Purse, an international relief organization, join South Carolina governor Carroll A. Campbell Jr. to tour parts of the state most heavily damaged by Hurricane Hugo in September.

Graham, who had just come from California where he had toured earthquake disaster sites with the Salvation Army said, "The devastation I've seen here is far greater than anything I saw there. Here, you have such unbelievable devastation over such a wide area."

William Tyndale's New Testament release—Yale University Press releases a reproduction of the New Testament as translated by William Tyndale. Available for the first time since the 16th century, the reproduction has been edited only to update antiquated spellings.

YFC and Young Life mandates—Dick Wynn, president of Youth for Christ, and Doug Burleigh, president of Young Life International, ratify six covenants which they urge their staffs to implement. These include mandates to pray for each other's organizations and to stop competing for staff, young people, and evangelistic turf.

Concerned Women for America wins—In a religious discrimination case, the U.S. Court of Appeals for the Fifth Circuit in New Orleans, LA, rules that a public library in Oxford, MS, may not prohibit a Concerned Women for America prayer chapter from using its facilities because of the religious content of the meetings.

Beverly LaHaye, founder and president of CWA, sees the decision as a significant step toward decreasing the widespread discrimination against religious groups that seek to use public facilities for meetings.

Satanic cults treatment program—Hartgrove Hospital in Chicago, IL, launches a formal treatment program for teenagers involved in satanic cults—one of the first of its kind in the country.

Pro-lifers make a symbolic statement—As more than 150,000 abortion-rights activists rally at the Lincoln Memorial, pro-lifers on the Ellipse erect the "Cemetery of the Innocents"—4,400 small white crosses to symbolize the number of babies aborted each day in the U.S.

A January 1990 survey by the Wirthlin Group shows that more than half of all Americans oppose the majority of abortions. The poll also finds that 49 percent misidentify themselves as pro-choice. The National Right to Life Committee model legislation for 1990 allows abortion in cases of rape, incest or danger to the mother's life. These circumstances cover only 2 percent of abortions performed in the U.S.

MA becomes second state to agree to homosexual rights—The Massachusetts Senate passes a bill banning discrimination against homosexuals in employment, credit, and housing following 17 years of controversy and debate. It is the second statewide gay-rights bill in the nation, after Wisconsin. To ensure passage, backers agree to compromise amendments. Among them: the state does not endorse homosexuality or recognize homosexual partnerships, and religious institutions are exempt.

CA compromises on evolution teaching—In a concession to Christians who believe the biblical account of creation, the California Board of Education adopts new textbook guidelines which omit the claim that the theory of evolution is a scientific fact. The guidelines retain a strong statement supporting the teaching of evolution as the accepted theory of the origin of mankind, but this new action sends a signal to publishers of science textbooks that backers of the biblical story of creation remain a strong force.

The Rev. Louis Sheldon, head of the Tradition Values Coalition in California, calls the compromise "a very significant victory" but acknowledges that it is only a start. Because of the large number of texts ordered by California schools, textbook decisions in this state influence what is taught in the rest of the nation. With 4.6 million students, California is the nation's largest textbook market.

THE YEAR IN REVIEW: JULY 1, 1989 TO JUNE 30, 1990 cont.

➤INTERNATIONAL

East German church leaders play key roles—Churches serve as forums and gathering places for large rallies of activists who spill out onto the streets to demonstrate for reforms leading to the opening of the Berlin Wall November 9. Church leaders are in the forefront of calls for freedom of travel and democratic elections.

West Berlin Christians take advantage of the historic events to show hospitality to their East German neighbors. Gertrud Vegener, West Berlin, opens her apartment to East Germans who line up at shopping centers, offering them refreshments and a place to rest. She passes out Christian literature and explains the Gospel. At least one East German woman responds by praying to receive Christ, according to *Baptist Press* correspondents in Germany.

Many congregations in West Berlin have partner congregations in East Berlin and on November 12 a number of East Berliners show up to worship with their fellow believers for the first time.

November 16–18, International Bible Society's partner in Germany distributes 20,000 Scriptures at Checkpoint Charlie and 8,000 more at southern border points.

Christians in Turkey declining—The number of Christians in Turkey is steadily shrinking. In 1915 there were 4.5 million; now the number is 150,000. Massacres, massive discriminations and persecutions by the Muslim majority have led to the death or exodus of the Christian minority.

Third world missionaries increase—Rev. Panya Baba, Nigerian church leader representing Third World missions at the Second International Congress on World Evangelization in Manila, Philippines, tells the congress that missionaries sent by churches in the Third World now number 20,000, up from 3,000 in 1974.

Bibles in Buddhist temples—The Bible Society in Thailand is visiting the 32,000 Buddhist temples in that nation to offer a free Bible to each temple library. Plans are to have a Bible in every temple by the end of 1990.

Philippines recognize SBC missionary—In a special meeting in Washington, DC, Philippine president Corazon Aquino honors Harold Watson, a Southern Baptist missionary, for his help in developing agriculture.

Watson established the Baptist Rural Life Center, an agricultural training center on the Philippine island of Mindanao. Watson also played a strong role in developing Sloping Agricultural Land Technology (SALT), which helps the country's resource-poor farmers. The awards ceremony is sponsored by the Philippine American Foundation which recognizes significant contributions to the Philippines by private sector organizations.

Watson and the Center have won numerous awards, including the Ramon Magsaysay Award for international understanding, considered by many in Asia to be as prestigious as a Nobel Prize.

TWR production facilities in USSR—Soviet officials grant Trans World Radio permission to set up radio production facilities in the Soviet Union.

"It's a new day and a new opportunity for production in cooperation with the Russian people themselves. This will enable us to provide better quality programming for the Soviet people which will more accurately reflect their everyday life and provide new formats not possible from the West," says Dr. Paul E. Freed, TWR president.

TWR plans to build at least three studios. A mobile recording van and several portable recording units will be available for program producers. TWR plans to broadcast programs for teenagers and the general population as well as live Sunday worship services for shut-ins who cannot attend church.

Lima's encounter with God—For 16 years the Rev. Alfredo Smith has guided "Lima's Encounter with God" program, alternating two-week evangelistic meetings with discipleship classes in the turbulent nation of Peru. As a result a small, struggling house fellowship has become the 4,000-member Lince Christian and Missionary Alliance Church.

This month Smith returns to his native Buenos Aires to work with a small C&MA church there. "I am asking the Lord for 5,000 converts in three years. I do not believe the Lord wants the church to grow through Christians transferring from other places. I want the church to increase through new conversions," says Smith.

DECEMBER 1989

➤NATIONAL

TV violence declines slightly—The January 1990 issue of *Moody Monthly* magazine reports that for the fourth year, the National Coalition on Television Violence has tracked a decline in TV violence.

The three major networks averaged 9.5 violent acts per hour during the fall 1989 season, down from the 9.9 average registered in 1987. The Fox TV network averaged 14 acts of violence per hour, similar to the record levels registered by the major networks in 1985.

NCTV researchers say that close to 30 percent of network prime-time programming continues to "inaccurately glamorize violence and promotes it as the best or only way to resolve conflict."

Pastor/congregation disputes increase—Conflicts between pastors and their congregations have become noisier and more public.

Speed Leas, of the Alban Institute, a Washington, DC, think tank which mediates such disputes with more than 200 mainline churches a year, says that for every pastor who's fired, another is struggling but staying on.

The battles are most often over leadership styles and unclear—or unmet—expectations. Half the time, Leas says, either "the pastor is too passive, not assertive enough," or "he's too assertive, he doesn't consult enough."

While most denominations do not keep statistics on clergy firings, a 1988 study by the Southern Baptist Sunday School Board finds that more than 2,100 Southern Baptist ministers were fired over an 18-month period—a 31 percent increase over a similar survey conducted in 1984. Another study by the Missouri Baptist Convention finds that at least 53 Southern Baptist pastors in MO have experienced forced terminations in the past three years.

Salvation Army bellringers face struggle—Complaints by retailers increasingly are driving out the familiar sound of Salvation Army bells. About 20 percent of shopping malls across the country ban the Salvation Army's bellringers—a trend that Army officials estimate will decrease holiday contributions by $100,000.

First Lady Barbara Bush sides with the Salvation Army. After reading that nearly half of the Washington area's malls ban the bellringers, Mrs. Bush stops by a Chevy Chase, MD, mall to tell bellringer Evelyn Barnes, "What great work you do. I'm a great fan of the Salvation Army."

Wauconda, IL, residents respond to atheist challenge—When atheist Robert Sherman threatens to sue the town of Wauconda, Illinois, unless crosses on the village's two water towers, a 45-year tradition, are removed, the town's 5,911 residents vote to replace the crosses with stars rather than pay an estimated cost of $41.00 to $82.00 per household to fight the lawsuit.

Following the vote, one by one, crosses begin to appear on the lawns, homes and businesses throughout the town. Soon more than 200 crosses dot the town in various sizes and shapes: red velvet crosses on garage doors, masking tape crosses in windows, crosses attached to CB and TV antennae etc.

Sherman, national spokesman for American Atheists Inc., says the display of crosses shows resentment toward atheists rather than Christian faith. The Rev. Byron Maher of Transfiguration Roman Catholic Church disagrees. "It's not attacking him at all. It is showing our Christianity. In fact, we've got

THE YEAR IN REVIEW: JULY 1, 1989 TO JUNE 30, 1990 cont.

countless people praying for him," says Maher.

➤INTERNATIONAL

Romanians celebrate religious freedom—In Timisoara's "Massacre Square" on December 23, with bullets still flying, Pastor Peter Dugulescu of First Baptist Church preaches in a large square and leads tens of thousands on their knees in the Lord's Prayer.

When Dugulescu and a Pentecostal ask the people to lead a nonviolent fight for liberty, the crowd responds by singing what has become known as the "Song of the Revolution":

We live at the end of an era, with fights, hate and war.

We look toward a happy heaven,

It is not very long and the Lord will return to us.

He comes again, he comes again, What an unspeakable joy.

It will be the end of bitter pains.

At Metropolitan Cathedral in Bucharest, Patriarch Teoctist Arapas of the Romanian Orthodox Church tells 500 Christmas worshipers, "We must thank God who gave us freedom after twenty-five years of terror." Romanian radio and television air church music for the first time in decades.

Twice on December 31 about 10,000 worshipers pack a sports area in Oradea. It is the first mass religious service in a public venue in years. For Joseph Tson of the Wheaton, IL, based Romanian Missionary Society, a former pastor in Oradea, it was the first of many opportunities to speak to Romanian crowds. Tson also calls the nation to turn to God on national TV. He returns to the U.S. with government approval for a seminary, Christian publishing house, newspaper and magazine.

Beijing students report multiple conversions—Chinese students in Beijing are turning to Christianity "by the dorm," two Chinese students report to News Network International. A dormitory usually houses 8 students.

"Since June 4, the rate at which students are turning to Christ is literally a dormitory at a time. Some departments within certain colleges have changed their whole atmosphere because so many have become Christian," according to the students.

The students are not free to relate specific details because they believe "a tough crackdown upon Christians, especially house church Christians, is expected very soon." Communist Party contacts have predicted an impending crackdown. During the last ten days of November, dormitories were unexpectedly raided by special units from the Public Security Bureau trained to spot anything "ideologically impure."

"A church opens in China every thirty-six hours," says Michael Chute, Baptist Press correspondent. The China Christian Council reports a total of 5 million Chinese Christians, but other organizations place the figure as high as 50 million.

Can a Jew not be a Jew?—Israel's Supreme Court rules that Messianic Jews are not entitled to automatic Israeli citizenship. The ruling clarifies the state's 1950 Law of Return—which grants automatic citizenship to virtually all Jews—by further defining what it means to be a Jew.

The December 25th, 100-page decision, says that "those who believe in Jesus are, in fact, Christians," and therefore as members of another faith are ineligible for automatic citizenship. Such believers, however, may apply for citizenship through normal immigration procedures.

JANUARY 1990

➤NATIONAL

International Year of Bible Reading—It is midnight, January 1. On the Mount of Olives, despite bitter cold winds and rain, Ken Connelly, professor at Pacific Coast Bible College, reads the first words of Genesis to officially begin the International Year of Bible Reading. The marathon of continuous Bible reading concludes at 3:30 p.m. January 3 with Thomas "Ed" Steele reading the final words of Revelation. Some 35 people participate, reading in English, Hebrew, German, Dutch, and French.

The U.S. Senate and the U.S. House of Representatives pass bills designating 1990 as the International Year of Bible Reading in the United States. The International Bible Reading Association in Tennessee sponsors the project. Bible readings are held in 50 additional countries throughout the year.

Christian ethics in business—Thousands of Christian-based companies today are run according to biblical principles, defying the conventional attitude that it is folly to mix business and religion. A study by management scholar Nabil A. Ibrahim of 152 such companies shows they grow significantly faster than other companies in their fields by every criterion examined, including return on assets, net sales, and number of employees.

CBN University becomes Regent University—Effective January 1, CBN University becomes known as Regent University to be "more symbolic of what our mission has always been—to represent God through the quality of our work in this nation and around the world," says Lawrence Walters, president of the school's alumni association.

Episcopalian surveys reveal differing viewpoints—Two separate polls reveal different levels of disagreement between Episcopalian laity and the denomination's leadership, but both polls indicate the two are moving in different directions.

Ninety percent of Episcopalian laity oppose both homosexual ordination and the blessing of homosexual unions, while the church leadership has tolerated the ordination of self-avowed, practicing homosexuals, according to an Episcopalians United for Revelation, Renewal, and Reformation survey of more than 100,000 Episcopalians on the six most hotly debated issues in the church. On theological issues, 91 percent say they oppose changing the statement, "Jesus Christ, the Way, the Truth, the Life" to "Jesus Christ, a Way, a Truth, a Life." More than 80 percent say evangelism should be the top priority, while 88 percent oppose the use of inclusive language in worship services, defined as changing "the teaching of the person of God from our Father to many female images."

Ted Nelson, chairman of the board of Episcopals United, asserts the survey confirms that the denomination's current leadership "does not reflect the thoughts, feelings or beliefs of those worshiping in our churches."

On another front, a Gallup Poll of Episcopalians concludes that 64 percent disapprove of church sanction for "relationships between members of the same sex," and 49 percent disapprove of "non-sexist language in the Psalms and the liturgy." Approval of the ordination of women as bishops runs 66 percent .

Sales tax bites the church—The Supreme Court rules January 17 that states may tax the sale of religious items. Most states tax the sale of religious goods within the state, but laws on mail-order sales vary.

The ruling means Jimmy Swaggart Ministries must pay a California tax bill of $183,000 on evangelistic items sold over an eight-year period, and it creates additional bookkeeping functions for mail-order ministries who sell Bibles and Christian books through televangelistic marketing.

The Justices see it as a commercial enterprise rather than spiritual. Wrote Justice Sandra Day O'Connor: "The tax is not a tax on the right to disseminate religious information, ideas or beliefs per se; rather it is a tax on the privilege of making retail sales of tangible personal property."

➤INTERNATIONAL

Dark Africa spreads light—Africa, once called the Dark Continent, holds a strategic place in contemporary world missions. Over the past twenty-five years, numerous indigenous, independent mission agencies have sprung up. Today there are approximately 17,000 African missionaries. Nigeria alone has 30 indigenous mission boards and 3,000 missionaries—making the country a leader in mission outreach.

THE YEAR IN REVIEW: JULY 1, 1989 TO JUNE 30, 1990 cont.

Oldest continuing interdenominational prayer week—January 7–14 marks the 143rd continuous year for the Universal Week of Prayer, sponsored by World Evangelical Fellowship and its predecessor.

One million Christians participate in the week-long nightly prayer gatherings in 4,700 locations in East and West Germany, Switzerland, and Austria according to the Information Service of the German Evangelical Alliance.

Religious freedom in Hungary—January 24 the Hungarian Parliament passes 304 to 1, with 11 abstentions, a law of freedom of conscience and religion which declares that such freedoms are a fundamental liberty.

Hungarian prime minister Miklos Hemeth apologizes to church leaders for past government policies which have formally forbidden religious practice for four decades, and reaffirms his commitment to religious freedom.

Churches no longer need permission for special activities, schools may teach religious instruction to public school children and restrictions on publishing no longer exist.

Soviets look at the Ten Commandments—Three professors from U.S. Christian colleges and a missions leader travel to Moscow to meet with two leading Soviet academics and a well-known journalist to plan a research project to study the impact of the Ten Commandments on individuals and society.

Russian officials will interview 10,000 people in the Soviet Union to examine their knowledge and understanding of the Ten Commandments. The Soviet researchers are looking for a connection between understanding of biblical values and a sense of fulfillment and purpose in individual lives.

Soviet Jews return to Israel—After more than a decade of trickling immigration, Israel is experiencing one of the largest influxes of Jews in history. During the first week of January 1,500 Jews arrive in Israel, most on direct flights from Moscow—more than all the Soviet Jews who immigrated to Israel in 1987.

The Israeli government estimates 500,000 Jews will enter Israel by 1991. According to a Religious News Service report, about 95 percent are expected to come from the Soviet Union.

FEBRUARY 1990

➤NATIONAL

Baptist memberships rise—The Baptist World Alliance grew by more than 1.5 million members in 1989, according to BWA statistics. The BWA membership at the end of 1989 included 136,154 churches (up 6,269 from 1988), and 35,875,005 baptized members (up 1,705,613 from 1988) according to J. Ralph McIntyre, director of the BWA's Division of Study and Research. The 144-member conventions range in size from the 14.8 million-member Southern Baptist Convention, to the 134-member Australasian Conference of Seventh Day Baptists.

Southern Baptists started 842 congregations in the US and Puerto Rico in 1988–1989, exceeding the SBC's Bold Mission Thrust goal for the period by 69. There are 42,735 SBC congregations; the denomination's goal is 50,000 by the year 2000.

Charismatic "shepherding" movement apologies—Bob Mumford, a key leader in launching Christian Growth Ministries, a charismatic discipleship or shepherding movement, publicly apologizes for the cult-like direction of the movement.

"Part of the motivation behind my public apology is the realization that a wrong attitude is still present in hundreds of independent church groups who are answerable to no one," says Mumford. He suggests that the movement had a noble purpose at its inception, but "people took something that began in the Spirit and attempted to perfect it in the flesh. Ends began to justify the means. The attitude became, 'I'm going to help you walk straight, even if I have to coerce you.' This is not the spirit of the gospel."

The movement reached its peak in the mid-1970s (with perhaps as many as

1,150,000 followers). According to its leaders, the movement was an attempt to address a perceived lack of discipline among members of charismatic groups. Local "shepherds," often self-appointed, laid down rules regulating personal conduct and decisions. As controversy spread over authoritarian styles and alleged abuses, respected Pentecostal and charismatic leaders, notably Jack Hayford of the Church on the Way in Van Nuys, CA, voiced objections. Hayford wrote in *Ministries Today* magazine that "multiplied hundreds of pastors, like myself, have spent large amounts of time over the past fifteen years picking up the pieces of broken lives that resulted from distortion of truth by extreme teachings and destructive applications on discipleship, authority, and shepherding."

Wheaton College offers MA in evangelism—Wheaton College Graduate School receives approval to add an accredited Master of Arts in evangelism to its curriculum.

"The purpose is to prepare Christians for ministries in evangelism," says James Kraakevik, director of the Billy Graham Center at Wheaton. Upon graduating, students will typically be involved in vocations in communications, churches, evangelistic organizations and parachurch agencies, as well as the secular marketplace.

Christian Management Institute—1,400 Christian managers attend the 13th annual Christian Management Institute at the Disneyland Hotel in Annaheim, CA.

Managers of Christian nonprofit organizations from across the U.S. choose from more than 125 workshops, learning skills in financial management, human resources, fund raising, marketing, information management, tax and legal issues, and church management.

Christian Ministries Management Association and the Evangelical Council for Financial Accountability sponsors the annual event.

➤INTERNATIONAL

Soviets crowd theatres to see *Jesus* film—Between August 1989 and February 1990 more than 560,000 people view *Jesus*—a two-hour motion picture based on the Gospel of Luke. In Bryansk, a city southwest of Moscow, the waiting list to see the film is a month long.

Jesus is the most translated film in the history of the motion picture industry. It is available in more than 150 languages and has been shown by more than 220 mission organizations in 166 countries. Since its release in October 1979, more than 330 million people have viewed the film with an estimated 30 million individuals indicating a decision to follow Jesus Christ.

Crackdown in Canton—The arrest of China's best-known house church leader, Lin Xiangao, on February 22 and the closing of his flourishing house church, the Damazhan Fellowship, has serious implications for the entire house church movement which claims a national membership of between 25 million and 50 million. The police release Lin on February 24 and allow him to return home, but the following day turn away Christians arriving for church services after posting a government notice on the door forbidding "illegal religious meetings." Officials confiscate Bibles, hymnals, cassettes and sound equipment.

Since 1980, when the church's first two converts were baptized, the Fellowship has baptized over 1,700 believers and has been regularly attended by some 1,000 Christians who crowd into the small house on any given day of the week for meetings. Since the Beijing massacre last June, many young people were attracted to the church, and on Saturday evenings over 80 percent of the congregation were youth, according to Anthony P.B. Lambert, correspondent for News Network International.

Lin has spent more than 21 of his 66 years in prison for his evangelistic activities.

Austria concerns—Individual consumption of alcohol in Austria is the highest in Europe. The Austrian abortion and suicide rates are among the highest in the world.

Bible societies organize in USSR—The Soviet Union's first Bible societies organize in Latvia and Moscow.

THE YEAR IN REVIEW: JULY 1, 1989 TO JUNE 30, 1990 cont.

Last June the American Bible Society reported a "memorandum of understanding" was signed by the Russian Orthodox Church and the United Bible Society. The goal was to work toward "the first-ever interconfessional Bible distribution organization" in the USSR.

In other Eastern Europe Bible society news, Armenian church leaders plan to open a Bible shop in the spiritual center of Etchmiazin—a first step toward organizing an Armenian Bible Society, and the Czechoslovakian Bible Society announces that 180,000 Bibles and New Testaments will be published each year by the government printing house.

Eastern Bloc mission leaders meet—Representatives of about 60 organizations with ministries in the Soviet Union meet in Dallas to share information and strategies for working in the rapidly changing communist bloc.

The 110 mission leaders present at the four-day meeting discuss literature distribution, discipleship and training, mass evangelism, and economic development for Soviet churches and groups, according to Ralph Mann of Mission Possible, one of the meeting organizers. Almost all the groups were unprepared for the dramatic changes in the country, Mann says, and they are rushing to respond to what many feel may be a limited opening for Western agencies.

Iranian evangelism—The Iranian Bible Training Center opens in London, England to train Iranian Christians to evangelize Iranians around the world. The Training Center offers a two-year program and is directed by Samuel Yeghnazar, who also leads a congregation that includes about 100 Iranian members.

MARCH 1990

➤NATIONAL

NAE reports record growth during the 1980s—Billy Melvin, National Association of Evangelicals executive director, reports a 58 percent increase in membership over the past ten years, the largest increase since the association's early years, at the association's 48th annual convention March 6–8 in Phoenix, AZ.

At the convention, NAE welcomes the Reformed Episcopal Church (100 churches with 6,500 people) and the Congregational Holiness Church (175 churches with 7,500 people) as its newest members. The additions bring NAE membership to 44 denominations and three denominational subunits representing a total 4.1 million communicants.

Melvin estimates that 30 million evangelicals have yet to be consolidated into an effective, national voice for biblical faith, and calls for NAE to reach out to more evangelical groups, including mainline evangelicals, black denominations, Southern Baptists, the Lutheran Church-Missouri Synod and fundamentalist churches.

"Without these important sectors of the Protestant community, NAE cannot move into the leadership vacuum that exists," says Melvin.

Spiritual life, top interest of church members—The primary interest of adults of most denominations seems to center on the spiritual life and on learning more about the Bible, reveals a three-and-a-half year research project conducted by the Search Institute of Minneapolis.

The study surveyed beliefs, attitudes, perspectives and behaviors of more than 11,000 members in 563 congregations in six denominations. Results show many of them have an undeveloped Christian faith and that the quality of Christian education is poor.

"High on most adult lists is developing interpersonal relationship skills—learning how to be a good spouse or parent, and improving proficiency at showing love and concern. For some, making friends at church comes high on the list.

"At the bottom of the list are study and action related to improving the lot of the poor and the disenfranchised. Direct help to those who are poor comes ahead, however, of socialpolitical activism designed to give a real chance, rather than temporary assistance, to the disenfranchised of the community," says Dr. Peter L. Benson, president of Search Institute and project director.

The DuPage Declaration—Evangelical leaders in mainline denominations issue *The DuPage Declaration: A Call to Biblical Fidelity* March 20 warning that their churches are drifting from the evangelical faith and calling for a genuine revival rooted in the Word of God.

The 21 signers (including members of Presbyterian, Episcopal, Methodist, United Church of Christ, Disciples of Christ, Lutheran and Catholic bodies) say their declaration is not intended to be a full confession of faith but summarizes through eight affirmations and denials a common position on critical theological and ethical standards currently under challenge by liberals in their denominations.

The document was drafted by United Church of Christ theologian Donald G. Bloesch, who teaches at Dubuque Seminary in IA, and adopted during a two-day consultation held at Wheaton, IL.

Pat Robertson organizes new political group—The Christian Coalition, a new political group, will focus on combating anti-Christian bias through the political system, focusing on the state and local levels.

The coalition, organized by former presidential candidate Pat Robertson, will be based in Virginia Beach, VA, and will recruit conservative Catholics and evangelical Christians with a three-pronged approach: to educate them as citizens, to make them citizen activists and lobbyists, and to groom them to be political candidates.

"We believe the Christian community in many ways missed the boat in the 1980s by focusing almost entirely on the White House and Congress when most of the issues that concern conservative Catholics and evangelicals are primarily determined in the city councils, school boards, and state legislatures," Ralph Reed, executive director of the Coalition, tells *Christianity Today*.

"We think the Lord is going to give us this nation back one precinct at a time, one neighborhood at a time, and one state at a time," says Reed.

"The time has come for us to take our eyes off the White House and focus on the grassroots," writes Billy McCormack, director of the Louisiana state chapter, in the organization's first newsletter.

World Council of Churches meets in Seoul—Evangelicals who attend WCC convocation on Justice, Peace, and the Integrity of Creation in Seoul, South Korea, March 5–13 come away believing there is no need to revise their perception of the WCC: that it is ideologically biased against the West, that it is hesitant to affirm the uniqueness of Jesus Christ, and that it emphasizes justice and social action at the expense of personal holiness and evangelism.

WCC general secretary, Emilio Castro, says that participants "reached a common understanding that without justice there is no ecological solution to the world's problems, and without peace there is little hope for justice or the environment."

U.S. theologian Ron Sider, an observer appointed by the World Evangelical Fellowship, is given full voting rights and is moderator of a drafting committee. Sider considers the theology articulated in Seoul "woefully inadequate" and "occasionally wrong." He cites a "pervasive unwillingness to place Jesus Christ, true God and true man, at the center of the Christian struggle for *shalom*," and he observes that participants "look for unity less in Jesus Christ than in the common struggle against oppression." Sider adds there was "almost no interest in discussing the role of personal sin and conversion."

Despite his negative critique of the Seoul assembly, Sider credits the WCC for what he believes is its genuine welcoming of evangelical participation. He believes that without such participation—and a more biblically solid theology that evangelicals could help develop—the WCC is destined for marginalization and irrelevance.

Average pastor salary is $56,695—The average 1989 salary of pastors of medium-size and large churches, according to a random

THE YEAR IN REVIEW: JULY 1, 1989 TO JUNE 30, 1990 cont.

survey by the Ft. Worth-based National Association of Church Business Administration, is $56,695. Figures for the average compensation package includes base salary, housing/utilities, retirement, and insurance, but not auto allowances or professional expenses. In the 700 churches with multiple staff that responded to the survey, clergy salaries range from $4,290 to $174,078.

Bowery Mission expands mission—The world-famous Bowery Mission in New York City opens a shelter for homeless women and children on March 15, branching out from its mission to men in the Bowery.

➤INTERNATIONAL

Billy Graham at Berlin's Brandenburg Gate—Standing at the Berlin Wall which divided East and West Germany for three decades, evangelist Billy Graham preaches to about 15,000 East and West Germans March 10. The event was the first ecumenical gathering uniting East and West Germany in more than 30 years.

Canadian church attendance dwindles—Canadian Protestant churches are rapidly losing membership as church attendance dwindles to 33 percent from an estimated 67 percent in 1946. Roman Catholics, which number perhaps half of the population, have an attendance of 43 percent, almost half of the 83 percent in 1946. Statistics suggest that 35 percent of the population now attend church, compared with close to 70 percent at the end of World War II. Projections are that weekly attendance figures will fall to 16 percent by 2025, according to *The Toronto Star*.

Vision 2000 leaders predict even lower numbers. In the 19 to 24 age group only 16 percent of Canadians attend church, leading to projections that if current trends continue, 95 percent of the country will be unchurched by the year 2000.

60 denominations and agencies launch Vision 2000 Canada—720 leaders meet in Ottawa, ON, March 16–20 to launch Vision 2000 Canada, a nationwide decade of evangelism which will involve Canadian churches in unprecedented evangelistic outreach. Participants map new strategies for evangelism in the changing Canadian society in an attempt to relate more effectively to the growing number of unchurched, secularized Canadians.

Romanians organize evangelical body—Delegates from five Protestant denominations and the evangelical wing of the dominant Romanian Orthodox Church form The Evangelical Alliance of Romania March 13.

Charter members are the Baptist Union, the (Plymouth) Brethren Assemblies, the Lutheran Evangelical Church, the Evangelical Church of Romania, the Pentecostal Church, and the Lord's Army. The six groups represent approximately 800,000 believers.

Concerns about regulation of religion remain. Instead of abolishing the Department of Cults, the National Salvation Front elevates it to ministry level. The Ministry is considering passage of a new religion law based on the pre-Communist 1928 law. The measure allows the Romanian Orthodox Church broad powers while severely restricting other denominations and religions.

Korean prisoner leads 200 to Christ—The former principal of a Korean Baptist church kindergarten, Ohm Hyun Suk, who took personal responsibility for an October 16 fire that killed six children and burned twenty-three others, leads more than 200 women to Christ during her three-month prison term.

Although she was not present at the time the fire broke out, Ohm turned herself in to authorities after she returned with her husband from a Christian retreat. It is customary in Korea for someone in a position of leadership to take blame for such a tragedy.

Prison officials say they are sorry to see her go because of the positive influence she had on the prisoners and the change in the prison atmosphere. In retrospect, Ohm says that some of her times in prison worshiping with murderers, thieves, and drug addicts who had found new life in Christ "was a little bit like heaven." Ohm says the experience changed her forever and that she wants to become South Korea's first woman chaplain to women prisoners.

Central America prime-time broadcast breaks records— "In the history of the church, I don't believe there has ever been a single day when two million people committed their lives to Jesus Christ," says Pat Robertson, Christian Broadcasting Network (CBN) founder, reporting the response to the third evening as more than 12.5 million view three prime-time CBN specials broadcast March 26–28 in Guatemala and El Salvador. The broadcasts drew 55 and 60 percent of the potential viewing audience in each country.

The local church, the Christian Broadcasting Network and Campus Crusade for Christ worked together in the evangelistic blitz in Guatemala, El Salvador and Nicaragua. The campaign featured the *Jesus* film, billboard and print advertisement, along with radio and television specials.

APRIL 1990

➤NATIONAL

Clorox boycott ends—Christian Leaders for Responsible Television (CLeaR-TV) ends its boycott of The Clorox Corporation eight months after identifying the company as one of two leading sponsors of prime-time sex, violence, and profanity on network television.

"Our intent has always been to support programs meeting standards we believe to be right. CLeaR-TV brought this inadequate implementation of our guidelines to our attention and helped us address the issue," says Clorox vice president David Goodman.

Don Wildmon, executive director of CLeaR-TV says there was a 32 percent drop in the amount of offensive television programs on network television between Spring and Fall 1989 monitoring periods. Network officials do not acknowledge that the CLeaR-TV boycott made a difference in their programming. But a top executive at NBC was quoted in the *Saturday Review* as saying: "We will always deny that we can be boycotted successfully . . . but if a boycott by a few million people were successful, it would shake up the programmers a lot. They'd be putting dresses on the girls in bikinis in a hurry."

The Mennen Company boycott continues.

Washington, DC politicans sponsor prayer vigil—Approximately 500 people attend an April 8 prayer vigil in response to a letter sent by the city's fire chief, police chief, and Department of Corrections director to churches, prayer groups, and media representatives asking people to gather "in the spirit of Christ" to ask for divine intervention. Bob Wilhite, director of the National Prayer Embassy in Washington, says "it was the first time DC leaders publicly acknowledged that we need God to intervene by calling a prayer meeting." Church-and-state separationists complain about the involvement of city officials in promoting the event.

Black church ministers to affluent whites—An all-black church in a low-income area of Oakland, CA, starts a church to reach affluent whites in Castro Valley. Knowing that Castro Valley residents were unlikely to attend his church, Pastor Jesse Davis Sr., of the 1,500-member Shiloh Baptist Church, started a home Bible study in Castro Valley last year and sent out 12,000 invitations to Castro Valley residents to the inaugural service of the new Canyons Community Church. The new church averages 80 at weekly services.

Christian music's growth potential—A study by the Barna Research Group finds that 2.5 million people are more likely to buy Christian music than Christian adult books. The study estimates that, given the right products and marketing, about 32 million adults will buy Christian music products during 1990, including a substantial number of non-Christians.

Clergy credibility wanes—The Princeton Religion Research Center reports that only

THE YEAR IN REVIEW: JULY 1, 1989 TO JUNE 30, 1990 cont.

55 percent of the public rates the clergy as having "very high" or "high" ethical standards as compared with 67 percent in 1985. In the last two years, the number of people willing to put clergy ethics in the top category of "very high" dropped from 22 percent to 12 percent . Yet clergy maintains their overall second-place ethical ranking compared to people in twelve other occupations. Pharmacists rank first (62 percent), physicians and dentists place third (52 percent), followed by college teachers (51 percent). At the bottom are ad practitioners (12 percent) and car salesmen (6 percent).

AIDS epidemic—With the spread of AIDS, concern for AIDS orphans is increasing. In New York City alone, if only 80 percent of the women already infected with AIDS die, they will leave behind more than 50,000 children. Many of these mothers are single parents. A deluge of children who will be put in orphanages because of the disease is expected.

Slightly more than 10 percent of churches in America have encountered somone with AIDS, according to a survey conducted by *Christianity Today*—a percentage that is likely to increase.

Says Jeff Collins, director of the Annapolis, MD, based AIDS ministry, Love and Action, "There isn't a church of any size in America that is going to be able to escape this problem. Our own sons and daughters are going to be coming down with AIDS. The church has got to behave as Jesus would behave in the midst of this epidemic. We need to minister to individuals who are bound by sin as Jesus would. We need to love them, whether they're gay or straight, and embrace them as Jesus would embrace them. We must let them know that God loves them very, very much."

Washington Pro-Life rally draws up to 350,000—In one of the largest rallies ever held in the nation's capital, up to 350,000 people participate in the Rally for Life '90 on April 28. The rally is the largest event in the history of the pro-life movement, exceeding by far the estimated 150,000 abortion-rights activists at the pro-choice Washington gathering last November.

While the park police estimates the crowd as low as 200,000, the National Right to Life Committee asserts that photos taken from the Washington Monument show the crowd to be in the 350,000 range.

Vice President Dan Quayle points out to the crowd that polls consistently show that most Americans object to lack of restrictions on abortion. "The great majority of Americans stand together against the terrible reality of unlimited abortion on demand," Quayle asserts.

➤INTERNATIONAL

East Germany elects church leader as prime minister—The future for East German Christians looks promising under the government of newly-elected Prime Minister of East Germany, Lothar De Maiziere.

De Maiziere was a key lay figure in the East German Protestant Church during the years that Communists controlled the country. DeMaiziere, 50, an attorney, was known for his defense of conscientious objectors and other dissidents.

Great Britain's "Spring Harvest"—65,000 people attend Britain's biggest spring event for Evangelicals during weeklong meetings in three locations between March 31 and April 26.

"Spring Harvest", the largest teaching event in Europe, has become an annual rallying point for many Protestants in a country where church membership has declined sharply in recent decades. One-third of the participants were Baptists, another third from the Church of England, and the rest from a variety of denominational backgrounds. 90,000 people are expected to attend the 1991 session.

Says Gordon Kuhrt, an Anglican archdeacon, "When I was ordained 23 years ago, only about 20 percent of those ordained by the Church of England were Evangelicals. Today it's around 50 percent."

Latin American Evangelicals sharpen focus—Evangelical leaders from more than 200 Protestant bodies, representing more than 20 million evangelical Christians in Latin America, meet April 23–27 in Acapulco. Latin America is experiencing a revival, according to Evangelist Luis Palau, who believes some Central American countries will be more than 50 percent Evangelical by the year 2000.

Cambodia legalizes Christianity —More than 700 Cambodian Protestants meet April 29 in Phnom Penh's government-owned Chenla Theater for the first officially-sanctioned public evangelistic crusade in more than 15 years of communist rule.

Protestant church groups are now able to meet freely for services in Phnom Penh, the capital. In January the Cambodian National Assembly issued a decree legalizing Christianity and acknowledging Christians' right to worship. However, churches are first required to submit lists of members. Less than one percent of Cambodians are Christians.

MAY 1990

➤NATIONAL

80 hours of Bible reading on U.S. Capitol steps—The entire Bible is read on the steps of the U.S. Capitol this month as part of the National Day of Prayer activities. More than 500 persons volunteer to read the Scriptures in 15-minute increments for a total of more than 80 hours. The reading begins at 5:30 A.M. on April 30 and concludes at 7:00 P.M. May 3.

One of the younger participants, Christopher Scott, 7, of Orlando, FL, recites from memory every verse in Ephesians.

The four-day event emphasizes President Bush's designation of 1990 as International Year of Bible Reading. Separately, a number of large prayer meetings convene on Capitol Hill and at other federal sites around Washington, including the Pentagon to commemorate the May 3 National Day of Prayer.

New Revised Standard Version appears in bookstores—The National Council of Churches releases the New Revised Standard Version (NRSV), the product of 17 years of work by an interfaith team of 30 Scripture experts.

The NRSV is both "the newest and the oldest" Bible because it uses the most ancient texts presently available, says biblical scholar Bruce Metzger, who headed the revision committee.

Bible influences top executives and educators—When the National College of Education, Evanston, IL, asks top executives of 1,000 major American companies and 12,000 U.S. university presidents what book affected their lives the most, 25 percent cite the Bible.

Charles Dicken's *Tale of Two Cities* was named by 4 percent, and the *Book of Mormon* by 2 percent. No other book was mentioned twice.

National Council of Churches restructures—In a three-day meeting in Pittsburg, PA, the NCC's Governing Board adopts a new constitution and amendments to the bylaws, elects new committees, and re-emerges on the final day as the General Board, NCC's new central policy-making body. Under restructure, four unit committees represent the NCC's operating entities: International Service and Witness, Prophetic Justice, Unity and Relationships, and Discipleship and Communication. A new Executive Coordinating Committee, representing members of the General Board and the four unit committees, will oversee day-to-day operations.

Seminary enrollment increases—The Association of Theological Schools reports U.S. seminary enrollment increases of 5.1 percent over the 1988–89 term. Numbers are based on reports from 203 accredited Protestant and Catholic seminaries with a total enrollment of 56,083 (including 3,814 blacks and 1,483 Hispanics—far too few to meet needs of the burgeoning Hispanic population, experts say). ATS officials say the increase may be attributed to an influx of "second career" students pursuing ordination after working in other fields and an increasing percentage of specialists preparing for non-pulpit ministries such as music, education, administration and counseling.

THE YEAR IN REVIEW: JULY 1, 1989 TO JUNE 30, 1990 cont.

Average age of today's seminarian: 31. The proportion of female students continues on the upswing; some analysts predict 25 percent of mainline Protestant pastors will be women by the end of the decade.

Priceless manuscript of the Four Gospels surfaces—Klaus C. Maurice, secretary general of West Germany's Cultural Foundation of the States, takes possession of a priceless manuscript of the Four Gospels dating from the 9th century, written in gold and encased in a jewel-encrusted gold and silver binding. An American soldier allegedly took it from a German mineshaft after World War II. Maurice agrees not to reveal the seller and to pay a $3 million finder's fee.

The Four Gospels were inscribed in gold in 840 A.D. by a ninth-century monk, probably for the imperial court. Later, the manuscript was given to the Quedlinburg cloister, a medieval castle town, where it remained for more than a thousand years. The town, which became part of East Germany after the war, will receive the gospels when Germany is reunited.

➤INTERNATIONAL

Nepal guarantees religious freedom—Speaking to more than 2,000 Christians meeting to celebrate the 30th anniversary of the Nepal Christian Fellowship May 7, leaders of Nepal's new interim government promise a new era of human rights and religious freedom in the new constitution which takes into account the religious sentiment of all citizens. Nepali Congress Party Leader Ganesh Man Singh commends the Christians for their contribution to the nation's history. Singh is known as the "father of democracy in Nepal". The government promises to release Christians in prison for their faith.

Until a change of government in April, Nepal was the only nation in the world with Hinduism as the state religion. Public demonstrations against the state brought about the change of government, although the country now faces political uncertainty as the new cabinet grapples with current problems, says Loknath Manaen, executive secretary of the Bible Society in Nepal.

Before 1950, no known Christians lived in Nepal, according to Nepalese Christian leaders.

Albania liberalizes religious activity—The Albania parliament adopts laws granting freedom of religious practice in the country on May 8. Albania, which twenty-three years ago stripped every building of religious symbols, has been the only country in the world to outlaw all faiths and declare itself officially atheistic.

Speculation is that Albania needs foreign assistance and wants a voice in the international community. Albania has requested a place in the Conference on Security and Cooperation in Europe. Albania has almost been an island unto itself since cutting off ties with Moscow in 1961 and China in 1976. Ties with the U.S. have been cut since 1946. Albania's borders were nearly completely closed to foreign travellers and Albanians wishing to leave. For decades there has been very little information about the Christian church in Albania.

More than 215,000 attend Luis Palau Romanian campaign—More than 215,000 attend Luis Palau's stadium rallies in three cities May 22–30. Altogether, more than 46,000 respond to Palau's invitation to commit their lives to Christ. The unexpected response forces counselors, trained to work one-on-one, to work with groups instead.

The results of the Romania campaign surpasses anything Palau has seen in more than twenty-three years of mass evangelistic campaigns in fifty-two countries, including Palau's historic campaign in five cities of the Soviet Union in September 1989.

In several messages, when the evangelist urges the country to include God in its new constitution, perhaps with a phrase such as "one nation under God," the crowds roar their approval with thunderous applause.

Bangladesh lifts Bible ban—The government of Bangladesh lifts a two-month ban on importation and possession of a Bengali version of the New Testament, the *Injil Sharif*. Officials had said the translation contains language offensive to the country's Muslim majority.

The country elects Michael Sushil Adhikari, a Baptist, as Prime Minister. Nearly 90 percent of Bangladesh's 110 million people are Muslim; most others are Hindu. Only 0.3 percent are Christian.

Suicide rate high in West Germany—One person commits suicide every half hour in West Germany. Every year approximately 11,600 people take their own lives, far more than the 8,500 killed in car accidents. West Berlin has one of the highest suicide rates in the world.

JUNE 1990

➤NATIONAL

SBC votes conservative for 12th straight year—Southern Baptist Convention delegates elect Rev. Morris Chapman, pastor of First Baptist Church, Wichita Falls, TX, president by a vote of 58–42 percent. The conservative victory marks the 12th year in a row of conservative control within the nation's largest (14.9 million members) Protestant denomination.

The election gives conservatives power to fill vacancies on the boards of twenty-four church agencies and six seminaries, and leaves moderates divided over whether to continue to fight for control or start funding alternative seminaries.

Tension continues between the conservatives, who believe in the in the inerrancy and infallibility of the Bible and practice strictly literal interpretation of the Bible, and moderates, who take a more liberal approach to Scripture.

"Whether or not the issue is settled in its most practical form is largely up to those who have been voting otherwise, who have insisted that we are not a group who have believed in the inerrancy and infallibility of the Bible," says Chapman. He does not believe the split in the denomination is as great as the vote indicates and maintains that at least 90 percent of Southern Baptists share his view of Scripture.

New program encourages ELCA congregations to win five converts per year for the next 20 years—Great Commission Network, a new conservative organization in the Evangelical Lutheran Church in America, adopts and distributes a "Statement of Vision" at St. Olaf College, Northfield, MN, June 4–6, and challenges each congregation to win five converts per year for the next 20 years to boost church membership by one million before 2010.

Organizers of the new group are pastors, theologians, seminarians and lay persons who are dissatisfied with liberal leanings in the 5.3 million-member denomination—especially on matters relating to sexuality, evangelism and use of gender-free language in Bible translations.

Presbyterian Church (USA) moves toward theological center—Delegates to the 202nd General Assembly of the Presbyterian Church (USA) affirm a number of values in theology and social justice and place new emphasis on contemporary concerns.

"Extremes on the left and right have been moving toward the theological center since the 1970s," Dr. John Mulder, president of Louisville Presbyterian Theological Seminary, said of the 2.9 million-member denomination. Says the Rev. Richard Dolan, Louisville, KY, "We're becoming much more of a middle-of-the-road church."

Symbolic of an emerging consensus amid diversity is the overwhelming vote for a proposed "Brief Statement of Faith," the first such statement since the 1983 merger of denominations that broke during the Civil War. The statement upholds traditional beliefs but also speaks of racial and sexual equality and uses some female imagery for God.

Key Supreme Court rulings—A review of top cases from the 1989–1990 Supreme Court sessions reflects another year of Court decisions of interest to the Christian community.

- *Abortion*: States can further restrict the rights of minors seeking abortions. The Court says states may require unwed girls under age eighteen to notify both

THE YEAR IN REVIEW: JULY 1, 1989 TO JUNE 30, 1990 cont.

parents before obtaining an abortion, but only if the state also provides a chance to "bypass" parental notification by getting a judge's approval.

- *Right to Die*: People who state their wish to end medical treatment while still competent have a constitutionally protected "right to die." The Court says states may block removal of life-sustaining equipment when the patient's treatment preferences haven't been stated clearly in advance.
- *Drunken Driving*: The Court endorses sobriety checkpoints and gives police power to record, videotape and use at trial police questioning of drunken driving suspects.
- *Church-State Relations*: States are justified in banning the religious use of the illegal drug peyote. Church advocates fear the ruling gives states greater freedom to regulate a range of religious practices.
- *Kiddie Porn*: States can prohibit the ownership of child pornography materials. States are able to ban production and distribution of the material, but the new ruling gives the green light to cracking down on ownership—enhancing prosecutor's tools in pornography cases.
- *Bible Clubs*: Public high schools with extracurricular programs must provide similar access to religious and political groups. Opponents to a 1984 federal law guaranteeing such access say it amounts to government endorsement of religion.
- *Capital Punishment*: Avenues of appeals for death row inmates narrow. The court limits inmates, whose cases already lost on appeal, from employing new court rules. Chief Justice William Rehnquist has campaigned for federal legislation to shorten the appeals process in death row cases.

Christian doctors approve ***in vitro*** **fertilization**—The Christian Medical and Dental Society (CMDS) gives its approval to *in vitro* fertilization and a number of other new reproductive technologies.

According to a report in *Christianity Today*, the group approves of such fertility enhancements in cases where the husband and wife provide the sperm and egg. The group says it "cannot speak with certainty" about artificial conception involving sperm or egg from a donor.

In its statement, the 7,000-member group opposes selective abortion to reduce the number of embryos a woman carries after having several fertilized eggs placed in her uterus. It also expresses displeasure with the discarding of embryos, experiments with embryos, and hiring surrogate mothers.

Evangelicals still shy about political involvement—Evangelical Christians make up one of the largest voting blocs in the U.S., but have less influence than smaller, more vocal groups, says Doug Wead, senior White House staff member.

Wead says that after a year in the White House, he is convinced "much of our ineffectiveness is of our own making." Wead believes many evangelicals are beginning to realize the necessity of becoming involved in the political system but that Christians feel a "bigoted backlash for speaking up."

"Much like the blacks of the 1960s, we are finding we must build from scratch to find a voice and place in government," Wead says. Wead calls government and media worthy mission fields where Christians can help bring understanding of the evangelical viewpoint.

➤INTERNATIONAL

Nepal frees religious prisoners, dismisses current cases—On June 15 Nepal's King Birendra grants amnesty to all religious prisoners and frees Christian leader Charles Mendies and 28 other believers, dismissing cases against approximately 200 others awaiting trial for religious activities.

Mendies is met at the prison gate by more than 300 fellow Christians who lead a victory parade through the streets of Kathmandu, waving a huge banner inscribed "Freedom of Religion in Nepal," singing Christian songs, and chanting "Jesus is Lord."

"This is a wonderful day! But we still have much work to do. We must make sure that Nepal's new constitution guarantees religious liberty for all the people, and specific laws must be changed to ensure that never again will Christians have to suffer arrest, imprisonment, and torture for practicing their faith," says Mendies.

Basic Youth Seminars expand to New Zealand—Bill Gothard, founder of the Institute of Basic Youth Conflicts, conducts the first overseas seminar in New Zealand after 25 years of continuous seminars in the U.S. The official roster of special events for the celebration of New Zealand's 150th year as a nation lists the seminar event.

Islam beats Christianity in the world's cities—Evangelistic efforts of Muslims are more effective on the cities of the world than evangelical Christianity is, according to Robert Douglas, director of the Zwemer Institute of Muslim Studies, a U.S. based evangelical organization.

"Islam always has been able to survive—and thrive—in the cities, whereas Christianity in the West tends to withdraw from the cities," says Douglas. Evangelicals may be frightened away from cities because of the comforts suburbs offer, and because cities are "gigantic, complex, and often scary places," adds Douglas. However he observes that cities are where most of the world's populations live, and disinterest in cities "is maybe just shorthand for saying we don't care about people."

Source: Various news sources with special appreciation to *Christianity Today* and *Church Around the World.*

THE 1990s: WHAT TO EXPECT

No one knows for certain how the future will unfurl. But history and trends give us clues. Here are some things likely to surface within the church and society during the next decade.

Life-style

- Rapid changes; an era of flexibility
- Time will be most valued resource; more important than money or career
- Contradiction of behavior and values
- Speed addiction; pace of life will not slow down
- 24-hour consumer services; rush deliveries, while-you-wait, on-site services reflecting "I want it now" demand; personalized marketing appeals
- "Sunday" distinctives will fade
- More frequent, shorter vacations
- Air travel will double
- Cable TV primary source for entertainment; 60 percent of households will have cable by 1993; 100 percent by 2000
- VCRs in virtually every home.

Arts

- Shift from sports to arts as a leisure activity
- Churches will increasingly incorporate drama and other art forms into worship styles
- Resurgence of classical music to replace gradual decline of rock
- Compilation music recordings; two or more artists

Family

- Family concerns will become increasingly crucial
- Divorce, though declining due to fewer and delayed marriage commitments, will be more acceptable
- Stepfamilies will outnumber traditional families; continuing increase in single parent homes
- Increasing relocation of families; fewer roots, more insecurities

THE 1990s: WHAT TO EXPECT cont.

- Increase in teenage suicides along with changing family structures; is now third leading cause of death among teens
- Health care, a top family concern
- Home environment will be zealously protected
- Television/video will play a central role in family activities

Education

- Shortage of qualified teachers
- Christian day schools will prosper as parents demand moral values and public schools struggle to incorporate values and ethics into curriculum
- Home school growth hazy; some predict an estimated two to three million home-schoolers by 2000
- Video education: elementary, college, and graduate levels
- Shift to "hands on" training rather than academics
- Decrease in college enrollments
- High educational costs will force Christian colleges to close or merge; more co-op programs among colleges
- More older students and "second careerists" will enroll in graduate schools and seminaries
- Theological education by extension; more informal, convenient training programs, weekend college and seminary classes
- More demand for geriatrics, computer literacy, counseling, information management, and minorities programs
- More English-language schools internationally

Career

- Corporations increasingly large or small squeezing out mid-sized companies
- Entrepreneurial spirit will live on
- Home-based employment
- Flexible work hours; job-sharing
- Employee child care services
- Women and minorities will outpace traditional white male leadership
- More frequent career changes
- Women will break through to top executive status
- Authoritative, militant style will give way to inspiration/teacher/coach/facilitator style
- Earlier retirement

Technology

- Voice-recognition computers; PCs will be smaller and as powerful as 1989's supercomputers
- Home computer shopping
- "Carry with" pocket-sized, cellular telephones
- Built-in car phones
- Electronic mail
- "Smart cars" able to adjust speed limits, calculate locations
- "Smart houses" programmed to perform household functions: turn on bath water, open garage doors, instant alert to fire/police stations, remote control instructions to begin cooking dinner

Church Life

- Declining membership in mainline churches; increases among Evangelicals and Fundamentalists

- More cooperation between Evangelicals and Pentecostals; denominational distinctives will fade
- Baby boomers will return to church with their children
- Growth of megachurches; congregations averaging 500 or more will increase by 30 percent
- Telemarketing evangelism outreach
- Shift away from a "home church" toward attending two or more churches
- Sunday schools and youth activities forced to compete with high-quality, hi-tech entertainment
- Services-oriented outreach: counseling, bookstores, travel groups, financial planning, day care, retirement centers
- Increasing need for divorce recovery, single-parent, blended-family programs
- Less lay involvement; more team and professional leadership
- Worship styles will change; look for more variety, less structure
- Faster-pace church services
- More reflective theology; rejection of pat answers
- Increase in women leadership, ordinations; diffusion of traditional roles
- Shorter tenure for pastors, burnout more common

Evangelism

- Televangelism decline
- Search for spiritual values will intensify
- More personalized, life-style evangelism
- Crusade evangelism will become more upbeat, entertaining, fast-moving; less sermonizing, more focus on needs of specific age groups, as well as social, economic, and family concerns
- More use of telemarketing techniques
- AD 2000 focus will provide impetus for a variety of evangelistic activities

Media

- More newsletters; fewer magazines
- Two, maybe three, high-volume general Christian magazines; most successful magazines will be more specialized, focused
- "Quick reading" print products
- Music products will flourish; books decline
- High definition television; interactive TV programs, more channels on cable systems

Missions

- Two-thirds World countries will take lead in number of missionaries, increasing from 30,000 in 1988 to 160,0000 in 2000
- Growth of Christianity strongest in Latin America, China, Africa, Europe
- Increase in number of charismatic mission groups
- Increase among Americans in short-term missionary commitments, tentmakers and professionals, rather than career commitment
- Focus on urban centers; cities will grow to unprecedented populations in developing countries
- AD 2000 programs will become increasingly aggressive
- Unified European market, free trade will simplify evangelism outreach; English will move toward the universal language

Social/Political

- Issues of the decade will be environment, economy, drugs, AIDS, medical costs, family, education, population control, poverty

THE 1990s: WHAT TO EXPECT cont.

- Churches will become more involved in social issues; strengthening of New Evangelicalism stance
- AIDS epidemic; cases will increase from 700,000 to 6 million people worldwide by 2000. Total number infected may approach 20 million; greatest increase among newborns
- Soaring drug and alcohol abuse
- Ethics in surrogacy, biotechnology, and biomedical increasingly complex
- Continuing pressure to establish a "wall of separation." Madalyn Murray O'Hair's American Atheists group's agenda includes having "In God We Trust" stricken from currency, nativity scenes banished from all government property, religious symbols excised from city and state seals, and religious groups' tax-exempt status removed.

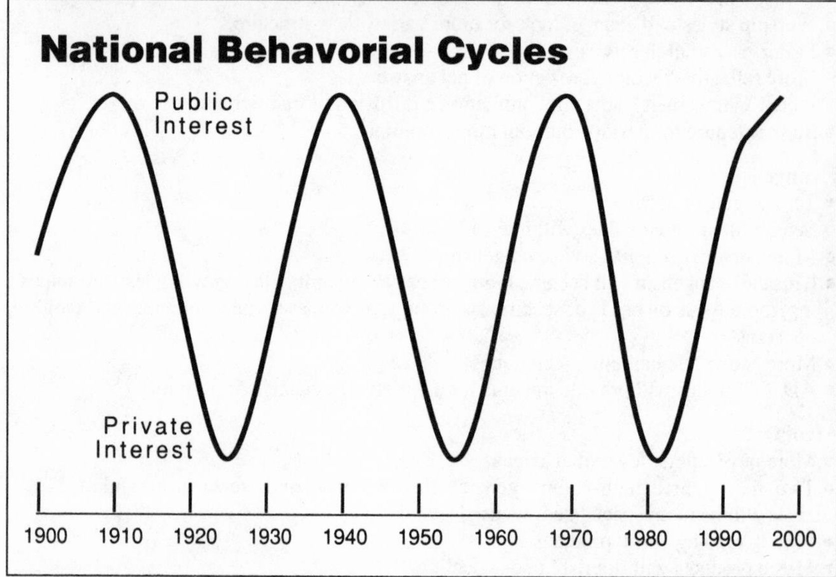

Source: *America 2000* by George Barna and adapted from *Cycles of American History*, by Arthur Schlesinger, Jr., Houghton Mifflin Company, Boston, 1986.

NEWS HIGHLIGHTS OF THE 1980s

1980 Popular speaker **Bill Gothard** steps down as president of the successful **Institute in Basic Youth Conflicts,** largely as a result of the way he handled charges of sexual immorality involving his brother, Steve, a ministry executive. **Seventh-day Adventists** strip Adventist theologian Desmond Ford of his credentials for debunking church doctrine.

1981 After twenty-two years of forced inactivity, China grants **Three-Self Patriotic Movement** permission to hold a major convention, opening the door to greater religious freedom. Colombian guerrillas kill missionary **Chet Bitterman,** and **Sandra Day O'Connor** becomes the first female Supreme Court justice, to the dismay of most Evangelicals, who question her position on abortion.

1982 A federal judge in Little Rock, Arkansas, rules that **creationism** is religious in nature, and thus strikes down a state law mandating that creation be given equal time with evolution in public school classrooms. **Billy Graham** preaches for the first time in the Soviet Union and is criticized for allegedly overlooking religious persecution.

1983 Exiled Philippine leader **Benigno Aquino** is shot and killed in Manila. He had returned to the country because of his Christian faith, according to some who knew him. Billy Graham's **Amsterdam '83** gathers 4,000 itinerant evangelists from around the world for instruction and inspiration.

1984 Aggressive **political activism** is adopted by many conservative evangelicals, who play a major role in the re-election of Ronald Reagan. After fierce debate, Congress rejects the School Prayer Amendment, but as a compromise passes the **Equal Access Act,** allowing voluntary student religious groups to meet at school.

1985 Tensions in the Southern Baptist Convention headline the SBC's annual meeting in Dallas, at which conservative **Charles Stanley** is re-elected president and a peace committee is formed to study the SBC turmoil. Church groups and Christian relief agencies put millions of dollars into projects to ease the **African famine.**

1986 Pat Robertson all but formally announces his bid for the presidency. The attorney general announces a major effort to crack down on illegal **pornography.** Pro-life groups approve the appointment of **Antonin Scalia** to the Supreme Court, and the Dutch Reformed Church in South Africa denounces **apartheid** as unjust.

1987 Televangelists' troubles begin when **Oral Roberts** announces in January that God would call him home if he does not raise $8 million for medical mission scholarships. **Jim Bakker** resigns from PTL amid revelations of sexual impropriety, and **Robertson** makes his presidential candidacy official.

1988 Abortion opponents consider the election of **George Bush** an important victory. Amid hope brought by **glasnost** comes the celebration of 1,000 years of Christianity in the Soviet Union. **Jimmy Swaggart** is defrocked amid revelations of sexual scandal. Christians take to the streets as part of the **rescue movement** and to protest the movie *The Last Tempation of Christ*.

1989 The **Berlin wall** crumbles as political reform sweeps Eastern Europe. The **abortion** battle heats up throughout the country as the Supreme Court's decision in *Webster v. Missouri* gives states freedom to set their own agenda. Federal Judge Robert Potter sentences **Jim Bakker** to a forty-five-year prison term for fraud.

Source: December 15, 1989, issue of *Christianity Today* Magazine. Used by permission.

WHAT PEOPLE ARE SAYING: JULY 1, 1989 TO JUNE 30, 1990

"We have never seen a year like 1989. Only the Reformation is remotely comparable to today's gale-force intellectual winds and loud crackling of institutional foundations. No year, even in the 16th century, ever swept so many people or such complex societies into a vortex of change. Nineteen eighty-nine has been the most startling, interesting, promising and consequential year, *ever*." **George F. Will** in *Newsweek*.

"Lord, please don't tease me; let me be a writer." **Frank Peretti,** author of *This Present Darkness* and *Piercing the Darkness,* with total sales of 2,159,021 as of June 1990.

"Bakker started out loving people and using things, but then he started loving things and using people." **Jerry Miller,** prosecutor at Jim Bakker's fraud trial.

"Because of Christ, this wheelchair has become the prison that has set me free." **Joni Eareckson Tada,** speaking at Billy Graham's Budapest crusade.

WHAT PEOPLE ARE SAYING: JULY 1, 1989 TO JUNE 30, 1990 cont.

"As long as God gives me breath, I expect to preach the Gospel." **Billy Graham,** November 7th, as he celebrates his 71st birthday.

"Long enough for you not to wait." **PTL aides James and David Taggart** to the cabbie who drove them to prison when asked how long they were going to be in for.

"Ones that deal with religion, especially those about downfallen church people like the Bakker and Swaggart matters. I am a deeply religious person myself, and I'm very bothered by anything that hurts people's conception of God. I have to report them, naturally, but it always brings me pain." **Dan Rather,** CBS news anchor, responding to Larry King asking him what stories were toughest for him to report.

"Most Alzheimer's caretakers will agree that a lot of people say they'll pray for you, but very few say they'll stay for you. My heart has been broken every day for ten years." **Delbert Bixler,** Sarasota, FL, who daily cares for his wife, diagnosed as having Alzheimer's Disease.

"Adoption is an alternative solution to some of the nation's most pressing family issues: teenage pregnancy, foster care, infertility, and welfare dependency." **Attorney General Richard Thornburgh.**

"When Christians meet, as Christians, to take counsel together, their purpose is not—or should not be—to ascertain what is the mind of the majority but what is the mind of the Holy Spirit—something which may be quite different." **England's Prime Minister Margaret Thatcher.**

"Andrew, if only the Christians would live according to their book [Bible], and the Muslims would live according to their book [Koran], we would not have all these problems." **Muslim head of the Hisbollah** to Brother Andrew, founder of Open Doors With Brother Andrew, Inc.

"By blood and origin, I am all Albanian. My citizenship is Indian. I am a Catholic nun. As to my calling, I belong to the whole world. As to my heart, I belong entirely to Jesus." **Mother Teresa,** quoted by Ruth A. Tucker in *Guardians of the Great Commission.*

"Nothing in Scriptural revelation precludes an evangelical and a secular humanist from standing together against race discrimination." **Carl F. H. Henry** in *Christianity Today.*

"We've been shaken, we've been jolted, but we're saying yes to life. And it's important for us to be shaken—rich, poor, and middle class. This quake shook us all, and now we have a common problem and need common solutions." **Rev. Cecil Williams,** pastor of Glide Memorial United Methodist Church, San Francisco, after the October 17 earthquake.

"If drug use isn't a sin, I don't know what it is. We've seen treatment programs run by churches that are every bit as effective as very expensive medical programs . . . If it's a spiritual problem, then the recovery should take place as much in churches as in hospitals." **William Bennett,** drug czar.

"There's no reason why gospel and contemporary Christian [music] should not achieve gold and platinum or even double plantinum status. We intend to make lyrics that say 'come pray with me' as pervasive in the popular music market in the 90s as those that say 'come lay with me' have been in the 80s." **Al Bell,** music pioneer and veteran record executive.

"The hated wall has lost its power." **Rev. William Downey,** hospital chaplain for the German Evangelical Church.

"About six years went by in six months." **Rev. Arthur Simon,** president of Bread for the World, commenting on changes in the Soviet Union and Eastern Europe.

"It is the task of the church to do this." **Gottfried Forck,** East Berlin's Protestant Bishop, commenting on prayer services for peace and reform in East Berlin and Leipzig which many observers feel have been catalysts for the mass demonstrations in East Germany and led to changes in the nation's government as well as opening of the Berlin Wall.

"I do not believe in abortion. But I will prefer to counsel a woman who has had a legal abortion rather than to bury one who has had an illegal one. I have done both." **Rev. Albert Demos,** dean of the Greek Orthodox Cathedral of New England.

"It's all because those soldiers on June 4th used real bullets to shoot the people . . . if they had used rubber bullets there would be no Christian revival among the students today." **A student at China's premier Beida University,** commenting on the turning of thousands of Chinese intellectuals to the Christian faith.

"Christianity is a religion for losers. The Ten Commandments are obsolete." **Ted Turner,** owner of Turner Network Television, America's fastest growing cable network with a 97% growth in 1988 and 1989.

"I would like to officially apologize to all Christians for saying that . . . . It was an uncalled-for statement." **Ted Turner's apology** on June 12, 1990, on a CNN program.

"I began to lose my faith and the more I lost it, the better I felt." **Ted Turner,** upon accepting "Humanist of the Year" citation from the American Humanist Association, a group that rejects traditional ideas of God and religion. Turner had just told the group that he was raised in a Christian home, and sent to a private Christian school, but turned away Christianity after prayers for his sister's health went unanswered.

"We need spiritual values, we need a revolution of the mind. This is the only way toward a new culture and new politics that can meet the challenge of our time.

"We have changed our attitude toward some matters—such as religion—which we used to treat in a simplistic manner . . . Now we not only proceed from the assumption that no one should interfere in matters of the individual's conscience; we also say that the moral values religion generated and embodied for centuries can help in the work of renewal in our country, too." **Mikhail Gorbachev** during his December 1989 meeting with Pope John Paul II in Rome.

"There is no connection between specific sin and the judgment of God, in the sense of retributive justice. . . . Sickness is often the proof of God's special favor." **Former U.S. Surgeon General C. Everett Koop.**

"If we want it, the love, the longing for understanding, spiritual and intellectual strength can permanently radiate outwards from our country. This is what we can offer as our individual contribution to world politics. . . .

"We are a small country but despite that we used to be the spiritual crossroads of Europe. Why should we not become this crossroads again? Would this not be another contribution to repay others for the assistance we shall need from them?" **Vaclav Havel,** president of Czechoslovakia, during his New Year's Day speech to his country.

"I will never turn away anyone who comes to me." **Rev. Uwe Holmer,** president of the East German Evangelist's Conference, replying to angry citizens protesting his hospitality to deposed East German leader Erich Honecker and his wife, Margot. The Holmers were not exempt from persecution under the Honecker regime; restrictions included denying the ten Holmer children a secondary or university education.

"We are arriving with our agenda of how to do things, forcing it upon them, and this is wrong." **Rev. Peter Dyneka,** president of the Slavic Gospel Association, warning U.S. Christians not to force their agenda on Soviets.

"I am now beyond eighty years of age. I would like to be called senior pastor." **Dr. W.A. Criswell,** author and pastor of First Baptist Church of Dallas, to his church's search committee a year after they started looking for a co-pastor.

"Homosexuality should not be singled out as a sin greater than all others. God calls us to love people, regardless of their lifestyle. God doesn't write these people off. Neither should we." **Stephen Hayner,** president of Inter-Varsity Christian Fellowship, on his concern about a strong homophobic element in the church that would exclude homosexuals from the same grace and love extended to other sinners.

"Power doesn't really bring the fulfillment that many think it does. . . . Inner security and true, real fulfillment comes by faith.

WHAT PEOPLE ARE SAYING: JULY 1, 1989 TO JUNE 30, 1990 cont.

It doesn't come by wielding power in a town where power is king. Fulfillment comes only by developing a personal relationship with God, which for me is personified by Christ." **James A. Baker III,** Secretary of State, at the National Prayer Breakfast.

"The issue for me is not whether women should be in ministry. . . . The issue is whether those in ministry, women or men, have been called by God to be there." **Mrs. Anne Graham Lotz,** speaking at Southeastern Baptist Theological Seminary in Wake Forest, NC.

"The major force in the growth of the church is still going to be the individual Christian sharing his or her faith with somebody else." **Wade Coggins,** retired executive director of Evangelical Foreign Missions Association.

"A credible message needs a credible messenger because charisma without character is catastrophe." **Dr. Peter Kuzmic,** Pentecostal theologian from Yugoslavia.

"God has ordained three institutions for the ordering of society: the family for the propagation of life, the state for the preservation of life, and the church for the proclamation of the gospel. These are not just voluntary associations that people can join or not as they see fit; they are organic sources of authority for restraining evil and humanizing society." **Charles Colson** in *Against the Night: Living in the New Dark Ages,* published by Servant Books.

"You have my blessing. It's about time somebody got going, so get on with it." **Billy Graham's** response to Luis Palau's vision to hold intensive citywide crusades in the US during the next decade.

"Why are people who identify God . . . as responsible for changing world events not taken seriously by the media?" **Barbara Reynolds,** Inquiry editor for *USA Today*.

"The biggest disease today is not leprosy or tuberculosis, but rather the feeling of being unwanted, uncared for and deserted by everybody. The greatest evil is the lack of love and charity." **Mother Teresa**

"Only 5 percent of the [drug and alcohol] addicts in America live on skid row. Many attend our churches regularly. Addicts are good actors and actresses, and our congregations are filled with actors and actresses." **Rev. Nelson Price,** pastor of Roswell Street Baptist Church, Marietta, GA, speaking at a seminar sponsored by the Southern Baptist Christian Life Commission in Birmingham, AL.

"Slavery was once legal in this nation, and critics now ask, 'Where was the church?' Hitler exterminated Jews in Germany, and critics ask, 'Where was the church?' I believe this society will one day look back at the horror of abortion, and critics will ask, 'Where was the church?'" **Pastor Joel Reiter,** Princeton, MN, Baptist Fellowship in *The Standard*.

"As Pascal said in the 16th century, the heart abhors a vacuum, and for want of a good object upon which to focus attention, it will certainly focus on the bad. There is a vacuum right now in the Soviet Union. It behooves us to move quickly to respond with appropriate assistance because others will move into the vacuum quickly." **Kent Hill,** director of the Institute on Religion and Democracy in Washington, DC, in *Christianity Today,* responding to the fear of church leaders—the onslaught of cults, Eastern mysticism, pornography, and drugs.

"Market-driven churches? Whatever happened to gospel-driven churches?" **Walter B. Shurden,** Macon, GA, in *Christianity Today.*

"We are not evangelicals, or fundamentalists, or charismatics, or ecumenists, or catholics, or protestants; we are children of God." **Stephen D. Watkins,** Providence, RI, in *Christianity Today*.

"It was not a revolution; it was a supernatural intervention of God on the Romanian people's behalf." **Nicolae Gheorghita,** Baptist pastor in Oradea, one of Romania's largest congregations, responding to the political changes in his country.

"The experiment we call atheism was worth it because it proved to this generation once and for all that the human soul clamors for God." **Luis Palau,** evangelist, at a Romanian press conference.

"As long as you keep the praise coming up, I'll keep the peace coming down." God's reassurance to **Catherine J. Jackson,** Winston-Salem, NC, as her husband lay dying in Duke Hospital.

"Jesus was at much greater risk in ministering to the lepers of his day than a person would be in ministering to an AIDS sufferer today." **W. Shepherd Smith, Jr.,** president of Americans for a Sound Aids Policy, Washington, DC.

"For centuries now, we have sent out missionaries. Should we not consider bringing missionaries from the Two-thirds World to the UK to help us? We need help from our Christian brothers and sisters overseas who understand the culture." **Bill Houston,** lecturer at All Nations Christian College addressing the Interaction Annual Conference in High Wycombe, England May 11–13, on the need to reach the Muslims, Hindus, and Buddhists living in the UK.

"That's what we need in the Soviet Union. I'd like to see your ministry active in our prisons." **Vadim Bakatin,** chief overseer of the Soviet prison system to Chuck Colson, chairman of Prison Fellowship.

"Norman Rockwell and The Brady Bunch Don't Live Here Anymore." Title of **article** in the June 1990 issue of *The Standard* on the changing face of the traditional American family.

"In a Calcutta home for the mentally ill, some men asked us to clip their fingernails. As I held one man's hand I realized his nails were already clipped. In that moment I knew I was not clipping fingernails. I was offering the gentle comfort of a human touch." **Clif Cartland** in the June–July, 1990 issue of *World Vision,* writing about his trip to Calcutta with Ministry of Money, a project of the Church of the Saviour, Washington, DC, which takes affluent North Americans to visit some of the poorest people in the world.

AWARDS: JULY 1, 1989 TO JUNE 30, 1990

1989 Horatio Alger Award—To **Robert Schuller,** founder and pastor at the Crystal Cathedral. Sponsored by the Horatio Alger Association, it is given to men and women who, through hard work and integrity, have overcome personal hardship and have achieved remarkable success in their field. In their triumph over adversity, winners of the Award exemplify the heroes of nineteenth century author Horatio Alger and are chosen to serve as role models to the nation's young people. Only two other living ministers have received this award: Norman Vincent Peale and Billy Graham.

Priscilla and Aquila Award—To **David Clowney,** assistant professor of philosophy at Glassboro State College in New Jersey. Clowney receives the first Priscilla and Aquila award from Christians for Biblical Equality for his resignation as assistant professor of Apologetics at Westminster Theological Seminary because he could no longer subscribe to the Westminster position that prohibits women from being ordained. The award was created for those who have "risked their necks" (Romans 16:3) for the sake of biblical feminism.

Prison Fellowship National Volunteer of the Year Award—To **Polly Scoutaris** of Albuquerque, NM, for more than twelve years of service and for continuing to work as a Prison

Fellowship volunteer despite assault and burglary by one of the men she and her husband had befriended.

The William Booth Award—To **Billy Graham** on October 12 in recognition for his forty years of God-honoring international ministry. The William Booth Award is the Salvation Army's most prestigious citation for service to God and others.

Hollywood Walk of Fame Star—To **Billy Graham** on October 15, the 1900th star on Hollywood Boulevard. Graham is the first clergyman ever to receive a star. He's preached to more than 100 million people in eighty-five countries—more people than anyone else in history. Graham's response: "We should put our eyes on the star, which is the Lord."

1989 Victory Awards—To **Joni Eareckson Tada and Skip Wilkins,** on November 7, two of six people to receive the 1989 Award from the National Rehabilitation Hospital in Washington, DC. The Award is given to people who overcome serious obstacles and go on to make important contributions to society. Joni learned to draw with a pencil held by her teeth after she became paralyzed from the shoulders down in a diving accident; Wilkins severed his spinal cord in a water skiing accident, but now stars in wheelchair athletics.

Faith and Freedom Award—To Miami pastor **Martin Anorga,** a native Cuban, for his radio broadcasts and publications on behalf of human rights and religious liberty in Cuba, from Presbyterians for Democracy and Religious Freedom.

1989 Hutch Award— To **Dave Dravecky,** San Francisco Giants pitcher, for his courage in battling back from cancer.

***Christian Herald* magazine's 1989 James 1:11 Award**—To **Randall A. Terry,** founder of Operation Rescue, a pro-life movement, at the grassroots level, which peacefully blocks abortion clinic doors to save babies' lives. The award is given annually to a "doer of the Word" leader. Operation Rescue closes its headquarters because of financial difficulties as a result of court-ordered fines, but Terry insists that "the rescue mission is not through. . . . The federal government cannot stop a movement of God."

Christian Leader of the Year—To **Oral Roberts,** by the International Christian Business Leaders to honor his healing ministry, his teaching on "seed-faith giving," the work of Oral Roberts University, the merging of healing and medicine through medical training, and his personal character.

Two Hungers Award—To **Leighton Ford** by Dr. Ted Yamamori, president of Food for the Hungry, at a reception at the National Religious Broadcasters convention. Ford is better known as an evangelist than as a man working to end hunger, but he teaches that Christians cannot meet spiritual needs while ignoring physical ones.

Vision: New England Awards—To **Robert and Betty Jacks,** laypeople who have led more than 400 people to Christ; the **Emmanuel Gospel Center,** a Boston ministry which supports urban churches; and **Bethany Congregational Church,** which has demonstrated creativity in caring for the needs of others; at the 30th Congress of the Evangelistic Association of New England in Boston, MA. The award is given to New Englanders who are outstanding models of evangelism.

Religious Freedom Award—To **Nicolae Gheorghita,** a world-renowned endocrinologist who left his profession to become a Baptist pastor in Romania. His church in Oradea near the Hungarian border is one of the country's largest congregations. The award is given annually by the Institute on Religion and Democracy.

Kerlan Award—To **Madeleine L'Engle,** author of a Newbery Award-winning *A Wrinkle* *in Time,* on April 17 at the University of Minnesota's Coffman Union. The award is given each year for recognition of singular attainments in the creation of children's literature. L'Engle's stories, though written for children, are popular with adults.

Helping Hands Award—To **Arthur "Gene" Dewey,** United Nations refugee authority and **Dr. David Hynd,** southern African physician, World Relief's 11th annual Helping Hands awards for continued service to the needy of the world. Dewey was instrumental in organizing a United Nations response to the African famine of 1984–85. Hynd's work in Swaziland has included the founding of hospitals, clinics, and colleges.

Religious Liberty Award—To **Jesse Helms,** Republican senator from NC for eighteen years, from the Southern Baptist Public Affairs Committee in Washington, DC, April 20. "Jesse Helms has got as much courage, if not more, than anyone I've seen in public life. I've seen him take [unpopular] stands again and again," says Richard Halverson, Senate chaplain.

Amy Writing Award—To **Glenn Tinder,** professor of political science at the University of Massachusetts at Boston, for his article, "Can We Be Good Without God?" a cover story in *The Atlantic* magazine, by the Amy Foundation. Tinder receives $10,000. To be considered for the competition, an article must address a public interest issue, show how a Bible quotation speaks to the issue, and be published in a non-religious periodical.

Achievement-Against-the-Odds Medallion—To **Alfredo Garcia,** pastor of Assemblies of God Victory Temple, San Antonio, TX, from President George Bush on May 4. The award is given for overcoming such obstacles as a criminal background and drug addiction to become a contributing asset to society.

William Booth Award—To **Rev. Dr. W.A. Criswell,** pastor of the 28,000-member First Baptist Church, Dallas, TX, for his long-time support of the Salvation Army and for his contributions to the spiritual welfare of the Dallas community. Criswell has written fifty-four books, addressed the Southern Baptist Convention six times and served as its president from 1968–1969.

Christian Council on Persons with Disabilities Awards—To the following churches at the International Congress on the Church and Disability, Grand Rapids, MI, on June 2: **Beverly Hills Baptist Church, Memphis, TN,** for their ministry to mentally handicapped members for the past ten years. They have 100 disabled attendees each meeting for the Sunday morning and evening and Wednesday services. **Georgetown Christian Reformed Church, Hudsonville, MI,** which has a multi-faceted ministry, including respite care programs that match church members with needs of disabled people. **Grace Evangelical Free Church, Walworth, WI,** a small church that commits sizeable financial and personal resources to its disabled attendees. **Crossroads Christian Church, Corona, CA,** focuses its ministry on developmentally disabled and deaf persons with an extensive program for each, including choir, respite care, field trips, social and Olympic events, support groups, outreach, and counseling. **Grace Community Church, Sun Valley, CA,** has over 200 volunteers to run an extensive program for all types of disabilities, including transportation, recreation, and deaf worship services. **Wealthy Park Baptist Church, Grand Rapids, MI,** has conducted a deaf worship service for over forty years with signing at both Sunday services. Awards are presented annually in an effort to promote active involvement of disabled people in the life of the church by the Christian Council on Persons with Disabilities.

TRANSITIONS: JULY 1, 1989 TO JUNE 30, 1990

APPOINTED

Bryant Kirkland, minister emeritus of New York's Fifth Avenue Presbyterian Church, to the American Bible Society's new post of chief executive officer. Kirkland is the first CEO in the Bible society's 173-year history.

David C. Fisher, as senior pastor of Boston's 180-year-old, 2,300-member Park Street Church. He succeeds the recently retired Paul Toms.

E. Brandt Gustavson, former executive vice president and chief operating officer of Trans World Radio begins his duties as executive director of National Religious Broadcasters, February 1. NRB, organized in 1944, represents more than 1100 radio and television stations, program producers, and others committed to maintaining high standards and accessibility for religious broadcasters in the US.

James L. Edwards as fourth president of Anderson University, succeeding Nicholson. Anderson University is affiliated with the Church of God—Anderson, IN.

James Osborne as national commander of the Salvation Army, November 1.

Richard J. Mouw as provost of Fuller Theological Seminary effective September 25.

Woodrow M. Kroll as general director and Bible teacher of Back to the Bible radio ministry.

Several evangelicals to the President's Drug Advisory Council: former Dallas Cowboys coach Tom Landry, gospel singer **Sandi Patti,** former American Red Cross president **Richard Schubert,** and federal judge **Paul Pressler,** a leader in the Southern Baptist Convention. The council will help promote the administration's drug policy.

Roland Lundy as president of Word, Inc. Lundy was previously executive vice-president of Word's records and music division.

Ted W. Engstrom as chairman of the Evangelical Council for Financial Accountability.

Tom Houston as International Director of the Lausanne Committee for World Evangelization.

Renovare, Inc., to bring "renewal to the Church of Jesus Christ in all her multifaceted expressions." Renovare, which means "to make new" in Latin, is Quaker author Richard Foster's vision.

CLOSINGS

City of Faith Medical Center at Oral Roberts University. The release of its last patient brings to an end Oral Roberts' dream that the 30-story hospital and 60-story clinic would become a leading world medical center combining medical skill and prayer.

Maranatha Christian Fellowship, a charismatic outreach with seventy churches in twenty-two nations around the world. "The Lord spoke to us and made it very clear what we were to do," says Bob Weiner, founder and president.

DEATHS

Albert C. Outler, 80, September 1 of a massive stroke. Prominent United Methodist theologian and ecumenist. Outler interpreted the theology of John Wesley for contemporary believers. He specialized in building Protestant-Catholic relations, becoming in 1971 the first non-Roman Catholic to be elected president of the American Catholic Historical Association.

Bill Vincent, 55, national director of L.I.F.E. (Life Institute for Evangelism) Ministries after a heart attack.

Cyrus N. Nelson, 80. Chairman of Gospel Light Publications, a major producer of church-school curriculum.

David C. Cook III, 77, retired president of the David C. Cook Foundation and Publishing Company, April 6. Cook, who retired in 1989 after nearly 55 years with the company his grandfather founded in 1875, was named president of the publishing company when his father died in 1932.

Frank J. Lindquist, 90, founder of North Central Bible College, Minneapolis, October 24. Lindquist was president of NCBC for 23 years.

J.O. Patterson, 77, presiding Bishop of the Church of God in Christ on December 28 in Memphis, TN, after an eight-month bout with cancer. Bishop Patterson led the 3.7 million-member Church of God in Christ, the largest black Pentecostal denomination in the U.S., for twenty years.

James Iley McCord, 70, of Parkinson's disease complications, at the Princeton Medical Center, Princeton, NJ, on February 19. McCord served as president of Princeton Theological Seminary and founder of its Center for Theological Inquiry.

John G. Mitchell, 97, founder and chairman of the board of Multnomah School of the Bible, on May 17. Mitchell's ministry began after he attended evangelistic meetings in Calgary, AB. Mitchell, who stuttered, preached his first sermon in three minutes. He recalled, "I told all I knew, and no one knew what I had said." To overcome his stuttering and "shorthand English," he walked the Canadian prairies, reading his Bible and praying aloud. In 1936 he became the founding vice president of Multnomah School of the Bible; in 1949 he was named chairman of the school's board of trustees, a position he held for the rest of his life.

Loraine Boettner, 88, scholar and writer, on January 3. Several of Boettner's books, most notably his treatment of the concept of predestination, have been widely read and highly regarded in evangelical circles.

Rev. Winfield Blair Sutphin, 71, nationally known television preacher of the 1950s, of pulmonary failure March 12. Sutphin made about 200 radio and television appearances on national radio and television networks on programs including "Lamp Unto My Feet" and "Midday Chapel."

Richard S. Beal, Sr., 101, on November 25. Instrumental in the 1943 founding of the Conservative Baptist Foreign Mission Society, Beal is considered one of the founding fathers of the Conservative Baptist movement.

Solomon Birnbaum, 98, influential Hebrew and Yiddish scholar who established the age and authenticity of the Dead Sea Scrolls, on December 28 in Toronto, ON. Dr. Birnbaum's book on the historical development of Yiddish from its beginning in the ninth century has become a standard resource for scholars of the language.

Walker Martin, 60, of a heart attack. Founder of the Southern California–based Christian Research Institute. An ordained Southern Baptist minister, Martin specialized in the study of cults and religious sects. His book *The Kingdom of the Cults* has been a best-seller for several years.

William Larimer Mellon Jr., 79, August 3 of cancer and Parkinson's disease in Haiti. Medical missionary and founder of Hospital Albert Schweitzer in Deschappelles, Haiti. Mellon and his wife, heir to his family's banking and oil fortune, decided to devote their lives to the poor after reading about Albert Schweitzer, a medical missionary who ran a hospital in Gabon.

John Thomas Walker, 64, September 30 of heart failure. Dean of the Washington National Cathedral and first black bishop in the nation's capital.

Richard J. Davis, 78, general director emeritus of SIM International, October 2 following a long illness. An SIM missionary since 1934, Davis became the fourth general director of SIM in 1962, a position he held until his retirement in 1975.

ELECTED

B. E. Underwood as general superintendent of the International Pentecostal Holiness Church. Underwood served for sixteen years as the church's director of world missions.

Ray Hughes, first general overseer of the Church of God in Cleveland, TN, as chairman of the Pentecostal World Conference (PWC) Advisory Committee, October 1.

Syngman Rhee, 58, Presbyterian minister from Korea, as president of the National Council of Churches effective January 1.

FOLDED

The Episcopalian, a thirty-year-old "independently edited, officially sponsored" monthly tabloid in March 1990. Replacing it will be Episcopal Life, owned and operated by the Episcopal Church and edited at denominational headquarters in New York.

Jerry Falwell's **Fundamentalist Journal.** Begun in 1982, the monthly magazine had a 70,000 circulation.

IMPRISONED

David and James Taggart, former PTL aides for income tax evasion. David, 32, receives eighteen years, five months; James, 35, receives seventeen years, nine months.

October 24, **Jim Bakker,** 49, PTL founder, to forty-five years in prison and $500,000 in fines on twenty-four counts of fraud and conspiracy.

INSTALLED

B. Edgar Johnson, general secretary of the Church of the Nazarene in Kansas City, MO, as the new president of the National Association of Evangelicals, March 8, during the NAE Convention in Phoenix, AZ.

RE-ELECTED

Jerry Rose, president of Chicago's TV-38, to his third term as president of National Religious Broadcasters.

RESIGNED

Robert A. Nicholson, as president of Anderson University, Anderson, IN, after forty-five years of service to the university.

J. Robertson McQuilken, 62, from the presidency of Columbia Bible College and Seminary June 30 after twenty-two years, to devote full-time to caring for his ill wife who struggles with dementia, saying the decision was rooted in his marriage vows forty-two years ago. "There are other people in the world who can successfully lead the school. There is only one who can successfully care for Muriel at this point. So love for both dictates the same answer!" McQuilken tells supporters.

John Guest, effective July 1, from his pastorate at St. Stephen's Episcopal Church in Sewickley, PA, to devote full-time to evangelism.

RETIRED

Mother Teresa, 79, whose work among the sick and dying in Calcutta earned her a Nobel Peace Prize on April 11. "I have been leading the Missionaries of Charity for forty years," said Mother Teresa, who would not comment further on her decision to step down. A Vatican spokesman said she was retiring for health reasons; she suffered a heart attack and serious infection last September. Since its founding, the Missionaries of Charity has grown to include 3,000 nuns in eighty-seven countries. A new superior general will be chosen in September.

Ben Armstrong, 66, Executive Director of National Religious Broadcasters, September 1 after twenty-three years of head of NRB. Armstrong had been the first and only executive director in NRB's history. Armstrong says he is not retiring, but is resigning to take advantage of consulting opportunities.

SENTENCED

On August 24, to an eight-year prison term, **Richard Dortch,** for his role in financial irregularities at PTL. Dortch pleads guilty to federal fraud and conspiracy charges and agrees to testify against Bakker. On April 25, Federal Judge Robert Potter of Charlotte, NC, reduces Dortch's sentence to two and a half years. Reason: Dortch's remorse and cooperation in fraud and conspiracy prosecutions. With good behavior, Dortch will likely be released in Spring 1992.

John Wesley Fletcher to three years probation after pleading guilty to charges of lying to a grand jury about the reasons he introduced PTL founder Jim Bakker to Jessica Hahn.

TOP 1989 NEWS STORIES: THREE PERSPECTIVES

How three different Christian authorities rank the top ten news stories of 1989:

***Christianity Today* Magazine News Staff**	**Bill Bray journalist and Christian newspaper publisher**	**Adult Sunday School Class, Bloomington, IN**
1. Decline of communism. The crumbling of the Berlin Wall was perhaps the most visible indication of sweeping political reform in Eastern Europe.	1. Lifting of the Russian Bible Import Ban. The USSR's willingness to end Bible import bans and allow new freedoms for evangelism and social outreach were greeted with disbelief and praise. They are the most dramatic changes for Christians in the wake of glasnost and perestroika in the Soviet empire.	1. The abortion issue—Supreme Court rulings and all.
2. Abortion. The Supreme Court's decision in *Webster v. Missouri* sent the abortion battle to the states.	2. Fear of Religious Persecution in China. The aftereffects of the Tienanmen Square massacre on the democracy movement in Beijing has had a sobering effect on evangelism among the 1.1 billion mainland Chinese.	2. Diminishing trust for televangelists.
3. Televangelists and accountability. The highly publicized trial and sentencing of Jim Bakker to 45 years in prison marked the end, religious broadcasters hope, of a troubled era.	3. Preparations for the A.D. 2000 Decade of Evangelism. Church and mission leaders from over 2,000 denominations began serious preparations to deal with the post-charismatic renewal movement.	3. The events in Poland specifically, and all of Eastern Europe as well.

4. Drugs. Issues related to drugs cleared a bigger place on the agenda of the church.	4. The Lausanne II World Congress on Evangelism in Manila. This congress was the focal point for Evangelicals planning the 1990s decade of evangelism. It featured the debut of the Third World Missions Association and related movements led by native missionary societies.	4. Awareness of world missions.
5. Crackdown in China. The flickerings of democracy in China were quickly snuffed out, raising concerns about the future of religious freedom in Hong Kong, which China will inherit in 1997.	5. The Jim Bakker Trial. The long mockery of the Christian community ended with the televangelist being sentenced to 45 years in prison. The TV scandals have had a wide and profound impact throughout the church on many different levels.	5. Disasters, and the relief projects by the church.
6. Moral Majority calls it quits. The organization that embodied the emergence of the Religious Right as a powerful political force closed shop.	6. The Fall of Arie Brouwer. This controversial general secretary of the National Council of Churches in the USA was ousted in a major attempt to salvage the ailing church body. The movement, which once spearheaded ecumenism in the USA and worldwide, has fallen along with the steady decline of the denominations which formed it.	6. Multiple family issues, including divorce, new definitions of "household," further fractioning of families, single partners, and so on.
7. NCC woes. The sudden and bitter resignation of the National Council of Churches' top executive highlighted a year of fundamental restructuring of the ecumenical organization.	7. The Ordination of Barbara Harris. Naming the first woman bishop of the Episcopal Church further polarized Anglicanism over theological feminism, and further divided Catholics and Protestants.	7. The plight of the homeless.

8. World evangelization. Two worldwide conferences highlighted an emphasis on reaching the world with the gospel.

9. Evaluating Bush. The jury is still out on the new President, who has sent out mixed signals on issues of importance to Christians.

10. Missionary dangers. The risks assumed by those who witness in the world's trouble spots were especially evident in 1989.

Christianity Today, December 15, 1989.

8. Hi-Tech Bibles Premier. Computerized electronic Bibles, scriptural research, and sermon preparation may do for preachers what the pocket calculators did for engineers. Clergy can now retrieve an entire exegetical library from a single laser disk.

9. Christian Fiction Tops Best-Seller Lists. For the first time in decades, religious fiction was back. Frank Peretti's books *Piercing the Darkness* and *This Present Darkness* rose to the top of all religious best-seller lists and some secular ones as well.

10. Operation Rescue. Christians began to work for the rights of the unborn and the abolition of abortion-on-demand through civil disobedience.

Note: Dallas, TX (EP)—This list depicts global trends as well as unique events. Says Bray, "1989 was a year in which Christians rediscovered evangelism. We were chastised and humbled by some events, and made hungry for God by others. Most of all, I think, we ended the decade with a fresh awareness of how much we need to relearn what it means to be spiritually militant for God."

EP News Service, January 12, 1990.

8. The increasing emphasis on "me" in America.

9. The unity of Europe and its prophetic ramifications.

10. Church-state issues in America, such as home schooling, religious displays in public places, and so on.

Note: These choices were selected by the individuals in the class as those having the greatest impact on the church. "The importance of any list is to help us use history as a window for the future. Events are changing so rapidly in the world that historical perspective is mandatory," said Dwain C. Illman, M.D., teacher of the class.

Christianity Today, February 19, 1990.

Declarations

THE LAUSANNE COVENANT

International Congress on World Evangelization,
Lausanne, Switzerland, July 1974

Introduction

We, members of the Church of Jesus Christ, from more than 150 nations, participants in the International Congress on World Evangelization at Lausanne, praise God for his great salvation and rejoice in the fellowship he has given us with himself and with each other. We are deeply stirred by what God is doing in our day, moved to penitence by our failures and challenged by the unfinished task of evangelization. We believe the gospel is God's good news for the whole world, and we are determined by his grace to obey Christ's commission to proclaim it to every person and to make disciples of every nation. We desire, therefore, to affirm our faith and our resolve, and to make public our covenant.

1. The Purpose of God

We affirm our belief in the one eternal God, Creator and Lord of the world, Father, Son and Holy Spirit, who governs all things according to the purpose of his will. He has been calling out from the world a people for himself, and sending his people back into the world to be his servants and his witnesses, for the extension of his kingdom, the building up of Christ's body, and the glory of his name. We confess with shame that we have often denied our calling and failed in our mission, by becoming conformed to the world or by withdrawing from it. Yet we rejoice that even when borne by earthen vessels the gospel is still a precious treasure. To the task of making that treasure known in the power of the Holy Spirit we desire to dedicate ourselves anew.

2. The Authority & Power of the Bible

We affirm the divine inspiration, truthfulness and authority of both Old and New Testament Scriptures in their entirety as the only written word of God, without error in all that it affirms, and the only infallible rule of faith and practice. We also affirm the power of God's Word to accomplish his purpose of salvation. The message of the Bible is addressed to all men and women. For God's revelation in Christ and in Scripture is unchangeable. Through it the Holy Spirit still speaks today. He illumines the minds of God's people in every culture to perceive its truth freshly through their own eyes and thus discloses to the whole Church ever more of the many-coloured wisdom of God.

3. The Uniqueness & Universality of Christ

We affirm that there is only one Saviour and only one gospel, although there is a wide diversity of evangelistic approaches. We recognise that everyone has some knowledge of God through his general revelation in nature. But we deny that this can save, for people suppress the truth by their unrighteousness. We also reject as derogatory to Christ and the gospel every kind of syncretism and dialogue which implies that Christ speaks equally through all religions and ideologies. Jesus Christ, being himself the only God-man, who gave himself as the only ransom for sinners, is the only mediator between God and people.

THE LAUSANNE COVENANT cont.

There is no other name by which we must be saved. All men and women are perishing because of sin, but God loves everyone, not wishing that any should perish but that all should repent. Yet those who reject Christ repudiate the joy of salvation and condemn themselves to eternal separation from God. To proclaim Jesus as "the Saviour of the world" is not to affirm that all people are either automatically or ultimately saved, still less to affirm that all religions offer salvation in Christ. Rather it is to proclaim God's love for a world of sinners and to invite everyone to respond to him as Saviour and Lord in the wholehearted personal commitment of repentance and faith. Jesus Christ has been exalted above every other name; we long for the day when every knee shall bow to him and every tongue shall confess him Lord.

4. The Nature of Evangelism

To evangelise is to spread the good news that Jesus Christ died for our sins and was raised from the dead according to the Scriptures, and that as the reigning Lord he now offers the forgiveness of sins and the liberating gift of the Spirit to all who repent and believe. Our Christian presence in the world is indispensable to evangelism, and so is that kind of dialogue whose purpose is to listen sensitively in order to understand. But evangelism itself is the proclamation of the historical, biblical Christ as Saviour and Lord, with a view to persuading people to come to him personally and so be reconciled to God. In issuing the gospel invitation we have no liberty to conceal the cost of discipleship. Jesus still calls all who would follow him to deny themselves, take up their cross, and identify themselves with his new community. The results of evangelism include obedience to Christ, incorporation into his Church and responsible service in the world.

5. Christian Social Responsibility

We affirm that God is both the Creator and the Judge of all. We therefore should share his concern for justice and reconciliation throughout human society and for the liberation of men and women from every kind of oppression. Because men and women are made in the image of God, every person, regardless of race, religion, colour, culture, class, sex or age, has an intrinsic dignity because of which he or she should be respected and served, not exploited. Here too we express penitence both for our neglect and for having sometimes regarded evangelism and social concern as mutually exclusive. Although reconciliation with other people is not reconciliation with God, nor is social action evangelism, nor is political liberation salvation, nevertheless we affirm that evangelism and socio-political involvement are both part of our Christian duty. For both are necessary expressions of our doctrines of God and man, our love for our neighbour and our obedience to Jesus Christ. The message of salvation implies also a message of judgment upon every form of alienation, oppression and discrimination, and we should not be afraid to denounce evil and injustice wherever they exist. When people receive Christ they are born again into his kingdom and must seek not only to exhibit but also to spread its righteousness in the midst of an unrighteous world. The salvation we claim should be transforming us in the totality of our personal and social responsibilities. Faith without works is dead.

6. The Church & Evangelism

We affirm that Christ sends his redeemed people into the world as the Father sent him, and that this calls for a similar deep and costly penetration of the world. We need to break out of our ecclesiastical ghettos and permeate non-Christian society. In the Church's mission of sacrificial service evangelism is primary. World evangelization requires the whole Church to take the whole gospel to the whole world. The Church is at the very centre of God's cosmic purpose and is his appointed means of spreading the gospel. But a church which preaches the cross must itself be marked by the cross. It becomes a stumbling block to evangelism when it betrays the gospel or lacks a living faith in God, a genuine love for people, or scrupulous honesty in all things including promotion and finance. The church is the community of God's people rather than an institution, and must not be identified with any particular culture, social or political system, or human ideology.

7. Cooperation in Evangelism

We affirm that the Church's visible unity in truth is God's purpose. Evangelism also summons us to unity, because our oneness strengthens our witness, just as our disunity undermines our gospel of reconciliation. We recognise, however, that organisational unity may take many forms and does not necessarily forward evangelism. Yet we who share the same biblical faith should be closely united in fellowship, work and witness. We confess that our testimony has sometimes been marred by sinful individualism and needless duplication. We pledge ourselves to seek a deeper unity in truth, worship, holiness and mission. We urge the development of regional and functional cooperation for the furtherance of the Church's mission, for strategic planning, for mutual encouragement, and for the sharing of resources and experience.

8. Churches in Evangelistic Partnership

We rejoice that a new missionary era has dawned. The dominant role of western missions is fast disappearing. God is raising up from the younger churches a great new resource for world evangelization, and is thus demonstrating that the responsibility to evangelise belongs to the whole body of Christ. All churches should therefore be asking God and themselves what they should be doing both to reach their own area and to send missionaries to other parts of the world. A reevaluation of our missionary responsibility and role should be continuous. Thus a growing partnership of churches will develop and the universal character of Christ's Church will be more clearly exhibited. We also thank God for agencies which labour in Bible translation, theological education, the mass media, Christian literature, evangelism, missions, church renewal and other specialist fields. They too should engage in constant self-examination to evaluate their effectiveness as part of the Church's mission.

9. The Urgency of the Evangelistic Task

More than 2,700 million people, which is more than two-thirds of all humanity, have yet to be evangelised. We are ashamed that so many have been neglected; it is a standing rebuke to us and to the whole Church. There is now, however, in many parts of the world an unprecedented receptivity to the Lord Jesus Christ. We are convinced that this is the time for churches and para-church agencies to pray earnestly for the salvation of the unreached and to launch new efforts to achieve world evangelization. A reduction of foreign missionaries and money in an evangelised country may sometimes be necessary to facilitate the national church's growth in self-reliance and to release resources for unevangelised areas. Missionaries should flow ever more freely from and to all six continents in a spirit of humble service. The goal should be, by all available means and at the earliest possible time, that every person will have the opportunity to hear, understand, and receive the good news. We cannot hope to attain this goal without sacrifice. All of us are shocked by the poverty of millions and disturbed by the injustices which cause it. Those of us who live in affluent circumstances accept our duty to develop a simple life-style in order to contribute more generously to both relief and evangelism.

10. Evangelism & Culture

The development of strategies for world evangelization calls for imaginative pioneering methods. Under God, the result will be the rise of churches deeply rooted in Christ and closely related to their culture. Culture must always be tested and judged by Scripture.

THE LAUSANNE COVENANT cont.

Because men and women are God's creatures, some of their culture is rich in beauty and goodness. Because they are fallen, all of it is tainted with sin and some of it is demonic. The gospel does not presuppose the superiority of any culture to another, but evaluates all cultures according to its own criteria of truth and righteousness, and insists on moral absolutes in every culture. Missions have all too frequently exported with the gospel an alien culture and churches have sometimes been in bondage to culture rather than to Scripture. Christ's evangelists must humbly seek to empty themselves of all but their personal authenticity in order to become the servants of others, and churches must seek to transform and enrich culture, all for the glory of God.

11. Education & Leadership

We confess that we have sometimes pursued church growth at the expense of church depth, and divorced evangelism from Christian nurture. We also acknowledge that some of our missions have been too slow to equip and encourage national leaders to assume their rightful responsibilities. Yet we are committed to indigenous principles, and long that every church will have national leaders who manifest a Christian style of leadership in terms not of domination but of service. We recognise that there is a great need to improve theological education, especially for church leaders. In every nation and culture there should be an effective training programme for pastors and laity in doctrine, discipleship, evangelism, nurture and service. Such training programmes should not rely on any stereotyped methodology but should be developed by creative local initiatives according to biblical standards.

12. Spiritual Conflict

We believe that we are engaged in constant spiritual warfare with the principalities and powers of evil, who are seeking to overthrow the Church and frustrate its task of world evangelization. We know our need to equip ourselves with God's armour and to fight this battle with the spiritual weapons of truth and prayer. For we detect the activity of our enemy, not only in false ideologies outside the Church, but also inside it in false gospels which twist Scripture and put people in the place of God. We need both watchfulness and discernment to safeguard the biblical gospel. We acknowledge that we ourselves are not immune to worldliness of thought and action, that is, to a surrender to secularism. For example, although careful studies of church growth, both numerical and spiritual, are right and valuable, we have sometimes neglected them. At other times, desirous to ensure a response to the gospel, we have compromised our message, manipulated our hearers through pressure techniques, and become unduly preoccupied with statistics or even dishonest in our use of them. All this is worldly. The Church must be in the world; the world must not be in the Church.

13. Freedom & Persecution

It is the God-appointed duty of every government to secure conditions of peace, justice and liberty in which the Church may obey God, serve the Lord Christ, and preach the gospel without interference. We therefore pray for the leaders of the nations and call upon them to guarantee freedom of thought and conscience, and freedom to practise and propagate religion in accordance with the will of God and as set forth in The Universal Declaration of Human Rights. We also express our deep concern for all who have been unjustly imprisoned, and especially for those who are suffering for their testimony to the Lord Jesus. We promise to pray and work for their freedom. At the same time we refuse to be intimidated by their fate. God helping us, we too will seek to stand against injustice and to remain faithful to the gospel, whatever the cost. We do not forget the warnings of Jesus that persecution is inevitable.

14. The Power of the Holy Spirit

We believe in the power of the Holy Spirit. The Father sent his Spirit to bear witness to his Son; without his witness ours is futile. Conviction of sin, faith in Christ, new birth and Christian growth are all his work. Further, the Holy Spirit is a missionary spirit; thus evangelism should arise spontaneously from a Spirit-filled church. A church that is not a missionary church is contradicting itself and quenching the Spirit. Worldwide evangelization will become a realistic possibility only when the Spirit renews the Church in truth and wisdom, faith, holiness, love and power. We therefore call upon all Christians to pray for such a visitation of the sovereign Spirit of God that all his fruit may appear in all his people and that all his gifts may enrich the body of Christ. Only then will the whole Church become a fit instrument in his hands, that the whole earth may hear his voice.

15. The Return of Christ

We believe that Jesus Christ will return personally and visibly, in power and glory, to consummate his salvation and his judgment. This promise of his coming is a further spur to our evangelism, for we remember his words that the gospel must first be preached to all nations. We believe that the interim period between Christ's ascension and return is to be filled with the mission of the people of God, who have no liberty to stop before the end. We also remember his warning that false Christs and false prophets will arise as precursors of the final Antichrist. We therefore reject as a proud, self-confident dream the notion that people can ever build a utopia on earth. Our Christian confidence is that God will perfect his kingdom, and we look forward with eager anticipation to that day, and to the new heaven and earth in which righteousness will dwell and God will reign forever. Meanwhile, we rededicate ourselves to the service of Christ and of people in joyful submission to his authority over the whole of our lives.

Conclusion

Therefore, in the light of this our faith and our resolve, we enter into a solemn covenant with God and with each other, to pray, to plan and to work together for the evangelization of the whole world. We call upon others to join us. May God help us by his grace and for his glory to be faithful to this our covenant! Amen, Alleluia!

“” FOCUS QUOTE

If both economic and human compassion aren't seen in the lives of those of us who follow Jesus, and enormous number of the poor will never have convincing enough evidence to believe the good news of the Kingdom of God. The tragedy of many of our churches is that they contribute to this credibility gap. —Tom Houston, International Director, Lausanne Committee for World Evangelization

---

LAUSANNE ADDRESS

Lausanne Committee for
World Evangelization
184A Cumnor Hill
Oxford OX2 9PJ
England

LAUSANNE SPONSORSHIPS

Since 1974 there have been numerous gatherings and publications sponsored by the Lausanne Committee for World Evangelization, or held in the unity of the Lausanne Covenant. What follows is a listing of the major congresses, consultations and publications that have been sponsored, singly or cooperatively, by the Lausanne Committee. More information on these events and resources can be obtained through the Lausanne Committee office.

International Congress on World Evangelization
Lausanne, Switzerland
July 1974
- Let the Earth Hear His Voice
  World Wide Publications; 1975
- The Lausanne Covenant: An Exposition and Commentary
  Lausanne Occasional Paper No. 3

Consultation on the Homogeneous Unit Principle
Pasadena, California, U.S.A.
June 1977
- The Pasadena Consultation,
  Lausanne Occasional Paper No. 1

Consultation on Gospel and Culture
Willowbank, Somerset Bridge, Bermuda
January 1978
- The Willowbank Report
  Lausanne Occasional Paper No. 2

Conference on Muslim Evangelization
Glen Eyrie, Colorado Springs, Colorado, U.S.A.
October 1978
- The Glen Eyrie Report
  Lausanne Occasional Paper No. 4
- The Gospel and Islam: A 1978 Compendium
  MARC; 1979

International Consultation on Simple Lifestyle
Hoddesdon, England
March 1980
- An Evangelical Commitment to Simple Lifestyle
  Lausanne Occasional Paper No. 20

Lausanne Consultation on World Evangelization
Pattaya, Thailand
July 1980
- Christian Witness to Refugees
  Lausanne Occasional Paper No. 5
- Christian Witness to the Chinese People
  Lausanne Occasional Paper No. 6
- Christian Witness to the Jewish People
  Lausanne Occasional Paper No. 7
- Christian Witness to Secularized People
  Lausanne Occasional Paper No. 8
- Christian Witness to Large Cities
  Lausanne Occasional Paper No. 9
- Christian Witness to Nominal Christians Among Roman Catholics
  Lausanne Occasional Paper No. 10
- Christian Witness to New Religious Movements
  Lausanne Occasional Paper No. 11
- Christian Witness to Marxists
  Lausanne Occasional Paper No. 12
- Christian Witness to Muslims
  Lausanne Occasional Paper No. 13
- Christian Witness to Hindus
  Lausanne Occasional Paper No. 14
- Christian Witness to Buddhists
  Lausanne Occasional Paper No. 15
- Christian Witness to Traditional Religionists of Asia and Oceania
  Lausanne Occasional Paper No. 16
- Christian Witness to Traditional Religionists of Latin America and Caribbean
  Lausanne Occasional Paper No. 17
- Christian Witness to People of African Traditional Religions
  Lausanne Occasional Paper No. 18
- Christian Witness to Nominal Christians among the Orthodox
  Lausanne Occasional Paper No. 19
- Christian Witness to the Urban Poor
  Lausanne Occasional Paper No. 22
- Christian Witness to Nominal Christians among Protestants
  Lausanne Occasional Paper No. 23
- Cooperating in World Evangelization: A Handbook on Church/Para-Church Relationships
  Lausanne Occasional Paper No. 24

Consultation on the Relationship Between Evangelism and Social Responsibility
Grand Rapids, Michigan, U.S.A.
June 1982
- Evangelism and Social Responsibility, Lausanne Occasional Paper No. 21
- The Church in Response to Human Need, Missions Advanced Research and Communication Center; 1983

International Prayer Assembly for World Evangelization
Seoul, Republic of Korea
June 1984
- Unleashing the Power of Prayer, Moody Press; 1989

Consultation on the Work of the Holy Spirit and Evangelization
Oslo, Norway
May 1985
- God the Evangelist
  Eerdmans, Grand Rapids & Paternoster, Exeter; 1987

Young Leaders Conference—Singapore '87
Republic of Singapore
June 1987

Consultation on Conversion
Hong Kong
January 1988
- Turning to God
  Eerdmans, Grand Rapids & Paternoster, Exeter; 1989

Younger Leaders Conference—Leadership '88
Washington, D.C., U.S.A.
June 1988
- Networking Directory
  LCWE; 1988
- Joining Together in the Gospel: Four Studies from Philippians
  LCWE; 1988

Lausanne II in Manila,
Second International Congress on World Evangelization
Manila, Philippines
July 1989
- The Challenge Before Us
  World Wide Publications; 1989
- The Whole Gospel for the Whole World
  Regal Books; 1989
- The Manila Manifesto: An Elaboration of the Lausanne Covenant Fifteen Years Later
  LCWE; 1989

Continuing Publications:
- *World Evangelization* magazine
- World Evangelization Information Service

THE MANILA MANIFESTO

Lausanne II in Manila
Second International Congress on World Evangelization
Manila, Philippines, July 1989

Introduction
In July 1974 the International Congress on World Evangelization was held in Lausanne, Switzerland, and issued the Lausanne Covenant. Now in July 1989 over 3,000 of us from about 170 countries have met in Manila for the same purpose, and have issued the Manila Manifesto. We are grateful for the welcome we have received from our Filipino brothers and sisters.

During the 15 years which have elapsed between the two congresses some smaller consultations have been held on topics like Gospel and Culture, Evangelism and Social Responsibility, Simple Lifestyle, the Holy Spirit, and Conversion. These meetings and their reports have helped to develop the thinking of the Lausanne movement.

A "manifesto" is defined as a public declaration of convictions, intentions and motives. The Manila Manifesto takes up the two congress themes, "Proclaim Christ until he comes" and "Calling the Whole Church to take the Whole Gospel to the Whole World." Its first part

THE MANILA MANIFESTO cont.

is a series of 21 succinct affirmations. Its second part elaborates these in 12 sections, which are commended to churches, alongside the Lausanne Covenant, for study and action.

TWENTY-ONE AFFIRMATIONS

1. We affirm our continuing commitment to the Lausanne Covenant as the basis of our cooperation in the Lausanne movement.
2. We affirm that in the Scriptures of the Old and New Testaments God has given us an authoritative disclosure of his character and will, his redemptive acts and their meaning, and his mandate for mission.
3. We affirm that the biblical gospel is God's enduring message to our world, and we determine to defend, proclaim and embody it.
4. We affirm that human beings, though created in the image of God, are sinful and guilty, and lost without Christ, and that this truth is a necessary preliminary to the gospel.
5. We affirm that the Jesus of history and the Christ of glory are the same person, and that this Jesus Christ is absolutely unique, for he alone is God incarnate, our sin-bearer, the conqueror of death and the coming judge.
6. We affirm that on the cross Jesus Christ took our place, bore our sins and died for our death; and that for this reason alone God freely forgives those who are brought to repentance and faith.
7. We affirm that other religions and ideologies are not alternative paths to God, and that human spirituality, if unredeemed by Christ, leads not to God but to judgment, for Christ is the only way.
8. We affirm that we must demonstrate God's love visibly by caring for those who are deprived of justice, dignity, food and shelter.
9. We affirm that the proclamation of God's kingdom of justice and peace demands the denunciation of all injustice and oppression, both personal and structural; we will not shrink from this prophetic witness.
10. We affirm that the Holy Spirit's witness to Christ is indispensable to evangelism, and that without his supernatural work neither new birth nor new life is possible.

“” FOCUS QUOTE

We determine to go on seeking that unity in truth for which Christ prayed.

—Manila Manifesto

---

11. We affirm that spiritual warfare demands spiritual weapons, and that we must both preach the word in the power of the Spirit, and pray constantly that we may enter into Christ's victory over the principalities and powers of evil.
12. We affirm that God has committed to the whole church and every member of it the task of making Christ known throughout the world; we long to see all lay and ordained persons mobilized and trained for this task.
13. We affirm that we who claim to be members of the Body of Christ must transcend within our fellowship the barriers of race, gender and class.
14. We affirm that the gifts of the Spirit are distributed to all God's people, women and men, and that their partnership in evangelization must be welcomed for the common good.
15. We affirm that we who proclaim the gospel must exemplify it in a life of holiness and love; otherwise our testimony loses its credibility.
16. We affirm that every Christian congregation must turn itself outward to its local

community in evangelistic witness and compassionate service.

17. We affirm the urgent need for churches, mission agencies and other Christian organizations to cooperate in evangelism and social action, repudiating competition and avoiding duplication.

18. We affirm our duty to study the society in which we live, in order to understand its structures, values and needs, and so develop an appropriate strategy of mission.

19. We affirm that world evangelization is urgent and that the reaching of unreached peoples is possible. So we resolve during the last decade of the twentieth century to give ourselves to these tasks with fresh determination.

20. We affirm our solidarity with those who suffer for the gospel, and will seek to prepare ourselves for the same possibility. We will also work for religious and political freedom everywhere.

21. We affirm that God is calling the whole church to take the whole gospel to the whole world. So we determine to proclaim it faithfully, urgently and sacrificially, until he comes.

A. The Whole Gospel

The gospel is the good news of God's salvation from the powers of evil, the establishment of his eternal kingdom and his final victory over everything which defines his purpose. In his love God purposed to do this before the world began and effected his liberating plan over sin, death and judgment through the death of our Lord Jesus Christ. It is Christ who makes us free, and unites us in his redeemed fellowship.

1. OUR HUMAN PREDICAMENT

We are committed to preaching the whole gospel, that is, the biblical gospel in its fulness. In order to do so, we have to understand why human beings need it.

Men and women have an intrinsic dignity and worth, because they were created in God's likeness to know, love and serve him. But now through sin every part of their humanness has been distorted. Human beings have become self-centered, self-serving rebels, who do not love God or their neighbour as they should. In consequence, they are alienated both from their Creator and from the rest of his creation, which is the basic cause of the pain, disorientation and loneliness which so many people suffer today. Sin also frequently erupts in anti-social behavior, in violent exploitation of others, and in a depletion of the earth's resources of which God has made men and women his stewards. Humanity is guilty, without excuse, and on the broad road which leads to destruction.

Although God's image in human beings has been corrupted, they are still capable of loving relationships, noble deeds and beautiful art. Yet even the finest human achievement is fatally flawed and cannot possibly fit anybody to enter God's presence. Men and women are also spiritual beings, but spiritual practices and self-help techniques can at the most alleviate felt needs; they cannot address the solemn realities of sin, guilt and judgment. Neither human religion, nor human righteousness, nor socio-political programs can save people. Self-salvation of every kind is impossible. Left to themselves, human beings are lost forever.

So we repudiate false gospels which deny human sin, divine judgment, the deity and incarnation of Jesus Christ, and the necessity of the cross and the resurrection. We also reject half-gospels, which minimize sin and confuse God's grace with human self-effort. We confess that we ourselves have sometimes trivilized the gospel. But we determine in our evangelism to remember God's radical diagnosis and his equally radical remedy.

2. GOOD NEWS FOR TODAY

We rejoice that the living God did not abandon us to our lostness and despair. In his love he came after us in Jesus Christ to rescue and re-make us. So the good news focuses on the historic person of Jesus, who came proclaiming the kingdom of God and living a life of

THE MANILA MANIFESTO cont.

humble service, who died for us, becoming sin and a curse in our place, and whom God vindicated by raising him from the dead. To those who repent and believe in Christ, God grants a share in the new creation. He gives us new life, which includes the forgiveness of our sins and the indwelling, transforming power of his Spirit. He welcomes us into his new community, which consists of people of all races, nations and cultures. And he promises that one day we will enter his new world, in which evil will be abolished, nature will be redeemed, and God will reign for ever.

This good news must be boldly proclaimed, wherever possible, in church and public hall, on radio and television, and in the open air, because it is God's power for salvation and we are under obligation to make it known. In our preaching we must faithfully declare the truth which God has revealed in the Bible and struggle to relate it to our own context.

We also affirm that apologetics, namely "the defense and confirmation of the gospel," is integral to the biblical understanding of mission and essential for effective witness in the modern world. Paul "reasoned" with people out of the Scriptures, with a view to "persuading" them of the truth of the gospel. So must we. In fact, all Christians should be ready to give a reason for the hope that is in them.

We have again been confronted with Luke's emphasis that the gospel is good news for the poor and have asked ourselves what this means to the majority of the world's population who are destitute, suffering or oppressed. We have been reminded that the law, the prophets and the wisdom books, and the teaching and ministry of Jesus, all stress God's concern for the materially poor and our consequent duty to defend and care for them. Scripture also refers to the spiritually poor who look to God alone for mercy. The gospel comes as good news to both. The spiritually poor, who, whatever their economic circumstances, humble themselves before God, receive by faith the free gift of salvation. There is no other way for anybody to enter the Kingdom of God. The materially poor and powerless find in addition a new dignity as God's children, and the love of brothers and sisters who will struggle with them for their liberation from everything which demeans or oppresses them.

We repent of any neglect of God's truth in Scripture and determine both to proclaim and to defend it. We also repent where we have been indifferent to the plight of the poor, and where we have shown preference for the rich, and we determine to follow Jesus in preaching good news to all people by both word and deed.

3. THE UNIQUENESS OF JESUS CHRIST

We are called to proclaim Christ in an increasingly pluralistic world. There is a resurgence of old faiths and a rise of new ones. In the first century too there were "many gods and many lords." Yet the apostles boldly affirmed the uniqueness, indispensability and centrality of Christ. We must do the same.

Because men and women are made in God's image and see in the creation traces of its Creator, the religions which have arisen do sometimes contain elements of truth and beauty. They are not, however, alternative gospels. Because human beings are sinful, and because "the whole world is under the control of the evil one," even religious people are in need of Christ's redemption. We, therefore, have no warrant for saying that salvation can be found outside Christ or apart from an explicit acceptance of his work through faith.

It is sometimes held that in virtue of God's covenant with Abraham, Jewish people do not need to acknowledge Jesus as their Messiah. We affirm that they need him as much as anyone else, that it would be a form of anti-Semitism, as well as being disloyal to Christ, to depart from the New Testament pattern of taking the gospel to "the Jew first . . . ." We therefore reject the thesis that Jews have their own covenant which renders faith in Jesus unnecessary.

What unites us is our common convictions about Jesus Christ. We confess him as the eternal Son of God who became fully human while remaining fully divine, who was our substitute on the cross, bearing our sins and dying our death, exchanging his righteousness for our unrighteousness, who rose victorious in a transformed body, and who will return in glory to judge the world. He alone is the incarnate Son, the Saviour, the Lord and the Judge, and he alone, with the Father and the Spirit, is worthy of the worship, faith and obedience of all people. There is only one gospel because there is only one Christ, who because of his death and resurrection is himself the only way of salvation. We therefore reject both the relativism which regards all religions and spiritualities as equally valid approaches to God, and the syncretism which tries to mix faith in Christ with other faiths.

Moreover, since God has exalted Jesus to the highest place, in order that everybody should acknowledge him, this also is our desire. Compelled by Christ's love, we must obey Christ's Great Commission and love his lost sheep, but we are especially motivated by "jealousy" for his holy name, and we long to see him receive the honour and glory which are due to him.

In the past we have sometimes been guilty of adopting towards adherents of other faiths attitudes of ignorance, arrogance, disrespect and even hostility. We repent of this. We nevertheless are determined to bear a positive and uncompromising witness to the uniqueness of our Lord, in his life, death and resurrection, in all aspects of our evangelistic work including inter-faith dialogue.

“” FOCUS QUOTE **We are ashamed of the suspicions and rivalries, the dogmatism over non-essentials, the power-struggles and empire-building which spoil our evangelistic witness.** —Manila Manifesto

---

4. THE GOSPEL AND SOCIAL RESPONSIBILITY

The authentic gospel must become visible in the transformed lives of men and women. As we proclaim the love of God we must be involved in loving service, and as we preach the Kingdom of God we must be committed to its demands of justice and peace.

Evangelism is primary because our chief concern is with the gospel, that all people may have the opportunity to accept Jesus Christ as Lord and Savior. Yet Jesus not only proclaimed the Kingdom of God, he also demonstrated its arrival by works of mercy and power. We are called today to a similar integration of words and deeds. In a spirit of humility we are to preach and teach, minister to the sick, feed the hungry, care for prisoners, help the disadvantaged and handicapped, and deliver the oppressed. While we acknowledge the diversity of spiritual gifts, callings and contexts, we also affirm that good news and good works are inseparable.

The proclamation of God's kingdom necessarily demands the prophetic denunciation of all that is incompatible with it. Among the evils we deplore are destructive violence, including institutionalized violence, political corruption, all forms of exploitation of people and of the earth, the undermining of the family, abortion on demand, the drug traffic, and the abuse of human rights. In our concern for the poor, we are distressed by the burden of debt in the Two-Thirds World. We are also outraged by the inhuman conditions in which millions live, who bear God's image as we do.

Our continuing commitment to social action is not a confusion of the Kingdom of God with a Christianized society. It is, rather, a recognition that the biblical gospel has inescapable social implications. True mission should always be incarnational. It necessitates

THE MANILA MANIFESTO cont.

entering humbly into other people's worlds, identifying with their social reality, their sorrow and suffering, and their struggles for justice against oppressive powers. This cannot be done without personal sacrifices.

We repent that the narrowness of our concerns and vision has often kept us from proclaiming the lordship of Jesus Christ over all of life, private and public, local and global. We determine to obey his command "to seek first the Kingdom of God and his righteousness."

B. The Whole Church

The whole gospel has to be proclaimed by the whole church. All the people of God are called to share in the evangelistic task. Yet without the Holy Spirit of God all their endeavors will be fruitless.

5. GOD THE EVANGELIST

The Scriptures declare that God himself is the chief evangelist. For the Spirit of God is the Spirit of truth, love, holiness and power, and evangelism is impossible without him. It is he who anoints the messenger, confirms the word, prepares the hearer, convicts the sinful, enlightens the blind, gives life to the dead, enables us to repent and believe, unites us to the Body of Christ, assures us that we are God's children, leads us into Christlike character and service, and sends us out in our turn to be Christ's witnesses. In all this the Holy Spirit's main preoccupation is to glorify Jesus Christ by showing him to us and forming him in us.

All evangelism involves spiritual warfare with the principalities and powers of evil, in which only spiritual weapons can prevail, especially the Word and the Spirit, with prayer. We therefore call on all Christian people to be diligent in their prayers both for the renewal of the church and for the evangelization of the world.

Every true conversion involves a power encounter, in which the superior authority of Jesus Christ is demonstrated. There is no greater miracle than this, in which the believer is set free from the bondage of Satan and sin, fear and futility, darkness and death.

Although the miracles of Jesus were special, being signs of his Messiahship and anticipations of his perfect kingdom when all nature will be subject to him, we have no liberty to place limits on the power of the living Creator today. We reject both the skepticism which denies miracles and the presumption which demands them, both the timidity which shrinks from the fulness of the Spirit and the triumphalism which shrinks from the weakness in which Christ's power is made perfect.

We repent of all self-confident attempts either to evangelize in our own strength or to dictate to the Holy Spirit. We determine in the future not to "grieve" or "quench" the Spirit, but rather to seek to spread the good news "with power, with the Holy Spirit and with deep conviction."

6. THE HUMAN WITNESS

God the evangelist gives his people the privilege of being his "fellow-workers." For, although we cannot witness without him, he normally chooses to witness through us. He calls only some to be evangelists, missionaries or pastors, but he calls his whole church and every member of it to be his witnesses.

The privileged task of pastors and teachers is to lead God's people (laos) into maturity and to equip them for ministry. Pastors are not to monopolize ministries, but rather to multiply them, by encouraging others to use their gifts and by training disciples to make disciples. The domination of the laity by the clergy has been a great evil in the history of the church. It robs both laity and clergy of their God-intended roles, causes clergy breakdowns, weakens the church and hinders the spread of the gospel. More than that, it is fundamentally unbiblical. We therefore, who have for centuries insisted on "the priesthood of all believers" now also insist on the ministry of all believers.

We gratefully recognize that children and young people enrich the church's worship and outreach by their enthusiasm and faith. We need to train them in discipleship and evangelism, so that they may reach their own generation for Christ.

God created men and women as equal bearers of his image, accepts them equally in Christ and poured out his Spirit on all flesh, sons and daughters alike. In addition, because the Holy Spirit distributes his gifts to women as well as to men, they must be given opportunities to exercise their gifts. We celebrate their distinguished record in the history of missions and are convinced that God calls women to similar roles today. Even though we are not fully agreed what forms their leadership should take, we do agree about the partnership in world evangelization which God intends men and women to enjoy. Suitable training must therefore be made available to both.

Lay witness takes place, by women and men, not only through the local church (see Section 8), but through friendships, in the home and at work. Even those who are homeless or unemployed share in the calling to be witnesses.

Our first responsibility is to witness to those who are already our friends, relatives, neighbors, and colleagues. Home evangelism is also natural, both for married and for single people. Not only should a Christian home commend God's standards of marriage, sex and family, and provide a haven of love and peace to people who are hurting, but neighbours who would not enter a church usually feel comfortable in a home, even when the gospel is discussed.

Another context for lay witness is the workplace, for it is here that most Christians spend half their waking hours, and work is a divine calling. Christians can commend Christ by word of mouth, by their consistent industry, honesty and thoughtfulness, by their concern for justice in the workplace, and especially if others can see from the quality of their daily work that it is done to the glory of God.

We repent of our share in discouraging the ministry of the laity, especially of women and young people. We determine in the future to encourage all Christ's followers to take their place, rightfully and naturally, as his witnesses. For true evangelism comes from the overflow of a heart in love with Christ. That is why it belongs to all his people without exception.

7. THE INTEGRITY OF THE WITNESSES

Nothing commends the gospel more eloquently than a transformed life, and nothing brings it into disrepute so much as personal inconsistency. We are charged to behave in a manner that is worthy of the gospel of Christ, and even to "adorn" it, enhancing its beauty by holy lives. For the watching world rightly seeks evidence to substantiate the claims which Christ's disciples make for him. A strong evidence is our integrity.

Our proclamation that Christ died to bring us to God appeals to people who are spiritually thirsty, but they will not believe us if we give no evidence of knowing the living God ourselves, or if our public worship lacks reality and relevance.

Our message that Christ reconciles alienated people to each other rings true only if we are seen to love and forgive one another, to serve others in humility, and to reach out beyond our own community in compassionate, costly ministry to the needy.

Our challenge to others to deny themselves, take up their cross and follow Christ will be plausive only if we ourselves have evidently died to selfish ambition, dishonesty and covetousness, and are living a life of simplicity, contentment and generosity.

We deplore the failures in Christian consistency which we see in both Christians and churches: material greed, professional pride and rivalry, competition in Christian service, jealousy of younger leaders, missionary paternalism, the lack of mutual accountability, the loss of Christian standards of sexuality, and racial, social and sexual discrimination. All this

THE MANILA MANIFESTO cont.

is worldliness, allowing the prevailing culture to subvert the church instead of the church challenging and changing the culture. We are deeply ashamed of the times when, both as individuals and in our Christian communities, we have affirmed Christ in word and denied him in deed. Our inconsistency deprives our witness of credibility. We acknowledge our continuing struggles and failures. But we also determine by God's grace to develop integrity in ourselves and in the church.

8. THE LOCAL CHURCH

Every Christian congregation is a local expression of the Body of Christ and has the same responsibilities. It is both "a holy priesthood" to offer God the spiritual sacrifices of worship and "a holy nation" to spread abroad his excellences in witness. The church is thus both a worshipping and a witnessing community, gathered and scattered, called and sent. Worship and witness are inseparable.

We believe that the local church bears a primary responsibility for the spread of the gospel. Scripture suggests this in the progession that "our gospel came to you" and then "rang out from you." In this way, the gospel created the church which spreads the gospel which creates more churches in a continuous chain-reaction. Moreover, what Scripture teaches, strategy confirms. Each local church must evangelize the district in which it is situated, and has the resources to do so.

We recommend every congregation to carry out regular studies not only of its own membership and program but of its local community in all its particularity, in order to develop appropriate strategies for mission. Its members might decide to organize a visitation of their whole area, to penetrate for Christ a particular place where people assemble, to arrange a series of evangelistic meetings, lectures or concerts, to work with the poor to transform a local slum, or to plant a new church in a neighboring district or village. At the same time, they must not forget the church's global task. A church which sends out missionaries must not neglect its own locality, and a church which evangelizes its neighborhood must not ignore the rest of the world.

In all this each congregation and denomination should, where possible, work with others, seeking to turn any spirit of competition into one of cooperation. Churches should also work with para-church organizations, especially in evangelism, discipling and community service, for such agencies are part of the Body of Christ, and have valuable, specialist expertise from which the church can greatly benefit.

The church is intended by God to be a sign of his kingdom, that is, an indication of what human community looks like when it comes under his rule of righteousness and peace. As with individuals, so with churches, the gospel has to be embodied if it is to be communicated effectively. It is through our love for one another that the invisible God reveals himself today, especially when our fellowship is expressed in small groups, and when it transcends the barriers of race, rank, sex and age which divide other communities.

We deeply regret that many of our congregations are inward-looking, organized for maintenance rather than mission, or preoccupied with church-based activities at the expense of witness. We determine to turn our churches inside out, so that they may engage in continuous outreach, until the Lord adds to them daily those who are being saved.

9. COOPERATION IN EVANGELISM

Evangelism and unity are closely related in the New Testament. Jesus prayed that his people's oneness might reflect his own oneness with the Father, in order that the world might believe in him, and Paul exhorted the Philippians to "contend as one person for the faith of the gospel." In contrast to this biblical vision, we are ashamed of the suspicions and rivalries, the dogmatism over non-essentials, the power-struggles and empire-building which spoil our evangelistic witness. We affirm that co-operation in evangelism is indispensable, first because it is the will of God, but also because the gospel of reconciliation is discredited by our disunity, and because, if the task of world evangelization is ever to be accomplished, we must engage in it together.

"Cooperation" means finding unity in diversity. It involves people of different temperaments, gifts, callings and cultures, national churches and mission agencies, all ages and both sexes working together.

We are determined to put behind us once and for all, as a hangover from the colonial past, the simplistic distinction between First World sending and Two-Thirds World receiving countries. For the great new fact of our era is the internationalization of missions. Not only are a large majority of all evangelical Christians now non-western, but the number of Two-Thirds World missionaries will soon exceed those from the West. We believe that mission teams, which are diverse in composition but united in heart and mind, constitute a dramatic witness to the grace of God.

FOCUS FACT

In AD 1900 only 9 percent of the world's population lived in cities; in AD 2000 it is thought that more than 50 percent will do so. This worldwide move into the cities has been called "the greatest migration in human history." —Manila Manifesto

Our reference to "the whole church" is not a presumptuous claim that the universal church and the evangelical community are synonymous. For we recognize that there are many churches which are not part of the evangelical movement. Evangelical attitudes to the Roman Catholic and Orthodox Churches differ widely. Some evangelicals are praying, talking, studying Scripture and working with these churches. Others are strongly opposed to any form of dialogue or cooperation with them. All evangelicals are aware that serious theological differences between us remain. Where appropriate, and so long as biblical truth is not compromised, cooperation may be possible in such areas as Bible translation, the study of contemporary theological and ethical issues, social work and political action. We wish to make it clear, however, that common evangelism demands a common commitment to the biblical gospel.

Some of us are members of churches which belong to the World Council of Churches and believe that a positive yet critical participation in its work is our Christian duty. Others among us have no link with the World Council. All of us urge the World Council of Churches to adopt a consistent biblical understanding of evangelism.

We confess our own share of responsibility for the brokenness of the Body of Christ, which is a major stumbling-block to world evangelization. We determine to go on seeking that unity in truth for which Christ prayed. We are persuaded that the right way forward towards closer cooperation is frank and patient dialogue on the basis of the Bible, with all who share our concerns. To this we gladly commit ourselves.

C. The Whole World

The whole gospel has been entrusted to the whole church, in order that it may be made known to the whole world. It is necessary, therefore, for us to understand the world into which we are sent.

10. THE MODERN WORLD

Evangelism takes place in a context, not in a vacuum. The balance between gospel and context must be carefully maintained. We must understand the context in order to address

THE MANILA MANIFESTO cont.

it, but the context must not be allowed to distort the gospel.

In this connection we have become concerned about the impact of "modernity," which is an emerging world culture produced by industrialization with its technology and urbanization with its economic order. These factors combine to create an environment, which significantly shapes the way in which we see our world. In addition, secularism has devastated faith by making God and the supernatural meaningless; urbanization has dehumanized life for many; and the mass media have contributed to the devaluation of truth and authority, by replacing word with image. In combination, these consequences of modernity pervert the message which many preach and undermine their motivation for mission.

In AD 1900 only 9 percent of the world's population lived in cities; in AD 2000 it is thought that more than 50 percent will do so. This worldwide move into the cities has been called "the greatest migration in human history"; it constitutes a major challenge to Christian mission. On the one hand, city populations are extremely cosmopolitan, so that the nations come to our doorstep in the city. Can we develop global churches in which the gospel abolishes the barriers of ethnicity? On the other hand, many city dwellers are migrant poor who are also receptive to the gospel. Can the people of God be persuaded to re-locate into such urban poor communities, in order to serve the people and share in the transformation of the city?

Modernization brings blessings as well as dangers. By creating links of communication and commerce around the globe, it makes unprecedented openings for the gospel, crossing old frontiers and penetrating closed societies, whether traditional or totalitarian. The Christian media have a powerful influence both in sowing the seed of the gospel and in preparing the soil. The major missionary broadcasters are committed to a gospel witness by radio in every major language by the year AD 2000.

We confess that we have not struggled as we should to understand modernization. We have used its methods and techniques uncritically and so exposed ourselves to worldliness. But we determine in the future to take these challenges and opportunities seriously, to resist the secular pressures of modernity, to relate the lordship of Christ to the whole of modern culture, and thus to engage in mission in the modern world without worldliness in modern mission.

FOCUS FACT

The great new fact of our era is the internationalization of missions. Not only are a large majority of all evangelical Christians now non-western, but the number of Two-Thirds World missionaries will soon exceed those from the West. —Manila Manifesto

---

11. THE CHALLENGE OF AD 2000 AND BEYOND

The world population today is approaching 6 billion. One third of them nominally confess Christ. Of the remaining four billion half have heard of him and the other half have not. In the light of these figures, we evaluate our evangelistic task by considering four categories of people.

First, there is the potential missionary work force, the committed. In this century this category of Christian believers has grown from about 40 million in 1900 to about 500 million today, and at this moment is growing over twice as fast as any other major religions group.

Secondly, there are the uncommitted. They make a Christian profession (they have been baptized, attend church occasionally and even call themselves Christians), but the notion of a personal commitment to Christ is foreign to them. They are found in all churches throughout the world. They urgently need to be re-evangelized.

Thirdly, there are the unevangelized. These are people who have a minimal knowledge of the gospel, but have had no valid opportunity to respond to it. They are probably within reach of Christian people if only these will go to the next street, road, village or town to find them.

Fourthly, there are the unreached. These are the two billion who may never have heard of Jesus as Savior, and are not within reach of Christians of their own people. There are, in fact, some 2,000 peoples or nationalities in which there is not yet a vital, indigenous church movement. We find it helpful to think of them as belonging to smaller "people groups" which perceive themselves as having an affinity with each other (e.g. a common culture, language, home or occupation). The most effective messengers to reach them will be those believers who already belong to their culture and know their language. Otherwise, cross-cultural messengers of the gospel will need to go, leaving behind their own culture and sacrificially identifying with the people they long to reach for Christ.

There are now about 12,000 such unreached people groups within the 2,000 larger peoples, so that the task is not impossible. Yet at present only 7 percent of all missionaries are engaged in this kind of outreach, while the remaining 93 percent are working in the already evangelized half of the world. If this imbalance is to be redressed, a strategic redeployment of personnel will be necessary.

A distressing factor that affects each of the above categories is that of inaccessibility. Many countries do not grant visas to self-styled missionaries, who have no other qualification or contribution to offer. Such areas are not absolutely inaccessible, however. For our prayers can pass through every curtain, door and barrier. And Christian radio and television, audio and video cassettes, films and literature can also reach the otherwise unreachable. So can so-called "tent-makers" who like Paul earn their own living. They travel in the course of their profession (e.g. business people, university lecturers, technical specialists and language teachers), and use every opportunity to speak of Jesus Christ. They do not enter a country under false pretenses, for their work genuinely takes them there; it is simply that witness is an essential component of their Christian lifestyle, wherever they may happen to be.

We are deeply ashamed that nearly two millennia have passed since the death and resurrection of Jesus, and still two-thirds of the world's population have not yet acknowledged him. On the other hand, we are amazed at the mounting evidence of God's power even in the most unlikely places of the globe.

Now the year 2000 has become for many a challenging milestone. Can we commit ourselves to evangelize the world during the last decade of this millennium? There is nothing magical about the date, yet should we not do our best to reach this goal? Christ commands us to take the gospel to all peoples. The task is urgent. We are determined to obey him with joy and hope.

12. DIFFICULT SITUATIONS

Jesus plainly told his followers to expect opposition. "If they persecuted me," he said, "they will persecute you also." He even told them to rejoice over persecution, and reminded them that the condition of fruitfulness was death.

These predictions, that Christian suffering is inevitable and productive, have come true in every age, including our own. There have been many thousands of martyrs. Today the situation is much the same. We earnestly hope that *glasnost* and *perestroika* will lead to complete religious freedom in the Soviet Union and other Eastern block nations, and that Islamic and Hindu countries will become more open to the gospel. We deplore the recent brutal suppression of China's democratic movement, and we pray that it will not bring further suffering to the Christians. On the whole, however, it seems that ancient religions are becoming less tolerant, expatriates less welcome, and the world less friendly to the gospel.

THE MANILA MANIFESTO cont.

In this situation we wish to make three statements to governments which are reconsidering their attitude to Christian believers.

First, Christians are loyal citizens, who seek the welfare of their nation. They pray for its leaders and pay their taxes. Of course, those who have confessed Jesus as Lord cannot also call other authorities Lord, and if commanded to do so, or to do anything which God forbids, must disobey. But they are conscientious citizens. They also contribute to their country's well-being by the stability of their marriages and homes, their honesty in business, their hard work and their voluntary activity in the service of the handicapped and needy. Just governments have nothing to fear from Christians.

Secondly, Christians renounce unworthy methods of evangelism. Though the nature of our faith requires us to share the gospel with others, our practice is to make an open and honest statement of it, which leaves the hearers entirely free to make up their own minds about it. We wish to be sensitive to those of other faiths, and we reject any approach that seeks to force conversion on them.

Thirdly, Christians earnestly desire freedom of religion for all people, not just freedom for Christianity. In predominantly Christian countries, Christians are at the forefront of those who demand freedom for religious minorities. In predominantly non-Christian countries, therefore, Christians are asking for themselves no more than they demand for others in similar circumstances. The freedom to "profess, practise and propagate" religion, as defined in the Universal Declaration of Human Rights, could and should surely be a reciprocally granted right.

We greatly regret any unworthy witness of which followers of Jesus may have been guilty. We determine to give no unnecessary offence in anything, lest the name of Christ be dishonored. However, the offence of the cross we cannot avoid. For the sake of Christ crucified we pray that we may be ready, by his grace, to suffer and even to die. Martyrdom is a form of witness which Christ has promised especially to honor.

Conclusion: Proclaim Christ until He Comes

"Proclaim Christ until he comes." That has been the theme of Lausanne II. Of course we believe that Christ has come; he came when Augustus was Emperor of Rome. But one day, as we know from his promises, he will come again in unimaginable splendor to perfect his kingdom. We are commanded to watch and be ready. Meanwhile, the gap between his two comings is to be filled with the Christian missionary enterprise. We have been told to go to the ends of the earth with the gospel, and we have been promised that the end of the age will come only when we have done so. The two ends (of earth space and time) will concide. Until then he has pledged to be with us.

So the Christian mission is an urgent task. We do not know how long we have. We certainly have no time to waste. And in order to get on urgently with our responsibility, other qualities will be necessary, especially unity (we must evangelize together) and sacrifice (we must count and accept the cost). Our covenant at Lausanne was "to pray, to play and to work together for the evangelization of the whole world." Our manifesto at Manila is that the whole church is called to take the whole gospel to the whole world, proclaiming Christ until he comes, with all necessary urgency, unity and sacrifice.

MEN, WOMEN AND BIBLICAL EQUALITY

The Bible teaches the full equality of men and women in creation and in redemption (Genesis 1:26-28, 2:23, 5:1, 2; 1 Corinthians 11:11, 12; Galatians 3:13, 28, 5:1).

The Bible teaches that God has revealed himself in the totality of Scripture, the authoritative Word of God (Matthew 5:18; John 10:35; 2 Timothy 3:16; 2 Peter 1:20, 21). We believe that Scripture is to be interpreted wholistically and thematically. We also recognize the necessity of making a distinction between inspiration and interpretation: Inspiration relates to the divine impulse and control whereby the whole canonical Scripture is the Word of God; interpretation relates to the human activity whereby we seek to apprehend revealed truth in harmony with the totality of Scripture and under the guidance of the Holy Spirit. To be truly biblical, Christians must continually examine their faith and practice under the searchlight of Scripture.

Biblical Truths

CREATION

1. The Bible teaches that both man and woman were created in God's image, had a direct relationship with God, and shared jointly the responsibilities of bearing and rearing children and having dominion over the created order (Genesis 1:26-28).

2. The Bible teaches that woman and man were created for full and equal partnership. The word "helper" (ezer), used to designate woman in Genesis 2:18, refers to God in most instances of Old Testament usage (e.g. 1 Samuel 7:12; Psalm 121:1, 2). Consequently the word conveys no implication whatsoever of female subordination or inferiority.

3. The Bible teaches that the forming of woman from man demonstrates the fundamental unity and equality of human beings (Genesis 2:21-23). In Genesis 2:18, 20 the word "suitable" (kenegdo) denotes equality and adequacy.

4. The Bible teaches that man and woman were co-participants in the Fall: Adam was no less culpable than Eve (Genesis 3:6; Romans 5:12-21; 1 Corinthians 15:21, 22).

5. The Bible teaches that the rulership of Adam over Eve resulted from the Fall and was therefore not a part of the original created order. Genesis 3:16 is a prediction of the effects of the Fall rather than a prescription of God's ideal order.

REDEMPTION

6. The Bible teaches that Jesus Christ came to redeem women as well as men. Through faith in Christ we all become children of God, one in Christ, and heirs to the blessings of salvation without reference to racial, social, or gender distinctives (John 1:12, 13; Romans 8:14-17; 2 Corinthians 5:17; Galatians 3:26-28).

COMMUNITY

7. The Bible teaches that at Pentecost the Holy Spirit came on men and women alike. Without distinction, the Holy Spirit indwells women and men, and sovereignly distributes gifts without preference as to gender (Acts 2:1-21; 1 Corinthians 12:7, 11, 14:31).

8. The Bible teaches that both women and men are called to develop their spiritual gifts and to use them as stewards of the grace of God (1 Peter 4:10, 11). Both men and women are divinely gifted and empowered to minister to the whole Body of Christ, under his authority (Acts 1:14, 18:6, 21:9; Romans 16:1-7, 12, 13, 15; Philippians 4:2, 3; Colossians 4:15; see also Mark 15:40, 41, 16:1-7; Luke 8:1-3; John 20:17, 18; compare also Old Testament examples: Judges 4:4-14, 5:7; 2 Chronicles 34:22-28; Proverbs 31:30, 31; Micah 6:4).

9. The Bible teaches that, in the New Testament economy, women as well as men exercise the prophetic, priestly and royal functions (Acts 2:17, 18, 21:9; 2 Corinthians 11:5; 1 Peter 2:9, 10; Revelation 1:6, 5:10). Therefore, the few isolated texts that appear to restrict the full redemptive freedom of women must not be interpreted simplistically and in contradiction to the rest of Scripture, but their interpretation must take into account their relation to the broader teaching of Scripture and their total context (1 Corinthians 11:2-16, 14:33-36; 1 Timothy 2:9-15).

10. The Bible defines the function of leadership as the empowerment of others for service rather than as the exercise of power over them (Matthew 20:25-28, 23:8; Mark 10:42-45; John 13:13-17; Galatians 5:13; 1 Peter 5:2, 3).

MEN, WOMEN AND BIBLICAL EQUALITY cont.

FAMILY

11. The Bible teaches that husbands and wives are heirs together of the grace of life and that they are bound together in a relationship of mutual submission and responsibility (1 Corinthians 7:3-5; Ephesians 5:21; 1 Peter 3:1-7; Genesis 21:12). The husband's function as "head" is to be understood as self-giving love and service within this relationship of mutual submission (Ephesians 5:21-33; Colossians 3:19; 1 Peter 3:7).

12. The Bible teaches that both mothers and fathers are to exercise leadership in the nurture, training, discipline and teaching of their children (Exodus 20:12; Leviticus 19:3; Deuteronomy 6:6-9, 21:18-21, 27:16; Proverbs 1:8, 6:20; Ephesians 6:1-4; Colossians 3:20; 2 Timothy 1:5; see also Luke 2:51).

FOCUS QUOTE

Nothing commends the gospel more eloquently than a transformed life, and nothing brings it into disrepute so much as personal inconsistency. We are charged to behave in a manner that is worthy of the gospel of Christ, and even to "adorn" it, enhancing its beauty by holy lives. For the watching world rightly seeks evidence to substantiate the claims which Christ's disciples make for him. A strong evidence is our integrity.—Manila Manifesto

---

Application

COMMUNITY

1. In the church, spiritual gifts of women and men are to be recognized, developed and used in serving and teaching ministries at all levels of involvement; as small group leaders, counselors, facilitators, administrators, ushers, communion servers, and board members, and in pastoral care, teaching, preaching, and worship.

In so doing, the church will honor God as the source of spiritual gifts. The church will also fulfill God's mandate of stewardship without the appalling loss to God's kingdom that results when half of the church's members are excluded from positions of responsibility.

2. In the church, public recognition is to be given to both women and men who exercise ministries of service and leadership.

In so doing, the church will model the unity and harmony that should characterize the community of believers. In a world fractured by discrimination and segregation, the church will dissociate itself from worldly or pagan devices designed to make women feel inferior for being female. It will help prevent their departure from the church or their rejection of the Christian faith.

FAMILY

3. In the Christian home, husband and wife are to defer to each other in seeking to fulfill each other's preferences, desires and aspirations. Neither spouse is to seek to dominate the other, but each is to act as servant of the other, in humility considering the other as better than oneself. In case of decisional deadlock, they should seek resolution through biblical methods of conflict resolution rather than by one spouse imposing a decision upon the other.

In so doing, husband and wife will help the Christian home stand against improper use of power and authority by spouses and will protect the home from wife and child abuse that sometimes tragically follows a hierarchical interpretation of the husband's "headship."

4. In the Christian home, spouses are to learn to share the responsibilities of leadership on the basis of gifts, expertise, and availability, with due regard for the partner most affected by the decision under consideration.

In so doing, spouses will learn to respect their competencies and their complementarity.

This will prevent one spouse from becoming the perennial loser, often forced to practice ingratiating or deceitful manipulation to protect self-esteem. By establishing their marriage on a partnership basis, the couple will protect it from joining the tide of dead or broken marriages resulting from marital inequities.

5. In the Christian home, couples who share a lifestyle characterized by the freedom they find in Christ will do so without experiencing feelings of guilt or resorting to hypocrisy. They are freed to emerge from an unbiblical "traditionalism" and can rejoice in their mutual accountability in Christ.

In so doing, they will openly express their obedience to Scripture, will model an example for other couples in quest of freedom in Christ, and will stand against patterns of domination and inequality sometimes imposed upon church and family.

We believe that biblical equality as reflected in this document is true to Scripture.

We stand united in our conviction that the Bible, in its totality, is the liberating Word that provides the most effective way for women and men to exercise the gifts distributed by the Holy Spirit and thus to serve God.

Gilbert Bilezikian
W. Ward Gasque
Stanley N. Gundry
Gretchen Gaebelein Hull
Catherine Clark Kroeger
Jo Anne Lyon
Roger Nicole

Source: Christians for Biblical Equality, Rosemount, MN.

THE DUPAGE DECLARATION: A CALL TO BIBLICAL FIDELITY

Preamble

We evangelical renewal leaders from North American mainline churches gathered at Wheaton in DuPage County, Illinois, March 19, 20, 1990 express our concern for the church of Jesus Christ in its drift away from the evangelical faith. What is needed, we believe, is a genuine revival rooted in the Word of God. We therefore, present this declaration: *A Call to Biblical Fidelity.*

This declaration represents our understanding of theological and moral issues that are now in dispute in our churches. It is not intended to be an exhaustive list of church doctrines and concerns.

It is offered in the spirit of Christ, our Savior and Judge, who calls each of us to confess our complicity in private and public sin, "For it is time for judgment to begin with the family of God"(1 Peter 4:17, NIV; cf. 2 Timothy 4:1-5). We resolve to serve him with total fidelity and obedience to his Word.

Declaration

I

We affirm the Trinitarian name of God—Father, Son and Holy Spirit.

We deny that these designations are mere metaphors drawn from the cultural experience of the past and may therefore be replaced by new symbols reflecting the cultural ethos of today.

II

We affirm that God has revealed himself fully and decisively in Jesus Christ as attested in Holy Scripture.

We deny that there are other revelations in nature or history that fulfill or complete this one revelation of God.

III

We affirm that there is only one way to salvation—God's way to us in Jesus Christ, which is apprehended by faith alone through God's grace.

We deny that other religions are pathways to salvation, or that one can be in a right relationship with God apart from repentance and faith in Jesus Christ.

IV

We affirm that Jesus Christ is God incarnate in human flesh, fully human and fully divine, different from all other human beings in kind, not simply in degree.

We deny that Jesus Christ is essentially the flower of humanity, a spiritual master, a paradigm of what all human beings can become.

V

We affirm that Holy Scripture is the written Word of God, the uniquely inspired testimony to God's self-disclosure in the history of biblical Israel culminating in Jesus Christ. The scriptures of the Old and New Testaments take precedence over experience, tradition and reason and are therefore our infallible standard for faith and practice.

We deny that Holy Scripture is a merely human document that records the religious experiences of a past people, that it is only an aid in understanding our experiences in the present rather than a rule that is used by the Spirit of God to direct the people of God in every age.

VI

We affirm the biblical guidelines for human sexuality: chastity outside of marriage, lifelong fidelity and holiness in marriage, and celibacy for the sake of the kingdom.

We deny that premarital or extramarital relations, trial marriages, cohabitation outside of marriage, homosexual relations and so-called homosexual unions, can ever be in genuine accord with the will and purpose of God for his people.

VII

We affirm the sanctity of human life at every stage based on our creation in the image of God and our election by God for service in his kingdom.

We deny, for example, that the personal choice of either parent takes precedence over the right of the unborn child to life in the service of God's glory. We deplore the continuing traffic of abortion as the slaughter of innocents, which can only be an abomination in the sight of God.

VIII

We affirm that the mission of the church is to spread the good news of salvation by word and deed to a lost and despairing humanity. This mission to proclaim the atoning death and resurrection of Jesus Christ to all nations calls people of faith to discipleship and obedience in the pursuit of personal and social holiness. We further affirm that the fruit of the gospel proclamation is justice, mercy and peace.

We deny that the mission of the church is the self-development of exploited peoples or the political liberation of oppressed people.

We invite pastors and lay people from the Body of Christ to join us in affirming this declaration.

Persons or groups desiring to affirm this declaration by adding their names may contact: James V. Heidinger II, Good News, P.O. Box 150, Wilmore, KY 40390.

Original signatories of the DuPage Declaration:

Timothy Bayly
Presbyterian Church (USA)

Richard M. Bowman
Christian Church
(Disciples of Christ)

J. Robert Campbell
Presbyterian Church (USA)

David M. Higbee
Independent Evangelical

James Mark Kushiner
Independent Evangelical

Richard Lovelace
Presbyterian Church (USA)

Kevin Perrotta
Roman Catholic

Gerald M. Sanders
United Church of Christ

Armand L. Weller
United Church of Christ

Waldo Werning
Lutheran

Parker Williamson
Presbyterian Church (USA)

Donald G. Bloesch
United Church of Christ

Ray Bringham
Church of God, Anderson

James V. Heidinger II
United Methodist Church

Paul D. Johnston
Presbyterian Church (USA)

Brad Long
Presbyterian Church (USA)

Betty Moore
Presbyterian Church (USA)

Kevin D. Ray
Christian Church
(Disciples of Christ)

Vernon Stoop, Jr.
United Church of Christ

Matthew J. Welde
Presbyterian Church (USA)

Todd Wetzel
Episcopal Church

The World in Review

STATUS OF THE CHRISTIAN WORLD

Year	*1900*	*1970*	*1980*	*1990*	*2000*
WORLD POPULATION					
1. Total population	1,619,886,800	3,610,034,400	4,373,917,500	5,297,042,000	6,259,642,000
2. Urban dwellers	232,694,900	1,354,237,000	1,797,479,000	2,414,450,100	3,160,381,900
3. Rural dwellers	1,387,191,900	2,255,797,400	2,576,438,500	2,882,591,900	3,099,260,100
4. Adult population	1,025,938,000	2,245,227,300	2,698,396,900	3,244,068,700	3,808,564,300
5. Literates	286,705,000	1,437,761,900	1,774,002,700	2,208,993,000	2,697,595,100
6. Nonliterates	739,233,000	807,465,400	924,394,200	1,035,075,700	1,110,969,200
WORLDWIDE EXPANSION OF CITIES					
7. Metropolises (over 100,000 population)	400	2,400	2,700	3,450	4,200
8. Megacities (over 1 million population)	20	161	227	330	433
WORLD POPULATION BY RELIGION					
9. Christians (total all kinds)	558,056,300	1,216,579,400	1,432,686,500	1,758,777,900	2,130,000,000
10. Muslims	200,102,200	550,919,000	722,956,500	934,842,200	1,200,653,000
11. Nonreligious	2,923,300	543,065,300	715,901,400	866,427,700	1,021,888,400
12. Hindus	203,033,300	465,784,800	582,749,900	705,345,900	859,252,300
13. Buddhists	127,159,000	231,672,200	273,715,600	323,349,500	359,092,100
14. Atheists	225,600	165,288,500	195,119,400	233,098,500	262,447,600
15. New-Religionists	5,910,000	76,443,100	96,021,800	117,589,100	138,263,800
16. Tribal religionists	106,339,600	88,077,400	89,963,500	99,424,000	100,535,900
17. Sikhs	2,960,600	10,612,200	14,244,400	18,152,800	23,831,700
18. Jews	12,269,800	15,185,900	16,938,200	17,719,800	19,173,600
19. Other religionists	400,907,100	246,406,600	233,620,300	221,314,200	143,503,600
GLOBAL CHRISTIANITY					
20. Total Christans as % of world	34.4	33.7	32.8	33.2	34.0
21. Affiliated church members	521,563,200	1,131,809,600	1,323,389,700	1,623,833,000	1,967,000,000
22. Practicing Christians	469,259,800	884,021,800	1,018,355,300	1,209,794,000	1,377,000,000
23. Pentecostals/Charismatics	3,700,000	72,600,000	158,000,000	372,651,300	562,526,000
24. Crypto-Christians	3,572,400	55,699,700	70,395,000	134,784,700	176,208,000
25. Avg. Christian martyrs per yr	35,600	230,000	270,000	260,000	500,000
MEMBERSHIP BY ECCLESIASTICAL BLOC					
26. Anglicans	30,573,700	47,557,000	49,804,000	53,820,200	61,037,200
27. Catholics (non-Roman)	276,000	3,134,400	3,439,400	3,822,800	4,334,100
28. Marginal Protestants	927,600	10,830,200	14,077,500	18,275,200	24,106,200
29. Nonwhite indigenous Christians	7,743,100	58,702,000	82,181,100	143,823,600	204,100,000
30. Orthodox	115,897,700	143,402,500	160,737,900	179,517,100	199,819,000
31. Protestants	103,056,700	233,424,200	262,157,600	324,240,100	386,000,000
32. Roman Catholics	266,419,400	672,319,100	802,660,000	962,632,600	1,144,000,000
MEMBERSHIP BY GEOGRAPHICAL REGION					
33. Africa	8,756,400	115,924,200	164,571,000	231,053,500	323,914,900
34. East Asia	1,763,000	10,050,200	16,149,600	84,455,900	128,000,000
35. Europe	273,788,400	397,108,700	403,177,600	408,392,800	411,448,700
36. Latin America	60,025,100	262,027,800	340,978,600	437,449,600	555,486,000
37. Northern America	59,569,700	169,246,900	178,892,500	189,460,500	201,265,200
38. Oceania	4,311,400	14,669,400	16,160,600	18,183,800	21,361,500

39. South Asia	16,347,200	76,770,200	106,733,200	143,176,000	185,476,700
40. USSR	97,002,000	86,012,300	96,726,500	107,614,800	118,101,000
CHRISTIAN ORGANIZATIONS					
41. Service agencies	1,500	14,100	17,500	21,000	24,000
42. Foreign-mission sending agencies	600	2,200	3,100	3,970	4,800
43. Institutions	9,500	80,500	91,000	99,200	103,000
CHRISTIAN WORKERS					
44. Nationals (all denominations)	1,050,000	2,350,000	2,950,000	3,923,000	4,500,000
45. Pentecostal/Charismatic national workers	2,000	237,300	420,000	934,500	1,133,000
46. Aliens (foreign missionaries)	62,000	240,000	249,000	285,250	400,000
47. Pentecostal/Charismatic foreign missionaries	100	3,790	34,600	85,500	167,000
CHRISTIAN FINANCE (IN US$, PER YEAR)					
48. Personal income of church members	270 billion	4,100 billion	5,878 billion	8,950 billion	12,700 billion
49. Personal income of Pentecostals/Charismatics	250,000,000	157 billion	395 billion	1,005 billion	1,550 billion
50. Giving to Christian causes	8 billion	70 billion	100.3 billion	157 billion	220 billion
51. Churches' income	7 billion	50 billion	64.5 billion	83.4 billion	100 billion
52. Parachurch and institutional income	1 billion	20 billion	35.8 billion	74.2 billion	120 billion
53. Ecclesiastical crime	300,000	5,000,000	30,000,000	874,500,000	2 billion
54. Income of global foreign missions	200,000,000	3.0 billion	5.0 billion	8.6 billion	12 billion
55. Computers in Christian use (total numbers)	0	1,000	3,000,000	54,000,000	340,000,000
CHRISTIAN LITERATURE					
56. New commercial book titles per yr	2,200	17,100	18,800	22,400	25,000
57. New titles including devotional	3,100	52,000	60,000	65,600	75,000
58. Christian periodicals	3,500	23,000	22,500	23,800	35,000
59. New books/articles on evangelization per year	300	3,100	7,500	11,000	16,000
SCRIPTURE DISTRIBUTION (ALL SOURCES)					
60. Bibles per year	5,452,600	25,000,000	36,800,000	51,410,000	70,000,000
61. New Testaments per year	7,300,000	45,000,000	57,500,000	76,865,000	110,000,000
CHRISTIAN BROADCASTING					
62. Christian radio/TV stations	0	1,230	1,450	2,160	4,000
63. Total monthly listeners/viewers	0	750,000,000	990,474,400	1,369,620,600	2,150,000,000
64. for Christian stations	0	150,000,000	291,810,500	451,859,400	600,000,000
65. for secular stations	0	650,000,000	834,068,900	1,155,597,300	1,810,000,000
CHRISTIAN URBAN MISSION					
66. Non-Christian megacities	5	65	95	150	202
67. New non-Christian urban dwellers per day	5,200	51,100	69,300	98,750	140,000
68. Urban Christians	159,600,000	660,800,000	844,600,000	1,094,713,000	1,393,700,000
69. Urban Christians as % of urban dwellers	68.8	47.8	46.3	45.0	44.5
70. Evangelized urban dwellers, %	72.0	80.0	83.0	88.0	91.0
WORLD EVANGELIZATION					
71. Unevangelized populations	788,159,000	1,391,956,000	1,380,576,000	1,252,557,000	1,038,819,000
72. Unevangelized as % of world	48.7	38.6	31.6	23.6	16.6
73. Unreached peoples (with no churches)	3,500	1,300	700	450	200
74. World evangelization plans since AD 30	250	510	620	910	1,400

Today's Global Human Need

THE MEGARICH: 0.05%
(400 billionaires, 50,000 multimillionaires, 2,500,000 millionaires)

50 million megarich hangers-on

THE RICH: 54% of world

Global Income or GWP
(Gross World Product):
$16.1 trillion p.a.
($3,040 per capita)

Third-World elites own $1 trillion in Western banks

Global average: $3040

THE POOR: 46% of world

Global Human Need
Total income of this 46% of world: $800 billion p.a. (5% of GWP)

Figures on edge of the globe:
Left edge: Per capita income p.a. (multiply by 4.3 for family income)
Right edge: Individual net worth

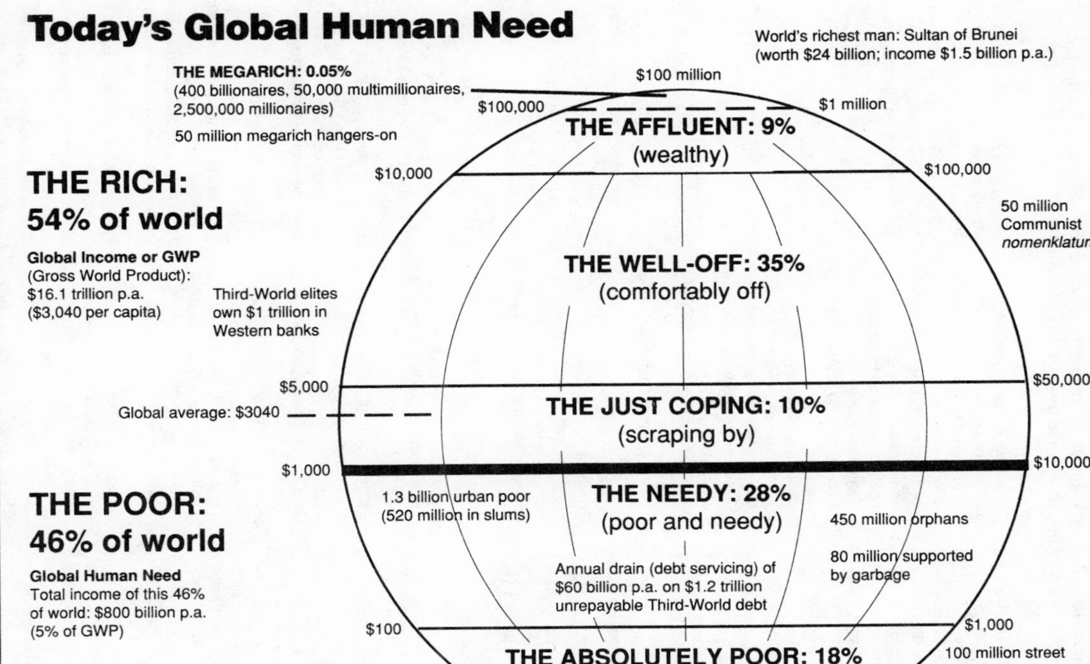

STRUCTURES OF SIN

Total cost of all organized "structures of sin": $5,200 billion p.a. (32% of GWP)

Computer crime
$44 billion p.a.
Tobacco
$290 billion p.a.
Tax cheating
$180 billion p.a.
Shoplifting
$90 billion p.a.
Drug traffic
$150 billion p.a.
Electronic warfare
$5 billion p.a.
Organized crime
$600 billion p.a.
Financial crime
$2 trillion p.a.
Financial fraud
$800 billion p.a.
Arms black-marketeers
$5 billion p.a.
Betting and gambling
$700 billion p.a.
Advertising
$120 billion p.a.
Pornography
$20 billion p.a.
Military
$950 billion p.a.
Military R&D
$80 billion p.a.
Absenteeism at work:
$6 billion p.a.
Total cost of all varieties of crime:
$3.2 trillion p.a.

Source: World Evangelization Database

Poverty, slums, disasters, deprivation, rights abuses, illness, disease, addiction:
Human need here focuses on the unfortunate victims involved (described by the detailed statistics).

The globe on page 77 gives an overview. It is divided into 2 halves. The lower half depicts the world of the Poor (the so-called "lower classes") divided into 2 main slices (with a megapoor minislice) and into several population segments. The statistics detail today's global human need.

The upper half of the globe depicts the world of the Rich (the "middle and upper classes"), divided into 3 main slices (with a megarich minislice) and into several population segments. The figures shown attached to this upper half briefly outline the so-called "structures of sin."

All statistics refer primarily to the year 1990 (usually mid-1990). All monies are given in U.S. dollars. Note also that *p.a.* means "per annum", "per year", "a year", "each year", "every year." These terms are used alternately to provide variety. Note further that the same global totals throughout these diagrams may be given rounded to 1, 2, 3, or 4 significant figures (e.g. world population is 5.3 billion, or 5.292 million, etc.). Partial totals may not always add up to global totals or 100.0% because of rounding.

HUMANS ON THE GLOBE OF MID-1990

5,292,180,000 population
91,201,500 population increase p.a. (1.72% p.a.; 93% in developing countries)
Median age 24.2 years
141.6 million births a year (2.67% p.a.)
50.5 million deaths a year (0.96% p.a.)
Life expectancy at birth 62.3 years

BASIC RIGHTS: FOOD, WATER, SHELTER, CARE

1.8 billion undernourished
950 million hungry (inadequate food for active working life)
550 million severely malnourished
500 million suffering from iron-deficiency anemia
400 million on verge of starvation
10 million babies born malnourished p.a.
Infant mortality (deaths under 1 year old) 68 per 1000 live births
Maternal mortality 500,000 p.a.
15 million annual hunger-related deaths of under 5s
20 million starvation-related deaths p.a.
1.3 billion without safe water to drink
2.2 billion without adequate safe water supply
3.0 billion with unsafe water and bad sanitation
25,000 a day killed by dirty water
1.1 billion without adequate shelter
100 million with no shelter whatsoever
50 million cave dwellers
1.1 billion without money to buy food
1.3 billion with scarce firewood
60 million abandoned children and infants
300 million homeless/family-less children
100 million megacity street children
450 million orphans
520 million slum dwellers or shanty dwellers
New slum dwellers increase at 70 million p.a.
80 million supported by garbage collection/recycling
1.5 billion with no access to medical care
2.4 billion poor (46% of world)
1,273 million urban poor (1.1 billion in Third World)
952 million absolutely poor (in absolute poverty; 18%)
Poorest 20% of world gets 1.6% of GWP
Working-age population: 60 million more p.a.
Exploited child labor: 50 million
80 million beggars
90 million unemployed workers
600 million underemployed labor
1 billion urban part-time street vendors
Physical quality of life index (global average): 68%
50 countries with less calorie supply than essential (2,600 per capita per day)

SOCIOPOLITICAL RIGHTS

10 million stateless (with no nationality)
12 million deportees (persons expelled) p.a.
4 billion unprotected from human rights abuses
Human rights: 45% violated
14 million permanently unsettled refugees
25 million emigrants/immigrants p.a.
154 countries not controlled by popular votes
2.8 billion disenfranchised (no control by vote; 54% of world)
1,035 million illiterate/nonliterate adults (29%)
880 million orate (nonreader) adults unable to read or write (25%)
9 million more illiterate adults p.a.
250 million with language handicaps
3.7 billion without political freedom
1,307 million in religious countries
1,579 million in secular countries
1,488 million under atheistic regimes
400 million under oppressive regimes
70 million under racist regimes
2.5 billion women denied full rights and equality
1 billion victims of corruption
750 million uneducated (no past schooling)
1.5 billion school-age children (ages 5-19)
1.0 billion with little or no access to schools (67% of those eligible)
620 million school-agers not in schools
360 million with no access to schools (24%)
24 million children reach school age p.a.
41% without access to electricity
43% without telephone access
67% without radio or TV
100 million prisoners in 12-month period
4 million political prisoners
1 million prisoners due to religion
800,000 prisoners of conscience
2.6 billion denied freedom of religion
4.2 billion denied full political freedom and civil rights
2 billion in countries frequently employing torture
100,000 prisoners being tortured
130 million citizens killed by own governments since 1900
1,692,400 political executions, 1948–1977
40,000 executed by governments each year
32 million slaves (bought and sold, including bonded labor, involun-

tary servitude)
510 million victims of crime p.a.
850,000 murders a year
5 million child victims of pedophile racketeers p.a.
22 million child-abuse incidents p.a.
200 million persons abused in childhood

FUNDAMENTAL FREEDOMS

3 billion denied freedom to travel in own country
4 billion denied freedom to travel abroad
3 billion denied freedom to assemble
3.5 billion denied freedom to teach ideas

DISASTERS AND DESERTIFICATION

1 million more desertification victims a year
10 million environmental refugees
850 million at risk through desertification
1,500 major earthquakes, 1900–1985, killing 1.8 million
80,000 earthquake victims (deaths) a year
350 major floods, 1960–1981, killing 175,000
10,000 flood victims (deaths) a year
210 major cyclones, 1960–1981, killing 536,000
250,000 environmental disaster victims p.a.
1 million poisoned by pesticides p.a.
625 million live in areas with unhealthy air
25,000 pollution deaths a day
1 million killed in man-made disasters p.a.
Traffic deaths 3 persons per 100 million vehicle miles

ILLNESS/DISEASE

42 million legally blind
28 million totally blind (nonsighted)
18 million with river blindness (85 million at risk)
320 million partially deaf (hearing-impaired)
130 million severely deaf
20 million totally deaf
10 million dumb (deaf-mutes)
10 million with dracunculiasis
13 million leprosy sufferers (lepers)
60 million diabetics
400 million new malaria cases p.a.
2.8 billion live at risk of malaria
5 million malaria deaths p.a.
270 million with elephantiasis
200 million with schistosomiasis (600 million at risk)
1 million a year bitten by venomous snakes
40,000 deaths p.a. from venomous snake bites
9 million with Parkinson's disease
10 million with tuberculosis (TB: 3 million deaths p.a.)
465 million iron-deficiency anemic women
100 million with chemosensory (taste and smell) disorders
3 million persons worldwide with artificial implants (pacemakers, prostheses)
300,000 persons kept alive by artificial kidneys
50,000 organ transplants a year
3,000 heart transplants a year
60,000 awaiting organ donors
51 million psychotics
10 million schizophrenics
950 million psychoneurotics
300 million arthritics
900 million experiencing chronic pain
1.6 billion disabled (handicapped)
340 million handicapped children
85 million severely handicapped children
3 million dwarfs (little people)
2 billion sick/ill persons (30% children)
Labor absenteeism: $6 billion p.a.
2.8 million children die p.a. from vaccine-preventable diseases
6 infectious diseases kill 4 million unimmunized children p.a.
4 billion persons not immunized
5 million diarrheal deaths of children under 5 p.a.
4 million children die of pneumonia p.a.
22 million prostitutes (9% male)
60 million AIDS carriers (growth rate 100% p.a.)
3 million AIDS cases
400,000 AIDS-related deaths a year
401,000 suicides a year
650 million tobacco smokers
2.6 million tobacco-related deaths p.a.
170 million alcoholics
55 million drug addicts (illicit drug users)
Leading causes of 50.5 million deaths p.a.:
  Parasitic diseases 16.8 million
  Circulatory diseases 13.3 million
  Cancer 4.3 million
  Perinatal diseases 3.3 million
  Injury and poisoning 2.7 million
  Cardiovascular disease 5 million
130 million severely mentally-retarded
220,000 Downs-syndrome (mongol) births p.a.
26 million epileptics
260,000 hemophiliacs (all males)
450,000 albinos (homozygous persons)
100 million albino-gene carriers

FINANCE

Money needed to provide those in poverty with adequate food, water, education, health: $500 billion p.a.

FOCUS FACT

This year:

- **250,000 children will be blind for lack of a 10 cent vitamin capsule or a handful of greens each day**
- **230,000 children will contract polio for want of immunization**
- **14 million children will die of common illnesses and malnutrition**
- **100 million children living on the streets of cities will be drawn to crime and corruption**

—Tom Houston, international director of Lausanne Committee for World Evangelization

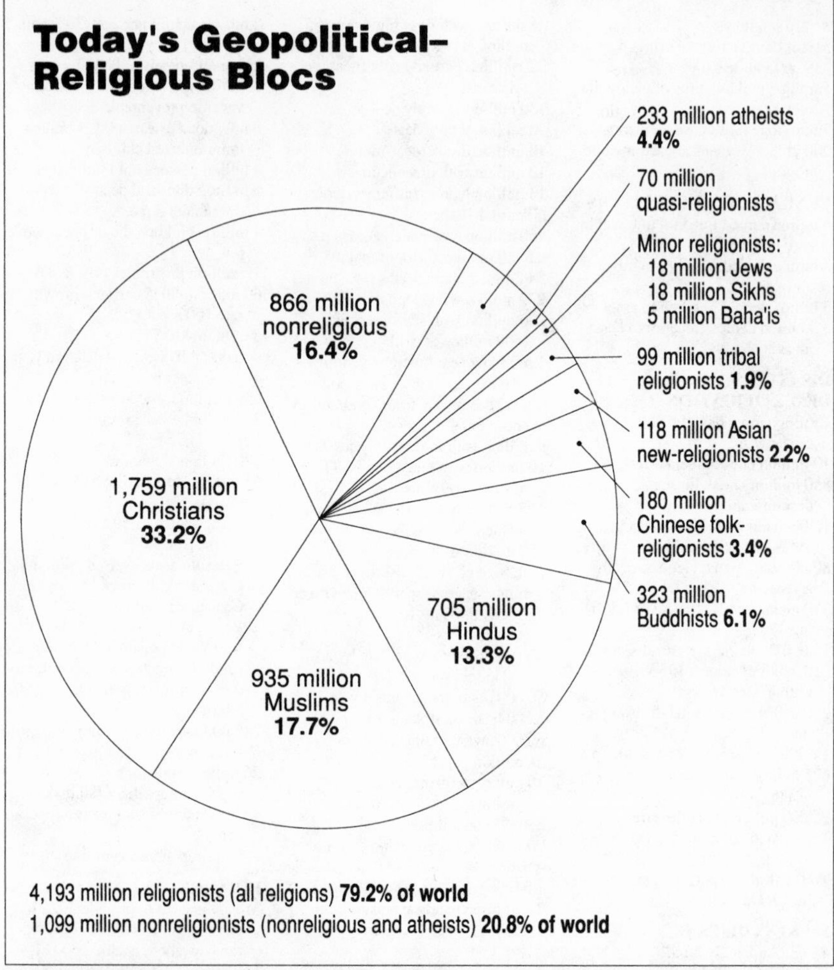

Source: World Evangelization database. Reproduced with permission from *Our Globe and How To Reach It* by David B. Barrett and Todd M. Johnson. Copyright © 1990 by the Foreign Mission Board of the Southern Baptist Convention. Published by New Hope, Birmingham, AL.

3 Worlds, 3 Megacontinents, 7 Continents, 9 Macro Regions, 25 Regions, 180 Nations, 251 Countries, 2,000 Provinces; With the Globe's 33 Major Religious and Antireligious Blocs

The statistics below enumerate the main varieties of political and religious segmentation of the world's population in use today. The various basic segments listed here can be grouped or regrouped in different ways depending on one's requirements. The pie chart shows the world's major religious blocs or segments.

Indented categories are part of (included in) preceding unindented categories. Figures in parentheses with a % sign are in all cases annual change (% increase, per year). All figures relate to the year 1990, usually to mid-1990, except for the Communist statistics which portray 1989 before the collapse of one-party Communism in Europe.

THE GLOBE IN MID-1990
5,292 million persons (1.72% p.a.)
  13% in First (Western) world
  33% in Second (Communist-related) world
  54% in Third (Nonaligned) world
91 million more people a year
Land area: 135.8 million sq km

WORLDS DEVELOPMENT
More developed regions: 51 countries

Less developed regions: 200 countries
1.2 billion in more developed regions
4.0 billion in less developed regions
Least developed countries (LDCs): 41
370 million in least developed countries

GEOPOLITICAL WORLDS (1989)
Western world: 35 countries
Communist world: 30 countries
Third World: 186 countries

CONTINENTS AND REGIONS
3 megacontinents
7 continents
9 macro regions (continental areas)
25 regions

COUNTRIES
251 countries in world (21 under 1,000 population, 230 over)
180 sovereign nations (172 being UN members, including observer states)
71 nonsovereign countries (dependencies)

GOVERNMENT (1989)
82 multiparty democratic states
50 one-party states (30 Marxist)
28 military regimes
20 autocracies/dictatorships
71 dependencies/colonies (17 million population)

IDEOLOGY (1989)
108 religious countries
113 secular countries
30 atheistic countries

FREEDOM OR REPRESSION (adherence to UN Universal Declaration on Human Rights)
79 politically free countries
87 partially politically free
85 politically not free

ASSOCIATIONS OF COUNTRIES (number of member countries in each)
UN 172, FAO 158, GATT 96, IAEA 113, IBRD 151, ICAO 157, IDA 136, IFAD 142, IFC 133, ILO 150, IMF 151, IMO 131, ITU 162, UNESCO 158, UNIDO 144, UPU 168, WHO 166, WIPO 199, WMO 160, WTO 150.

PROVINCES
2,000 major civil divisions (MCDs)

MULTINATIONALS
10,500 transnational corporations (TNCs)
4,800 TNCs in association in Global T-Net
262 supranationals or intergovernmental organizations (IGOs)
3,500 international nongovernmental organizations (NGOs)
International electronic fund transfers $14 billion a day
International foreign exchange transactions p.a. $95 trillion
50 million internationals (persons living abroad)

WORLD COMMUNISM (situation in mid-1989)
122 Communist, Leninist, or Marxist parties (in 130 countries)
88.7 million Communist party members
16 Communist-ruled (Leninist) states (with 83 million party members)
30 Marxist-ruled (including Communist-ruled) states
12 international Communist front organizations with 1,400 affiliates (agencies)
1.7 billion persons under Marxist regimes

RELIGION
(30,000 religions, analyzable into 33 major religious and antireligious blocs)

ADHERENCE TO RELIGION IN 1990
4,193 million religionists (all religions) (annual increase 1.9% p.a.)
2,000 million popular-religionists
430 million New Age/occult/neo-Hindu cultists
720 million Christian popular-religionist-pietists
70 million quasi-religionists, including 6.9 million Freemasons (males)
1,099 million nonreligionists (2.8% p.a.)
866 million nonreligious (2.8% p.a.)
233 million atheists (1.7% p.a.)

ADHERENTS OF NON-CHRISTIAN RELIGIONS
2,434 million non-Christian religionists (annual increase 2.3% p.a.)

GREAT WORLD RELIGIONS
935 million Muslims (2.7% p.a.)
780 million Sunnis (2.7% p.a.)
145 million Shias (Shiites) (2.9% p.a.)
18 million Ismailis (3.4% p.a.)
10 million Admadis (4.2% p.a.)
705 million Hindus (2.3% p.a.)
493 million Vaishnavites (2.3% p.a.)
175 million Shaivites (2.3% p.a.)
20 million Saktists (2.2% p.a.)
12 million Neo-Hindus (3.3% p.a.)
4 million Reformed Hindus (2.5% p.a.)
323 million Buddhists (1.7% p.a.)
182 million Mahayana (1.7% p.a.)
122 million Theravada (1.7% p.a.)
19 million Tantrayana (Lamaists) (1.7% p.a.)

OTHER MAJOR RELIGIONS
180 million Chinese folk-religionists (0.8% p.a.)
118 million Asian New-Religionists (2.3% p.a.)
99 million tribal religionists (0.2% p.a.)

MINOR RELIGIONS
18 million Jews (1.1% p.a.)
18 million Sikhs (2.9% p.a.)
8 million non-Christian Spiritists (5.5% p.a.)
5 million Baha'is (3.6% p.a.)
3 million Shintoists (-1.7% p.a.)
3 million Jains (2.0% p.a.)

CHRISTIANS AND NON-CHRISTIANS
1,759 million Christians (2.2% p.a.)
3,533 million non-Christians (1.7% p.a.)

FOCUS FACT

There are 30,000 Christian clergy of all types in West Germany, but 90,000 registered witches and fortune tellers.—*Theological News 1989*

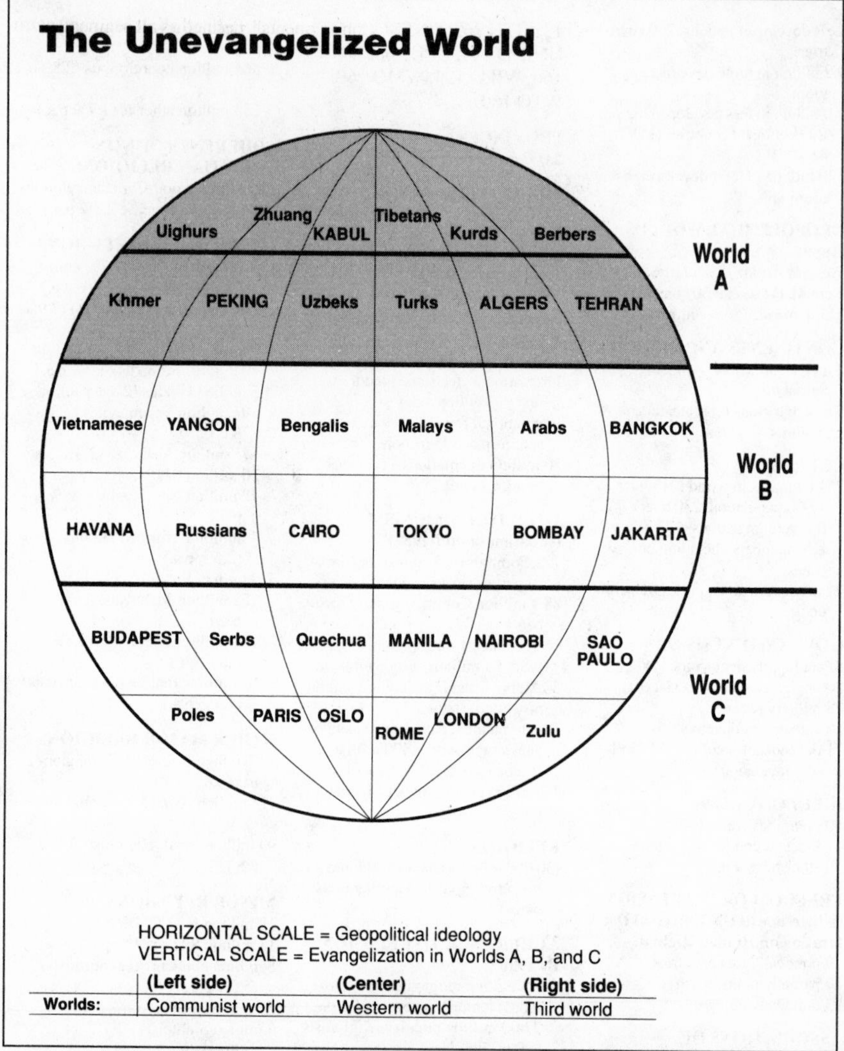

Reproduced with permission from *Our Globe and How To Reach It* by David B. Barrett and Todd M. Johnson. Copyright © 1990 by the Foreign Mission Board of the Southern Baptist Convention. Published by New Hope, Birmingham, AL.

In 3,030 major unevangelized population segments

The globe is divided here into some 15,000 distinct population segments, of 3 major varieties: ethnolinguistic peoples, metropolises (mother cities of over 100,000 population), and countries.

The 3 varieties of segment overlap because they are 3 different ways of dividing up the same one world. This segmented globe in turn can be subdivided into our 3 categories of world—Worlds A, B, and C. This superimposing on one schema (segments) on another (3 worlds) is done for purposes of illustration only, since most segments are composed each of a mixture of unevangelized persons, evangelized non-Christians, and Christians. For purpose of illustration also, we name a few segments below: a few megapeoples (in lower-case letters), and a few megacities (in capital letters), placing these segments where the majority of their individuals are located. In this schema, therefore, "evangelized non-Christian population segments," defined as segments with church members under 50%, are listed for convenience under World B; and "christianized population segments", defined as all segments with church members of 50% or over, are listed for convenience under World C.

The globe therefore gives a detailed representation of the nature of the unfinished Christian task. This task's main secular feature ought to be to rectify the grossly disproportionate spread of life's blessings—health, wealth, shelter, food, rights, justice—around the world. This disproportion is briefly sketched here in this series of global diagrams. From the Christian point of view, the major unfinished task is to spread the blessings of Christ throughout the segments of World A, the unevangelized world, here shown shaded gray for emphasis.

A. THE UNEVANGELIZED WORLD

1,253 million unevangelized persons (all being also unreached persons)

MACRO SEGMENTS

3,030 unevangelized population segments:
2,000 unreached peoples (1.0 billion population)
1,000 unevangelized metropolises
30 closed countries increasing by 2 a year including:
450 completely unreached peoples (with no churches)
150 unreached megapeoples
85 anti-Christian megacities

MICRO SEGMENTS

17,000 unreached people groups (minipeoples) in 1974, decreasing to 12,000 by 1990
50,000 unreached micropeoples
300,000 unreached sociopeoples

B. THE EVANGELIZED NON-CHRISTIAN WORLD

2,280 million evangelized non-Christians (of whom 0.5 billion are unreached, and 1.7 billion reached)

MACRO SEGMENTS

4,870 evangelized non-Christian population segments:
4,000 peoples
800 metropolises
76 countries (50 closed/restricted-access) including:
70 non-Christian megacities

MICRO SEGMENTS

150,000 micropeoples
700,000 sociopeoples

C. THE CHRISTIAN WORLD

1,759 million Christians (all reached)

MACRO SEGMENTS

7,100 christianized population segments:
5,500 peoples
1,450 metropolises
145 countries over 60% Christians (39 restricted-access, 10 closed) including:
167 mainly-Christian megacities
9,500 reached peoples (with own churches) in Worlds B and C

MICRO SEGMENTS

50,000 micropeoples
1 million sociopeoples
48,000 reached minipeoples, now coalesced into 12,000 agglomerated christianized minipeoples

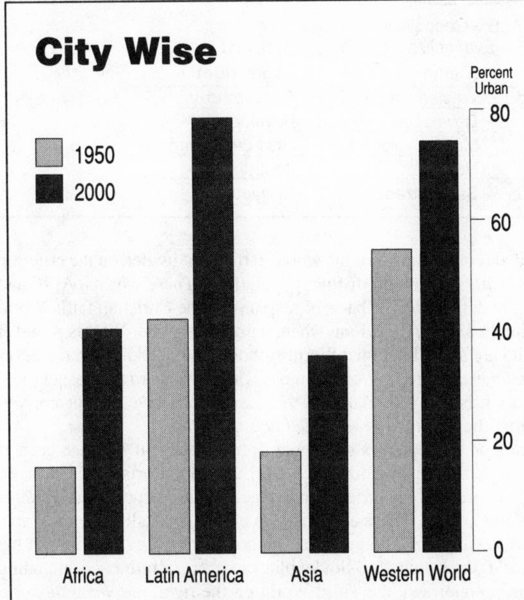

The urban population has doubled since 1950 in the more developed parts of the world. In the developing countries it has quadrupled. Overall the urban population has increased tenfold in the last 60 years, while the rural population has only doubled.

In the 1990s for the first time in the history of the world, more people will be living in cities than in villages or rural areas.

The United Nations expects that by A.D. 2000, 17 of the world's 20 largest cities will be in the Third World. In 1980 there were only 11. Mexico City and São Paulo, Brazil, are expected to top the list with about 25 million people each.

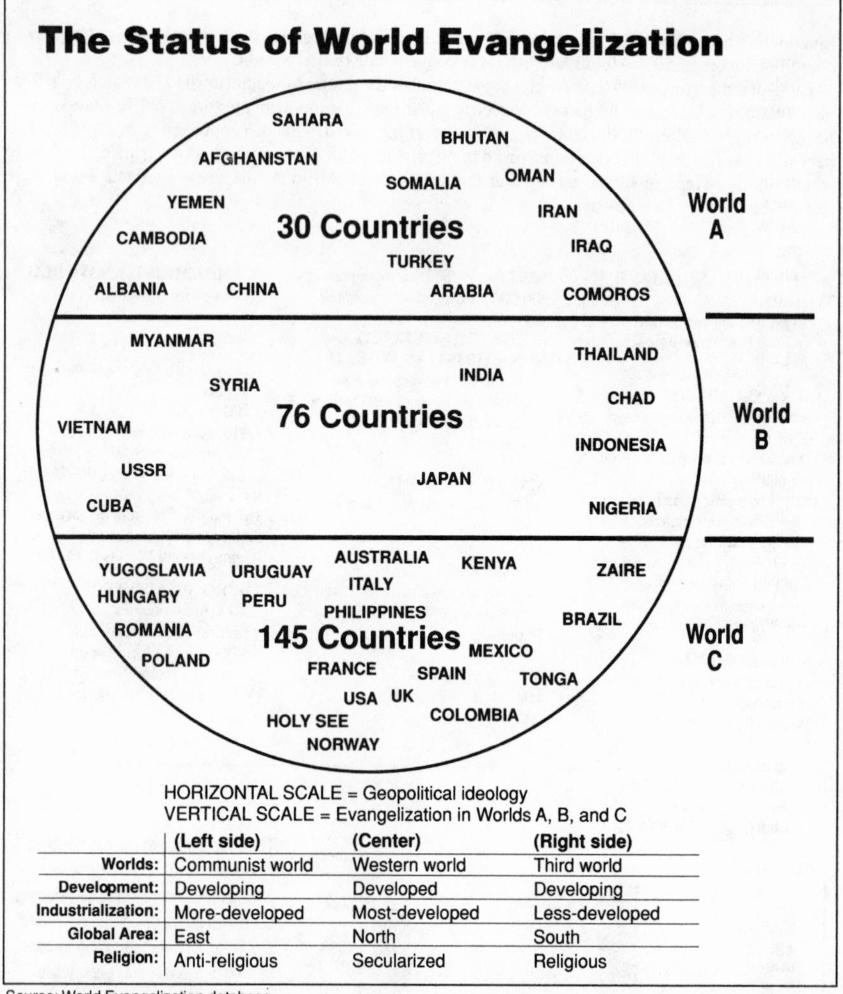

	(Left side)	(Center)	(Right side)
Worlds:	Communist world	Western world	Third world
Development:	Developing	Developed	Developing
Industrialization:	More-developed	Most-developed	Less-developed
Global Area:	East	North	South
Religion:	Anti-religious	Secularized	Religious

Source: World Evangelization database

Today's globe is shown here as a detailed representation of the whole earth. It is divided on the criterion of demographic evangelization into 3 worlds each with distinct populations. These worlds, A, B, and C, are not geographically defined but are defined on the basis of response to the Christian faith. World C consists of all persons who individually are *Christians* anywhere across the globe. Worlds A and B consist of all persons, individually, who are non-Christians: World A those who in addition have never heard the gospel or heard of Jesus (the *unevangelized*), World B those who have heard the gospel (who have heard, with understanding about Christianity, Christ, and the gospel) but have not, or not yet, accepted it or become disciples of Christ (here termed *evangelized non-Christians*).

Onto this 3-world division, countries or metropolises or people do not easily fit because each is composed of a mixture of unevangelized persons, evangelized non-Christians and Christians. However, for purposes of illustration we add a few names of countries below, placing these population segments where the majority of their individuals are located. These countries are placed vertically according to a numerical scale of evangelization: most-evangelized countries at the bottom, least-evangelized at the top; also, on the left the Communist world (the whole Sino-Soviet bloc or sphere of influence, including Eastern Europe and other ex-Communist countries), the Third World on the right, the Western world inbetween. Note that to illustrate today's global mission, Worlds A and B do have Christian activities in their midst, and therefore have some Christian workers and some foreign missionaries present.

Note also that World C is not defined as precisely the same as "Christendom", "the Christian West" nor "the christianized world" nor does it include North America or Europe in their entirety. Non-Christians or atheists or agnostics in heavily-evangelized countries like the USA or Norway or Britain, for example, fall (on our definition) into World B.

A parallel but slightly differing definition of evangelization divides the world into 2 dichotomous categories of the state of being reached by the gospel: the *unreached world* (top half of the globe, covering World A and 0.5 billion persons in World B), and the *reached world* (bottom half of the globe, covering World C and 1.6 billion persons in World B). This expounds the concept of "individual evangelization" (persons who individually have received the opportunity to respond to the gospel if they wish to by joining a local church of their own culture), by contrast with "demographic evangelization" (families, groups, or people as a whole hearing and understanding the gospel.

THE GLOBE

THE HUMAN BACKDROP

5.3 billion persons
Land area 135.8 million sq km (11% arable)
Density 39 people per sq km
2,260 million urban dwellers
3,032 million rural dwellers
3,577 million adults (ages 15 and over) (67.6%)
1,011 million youth (ages 15-24) (19.1%)
704 million adolescents (teenagers, ages 13-19)
1,715 million children under 15 (32.4%)
630 million children under 5 (infants and babies; 11.9%)
487 million elderly (60 and over, 9.2%)
34 million elderly aged 80 or over
1,318 million women ages 15-49 (24.9%)
141.6 million births p.a. (388,000 a day)
190 live births per 1000 females
2,542 million literates (71% of adults)
1,035 million nonliterates (29% of adults)
Global income (GWP) US $16,100 billion p.a.
Growth of GWP 3.0% per year
Average income per person $3,040
Average family income $13,070
687 million telephones (95% direct-dial)
750 million TV sets
93 million computers

EVANGELIZATION

4.0 billion evangelized persons (4,039,623,000; 76.3% of world)
3.5 billion reached persons
1.8 billion unreached persons
1.3 billion unevangelized persons (23.7% of world)
Urban dwellers 88% evangelized
270 million unevangelized urbanites
364,000 newly-evangelized every day
500 million evangelized but unreached non-Christians
133 million newly-evangelized every year

CHURCH EXPANSION

Christians and churches exist in all 251 countries
38.7 million more Christians each year
35.7 million more church members each year
50,000 new churches each year

VERTICAL SCALE: Evangelization in Worlds A, B, C
(percentages "p.a." in parenthesis are annual rates)

A. THE UNEVANGELIZED WORLD

(30 countries each less than half evangelized, meaning E is 50% or less)
1,252,557,000 unevangelized persons (-0.1% p.a.)
23.7% of global population
5.0% of global income
3.0% of all telephones
3.0% of all TV sets
0.6% of all computers

B. THE EVANGELIZED NON-CHRISTIAN WORLD

(76 countries over half evangelized [E is greater than 50%] but with church members less than 60%)
2,280,845,000 evangelized non-Christians (4.5% p.a.)
500 million evangelized but unreached non-Christians
43.1% of global population
33% of global income
17.0% of all telephones
19.0% of all TV sets
11.4% of all computers

C. THE CHRISTIAN WORLD

(145 countries with church members 60% or over, all also having E 95% or over)
1,758,778,000 Christians (2.2% p.a.)
33.2% of global population
Christians receive, own and/or use:
- 62% of global income
- 80% of all telephones
- 78% of all TV sets
- 88% of all computers (56% of all being owned and operated by Christians)

Christians spend:
- 99.9% of Christian income on themselves
- 0.09% on the Evangelized Non-Christian World
- 0.01% on the Unevangelized World

“” FOCUS QUOTE

East Europeans are saying that while it took the Poles 10 years to achieve freedom, Hungary made it in 10 months, East Germany in 10 weeks, Czechoslovakia in 10 days, and Romania in 10 hours. But who really caused these things to come to pass? Who else but God? Who else could have done it?
–Thomas Wang in *AD2000 and Beyond* magazine, May-August 1990 issue.

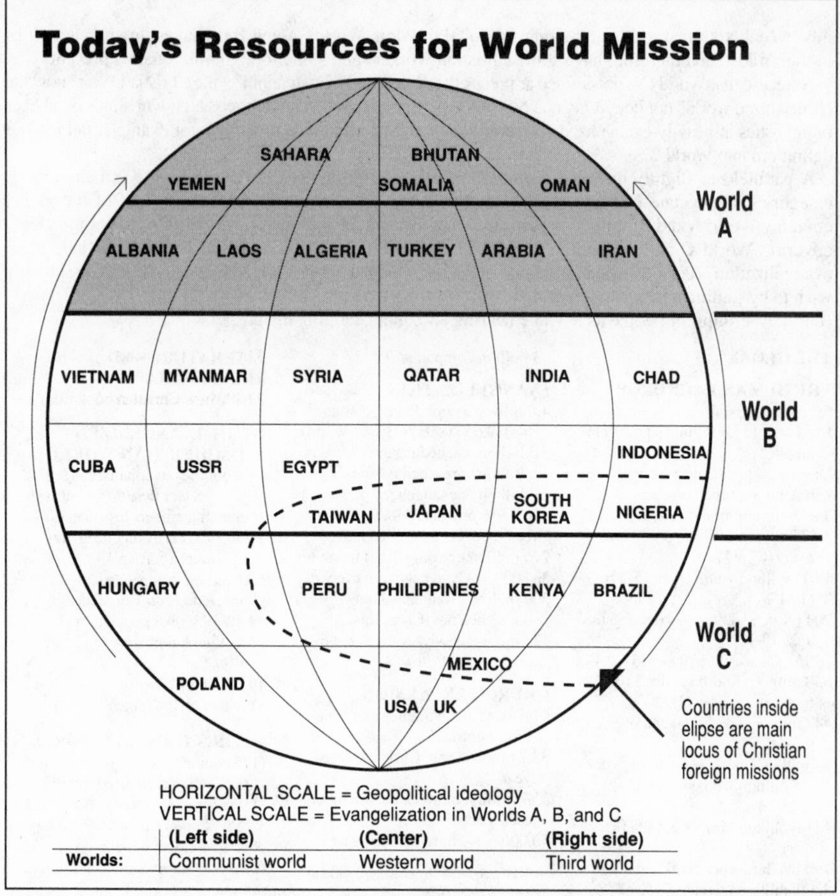

Churches, workers, institutions, agencies, media, literature, radio / TV, money, computers, networks, plans

This table enumerates the entire extent of global Christian resources of all kinds. Several of these are then shown as they are utilized today, divided among the 3 worlds, A, B, and C.

The present situation is that the vast bulk of these resources benefit only the Christian world. Even in foreign missions, 85% of personnel and money are devoted to Christian lands, such as missionaries from the U.S. to Brazil or Kenya or the Philippines (see inner ellipse in globe at bottom).

It is obvious that all segments of the earth have a right to their fair share of resources of all kinds. The least that Christians can do is to ensure that the resources which are under their own direct control—the spiritual resources catalogued below—get properly shared with all. To redress the present situation Christians will need to concentrate on World A far more, hence it is shown shaded gray and its segments are shown in bold on the globe. The faint lines of the other 2 worlds B and C suggest the far less significant share of global resources that these worlds should now be deliberately restricted to. The 2 thin arrows then show the new directions in which these ample resources need to be redirected or redeployed.

THE GLOBE

5.3 billion persons

GLOBAL CHRISTIAN RESOURCES IN 1990

CHRISTIAN PERSONS

1,759 million Christians (99.8% lay persons)
1,622 million professing Christians
137 million crypto-Christians (7.8% of all Christians)
135 million nominal Christians (7.7% of all Christians)
1,623,833,000 affiliated Christians (church members)
620 million Christian children under 15
230 million Christian infants under 5
1,095 million urban Christians (48.5% of all urbanites)
1.0 billion literate adult Christians
1,210 million practicing Christians
480 million weekly-worshipping Christians
900 million Christian regulars for Christian radio/TV
1,755 million lay persons (99.8% of all Christians)
25 million lay persons (lay Christians) residing abroad
120 million Christian pilgrims on move every year
250 million Christian foreign tourists a year
2,900 million Christian domestic tourists a year

INTERCESSION

36 worldwide intercessory networks (22 active)
20 million in full-time prayer ministry
10 million weekly prayer groups
170 million praying daily for world mission
2,100 religious institutes (orders, societies for the full-time religious life centered on prayer)
7,000 monasteries, ashrams, convents, abbeys, priories

ORGANIZATIONS

2.6 million worship centers (local churches)
23,500 distinct denominations
6,000 major councils of churches
3,970 foreign mission boards or societies
5,000 home mission boards, agencies, or societies
400 medical missions (foreign mission agencies)
21,000 parachurch or service agencies
400,000 base ecclesial communities (BECs)

INSTITUTIONS

99,200 major Christian/church-related institutions
500,000 minor Christian institutions
145,000 Christian primary/elementary schools
45,000 Christian secondary/high schools
300 million pupils
1,300 Christian universities and colleges
4,600 seminaries/theological colleges
4,500 Christian hospitals
29,500 Christian medical centers
50 million medical consultations a year (in Christian centers)
1,500 Christian-owned presses and publishers
350 ecumenical centers
950 church-related research centers

FINANCE

Christians by income: 58% rich (11% affluent, 37% well-off, 10% just coping), 42% poor (29% needy, 13% absolutely poor)
Church of the Rich: 942 million members
Church of the Affluent: 179 million members
Church of the Poor: 682 million members
Church of the Absolutely Poor: 211 million members
Personal income of Christians (church members) $8,950 billion p.a.
Personal income per capita of Christians, $5,510
Average Christian family income $19,280
Stewardship: giving per church member per week $1.85
Church/agency income $157 billion a year
Churches' Income $83.4 billion p.a.
Parachurch/institutional income $74.2 billion p.a.
$5 billion a year on new religious buildings (Christian)
Foreign missions giving per church member per week $0.10
Foreign missions $8.6 billion a year
Christian broadcasting (radio/TV) $5 billion p.a.

FULL-TIME PERSONNEL

950,000 ordained clergy, ministers, pastors, priests (5% women)
4,208,250 full-time Christian workers (36% women; 93% citizens)
1.5 million full-time women workers
50,000 ordained women clergy/ministers
470,000 monks including friars
1,045,000 nuns (sisters)
1 million professional theologians
20,000 professional missiologists
15 million Christian schoolteachers
1 million seminarians
30 million Christian students
100,000 TEE extension students in 120 countries
285,250 foreign missionaries
38,000 foreign missionaries from Third-World countries
800,000 home missionaries
3,923,000 national (citizen) workers
180,000 short-term foreign missionaries

LITERATURE AND PRINT MEDIA

22,400 new Christian book titles a year
100 million copies of new Christian books printed p.a.
11,000 books/articles on mission a year
3,000 new scholarly research books on Christian faith p.a.
13,000 major religious (Christian) libraries
23,800 religious (Christian) periodicals
51.4 million Bibles distributed a year
76.9 million New Testaments a year
1,430 million scriptures (all varieties) distributed p.a.
3 billion Christian books printed p.a.
4 billion Christian tracts a year

ELECTRONIC MEDIA AND AUDIOVISUALS

2,160 Christian radio/TV stations
900 national/international Christian broadcasting agencies
100,000 full-time personnel in Christian broadcasting
3 billion a year view *Jesus* and other Christian films

MASS EVANGELISM

2,500 evangelistic mass campaigns a year
1,300 metropolises each year hold citywide evangelistic campaigns

COMPUTERS

54 million Christian-owned computers (worth $310 billion)
145 million Christian-owned screens/terminals
16,800 new Christian-owned computers a day
6,000 MIPS new Christian-purchased computer power a day
1.2 million electronic mail systems (95% secular)
450 secular commercial databases
5,000 secular electronic bulletin boards (BBS) active

200 million Christian computer users
50 million Christian computer professionals

NETWORKS AND GLOBAL PLANS

4,000 Great Commission networks
56 Great Commission global networks
9 Great Commission global meganetworks
410 current global plans
260 current global plans making progress
78 global megaplans
33 global gigaplans
Plan expenditures $45 billion

A. THE UNEVANGELIZED WORLD

Present cost of Christian foreign missions: $0.1 billion a year
30 restricted-access (closed) countries
3,000 foreign missionaries (1.0%)
No citywide evangelistic campaigns
30,000 full-time Christian workers
50,000 lay Christians residing abroad in closed countries
0.1% of all Christian literature
0.01% of all Christian radio/TV

B. THE EVANGELIZED NON-CHRISTIAN WORLD

Per capita income of non-Christians: $1,350 p.a.
Present cost of Christian foreign missions: $1 billion a year
23,000 foreign missionaries (8.1%), 5,000 being in 50 restricted-access countries
200 cities per year have citywide evangelistic campaigns
200,000 full-time Christian workers, 50,000 being in 50 restricted-access countries
0.9% of all Christian literature
0.1% of all Christian radio/TV

C. THE CHRISTIAN WORLD

Present cost of home Christianity: $140 billion a year
Foreign missions to other Christian lands: $7.5 billion a year
259,250 foreign missionaries to other Christian lands (90.9%), 4,000 being in 39 restricted-access countries
1,100 cities per year have citywide evangelistic campaigns
4.0 million full-time Christian workers (95%) work in World C, including 200,000 in 39 restricted-access countries
500 million lay Christians live in 39 restricted-access heavily-Christian countries
99% of all Christian literature is consumed by World C
99.9% of all Christian radio/TV output is directed at World C

GROWTH IN PARACHURCH AGENCIES

Six Years of Parachurch Growth

1982	2,402
1984	2,989
1986	3,580
1988	4,074

Source: 1989 MARC Europe Handbook.

HISTORICAL PROFILE OF PARACHURCH GROWTH

More than 57 percent of today's parachurch agencies have been established in the last thirty years:

Pre-1900	19 percent
1900–1960	24 percent
1960–1990	57 percent

Source: 1989 MARC Europe Handbook.

FOCUS FACT

The United Nations calls the decade of the 1980s the "Lost Generation," citing an increase in illiteracy and dim prospects for the 1990s. In Benin they have not taught school for two years. In Zaire they have fired 20 percent of the teachers. The 37 poorest nations in the world have decreased their educational budgets by 25 percent in the past decade.

SEVEN MARKS OF AN AD 2000 MISSION

1. Be a networker.
2. Communicate why your mission makes a difference.
3. Celebrate diversity and distinctives within biblical norms. Learn to appreciate the mosaic that is the body of Christ.
4. Know who you are and constantly clarify your values. . . . Be characterized by intense activity interspersed with intense reflection.
5. Be motivational, but control-oriented. Commitment must be to personal growth, not organizational ascendancy.
6. Develop programs and products that make a difference. Get rid of the marginal programs.
7. **Reallocate:** Until you assign time, people, and money to it, you haven't got anything but a good intention.
   Renew: More plans and visions within organizations fail because of their competition with established programs than for any other reason.
   Recruit: Recruit to your vision.
   Report: Report back exactly what happens.

Source: Rev. Paul McKaughan, executive director, Evangelical Foreign Missions Association. Condensed from *AD2000 and Beyond* magazine, May-August 1990 issue. See the Missions section of the *Almanac of the Christian World* for more information on the AD2000 movement.

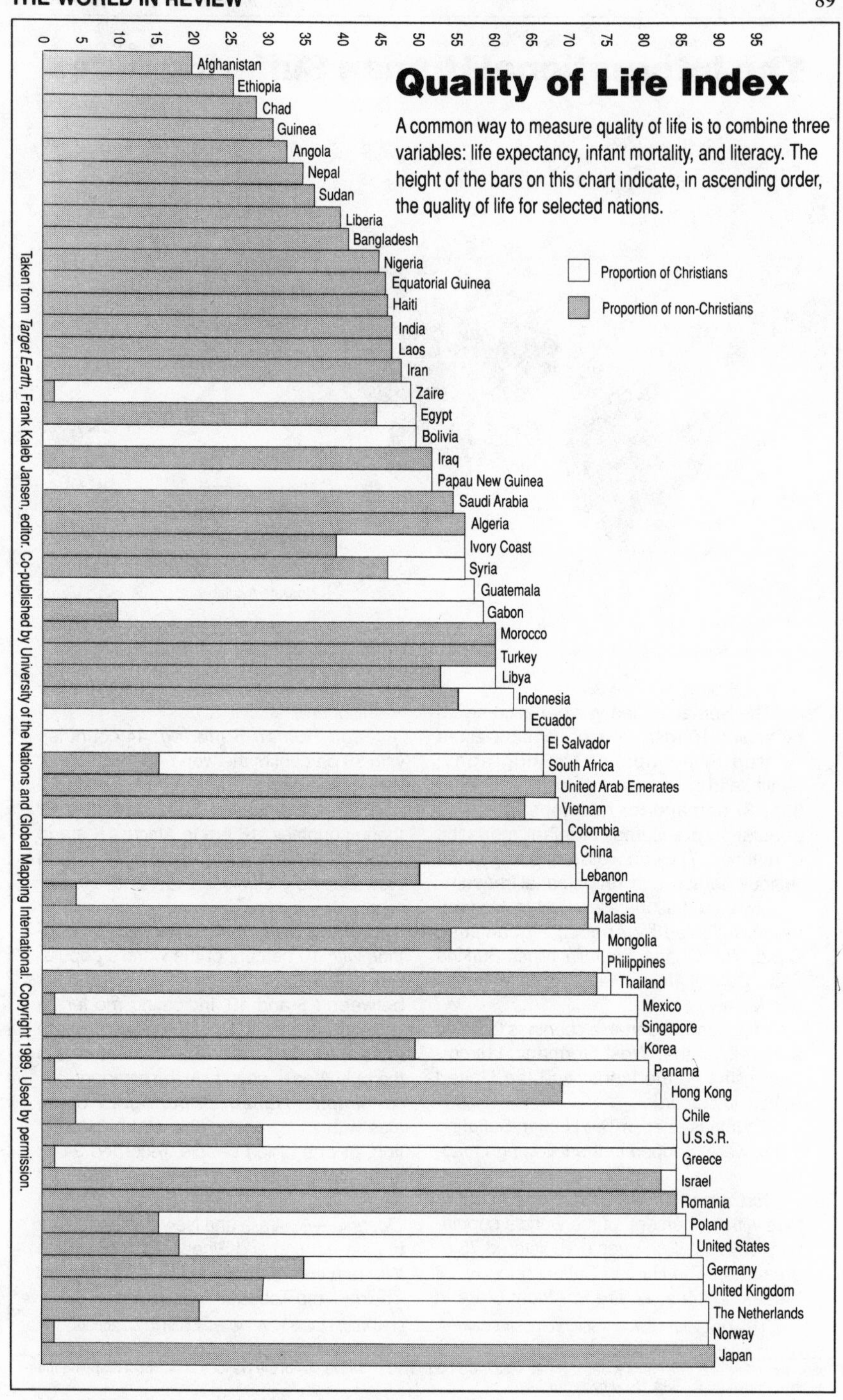
0
5
10
15
20
25
30
35
40
45
50
55
60
65
70
75
80
85
90
95
Quality of Life Index
A common way to measure quality of life is to combine three variables: life expectancy, infant mortality, and literacy. The height of the bars on this chart indicate, in ascending order, the quality of life for selected nations.
Proportion of Christians
Proportion of non-Christians
Afghanistan
Ethiopia
Chad
Guinea
Angola
Nepal
Sudan
Liberia
Bangladesh
Nigeria
Equatorial Guinea
Haiti
India
Laos
Iran
Zaire
Egypt
Bolivia
Iraq
Papau New Guinea
Saudi Arabia
Algeria
Ivory Coast
Syria
Guatemala
Gabon
Morocco
Turkey
Libya
Indonesia
Ecuador
El Salvador
South Africa
United Arab Emerates
Vietnam
Colombia
China
Lebanon
Argentina
Malasia
Mongolia
Philippines
Thailand
Mexico
Singapore
Korea
Panama
Hong Kong
Chile
U.S.S.R.
Greece
Israel
Romania
Poland
United States
Germany
United Kingdom
The Netherlands
Norway
Japan

The International Human Suffering Index

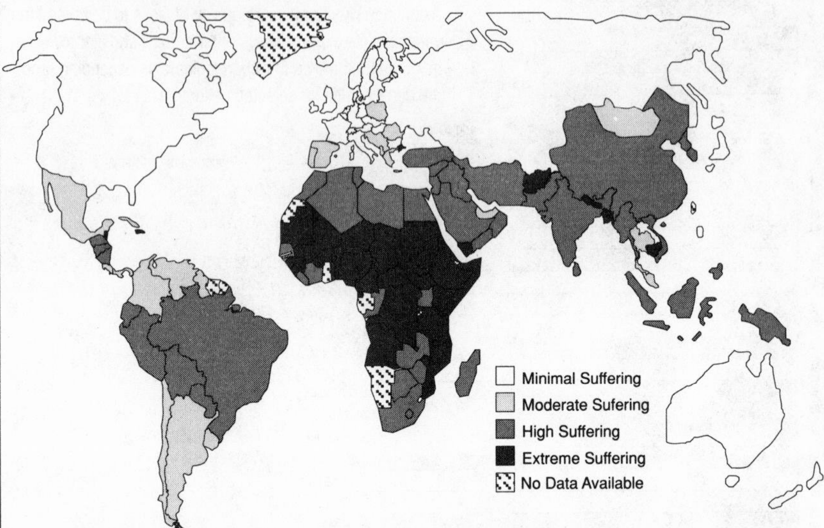

By Sharon Camp and Joseph Speidel

The Human Suffering Index is compiled by adding 10 measures of human welfare related to economics, demography, health, and governance: **1**) income, **2**) inflation, **3**) demand for new jobs, **4**) urban population pressures, **5**) infant mortality, **6**) nutrition, **7**) clean water, **8**) energy use, **9**) adult literacy, and **10**) personal freedom.

Living conditions are worst in Mozambique, followed by Angola, Afghanistan, Chad, Mali, Ghana, Somalia, Niger, Burkina Faso, Central African Republic, Zaire, Benin, and Malawi.

The most comfortable countries to live in are Switzerland, West Germany, Luxembourg, the Netherlands, and the United States, in that order.

Countries rated in The Human Suffering Index were grouped in the following Quadrants:

Extreme Human Suffering: 30 countries with 11 percent of the world's population, or 519 million people, registered 75 or greater on The Human Suffering Index. Of these countries, 24 are in Africa; 6 are in Asia. None is in Europe or the Western Hemisphere.

High Human Suffering: 44 countries with 58 percent of the world's population, or 2.85 billion people, registered between 50 and 74 on the Human Suffering Index. Of these countries, 16 are in Africa; 16 are in Asia; 11 are in Latin America; 1—Papua New Guinea—is in Oceania; none is in Europe.

Moderate Human Suffering: 29 countries with 10 percent of the world's population, or 491 million people, recorded an index between 25 and 49, indicating moderate levels of suffering. Of these countries, 10 are in Asia; 11 are in Latin America. Mauritius is the only African country in the category.

Minimal Human Suffering: 27 countries with 21 percent of the world's population, or one billion people, recorded 24 or lower on The Human Suffering Index. Of these countries, 20 are in Europe; 2 are in Oceania—Australia and New Zealand; 2 are in Asia—Japan and Singapore; 3 are in the Western Hemisphere —U.S., Canada, and Trinidad and Tobago.

BOOKS CHRISTIAN LEADERS WOULD LIKE GORBACHEV TO READ

ACW asked seven Christian leaders what book they would like Mikhail Gorbachev to read. The answers:

Charles Colson, chairman of Prison Fellowship Ministries, author and special counsel to President Richard M. Nixon from 1969 to 1973: *Mere Christianity* by C.S. Lewis

Peter Deyneka, director of Slavic Gospel Mission: *Mere Christianity* by C. S. Lewis

Mark Elliott, director of Institute for the Study of Christianity and Marxism, Billy Graham Center: *The Puzzle of the Soviet Church, An Inside Look at Christianity and Glasnost* by Kent Hill

Harold Myra, president of Christianity Today, Inc.: *The Brothers Karamazov* by Fyodor Dostoyevski

Luis Palau, evangelist: *Peace with God* by Billy Graham

Pat Robertson, chairman of the board, The Christian Broadcasting Network Inc.: *The Secret Kingdom* by Pat Robertson

Robert H. Schuller, founding pastor, Crystal Cathedral: *Tough Times Never Last But Tough People Do* by Robert H. Schuller

Nations with Highest Inflation

Countries with the highest inflation rates in 1988, when the U.S. inflation rate was 4.4%.

1,722% Peru
980% Brazil
388% Argentina
243% Yugoslavia
86% Ecuador

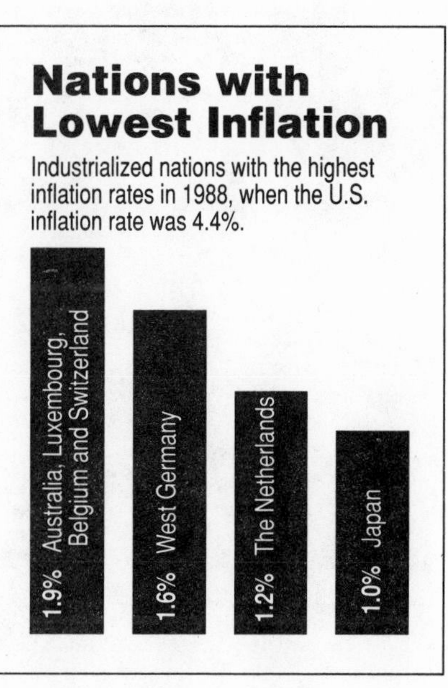

Countries of the World

Statistics . . . Peoples . . . Literacy . . . Economy . . . Politics . . . Religion

COUNTRIES OF THE WORLD
With population of 12,000,000 or more

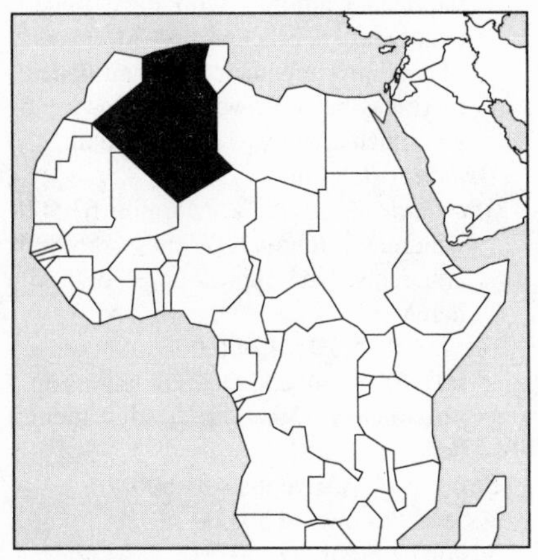

ALGERIA

Area 2,381,000 sq.km. Agriculturalized on the Mediterranean coast, in the Atlas mountains and oases. 80% in Sahara Desert.

Population 25,700,000. Annual growth 3.2%. People per sq.km. 11; 90% near the coast. About 1.7 million Algerians are migrants in Europe.

Peoples

Arab-Berber 70%. Speaking Arabic.

Berber (8 groups) 20%. Kabyle 2,700,000; Shawiya 1,100,000; Mzab (5 groups) 100,000; Tuareg 15,000.

European 0.8%. French 120,000; Russian 10,000, etc.

Literacy 38%. *Official language:* Arabic. French and, increasingly, English widely used. 25% speak one of the Berber dialects. *All languages* 15. *Bible translations* 1 Bible, 2 New Testaments, 5 portions.

Capital: Algiers 1,650,000. Urbanization 52%.

Economy: Heavily dependent on oil exports. Over 50% of work force is in agriculture, but its potential has not been effectively exploited. Income/person $2,760 (15% of USA).

Politics: French colony for 132 years. Independence in 1962 after a bitter war of liberation. The 28 year one-party rule of the National Liberation Front with its strong socialist policies is being threatened by the rise of Islamic fundamentalist parties. The likely future is an Islamic democratic government.

Religion: Since independence, the government has actively encouraged the development of an Islamic Arab socialist state. Proselytism is not allowed.

Muslim 99.5%. Increasing tendency to a more orthodox and radical expression of Ibadi Islam.

Christian 0.3%. Nominal 0.05%. Affiliated 0.25%.

Roman Catholic 0.24%. 53,000 adherents.

Orthodox 0.01%, 2,400 adherents.

Protestant 0.01%. 2,900 adherents; 1,100 members. 70% are expatriates.

Cross-cultural Christians witnessing in Algeria: 30 (1:750,000) in 5 agencies.

ARGENTINA

Area 2,777,000 sq.km. Latin America's second largest country with a great range of climate, rainfall and topography.

Population 31,900,000. Annual growth 1.4%. People per sq.km. 11.

Peoples

European 87%. A fusion of many nationalities, but largely Spanish, Italian and other East and West Europeans. Many minorities have retained a considerable degree of national identity.

Mestizo 10%. Largely Paraguayan, Bolivian and Chilean.

Amerindian 1.9%. Quechua 300,000; Mapuche 50,000; Lowland peoples (9) 208,000, mostly in the Chaco in the far north and Patagonia in the far south.

Literacy 93%. *Official language:* Spanish. *All languages* 21. *Bible translations* 1 Bible, 4 New Testaments, 6 portions.

Capital: Buenos Aires 11,400,000. Other major cities: Cordoba, 1,140,000; Rosario 1,000,000. Urbanization 82%.

Economy: Largely based on agriculture, but with much industry. There has been a steady, and at times catastrophic, fall in living standards this century. Once wealthy but now there is widespread poverty and unemployment. Hyperinflation has been the product of successive governments failing to curb overspending on a bloated bureaucracy and state/military-run industries. Income/person $2370 (13% of USA).

Politics: Independent from Spain in 1816. Peronist misrule, inflation and increasing leftist urban terrorism provoked the 1976 military takeover. The military government's incompetence, military adventurism and bad record on human rights led to the restoration of democratic rule in 1983. Successive democratic governments have been unable to contain the national economic crises.

Religion: Roman Catholicism is the official religion, but the new government has declared total freedom of conscience.

Non-religious/Atheist 1.8%.

Jews 2%. The fifth largest group of Jews in the world.

Muslim 0.2%. Mainly Palestinian and Lebanese.

Christian 95.5%. Affiliated 93.6%.

Roman Catholic 86.5%. Practicing 63%. 26,500,000 adherents; 17,200,000 members. There are over 1.7 million baptized Catholics who have joined evangelical or other groups. After years of declining attendances and influence, there has been a reversal of this trend and much activity to win the youth.

Orthodox (6 groups) 0.5%.

Marginal groups 1.1%. Mormon 63,500 adherents; Jehovah Witness, 56,500 adherents; New Apostolic 38,000 adherents.

Protestant 5.5%. 1,680,000 adherents; 603,700 members. Denominations approximately 150; Largest adult members:

Seventh-Day Adventists 53,600
Assemblies of God 50,000
Vision de Futuro (?) 50,000
Brethren 40,000
Southern Baptist Convention 36,500
Christian Assemblies 36,000
Anglican 19,000

Evangelical 4.7% of population.

Missionaries to Argentina 590 (1:52,000 people) in 58 agencies. Missionaries from Argentina estimated 50.

AUSTRALIA

Area 7,687,000 sq.km. This island continent is largely grassland and desert in the interior but better watered in the east, southeast and southwest coastal regions, where most live in highly concentrated urban areas.

Population 16,800,000. Annual growth 1.6%. Immigration 0.8%. People per sq.km. 2.2.

Peoples

British origin 82.6%.

Other European 13%.

Middle Eastern 2%. Arab-speaking 250,000.

Asian 1.3%. Chinese, Vietnamese, Indian.

Australian Aborigine 1.1%. 172,000. (In 1780 approximately 300,000 speaking 260 languages.) About 50,000 are still nomadic.

Literacy 99%. *Official language:* English. Nearly 10% of the population do not use English as their first language. *All indigenous living languages* 121. *Bible translations* 1 Bible, 2 New Testaments, 28 portions.

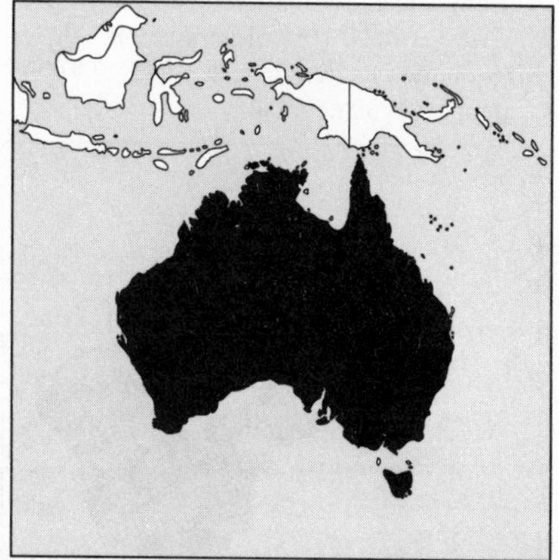

Capital: Canberra 260,000. Other cities: Sydney 3,500,000; Melbourne 3,000,000; Brisbane 1,160,000; Adelaide 1,000,000; Perth 980,000. Urbanization 86%.

Economy: Wealthy mixed economy based on industry, agriculture and mining, but world recession and severe droughts slowed the economy in the '80s. Income/person $10,900 (77% of USA).

Politics: Parliamentary democracy, independent of Britain in 1901.

Religion: A secular state with freedom of religion.

Non-religious/Atheist, etc. 21.8%.

Muslim 1.5%. Predominantly Turks, Arabs and Yugoslavs.

Jews 0.4%.

Chinese religions 0.3%.

Christian 76%. Affiliated 73.1%. Weekly church attendance is nearer 12% of the population.

Roman Catholic 26.7%. 4,100,000 adherents; 2,860,000 members. High proportion of continental European nationalities.

Orthodox 3.1%. Over 28 denominations mainly from Eastern Europe and Middle East.

Marginal groups 1.1%. 182,000 adherents; 99,000 members. Over 54 cults. Largest (adherents): Jehovah's Witnesses 79,000; Mormons 47,000.

Protestant 42%. A further 10% nominal Protestants. 6,630,000 adherents; 1,890,000 members. Denominations 150. Largest (adherents):

Anglican Church 3,860,000
Uniting Church 1,460,000
Presbyterian Church (continuing) 213,000
Baptist Union 204,000
Lutheran Church 114,050
Churches of Christ 92,000
Salvation Army 75,000
Methodist Church (continuing) 67,000
Seventh-Day Adventist Church 54,000
Assemblies of God 35,500
Congregational Union 25,000
Brethren 22,000

Evangelical 17% of population.

Missionaries to Australia (cross-cultural) approximately 600 (1:26,000 people). Missionaries from within Australia 2,690 (1:2,460 Protestants) in 62 agencies.

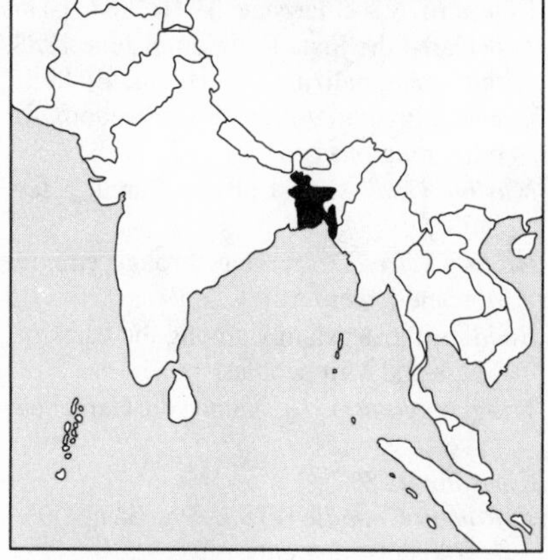

BANGLADESH

Area 144,000 sq.km. Occupying the delta and floodplains of the Ganges and Brahmaputra rivers, with high rainfall and frequent flooding.

Population 117,900,000. Annual growth 2.8%. People per sq.km. 819.

Peoples

Bengali 98%.

Bihari 1%. Mostly in refugee camps.

Tribal peoples 0.7%. 640,000 people in 28 tribes. Largest: Chakma 300,000.

Literacy 25%. *Official languages:* Bengali; English used widely. *All languages* 33. *Bible translations* 13 Bibles, 3 New Testaments, 8 portions.

Capital: Dhaka 5,300,000. Other cities: Chittagong 1,900,000. Urbanization 13%.

Economy: One of the world's poorest nations, suffering from gross overpopulation and periodic natural disasters such as devastating floods and cyclones. There seems little hope that the poverty of this unhappy land will ever be substantially alleviated. Income/person $160 (1% of USA).

Politics: Formerly East Pakistan; independent in 1971 after bitter civil war and defeat of Pakistan by Indian and Bangladesh forces. Corruption, instability, assassinations and 18 coups have marred the years since then. The military took over the government in 1982 but is unable to cope with the serious problems the country faces.

Religion: A secular state 1971-1988. Islam declared the State Religion in June 1988, thus marginalizing the Hindu, Buddhist and Christian minorities. Freedom for other religions has been promised.

Muslim 87%. Almost all are Sunni, a few Shi'a.

Hindu 11.7%. Decreasing through emigration and lower fertility.

Buddhist 0.6%. Mainly among the Chakma, Magh and Mru peoples.

Tribal religions 0.1%. Among the Garo, Santal, etc.

Christian 0.38%.

Roman Catholic 0.18%. Practicing 59%. 190,000 adherents.

Protestant 0.18%. 188,000 adherents; 72,600 members. Denominations 25. Largest (adult members):

Baptist Union of Bangladesh (Baptist Missionary Society) 11,500
Garo Baptist Union 10,000
Bawm Evangelical Christian Church 9,600
All One in Christ Fellowship 7,100
Evangelical Lutheran Church 5,000
Church of Bangladesh (Anglican-Presbyterian) 4,400
Seventh-Day Adventist Church 4,200
Assemblies of God 2,400
Bangladesh Baptist Union 1,790

Evangelical 0.10% of population.

Missionaries to Bangladesh 440 (1:230,000 people) in 30 agencies.

BRAZIL

Area 8,512,000 sq.km. One half of the land surface and population of South America. The world's fifth largest country (36 times the size of the United Kingdom).

Population 150,300,000. Annual growth 2.0%. People per sq.km. 16.

Peoples: Brazil is a "melting pot" of the nations, with much intermarriage, so percentages given below are not meant to indicate rigid categories.

European 54%. Portuguese 15%, Italian 11%, Spanish 10%, German 3%.

African 11%. Descendants of slaves brought from West Africa and Angola.

Mixed race 33%. Mestizo and Mulatto.

Asian 1.5%. Japanese 1,000,000; Chinese 60,000; Arab, etc.

Amerindian 0.1%. In 1900 there were 500,000 in 230 tribes, but now there are less than 100,000 in 140 tribes and still decreasing through the encroachments of civilization, loss of land and disease.

Literacy 78%. *Official language:* Portuguese. *All languages* 152. *Bible Translations* 1 Bible, 18 New Testaments, 38 portions.

Capital: Brasilia 1,700,000. Other major cities: Sao Paulo 16,412,000; Rio de Janeiro 12,525,000; Recife 2,900,000; Porto Alegre 3,073,000; Belo Horizonte 3,785,000; Curitiba 2,827,000; Salvador 2,000,000; Fortaleza 1,900,000. Urbanization 71%.

Economy: Vast economic potential in the developing hinterland of the north and west, rapid growth and industrialization in the '60s and '70s in the south made Brazil one of the leading industrial and trading nations in the world. Lack of oil reserves, rampant inflation and crippling international debt has blunted growth and brought economic hardship to many. In 1989 the new government instituted stringent reforms and have greatly reduced the rate of inflation. Income/person $2,020 (11% of USA). Inflation in December 1989 alone 54%.

Politics: A republic with authoritarian military government since 1964. There was a return to a fully democratic government in 1985.

Religion: Complete freedom of religion.

Non-religious/Atheist 1.4%. Secularism is on the increase in the middle and upper classes.

Buddhist 0.3%.

Muslim 0.1%.

Spiritist 30-35% (estimate). Probably 14% of all Brazilians are openly associated and more than 60% dabble in the various forms of spiritism of European, Amerindian and especially African origin while still claiming to be Christian.

Christian 93%.

Roman Catholic 73.1%. Practicing 12%. 101,000,000 adherents; 60,707,000 members. There are 18 million baptized Catholics who have joined evangelical or other groups.

Other Catholic (2) 2%. 2,770,000 adherents.

Marginal groups (58) 0.52%. 724,000 adherents. Jehovah Witnesses 474,000 adherents; Mormons 161,800 adherents.

Protestant 17.4%. 24,120,000 adherents; 10,377,000 members. Denominations 350. Largest (adult members):

Assemblies of God 5,000,300
Christian Congregation 1,253,000
Baptist Convention (Southern Baptist Convention) 602,000
Conference of Lutheran Churches 580,000
Brazil for Christ 450,000
Seventh-Day Adventist Church 403,000
Cruzada Nacional (ICFG) 250,000
Presbyterian Church 149,000
Evangelical Lutheran Church 128,000
Union of Evangelical Congregational Churches (Evangelical Union of South America) 115,000
All other churches 1,445,000

Evangelical 16% of population.

Missionaries to Brazil 2,600 (1:53,000 people) in 139 agencies.

Missionaries from within Brazil 840 (1:28,700 Protestants) in about 35 agencies.

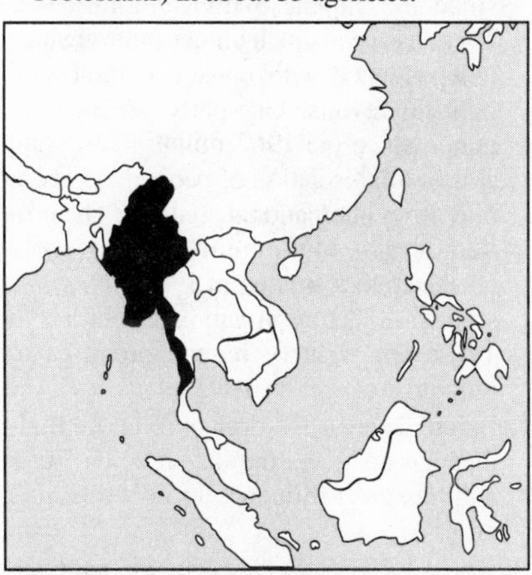

BURMA (Union of Myanmar)

Area 678,000 sq.km. Isolated from India, China and Thailand by a ring of mountains.

Population 41,700,000. Annual growth 2.3%. People per sq.km. 62.

Peoples

Bhama 65.1% and related *Mogh* (Arakanese) 5%.

Ethnic minorities (with their own states within Union) 24.1%. Karen 4,000,000; Shan 2,660,000; Kachin 860,000; Mon 720,000; Chin 720,000; Kayah 190,000.

Other ethnic minorities 2.2%. Palaung 266,000; Lisu 200,000; Wa 150,000; Lahu 100,000; Akha 60,000; Lushai (Mizo) 40,000; Naga 30,000, etc.

Immigrant minorities 3.6%. Chinese 750,000; Bangladeshi/Indian 300,000.

Literacy 78%. *Official language:* Burmese. *All languages* 90. *Bible translations* 12 Bibles, 10 New Testaments, 16 portions.

Capital: Yangon (Rangoon) 2,900,000. Other major city: Mandalay 725,000. Urbanization 24%.

Economy: Very poor due to years of unrest, inefficient socialism and excessive isolationist policies of the government. Huge illegal trade in opium breeds corruption at every level in the country. Some economic relaxations since 1980. Income/person $180 (1% of USA). Inflation 9.2%

Politics: The country has known little peace since the Japanese invasion in 1942. There has been much unrest and war since independence with constant ethnic and political revolts. One-party socialist republic since the 1962 military coup and almost total isolation of people and economy from international contacts. The pro-democracy movement was severely crushed and restricted in 1989, yet won a surprising victory in national elections in 1990. The military regime promises to relinquish power by 1992.

Religion: There is freedom of religion. Buddhism is no longer the state religion, but it still has great influence in governmental affairs.

Buddhist 87%. Shot through with animist practices. Mainly Burmese, Shan, Mon and many Arakanese.

Animist 2%. Many Buddhists are more animist than Buddhist. Karen and many smaller tribes

Muslim 3.6%. Bengali and Arakanese.

Hindu 0.9%. Indian.

Christian 5.9%. 95% from Animistic and 5% from Buddhist background; only 2% of Christians from Bhama majority.

Roman Catholic 1.2%. Practicing 63%. 442,000 adherents; 289,000 members.

Protestant 4.7%. 1,730,000 adherents; 668,000 members. Denominations 43. Largest (adult members):

Burma Baptist Convention 422,000
Assemblies of God 66,000
Church of Christ (Overseas Missionary Fellowship) 56,000
Anglican Church 20,000
Methodist Churches (2) 20,000
Presbyterian Church 11,900

Evangelical 3.1% of population.

Missionaries to Burma 2. Missionaries from within Burma approximately 1,000 (1:1,700 Protestants).

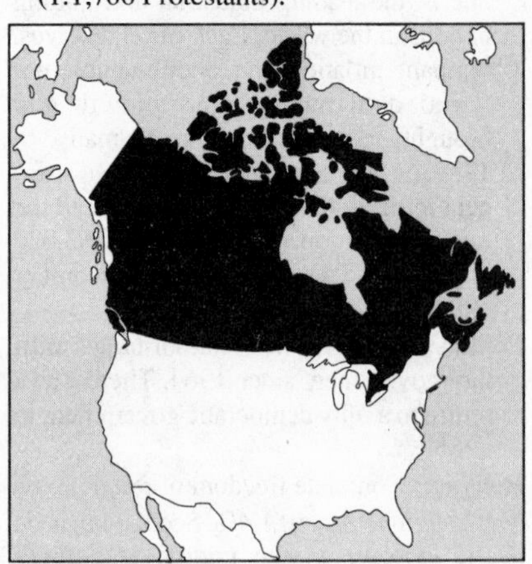

CANADA

Area 9,980,000 sq.km. The world's second largest country. Much is cold arctic tundra or sparsely populated forest.

Population 26,500,000. Annual growth 0.8%, of this immigration 0.6%. 80% of population live within 150 km. of the 7,000 km. USA border. People per sq.km. 2.7.

Peoples: A mosaic of many nations and peoples often retaining much of their original culture.

British 42%. Majority in east, center and west.

French 29%. Majority in Quebec Province. Although Canada is officially bilingual with equal rights for all, the French minority includes a considerable separatist segment.

Other European 19%. German 1,560,000; Italian 830,000; Ukrainian 659,000; Dutch 490,000; Polish 366,000; Norwegian 195,000; Hungarian 146,000; Greek 140,000; Swedish 122,000; Yugoslav 122,000; Danish 98,000; Portuguese 98,000; Czech 73,000; Russian 70,000; Finnish 70,000; Belgian 50,000, etc.

Indigenous 5%. Amerindians (registered 340,000 in 61 tribes on reservations; non-registered 1,000,000), Eskimo 30,000.

Asian 3%. Indo-Pakistanis 350,000; Chinese 301,000; Vietnamese 90,000; Japanese 50,000; Korean 40,000.

Middle Eastern 1.1%. Mainly Arabic speaking.

African 0.8%. 200,000 North American, West Indian and African.

Latin American 0.8%. 200,000.

Literacy 99%. *Official languages:* English, French. *All indigenous languages* 70. *Bible translations* 2 Bibles, 2 New Testaments, 35 portions.

Capital: Ottawa 850,000. Major cities: Toronto 3,300,000; Montreal 3,300,000; Vancouver 1,350,000. Urbanization 76%.

Economy: One of the world's leading industrial nations. The USA is Canada's main trading partner. This interdependence moderates trends towards an economic nationalism. Income/person $15,080 (82% of USA).

Politics: Parliamentary and federal monarchy. Independent of Britain in 1867. Though the world's longest undefended border runs between Canada and the USA, Canada's own cultural and political identity leads to an independent line in foreign affairs to its NATO ally. Quebec separatism has become a dominant national issue.

Religion: Freedom of religion.

Non-religious/Atheist 7.5%.

Muslim 1.5%. Pakistani, Arab,etc.

Jews 1.4%. Some from North Africa and USSR.

Hindu 0.5%. Mostly Indian.

Sikh 0.2%.

Baha'i 0.2%

Animist 0.1%. Increasing again among Amerindians.

Christian 88%. Nominal 23.2%. Affiliated 64.8%.

Roman Catholic 39.6%. Practicing 40%. 10,060,000 adherents. Majority of French, Spanish, Italian, Portuguese, etc.

Orthodox 2.4%. 612,000 adherents. Denominations 31+. Mostly ethnic minorities of East European, Greek and Middle Eastern origin.

Marginal groups 2.3%. Over 34 cults. Largest (adult members): Mormons 90,000; Jehovah's Witnesses 77,003.

Protestant 20.6%. (A further 15% nominal.) 5,220,000 adherents; 2,880,000 members. Denominations 180. Largest (adult members):

United Church 983,000
Anglican Church 588,000
Pentecostal (30 groups) 266,000
Lutheran (8 groups) 223,000
Presbyterian (5 groups) 210,000
Baptist (11 groups) 205,000
Mennonite (12 groups) 64,000

Evangelical 6.5% of population.

Missionaries to Canada approximately 300 (Mostly from the USA).

Missionaries from within Canada approximately 4,000 (1:1,300 Protestants) in over 50 agencies. Of these 420 serve in crosscultural work in Canada.

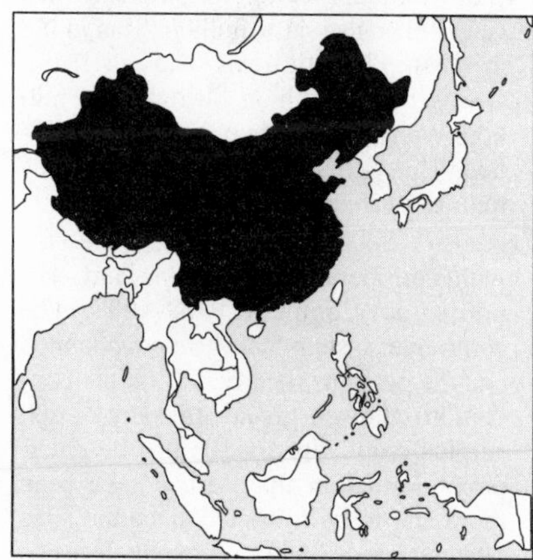

CHINA

Area 9,561,000 sq.km. The third largest country in the world. Taiwan, Hong Kong and Macao are not included here.

Population 1,119,300,000. By far the largest nation in the world; 21% of world's population. Most live in the better-watered central and eastern coastal provinces. Annual growth 1.4%. People per sq.km. 117.

Peoples

Chinese (Han) 93%. Eight major languages and 600 dialects but one written language common to all. Putunghua (Mandarin) 748 million, Wu 90 million, Yueh (Cantonese) 54 million, Xiang (Hunanese) 53 million, Hakka 43 million, Minnan 32 million, Gan 26 million, Minpei 13 million.

Ethnic minorities 7%. 55 minorities officially recognized. Largest: Zhuang 14 million, Hui 7.6 million, Uighur 6.3 million, Yi 5.7 million, Hmong (Miao) 5.3 million, Manchu 4.5 million, Tibetan 4 million, Mongol 3.4 million, Bouyei-Tai 3.2 million, Tujia 3 million, Korean 1.8 million, Dong 1.5 million, Bai 1.2 million, Hani 1.1 million. Many smaller minorities live in the mountainous south and southwest.

Literacy 76%. *Official language:* Putunghua (Mandarin Chinese); local languages in the five Autonomous Regions. *All languages* 115. *Bible translations* 13 Bibles, 10 New Testaments, 23 portions.

Capital: Beijing (Peking) 9.2 million. Other cities: Shanghai 11.9 million, Tianjin 7.8 million, Chongqing 6.5 million, Guangzhou 5.6 million, Shenyang 5.1 million, Wuham 4.2 million, Nanjing 3.6 million. Thirty-eight other cities of over one million inhabitants. Urbanization 21%.

Economy: Socialist centralized economy, with considerable relaxations and economic development 1978-1989. The commune system has been dismantled and the peasants (nearly 80% of the population) allowed greater freedom to sell surplus crops. Small-scale private enterprises started in that period have been more and more restricted since the June 1989 clamp-down. The economy is in crisis once more. Income/person $300 (2% of USA).

Politics: This great and ancient nation has regained its place of importance in the world after nearly two centuries of decline and humiliation at the hands of the Western powers and Japan. Since the final conquest of mainland China in 1949, the Communist Party has remoulded the nation along Marxist lines. The Cultural Revolution (1966-76) was the culmination of this policy. It caused immeasurable suffering and economic chaos. Intellectuals and religious believers were cruelly persecuted. The loss of life was enormous. After the death of Mao in 1976 the radical leftists were discredited and removed from power. A more pragmatic leadership initiated a series of economic, political and cultural reforms and developed links with other nations, but all within definite limits. The Communist party still maintains strict control over every aspect of life. In the latter half of 1983 a series of campaigns were initiated against crime, leftists, and "spiritual" pollution to counter growing corruption, dissident Western influences and revivals of religion. After a further period of relaxation, the student protest movement in Beijing in 1989 provoked a massacre in Tiananmen Square, repression of all protest, and a return to hard-line Marxist policies. The political situation remains tense and the aging leadership is unlikely to retain the status quo.

Religion: The elimination of all religious groups has always been the ultimate aim of the Marxist government. In the '50s the government engineered the infiltration, subversion and control of all organized Christianity. By 1958 this had been achieved through the Three Self Patriotic Movement among Protestants and the Catholic Patriotic Association among Catholics. During the Cultural Revolution even these front structures were moribund, and all religious activity forced underground. In 1978 restrictions were eased and the Three Self Patriotic Movement and Catholic Patriotic Association resurrected as a means of regaining governmental control of the thousands of house churches. This has been only partially successful. Recent government policy has been to tolerate religious belief and allow worship under government supervision. There has been a marked increase in pressure and persecution for unregistered churches since June 1989.

All figures are estimates.

Atheist 12%. Communist Party members nearly 40 million.

Non-religious 50%(?). The atheistic education system ensures that most young people have no religious knowledge.

Chinese religions (Taoism, Buddhism, Confucianism) 28%(?).

Animist 2%. Among tribal peoples of the south, etc.

Muslim 2.4%. Ten national minorities are Muslim.

Christian 5%(?). The official estimate for all Christians is 6 million. House church and overseas researchers estimate 30 million to 50 million.

Roman Catholic 0.6%. Divided between the official CPA and those remaining loyal to the Vatican (over 50%). 6,600,000 adherents(?).

Marginal groups (3+) 0.1%. Various groups that are unitarian, "shouters," etc. 1,000,000 adherents(?).

Protestant 4.3%. 45,000,000 adherents, possibly subdivided thus:

Three Self Patriotic Movement 3,000,000 adherents

Three Self Patriotic Movement-related meeting points 9,000,000 adherents

Home meetings 33,000,000 adherents. Personnel in China-related ministries estimate 600 but working from other lands.

COLOMBIA

Area 1,139,000 sq.km. NW corner of South America. The fourth largest country in the continent. Mountains in west, plains and forests in east.

Population 31,800,000. Annual growth 2.0%. People per sq.km. 28. Only 3% live in the eastern half of the country.

Peoples

Spanish-speaking 97.4%. Approximate composition: Mestizo (Eurindian) 49%, Mulatto (Eurafrican) 21%, European 20%, African 7%.

Amerindians 1.6%. Approximately 100 tribes in about 10 language families. Largest: Guajiro 100,000; Paez 40,000; Catio 20,000; Guahibo 20,000.

Other 1%. Lebanese 120,000; Chinese 5,000, etc.

Literacy 84%. *Official language:* Spanish. *All languages* 75. *Bible translations* 1 Bible, 12 New Testaments, 29 portions.

Capital: Bogota 7 million. Other cities: Medellin 300,000, Cali 200,000, Barranquilla 1,500,000. Urbanization 67%.

Economy: Major export earners: coffee (legal) and cocaine (illegal). Income/person \$1,220 (7% of USA). A great difference between incomes of rich and poor, but a growing middle class.

Politics: Independent from Spain in 1819. A democratic republic, but with several dictatorships and civil wars this century. The period of anarchy and civil war 1948-60 became known as "La Violencia," during which 300,000 died. The country is plagued by crime, Communist guerrilla movements, and narcotics terrorists. The latter became so powerful through intrigue, corruption and murder that the integrity of the State was threatened. In 1990 the Presidential candidate most opposed to the drug barons was elected.

Religion: The Roman Catholic Church is the state church, and is accorded a privileged position. Since 1974 there has been considerable freedom for Evangelicals to evangelize, though policy towards foreign missions has been somewhat restrictive.

Non-religious/Atheist 1.2%.

Tribal religions 1.1%.

Muslim 0.2%.

Baha'i 0.1%.

Christian 97.4%.

Roman Catholic 93%. 27,250,000 adherents; 14,000,000 members.

Marginal groups (8) 1.1%. 330,000 adherents; 114,000 members. Largest (adherents): Unitarian Pentecostals 190,000; Jehovah's Witnesses 96,400; Mormons 39,500.

Protestant 3.1%. 900,000 adherents; 284,000 members. Denominations 97+. Largest (adult members):

Seventh-Day Adventist Church 76,000

International Church of Foursquare Gospel 35,000

Christian Crusade Church 21,000

Christian & Missionary Alliance 16,400

Panamerican Mission 15,000

Assemblies of God 11,500

Amerindian churches (New Tribes Mission) 10,000

Southern Baptist Convention 9,300

Association of Evangelical Churches of East (The Evangelical Alliance Mission) 9,000

Missionary Evangelical Union (Gospel Missionary Union) 7,900

Evangelical 2.4% of population.

Missionaries to Colombia 1,150 (1:25,500 people) in 70 agencies. Missionaries from within Colombia approximately 40 (1:22,500 Protestants).

CZECHOSLOVAKIA

Area 128,000 sq.km. Landlocked state in central Europe.

Population 15,600,000. Annual growth 0.2%. People per sq.km. 121.

Peoples

Czech 62.5%. In center and west.

Slovak 29%. In east.

Other minorities 8.5%. Magyar (Hungarian) 620,000; Gypsy 385,000; Polish 80,000; German 77,000.

Literacy 99%. *Official languages:* Czech, Slovak. *All languages* 8. *Bible translations* 6 Bibles, 1 portion.

Capital: Prague 1,300,000. Urbanization 74%.

Economy: Highly industrialized and efficient before the Communist takeover. The efficient industrialized economy before World War II was devastated by both the war and four decades of Communist economics. The long and painful restoration of a free market has begun. Income/person $5,800 (31% of USA).

Politics: A federal republic of two nations—Czechs (Bohemia, Moravia and parts of Silesia) in the west and Slovaks in the east. Although a minority party, the Communists seized power in 1948. The liberalizing policies of the Dubcek Government (1966-68) were ended by the Russian invasion of 1968. The sudden and dramatic collapse of the hard-line Communist regime in November 1989 opened the way for democratic multiparty elections in June 1990. The broad-based Civic Forum and the Slovak Public Against Violence parties came away with the biggest share of the convincing election victory, and under the popular leadership of President Vaclav Havel have tried to form a non-communist, coalition basis for freeing up the country's institutions and industry.

Religion: The remarkable freedom of the

"Prague Spring" of 1968 has been replaced by increasing repression and persecution of the churches to almost Stalinist proportions. Since 1984, the Catholic leadership has taken a much stronger stance against the repressive policies of the authorities. Harsh control, repression and persecution of Christians and churches characterized the Communist period. The new non-Communist government is drafting laws granting freedom of religion.

Non-religious/Atheist 21.3%.

Jews 0.1%. 4,000 left of the 360,000 in 1938.

Christian 78.6%.

Roman Catholic 68%. 10,540,000 adherents. Only 1 million attend church regularly.

Other Catholic 3.2%. 501,000 adherents. Mainly the Czech Hussite Church which broke away from Rome in 1920.

Orthodox 1.2%. 181,000 adherents.

Protestant 6%. 935,000 adherents; 570,000 members. Denominations 16. Largest (adult members):

Slovak Evangelical Lutheran Church 369,000

Slovak Reformed Church est. 130,000

Evangelical Church of Czech Brethren 200,000

United Methodist Church 10,000

Moravian Church 9,700

Seventh-Day Adventist Church 7,800

Church of Brethren (Congregational) 8,000

Brethren est. 5,400

Pentecostal Church (Assemblies of God) 4,600

Evangelical 2.1% of population.

Silerian Lutheran Church 46,000

EGYPT

Area 1,001,000 sq.km. 96% desert, and only 3% arable land along the banks of the Nile and around the Western Desert oases.

Population 56,300,000. Annual growth 2.8%. People per sq.km. 45; in fertile areas 1,875 people/sq.km. The rapid loss of cultivable land bodes ill for the future.

Peoples

Egyptian 86.4%. Speaking Arabic, but essentially the same people of ancient and biblical history.

Arab 6.3%. Lebanese, Sudanese, Yemeni, Palestinian, etc.

Nubian 3%. Mostly living in the southern part of the country.

Bedouin 2%. Many still nomadic in Sinai, etc.

Berber 2%. Most now Arabized, but a few still speaking a Berber dialect at the Siwa Oasis.

Other minorities 0.3%. Westerner, Armenian, Greek, etc.

Literacy 48%. *Official language:* Arabic. *All languages* 6. *Bible translations* 2 Bibles, 1 New Testament, 2 portions.

Capital: Cairo est. 12,000,000. Other major cities: Alexandria 3,162,000. Thirteen other cities with over 100,000 people. Rapid urbanization—now at 48%.

Economy: Poor, crippled by high birth rate and lack of agricultural land, but somewhat alleviated by USA aid, and remittances from 1.8 million Egyptians resident abroad, but this number and source of income is rapidly diminishing. Income/person $710 (4% of USA).

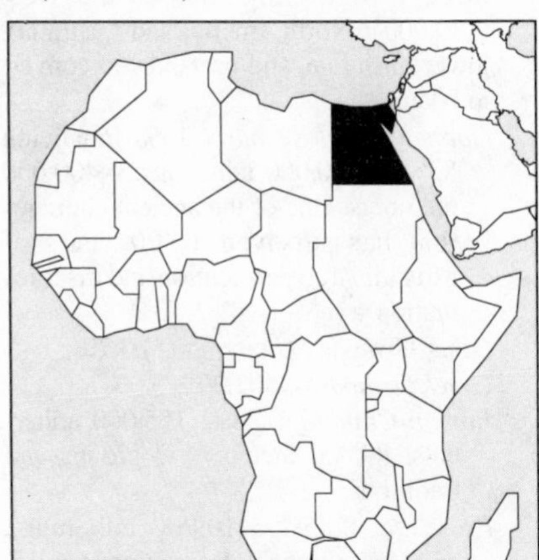

Politics: President Sadat's diplomacy (1970-81) ended the dominance of the USSR and won control of the valuable Suez Canal and Sinai oilfields from Israel as an outcome of the 1973 Yom Kippur War. The generally popular peace treaty with Israel in 1979 was bitterly opposed by many Arab nations and Muslim fundamentalists within the country and led to Egypt's isolation in the Middle East and Sadat's assassination. The present government of President Mubarak is cautiously introducing political liberizations and seeking rapprochement with other Arab states. The economic woes of the land are causing many to turn to fundamentalist Islamic political movements.

Religion: Islam is the state religion. Fundamentalist Muslims are pressing for the full Islamization of society. Christians are free to worship but not to openly evangelize Muslims. The 1981 clampdown on both Muslim fundamentalists and Christian leaders had its roots in tensions caused by enforced conversions to Islam and successful evangelism by Christians.

Muslim 82.4%. Cairo is the intellectual capital of Islam. Muslim fundamentalism has become a significant force over the last 10 years.

Non-religious/Atheist 0.4%.

Christian 17.2%. Though officially only 6%. Gradual erosion of this percentage through high emigration to the West (130,000 in North America and Australia), lower birth rate, and pressures to convert to Islam.

Coptic Orthodox Church 15%. Practicing 83%. 7,600,000 adherents; 4,400,000 members. One of the ancient churches that has survived 1,300 years of Muslim Arab persecution and discrimination.

Other Orthodox Churches (5) 0.7%.

Greek Orthodox 350,000

Roman Catholic 0.33%. 155,000 adherents; 89,000 members. 7 groups and traditions.

Protestant 0.85%. 410,000 adherents; 154,000 members. Denominations 46. Largest (adult members):

Coptic Evangelical Church 88,000
Assemblies of God 13,000
Brethren (2 groups) 10,400
Free Methodist Church 9,000

Protestant Evangelical 0.69% of population, but possibly 3% if Orthodox included.

Missionaries to Egypt estimated 150 (1:322,000 people) in 27 agencies. Missionaries from Egypt 25 (1:16,400 Protestants) in 3 agencies.

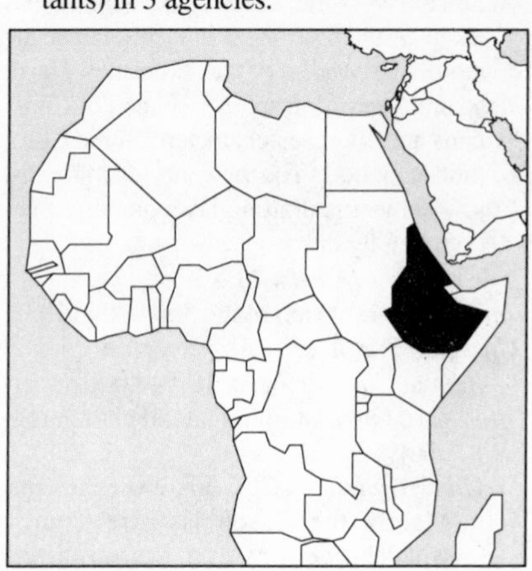

ETHIOPIA

Area 1,222,000 sq.km. Fertile mountain plateau surrounded by the deserts of the Red Sea coast, and the Somali, Kenya and Sudan borders.

Population 50,800,000. Annual growth 2.1%. People per sq.km. 42.

Peoples: There are over 200 major dialects spoken, but the 1974 revolution has stimulated a greater sense of national identity in this diversity.

Semitic origin 36%. Amharas (4 groups) 8,840,000 in Central and Northern Highlands; Tigrinya 2,120,000 in Central Eritrea; Tigre 700,000 in Northern Eritrea; and Gurage (4) 1,000,000 in Southern Highlands. They originally came from Arabia, conquering and mixing with the local Hamitic peoples.

Cushitic 57%. Over 52 peoples in the east, center and south.

Oromo 14,000,000 (Wolayta 3,400,000; Wallega 1,650,000; Arusi 1,050,000; Konso 400,000; and at least 14 other smaller groups.)

Somali 2,000,000—but about 500,000 are refugees in Somalia.

Other significant peoples: Sidamo 1,000,000; Hadiya 950,000; Kambalfa 460,000; Gideo 390,000; Kafa

230,000; Afar 200,000; Awiya 160,000; Boran 150,000; Beja 90,000; Ari 60,000; She 50,000; Burji 30,000; Bako 25,000; Banna 25,000.

Nilotic-Sudanic 6%. Twenty-two peoples largely in south and west: Gumuz 250,000; Berta 140,000; Murle 140,000; Anuak 130,000; Ma'en 130,000; Nuer 130,000; Masengo 100,000; Nara 100,000; Tirma 50,000; Koma 43,000; Turkana 30,000; Mabaan 7,000; etc., and Kunama (Eritrea) 200,000.

Falasha Jew 15,000. Black Jews who still practice Old Testament animal sacrifices.

Foreign 0.8%. Arab 90,000; Eastern European; Westerner, etc.

Literacy 20%. *Official language:* Amharic, 65% of population are able to speak it. *All languages* over 100. *Bible translations* 5 Bibles, 6 New Testaments, 10 portions.

Capital: Addis Ababa 1,845,000. Other major city: Asmara 550,000. Urbanization 15%.

Economy: A semi-feudal society radically transformed by the changes and upheavals following the 1974 revolution. The country's economy has been devastated by drought, war and ruinous Marxist collectivisation attempts. In desperation the government has opted to open up the economy by drastic liberalizing reforms. Terrible famines in 1984/85 and 1989/90 have caused the death of over 1 million people.

Politics: The government of Emperor Haile Selassie was overthrown in 1974 by the army, but the Provisional Military Administrative Council did not gain full political control until 1976. The Marxist-oriented government has had to contend with six separatist movements—the major ones being in the Ogaden in the east and Eritrea and Tigre Provinces in the north; bitter fighting still continues. Economic necessity and world events have forced the government to renounce Marxism, and seek more ties with the West. The isolation of the government is such that its survival is in doubt. The two most successful guerilla movements in Eritrea and Tigre in the north are strongly Marxist in ideology.

Religion: During the Marxist period 1974-90, all religions were opposed and Christians especially subjected to much persecution, and limitations. These pressures are now reduced.

Non-religious/Atheist 3%.

Tribal religions 10%. Mainly among the peoples of the south and west.

Muslim 35%. Strong in the north (Tigre), east (Afars), and southeast (Somalis and Oromo groups).

Christian 52%. Majority among Amharas, Tigre and many Oromo peoples of the Highlands.

Ethiopian Orthodox Church 41%. 14,600,000 adherents; 8,600,000 members.

Roman Catholic 0.7%. 242,000 adherents; 140,000 members.

Protestant 10%. 3,580,000 adherents; 1,700,000 members. Denominations 36. Largest (adherents):

Kale Hiywot Church (KHC) 1,200,000
Mekane Yesu Church (ECMY) 816,000
Full Gospel Believers' Church 100,000
Seventh-Day Adventist Church 35,000
Assemblies of God 30,000
Mulu Wengel Church 19,000
Yihiywot Birhan Church 15,000
Meseret Kristos Church 6,000
Emmanuel Baptist Church 3,200
Evangelical Church of Eritrea 2,500

Evangelical 9.6% of population. There are also Orthodox Christians who are evangelical.

Missionaries to Ethiopia approximately 400 (1:89,000 people). Missionaries from within Ethiopia approximately 50 (1:71,600).

FRANCE

Area 551,000 sq.km. The largest country in Western Europe.

Population 56,300,000. Annual growth 0.4%. People per sq.km. 102.

Peoples

Indigenous 90.2%.

French 79%.

Minorities 10%. Alsatian 1,465,000; Breton 1,302,000; Flemish 380,000, Corsican 290,000; Basque 160,000.

Other minorities 2%. Jews 750,000; West Indian Antillean 230,000; Gypsy 160,000.

Foreign residents 9%.

North African/Middle Easterner 4%. Algerian 1,172,000; Moroccan 640,000; Tunisian 298,000; Turk 160,000; Irani 30,000.

European 3.2%. Portuguese 857,000; Italian 469,000; Spanish 430,000; Armenian 210,000; Polish 100,000; Yugoslavian 70,000.

Asian 1.2%. Vietnamese 250,000; Chinese 190,000; Laotian 100,000; Cambodian 70,000.

African 0.5%. Mostly from Francophone West Africa. Malian 20,000.

Literacy 98%. *Official language:* French.

Capital: Paris 10,413,000. The capital dominates the life of the country. Other major cities: Lyon 1,300,000; Marseille 1,230,000; Lille 1,100,000. Urbanization 79%.

Economy: Economic stability and growth gave the nation one of the highest standards of living in Europe. Oil price rises and world recession have bitten deep into those standards. Income/person $12,860 (70% of USA). Inflation 10%.

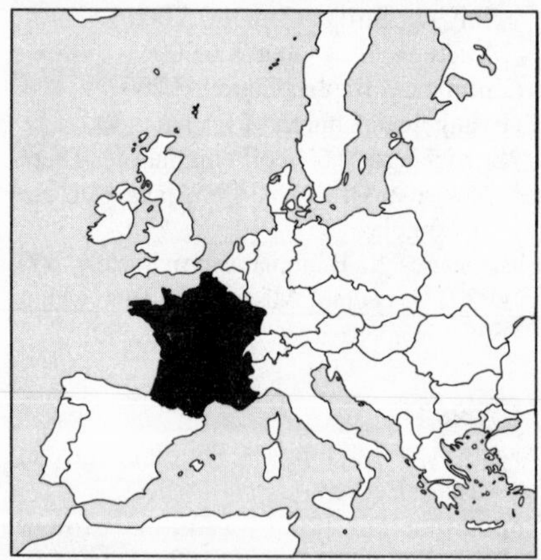

Politics: Democratic republic with strong executive presidency. A member of the European Community, and pressing for economic union within the EEC.

Religion: Secular state with freedom of religion.

Non-religious/Atheist 16.0%. Many were baptized as Christians.

Muslim 4.6%. North African, African, Turk, etc.

Jews 1.1%.

Christian 78%.

Roman Catholic 74%. Regular practicing 6%. 40,500,000 adherents; 29,800,000 members.

Other Catholic 0.2%. Over 73 small groups.

Orthodox groups (17) 0.8%.

Marginal groups 0.6%. Over 25 cults. Largest (adherents): Jehovah's Witnesses 166,100; Mormons 13,100.

Protestant 2%. 1,140,000 adherents; 655,000 members. Denominations 60 (also many independent congregations). Some of the largest (adult members):

Reformed Church 274,000
Lutheran Churches (3 groups) 145,000
Assemblies of God 75,000
Reformed Church of Alsace & Lorraine 47,000
Gypsy Pentecostal Church 15,600
Free Pentecostal Church 8,000
Federation of Baptist Churches 3,800
Brethren 3,200

Evangelical 0.63% of population.

Missionaries to France 905 (1:60,000 people) in 80 agencies. Missionaries from France 373 (1:3,100 Protestants) in 32 agencies.

GERMANY

The Federal Republic of Germany and German Democratic Republic

Note: Statistics partly amalgamated, paralleling the ongoing reunification process.

Area 356,000 sq.km. (30% of which was the area of former East Germany). The full union of the two Germanies is still subject to finalization as of June 30, 1990. People per sq.km. 219.

Population 78,100,000 (of which 21% are of former East Germany). A further 3.5 million Germans live in Eastern Europe, Americas and Namibia.

Peoples

German 93%. Massive immigration of

USSR and Eastern Europe Germans during 1989/90—possibly 300,000 over that period.

Other minorities 2%. Danes, Sorbs, Wends, etc.

Foreign 7% Migrant "guest workers" and their families from:

S. European: Yugoslavs 613,000; Italians 565,000; Greeks 292,000; Spaniards 166,000; Portuguese 99,000.

Middle Eastern/North African: Turks 1,552,000; Moroccans 44,000; Iranians 33,000; Tunisians 25,000, etc.

Asian: Chinese 40,000; Tamils from Sri Lanka 30,000; Vietnamese 26,000; Pakistanis and Indians 16,000, Koreans 14,000; Indonesians 9,000; Japanese 6,000.

Literacy 99%. *Official language:* German.

Capital: Bonn (West) 515,000; East Berlin (East) 1,200,000. The new capital of the reunited Germany will probably be Berlin. Other major city complexes: Ruhr Area 8,850,000; Hamburg 2,810,000; Stuttgart 2,790,000, Frankfurt 2,680,000; Munich 2,310,000. Urbanization 85%.

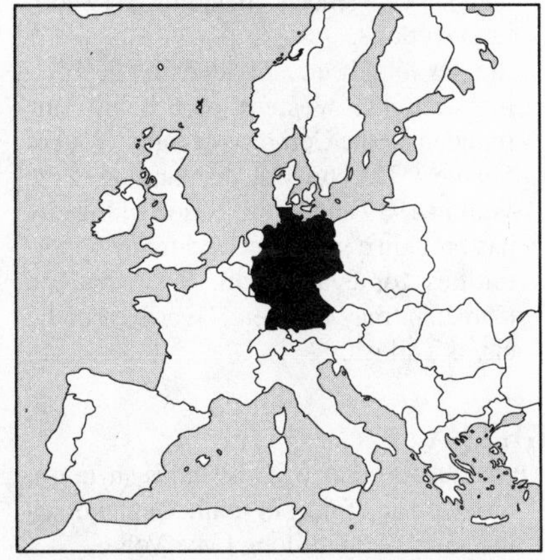

Economy: Highly industrialized and strong export-oriented economy with enormous trade surpluses. A leading member of the European Community and committed to the financial integration of the EC. Now facing the enormous cost of incorporating East Germany and rebuilding its shattered economy. The ecological disaster of Communist-run industries will take many decades to rectify. Income/person: W - $14,460 (79% of USA); E - $6,000 (33% of USA).

Politics: Germany lost much of her eastern territories to the USSR and Poland at the end of World War II. The remaining third of the country was occupied by the Russians, who still maintain a large military presence. The collapse of the hard-line Honecker regime opened the way for democratic elections in Spring 1990, rejection of Socialism and Marxism and a rapid move toward reunification with West Germany, which began with monetary reunification on July 1, 1990. Political reunification is projected to begin in December 1990.

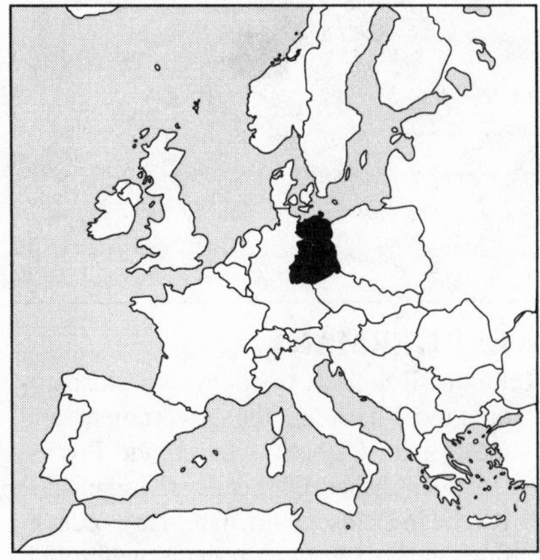

EAST GERMANY

(German Democratic Republic)

Religion: After 40 years of subtle pressures on the numerically strong Protestant church, there has been complete religious freedom since 1989.

Non-religious/Atheist 38.7%.

Christian 61.5%. Nominal 16.4%. Affiliated 45.1%.

Roman Catholic 7.4%. Practicing 20%. 1,250,000 adherents; 1,000,000 members.

Marginal groups 0.87%. 147,000 adherents. New Apostolic 105,00 adherents, etc.

Protestant 36.7%. 6,200,000 adherents; 4,910,000 members. Denominations 19. Eight regional churches in two major groups (adherents):

EKU (Lutheran/Reformed) 3,000,000
VELK (Lutheran) 2,900,000
Free Churches (adult members):
Methodist Church 35,000
Free Church Union (Baptist) 22,000
Seventh-Day Adventist Church 10,000
Independent Lutheran 10,000
Reformed Church 8,400
Brethren 6,000
Evangelical 11% of population.

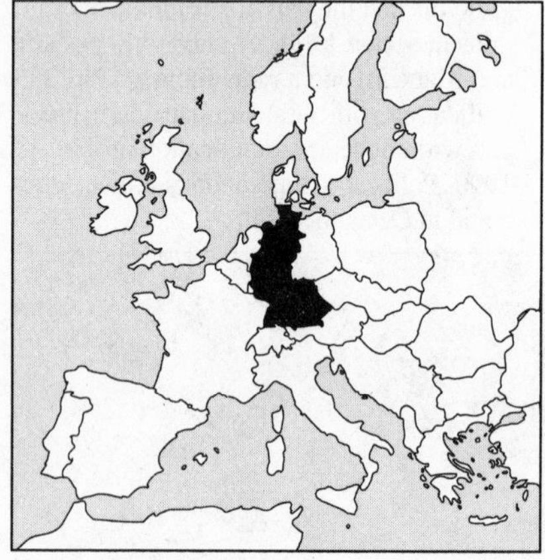

WEST GERMANY

Religion: Religious freedom, but close co-operation between the government and the Roman Catholic Church and Protestant Established Churches, Evangelische Kirche in Deutschland, in religious education, radio, TV, church taxation through state channels, etc.

Non-religious/Atheist 5%.

Muslim 3%. Almost entirely immigrant minorities.

Jews 32,000 (564,000 in 1932 before the Nazi pogroms).

Christian 92%. Affiliated 86%. Only a minority of the population is involved in Christian activities.

Roman Catholic 42%. 25,600,000 adherents; 19,700,000 members. 70% hardly ever attend church.

Other Catholic groups (43) 0.1%.

Orthodox Churches (13) 0.8%. 485,000 adherents. Greeks, East Europeans.

Marginal groups (34) 1.5%. 892,000 adherents; 515,000 members. Largest (adherents): New Apostolic Church 482,000; Jehovah's Witnesses (2 groups) 245,000; Mormons 27,500.

Protestant (162 groups) 43%. 25,700,000 adherents; 6,670,000 members. There are two major groupings. *Evangelische Kirche in Deutschland (EKD)* 17 territorial or State Churches. 24,500,000 adherents. Regular church attendance 1,400,000 (5.5% of those affiliated). *Free churches* 1,200,000 adherents; 420,000 members. Total weekly church attendance 700,000. Denominations 150. Largest (adult members):

Baptist Union 67,500
Independent Lutheran Church 37,000
Methodist Church 33,500
Brethren 32,000
Seventh-Day Adventist Church 25,000
Free Evangelical Churches 24,000
Association of Free Pentecostal Churches 19,000
Mennonite Churches (2) 15,800
Conservative Evangelical 7% of population.

Missionaries to Germany 680. Missionaries from Germany 2,686 (1:9,600 Protestants) in 62 agencies, including 311 short-term workers.

Berlin has long been a divided and depressing city, the western part being surrounded by the Communist-built "Wall of Shame." The euphoric dismantling of the Wall in 1989 and reunification of the city has brought a new hope and many opportunities for evangelism. Pray that the Christians may use them. Over 10% of the city is Turkish.

GHANA

Area 238,500 sq.km. Grasslands in north, farmland and forest in south. Center dominated by 520 km.-long Lake Volta.

Population 15,000,000. Annual growth 3.1%. People per sq.km. 63. Higher density in south.

Peoples: About 100 ethnic groups and 3 major language divisions.

Kwa 75%. 5 major sub-groups in center and south.

Akan (25 groups): Ashanti 1,900,000;

Fante 1,700,000; Brong 708,000, etc., most speak dialects of Twi.

Ewe (3) 1.9 million in southeast.

Ga-Adangme (4) 1.3 million around Accra.

Guan (13) 510,000 in center and north.

C. Togo (14) 125,000 on eastern border.

Gur 22%. 5 major sub-groups in north.

Mole-Dagbani (13). Dagomba 460,000; Dagari-Birifor 420,000; Frafra 400,000; Kusasi 256,000.

Gurma (5). Konkomba 450,000; Bimoba 68,000, etc.

Grusi (5). Sisaala 300,000; Kasena 78,000, etc.

Mande 0.9%. 2 small groups.

Foreign 2%.

Literacy 35%. *Official language:* English. *All languages* 60. *Bible translations* 4 Bibles, 9 New Testaments, 14 portions.

Capital: Accra 1,800,000. Other cities: Kumasi 800,000; Sekondi-Takoradi 255,000. Urbanization 32%.

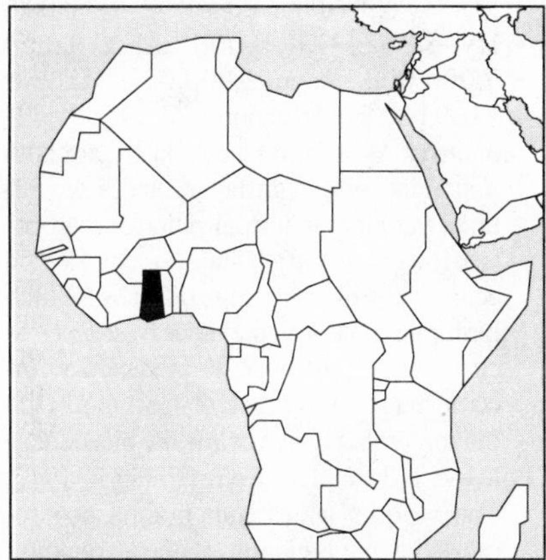

Economy: Slowly recovering from almost total collapse in 1982. Earlier government overspending, mismanagement and corruption reduced this once prosperous land to poverty. Main exports are cocoa, gold and timber. Living standards were reduced by uncontrolled inflation, periods of drought and enforced repatriation of Ghanaians from Nigeria 1983-85. Since 1984 Ghana has begun to recover and the shattered economic infrastructure slowly repaired. Income/person $390 (2% of USA).

Politics: Independent from Britain in 1957. Nkrumah's "socialist" experiment was a disaster from which the nation will take years to recover. There have been five military regimes and three short-lived civilian governments since Nkrumah's overthrow in 1966. The government has had close links with Libya and retained power despite early unpopularity and harshness of leftist elements to political opponents. The government has become more relaxed and pragmatic in international relations since 1984.

Religion: Secular state with religious freedom, but some members of the military government are hostile to Christianity and have sought to hamper the spread of the gospel.

African traditional religions 31%. Mainly among peoples on the northern border.

Muslim 17%. Sunni 9%, Ahmaddiya 8%. The majority among the Dagomba, Gonja and Wali; growing minority among other northern peoples.

Christian 52%. Nominal 5%. Affiliated 47%. Note that figures are very tentative for some denominations.

Roman Catholic 11.3%. Practicing 35%. 1,430,000 adherents; 758,000 members.

African marginal groups (700+) 12%. 1,500,000 adherents.

Foreign marginal groups (14) 1.2%. 157,000 adherents; 47,430 members. Largest: Jehovah's Witnesses 27,730 members.

Protestant 22.4%. Denominations 60+. 2,090,000 adherents; 1,000,000 members. Largest (adult members):

Methodist Church 186,966
Church of Pentecost 159,915
Presbyterian Church 132,860
Evangelical Presbyterian Church 76,400(?)
Anglican Church 64,000(?)
Seventh-Day Adventist Church 56,000
Apostolic Church 32,000(?)
Christ Apostolic Church 30,000(?)
Assemblies of God 20,000

Southern Baptist Convention 19,000
African Methodist Episcopal Zion 17,000
Evangelical 9% of population.

Missionaries to Ghana 380 (1:33,400 people) in 50 agencies. Missionaries from within Ghana 25(?) (1:83,600 Protestants).

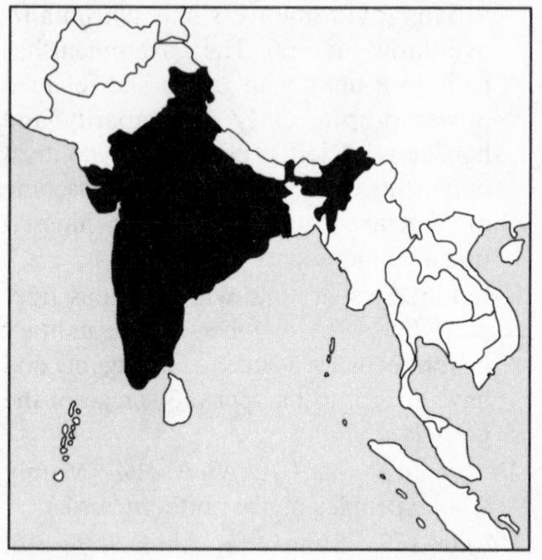

INDIA

Area 3,204,000 sq.km. 22 union states and 9 union territories. Geographically India dominates South Asia and the Indian Ocean.

Population 853,400,000. Annual growth 2.2%; 18.5 million increase every year. People per sq.km. 266. Nearly 16% of the world's population is Indian, living on 2.4% of the world's land surface.

Peoples: The great racial, ethnic, religious and linguistic diversity makes a simple subdivision of the population difficult.

Ethno-Linguistic:

Indo-Aryan 72%. In Northern and Central India.

Dravidian 25%. Majority in Southern India.

Sino-Tibetan 3%. Northern border and Northeast India.

Caste: A system that pervasively influences every religion in India, to a lesser or greater extent, but which is fundamental to Hinduism. Caste discrimination is forbidden by the constitution, but it is socially important for over 80% of the population.

Caste Hindus 64%. (Brahmin, Kshatriya, Vaisya, Sudra).

Harijan (Outcastes, Untouchables) 14%. Classified by the government as "Scheduled Castes."

Tribal peoples 7%. *Muslims* 12%. *Christians* 3%, etc., are considered outside the caste structure. The former are classified as "Scheduled Tribes."

Literacy 36%. *Official languages* 14; Hindi 31%, Telugu 8%, Tamil 7%, Urdu 5%, Gujarati 4.6%, Kannada 4%, Malayalam 4%, Oriya 4%, Punjabi 2.5%, Assamese 1.6%, Kashmiri 0.5%. *Nationally used languages:* Hindi and English; the latter being important in education. *All languages* 1,658 (1971 census). 329 listed by Summer Institute of Linguistics. Those with over 5,000 speakers number 350. *Bible translations* 36 Bibles, 25 New Testaments, 54 portions. At least 13 New Testaments need a major revision.

Capital: Delhi 6,600,000. Other major cities: Calcutta 10,200,000, Bombay 10,000,000, Madras 6,900,000, Bangalore 4,000,000, Hyderabad 3,000,000, Ahmedabad 3,000,000, Pune 2,000,000, Kanpur 2,000,000. Urbanization 23%.

Economy: Agriculture and industry are both important. 74% of the labor force is agricultural, but rapid industrialization and urbanization is taking place. Remarkable economic growth has been offset by the high birth rate, illiteracy, prejudice, resistance to change, and bureaucratic inefficiency. Income/person $300 (2% of USA). Yet 300 million probably live below the breadline.

Politics: Independent from Britain in 1947. The world's largest functioning democracy. Troubled relations with surrounding nations; two wars with Pakistan and one with China. Internal tensions have arisen because of regional, caste, and religious loyalties that have sometimes broken out into violence and rioting. The Sikh separatist movements in the Punjab and the Muslim independence movement in Kashmir have developed into virtual guerilla warfare and threaten the unity of the country.

Religion: India is a secular state that grants

freedom to all religions to practice and propagate their faith. In practice there has been strong pressure from Hindu militants to prevent proselytization at a state and central level. Several states have discriminatory legislation against religious minorities, but the federal government has not followed this course. The 1989 elections brought in a new government coalition in which Hindu nationalist parties participate—a fact which could increase pressures on Christians and Muslims.

Hindu 82%. Figure somewhat raised by the automatic inclusion of many of the tribal animists. Hinduism is a social system and philosophy and readily absorbs elements of any religion with which it comes into contact. Popular Hinduism is idolatrous. Intellectual Hinduism is philosophical and mystical and has a growing appeal to Western countries. India suffers under its fatalism, castism, 200 million holy cows, 33 million gods, etc., to its economic and spiritual detriment.

Muslim 11.8% (Muslims claim 13%). A widespread minority, but a majority in Kashmir and Lakshadweep, and growing among Harijans.

Sikhs 1.92%. Majority in Punjab. Many in armed forces.

Tribal religions approximately 1.5%. Among scheduled tribes.

Buddhist 0.7%. A small minority in the land of its origin. Majority among Tibetans, several Northeastern tribes and growing among Harijans in Maharashtra.

Jain 0.47%.

Other religions and persuasions 0.4%. *Baha'i, Zoroastrian* 75,000; *Jews* 6,000.

Christian 2.61% officially (churches claim 3.6%). A great variation in percentages in the different states.

Roman Catholic 1.55%. Strongest in the south and in Goa. Practicing 70%. 11,700,000 adherents.

Syrian Orthodox 0.24%. 1,840,000 adherents. Predominantly in Kerala, southwest India; descended from churches planted by the Apostle Thomas in the first century.

Protestant 1.79%. More numerous in the south and northeast. 13,400,000 adherents; 5,480,000 members. Denominations 320+. Largest (adult members):

Church of South India (CSI) 600,000
United Lutheran Church 464,000
Council of Baptist Churches in N.E. 400,444
Methodist Church of South Asia 400,000
Salvation Army 400,000
Church of North India (CNI) 324,000
Mar Thoma Syrian Church 270,000
Presbyterian Church of N.E. 201,000
Telugu Baptist Churches 128,000
Seventh-Day Adventist Church 124,000
Independent Pentecostal Church of God 105,000
Baptist Convention of Northern areas 84,500
Christian Assemblies/Brethren 71,000
Church of God (Cleveland) 43,000
Assemblies (Bakht Singh) approximately 42,000

Evangelical 0.7% of population.

Missionaries to India 900 (1:850,000 people), with a rapid reduction in numbers. Missionaries from within India 4,200 in about 120 agencies. Not all are in cross-cultural ministries.

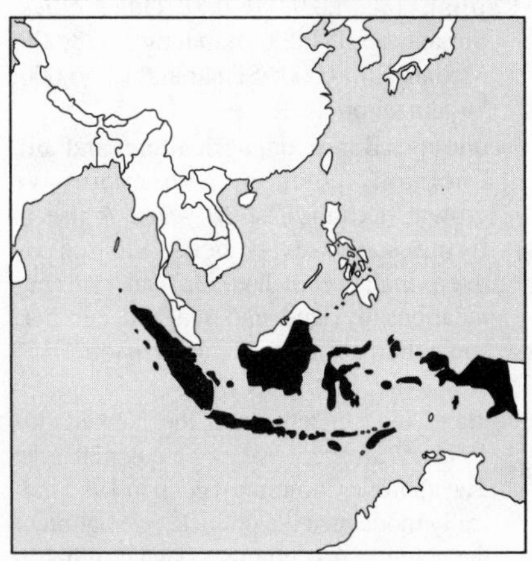

INDONESIA

Area 1,920,000 sq.km. 13,500 islands of which 3,000 are inhabited and cover 9,500,000 sq.km. of the Indian/Pacific Oceans, 27 provinces.

Population 188,300,000. The world's fifth most populous nation. Annual growth

2.0%. People per sq.km. 98; varying from Java's 700 to Irian Jaya's two.

Peoples. Major races:

Malay 94%. Seventeen languages with more than one million speakers of which the largest are: Javanese 42%, Sundanese 13.6%, Madurese 7%, Minangkabau 3.3%, Batak 2.9%, Sumatran Malay 2.9%, Bugis 2.8% Balinese 2.1%.

Chinese 4%. Many are becoming integrated into the Indonesian majority. Only 20% still use Chinese dialects. Scattered throughout the nation.

Irianese/Papuan peoples 1.2%. In Timor, Alor, Halmahera and Irian Jaya.

Other 0.8%. Arabs, Indians, Europeans, mixed race.

Literacy 64%; rising rapidly. *Official language:* Indonesian. Its increasing use is both unifying the nation and lessening the importance of smaller languages to the younger generation. *All languages* 583; 17 spoken by more than one million speakers; 238 spoken in Irian Jaya. *Bible translations* 8 Bibles, 21 New Testaments, 39 portions.

Capital: Jakarta 9,086,000. Other cities: Surabaya 3,054,000; Bandung 1,878,000; Medan 1,600,000; Semarang 1,056,000. Urbanization 24%.

Economy: Based on agriculture and oil. Enormous potential with impressive growth over the last 20 years. A rise in living standards is being slowed by overpopulation in Java, difficult communications by land and sea and cumbersome bureaucracy. Income/person $450 (2.5% of USA).

Politics: Independent from the Netherlands 1945-49 after 350 years of colonial rule. The abortive Communist coup in 1965 radically moderated the political orientation of the country. A strong presidential military-civilian government. President Suharto seeks to balance tendencies to religious extremisms and local secessionist nationalisms in this culturally diverse nation.

Religion: Monotheism and communal peace are the bases of the government ideology of "Pancasila." All are free to choose to follow Islam, Hinduism, Buddhism, or Christianity; but the numerical and political strength of Islam is frequently exercised to give it preferential treatment and limit Christian expansion. There are, therefore, some restrictions on open proselytism.

Muslim 78-80%. This figure needs to be qualified. 29% of the electorate voted in 1982 for parties that seek to make Indonesia an Islamic state. 43% could be defined as Quranic Muslims, living by many of Islam's tenets. A further 35% are statistical Muslims, who, though enumerated as Muslims for the census, are actually followers of the Javanese mystical religion that predates Islam, or else animists who have (to a lesser or greater extent) accepted some of the outward aspects of Islam. Islam is strongest in Sumatra, Java and in many coastal areas in the east.

Animist 5.1%. Discouraged by the government but strong among some peoples in Irian Jaya, East Timor, Sumba, and inland Sumatra, Kalimantan, Sulawesi, etc. Folk Islam followed by the majority is strongly influenced by animism.

Hindu 3.1%. Majority on Bali and among Tengger in East Java.

Buddhist/Chinese religions 1.22%. Mainly Chinese.

Non-religious/Atheist 1.4%. Mainly Chinese and underground Communists.

Christian 11.2%. Church figures indicate 13.2%. A large number of known "sympathizers" would further increase this total.

Roman Catholic 3.5%. In the majority on Flores and East Timor. Practicing 74%. 4,900,000 adherents; 2,600,000 members.

Foreign and indigenous marginal groups 0.1%.

Protestant 9.7%. 16,100,000 adherents; 7,100,000 members.

Denominations 250+. Largest (adherents):

Regional Reformed Churches (32) (Dutch and Swiss missions) 5,600,000

Pentecostal Churches (72) 4,200,000

Lutheran Churches (13)

(German and Scandinavian missions) 3,000,000
KINGMI (Christian & Missionary Alliance) 325,000
Seventh-Day Adventist Church 168,000
GIIJ (Unevangelized Fields Mission, Asia Pacific Christian Mission, RBMU International) 100,000
GMI (Methodist) 94,000
Churches related to WEC International-Indonesian
Missionary Fellowship 30,000
Churches related to The Evangelical Alliance Mission 20,000
Evangelical 4.3% of population.

Missionaries to Indonesia 700 (1:269,000 people)

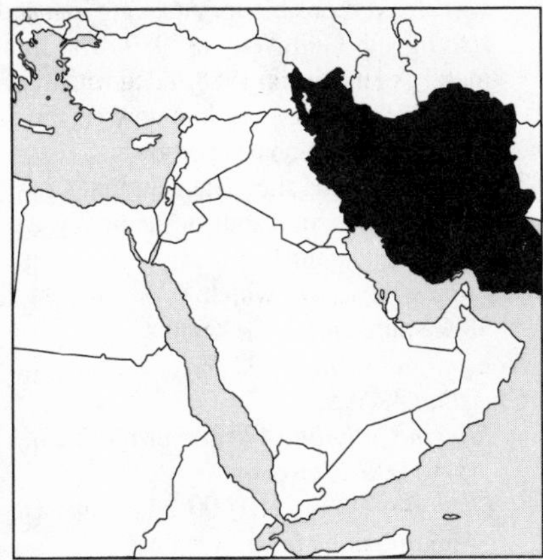

IRAN

Area 1,648,000 sq.km. A central desert ringed by mountains.

Population 55,700,000. Annual growth 3.4%. People per sq.km. 34.

Peoples: Over 45 peoples/tribes speaking at least 23 distinct languages. Many are small nomadic groups.

Indo-Iranic (22) 76.8%. Persian (speaking Farsi) 22,300,000, the dominant people. Kurds 3,800,000; also the related Luri-Bakhtiari peoples 3,400,000.

Turkic (18) 21%. Azerbaijani 7,600,000; Turkoman 710,000; Afshar 370,000; Qashqa'i 230,000, etc.

Arab (2) 1.5%. *Other* (5) 0.7%. Armenian 150,000 estimated; Assyrian 40,000 estimated; Jews 50,000. Non-Muslim groups decreasing by emigration since the revolution.

Literacy 44%. *Official language:* Farsi. *All languages* 31. *Bible translations* 4 Bibles, 4 portions.

Capital: Tehran 6,700,000. Other cities: Rai 1,100,000, Qazvin 1,000,000, Isfahan 1,000,000, Mashad 1,000,000. Urbanization 50%.

Economy: Material progress under the Shah was reversed by the religious bigotry, national paranoia, and violence that followed the 1979 revolution. The eight-year Gulf War severely strained the oil-based economy. The diplomatic isolation of the country further prolongs the long economic recovery. Income/person $2,500 in 1982.

Politics: The progressive, West-leaning, but unpopular Shah was deposed in the Shi'ite Muslim Revolution, and a theocratic Islamic Republic formed in 1979. Regional loyalties and anarchy brought the country close to civil war and ruin. The invasion by Iraq in 1980 was the start of the bitter eight year Gulf War. The casualties were high with over one million killed, 80% of which were Iranian. The death of the Ayatollah Khomeini in 1989 has only led to a slight moderation of the political extremes of the revolutionary period.

Religion: Shi'a Islam is the state religion. All deviations from Islam are liable to mean severe persecution. Other religious minorities tolerated.

Muslim 98%. Shi'a 91%, Sunni 7% (Kurds, Baluchis and Turkoman). Iran is the power house for exporting Shi'ite revolution to the Middle East and beyond.

Baha'i 0.8%. 340,000 followers of a Persian world religion founded in 1844. Severely persecuted as a heresy of Islam.

Parsi (Zoroastrian) 0.09%. 39,000 followers of Persia's ancient pre-Islamic religion.

Jews 0.09%. 40,000 estimated. Farsi-speaking Jews, many of whom are descendants of those exiled to Persia at the time of Daniel.

Christian 0.4%.

Orthodox Churches (4) 0.34%. 153,000

adherents, 100,000 members. Largest (adherents):

Armenian Apostolic Church 140,000
Nestorian Church (Assyrians) 12,000
Roman Catholic 0.03%. 17,000
(3 different rites—Chaldean, Latin and Armenian.)

Protestant 0.02%. 8,700 adherents; 3,990 members. Denominations 20. Largest (adult members):

Evangelical Church (Presbyterian) 2,730
Pentecostal Churches 1,800
Episcopal (Anglican) 1,200
Evangelical 0.02% of population.

Missionaries to Iran 0.

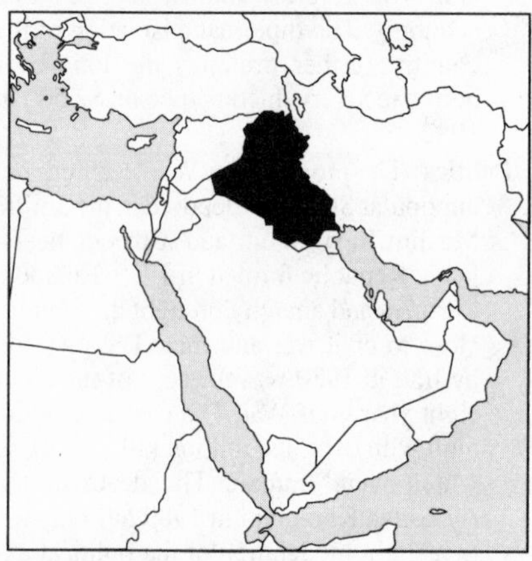

IRAQ

Area 435,000 sq.km. The site of the biblical Assyrian and Babylonian Empires.

Population 18,800,000. Annual growth 3.8%. People per sq.km. 36.

Peoples: Ethnic and religious diversity is responsible for much of Iraq's agonizing recent history.

Arabs 77%. Almost all Muslim; Shi'a 54%, Sunni 23%. Migrant Egyptians 300,000.

Kurds 18%. Mostly Sunni Muslim, but 135,000 are Yezidis, followers of a syncretic form of Islam. The Kurds have been fighting intermittently for autonomy or independence in their northern mountains since 1919. The government took vengeful action on the dissident Kurds after the end of the Gulf War with heavy casualties being inflicted.

Other minorities 5%. Turkoman 386,000; Luri 230,000; Farsi 120,000; Assyrian 60,000; Romany 50,000; Armenian 40,000; Chaldean 35,000; Circassian 9,000.

Literacy 41%. *Official languages:* Arabic, Kurdish in Kurdish districts. *All languages* 18. *Bible translations* 3 Bibles, 1 New Testament, 1 portion.

Capital: Baghdad 6,492,000. Other city: Basra 1,000,000. Urbanization 76%.

Economy: Oil-based economy (since Genesis 11!); profits are used for industrialization. The war with Iran since 1980 has been a serious economic setback.

Politics: A violent revolution in 1958 overthrew the monarchy. The Baathist government has proved cruel in both repression of ethnic minorities, any potential dissent, and was also responsible for attacking Iran and starting the Gulf War in 1980. The final months of the war in 1988 ended with moderate victories for Iraq. Iraq now perceives itself to be a regional superpower.

Religion: Islam is the state religion. Christians are tolerated, but occasionally discriminated against.

Muslim 95.8%. Of which 62% are Shi'a, 38% Sunni and 0.9% Yezidis.

Non-religious/Atheist 0.5%.

Christian 3.4%.

Roman Catholic (4 different rites) 2.6%. 410,000 adherents.

Orthodox 0.7%. 110,000 adherents. Denominations 6.

Protestant 0.02%. 4,200 adherents; 1,960 members. Denominations 12. Largest (adult members):

Arab Evangelical Church 585
Episcopal Church 180
Evangelical 0.02% of population.

Missionaries to Iraq 0.

ITALY

Area 301,000 sq.km. A long peninsula that dominates the central Mediterranean Sea.

Population 57,600,000. Annual growth 0%. People per sq.km. 192.

Peoples

Italian 95.2%. Deep cultural differences exist between the wealthier, and more radical northerners and the poorer, more

conservative southerners.
Sardinian 2.2%. Speaking many Sard dialects.
Tyrolean 0.5%. In the northeast, speaking German.
Friulian/Ladin 0.8%. In the north.
Other European 0.5%. Albanian 260,000; French 70,000; British 25,000; Greek 15,000; Gypsy 12,000.
Middle Eastern 0.35%. Almost all Muslim.
Literacy 94%. *Official language:* Italian.

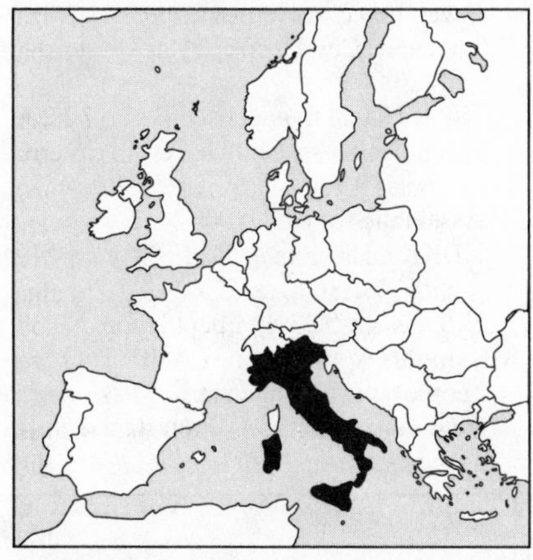

Capital: Rome 3,839,000. Other cities: Milan 6,940,000; Naples 4,116,000; Turin 2,171,000; Genoa 1,195,000; Florence 1,106,000. Urbanization 72%.

Economy: Highly centralized and inefficient government could have brought economic ruin had it not been for the drive of the private industrial sector and the initiative of the 'black' (illegal) economy. The north is very industrialized. Income/person $10,420 (57% of USA). Inflation 14%.

Politics: United as a single state in 1870. Republican democracy since 1946. Weak and unstable succession of 45 governments since the war but with an underlying social stability. National frustration was expressed in the '70s by anarchy, terrorism and increasing support for the Communist party, one of the largest and most democratic outside the Eastern Bloc.

Religion: Roman Catholicism ceased to be the state religion in 1984. All religions have equal freedom before the law.
Non-religious/Atheist 18.3%. Almost all were baptized in the Catholic Church.
Muslim 0.35%.
Jews 39,000.
Christian 81.1%. Affiliated 80%.
Roman Catholic 78.9%. Practicing 15%. 45,300,000 adherents.
Orthodox 0.07%. 38,000 adherents.
Marginal groups 0.5%. 284,000 adherents. Over 6 cults. Largest (adherents): Jehovah's Witnesses 251,000; New Apostolic Church 20,000; Mormons 12,000.
Protestant 0.78%. 450,000 adherents; 300,000 members. Denominations 22 larger and 125 small groups. Largest (adult members):
Assemblies of God 190,000
Waldensian/Methodist Church 31,000
Brethren assemblies 15,000
Salvation Army 12,000
Lutheran Church 10,000
Seventh-Day Adventist Church 5,300
Baptist Union 4,250
Evangelical 0.6% of population.
Missionaries to Italy 420 (1:137,000 people) in 57 agencies. Missionaries from Italy approximately 20 (1:22,500 Protestants).

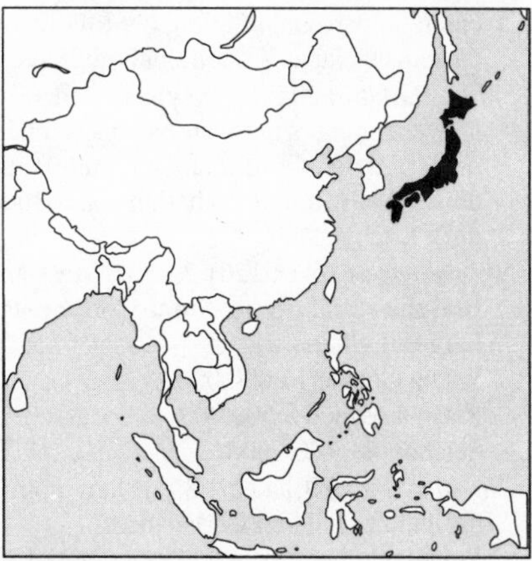

JAPAN

Area 372,300 sq.km. A 3,000 km. arc of four large islands (Honshu, Hokkaido, Shikoku, Kyushu) and 3,000 small islands in Northwest Pacific. Mountainous; only 13% can be cultivated.

Population 123,800,000. Annual growth

0.5%. People per sq.km. 332. Concentrated on the narrow coastal plains.

Peoples

Indigenous 99.3%. Japanese; Ainu 20,000 (19 dialects; dying language).

Foreign 0.7%. Korean 720,000; Chinese 55,000

Literacy 100%. *Official language:* Japanese. *Bible translations* 3 Bibles, 1 portion.

Capital: Tokyo. Major conurbations: Tokyo-Yokohama-Kawasaki 21,600,000, Osaka-Kobe 10,000,000, Fukuoko-Kita-Kyushu 3,100,000, Nagoya 2,200,000, Kyoto 1,500,000, Sapporo 1,500,000, Hiroshima 1,000,000. Urbanization 78%.

Economy: The world's most powerful export-oriented economy despite lack of oil and raw materials. Inflation 3%. Income/person $15,770 (86% of USA).

Politics: Stable democratic constitutional monarchy since 1947.

Religion: Freedom of religion is guaranteed to all by the constitution. In practice social and family pressures restrict that freedom. There has been a significant rise in officially approved Shinto practices since the death of Emperor Hirohito in 1989.

Non-religious/Atheist 12.3%-60%. Many claim no personal religion, but follow the customs of Japan's traditional religions.

Shinto/Buddhist 20-60% Polytheistic, ancestor-venerating Shintoism has been much modified by Confucianism and Buddhism. Many follow both Shinto and Buddhist teachings.

New religions (over 120) 23.5%. Most are Buddhist and some Shinto offshoots. Largest (adherents):
Sokka Gakkai 17,000,000
Risshokoseikai 5,500,000
Seichonoie 3,700,000

Christian 2%. Affiliated 1.3%. Many nominal and backsliding Christians.

Roman Catholic 0.34%. Practicing 34%. 405,000 adherents; 283,000 members.

Orthodox (2) 0.02%. Greek Orthodox 24,700 adherents.

Marginal groups (10+) 0.51%. 610,000 adherents; 430,000 members. Some claimed figures appear inflated! Largest (adherents): Unification Church (Moonies) 270,000; Spirit of Jesus Church (Unitarian) 120,000; Jehovah's Witnesses 92,022; Mormons 71,000; Original Gospel Movement 47,000.

Protestant 0.44%. 534,000 adherents, 309,000 members. Denominations 120+. Largest (adherents):
United Church 192,000
Southern Baptist Convention 26,500
Presbyterian Church of Christ 12,300
Seventh-Day Adventist Church 11,500
Immanuel Church (Wesleyan Missionary) 10,500
NIKK (Japan Evangelistic Band) 10,200
Japan Holiness Church (OMS International) 9,720
Assemblies of God 9,000
NDKK (The Evangelical Alliance Mission) 7,100

Evangelical 0.23% of population.

Missionaries to Japan 2,570 (1:47,000 people) in 140 agencies. Missionaries from Japan 260 (300 Protestants) in 48 agencies.

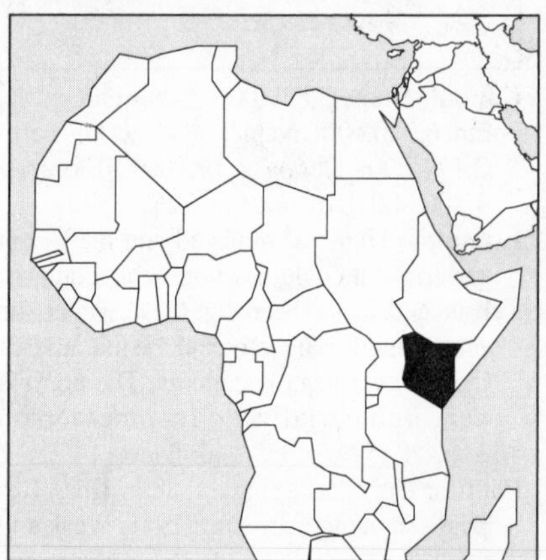

KENYA

Area 582,600 sq.km. Much of the north and east is desert. Most people live in the better watered plateaus of the south and west. Only 9.5% of the land is cultivated.

Population 25,100,000. Annual growth 4.1%. The highest natural incrase in the world. People per sq.km. 43.

Peoples: About 65 ethnic groups.

Bantu peoples 67%. Over 30 peoples:

Kikuyu 4,200,000; Luyia 2,200,000; Kamba 2,200,000; Gusii 1,200,000; Meru 1,100,000; Mijikenda (9 peoples) 969,000; Embu 250,000; Kuria 120,000; Mbere 100,000; Pokomo 60,000.

Nilotic peoples 29.5%. Over 16 peoples: Luo 2,900,000; Kalenjin (5 groups) 2,000,000; Maasai 280,000; Turkana 260,000; Samburu 100,000; Sabaot 95,000.

Cushitic peoples 2.6%. Two major groups: Somali (6) 430,000; Oromo-Boran (5) 130,000.

Other 0.9%. Asian 80,000; Arab 40,000; European 40,000.

Literacy 65%. *Official languages:* English, Swahili. *All languages* 55. *Bible translations* 14 Bibles, 5 New Testaments, 9 portions.

Capital: Nairobi 1,830,000. Other major city: Mombasa 520,000. Urbanization 19%.

Economy: Predominantly agricultural. Good growth following independence was not maintained after 1976 due to world recession, lack of oil, drought and a high population growth. Income/person $340 (2% of USA).

Politics: Independent from Britain in 1963. One-party republic. Relatively stable despite complex tribal divisions that make all political decisions a delicate balancing act.

Religion: Freedom of religion. Government very sympathetic to Christianity. Many Christians in high leadership positions, including the President.

African traditional religions 12.8%

Muslim 6%. Majority among coastal Swahili/Arab, Pokomo, Digo and Northeast desert Somali, Boran, etc.

Baha'i 1.1%.

Hindu/Sikh/Jain 0.3%.

Christian 80%. Nominal 15%. Affiliated 65%.

Roman Catholic 20.5% (officially 29%). 4,143,000 adherents; 2,200,000 members.

Orthodox Church 2.2% (officially 2.7%). Indigenous groups linked with Greek Orthodox and Coptic Churches.

Marginal groups 13% (officially 23%). 2,600,000 adherents; 1,200,000 members. Over 152 groups, some close to mainstream Christian doctrine, others very syncretic.

Protestant 29.3%. 5,925,000 adherents; 2,500,000 members. Denominations 60+. Largest (adult members):

Africa Inland Church 540,000
Anglican Church (CMS) 520,000
Presbyterian Church (CofS) 380,000
Pentecostal Assemblies of Canada 192,000
Seventh-Day Adventist Church 190,000
Pentecostal Evangelical Fellowship (Elim) 105,000
Full Gospel Churches (FFFM) 90,000
Methodist Church 80,000
Salvation Army 49,000
Southern Baptist Convention 27,000
Assemblies of God 25,000
African Gospel Church (WGM) 15,000

Evangelical 26.5% of population.

Missionaries to Kenya 1,850 (1:11,000 people) in about 100 agencies. Missionaries from within Kenya est. 100 (1:59,000 Protestants).

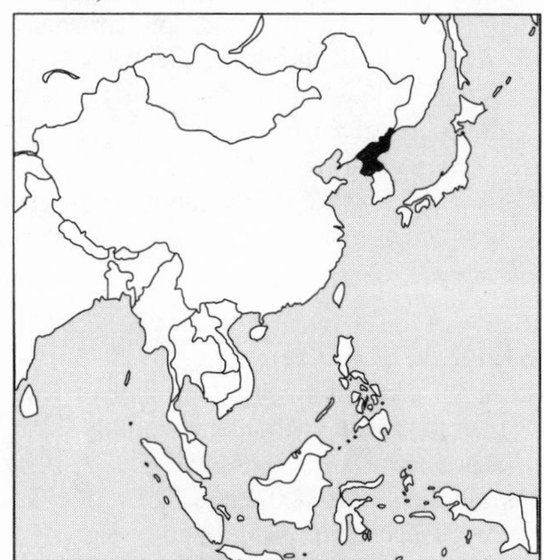

KOREA, NORTH

Area 121,000 sq.km. The larger part of the Korean peninsula, but climate more rigorous.

Population 23,000,000. Annual growth 2.4%. People per sq.km. 190. Two and a half million people died in Korean War, two million more fled from the north to the south at that time.

Peoples

Korean 99.3%.

Chinese, Russian 0.7%.

Literacy 91%. *Official language:* Korean.

Capital: Pyongyang 1,501,000. Urbanization 64%.

Economy: Heavily industrialized and very centralized socialist economy. The revolutionary changes in the Communist world since 1989 have reinforced the isolationism of the present regime. Income/ person $620 (5% of USA).

Politics: Occupied by Japan 1910-45. On Russian insistence, Korea was partitioned after World War II. A Communist regime was installed in 1948 in the North. North Korea invaded South Korea in 1949. The Korean War dragged on until 1953. The large North Korean armed forces continue to threaten a second invasion. One of the most oppressive Communist regimes in the world. There are occasional hints of a reunification of the Koreas, but the fortified border between them is one of the most impenetrable in the world.

Religion: All religions have been harshly repressed. Many thousands of Christians were murdered during and after the Korean War. Religious affiliations are unknown, so the figures given are estimates.

Non-religious/Atheist 60%.

Korean religions 39% (Buddhism, Animism, Confucianism, etc.)

Christian 1%.

KOREA, SOUTH

Area 98,500 sq.km. Southern half of Korean peninsula. Mountainous; only 22% is arable.

Population 43,700,000. Annual growth 1.3%. People per sq.km. 445.

Peoples

Korean 99.8%. An ancient and cultured nation.

Other 0.2%. United States military and Chinese (30,000).

Literacy 92%. *Official language:* Korean.

Capital: Seoul 10,028,000. Other major cities: Pusan 3,781,000; Taegu 1,848,000; Inchon 1,158,000. Urbanization 64%.

Economy: Rapid industrialization and growth since the Korean War. The economy has reached "take off" with high export earnings. The permanent state of confrontation and military preparedness before invasion threats from the North are a strain on the economy. Income/person $2,690 (15% of USA).

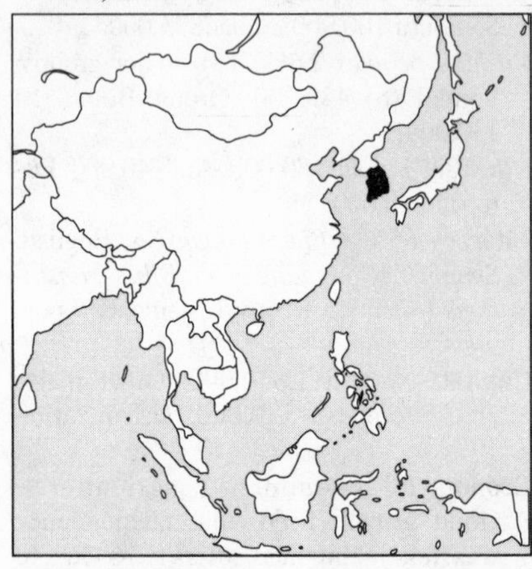

Politics: The Japanese occupation (1910-45), the Russian-imposed division of Korea (1945-48) and the Korean War in which the Communist North invaded the South (1950-53) have molded the attitudes and politics of South Korea. The military-civilian government allowed free elections in 1988 resulting in more democratic government.

Religion: There is complete religious freedom unless that freedom is used by religious leaders to attack government policies. The government has been favorable to Christianity, seeing this as an ideological bulwark against the Communist threat.

No professed religion 14%. Including secularists, non-religious and many Shamanists (animist).

Buddhist 33%. Strong until 15th century, and with post-war resurgence.

Confucian 12%. Official religion until 1910. Both Buddhism and Confucianism have made a deep impact on Korean culture.

New religions 10.6%. Over 250 syncretic non-Christian religions, most of recent origin.

Muslim 0.1%. A growing movement among Koreans.

Christian 30%.

Roman Catholic 4.4%. Practicing 66%. 1,900,000 adherents; 1,060,000 members.

Foreign and indigenous marginal (at least 13 groups) 1.6%. 660,000 adherents; 220,000 members. Largest (adherents): Unification Church (Moonies) 500,000; Jehovah's Witnesses 77,428; Mormons 36,000.

Protestant 24%. 10,200,000 adherents; 4,370,000 members. Denominations 61. Largest (adherents):

Presbyterian Church in Korea (Haptong) 1,389,200

Presbyterian Church of Korea (Tonghap) 1,373,600

Methodist Church (4 groups) 1,007,600

Southern Baptist Convention (4 groups) 505,300

Full Gospel C. Church (Cho) 500,000

Korean Evangelical Church (OMS) (3 groups) 461,000

Christian Assemblies of God (6 groups) 293,200

Presbyterian Church in ROK 273,700

Koryo Presbyterian Church 250,800

Seventh-Day Adventist Church 134,500

Other Presbyterian (28 groups) 3,231,200

Evangelical 18% of population.

Missionaries to Korea 610 (1:70,000 people) in 60 agencies. Missionaries from Korea 360 (1:28,300 Protestants) in 17 sending agencies working in 37 countries. Just over half are cross-cultural missionaries.

MALAYSIA

Area 330,000 sq.km. Two distinct parts: Peninsular (West) Malaysia on the Kra peninsula of mainland Asia (PM), and East Malaysia (EM) consisting of the territories of Sarawak and Sabah on the northern third of the island of Borneo.

Population 17,800,000 (83% in PM). Annual growth 2.5%. People per sq.km. 54.

Peoples

Malay 48%. This figure includes some Muslim Orang Asli and all Indonesians (Javanese 136,000; Banjarese 45,000; Minangkabau 12,000, etc.). Predominantly rural, but influential in politics and civil service. A majority in PM only.

Chinese 36%. Speaking over 9 major dialects; majority Hokkien, Cantonese, Hakka and Teochew. Influential in commerce and business.

Indian 9%. Tamil 1,040,000; Punjabi 40,000; Malayali 36,000; Telugu 30,000, etc. Mainly poor estate workers or urban.

Orang Asli 7% ("Original People" tribal groups). In PM 75,000, EM 873,000 in about 80 tribes.

Literacy 59%. *Official language:* Malay. *All languages* 117. *Bible translations* 9 Bibles, 9 New Testaments, 12 portions.

Capital: Kuala Lumpur 1,397,000. Urbanization 35%. Chinese and Indian majority in urban areas.

Economy: Vigorous growth since independence through the development of oil, mining, agriculture and industry. Income/person $1,800 (10% of USA).

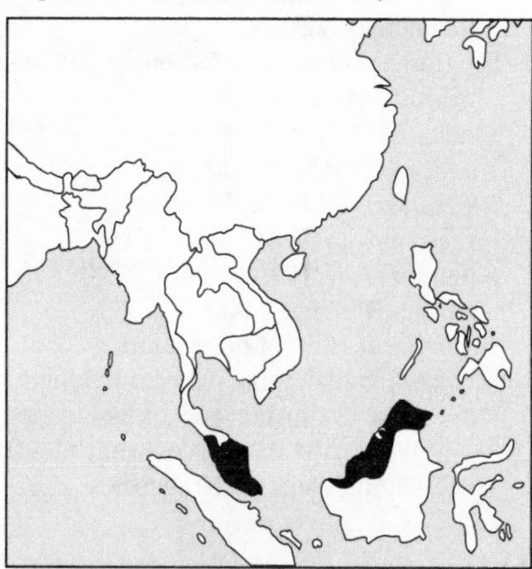

Politics: Independent from Britain in 1957 as the Federation of Malaya. Sabah and Sarawak joined to form the Federation of Malaysia in 1963. Recent years have been dominated by the efforts of the politically powerful Malays to extend their influence over the non-Malay half of the population in educational, economic and religious life. These have strained inter-ethnic relationships.

Religion: Sunni Islam is the official and favored religion in PM, and there is continual pressure to apply the same in EM where Islam is a minority. It is illegal to proselytize Muslims, but considerable effort is expended to induce animistic tribal people and Chinese to become Muslim.

Muslim 53%. Malays, some Indians and a few ethnic minorities in EM.

Buddhist and Chinese religions 28%.

Hindu 7%. Almost entirely Indian.

Animist 3%(?). Many tribal animists are classified as "Muslim."

Non-religious/Atheist, other 3%.

Christian 7%. Affiliated 5%. The Church statistical situation is confusing and unclear for many denominations!

Roman Catholic 2.9%. Practicing 60%. 460,000 adherents; 244,000 members. Mainly Chinese and Eurasian.

Marginal groups (6+) 0.1%. 14,500 adherents.

Protestant 2%. 320,000 adherents; 150,000 members. Denominations 48. Largest (adult members):

S.I. Borneo (Overseas Missionary Fellowship) 50,000
Methodist Church 40,000
Anglican Church 20,000
Assemblies of God 7,500
Protestant Church of Sabah 7,200
Southern Baptist Convention 4,700
Christian Brethren 2,000

Evangelical 1.2% of population.

Missionaries to Malaysia estimated 150, fairly rapid reduction in numbers. Missionaries from within Malaysia estimated 40 (1:8,000 Protestants) in 10 agencies.

MEXICO

Area 1,973,000 sq.km. Latin America's fourth largest country. Much of the country is arid or semi-arid; only 11% of the land is arable.

Population 88,800,000. Annual growth 2.4%. People per sq.km. 45. Massive illegal emigration to USA hardly alleviates the explosive population growth. Five million Mexicans live in the USA, increasing by 800,000 illegals per year.

Peoples

Spanish/Amerindian (Mestizo) 55%.

Amerindian 29%. 21.3% speaking Spanish only. Six million Indians still speak 236 languages. Major groupings: Aztec 4,800,000; Maya 2,700,000; Otomi 2,100,000; Zapotec 1,800,000; Mixtec 1,600,000; Totonac 240,000; Mazahua 160,000; Mazatec 160,000, etc.

Spanish and other European 15.3%.

African origin 0.5%. *Other* 0.2%.

Central American refugees 150,000.

Literacy 80%. *Official language:* Spanish, the world's largest Spanish-speaking nation. *All languages* 237. *Bible translations* 2 Bibles, 71 New Testaments, 41 portions.

Capital: Mexico City 18,535,000. Other cities: Guadalajara 3,483,000; Monterrey 2,622,000; Puebla 1,022,000. Urbanization 72%.

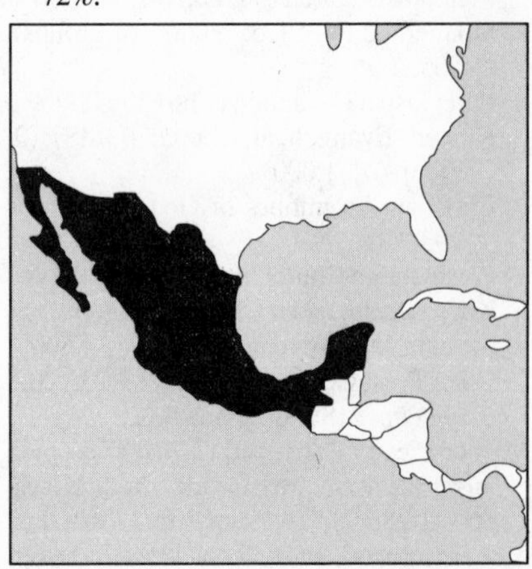

Economy: Mixed but very dependent on oil since 1975. Rapid population growth and overspending of new wealth led to massive international debts ($85 billion in 1985). The radical correctives imposed increased unemployment to 40% and inflation to 80% with a rise in urban and rural poverty. Recession and the lack of confidence in the economy have been checked by firm action by the government since 1989, with some visible improvement. Income/person $1,820 (10% of USA).

Politics: Independent from Spain in 1821.

Republic with what is virtually a one-party democracy since 1910. Pressures for more democratic multiparty politics led to a more open election in 1988.

Religion: Secular state with freedom of conscience and practice of religion, but with careful legal controls on Catholics, Protestants and others.

Non-religious/Atheist 3.4%.

Jews 0.1%, 57,000.

Baha'i 28,000.

Muslim 25,000.

Christian 96.4%. Nominal 4%. Affiliated 92.4%. Doubly affiliated 2.4%.

Roman Catholic 88% (officially 90.5%, but with many defections to other beliefs). 70,800,000 adherents; 37,500,000 members.

Marginal groups (16) 1%. Largest (adherents): Jehovah's Witnesses 388,000; Mormons 295,000.

Protestant 4%. 3,200,000 adherents; 1,300,000 members. Denominations 250. Largest (adult members):

Union of Ind. Evangelicals (Pentecostal) 270,000
Seventh-Day Adventist Church 210,000
Assemblies of God 120,000
Southern Baptist Convention 65,000
Presbyterian Church 53,000
Church of God (Cleveland) 29,000
Church of the Nazarene 21,700

Evangelical 3.1% of population.

Missionaries to Mexico 1,700 (1:47,000 people) in 84 agencies. Missionaries from Mexico approximately 98 (1:33,000 Protestants) in 3+ agencies.

MOROCCO

Area 447,000 sq.km. Northwest corner of Africa. A further 160,000 sq.km. of former Spanish Sahara claimed and occupied by Morocco in 1976. Fertile coastal areas, barren Atlas mountains inland and Sahara Desert to south and southeast.

Population 26,300,000. Annual growth 2.6%. People per sq.km. 59. Nearly one million Moroccans live and work in Europe.

Peoples

Arabic-speaking 65%. Culturally Arab, but predominantly Berber with Arab admixture.

Berber-speaking 34%. Three main languages: Shluh (speaking Shilha) 4,100,000 in south; Beraber (speaking Tamazight) 2,500,000 in center; Riff 1,360,000 in north. There are numerous tribal dialects and sub-dialects. Also Black Berber Haratine and Tuareg of the Sahara.

Other 1%. French 100,000; Spanish 20,000; Jewish 20,000, etc.

Literacy 24%. *Official language:* Arabic, French and English are widely used. *All languages* 5. *Bible translations* 1 Bible, 3 portions.

Capital: Rabat 1,212,000. Other cities: Casablanca 3,000,000; Marrakech 1,700,000; Fez 1,200,000. Urbanization 49%.

Economy: Mainly agricultural, but phosphate deposits in Morocco and the Sahara are large and important with 70% of world's proven reserves. The cost of the Sahara War has strained the economy. Income/person $620 (3% of USA).

Politics: Independent kingdom in 1956. Formerly French and Spanish protectorates. A limited democracy with an executive monarchy. The dominant political issue since 1974 has been the occupation of the Western Sahara and the subsequent warfare to retain it.

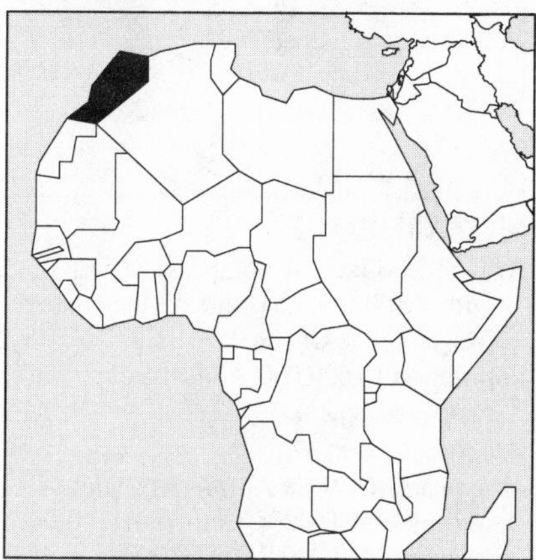

Religion: Islam is the state religion. The government is committed to the preservation of Islam as the religion of all Moroccans. Other religious groups are tolerated so long as they confine their ministry to expatriate communities.

Muslim 99.6%. Almost entirely Sunni.

Jews 0.1%. 20,000 Sephardic Jews, the remnant of a large community that has emigrated to Israel.

Christian 0.27%. Foreign 97%. Moroccan 3%.

Roman Catholic 0.25%. Practicing 10%. 60,000 adherents; 33,600 members. French, Spanish, etc. Only 500 Moroccans.

Protestant 0.01%. 3,460 adherents; 1,780 members. About 60% Moroccan. Denominations 10. Largest (adherents):

Indigenous fellowships 1,250

French Reformed Church 1,000

Anglican Church 800

Christian expatriates in Moroccan ministries inside and outside country approximately 100.

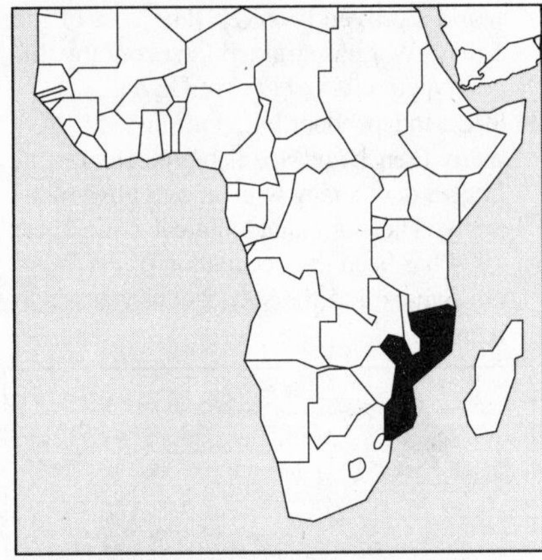

MOZAMBIQUE

Area 802,000 sq.km. Southeast African state with 2,800 km. coastline on the strategic Mozambique Channel.

Population 15,600,000. Annual growth 2.6%. People per sq.km. 19.

Peoples

African peoples 99%. *Northern peoples* 44%. Makua 4,300,000; Lomwe 1,200,000; Makonde 320,000; Yao 250,000.

Central peoples 22%. Sena-Nyungwe 1,600,000; Shona-Ndua 1,100,000; Nyanja 350,000.

Southern peoples 33%. Tsonga (Shangaan) 1,600,000; Ronga (Tswa) 600,000; Chopi 800,000; Tonga 10,000.

Other 1%. Portuguese 30,000, Mixed race 30,000.

Literacy 24%. *Official language:* Portuguese. *All languages* 23. *Bible translations* 8 Bibles, 2 New Testaments, 6 portions.

Capital: Maputo 1,040,000. Urbanization 20%.

Economy: Subsistence economy despite fertile agricultural land and rich mineral deposits. Restrictive colonial exploitation, followed by overhasty application of Marxist economic theories, limited the development of resources and infrastructure. Drought, floods and widespread guerrilla warfare have further impoverished the country. It is possibly the poorest country in the world. Income/person $150 (0.7% of USA).

Politics: A Portuguese colony for 470 years. Independent in 1975 as a Marxist-Leninist state after a long and bitter war of independence. Widespread opposition to the central government's policies stimulated a dirty guerrilla war that has made chaos, a state of armed anarchy and starvation a way of life to most people. Over one million people have been killed or have died as a result. The government has openly abandoned its Marxist ideology.

Religion: Marxist-Leninist ideology is propagated and promoted. Until 1982 government policy was "all-out war on the churches" and "destruction of religious superstitions." The collapse of the economy and desperate straits of the country have caused the government to declare freedom of religion.

Non-religious/Atheist est. 5%.

Muslim 13%. The majority among the Yao in northwest and coastal Makonde and Makua.

African traditional religions 59.5%.

Christian 21%.

Roman Catholic 13%. 1,562,000 adherents. The Church suffered a serious decline after independence because of its links with the colonial regime.

Marginal groups (100+) 0.4%. 56,000 adherents.

Protestant 6.4%. 890,000 adherents, 379,000 members. Denominations 30. Largest (adherents):

United Baptist (Africa Evangelical Fellowship, Scandinavian Baptist) 160,000

Pentecostal Assemblies of God 75,000

Presbyterian Church (Swiss Mission) 70,000

Anglican Church 65,000

United Methodist Church 60,000

Seventh-Day Adventist Church 57,000

Assemblies of God 35,000

Church of the New Covenant 25,000

Church of the Nazarene 22,000

Free Methodist Church 15,000

Evangelical 4.5% of population.

Missionaries to Mozambique estimated 100.

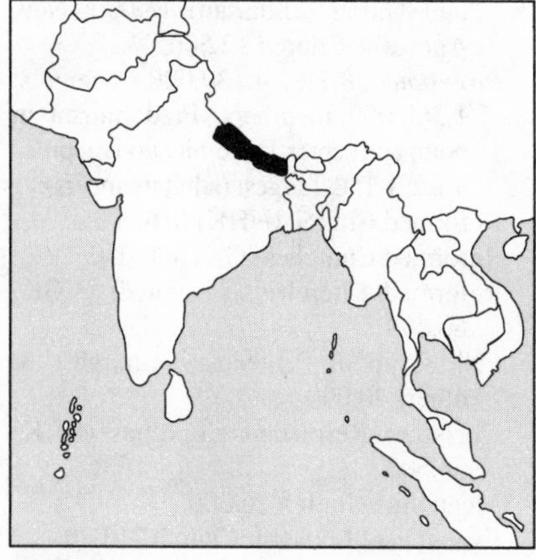

NEPAL

Area 141,000 sq.km. A mountain-ringed Himalayan state between China (Tibet) and India.

Population 19,200,000. Annual growth 2.5%. People per sq.km. 136. Very unevenly distributed. Most live on the over-populated hills and in the Kathmandu valley; many are migrating to the lowland Terai in the south.

Peoples: Over 30 major ethnic groups; numberous smaller groups. Two main ethnic components, with considerable intermingling:

Indo-Aryan (from south and west) 79%. Nepali 8,800,000; Maithili 1,830,000; Bhojpuri 1,120,000; Tharu 686,000; Awadhi 438,000; Rajbansi 77,000; Dhanwar 14,000; also eight other languages.

Tibeto-Burman (from north and east) 20%. Thamang 768,000; Newari 630,000; Magar 400,000; Rai (21 dialects) 321,000; Gurung 238,000; Limbu 236,000; Sherpa 110,000; Sunwar 29,000; also 34 other languages.

Other 1%. Santali 29,000; Munda; Indian; European.

Literacy 20%. *Official language:* Nepali, the first language of 55% of the population. *All languages* 76. *Bible translations* 6 Bibles, 1 New Testament, 21 portions.

Capital: Kathmandu 430,000. Urbanization 6%.

Economy: An isolated subsistence economy. The difficult terrain and high population density in habitable regions, slow development of roads, agriculture and social projects. Main foreign exchange earners are tourism, agriculture and Gurkha soldiers. Heavily dependent on foreign aid. The economic confrontation with India in 1989-90 has had disastrous economic and ecological results on the already impoverished land. Income/person $160 (1% of USA) with 40% living below the poverty line (1% of USA).

Politics: Political isolation from the outside world ended in 1951. The strong executive powers invested in the king in the partyless government system was brought to an end through popular resistance in 1989/90. The aim is to have a multiparty democracy with a constitutional monarch.

Religion: The world's only Hindu kingdom. Hinduism is the state religion. Open Christian evangelism is illegal. On June 15, 1990, King Birendra granted amnesty to all religious prisoners. Christians continue to work with the government to incorporate religious freedom into the new constitution.

Hindu 89%. Much intertwined in Buddhism and a strong, underlying animism. A complex caste system exists despite its illegality since 1963.

Buddhist 7%. Lamaistic Buddhism is dominant among the Tibeto-Burman peoples. The Buddha was born in Nepal.

Muslim 3.5%. Predominantly in the Terai.

Christian 0.3%. Almost entirely Protestant Evangelicals.

Roman Catholic about 250 adherents.
Protestant 0.4%. 60,000 adherents; 40,000 members.

Missionaries to Nepal approximately 600 (1:26,700 people) in two large inter-mission fellowships and several independent agencies.

NETHERLANDS

Area 41,000 sq.km. Over 30% is below sea level.

Population 15,000,000. Annual growth 0.4%. People per sq.m. 365.

Peoples

Indigenous 91.2%. Dutch 12,800,000; Frisian 460,000; Gypsies 1,200.

Ex-colonial 4.1%. Dutch-Indonesian 320,000; Surinamese 260,000; South Molukkan 45,000; Antilles 33,000.

Immigrant communities 4.6%. Other European Economic Community countries 160,000; Turkish 150,000; North African 105,000; Chinese 45,000; Yugoslav 14,000.

Literacy 100%. *Official language:* Dutch (Nederlands).

Capital: Amsterdam 1,000,000. Other cities: The Hague (seat of government) 700,000; Rotterdam (the world's busiest seaport) 1,100,000. Urbanization 88%.

Economy: A strong industrial and trading economy. A member of the European Economic Community. Income/person $11,860 (64% of USA).

Politics: Stable democratic constitutional monarchy.

Religion: Complete freedom of religion, but with a strong and steady secularization of society.

Non-religious 28%. Also includes nominal Christians who have no affiliation to a church.

Muslim 2.1%. North African, Turk, Indonesian and some Surinamese.

Hindu 0.7%. Surinamese Asian and Sri Lankan Tamil.

Jews 0.2%. Before World War II it was 1.4%.

Christian 69%. About half attend church.

Roman Catholic 39.2%. 5,650,000 adherents; 3,955,000 members. Predominantly in southern provinces.

Marginal groups 1%. 133,000 adherents; 82,000 members. Largest (adherents): Jehovah's Witnesses 46,700; Protestant Union (unitarian) 18,000; New Apostolic Church 12,500.

Protestant 28.7%. 4,130,000 adherents; 1,360,000 members. Predominant in north and center. Denominations approximately 150. Largest (adult members):

Reformed Church (NHK) 616,000
Reformed Churches (GK) 480,050
Reformed Churches (Liberated) (VGK) 60,850
Fellowship of Pentecostal Churches & others 40,000
Christian Reformed Churches (CRK) 38,500
Mennonite Church 26,300
Evangelical Lutheran Church 21,070
Netherlands Reformed Churches (NRK) 17,600
Remonstrant Brotherhood 13,000
Baptist Union 12,000
Free Evangelical Churches 7,450

Evangelical 8% of population.

Missionaries to Netherlands approximately 160. Missionaries from Netherlands 1,100 (1:3,800 Protestants) in over 75 agencies. Over 85% are evangelical.

NIGERIA

Area 924,000 sq. km. Tropical forest in south, merging into savannah in the north. Divided into 21 states to minimize the impact of ethnic loyalties on national politics.

Population est. 118,600,000. No reliable census since independence; the northern population is likely to be overestimated. Annual growth 2.9%. People per sq.km. 128. Africa's most populous state.

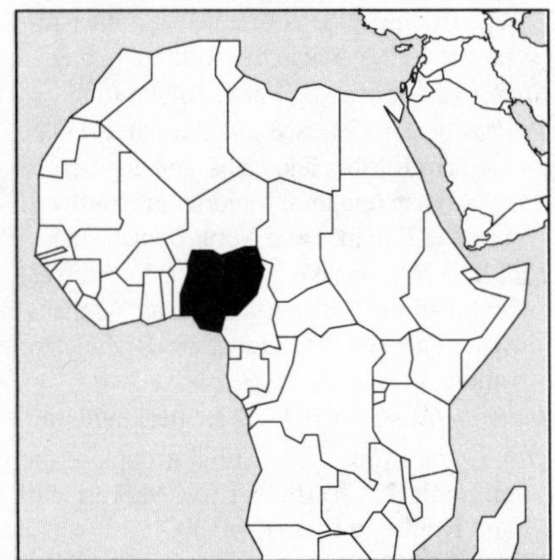

Peoples: Over 426 known. The major groups are: Yoruba 17.8%, Ibo 17.5%, Hausa 16.8%, Fulani 10.3%, Tiv 5.6%, Kanuri 4.7%.

Literacy 30%. *Official language:* English. *Trade languages:* Hausa in north and center, Yoruba in southwest, Ibo in southeast. *All languages* 408, though some say 510. *Bible translations* 15 Bibles, 33 New Testaments, 48 portions.

Capital: Lagos estimated 4-5 million, capital being transferred to Abuja in central Nigeria. Other major cities: Ibadan 4,000,000; Ado-Ekiti 1,400,000; Port Harcourt 500,000. Twenty-five cities of over 100,000 people. Urbanization 28%.

Economy: Rich in agricultural land and mineral resources. Vast oil wealth in the '70s raised educational and living standards, but also stimulated gross misuse of public funds. Grandiose prestige projects, spectacular corruption, incompetent management and neglect of agriculture were the result. The collapse of oil prices then quickened both the collapse of the economy and the fall of the corrupt civilian government in 1983. Solutions to Nigeria's economic woes are not yet in sight. Income/person $360 (2% of USA), but the cost of living is high.

Politics: Independent from Britain as a federal state in 1960. Colonial history further polarized the widely differing cultural, religious and educational systems between the Muslim feudal north and the traditional religion/Christian capitalist south. These differences underlie the tensions, coups and Biafra Civil War (1967-70), and attempts by the Muslim north to retain political control. The civilian government ousted in 1983 was predominantly Muslim, as was the military regime that followed. The latter found it difficult to cope with the economic crisis, and there was widespread disillusionment, which led to another coup in 1985. The new military government appears to be more vigorous in dealing with the inherent malaise in the structure and economy. The expressed intention is a handover to a civilian government in 1992.

Religion: Freedom of religion, but most post-independence governments giving preferential treatment to Islam. The Christian South and Middle Belt have become increasingly restive with Muslim gerrymandering to retain power. Statistics for religions and churches given below are nearly all estimates.

Muslim 36%. Muslims claim up to 60%, non-Muslims as low as 30%. Dominant in federal and military leadership until 1985, and in northern states.

Traditional religions 15%. The majority in numerous peoples in the Middle Belt, but influential in both Muslim peoples of north and west, and Christian peoples of the south.

Christian 49%. Nominal 18%. Affiliated 31%. Large numbers claim to be Catholic, Protestant, etc. but are not affiliated to any church. All statistics are approximate but given to indicate the growth of the Church.

Roman Catholic 6.6%. (12% claim to be Roman Catholic.) Practicing 40%. 6,040,000 adherents; 3,323,000 members.

Indigenous marginal groups (800+) 5%. 4,560,000 adherents. A profusion of syncretistic denominations.

Foreign marginal groups (20+) 0.4%. Over 20 cults. Largest (adult members): Jehovah's Witnesses 113,360.

Protestant 19%. (28% would claim to be Protestant). 17,584,000 adherents; 5,800,000 members. Denominations 140+. Largest (adult members):

Anglican Church 1,000,000

Evangelical Churches of West Africa (Sudan Interior Mission) 650,000

TEKAN (The SUM Fellowship) est. 400,000

Nigerian Baptist Convention (Southern Baptist) 400,000

Christ Apostolic Church est. 400,000

Nigerian Christian Fellowship est. 350,000

Apostolic Church 320,000

Assemblies of God 275,000

Church of God Mission est. 250,000

Gospel Faith Mission est. 200,000

Methodist Church 160,000

Qua Iboe Church 83,000

Evangelical 14% of population.

Missionaries to Nigeria estimated 950 (1:96,000 people) in about 60 agencies. Missionaries from within Nigeria estimated 740 (1:23,500 Protestants) in about 10 agencies. About 60 of these are outside Nigeria.

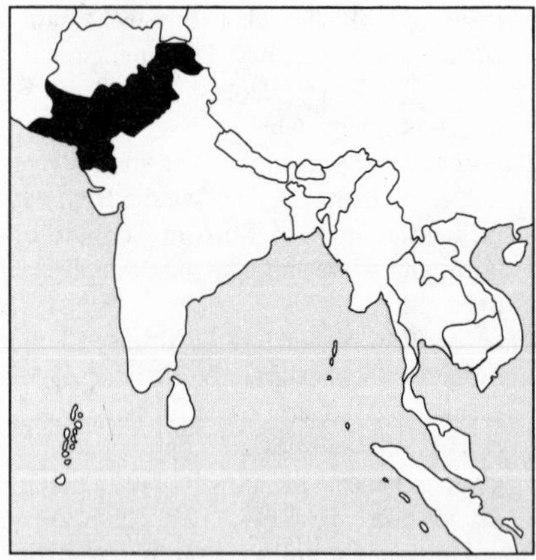

PAKISTAN

Area 804,000 sq.km. Arid mountains in the north and west. Sind desert in southwest. Vast irrigation schemes in the fertile Indus valley.

Population 113,600,000. Annual growth 2.9%. People per sq.km. 141. Over half the population lives in the Punjab.

Peoples

Punjabi 60%. Speaking Punjabi and Urdu. Their dominance is resented by other minorities. They live in the northern plains.

Sindhi 12%. Speaking Sindhi. In the south.

Pushtu-Afghan 15%. Speaking Pushtu and Dari. Numerous tribes and clans, and augmented by Afghan refugees. Majority in Northwest Frontier Province and North Baluchistan.

Baluch 3.5%. Speaking Baluchi. In the west and also in East Iran and South Afghanistan. The 800,000 Dravidian Brahui live among them.

Indian refugees (of 1947) 8%. Speaking Urdu.

Other minorities 1.5%. Tribal groups in the far north (27) 700,000; Tribal Mawari Bhil and Kohli (16 tribes) 700,000.

Literacy 18%. *Official languages:* Urdu, English. Urdu is becoming widely used by all. *All languages* 50. *Bible translations* 6 Bibles, 1 New Testament, 8 portions.

Capital: Islamabad 335,000. Other cities: Karachi est. 16,000,000; Lahore 3,600,000; Rawalpindi 2,000,000; Faisalabad 1,600,000; Peshawar 1,000,000. Urbanization 29%.

Economy: Predominantly agricultural. A large textile industry. Remittances from Pakistanis living and working in Europe, North America and Middle East are the largest source of foreign currency. The large army, and influx of millions of refugees from Afghanistan and Iran, have strained the country's resources. Income/person $390 (3% of USA).

Politics: Independent from Britain at the partition of India in 1947. Constant instability and three wars with India over Kashmir and East Pakistan. (The latter became independent as Bangladesh in 1971.) The military regime of President Zia ended with his death, and an elected government under Miss Benazir Bhutto came to power. Regional politics, ethnic violence and continued tensions with India have hindered all efforts to improve the social and economic life of the country.

Religion: Islamic republic, but continual tensions between fundamentalists and moderates have arisen over the avowed intent of the previous government to Islamize the structures of society. Minority religions are safeguarded in the constitution, but the situation is both delicate and unclear for non-Muslims.

Muslim 96.6%. Sunni 70%, Shi'a 27% (including the unorthodox Ismaili), Ahmaddiya 3%. The latter are not considered Muslims by the government and are persecuted, and many driven underground.

Hindu 1.6%. Tribal peoples of Sind and some Sindhis and Punjabis.

Christian 1.6%. Affiliated 1.5%.

Roman Catholic 0.5%. Practicing 37%. 471,000 adherents; 254,000 members. Punjabis and also Goanese in Karachi.

Protestant 1%. 974,000 adherents; 445,000 members. Denominations 44. Figures very approximate. Largest (adherents):

Church of Pakistan 400,000
United Presbyterian Church 250,000
National Virgin Church (ex-Presbyterian) 52,000
Salvation Army 50,000
United Church in Pakistan (Lahore Church Council) 42,000
National Methodist Church 32,000
Association of Reformed Presbyterian Churches 25,000
Full Gospel Assemblies (Swedish Free Mission) 12,000
Pakistan Christian Fellowship (International Christian Fellowship) 2,600
Indus Christian Fellowship (Conservative Baptist Foreign Missionary Society) 2,500
International Missions (International Mission,Inc.) 2,500
Evangelical Alliance Churches (The Evangelical Alliance Mission) 1,100

Evangelical 0.2% of population.

Missionaries to Pakistan 680 (1:146,000 people) in about 40 agencies. Missionaries from within Pakistan estimated 10.

PERU

Area 1,285,000 sq.km. Andean state. Three zones—dry coastal plain in the west where most of the cities and industry are located, high plateau which is agricultural, and upper Amazon jungles in the east.

Population 21,900,000. Annual growth 2.1%. People per sq.km. 17.

Peoples

Spanish-speaking 45% (majority Mestizo, minority white and black).

Amerindian 54%. *Highland peoples*: Quechua 9,200,000; Aymara 1,000,000; *Lowland peoples* 330,000 speaking 41 languages.

Other minorities 1%. Japanese 65,000; Chinese 60,000; other European, etc.

Literacy 88%. *Official languages:* Spanish, Quechua. *All languages* 86. *Bible Translations* 2 Bible, 19 New Testaments, 24 portions.

Capital: Lima 5,627,000 including the port city of Callao. Other city: Arequipa 700,000. Urbanization 67%.

Economy: The combined effects of sudden climatic changes, world recession and destructive terrorism have brought the country to its knees and hindered necessary social and land reforms. The disastrous economic policies of the left-wing populist government has further devastated the country. Income/person $1,430 (8% of USA).

Politics: Fully independent from Spain in 1824. Return to democratic government since 1980, but a Maoist guerrilla movement has brought increasing instability and an atmosphere of fear through spectacular acts of terrorism. The socialist government elected in 1985 was unable to cope with the nation's problems. In 1990 a moderate government was elected.

Religion: Religious freedom guaranteed in 1978 constitution, but in practice the Catholic Church still tends to be favored and exercises a decisive influence.

Non-religious/Atheist 1%.

Animist 1%. Though at least 30% of nominal Catholics are in reality Christo-pagan.

Christian 98%. Affiliated 94%.

Roman Catholic 89.1%. Practicing 20%. 17,400,000 adherents.

Marginal groups (10) 0.86%. 167,000 adherents. Largest (adherents): Jehovah's Witnesses 75,080; Mormons 60,000.

Protestant 3.6%. 692,000 adherents; 285,000 members. Denominations 85. Largest (adult members):

Assemblies of God 97,000
Seventh-Day Adventist Church 60,000
Iglesia Evangelica Peruana (Evangelical Union of South America, SIM) 40,000
Christian & Missionary Alliance 15,000
Church of the Nazarene 12,400
Southern Baptist Convention 8,500
Church of God (Cleveland) 7,330
Evangelical Churches of NE (RBMU International) 4,000
Brethren 3,500

Evangelical 3% of population.

Missionaries to Peru 890 (1:21,900 people) in 60 agencies. Missionaries from within Peru estimated 110 (1:6,300 Protestants).

PHILIPPINES

Area 300,000 sq.km. 73 provinces; 7,250 islands, of which over 700 are inhabited, the largest being Luzon (116,000 sq.km.) in the north and Mindanao (95,000 sq.km.) in the south.

Population 66,700,000. Annual growth 2.9%. People per sq.km. 222. Over 400,000 Filipinos working in 103 nations and on ships. About one million have emigrated to the USA.

Peoples

Malayo-Indonesian Filipinos 95%. Major languages: Cebuano 24.4%, Tagalog 23.8%, Ilocano 11.1%, Hiligaynon 10%, Bicol (many dialects) 7%, Waray 4.6%, Kapampangan 3.4%, Maranao 2.8%, Pangasinan 2.3%, Magindanao 2.2%, Tausug 1.5%, Samal 1%.

Tribal peoples 2.8%. In the more inaccessible mountainous areas of Luzon (46 tribes) 930,000; Mindanao (22 tribes) 490,000; Mindoro (6 tribes) 50,000; Palawan (6 tribes) 30,000.

Chinese 1%. Important in the commercial world.

Other 1%. USA citizens, Vietnamese, etc.

Literacy 88%. *Official languages:* Filipino (based on Tagalog), English. *All languages* 151. *Bible translations* 9 Bibles, 26 New Testaments, 55 portions.

Capital: Metro-Manila 10,000,000. Urbanization 37%.

Economy: A mixed agricultural and industrial economy. Serious economic difficulties have worsened under the combined impact of the oil crisis, decline of export income, widespread corruption, social and political unrest and a series of natural disasters. Loss of international confidence in the country's future since 1983 has caused hardship, with rising unemployment, 50% inflation rate and widespread poverty. Income/person $590 (3% of USA).

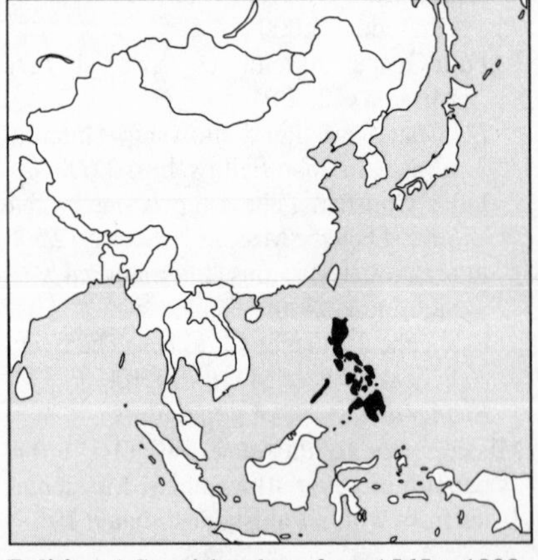

Politics: A Spanish colony from 1565 to 1898; hence the Catholic majority and many Spanish customs. Ruled by the USA until independence in 1946. Martial law imposed in 1971 to combat Communist subversion, and the country became virtually a one-party republic. Political manipulation, mismanagement and abuse of civil liberties stimulated antipathy to the government and led to its downfall in 1986. The government of Cory Aquino has proved relatively ineffective in controlling the economy or curbing the Communist guerillas, but has survived seven coup attempts. The Republic is a member of ASEAN and is an important ally of the USA.

Religion: Freedom of religion. Asia's only country with a Catholic majority.

Non-religious/Atheist 1.5%.

Animist 1%. Many nominal Catholics are still animist at heart. Majority among many of the tribal peoples.

Muslim 8.4%. Sunni Islam. Almost all in Southwest Mindanao, Sulu Island and Palawan. Strong among the Magindanao, Maranao, Ilanon, Samal and Tausug; less strong, but in the majority among eight other peoples.

Christian 89.2%. Many Christo-pagan.

Roman Catholic 63.6%, though a further 12% were baptized Catholic, but have left the Church. 36,150,000 adherents; 19,240,000 members.

Indigenous Catholic groups 8%. 4,500,000 adherents; 2,600,000 members. Over 120 groups have broken away from Rome. Largest (adherents): Philippine Independent Church 4,200,000.

Indigenous marginal groups 6.1%. Over 280 groups. 3,433,000 adherents; 1,850,000 members. Largest (adherents): Iglesia ni Cristo 1,400,000.

Foreign marginal groups 0.7%. 388,000 adherents; 185,000 members. Most rapidly growing and largest (adherents): Jehovah's Witnesses 237,000; Mormons 76,000.

Protestant 10.7%. 6,010,000 adherents; 2,600,000 members. Denominations 140. Largest (adult members):

Seventh-Day Adventist Church 290,000
United Church 260,000
Christian & Missionary Alliance 185,000
United Methodist Church 166,000
Southern Baptist Convention 89,000
Assemblies of God 60,000
March of Faith 55,000
Convention of Philippino Baptist Churches 54,000
International Church of Foursquare Gospel 48,000
Evangelical Methodist Church 40,000
Episcopal Church 33,000
ABCOP (Overseas Missionary Fellowship, Send International) 16,000
Conservative Baptist Association 15,000

Evangelical 6.4% of population.

Missionaries to Philippines approximately 2,300 (1:24,700 people) in about 120 agencies. Missionaries from within the Philippines approximately 670 (1:9,000 Protestants) of which over 180 are serving in other lands.

POLAND

Area 313,000 sq.km. Poland has the misfortune of being sandwiched between Germany and Russia.

Population 38,400,000. Annual growth .6%. People per sq.km. 122.

Peoples

Poles 96.6%. Over 10 million emigrants (65% in USA).

Minorities 3%. Ukrainian 256,000; Pomeranian 220,000; Byelorussian 220,000; German 73,000; Gypsy 70,000.

USSR Military, etc. 0.4%.

Literacy 98%. *Official language:* Polish. *All languages* 7. *Bible translations* 4 Bibles, 1 portion.

Capital: Warsaw 1,770,000. Other major cities: Lodz 945,000, Cracow 800,000. Urbanization 61%.

Economy: The courage of the new government in radically tackling the chaos left by 45 years of Communist mismanagement is setting the land on the painful path to recovery. Income/person $1920 (10% of USA).

Politics: A well-remembered tragic history of wars and partition among powerful neighbors over the last 200 years. One quarter of the population died in World War II. The Soviet army imposed a communist regime in 1945. Popular discontent caused gradual liberalizations during 1980-81. The Solidarity movement forced negotiations with the Communist regime in 1988/89 and in the subsequent partially democratic elections, came to power as part of an ambitious Communist/Solidarity coalition government in June 1989. This show of strength and resilience by Solidarity marks a watershed for eastern Europe, and furthermore appears to have initiated dramatic changes of government in nearly every continent of the world. More recently, a jolting shift to a market economy and dissatisfaction with many of the effects thus far have tested Solidarity's cohesiveness. To be successful, the reforms will need to address cooperation of professionals and workers, the relationship of Solidarity to the government, and the critical role of Lech Walesa.

Religion: The Roman Catholic Church is too strong for the Communists to dominate or destroy, so there is more religious freedom than in any other Communist state. The Protestants have more freedom than for centuries because they are considered a counterbalance to the Roman Catholics.

Non-religious/Atheist 10%.

Jews 12,000 (3,500,000 in 1939).

Christian 89.8%

Roman Catholic 87.3%. Practicing 65%. 32,800,000 adherents; 21,600,000 members.

Orthodox 1.6%. 606,000 adherents; 375,000 members. Denominations 3.

Protestant 0.45%. 171,000 adherents; 110,000 members. Denominations 24. Largest (adult members):

Lutheran Church (German) 60,000
United Evangelical Church 20,000
Assemblies of God 8,500
Baptist Union 4,200

Evangelical 0.2% of population (0.5% including the members of Oasis).

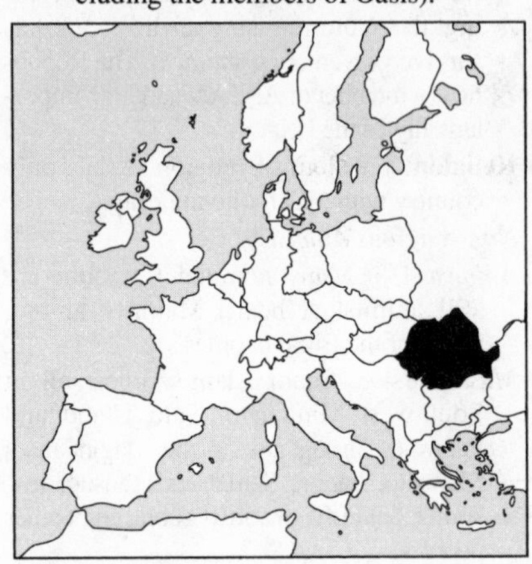

ROMANIA

Area 237,000 sq.km. Area is much reduced by Russian seizure of Bessarabia in 1940 (now the Moldavian Soviet Socialist Republic).

Population 23,300,000. Annual growth 0.5%. People per sq.km. 98.

Peoples

Romanian 84%. A Latin people descended from Romans settled in Dacia.

Hungarian 8.5%. In Transylvania.

Minorities 7.5%. Gypsy 700,000; German 300,000; Jew 106,000; Turk 100,000; Ukrainian 67,000; Serbian 65,000; etc.

Literacy 98%. *Official languages:* Romanian, Hungarian.

Capital: Bucharest 2,200,000. Urbanization 51%.

Economy: The Communist regime impoverished the country and brought its population to poverty and despair. The newly elected government is committed to set up a market economy, but the social and economic dislocations will be traumatic. Income/person est. $1,988 (11% of USA).

Politics: The Russian-supported Communist

coup in 1947 brought 43 years of tyranny and suffering to the country. The final collapse of Communism in December 1989 was sudden and violent. The May 1990 multiparty elections were neither peaceful nor acceptable to many, for many former Communists were elected as members of the National Salvation Front Party. Its subsequent human rights record is hardly a guarantee for the institution of full democracy.

Religion: Communist persecution of Christians was the most severe of any Eastern European country apart from Albania. Freedom of religion is promised, but the attitude of the Romanian Orthodox Church has been hostile to other Christian groups.

Non-religious/Atheist 14%.

Muslim 1.2%. Predominantly Turks, some Bulgars and Gypsies.

Jews 0.5%. Steadily declining through emigration to Israel.

Christian 84.2%.

Orthodox 67.4%; 15,400,000 adherents; 10,700,000 members. Denominations 6. Largest (adherents):

Roman Catholic 5.5%. 1,244,000 adherents; 900,000 members.

Marginal groups 0.3%. 66,000 adherents; 48,000 members.

Protestant 11%. 2,500,000 adherents; 1,500,000 members. Denominations 14 legally acknowledged. Largest (adult members):

Reformed Church 520,000
Baptist Union 340,000(?)
Church of God 230,000
Assemblies of God 170,000
Lutheran Church 94,500
Brethren 63,000 (?)
Seventh-Day Adventist Church 57,000

Evangelical 7.8% of population (11% if the Lord's Army Christians are included).

RUSSIA

Area 22,402,000 sq.km. The world's largest country; nearly 11,000 km. from east to west and 4,000 km. from north to south. The USSR straddles 11 time zones. 24% of the USSR lies in Europe and 76% in Asia (Siberia).

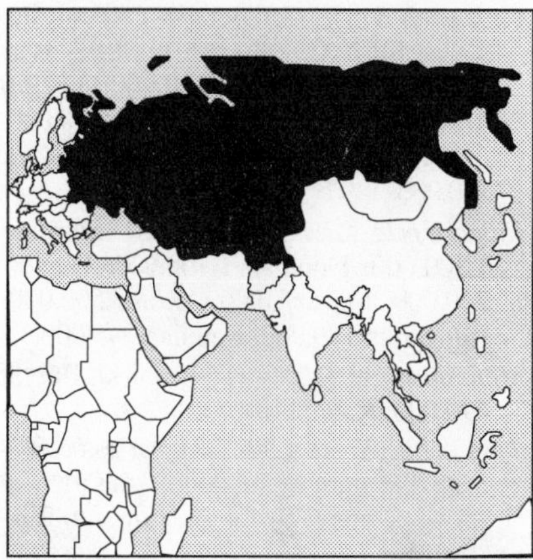

Population 291,900,000. Annual growth 1.0 The Slavic population is almost static, but some groups, particularly the Turkic peoples of Central Asia, are growing at over 3%. Large areas are uninhabited. 25% of the population lives in Siberia. People per sq.km. 13.

Peoples: An extraordinary mosaic of peoples came under Russian domination over the past several centuries. There are approximately 154 ethnic groups.

Indo-European 78.2%.

Slavic 72.8% (8 peoples). Russian 138,000,000; Ukrainian 43,000,000; Byelorussian 10,000,000; Polish 1,150,000.

Baltic 1.6%. Lithuanian 3,020,000; Latvian 1,518,000.

Iranian 1.3% (12 peoples). Tajik 3,400,000; Talysh 150,000; Kurdish 140,000.

Other 2.8%. Armenian 4,500,000; Romanian (Moldavian) 3,260,000; German 2,040,000; Ossetian 590,000; Greek 360,000;

Gypsy (Jati, Romany) 337,000.

Altaic 16.5%.

Turkic 16% (24 peoples). Uzbek 15,000,000; Kazakh 7,800,000; Tatar 7,400,000; Azeri 6,500,000; Turkmen 2,430,000; Kirghiz 2,290,000; Chuvash 1,900,000; Bashkir 1,500,000; Karakalpak 350,000; Yakut

350,000; Crimean Turks 330,000; Uighur 250,000; Kumyk 226,000; Karachay 225,000; Tuvin 200,000; Gagauz 200,000.

Caucasian 2.5% (33 peoples). Georgian 3,900,000; Chechen 800,000; Avar 528,000; Karbardian 420,000; Lezgin 415,000; Dargin 310,000; Ingush 200,000; Adygey (Circassian) 120,000; Lak 110,000.

Finno-Ugric 1.7% (17 peoples). Mordvin 1,300,000; Estonian 1,100,000; Udmurt 770,000; Mari 670,000; Komi 500,000; Hungarian 180,000; Karelian 145,000.

Mongolian etc. 0.28% (12 peoples). Buryat 390,000; Kalmyk 160,000.

Jews 0.7%. About 1,900,000, but some estimate the number at double this due to strong pressures by the authorities to Russify them.

Other 0.16%. Over 10 other Siberian peoples totalling 31,000; Chinese 55,000; Korean 400,000.

Literacy 99%. It was 25% before the revolution. *Official language:* Russian spoken as first language by 56% of the population. Local languages are officially recognized in the various constituent Soviet Socialist Republics and Autonomous Regions. Sixty-five languages are recognized as literary languages for use in the media. *All languages* 138. *Bible translations* 25 Bibles, 5 New Testaments, 34 portions.

Capital: Moscow 8,600,000. Other major cities: Leningrad 5,000,000; Kiev 2,500,000; Tashkent 2,100,000; Baku 1,700,000; Kharkov 1,600,000. There are 26 cities with populations over one million. Urbanization 66%.

Economy: Highly centralized socialist economy, with very little private ownership. The "command" economy is both cumbersome and inefficient. Vast mineral wealth as well as an extensive agricultural output make the USSR the world's leading producer of wheat, butter, iron ore etc. The extremes of climate and collectivized agriculture make for low and erratic production figures. Over 15% of the nation's resources are spent on the armed forces. Income/person $6,350 (45% of USA).

Politics: The USSR came into being following the Bolshevik revolution in 1917 and currently consists of 15 federative socialist republics. The type of Marxism commonly attributed to the Soviet Union is one that was adapted ideologically by Vladimir Lenin and translated bureaucratically by Josef Stalin. The monolithic governmental structure has been dominated since shortly after 1917 by the Communist Party, which has viewed itself as the vanguard of change in lieu of the alleged eventual, if not imminent, self-destruction of the capitalist system. The pace of change in the Soviet Union has accelerated, however, since Mikhail Gorbachev became General Secretary in March 1985. Through his policies of *glasnost* (openness) and *perestroike* (restructuring), Gorbachev has attempted to rally all sectors of Soviet society to come to grips with the problems facing the country in light of the contemporary world situation, and he is widely regarded as a significant catalyst for change in Europe. In time, he has encountered opposition from radical social reformers and from conservative party bureaucrats. Moreover, ethnic conflicts in the central Asian republics as well as moves toward autonomy by the Baltic republics have heightened the sense of drama in a country already burdened with a grave economic condition. A multiparty system has been sanctioned in principle, and in practice splits in the Communist Party appear imminent as the more radical reformers are increasingly dissatisfied with the nature and pace of the current reform program. Because of the complexity of this country's situation, lasting beneficial effects due to fundamental change in the economy or government are likely to involve profound social upheaval and will probably require several years or more to get established.

Religion: Marxism-Leninism is the official state ideology, of which atheism is an inseparable part. The strong opposition of the

Communist Party to any religion makes mockery of the constitutional right of a citizen to profess a faith. There have been periods of severe persecution, with the closure of most churches, and imprisonment and murder of church leaders and believers. Persecution continues today, and is particularly severe against all who do not comply with the demands of the authorities. The state uses every means at its disposal to prevent evangelism and destroy the Church by rigid controls, discriminatory legislation, infiltration of agents, and also by intimidation and manipulation of church leadership even in the churches that have official recognition. All statistics are estimates (possibly conservative). Even if the figures were accurately known it would be unwise to publicize them.

Non-religious/Atheist 52% and possibly up to 75%. For many, especially young people, it is inexpedient to profess any religion.

Muslim 18% ethnically; by profession around 12%; a large minority would claim to be atheist. Muslims are in the majority in six republics (Azerbaijan, Kazakhstan, Kirgizia, Tajikistan, Turkmenisten and Uzbekistan), nine autonomous republics and four autonomous regions. 75% of Muslims live in Soviet Central Asia adjoining Iran, Afghanistan and China. The majority are Sunni Muslim. The Azeri, Kurds and Talysh are Shi'a. Official Islam is government controlled by spiritual directorates in four different regions. There is a strong fundamentalist underground Islamic movement.

Jews 1.2%. Possibly over half are atheists. Two major groups: Western, and Eastern (Crimea, Georgia and Central Asia). They have suffered much persecution over the past 15 years, especially the many who have applied for emigration to Israel.

Shamanist 0.1%. Many of the smaller tribal peoples of North Russia and Siberia are still animist—especially the Yakut, Chukchi, and also the Tungus and Samoyed peoples.

Buddhist 0.1%. The majority would not be practicing Buddhists. Mahayana Buddhism among the Buryats, Kalmyks and Tuvinians. Some Koreans are also Buddhist. Officially recognized, but with a long history of repression by the Soviet authorities. Between 1933 and 1938 all 120 Buddhist monasteries were destroyed.

Christian 33%. Active adherents possibly 22%. Many are still baptized as children. Actual figures are only general estimates.

Orthodox 16.4%. 45,600,000 adherents (?). Over 43 national or breakaway denominations. Largest (adherents):

Russian Orthodox 37,000,000 (?)
Armenian Orthodox 3,000,000
Georgian Orthodox 2,500,000
Other Orthodox groups 2,700,000 (?)

Roman Catholic 3.2%. 9,000,000 adherents (?). Many Uniate Catholics have been compelled to be classified as Russian Orthodox.

Protestant 2.6%. 7,300,000 adherents; 2,800,000 members. Some officially sanctioned denominations, many unregistered groups, all totalling possibly 100. Largest (adherents):

AUCECB (registered) 3,000,000
Evangelical Lutheran Church of Latvia 350,000
Evangelical Lutheran Church of Estonia 250,000
Reformed Church of Transcarpathia 70,000
Other unregistered groups (?) 1,500,000

Evangelical 2.5% of population. Higher if evangelical Orthodox and Catholic included.

SOUTH AFRICA

Area 1,222,000 sq.km. This includes: 1. Walvis Bay (an enclave on Namibian coast 1,124 sq.km). 2. Four independent states: Transkei 45,000 sq.km., Bophuthatswana 40,000 sq.km., Ciskei 9,000 sq.km., and Venda 6,500 sq.km. These "TBVC" states are not internationally recognized so are included here as part of South Africa.

Population 32,100,000. Annual growth 2.4% (White 1.2%, Black 2.8%). People per sq.

km. 27. TBVC states 5,100,000, National states ("Homelands") 7,100,000. 52% of the Black population lives in the ten enclave states created by the government.

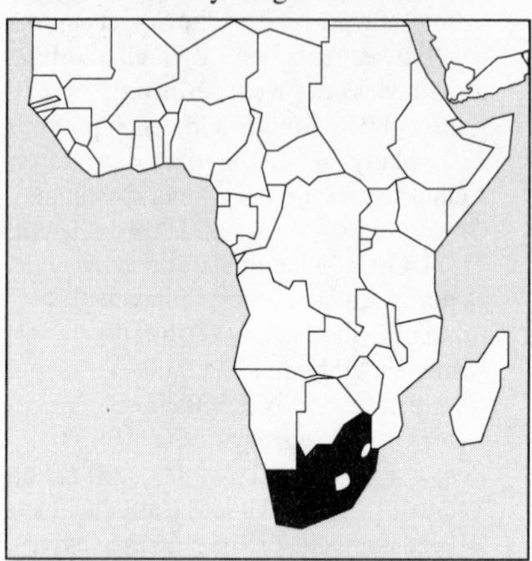

Peoples

Black 73%. *Nguni* (5) Zulu 6,600,000; Xhosa 5,900,000; Swazi 1,000,000; South Ndebele 477,000.

Sotho (3) North Sotho/Pedi 2,800,000; East Sotho/Tswana 2,400,000; South Sotho 2,200,000; North Ndebele 340,000.

Other (2) Tsonga/Shangaan 1,200,000, Venda 594,000.

White 15%. Afrikaners 2,700,000, English speaking 1,800,000. Portuguese 650,000; German 45,000; Greek 40,000.

Colored (Mixed race) 9%. Predominantly descendants of slaves with Black, Khoi-Khoi (Hottentot), European and Asian blood. Ninety percent live in the Western Cape Province. The Cape Malays are considered part of this community.

Asian 3%. Indians 77% in Durban area of Natal, Chinese 11,000.

Literacy 89%. *National languages:* Afrikaans, English. The 10 national independent states also use their majority language as the official language. *All languages* 28. *Bible translations* 17 Bibles, 1 New Testament, 1 portion.

Capitals: Pretoria (administrative) 865,000; Cape Town (legislative) 1,740,000; Bloemfontein (judicial) 220,000. *Other major cities:* Johannesburg/Soweto 3,500,000 (6,600,000 live in the Witwatersrand and South Transvaal industrial complex); Durban 1,100,000; Port Elizabeth 680,000. Urbanization 56% (Asians 91%, Whites 89%, Coloreds 77%, Blacks 31%).

Economy: The richest and most industrialized country in Africa (25% of GNP, 40% of industrial output). The world's biggest exporter of non-petroleum minerals—especially gold, platinum, chrome, diamonds and coal. Lack of water and erratic rainfall could limit growth. World recession, drought and worldwide opposition to the racial policies have further stimulated government overspending on the cumbersome administration of separate development (apartheid) and defense. Inflation and a severe decline in the economy since 1982 have been the result. Inflation 25% ('85). Income/person $2,450 (18% of USA). Whites, on average, earn three times that of Blacks.

Politics: The Union of South Africa was formed in 1910. A White minority parliamentary republic created in 1961. The constitution of 1984 instituted a strong presidency and a limited sharing of power with the Colored and Asian minorities, but created serious rifts in both the Afrikaner and other communities. The exclusion of Blacks (especially the urban population) from national politics and the compartmentalization of the races are the major unresolved issues which dominate every aspect of national life. Changes are coming, but too fast for the fearful Whites and far too slow for the frustrated Blacks. The deteriorating security situation, adverse world publicity and the economic crisis make more rapid changes essential. The economic and strategic importance of South Africa ensure that internal stresses have serious international consequences, both for surrounding Black states and the superpowers. The 10 national states are enclaves within South Africa. All are overpopulated and very dependent economically on South Africa. They are the theoretical home for the 11 million Blacks in the White areas of

South Africa (87% of the territory). Four have opted for political independence: Transkei 1976, Bophuthatswana 1977, Venda 1979, Ciskei 1981. All but Bophuthatswana are one-party states.

Religion: Freedom of religion. The racial issue has led to a rising level of church-state confrontations and divisions within denominations. Official statistics omit the four independent states, which are here included:

African traditional religions approximately 20%. The more strongly so being Shangaan 49%, Venda 46%, Xhosa 25%, Zulu 25%.

Non-religious/Atheist, etc. 5%.

Hindu 1.8%. Indians, mainly in Natal.

Muslim 1.1%. Cape Malays and Indians.

Jews 0.42%. Over 130,000 mainly in Rand area of South Transvaal.

Christian 71.6%. Affiliated approximately 61%, (including TBVC states). Church statistics below are based on 1980 government census which excludes TBVC states and are thus not affiliated figures as elsewhere. Numbers of Christians will also now be lower than indicated in 1980 for older, mainline denominations and higher for rapidly growing younger churches.

Roman Catholic 10.1%. 3,200,000 adherents. Growing among Blacks.

Orthodox 0.13%. Mostly Greeks.

African Independent Churches 22%. Over 3,700 groups. Largest (adherents):

Zion Christian Church 1,250,000

Nazarite Baptist Church approximately 500,000

St. John's Apostolic Faith Mission 400,000

Foreign marginal groups 0.5%. Largest (adherents): Jehovah's Witnesses 103,750; Mormons 9,000.

Protestant 40%. Approximately 12,800,000 adherents. Denominations probably 160. Largest (adherents of all races):

Nederduitse Gerefermeeerde Kerk (Dutch Reformed) 3,478,000

Methodist Church 2,113,000

Church of the Province of South Africa (Anglican) 1,517,000

Lutheran Churches 835,000

Presbyterian Church 499,000

Congregational Church (UCCSA) 407,000

Apostolic Faith Mission 303,000

Baptist Church 255,000

Full Gospel Church of God 169,000

Assemblies of God (various) 133,000

Church of England in South Africa 96,000

Other Pentecostal Churches 764,000

Evangelical 15% of population.

Missionaries to South Africa approximately 1,310 in over 80 agencies. Missionaries from within South Africa approximately 1,020 of which 240 serve outside South Africa (1:12,500 Protestants).

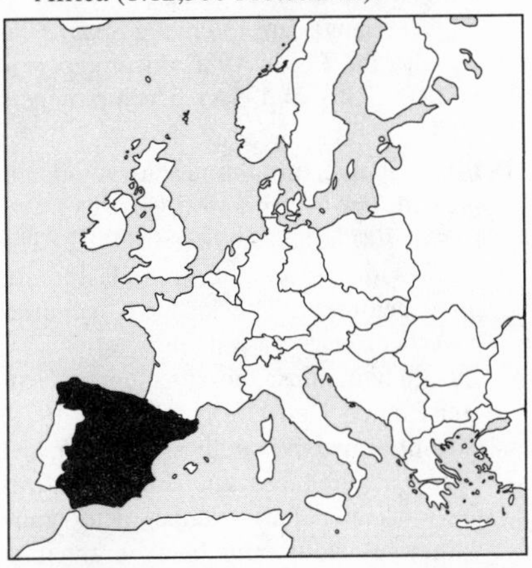

SPAIN

Area 505,000 sq.km. The major part of the Iberian peninsula, and including the Canary Islands off Northwest Africa, and the enclaves of Ceuta and Melilla on the North African coast.

Population 39,300,000. Annual growth 0.3%. People per sq.km. 78.

Peoples

Spanish 96%. Castilian 27,000,000; Catalan 6,900,000, Galician 3,200,000.

Basque 2.3%. Most in the four Atlantic provinces adjoining France. Many more Basques are being culturally absorbed into the Castilian majority. There is a strong separatist movement.

Gypsy 0.2%. Some claim that there may be 200,000.

Foreign 1%. German, French, Portuguese, British, Latin American, etc.

Literacy 93%. *Official language:* Castilian Spanish. Regionally official: Basque,

Catalan, Galician. Spanish is now the third most widely spoken language in the world. *All languages* 5. *Bible translations* 3 Bibles, 2 portions.

Capital: Madrid 4,000,000. Other major cities: Barcelona approximately 3,000,000; Valencia 1,000,000; Bilbao 1,000,000; Seville 1,000,000. Urbanization 91%.

Economy: The devastation caused by instability and the 1936-39 civil war impoverished the country. Steady growth through tourism and industry since 1968. Further radical changes are following Spain's entry into the EC in 1986. Income/person $6,010 (33% of USA). Unemployment 19%.

Politics: Spain's tumultuous past molds the present. The Muslim Moorish occupation lasted 700 years, ending in 1492. The worldwide Spanish Empire lasted for three centuries. The last two centuries have been ones of instability, civil wars and dictatorships; the latter under General Franco lasted from 1939 to 1975. Constitutional monarchy since 1975, and a gradual democratization and liberalization since then. Parliamentary democracy with more autonomy being granted to regions—especially for the Catalans and Basques. The left-wing ETA Basque terrorist campaign for full independence has plagued Spain since 1961.

Religion: Severe discrimination against, and even open persecution of, non-Catholics followed Franco's victory in the civil war. Traditional Catholicism became dominant. Gradual easing of discriminatory laws culminated in religious freedom being guaranteed in the 1978 constitution.

Non-religious/Atheist 4%. Rapid secularization with many baptized Catholics no longer linked to the church.

Christian 96%. Affiliated 94%.

Roman Catholic 93.6%. Practicing 25%.

Marginal groups 0.35%. 135,000 adherents; 57,000 members. Rapid growth. Largest (adult members): Jehovah's Witnesses 56,700; Mormons 7,200.

Protestant 0.5%. 193,000 adherents; 63,700 members. Denominations 20. Largest (adult members):

Filadelfia Church (gypsies) 13,500

Brethren 12,000

Evangelical Baptist Union (Southern Baptist) 7,500

Seventh-Day Adventist Church 5,000

Federation of Independent Churches (The Evangelical Alliance Mission) 3,800

Assemblies of God 1,850

Evangelical 0.34% of population.

Missionaries to Spain 610 (1:63,400 people) in 88 agencies. Missionaries from Spain approximately 10 (1:19,300 Protestants).

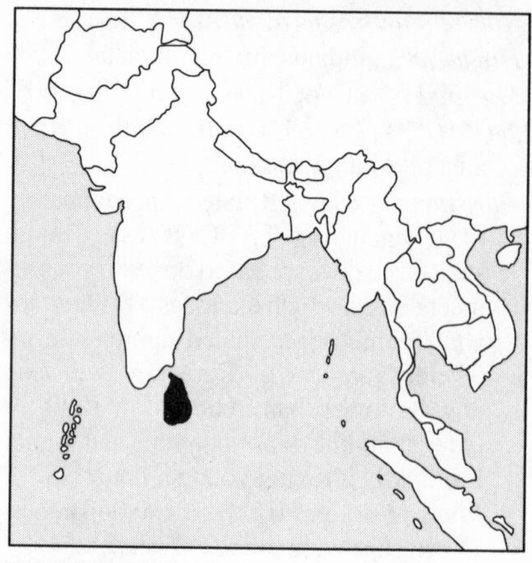

SRI LANKA

Area 65,600 sq.km. Large island 80 km. southeast of the southern tip of India.

Population 17,200,000. Annual growth 1.6%. People per sq.km. 264.

Peoples

Sinhalese 72%. An Aryan people; largely Buddhist. Many castes—unusual for Buddhist societies.

Tamil 20%. (Lanka Tamils residents for over 1,000 years, mainly in north and east) 1,770,000; Indian Tamils (imported laborers in 19th and 20th centuries; mainly in highland tea plantations). The majority are Hindu.

Moor 6%. Arab-Tamil descent 950,000, Tamil descent 28,000.

Burgher 0.3%. European-Asian descent. Once privileged; many emigrating to Australia. Nearly all live in Colombo.

Veddah: Only 140 left of the aboriginal people.

Literacy 90%. *Official language:* Sinhala. Tamil and English are recognized as national languages. *All languages* 5. *Bible translations* 3 Bibles.

Capital: Colombo 991,000. Urbanization 24%.

Economy: Agricultural with tea and rubber the most important export commodities. Increasing industrialization since 1977. Subsequent rapid progress has been marred by the impact of the communal violence. Inflation, the cost of living and foreign debt are soaring. Tourism and trade are adversely affected. Income/person $320 (2% of USA).

Politics: Independence gained in 1948, as a parliamentary democracy, after 450 years of successive colonial administrations by the Portuguese, Dutch and British. Attempts to Sinhalize national life in 1956 and the attendant discrimination against ethnic and religious minorities provoked increasing communal violence and efforts by extremists to fight for an independent Tamil state in the north and east. The increasing scale of violence led to massacres, a massive refugee problem and civil war. The Indian armed forces intervened in 1987 to supress the Tamil Tiger guerilla movement with only partial success. The Indian peacekeeping force was asked by the government to leave in 1989. Renewed fighting betwen the government and Tamil Tigers continues.

Religion: Buddhism is the state religion and, as such, is protected and promoted. Although freedom for other religions is assured, there has been some discrimination against minority religions in taxation, employment and education.

Buddhist 69.3%. Almost entirely of the Sinhala community. Resurgence since 1956, and actively seeking the conversion of Christians, and stimulating Buddhist missionary activity around the world.

Hindu 15.4%. Almost entirely Tamil.

Muslim 7.6% Moors and Malays.

Christian 7.4%. Affiliated 7%.

Roman Catholic 6.3%. 1,030,000 adherents; 577,000 members. Influential through a variety of social programs.

Protestant 0.75%. 124,000 adherents; 59,600 members. Denominations 30. Largest (adult adherents):

Church of Ceylon 48,800
Methodist Church 26,200
Salvation Army 5,500
Church of South India (Tamil) 5,300
Independent Indigenous Churches 5,000
Ceylon Pentecostal Mission 5,000
Assemblies of God 3,500
Baptist Union 3,200
Apostolic Church 3,100
Fellowship of Free Churches (Pentecostal) 2,500
Foursquare Gospel Church 1,750
Apostolic Church 1,250
Seventh-Day Adventist Church 1,000

Evangelical 0.2% of population.

Missionaries to Sri Lanka estimated 90 (10,182,000 people) in 20 agencies. Missionaries from within Sri Lanka estimated 12 (Ceylon Pentecostal Mission which began in 1923 in Ceylon has established churches in India, Malaysia, United Kingdom, France, Canada, USA, Mexico).

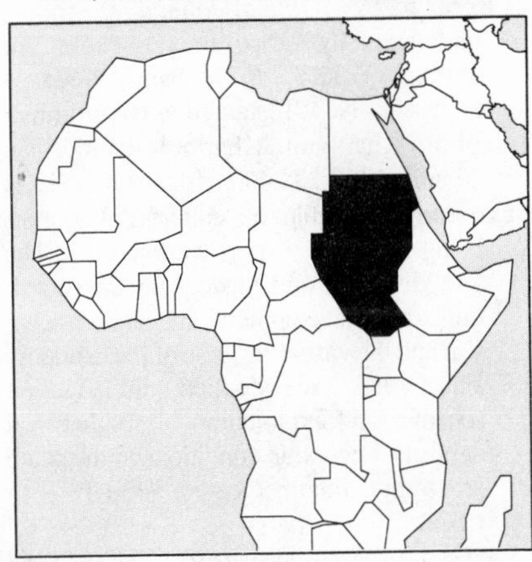

SUDAN

Area 2,506,000 sq.km. Africa's largest country. Desert in north, merging into tropical bush in south.

Population 25,300,000. Annual growth 2.8%. People per sq.km. 10. About 40% of the population is nomadic or semi-nomadic.

Peoples: Over 56 distinct ethnic groups, 597 sub-groups. Many language families—

Semitic, Cushitic, Nilotic, Nilo-Saharan, etc., too complex and unclear for breakdown here.

Sudanese Arab 51%. Predominant in center and north.

Other African peoples 49%.

Southern provinces 25%. Dinka 1,466,000; Nuer 800,000; Azande 360,000; Lotuko 200,000; Shilluk 190,000; Thuri 170,000; Toposa 160,000; Murle 70,000, etc.

North/northeastern peoples 8%. Beja 1,100,000; Nubians 450,000; Tigre 190,000.

Darfur 5%. Fur 400,000; Masalit 125,000; Zaghawa 120,000; Daju 80,000, Tama 60,000, etc.

West Africans 6%. Fulani 100,000, etc.

Kordofan peoples 5%. Nuba tribes (100 tribes speaking 37 languages) 900,000.

Refugees number 1-1.5 million. The majority from Ethiopia, many from Chad, some from Uganda. Just over half use Arabic as trade language.

Literacy 20%. *Official language:* Arabic, understood by 80% of the population. *All languages* 137. *Bible translations* 4 Bibles, 14 New Testaments, 10 portions.

Capital: Khartoum. Khartoum-Omdurman conurbation 2,258,000. Urbanization 21%.

Economy: Agricultural; cotton and peanuts being the major export commodities. The vast distances and inadequate transportation hinder development. The renewed civil war and the virtual collapse of the economy since 1983 have stopped big irrigation schemes and exploitation of southern oil deposits. Economic conditions in the south are tragic. Income/person $400 (3% of USA).

Politics: Independent from Britain and Egypt in 1956. Bitter fighting between Arab northerners and southern secessionists 1955-1972. After 12 years of uneasy peace, and a degree of autonomy for the south, fighting has broken out again. The erratic, and increasingly unstable, West-leaning government of President Nimeiry collapsed in 1985. Successive governments since then have been riven with religious differences on the national application of Islamic law, and thus unable to open peace negotiations with the Southerners.

Religion: The strenuous efforts by Muslim northerners to impose Islam and Arab culture on the southerners has been one of the root causes for the present conflict. An Islamic republic—declared in 1983, with the imposition of Islamic sharia law on all citizens—provoked anger among non-Muslims and vociferous anti-Christian propaganda and actions by Muslim fundamentalists. Muslim efforts to Islamize the southerners have been both crude and forceful.

Muslim 74%. Sunni Islam, with several powerful Sufi religious orders, the largest being Ansar, the followers of the famous Mahdi. Almost the entire northern population is Muslim.

Traditional religions 15%. Predominantly among southern tribes, Nuba Mountain peoples and some Darfur peoples.

Non-religious/Atheist 1.2%. Mainly urban intellectuals.

Christian 9.8%. Affiliated 9.1%. Most statistics are approximate.

Roman Catholic 5.2%. 1,100,000 adherents; 640,000 members.

Orthodox 0.8%. 170,000 adherents. Mainly Coptic in Nile Valley, and among Ethiopian refugees.

Protestant 3.1%. 650,000 adherents; 190,000 members. Denominations 11, largest (adherents):

Episcopal Church 520,000 (Anglican) (?)

Presbyterian Church 55,000 (?)

Sudanese Church of Christ (SUM) 40,000

Sudan Interior Church (Sudan Interior Mission) 9,000

Africa Inland Church (Africa Inland Mission) 4,000 (?)

Evangelical 1.6% of population.

Foreign Christian workers approximately 200 (1:110,000 people).

TAIWAN

Area 36,000 sq.km. A mountainous island 300 km. off coast of mainland China.

Population 20,200,000. Annual growth 1.1%. People per sq.km. 561.

Peoples

Han Chinese 98% speaking three major languages.

Taiwanese (Hoklo, Minnan) 14,200,000. Over 300 years on Taiwan. Rural majority.

Hakka 2,100,000. About 200 years on Taiwan.

Mandarin 2,500,000. Refugees from Mainland China 1945-50. Predominantly urban.

Malayo-Polynesian mountain peoples (11) 1.7%. Largest: Ami 104,000; Paiwan 53,000; Tayal 46,000; Bunun 32,000; Sediq 20,000.

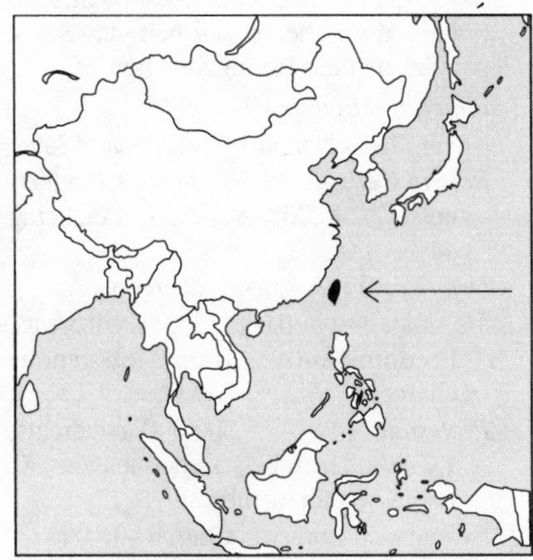

Literacy 90%. *Official language* and language of education: Mandarin. Hoklo is widely spoken. *All languages* 14. *Bible translations* 4 Bibles, 5 New Testaments, 1 portion.

Capital: Taipei 2,500,000. Major city: Kaoshiung 1,300,000. Urbanization 73%.

Economy: Rapid industrialization and economic growth to become one of the world's leading exporting states. Income/person $3,000 (21.3% of USA).

Politics: Under Japanese rule 1895-1945. After the fall of mainland China to the Communists in 1949, Taiwan became the refuge of the Nationalist Chinese government. A one-party republic dominated by mainlanders, but increasing Taiwanese participation in economic and political life is lessening communal tensions. International political isolation of Taiwan led to the loss of UN membership in 1971. Both Chinese governments seek reunification on their own terms.

Religion: Secular state with freedom of religion. The strong anti-communist stance of the government, and efforts to unify the country under one language, have placed it in conflict with some denominations—chiefly the large Presbyterian Church, whose membership is predominantly Taiwanese.

Non-religious/Atheist 20-30%. Many younger people are secular and abandon their family religions.

Chinese religions 60-70%. Blend of Confucianism, Taoism and Buddhism, with strong emphasis on veneration of ancestors.

Muslim 0.5%. Post-war immigrant Hui.

Tribal religions 0.5%. Minority of mountain peoples.

Christian 5%.

Roman Catholic 1.4%. Practicing 50%. 275,000 adherents; 151,000 members.

Marginal groups 0.26%. 52,000 adherents; 35,000 members. Largest (adult members): True Jesus Church 27,300; Mormons 6,100.

Protestant 3.5%. 670,000 adherents; 347,000 members. Denominations 70, also numerous independent congregations. Largest (adult members):

Presbyterian Church of Taiwan 95,000
Assembly Hall (W. Nee) 48,000
Southern Baptist Convention 12,000
Seventh-Day Adventist Church 6,078
Taiwan Holiness Church (OMS International) 4,495
Taiwan Lutheran Church 4,239
Free Methodist Church 3,800
Methodist Church 3,000
Assemblies of God 2,700
Chinese Evangelical Lutheran Church 2,000

Evangelical 2.5% of population.

Missionaries to Taiwan 863 (1:22,000 people) in over 80 agencies. Missionaries from Taiwan 10 (1:67,000 Protestants). Many others have gone as "tentmaking" missionaries, or to pastor overseas Chinese congregations.

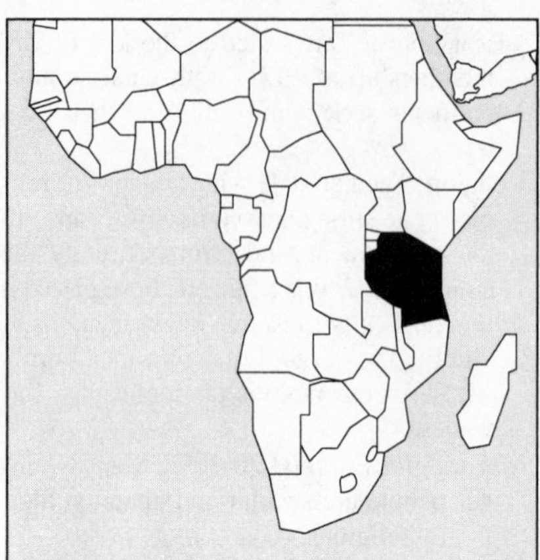

TANZANIA

Area 946,000 sq.km. Mainland Tanganyika and Zanzibar (two offshore islands) 2,650 sq.km.

Population 27,300,000. Zanzibar 728,000. Annual growth 3.6%. People per sq.km. 29.

Peoples: Over 126 distinct ethnic groups.

African peoples 99%. Tribalism has not been as divisive a force as in many lands. Major groups: Sukuma 2,820,000; Rufiji (4 groups) 1,950,000; Rukwa (3) 1,090,000; Makonde 890,000; Chagga 800,000.

Other 1%. Hutu refugees from Burundi, 100,000 (?); Indian 70,000 and decreasing, Westerners, etc.

Literacy 85%. *Official languages:* Swahili, English. The use of Swahili is so widespread, it is even replacing local languages in some areas. *All languages* 115. *Bible translations* 11 Bibles, 18 New Testaments, 15 portions.

Capital: Dar es Salaam 1,500,000. Capital designate. Dodoma. Urbanization 19%.

Economy: Agricultural subsistence economy. Inefficient, centralized bureaucracy and an over-zealous nationalization of businesses and collectivization of rural communities into "ujamaa" villages have been detrimental. Lowered production, and a run-down of industry and services, together with severe drought in the '80s have seriously reduced living standards. Income/person $220 (1% of USA).

Politics: Tanganyika gained independence from Britain in 1961, Zanzibar in 1963. The two countries united as a one-party federal socialist republic in 1964, though Zanzibar has retained a considerable degree of autonomy. The retirement of the respected President Nyerere may eventually lead to a shift away from his socialist dream. There is considerable pressure for change and liberalization in Zanzibar.

Religion: Religious freedom; the government encourages religious education in schools, though Islam is gaining in political influence.

Muslim 32.5%. The majority in Zanzibar (98%), along the coastal belt, and some peoples on the Mozambique border.

Traditional religions 19%.

Christian 47.7%. Nominal 12%. Affiliated 34%.

Roman Catholic 18.5%. 4,000,000 adherents; 2,200,000 members. Practicing 44%.

Orthodox 0.1%. 15,000 adherents.

Marginal groups 0.6%. 130,000 adherents. Predominantly African indigenous churches.

Protestant 14.8%. 3,200,000 adherents; 1,271,000 members. Denominations 30. Largest (adult members):

Evangelical Lutheran Church 436,000
Anglican Church 306,000
Africa Inland Church (African Inland Mission) 200,000
Moravian Church 79,500
Seventh-Day Adventist Church 53,000
Pentecostal Churches in Tanzania (ex-Swedish) 42,000
Tanzania Assemblies of God (AoG) 18,000
Pentecostal Assemblies of Tanzania (Pentecostal Assemblies of Canada) 15,000
Brethren Assemblies 12,000

Evangelical 9% of population.

Missionaries to Tanzania approximately 660 (1:33,000 people) in about 60 agencies. Missionaries from within Tanzania approximately 10.

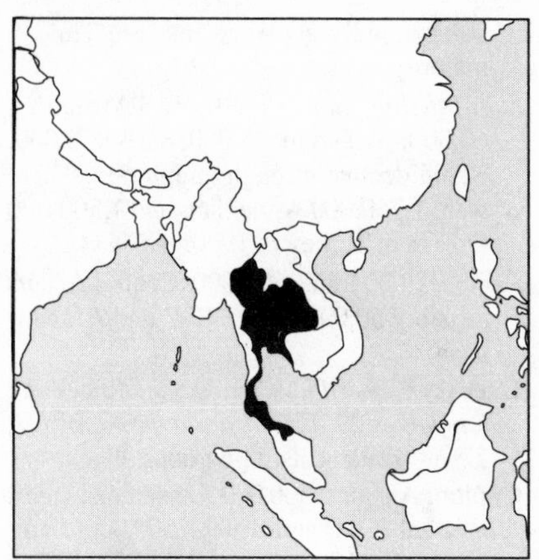

THAILAND

Area 514,000 sq.km. A fertile and well-watered land.

Population 56,600,000. Annual growth 1.7%. People per sq.km. 110.

Peoples: Four major peoples and numerous smaller groups.

Thai 80%. Four main groups. Central 19,000,000; Northern 6,000,000; Southern 4,000,000; Lao 12,500,000. The latter live in the northeast.

Chinese 12% or more. Thai-speaking 80%. A minority still use over six Chinese languages, mostly Chaochow.

Malay 3.2%. In the extreme south adjoining Malaysia.

Khmer 2.8%. Two main languages.

Tribal peoples 2%. Over 48 indigenous groups, most in the mountainous border regions. Six main groups: Mon-Khmer peoples (15 groups) 340,000; Karen (6) 280,000; Tai (9) 210,000; Miao-Yao (3) 156,000; Tibeto-Burman (10) 73,000; Austronesian (4) 8,000.

Refugees 1%. Kampucheans around 300,000; Laotians and Vietnamese 250,000; Burmese 15,000.

Literacy 84%. *Official language:* Thai. *All languages* 61. *Bible translations* 6 Bibles, 7 New Testaments, 10 portions.

Capital: Krung Thep (Bangkok) 6,043,000. Urbanization 17%.

Economy: Productive agricultural economy. Main exports are rice, pineapples, tapioca and rubber. The depletion of forest cover is worsening the cycle of droughts and floods. Rapid industrialization and development of mineral resources. The government is making a determined effort to eradicate the drug trafficking from the "Golden Triangle" in the far northwest of the country. Income/person $840 (5% of USA).

Politics: Never ruled by any Western power. Constitutional monarchy, with the popular king having a strong unifying and stabilizing role. The succession of stable governments, growth in the economy and the world collapse of Communism has boosted Thai importance and prospects.

Religion: Buddhism is the state religion, but there is freedom and all religions are seen as a bulwark against Communist ideology.

Buddhist 92%. Thai, Lao, Shan, some Chinese, etc. Much syncretism with spirit worship.

Muslim 4%. Malays and some Thai in the far south.

Chinese religions 1.6%. Many Chinese are included with the Buddhist figure.

Animist 1.4%. Among tribal peoples.

Christian 1%. Affiliated 0.72%.

Roman Catholic 0.4%. 212,000 adherents; 114,000 members. Stronger among Chinese and in Bangkok.

Protestant 0.31%. 167,000 adherents; 81,000 members. Denominations 33. Largest (adult members):

Church of Christ in Thailand (Presbyterian, Baptist, etc.) 35,000

Karen Baptist Convention 8,500

Seventh-Day Adventist Church 6,800

Lahu Church 4,000

Church Fellowships relating to Overseas Missionary Fellowship 3,200

Church Fellowships relating to WEC International 2,200

Gospel Church of Thailand (Christian & Missionary Alliance) 2,110

Thailand Baptist Churches Association (Southern Baptist) 2,100

Evangelical 0.2% of population.

Missionaries to Thailand approximately 1,030 (1:51,000 people) in 70 agencies. Missionaries from within Thailand approximately 14.

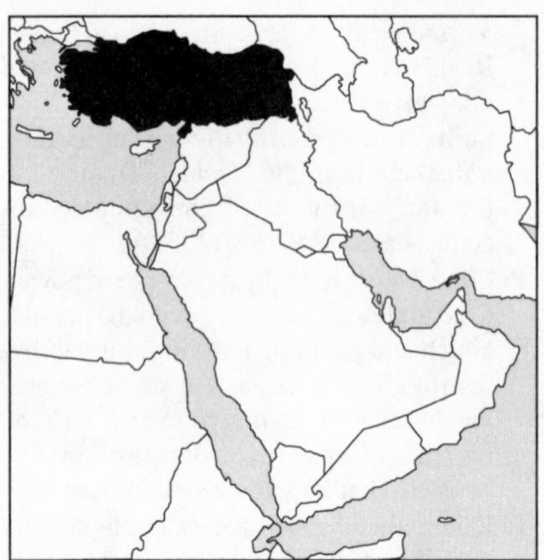

TURKEY

Area 781,000 sq.km. The country straddles two continents; 3% in Europe (Thrace), 97% in Asia (Anatolia), and controls the Bosphorus and the Dardanelles, the vital sea link between the Black Sea and Mediterranean. Its strategic position has made the area of prime importance through history.

Population 56,600,000. Annual growth 2.2%. People per sq.km. 73.

Peoples: There has been continued pressure on the ethnic minorities to conform to Turkish culture. Ethnic populations are therefore hard to assess.

Turks 80.2%. A Central Asian people that conquered and largely absorbed the indigenous peoples of the land from the eleventh century onward. The Turks are ethnically diverse, but culturally fairly homogenous. Distinctive sub-groups: Azeri 530,000 in the east, Yoruk 320,000 on the west coast.

Kurds 16%. An Indo-Iranian people in southeast Anatolia, probably related to the ancient Medes. Their ethnic identity is denied by the Turks, and by 1990 there was a growing insurgency problem in the Kurdish area.

Arabs 1.4% in South Anatolia adjoining Syria.

Muslim minorities 1.1%. Adygey 130,000; Laz 92,000; Georgian 90,000; Serbo-Croat 61,000; Albanian 61,000; Bulgarian 27,000; Gypsy 20,000, all of whom are being rapidly absorbed into the Turkish majority.

Non-Muslim minorities 0.3%. Armenian 60,000; Assyrian 25,000; Greek 8,000. Rapid decline through emigration. There were 1,750,000 Armenians and 1,500,000 Greeks in Turkey in 1900.

Refugees 1%. Iranis 600,000; Central Asians possibly 50,000 from USSR and Afghanistan.

Literacy 62%. *Official language:* Turkish. *All languages* 29. *Bible translations* 7 Bibles, 2 New Testaments, 11 portions.

Capital: Ankara 2,300,000. Other major cities: Istanbul (Constantinople) 5,500,000; Izmir (Smyrna) 1,500,000; Adana 780,000; Bursa 620,000. Urbanization 53%. Rapid growth of cities with huge slum areas in which 65% of Ankara's population and 45% of Istanbul's live.

Economy: Political instability and social unrest together with world recession led to economic crises between 1973 and 1983. Steady recovery since then, but the land is only partially industrialized. Remittances from Turks in Europe are an important source of foreign exchange. Income/person $1,200 (7% of USA).

Politics: The Turkish Ottoman Empire once stretched across North Africa, Arabia, Western Asia and Southeast Europe. Its demise and final fragmentation in World War I led to revolution and the formation of a republic in 1923. Periods of social disorder and military rule gave way to a democratic government in 1983, but with the military still retaining considerable power. Turkey is a member of NATO, but is in dispute with fellow-NATO member Greece for long-standing historic reasons and over territorial rights in the Aegean Sea and the division of Cyprus. Application has been made to join the EC.

Religion: Turkey's Ottoman Empire was for centuries the guardian of all the holy places of Islam and its chief protaganist. Since the sweeping reforms of the 1920s Turkey has officially been a secular state. In recent years Islam has become a more important political factor, making the lot of non-Muslim minorities more difficult despite the constitutional guarantee of religious freedom.

Muslim 99.5%. Sunni Muslims 85%. Alevi Shi'a 14% predominantly among Kurds. There are also Yezidis (a divergent syncretic sect) among the Kurds.

Christian 0.3%. Rapid decline. Almost entirely confined to national and foreign minorities.

Orthodox 0.23%. 120,000 adherents. Denominations 10. Largest (adherents): Armenian Orthodox Church 60,000; Greek Orthodox Church 23,000 (?); Syrian Orthodox Church 21,000.

Roman Catholic 0.02%. 15,000 adherents. Predominantly foreign residents and Assyrians.

Protestant 0.02%. 13,100 adherents; 4,500 members. Predominantly foreign residents and Armenians.

Evangelical only about 750 indigenous believers, mostly Armenian, Assyrian and Greek. Maybe 250 believers from a Muslim background.

Foreign Christians serving in Turkey approximately 100 (1:500,000 people).

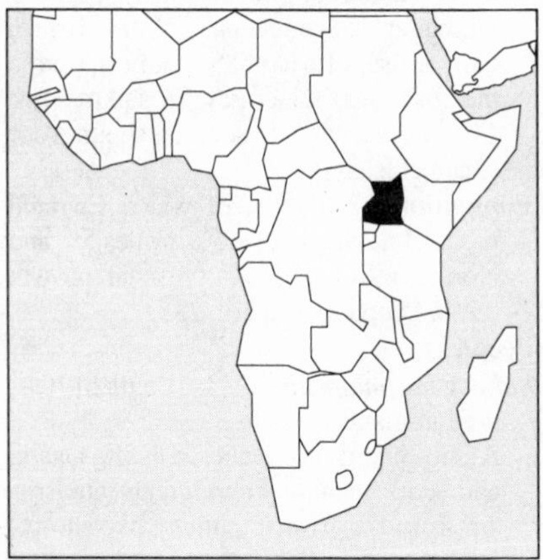

UGANDA

Area 236,000 sq.km. Much of the land is fertile and well watered. The climate is temperate in the highlands. Long known as the "Pearl of Africa."

NOTE: All following statistics are reasonable estimates; the anarchy and devastation since 1976 having been so great that accurate statistics are not available.

Population 17,600,000. Annual growth 3.4%. People per sq.km. 74. No one can estimate with accuracy the numbers who perished during Amin's dictatorship, and the subsequent civil wars, famines and tribal killings. Estimates vary from 800,000 to 2,000,000; 300,000 of these have been since 1981. Many more have fled into Kenya, Sudan and Zaire.

Peoples: Over 40 ethnic groups; three major divisions:

Bantu 65% (over 16 groups, mainly in west, southwest and south): Ganda 2,350,000; Ankole 1,200,000; Soga 1,175,000; Chiga 1,040,000; Toro-Nyoro 910,000; Nyaruanda 860,000; Luhya 400,000; Rundi 300,000; Konjo 250,000; Gwere 240,000, etc.

Nilotic 27% (12, mainly in the north and center): Teso 1,220,000; Lango 800,000; Acholi 630,000; Karamajong 300,000; Alur 280,000; Padhola 230,000; Kakwa 90,000, etc.

Sudanic 6.4% (over 10): Lugbara 544,000; Madi 176,000, etc.

Other 1.6%. Kenyans, etc.

Literacy 40%. *Official language:* English, spoken by about 10% of the population. *All languages* 43. *Bible translations* 16 Bibles, 3 New Testaments, 10 portions.

Capital: Kampala 500,000. Urbanization 14%.

Economy: The fertility of the soil could have provided a healthy economic future. The expulsion in 1972 of the Asian community, who had played such a vital role in the economy, and the chaos in the years following, have reduced the land to poverty. Many areas have been laid waste by marauding soldiers—especially in the West Nile District and Luwero Triangle northwest of Kampala. However by 1990 a slow recovery was under way. Income/person $560 (4% of USA).

Politics: Independence from Britain in 1962. An attempt at delicately balancing the political powers of the southern Bantu kingdoms and northern Nilotic peoples ended in

1967, when the Northerner Milton Obote took complete control, favoring his own tribe, the Lango. Anarchy increased until Idi Amin seized power in 1971. The crazed dictatorship of Amin brutalized the country as the army pillaged and murdered with impunity. Amin's invasion of northwest Tanzania in 1978 provoked a vigorous response, and in 1979 Tanzanian and Ugandan exile troops deposed the military regime. Sadly, bitter tribal and political rivalries have continued with much bloodshed and civil war. The Museveni government is a military-civilian regime that has allowed a limited degree of democracy.

Religion: Under Amin there were restrictions and intense persecution of Christians (often for reasons of tribalism). For a time the Muslim minority was favored. There is now freedom of religion. Most figures below are rough estimates.

Traditional religions 12%. Throughout the country, but only in a majority in four or five northeastern peoples, the Karamajong, Pokot, etc.

Muslim 5%. Most live in the northwest, but there are some sprinkled all over the country. No group has a Muslim majority, but there are large minorities among the Kakwa, Madi and Soga. Somewhat discredited since the fall of Amin.

Baha'i 2.8%.

Christian 80%. Nominal 9%, affiliated 71%.

Roman Catholic 42.3%. 6,211,000 adherents; 3,540,000 members.

Orthodox 0.14%. 20,000 adherents.

African Indigenous Churches 0.9%. 130,000 adherents; 71,000 members.

Protestant 27.6%. 4,068,000 adherents; 1,010,000 members. Largest (adherents):

Anglican Church (CMS, Bible Churchman's Missionary Society, Africa Inland Mission) 3,700,000

Pentecostal Assemblies of God 80,000 (?)

Elim Pentecostal Fellowship 60,000 (?)

Church of the Redeemed 50,000 (?)

Baptist Union (Southern Baptist, Conservative Baptist Foreign Missionary Society) 30,000

Evangelicals 24.9% of population.

Missionaries to Uganda 190 (1:77,000 people) in 28 agencies. Missionaries from within Uganda 100 (?). Many are exiles serving the Lord in other lands.

UNITED KINGDOM

Area 244,000 sq.km. Two main islands: Britain and the northeast of Ireland. A union of four kingdoms: England 53%, Scotland 32.4%, Wales 8.5%, and Northern Ireland 5.8%. Also three small autonomous states which are dependencies of the British Crown: Isle of Man 588 sq.km. (island in the Irish Sea); Guernsey 78 sq.km. (five Channel Islands); Jersey 116 sq.km. (one Channel Island).

Population 57,400,000 of which England has 83.1%, Scotland 9.2%, Wales 5% and Northern Ireland 2.7%. Annual growth 0.2%. People per sq.km. 235.

Peoples

Indigenous majorities 93%. English 76%, predominantly Anglo-Saxon; Scots 8%, Anglo-Saxon and Gaelic; Irish 5%, Gaelic and Scots (including immigrants into Britain from the Irish Republic); Welsh 4%, predominantly Celtic.

Indigenous minorities 0.9%. Jews 410,000; Gypsies 85,000.

Immigrant minorities 6%. *South Asians* 2.5%. Indian origin 700,000; Pakistani 250,000; Bangladeshi 200,000. Also refugees from East Africa 200,000. *West Indians* 1.9%. From many Caribbean countries; almost all are Blacks. *Other* 1.3%. Greeks 200,000; Italians 200,000; Arabs 150,000; Chinese 125,000; Africans 90,000; Turks, 55,000; Vietnamese 20,000.

Literacy 95%. *Official language:* English; in Wales both English and Welsh. English has become the primary language of 700 million in the world, and become the major language of international communication. *All languages* 7 indigenous, many more immigrant languages (at least 128 in London alone). *Bible translations* in indigenous languages 4 Bibles, 2 portions. There have been more translations of the Scriptures into English than in any other language.

Capital: London 10,100,000. Other major cities: Birmingham 2,800,000; Manchester 2,600,000; Bradford-Leeds 2,100,000; Glasgow 1,850,000; Liverpool 1,520,000; Newcastle-upon-Tyne 1,150,000. Urbanization 76%.

Economy: An industrialized economy—the world's first. Renewed economic growth in the '80s after years of decline through poor management, labor unrest, and the extent of public ownership in industry. The government has vigorously sought to rectify these with some success. Exploitation of North Sea oil has helped to stimulate recovery. The basic underlying ill-health of the economy is cause for concern. Income/person $10,430 (57% of USA).

Politics: Parliamentary, constitutional monarchy. The United Kingdom was formed in 1801 as a Union of Great Britain and Ireland. Southern Ireland formally seceded from the Union in 1921. The British Empire which once covered one quarter of the world has become 60 independent states, most being members of the British Commonwealth. Since 1945 the transition from a world power to a European state linked to its own continent has not been easy. The UK is a member of NATO and of the EC.

Religion: Complete religious freedom. The Church of England (Anglican) is recognized as the Established Church in England, and the Church of Scotland (Presbyterian) in Scotland. The Sovereign is recognized as the titular head of the Church of England.

Non-religious/Atheist: 26%. Many nominal "Christians" are actually secularists.

Muslim 2.7%. The actual number of Muslims is disputed, but is between 1 and 1.5 million, predominantly South Asians, but also Arabs, Turks, etc.

Jews 0.7%. Gradually declining.

Hindu 0.5%. *Sikh* 0.5%. Predominantly Indian.

Buddhist 0.2%. Chinese, etc.

Christian 69.4%. Nominal 20%. Affiliated 49.9%. Regular adult church attendance 11%; but with wide regional differences. See below:

Roman Catholic 9%. 5,100,000 adherents; 2,315,000 members. Predominantly lower class and many of Irish extraction. Highest percentage in northwest and London area.

Orthodox Churches 0.7%. 372,000 adherents; 125,000 members. Denominations 12. Predominantly Greek Cypriot, also many Eastern European refugee minorities.

Marginal 2.6%. 1,400,000 adherents; 348,000 members. Groups 14+. Largest (adult members): Jehovah's Witnesses 97,945; Mormons 67,000; Spiritualist 53,000; Scientology 45,000.

Protestant 48% including nominals. 31,200,000 adherents; 4,900,000 members. Many baptized Anglicans no longer attend church, hence the large adherent figure. Denominations 250+. Largest (adult members):

All Anglican/Episcopal (8) 2,058,000
All Presbyterian/United Reformed (14) 1,483,000
All Methodists (6) 484,700
All Baptists (10+) 226,000
All "house" churches 120,000
All other Pentecostal Churches (15+) 95,000
Other independent churches 85,000 (?)
All West Indian Churches (numerous) 80,000
Brethren assemblies 65,000 (?)

Evangelical 7% of population.

Missionaries from within UK 5,800 (1:5,300

Protestants) in 102 agencies. Missionaries to UK estimated 580, increasingly so from the Third World and USA.

VENEZUELA

Area 912,000 sq.km., with a long Caribbean coastline. A further 230,000 sq.km. of Guyana to the east is claimed by Venezuela.

Population 19,600,000. Annual growth 2.4%. People per sq.km. 21.

Peoples

Spanish-speaking 96%. Approximate composition: Mestizo 64%, European 22%, African 10%. The large Italian community has been almost entirely absorbed into the majority.

Amerindian 2.8%. Over 30 tribes. Largest: Guajiro 50,000; Warao 15,000; Piaroa 12,000; Yanomano 10,000; Carib 10,000.

Other 1.2%. Arabs 100,000; Chinese 25,000; Jews 20,000, etc.

Literacy 86%. *Official language:* Spanish. *All languages* 37. *Bible translations* 1 Bible, 6 New Testaments, 11 portions.

Capital: Caracas 4,500,000. Other major cities: Maracaibo 1,050,000; Valencia 840,000; Barquisimeto 600,000. Urbanization 83%.

Economy: Oil has been the main foreign exchange earner, but the nation's prosperity was reduced by huge foreign debt and misuse of wealth, and in 1988/9 the economy went into severe recession. There is an unhealthy gap between the rich and the poor. Income/person $3,230 (18% of USA).

Politics: Independent from Spain in 1821. A succession of revolutions and harsh dictatorships ended in 1958. Since then there has been a stable democratic government. It is the first Latin American country to have a political party recognized as one founded by Evangelicals on reformation principles.

Religion: Religious freedom is guaranteed in the constitution. The Catholic Church regained official recognition in 1964 after years of strained Church-State relations, and has a pervasively influential position.

Non-religious/Atheist 1.5%.

Muslim 0.4%. Predominantly Arab, but also an inflow of Iranis.

Animist and Spiritist 2.2%. Among tribal Amerindians and also the Spanish-speaking majority.

Christian 95.8%. Affiliated 93.5%.

Roman Catholic 90%. Practicing approximately 10%. 15,587,000 adherents.

Orthodox 0.09%. 16,000 adherents. Romanians, Greeks, Russians, Ukrainians etc., in 6 denominations.

Marginal groups 0.7%. 113,000 adherents; 35,400 members. Largest (adult members): Jehovah's Witnesses 25,300; Mormons 8,300.

Protestant 2.6%. 450,000 adherents; 187,000 members. Denominations 74 with many independent churches. Largest (adult members):

Seventh-Day Adventist Church 32,000
Assemblies of God 14,500
OVICE/AIEO (The Evangelical Alliance Mission/ORM) 13,100 (?)
Brethren 10,000 (?)
Southern Baptist Convention 8,300
The Native Church 7,500
International Church of Foursquare Gospel 4,000
Tribal Churches (New Tribes Mission) 3,800 (?)

Evangelicals 2.1% of population.

Missionaries to Venezuela 510 (1:34,000 people) in about 36 agencies. Missionaries from within Venezuela 12 (?).

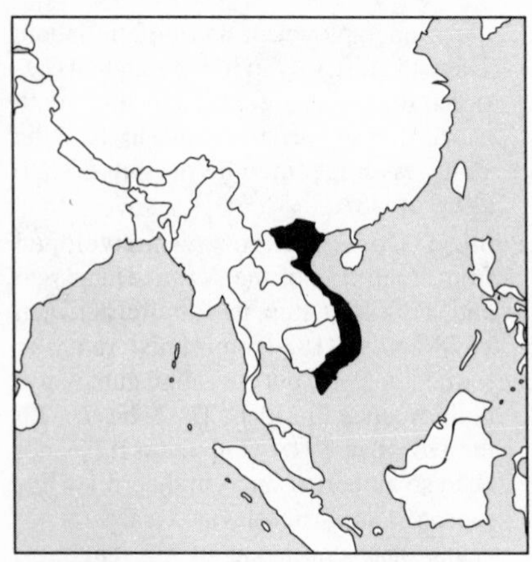

VIETNAM

Area 330,000 sq.km. Occupying the entire 2,000 km. eastern and southern coastline of Indochina.

Population 68,500,000. Annual growth 2.6%. People per sq.km. 208. Possibly 1,500,000 have fled Vietnam since 1975.

Peoples

Vietnamese 86%. Predominantly coastal people; large cultural differences between northern and southern Vietnamese.

Northern ethnic minorities 7.2%. Predominantly Sino-Tibetan; Thai-Tai (19 groups) 2,500,000; Muong 800,000; Hmong (Meo) 350,000; Yao 150,000; Nung 100,000.

Southern ethnic minorities 5.6%. About 40 different groups. Predominantly Austro-Asiatic and Austronesian (Malay) in Southern Highlands. Khmer 500,000; Cham 233,000; Jarai 200,000; Mnong 186,000; Koho 100,000; Hrey 100,000; Bru 70,000, etc.

Chinese 1%. About two-thirds fled to China and the West since 1975.

Literacy 55%. *Official language:* Vietnamese. *All languages* 62. *Bible translations* 2 Bibles, 11 New Testaments, 19 portions.

Capital: Hanoi 1,299,000. Other cities: Ho Chi Minh City (Saigon) 2,703,000, Danang 2,513,000. Urbanization 19%.

Economy: The destructive Vietnam wars have played havoc with the economy. High military expenditure, rigid socialist policies and world isolation prevent much progress. Widespread hunger and poverty. There was some private enterprise and agriculture permitted in 1989.

Politics: Communist republic declared in North Vietnam in 1945. There has been continuous warfare since 1941, under the Japanese, against the French, South Vietnam, USA and all surrounding lands. North Vietnam finally conquered the South in 1975, and Kampuchea in 1978-89. Vietnam's withdrawal from Kampuchea (Cambodia) in 1989 may end her diplomatic isolation. Worldwide rejection of Communism has scarcely affected Vietnam.

Religion: Government policy is the steady erosion of the influence of all religions in national affairs, and control of all organized religious movements. Pressures on Christians continue to be severe. Statistics below are approximations.

Non-religious/Atheist 22.5%.

Buddhist 54%. Numerous sects, and strongly permeated with Confucianism, animism and magic.

New religions 11%. Hoa Hao 1,800,000 (Buddhist offshoot), Cao Dai (Buddhist-Catholic syncretism) 3,600,000, etc.

Animist 4%. Minority ethnic groups.

Muslim 1%. Mainly Cham.

Christian 7.5%.

Roman Catholic 7%. 4,200,000 adherents.

Protestant 0.5%. 316,000 adherents; 106,000 members. Main groups (est. members):

Evangelical Church (South) 80,000
Evangelical Church (North) 10,000
Other mountain churches 5,000
Seventh-Day Adventist Church 3,600
Baptist Churches 1,900

Evangelical 0.5% of population.

YUGOSLAVIA

Area 256,000 sq.km. A Balkan state bordering on the Adriatic Sea.

Population 23,800,000. Annual growth 0.6%. People per sq.km. 93.

Peoples

Serbo-Croatian-speaking 70%. Four distinct Slavic peoples: *Serbian* 39.4%. Predominant in center and east, and mainly Orthodox. *Croatian* 21%. Mainly in northwest and along Dalmatian coast. Predominantly Catholic. *Bosnian* 6%. Serbian Muslims, but officially considered an ethnic entity in the central republic of Bosnia. *Montenegrin* 2.6%. Mainly in the south coastal republic of Montenegro. *Slovene* 8%. A Slavic people in the northwestern republic of Slovenia.

Albanian 7.8%. Majority in the Kosovo region adjoining Albania and many in Montenegro and Macedonia. Mainly Muslim; descendants of the ancient Illyrians.

Macedonian 6%. A Slavic people related to the Bulgarians in the far southern republic of Macedonia. Predominantly Orthodox.

Hungarian 2%. A large minority in Vojvodina region. Many are Catholic or Reformed Protestant.

Other minorities 7.2%. Romany Gypsies, maybe 300,000; Rumelian Turks 125,000; Bulgarians 36,000; Ukranians 30,000, etc.

Literacy 90%. *Official languages:* Serbo-Croatian, Slovene and Macedonian and, locally, six other languages. *All languages* 20. *Bible translations* 8 Bibles, 3 New Testaments, 3 portions.

Capital: Belgrade 1,600,000. Other major city: Zagreb 1,200,000. Urbanization 37%.

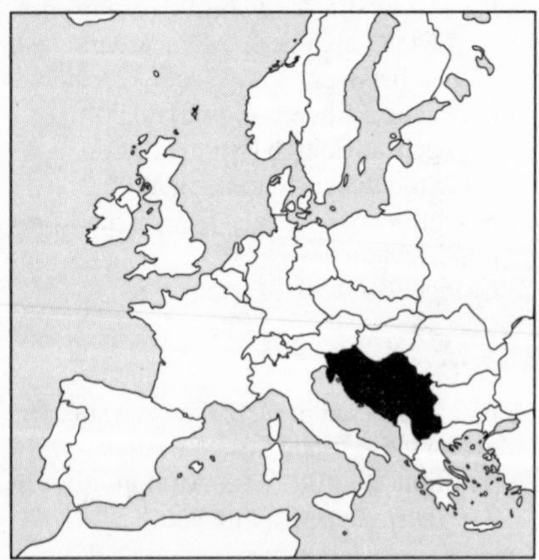

Economy: The world recession in 1979 exposed the inbuilt weaknesses of a bloated bureaucracy and excessive regionalization. There is a massive international debt, much unemployment and high inflation. The wide disparity in living standards between the wealthier north and poor south has further strained the fragile unity of the state. Average income/person $2,620 (19% of USA).

Politics: Modern Yugoslavia developed from fragments of the Austro-Hungarian and Turkish Ottoman Empire between 1878 and 1918. Communist republic formed in 1945, but non-aligned in world politics since President Tito's break with the USSR in 1948. Communism has not been so authoritarian as in other East European states. Yugoslavia is a federal socialist state consisting of six republics, two autonomous regions, three religions, eight major national groups and two alphabets! The fragmented and fierce nationalism of the various ethnic groups helped trigger off World War I, provoked intense civil war in World War II, and poses a flash-point for possible future conflict. Since Tito's death a complex collective leadership and devolution of power to the constituent republics has barely managed to keep the country together and has hampered development and economic reform. Slovene, Croatian and, above all, Albanian nationalism are the most sensitive issues today.

Religion: Atheism is actively promoted by the state in the education system. There is considerable religious freedom, though active proselytization is discouraged. There are restrictions on churches' social and cultural ministries, and some discrimination against Christians in job opportunities.

Non-religious/Atheist 18%. The Communist party has 2,200,000 members.

Muslim 11%. Bosnians, 80% of Albanians, Gypsies, Turks. Most are Sunni Muslims, a few are Shi'a. There are 2,250 functioning mosques.

Christian 71%. Affiliated 67%. Many are baptized, but do not attend church.

Orthodox 36.7%. 8,480,000 adherents Denominations 7. Mainly Serbians and Macedonians, a few Albanians.

Roman Catholic 29.7%. 6,680,000 adherents. Mainly Slovenes, Croats and Hungarians and some Albanians.

Protestant 0.7%. 162,000 adherents; 96,000 members. Denominations approximately 40. Largest (adult members):

Lutheran Churches (3) 42,000
Reformed Church (Hungarian) 20,000
Pentecostal Churches (4) (?) 11,300
Seventh-Day Adventist Church 10,600
Baptist Church 3,650
Methodist Church (Macedonian & Hungarian) 1,850

Evangelicals 0.16% of population.

Foreign Christians serving Yugoslavians estimated 25. Missionaries from within Yugoslavia estimated 10.

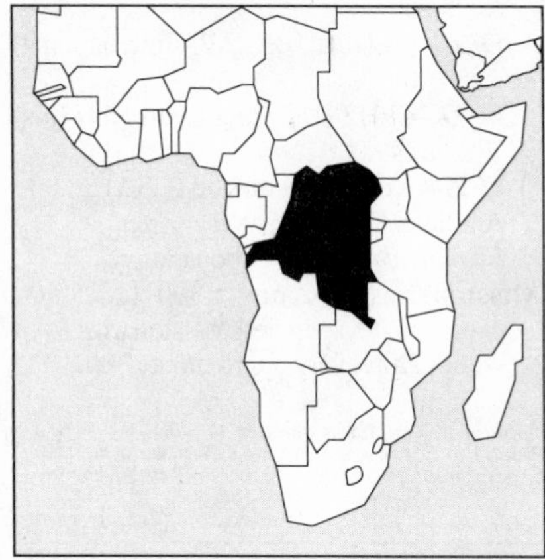

ZAIRE

Area 2,345,000 sq.km. Covering much of Central Africa's rain forest. The heavy rainfall and extensive river systems complicate communications.

Population 36,000,000. Annual growth 3.1%. People per sq.km. 15. Large areas are sparsely populated.

Peoples: An estimated 200 ethnic groups, and many more sub-groups.

Bantu peoples 80%. Center and south. Over 32 peoples with more than 100,000. Largest: Luba group 6,173,000; Mongo group 5,600,000; Kongo 4,000,000; Bemba 1,700,000; Songe 800,000; Tetela 650,000; Chokwe 550,000; Bbadha 500,000.

Adamawa Eastern 10%. Northern borderlands. Three peoples with over 100,000 each are: Zande 1,500,000; Ngbaka 800,000; Ngbandi 250,000.

Sudanic 6.7%. Northeast corner. Two peoples with 100,000 and over. Mangbetu 500,000; Lugbara 100,000.

Nilotic 2%. One major people on Uganda border: Alur 700,000.

Pygmy 0.4%. Many small groups in the northern forests.

Other 0.7%. Foreigners, Westerners, other Africans, etc.

Literacy 45%. *Official language:* French. *Trade languages:* Lingala-Bangala in north and northwest, Swahili in east and south, Luba in center and Kongo-Tuba in west. *All languages* 192. *Bible translations* 20 Bibles, 12 New Testaments, 33 portions.

Capital: Kinshasa 4,200,000. Other major cities: Kananga 1,500,000; Lubumbashi 700,000; Kisangani 500,000. Urbanization 40%.

Economy: Vast mineral resources and agricultural potential. Post-independence chaos, widespread maladminstration and corruption have enriched the powerful elite, but impoverished the nation. The road system hardly functions, trade is reduced to a trickle and profitable agricultural estates have reverted to forest. Africa's potentially most wealthy nation can no longer feed its own people, and is dependent on foreign aid. Some economies introduced since 1983 have brought slight improvements. Income/person $160 (1% of USA).

Politics: In 1960 Belgium hastily granted independence to an ill-prepared people, which led to eight years of violence, anarchy and secessionist wars. A military coup in 1965 brought General Mobutu to national leadership as an autocratic President of a one-party state. A measure of peace and stability has been restored. The sheer size, ethnic complexity and lack of communications in the country could imperil its future unity. In 1990 widespread antigovernment protests forced Mobutu to concede some form of multiparty political system in the future.

Religion: In 1972 the President decreed that only six organized religions were permitted to operate and own property: Catholic, one Protestant Church (ECZ), Kimbanguist Church, Orthodox, Muslims and Jews. The authenticity program of the government between 1971 and 1978 placed increasing controls and limitations on Christian institutions and activities. Economic and social disasters forced a dramatic reversal, so that by 1980 there was considerable religious freedom once more, though with a continued subtle pressure that equates Christian commitment with a denial of national heritage. Zaire's size and lack of statistics and communications prevent accuracy in many of the following figures—especially for the African Independent Churches.

Traditional religions 8-12%. Pockets of peoples and areas where the response to the gospel has been less.

Muslim 1.4%. Sunni Muslims predominantly in eastern towns.

Christian 88-92%. Practicing 62%.

Roman Catholic 42%. 14,000,000 adherents; 8,100,000 members.

African Indigenous Churches 15-19%. (?) Approximately 6,000,000 adherents. Kimbanguist Church 4,800,000 (?)

Protestant 28%. 9,270,000 adherents; 3,100,000 members. Almost all of the 83 Protestant Churches are member communities of the Eglise du Christ au Zaire (ECZ). Most are evangelical, some more liberal, and others marginal in their theology. Some of the larger communities (adult members):

ECZ—Disciples of Christ 330,000 (?)
ECZ—Presbyterian 320,000
ECZ—CECA (Africa Inland Mission) 310,000
ECZ—Pentecostal (ZEM, UK) 151,000
ECZ—Baptist (Canadian Baptist Overseas Mission Board) 135,000
ECZ—Baptist (Baptist Missionary Society, UK) 120,000
ECZ—Methodist (UMC) 115,000
ECZ—CEAZ (Christian & Missionary Alliance) 98,374
ECZ—CECCA (WEC International) 78,000
ECZ—CADELU (RBMU International) 50,000
ECZ—CEHZ (Unevanglized Fields Mission) 49,000 (?)
ECZ—Assemblies of God (USA) 38,000
Anglican Church 72,000

Evangelical 17.6% of population.

Missionaries to Zaire 1,300 (1:25,500 people) in 85 agencies. Missionaries from within Zaire, very approximate 300.

FOCUS FACT

Operation World, a 500-page combination resource book and prayer diary, is loaded with background facts and figures including populations, peoples, economies, politics, religions and churches throughout the world. Gives specific situations to pray for daily. To receive a copy send $7.95 (postage paid) to: Send the Light, PO Box 28, Industrial Park Road, Waynesboro, GA 30830

Calendars & Special Events

1991 CHURCH CALENDAR

JANUARY

1/Tuesday	New Year's Day Feast of the Holy Name of Our Lord Jesus Christ The Circumcision and the Name of Jesus
2/Wednesday	
3/Thursday	
4/Friday	
5/Saturday	
6/Sunday	The Epiphany of Our Lord Jesus Christ
7/Monday	
8/Tuesday	
9/Wednesday	
10/Thursday	William Laud, Archbishop of Canterbury, 1645
11/Friday	
12/Saturday	
13/Sunday	First Sunday after Epiphany Hilary, Bishop of Pointiers, 367
14/Monday	
15/Tuesday	
16/Wednesday	
17/Thursday	Anthony, Abbot in Egypt, 356
18/Friday	Week of Prayer for Christian Unity begins The Confession of Saint Peter the Apostle
19/Saturday	Wulfstan, Bishop of Worcester, 1095
20/Sunday	Second Sunday after Epiphany Ecumenical Sunday Fabian, Bishop and Martyr of Rome, 250
21/Monday	Martin Luther King's Birthday observed Agnes, Martyr at Rome, 304
22/Tuesday	Vincent, Deacon of Saragossa and Martyr, 304
23/Wednesday	Phillips Brooks, Bishop of Massachusetts, 1893
24/Thursday	
25/Friday	The Conversion of Saint Paul the Apostle
26/Saturday	Timothy and Titus, Companions of Saint Paul
27/Sunday	Third Sunday after Epiphany National Association of Evangelicals Sunday John Chrysostom, Bishop of Constantinople, 407
28/Monday	Thomas Aquinas, Priest and Friar, 1274
29/Tuesday	

1991 CHURCH CALENDAR cont.

30/Wednesday	
31/Thursday	

FEBRUARY

1/Friday	
2/Saturday	Groundhog Day The Presentation of Jesus in the Temple The Purification of Mary
3/Sunday	Fourth Sunday after Epiphany Anskar, Archbishop of Hamburg, Missionary to Denmark and Sweden, 865
4/Monday	Cornelius the Centurion
5/Tuesday	The Martyrs of Japan, 1597
6/Wednesday	
7/Thursday	
8/Friday	
9/Saturday	
10/Sunday	Last Sunday after Epiphany
11/Monday	
12/Tuesday	Shrove Tuesday, Lincoln's Birthday
13/Wednesday	Ash Wednesday, Lent begins Absalom Jones, Priest, 1818
14/Thursday	St. Valentine's Day Cyril, Monk, and Methodius, Bishop, Missionaries to the Slavs, 869, 885
15/Friday	Thomas Bray, Priest and Missionary, 1730
16/Saturday	
17/Sunday	Brotherhood Week begins
18/Monday	Washington's Birthday observed
19/Tuesday	
20/Wednesday	
21/Thursday	
22/Friday	
23/Saturday	Polycarp, Bishop and Martyr of Smyrna, 156
24/Sunday	Saint Matthias the Apostle
25/Monday	
26/Tuesday	
27/Wednesday	George Herbert, Priest, 1633
28/Thursday	

MARCH

1/Friday	World Day of Prayer David, Bishop of Menevia, Wales, c. 544
2/Saturday	Chad, Bishop of Lichfield, 672
3/Sunday	John and Charles Wesley, Priests, 1791, 1788
4/Monday	
5/Tuesday	
6/Wednesday	
7/Thursday	Perpetua and her Companions, Martyrs at Carthage, 202
8/Friday	

9/Saturday	Gregory, Bishop of Nyssa, c. 394
10/Sunday	
11/Monday	
12/Tuesday	Gregory the Great, Bishop of Rome, 604
13/Wednesday	
14/Thursday	
15/Friday	
16/Saturday	
17/Sunday	Patrick, Bishop and Missionary of Ireland, 461
18/Monday	Cyril, Bishop of Jerusalem, 386
19/Tuesday	Saint Joseph, husband of Mary
20/Wednesday	Spring begins Cuthbert, Bishop of Lindisfarne, 687
21/Thursday	Thomas Ken, Bishop of Bath and Wells, 1711
22/Friday	James DeKoven, Priest, 1879
23/Saturday	Gregory the Illuminator, Bishop and Missionary of Armenia, c. 332
24/Sunday	Palm Sunday, Holy Week begins
25/Monday	The Annunciation of Our Lord Jesus Christ to the Blessed Virgin Mary
26/Tuesday	
27/Wednesday	Charles Henry Brent, Bishop of the Philippines and of Western New York, 1929
28/Thursday	Maundy Thursday
29/Friday	Good Friday John Keble, Priest, 1866
30/Saturday	First Day of Passover
31/Sunday	Easter John Donne, Priest, 1631

APRIL

1/Monday	Frederick Denison Maurice, Priest, 1872
2/Tuesday	James Lloyd Breck, Priest, 1876
3/Wednesday	Richard, Bishop of Chichester, 1253
4/Thursday	
5/Friday	
6/Saturday	
7/Sunday	Daylight Saving Time begins
8/Monday	William Augustus Muhlenberg, Priest, 1877
9/Tuesday	William Law, Priest, 1761
10/Wednesday	
11/Thursday	George Augustus Selwyn, First Missionary Bishop of New Zealand, 1878
12/Friday	
13/Saturday	
14/Sunday	
15/Monday	
16/Tuesday	
17/Wednesday	
18/Thursday	
19/Friday	Alphege, Archbishop of Canterbury and Martyr, 1012
20/Saturday	
21/Sunday	Anselm, Archbishop of Canterbury, 1109

1991 CHURCH CALENDAR cont.

22/Monday	
23/Tuesday	
24/Wednesday	
25/Thursday	Saint Mark the Evangelist
26/Friday	
27/Saturday	
28/Sunday	
29/Monday	Catherine of Siena, 1380
30/Tuesday	

MAY

1/Wednesday	Saint Philip and Saint James, Apostles
2/Thursday	National Day of Prayer
	May Fellowship Day
	Athanasius, Bishop of Alexandria, 373
3/Friday	
4/Saturday	Monica, Mother of Augustine of Hippo, 387
5/Sunday	
6/Monday	
7/Tuesday	
8/Wednesday	Dame Julian of Norwich, c. 1417
9/Thursday	Ascension Day
	Gregory of Nazianzus, Bishop of Constantinople, 389
10/Friday	
11/Saturday	
12/Sunday	Mother's Day
	Rural Life Sunday
13/Monday	
14/Tuesday	
15/Wednesday	
16/Thursday	
17/Friday	
18/Saturday	
19/Sunday	Whit Sunday, Pentecost
	Dunstan, Archbishop of Canterbury, 988
20/Monday	Alcuin, Deacon and Abbot of Tours, 804
21/Tuesday	
22/Wednesday	
23/Thursday	
24/Friday	Jackson Kemper, First Missionary Bishop in the United States, 1870
25/Saturday	Bede, the Venerable, Priest, and Monk of Jarrow, 735
26/Sunday	Holy Trinity Sunday
	Augustine, First Archbishop of Canterbury, 605
27/Monday	Memorial Day observed
28/Tuesday	
29/Wednesday	
30/Thursday	
31/Friday	The Visitation of the Blessed Virgin Mary

JUNE

1/Saturday — Justin, Martyr at Rome, c. 167
2/Sunday — Suffering Church Sunday
The Martyrs of Lyons, 177
3/Monday — The Martyrs of Uganda, 1886
4/Tuesday
5/Wednesday — Boniface, Archbishop of Mainz, Missionary to Germany, and Martyr, 754
6/Thursday
7/Friday
8/Saturday
9/Sunday — Children's Day
Columba, Abbot of Iona, 597
10/Monday — Ephrem of Edessa, Syria, Deacon, 373
11/Tuesday — Saint Barnabas the Apostle
12/Wednesday
13/Thursday
14/Friday — Flag Day
Basil the Great, Bishop of Caesarea, 379
15/Saturday
16/Sunday — Father's Day
Joseph Butler, Bishop of Durham, 1752
17/Monday
18/Tuesday — Bernard Mizeki, Catechist and Martyr in Rhodesia, 1896
19/Wednesday
20/Thursday
21/Friday — Summer begins
22/Saturday — Alban, First Martyr of Britain, c. 304
23/Sunday
24/Monday — The Nativity of Saint John the Baptist
25/Tuesday
26/Wednesday
27/Thursday
28/Friday — Irenaeus, Bishop of Lyons, c. 202
29/Saturday — Saint Peter and Saint Paul, Apostles
30/Sunday

JULY

1/Monday
2//Tuesday — The Visitation
3/Wednesday
4/Thursday — Independence Day
5/Friday
6/Saturday
7/Sunday
8/Monday
9/Tuesday
10/Wednesday
11/Thursday — Benedict of Nursia, Abbot of Monte Cassino, c. 540
12/Friday

1991 CHURCH CALENDAR cont.

13/Saturday	
14/Sunday	
15/Monday	
16/Tuesday	
17/Wednesday	William White, Bishop of Pennsylvania, 1836
18/Thursday	
19/Friday	
20/Saturday	
21/Sunday	
22/Monday	Saint Mary Magdalene
23/Tuesday	
24/Wednesday	Thomas à Kempis, Priest, 1471
25/Thursday	Saint James the Apostle
26/Friday	The Parents of the Blessed Virgin Mary
27/Saturday	William Reed Huntington, Priest, 1909
28/Sunday	
29/Monday	Mary and Martha of Bethany
30/Tuesday	William Wilberforce, 1833
31/Wednesday	Joseph of Arimathaea

AUGUST

1/Thursday	
2/Friday	
3/Saturday	
4/Sunday	
5/Monday	
6/Tuesday	The Transfiguration of Our Lord Jesus Christ
7/Wednesday	John Mason Neale, Priest, 1866
8/Thursday	Dominic, Priest and Friar, 1221
9/Friday	
10/Saturday	Laurence, Deacon and Martyr at Rome, 258
11/Sunday	Clare, Abbess at Assisi, 1253
12/Monday	
13/Tuesday	Jeremy Taylor, Bishop of Down, Connor, and Dromore, 1667
14/Wednesday	
15/Thursday	Saint Mary the Virgin, Mother of Our Lord Jesus Christ
16/Friday	
17/Saturday	
18/Sunday	William Porcher DuBose, Priest, 1918
19/Monday	
20/Tuesday	Bernard, Abbot of Clairvaux, 1153
21/Wednesday	
22/Thursday	
23/Friday	
24/Saturday	Saint Bartholomew the Apostle
25/Sunday	Louis, King of France, 1270
26/Monday	
27/Tuesday	
28/Wednesday	Augustine, Bishop of Hippo, 430

29/Thursday
30/Friday
31/Saturday Aidan, Bishop of Lindisfarne, 651

SEPTEMBER

1/Sunday
2/Monday Labor Day
The Martyrs of New Guinea, 1942
3/Tuesday
4/Wednesday
5/Thursday
6/Friday
7/Saturday
8/Sunday
9/Monday
10/Tuesday
11/Wednesday
12/Thursday John Henry Hobart, Bishop of New York, 1830
13/Friday Cyprian, Bishop and Martyr of Carthage, 258
14/Saturday Holy Cross Day
15/Sunday
16/Monday Ninian, Bishop in Galloway, c. 430
17/Tuesday
18/Wednesday Yom Kippur
Edward Bouverie Pusey, Priest, 1882
19/Thursday Theodore of Tarsus, Archbishop of Canterbury, 690
20/Friday John Coleridge Patteson, Bishop of Melanesia, and his Companions, Martyrs, 1871
21/Saturday Saint Matthew, Apostle and Evangelist
22/Sunday
23/Monday Autumn begins
24/Tuesday
25/Wednesday Sergius, Abbot of Holy Trinity, Moscow, 1392
26/Thursday Lancelot Andrewes, Bishop of Winchester, 1626
27/Friday
28/Saturday
29/Sunday Saint Michael and All Angels
30/Monday Jerome, Priest and Monk of Bethlehem, 420

OCTOBER

1/Tuesday Remigius, Bishop of Rheims, c. 530
2/Wednesday
3/Thursday
4/Friday Francis of Assisi, Friar, 1226
5/Saturday
6/Sunday World Communion Sunday
William Tyndale, Priest, 1536
7/Monday
8/Tuesday
9/Wednesday Robert Grosseteste, Bishop of Lincoln, 1253

1991 CHURCH CALENDAR cont.

10/Thursday	
11/Friday	
12/Saturday	
13/Sunday	Laity Sunday
14/Monday	Columbus Day
15/Tuesday	Samuel Isaac Joseph Schereschewsky, Bishop of Shanghai, 1906
16/Wednesday	Hugh Latimer and Nicholas Ridley, Bishops, 1555, and Thomas Cranmer, Archbishop of Canterbury, 1556
17/Thursday	Ignatius, Bishop of Antioch and Martyr, c. 115
18/Friday	Saint Luke the Evangelist
19/Saturday	Henry Martyn, Priest and Missionary to India and Persia, 1812
20/Sunday	
21/Monday	
22/Tuesday	
23/Wednesday	Saint James of Jerusalem, Brother of Our Lord Jesus Christ and Martyr, c. 62
24/Thursday	
25/Friday	
26/Saturday	Alfred the Great, King of the West Saxons, 899
27/Sunday	Reformation Sunday Daylight Saving Time ends
28/Monday	Saint Simon and Saint Jude, Apostles
29/Tuesday	James Hannington, Bishop of Eastern Equatorial Africa, and his Companions, Martyrs, 1885
30/Wednesday	
31/Thursday	Reformation Day

NOVEMBER

1/Friday	All Saints Day World Community Day
2/Saturday	Commemoration of All Faithful Departed
3/Sunday	International Bible Sunday Richard Hooker, Priest, 1600
4/Monday	
5/Tuesday	General Election Day
6/Wednesday	
7/Thursday	Willibrord, Archbishop of Utrecht, Missionary to Frisia, 739
8/Friday	
9/Saturday	
10/Sunday	Stewardship Day Leo the Great, Bishop of Rome, 461
11/Monday	Veterans Day Martin, Bishop of Tours, 397
12/Tuesday	Charles Simeon, Priest, 1836
13/Wednesday	
14/Thursday	Consecration of Samuel Seabury, First American Bishop, 1784
15/Friday	
16/Saturday	Margaret, Queen of Scotland, 1093
17/Sunday	Bible Sunday

	Hugh, Bishop of Lincoln, 1200
18/Monday	Hilda, Abbess of Whitby, 680
19/Tuesday	Elizabeth, Princess of Hungary, 1231
20/Wednesday	
21/Thursday	
22/Friday	
23/Saturday	Clement, Bishop of Rome, c. 100
24/Sunday	Last Sunday after Pentecost Thanksgiving Sunday
25/Monday	
26/Tuesday	
27/Wednesday	
28/Thursday	Thanksgiving Day
29/Friday	
30/Saturday	Saint Andrew the Apostle

DECEMBER

1/Sunday	First Sunday of Advent Nicholas Ferrar, Deacon, 1637
2/Monday	Channing Moore Williams, Missionary Bishop in China and Japan, 1910
3/Tuesday	
4/Wednesday	John of Damascus, Priest, c. 760
5/Thursday	Clement of Alexandria, Priest, c. 210
6/Friday	Nicholas, Bishop of Myra, c. 342
7/Saturday	Ambrose, Bishop of Milan, 397
8/Sunday	Second Sunday of Advent
9/Monday	
10/Tuesday	
11/Wednesday	
12/Thursday	
13/Friday	
14/Saturday	
15/Sunday	Third Sunday of Advent
16/Monday	
17/Tuesday	
18/Wednesday	
19/Thursday	
20/Friday	
21/Saturday	Saint Thomas the Apostle
22/Sunday	Fourth Sunday of Advent Winter begins
23/Monday	
24/Tuesday	
25/Wednesday	Christmas Day
26/Thursday	Saint Stephen, Deacon and Martyr
27/Friday	Saint John, Apostle and Evangelist
28/Saturday	The Holy Innocents
29/Sunday	
30/Monday	
31/Tuesday	

1991 EVENTS CALENDAR

January 6–13

Universal Week of Prayer

Harry Genet, World Evangelical Fellowship, P.O. Box WEF, Wheaton, IL 60189 708-668-0440

January 8–11

Fellowship of Christian Educators Vocational Staff Conference, Orlando, FL

Jack L. Clark, The Fellowship of Christian Educators, ON345 Willow Road, Wheaton, IL 60187 708-665-4667

January 8–11

National Youth Leader's Convention, Joplin, MO

Dick Gibson, Christ in Youth 417-781-2273

January 18–20

Missions Fest '91,Calvary Temple, Winnipeg, MB

Ike Bergen, Missions Fest '91, 228 Notre Dame Avenue, Suite 606, Winnipeg, MB R3B 1N7 Canada 204-667-0153

January 18–25

Week of Prayer for Christian Unity, sponsored by World Council of Churches and the Pontifical Council for Promoting Christian Unity

James T. Gardiner, Graymore Ecumenical Institute, 475 Riverside Drive, New York, NY 10115 312-870-2330

January 21–25

Federal Seminar for College Students, Washington, DC

Don Brown, National Association of Evangelicals, 450 Gundersen Drive, Carol Stream, IL 60188 708-665-0500

January 23–26

Institute for Successful Church Leadership, Crystal Cathedral, Garden Grove, CA

Robert Schuller Institute, 12141 Lewis Street, Garden Grove, CA 92640 714-971-4133

January 25–27

Missions Fest '91, Calgary, AB

Roy Krohn, Missions Fest '91, 110-11th Avenue SW, Suite 200, Calgary, AB T2R 0B8 Canada 403-237-7722

January 26–30

48th annual National Religious Broadcasters Convention and Exposition (NRB 91), Washington, DC

National Religious Broadcasters, P.O. Box 1926, Morristown, NJ 07962-1926 201-428-5400

January 27

National Association of Evangelicals Sunday

Don Brown, National Association of Evangelicals, 450 Gundersen Drive, Carol Stream, IL 60188 708-665-0500

January and February

Afro-American Evangelicals Museum Exhibit, Billy Graham Center, Wheaton, IL

Billy Graham Center Museum, Wheaton College, Wheaton, IL 60187 708-260-5909

February 1–3

Missions Fest '91, Vancouver, BC

Richard Dodding Missions Fest, P.O. Box 80864, Burnaby, BC V5H 3Y1 Canada 604-524-9944

February 7–29

7th Assembly of the World Council of Churches (Held every 10 years), Canberra, Australia

Rev. Joan B. Campbell, World Council of Churches, 475 Riverside Drive, Room 1062, New York, NY 10115 212-870-2533

February 10–March 31

50 Days to Welcome Christ to My Church

The Chapel of the Air, P.O. Box 30, Wheaton, IL 60189 708-668-7292

February 19–21

First National Conference for Ministry Wives, Orlando, FL

Dr. Michael Duduit, Preaching Magazine, 1529 Cesery Blvd., Jacksonville, FL 32211 904-743-5994

February 19–21
National Conference on Preaching, Orlando, FL
Dr. Michael Duduit, Preaching Magazine, 1529 Cesery Blvd., Jacksonville, FL 32211 904-743-5994

March 1
World Day of Prayer
Don Brown, National Association of Evangelicals, 450 Gundersen Drive, Carol Stream, IL 60188 708-665-0500

March 5–7
49th Annual Convention, National Association of Evangelicals, St. Louis, MO
Don Brown, National Association of Evangelicals, 450 Gundersen Drive, Carol Stream, IL 60188 708-665-0500

March 31–April 6
National Religious Books Week
Doug Ross, Evangelical Christian Publishers Association, 950 W. Southern Avenue, Suite 102, Tempe, AZ 85282 602-966-3998

March through May
Sacred Arts Museum Exhibit, Billy Graham Center, Wheaton, IL
Billy Graham Center Museum, Wheaton College, Wheaton, IL 60187 708-260-5909

April 15–20
Institute of Biblical Counseling with Larry Crabb and Dan Allender, Coral Ridge Presbyterian Church, Fort Lauderdale, FL
Coral Ridge Presbyterian Church, 5555 North Federal Highway, Fort Lauderdale, FL 33308 305-771-8840

May 2
National Day of Prayer
National Day of Prayer Task Force, P.O. Box 6826, San Bernardino, CA 92412 714-882-9932

May 6–8
Evangelical Press Association Convention, Pheasant Run Resort, St. Charles, IL
Gary Warner, Evangelical Press Association, P.O. Box 4550, Overland Park, KS 66204 913-381-2017

May 21–26
Christian and Missionary Alliance 94th General Council, Denver, CO
Bobbie Reed Christian and Missionary Alliance, P.O. Box 35000, Colorado Springs, CO 80935-3500 719-599-5999

June 2
Suffering Church Sunday
Open Doors with Brother Andrew, P.O. Box 27001, Santa Ana, CA 92799 714-531-6000

June 11–13
Prison Ministry Conference, Wheaton College, Wheaton, IL
Institute for Prison Ministries, Wheaton College, Wheaton, IL 60187 708-260-3727

June 13–15
Evangelicals, Voluntary Associations and American Public Life Conference, Billy Graham Center at Wheaton College
Institute for the Study of American Evangelicals, Wheaton College, Wheaton, IL 60187 708-260-5437

June 17–21
107th Annual Conference of the Evangelical Free Church of America, Hartford, CT
Evangelical Free Church of America, 1515 E. 66th Street, Minneapolis, MN 55423 612-866-3343

June 21–17
Biennial General Convention of the Pentecostal Church of God, Tampa, FL
Ronald R. Minor, Pentecostal Church of God, P.O. Box 850, Joplin, MO 64802 417-624-7050

June 26–29
High Praises Family Conference, Tulsa, OK
Lisa Taylor, Carman Ministries, P.O. Box 701050, Tulsa, OK 74170 918-258-HPFC

June 26–30
113th Annual Meeting of the Baptist General Conference, Bethel College, St. Paul, MN
Calvin E. Fernlund, Baptist General Conference, 2002 S. Arlington Heights Road, Arlington Heights, IL 60005 800-323-4215

June through August
Prison Ministry Museum Exhibit, Billy Graham Center, Wheaton, IL
Billy Graham Center Museum, Wheaton College, Wheaton, IL 60187 708-260-5909

July 1–5
Joni and Friends Family Retreat, Spruce Lake Retreat Center, PA
John Wern, Joni and Friends, P.O. Box 3333, Agoura Hills, CA 91301 818-707-5664

July 13–18
Christian Booksellers Association Convention, Orlando, FL
Dorothy Hull, Christian Booksellers Association, 2620 Venetucci Blvd., Colorado Springs, CO 80906-4000 719-576-7880

July 17–20
ACMC '91, Wheaton College, Wheaton, IL
Kenneth Campbell, Association of Church Mission Committees, P.O. Box ACMC, Wheaton, IL 60189-8000 708-260-1660

August 19–21
2nd Annual Church Planting Executives Conference, International Bible Society, Colorado Springs, CO
Tom Youngblood, International Bible Society, P.O. Box 62970, Colorado Springs, CO 80962-2970 800-448-0456

September 22–25
Christian Stewardship Association 29th Annual Conference, Minneapolis, MN
Edward J. Hales, Christian Stewardship Association, 917 Beville Road, Suite C, South Daytona, FL 32119 904-760-3170

October 9–12
Possibility Thinking Women's Conference, Crystal Cathedral, Garden Grove, CA
Robert Schuller Institute, 12141 Lewis Street, Garden Grove, CA 92640 714-971-4133

October 27–November 3
Pornography Awareness Week
Tim Wildmon, American Family Association, P.O. Drawer 2440, Tupelo, MS 38803 601-844-5036

November 3
International Bible Sunday
International Bible Society, P.O. Box 62970, Colorado Springs, CO 80962-2970 719-488-9200

November 3–9
National Religious Books Week
Doug Ross, Evangelical Christian Publishers Association, 950 W. Southern Avenue, Suite 102, Tempe, AZ 85282 602-966-3998

THREE-YEAR CALENDAR OF MOVABLE HOLIDAYS

Year	*Ash Wednesday*	*Easter*	*Pentecost*	*Labor Day*	*Election Day*	*Thanksgiving*	*1st Sunday Advent*
1991	Feb 13	Mar 31	May 19	Sep 2	Nov 5	Nov 28	Dec 1
1992	Mar 14	Apr 19	Jun 7	Sep 7	Nov 3	Nov 26	Nov 29
1993	Feb 24	Apr 11	May 30	Sep 6	Nov 2	Nov 25	Nov 28

1991 Calendar

JANUARY

S	M	T	W	T	F	S
		1	2	3	4	5
6	7	8	9	10	11	12
13	14	15	16	17	18	19
20	21	22	23	24	25	26
27	28	29	30	31		

FEBRUARY

S	M	T	W	T	F	S
				1	2	3	4
5	6	7	8	9	10	11
12	13	14	15	16	17	18
19	20	21	22	23	24	25
26	27	28				

MARCH

S	M	T	W	T	F	S
			1	2	3	4
5	6	7	8	9	10	11
12	13	14	15	16	17	18
19	20	21	22	23	24	25
26	27	28	29	30	31	

APRIL

S	M	T	W	T	F	S
1	2	3	4	5	6	7
8	9	10	11	12	13	14
15	16	17	18	19	20	21
22	23	24	25	26	27	28
29	30					

MAY

S	M	T	W	T	F	S
					1	2
3	4	5	6	7	8	9
10	11	12	13	14	15	16
17	18	19	20	21	22	23
24	25	26	27	28	29	30
31						

JUNE

S	M	T	W	T	F	S
				1	2	3
4	5	6	7	8	9	10
11	12	13	14	15	16	17
18	19	20	21	22	23	24
25	26	27	28	29	30	

JULY

S	M	T	W	T	F	S
1	2	3	4	5	6	7
8	9	10	11	12	13	14
15	16	17	18	19	20	21
22	23	24	25	26	27	28
29	30	31				

AUGUST

S	M	T	W	T	F	S
		1	2	3	4	5
6	7	8	9	10	11	12
13	14	15	16	17	18	19
20	21	22	23	24	25	26
27	28	29	30	31		

SEPTEMBER

S	M	T	W	T	F	S
1	2	3	4	5	6	7
8	9	10	11	12	13	14
15	16	17	18	19	20	21
22	23	24	25	26	27	28
29	30					

OCTOBER

S	M	T	W	T	F	S
	1	2	3	4	5	6
7	8	9	10	11	12	13
14	15	16	17	18	19	20
21	22	23	24	25	26	27
28	29	30	31			

NOVEMBER

S	M	T	W	T	F	S
			1	2	3	4
5	6	7	8	9	10	11
12	13	14	15	16	17	18
19	20	21	22	23	24	25
26	27	28	29	30		

DECEMBER

S	M	T	W	T	F	S
1	2	3	4	5	6	7
8	9	10	11	12	13	14
15	16	17	18	19	20	21
22	23	24	25	26	27	28
29	30	31				

1992 Calendar

JANUARY

S	M	T	W	T	F	S
			1	2	3	4
5	6	7	8	9	10	11
12	13	14	15	16	17	18
19	20	21	22	23	24	25
26	27	28	29	30	31	

FEBRUARY

S	M	T	W	T	F	S
						1
2	3	4	5	6	7	8
9	10	11	12	13	14	15
16	17	18	19	20	21	22
23	24	25	26	27	28	29

MARCH

S	M	T	W	T	F	S
1	2	3	4	5	6	7
8	9	10	11	12	13	14
15	16	17	18	19	20	21
22	23	24	25	26	27	28
29	30	31				

APRIL

S	M	T	W	T	F	S
			1	2	3	4
5	6	7	8	9	10	11
12	13	14	15	16	17	18
19	20	21	22	23	24	25
26	27	28	29	30		

MAY

S	M	T	W	T	F	S
					1	2
3	4	5	6	7	8	9
10	11	12	13	14	15	16
17	18	19	20	21	22	23
24	25	26	27	28	29	30
31						

JUNE

S	M	T	W	T	F	S
	1	2	3	4	5	6
7	8	9	10	11	12	13
14	15	16	17	18	19	20
21	22	23	24	25	26	27
28	29	30				

JULY

S	M	T	W	T	F	S
			1	2	3	4
5	6	7	8	9	10	11
12	13	14	15	16	17	18
19	20	21	22	23	24	25
26	27	28	29	30	31	

AUGUST

S	M	T	W	T	F	S
						1
2	3	4	5	6	7	8
9	10	11	12	13	14	15
16	17	18	19	20	21	22
23	24	25	26	27	28	29
30	31					

SEPTEMBER

S	M	T	W	T	F	S
		1	2	3	4	5
6	7	8	9	10	11	12
13	14	15	16	17	18	19
20	21	22	23	24	25	26
27	28	29	30			

OCTOBER

S	M	T	W	T	F	S
				1	2	3
4	5	6	7	8	9	10
11	12	13	14	15	16	17
18	19	20	21	22	23	24
25	26	27	28	29	30	31

NOVEMBER

S	M	T	W	T	F	S
1	2	3	4	5	6	7
8	9	10	11	12	13	14
15	16	17	18	19	20	21
22	23	24	25	26	27	28
29	30					

DECEMBER

S	M	T	W	T	F	S
	1	2	3	4	5	6
7	8	9	10	11	12	13
14	15	16	17	18	19	20
21	22	23	24	25	26	27
28	29	30	31			

1993 Calendar

JANUARY

S	M	T	W	T	F	S
					1	2
3	4	5	6	7	8	9
10	11	12	13	14	15	16
17	18	19	20	21	22	23
24	25	26	27	28	29	30
31						

FEBRUARY

S	M	T	W	T	F	S
	1	2	3	4	5	6
7	8	9	10	11	12	13
14	15	16	17	18	19	20
21	22	23	24	25	26	27
28						

MARCH

S	M	T	W	T	F	S
	1	2	3	4	5	6
7	8	9	10	11	12	13
14	15	16	17	18	19	20
21	22	23	24	25	26	27
28	29	30	31			

APRIL

S	M	T	W	T	F	S
				1	2	3
4	5	6	7	8	9	10
11	12	13	14	15	16	17
18	19	20	21	22	23	24
25	26	27	28	29	30	

MAY

S	M	T	W	T	F	S
						1
2	3	4	5	6	7	8
9	10	11	12	13	14	15
16	17	18	19	20	21	22
23	24	25	26	27	28	29
30	31					

JUNE

S	M	T	W	T	F	S
		1	2	3	4	5
6	7	8	9	10	11	12
13	14	15	16	17	18	19
20	21	22	23	24	25	26
27	28	29	30			

JULY

S	M	T	W	T	F	S
				1	2	3
4	5	6	7	8	9	10
11	12	13	14	15	16	17
18	19	20	21	22	23	24
25	26	27	28	29	30	31

AUGUST

S	M	T	W	T	F	S
1	2	3	4	5	6	7
8	9	10	11	12	13	14
15	16	17	18	19	20	21
22	23	24	25	26	27	28
29	30	31				

SEPTEMBER

S	M	T	W	T	F	S
			1	2	3	4
5	6	7	8	9	10	11
12	13	14	15	16	17	18
19	20	21	22	23	24	25
26	27	28	29	30		

OCTOBER

S	M	T	W	T	F	S
					1	2
3	4	5	6	7	8	9
10	11	12	13	14	15	16
17	18	19	20	21	22	23
24	25	26	27	28	29	30
31						

NOVEMBER

S	M	T	W	T	F	S
	1	2	3	4	5	6
7	8	9	10	11	12	13
14	15	16	17	18	19	20
21	22	23	24	25	26	27
28	29	30				

DECEMBER

S	M	T	W	T	F	S
			1	2	3	4
5	6	7	8	9	10	11
12	13	14	15	16	17	18
19	20	21	22	23	24	25
26	27	28	29	30	31	

1994 Calendar

JANUARY

S	M	T	W	T	F	S
						1
2	3	4	5	6	7	8
9	10	11	12	13	14	15
16	17	18	19	20	21	22
23	24	25	26	27	28	29
30	31					

FEBRUARY

S	M	T	W	T	F	S
		1	2	3	4	5
6	7	8	9	10	11	12
13	14	15	16	17	18	19
20	21	22	23	24	25	26
27	28					

MARCH

S	M	T	W	T	F	S
		1	2	3	4	5
6	7	8	9	10	11	12
13	14	15	16	17	18	19
20	21	22	23	24	25	26
27	28	29	30	31		

APRIL

S	M	T	W	T	F	S
					1	2
3	4	5	6	7	8	9
10	11	12	13	14	15	16
17	18	19	20	21	22	23
24	25	26	27	28	29	30

MAY

S	M	T	W	T	F	S
1	2	3	4	5	6	7
8	9	10	11	12	13	14
15	16	17	18	19	20	21
22	23	24	25	26	27	28
29	30	31				

JUNE

S	M	T	W	T	F	S
			1	2	3	4
5	6	7	8	9	10	11
12	13	14	15	16	17	18
19	20	21	22	23	24	25
26	27	28	29	30		

JULY

S	M	T	W	T	F	S
					1	2
3	4	5	6	7	8	9
10	11	12	13	14	15	16
17	18	19	20	21	22	23
24	25	26	27	28	29	30
31						

AUGUST

S	M	T	W	T	F	S
	1	2	3	4	5	6
7	8	9	10	11	12	13
14	15	16	17	18	19	20
21	22	23	24	25	26	27
28	29	30	31			

SEPTEMBER

S	M	T	W	T	F	S
				1	2	3
4	5	6	7	8	9	10
11	12	13	14	15	16	17
18	19	20	21	22	23	24
25	26	27	28	29	30	

OCTOBER

S	M	T	W	T	F	S
						1
2	3	4	5	6	7	8
9	10	11	12	13	14	15
16	17	18	19	20	21	22
23	24	25	26	27	28	29
30	31					

NOVEMBER

S	M	T	W	T	F	S
		1	2	3	4	5
6	7	8	9	10	11	12
13	14	15	16	17	18	19
20	21	22	23	24	25	26
27	28	29	30			

DECEMBER

S	M	T	W	T	F	S
				1	2	3
4	5	6	7	8	9	10
11	12	13	14	15	16	17
18	19	20	21	22	23	24
25	26	27	28	29	30	31

1995 Calendar

JANUARY

S	M	T	W	T	F	S
1	2	3	4	5	6	7
8	9	10	11	12	13	14
15	16	17	18	19	20	21
22	23	24	25	26	27	28
29	30	31				

FEBRUARY

S	M	T	W	T	F	S
			1	2	3	4
5	6	7	8	9	10	11
12	13	14	15	16	17	18
19	20	21	22	23	24	25
26	27	28				

MARCH

S	M	T	W	T	F	S
			1	2	3	4
5	6	7	8	9	10	11
12	13	14	15	16	17	18
19	20	21	22	23	24	25
26	27	28	29	30	31	

APRIL

S	M	T	W	T	F	S
						1
2	3	4	5	6	7	8
9	10	11	12	13	14	15
16	17	18	19	20	21	22
23	24	25	26	27	28	29
30						

MAY

S	M	T	W	T	F	S
	1	2	3	4	5	6
7	8	9	10	11	12	13
14	15	16	17	18	19	20
21	22	23	24	25	26	27
28	29	30	31			

JUNE

S	M	T	W	T	F	S
				1	2	3
4	5	6	7	8	9	10
11	12	13	14	15	16	17
18	19	20	21	22	23	24
25	26	27	28	29	30	

JULY

S	M	T	W	T	F	S
						1
2	3	4	5	6	7	8
9	10	11	12	13	14	15
16	17	18	19	20	21	22
23	24	25	26	27	28	29
30	31					

AUGUST

S	M	T	W	T	F	S
		1	2	3	4	5
6	7	8	9	10	11	12
13	14	15	16	17	18	19
20	21	22	23	24	25	26
27	28	29	30	31		

SEPTEMBER

S	M	T	W	T	F	S
					1	2
3	4	5	6	7	8	9
10	11	12	13	14	15	16
17	18	19	20	21	22	23
24	25	26	27	28	29	30

OCTOBER

S	M	T	W	T	F	S
1	2	3	4	5	6	7
8	9	10	11	12	13	14
15	16	17	18	19	20	21
22	23	24	25	26	27	28
29	30	31				

NOVEMBER

S	M	T	W	T	F	S
			1	2	3	4
5	6	7	8	9	10	11
12	13	14	15	16	17	18
19	20	21	22	23	24	25
26	27	28	29	30		

DECEMBER

S	M	T	W	T	F	S
					1	2
3	4	5	6	7	8	9
10	11	12	13	14	15	16
17	18	19	20	21	22	23
24	25	26	27	28	29	30

1996 Calendar

JANUARY

S	M	T	W	T	F	S
	1	2	3	4	5	6
7	8	9	10	11	12	13
14	15	16	17	18	19	20
21	22	23	24	25	26	27
28	29	30	31			

FEBRUARY

S	M	T	W	T	F	S
				1	2	3
4	5	6	7	8	9	10
11	12	13	14	15	16	17
18	19	20	21	22	23	24
25	26	27	28	29		

MARCH

S	M	T	W	T	F	S
					1	2
3	4	5	6	7	8	9
10	11	12	13	14	15	16
17	18	19	20	21	22	23
24	25	26	27	28	29	30
31						

APRIL

S	M	T	W	T	F	S
	1	2	3	4	5	6
7	8	9	10	11	12	13
14	15	16	17	18	19	20
21	22	23	24	25	26	27
28	29	30				

MAY

S	M	T	W	T	F	S
			1	2	3	4
5	6	7	8	9	10	11
12	13	14	15	16	17	18
19	20	21	22	23	24	25
26	27	28	29	30	31	

JUNE

S	M	T	W	T	F	S
						1
2	3	4	5	6	7	8
9	10	11	12	13	14	15
16	17	18	19	20	21	22
23	24	25	26	27	28	29
30						

JULY

S	M	T	W	T	F	S
	1	2	3	4	5	6
7	8	9	10	11	12	13
14	15	16	17	18	19	20
21	22	23	24	25	26	27
28	29	30	31			

AUGUST

S	M	T	W	T	F	S
				1	2	3
4	5	6	7	8	9	10
11	12	13	14	15	16	17
18	19	20	21	22	23	24
25	26	27	28	29	30	31

SEPTEMBER

S	M	T	W	T	F	S
1	2	3	4	5	6	7
8	9	10	11	12	13	14
15	16	17	18	19	20	21
22	23	24	25	26	27	28
29	30					

OCTOBER

S	M	T	W	T	F	S
	1	2	3	4	5	6
7	8	9	10	11	12	13
14	15	16	17	18	19	20
21	22	23	24	25	26	27
28	29	30	31			

NOVEMBER

S	M	T	W	T	F	S
					1	2
3	4	5	6	7	8	9
10	11	12	13	14	15	16
17	18	19	20	21	22	23
24	25	26	27	28	29	30

DECEMBER

S	M	T	W	T	F	S
1	2	3	4	5	6	7
8	9	10	11	12	13	14
15	16	17	18	19	20	21
22	23	24	25	26	27	28
29	30					

Ready-Reference Calendar

For ascertaining any day of the week for any given time from 1800 to 2050 inclusive.

Common Years, 1800 to 2050	JAN	FEB	MAR	APR	MAY	JUN	JUL	AUG	SEP	OCT	NOV	DEC
1801 1829 1857 1885 1914 1942 1970 1998 2026 1807 1835 1863 1891 1925 1953 1981 2009 2037 1818 1846 1874 1903 1931 1959 1987 2015 2043	4	7	7	3	5	1	3	6	2	4	7	2
1802 1830 1858 1886 1915 1943 1971 1999 2027 1813 1841 1869 1897 1926 1954 1982 2010 2038 1819 1847 1875 1909 1937 1965 1993 2021 2049	5	1	1	4	6	2	4	7	3	5	1	3
1803 1831 1859 1887 1921 1949 1977 2005 2033 1814 1842 1870 1898 1927 1955 1983 2011 2039 1825 1853 1881 1910 1938 1966 1994 2022 2050	6	2	2	5	7	3	5	1	4	6	2	4
1805 1833 1861 1889 1907 1935 1963 1991 2019 2047 1811 1839 1867 1895 1918 1946 1974 2002 2030 1822 1850 1878 1901 1929 1957 1985 2013 2041	2	5	5	1	3	6	1	4	7	2	5	7
1800 1823 1851 1879 1913 1941 1969 1997 2025 1806 1834 1862 1890 1919 1947 1975 2003 2031 1817 1845 1873 1902 1930 1958 1986 2014 2042	3	6	6	2	4	7	2	5	1	3	6	1
1809 1837 1865 1893 1911 1939 1967 1995 2023 1815 1843 1871 1899 1922 1950 1978 2006 2034 1826 1854 1882 1905 1933 1961 1989 2017 2045	7	3	3	6	1	4	6	2	5	7	3	5
1810 1838 1866 1894 1917 1945 1973 2001 2029 1821 1849 1877 1900 1923 1951 1979 2007 2035 1827 1855 1883 1906 1934 1962 1990 2018 2046	1	4	4	7	2	5	7	3	6	1	4	6
Leap Year, 1804 to 2048		29										
1804 1832 1860 1888 1928 1956 1984 2012 2040	7	3	4	7	2	5	7	3	6	1	4	6
1808 1836 1864 1892 1904 1932 1960 1988 2016 2044	5	1	2	5	7	3	5	1	4	6	2	4
1812 1840 1868 1896 1908 1936 1964 1992 2020 2048	3	6	7	3	5	1	3	6	2	4	7	2
1816 1844 1872 1912 1940 1968 1996 2024	1	4	5	1	3	6	1	4	7	2	5	7
1820 1848 1876 1916 1944 1972 2000 2028	6	2	3	6	1	4	6	2	5	7	3	5
1824 1852 1880 1920 1948 1976 2004 2032	4	7	1	4	6	2	4	7	3	5	1	3
1828 1856 1884 1924 1952 1980 2008 2036	2	5	6	2	4	7	2	5	1	3	6	1

1	2	3	4	5	6	7
Monday 1	Tuesday 1	Wednesday . 1	Thursday 1	Friday 1	Saturday 1	SUNDAY 1
Tuesday 2	Wednesday . 2	Thursday 2	Friday 2	Saturday 2	SUNDAY 2	Monday 2
Wednesday . 3	Thursday 3	Friday 3	Saturday 3	SUNDAY 3	Monday 3	Tuesday 3
Thursday 4	Friday 4	Saturday 4	SUNDAY 4	Monday 4	Tuesday 4	Wednesday . 4
Friday 5	Saturday 5	SUNDAY 5	Monday 5	Tuesday 5	Wednesday . 5	Thursday 5
Saturday 6	SUNDAY 6	Monday 6	Tuesday 6	Wednesday . 6	Thursday 6	Friday 6
SUNDAY 7	Monday 7	Tuesday 7	Wednesday . 7	Thursday 7	Friday 7	Saturday 7
Monday 8	Tuesday 8	Wednesday . 8	Thursday 8	Friday 8	Saturday 8	SUNDAY 8
Tuesday 9	Wednesday . 9	Thursday 9	Friday 9	Saturday 9	SUNDAY 9	Monday 9
Wednesday 10	Thursday ... 10	Friday 10	Saturday ... 10	SUNDAY ... 10	Monday 10	Tuesday 10
Thursday ... 11	Friday 11	Saturday ... 11	SUNDAY ... 11	Monday 11	Tuesday 11	Wednesday 11
Friday 12	Saturday ... 12	SUNDAY ... 12	Monday 12	Tuesday 12	Wednesday 12	Thursday ... 12
Saturday ... 13	SUNDAY ... 13	Monday 13	Tuesday 13	Wednesday 13	Thursday ... 13	Friday 13
SUNDAY ... 14	Monday 14	Tuesday 14	Wednesday 14	Thursday ... 14	Friday 14	Saturday ... 14
Monday 15	Tuesday 15	Wednesday 15	Thursday ... 15	Friday 15	Saturday ... 15	SUNDAY ... 15
Tuesday 16	Wednesday 16	Thursday ... 16	Friday 16	Saturday ... 16	SUNDAY ... 16	Monday 16
Wednesday 17	Thursday ... 17	Friday 17	Saturday ... 17	SUNDAY ... 17	Monday 17	Tuesday 17
Thursday ... 18	Friday 18	Saturday ... 18	SUNDAY ... 18	Monday 18	Tuesday 18	Wednesday 18
Friday 19	Saturday ... 19	SUNDAY ... 19	Monday 19	Tuesday 19	Wednesday 19	Thursday ... 19
Saturday ... 20	SUNDAY ... 20	Monday 20	Tuesday 20	Wednesday 20	Thursday ... 20	Friday 20
SUNDAY ... 21	Monday 21	Tuesday 21	Wednesday 21	Thursday ... 21	Friday 21	Saturday ... 21
Monday 22	Tuesday 22	Wednesday 22	Thursday ... 22	Friday 22	Saturday ... 22	SUNDAY ... 22
Tuesday 23	Wednesday 23	Thursday ... 23	Friday 23	Saturday ... 23	SUNDAY ... 23	Monday 23
Wednesday 24	Thursday ... 24	Friday 24	Saturday ... 24	SUNDAY ... 24	Monday 24	Tuesday 24
Thursday ... 25	Friday 25	Saturday ... 25	SUNDAY ... 25	Monday 25	Tuesday 25	Wednesday 25
Friday 26	Saturday ... 26	SUNDAY ... 26	Monday 26	Tuesday 26	Wednesday 26	Thursday ... 26
Saturday ... 27	SUNDAY ... 27	Monday 27	Tuesday 27	Wednesday 27	Thursday ... 27	Friday 27
SUNDAY ... 28	Monday 28	Tuesday 28	Wednesday 28	Thursday ... 28	Friday 28	Saturday ... 28
Monday 29	Tuesday 29	Wednesday 29	Thursday ... 29	Friday 29	Saturday ... 29	SUNDAY ... 29
Tuesday 30	Wednesday 30	Thursday ... 30	Friday 30	Saturday ... 30	SUNDAY ... 30	Monday 30
Wednesday 31	Thursday ... 31	Friday 31	Saturday ... 31	SUNDAY ... 31	Monday 31	Tuesday 31

NOTE: To ascertain any day of the week, first look in the table for the year required. Then under the months find the figure that corresponds to the number below at the head of the columns of the days. **For example:** To know on what day of the week July 4, 1918, fell, look in the table of years for 1918, and in a parallel line under July is figure 1, which directs to column 1 where it will be seen that July 4 fell on Thursday.

Ready-Reference Calendar

Arts

DRAMA GROUPS AVAILABLE FOR 1991 PERFORMANCES

Group/Affiliation	*Address*	*Contact*
General		
A.D. Players	2710 West Alabama, Houston, TX 77098	
Acacia Theatre Company	924 E. Juneau Ave., #209, Milwaukee, WI 53202	Therese Hummel, Mng Dir.
Asbury College Perf. Troupe	Asbury College, Wilmore, KY 40390	
Bane, Randall	Box 412861, Kansas City, MO 64141	
Capt. Ken's Marionette Ministry	P.O. Box 441, Phoenixville, PA 19460	
Chancel Players	Malone College, 515-25th St. NW, Canton, OH 44709	Alan Hedges
CHART	LaSalle St. Church, 1136 N. LaSalle St., Chicago, IL 60616	
Clown Connection	Eastern College, St. Davids, PA 19087	Rev. Ian J. Scott, Chaplain
Dramatic Word	P.O. Box 903, Salem, OR 97308	
Fountain Square Fools	607 Sycamore Street, Cincinnati, OH 45202	
Genesians	Bethel College, 1001 W. Mckinley Ave., Mishawaka, IN 46545	
Inst. of Perf. Arts and Ministries	Regent Univ., CBN Ctr, Virginia Beach, VA 23464	Professor D.R. Graves
King's Players	Baptist Bible College, 538 Venard, Clarks Summit, PA 18411	
L.I.F.E. Players	Redlands Comm. Church, 2327 Broadway, Grand Junction, CO 81503	Margene Terry
Movenaco Players	Mt Vernon Nazarene College, Mt Vernon, OH 43050	Daniel Behr, Drama Dir.
Power Source	Trinity Bible Coll., 50 S. Sixth Ave., Ellendale, ND 58436	Dr. Sharon Carbaugh, Chairman, Music/Drama Department
Soul Patrol	Trinity Bible College, 50 S. Sixth Ave., Ellendale, ND 58436	Dr. Sharon Carbaugh, Chairman, Music/Drama Department
Taproot Theatre Company	915 Pleasant View Rd, Chanhassen, MN 55317	David and Heidi Vogel
Transformed!	Eastern College, St. Davids, PA 19087	Rev. Ian J. Scott, Chaplain
Dance		
Ballet Magnificate	School & Studios, 4455 N. State, Jackson, MS 39206	Jeff Bieber, Tour Director
Beckman, Betsey	16001 Larch Way, Lynnwood, WA 98037	
Craighill, Mary	c/o St. Mark's Dance Co., 301 A St., S.E., Wash., DC 20003	
Crystal Cathedral	12141 Lewis St., Garden Grove, CA 92669	Dorie Lee Mattson, Dir. of Dance
Hosanna Sacred Dance	1318 S. Reisner St., Indianapolis, IN 46221	Kenneth Tolle, Artistic Dir.
Impact Productions	807 S. Xanthus Place, Tulsa, OK 74104	Andrea Jobe, Artistic Dir.
Praise His Name in the Dance	2327 Julianna Circle, Dallas, TX 75229	Judith Jenkins
Vine Dance Theatre, The	P.O. Box 6482, FDR Station, NY, NY 10150	Kathleen LaCamera, Art. Dir.
Media Arts		
Maranatha Productions, Inc.	P.O. Box 210, Dixon, IL 61021	Bette Bluemker, Adm. Asst
Multi		
Academy of Performing Arts	180 1/2 Hespeler Road, P.O. Box 1324, Cambridge, ON N1R 7G6	Colin Harbinson, Director
Because He Cares, Inc.	P.O. Box 71, Akron, OH 44309-0071	Yvonne M. Brake
Felshp of Artists for Cultrl Evang.	1605 Elizabeth Street, Pasadena, CA 91104	Gene Totten, Co-Director
Foundtn for Relig. and the Arts	P.O. Box 6482, FDR Station, NY, NY 10150	Kathleen LaCamera, Exe. Dir.
LaRue, Donna	7 Sherbron Court, Somerville, MA 02145	
Natl Assn of Pastoral Musicians	225 Sheridan Street, N.W., Washington, DC 20011	Thomas Wilson, Assoc. Dir.
Pacific School of Religion	1798 Scenic Avenue, Berkeley, CA 94709	Carol Voisin, Dir. Special Studies

Ricky Smith Mime Productions	P.O. Box 782 DTS, Omaha, NE 68101	Liz Smith, Road Manager
Slack, Susanne Swing	2360 Street de Ville, Atlanta, GA 30345	
Son's Shadow, The	Gaye Dimmick, 4028 Langhorne Ave., Charlotte, NC 28205	
Music		
Christian Musicians United, Inc.	91-16 86th Street, Woodhaven, NY 11421	Sal Baldino, President
Maranatha Music	P.O. Box 31050, Laguna Hills, CA 92654	Grace Marestaing, Prod. Mgr
Music Ministry	Camp. Crusade for Christ, 22912 Mill Creek Dr. #A, Laguna Hills, CA 92653	Janice Kaszycki, Assoc. Natl Dir.
Quail Ministries	203 Brightwood Avenue, Torrington, CT 06790	Michael Blanchard, Dir. of Minis.
Redemption	Trinity Bible Coll., 50 S. Sixth Ave., Ellendale, ND 58436	Dr. Sharon Carbaugh, Chairman, Music/Drama Department
Vision	Trinity Bible Coll., 50 S. Sixth Ave., Ellendale, ND 58436	Dr. Sharon Carbaugh, Chairman, Music/Drama Department
Music and Theatre		
Dept of Theatre and Speech	Northwestern College, Orange City, IA 51041	
Opera/Music Theatre		
Christian Arts, Inc.	1755 W. End Avenue, New Hyde Park, NY 11040	Derek deCambra, Artistic Dir.
Refreshment Committee	801 Dayton Avenue, St. Paul, MN 55104	
Theatre		
Covenant Players	1741 Fiske Place, P.O. Box 2900, Oxnard, CA 93033	Helen H. Marshall, Dir. of Dev.
Dort College Theatre Department	Dort College, 4th Avenue, Sioux Center, IA 51250	Verne Meyer, Theatre Dpt Chrmn
Dramatic Word	P.O. Box 903, Salem, OR 97308	Art Obendorf, Booking Coord.
Eastern Nazarene Theatre Prog.	Eastrn Nazarene Coll., 23 E. Elm Av., Quincy, MA 02120	Dr. Ronda Rice Winderl, Art Dir.
Fisherpeople Drama Ministry	598 Crestview Avenue, Akron, OH 44320	Bob and Susanne Crowley
Friends of John Wesley	1716 1/4 Sierra Bonita, Pasadena, CA 91104	Roger Nelson, Director
Friends of The Groom	83 Gatch Street, Milford, OH 45150	
Garold Andersen	Box 144, Guymon, OK 73942	
Globe Players	NW Nazarene Coll., 623 Holly St., Nampa, ID 83686	
Kent D. Berg	143 S. Elmwood, Oak Park, IL 60302	
Lampost Theatre Co.	Iowa Christian Theater, Inc., P.O. Box 322, 1121 E. Main, Washington, IA 52353	
Margaret Anderson	400 W. 45th Street, #3E, New York, NY 10185	
Master Arts Players	P.O. Box 9336, Grand Rapids, MI 49509	
Mosca, Bernie	Stuart Scadron-Wattles, P.O. Box 1324, 180 1/2 Hespeler Rd., Cambridge, ON	
Orlando Theatre Project	1007 La Quinta Drive, Orlando, FL 32809	
Potters Cast	Green Acres Bapt. Church, 1612 Leo Lynn, Tyler, TX 75701	Ken Brumley, Singles Minister
Pure Heart Players	Trinity Bible Coll., 50 S. Sixth Ave., Ellendale, ND 58436	
Robert Macklin	4100 1/2 Los Feliz Blvd., Los Angeles, CA 90027	
SAK Entertaiment	1005 LaQuinta Drive, Orlando, FL 32809	Terry Olson, President
Simple Rhyme Repertory Co.	12 Manakin Place, Willingboro, NJ 08046	Hank Stadler
Spg Arbor Coll. Readers Theatre	Spring Arbor College, Spring Arbor, MI 49283	Esther Lee Maddox
St. Luke Productions	P.O. Box 761, Beaverton, OR 97075	Leonardo Defilippis, Prod./Dir.

Source: Christians in the Arts Networking, Inc. (CAN) and Christians in the Theatre Arts (CITA).

DRAMA RESOURCES

Agape Drama Press, Ltd., Box 1313, Englewood, CO 80110

Augsburg Publishing House, 426 S. Fifth Street, Minneapolis, MN 55415

Baker's Plays, 100 Chauncy St., Boston, MA 02111

Bethany Press, Box 179, St. Louis, MO 63166

Broadman Press, Baptist Convention Press, 127 Ninth Avenue N., Nashville, TN 37234

Christian Board of Publication, P.O. Box 179, St. Louis, MO 63166

Coach House Press, Inc., 53 West Jackson Blvd., Chicago, IL 60604

Contemporary Drama Service, Box 7710-B5, Colorado Springs, CO 80933

Continental Ministries (Jeremiah

People), P.O. Box 1996, Thousand Oaks, CA 91360

Creative Arts Productions, Box 7008, Santa Cruz, CA 95061

C.S.S. Publishing Company, 628 South Main Street, Lima, OH 45804

Dramatic Publishing Co., 4150 N. Milwaukee Avenue, Chicago, IL 60641

Dramatists Play Service, 440 Park Avenue South, New York, NY 10016

Edna Means Dramatic Service, 610 Harmon Street, Tama, IA 52339

Eldridge Publishing Company, P.O. Drawer 216, Franklin, OH 45005

Friendship Press, P.O. Box 37844, Cincinnati, OH 45237

Hansen Drama Shop, 459 South Seventh East, Salt Lake City, UT 84102

Heuer Publishing Company, Drawer 248, Cedar Rapids, IA 52406

Horizon Gate Productions, P.O. Box 1740, #52, La Mesa, CA 92401

I.E. Clark, Inc., P.O. Box 246, Schulenburg, TX 78956-0246

The Jeremiah People, Box 1996, Thousand Oaks, CA 91360 (Sketch books)

Judson Press, Valley Forge, PA 19481

Laudamus Press, 1821 Fourth Street, N.W., Ankeny, IA 50021

Lillenas Publishing Co., Box 419527, Kansas City, MO 64141

Lutheran Church Press, 2900 Queen Lane, Philadelphia, PA 19129

National Council of Church of Christ, Dept. of Worship and Arts, 475 Riverside Drive, New York, NY 10027

On Stage, P.O. Box 25365, Chicago, IL 60625-0365

Performance Publishing Company, 978 McLean Blvd. North, Elgin, IL 60120

Pioneer Drama Service, Inc., 2172 Colorado Blvd. South, P.O. Box 22555, Denver, CO 80222

Russell House, 522 East Chase Avenue, Suite A, El Cajon, CA 92020

Ruth Vaughn, Inc., P.O. Box 1575, Bethany, OK 73008

Samuel French, Inc., 45 W. 25th Street, New York, NY 10010

Willow Creek Community Church, 67 East Algonquin Road, South Barrington, IL 60010 (Sketch books)

Source: Steve Pederson, Drama Director, Willow Creek Community Church, South Barrington, IL and *Christian Drama.* Used by permission.

“ ” FOCUS QUOTE

Drama, narrative art, dance and mime are as old as our civilization. These are present ways of holding up—in a playful manner—a mirror to the audience's face, to make them think about themselves, about situtations in life and about faith, without them having intended to do so. That's the real art of communication.

Christians shouldn't put themselves above the society in which they live. Jesus never did that. He was the best narrator of his time, and he used the best visual pictures to explain the Good News of God.—Geoffrey Stevenson in *Tema Info,* publication of The European Missionary Association

ARTS ORGANIZATIONS

Artists in Christian Testimony, 9521 Business Center Drive, Bldg. 9, Suite A, P.O. Box 1002, Cucamonga, CA 91730

Christians in the Arts Networking, Inc., P.O. Box 1941, Cambridge, MA 02238-1941

Fellowship of Artists for Cultural Evangelism, 1605 E. Elizabeth Street, Pasadena, CA 91104

Fellowship of Christian Magicians, P.O. Box 1027, Wheaton, IL 60189-5169

Christians in Theatre Arts, 14 Blackburn Street, Greenville, SC 29607

Christians in the Visual Arts (C.I.V.A.), Wheaton College, Wheaton, IL 60187

BOOKLIST: A TECHNICAL DRAMA REFERENCE LIBRARY

SCENERY DESIGN AND CONSTRUCTION

Scene Technology by Richard L. Arnold. Prentice-Hall

Scenography and Stage Technology by Willard Bellman. Thomas Crowell

Handbook of Technical Practice for the Performing Arts by Ned Bowman. Scenographic Media

Scenery for the Theatre by Harold Burris-Meyer and Edward Cole. Little, Brown, and Company

Stage Scenery by A.S. Gillette. Harper and Row, Publishers

Stage Scenery, Its Construction and Rigging by A.S. Gillette and J. Michael Gillette. Harper and Row, Publishers

Scene Design and Stage Lighting by W. Oren Parker and Harvey K. Smith. Holt, Rinehart and Winston

Designing and Painting for the Theatre by Lynn Pecktal. Holt, Rinehart and Winston

Essentials of Stage Scenery by Samuel Selden and Tom Rezzuto. Appleton-Century-Crofts

STAGE MANAGEMENT

The Stage Manager's Handbook by Bert Gruver. Drama Book Specialists

Stage Management: A Guidebook of Practical Techniques by Lawrence Stern. Allyn and Bacon

THE THEATRE FACILITY

Theatres and Auditoriums by Harold Burris-Meyer and Edward Cole. Reinhold

The Shapes of Our Theatre by Jo Meilziner. Clarkson N. Potter

MAKEUP

Stage Makeup by Herman Buchman. Watson-Guptill

Stage Makeup by Richard Corson. Prentice-Hall

LIGHTING

Lighting the Stage: Art and Practice by Willard F. Bellman. Crowell

Designing with Light by J. Michael Gillette. Mayfield

Scene Design and Stage Lighting by W. Oren Parker and Harvey K. Smith. Holt, Rinehart and Winston

Stage Lighting by Richard Pilbrow. Van Nostrand Reinhold

Essentials of Stage Lighting by H.D. Sellman. Appleton-Century-Crofts

SOUND

Sound in the Theatre by Harold Burris-Meyer, Vincent Mallory and Lewis Goodfriend. Theatre Arts Books

Stage Sound by David Collison. Drama Book Specialists

Source: Bill Jenkins in *Christian Drama,* February 1988 issue. Used by permission.

PRAISE HIS NAME, TWO, THREE, FOUR

Our church has seen several movements—the charismatic, the church-growth, and the small-group movements, to name a few. Still, we weren't prepared for the latest: the Movement movement.

It started innocently with a women's aerobics class, which was followed by some innocent swaying to praise choruses and fast-moving hymns. But it started to get out of hand when our intern from the seminary arrived, all excited about his class in "Theo-Kinetics." He proposed a Sunday morning dance troupe to "recapture the intuitive in worship." Then denominational headquarters, never wanting to be out of step (so to speak), issued a denominationwide study curriculum, "Motion and Mission."

But local congregations aren't always moving at the same speed as seminary professors and denominational hierarchs. After the worship-dance group's first Sunday-morning performance, the issue came to the board. Some favored the new expression, citing Jeremiah 31:13. Others ridiculed it as "discipleship in Danskin." It finally came to a motion (of course).

As expected, the board voted for a compromise between the progressives and conservatives. Worship dance is permissible, but for men only. That left our head ushers, Frank and Wilber, with the job of leading the men in an expressionistic interpretation of "All Hail the Power" as part of the call to worship. They resigned immediately.

Now we need a study from the seminary or headquarters on "Finding Ushers for Ministry."

Eutychus, *Christianity Today*, December 15, 1989

TOP 10 CHRISTIAN FILMS OF 1989

1. **A Man Called Norman,** Focus on the Family
2. **Without Reservation,** Gospel Films/Mars Hill Productions
3. **Thin Ice,** Gospel Films/Rick Garside Productions
4. **Twice Pardoned,** Focus on the Family
5. **Wait of the World,** Gospel Films/John Schmidt Productions
6. **The Pretender,** Christiano Brothers Films
7. **Fury to Freedom,** Gospel Films/Erik Jacobsen Productions
8. **Superchristian II,** Gospel Films/John Schmidt Productions
9. **The Estate Sale,** Word Films/White Lion Productions
10. **Never Ashamed,** Ed McDougal Productions

Source: Visual Media Center, Fresno Bible House, Fresno, CA

TOP 10 VIDEOS OF 1989

Rentals

1. *A Distant Thunder,* Mark IV Pictures
2. *A Thief in the Night,* Mark IV Pictures
3. *Image of the Beast,* Mark IV Pictures
4. *The Prodigal Planet,* Mark IV Pictures
5. *The Cross and the Switchblade,* Vanguard Video
6. *McGee and Me! The Big Lie,* Focus on the Family (Tyndale)
7. *Carman Live . . . Radically Saved!* by Carman, Benson Videos
8. *Do You Hear Me?!* by Mike Warnke, DaySpring (Word)
9. *The God Makers,* Jeremiah Films
10. *The Hiding Place,* World Wide Publications

Sales

1. *McGee and Me! The Big Lie,* Focus on the Family (Tyndale)
2. *McGee and Me! The Not-So-Great Escape,* Focus on the Family (Tyndale)
3. *McGee and Me! A Star in the Breaking,* Focus on the Family (Tyndale)
4. *The Greatest Adventure Vol. 7, The Nativity,* Hanna-Barbera Productions (Sparrow/Star Song)
5. *The Amazing Book,* Anthony Paul Productions (Multnomah Press)
6. *McGee and Me! Skate Expectations,* Focus on the Family (Tyndale)
7. *The Greatest Adventure Vol. 8, Creation,* Hanna-Barbera Productions (Sparrow/Star Song)
8. *The Greatest Adventure Vol. 4, Noah's Ark,* Hanna-Barbera Productions (Sparrow/Star Song)
9. *McGee and Me! Twister and Shout,* Focus on the Family (Tyndale)
10. *The Greatest Adventure Vol. 2, David & Goliath,* Hanna-Barbera Productions (Sparrow/Star Song)

This list is based on actual rentals and sales in Christian retail stores in the United States and Canada during 1989.

CROWN AWARDS

Academy of Christian Cinemagraphic Arts. Sposored by Christian Film and Video Association, Inc.

Year Category	Film	Actor/Actress/ Director	Production Company
1977			
Best Actor	Sammy	Eric Buhr	Heartland Productions
Best Actress	All The King's Horses	Dee Wallace	Mark IV Pictures
Best Children's	Sammy		Heartland Productions
Best Documentary	World That Perished		Films For Christ
Best Film	All The King's Horses		Mark IV Pictures
Best Missionary	For All Men		Harvest Productions
Best Soul Winning	Senior Year		Ken Anderson Films
Outstanding Personality in the Film Industry		Ken Anderson	
Pioneer in Christian Film Production		Irwin Moon	
1978			
Best Actor	Pilgrim's Progress	Peter Thomas	Ken Anderson Films
Best Actress	Distant Thunder	Patty Dunning	Mark IV Pictures
Best Children's	Great Banana Pie Caper		Quadros Communications
Best Cinematography	Pilgrim's Progress	Max Anderson, Roger Boller	Ken Anderson Films
Best Director	Pilgrim's Progress	Ken Anderson	Ken Anderson Films
Best Documentary	Eldridge Cleaver		Gospel Films
Best Effects	Pilgrim's Progress		Ken Anderson Films
Best Film	Pilgrim's Progress		Ken Anderson Films
Best Historical	Megiddo		Cathedral Films
Best Missionary	Survivor No. 3		Moody Institute of Science
Best Musical Score	Pilgrim's Progress	Tim Simonec	Ken Anderson Films
Best Series	Faith For Today		Gateway Films
Best Soul Winning	Distant Thunder		Mark IV Pictures
Best Stewardship	Gift of Love		Christian Communications
Best Supporting Actor	The Prize	Chuck Woolery	Outreach Films
Best Supporting Actress	Distant Thunder	Sally Johnson	Mark IV Pictures
Best Youth	Nite Song		Heartland Productions
1979			
Best Actor	John Hus	Rod Colbin	Gateway Films
Best Actress	Crossfire	Jane Klint	Quadrus Communications
Best Biblical	Man From Tarsus		Harvest Productions
Best Children's	The Wacky Weirdos of Willoughby Castle		Quadrus Communications
Best Christian Living	Strike the Original Match		New Liberty Enterprises
Best Cinematography	Crossfire	Tim Dabner	Quadrus Communications
Best Director	Deceived	Mel White	Mel White Productions
Best Documentary	Deceived		Mel White Productions
Best Film of the Year	John Hus		Gateway Films
Best Musical Score	Christiana	Tim Simonec	Ken Anderson Films
Best Series	Focus On The Family		Word, Inc.
Best Soul Winning	Paradise Trail		Mark IV Pictures
Best Supporting Actor	John Hus	Regis Cordic	Quadrus Communications
Best Supporting Actress	Christiana	Tina Heath	Ken Anderson Films
Best Youth	Crossfire		Quadrus Communications
Outstanding Contribution to the Film Ministry		Mel White	
1980			
Best Actor	Ordinary Guy	Richard Foster	Day Star Productions
Best Actress	Heaven's Heroes	Heide Vaughn	Mark IV Pictures
Best Art Director	Stolen Watermelon	John Miller	Ken Anderson Films

Year Category	*Film*	*Actor/Actress/ Director*	*Production Company*
Best Biblical	I, Paul		Gateway Films
Best Children's	Goosehill Gang/The Vanishing Schoolmate		Family Films
Best Cinematography	Sports Galaxy	Bob Cording	Omega Films
Best Direction	Heaven's Heroes	Don Thompson	Mark IV
Best Documentary	Assignment: Life		New Liberty Enterprises
Best Editing	Assignment: Life	Carrie Matrisciana	New Liberty Enterprises
Best Evangelistic	Heaven's Heroes		Mark IV Pictures
Best Film of the Year	Ordinary Guy		Day Star Productions
Best Film Series	Goosehill Gang		Family Films
Best Missionary	Telling Kelli		Harvest Productions
Best Musical Score	Music Box	Charles R. Johnson	White Lion Pictograph
Best Screen Play	Touch of The Master's Hand	Jimmy Murphy	Ken Anderson Films
Best Special Effects	Whitcomb's War	Timothy Doughton	Heartland Productions
Best Stewardship	Energy in a Twilight World		Moody Institute of Science
Best Supporting Actor	Heaven's Heroes	James O'Hagen	Mark IV Pictures
Best Supporting Actress	Whitcomb's War	Joanne Talarico	Heartland Productions
Best Youth	Super Christian		Gospel Films, Inc. (John Schmidt Prodctns)
Founder's Award		Harvey W. Marks, CFDA Exec. Sec.	
President's Award	The Spirit Controlled Temperment		Family Life Distributors
President's Award	Reflections of His Love		World Wide Pictures
1981			
Best Actor	Brother Enemy	William Wellman, Jr.	Heartland Productions
Best Actress	Early Warning	Delana Michaels	Missionary Enterprises
Best Biblical	Daring Daniel		Ken Anderson Films
Best Children's	Treehouse Ghosts		Family Films
Best Cinematography	Hudson Taylor	Heather Edmondson	Ken Anderson Films
Best Director	Hudson Taylor	Ken Anderson	Ken Anderson Films
Best Documentary	Some Through Fire		Ken Anderson Films
Best Editing	Football Fever	Bob Cording	Omega Films
Best Evangelistic	Brother Enemy		Heartland Productions
Best Film	Kevin Can Wait		John Schmidt Productions
Best Film Series	Marriage Enrichment		New Day Productions
Best Missionary	Hudson Taylor		Ken Anderson Films
Best Music	Kevin Can Wait	David Maddux	John Schmidt Productions
Best Screen Play	Kevin Can Wait	John Schmidt	John Schmidt Productions
Best Special Effects	Years of Beast	Dan Quick	Gospel Films
Best Supporting Actor	Kevin Can Wait	David Prince	John Schmidt Productions
Best Supporting Actress	Hudson Taylor	Marie Brady	Ken Anderson Films
Best Youth	Kevin Can Wait		John Schmidt Productions
Founder's Award		Leonard Skibitzke	
1982			
Information not available			
1983			
Information not available			
1984			
Best Actor	Never Ashamed	Timothy Elwell	Edward T. McDougal Films
Best Actress	Fanny Crosby	Wenda Shereos	Ken Anderson Films
Best Children's	Honesty		Gospel Films, Inc.
Best Children's	Sunshine Factory		Gospel Films, Inc.
Best Director	Fanny Crosby	Ken Anderson	Ken Anderson Films
Best Evangelistic	Never Ashamed		Edward T. McDougal Films
Best Film of the Year	Never Ashamed		Edward T. McDougal Films
Best Missionary	Mud, Sweat, Cheers		Ken Anderson Films
Best Series	Evidence for Faith		Word Films
Best Supporting Actor	Never Ashamed	Jon Jancovic	Edward T. McDougal Films
Best Supporting Actress	Fanny Crosby	Cathy Shipley	Ken Anderson Films
Best Youth	Never Ashamed		Edward T. McDougal Films
Founder's Award	The Healing		Heartland Productions
President's Award	Christian European		Visual Media Association

Year Category	Film	Actor/Actress/ Director	Production Company
1985			
Best Actor	Fury To Freedom	Tom Salardi	Gospel Films, Inc.
Best Actress	Fury To Freedom	Joy Vogel	Gospel Films, Inc.
Best Children's	Hoomania		Gospel Films, Inc.
Best Cinematography	Journey of Life	Robert Miller and Don Valentine	
Best Director	Fury to Freedom	Eric Jacobson	Gospel Films, Inc.
Best Evangelistic	Fury To Freedom		Gospel Films, Inc.
Best Film of the Year	Fury To Freedom		Gospel Films, Inc.
Best Film Series	Love Is A Decision		Zondervan/Miller
Best Missionary	The Search		Harvest Films
Best Supporting Actor	Harley	Eli Cummings	Kuntz Brothers
Best Supporting Actress	Fractured Families	Tammy Taylor	Life Productions
Best Youth	They Lied To Us		Life Productions
Founder's Award		John Schmidt	John Schmidt Productions
1986			
Best Actor	Wait of the World	Jim Schmidt	John Schmidt Productions
Best Actress	Consider It All Joy	Bonnie Hawley	Victory Internatl Productns
Best Children's	Badrock Valley Gang		Ken Anderson Films
Best Cinematography	Wait of the World	Jack Tankard and Roger Boller	John Schmidt Productions
Best Director	Wait of the World	John Schmidt	John Schmidt Productions
Best Evangelistic	Golden Dolphin		Ken Anderson Films
Best Film of the Year	Wait of The World		Gospel Films, Inc.
Best Film Series	Turn Your Heart Toward Home		Word, Inc.
Best Missionary	The Calling		Gospel Films, Inc.
Best Supporting Actor	Wait of the World	Eddie Hailey	John Schmidt Productions
Best Supporting Actress	Wait of the World	Loren Cedar	John Schmidt Productions
Best Youth	Second Step		Ken Anderson Films
Founder's Award		Edward T. McDougal	Edward T. McDougal Films
President's Award		Kenneth Curtis	Gateway Films
1987			
Best Actor	Gold Through the Fire	Charles Harlan	Edward T. McDougal Films
Best Actress	Love Note	Sally Murphy	Ken Anderson Films
Best Children's	Bible Walk		Educational Evangelism/ Word, Inc.
Best Cinematog./Editing	Distinctively Human		Moody Institute of Science
Best Director	Gold Through the Fire	Edward T. McDougal	Edward T. McDougal Films
Best Documentary	A Winnable War		Focus on the Family
Best Evangelistic	Twice Pardoned		Focus on the Family
Best Film of the Year	Gold Through The Fire		Edward T. McDougal Films
Best Film Series	Twice Pardoned		Focus on the Family
Best Individual Non-Dramatic Presentation	Twice Pardoned	Harold Morris	Focus on the Family
Best Supporting Actor	Gold Through the Fire	Kris Wolff	Edward T. McDougal Films
Best Supporting Actress	Thin Ice	Alyson Davis	Gospel Films, Inc.
Best Youth	Love Note		Ken Anderson Films
Founder's Award		Wendell Moody	
President's Award		Heinz Fussle	
1988			
Best Cinematography	God's Outlaw	Mike Reed	Gateway Films
Best Evangelistic	Without Reservation		Gospel Films, Inc.
Best Film of the Year	A Man Called Norman		Focus on the Family
Best Film Series	The Homebuilders		Word Films
Best Individual Non-Dramatic Presentation	A Man Called Norman	Mike Adkins	Focus on the Family
Best Original Form Video-Children	Gerbert		E-Film and Video
Best Original Form Video-Dramatic	God's Outlaw		Gateway Films
Best Video of the Year	This Is The Day		Moody Institute of Science
Best Youth	Without Reservation		Gospel Films, Inc.

MAGAZINES

II Chronicles Magazine, P.O. Box 42, Medford, OR 97501
Oregon Christian Arts Group. Arts, Semimonthly, 5,000 circ. $10.00/2 yrs

Christian Conjurer, 1705 Barbara Lane, Connersville, IN 47331
Fellowship of Christian Magicians, Inc. Drama, Digest, 6/year, $12.00 membership

Image: A Journal of the Arts and Religion, 526 Ziela Ave., Front Royal, VA 22630 703-635-9217

SACRED ARTS AWARDS

Co-Sponsored by First Presbyterian Church of Wheaton and Billy Graham Center Museum

Award	*Year*	*Artist*	*Title*
Best Collegiate Award	1980	Sarah Travis	Astral Dream
Best High School Award	1980	Greg McCallum	Baptismal Bowl
	1981	Andrew Ayers IV	Drawing
Best of Show	1985	Vivian Wright	Resurrection Triptych
	1986	R. Earl Cleveland	Prophecy
	1987	Vladislav Andrejev	Illuminated & Handwritten Gospel
	1988	James F. Darrow	Apostles Creed
	1989	Michael Mallard	The Darkness of Excessive Light
	1990	Donald J. Forsythe	A Wise Virgin/A Foolish Virgin
Best Photograph	1985	Patricia Phelps Wheless	Aunt Margaret's Room
BGC Museum Purchase Award	1986	Joan Bohlig	Fully Interlocking Puzzle
	1987	David L. Gould	Untitled #099
	1988	Charles Rohrbacher	Mystical Supper
	1988	Chris Anderson	Historical Dislocations
	1988	Forge Toro	Baby Christ in Glory
	1988	Lynda L. Oren	Diptych
	1988	Raymond N. Calvert	Missa III
	1989	Fred DelGuidice	Mercy Seat/Bread of Life
	1989	Fred DelGuidice	No Mercy
	1989	Kayano Umehara	Me and You
	1989	Mark Ritchie	Celtic Cross
	1990	Guy Chase	Tablet for a New Law
	1990	Vladimir P. Kozhemiakov	The Head
First Prize	1982	Clara Harmelin Von Tascha	Creation of Eve
	1983	Arlene Fitterer	Genesis
	1984	Community Presbyterian Ch. of Clarendon Hills	The Earth is the Lord's and the Fullness Thereof
	1990	David Harmon	About Joel 2
First Purchase Award	1980	Pat Koutny	Incarnation (Birth of Christianity)
	1981	Gregg Oakes	Paths of Life
High School Award	1982	Greg McCallum	Christ
	1983	Susan Eriksen	Blessed Be the Name of the Lord
Honorable Mention	1980	Jean Covert	This Do In Remembrance of Me
	1980	Sue Jorden	Palm Sunday
	1981	Barbara Brien	Apocalypse 6:18
	1981	Carol Friedle	The World Was Made By Him
	1981	Clara Hamelin Von Tascha	The Baptism
	1981	Dorothy Turner	Bread and Wine
	1981	Gregg Oakes	The Parable of the Farmer

Award	*Year*	*Artist*	*Title*
	1981	Jacqueline DeClute	Untitled
	1981	Joseph Heyd	Jonah and the Whale
	1981	Judith Hensel	Temptation of St. Anthony
	1981	Lee Jens	Christ Among the Crowd
	1981	Linda Nurmet	You Will Know Them
	1981	Sister Richard Mehren	Corpus
	1981	Thom Kapheim	Birth Rite
	1982	Alfred W. Heston	Christus
	1982	Barbara Tribes	Then he opened their minds to understand the Scriptures—Luke 24:45
	1982	Edward Dlugopolski	Entombment
	1982	Edward Dlugopolski	Humann Esterrare
	1982	Grover Boone	Trinity
	1982	Janet Nisbett LaPage	And God Said, Let the Earth Be Filled with Living Creatures
	1982	Judith & Liz Hoying Dioszegi	Pentecost Holy Spirit
	1982	Mary Sabo	Untitled
	1982	Sister Dorothy Bock	Fire Bread
	1982	Sister Helena Steffens-Meier	Shekinah
	1982	Sister Maureen McLain	St. Nicholas Church
	1982	Thomas Holzaepfel	Three Days and Three Nights
	1983	Alex Elkind	And His Name Will Be Called Prince of Peace
	1983	Frank Brun	Untitled Christ
	1983	Kennet J. Hempel	Seven Wise and Seven Foolish
	1983	Lou Ann Burkhardt	And They Shall Be Filled
	1983	Louis E. Ransom	Small Altar Cross
	1983	Terry Groh	Untitled
	1983	William C. Hill	The 19th Day of Daniel's Prayer
	1984	Dorothy Turner	Glory to God
	1984	John A. Slavik	Shoe of a Fisherman
	1984	Joseph Lipinski	Prophet IV
	1984	Marilyn Kayton	Jacob's Coat
	1984	Pat Koutny	Angels
	1984	Peg Sindelar	Garden of Eden
	1984	Thomas Manley	Jesus the Compassionate
	1984	Tim Botts	Cicles
	1984	William Lankton	Wings of Peace
	1985	Carmelo Gannello	Testimony Time
	1985	Irene Elios	Jericho
	1985	Jeff Thompson	Centerpiece
	1985	John M. Bohlig	Wolf in Sheep's Clothing
	1985	Joseph Heyd	Cloud/Moses/Sinai
	1985	Ruth Meredith	Archangel Gabriel
	1986	Dhimitri Zonia	Adam and Eve
	1986	Kay Wahlgren	Genesis
	1986	Mary Hecht	Homage to Lipchitz: The Sacrifice
	1986	Maureen Hubbard Cribbs	Ode to Psalm 24, Verses 1 & 2
	1986	William Frederick	Chalice
	1987	Beva Farmer	Icon of Shadrach, Meshach & Abednego
	1987	Erica L. Schwartz	Christ and Lazarus
	1987	Lynda L.Oren	Genesis Series
	1987	Marvin Jarboe	Job
	1987	William Frederick	Lectionary Cover

Award	*Year*	*Artist*	*Title*
	1988	Cathie Boucher	Jesus Christ Our Lord
	1988	Dan Spahn	Beatitude
	1988	Donald Forsythe	In the Day of Judgment
	1988	Jeff Thompson	Seven Stones
	1988	Jonathan Blocher	Isaiah 41:10
	1988	Lynda L. Oren	Servant's Basket
	1989	Arthur Geisert	Ark
	1989	Bill Bippes	Untitled
	1989	Don Schol	After Eden
	1989	Jerry Dienes	The Temptation Diptych
	1989	Kayano Umehara	Me and You
	1989	Lewis Toby	Madonna
	1989	Sandra Bowden	Sanctus
	1989	William Weber	For the yolk I will give you is easy —Matthew 11:30
	1990	Aaron Benson	Revelation
	1990	Laurence Conn	Christ and St. John on the Island of Patmos
	1990	Karen Engelke	"For still the vision awaits its time"
	1990	Edward Knippers	Lamentation (Angel at the Crucifixion)
	1990	Irina Sukhanova-Oksengendler	Archangel Michael
	1990	Forge Toro	Pray for the Peace of Jerusalem
Judge's Award	1989	Pat Groenenboom	Demons at the Entrance
McCormick Memorial Award	1985	Jonathan Flew	The Fisherman
	1986	Theresa Verdine	Altar to Unborn Children
	1987	Dhimitri Zonia	Genesis
	1988	Forge Toro	Baby Christ in Glory
	1989	Fred DelGuidice	No Mercy
Purchase Award—Photography	1986	Patricia Phelps Wheless	Meet Me In Heaven
R.H. Love Award	1990	Lynda Lowe Oren	Sparrow's Reliquary/Survivor's Reliquary
Second Prize	1982	Gregg Oakes	Trinity at Gethsemane
	1983	Gregory Piro	Bible Cover
	1990	Lucinda Hubing	Worship
Second Purchase Award	1980	Sarah Travis	Astral Dream
	1981	Mary Kingsbury Dowse	The Sleeping Church
Tenth Anniversary Award	1989	Arthur Geisert	Ark
Theme Prize (Celebration)	1984	Ruth Meredith	Noah's Ark
Theme Prize (Peace)	1983	Jacqueline Dodson	Peaceful Doves
Theme Prize (Pentecost)	1982	Dorothy Turner	Flame
	1982	Dorothy Turner	Rainbow
Third Prize	1982	Thomas Holzaepfel	Jonah and the Cross
	1990	Timothy Young	Acts 2:2
Visitor's Choice Award	1982	Comm. Presb. Ch./Clarndn Hls	Antependia & Banners
	1983	Paul Higdon	To Guide Our Feet Unto the Way of Heaven
	1984	Tim Botts	Oh Lord, What a Variety You Have Made
	1985	Carol Cameron	Aventine
	1986	Kay Wahlgren	Genesis
	1987	Lynda L. Oren	Genesis Series
	1988	Steven Rockwell	Easter
	1989	Mark Smothers	In the Twinkling of an Eye
	1990	Joseph DeVelasco	Satan Bound

1991 GOSPEL MUSIC FESTIVALS

January 7-11 **Music Florida** Orlando, FL. Contact: Kempke's Music, 2005 Tree Fork Lane, Suite 105, Longwood, FL 32750 407-831-0333

April 25-27 **Hosanna '90** Grace Brethren Worship Center, Westerville, OH. Contact: Susan Zartman, 8225 Worthington, Galena Road, Westerville, OH 43081 614-431-8221

Spring **Christian Artists' Songship** Dallas, TX; Anaheim, CA; Minneapolis, MN. Contact: Christian Artists Corporation, P.O. Box 1984, Thousand Oaks, CA 91358 800-827-0099

June 20-22 **Atlanta Fest** Six Flags Over Georgia, Atlanta, GA. Contact: Tiley and Associates, P.O. Box 6271, Marietta, GA 30067 404-955-8669

June 24-28 **Music Texas** Ft. Worth, TX. Contact: Kempke's Music, 2005 Tree Fork Lane, Suite 105, Longwood, FL 32750 407-831-0333

June 27-28 **Creation Festival** Agape Campground, Mt. Union, PA. Contact: Come Alive Ministries, P.O. Box 86, Medford, NJ 08055 800-327-6921

July 8-12 **Church Music in the Smokies** Grand Hotel, Pigeon Forge, TN. Contact: J & J Music, 234 N. Craft Highway, Chickasaw, AL 36611 800-456-4966

July 18-20 **Jesus Northwest** Clark County Fair, Vancouver, WA. Contact: People's Church, P.O. Box 7718, Salem, OR 97303 503-393-1616

July 28-31 **Kingdom '90 Youth Conference** Location to be announced. Contact: Regal Ventures, P.O. Box 1010, Kings Mountain, NC 28086 704-739-3838

September 30-October 5 **National Quartet Convention** Nashville, TN. Contact: National Quartet Convention, 54 Music Square West, Nashville, TN 37203 615-320-7000

Source: Gospel Music Association

50 TOP CHRISTIAN SONGS OF 1989

1. "Forever Friends" by Sandi Patti, Word
2. "Farther On" by Russ Taff, Myrrh
3. "More To This Life" by Steven Curtis Chapman, Sparrow
4. "The Throne" by Michael W. Smith, Reunion
5. "Healing" by Deniece Williams, Sparrow
6. "I Can Begin Again" by Larnelle Harris, Benson
7. "My Turn Now" by Steven Curtis Chapman, Sparrow
8. "Perfect Union" by Matthew Ward, Live Oak
9. "Testimony" by Kim Hill, Reunion
10. "Back To Who I Am " by Paul Smith, DaySpring
11. "Lost Without You" by BeBe & CeCe Winans, Sparrow
12. "Sweet Victory" by Twila Paris, Star Song
13. "Jesus, It's You" by Mylon & Broken Heart, Star Song
14. "Look What God Is Doing" by Scott Wesley Brown, DaySpring
15. "We Need Each Other" by Trace Balin, DaySpring
16. "The Hunger Stays" by Margaret Becker, Sparrow
17. "Neverending Love" by Twila Paris, Star Song
18. "If I Stand" by Rich Mullins, Reunion
19. "What About the Love? " by Amy Grant, Myrrh

20. "'Tis So Sweet To Trust in Jesus" by Amy Grant, Myrrh
21. "Strong Medicine" by Bryan Duncan, Modern Art
22. "Do You Feel Their Pain?" by Steve Camp, Sparrow
23. "If God Is For Us" by DeGarmo & Key, Power Discs
24. "Homeless Few" by Petra, Star Song
25. "Light Your World" by Newsong, DaySpring
26. "Could It Be?" by Michael Card, Sparrow
27. "It's Alright" by Paul Smith, DaySpring
28. "True Friend " by Twila Paris, Star Song
29. "Sweet Love" by First Call, Myrrh
30. "I Miss the Way" by Michael W. Smith, Reunion
31. "Is It Right?" by Jerome Olds, Star Song
32. "I Wish" by Billy Sprague, Reunion
33. "Your Steadfast Love " by Kelly Willard & Lenny LeBlanc, Alleluia
34. "Yahweh Is For Us" by Maranatha Singers with Randy Stonehill, Maranatha! Music
35. "Streets of Innocence" by Margaret Becker, Sparrow
36. "In It After All" by Larnelle Harris, Benson
37. "Bigger Than Life" by Paul Smith, DaySpring
38. "Every Moment" by Deniece Williams, Sparrow
39. "Untouched by Human Hands" by Wayne Watson, DaySpring
40. "The Calling of Love" by Sheila Walsh, Myrrh
41. "The Boss" by Imperials, Myrrh
42. "The Light Has Come" by Tramaine Hawkins, Sparrow
43. "I Will Be With You" by Maranatha Singers with Denny Correll, Maranatha! Music
44. "Living Dangerously in the Hands of God" by Steve Camp, Sparrow
45. "Perfect" by Benny Hester, Frontline
46. "On the Other Side" by Michael W. Smith, Reunion
47. "Here's My Heart" by David & The Giants, Giant
48. "Tearin' Down the Walls" by Geoff Moore & the Distance, Sparrow
49. "Feel Every Heartbeat" by Holm, Sheppard, Johnson, DaySpring
50. "Hand in Hand" by DeGarmo & Key, Power Discs

Source: Compiled from airplay reports from leading Christian radio stations throughout the U.S. Reprinted from the December 18, 1989 issue of *The CCM Update*. Copyright © 1989 by CCM Publications, Inc. Used by permission.

TOP 20 BEST-SELLING CHRISTIAN RECORDS/CD'S OF 1989

1. *Sandi Patti and the Friendship Company* by Sandi Patti, Word Records
2. *i 2 (EYE)* by Michael W. Smith, Reunion (Word)
3. *Lead Me On* by Amy Grant, Myrrh (Word)
4. *Revival in the Land* by Carman, Benson Records
5. *The Collection* by Amy Grant, Myrrh (Word)
6. *Make His Praise Glorious* by Sandi Patti, Word Records
7. *Thank You* by Ray Boltz, Diadem (Spectra)
8. *The Acapella Project* by Glad, Benson Records
9. *Carman Live . . . Radically Saved!* by Carman, Benson Records
10. *Hymns Just for You* by Sandi Patti, Helvering Productions (Benson)
11. *On Fire!* by Petra, Star Song (Sparrow/Star Song)
12. *The Finest Moments* by Sandi Patti, Word Records
13. *The Way Home* by Russ Taff, Myrrh (Word)
14. *Our Hymns* by various artists, Word Records
15. *Michael W. Smith Christmas* by Michael W. Smith, Reunion (Word)
16. *Heaven* by BeBe & CeCe Winans, Sparrow Records
17. *Take 6* by Take 6, Reunion (Word)
18. *More Than Wonderful* by Sandi Patti, Impact (Benson)

19. *The Mission* by Steve Green, Sparrow Records
20. *Petra Praise . . . the Rock Cries Out* by Petra, DaySpring (Word)

This list is based on actual sales in Christian retail stores in the United States and Canada during 1989. Distributed by Evangelical Christian Publishers Association. Reprinted by permission from the March 1990 issue of Bookstore Journal, official trade publication of the Christian Booksellers Association.

20 BEST-SELLING CHRISTIAN RECORDS OF THE 80s

1. *Age to Age* by Amy Grant, Myrrh (Word)
2. *More Than Wonderful* by Sandi Patti, Impact (Benson)
3. *Hymns Just for You* by Sandi Patti, Helvering Productions (Benson)
4. *The Collection* by Amy Grant, Myrrh (Word)
5. *Morning Like This* by Sandi Patti, Word Records
6. *Songs From the Heart* by Sandi Patti, Impact (Benson)
7. *Straight Ahead* by Amy Grant, Myrrh (Word)
8. *Michael W. Smith Project* by Michael W. Smith, Reunion (Word)
9. *Unguarded* by Amy Grant, Myrrh (Word)
10. *Music Machine* by Candle, Birdwing (Sparrow)
11. *More Power to Ya* by Petra, Star Song
12. *Lead Me On* by Amy Grant, Myrrh (Word)
13. *For God and God Alone* by Steve Green, Sparrow Records
14. *Make His Praise Glorious* by Sandi Patti, Word Records
15. *Not of This World* by Petra, Star Song
16. *Heed the Call* by The Imperials, DaySpring (Word)
17. *Priority* by The Imperials, DaySpring (Word)
18. *Carman Live. . .Radically Saved!* by Carman, Benson Records
19. *Michael W. Smith 2* by Michael W. Smith, Reunion (Word)
20. *i2 (EYE)* by Michael W. Smith, Reunion (Word)

This list was compiled from *Bookstore Journal's* music best-seller lists of the 1980s—not actual sales. Titles received 10 points for each No. 1 placement, nine points for each No. 2, etc. From *Bookstore Journal,* Official Trade Publication of the Christian Booksellers Association. Reprinted by permission.

25 TOP CONTEMPORARY CHRISTIAN ALBUMS OF ALL TIME

1. *Only Visiting This Planet* by Larry Norman. Producer: Larry Norman. MGM/Verve 1972
2. *Slow Train Coming* by Bob Dylan. Producer: Jerry Wexler and Barry Beckett. Columbia 1979
3. *Welcome to Paradise* by Randy Stonehill. Producer: Larry Norman. Solid Rock 1976
4. *White Horse* by Michael Omartian. Producer: Michael Omartian. ABC/Dunhill 1974
5. *Age to Age* by Amy Grant. Producer: Brown Bannister. Myrrh 1982
6. *With Footnotes* by 2nd Chapter of Acts. Producer: Buck Herring. Myrrh 1974
7. *Love Song* by Love Song. Producer: Love Song and Freddie Piro. Good News 1972
8. *For Him Who Has Ears to Hear* by Keith Green. Producer: Bill Maxwell. Sparrow 1977
9. *Unguarded* by Amy Grant. Producer: Brown Bannister. Myrrh 1985
10. *Medals* by Russ Taff. Producer: Jack Joseph Puig and Russ Taff. Myrrh 1985
11. *Love Broke Through* by Phil Keaggy. Producer: Buck Herring. New Song 1976
12. *Victims of the Age* by Mark Heard. Producer: Mark Heard. Home Sweet Home 1982
13. *The Turning* by Leslie Phillips. Producer: T-Bone Burnett. Myrrh 1987
14. *Romeo Unchained* by Tonio K. Producer: Rick Neigher, Bob Rose, Howard Steele, T Bone Burnett. What? 1987

15. *October* by U2. Producer: Steve Lillywhite. Island 1981
16. *Truth Decay* by T Bone Burnett. Producer: Reggie Fisher. Takoma 1980
17. *The Joshua Tree* by U2. Producer: Daniel Lanois and Brian Eno. Island 1987
18. *Humans* by Bruce Cockburn. Producer: Eugene Martynec. Millenium 1980
19. *Shotgun Angel* by Daniel Amos. Producer: Jonathan David Brown. Maranatha! Music 1977
20. *Horrendous Disc* by Daniel Amos. Producer: Larry Norman. Solid Rock 1981
21. *Straight On* by DeGarmo & Key. Producer: Joe Hardy, Eddie DeGarmo, Dana Key. Lamb & Lion 1979
22. *Meltdown* by Steve Taylor. Producer: Jonathan David Brown. Sparrow 1985
23. *I Want To Be a Clone* by Steve Taylor. Producer: Jonathan David Brown. Sparrow 1984
24. *Awaiting Your Reply* by Resurrection Bank. Producer: Resurrection Band. Star Song 1978
25. *Matters of the Heart* by Bob Bennett. Producer: Jonathan David Brown. Priority 1982

Source: This listing represents the opinions of writers and contributors to *Contemporary Christian Music* magazine, as of June 1988. Copyright © 1988 by CCM Publications, Inc. Used by permission.

“” FOCUS QUOTE **The creative men and women are in the church. Some express their art through music, the only art fully accepted by the church. But others sit quietly alone; waiting to be affirmed, encouraged, supported. They are waiting for the body of Christ to understand and find room for the novel, the film, and play, the masterpiece ruminating within that could reach beyond the subculture and challenge the basic assumptions of our secular age and point the world toward ultimate truth.**

Until the church goes beyond just lip service to encourage and invest some of her resources, her members, and even her own children in the pursuit of redeeming art, I fear the body of Christ will be left with only the shrill, small voice of reaction to art instead of the clear, powerful voice of the Creator of art.—Max McLean in *Christianity Today,* September 8, 1989 issue.

DEVELOPMENT OF CHURCH MUSIC THROUGH THE CENTURIES

Gladys Christensen

Introduction

Period	*Form*	*Characteristics*	*Example*
Old Testament	Psalms	Hebrew poetry for temple worship. Responsorial usage allows people to respond with Amen, Hallelujah or His mercy endureth forever.	Psalm 136
		Antiphonal use involves two choruses alternately on psalm verse or half verse.	Psalm 142
New Testament	Canticles	Scriptural songs other than Psalms include: Magnificat, Benedictus	Luke 1
		Gloria in Excelsis, Nunc Dimittis,	Luke 2
		Agnus Dei	John 1
		Basis for Mass, Holy Communion, Morning and Evening Prayer services.	

Period	*Form*	*Characteristics*	*Example*
Early Christian	Hymns	Free texts on scriptural themes include: Te Deum, Gloria Patri, Sanctus—Text expanded from Holy, Holy, Holy.	Isaiah 6
	Chant	Monotone recitation of scripture and liturgy by priest.	
		Plainsong—A single, undulating melodic line sung in unison. Text governs free rhythm.	
		Psalm tones—Melodic formulae for choir or soloist to sing the psalms.	
		Antiphon—A psalm portion which precedes and follows the entire psalm.	

Development of Choral Music

Period	*Movement/ Form*	*Person/Contribution*	*Example*
from 9th c.	ORGANUM	A *cantus firmus* (liturgical chant) accompanied by one or more additional voices at interval of 4th or 5th. Strict Style: Note against note	
	SEQUENCE/ TROPE	Practice of setting a free text to melismatic passage (syllabic).	
12th c.	MASS	**Leonin** writes earliest musical setting of mass.	
12-13th c.		**Perotin.** Development includes the upper voices moving more quickly than tenor.	
	MOTET	Given song in tenor is accompanied by upper parts singing own text (1250).	
14th c.	MASS	**Guillaume Machault.** First polyphonic (more than one voice) setting of ordinary (unchanging parts).	Messe de Notre Dame
15th c.	MASS, MOTET, HYMNS, ANTIPHONS	Development of polyphonic choral music and composition techniques by:	
		John Dunstable. England	
		Johannes Okenghem. Netherlands, Belgium, France	
		Josquin des Pres. Belgium, Italy, France	
16th c.	MASS, MOTET, MAGNIFICAT	**Orlando Lassus** perfects the motet form; expressive settings.	Penitential Psalms (1565)
		Giovanni Perluigi (Palestrina) devotes entire life to church music; carries out reforms to preserve integrity of text.	

Period	*Movement/ Form*	*Person/Contribution*	*Example*
		Adrian Willaert. Venetian polychoral style (1550) places divided chorus in opposite galleries of St. Marks cathedral.	
	CONCERTATO STYLE	Instruments with voices or contrasting choral or instrumental groups. Andrea and Giovanni Gabrielli develop style.	
	ORATORIO	Opera on sacred text. Multi-movement work utilizes chorus, solo or both. No action, scenery or costumes.	
		San Felippo dei Neri (c. 1550) institutes popular service in Oratory (Prayer chapel) Laude (devotional songs) provide basis for semi-dramatic work on sacred theme.	
c. 1600	MONODY	**Claudio Monteverdi.** Composition includes melodic writing in recitative style: a narrative text sung by solo voice with chordal accompaniment.	
16th c.	ENGLISH CHORAL MUSIC		
	ANTHEM	**Christopher Tye** writes the first English motet (c. 1550). Syllabic, more chordal, straightforward rhythm.	
		Thomas Tallis. A founder of English cathedral music. Latin masses and motets.	
		William Byrd develops the verse anthem to include choral and solo sections.	
		Latin masses and motets.	
17th c.	CANTATA Italy	Smaller version of oratorio.	
		Giacomo Carissimi. His cantatas establish older form consisting of two or more arias with recitative, no chorus.	
		Carissimi composes twelve oratorios on O.T. themes. Soloist carries out narrative. Music descriptive of text.	Jephte (c. 1650)
	VERSE ANTHEM		
	England	**Henry Purcell** adds instrumental sections to chorus and solo sections.	

Period	*Movement/ Form*	*Person/Contribution*	*Example*
	DRAMATIC CONCERTATO		
	Germany	**Heinrich Schutz.** Venetian influence: instruments with voices. Recitative is pictorial setting of text—perfect union of words and music in German. Continuo required. Not based on chorale or cantus.	Symphoniae Sacra (1629,-47,-50) The Seven Words of Christ on the Cross (1664) Passion Settings (1666)
17-18th c.	CHORALE CANTATA	**Dietrich Buxtehude** institutes evening concerts of sacred music during Advent. Writes chorale cantatas and motets for solo and chorus. Instrumental accompaniment.	Wachet Auf In Dulci Jubilo
		J. S. Bach. Cantatas for specific services include chorus, solo recitative, arias, duets. Instrumental accompaniment. Freely composed texts. Chorale tune harmonized at conclusion.	Magnificat, Passions, Mass, Motets (from 1723) Christmas Oratorio a series of cantatas (1733-34)
	ORATORIO		
	England	**George F. Handel.** Dramatic Biblical text. Includes chorus, recitative, aria, duet, instrumental accompaniment.	Israel in Egypt (1738) Messiah (1741) Jephtha (1751)
		Anthem collections are high point of Baroque development.	
	CLASSIC-ROMANTIC DEVELOPMENTS	Development of opera and symphony expands the resources of sacred choral composition.	
	MASS	**Haydn, Mozart, Beethoven, Schubert and Bruckner** compose concert settings of the mass.	
18th c.	Germany/ Austria	**Joseph Haydn.**	Seven Last Words (1785 orch) (1794 text)
		New impetus to oratorio. Free text.	Creation (1798)
		Wolfgang A. Mozart	Solemn Vespers (1780) Requiem (Mass for Dead) (1791)

Period	*Movement/ Form*	*Person/Contribution*	*Example*
19th c.		**Ludwig van Beethoven**	Christ on the Mount of Olives (1803)
			Missa Solemnis (1818-23)
		Felix Mendelssohn	St. Paul (1836)
			Elijah (1846)
	France	**Hector Berlioz**	Requiem (1837)
			Te Deum (1848-49)
			L'Enfance du Christ (1854)
	Germany	**Johannes Brahms.** Musical settings of Scriptures on themes of comfort and eternal life.	A German Requiem (1857-1868)
	Austria	**Anton Bruckner**	Te Deum (1884)
	Italy	**Giuseppe Verdi**	Requiem Mass (1874)
	France	**Claude Debussy**	The Prodigal Son (1884)
		Gabriel Fauré	Requiem (1887)
		Cesar Franck	The Beatitudes (1899)
19-20th c.	England	**Charles Stanford**	
		Charles H. H. Parry. Anthems and service music of high quality set a new standard.	
	America	**Charles Ives.** Psalm settings	Psalm 67
20th c.	Representative Choral Works		
	France	**Arthur Honneger**	Symphonic Psalm King David (1923)
		Francis Poulenc	Gloria (1961)
	England	**Ralph Vaughan Williams**	Hodie (1954)
		William Walton	Belshazzar's Feast (1931)
		Benjamin Britten	A Ceremony of Carols (1942)
			Festival Te Deum (1945)
		Andrew Lloyd Webber	Requiem (1984)
		John Rutter. Carol Arrangements	Requiem (1978)

Period	Movement/ Form	Person/Contribution	Example
	America	**Igor Stravinsky**	Symphony of Psalms (1930) Mass (1948)
		Leo Sowerby	Forsaken of Man
		Randall Thompson	Peaceable Kingdom (1936)
		Leonard Bernstein.	Chichester Psalms (1965)
		A theatre piece including singers, players, dancers. Text added to traditional mass.	Mass (1972)
	Poland	**Krzysztof Penderecki**	Passion according to St. Luke (1965)
Development of Congregational Music			
3rd c.	Greek and Latin Hymnody	**Clement of Alexandria** writes earliest extant hymn.	Shepherd of Tender Youth
4th c.		**Ambrose—Bishop of Milan** encourages congregational singing; writes hymns.	O Splendor of God's Glory
6th c.		**Gregory the Great—Rome.** Under his papal reign, the Schola Cantorum codifies chant and psalm tones. Writes hymns.	Father, We Praise Thee
8-13th c.		Period of rich development. Many hymns, translated to English, are still in use.	Come, Ye Faithful
			All Glory, Laud and Honor
13-15th c.	Carol	From carola—ring dance: a narrative dance song for any season.	In Dulci Jubilo (Christmas)
			O Sons and Daughters of the King (Easter)
		St. Francis of Assisi develops practice of singing Nativity songs around a manger scene (1223).	
16th c.	Metrical psalmody	The psalms in meter or verse.	
	GERMAN REFORMATION	**Martin Luther** versifies psalms (1523). Translates Latin hymns to German. Encourages original hymns for congregational worship. Adapts music from quality folk songs and Latin chant.	Psalm 46 "God is our refuge and strength" becomes A Mighty Fortress or A Sure Stronghold
			Veni, Creator Spiritus becomes Komm, Gott Schopfer

Period	*Movement/ Form*	*Person/Contribution*	*Example*
	Chorale	German congregations sing hymns in unison.	
	GENEVAN REFORMATION	**John Calvin** begins to versify psalms (1539). Enlists poet Marot to continue the work in French. Publishes psalter in 1543. Bourgeois writes musical settings.	Psalms of David (1551) "Old Hundredth" tune set to Psalm 100
	English Psalmody	**Thomas Sternhold** revises his own versification modelled on Marot (1549).	
		John Hopkins enlarges psalter in 1562 to include all psalms. Printed with melodies. This is adopted as official psalter by those who flee to Geneva with Knox.	
	ANGLICAN REFORMATION Service Settings	**John Merbecke** sets service of Holy Communion in four-part harmony, one note for one syllable (1549).	Kyrie, Credo, Sanctus and Benedictus, Lord's Prayer, Agnus Dei, Gloria in Excelsis
	Anglican Chant	Method devised for singing psalms of canticles. Symbols indicate when to change pitch in verses of variable length.	
	NEW WORLD		
	American Psalmody	Genevan and English psalters brought to America. Bay Psalm Book printed in America (1640).	
17th c.	ENGLAND		
	English Hymnody	**Bishop Thomas Ken** desires that people praise God in own words—not only in psalms and canticles. Doxology is final stanza of his hymn.	All Praise to Thee, My God This Night (1674)
18th c.		**Isaac Watts** versifies psalms in freer translations than in previous psalters. Collection of original hymns.	
		Hymns and Spiritual Songs (1707)	
		Psalms of David Imitated (1719)	Psalm 72 Jesus Shall Reign Psalm 90 O God, Our Help
		Charles Wesley writes hymns with freer texts based on psalms and N.T. themes. Publishes two major collections:	
		Foundery Collection (1742)	
		Hymns for the Use of the People Called Methodists (1780)	Contains original 18 stanzas of O For A Thousand Tongues

Period	*Movement/ Form*	*Person/Contribution*	*Example*
	AMERICA	Moravian missionary movement settles in Bethlehem, Pennsylvania (1741). Introduces classical music traditions and instrumentation.	
		Wm. Billings publishes collection of psalms which include fuguing tunes.	New England Psalm Singer (1770) When Jesus Wept
19th c.	Gospel music	Outgrowth of Kentucky revival (1800)	
	White spirituals	Shape note hymns—System of teaching reading. Collections provide tunes in use today:	Southern Harmony (1835) contains tunes for Amazing Grace, What Wondrous Love The Sacred Harp (1844) tune "Beach Spring"
	ENGLAND OXFORD MOVEMENT	Return to Catholic traditions (1833) Emphasis on content and reverence in worship.	
		John Keble writes poetry for church year	Sun of My Soul
		Many hymns from Greek or Latin are translated to poetic English by **Edward Caswall** and **John M. Neale**	Jesus, the Very Thought of Thee All Glory, Laud and Honor
	REVIVAL MOVEMENTS		
	(England and America)	Musicians join evangelists: write gospel songs, sing, and direct singing (from 1873)	
		Ira D. Sankey with Dwight Moody	Composes tune: Hiding in Thee
		Phillip Bliss with Maj. Whittle	Tune: When Peace Like a River
		Homer Rodeheaver with Billy Sunday	Tune: Then Jesus Came
		Prolific writer **Fanny Crosby** writes 8000 gospel hymns	To God Be the Glory, Blessed Assurance
20th c.	Evangelistic crusades	**Cliff Barrows** and **George Beverly Shea** with Billy Graham	
	Solo artist	**Ken Medema** composes and sings of social justice	

Period	*Movement/ Form*	*Person/Contribution*	*Example*
20th c. trends	Hymnals	Inclusion of hymns, chant, chorales, spiritual songs from a wide variety of religious sources, ethnic and racial backgrounds. Themes include nature, environment, space, social concerns.	Earth and All Stars O Young and Fear-less Prophet
		Gospel songs stress personal experience and conviction. Emphasis on the individual rather than institutional church. Exhortation to fellow man.	I Am Thine, O Lord
		Folk songs: Songs in the common, pictorial language of the people, traced to racial or national origin.	What Wondrous Love (USA)
		Spirituals (Afro-American): Black folk songs about the tasks of day or a better day in heaven.	Swing Low, Sweet Chariot
	Scripture songs	Literal Scripture passages set to simple, folklike melodies.	
	Psalm singing	Renewed interest in recitation of psalms on musical tones.	

Contemporary Popular Music

Period	*Style*	*Performing Artist or Group/Contribution*	*Example*
	Inspirational	Sandi Patti; Steve Green; Larnelle Harris; Evie Tornquist; Bill and Gloria Gaither. Lyrics tend to be praise-oriented.	Jesus, We Just Want to Thank You; We Shall Behold Him; He Touched Me; The Father Hath Provided.
	Rock	Petra; Michael W. Smith; White Heart; Russ Taff; Rick Cua; Allies. Formula of two bars in blues or ballad style; both melody and harmony subject to beat. Development includes physical movement and high volume level. Ranges from "hard" to "soft." Lyrics often address social issues or personal morality and salvation.	Beat the System; I Can, I Will; The Devil Is a Liar.
	Contemporary	Imperials; Amy Grant; Twila Paris; Michael Card; First Call. Softer sound than rock, often highlights solo singer with acoustic instrumentation. Lyrically, is a combination of rock and inspirational forms.	Great Is the Lord; El Shaddai.

Period	*Movement/ Form*	*Person/Contribution*	*Example*
	Southern Gospel	Hemphills; The Cathedrals; Florida Boys; Nelsons. Usually quartet harmonies, family groups. Lyrics often stress heavenly rewards and rely heavily on clever phrase turns.	He's Still Working On Me; When He Was On the Cross (You Were On His Mind); I'll Fly Away.
	Traditional Black Gospel	Aretha Franklin; Shirley Caesar; Al Green. Spiritual and gospel songs, often sung by a choir, but with more emphasis on rhythm than church music or hymns.	One Lord, One Faith, One Baptism; Celebration; We Sing Praises.
	Contemporary Black Gospel	The Winans; The Clark Sisters; Andrae Crouch. Combines elements of rock with rhythm and blues. Increasingly known as "Urban Contemporary."	Let My People Go; No Time to Lose; Give Me More Love In My Heart.

About the author: Gladys Christensen has completed 35 years of teaching in the Wheaton Conservatory of Music, Wheaton College, IL. She holds the Associate certificate of the American Guild of Organists. She has extensive experience as a church organist and accompanist for cantata and oratorio performances. Contemporary Popular Music information provided by John Styll, editor, *Contemporary Christian Music* Magazine.

POPULAR MUSIC DEFINITIONS

Dave Hart

The world of popular music is becoming more complicated. Many people are getting lost in the sheer volume of classifications, sub-divisions, terms, styles, genres, etc. It can literally boggle the mind. In an effort to sort through the musical mush, a brief list of modern musical terms and their definitions follow:

Acid Rock. A term used to describe the hard-edged electronic music created by "hippies" in the late 1960s and early 1970s. The music was supposed to reproduce the feelings and attitudes of the drug culture, particularly the psychedelic experiences of LSD (i.e. acid). It is sometimes still used today to refer to hard rock and heavy metal, but the term is generally considered old-fashioned and is rarely used by professional musicians or today's youth.

Blues. The mournful melodies of the African slaves became known as the blues sometime after the Civil War. During the 1920s and on into the 1940s, performers began to move from the rural clubs of the south (often known as road houses) to the clubs of the northern big cities like Chicago and Detroit. There it became a basic element in the development of big band jazz and other forms of popular music of the post-World War era. The sound was "rediscovered" in the early 1960s by young white musicians in America and Europe, becoming a major influence on the sound and direction of rock music.

Classical. Generally refers to vocal and instrumental compositions of 18th and 19th century Europe. Classical music includes operas, symphonies, chorales, sonatas, and chamber music. The many inspiring religious works of the period have led some people to believe that all classical music is of a Christian spiritual nature. However, many composers of this period were quite secular in their orientations, including some with notoriously immoral life-styles and others who used occult and mystical themes to inspire the direction of their compositions.

Contemporary Christian Music (CCM). A generic term used to describe any popular music style with Christian lyrics and intent. CCM usually distinguishes itself from traditional church music forms such as classical music, church hymns, or Gospel music. The bulk of CCM reflects pop music and adult contemporary styles, but includes rock, heavy metal, new wave, jazz, and improvisational/experimental styles as well. Generally the production quality, sound and look of contemporary Christian artists is on a par with secular artists, but with a Christian message or worldview.

Country Music. Derived from English and Irish folk music, which then developed into early American folk music, bluegrass, hillbilly mountain music, and country and western with its distinctive southern twang. In the 1940s, it was combined with big band styles (including blues, jazz, even polkas) in what was known as Western swing. In the 1950s, it reflected the blues in honky tonk music, and later included a light rock feel known as rockabilly. By the 1970s country rock (played by rock musicians) and outlaw country (played by country artists) was essentially the same sound. The popularity of country during the Urban Cowboy craze of the late 1970s resulted in country music that was virtually indistinguishable from pop music and Top 40 radio. Lately there is a move to return to country roots with basic story telling, Southern accents, and the twang of steel guitars.

Dance Music. A generic term for any popular music with enough rhythm and beat to get the toes tapping and the body moving. Rock and roll was always designed for dancing. Dance craze's came and went in the 1960s, most notably the Twist, one of the first popular dances that could be done without the necessity of a dance partner. For awhile everybody "boogied" especially to the funky rhythms of black dance music in the early 1970s. Some of this music was reclaimed by white gays in what was to become known as disco.

As disco died, punks brought a violent form of body bashing known as slam dancing. But more commercial forms of New Wave brought back opportunities for couples to dance again. Black musicians dared to be different with break dancing, which included a lot of gymnastics and spinning on shoulders and heads. The Latin rhythms of Cuban, Mexican, and South American music introduced a spicy flavor to dancing called Salsa. The latest trend along those lines is called Lambada, which is unabashedly described as sex with your clothes on. Most of today's youth find their dance music in white pop, the current derivatives of New Wave music, and current versions of R & B, funk, and Rap/Hip Hop from the black music scene.

Disco. The Dance club phenomenon of the mid-1970s was best exemplified in the 1977 film "Saturday Night Fever," featuring the music of the Bee Gees. Before that time, disco was stigmatized as music for blacks and gays. Many music critics of the time despised disco because it was coldly electronic and over-produced, with little real passion, warmth, or romance. Disco fever burned itself out by 1980, but dance music continued in the form of commercial New Wave and pop music.

Funk. A term applied to black dance music in the 1970s. It was characterized by a minimum of melody and a maximum of syncopated rhythms. The derivative word *funky* originally meant dirty or sexy. The word came to be applied to anything that was current and dynamic—synonymous with words like groovy, hip, and happening.

Fusion. The term simply means the merging of any two ideas. In music, it refers to combining two or more distinctive styles, such as a jazz-rock fusion, which combined brass horns with electric guitar. The 1970s also saw attempts at classical-rock fusion and funk-rock fusion. Some music critics speculate that these ponderous styles of music and the electronic excesses of this era were so complex and sophisticated that they led to the severe decline in the music industry at that time. Since then music producers have tried to keep things simpler.

Gospel. Today the secular music industry refers to almost all modern Christian

POPULAR MUSIC DEFINITIONS cont.

music as gospel music. But traditionally, the term refers to the sounds of the black church. It takes two basic forms. One is the plaintive spiritual which parallels blues and soul music in secular terms. The other form is the high energy call and response that so many black choirs are famous for. It is this sound that gave rise to rhythm and blues, and later, what we call rock and roll. In addition to Black Gospel, many people enjoy what they call Southern Gospel. This refers to music derived from country/western and American folk styles popular in white churches in the south, typically performed by quartets and family groups.

Heavy Metal. This style features bombastic power chords, screaming electric guitars, throat-wrenching vocals and a demolition-derby approach to drumming. Devoted fans often treat heavy metal as a way of life. Today heavy metal can generally be divided into three basic categories. Each retains the extreme volume but may appeal to different audiences:

Black Metal. A demons-and-drama approach to rock music. This style combines the grossest images of a horror movie with loud, driving music to provide the ultimate in blood curdling entertainment. Magic, Satanism, mutilations, murder, and mayhem are reflected in their stage shows, lyrics, costumes and props. (Best examples: King Diamond, Slayer, W.A.S.P.)

Party/Glam Metal. Sex, drugs and partying are the main themes. This music expresses the idea to live for today and don't think about tomorrow. It gives the impression that there is no price to pay for an irresponsible life-style. It is sometimes called glam metal (short for glamorous) because of the feminine make-up and brightly colored costumes, although many groups today have feigned that look. (Best examples: Bon Jovi, Def Leppard, Warrant, Skid Row.)

Thrash Metal. A synthesis of punk rhythms and the screaming electric guitars of heavy metal. Sometimes called speed metal or metal hardcore. Themes are best summed up as "67 ways to die," because so much of it focuses on anger, hatred, fatalism, gore, death, and a negative attitude toward authority. Fans participate in "moshing," which include the mosh pit (the heavy metal version of what punkers call slam dancing), headbanging (vigorous shaking of the head to the rhythm of the music), and stage-diving (a dangerous practice of throwing oneself from the stage into the crowd—sometimes they land on people, sometimes on the floor.) (Best examples: Metallica, Megadeth, Anthrax.)

Jazz. Originally a Creole Indian word for sex. It applies to many forms of improvisational music, both vocal and instrumental. The form started with a style in New Orleans which improvised on popular ragtime melodies. It came to be known as Dixieland Jazz. Big Bands were sometimes distinguished from popular orchestras by their experimental styles. These were variously referred to as swing (1930s), bebop (1940s), and "cool," hard-bop, or modal playing (1950s). Progressive jazz represents the most experimental efforts to stretch the structure and form of popular music. Fifty years ago, jazz musicians were considered less than reputable, and the music was often forbidden in the church. Today's jazz stylings tend to be considered smooth and sophisticated and are more accepted in church circles than the angry, raw styles of rock music.

MTV. Music Television was an inevitable product of the advent of cable TV. Many predicted its early demise when it first aired in 1981. Instead it began to shape and influence music and our culture in a strong fashion. It often makes or breaks a new artist, and the music industry depends on music videos heavily to influence concert and record sales. MTV has also shaped fashions and clothing styles. It has changed the way commercials are filmed and viewed, as well as influencing the pace and feel of movies and other TV programs.

New Age. A generic term for almost any kind of soft, light, improvisational jazz or instrumental music. Its gentle, soothing tones were designed to calm the nerves of Wall Street Wizards and Yuppie jet-setters living in the fast lane. Light, airy instrumentals might also be accompanied by the sounds of nature such as ocean waves, bubbling brooks, soft rainfall, or gentle breezes. Some of this music is specifically designed to help those in the New Age movement to achieve meditative states, but much of it is just talented musicians exploring melodic jazz stylings.

New Wave. Also called new music, it is a wide-spread but almost meaningless musical term. It generally represents those who shifted from the raw, angry sounds of punk to the more commercial use of electronic synthesizers in performing music in the late 1970s. It was essentially pop music with the punk trappings of alienated lyrics and ultramodern fashions. Eventually, it became a catch-all phrase for any new musical scene that emerged after 1976 that wasn't strictly punk or heavy metal. Today this music is generally referred to as Modern Rock and tends to emphasize electronic synthesizers, hollow vocals, and an often bleak perspective of life. It may also be referred to as:

Alternative Music. A term that generally referred to new music and punk that was played on local college radio formats. This music was considered too abrasive, offensive, political, "underground," and elitist in the early to mid-1980s to get airplay on regular radio stations.

Dark Music. Refers to a somber dark style of new music characterized by eerie, haunting melodies, black clothing, and hopelessness. Themes of lost loves and death fantasies only serve to emphasize the dreary despair and a helpless resignation to a bleak future.

Gothic Rock. A more aggressive approach to the doom and gloom mentality of Dark music. The dark clothes and capes accent stark white faces and dark make-up, suggesting a New Wave Halloween party. The music may vary from somber to frantic, and focus on themes of death and the occult. Like Black Metal, the musical performances are often accompanied by theatrical stage props to enhance the eerie horror movie atmosphere. There are entire clubs in Europe and America that cater to this scene.

Post-Modern. Also called post-punk or post-mod. It often reflects the political and social sensibilities of punk with more "accessible" or commercial music styles. This style usually gets airplay on radio and MTV.

Pop. Short for popular music. It represented a move from the more complex concert structures of opera and classical music to a focus on a single tune. Early pop hits in the 1930s were pushed by "drummers" (salesmen) of printed music and later popularized through the movies. Patriotic propaganda was pushed by pop tunes during World War II and the pop charts were developed during this time. Pop music became more accessible during the post-war era and the pop charts reflected the rise in record sales.

Pop music is sometimes contrasted to rock music in its emphasis on piano and keyboard arrangements and a focus on romantic themes, whereas rock emphasizes the electric guitar and more confrontational lyrics. But in general, pop music continues to be no better defined than whatever is popular on the radio and the Top 40 sales charts. Today those charts predominantly reflect the sales of CDs (compact discs) and cassette tapes, as vinyl records are becoming a thing of the past.

Punk Rock. Originated in England in the 1970s primarily as a protest against the music industry, which punks claimed had lost its revolutionary edge. The music is raw and angry, stressing the pounding rhythms rather than any kind of melodic form. The musicians were usually untrained and the music simple (three chords and a drum), vocals were abrasive (shouting of obscenities and hatred) and rhythms were very fast (often a hundred or more beats a minute, give or take a few). Punk was never widely popular, although it did receive some sensational attention for awhile in the late 1970s.

POPULAR MUSIC DEFINITIONS cont.

Today punk has gone underground, which means that it is not part of the usual circles in the music industry. There are still punk bands and punk clubs, but most of the look and sound has been absorbed by the Thrash Metal scene. Punks are gaining some attention again in the form of Skinheads—a particular type of punk who shaves his head and tends to subscribe to white supremacy ideas.

Rap. Also known as Hip Hop and Bass Music. It originated on the streets of New York City with rappers speaking in rhymes over the back beat of a beat box. As stereo systems were added at dances, the sounds were enhanced by running the stereo needle quickly over records in a style called scratching. The songs usually reflect street life for blacks in the inner city, including boasting, sexual conquests (often in graphic detail), gang life, violence, and drugs. Rap is often fused with pop/dance styles in a form called House Rap, where verses are rapped and the choruses are sung.

Reggae. Jamaican dance music, related to Afro-Caribbean styles like mento, calypso, and ska. The acoustic versions are generally pleasant because the rhythms duplicate the heartbeat. By the 1970s virtually all Reggae lyrics were influenced by Rastafarian beliefs. Among other things, Rastas believe in smoking marijuana ("de ganja") as a way to attain spiritual wisdom, and the belief that Haile Selassie, emperor of Ethiopia, is Christ returned to earth.

Rock and Roll. Originally a blues term for sexual intercourse. Rock and roll was simply the white version of rhythm and blues. Early rock and roll in the mid-1950s was influenced by country music and folk as well as southern black music. After the British Invasion of the mid-1960s, the music simply became known as rock. Drugs, sex, and rock and roll became the anthem of the younger generation in the 1960s. The music is more graphic and intense than ever with themes of passionate love, casual sex, rebellion toward authority, and seeking the endless party. Today there are also some messages of social responsibility, but that is countered with an increase in violence, references to the occult, and a good deal of macho sexism.

Rhythm and Blues. R & B is the black version of rock and roll. It is more energetic than the blues and covers a wider variety of topics in its lyrics. It was called "race music" for some time, but it gradually grew more respectable and evolved into soul, funk, disco and other "black" music dance styles. It is largely derived from the Gospel "shout" style and was essential in the development of rock and roll.

Source: Dave Hart is research analyst with Al Menconi Ministries. He is also a popular youth speaker nationally on the topic of the influence of rock music. And he is the pastor of Sanctuary, San Diego, a church that ministers to heavy metal fans. Reprinted with permission from Al Menconi Ministries. Dave is the associate editor of *Media Update*, the ministry's bimonthly publication that teaches parents and youth workers how to effectively deal with young people and their music. For a free sample copy, contact Al Menconi Ministries, P.O. Box 969-F, Cardiff, CA 92007-0810, (619) 436-8676.

INSTRUMENTS TEENS LIKE TO PLAY

1. Synthesizer/keyboards 34%
2. Woodwinds 32%
3. Acoustic piano 31%
4. Brass 21%
5. Guitar 13%

Source: American Music Conference, survey of 1,313 teens

FOCUS FACT

Award for the most prolific hymn writer goes to Fanny Crosby (1820-1915), who wrote more than 8,000 hymns. Charles Wesley (1707-1788) is runner-up with 6,000 hymns to his credit.

AMERICA'S FAVORITE HYMNS

1. Amazing Grace
2. How Great Thou Art
3. In the Garden
4. The Old Rugged Cross
5. What a Friend We Have in Jesus
6. A Mighty Fortress
7. Blessed Assurance
8. He Lives
9. Victory in Jesus
10. Holy, Holy, Holy

"Amazing Grace"is the most popular hymn in America, according to a survey of 10,000 newspaper readers, ages 5 to 96, taken by George Plagenz , nationally syndicated religion columnist. Voters represent 32 denominations.

President and Mrs. Bush were among those who took part in the survey. Mrs. Bush chose "Nearer My God to Thee" as her favorite hymn. It ranked 19th in the poll.

President Bush chose "Eternal Father Strong to Save," which Mr. Plagenz said was "not among the leaders."

NEW RELEASES: EASTER CHURCH MUSIC

Arrangement

Crown Him with Many Crowns
Matthew Bridges, Godfrey Thring, George Elvey, arranged/Ovid Young
Word Music, $1.10

This traditional hymn for SATB choirs has been arranged into an anthem with parts for brass and percussion.

No Wonder
Niles Borop, Barbi and Terri Franklin, arranged/Russell Mauldin
The Benson Company, $0.95

This moderately difficult choral arrangement is for adult SATB choirs and can be performed in five minutes.

Organ Music for Festive Occasions
L. Dean Bye
Cathedral Music Press, $4.95

This moderately difficult instrumental music is designed for organ or organ and trumpet.

Cantata

A Symphony of Praise
Tom Fettke
Sparrow Records, $4.95

This moderately difficult cantata for adult choirs combines inspirational and traditional praise music. It can be performed in 47 minutes.

Behold the Man
Arranged by Joseph Linn
Lillenas Publishing Company, $4.59

This easy cantata for adult SATB choirs, with a four-part hymnal-style format, can be performed in 30 minutes. It features a mixture of contemporary favorites, hymns, gospel songs, and scriptural narrations.

Forever Life
Don Marsh
Pathway Music, $4.50

This 30-minute cantata for adult SATB choirs celebrates life eternal. It is moderately easy to learn and includes optional narration.

Glorious Morning
David Culross
Music Marketplace/Paragon, $4.95

This moderately difficult cantata for SATB adult choirs contains traditional favorites and popular songs that can be performed in 35 minutes.

Hallelujah! Hallelujah!
Phil and Lynne Brower
Singspiration, $5.50

This challenging cantata for adult SATB choirs features audience involvement recounting the events of the first Easter. It can be performed in 45 minutes.

NEW RELEASES: EASTER CHURCH MUSIC cont.

Into His Presence
Ed Kee
Brentwood Music, $4.50

This easy cantata for adult SATB choirs with congregational participation can be performed in 25 minutes.

No Wonder . . . We Call Him Our Savior
Dave Clark and Russell Mauldin
The Benson Company, $4.95

This moderately difficult cantata for adult SATB choirs includes narration, a solo, and a duet and can be performed in 36 minutes.

Raise Your Joys and Triumphs High
Dave Williamson
Brentwood Music, $4.95

This moderately easy adult cantata features traditional hymns and a joyous praise anthem. It can be performed in 40 minutes.

The Miracle of Easter
Joe Parks
Singspiration, $3.50

This easy-to-learn cantata for adult SATB choirs is a mini-musical about Christ's resurrection and can be performed in 20 minutes.

The Passion of Our Lord
Eugene Butler
Fred Bock Music Company, $4.95

This 45-minute adult cantata recounts our Lord's passion and death. It is moderately easy to learn.

Children's Musical

Biblical Easter and Spring Performances
Compiled by Rebecca Daniel
Shining Star Publications, $7.95

Original Easter plays, musicals and programs combine with choral readings, poems, and stories in this performance book for 5 to 13-year-olds.

His Only Forgotten Son
Shirly Garvais
Adventures, Inc., $2.95

This moderately difficult children's musical contains the Easter theme and a lesson about what can happen when we forget Jesus. It can be performed in 35 to 40 minutes.

The Boy Who Believed
Claire Cloninger, arranged by Joseph Linn
Word Music, $4.95

This children's Easter musical can be performed in unison or two parts.

Musical

He's Living Today
John W. Peterson
John W. Peterson Music Company, $4.95

This moderately difficult musical for SATB adult choirs includes optional narration and can be performed in 38 minutes.

The Father Hath Provided
Dennis and Nan Allen, orchestrated by Camp Kirkland
Word Music, $4.95

This moderately easy musical is for adult SATB choirs and can be performed in 35 minutes.

The Promise
Jan Dargatz and Gary Rhodes
Word Music, $5.95

Together with an original story line, this pageant features traditional and contemporary hymns on the life of Jesus Christ, complete with overture, medley, and finale. For adult SATB choirs, it is moderately difficult to learn and can be performed in 75 minutes.

Octavo

Alleluia
David Lantz III
GlorySound, $0.95

In this moderately difficult octavo for adult SATB choirs, the word alleluia creates a sustained and gradually building anthem. Performance time is three minutes.

Alleluia!
L. Dean Bye
Cathedral Music Press, $1.35

This moderately difficult SATB octavo for adult choirs can include congregational participation.

Behold He Is Risen
Dave Clark and Don Koch, arranged by John Lee
Singspiration, $0.90

This moderately difficult octavo for adult SATB choirs can be performed in four minutes.

Christ Arose
Robert Lowry, arranged by Don Wyrtzen
Singspiration, $0.90

This newly arranged octavo for adult SATB choirs is moderately difficult to learn and can be performed in three minutes.

Easter
Arranged by Camp Kirkland
Alexandria House, $2.50

This moderately difficult adult choir octavo is part of the "Camp Kirkland Signature"series. Featuring Bill and Gloria Gaither's "Resurrection," a worship song from Randy Vader and Jay Rouse, and a hymn medley, it can be performed in approximately 15 minutes.

Easter
John Leavitt
Augsburg Fortress, $1.25

This moderately difficult octavo for adult SATB choirs can be performed in five minutes. Optional parts include two trumpets and horn, two trombones, timpani, xylophone, glockenspiel, suspended cymbal, and triangle.

Fanfare for Easter Day
Benjamin Harlan
GlorySound, $0.95

This moderately difficult octavo for SATB choirs, two trumpets, and an organ incorporates the hymn "Christ the Lord Is Risen Today" and can be performed in two to four minutes.

Gloria!
William Bay
Cathedral Music Press, $1.10

This SATB adult octavo with tenor or soprano solo is moderately difficult.

He Died for Me
Joe Parks
Singspiration, $0.90

This easy octavo for adult SATB choirs contains music for a complete service, including a call to worship, anthem, prayer response, and benediction.

He Is Risen
Craig Smith, arranged by Don Wyrtzen
Singspiration, $0.95

Reflecting the excitement of Luke 24:6-8, this moderately difficult octavo for adult SATB choirs can be performed in three minutes.

He Is Risen!
Nancy Price and Don Besig
Harold Flammer, $0.95

Incorporating the hymn tune "Regent Square," this easy octavo for adult SATB choirs can be performed in about two minutes.

Hear the Sound of Joy
Lodovico Viadana and Hal Hopson
Harold Flammer, $0.95

Incorporating the hymn tune "Regent Square," this easy octavo for adult SATB choirs can be performed in about two minutes.

Jesus Christ Is Risen Today
Llanfair, arranged by William Bay
Cathedral Music Press, $1.50

This moderately difficult adult SATB octavo includes a trumpet part and optional brass and congregational participation.

Jesus Is Our King
Sherrell Prebble
Cathedral Music Press, $1.35

This octavo for SATB adult choirs is moderately difficult to learn. Congregation, piano, gutar, and trumpet parts are included.

Let Your Alleluias Rise
K. Lee Scott
Augusburg Fortress, $0.95

This moderately difficult *a cappella* octavo for adult choirs includes tenor or soprano solo and can be performed in about five minutes.

O Lord, I Will Praise You
Gloria Gaither, Michael W. Smith, Phill McHugh,Tom Fettke, and Jean Sibelius, arranged by Tom Fettke
Word Music, $1.10

This is an octavo for SATB choirs.

NEW RELEASES: EASTER CHURCH MUSIC cont.

Rejoice!
Abel Goemanne
Harold Flammer, $0.95
This moderately difficult octavo for adult SATB choirs can be performed in three minutes.

Shout to the Lord
Jane Marshall
Augsburg Fortress, $1.15
Three minutes long, this moderately difficult octavo for adult SATB choirs can be performed *a capella*.

The Victor
Jamie Owens Collins, Tom Fettke, and Doug Holck
Lillenas Publishing Company, $0.90
This moderately difficult contemporary octavo for adult SATB choirs celebrates Christ's victory over death. It can be performed in three minutes.

Wave the Palms and Shout Hosanna!
Joe Parks
Singspiration, $0.90
This easy-to-learn octavo for adult SATB choirs re-creates the joyful crowds that celebrated Jesus' triumphal entry. Designed for Palm Sunday, it can be performed in about three minutes.

Source: *Bookstore Journal,* Official Trade Publication of the Christian Booksellers Association. Copyright © 1990. Reprinted by permission.

MUSIC ORGANIZATIONS

American Choral Directors Association 2834 W. Kingsley Road, Garland, TX 75041

American Guild of Organists P.O. Box 26811, Richmond, VA 23261

Choral Conductors Guild 519 N. Halifax, Daytona Beach, FL 32018

Choristers Guild 2111 Samson Street, Philadelphia, PA 19103

Church Music Publishers Association P.O. Box 158992, Nashville, TN 37215

Contemporary Christian Music 1913 21st Avenue South, Nashville, TN 37212

Gospel Music Association P.O. Box 23201, Nashville, TN 37202

Hymn Society of America Texas Christian University, Fort Worth, TX 76129

Menconi Ministries P.O. Box 306, Cardiff, CA 92007

Music Educators National Association 1902 Association Drive, Reston, VA 22091

Music Publishers Association 110 E. 59th Street, New York, NY 10022

National Association of Schools of Music 11250 Roger Bacon Drive, Suite 21, Reston, VA 22091

National Music Publishers Association 205 E. 42nd Street, New York, NY 10017

Presbyterian Association of Musicians 1000 E. Moreland Street, Charlotte, NC 28204

Retail Sheet Music Dealers Association 1407 E. Harry, Wichita, KS 67211

Standing Commission on Church Music of the Episcopal Church 815 2nd Avenue, New York, NY 10017

1989 CASHBOX AWARDS

Award	*Artist*
Contemporary Gospel Album of the Year	Amy Grant *Lead Me On*
Contemporary Gospel Female Vocalist of the Year	Amy Grant
Contemporary Gospel Group of the Year	BeBe & CeCe Winans
Contemporary Gospel Male Vocalist of the Year	Michael W. Smith
Contemporary Gospel Producers of the Year	Brown Bannister
Contemporary Gospel Single of the Year (tie)	Steve Camp "Do You Feel Their Pain?"
Contemporary Gospel Single of the Year (tie)	Larnelle Harris "I Can Begin Again"
Inspirational Female Vocalist of the Year	Twila Paris

Inspirational Male Vocalist of the Year	Steven Curtis Chapman
New Contemporary Gospel Artist of the Year	Kim Hill
New Inspirational Artist of the Year	Bruce Carroll
New Southern Gospel Female Vocalist of the Year	Sheri Easter
New Southern Gospel Group of the Year	The Bishops
New Southern Gospel Male Vocalist of the Year	Carroll Roberson
Southern Gospel Album of the Year	The Cathedrals *Goin' in Style*
Southern Gospel Duet of the Year	Jeff & Sherri Easter
Southern Gospel Female Vocalist of the Year	Sheri Easter
Southern Gospel Group of the Year	Gold City
Southern Gospel Horizon Award of the Year	The McGruders
Southern Gospel Producers of the Year	Eddie Crook
Southern Gospel Single of the Year	The McKameys "God on the Mountain"
Southern Gospel Male Vocalist of the Year	Kirk Talley

DOVE AWARDS

Sponsor: The Gospel Music Association

Song of the Year

1970 **Jesus is Coming Soon** R. E. Winsett; R. E. Winsett Music Company
1971 **The Night Before Easter** Don Sumner/Dwayne Friend; Gospel Quartet Music Co.
1972 No awards given
1973 **The Lighthouse** Ron Hinson; Journey Music
1974 **Why Me Lord?** Kris Kristofferson; Resasca Music
1975 **Because He Lives** Bill Gaither; Gaither Music Co.
1976 **One Day At a Time** Marijohn Wilkin/Kris Kristofferson; Buckhorn Music
1977 **Statue of Liberty** Neil Enloe; Enloe Music
1978 **Learning to Lean** John Stallings; Heartwarming Music
1979 **Rise Again** Dallas Holm; Dimension Music
1980 **He's Alive** Don Francisco; New Pax Music
1981 **Praise The Lord** Brown Bannister/Mike Hudson; Home Sweet Home Music/Bug and Bear Music
1982 **We Shall Behold Him** Dottie Rambo; John T. Benson Publishing
1983 **El Shaddai** Michael Card/John Thompson; Whole Armour Publishing
1984 **More Than Wonderful** Lanny Wolfe; Lanny Wolfe Music Co.
1985 **Upon This Rock** Gloria Gaither/Dony McQuire; Gaither Music Co./It's-N-Me Music/Lexicon Music
1986 **Via Dolorosa** Billy Sprague/Niles Borop; Meadowgreen Music/Word Music
1987 **How Excellent Is Thy Name** Dick Tunney, Melodie Tunney & Paul Smith; Word Music & Marquis III/Laurel Press/Pamela Kay Music
1988 **In The Name of The Lord** Phil McHugh, Gloria Gaither, Sandi Patti Helvering; River Oaks Music/Sandi's Songs, BMI/Gaither Music Co.
1989 **Friend of a Wounded Heart** Wayne Watson and Claire Cloninger; Word Music
1990 **Thank You** Ray Boltz; Gaither Music

Songwriter of the Year

1970 **Bill Gaither**
1971 **Bill Gaither**
1972 No awards given
1973 **Bill Gaither**
1974 **Bill Gaither**
1975 **Bill Gaither**
1976 **Bill Gaither**
1977 **Bill Gaither**
1978 **Bill Gaither**
1979 **Dallas Holm**
1980 **Don Francisco**

DOVE AWARDS cont.

1981 **Gary Chapman**
1982 **Dottie Rambo**
1983 **Michael Card**
1984 **Lanny Wolfe**
1985 **Michael W. Smith**
1986 **Gloria Gaither**
1987 **Dick & Melodie Tunney**
1988 **Larnelle Harris**
1989 **Steven Curtis Chapman**
1990 **Steven Curtis Chapman**

Male Vocalist of the Year

1970 **James Blackwood**
1971 **James Blackwood**
1972 No awards given
1973 **James Blackwood**
1974 **James Blackwood**
1975 **James Blackwood**
1976 **James Blackwood**
1977 **Johnny Cook**
1978 **James Blackwood**
1979 **Dallas Holm**
1980 **Dallas Holm**
1981 **Russ Taff**
1982 **Russ Taff**
1983 **Larnelle Harris**
1984 **Russ Taff**
1985 **Steve Green**
1986 **Larnelle Harris**
1987 **Steve Green**
1988 **Larnelle Harris**
1989 **Wayne Watson**
1990 **Steven Curtis Chapman**

Female Vocalist of the Year

1970 **Vestal Goodman**
1971 **Ann Downing**
1972 No awards given
1973 **Sue Chenault**
1974 **Sue Chenault**
1975 **Sue Chenault Dodge**
1976 **Jeanne Johnson**
1977 **Joy McQuire**
1978 **Evie Tornquist**
1979 **Evie Tornquist**
1980 **Cynthia Clawson**
1981 **Cynthia Clawson**
1982 **Sandi Patti**
1983 **Sandi Patti**
1984 **Sandi Patti**
1985 **Sandi Patti**
1986 **Sandi Patti**
1987 **Sandi Patti**
1988 **Sandi Patti**
1989 **Sandi Patti**
1990 **Sandi Patti**

Male Group of the Year

1970 **Imperials**
1971 **Oak Ridge Boys**
1972 No awards given
1973 **Oak Ridge Boys**
1974 **Blackwood Brothers**
1975 **Blackwood Brothers**
1976 **Imperials**
1977 **Imperials**
1978 **Cathedral Quartet**
1979 **Imperials**
1980 **Imperials**

Mixed Group of the Year

(Category changed to "Group of the Year" in 1981)

1970 **Speer Family**
1971 **Speer Family**
1972 No awards given
1973 **Speer Family**
1974 **Speer Family**
1975 **Speer Family**
1976 **Speer Family**
1977 **Speer Family**
1978 **Speer Family**
1979 **Dallas Holm and Praise**
1980 **Bill Gaither Trio**

Group of the Year

1981 **Imperials**
1982 **Imperials**
1983 **Imperials**
1984 No award—category changed
1985 No award—category changed
1986 No award—category changed
1987 **First Call**
1988 **First Call**
1989 **Take 6**
1990 **BeBe and CeCe Winans**

Album of the Year

Recording artist listed first, producer/producers listed second, record company third

1970 **It's Happening** Oak Ridge Boys; Bob MacKenzie; Heartwarming Music
1971 **Fill My Cup, Lord** Blackwood Brothers; Darol Rice; RCA Victor
1972 No awards given
1973 **Light** Oak Ridge Boys; Bob MacKenzie; Heartwarming Music
1974 **Street Gospel** Oak Ridge Boys; Bob MacKenzie; Heartwarming Music
1975 **Big and Live** Kingsman Quartet; Marvin Norcross; Canaan Records
1976 **I Just Feel Like Something Good Is About To Happen** Speer Family; Bob MacKenzie; Heartwarming Music

Rock Album of the Year

1988 **Crack The Sky** Mylon LeFevre & Broken Heart; Joe Hardy & Mylon LeFevre, Producers; Myrrh Records
1989 **Russ Taff** Russ Taff; Jack Joseph Puig; Myrrh Records
1990 **The Way Home** Russ Taff; Russ Taff and James Hollihan; Sparrow Records

Rock Recorded Song of the Year

1989 **Won By One** Mylon and Broken Heart; Scott Allen, Trent Arganti, Kenneth Bentley, Ben Hewitt
1990 **The River Unbroken** Russ Taff; Darryl Brown and David Batteau; Myrrh Records

Contemporary Gospel Album of the Year

Recording artist listed first; producer/producers second; record company third

1977 **No Shortage** Imperials; Bob MacKenzie/Gary Paxton; Impact
1978 **Reba** Lady Reba Rambo Gardner; Phil Johnson; Greentree
1979 **Transformation** Cruse Family; Ken Harding; Canaan Records
1980 **All That Matters** Dallas Holm and Praise; Phil Johnson; Greentree
1981 **One More Song For You** Imperials; Michael Omartian; Dayspring Records
1982 **Priority** Imperials; Michael Omartian; Dayspring Records
1983 **Age To Age** Amy Grant; Brown Bannister; Myrrh Records
1984 **Side By Side** Imperials; Keith Thomas/Neal Joseph; Dayspring Records
1985 **Straight Ahead** Amy Grant; Brown Bannister, Myrrh Records
1986 **Medals** Russ Taff; Russ Taff/Jack Puig; Myrrh/Word Records
1987 **The Big Picture** Michael W. Smith; Michael W. Smith, John Potoker; Reunion Records
1988 **Watercolour Ponies** Wayne Watson; Wayne Watson & Paul Mills; Dayspring Records
1989 **Lead Me On** Amy Grant; Brown Bannister; Myrrh Records
1990 **Heaven** BeBe and CeCe Winans; Keith Thomas; Sparrow Records

Contemporary Recorded Song of the Year

1989 **His Eyes** Steven Curtis Chapman; Steven Curtis Chapman and James Isaac Elliott
1990 **Heaven** BeBe and CeCe Winans; Keith Thomas and Benjamin Winans; Sparrow Records

Inspirational Album of the Year

Recording artist listed first; producer/producers listed second; record companies listed last

1977 **Jesus, We Just Want To Thank You** Bill Gaither Trio; Bob MacKenzie; Heartwarming Music
1978 **Ovation** Couriers; Jesse Peterson; Tempo
1979 **Pilgrim's Progress** Bill Gaither Trio; Bob MacKenzie/John W. Thompson; Impact Records
1980 **Special Delivery** Doug Oldham; Joe Huffman; Impact Records
1981 **You're Welcome Here** Cynthia Clawson; JEN Productions; Triangle
1982 **Joni's Song** Joni Earecksen; Kurt Kaiser; Word Records
1983 **Lift Up The Lord** Sandi Patti; Greg Nelson; Impact Records
1984 **More Than Wonderful** Sandi Patti; John Helvering, David Clydesdale/Greg Nelson/Sandi Patti Helvering; Impact Records

DOVE AWARDS cont.

1985 **Songs From The Heart** Sandi Patti; Greg Nelson/Sandi Patti Helvering; Impact Records
1986 **I've Just Seen Jesus** Larnelle Harris; Greg Nelson; Impact/Benson Records
1987 **Morning Like This** Sandi Patti; Greg Nelson & Sandi Patti Helvering; Word Records
1988 **The Father Hath Provided** Larnelle Harris; Greg Nelson; Benson Records
1989 **Make His Praise Glorious** Sandi Patti; Greg Nelson and Sandi Patti; Word Records
1990 **The Mission** Steve Green; Greg Nelson; Sparrow Records

Inspirational Recorded Song of the Year

1989 **In Heaven's Eyes** Sandi Patti; Phill McHugh
1990 **His Strength Is Perfect** Steven Curtis Chapman; Steven Curtis Chapman and Jerry Salley; Sparrow Records

Traditional Album of the Year

Category changed to Southern Gospel with 18th annual. Includes Country, Folk and/or Bluegrass). Recording artist listed first, producer/producers listed second, record company listed third

1977 **Between the Cross & Heaven** Speer Family; Joe Huffman; Heartwarming Music
1978 **Then & Now** Cathedral Quartet; Ken Harding; Canaan Records
1979 **Kingsmen Live In Chattanooga** Kingsmen; Joe Huffman/Eldridge Fox; Heartwarming Music
1980 **From Out Of The Past** Kingsmen; Joe Huffman/Eldridge Fox; Heartwarming Music
1981 **Workin'** Hemphills; Jerry Crutchfield; Heartwarming Music
1982 **One Step Closer** Rex Nelon Singers; Ken Harding; Canaan Records
1983 **Feeling At Home** Rex Nelon Singers; Ken Harding; Canaan Records
1984 **We Shall Behold The King** Rex Nelon Singers; Ken Harding; Canaan Records
1985 **The Best Of And A Whole Lot More** Rex Nelon Singers; Ken Harding; Canaan Records
1986 **Excited** Hemphills; W. Hilton/T. Hemphill; Heartwarming Music
1987 **The Master Builder** The Cathedrals; William Gaither and Gary McSpadden; Riversong Records

Southern Gospel Album of the Year

1988 **Symphony of Praise** The Cathedrals; Lari Goss; Riversong Records
1989 **Goin' In Style** The Cathedrals; Lari Goss; Homeland Records
1990 **I Just Started Living** Cathedrals; Lari Goss; Homeland Records

Southern Gospel Recorded Song of the Year

1989 **Champions Of Love** The Cathedrals; Phil Cross and Carolyn Cross
1990 **I Can See The Hand of God** Cathedrals; Steven Curtis Chapman, Jim Chapman III; Homeland Records

Country Gospel Album of the Year

1988 **An Evening Together** Steve & Annie Chapman; Ron Griffin & Steve Chapman; Star Song Records
1989 **Richest Man In Town** Bruce Carroll; Bubba Smith; New Canaan Records
1990 **Heirloom**; Heirloom; Michael Sykes and Trent Hemphill;Benson Records

Country Recorded Song of the Year

1989 **Above and Beyond** Bruce Carroll; Bruce Carroll and Paul Smith
1990 **'Tis So Sweet To Trust In Jesus** Amy Grant; Word Records

Contemporary Black Gospel Album of the Year

Recording artist listed first, producer/producers second, record company third

1981 **Give Me More Love In My Heart** Larnelle Harris; Howard McCrary/Paul Johnson; Benson
1982 **Walter Hawkins & Family Live** Walter Hawkins Family; Walter Hawkins; Light Records

1983 **I'll Never Stop Loving You** Leon Patillo, Skip Konte; Myrrh Records
1984 **Come Together** Bobby Jones and New Life; Tony Brown, Myrrh Records
1985 **No Time To Lose** Andrae Crouch; Bill Maxwell; Light Records
1986 **Let My People Go** The Winans; Marvin Winans; Qwest Records
1987 **Heart & Soul** The Clark Sisters; Norbert Putnam and Twinkie Clark; Rejoice Records
1988 **Decisions** The Winans; Marvin Winans, Barry Hankerson, Carvin & Michael Winans; Qwest Records
1989 **Take 6** Take 6; Mark Kibble, Claude V. McKnight III, Mervyn E. Warren; Reunion Records
1990 **Will You Be Ready?** Commissioned Fred Hammand and Michael Brooks; Light Records

Contemporary Black Gospel Recorded Song of the Year

1989 **If We Ever** Take 6
1990 **With My Whole Heart** BeBe and CeCe Winans; Patrick Henderson and Louis Brown III; Sparrow Records

Soul Album of the Year

Recording artist first, producer/producers second, record company third

1978 **This Is Another Day** Andrae Crouch and The Disciples; Bill Maxwell; Light Records
1979 **Live In London** Andrae Crouch and The Disciples; Bill Maxwell/Andrae Crouch; Light Records

Black Gospel Album of the Year

Recording artist listed first, producer/producers second, record company third

1980 **Love Alive II** Walter Hawkins and the Love Center Choir; Walter Hawkins; Light Records

Traditional Black Gospel Album of the Year

Recording artist listed first, producer/producers second, record company third

1981 **Incredible** Teddy Huffam and The Gems; Ken Harding; Canaan Records
1982 **Go** Shirley Caesar; Tony Brown/Shirley Caesar; Myrrh Records
1983 **Precious Lord** Al Green; Al Green; Myrrh Records
1984 **We Sing Praises** Sandra Crouch; Sandra Crouch; Light Records
1985 **Sailin'** Shirley Caesar; Sanchez Harley/Shirley Caesar/David Lehman; Myrrh Records
1986 **Celebration** Shirley Caesar; Dave Lehman/Shirley Caesar; Rejoice Records
1987 **Christmasing** Shirley Caesar; Norbert Putnam; Rejoice Records
1988 **One Lord, One Faith, One Baptism** Aretha Franklin; Aretha Franklin; Arista Records
1989 **Live . . . In Chicago** Shirley Caesar; Bubba Smith and Shirley Caesar; Rejoice Records
1990 **Saints In Praise** West Angeles Church Of God In Christ Mass Choir; Patrick Henderson; Sparrow Records

Traditional Black Gospel Recorded Song of the Year

1989 **Hold My Mule** Shirley Caesar; Shirley Caesar Williams
1990 **Wonderful** Beau Williams; Virginia David and Theodore Fry; Light Records

Inspirational Black Gospel Album of the Year

Recording artist listed first, producer/producers second, record company third

1981 **Rejoice** Shirley Caesar; Tony Brown/Ken Harding; Myrrh Records
1982 **Edwin Hawkins Live** Oakland Symphony Orchestra and Edwin Hawkins; Gil Askey; Myrrh Records
1983 **Touch Me Lord** Larnelle Harris; Greg Nelson; Impact Records

Instrumentalist of the Year

1970 **Dwayne Friend**
1971 **Dwayne Friend**
1972 No awards given
1973 **Tony Brown**
1974 **Henry Slaughter**
1975 **Henry Slaughter**

DOVE AWARDS cont.

1976 **Henry Slaughter**
1977 **Henry Slaughter**
1978 **Henry Slaughter**
1979 **Dino Kartsonakis**
1980 **Dino Kartsonakis**
1981 **Dino Kartsonakis**
1982 **Dino Kartsonakis**
1983 **Dino Kartsonakis**
1984 **Phil Driscoll**
1985 **Phil Driscoll**
1986 **Dino Kartsonakis**

Instrumental Album of the Year

1987 **Instrument of Praise** Phil Driscoll; Lari Goss, Phil Driscoll, Ken Pennel; Benson Records
1988 **The Wind & The Wheat** Phil Keaggy; Phil Keaggy, Tom Coomes; Colours (Maranatha! Music)
1989 **A Symphony Of Praise** Sandi Patti; David T. Clydesdale; Word Records
1990 **One of Several Possible Musiks** Kerry Livgren; Kerry Livgren; Sparrow Records

Worship and Praise Album of the Year

Recording artist listed first, producer second, record company third

1981 **The Lord's Prayer** Dony McGuire; Light Records
1982 **Exaltation** Ronn Huff
1983 **Light Eternal** Billy Ray Hearn; Birdwing Records
1984 **Celebrate The Joy** David T. Clydesdale; Impact Records
1985 **The Praise In Us** Neal Joseph; Myrrh Records
1986 **I've Just Seen Jesus** William J. Gaither/Randy Vader; Gaither Music Records
1987 **Hymns** 2nd Chapter of Acts; Buck Herring; Live Oak Records
1988 **The Final Word** Michael Card; Norbert Putnam; Sparrow Records
1989 **Praise 10** Maranatha Singers Smitty Price and Tom Coomes; Maranatha Music Records
1990 **Our Hymns** Various Artists Word Records

Musical Album of the Year

Recording artist listed first, creator second, record company third

1981 **The Messiah** Billy Ray Hearn; Irving Martin; Sparrow Records
1982 **The Love Story** Phil Brower/Don Wyrtzen; New Dawn Records
1983 **The Day He Wore My Crown** David T. Clydesdale; Impact Records
1984 **Dreamer** Cam Florida; Christian Artist Records
1985 **The Race Is On** Steve Taylor; Word Records
1986 **Come Celebrate Jesus** Neal Joseph/Don Marsh; Word Records
1987 **A Mighty Fortress** Steve Green, Dwight Liles, Niles Borop, Creators; Sparrow Records
1988 **A Son! A Savior!** Various; Claire Cloninger, Gary Rhodes & Bob Krogstad; Word Music
1989 **In His Presence; The Risen King** Dick and Melodie Tunney; Dick and Melodie Tunney; Genevox Records
1990 **Friends Forever/Part 2** Billy Sprague; Jim Weber, Nan Gurley and Billy Sprague; Word/Meadowgreen Music

Children's Music Album of the Year

Recording artist listed first, creator second, record company third

1981 **Very Best of The Very Best For Kids** Robert MacKenzie; Word Records
1982 **Kids Under Construction** Bob MacKenzie/Ronn Huff; Paragon Records
1983 **Lullabies & Nursery Rhymes Vol 1** Tony Salerno/Fletch Wiley; Birdwing Records
1984 **Music Machine II** Fletch Wiley/Tony Salerno/Ron Kreuger; Birdwing Records
1985 **Ten New Songs With Kids For Kids About Life** Ron W. Griffin; Word Records
1986 **Bullfrogs & Butterflies Part II** Tony Salerno; Birdwing Records
1987 **God Likes Kids** Joel & Labreeska Hemphill; Benson Records

1988 **Bullfrogs & Butterflies Part III** The Agapeland Singers & Candle; Tony Salerno; Sparrow Records
1989 **Wise Guys and Starry Skies** Kathie Hill; Sparrow Records
1990 **The Friendship Company** Sandi Patti; Sandi Patti; Word Records

Artist of the Year

1981 **Imperials**
1982 **Sandi Patti**
1983 **Amy Grant**
1984 **Sandi Patti**
1985 **Sandi Patti**
1986 **Amy Grant**
1987 **Sandi Patti**
1988 **Sandi Patti**
1989 **Amy Grant**
1990 **Steven Curtis Chapman**

Short Form Video of the Year

Title, Artist, Producer, Director
1987 **Famine in Their Land** The Nelons; Robert Deaton, George Flanigen; Word Record & Music Group
1988 **Stay For A While** Amy Grant; Marc Ball; Jack Cole, Scene Three Productions
1989 **Lead Me On** Amy Grant; Tina Silvey; Andrew Doucette
1990 **I Miss The Way** Michael W. Smith; Fire By Night Productions, Steve Yake

Long Form Video of the Year

Title, Artist, Producer, Director
1987 **Limelight** Steve Taylor; John Anneman, Steve Taylor; Sparrow Records
1988 **The Big Picture Tour Video** Michael W. Smith; Brian Shipley; Stephen Bowlby
1989 **Carman Live . . . Radically Saved** Carman; Cindy DuPree; George J. Flanigen IV and Robert Deaton;
1990 **On Fire** Petra; FirstBorne Productions, Steve Yake, director

Contribution to Gospel Music by a Secular Artist

Recording artist listed first, producer/producers second, record company third
1976 **Sunday Morning with Charley Pride** Charley Pride; Jerry Bradley; RCA Records
1978 **Home Where I Belong** B.J. Thomas; Myrrh Records
1979 **First Class** The Boones; Chris Christian; Lamb & Lion
1980 **Slow Train Coming** Bob Dylan; Jerry Wexler-Barry Beckett; Columbia Records
1981 **With My Song** Debbie Boone; Brown Bannister; Lamb & Son
1982 **Amazing Grace** B. J. Thomas; Pete Drake; Myrrh Records
1983 **He Set My Life To Music** Barbara Mandrell; Tom Collins; MCA Records
1984 **Surrender** Debbie Boone; Brown Bannister; Lamb & Lion
1985 **You Were Loving Me** Lulu Roman Smith; Gary McSpadden; Canaan Records
1986 **No More Night** Glen Campbell; Glen Campbell/Ken Harding; Word Records

Horizon Award

1988 **BeBe & CeCe Winans**

Choral Collection Album of the Year

1989 **Sandi Patti Choral Praise** Sandi Patti; Greg Nelson; Word Music Records
1990 **The A Capella Collection** Greg Nelson Singers; Greg Nelson; Wordsong

Metal Album of the Year

1989 **In God We Trust** Stryper; Stryper and Michael Lloyd; Enigma Records
1990 **Triumphant Return** White Cross; Rex Carroll and Joey Powers; Pure Metal Records

Metal Recorded Song of the Year

1989 **In God We Trust** Stryper; Stryper
1990 **In Your Face** Shout; Ken Tamplin; Frontline Records

New Artist of the Year

1989 **Take 6**
1990 **David Mullen**

Impact Award

1990 **Sparrow Records**

DOVE AWARDS cont.

International Award

1990 **Phil and John, U.K.** Word

Lifetime Achievement Award

1990 **How Great Thou Art** accepted by Hal Spencer

Gospel Music Hall of Fame Inductees

Living

1970 "Pappy" Jim Waites
1971 Albert E. Brumley
1972 Le Roy Abernathy
1973 James Blackwood, Sr.
1974 Brock Speer
1975 Mosie Lister
1976 Eva Mae LeFevre
1977 George Beverly Shea
1978 Connor B. Hall
1979 John T. Benson, Jr., Ira Stanphill
1980 Thomas A. Dorsey
1981 William (Bill) Gaither
1982 Hovie Lister
1983 Ralph Carmichael
1984 John W. Peterson
1985 W. J. "Jake" Hess
1986 Cliff Barrows

Deceased

1970 G. T. "Dad" Speer
1971 Lena Brock Speer, James D. Vaughan
1972 Denver Crumpler
1973 G. Keffer Vaughan
1974 Fanny Crosby
1975 George Bennard
1976 James "Big Chief" Wetherington
1977 Mahalia Jackson
1978 Ira Sanky
1979 Clarice Baxter
1980 John T. Benson, Sr.
1981 Marvin Norcross
1982 Cleavant Derricks
1983 Tim Spencer
1984 Urias LeFevre

In 1973 a special resolution was passed to induct the following persons into the Gospel Music Hall of Fame.

Deceased

J. R. Baxter, Jr.
E. M. Bartlett
John Daniel
Adger M. Pace
Homer Rodeheaver
A. J. Showalter
V. O. Stamps
Frank Stamps
W. B. Walbert
R. E. Winsett

In 1982 a special resolution was passed to induct the following persons into the Gospel Music Hall of Fame.

Deceased

Charles Gabriel
Haldor Lillenas
B. B. McKinney
Lowell Mason
John Newton

In 1984 a special resolution was passed to induct the following persons into the Gospel Music Hall of Fame.

Living

Rev. James Cleveland
John Wallace "Wally" Fowler
W. B. Nowlin
J. D. Sumner
P. J. Zondervan

Deceased

D. P. "Dad" Carter
Paul Heinecke
Lloyd Orrell
Clara Ward
Ethel Waters

In 1989 a special resolution was passed to induct J.G. Whitfield into the Gospel Music Hall of Fame.

GRAMMY AWARDS, RELIGIOUS CATEGORIES

Grammy winners are selected annually by the voting members of The Recording Academy, who number nearly 6000 creative contributors to the fields of recording. Their criteria for judging are artistic and/or technical excellence. Although Grammy winners were first selected in 1958 it was not until 1961 that a religious recording category was created.

Year	*Category*	*Artist*	*Song/Album*	*Label*
1961	Best Gospel or Other Religious Recording	Mahalia Jackson	Everytime I Feel the Spirit	Columbia
1962	Best Gospel or Other Religious Recording	Mahalia Jackson	Great Songs of Love and Faith	Columbia
1963	Best Gospel or Other Religious Recording (Musical)	Soeur Sourire (The Singing Nun)	Dominique	Philips
1964	Best Gospel or Other Relig. Rec.	Tennessee Ernie Ford	Great Gospel Songs	Capitol
1965	Best Gospel or Other Religious Recording (Musical)	George Beverly Shea & the Anita Kerr Singers	Southland Favorites	RCA
1966	Best Sacred Recording (Musical)	Porter Wagoner and The Blackwood Brothers	Grand Old Gospel	RCA
1967	Best Gospel Performance	Porter Wagoner and The Blackwood Brothers	More Grand Old Gospel	RCA
	Best Sacred Performance	Elvis Presley	How Great Thou Art	RCA
1968	Best Gospel Perf.	Happy Goodman Family	The Happy Gospel of The Happy Goodmans	Word
	Best Sacred Perf.	Jake Hess	Beautiful Isle of Somewhere	RCA
	Best Soul Gospel Perf.	Dottie Rambo	The Soul of Me	Heartwarming
1969	Best Gospel Perf.	Porter Wagoner and The Blackwood Brothers	In Gospel Country	RCA
	Best Sacred Perf.	Jake Hess	Ain't That Beautiful Singing	RCA
	Best Soul Gospel	Edwin Hawkins Singers	Oh Happy Day	Buddah
1970	Best Gospel Perf.	Oak Ridge Boys	Talk about The Good Times	Heart Warming
	Best Sacred Perf.	Jake Hess	Everything is Beautiful	RCA
	Best Soul Gospel Perf.	Edwin Hawkins Singers	Every Man Wants To Be Free	Buddah
1971	Best Gospel Perf. (Other Than Soul Gospel)	Charley Pride	Let Me Live	RCA
	Best Sacred Perf.	Charley Pride	Did You Think To Pray	RCA
	Best Soul Gospel Perf.	Shirley Caesar	Put Your Hand in the Hand of the Man From Galilee	Hob
1972	Best Gospel Perf.	Blackwood Brothers	Love	RCA
	Best Inspir. Perf.	Elvis Presley	He Touched Me	RCA
	Best Soul Gospel Perf.	Aretha Franklin	Amazing Grace	Atlantic
1973	Best Gospel Perf.	Blackwood Brothers	Release Me (From My Sin) (Album)	Skylite
	Best Inspir. Perf.	Bill Gaither Trio	Let's Just Praise The Lord (Album)	Impact
	Best Soul Gospel Perf.	Dixie Hummingbirds	Loves Me Like A Rock (Single)	ABC
1974	Best Gospel Perf.	Oak Ridge Boys	The Baptism of Jesse Taylor (Single)	Columbia
	Best Inspir. Perf.	Elvis Presley	How Great Thou Art (Track)	RCA
	Best Soul Gospel Perf.	James Cleveland and the So. Calif. Comm. Choir	In the Ghetto (Album)	Savoy
1975	Best Gospel Perf.	Imperials	No Shortage (Album)	Impact
	Best Inspir. Perf.	The Bill Gaither Trio	Jesus, We Just Want To Thank You (Album)	Impact
	Best Soul Gospel Perf.	Andrae Crouch and the Disciples	Take Me Back (Album)	Light
1976	Best Gospel Perf.	Oak Ridge Boys	Where The Soul Never Dies (Single)	Columbia
	Best Inspir. Perf.	Gary S. Paxton	The Astonishing, Outrageous, Amazing, Incredible, Unbelievable, Different World of Gary S. Paxton (Album)	Newpax
	Best Soul Gospel Perf.	Mahalia Jackson	How I Got Over (Album)	Columbia
1977	Best Gospel Perf., Contemp./Inspir.	Imperials	Sail On (Album)	Dayspring/Word
	Best Gospel Perf., Tradtnl	Oak Ridge Boys	Just A Little Talk With Jesus (Track)	Rockland Road
	Best Inspr. Perf.	B.J. Thomas	Home Where I Belong (Album)	Myrrh/Word
	Best Soul Gospel Perf., Contemp.	Edwin Hawkins and The Edwin Hawkins Singers	Wonderful! (Album)	Birthright

Year	*Category*	*Artist*	*Song/Album*	*Label*
	Best Soul Gospel Perf., Tradtnl	James Cleveland	James Cleveland Live at Carnegie Hall (Album)	Savoy
1978	Best Gospel Perf., Contemp./Inspir.	Larry Hart	What A Friend (Track)	Genesis
	Best Gospel Perf., Traditional	The Happy Goodman Family	Refreshing (Album)	Canaan
	Best Inspr. Perf.	B.J. Thomas	Happy Man (Album)	Myrrh
	Best Soul Gospel Perf., Contemp.	Andrae Crouch and The Disciples	Live in London (Album)	Light
	Best Soul Gospel Perf., Tradtnl	Mighty Clouds of Joy	Live and Direct (Album)	ABC
1979	Best Gospel Perf. Contemp./Inspir.	Imperials	Heed The Call (Album)	Dayspring
	Best Gospel Perf., Traditional	The Blackwood Brothers	Lift Up The Name of Jesus (Album)	Skylite
	Best Inspr. Perf.	B.J. Thomas	You Gave Me Love (When Nobody Gave Me a Prayer) (Album)	Myrrh
	Best Soul Gospel Perf., Contemp.	Andrae Crouch	I'll Be Thinking of You (Album)	Light
	Best Soul Gospel Perf., Tradtnl	Mighty Clouds of Joy	Changing Times (Album)	Epic
1980	Best Gospel Perf., Contemp./Inspir.	Reba Rambo, Dony McGuire, B.J. Thomas, Andrae Crouch, The Archers, Walter and Tramaine Hawkins, Cynthia Clawson	The Lord's Prayer (Album)	Light
	Best Gospel Perf., Traditional	Blackwood Brothers	We Come to Worship (Album)	Voice Box
	Best Inspir. Perf.	Debby Boone	With My Song I Will Praise Him (Album)	Lamb & Lion
	Best Soul Gospel Perf., Contemp.	Shirley Caesar	Rejoice (Album)	Myrrh
	Best Soul Gospel Perf., Tradtnl	James Cleveland and The Charles Fold Singers	Lord, Let Me Be An Instrmt (Album)	Savoy
1981	Best Gospel Perf. Contemp./Inspir.	Imperials	Priority (Album)	Dayspring/Word
	Best Gospel Perf., Traditional	J.D. Sumner, James Blackwood, Hovie Lister, Rosie Rozell, Jake Hess	The Masters V (Album)	Skylite
	Best Inspr. Perf.	B.J. Thomas	Amazing Grace (Album)	Myrrh/Word
	Best Soul Gospel Perf., Contemp.	Andrae Crouch	Don't Give Up (Album)	W.B.
	Best Soul Gospel Perf., Tradtnl	Al Green	The Lord Will Make A Way (Album)	Hi-Myrrh/Word
1982	Best Gospel Perf., Contemp./Inspir.	Amy Grant	Age To Age (Album)	Myrrh/Word
	Best Gospel Perf., Traditional	Blackwood Brothers	I'm Following You (Album)	Voice Box
	Best Inspr. Perf.	Barbara Mandrell	He Set My Life to Music (Album)	Songbird/MCA
	Best Soul Gospel Perf., Contemp.	Al Green	Higher Plane (Album)	Myrrh/Word
	Best Soul Gospel Perf., Tradtnl	Al Green	Precious Lord (Album)	Myrrh/Word
1983	Best Gospel Perf. by Duo or Group	Sandi Patti and Larnelle Harris	More Than Wonderful (Track)	Impact/Benson
	Best Gospel Perf., Female	Amy Grant	Ageless Medley (Single)	Myrrh/Word
	Best Gospel Perf., Male	Russ Taff	Walls of Glass (Album)	Myrrh/Word
	Best Inspr. Perf.	Donna Summer	He's A Rebel (Track)	Mercury/ Polygram
	Best Soul Gospel Perf., Duo/Group	Bobby Jones with Barbara Mandrell	I'm So Glad I'm Standing Here Today (Track)	Myrrh/Word
	Best Soul Gospel Perf., Female	Sandra Crouch	We Sing Praises (Album)	Light/Lexicon
	Best Soul Gospel Perf., Male	Al Green	I'll Rise Again (Album)	Myrrh/Word
1984	Best Gospel Perf. by Duo or Group	Debby Boone and Phil Driscoll	Keep The Flame Burning (from Debby Boone Surrender)	Lamb and Lion/ Sparrow
	Best Gospel Perf., Female	Amy Grant	Angels (from Straight Ahead)	Myrrh/Word
	Best Gospel Perf., Male	Michael W. Smith	Michael W. Smith (Album)	Reunion/Word
	Best Inspr. Perf.	Donna Summer	Forgive Me (from Cats without Claws)	Geffen/Warner Brothers
	Best Soul Gospel Perf., Duo/Group	Shirley Caesar & Al Green	Sailin' on the Sea of Your Love (from Shirley Caesar Sailin)	Myrrh/Word
	Best Soul Gospel Perf., Female	Shirley Caesar	Sailin' (Album)	Myrrh/Word
	Best Soul Gospel Perf., Male	Andrae Crouch	Always Remember (from No Time To Lose)	Light/Lexicon
1985	Best Gospel Perf. by Duo or Group	Larnelle Harris and Sandi Patti	I've Just Seen Jesus (from I've Just Seen Jesus)	Impact/Benson
	Best Gospel Perf., Female	Amy Grant	Unguarded (Album)	Myrrh/Word

Year	Category	Artist	Song/Album	Label
	Best Gospel Perf., Male	Larnelle Harris	How Excellent is Thy Name (from I've Just Seen Jesus)	Benson
	Best Inspr. Perf.	Jennifer Holliday	Come Sunday (from Say You Love Me)	Geffen
	Best Soul Gospel Perf., Duo/Group	The Winans	Tomorrow (Album)	Light
	Best Soul Gospel Perf., Female	Shirley Caesar	Martin (Single)	Rejoice/Word
	Best Soul Gospel Perf., Male	Marvin Winans	Bring Back The Days of Yea and Nay (from Tomorrow)	Light
1986	Best Gospel Perf. by a Duo, Group, Choir or Choirs	Sandi Patti and Deniece Williams	They Say (from So Glad I Know)	Sparrow
	Best Gospel Perf., Female	Sandi Patti	Morning Like This (Album)	Word
	Best Gospel Perf., Male	Philip Bailey	Triumph (Album)	Myrrh/Word
	Best Soul Gospel Perf. by a Duo, Group, Choir or Chorus	The Winans	Let My People Go (Album)	Qwest
	Best Soul Gospel Perf., Female	Deniece Williams	I Surrender All (from So Glad I Know)	Sparrow
	Best Soul Perf., Male	Al Green	Going Away (Single)	A&M
1987	Best Gospel Perf. by a Duo, Group, Choir or Chorus	Mylon LeFevre and Broken Heart	Crack The Sky (Album)	Myrrh/Word
	Best Gospel Perf., Female	Deniece Williams	I Believe In You (from Water Under The Bridge)	Columbia/CBS
	Best Gospel Perf., Male	Larnelle Harris	The Father Hath Provided (Album)	Benson
	Best Soul Gospel Perf. by a Duo, Group, Choir or Chorus	The Winans and Anita Baker	Ain't No Need To Worry (Single)	Qwest
	Best Soul Gospel Perf., Female	Cece Winans	For Always (from Bebe and Cece Winans)	Sparrow
	Best Soul Gospel Perf., Male	Al Green	Everything's Gonna Be Alright (from Soul Survivor)	A&M
1988	Best Gospel Perf. by a Duo, Group, Choir or Chorus	The Winans	The Winans Live at Carnegie Hall	Qwest
	Best Gospel Perf., Female	Amy Grant	Lead Me On	A&M
	Best Gospel Perf., Male	Larnelle Harris	Christmas (Album)	Benson
	Best Soul Gospel Perf. by a Duo, Group, Choir or Chorus	Bebe Winans	Abundant Life (Track/Ron Winans Family and Friends Choir)	Selah
	Best Soul Gospel Perf., Female	Aretha Franklin	One Lord, One Faith, One Baptism	Arista
	Best Soul Gospel Perf., Male	Take 6	Take Six (Album)	Reprise
1989	Best Gospel Perf. by a Duo, Group, Choir or Chorus	Take 6	The Savior Is Waiting (Track/Our Hymns/Various Artists)	Word
	Best Gospel Perf., Female	Cece Winans	Don't Cry	Capitol
	Best Gospel Perf., Male	Bebe Winans	Meantime (Track/Heaven)	Capitol
	Best Soul Gospel Perf. by a Duo, Group, Choir or Chorus	Daniel Winans and Choir	Let Brotherly Love Continue	Rejoice
	Best Soul Gospel Perf., Male	Al Green	As Long as We're Together (Single)	A&M

STELLAR GOSPEL MUSIC AWARDS

Sponsor: Central City Productions

Year	Award	Artist
1986	Album of the Year—Contemporary	The Winans
1986	Album of the Year—Traditional	Shirley Caesar
1986	Best New Artist of the Year	Calvin Bridges
1986	Choir of the Year	Rev. Milton Brunson and The Thompson Community Singers
1986	Excellence Award for Gospel Performance by a Group—Contemporary	The Winans
1986	Excel. Award for Gospel Perf. by a Group—Traditional	The Williams Brothers
1986	Excel. Award for Single Gospel Artist/ Female Contemporary	Tramaine Hawkins
1986	Excel. Award for Single Gospel Artist/	

Female Traditional	Shirley Caesar
1986 Excel. Award for Single Gospel Artist/ Male Contemporary	Walter Hawkins
1986 Excel. Award for Single Gospel Artist/Male Traditional	Howard Smith
1986 Most Notable Achievement Award	Andrae Crouch
1986 Producer of the Year	Andrae Crouch
1986 Producer of the Year	Sandra Crouch
1986 Significant Contributions to Gospel Music	Clara Ward
1986 Song of the Year	Sandra Crouch
1987 Album of the Year—Contemporary	Let My People Go by The Winans
1987 Album of the Year—Traditional	Celebration by Shirley Caesar
1987 Best New Artist of the Year	Calvin Bridges
1987 Choir of the Year	Rev. Milton Brunson and The Thompson Community Singers
1987 Excel. Award for Gospel Artist/Female Contemporary	Tramaine Hawkins
1987 Excel. Award for Gospel Perf. by a Group— Contemporary	The Winans
1987 Excel. Award for Gospel Perf. by a Group—Traditional	The Williams Brothers
1987 Excel. Award for Single Gospel Artist/ Female Traditional	Shirley Caesar
1987 Excel. Award for Single Gospel Artist/ Male Contemporary	Walter Hawkins
1987 Excel. Award for Single Gospel Artist/Male Traditional	Howard Smith
1987 For Significant Contributions to Gospel Music	Clara Ward
1987 Most Notable Achievement Award	Andrae Crouch
1987 Producer of the Year	Sandra Crouch and Andrae Crouch
1987 Song of the Year	Completely Yes by Sandra Crouch
1988 Album of the Year—Contemporary	Be Encouraged
1988 Album of the Year—Traditional	Rev. Milton Brunson
1988 Best Inspr. Soul Gospel Perf.	Aretha Franklin
1988 Best New Artist	Take 6
1988 Best Perf. by Group or Duo—Contemporary	Take 6
1988 Best Perf. by Group or Duo—Traditional	The Williams Brothers
1988 Best Solo Perf. by Female—Contemporary	Vanessa Bell Armstrong
1988 Best Solo Perf. by Female—Traditional	Shirley Caesar
1988 Best Solo Perf. by Male—Contemporary	Larnelle Harris
1988 Best Solo Perf. by Male—Traditional	Calvin Bridges
1988 Choir of the Year	New Jersey Mass Choir
1988 Song of the Year	William and Gloria Gaither
1989 Album of the Year—Contemporary	Bebe and Cece Winans
1989 Album of the Year—Traditional	The Mississippi Mass Choir
1989 Best Gospel Music Video	The Mississippi Mass Choir
1989 Best Inspirational Gospel Performance	Bebe and Cece Winans
1989 Best New Artist	The Mississippi Mass Choir
1989 Best Perf. by a Group or Duo-Contemporary	Bebe and Cece Winans
1989 Best Perf. by Group or Duo—Traditional	The Jackson Southernaires

1989 Best Solo Perf. by Female—Contemporary	Tramaine Hawkins
1989 Best Solo Perf. by Female—Traditional	Myrna Summers
1989 Best Solo Perf. by Male—Contemporary	Daryl Coley
1989 Best Solo Perf. by Male—Traditional	Reverend James Moore
1989 Choir of the Year	The Mississippi Mass Choir
1989 Song of the Year	Bebe and Cece Winans

Bible

TOP 10 BEST-SELLING BIBLES OF 1989

Study Bibles

1. *The NIV Student Bible,* Zondervan
2. *The NIV Study Bible,* Zondervan
3. *Life Application Bible (TLB),* Tyndale
4. *The Adventure Bible (NIV),* Zondervan
5. *Thompson Chain-Reference Bible (KJV),* Kirkbride
6. *Disciple's Study Bible (NIV),* Holman
7. *The Open Bible (NKJV),* Nelson
8. *Scofield Reference Bible/New Scofield Reference Bible (KJV),* Oxford
9. *Thompson Chain-Reference Bible (NIV),* Kirkbride, Zondervan
10. *The Open Bible (KJV),* Nelson

General Versions and Translations

1. *New International Version,* Various Publishers
2. *King James Version,* Various Publishers
3. *New King James Version/ The Bible,* Nelson
4. *The Living Bible/The Book,* Tyndale
5. *New American Standard Version,* Various Publishers
6. *New Century Version,* Word
7. *Today's English Version/Good News Bible,* Nelson
8. *The Amplified Bible,* Zondervan
9. *Spanish Bibles,* Various Publishers
10. *Interlinear and Parallel Texts,* Various Publishers

SO MUCH TIME TO READ THE BIBLE

How much time does it take to read from Genesis to Revelation? If you would read the Bible at standard pulpit speed (slow enough to be heard and understood), the reading time would be seventy-one hours. If you would break that down into minutes and divide it into 365 days, you could read the entire Bible, cover to cover, in only twelve minutes a day. Is this really too much time to spend reading about God?

BIBLE RESOURCES FOR THE DEAF

The Canadian Bible Society is now making the American Sign Language (ASL) translation of the Bible available to deaf people so that they can understand and relate to the Scriptures. If interested in obtaining a copy of the video, write to: Deaf Missions, Rural Route 2, Box 26, Council Bluffs, IA 50503 or Canadian Bible Society, 10 Carnforth Road, Toronto, ON M4A 2S4, Canada.

A program to train deaf people for Christian leadership is being established in Washington, DC, in cooperation with the Washington Community Fellowship and Eastern Mennonite College in Harrisonburg, VA. Nancy Marshall, director of the program, points out that the location will make it available to students at Gallaudet University, the leading school for deaf persons.

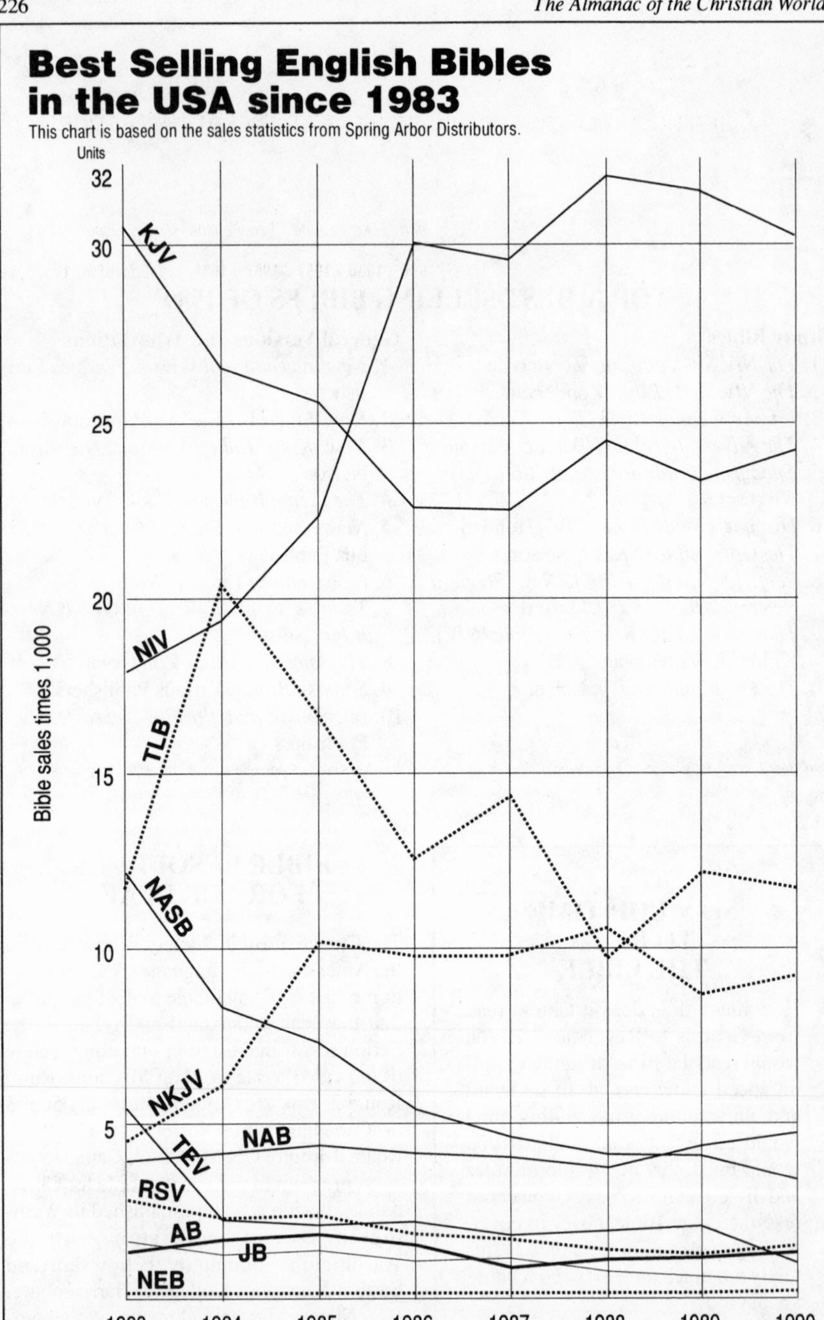

Taken from *Words About the Word* by John R. Kohlenberger III. Copyright © 1987 by John R. Kohlenberger. Used by permission of Zondervan Publishing House.

SPRING ARBOR DISTRIBUTORS BIBLE TRANSLATION TRENDS (UNIT SALES) in 1,000s

	Jan-June	*Jul-Dec*	*Jan-June*	*Jul-Dec*	*Jan-June*	*Jul-Dec*	*Jan-June*	*Jul-Dec*	*Jan-June*	*Jul-Dec*	*Jan-June*	*Jul-Dec*	*Jan-June*	*Jul-Dec*	*Jan-Jun*
Versions	**1983**	**1983**	**1984**	**1984**	**1985**	**1985**	**1986**	**1986**	**1987**	**1987**	**1988**	**1988**	**1989**	**1989**	**1990**
NI	16.5	17.9	20.8	19.5	22.6	22.3	22.9	30.0	30.9	29.8	31.6	31.9	31.9	31.5	30.1
KJ	31.7	30.6	38.3	26.5	26.2	25.4	25.2	23.5	23.8	23.4	23.1	24.6	22.7	23.6	24.2
LI	11.1	11.9	11.8	20.4	18.4	16.7	14.7	12.5	14.0	14.1	12.6	9.9	12.0	12.2	11.9
NK	4.6	4.5	5.9	6.1	6.3	10.1	10.2	9.8	9.4	9.8	8.8	10.7	9.5	8.9	9.1
NB	4.2	3.9	3.2	4.2	5.1	4.4	4.3	4.1	2.9	4.0	4.5	3.8	4.5	4.3	4.9
NS	13.1	12.2	12.9	8.4	7.8	7.3	6.6	5.3	4.8	4.7	4.0	4.2	3.8	4.1	3.2
IC/NC	0.0	0.0	0.0	0.0	0.0	0.0	0.0	1.3	1.5	2.0	2.2	2.6	2.1	2.7	2.2
TE	6.5	5.5	4.4	2.3	2.2	2.1	2.3	1.9	1.8	2.0	3.6	3.1	3.8	2.7	4.2
SP	0.0	0.0	0.0	0.0	.7	1.0	1.1	1.4	1.4	1.4	1.4	1.9	2.1	2.2	2.2
PR	0.0	0.0	0.0	0.0	0.0	0.0	2.6	2.1	2.0	1.8	1.8	1.5	1.6	1.7	1.6
RS	3.2	2.9	2.6	2.5	2.4	2.6	2.5	1.9	1.8	1.8	1.5	1.6	1.5	1.4	1.5
AM	2.3	2.8	2.6	2.2	2.0	1.9	1.9	1.6	1.1	.9	1.3	1.2	1.3	1.3	1.4
OE	0.0	0.0	0.0	0.0	0.0	0.0	1.2	1.0	1.5	1.6	1.4	1.1	1.1	1.1	1.4
FL	0.0	0.0	0.0	0.0	0.0	0.0	.9	.9	1.0	1.0	.9	.8	.8	.9	.9
JB/NJ	2.1	1.7	1.7	1.3	1.2	1.4	1.2	1.1	1.2	1.2	.9	.7	.8	.6	.4
IL	0.0	0.0	0.0	0.0	0.0	0.0	1.2	.5	.7	.6	.6	.5	.5	.5	.5
RE/NE	0.0	0.0	0.0	0.0	0.0	0.0	0.0	0.0	0.0	0.0	0.0	0.0	0.0	.3	.3

Key to Versions:

JB/NJ Jerusalem/New Jerusalem
NS New American Standard
TE Today's English
KJ/NJ King James Version
OE Other English Versions
AM Amplified Bible
LI Living Bible
PR Parallel Bibles
FL Foreign Language
NB New American Bible
RE/NE Revised English/New English
IC/NC New Century Version/ICV
NI New International Version
RS Revised Standard
IL Interlinear Bibles
NK New King James
SP Spanish Bibles

Notes on Bible Translation Trends from Spring Arbor Distributors:

—Spring Arbor does not claim to stock every Bible in print. We do, however, stock some 3,500 Bibles, testaments and Scripture portions.

—Our statistics honestly report unit sales we have experienced in our warehouse over a given period of time.

—Our statistics are affected by product availability, special promotions run by publishers and/or Spring Arbor, publisher advertising and other factors.

—We do not pretend that our translation ranking speaks for all wholesalers or all markets into which Bibles are sold. It simply indicates the trends experienced by one major wholesaler.

12/88

HOW TO SELECT A BIBLE

Determine the textual content ("canon")

1. Old and New Testaments (most Protestants)
2. Old Testament and New Testament with Apocrypha (most Catholics)
3. Old Testament only (most Jewish)
4. New Testament only

Determine the needs

1. Determine reading level
   a. Age
   b. Education: secular and ecclesiastical
   c. Literacy or literary appreciation
   d. Familiarity with ecclesiastical vocabulary

2. Purpose
   a. Reading
      1) General study
      2) Devotional
      3) Public reading
   b. Detailed analysis: word study and diagramming
   c. Comparison: in general or within a congregation
   d. Communication: Preaching, teaching, writing
   e. Gift
   f. Conformity within a congregation

Determine the options

1. For children (through junior high)
2. For those with limited reading ability and little or no church background
3. For youth and adults with no reading difficulty but little or no church background
4. For youth and adults from a conservative church background
5. For youth and adults from a mainline or liberal church background
6. For youth and adults from a Catholic background
7. For youth and adults from a Jewish background
8. For those with an appreciation of literature and literary English
9. For those who want to do word and sentence analysis

Determine study features, if desired

1. Introductions and outlines
2. Cross references
3. Textual notes:
   a. Simple explanations
   b. Topical synthesis
   c. Interpretive: note theological and/or critical preference
4. Concordance
5. Topical index
6. Dictionary
7. Maps
8. Illustrations and charts
9. Essays, articles, and other helps
10. Historical and harmony charts and outlines

Determine the layout (if there are options in the version)

1. Verse format or paragraph format
2. One-column or two-column
3. Type size and color (red-letter)
4. Trim size (book dimensions)

Determine the binding quality

1. Paperback and kivar (low cost)
   a. For awards and other giveaways
   b. For collecting translations for comparative study
   c. For economic necessity
2. Cloth (economy and durability)
   a. A permanent version
   b. Can stand on a shelf
3. Imitation and bonded leather (economy)
   a. A permanent version
   b. Flexible

c. For economic necessity (vs. genuine leather)
4. Leather (durability and beauty)
   a. A permanent version
   b. Genuine leathers are most durable, but also most expensive

FOCUS QUOTE

The Bible is the constitution of Christianity. —Billy Graham

HOW BIBLICALLY LITERATE ARE WE?

Many Americans are biblically illiterate. Recent surveys show that a large percentage could not correctly answer basic questions about the Bible.

	Percent
Is the Book of Isaiah:	
In the Old Testament	62
In the New Testament	10
Don't know	28
Is the expression "God helps those who help themselves" in the Bible?	
Yes	41
No	31
Don't know	28
Is the Book of Jonah part of the Bible?	
Yes	48
No	27
Don't know	25
Is the Book of Thomas part of the Bible?	
Yes	21
No	52
Don't know	27
In what city was Jesus Christ born?	
Bethlehem	61
Jerusalem	18
Nazareth	8
Named another city or area	2
Don't know	10
How many apostles were there?	
Twelve	70
Incorrect number	14
Don't know	16

Barna Research Group, Glendale, CA.

	Percent
Can you name five of the Ten Commandments?	
All five correct	42
Four correct	21
Three correct	14
Two correct	8
One correct	2
Don't know	13

Gallup Survey for *Christianity Today.*

Will you tell me the names of the first four books of the New Testament of the Bible—that is, the four Gospels?	
All four correct	46
Three correct	4
Two correct	2
One correct	2
None correct	3
Don't know	43
Who delivered the Sermon on the Mount?	
Jesus	42
Incorrect answer	24
Don't know	34
Where was Jesus born?	
Bethlehem	70
Incorrect answer	17
Don't know	13

Gallup Survey for the Robert H. Schuller Ministries.

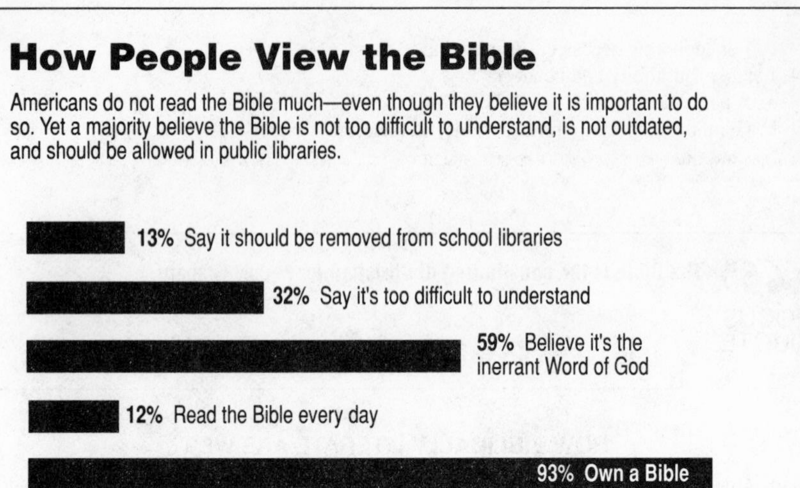

Barna Research Group, Glendale, CA.

HOW PEOPLE INTERPRET THE BIBLE

The question of biblical inerrancy and authority has been debated for centuries and has never resulted in an absolute consensus of opinion on whether the Scriptures are historically reliable.

Which of the following statements comes closest to describing your feelings about the Bible?
The Bible is the actual word of God and is to be taken literally, word for word.
The Bible is the inspired word of God. It contains no errors, but some verses are to be taken symbolically rather than literally.
The Bible is the inspired word of God, but it may contain historical and scientific errors.
The Bible was not inspired by God, but it represents humankind's best understanding of God's nature.
The Bible is an ancient book of human fables, legends, history and moral precepts.
No opinion.

	Literal word of God %	*Inspired word of God* %	*Inspired word with errors* %	*Human Document* %	*Ancient Lit.* %	*No Opinion* %
National	31	24	22	7	10	6
Men	38	23	21	8	13	7
Women	34	26	22	6	7	5
Whites	29	25	23	8	10	5
Blacks	45	23	14	4	4	10
Protestants	37	27	22	5	5	4
Catholics	26	28	26	8	7	5

Gallup Survey for the National Catholic Evangelization Association. Taken from *100 Questions and Answers.* Published by Princeton Religion Research Center.

HOW OFTEN DO PEOPLE READ THE BIBLE?

How often do you read the Bible?

	Daily %	*Weekly* %	*Monthly* %	*Less than Monthly* %	*Never* %
Adults	11	22	14	26	22
Teens	10	30	18	22	20

One-third of adult Americans (33%) read the Bible at least once a week, with one in nine a daily reader. One in seven (14%) reads the Bible at least once a month, about one in four (26%) less than monthly, and one in five (22%) never reads scriptures. These figures are virtually unchanged from earlier surveys.

The Bible is near the top of many teens' book lists. A majority of American teens (58%) say they read the Bible at least monthly, according to a Gallup Youth Survey. This finding represents a slight increase in Bible reading since 1983, when 55% of all teens reported reading scriptures at least monthly.

One teen in ten (10%) reports daily Bible reading. Thirty percent of teens say they read the Bible at least once a week, and 18% at least monthly. Twenty-two percent say they read it less often than once a month. One teen in five (20%) rarely or never reads the Bible.

Gallup Poll public service, in conjunction with the Layman's National Bible Committee. Taken from *100 Questions and Answers*. Published by Princeton Religion Research Center. Copyright © 1989 by George Gallup, Jr., and Sarah Jones. Used by permission.

FOCUS QUOTE

A Bible that's falling apart probably belongs to someone who isn't. Christian Johnson

PEOPLE BELIEVE THE BIBLE BEST CURE FOR DEPRESSION

Eight in ten Americans (81%) report bouts with depression, which best-selling psychiatrist M. Scott Peck says often accompanies mental and spiritual growth needed to adapt successfully to life events.

While most turn to a hobby, television, reading, or music to overcome depression, spiritual activities—prayer, meditation and Bible reading—are cited as the most effective means for dealing with depressive disorder.

Money and bills, job, family and health problems are most often causes of depression or discouragement, followed by general frustrations, problems with children, the state of the economy, world affairs, and one's social life.

Please tell me whether you frequently or occasionally do the following when you feel discouraged or depressed. (Based on the 81% who are ever depressed or discouraged.)

A—Frequently or occasionally engage in these activities %
B—Very or somewhat effective %

	A	*B*
Spend more time alone, with a hobby, TV, reading,or listening to music	77	84
Seek out friends to talk with	68	90

	A	B
Seek out family members to talk with	66	88
Eat more/less	64	31
Spend more time in prayer, meditation or reading the Bible	48	94
Spend more time exercising	40	92
Shop more, spend money	31	47
Spend more hours at work	29	77
Seek out pastor, religious leader	27	87
Spend more time sleeping	26	59
Seek help from a doctor or professional counselor	14	71
Drink more alcohol	10	37
Rely more heavily on medication	6	58

Gallup Survey for the Christian Broadcasting Network, Inc. Taken from *100 Questions and Answers.* Published by Princeton Religion Research Center.

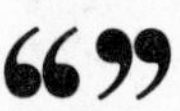

FOCUS QUOTE

God walks in the Holy Scriptures, seeking men. —St. Ambrose

THE BIBLE TALKS ABOUT LIFE, RELATIONSHIPS, THE FUTURE

The Bible Talks about Life

Let him have all your worries and cares, for he is always thinking about you and watching everything that concerns you. *1 Peter 5:7*

AGITATION

"I am leaving you with a gift—peace of mind and heart! And the peace I give isn't fragile like the peace the world gives. So don't be troubled or afraid." *John 14:27*

Don't worry about anything; instead, pray about everything; tell God your needs and don't forget to thank him for his answers. If you do this you will experience God's peace, which is far more wonderful than the human mind can understand. His peace will keep your thoughts and hearts quiet and at rest as you trust in Christ Jesus. *Philippians 4:6, 7*

ANGER

If you are angry, don't sin by nursing your grudge. Don't let the sun go down with you still angry—get over it quickly; for when you are angry you give a mighty foothold to the devil. *Ephesians 4:26, 27*

Dear brothers, don't ever forget that it is best to listen much, speak little, and not become angry; for anger doesn't make us good, as God demands that we must be. *James 1:19, 20*

DEPRESSION

I waited patiently for God to help me; then he listened and heard my cry. He lifted me out of the pit of despair, out from the bog and the mire, and set my feet on a hard, firm path and steadied me as I walked along. He has given me a new song to sing, of praises to our God. *Psalm 40:1-3*

Yes, the Lord hears the good man when he calls to him for help, and saves him out of all his troubles. . . . The good man does not escape all troubles—he has them too. But the Lord helps him in each and every one. *Psalm 34:17, 19*

DISCOURAGEMENT

"Let not your heart be troubled. You are trusting God, now trust in me. There are many homes up there where my Father lives, and I am going to prepare them for your coming. When everything is ready, then I will come and get you, so that you can always be with me where I am." *John 14:1-3*

Be strong! Be courageous! Do not be afraid of them! For the Lord your God will be with you. He will neither fail you nor forsake you. *Deuteronomy 31:6*

ETERNAL LIFE

Jesus told her, "I am the one who raises the dead and gives them life again. Anyone who believes in me, even though he died like anyone else, shall live again. He is given eternal life for believing in me and shall never perish. Do you believes this, Martha?" *John 11:25, 26*

For we know that when this tent we live in now is taken down—when we die and leave these bodies—we will have wonderful new bodies in heaven, homes that will be ours forevermore, made for us by God himself, and not by human hands. How weary we grow of our present bodies. . . . We want to slip into our new bodies so that these dying bodies will, as it were, be swallowed up by everlasting life. This is what God has prepared for us and, as a guarantee, he has given us his Holy Spirit. *2 Corinthians 5:1, 2, 4, 5*

Yet what we suffer now is nothing compared to the glory he will give us later. *Romans 8:18*

FEAR

Fear not, for I am with you. Do not be dismayed. I am your God. I will strengthen you; I will help you; I will uphold you with my victorious right hand. *Isaiah 41:10*

He does not fear bad news, nor live in dread of what may happen. For he is settled in his mind that Jehovah will take care of him. That is why he is not afraid, but can calmly face his foes. *Psalm 112:7, 8*

You are my hiding place from every storm of life; you even keep me from getting into trouble! You surround me with songs of victory. *Psalm 32:7*

FRUSTRATION

You need to keep on patiently doing God's will if you want him to do for you all that he has promised. *Hebrews 10:36*

He will keep in perfect peace all those who trust in him, whose thoughts turn often to the Lord! Trust in the Lord God always, for in the Lord Jehovah is your everlasting strength. *Isaiah 26:3, 4*

GUILT

But if we confess our sins to him, he can be depended on to forgive us and to cleanse us from every wrong. [And it is perfectly proper for God to do this for us because Christ died to wash away our sins.] *1 John 1:9*

I've blotted out your sins; they are gone like morning mist at noon! Oh, return to me, for I have paid the price to set you free. *Isaiah 44:22*

Come, let's talk this over! says the Lord; no matter how deep the stain of your sins, I can take it out and make you as clean as freshly fallen snow. Even if you are stained as red as crimson, I can make you white as wool. *Isaiah 1:18*

So overflowing is his kindness towards us that he took away all our sins through the blood of his Son, by whom we are saved. *Ephesians 1:7*

And I will be merciful to them in their wrongdoings, and I will remember their sins no more. *Hebrews 8:12*

IMPATIENCE

Rest in the Lord: wait patiently for him to act. Don't be envious of evil men who prosper. *Psalm 37:7*

Now as for you, dear brothers who are waiting for the Lord's return, be patient, like a farmer who waits until the autumn for his precious harvest to ripen. Yes, be patient. And take courage, for the coming of the Lord is near. *James 5:7, 8*

INSECURITY

What can we ever say to such wonderful things as these? If God is on our side, who can ever be against us? Since he did not spare even his own Son for us but gave him up for us all, won't he also surely give us everything else? *Romans 8:31, 32*

I am holding you by your right hand—I, the Lord your God—and I say to you, Don't be afraid; I am here to help you. *Isaiah 41:13*

That is why we can say without any doubt or fear, "The Lord is my Helper and I am not

THE BIBLE TALKS ABOUT LIFE, RELATIONSHIPS, THE FUTURE cont.

afraid of anything that mere man can do to me." *Hebrews 13:6*

INSULT

"Happy are those who are persecuted because they are good, for the Kingdom of Heaven is theirs. When you are reviled and persecuted and lied about because you are my followers—wonderful! Be happy about it! Be very glad! for a tremendous reward awaits you up in heaven. And remember, the ancient prophets were persecuted too. . . . But I say: Love your enemies! Pray for those who persecute you! In that way you will be acting as true sons of your Father in heaven. For he gives his sunlight to both the evil and the good, and sends rain on the just and on the unjust too." *Matthew 5:10-12, 44, 45*

JEALOUSY

And by all means don't brag about being wise and good if you are bitter and jealous and selfish; that is the worst sort of lie. For jealousy and selfishness are not God's kind of wisdom. Such things are earthly, unspiritual, inspired by the devil. For wherever there is jealousy or selfish ambition, there will be disorder and every other kind of evil. *James 3:14-16*

So do not be dismayed when evil men grow rich and build their lovely homes. For when they die they carry nothing with them! Their honors will not follow them. *Psalm 49:16, 17*

LONELINESS

I will lie down in peace and sleep, for though I am alone, O Lord, you will keep me safe. *Psalm 4:8*

For the mountains may depart and the hills disappear, but my kindness shall not leave you. My promise of peace for you will never be broken, says the Lord who has mercy upon you. *Isaiah 54:10*

"No, I will not abandon you or leave you as orphans in the storm—I will come to you." *John 14:18*

LOW SELF-ESTEEM

So God made man like his Maker. Like God did God make man; man and maid did he make them. *Genesis 1:27*

"The second is: 'You must love others as much as yourself.' No other commandments are greater than these." *Mark 12:31*

As God's messenger I give each of you God's warning: Be honest in your estimate of yourselves, measuring your value by how much faith God has given you. Just as there are many parts to our bodies, so it is with Christ's body. We are all parts of it, and it takes every one of us to make it complete, for we each have different work to do. So we belong to each other, and each needs all the others. *Romans 12:3-5*

PAIN

"Father, Father," he said, "everything is possible for you. Take away this cup from me. Yet I want your will, not mine." *Mark 14:36*

These troubles and sufferings of ours are, after all, quite small and won't last very long. Yet this short time of distress will result in God's richest blessing upon us forever and ever! . . . I was given a physical condition which has been a thorn in my flesh, a messenger from Satan to hurt and bother me, and prick my pride. Three different times I begged God to make me well again. Each time he said, "No. But I am with you; that is all you need. My power shows up best in weak people." Now I am glad to boast about how weak I am; I am glad to be a living demonstration of Christ's power. Since I know it is all for Christ's good, I am quite happy about "the thorn," and about insults and hardships, persecutions and difficulties; for when I am weak, then I am strong—the less I have, the more I depend on him. *2 Corinthians 4:17; 12:7-10*

SICKNESS

Is anyone sick? He should call for the elders of the church and they should pray over him and pour a little oil upon him, calling on the Lord to heal him. And their prayer, if offered in faith, will heal him, for the Lord will make him well; and if his sickness was caused by some sin, the Lord will forgive him. *James 5:14, 15*

He nurses them when they are sick and soothes their pains and worries. *Psalm 41:3*

SUFFERING AND DEATH

And now, dear brothers, I want you to know what happens to a Christian when he dies so that when it happens, you will not be full of sorrow, as those are who have no hope. For since we believe that Jesus died and then came back to life again, we can also believe that when Jesus returns, God will bring back with him all the Christians who have died. *1 Thessalonians 4:13, 14*

The Lord is close to those whose hearts are breaking. *Psalm 34:18a*

But I am telling you this strange and wonderful secret: we shall not all die, but we shall all be given new bodies! It will all happen in a moment, in the twinkling of an eye, when the last trumpet is blown. For there will be a trumpet blast from the sky and all the Christians who have died will suddenly become alive, with new bodies that will never, never die; and then we who are still alive shall suddenly have new bodies too. For our earthly bodies, the ones we have now that can die, must be transformed into heavenly bodies that cannot perish but will live forever. When this happens, then at last this Scripture will come true— "Death is swallowed up in victory." O death, where then your victory? Where then your sting? *1 Corinthians 15:51-55*

TEMPTATION

But remember this—the wrong desires that come into your life aren't anything new and different. Many others have faced exactly the same problems before you. And no temptation is irresistible. You can trust God to keep the temptation from becoming so strong that you can't stand up against it, for he has promised this and will do what he says. He will show you how to escape temptation's power so that you can bear up patiently against it. *1 Corinthians 10:13*

Happy is the man who doesn't give in and do wrong when he is tempted, for afterwards he will get as his reward the crown of life that God has promised those who love him. And remember, when someone wants to do wrong it is never God who is tempting him, for God never wants to do wrong and never tempts anyone else to do it. . . . So give yourselves humbly to God. Resist the devil and he will flee from you. *James 1:12, 13; 4:7*

For since he himself has now been through suffering and temptation, he knows what it is like when we suffer and are tempted, and he is wonderfully able to help us. *Hebrews 2:18*

WEARINESS

But they that wait upon the Lord shall renew their strength. They shall mount up with wings like eagles; they shall run and not be weary; they shall walk and not faint. *Isaiah 40:31*

"Come to me and I will give you rest—all of you who work so hard beneath a heavy yoke. Wear my yoke—for it fits perfectly—and let me teach you; for I am gentle and humble, and you shall find rest for your souls; for I give you only light burdens." *Matthew 11:28-30*

WORRY

He will keep in perfect peace all those who trust in him, whose thoughts turn often to the Lord! Trust in the Lord God always, for in the Lord Jehovah is your everlasting strength. *Isaiah 26:3, 4*

Let him have all your worries and cares, for he is always thinking about you and watching everything that concerns you. *1 Peter 5:7*

Then turning to his disciples he said, "Don't worry about whether you have enough food to eat or clothes to wear. For life consists of far more than food and clothes. And besides, what's the use of worrying? What good does it do? Will it add a single day to your life? Of course not! And if worry can't even do such little things as that, what's the use of worrying over bigger things? Look at the lilies! They don't toil and spin, and yet Solomon in all his glory was not robed as well as they are. And if God provides clothing for the flowers that are here today and gone tomorrow, don't you suppose that he will provide clothing for you, you doubters?" *Luke 12:22-28*

THE BIBLE TALKS ABOUT LIFE, RELATIONSHIPS, THE FUTURE cont.

The Bible Talks about Relationships

There are "friends" who pretend to be friends, but there is a friend who sticks closer than a brother. *Proverbs 18:24*

FRIENDS

Be with wise men and become wise. Be with evil men and become evil. *Proverbs 13:20*

Don't be selfish; don't live to make a good impression on others. Be humble, thinking of others as better than yourself. Don't just think about your own affairs, but be interested in others, too, and in what they are doing. *Philippians 2:3, 4*

INJUSTICE

Do what is right; then if men speak against you, calling you evil names, they will become ashamed of themselves for falsely accusing you when you have only done what is good. Remember, if God wants you to suffer, it is better to suffer for doing good than for doing wrong! Christ also suffered. He died once for the sins of all us guilty sinners, although he himself was innocent of any sin at any time, that he might bring us safely home to God. *1 Peter 3:16-18*

After you have suffered a little while, our God, who is full of kindness through Christ, will give you his eternal glory. He personally will come and pick you up, and set you firmly in place, and make you stronger than ever. To him be all power over all things forever and ever. Amen. *1 Peter 5:10, 11*

LOVE

"I have loved you even as the Father has loved me. Live within my love. When you obey me you are living in my love, just as I obey my Father and live in his love. I have told you this so that you will be filled with my joy. Yes, your cup of joy will overflow! I demand that you love each other as much as I love you. And here is how to measure it—the greatest love is shown when a person lays down his life for his friends; and you are my friends if you obey me. I no longer call you slaves, for a master doesn't confide in his slaves; now you are my friends, proved by the fact that I have told you everything the Father told me. You didn't choose me! I chose you! I appointed you to go and produce lovely fruit always, so that no matter what you ask for from the Father, using my name, he will give it to you." *John 15:9-16*

"For God loved the world so much that he gave his only Son so that anyone who believes in him shall not perish but have eternal life." *John 3:16*

God showed how much he loved us by sending his only Son into this wicked world to bring to us eternal life through his death. In this act we see what real love is: it is not our love for God, but his love for us when he sent his Son to satisfy God's anger against our sins. . . . We know how much God loves us because we have felt his love and because we believe him when he tells us that he loves us dearly. God is love, and anyone who lives in love is living with God and God is living in him. And as we live with Christ, our love grows more perfect and complete; so we will not be ashamed and embarrassed at the day of judgment, but can face him with confidence and joy, because he loves us and we love him too. . . . If anyone says "I love God," but keeps on hating his brother, he is a liar; for if he doesn't love his brother who is right there in front of him, how can he love God whom he has never seen? And God himself has said that one must love not only God, but his brother too. *1 John 4:9-21*

Love is very patient and kind, never jealous or envious, never boastful or proud, never haughty or selfish or rude. Love does not demand its own way. It is not irritable or touchy. It does not hold grudges and will hardly even notice when others do it wrong. It is never glad about injustice, but rejoices whenever truth wins out. If you love someone you will be loyal to him no matter what the cost. You will always believe in him, always expect the best of him, and always stand your ground in defending him. . . . There are three things that remain—faith, hope, and love—and the greatest of these is love. *1 Corinthians 13:4-7, 13*

MARRIAGE

Honor Christ by submitting to each other. You wives must submit to your husbands' leadership in the same way you submit to the Lord. . . . And you husbands, show the same kind of love to your wives as Christ showed to the Church when he died for her, to make her holy and clean, washed by baptism and God's Word; so that he could give her to himself as a glorious Church without a single spot or wrinkle or any other blemish, being holy and without a single fault. That is how husbands should treat their wives, loving them as parts of themselves. For since a man and his wife are now one, a man is really doing himself a favor and loving himself when he loves his wife. *Ephesians 5:21, 22, 25-28*

Wives, fit in with your husbands' plans; for then if they refuse to listen when you talk to them about the Lord, they will be won by your respectful, pure behavior. Your godly lives will speak to them better than any words. Don't be concerned about the outward beauty that depends on jewelry, or beautiful clothes, or hair arrangement. Be beautiful inside, in your hearts, with the lasting charm of a gentle and quiet spirit which is so precious to God. That kind of deep beauty was seen in the saintly women of old, who trusted God and fitted in with their husbands' plans. Sarah, for instance, obeyed her husband Abraham, honoring him as head of the house. And if you do the same, you will be following in her steps like good daughters and doing what is right; then you will not need to fear [offending your husbands]. You husbands must be careful of your wives, being thoughtful of their needs and honoring them as the weaker sex. Remember that you and your wife are partners in receiving God's blessings, and if you don't treat her as you should, your prayers will not get ready answers. *1 Peter 3:1-7*

A man should leave his father and mother, and be forever united to his wife. The two shall become one—no longer two, but one! And no man may divorce what God has joined together. Anyone who divorces his wife, except for fornication, and marries another, commits adultery. *Matthew 19:5, 9*

When a man divorces his wife to marry someone else, he commits adultery against her. And if a wife divorces her husband and remarries, she, too, commits adultery. *Mark 10:11, 12*

PARENTS AND CHILDREN

Children, obey your parents; this is the right thing to do because God has placed them in authority over you. Honor your father and mother. This is the first of God's Ten Commandments that ends with a promise. And this is the promise: that if you honor your father and mother, yours will be a long life, full of blessing. And now a word to you parents. Don't keep on scolding and nagging your children, making them angry and resentful. Rather, bring them up with the loving discipline the Lord himself approves, with suggestions and godly advice. *Ephesians 6:1-4*

The Bible Talks about the Future

Your words are a flashlight to light the path ahead of me, and keep me from stumbling. *Psalm 119:105*

ASTROLOGY, HOROSCOPES, AND THE OCCULT

So why are you trying to find out the future by consulting witches and mediums? Don't listen to their whisperings and mutterings. Can the living find out the future from the dead? Why not ask your God? *Isaiah 8:19*

Call out the demon hordes you've worshiped all these years. Call on them to help you strike deep terror into many hearts again. You have advisors by the ton—your astrologers and stargazers, who try to tell you what the future holds. But they are as useless as dried grass burning in the fire. They cannot even deliver themselves! You'll get no help from them at all. Theirs is no fire to sit beside to make you warm! *Isaiah 47:12-14*

DIRECTION FOR LIFE

I will bless the Lord who counsels me; he gives me wisdom in the night. He tells me what to do. I am always thinking of the Lord; and because he is so near, I never need to stumble or to fall. *Psalm 16:7, 8*

THE BIBLE TALKS ABOUT LIFE, RELATIONSHIPS, THE FUTURE cont.

And if you leave God's paths and go astray, you will hear a Voice behind you say, "No, this is the way; walk here." *Isaiah 30:21*

He will teach the ways that are right and best to those who humbly turn to him. And when we obey him, every path he guides us on is fragrant with his lovingkindness and his truth. *Psalm 25:9, 10*

And remember, it is a message to obey, not just to listen to. So don't fool yourselves. For if a person just listens and doesn't obey, he is like a man looking at his face in a mirror; as soon as he walks away, he can't see himself any more or remember what he looks like. But if anyone keeps looking steadily into God's law for free men, he will not only remember it but he will do what it says, and God will greatly bless him in everything he does. *James 1:22-25*

MONEY MANAGEMENT

And it is he who will supply all your needs from his riches in glory, because of what Christ Jesus has done for us. *Philippians 4:19*

He who loves money shall never have enough. The foolishness of thinking that wealth brings happiness! *Ecclesiastes 5:10*

Do you want to be truly rich? You already are if you are happy and good. After all, we didn't bring any money with us when we came into the world, and we can't carry away a single penny when we die. So we should be well satisfied without money if we have enough food and clothing. But people who long to be rich soon begin to do all kinds of wrong things to get money, things that hurt them and make them evil-minded and finally send them to hell itself. For the love of money is the first step toward all kinds of sin. Some people have even turned away from God because of their love for it, and as a result have pierced themselves with many sorrows. *1 Timothy 6:6-10*

TRUST

Trust the Lord completely; don't ever trust yourself. In everything you do, put God first, and he will direct you and crown your efforts with success. *Proverbs 3:5, 6*

I know how to live on almost nothing or with everything. I have learned the secret of contentment in every situation, whether it be a full stomach or hunger, plenty or want; for I can do everything God asks me to with the help of Christ who gives me the strength and power. *Philippians 4:12, 13*

The Bible Talks about Faith

Faith comes from listening to this Good News—the Good News about Christ. *Romans 10:17*

BEING BORN AGAIN

Jesus replied, "With all the earnestness I possess I tell you this: Unless you are born again, you can never get into the Kingdom of God. . . . What I am telling you so earnestly is this: Unless one is born of water and the Spirit, he cannot enter the Kingdom of God. Men can only reproduce human life, but the Holy Spirit gives new life from heaven; so don't be surprised at my statement that you must be born again." *John 3:3, 5-7*

All honor to God, the God and Father of our Lord Jesus Christ; for it is his boundless mercy that has given us the privilege of being born again, so that we are now members of God's own family. *1 Peter 1:3*

The person who has been born into God's family does not make a practice of sinning, because now God's life is in him; so he can't keep on sinning, for this new life has been born into him and controls him—he has been *born again*. *1 John 3:9*

FINDING GOD

"His purpose in all of this is that they should seek after God, and perhaps feel their way toward him and find him—though he is not far from any one of us. For in him we live and move and are! As one of your own poets says it, 'We are the sons of God.'" *Acts 17:27, 28*

For I know the plans I have for you, says the Lord. They are plans for good and not for evil, to give you a future and a hope. In those days when you pray, I will listen. You will find me when you seek me, if you look for me in earnest. *Jeremiah 29:11-13*

KNOWING GOD

How can we describe God? With what can we compare him? With an idol? . . . It is God who sits above the circle of the earth. (The people below must seem to him like grasshoppers!) He is the one who stretches out the heavens like a curtain and makes his tent from them. He dooms the great men of the world and brings them all to naught. They hardly get started, barely take root, when he blows on them and their work withers and the wind carries them off like straw. "With whom will you compare me? Who is my equal?" asks the Holy One. Look up into the heavens! Who created all these stars? As a shepherd leads his sheep, calling each by its pet name, and counts them to see that none are lost or strayed, so God does with stars and planets! *Isaiah 40:18, 22-26*

Dear friends, let us practice loving each other, for love comes from God and those who are loving and kind show that they are getting to know him better. But if a person isn't loving and kind, it shows that he doesn't know God—for God is love. *1 John 4:7, 8*

KNOWING JESUS CHRIST

Before anything else existed, there was Christ, with God. He has always been alive and is himself God. He created everything there is—nothing exists that he didn't make. Eternal life is in him, and this life gives light to all mankind. His life is the light that shines through the darkness—and the darkness can never extinguish it. God sent John the Baptist as a witness to the fact that Jesus Christ is the true Light. John himself was not the Light; he was only a witness to identify it. Later on, the one who is the true Light arrived to shine on everyone coming into the world. But although he made the world, the world didn't recognize him when he came. Even in his own land and among his own people, the Jews, he was not accepted. Only a few would welcome and receive him. But to all who received him he gave the right to become children of God. All they needed to do was to trust him to save them. All those who believe this are reborn!—not a physical rebirth resulting from human passion or plan—but from the will of God. And Christ became a human being and lived here on earth among us and was full of loving forgiveness and truth. And some of us have seen his glory—the glory of the only Son of the heavenly Father! *John 1:1-14*

Christ is the exact likeness of the unseen God. He existed before God made anything at all, and, in fact, Christ himself is the Creator who made everything in heaven and earth, the things we can see and the things we can't; the spirit world with its kings and kingdoms, its rulers and authorities; all were made by Christ for his own use and glory. He was before all else began and it is his power that holds everything together. He is the Head of the body made up of his people—that is, his Church—which he began; and he is the Leader of all those who arise from the dead, so that he is first in everything; for God wanted all of himself to be in his Son. . . . You were dead in sins, and your sinful desires were not yet cut away. Then he gave you a share in the very life of Christ, for he forgave all your sins, and blotted out the charges proved against you, the list of his commandments which you had not obeyed. He took this list of sins and destroyed it by nailing it to Christ's cross. *Colossians 1:15-19; 2:13, 14*

God's Son shines out with God's glory, and all that God's Son is and does marks him as God. He regulates the universe by the mighty power of his command. He is the one who died to cleanse us and clear our record of all sin, and then sat down in highest honor

FOCUS QUOTE

The Bible is meant to be bread for our daily use; not just cake for special occasions.

THE BIBLE TALKS ABOUT LIFE, RELATIONSHIPS, THE FUTURE cont.

beside the great God of heaven. . . . but of his Son he says, "Your kingdom, O God, will last forever and ever; its commands are always just and right." *Hebrews 1:3, 8*

KNOWING THE HOLY SPIRIT

He has put his brand upon us—his mark of ownership—and given us his Holy Spirit in our hearts as guarantee that we belong to him, and as the first installment of all that he is going to give us. *2 Corinthians 1:22*

But you are not like that. You are controlled by your new nature if you have the Spirit of God living in you. (And remember that if anyone doesn't have the Spirit of Christ living in him, he is not a Christian at all.) Yet, even though Christ lives within you, your body will die because of sin; but your spirit will live, for Christ has pardoned it. And if the Spirit of God, who raised up Jesus from the dead, lives in you, he will make your dying bodies live again after you die, by means of this same Holy Spirit living within you. *Romans 8:9-11*

"If you love me, obey me; and I will ask the Father and he will give you another Comforter, and he will never leave you. He is the Holy Spirit, the Spirit who leads into all truth. The world at large cannot receive him, for it isn't looking for him and doesn't recognize him. But you do, for he lives with you now and some day shall be in you. . . . But when the Father sends the Comforter instead of me—and by the Comforter I mean the Holy Spirit—he will teach you much, as well as remind you of everything I myself have told you." *John 14:15-17, 26*

PRAYER

Admit your faults to one another and pray for each other so that you may be healed. The earnest prayer of a righteous man has great power and wonderful results. *James 5:16*

"But if you stay in me and obey my commands, you may ask any request you like, and it will be granted!" *John 15:7*

"Ask, and you will be given what you ask for. Seek, and you will find. Knock, and the door will be opened. For everyone who asks, receives. Anyone who seeks, finds. If only you will knock, the door will open." *Matthew 7:7, 8*

If we confess our sins to him, he can be depended on to forgive us and to cleanse us from every wrong. *1 John 1:9*

FOCUS QUOTE

Trying to absorb the depths of the Bible is like trying to mop up the ocean floor with a sponge.

BIBLE READING GUIDES

Read your Bible through in one year.

Topically (Used by permission of the National Association of Evangelicals.)

God's Power
Jan 1 Ex 7:14-24
2 Ex 8:1-19
3 Jb 9:1-12
4 Ps 66:1-7
5 Is 44:18-28
6 Jer 10:12-16
7 Ez 17:11-24
Sustainer
8 Hb 3:1-15
9 Gn 45:4-15
10 1 Kgs 17:1-16
11 1 Kgs 19:1-8
12 Ez 34:11-16, 25-31
13 Mt 6:25-34
14 Acts 17:22-28
Master of All
15 Col 1:15-19
16 Dt 2:16-25
17 1 Sm 2:1-10
18 Jb 12:13-25
19 Jb 26
20 Jb 37
21 Is 41:1-10
Our Victory
22 Mt 8
23 Dt 7:17-26
24 Dt 20:1-4
25 Ps 27
26 Ps 28
27 Is 33:13-22
28 Is 41:8-16
Our Deliverer
29 1 Cor 15:51-58
30 Jgs 6:11-18
31 2 Chr 20:5-17
Feb 1 Ps 40:1-5
2 Is 11:10-16
3 Is 51:1-11
4 Acts 12:1-17
Accessible
5 Acts 16:25-40
6 Is 55:1-9
7 Mt 28:16-20
8 Lk 11:5-13
9 Eph 2:11-22
10 Heb 4:12-16
11 Heb 10:11-25
Our Conqueror
12 Jas 5:13-18
13 Is 31:1-5
14 Is 49:22-26
15 Jer 51:27-33
16 Na 1:7-15

17 Na 2
18 Zec 9:9-17
Our Help in Spiritual Warfare
19 Rom 7:13-25
20 Ps 18:31-50
21 Rom 6:15-23
22 Rom 8:26-39
23 2 Cor 10:1-12
24 Eph 6:10-20
25 2 Tm 1:3-14
Redeems Israel
26 2 Tm 2:1-19
27 Is 43:14-21
28 Is 49:-7
Mar 1 Is 60:5-22
2 Jl 3:9-21
3 Am 9:5-15
4 Zep 3:6-13
Reconciles
5 Zec 12:1-3:1
6 Jb 33:19-33
7 Hos 2:14-23
8 Zec 13
9 Gal 3:23-4:7
10 Col 1:21-29
11 Heb 9:11-22
12 Heb 9:11-22
Restores
13 Ez 37:15-28
14 Hos 14
15 Jl 2:18-32
16 Zep 3:9-20
17 Zec 8
18 Lk 15:11-24
19 Acts 26:1-23
Our Response in Humility
20 Ps 131
21 Mk 9:33-37, 10:13-16
22 Lk 18:9-14
23 Rom 12:3-13
24 1 Cor 1:18-31
25 Phil 3:1-11
26 1 Pt 5:1-11
God's Love
27 Ps 107:1-3, 17-22
28 Ps 136:1-3, 23-26
29 Mt 18:10-14
30 Jn 10:1-18
31 Jn 12:20-36
Apr 1 Rom 5:1-11
2 Eph 4:25-5:2
Our Substitute
3 Ps 22
4 Is 53
5 Rom 15:1-13
6 2 Cor 5:11-21
7 Gal 3:10-14
8 Heb 2:9-18
9 1 Pt 2:18-25
Our Salvation
10 Is 12:1-6
11 Is 61
12 Lk 15:1-10
13 Lk 19:1-10
14 Acts 4:1-12
15 Acts 28:2-31
16 Eph 1:3-14
Blessings in Path of Life
17 Dt 7:6-11
18 Ps 18:20-24
19 Ps 19:7-14
20 Ps 92:5-15
21 Is 26:7-15
22 Is 58:6-14
23 Mal 3:6-12
Eternal Life
24 Ps 23
25 Jn 6:25-40
26 Jn 6:50-69
27 Jn 17:1-5
28 1 Thes 4:13-18
29 1 Jn 5:6-12
30 Rv 22
Kingdom of God
May 1 Ps 145
2 Mt 18:21-35
3 Mt 20:1-16
4 Mt 25:1-13
5 Mt 25:14-30
6 Mk 4:1-20
7 Lk 14:16-24
Great Hope
8 Ps 16
9 Ps 130
10 Jer 17:5-18
11 Jn 14:1-7
12 1 Cor 15:12-28
13 Heb 6:9-20
14 1 Pt 1:3-12
God's Sovereignty
15 Jb 36:22-33
16 Ps 47
17 Is 60:1-9
18 Jer 27
19 Jer 51:15-24
20 Dn 4:10-37
21 Rv 19:5-16
God's Uniqueness
22 Dt 10:12-22
23 Dt 32:34-43
24 Ps 148
25 Is 40:12-26
26 Is 44:1-8
27 Is 45:14-25
28 Jer 10:1-10
A Jealous God
29 Ex 20:1-7
30 Ex 34:11-17
31 Dt 4:15-24
Jun 1 Dt 29:16-29
2 Is 31
3 Ez 23:22-35
4 Mt 10:34-42
Penitence Required
5 Ps 52
6 Ez 18:21-32
7 Dn 9:3-19
8 Hos 14
9 Mt 3:7-10
10 Lk 13:1-9
11 Acts 2:22-42
God's Patience
12 Ps 86
13 Ps 103:6-14
14 Is 30:15-26
15 Jer 15:15-21
16 Jl 2:12-19
17 Rom 2:1-11
18 2 Pt 3:8-18
Source of Rest
19 Ps 4
20 Ps 116
21 Prv 3:21-27
22 Is 28:5-13
23 Mt 11:25-30
24 2 Thes 1:5-12
25 Heb 4:1-11
God of Mercy
26 Nm 21:4-9
27 Dt 4:25-31
28 Jer 31:15-20
29 Jon 4
30 Rom 9:14-26
Jul 1 Rom 11:17-32
2 1 Tm 1:12-17
God of Grace
3 Is 54
4 Mi 7:8-20
5 Acts 11:1-18
6 Rom 3:21-26
7 Rom 5:12-21
8 Eph 1:3-14
9 Ti 2:11-14
Eternal God
10 Gn 21:25-34
11 Ex 3:7-17
12 Ps 102:23-28
13 Is 48:9-13
14 1 Tm 6:11-16
15 Heb 1:1-12
16 Rv 1:4-8, 12-18
Wise God
17 Jb 28:12-28
18 Ps 104:24-35
19 Prv 120:33
20 Prv 3:13-26
21 Prv 8:22-36
22 Dn 2:17-23
23 1 Cor 2:6-16
God of Great Glory
24 Ex 24:9-18
25 1 Kgs 8:1-13
26 Ps 24:1-11
27 Is 30:29-33
28 Ez 1:15-28
29 Rv 4
30 Rv 15
Worthy of Worship
31 Dt 6:4-17
Aug 1 1 Chron. 16:7-36
2 Ps 135
3 Ps 149
4 Ps 150
5 Lk 4:1-13
6 Jn 4:5-24
Our Love for God
7 Dt 30:1-10
8 Ps 31:19-24
9 Ps 63:1-8
10 Mk 12:28-34
11 Lk 7:36-50
12 1 Jn 5:1-5
13 Rv 2:1-7
Our Love for Mankind
14 Mt 25:31-46
15 Lk 10:25-37
16 Jn 15:12-15
17 Rom 12:9-21
18 1 Cor 8
19 1 Cor 13
20 1 Jn 4:7-21
Love Shown in Obedience
21 Lv 26:3-13
22 Jos 22:1-6
23 Is 56:1-8
24 Jn 14:12-24
25 Jn 15:1-11
26 Rom 13:1-4
27 2 Cor 6:14-7:1
God's Forgiveness
28 Ps 32:1-7
29 Ps 130
30 Jer 31:23-34
31 Jer 33:1-11
Sep 1 Ez 36:22-36
2 Mi 7:9-2
3 Col 2:8-15
God's Fatherhood
4 Ps 68:1-10
5 Jer 3:19-25
6 Hos 11
7 Mt 7:7-12
8 Jn 5:19-29
9 Gal 4:1-7
10 Heb 12:1-11
God's Faithfulness
11 Gn 7:1-5; 8:1-22
12 Gn 45:1-8
13 Neh 9:5-15
14 Ps 147:7-20
15 Is 49:5-13
16 Lk 12:22-34
17 Jn 14:15-31
God's Protection
18 Ex 15:1-13
19 Ps 62:1-8
20 Ps 91
21 Is 43:1-7
22 Jn 17:15-26
23 Acts 23:16-30
24 2 Tm 4:16-22
Salvation Through Faith
25 Jn 3:14-18
26 Acts 13:26-39
27 Rom 1:8-17
28 Rom 4:1-15
29 Gal 3:21-29
30 Eph 2:1-10
Oct 1 Heb 7:15-25
Live by Faith
2 1 Sm 17:31-49
3 Ps 40:1-10
4 Prv 3:1-8
5 Rom 4:16-25
6 Gal 3:1-9
7 Heb 11:1-16
8 Heb 11:17-40
Result of Faith: Contentment
9 Ps 34:1-10
10 Ps 37:8-19
11 1 Cor 7:17-24
12 2 Cor 12:1-10
13 Phil 4:4-13
14 1 Tm 6:3-10
15 Heb 12:28-13:8
Result of Faith: Meekness
16 Mt 5:38-48
17 Eph 4:1-16
18 Col 3:12-17
19 1 Thes 5:12-22
20 2 Tm 2:20-26
21 Ti 3:1-11
22 Jas 3:13-18
Gives Us Joy
23 Ps 126
24 Is 12:1-6
25 Lk 6:17-23
26 2 Cor 6:1-10
27 Phil 4:1-4
28 Jas 1:1-8
29 1 Pt 1:3-9
Makes Us Patient
30 Ps 37:1-9
31 Lam 3:19-27
Nov 1 2 Cor 4:7-18
2 1 Thes 1
3 2 Tm 2:1-7
4 Jas 5:7-11
5 2 Pt 1:1-11
Fills Us with Thanksgiving
6 Ps 33:1-6, 18-22
7 Ps 71
8 Ps 136:1-3, 23-26
9 Ps 138
10 2 Cor 9:6-15
11 Phil 1:3-11
12 Col 2:1-7
Gives Us Courage
13 Jos 1:1-9
14 Dn 3:1-18
15 Jn 16:16-24
16 Acts 5:17-42
17 2 Cor 5:1-10
18 Phil 1:15-30
19 1 Pt 4:7-14
Motivates Us to Discipline
20 Ps 119:33-40
21 Mt 16:24-28
22 1 Cor 8:1-13
23 1 Cor 9:19-27
24 1 Cor 10:23-32
25 Phil 3:7-16
26 2 Thes 3:6-15
Call to Perseverance
27 Hos 12:2-9
28 Mt 24:3-14
29 2 Cor 4:7-18
30 Gal 6:1-10
Dec 1 1 Tm 6:11-21
2 2 Tm 4:1-18
3 Rv 3
Purity of Heart
4 Ps 82
5 Prv 2
6 Ez 18:1-9
7 Mi 6:1-8
8 Mal 3:13-38
9 Jas 4:1-10
10 1 Pt 3:1-7
The New Man
11 Ps 24:1-6
12 Ps 40:6-12
13 Is 1:10-20
14 Mal 3:1-5
15 Mt 5:27-42
16 1 Cor 10:1-15
17 1 Pt 1:13-25
Christlikeness
18 Ez 11:14-21
19 Jn 3:1-8, 19-21
20 Rom 8:1-8
21 Gal 5:16-23
22 Phil 3:17-21
23 Col 3:7-17
24 1 Pt 2:1-10
25 Ps 1
26 Jn 13:1-17
27 Rom 6:1-14
28 Rom 7:1-12
29 2 Cor 3:4-1
30 Eph 4:17-32
31 1 Jn 3

Chronologically

Jan 1 Gn 1-5
2 Gn 6-11
3 Gn 12-16
4 Gn 17-22
5 Jb 1-7
6 Jb 8-14
7 Jb 15-18
8 Jb 19-24
9 Jb 25-31
10 Jb 32-37
11 Jb 38-42
12 Gn 23-28
13 Gn 29-33
14 Gn 34-38
15 Gn 39-45
16 Gn 46-50
17 Ex 1-5
18 Ex 6-10
19 Ex 11-14
20 Ex 15-19
21 Ex 20-25
22 Ex 26-31
23 Ex 32-36
24 Ex 37-40
25 Ps 90
26 Lv 1-6
27 Lv 7-12
28 Lv 13-17
29 Lv 18-23
30 Lv 24-27
31 Nm 1-6
Feb 1 Nm 7-11
2 Nm 12-16
3 Nm 17-21
4 Nm 22-26
5 Nm 27-31
6 Nm 32-36
7 Dt 1-4
8 Dt 5-9
9 Dt 10-15
10 Dt 16-22
11 Dt 23-28
12 Dt 29-34
13 Ps 91
14 Jos 1-6
15 Jos 7-12
16 Jos 13-18
17 Jos 19-24
18 Jgs 1-5
19 Jgs 6-12
20 Jgs 13-16
21 Jgs 17-21
22 Ruth 1-4
23 1 Sm 1:1-16:13
24 Ps 23
25 1 Sm 16:14-19:11
26 Ps 59
27 1 Sm 19:12-21:15
28 Ps 34, 56
Mar 1 1 Sm 22:1-2
2 Ps 57, 142
3 1 Sm 22:3-23
4 Ps 52
5 1 Sm 23:1-29
6 Ps 54, 63
7 1 Sm 24-31
8 2 Sm 1-7
9 Ps 30
10 2 Sm 8:1-14
11 Ps 60
12 2 Sm 8:15-12:14
13 Ps 51, 32
14 2 Sm 12:15-15:37
15 Ps 3, 69
16 2 Sm 16:1-20:26
17 Ps 64, 70
18 2 Sm 21:1-22:51
19 Ps 18
20 2 Sm 23-24
21 Ps 4
22 Ps 5
23 Ps 6
24 Ps 7
25 Ps 8
26 Ps 9
27 Ps 11
28 Ps 12
29 Ps 13
30 Ps 14
31 Ps 15
Apr 1 Ps 16
2 Ps 17
3 Ps 19
4 Ps 20
5 Ps 21
6 Ps 22
7 Ps 24
8 Ps 25
9 Ps 26
10 Ps 27
11 Ps 28
12 Ps 29
13 Ps 31
14 Ps 35
15 Ps 36
16 Ps 37
17 Ps 38
18 Ps 39
19 Ps 40
20 Ps 41
21 Ps 53
22 Ps 55
23 Ps 58
24 Ps 61
25 Ps 62
26 Ps 65
27 Ps 68
28 Ps 72
29 Ps 86
30 Ps 101
May 1 Ps 103
2 Ps 108
3 Ps 109
4 Ps 110
5 Ps 138
6 Ps 139
7 Ps 140
8 Ps 141
9 Ps 143
10 Ps 144
11 Ps 145
12 1 Kgs 1-4
13 Prv 1-5
14 Prv 6-10
15 Prv 11-15
16 Prv 12-20
17 Prv 21-26
18 Prv 27-31
19 Sg 1-4
20 Sg 5-8
21 1 Kgs 5-11
22 Eccl 1-4
23 Eccl 5-9
24 Eccl 10-12
25 1 Kgs 1-5
26 1 Kgs 6-10
27 2 Kgs 1-5
28 2 Kgs 6-10
29 2 Kgs 11-14:25
30 Jon 1-4
31 2 Kgs 14:26-29
Jun 1 Am 1-9
2 2 Kgs 15-20
3 2 Kgs 21-25
4 Ps 1
5 Ps 2
6 Ps 10
7 Ps 33
8 Ps 43
9 Ps 66
10 Ps 67
11 Ps 71
12 Ps 89
13 Ps 92
14 Ps 93
15 Ps 94
16 Ps 95
17 Ps 96
18 Ps 97
19 Ps 98
20 Ps 99
21 Ps 100
22 Ps 102
23 Ps 104
24 Ps 105
25 Ps 106
26 Ps 111
27 Ps 112
28 Ps 113
29 Ps 114
30 Ps 115
Jul 1 Ps 116
2 Ps 117
3 Ps 118
4 Ps 119
5 Ps 120
6 Ps 121
7 Ps 122
8 Ps 123
9 Ps 124
10 Ps 125
11 Ps 127
12 Ps 128
13 Ps 129
14 Ps 130
15 Ps 131
16 Ps 132
17 Ps 133
18 Ps 134
19 Ps 135
20 Ps 136
21 Ps 146
22 Ps 147
23 Ps 148
24 Ps 149
25 Ps 150
26 1 Chr 1-5
27 1 Chr 6-10
28 1 Chr 11-16
29 Ps 42
30 Ps 44
31 Ps 45
Aug 1 Ps 46
2 Ps 47
3 Ps 48
4 Ps 49
5 Ps 50
6 Ps 73
7 Ps 74
8 Ps 75
9 Ps 76
10 Ps 77
11 Ps 78
12 Ps 79
13 Ps 80
14 Ps 81
15 Ps 82
16 Ps 83
17 Ps 84
18 Ps 85
19 Ps 87
20 Ps 88
21 1 Chr 27-23
22 1 Chr 24-29
23 2 Chr 1-4
24 2 Chr 5-9
25 2 Chr 10-16
26 2 Chr 17-21
27 Ob
28 2 Chr 22
29 Jl 1-3
30 2 Chr 23:1-26:8
31 Is 1-5
Sep 1 2 Chr 26:9-23
2 Is 6
3 2 Chr 27-32
4 Is 7-11
5 Is 12-16
6 Is 17-21
7 Is 22-26
8 Is 27-31
9 Is 32-37
10 Is 38-42
11 Is 43-47
12 Is 48-52
13 Is 53-58
14 Is 59-66
15 Hos 1-5
16 Hos 6-10
17 Hos 11-14
18 Mi 1-4
19 Mi 5-7
20 Na 1-3
21 2 Chr 33-34
22 Zep 1-3
23 2 Chr 3-5
24 Hb 1-3
25 Jer 1-5
26 Jer 6-10
27 Jer 11-17
28 Jer 18-23
29 Jer 24-28
30 Jer 29-34
Oct 1 Jer 35-39
2 Jer 40-45
3 Jer 46-49
4 Jer 50-52
5 Lam 1-5
6 2 Chr 36:1-8
7 Dn 1-6
8 Dn 7-12
9 2 Chr 36:9-21
10 Ps 137
11 Ez 1-6
12 Ez 7-12
13 Ez 13-19
14 Ez 20-24
15 Ez 25-31
16 Ez 32-37
17 Ez 38-43
18 Ez 44-48
19 Est 1-5
20 Est 6-10
21 2 Chr 36:22-23
22 Ezr 1:1-5:1
23 Hg 1-2
24 Zec 1-5
25 Zec 6-9
26 Zec 10-14
27 Ps 107, 126
28 Ezr 5:2-10:44
29 Neh 1-7
30 Neh 8-13
31 Mal 1-4
Nov 1 Mt 1-4
2 Mt 5-9
3 Mt 10-13
4 Mt 14-16
5 Mk 1-4
6 Mk 5-9
7 Mk 10-13
8 Mk 14-16
9 Lk 1-4
10 Lk 5-9
11 Lk 10-14
12 Lk 15-19
13 Lk 20-24
14 Jn 1-4
15 Jn 5-9
16 Jn 10-14
17 Jn 15-18
18 Jn 19-21
19 Acts 1-4
20 Acts 5-10
21 Acts 11-14
22 Jas 1-5
23 Acts 15
24 Gal 1-6
25 Acts 16
26 Phil 1-4
27 Acts 17:1-10
28 1 Thes 1-5
29 2 Thes 1-3
30 Acts 17:11-18:11
Dec 1 1 Cor 1-5
2 1 Cor 6-11
3 1 Cor 12-16
4 2 Cor 1-4
5 2 Cor 5-9
6 2 Cor 10-13
7 Acts 18:12-20:1
8 Eph 1-6
9 Rom 1-5
10 Rom 6-11
11 Rom 12-16
12 Acts 20-23
13 Acts 24-28
14 Col 1-4
15 Heb 1-5
16 Heb 6-10
17 Heb 11-13
18 Ti 1-3
19 Phlm
20 1 Tm 1-6
21 2 Tm 1-4
22 1 Pt 1-5
23 2 Pt 1-3
24 1 Jn 1-5
25 2 Jn
26 3 Jn
27 Jude
28 Rv 1-6
29 Rv 7-12
30 Rv 13-17
31 Rv 18-22

A. B. Davis

Weekly Psalms (Used by permission of the National Association of Evangelicals.)

Jan 1 Ps 1-3
2 Jn 1:1-18
3 Gn 1-4
4 Gn 5-8
5 Gn 9-12
6 Gn 13-16
7 Gn 17-19
8 Ps 4-7
9 Gn 20-22
10 Jb 1-4
11 Jb 5-8
12 Jb 9-12
13 Jb 13-16
14 Jb 17-20
15 Ps 8-11
16 Jb 21-24
17 Jb 25-28
18 Jb 29-32
19 Jb 33-36
20 Jb 37-39
21 Jb 40-42
22 Ps 12-14
23 Gn 23-26
24 Gn 27-30
25 Gn 31-34
26 Gn 35-38
27 Gn 39-42
28 Gn 43-46
29 Ps 15-17
30 Gn 47-50
31 Ex 1-3
Feb 1 Ex 4-6
2 Ex 7-9
3 Ex 10-12
4 Ex 13-15
5 Ps 18-20
6 Ex 16-18
7 Ex 19-21
8 Ex 22-24
9 Ex 25-27
10 Ex 26-30
11 Ex 31-33
12 Ps 21-23
13 Ex 34-37
14 Ex 38-40
15 Lv 1-3
16 Lv 4-6
17 Lv 7-9
18 Lv 10-12
19 Ps 24-26
20 Lv 13-15
21 Lv 16-18
22 Lv 19-21
23 Lv 22-24
24 Lv 25-27
25 Nm 1-3
26 Ps 27-29
27 Nm 4-6
28 Nm 7-10
Mar 1 Nm 11-12
2 Nm 13-15
3 Nm 16-18
4 Nm 19-21
5 Ps 30-32
6 Nm 22-24
7 Nm 25-27
8 Nm 28-30
9 Nm 31-33
10 Nm 34-36
11 Dt 1-3
12 Ps 33-35
13 Dt 4-6
14 Dt 7-9
15 Dt 10-12
16 Dt 13-15
17 Dt 16-18
18 Dt 19-21
19 Ps 36-38
20 Dt 22-24
21 Dt 25-27
22 Dt 28-30
23 Dt 31-34
24 Jos 1-3
25 Jos 4-6
26 Ps 39-41
27 Jos 7-9
28 Jos 10-12
29 Jos 13-15
30 Jos 16-18
31 Jos 19-21
Apr 1 Jos 22-24
2 Ps 42-44
3 Jgs 1-3
4 Jgs 4-6
5 Jgs 7-9
6 Jgs 10-12
7 Jgs 13-15
8 Jgs 16-18
9 Ps 45-47
10 Jgs 19-21
11 Ru 1-4
12 1 Sm 1-3
13 1 Sm 4-6
14 1 Sm 7-9
15 1 Sm 10-13
16 Ps 48-50
17 1 Sm 14-16
18 1 Sm 17-19
19 1 Sm 20-22
20 1 Sm 23-25
21 1 Sm 26-28
22 1 Sm 29-31
23 Ps 51-53
24 2 Sm 1-3
25 2 Sm 4-6
26 2 Sm 7-9
27 2 Sm 10-12
28 2 Sm 13-15
29 2 Sm 16-18
30 Ps 54-56
May 1 2 Sm 19-21
2 2 Sm 22-24
3 1 Kgs 1-4
4 Prv 1-3
5 Prv 4-6
6 Prv 7-9
7 Ps 57-59
8 Prv 10-12
9 Prv 13-15
10 Prv 16-18
11 Prv 19-21
12 Prv 22-24
13 Prv 25-27
14 Ps 60-62
15 Prv 28-31
16 Sg 1-4
17 Sg 5-8
18 1 Kgs 5-7
19 1 Kgs 8-11
20 Eccl 1-4
21 Ps 63-6
22 Eccl 5-8
23 Eccl 9-12
24 1 Kgs 12-14
25 1 Kgs 15-17
26 1 Kgs 18-20
27 1 Kgs 21-22; 2 Kgs 1
28 Ps 66-68
29 2 Kgs 2-4
30 2 Kgs 5-7
31 2 Kgs 8-10
Jun 1 2 Kgs 11:1-14:25
2 Jon
3 2 Kgs 14:26-29; Am 1-3
4 Ps 69-71
5 Am 4-6
6 Am 7-9
7 2 Kgs 15-17
8 2 Kgs 18-21
9 2 Kgs 22-25
10 1 Chr 1-3
11 Ps 72-74
12 1 Chr 4-6
13 1 Chr 7-9
14 1 Chr 10-12
15 1 Chr 13-16
16 1 Chr 17-19
17 1 Chr 20-22
18 Ps 75-77
19 1 Chr 23-25
20 1 Chorn. 26-29
21 2 Chr 1-3
22 2 Chr 4-8
23 2 Chr 7-9
24 2 Chr 10-12
25 Ps 78-80
26 2 Chr 13-15
27 2 Chr 16-18
28 2 Chr 19-22
29 Jl 1-3; Ob
30 2 Chr 23:1-26:8
Jul 1 Is 1-3
2 Ps 81-83
3 Is 4:6; 2 Chr 26:9-23
4 2 Chr 27-29
5 2 Chr 30-32
6 Is 7-9
7 Is 10-12
8 Is 13-15
9 Ps 84-86
10 Is 16-18
11 Is 19-21
12 Is 22-24
13 Is 25-27
14 Is 28-30
15 Is 31-33
16 Ps 87-90
17 Is 34-36
18 Is 37-39
19 Is 40-42
20 Is 43-45
21 Is 46-48
22 Is 49-51
23 Ps 91-93
24 Is 52-54
25 Is 56-57
26 Is 58-60
27 Is 61-63
28 Is 64-66
29 Hos 1-3
30 Ps 94-96
31 Hos 4-6
Aug 1 Hos 7-9
2 Hos 10-12
3 Hos 13-14; Mi 1
4 Mi 2-4
5 Mi 5-7
6 Ps 97-99
7 Na 1-3
8 2 Chr 33-34; Zep 1
9 Zep 2-3; 2 Chr 35
10 Heb 1-3
11 Jer 1-3
12 Jer 4-6
13 Ps 100-102
14 Jer 11-12, 26
15 Jer 7-9
16 Jer 10, 14-15
17 Jer 16-18
18 Jer 19-20, 35
19 Jer 25, 36, 45
20 Ps 103-105
21 Jer 46-49
22 Jer 13, 22-23
23 Jer 24, 27-28
24 Jer 29, 50-51
25 Jer 30-33
26 Jer 21, 34, 37
27 Ps 106-108
28 Jer 38-39, 52
29 Jer 40-42
30 Jer 43-44; Lam 1
31 Lam 2-5
Sep 1 2 Chr 36:1-8, Dn 1-3
2 Dn 4-6
3 Ps 109-111
4 Dn 7-9
5 Dn 10-12
6 2 Chr 36:9-21, Ez 1-3
7 Ez 4-6
8 Ez 7-9
9 Ez 10-12
10 Ps 112-114
11 Ez 13-16
12 Ez 17-20
13 Ez 21-24
14 Ez 25-28
15 Ez 29-32
16 Ez 33-36
17 Ps 115-117
18 Ez 37-40
19 Ez 41-44
20 Ez 45-48
21 2 Chr 36:22-23; Ezr 1-3
22 Ezr 4; Hg 1-2
23 Zec 1-3
24 Ps 118-119:16
25 Zec 4-6
26 Zec 7-9
27 Zec 10-12
28 Zec 13-14
29 Ezr 5-7
30 Ezr 8-10
Oct 1 Ps 119:17-72
2 Est 1-3
3 Est 4-6
4 Est 7-10
5 Neh 1-3
6 Neh 4-6
7 Neh 7-9
8 Ps 119:73-120
9 Neh 10-13
10 Mal
11 Mt 1-3
12 Mt 4-7
13 Mt 8-10
14 Mt 11-13
15 Ps 119:121-176
16 Mt 14-16
17 Mt 17-19
18 Mt 20-22
19 Mt 23-25
20 Mt 26-28
21 Mk 1-4
22 Ps 120-122
23 Mk 5-8
24 Mk 9-12
25 Mk 13-16
26 Lk 1-4
27 Lk 5-8
28 Lk 9-12
29 Ps 123-125
30 Lk 13-16
31 Lk 17-20
Nov 1 Lk 21-24
2 Jn 1-3
3 Jn 4-6
4 Jn 7-9
5 Ps 126-128
6 Jn 10-12
7 Jn 13-15
8 Jn 16-18
9 Jn 19-21
10 Acts 1-4
11 Acts 5:1-8:3
12 Ps 129-131
13 Acts 8:4-11:18
14 Acts 11:19-14:28
15 Jas
16 Gal
17 Acts 15-17:10
18 Phil
19 Ps 132-134
20 1 Thes
21 2 Thes, Acts 17:11-18:11
22 1 Cor 1-3
23 1 Cor 4-7
24 1 Cor 8:1-11:1
25 1 Cor 11:2-14:40
26 Ps 135-137
27 1 Cor 15-16
28 2 Cor 1-5
29 2 Cor 6-9
30 2 Cor 10-13
Dec 1 Acts 18:12-19:41; Eph 1-2
2 Eph 3-6
3 Ps 138-140
4 Rom 1-3
5 Rom 4-6
6 Rom 7-9
7 Rom 10-12
8 Rom 13-1
9 Acts 20-226
10 Ps 141-143
11 Acts 23-25
12 Acts 26-28
13 Col
14 Heb 1-4
15 Heb 5-8
16 Heb 9-11
17 Ps 144-146
18 Heb 12-13; Ti
19 Phlm
20 1 Tm, 2 Tm
21 1 Pt
22 1 Jn
23 2 Pt; 2, 3 Jn; Jude
24 Ps 147-148
25 Rv 1-3
26 Rv 4-7
27 Rv 8-10
28 Rv 11-14
29 Rv 15-18
30 Rv 19-22
31 Ps 149-150

CLASSIC DEVOTIONAL BOOKS

Recommended by Robert Kregel, Chairman of the Board, Kregel Publications.

Listed below are some of the finest classic devotionals and biographies in print. Unless otherwise indicated, each title is published by several publishers.

Beyond Humiliation, by J. Gregory Mantle, Bethany House Publishers

The Christian's Secret of a Happy Life, by Hannah Whitehall Smith

God's Best Secrets, by Andrew Murray, Zondervan Publishing House

The Greatest Thing in the World, by Henry Drummond

He That Is Spiritual, by Lewis Sperry Chafer, Zondervan

Hinds' Feet on High Places, by Hannah Humard

How to Live a Victorious Life, by an Unknown Christian, Zondervan

The Kneeling Christian, by an Unknown Christian, Zondervan

The Knowledge of the Holy, by A. W. Tozer, Harper & Row, Publishers

Memoirs and Remains of Robert Murray McCheyne, by Andrew Bonar, Banner of Truth

Morning and Evening, by Charles Spurgeon, Zondervan and Henrickson Publishers

My Utmost for His Highest, by Oswald Chambers

Our Lord Prays for His Own, by Marcus Rainsford, Kregel Publications

Pilgrim's Progress, by John Bunyan

The Pursuit of God, by A. W. Tozer, Christian Publications

A Serious Call to a Devout and Holy Life, by William Law

Spiritual Leadership, by J. Oswald Sanders, Moody Press

The Spiritual Man, by Watchman Nee, Christian Fellowship Publishers

With Christ in the School of Prayer, by Andrew Murray

BIBLE SOFTWARE PROGRAMS

1200 various machine-readable Bible Translations in most languages, United Bible Societies: Translation Department, Attn: Harold Scanlin, 1865 Broadway, New York, NY 10023

"Ask God" Expert System Bible Software, Business Solutions, 15395 SE 30th Place, Suite 310, Bellevue, WA 98007, 206-644-2015

"Atari Bible Concordance" Bible Study Software, SpiritWare, 15th Avenue Bible Church, 15211 15th Ave. NE, Seattle, WA, 98155, 206-685-1854

"Bible Library" on CD-ROM Software, Ellis Enterprises, Inc., 4205 McAuley Blvd., Suite 315, Oklahoma City, OK 73120, 405-749-0273

"Bible Scholar" Bible Research Software, Scholar Systems, Inc., 2313 Overland, Boise, ID 83705, FAX 208-336-3844, 208-343-6262

"Bible Search" Bible Study Software, SOGWAP Company, 115 Bellmont Road, Decatur, IN 46733, 219-724-3900

"Bible Word" Greek NT, LXX, Hebrew OT Bible Research Software; "On-Line Bible" Research Software, Hermeneutika Computer-Aided Bible Research Software Company, P.O. Box 98563, Seattle, WA 98198, 1-800-55BIBLE (1-800-552-4253), 206-824-3927, FAX 206-824-2757

"BibleQuest KJV" Bible Study Software, InfoQuest Technologies, Inc., Pleasant Grove, UT 84062, 801-375-8855, 800-336-6644

"BibleQ" Game with 1200 Questions & Answers; "Daily Bread" TSR Software program with "Verse of the Day" at bootup, SmithSoft, 557 Plantation Road, Pelican Lake, WI 54463, 715-487-5484

"BookMaster" Bible Study Software, Koala-T Software/BookMaster Bible, 3255 Wing Street, Suite 220, San Diego, CA 92110, 800-642-1144

"CDWord Interactive Bible Library" CD-ROM Bible Research Software, CDWord Library, Inc., Two Lincoln Centre, 5420 LBJ Freeway LB7, Dallas, TX 75240-6215, 214-770-2414

"Christian Marriage Analysis," "Christian Personality Profile," & "Stress & Coping Strength" Christian Counseling Software, Wellness Publications, Inc., P.O. Box 2397, Holland, MI 49422-2397, 616-396-5477

"CompuBible" Bible Research Software, NASSCO, P.O. Box 65600, Lubbock, TX 79464, 800-288-2044, 806-791-5138

"EB-2000" Selectronics Electronic Handheld/Pocket Bible Hardware, Chapel Hill Marketing, Inc., 1506 E. Franklin St., The Center, Suite 100, Chapel Hill, NC 27514, 919-933-7674

"EveryWord" KJV and TEV Bible Scripture Study Software, ECHO Microtek, P.O. Box 1088, Orem, UT 84057, 801-226-7800, 801-226-7897

"FABS Reference Bibles" & "Theological/Religious Abstracts" on CD-ROM, FABS International, P.O.Box 427, DeFuniak Springs, FL 32433, 904-892-6257 (Foundation for Advanced Biblical Studies)

"FancyFont" Greek/Hebrew Fonts for Microsoft Word + "WysiFonts" Greek/Hebrew Fonts for Microsoft Windows, SoftCraft, 16 North Carroll St, Suite 500, Madison, WI 53711, 608-257-3300

"FindIT TEV" Bible Software, Canadian Bible Society Central Stock Depot, Suite 100, 10 Carnforth Road, Toronto, Ontario, Canada M4A 2S4, 416-757-4171

"FindIT Bible" Study Software (many translations: English, French, Spanish, et al.), Murray & Gillespie Computer Solutions, 90 Nolan Court, Unit 22, Markham, Ontario L3R 4L9, Canada, FAX 416-477-8506, 416-477-0260

"Folio KJV" Bible Study Software based upon "Folio Views" Software, InfoBasix Corporation, 9587 South Grandview Drive, Sandy, UT 84092, 801-944-8716

"Franklin KJV or RSV" Handheld/Pocket Electronic Bible Hardware, Franklin Computer Corporation, 122 Burrs Road, Mt. Holly, NJ 08060, Sales Dept: 609-261-4800, FAX 609-261-1631

"GodSpeed" Bible Research Software, Kingdom Age Software, 3368 Governor Dr., Suite F-197, San Diego, CA 92122, 619-586-1082

"GramCord Scholar," Greek NT Grammatical Research Software plus Greek & Hebrew Multilingual Word Processor Software, GramCord Institute, 2065 Half Day Road, Deerfield, IL 60015, 312-223-3242

Greek, Hebrew, English Bible Texts (ASCII) on disk, University of Pennsylvania Computer Center for Analysis of Texts (CCAT/CATSS), Attn: Dr. Robert Kraft, Box 36, College Hall, Philadelphia, PA 19104-6303, 215-898-1597

Greek Literature from Homer through AD600 on CD-ROM (over 600 MB of data), TLG Project—Thesaurus Linguae Graecae, Dr. Theodore F. Brunner, 156 Humanities Hall, University of California, Irvine, Irvine, CA 92717, 714-856-7031, 714-856-6404

"Greek MemCards" & "Hebrew MemCards" Biblical Vocabulary Learning Software, Memorization Technology, P.O. Box 60788, Palo Alto, CA 94306, 415-857-9220

"Greek Tutor" academic NT Greek Language/Grammar Learning Software, Dr. John Hurd, Trinity College, 6 Hoskins Ave., Toronto, Quebec, Canada M5S 1H8, 416-978-3056

"HyperBible," Thompson Chain Reference HyperText Bible Software, Beacon Technology, Inc., 5369 Camden Ave., Suite 230, San Jose, CA 95124, 800-777-1841, 408-723-4884

HyperCard "BibleStack" Bible Software (Mac), Holy Mountain Software, 2775 Fountain Circle, Sarasota, FL 34235, 813-951-0246

"Interlinear Text" Bible/Text Processing Software for Linguistic Translation Work & TextBase Management, SIL/Wycliffe: IT & IT Formatter SIL—Academic Computing, 7500 West Camp, Wisdom Road, Dallas, TX 75236, 214-709-2418, 214-296-3105

Japanese Bible Study VideoDisc CD Software, Japanese Bible Society Kyobashi, P.O. Box 6, Tokyo, Japan, 81-3-567-1986, FAX 81-3-567-4436

Jewish Culture Software including Biblical Hebrew Vocabulary Software, Davka Corporation, 845 N. Michigan Ave., Suite 843, Chicago, IL 60611, 800-621-8227, 312-944-4070

"Kingdom Games" Christian Bible Games Software, Castle Enterprises, Route 2, Box 299, North Manchester, IN 46962, 219-982-2045

"Lamp" Bible Study Software, Andrews

University, The LAMP, Berrien Springs, MI 49104

"LaserGreek," "LaserHebrew," Fonts for over 200 other Languages in Postscript, Macintosh, Linguist's Software, Inc., P.O. Box 580, Edmunds, WA 98020-0580, 206-775-1130

"LBase" Biblical/General Text Linguistic Database/TextBase Management & Search/Display Software (including Greek & Hebrew & Coptic Fonts) plus: CD-ROM accessing Software, Silver Mountain Software, Attn: John Baima, 7246 Cloverglen Drive, Dallas, TX 75249, 214-709-8987

"Lexegete" Lectionary Sermon Exegetical Helps Software, Tischrede Software, P.O. Box 9594, North Dartmouth, MA 02747, 617-994-7907

"Lion-Hearted Games" Christian Role-Playing/Adventure Games Software, Shaddox Interstellar Enterprises, P.O. Box 267, Goldendale, WA 98620, 509-773-3078

"Master Search Bible" Research Library on CD-ROM with Accessing Software, TriStar Publishing, P.O. Box 7515, Fort Washington, PA 19034, 800-872-2828, 800-29BIBLE

"MegaWord Gold" & "MegaWord Silver" Bible Research Software, Paraclete Software, 1000 E. 14th Street, Suite 425, Plano, TX 75074, 214-578-8185, 800-825-6342

"Multi-Lingual Scholar" Business/Academic Multilingual Word Processing Software, Gamma Productions, Inc., 710 Wilshire Blvd, Suite 609, Santa Monica, CA 90401, FAX 213-395-4214, 213-394-8622

"NASB Computer Bible" Study Software, Foundation Press Publications, Inc., 1121 N. Kraemer Place, P.O. Box 6439, Anaheim, CA 92806, 714-630-6450

"NIV On-Line Bible" Research Software, ROCKware Publishing, 57 Bater Road, Coldwater, MI 49036, 517-369-6035

"NIV PC" Bible Research Software & "MacBible" Bible Research Software & "ScriptureFonts" Greek & Hebrew Fonts for WordPerfect, Zondervan Corporation, 1415 Lake Drive SE, Grand Rapids, MI 49506, 616-698-6900, 800-727-3060

"On-Line Bible" Bible Research Software, Timnathserah, Inc., R.R. 2, West Montrose, Ontario, N0B 2V0, Canada, 519-664-2266

"PassageWay" Bible Study Software, PassageWay Bible, P. O. Box 3789, Pensacola, FL 32526, 904-456-1595

"Pastor's Story File & Parables," "Auto-Illustrator," 3700 indexed stories with cross-references + Subscription Software, Saratoga Press, 14200 Victor Place, Saratoga, CA 95070, 408-867-4211

"Pauline Epistles HyperText" Bible Study, Ray Hamilton, P.O. Box 308, Greenleaf, ID 83626, 208-454-2914

"PC Study Bible" Bible Research Software, BibleSoft, 22014 7th Ave., South Seattle, WA 98198, 206-824-0656

"PC-Translator" Language Translation Software (several languages to & from English), Linguistic Products, P.O. Box 8263, The Woodlands, TX 77387, 713-363-9154, FAX 713-298-1911

"PHI Demonstration CD-ROM": including CCAT Greek, Hebrew, English Bible texts on CD-ROM, Packard Humanities Institute, 300 Second Street, Los Altos, CA 94022, 415-948-0150

"QuickVerse" Bible Software, "Membership Plus" Church Organization Software, Parsons Technology, 375 Collins Road NE, Cedar Rapids, IA 52402, FAX 319-395-0217, 800-369-5000

"Scripture Scanner II" Bible Study Software, Omega Software, Inc., P.O. Box 355, Round Rock, TX 78680-0355, 512-255-9569

"SeedMaster" Bible Research Software, White Harvest Software, Inc., P.O. Box 97153, Raleigh, NC 27624-7153

"Translate" Software for Language Translation (Spanish to English), FinalSoft Corporation, 3900 NW 79th Avenue, Suite 215, Miami, FL 33166-9791, 800-232-8228, FAX 305-477-0680, 305-477-2703

"TurboFonts" Greek/Hebrew Fonts for Display & Print, Image Processing Software, Inc., 6409 Appalachian Way, P.O. Box 5016, Madison, WI 53705, 608-233-5033

"WORD Processor," "VerseSearch" Bible Research Software, Bible Research Systems, 2013 Wells Branch Parkway #304, Austin, TX 78728, 512-251-7541

"WordSearch" Bible Study Software & "InfoSearch" Sermon Illustration & Current Christian Abstracts & Music Hymnal DataBase Management & Quarterly Subscription Software, NavPress, P.O. Box 6000, Colorado Springs, CO 80934, 800-888-9898, 719-598-1212

Source: Hermeneutika Company, Computer-Aided Bible Research Software, over 400 Products, Mail Order, Discount Software for Bible Research, Bible Study, Writing, Education. Compiled by Mark Rice.

BIBLE CORRESPONDENCE COURSES

See the Education section of the *Almanac of the Christian World.*

FOCUS QUOTE

Whatever truth you have chosen, read only a small portion of it, endeavoring to taste and digest it, to extract the essence and substance thereof, and proceed no farther while any savor or relish remains in the passage. When this subsides, take up your book again and proceed as before, seldom reading more than half a page at a time. For it is not the quantity you read, but the manner of reading that yields the profit.—Madame Guyon (1646-1717)

THE BIBLE IN WORLD LANGUAGES

Translation and Distribution Statistics

	Portions	*Testaments*	*Complete Bibles*	*Total*
Africa	228	206	119	553
Asia	225	158	96	479
Australia/New Zealand/Pacific	152	125	26	303
Europe	105	24	58	187
North America	43	19	7	69
Caribbean/Latin America	144	183	7	334
Constructed Languages	2	0	1	3
Total	899	715	314	1928

United Bible Societies

WHERE TO OBTAIN BIBLES IN VARIOUS LANGUAGES

American Bible Society, 1865 Broadway, New York NY 10023

Bibles for India, 4221 Richmond NW, Grand Rapids, MI 49504

Bibles for the World, Inc., 116 N. Schmale Rd., Carol Stream, IL 60188

Bible Literature International, P.O. Box 477, Columbus, OH 43216

Christian Literature and Bible Center, 1006 Oak Cliff Dr., Toccoa, GA 30577

Christian Literature Crusade, PO Box 1449, Fort Washington, PA 19034

Christian Literature International, P.O. Box 777, Canby, OR 97013

Gideons International, 2900 Lebanon Rd., Nashville, TN 37214

International Bible Society, 144 Tices Ln., East Brunswick, NJ 08816

Living Bibles International, 351 Main Place, Carol Stream, IL 60188

Multi-Language Media, P.O. Box 548, Waynesboro, GA 30830

The Bible League, 16801 Van Dam Rd., South Holland, IL 60473

World Literature Crusade, 20232 Sunburst Ave., Chatsworth, CA 91311

World Missionary Press, P.O. Box 120, New Paris, IN 46553

FOCUS QUOTE

The Bible is a stream wherein the elephant may swim and the lamb may wade. —Pope Gregory the Great

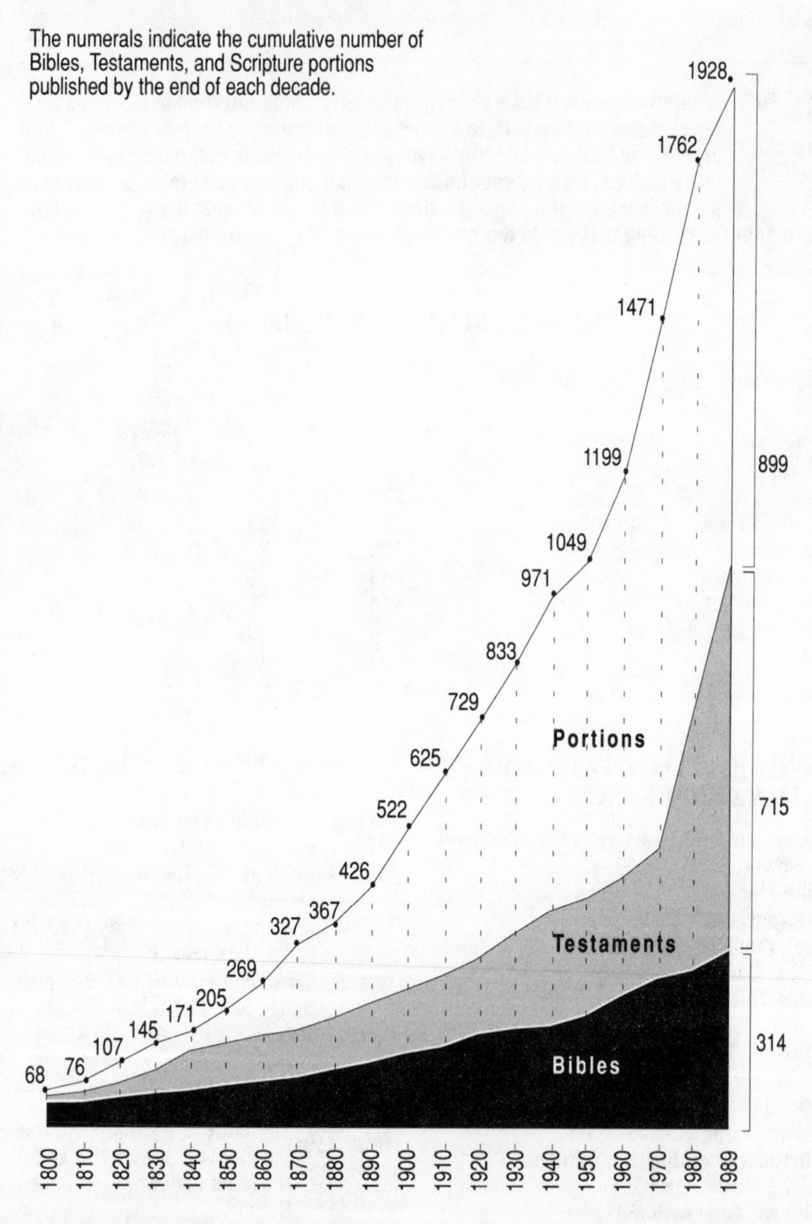

United Bible Societies

GUTENBERG BIBLE CENSUS

The Gutenberg Bible, printed in 1456 by Johann Gutenberg, is believed to be the first Bible printed with movable type. There are 48 known copies of the Gutenberg Bible in existence today. This list comes from the Pierpont Morgan Library, New York City. Copies are arranged roughly according to the quantity of sheets in first setting each contains. Copies printed on vellum precede those printed on paper.

In 1978, University of Texas at Austin purchased a Gutenberg Bible for $2.4 million (#30 on list). In December 1987, Maruzen Book Co., Tokyo, purchased a copy for $5.4 million (#39 on list).

Vellum Copies

1. Bibliotheque Nationale, Paris, France
2. Henry E. Huntington Library, San Marino, CA
3. Deutsches Buch-und Schrift Museum der Deutschen Bucherei, Leipzig, West Germany
4. Landesbibliothek, Fulda, West Germany
5. Karl-Marx Universitatsbibliothek, Leipzig, East Germany
6. Universitatsbibliothek, Gottingen, West Germany
7. Staatsbibliothek Preussischer Kulturbesitz, Berlin, West Germany
8. Library of Congress, Washington, D.C.
9. Pierpont Morgan Library, New York, NY
10. British Library (Grenville), London, England
11. Biblioteca Apostolica Vaticana (Barberini Collection), Vatican Library, Italy
12. Lambeth Palace Library, London, England

Paper Copies

13. Bayerische Staatsbibliothek, Munich, West Germany
14. Stadt-und Universitatsbibliothek, Frankfurt-am-Main, West Germany
15. Hofbibliothek, Aschaffenburg, W. Germany
16. Gutenberg Museum, Mainz, W. Germany
17. Wurttembergische Landesbibliothek, Stuttgart, West Germany
18. Gabriel Wells (bookseller), New York, NY
19. Karl-Marx Universitatsbibliothek, Leipzig, East Germany
20. Bibliotheque Mazarine, Paris, France
21. Eton College Library, Eton, England
22. Bodleian Library, Oxford, England
23. The John Rylands Library, Manchester, England
24. Harvard College Library, Cambridge, MA
25. Biblioteka Seminarium Duchownego, Pelplin, Poland
26. The Scheide Library, Princeton, NJ
27. British Library (George III), London, England
28. Pierpont Morgan Library, New York, NY
29. Osterreichische Nationalbibliothek, Vienna, Austria
30. University of Texas Library, Austin, TX
31. Bibliotheca Bodmeriana, Cologny, Switzerland
32. Biblioteca Nacional, Lisbon, Portugal
33. University Library, Cambridge, England
34. Yale University Library, New Haven, CT
35. Biblioteca Publica Provincial, Burgos, Spain
36. New York Public Library, New York, NY
37. National Library of Scotland, Edinburgh, Scotland
38. Pierpont Morgan Library, New York, NY
39. Maruzen Book Company, Tokyo, Japan
40. Biblioteca Apostolica Vaticana (DeRossi Collection), Vatican Library, Italy
41. Stadtbibliothek, Trier, West Germany
42. Landesbibliothek, Kassel, W. Germany
43. Bibliotheque Municipale, St. Omer, France
44. Bibliotheque Nationale, Paris, France

45a* Bibliotheque Universitaire, Mons, Belgium

45b* Indiana University Library, Bloomington, IN

46. Gutenberg Museum, Mainz, W. Germany

47. Kongelige Bibliotek, Copenhagen, Denmark
48. Biblioteca Universitaria, Seville, Spain

*The Mons partial Vol. I, the Bloomington New Testament, some large fragments of Vol. I owned since the last century by the Counts Von Seilern, ten leaves added to the Scheide copy and a number of separate leaves now scattered were once parts of a single copy, according to Paul Needham.

A rare-book collector met a guy who said he'd just thrown out an old Bible that had been packed away for generations. "Somebody named Guten-something had printed it," the man explained.

"Not Gutenberg!" gasped the book lover. "You've just thrown away one of the most famous books ever printed. One copy recently sold at an auction for over $4 million!"

The other man was still unmoved. "My copy wouldn't have brought a dime," he said. "Some guy named Martin Luther scribbled notes all over it."

Tal D. Bonham, *The Treasury of Clean Jokes*. Published by Broadman.

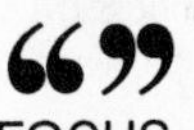
FOCUS QUOTE

All things desirable to men are contained in the Bible. —Abraham Lincoln

ENGLISH BIBLE VERSIONS THROUGH 20TH CENTURY

J. H. Skilton

Date AD	*Version (italics = Catholic Version)*	*Translator*
ANGLO-SAXON VERSIONS		
Late 7th cent.	English verse (oral)	Caedmon
	John's Gospel, + ?	Bede
	Psalms; entire Bible?	Aldhelm (640-709)
	Anglo-Saxon Psalter glosses	
Late 9th cent.	Ten Commandments	Alfred the Great (849-901)
	Ex. 21-23	
	Acts 15	
	Scripture refs. in Gregory's "De Cura Pastorali"	
c.950	Anglo-Saxon gloss of the Lindisfarne Gospels	
	Anglo-Saxon gloss of the Rushworth Gospels	
11th cent.	Parts of the OT	Aelfric
	Four Gospels into continuous English text	
MIDDLE ENGLISH VERSIONS		
c.1300	Metric Psalter	
	Prose Psalter	Richard Rolle of Hampole c.1380-1383
	Wyclif Bible	Nicholas of Hereford and Wyclif (?)
	Revision of Wyclif's Bible	John Purvey

SIXTEENTH-CENTURY VERSIONS

1525/6	NT	William Tyndale
1530	Pentateuch	Tyndale
1531	Jonah	Tyndale
	Isaiah	George Joye
1534	OT selections	Tyndale
	NT revision	
	Psalms	Joye
	Lamentations	
	Jeremiah	
	Song of Moses at the Red Sea	
	Revision (unauthorized) of Tyndale's NT	
1535	NT revision	Tyndale
	First complete Bible in English	Miles Coverdale
1537	The Matthew Bible	John Rogers? ('Thomas Matthew')
1538	Parallel English-Latin NT (Vulgate)	Coverdale
1539	Revision of the Matthew Bible	Richard Taverner
	The Great Bible	Coverdale, for Thomas Cromwell
1540	2nd edition of the Great Bible	Preface by Archbp. Cranmer
1545	Revised Primer ("Primer of Henry VIII")	
1557	Geneva NT	William Whittingham
1560	Geneva Bible	Various (including Whittingham)
1568	The Bishops' Bible	Matthew Parker and others
1572	Revised folio edition of the Bishops' Bible	
1582	*Rheims NT*	*Gregory Martin, William Allen and others*

SEVENTEENTH-CENTURY VERSIONS

1609-1610	*Douay OT*	*Gregory Martin and others*
1611	Authorized (King James) Version	Fifty-four translators
1613	Revision of AV	
1616-1623	Pentateuch	Henry Ainsworth
	Song of Solomon	
	Psalms	

EIGHTEENTH-CENTURY VERSIONS

1718-1719	*NT*	*Cornelius Nary*
1729	Greek and English NT	William Mace
1730	NT	*Robert Witham*
1738	*Fifth edition of Rheims NT*	
1745	The Primitive NT	William Whiston
1749-1772	*Two rev. of Douay OT, five rev. of Rheims NT*	*Richard Challoner*
1755	Revision of AV	John Wesley
1764	NT	Richard Wynne
	Bible	Anthony Purver
1768	Liberal translation of the NT	E. Harwood

1770	NT	John Worsley
1783-1810	*Revisions of Rheims and Douay texts*	*Bernard MacMahon*

NINETEENTH-CENTURY VERSIONS

1822	Paul's Epistles	Thomas Belsham (Unitarian)
1832	Paul's Epistles	Charles Eyre (Unitarian)
1833	NT	Rodolphus Dickinson
1840	NT	Samuel Sharpe (Unitarian)
1849-1860	*Annotated revision of Douay-Rheims text*	*Bishop Francis Patrick Kenrick*
1855	Gospels	Andrew Norton
1858	NT	Leicester Ambrose Sawyer
1862	OT & NT	Robert Young
1863	Gospels	G. W. Braineld
1869	NT	Henry Alford
	OT & NT	Robert Ainslie
1871	NT	J. N. Darby
1872	NT	J. B. Rotherham
1875	NT	Samuel Davidson
1881	Revised version of the AV NT	British & American companies
1882	Romans	Ferrar Fenton
1883	Paul's Epistles	Fenton
1885	RV complete Bible	British & American companies
1890	Bible	J. N. Darby
1895	Current English NT	Fenton

TWENTIETH-CENTURY VERSIONS

1898-1901	The Twentieth Century NT	Twenty lay scholars
1901	American Standard Edition (of RV)	American scholars
1903	Bible in Modern English	Fenton
	NT in Modern Speech	R. F. Weymouth
1913	NT	James Moffatt
1923	American translation of the NT	E. J. Goodspeed
	Riverside NT	W. G. Ballantine
1924	OT	Moffatt
	Centenary translation of the NT	Helen B. Montgomery
1927	American translation of the OT	A. R. Gordon, T. J. Meek, Leroy Waterman, J. M. Powis Smith
1935	*Westminster Version of the Sacred Scriptures, NT*	*Various Catholic scholars*
	Revision of Challoner's edition of the Rheims NT	*J. A. Carey*
1937	NT	C. B. Williams
	NT	*F. A. Spencer*
1941	The NT in Basic English	S. H. Hooke
	Revision of Challoner-Rheims NT	*Confraternity of Christian Doctrine*
1945	Berkeley Version of the NT	Gerrit Verkuyl
	NT (trans. from Vulgate)	*Monsignor R. A. Knox*
1946	Revision of American RV NT (RSV)	International Council of Religious Education
1947-1957	NT	J. B. Phillips

1948	The Letchworth Version (NT) in Modern English	T. F. & R. E. Ford
1949	Bible in Basic English	S. H. Hooke
	OT	*R. A. Knox*
1952	Entire RSV Bible	
	Plain English NT	C. K. Williams
1954	*NT*	*J. A. Kleist & J. L. Lilly*
1955	Authentic NT	H. J. Schonfield
	Revision of Knox's OT	
1956-1959	Expanded Translation of the Greek NT	K. S. Wuest
1958	The Amplified NT	F. E. Siewert & Lockman Foundation
1959	The Berkeley Bible	Gerrit Verkuyl
1961	The New English Bible NT	Representatives of major British churches & Bible societies
1962	The Amplified OT (I)	F. E. Siewert & Lockman Foundation
1962-1971	The Living Bible	K. N. Taylor
1963	The NT in the Language of Today	W. F. Beck
	New American Standard Bible (rev. of the American RV)	Evangelical scholars
1964	The Amplified OT (II)	F. E. Siewert & Lockman Foundation
1965	*Catholic edition of RSV*	
1966	Today's English Version (Good News for Modern Man) NT	American Bible Society
	Jerusalem Bible	*Catholic scholars*
1968-9	New translation, NT	William Barclay
1969	The New Berkeley (Modern Language) Bible	Verkuyl
1970	The New English Bible OT	Representatives of major British churches, etc.
	The New American Bible	*Bishops' committee of the Confraternity of Christian Doctrine*
1972	New International Version (NT)	Evangelical scholars & International Bible Society
1973	The Translator's NT	British & Foreign Bible Society
1976	Complete Good News Bible	American Bible Society
1979	New International Version Holy Bible	Evangelical scholars & International Bible Society

The People's Study Bible: The Living Bible Harold Lindsell, Ph.D., D.D., General Editor, Tyndale House Publishers, Inc., Wheaton, IL, c1986: p.p. 1823-1826. From *New Bible Dictionary*; used by permission of InterVarsity Press.

20TH-CENTURY ENGLISH BIBLE VERSIONS

The translations are arranged under the date the entire Bible was published. Earlier parts of the translation are listed under this date. If only the New Testament has been translated, it is, of course, listed under its date. If no complete New Testament or Old Testament exists, then the date of the first portion is used. The compilers are aware that there may be other translations not listed, especially those of individual books, particularly the Psalms. Annotations are included for those that the compilers were able to examine. Reference is made to

20TH-CENTURY ENGLISH BIBLE VERSIONS cont.

the appropriate chapter when that translation has been treated in the book. Reprints of pre-twentieth-century Bibles are not included in the list.

The compilers were especially indebted to the following two works in putting together this bibliography: Margaret T. Hills, editor, *The English Bible in America: A Bibliography of Editions of the Bible and the New Testament Published in America, 1777–1957* (New York: The American Bible Society and the New York Public Library, 1961). A. S. Herbert, *Historical Catalogue of Printed Editions of the English Bible, 1525–1961* (London: The British and Foreign Bible Society; New York: The American Bible Society, 1968).

1900 **Hayman's Epistles** The Epistles of the New Testament. An attempt to present them in current and popular idiom by Henry Hayman. London: A. and C. Black.

1901 **The American Standard Version** The Holy Bible containing the Old and New Testaments translated out of the Original Languages. The Version set forth A.D. 1677, compared with the most ancient authorities and revised A.D. 1881–1885. Newly edited by the American Revision Committee. A.D. 1901 Standard Edition, New York: Thomas Nelson and Sons.

1901 **Modern American Bible** The New Testament; The Books of the Bible in Modern American Form and Phrase with Notes and Introduction by Frank Schell Ballantine. New York: Thomas Whittaker, 1899–1901

Part I: S. Mark (1899?). Part II: S. Matthew, S. Peter, S. Jude, and S. James (1899?). Part III: S. Luke (Gospel-Acts) (1899?). Part IV: S. Paul (including Hebrews) (1901?). Part V: S. John (Gospel, Letters, Revelation) (1901?). Based on Textus Receptus and later Greek Texts. Preceded this by translation of the Four Gospels (Good News—The Four Gospels in a Modern American Dress, 1897). Revised 1909.

1901 **Moffatt's Historical New Testament** The Historical New Testament; A New Translation, by James Moffat. Edinburgh: T. & T. Clark.

The books are chronologically arranged. A different translation from Moffat's later translation.

1901 **Way's Epistles** The letters of St. Paul to Seven Churches and Three Friends. Translated by Arthur S. Way. London: The Macmillan Company.

Arthur S. Way, a classical scholar, translated the Letters of St. Paul, the first edition of which appeared in 1901 and a second thoroughly revised edition, which included Hebrews, was published in 1906 and reprinted in 1951.

1901 **Young People's Bible** or, the Scriptures Corrected, Explained, and Simplified, by Harriet Newell Jones, with Introduction by Rev. Malcolm MacGregor. Philadelphia: American Book and Bible House.

1902 **Emphasized Bible (Rotherham)** a new translation designed to set forth the exact meaning, the proper terminology, and the graphic style of the sacred originals; arranged to show at a glance narrative, speech, parallelism, and logical analysis, also to enable the student readily to distinguish the several divine names; and emphasized throughout after the idioms of the Hebrew and Greek tongues. By Joseph Bryant Rotherham.

Old Testament (1902), New York, Chicago, Toronto: Fleming H. Revell Company, 3 vols. Vol I: Genesis-Ruth. Vol. II: 1 Samuel-Psalms. Vol. III: Proverbs-Malachi.

New Testament (1897), is rewritten edition of the version first printed in 1872 and reissued in a revised form in 1878. Gospel according to Matthew (1868). Greek text of Tregelles. In 1916, published four volumes in one.

1902? **Godbey's New Testament** Translation of the New Testament from the original Greek. By Rev. W. B. Godbey. Cincinnati: M. W. Knapp, Office of God's Revivalist.

Based on Tischendorf's edition of the Codex Sinaiticus. Dedicated to "The Holiness People of all lands."

1902 **Twentieth Century New Testament.** A translation into Modern English. Made from the original Greek. New York: Fleming H. Revell Company.

Part I: The Five Historial Books (undated, 1898?). Part II: Paul's Letters to the Churches (1900). Part III: The Pastoral, Personal and General Letters, and the Revelation (1901). Based on Westcott and Hort's Greek text.

One-volume edition (revised) in 1904. Reprinted frequently.

1903 **Fenton's Bible** The Holy Bible in Modern English, containing the complete sacred Scriptures of the Old and New Testaments, translated into English direct from the original Hebrew, Chaldee, and Greek, by Ferrar Fenton.

1882, Romans; 1884, Epistles; 1895, New Testament; 1903, whole Bible. New Testament and four parts of Old Testament.

First edition of New Testament in Modern English 1895, revised 1900. Vol. I: Pentateuch, 1901? Vol. II: Joshua–II Kings, 1902? Vol. III: Isaiah, Jeremiah, Ezekiel, Minor Prophets, Prophets, 1902?

Ferrar Fenton was a London businessman who devoted some twenty years of his life to fulfill a pledge of making the Scriptures intelligible "through the use of modern English." This work by an amateur was popular for a time, but "its erroneous and inaccurate renderings have rather damaged its earlier favor" (Price).

A little from God is better than a great deal from men. What is from men is uncertain, and is often lost and tumbled over and over by men; but what is from God is fixed as a nail in a sure place. —John Bunyan

---

1903 **Weymouth's New Testament** The New Testament in Modern Speech. An Idiomatic Translation into Every Day English from the text of The Resultant Greek Testament by Richard Francis Weymouth.

The text was revised in the 1924 edition by the Rev. S. W. Green, The Rev. Prof. A. J. D. Farrer, and the Rev. Prof. H. T. Andrews, and again in 1929 by the Rev. Prof. James Alexander Robertson.

1904 **Worrell's New Testament** The New Testament Revised and Translated by A. S. Worrell, with Notes and Instructions designed to aid the earnest Reader in obtaining a clear Understanding of the Doctrines, Ordinances and primitive Assemblies as revealed in these Scriptures. Louisville, Ky: A. S. Worrell.

Based on the Greek text underlying the ERV and on Westcott and Hort as modified by Scrivener and others. "Baptize" is translated "immerse"; "church" is "assembly" or "congregation." Claims great fidelity to the Greek. "To handle the tenses carelessly," writes the translator, "is to trifle with the word of God. . . . It is the business of the translator to translate with scrupulous exactness." Contains some textual variants, alternate renderings and explanatory notes.

1905 **Lloyd's New Testament** The Corrected English New Testament. A Revision of the "Authorized" Version (By Nestle's Resultant Text). Prepared with the Assistance of

20TH-CENTURY ENGLISH BIBLE VERSIONS cont.

Eminent Scholars and Issued by Samuel Lloyd, a Life Governor of the British and Foreign Bible Society as His Memorial of the Society's Centenary, 1904. London: Samuel Bagster & Sons, Ltd.

The corrections are of two kinds: (1) the removal of textual defects in the underlying Greek and (2) a modernization of the English. Because of the large extent to which the Authorized Version had failed, Lloyd proposed that the Bible Society produce a new revision as a memorial to its centenary. When this was not accepted, he, with the cooperation of a number of biblical scholars, independently produced this version of the New Testament as an illustration of the kind of revision needed. He attempted "to show the possibility of popularizing without demeaning the Sacred Scriptures and of correcting without defacing the Version so worthily beloved."

1906 **Forster** St. John's Gospel, Epistles, and Revelation, translated by Henry Langstaff Forster. Adelaide: Hunkin, Ellis and King.

The Revelation (1903). Tasmania: Henry Langstaff Forster.

1907 **Bourne's Gospels** The Fourfold Portrait of the Heavenly King, translated by "Interpreter" i.e., A. E. Bourne. London: E. Stock.

A new translation of the Gospels.

1907 **Moulton's Modern Reader's Bible** The Books of the Bible with Three Books of the Apocrypha presented in Modern Literary Form; edited with Introductions and Notes, by Richard G. Moulton. New York: The Macmillan Company.

1908 **Rutherford's Epistles** Paul's Epistles to the Thessalonians and to the Corinthians. A New Translation by W. G. Rutherford, London.

1909 **The Bible in Modern English** The Bible in Modern English. A Rendering from the Originals by an American, making use of the best scholarship and the latest research at home and abroad. Perkiomen, PA.

1909 **Weaver New Testament** New Testament in Modern Historical and Literary Form for the church, the school and the home, embracing the life of Jesus Christ in the words of Matthew, Mark, Luke, and John, and the Church of the Apostles according to the Acts, the Epistles and Revelation, historically harmonized. Translated by S. Townsend Weaver. Philadelphia: University Literature Extension.

"" FOCUS QUOTE **One of the many divine qualities of the Bible is this: that it does not yield its secrets to the irreverent and censorious.** —J. I. Packer

---

1910 **Cunard's** The first judgment of the Christians by the Spirit, Alpha and Omega. An Authorized Revision of St. Matthew and the History of this Planet, from the First Strata to the End. Written for the Spirit at Command by F. W. Cunard. Liverpool: Cunard & Sons.

1912 **Improved Bible Union Version** The Holy Bible containing the Old and New Testaments. An Improved Edition (Based in Part on the Bible Union Version). Philadelphia: American Baptist Publication Society.

The Bible Union Version was an "immersion" version begun in the middle of the nineteenth century, but of which the Old Testament was never fully completed. The New Testament of that version used "immersion" for "baptism." The Improved Version has "baptism (immersion)," "baptize (immerse)," and "baptized (immersed)." The poetic portions of the Old Testament, including those of the prophets, are printed in poetic form.

1914 **Numeric New Testament** The New Testament from the Greek text as established by Bible Numerics. Edited by Ivan Panin. New Haven: Bible Numerics Company.
Based on the number value of the Greek and Hebrew letters. Awkward in many places. Second edition, 1935 and reprinted several times.

1914 **Cunnington's New Testament** The New Covenant, commonly called the New Testament of our Lord and Saviour Jesus Christ. A revision of the version of A.D. 1611 by E. E. Cunnington. London: G. Routledge & Sons.
Other editions appeared, e.g., in 1919 by T. Foster Unwin, London, under the title The Adelphi New Testament; and in 1926 with the title The Western New Testament.

FOCUS QUOTE

The Scriptures teach us the best way of living, the noblest way of suffering, and the most comfortable way of dying. —John Flavel

1916 **McFadyen** The Psalms in Modern Speech and Rhythmical Form by John Edgar McFadyen. London: James Clarke & Company.
The Wisdom Books, also Lamentations and the Song of Songs, in Modern Speech and Rhythmical form by John Edgar McFadyen, 1917. Isaiah in Modern Speech, 1918. Jeremiah in Modern Speech, 1919.

1917 **Jewish Publication Society Bible** The Holy Scriptures According to the Masoretic Text. A New Translation with the Aid of Previous Versions and with Constant Consultation of Jewish Authorities. Philadelphia: The Jewish Publication Society.
Jewish Publication Society Version. Psalms, 1903.

1918 **Anderson New Testament** The New Testament. Translated from the Sinaitic Manuscript Discovered by Constantine Tischendorf at Mount Sinai, by H. T. Anderson. Cincinnati: The Standard Publishing Company.

1919 **The Messages of the Bible** The Messages of the Bible, edited by Frank K. Sanders and Charles F. Kent. 12 vols. New York: Charles Scribner's Sons, 1898-1919.
Brief introductions of each book and free rendering in paraphrase.

1921 **Pym** Mark's Account of Jesus. Cambridge: W. Heffer and Sons. "Common Speech" by T. W. Pym.

1921 **Shorter Bible** The Shorter Bible, translated and arranged by Charles Foster Kent with the Collaboration of Charles Cutler Torrey, Henry A. Sherman, Frederick Harris, Ethel Cutler. New York: Charles Scribner's Sons.
New Testament, 1918. Old Testament, 1921. About two-thirds of the Old Testament and one-third of the New Testament are omitted.

1922 **Plainer Bible** A Plainer Bible for Plain People in Plain America (New Testament), from the original Greek by Chaplain [Frank Schell] Ballentine. Jersey City, N.J.: Plainer Bible Press.
See 1901, Modern American Bible.

20TH-CENTURY ENGLISH BIBLE VERSIONS cont.

1923 **Riverside New Testament** The Riverside New Testament; a translation from the original Greek into the English of today, by William G. Ballantine. Boston: Houghton, Mifflin.

An eclectic rendering of Nestle's Greek text by William G. Ballantine, a former President of Oberlin College, who confesses his indebtedness to other versions, such as Weymouth's, Moffatt's and The Twentieth Century New Testament. Produced in a very readable form with an index, this version was first published in 1923, and revised in 1934.

1923 **Robertson** A Translation of Luke's Gospel with Grammatical Notes by A. T. Robertson. New York: George H. Doran Company.

1924 **Labor Determinative Version** The New Covenant: a Mutual Arrangement or Testament for a true civilization founded upon brotherly labor, following the Greek title which is usually rendered the New Testament, translated out of the Greek as a Labor Determinative Version, and diligently compared with former translations herein revised for the recovery of Biblical labor standards. Jackson, Michigan: Home of the American Labor Determinative Revision Committee.

1924 **Montgomery's Centenary Translation** Centenary Translation of the New Testament in Modern English. Translated by Helen Barrett Montgomery. Philadelphia: Judson Press. 2 vols.

In commemoration of the centenary of the American Baptist Publication Society, Mrs. Helen Barrett Montgomery of Rochester, N.Y., and a graduate of Wellesley College, published this translation. Many of her colloquial paragraph and chapter headings are striking, such as "Play the Game," "A 'Close-up' of Sin," "Paul's Swan Song" and "Orchestrate Your Virtues."

1925 **Askwith's Psalms** The Psalms Books IV and V. Rendered into English in Rhythm Consonant with that of the Original Hebrew by E. H. Askwith. London: M. Hopkinson and Company.

1925 **People's New Covenant** The People's New Covenant. Translated from the Metaphysical Standpoint by Arthur E. Overbury. Monrovia, Calif.: Arthur E. Overbury.

This version is based on the premise of Scientific Statement of Being, as given in *Science and Health* by Mary Baker Eddy.

1925 **Children's Bible** The Children's Bible. Selections from the Old and New Testaments. Translated and arranged by Henry A. Gherman and Charles Foster Kent. New York: Charles Scribner's Sons.

A translation in readable, simple English of selections from the Old Testament and New Testament. Includes not only narratives, but poetic and didactic selections.

1926 **Moffatt** A New Translation of The Bible, Containing the Old and New Testaments, by James Moffatt. New York and London: Harper and Brothers.

New Testament, 1913. New edition, revised, 1917. Old Testament, 1924-25, in 2 vols. Vol. I: Genesis-Esther (1924). Vol. II: Job-Malachi (1925). Revision of complete Bible in 1935.

1927 **Kent's Student's Old Testament** The Student's Old Testament Logically and Chronologically Arranged and translated by Charles Foster Kent. New York: Charles Scribner's Sons, 1904-27.

Six vols. I: Narratives of the Beginnings of Hebrew History from the Creation to the

Establishment of the Hebrew Kingdom, 1904. II: Israel's Historical and Biographical Narratives from the Establishment of the Hebrew Kingdom to the End of the Maccabean Struggle, 1905. III: The Sermons, Epistles, and Apocalypses of Israel's Prophets from the Beginning of the Assyrian Period to the End of the Maccabean Struggle, 1910. IV: Israel's Laws and Legal Precedents from the Days of Moses to the Closing of the Legal Canon, 1907. V: The Songs, Hymns, and Prayers of the Old Testament, 1914. VI: Proverbs and Didactic Poems, 1927.

1927 **Smith-Goodspeed** The Bible. An American Translation. The Old Testament Translated by J. M. Powis Smith and a Group of Scholars. The New Testament Translated by Edgar J. Goodspeed. Chicago: The University of Chicago Press.

Revised, 1935. The New Testament, An American Translation, 1923. The Old Testament, An American Translation, 1927. The Apocrypha, An American Translation, 1938. Reprinted, with Apocrypha included, 1939.

1927 **Christian's Bible** New Testament. Strasburg, Pa.: George N. Le Fevre.

A translation from the Greek, chiefly from B and Aleph. Not simply a translation of the Words, but under the guidance of the Holy Ghost, His thoughts as recorded. George Le Fevre is considered the translator as well as publisher.

1928 **Czarnomska Version** The Authentic Literature of Israel freed from the Disarrangements, Expansions, and Comments of Early Native Editors, edited with an introduction by Elizabeth Czarnomska. New York: The Macmillan Company, 1924-28.

“” FOCUS QUOTE

He who hath heard the Word of God can bear his silences. —St. Ignatius

1928 **Spiritualist's Matthew** The Good Message according to Matthew. For the use of Christian Spiritualists, an entirely new and accurate translation edited by J. W. Potter. London: Society of Communion.

1929 **Gowen's Psalms** The Psalms; or, the Book of Praises. A New Transcription and Translation arranged Strophically and Metrically from a critically constructed text, with introduction, textual notes, and glossary by Herbert H. Gowen. London: Mowbray.

1930 **Loux's Mark** Mark: To Every Man His Work, His Pay, His Rest. Translated by DuBois H. Loux. Jackson, Mich.: Privately printed.

1931 **Wales's Psalms** The Psalms. A Revised Translations, by Frank H. Wales. London: Oxford University Press.

1932 **Chaplain Ballentine** Our God and Godhealth, our Healer. Godhealth's Messenger and Godhealth's Message of Life and Light and Love and Law, the wisdom of the ages: translated from the original Greek, reinterpreted in the thought-forms, language, and idioms of America today, and arranged for reading with sustained interest from beginning to end as a modern novel, by Chaplain [Frank Schell] Ballentine. Collegeville, Pa.: The Craigie Publishing Company.

1932 **Kleist's Memoirs of St. Peter** The Memoirs of St. Peter, or the Gospel according to St. Mark, translated into English sense-lines. By James A. Kleist, S. J. Milwaukee: Bruce Publishing Company.

20TH-CENTURY ENGLISH BIBLE VERSIONS cont.

Translated into sense-lines, which it is maintained is the form that resembles the original itself.

1933 **Torrey's Four Gospels** The Four Gospels, a New Translation by Charles Cutler Torrey. New York and London: Harper and Brothers.

Its purpose is to show that the Gospels of Matthew, Mark, and John were composed in Aramaic.

1934 **Royds' Epistles and Gospels** The Epistles and Gospels for the Sundays & chief holy days of the Christian year. A new translation by Thomas Fletcher Royds. Oxford: Basil Blackwell.

New Testament into modern English: "such English as intelligent village schoolchildren can understand without much explaining of long words." Nestle Greek text. Not continuous text. Good straightforward translation.

1934 **Old Testament in Colloquial English** The Books of the Old Testament in Colloquial English, 1920-34.

Listed in E. H. Robertson's *The New Translations of the Bible*.

1934 **Wade** The Documents of the New Testament. Translated and Historically Arranged with Critical Introduction by G. W. Wade. London: Thomas Murby & Company. Copies of Mark, Luke, and John issued separately in 1936.

Claims to be "an accurate, yet not literal" translation. Avoids ambiguity by presenting what the translator judges to be the most probable meaning. Literary relationships are indicated in the Synoptics, Acts, and 2 Peter–Jude. Westcott and Hort text.

1935 **Westminster Version** The Westminster Version of the Sacred Scriptures, general editor, Cuthbert Lattey. Introductions and commentaries with translation.

New Testament, 1935. Smaller edition in 1948, translations with brief introductions by Father Lattey.

New Testament in parts from 1913-35, edited by Cuthbert Lattey and J. Keating.

Malachi, 1934—Lattey. Ruth, 1935—Lattey. Nahum and Habakkuk, 1937—Bevenot. Jonah, 1938—T. E. Bird. Psalms 1–41, 1939—Lattey. Psalms, 1944—Lattey. Daniel, 1948—Lattey. Obadiah, Micah, Zephaniah, Haggai, Zechariah, 1953—Sebastian Bullough.

An excellent translation by English Roman Catholic scholars under the editorship of Cuthbert Lattey, S.J., based on the original texts in both Testaments. An independent venture; not an "official" translation.

1937 **Cornish's St. Paul from the Trenches** Translated by Gerald Warre Cornish. Two epistles of Corinthians, part of Ephesians.

For the story behind this expanded version see F. F. Bruce, *The English Bible*, New and Revised Edition, p. 22 (New York: Oxford Press).

1937 **Greber's New Testament** The New Testament. A New Translation and Explanation Based on The Oldest Manuscripts, by Johannes Greber. New York: John Felsberg, Inc. The English translation was made by a professional translator and corrected by a committee of American clergymen. A somewhat eccentric translation. It is based mainly on Codex Bezae, but at times the translator has given a version with no MS authority. Originally published in German but subsequently translated into English. Translator is a former Roman Catholic priest who came to believe in communication with the world of divine spirits.

1937 **Martin's New Testament** The New Testament critically reconstructed and retranslated, by William Wallace Martin. Nashville, Tenn.: Parthenon Press.

Epistles in 2 vols. Part I: Press of Marshall and Bruce Company, Nashville, 1929. Part II: Press of the Methodist Episcopal Church, Nashville, 1930.

The twenty-one canonical Epistles have been reconstructed into thirty-six, including as authors Apollos, Barnabas, and John, son of Zebedee (as the writer of the Epistle of James).

The Psalms Complete: Their Prayers, their Collects, their Praises, in three Books. Separated, arranged, and translated by Willism Wallace Martin. Nashville, Tenn.: Marshall & Bruce Company.

The Book of Job in Two Versions: A Judean Version, an Ephramaean Version; and The Book of Ecclesiastes. Nashville, Tenn.: Methodist Publishing House. Isaian Prophecies. Nashville, Tenn.: Parthenon Press.

Jeremiah–Ezekiel Prophecies. Nashville, Tenn.: Parthenon Press.

The Book of Genesis Complete. The Ephramaean Version . . .Judean Version. Nashville, Tenn.: Parthenon Press.

Twelve Minor Prophets. Nashville, Tenn.: Parthenon Press.

FOCUS QUOTE

The amazing wealth of the Bible is precisely what makes it a difficult book to study. —Paul Tournier

---

1937 **Spencer's New Testament** The New Testament of Our Lord and Saviour Jesus Christ; translated into English from the original Greek by the Very Rev. Francis Aloysius Spencer, O.P.; edited by Charles J. Callan, O.P., and John A. McHugh, O.P. New York: The Macmillan Company.

After publishing a new translation of the Gospels from the Latin in 1898, Father Francis Aloysius Spencer was moved to attempt a new translation from the Greek. The four Gospels were published in 1901 and the rest of the NT finished with notes shortly before Spencer's death in 1913. The whole NT, however, was not published until 1937, under the editorship of Charles J. Callan and John A. McHugh, and has been reprinted several times since. The words of Christ are printed in italics, quotations from the OT are put in small capitals, and Vulgate readings that differ from the Greek are given in brackets or footnotes.

1937 **Williams's New Testament** The New Testament; a translation in the language of the people, by Charles B. Williams. Boston: Bruce Humphries. Slightly revised edition, Chicago: Moody Press, 1950. Verse numbers inserted in the text. Westcott and Hort Greek text.

A Greek professor from Union University (Jackson, Tenn.), Charles B. Williams's aim was to reproduce as far as possible the exact shades of meaning in the Greek tenses. To do this requires the use of auxiliaries and the like in English and can result in overtranslation and in the use of language that is hardly the "language of the people."

1938 **Book of Books** A Translation of the New Testament Complete and Unabridged. London: R.T.S. The Lutterworth Press, The United Society for Christian Literature. R. Mercer Wilson, General Secretary, The United Society for Christian Literature translated this NT to celebrate the centenary of the *Annotated Paragraph Bible,* which he

20TH-CENTURY ENGLISH BIBLE VERSIONS cont.

follows in the arrangement of his text, and the fourth centenary of the setting up of the English Bible in the churches. Rather straightforward simple translation.

1938 **Buttenweiser's Psalms** The Psalms. Chronologically Treated with a New Translation by Moses Buttenweiser, Prof. Emeritus of Biblical Exegesis, Hebrew Union College. Chicago: The University of Chicago Press.

1938 **Clementson's New Testament** The New Testament. A Translation by Edgar Lewis Clementson. Pittsburgh: The Evangelization Society of the Pittsburgh Bible Institute.

1939 **Oesterley Psalms** The Psalms. Translated with Text-Critical and Exegetical Notes by W. O. C. Oesterley. London: S.P.C.K.; New York: The Macmillan Company. 2 vols.

1940 **Dakes's Gospels** Christ Jesus: The Authentic Story of the Founder of Christianity as told by Matthew, Mark, Luke and John in the Four Gospels. Translated from the original Greek by John A. Dakes. Chicago: Avalon Publishing Company.

Dakes was a Greek businessman who felt "that a translation made by a Greek who had learned the original language of the Gospels in the schools of Greece might prove helpful." Certain Greek words are transliterated, such as *petros* and *petra* in Matthew 16:18, *ecclesia, aeonian,* and *Logos*. A glossary appears at the back of the book.

1940 **St. Mark in Current English** By Mary L. Matheson. Melbourne: National Council of Religious Education of Australia.

1944 **Callan's Psalms** The Psalms. Translated from the Latin Psalter, in the Light of the Hebrew, of the Septuagint and Peshitta Versions, and of the Psalterium Juxta Hebraeos of St. Jerome. With Introductions, Critical Notes, and Spiritual Reflections by Charles J. Callan. New York: Joseph F. Wagner.

1944 **Wand's New Testament Letters** The New Testament Letters, prefaced and paraphrased by J. W. C. Wand. Brisbane, Australia. Revised edition published in England, 1946.

Romans–Jude. According to the Introduction, the work "may be called either a free translation or a close paraphrase." "I have tried," says Bishop Wand, "to put the Epistles into the kind of language a Bishop might use in writing a monthly letter for his diocesan magazine."

1945 **Stringfellow's New Testament** New Testament. A Translation, Harmony and Annotations by Erwin Edward Stringfellow. . . . Planographed by John S. Swift Company, Inc.

Vol. I: The Gospels (1943). Vol. II: Acts–Revelation (1945). Dubuque, Iowa: Wm. C. Brown Company

Westcott and Hort text.

1946 **Lenski** The Interpretation of [the New Testament] . . . R. C. H. Lenski. Columbus, Ohio: Lutheran Book Concern, 1931–46.

Twelve vols. Commentary with independent translation by a noted Lutheran scholar.

1947 **Eerdmans's Psalms** The Hebrew Books of Psalms by B. D. Eerdmans. Oudtestamentliche Studien, IV. Leiden: E. J. Brill.

1947 **Swann's New Testament** The New Testament. Translated from the Greek text of Westcott and Hort. By Rev. George Swann, Louisville, Ky.: Pentecostal Publishing Company. Second ed., 1949.

Third ed.

1948 **Letchworth New Testament** The New Testament. Letchworth Version in Modern English, by T. F. Ford and R. E. Ford. Letchworth, Herts: Letchworth Printer, Ltd.

A translation of the TR Greek text into current English, mainly using words of Anglo-Saxon origin, and free from colloquialisms and slang expressions. Seeks to maintain in modern dress the simple, dignified style of writing associated with the classical English versions.

1949 **Basic Bible** Containing the Old and New Testaments in Basic English. Cambridge: The University Press and Evans Bros. New York: Dutton.

The New Testament in Basic English, 1940. Whole Bible, 1949. Selections, 1933; Micah and Habakkuk, 1934; Mark, 1945; John, 1938.

Basic English is a system of simplified English with a primary vocabulary of 850 words devised by C. K. Ogden as an international auxiliary language and as an aid in learning English. In 1940 a committee under the direction of S. H. Hooke of the University of London produuced an independent translation of the New Testament, using the 850 words in the primary vocabulary of Basic English to which 50 special Bible words and 100 others were added.

1949 **Leslie's Psalms** The Psalms. Translated and Interpreted in the Light of Hebrew Life and Worship by Elmer A. Leslie. New York and Nashville: Abingdon-Cokesbury Press.

“” FOCUS QUOTE

I am sorry for men who do not read the Bible every day. I wonder why they deprive themselves of the strength and the pleasure. —Woodrow Wilson

---

1951 **Authentic Version** The New Testament. Plattsburg, Mo.: Brotherhood Authentic Bible Society.

Anonymous translator: "Believing that I have been given divine authority through the Holy Spirit to bring the true translation of the original Greek text, and that which has been given me through the inspiration of the Holy Spirit, I have diligently and carefully compared with the original Greek text by the use of the best Greek dictionaries and former translations, some out of the Greek and some Latin: and find that what the Spirit has given me is according to the Original Greek." Modern speech version.

1951 **Vernon's Mark** The Gospel of St. Mark: A New Translation in Simple English, translated by Edward Vernon.

For the average intelligent child of twelve years old and upwards.

1952 **New Testament in Plain English** The New Testament; a new translation in plain English by Charles Kingsley Williams. London: S.P.C.K., Longmans, Green and Company. The Life of Our Lord Jesus Christ according to St. Luke, together with some passages from the other Gospels, newly done into very simple English from the Greek of The Revised Version, 1933. Matthew, 1934.

"Plain English" is a simplified form of the English language based on a list of 1,500 "fundamental and common words that make up ordinary English speech," plus some 160 or 170 others that are explained in a glossary at the end of the volume. The translation is based on Souter's Greek Text (Oxford Press, 1910).

1952 **Penguin Bible (Rieu)** The Four Gospels, a New Translation from the Greek by E. V. Rieu. London and Melbourne: Penguin Books.

20TH-CENTURY ENGLISH BIBLE VERSIONS cont.

Acts of the Apostles by Saint Luke, by C. H. Rieu, son of E. V. Rieu.

E. V. Rieu justifies his translation on the basis that it is from the literary standpoint more in harmony with the Greek Gospels than the KJV, whose translators "mistook fidelity to the idiom of the Greek for fidelity to its meaning" and "felt the sanctity and importance of the original so keenly that the use of normal language would have seemed a kind of sacrilege." Accurate and readable.

1952 **Revised Standard Version** The Holy Bible, being the Version Set Forth A.D. 1611. Revised 1881 and 1901 and Revised 1952. New York, Toronto, Edinburgh: Thomas Nelson and Sons.

New Testament, 1946. Old Testament with Complete Bible, 1952. Apocrypha, 1957.

1954 **Kissane's Psalms** The Books of Psalms. Translated from a Critically Revised Hebrew Text with a Commentary by Monsignor Edward J. Kissane. Dublin: Brown and Nolan, Ltd. Vol. I, 1953; Vol. II, 1954.

1954 **Kleist and Lilly's New Testament** The New Testament rendered from the original Greek with Explanatory Notes. Milwaukee: Bruce Publishing Company.

The Four Gospels translated by James A. Kleist, S.J., and the Acts to Revelation by Joseph L. Lilly, C. M. Made from 1943 Bover Greek Text into modern popular English. An independent modern American translation.

1954 **Kleist and Lynam's Psalms** The Psalms in Rhythmic Prose. By James A. Kleist, S.J., and Thomas James Lynam, S.J. Milwaukee: Bruce Publishing Company.

Based on Latin text of the Pontifical Biblical Institute, Rome.

1954 **Moore's New Testament** A New, Independent, Individual Translation from the Greek, by George Albert Moore, Colonel, U.S.A. Chevy Chase, MD.: The Country Dollar Press.

Based on Souter's 1950 Greek text. Gospels issued separately in 1953.

1955 **Fides Translation (Psalms)** The Psalms. Introduction and Notes by Mary Perkins Ryan. Chicago: Fides Publishers Association.

Made in accordance with the new Roman Psalter.

1955 **Knox** The Holy Bible; a translation from the Latin Vulgate in the light of the Hebrew and Greek originals. Authorized by the hierarchy of England and Wales and the hierarchy of Scotland. Translated by Monsignor Knox. London: Burns and Oates.

Old Testament. New York: Sheed and Ward, 1948-50, 2 vols. Vol. I: Genesis-Esther. Vol. II: Job-Maccabees.

New Testament. Newly Translated from the Vulgate Latin at the Request of their Lordships, the Archbishops of England Wales. New York: Sheed & Ward, British Trial Edition, 1944.

1955 **Schonfield's Authentic New Testament** The Authentic New Testament, edited and translated from the Greek for the general reader by Hugh J. Schonfield. London: D. Dobson.

This is a work of high quality by the distinguished Jewish Scholar, Dr. Hugh J. Schonfield, who approaches these documents "as if they had recently been recovered from a cave in Palestine or beneath the sands of Egypt, and had never previously been given to the public." Much helpful information on the Jewish references in the New Testament is given in the Notes and Introduction.

1956 **Laubach's Inspired Letters** The Inspired Letters in Clearest English. Prepared by Frank C. Laubach. New York: Thomas Nelson and Sons.

Romans–Jude. Written in short, clear sentences with a limited vocabulary of about two thousand words, this translation is intended as a preparation for the reading of the RSV for beginning students of English. The Gospels and Acts, the translator feels, are simple enough in the RSV. By the world's leader in the fight against illiteracy.

1957 **Concordant Version** International Edition. The Sacred Scriptures. An Idiomatic, Consistent, Emphasized Version. Los Angeles: Concordant Publishing concern.

Old Testament—Half title: Concordant Version of the Hebrew Scriptures. In a Beginning, commonly called "Genesis."

[The New Testament] Concordant Version, 1919-26. One-volume reprint, 1931.

This version is based on the belief that "every word in the original should have its own English equivalent." It is said to aim "at truth and accuracy rather than literary elegance." It shows the eccentricities "of a self-taught and opinionated 'one man' translator who has certain peculiar views to proclaim yet is 'reverent, careful, and thorough.' "

1957 **Lamsa's** The Holy Bible from ancient Eastern manuscripts. Containing the Old and New Testaments, translated from the Peshitta, the authorized Bible of the church of the East, by George M. Lamsa. Philadelphia: A. J. Holman Company.

The Four Gospels according to the Eastern Version, 1933.

The Book of Psalms according to the Eastern Version, 1939.

The New Testament, 1940.

George M. Lamsa's translation purports to be produced "from original Aramaic sources." Lamsa's original claims for his work are generally questioned. The Peshitta is not to be identified with the "original Aramaic." Lamsa also adapted some questionable renderings such as "rope" for "camel" in Matthew 19:24, et al.

“” FOCUS QUOTE **Nobody ever outgrows Scripture; the book widens and deepens with our years.** —Charles Haddon Spurgeon

---

1958 **Hudson** The Pauline Epistles: Their Meanings and Message. Introduction, Translation, Marginal Analysis, and Paraphrase by James T. Hudson. London: James Clarke & Company, Ltd.

"New translation with the missing steps in Paul's thought supplied in brackets." Omits Hebrews.

1958 **Meissner's Gospels** New Testament Gospels, a Modern Translation by Lawrence Meissner. Portland, Oreg.

All the verses, 40 percent fewer words.

1958 **Phillips's New Testament** New Testament in Modern English. New York: The Macmillan Company letters to Young Churches; a translation of the New Testament Epistles, by J. B. Phillips; with an introduction by C. S. Lewis, 1951. A corrected edition, 1957. First published in England, 1947. The Gospels, translated into modern English by J. B. Phillips, c. 1951. First published in 1952. The Young Church in Action; a Translation of the Acts of the Apostles by J. B. Phillips, 1955. Book of Revelation, 1957. Gospels, a corrected edition, 1958. Four Prophets: Amos, Hosea, First Isaiah, Micah;

20TH-CENTURY ENGLISH BIBLE VERSIONS cont.

a modern translation from the Hebrew, by J. B. Phillips, 1963. Second revised edition of the New Testament, 1973.

1958 **Tomanek's New Testament** The New Testament of Our Lord and Savior Jesus Anointed, by James L. Tomanek. Pocatello, Ida.: Arrowhead Press.

1959 **Cressman** St. Mark. Toronto: Full Gospel Publishing House. Mark, 2nd ed., 1960. John, American Bible Society, 1962. Simplified English for Liberians by Annie Cressman of the Assemblies of God Mission.

1959 **Modern Language Bible (Berkeley)** The Holy Bible, the Berkeley Version in Modern English, containing the Old and New Testaments. Translated afresh from the original languages and diligently compared with previous translations, with numerous helpful nondoctrinal notes to aid the understanding of the reader. Gerrit Verkuyl, editor-in-chief and translator of the New Testament section. Grand Rapids: Zondervan Publishing House.

Berkeley Version of the New Testament, 1945. Berkeley, Calif.: James J. Gillick & Company. Grand Rapids: Zondervan Publishing House, 1950, 1953.

1960 **The Children's "King James"** The Children's "King James" Bible: New Testament. Jay Green is responsible for the wording; "Peter" Palmer for the stories. Evansville, Ind.: Modern Bible Translations.

Not KJV of 1611, but a modern version using the same text the KJ translation used.

1961 **New World Translation—Jehovah's Witnesses** New World Translation of the Holy Scriptures, rendered from the original languages by the New World Bible Translation Committee. Revised. Brooklyn: Watchtower Bible and Tract Society of New York.

The New World Translation of the Christian Greek Scriptures, 1950.

Based on Westcott and Hort, supplemented by Nestle, Bover, Merk.

New World Translation of the Hebrew Scriptures, 1953–60. Issued in five vols. Genesis–Ruth, 1953; 1 Samuel–Esther, 1955; Job–Song of Solomon, 1957; Isaiah–Lamentations, 1958; Ezekiel–Malachi, 1960. Based on 3rd ed. Kittel, 1951.

1961 **Noli's Greek Orthodox New Testament** The New Testament of our Lord and Savior Jesus Christ. Translated into English from the approved Greek text of the Church of Constantinople and the Church of Greece, by Fan S. Noli. Boston: Albanian Orthodox Church in America.

1961 **One Way** One Way: The Jesus People New Testament. A Translation in Modern English. Pasadena, Calif.: Compass Press.

This is the same as Norlie's The New Testament in Modern English, 1951.

1961 **Simplified New Testament (Norlie)** Simplified New Testament in Plain English for Today's Reader. A New Translation from the Greek by Olaf M. Norlie. With the Psalms for Today, a new translation in current English by R. K. Harrison. Grand Rapids: Zondervan Publishing House.

Dr. Olaf M. Norlie of St. Olaf College designed this translation particularly for teenagers. It is rendered in plain, lucid, and straightforward English.

An earlier translation of Norlie was published by the author in 1951 in Northfield, Minn., with the title: The New Testament . . . in Modern English translated from the original Greek and supplied with an outline by Olaf Morgan Norlie. Still earlier, in 1943, a translation of the Gospel of John was published in mimeographed form in San Antonio, Tex., by the Life Builders Press.

1961 **Wuest's Expanded New Testament** Expanded Translation of the Greek New Testament by Kenneth S. Wuest. Grand Rapids: Wm. B. Eerdmans Publishing Company.

Vol. 1: Gospels (1956). Vol. 2: Acts through Ephesians (1958). Vol. 3: Philippians through Revelation (1959).

Kenneth S. Wuest endeavors to reproduce for the English readers the nuances of the Greek text, both philologically and theologically. Bible scholars may feel that he at times overtranslates and finds shades of meaning not actually in the Greek text. He does for all parts of speech what Williams does for verbs.

“” FOCUS QUOTE

In this little Book is contained all the wisdom of the world. —George Heinrich Ewald

---

1962 **Children's Version** The Children's Version of the Holy Bible. New York: McGraw Hill.

Printed in large, Caledonia type for easy reading. The text is arranged in paragraphs, though the verse numbers are retained in small type interspersed through the text. Difficult words, names, and places are diacritically marked and some are phonetically pronounced. The text is a simplification and modernization of the KJV. The preface is by Jay P. Green.

1963 **Gelineau's Psalms** The Psalms: A New Translation. Translated from the Hebrew and arranged for Singing to the Psalmody of Joseph Gelineau. Philadelphia: The Westminster Press.

1963 **The Holy Name Bible** The Holy Name Bible containing the Holy Name Version of the Old and New Testaments. Revised by A. B. Traina. Irvington, N.J.: The Scripture Research Association, Inc.

The New Testament of our Messiah and Saviour Yahshua. Sacred Name Version, 1950.

This translation is understood to have been made by A. B. Traina and reprinted at his expense. The version attempts to restore Semitic proper names to their Aramaic or Hebrew form and to clear up difficulties in the text in the light of possible Semitic background.

1964 **Anchor Bible** Anchor Bible, edited by William F. Albright and David N. Freedman. Individual translators for books. Garden City, N.J.: Doubleday & Company.

1964 **Hadas's Psalms** The Book of Psalms for the Modern Reader: A New Translation by Gershon Hadas. New York: Jonathan David.

1965 **Amplified Bible** The Amplified Bible, containing the Amplified Old Testament and the Amplified New Testament. Grand Rapids: Zondervan Publishing House.

The Amplified New Testament. Zondervan Publishing House, 1958–65. Old Testament: Part I (1964), Genesis–Esther; Part II (1962), Job–Malachi. Zondervan Publishing House. Translation by Frances E. Siwert.

1965 **Bruce's Expanded Paraphrase** An Expanded Paraphrase of the Epistles of Paul. Printed in parallel with the Revised Version, with fuller references by Drs. Scrivener, Moulton & Greenup, by F. F. Bruce. Exeter: Paternoster Press.

American edition has title: The Letters of Paul: Expanded Paraphrase.

This paraphrase is designed, as Bruce states, “to make the course of Paul's argument as clear as possible.” The “expanded paraphrase” is printed alongside the Revised

20TH-CENTURY ENGLISH BIBLE VERSIONS cont.

Version of 1881, "for the convenience and interest of readers who may care to compare and contrast two renderings produced on directly opposite principles."

1966 **The Bible in Simplified English** Listen . . . The Lord is Speaking: The Bible in Simplified English. Collegeville, Minn.: The Liturgical Press.

The authorized English edition of the Katholische Schulbibel, which is an abridged selection of biblical passages rearranged to provide a chronological history of the biblical period. The poetic books, duplicated historical material, and Epistles are not included. Written in simple English, this is intended for beginners in the study of the Bible.

1966 **Burke** God Is For Real, Man: Interpretations of Bible Passages and Stories as Told by Some of God's Bad-tempered Angels with Busted Haloes to Carl F. Burke. New York: Association Press.

1969 edition entitled God Is Beautiful, Man.

Free treatment of selected Bible passages in American downtown slang by young people of the inner city.

1966 **Jerusalem Bible** General editor, Alexander Jones. Garden City, New York, and London: Doubleday and Darton, Longman and Todd.

1966 **Living Scriptures** The Living Scriptures, a New Translation in the King James Tradition. Edited by Jay P. Green. Marshatton, Del.: National Foundation for Christian American Bible Society. New York: The Macmillan Company.

1967 **Dale's New World** New World: The Heart of the New Testament in Plain English, by Alan T. Dale. London: Oxford University Press, c. 1967, 1968.

1967 **Liverpool Vernacular Gospels** The Gospels in Scouse, translated by Dick Williams and Frank Shaw. Revised edition, London: White Lion Publishers, 1977.

"A rollicking, carefree interpretaion of some Gospel passages in the Liverpool vernacular."

1968 **Cotton Patch Version** The Cotton Patch Version of Paul's Epistles, by Clarence Jordan. New York: Association Press.

The Cotton Patch version of Luke and Acts, 1969. The Cotton Patch Version of Matthew and John, 1970. First eight chapters of John only. The Cotton Patch Version of Hebrews and the General Epistles, 1973.

A local dialect version rather than merely an English version. Intended for the South, especially the area around Atlanta. This version goes to the limit of the spectrum in translating ideas and substitutes local place names for biblical ones. Based on Nestle-Aland, 23rd ed., 1957. By the founder of an interracial farming community in Americus, Georgia, with a Ph.D. in Greek from Southern Baptist Theological Seminary.

1968 **Hanson's Psalms in Modern Speech** The Psalms in Modern Speech for Public and Private Use, by Richard S. Hanson. Philadelphia: Fortress Press.

3 vols. Vol. 1: Psalms 1–41. Vol. 2: Psalms 42–89. Vol. 3: Psalms 90–150.

A fresh poetic rendering of "the Hymnbook of Ancient Israel," with special attention to its liturgical usage. Contains an informative "Introduction," introductory notes to many of the Psalms, and footnotes explaining deviations from previous translations.

1968 **Restoration of Original Name New Testament** The New Testament of Our Master and Saviour Yahvahshua the Messiah (commonly called Jesus Christ): Restoration of Original Name New Testament. Junction City, Oreg.: Missionary Dispensary Bible Research.

Rotherham's version but with changes made principally by returning to the Hebrew form of God's name and by replacing Lord and God in the New Testament by YAHVAH or, for the latter, Elohim when it is used with God.

1969 **Barclay's New Testament** The New Testament: a new translation by William Barclay. London, Cleveland: Collins.

Gospels and Acts, 1968. Letters and The Revelation, 1969.

1969 **Children's New Testament** Translated by Gleason H. Ledyard. Waco, Tex.: Word Books.

1970 **King James II New Testament** Translated by Jay P. Green. Byron Center, Mich.: Associated Publishers.

1970 **The Mercier New Testament** The Mercier New Testament: A Version of the New Testament in Modern English. Part I: Matthew, Mark, Luke, John. Prepared by Kevin Condon. Cork: Mercier Press. (Identical with The Alba House New Testament.)

A fresh Catholic translation from the Greek in plain, simple, modern English. Patterned after the German Das Neue Testament fur Menschen unserer Zeit (1964). Not meant to compete with the standard English versions, but to lead to a greater appreciation and use of them. Illustrated by a hundred carefully selected photographs.

“” FOCUS QUOTE

I read my Bible to know what people ought to do, and my newspaper to know what they are doing. —Cardinal John Henry Newman

---

1970 **New American Bible** Translated from the original languages, with the critical use of all the ancient sources, by members of the Catholic Biblical Association of America. New York: P. J. Kenedy.

The New Testament of Our Lord and Savior Jesus Christ translated from the Latin Vulgate. A revision of the Challoner-Rheims Version edited by Catholic Scholars under the patronage of the episcopal committee of the Confraternity of Christian Doctrine. Paterson, NJ.: St. Anthony Guild Press, 1941. (The NT in the NAB is a new translation from the Greek text.)

Genesis, 1948; Vol. I (Genesis–Ruth), 1952; Vol. III (Sapiential or Wisdom Books), 1955; Vol. IV (Prophetic Books), 1961; Vol. II (Samuel–Maccabees), 1969.

1970 **New English Bible** The New English Bible with the Apocrypha. Oxford University Press and Cambridge University Press.

New Testament, 1961; 2nd ed., 1970. The Old Testament and Apocrypha, 1970.

1971 **Blackwelder's Exegetical Translation** Letters from Paul. An Exegetical Translation by Boyce W. Blackwelder. Anderson, Ind.: Warner Press.

Based on Nestle's 4th ed., 1904. At times reads more like a condensed commentary than a translation. Sacrifices literary quality for exegetical values. Uses brackets in place of italics to indicate words or expressions that are added to complete the meaning of the Greek. Does not include Hebrews. By the chairman of the Department of NT at Anderson College, Anderson, Ind.

1971 **Living Bible** The Living Bible, Paraphrased. Wheaton, Ill.: Tyndale House.

20TH-CENTURY ENGLISH BIBLE VERSIONS cont.

Living History of Israel, a paraphrase of Joshua, Judges, 1 and 2 Samuel, 1 and 2 Kings, 1 and 2 Chronicles, Ezra, and Nehemiah, 1970. Living Prophecies: the Minor Prophets paraphrased with Daniel and the Revelation, 1965, 1967. Living New Testament Paraphrased, 1967. Living Letters: the Paraphrased Epistles, c. 1962, 1967.

1971 **New American Standard Bible** Carol Stream, Ill.: Creation House.
New Testament Pilot ed., La Habra, Calif. Produced and published by the Lockman Foundation, 1963.

1972 **The Bible in Living English** Translated by Stephen T. Byington. Brooklyn, NY: Watchtower Bible and Tract Society of New York, Inc.

1973 **A Child's Bible** A Child's Bible in Colour: The Old Testament, rewritten for children by Anne Edwards. The New Testament, rewritten for children by Shirley Steen. London and New York: Pan Books and Paulist Press.

1973 **Common Bible** Common Bible: The Holy Bible; Revised Standard Version, containing the Old and New Testament with Apocrypha/Deuterocanonical Books. New York: William Collins Sons.

1973 **New International Version** The Holy Bible, New International Version: The New Testament. Grand Rapids: Zondervan Bible Publishers.

1973 **The Psalms** The Psalms: An Exploratory Translation by Mother Maus [Lydia Gysi].
New Pagnell, Bucks.: Green Orthodox Monastery of the Assumption.

1973 **The Translator's New Testament** The Translator's New Testament. London: The British and Foreign Bible Society.
Under the direction of W. D. McHardy a team of thirty-five Bible scholars and eighteen missionary linguists prepared this translation in order "to make available, to those translators of the New Testament into their own mother tongue who depend on English for access to the sources of biblical scholarship, such help as is necessary for the making of effective translations in the languages of today." Includes Notes and a Glossary. Based on the United Bible Societies" Greek Text, 1966.

1973 **The Better Version of the New Testament** The Better Version of the New Testament based on the Greek text according to eminent scholars and according to certain fundamental principles and rules of biblical interpretation, by Chester Estes. Muscle Shoals, Ala.

1974 **Klingensmith New Testament** The New Testament in Everyday English, by Don J. Klingensmith, Fargo, N. Dak.: Kayes Inc.
A translation of the "simple Greek' into the simple words of everyday English. Leaves out chapter and verse divisions. In the Gospels the Pharisees are the Orthodox, the Sadducees are Liberals, scribes are scholars, disciples are students, hypocrites are stage players, Gehenna is a junk yard, and repentance is a change of thinking.

1975 **The Word Made Fresh** A paraphrase of selected portions of the Bible by Andrew Edington. 3 vols. Atlanta: John Knox.

1976 **Train Up a Child** Train Up a Child. Pt 1, Genesis, paraphrased for children by Ben Nutt. Chicago: Adams Press.

1976 **Concise Jewish Bible** Edited and translated by Philip Birnbaum. New York: Sanhedrin Press.

1976 **Beck's: An American Translation** The Holy Bible in the Language of Today, An American Translation by William F. Beck. Stylistic alterations and other changes dictated by the latest MS evidence made by Elmer B. Smick and Erich H. Kiehl. Nashville: Hollman Bible Publishers.

The New Testament in the Language of Today, St. Louis: Concordia Publishing House, 1963.

A refreshing translation by a Lutheran scholar in simple, precise English. It is printed in readable type with orderly paragraphing and lively headings. OT quotations are printed in italics. Makes an attempt to date the events of the NT. In John 8:57 it follows P75 and a few other MSS in its translation "and Abraham has seen you?" "Grace" (*charis*) is usually translated as love, and "justify" as make righteous. Contains approximately twenty-five textual notes in the NT. A numbered list of OT references is given at the close of each book.

1976 **Good News Bible** The Bible in Today's English Version, New York: The American Bible Society, 1976.

Good News for Modern Man. The New Testament in Today's English Version. New York: American Bible Society, 1966, 1971, 1976.

Psalms for Modern Man, 1970. Job for Modern Man, 1971. Wisdom for Modern Man (Proverbs & Ecclesiastes), 1972.

1976 **Renaissance New Testament** The Renaissance New Testament, by Randolph O. Yeager. Bowling Green, Ky.: Renaissance Press.

Contents, v. 1. Matthew I-VIII.

1976 **New Life Testament** The New Life Testament. Translated by Gleason H. Ledyard. Canby, Oreg.: Christian Literature International.

1976 **The Gospel Jesus** The Gospel Jesus: The Story in Modern English by Ronald Cox. Nole Plaza, Ind.: Our Sunday Visitor.

1977 **The Song of Songs** The Song of Songs: Love poems from the Bible, translated from the original Hebrew by Marcia Falk. 1st ed. New York: Harcourt Brace Jovanovich.

1977 **The Psalms** The Psalms translated [from the Hebrew] by Peter Levi, with an introduction by Nicholas de Lange. Harmondsworth: Penguin.

1977 **The Gospels in Scouse** The Gospels in Scouse by Dick Williams and Frank Shaw, illustrated by Derek Alden, introduction by David Sheppard. Rev. ed. London: White Lion Publishers.

1977 **Marrow Gospels** The Four Gospels; newly translated from the Greek. Luton, England: White Crescent Press.

For the most part uses the Greek text of The British and Foreign Bible Society.

1977 **The Psalms** The Psalms, a New Translation for Worship prepared by David L. Frost and a panel of Hebrew and Biblical Scholars. London: Collins Liturgical.

1977 **Christian Counselor's New Testament** The Christian Counselor's New Testament; a new translation in everyday English with notations . . . by Jay E. Adams. Grand Rapids: Baker Book House, 1977. NT in Everyday English, 1979.

1977 **The Holy Bible for Children** The Holy Bible for Children: A Simplified Version of the Old and New Testaments edited by Allan Hart Johsmann. Illustrations and maps by Don Kueker. St. Louis: Concordia.

A simplified retelling of selected portions of the books of the Bible.

20TH-CENTURY ENGLISH BIBLE VERSIONS cont.

1978 **The Holy Name Bible** The Holy Name Bible, containing the Holy Name Version of the Old and New Testaments. Brandywine, Md.

1978 **The New International Version** The Holy Bible, New International Version, Grand Rapids: Zondervan Bible Publishers.

The Holy Bible, New International Version: The New Testament, Grand Rapids: Zondervan Bible Publishers.

1978 **New Testament for the Deaf** The New Testament: English Version for the Deaf, translated from the Greek Text. Grand Rapids: Baker Book House.

1979 **The Psalms** The Psalms: A New Translation by Bonaventure Zerr. New York: Paulist Press.

1979 **Ephesians** Ephesians by R. Paul Caudill. Nashville: Broadman Press.

1979 **Lattimore's Gospels and Revelation** The Four Gospels and the Revelation. Newly translated from the Greek by Richmond Lattimore. New York: Farrar, Straus and Giroux.

1979 **Sasson's Ruth** Ruth: A New Translation with a Philological Commentary and a Formalist Folklorist Interpretation by Jack M. Sasson. Johns Hopkins University Near Eastern Studies. Baltimore: Johns Hopkins University Press.

1979 **Mitchell's Job** Into the Whirlwind: A Translation of the Book of Job, by Stephen Mitchell. Garden City, N.J.: Doubleday.

1982 **New Jewish Version** The Writings, Kethubim: The third section of A New Translation of the Holy Scriptures according to the Masoretic Text. Philadelphia: The Jewish Publication Society of America.

The Torah: The Five Books of Moses, the first section, 1962. 2nd rev. ed., 1973. The Five Megilloth and Jonah; a new translation. Introductions by H. L. Ginsberg, with drawings by Ismar David, 1969. Psalms 1972, Isaiah 1973, Jeremiah 1974.

The Prophets, Nevi'im. Second section of a new translation, 1978.

1982 **The New King James** Holy Bible. The New King James Version, Nashville, Camden, New York: Thomas Nelson Publishers, 1979.

The New King James Bible New Testament, Nashville, Camden, New York: Thomas Nelson Publishers.

1982 **The Reader's Digest Bible** The Reader's Digest Bible condensed from the Revised Standard Version, Old and New Testament, Pleasantville, NY: The Reader's Digest Association.

1983 **First Corinthians** First Corinthians: a translation with notes by R. Paul Caudill. Nashville: Broadman Press.

1983 **In the Beginning** In the Beginning: A New Translation of the Book of Genesis. Edited and translated by Everett Fox. New York: Schocken.

1983 **International Children's Version: New Testament** Sweet Publishing.

1983 **New Testament in Scots** New Testament in Scots, edited and translated by William L. Lorimer. Edinburgh, Southside: Canongate.

1984 **The Five Scrolls** Ed. Herbert Bronstein and Albert Friedlander. New York: CCAR.

1984 **New Testament into Everyday American English** Julian G. Anderson, ed. Naples, FL: Julian G. Anderson

1984 **The New World Translation** The New World Translation of the Holy Scriptures with references, rendered from the original languages, by the New World Bible Translation Committee, revised. Watchtower Bible and Tract Society of New York, International Bible Students Association.

Revised edition of New World Translation published in 1981.

1984 **The Psalms** The Psalms: A New Translation for Prayer and Worship translated by Gary Chamberlain. Nashville, TN: Upper Room.

1984 **The Psalter** The Psalter. Monks of the Brotherhood of Saint Francis, ed. Cambridge, NY: New Skete Monastery.

1984 **The Word** The Word: New Century Version, NT. Translated by the World Bible Translation Center.

1985 **New Jerusalem Bible** Henry Wansbrough, ed. London: Darton, Longman and Todd and Garden City, NY: Doubleday and Company.

A revision of the New Jerusalem Bible published in 1966.

1985 **One Gospel** Taken literally from the four gospels in the Authorized KJV by the Bible compiled by R. Lewis Pryor. Jefferson, NC: McFarland.

1985 **The Original New Testament** by Hugh J. Schonfield. New York: Harper and Row.

1985 **The Psalms** Translated by Peter Levi, with an introduction by Nicholas de Lange. New York: Penguin Books.

1985 **Tanakh** A Translation of the Holy Scriptures according to the Traditional Hebrew Text. Philadelphia: Jewish Publication Society. Was called the New Jewish Version before the complete Hebrew Scripture was published.

Published in three stages: The Torah, 1962; The Prophets (Nevi'im), 1978; and The Writings (Kethuvim), 1982. Brought together in 1985 as the complete English Tanakh (Torah, Nevi'im, Kethuvim).

Some parts of these three sections were published separately: The Five Megillot and Jonah, 1969; Psalms, 1973; Isaiah, 1973; Jeremiah, 1974; Job, 1980.

1986 **The Navarre Bible** St. Mark, 1986; St. John, 1987. Houston: Lumen Christi.

1986 **New American Bible New Testament** Revised edition. Collegeville, MN: Liturgical Press.

Revision of the NAB New Testament published in 1970.

1986 **The Psalms** A new version by Roy Koeblitz. Palm.

1987 **The Holy Bible** English version for the deaf; translated from the original languages. Grand Rapids, MI: Baker Book House.

1988 **The Book of Isaiah** A New Translation with Interpretive Keys from the Book of Mormon, by Avraham Giliadi. Salt Lake City, UT: Deseret Book.

1988 **Christian Community Bible** Translated, presented and commented for the Christian communities of the Philippines and the Third World, and for those who seek God. 2d ed. Quezon City: Claretian Publications; Makati: Saint Paul Publications; Manila: Divine Word Publications.

20TH-CENTURY ENGLISH BIBLE VERSIONS cont.

1988 **New Testament** McCord's New Testament translation of the everlasting Gospel; translated by Hugo McCord. Freed-Hardeman College.

1988 **New Century** The Everyday Bible: New Testament. Minneapolis, MN: World Wide Publishers.

1988 **God's Word to the Nations** The New Testament. Ed. Phillip B. Giessler. Luther Bible Society Revision Committee Staff. Cleveland, OH: Biblion Publishers.

1988 **The Holy Gospel of John** A New Translation by P. Levi. Wilton, CT: Morehouse-Barlow.

1989 **God's New Covenant** A New Testament Translation. Translated from the Greek by Heinz W. Cassirer. Grand Rapids, MI: Eerdmans.

1989 **Revised English Bible with the Apocrypha** Oxford and Cambridge: Oxford University Press and Cambridge University Press.
A revision of the New English Bible published in 1970.

"" FOCUS QUOTE **The Bible was never intended to be a book for scholars and specialists only. From the very beginning it was intended to be everybody's book, and that is what it continues to be.** —F.F. Bruce

THE STORY OF THE BIBLE

"Behind and beneath the Bible, above and beyond the Bible, is the God of the Bible."

The Bible is God's written revelation of his will to men.

Its central theme is salvation through Jesus Christ.

The word *Bible* comes from the Greek word *biblos*, which means "book."

The Bible contains sixty-six books, written by forty authors, covering a period of approximately sixteen hundred years. The authors were kings and princes, poets and philosophers, prophets and statesmen. Some were learned in all the arts of the times and others were unschooled fishermen. Other books soon are out of date, but this Book spans the centuries.

The Old Testament was written mostly in Hebrew (a few short passages in Aramaic). About a hundred years (or more) before the Christian Era the entire Old Testament was translated into the Greek language. The New Testament was written in Greek.

The word *testament* means "covenant" or "agreement." The Old Testament is the covenant God made with man about his salvation before Christ came. The New Testament is the agreement God made with man about his salvation after Christ came.

In the Old Testament we find the covenant of law. In the New Testament we find the covenant of grace, which came through Jesus Christ. One led into the other (Galatians 3:17-25).

The Old commences what the New completes.

The Old gathers around Sinai—the New around Calvary.

The Old is associated with Moses—the New with Christ (John 1:17).

The Old Testament begins with God (Genesis 1:1). The New Testament begins with Christ (Matthew 1:1).

From Adam to Abraham we have the history of the human race. From Abraham to Christ we have the history of the chosen race. From Christ on we have the history of the church.

Interesting Facts

OLD TESTAMENT BOOKS

Law—five
History—twelve
Poetry—six
Prophecy—sixteen (Major, four; Minor, twelve)

NEW TESTAMENT BOOKS

The New Testament was written to reveal to us the character and teaching of Jesus Christ, the mediator of the New Covenant, by at least eight men, four of whom—Matthew, John, Peter, and Paul—were apostles; two—Mark and Luke—were companions of the apostles; and two—James and Jude—were brothers of Jesus. The books were written at various times during the second half of the first century.

The books in the New Testament may be grouped this way:

Gospels—four
History—one
Prophecy—one
Letters—twenty-one (Pauline, thirteen; General, eight)

The major themes of the New Testament are God, man, sin, redemption, justification, sanctification, glorification. In two words—*grace, glory.* In one word—*Jesus.*

OLD TESTAMENT—PRINCIPAL FACTS

1. Creation (Genesis 1:1–2:3)
2. Fall of man (Genesis 3)
3. Flood (Genesis 6–9)
4. Babel (Genesis 11:1-9)
5. Call of Abraham (Genesis 11:10–12:3)
6. Descent into Egypt (Genesis 46–47)
7. Plagues (Exodus 7–12)
8. Passover and Exodus (Exodus 12)
9. Giving of the Law (Exodus 19–24)
10. Wilderness wanderings (Numbers 13–14)
11. Conquest of the Promised Land (Joshua 11)
12. Dark ages of the chosen people (Judges)
13. Anointing of Saul as king (1 Samuel 9:27–10:1)
14. Golden age of Israel under David and Solomon, united kingdom (2 Samuel 5:4-5; 1 Kings 10:6-8)
15. The divided kingdom—Israel and Judah (1 Kings 12:26-33)
16. The Captivity (2 Kings 17; 25)
17. The Return (Ezra)

NEW TESTAMENT—PRINCIPAL FACTS

1. Early life of Christ
2. Ministry of Christ
3. Church in Jerusalem
4. Church extending to the Gentiles
5. Church in all the world

How to Study the Bible

Many say, "The Bible is so great. I don't know where to begin and don't know how to go on." This is often said quite earnestly and sincerely. And it is true that, unless we have some method, we will surely lose the very best results, even though we may spend much time with the Book.

G. Campbell Morgan once stated, "The Bible can be read from Genesis 1 to Revelation 22 at pulpit rate in seventy-eight hours." A lawyer challenged him on that. Morgan told him to go on and try it before he challenged. The lawyer went home and read the Bible in less than eighty hours.

Do you want to read the Bible through? Leave eighty hours for it. Plot out that time. How much time can you give each day? How many days a week? This is a highly practical proposition and should be seized by the very busiest. We are all busy and must take time for it. Unless we do, we will never come into any worthy knowledge of the Word, for it is impossible from pulpit ministry to get that knowledge of the Word that is possible and is indeed needful. The Bible reveals the will of God so as to lead man into it. Each book has a direct teaching. Find out what it is and shape your life by it.

Remember, the books of the Bible were

given to us by forty different men over a period of about sixteen hundred years. All these are brought together and are called "the Book." We can begin at Genesis and read on through to the end. There is no jar. We can pass from one style of literature to another as easily as though we were reading a story written by one hand and produced by one life, and indeed we have here a story produced by one Mind (2 Peter 1:21), though not written by one hand.

While divine, the Bible is human. The thought is divine and the revelation is divine, but the expression of the communication is human. *It was the Holy Spirit* [divine element] *within these godly men* [human element] *who gave them true messages from God* (2 Peter 1:21).

So we have here a book unlike all others. The Book—a divine revelation, a progressive revelation, a revelation of God to man communicated through men—moves on smoothly from its beginnings to its great end. In Genesis we have beginnings, in Revelation we have endings, and from Exodus to Jude we see how God carried out his purpose.

The Old Testament is the foundation; the New Testament is the superstructure. A foundation is of no value unless a building is built upon it. A building is impossible unless there is a foundation. So the Old Testament and New Testament are essential to one another. As Augustine said:

The New is in the Old contained,
The Old is in the New explained.

One Book, One History, One Story

The Bible is one book, one history, one story, his story. Behind ten thousand events stands God, the builder of history, the maker of the ages. Eternity bounds one side, eternity bounds the other side, and time is in between: Genesis—origins, Revelation—endings, and all the way between, God is working things out. You can go down into the minutest detail everywhere and see that there is one great purpose moving through the ages: the eternal design of the Almighty God to redeem a wrecked and ruined world.

The Bible is one book, and you cannot take it in pieces and expect to comprehend the magnificence of divine revelation. Don't suppose reading little scraps can ever be enough—we would scorn reading any other book, even the lightest novel, in this fashion. God has taken pains to give a progressive revelation, and we should take pains to read it from beginning to end. We must see it in its completeness, doing deep and consecutive work on the Bible itself. We must get back to the Book.

The Bible is not a book of texts—it is a story, a revelation, to be begun and pursued and ended as we start and continue other books. Don't divide it into short devotional paragraphs and think you have understood its messages. It may be excusable for someone who can hardly read to open the Bible and take whatever his eyes light upon as the message of God. Many people do that, but the Bible shouldn't be misused in that manner. We must come to it in a commonsense fashion. Believe that every book is about something, and read and reread until you find out what that something is.

First read the Book, not books about the Book, nor turn to the commentaries. They will come in good time, perhaps, but give the Book a chance to speak for itself and to make its own impression, to bear its own testimony.

The Word of God is alive, and every part is necessary to the perfection of the whole. We don't say that every part is equally important. If you were to ask me whether I would give up my finger or my eye, of course I would part with my finger. So with the Word of God. All is necessary to make a perfect whole, but some portions are more precious than others. You can't take away the Song of Solomon and have a perfect revelation. No one says the Song of Solomon is comparable with John's Gospel, but both are parts of an organism, and that organism is not complete if any part is missing.

Christ, the Living Word

The Old Testament is an account of a nation (the Jewish nation). The New Testament is an account of a Man (the Son of man). The nation was founded and nurtured by God in order to bring this man into the world (see Genesis 12:1-3).

God himself became a man so that we might know what to think of when we think of God (John 1:14; 14:9). His appearance on the earth is the central event of all history. The Old Testament sets the stage for it. The New Testament describes it.

As a man, Christ lived the most perfect life ever known. He was kind, tender, gentle, patient, and sympathetic. He loved people. He worked marvelous miracles to feed the hungry. Crowds—weary, pain-ridden, and heartsick—came to him, and he gave them rest (Matthew 11:28-30). It is said that if all the deeds of kindness that he did were written, the world could not contain the books (John 21:25).

Then he died—to take away the sin of the world and to become the Savior of mankind.

Then he rose from the dead. He is alive today. He is not merely a historical character but a living Person—the most important fact of history and the most vital force in the world today. And he promises eternal life to all who come to him.

The whole Bible is built around the story of Christ and his promise of everlasting life. It was written only so that we would believe and understand, know and love, and follow him.

Apart from any theory of inspiration or any theory of how the Bible books came to their present form or how much the text may have suffered in passing through the hands of editors and copyists or what is historical and what may be poetical—assume that the Bible is just what it appears to be. Accept the books as we have them in our Bible as units. Study them to know their contents. You will find there is a unity of thought that indicates that one Mind inspired the writing of the whole series of books, that it bears on its face the stamp of its Author, that it is in every sense the *Word of God.*

Source: *What the Bible Is All About*, Living Bible Edition, Henrietta C. Mears, Copyright © 1953, 1954, 1960, 1966, 1983 by Gospel Light Publications. Living Bible edition copyright © 1987 by Tyndale House Publishers, Inc. Used by permission.

“” FOCUS QUOTE

It is not possible ever to exhaust the mind of the Scriptures. It is a well that has no bottom. —St. John Chrysostom

OVERVIEW OF THE BOOKS OF THE BIBLE

THE OLD TESTAMENT

The first five books of the Bible tell the origins of the Jewish race and culture.

Genesis: The book of beginnings describes creation, the first rebellions against God, and God's choosing of Abraham and his offspring.

Exodus: God rescued the Israelites from slavery in Egypt and led them to the Sinai Desert. There, he gave Moses the laws to govern the new nation.

Leviticus: God set up laws for the Israelites, mostly regarding holiness and worship.

Numbers: Because of their rebellion and disobedience, the Israelites had to wander in a wilderness for 40 years before entering the promised land.

Deuteronomy: Just before his death, Moses made three emotional farewell speeches, recapping history and warning the Israelites against further mistakes.

HISTORY BOOKS

The next 12 books continue the history of the Israelites: they moved into the land of Canaan and established a kingdom that lasted almost 500 years.

Joshua: After Moses' death, Joshua commanded the armies that conquered much of the territory in the promised land.

Judges: The new nation fell into a series of dismal failures. God raised up leaders called "judges."

Ruth: This story of love and loyalty between

OVERVIEW OF THE BOOKS OF THE BIBLE cont.

two widows shines out brightly in an otherwise dark period.

1 Samuel: Samuel became a transition leader between the time of the judges and that of the kings. He appointed Israel's first king, Saul. After his own failure, Saul tried violently to prevent God's king-elect David from taking the throne.

2 Samuel: David, "a man after God's own heart," brought the nation together. But after committing adultery and murder, he was haunted by family and national crises.

1 Kings: Solomon succeeded David, with mixed success. At his death, a civil war tore apart the nation. Successive kings were mostly bad, and the prophet Elijah had dramatic confrontations with King Ahab.

2 Kings: This book continues the record of the rulers of the divided kingdom. None of the Northern kings followed God consistently, and so Israel was finally destroyed by an invader. The South, Judah, lasted much longer, but finally Babylon conquered Judah and deported its citizens.

1 Chronicles: The book opens with the most complete genealogical record in the Bible, then adds many incidents from the life of David (often the same as those in 2 Samuel).

2 Chronicles: Often paralleling the books of Kings, this book records the history of the rulers of Judah, emphasizing the good kings.

Ezra: After being held captive in Babylon for decades, the Jews were allowed to return to their homeland. Ezra, a priest, emerged from one of the first waves of refugees.

Nehemiah: Nehemiah returned from the Babylonian captivity after the temple had been rebuilt. He concentrated on restoring the protective wall around Jerusalem and joined Ezra in leading a religious revival.

Esther: This story is set among captive Jews in Persia. A courageous Jewish queen foiled a plan to exterminate her people.

BOOKS OF POETRY

Almost one-third of the Old Testament was originally written in poetry. These books concentrate on questions about pain, God, life, and love.

Job: The best man of his day suffered the greatest personal tragedy. The entire book deals with the question, "Why?"

Psalms: These prayers and hymns cover the full range of human emotion; together, they represent a personal journal of how to relate to God. Some were also used in public worship services.

Proverbs: The proverbs offer advice on every imaginable area of life. The style of wise living described here leads to a fulfilled life.

Ecclesiastes: A life without God, 'under the sun,' leads to meaninglessness and despair, says the Teacher in a strikingly modern book.

Song of Songs: This beautiful poem celebrates romantic and physical love.

BOOKS OF THE PROPHETS

During the years when kings ruled Israel and Judah, God spoke through prophets. Though some prophets did predict future events, their primary role was to call God's people back to him.

Isaiah: The most eloquent of the prophets, Isaiah analyzed the failures of all the nations around him and pointed to a future Messiah who would bring peace.

Jeremiah: Jeremiah led an emotionally tortured life, yet held to his stern message. He spoke to Judah in the last decades before Babylon destroyed the nation.

Lamentations: All Jeremiah's warnings about Jerusalem came true, and Lamentations records five poems of sorrow for the fallen city.

Ezekiel: Ezekiel spoke to the Jews who were captive in Babylon. He often used dramatic stories and "enacted parables" to make his points.

Daniel: A captive in Babylon, Daniel rose to the office of prime minister. Despite intense political pressure, he lived a model life of integrity and left highly symbolic prophecies about the future.

Hosea: By marrying a loose-living wife,

Hosea lived out his message: that Israel had committed spiritual adultery against God.

Joel: Beginning with a recent catastrophe in Judah (a locust plague), Joel foretold God's judgment on Judah.

Amos: A country boy, Amos preached to Israel at the height of its prosperity. His grim warnings focused on materialism.

Obadiah: Obadiah warned Edom, a nation bordering Judah.

Jonah: Jonah reluctantly went to Nineveh and found Israel's enemies responsive to God's message.

Micah: Micah exposed corruption in every level of society, but closed with a promise of forgiveness and restoration.

Nahum: Long after Jonah had stirred Nineveh to repentance, Nahum foretold the mighty city's total destruction.

Habakkuk: Habakkuk addressed his book to God, not people. In a frank dialogue with God, he discussed problems of suffering and justice.

Zephaniah: Zephaniah focused on the coming day of the Lord, which would purge Judah, resulting in a remnant used to bless the entire world.

Haggai: After returning from the Babylonian captivity, the Jews began rebuilding the temple of God. But before long they set aside that task to work on their own homes. Haggai reminded them to put God first.

Zechariah: Writing around the same time as Haggai, Zechariah also urged the Jews to work on the temple. He used a more uplifting approach, describing how the temple would point to the coming Messiah.

Malachi: The last Old Testament prophet, Malachi faced a nation that had grown indifferent. He sought to stir them from apathy.

THE NEW TESTAMENT

History Books The word gospel means "good news." Almost half the New Testament consists of four accounts of the life of Jesus and good news he brought to earth. Each of these four books, or Gospels, has a different focus and a different audience; taken together, they give a complete picture of Jesus' life and teaching. About a third of their pages are devoted to the events of his last week on earth, including the crucifixion and resurrection.

Acts continues the history into the period after Jesus left earth.

Matthew: Written to a Jewish audience, this Gospel links the Old and New Testaments. It presents Jesus as the Messiah and King promised in the Old Testament. Matthew emphasizes Jesus' authority and power.

Mark: Mark probably had pragmatic Roman readers in mind. His Gospel stresses action and gives a straightforward, blow-by-blow account of Jesus' work on earth.

Luke: A doctor, Luke was also a fine writer. His Gospel provides many details of human interest, especially in Jesus' treatment of the poor and needy. A joyful tone characterizes Luke's book.

John: John has a different, more reflective style than the other Gospels. Its author selected seven signs that point to Jesus as the Son of God and wove together everything else to underscore that point.

Acts: Acts tells what happened to Jesus' followers after he left them. Peter and Paul soon emerged as leaders of the rapidly spreading church.

THE LETTERS

The young church was nourished by apostles who set down their beliefs and messages in a series of letters. The first 13 such letters (Romans through Philemon) were written by the apostle Paul, who led the advance of Christianity to non-Jewish people.

Paul's Letters:

Romans: Written for a sophisticated audience, Romans sets forth theology in a logical, organized form.

1 Corinthians: A very practical book, 1 Corinthians takes up the problems of a tumultuous church in Corinth: marriage, factions, immorality, public worship, and lawsuits.

2 Corinthians: Paul wrote this follow-up letter to defend himself against a rebellion led by certain false apostles.

OVERVIEW OF THE BOOKS OF THE BIBLE cont.

Galatians: A short version of the message of Romans, this book addresses legalism. It shows how Christ came to bring freedom, not bondage to a set of laws.

Ephesians: Although written in jail, this letter is Paul's most optimistic and encouraging. It tells of the advantages a believer has in Christ.

Philippians: The church at Philippi ranked among Paul's favorites. This friendly letter stresses that joy can be found in any situation.

Colossians: Written to oppose certain cults, Colossians tells how faith in Christ is complete. Nothing needs to be added to what Christ did.

1 Thessalonians: Composed early in Paul's ministry, this letter gives a capsule history of one church, as well as Paûl's direct advice about specific problems.

2 Thessalonians: Stronger in tone than his first letter to the Thessalonians, the sequel goes over the same topics, especially the church's questions about Christ' second coming.

1 Timothy: As Paul neared the end of his life, he chose young men such as Timothy to carry on his work. His two letters to Timothy form a leadership manual for a young pastor.

2 Timothy: Written just before Paul's death, 2 Timothy offers Paul's final words to his young assistant.

Titus: Titus was left in Crete, a notoriously difficult place to nurture a church. Paul's letter gave practical advice on how to go about it.

Philemon: Paul urged Philemon, owner of runaway slave Onesimus, to forgive his slave and accept him as a brother in Christ.

OTHER LETTERS

Hebrews: No one knows who wrote Hebrews, but it probably first went to Christians in danger of slipping back into Judaism. It interprets the Old Testament, explaining many Jewish practices as symbols that prepared the way for Christ.

James: James, a man of action, emphasized the right kind of behavior for a believer. Someone who calls himself a Christian ought to act like it, James believed, and his letter spells out the specifics.

1 Peter: Early Christians often met violent opposition, and Peter's letter comforted and encouraged Christians who were being persecuted for their faith.

2 Peter: In contrast to Peter's first letter, this one focused on problems that sprang up from the inside. It warns against false teachers.

1 John: John could fill simple words—light, love, life—with deep meaning, and in this letter, he elegantly explains basic truths about the Christian life.

2 John: Warning against false teachers, John counseled churches on how to respond to them.

3 John: Balancing 2 John, this companion letter mentions the need to be hospitable to true teachers.

Jude: Jude gave a brief but fiery expose of heretics.

Revelation: A book of visions and symbols, Revelation is the only New Testament book that concentrates on prophecy. It completes the story, begun in Genesis, of the cosmic battle between good and evil being waged on earth. It ends with a picture of a new heaven and new earth.

A CHRONOLOGY OF OLD AND NEW TESTAMENT EVENTS

Old Testament (B.C.)

2166 .... Abram born
2091 .... Abram enters Canaan
2066 .... Isaac born
2006 .... Jacob and Esau born
1991 .... Abraham dies
1929 .... Jacob flees to Haran

1915 .... Joseph born
1898 .... Joseph sold into slavery
1886 .... Isaac dies
1885 ...... Joseph begins to rule in Egypt
1876 ...... Jacob's family comes to Egypt
1859 .... Jacob dies
1805 .... Joseph dies
1526 .... Moses born
1446 .... Exodus from Egypt
1406 .... Israel enters Canaan
1375-1050 .... Judges' rule
1367-1327 .... Othniel
1309-1229 .... Ehud
1209-1169 .... Deborah
1162-1122 .... Gideon
1105 .... Samuel born
1078-1072 .... Jepthath
1075-1055 .... Samson

United Kingdom

1050-1010 .... Saul's rule
1010-970 .... David's rule
970-930 .... Solomon's rule

Divided Kingdoms

JUDAH (KINGS/PROPHETS)

930-913 .... Rehoboam
910-869 .... Asa
872-848 .... Jehoshaphat
855-840 .... Obadiah
853-841 .... Jehoram
841-835 .... Athaliah
835-796 .... Joash
810-750 .... Joel
792-740 .... Azzariah (Uzziah)
750-735 .... Jotham
742-687 .... Micah
740-681 .... Isaiah
735-715 .... Ahaz
715-686 .... Hezekiah
697-642 .... Manasseh
664-612 .... Nahum
640-609 .... Zephaniah
640-609 .... Josiah
627-586 .... Jeremiah
609-598 .... Jehoiakim
605-589 .... Habakkuk
597 .... Jehoiachin
597-586 .... Zedekiah
c.587 .... Obadiah

586 .... Fall of Jerusalem

ISRAEL (KINGS/PROPHETS)

930-909 .... Jeroboam I
909-908 .... Nadab
908-886 .... Baasha
886-885 .... Elah
885 .... Zimri, Timri
885-874 .... Omri
875-848 .... Elijah
874-853 .... Ahab
852-841 .... Joram
848-797 .... Elisha
841-814 .... Jehu
814-798 .... Jehoahaz
798-782 .... Jehoash
793-753 .... Jeroboam II
785-775 .... Jonah
760-750 .... Amos
753-752 .... Zechariah
752 .... Shallum
752-742 .... Menahem
752-732 .... Pekah
750-715 .... Hosea
732-722 .... Hoshea
722 .... Fall of Northern Kingdom

CAPTIVITY

586 .... Babylonian Captivity

Prophets in exile:
605-530 .... Daniel
593-571 .... Ezekiel

Recovery

538 ... First group returns with Zerubbabel
537 .... Rebuilding of Temple begins
520 .... Haggai
520-480 .... Zechariah
516 .... Rebuilding of Temple finished
458 ...... Second group returns with Ezra
445 ...... Nehemiah comes to Jerusalem, begins first governorship
440-430 .... Malachi
433 .. Nehemiah begins second governorship
432-6 B.C. .... Between the Testaments

New Testament Events

6/5 B.C. .... Christ's birth
A.D. 6/7 .... Jesus in the temple
26 .... John the baptist begins his ministry

26/27 . . . . Christ is baptized, begins his ministry
30 . . . . Christ is crucified, resurrected, and enthroned
30 . . . . Pentecost
34/35 . . . . Paul's conversion
44 . . . . James, the apostle, is martyred
46-48 . . . . . Paul's first missionary journey
49/50 . . . . Jerusalem council
50-52 . . Paul's second missionary journey
53-57 . . . . . Paul's third missionary journey
59-62 . . . . . . Paul's imprisonment in Rome
67 . . . . Paul's second imprisonment
65-67 . . . . Peter martyred
68 . . . . Paul martyred
90-95 . . . . John exiled
c.100 . . . . John dies

New Testament Books

45-50 . . . . James
49 or 56 . . . . Galatians
50's . . . . Mark
50, 51 . . . . 1 & 2 Thessalonians
55, 56 . . . . 1 & 2 Corinthians
56/57 . . . . Romans
60 . . . . Luke
60's . . . . Matthew
60/61 . . . . Colossians, Philemon, Ephesians
61/62 . . . . Philippians
63 . . . . 1 Timothy
63 . . . . 1 Peter
64-68 . . . . Hebrews
64-72 . . . . Acts
65 . . . . Titus
65-67 . . . . 2 Peter
67 . . . . 2 Timothy
70-80 . . . . Jude
85-90 . . . . John, Epistles of John
95 . . . . Revelation

The People's Study Bible: The Living Bible Harold Lindsell, Ph.D., D.D., General Editor, Tyndale House Publishers, Inc., Wheaton, IL, © 1986: p.p. 1823-1826. From *New Bible Dictionary*; used by permission of InterVarsity Press.

IMPORTANT BIBLE WORDS

Certain words and ideas are found over and over again in the Bible because they refer to significant concepts that governed the lives of God's people. These words have come down through the centuries as aspects of church life and thought and, today also, reflect the essence of what Christians believe. The entries here are the most important words found in the Bible and in Christian theology.

Adoption The process through which a person who does not belong to a given family is formally brought into it and made a full, legal family member with the rights and responsibilities of that position. The practice of adoption was not common among the Jews, but was more widespread in the Greek and Roman world. The apostle Paul used the term to illustrate the truth that believers have been given the status of "sonship" in the heavenly family; they can call God "Father" (Romans 8:15; Galatians 4:6). Adoption makes it clear that our sonship is conferred on us, in distinction from Christ's, which is inherent.

Apostle "Someone who is sent," often "a messenger." In the New Testament the word refers particularly to twelve apostles whom Jesus selected to be with him and whom he sent out to preach and to cast out demons (Mark 3:14-15). Other individuals than the Twelve bore that title—for example, Paul and Barnabas (Acts 14:14). Apostles were important figures in the early church (1 Corinthians 12:28). They were appointed by Christ, not by men (Galatians 1:1), and they gave authoritative witness to what God had done in Christ (Acts 1:22).

Assurance Certainty of salvation, because of the promises of God and the effectiveness of Christ's atonement (1 John 5:13). The word does not occur often in the Bible, but the idea is more frequent. It is basic that people do not deserve their salvation because of their own efforts; that would leave them always uncertain, never knowing whether they had been good enough. But Christ did all that was needed, and we can rely on his perfect work. Further, believers have evidence of God's power in their lives (1 John

2:3-5; 3:19-21). Our assurance rests on the certainty that what God has begun he will complete (Philippians 1:6).

Atonement Literally "at-one-ment," the making at one of those who have been separated. The word is used of Christ's dying to bring God and sinners together. Sin had separated them (Isaiah 59:2) and made them enemies (Colossians 1:21); it was thus a very serious matter. A many-sided act was required to remove that sin; words like *redemption* and *reconciliation* bring out significant aspects of Christ's saving work. Whatever had to be done about sin, Christ's death did, and thus opened up salvation for sinners.

"" FOCUS QUOTE **I know the Bible is inspired because it finds me at a greater depth of my being than any other book.** —Samuel Taylor Coleridge

---

Christ English form of a Greek word meaning "anointed"; "Messiah" is the English form of the Hebrew word with the same meaning. In Old Testament days God anointed people for special service, especially the king (2 Samuel 1:14; 23:1) and the priest (Leviticus 4:3). Eventually the understanding developed that an outstanding "anointed one" would appear, who would do God's will in a very special way (Daniel 9:25-26). This great One is often referred to without the use of the term *anointed* (Isaiah 9:6-7; 11:1-9). The New Testament shows that Jesus was this chosen One, God's Messiah (John 4:25-26; cf. Matthew 23:10; Mark 9:41).

Conversion The decisive act in which a sinner turns away from sin in genuine repentance and accepts the salvation that Christ offers. The imagery in conversion is that of turning. A person is going along a road and realizes that he or she is on the wrong track. They will never reach the destination if they continue in that direction. So the person "turns," or "is converted." He or she ceases to go in the wrong direction and begins going in the right one. Conversion changes the direction of one's course of life from the wrong way to the right way, the way that God wants.

Covenant A solemn agreement, such as the pact between Jacob and Laban (Genesis 31:44). God's love and grace are shown in his readiness to make covenants with people. When God promised Noah that he would not again destroy the world with a flood, he made a covenant with him (Genesis 6:18; 9:9-17). A very important covenant existed between God and Israel (Exodus 24:1-8), which is pictured in the book of Hebrews as the "old covenant." When the people repeatedly broke that covenant, God promised a new covenant based on forgiveness and the writing of his law on people's hearts (Jeremiah 31:31-34). Jesus inaugurated this new covenant with his blood (Mark 14:24; 1 Corinthians 11:25).

Disciple In Bible times, a student. Whereas a student today studies a subject (law, architecture, or whatever), a disciple in olden days learned from a teacher. Attachment to a specific teacher was the essence of discipleship. The Pharisees and John the Baptist had disciples (Mark 2:18). The Jews saw themselves as disciples of Moses (John 9:28). The term is used often in the Gospels and Acts of the followers of Jesus. They learned from him and attached themselves wholeheartedly to him. It meant putting Christ before family and possessions. It meant taking up the cross (Luke 14:26-33). Today, too, to be a disciple of Jesus means total commitment.

Doctrine "Teaching"; used of the content rather than the act of teaching. The Greek word may be used of the doctrines of men (Matthew 15:9), but, more important, refers to the teaching of Jesus (Matthew 7:28) and later the teaching of his followers. "My teaching," Jesus said, "is not my own. It comes from him who sent me" (John 7:16; i.e., it is from God). The word was used of Christian doctrine (Acts

IMPORTANT BIBLE WORDS cont.

2:42), to which believers are to be wholeheartedly committed (Romans 6:17). It is important to "continue" in the doctrine (2 John 9) and to be able both to teach it and to refute those who oppose it (Titus 1:9).

Election Chosen by God. The idea of election goes back to Abraham (Genesis 12:1-3). God chose to make a nation of that patriarch's descendants. He chose Israel to be his people. He worked his purposes out through that one nation and in due course sent his Messiah as a Jew. After that, God continued to choose, or elect, people in accordance with his purpose (Romans 9:11), grace (Romans 11:5), love (1 Thessalonians 1:4), and foreknowledge (1 Peter 1:2). The "elect" can rely on God's concern for them (Luke 18:7) and on their sure salvation (Romans 8:33). They are to live lives befitting their status (Colossians 3:12-14). Mystery is inherent in the concept of election, because we also know that God desires the salvation of all persons (1 Timothy 2:4).

Expiation See *Propitiation*

Faith Relying on what God has done rather than on one's own efforts. In the Old Testament, *faith* is rarely mentioned. The word *trust* is used frequently, and verbs like *believe* and *rely* are used to express the right attitude to God. The classic example is Abraham, whose faith was reckoned as righteousness (Genesis 15:6). At the heart of the Christian message is the story of the cross: Christ's dying to bring salvation. Faith is an attitude of trust in which a believer receives God's good gift of salvation (Acts 16:30-31) and lives in that awareness thereafter (Galatians 2:20; cf. Hebrews 11:l).

Gospel "Good News." Our word *gospel* comes from two Old English words. There is no good news like the good news that God sent his Son to die on a cross to get rid of our sins. 1 Corinthians 15:1-11 summarizes the good news or gospel, that the apostle Paul preached. The term emphasizes the truth that salvation is entirely of grace. From its use for the central Christian message, the word came to be used as the title of each of the four books (Matthew, Mark, Luke, John) that tell the story of Jesus' life and atoning death.

Grace God's unmerited favor. The Greek words for *joy* and *grace* are related; grace causes joy. In the Christian understanding, nothing brings joy like the good news of what God has done in Christ to bring us salvation. Salvation by grace is "through faith—and this not from yourselves, it is the gift of God—not by works. . ." (Ephesians 2:8-9). God's grace also brings about qualities of conduct in the believer (2 Corinthians 9:8; 12:9; Ephesians 4:7). The word *grace* came to be used as a kind of prayer ("grace to you") in Christian greetings at the beginning and end of some of the New Testament letters (2 Corinthians 1:2; 13:14).

Heaven The abode of God (1 Kings 8:30) and of the angels (Mark 13:32); believers will be there in due course (1 Peter 1:4). The New Testament uses striking imagery to bring out the wonder and loveliness of heaven (gates of pearl and a street of gold—Revelations 21:21). Heaven means eternal joy in the presence of God.

Hell The abode of Satan and his angels (Matthew 25:41), described in the Bible with the imagery of eternal fire, outer darkness, being lost, perishing, and the like. It is impossible to envisage a state that can be described in so many different ways. Clearly it is horrible and is to be avoided at all costs (Mark 9:43).

Incarnation Literally, "en-flesh-ment" (Latin *carnis*— "flesh"); the doctrine that the Son of God became human (John 1:14). Jesus did not play at becoming a man but took on our flesh with all its problems and weaknesses. Incarnation, in the Christian understanding, means that Christ was both God and human.

Justification Legal term meaning "acquittal," a declaration that someone is in the right.

Sinners are in the wrong before God. They have broken his laws, they deserve punishment, but on the cross Christ took their place. Now, when they put their trust in Christ, they are declared to be in the right, acquitted, justified. The cross shows God to be just, not simply in the fact that he forgives, but in the way he forgives. To pass over sins would show mercy, but it would not show justice. Forgiveness by the way of the cross shows both (Romans 3:25-26).

“” FOCUS QUOTE **Every Christian must refer always and everywhere to the Scriptures for all his choices, becoming like a child before it, seeking in it the most effective remedy against all his various weaknesses, and not daring to take a step without being illuminated by the divine rays of those words.** —Pope John Paul II

Kingdom of God An expression first used by Jesus, although the idea that God reigns is everywhere in the Old Testament. The coming of the kingdom of God was the most frequent topic in the teaching of Jesus (Mark 1:15). It expresses the truth that God is a great God who does what he wills in human affairs. Specifically he wills to save people through the life, death, resurrection, and ascension of Jesus. In one sense the kingdom of God is a present reality. People enter it now (Matthew 21:31). In another sense it is future (Matthew 16:28). God's control is plain in both aspects, and in the end his sovereign will be perfectly done (1 Corinthians 15:28).

Last Judgment The evaluation of all humankind on the basis of works at Christ's return (Matthew 25:31-32). The wicked will be condemned because of their evil deeds. Salvation is by grace and through faith (Ephesians 2:8); the last judgment will test what believers have done with their lives (1 Corinthians 3:13-15). Some will be rewarded (Luke 19:16-19). Thus, although our salvation depends on what Christ has done, our eternal reward is related to the use we have made of God's gifts to us.

Love God's benevolent concern for humankind. All religions have some idea of the importance of love. Christian theology stresses the importance of love because God has revealed that he is love (1 John 4:8, 16). Love is both what God is and what he has done; God always acts in love. Love is a transitive reality—that is, it requires an object. In the Bible, love is described as personal (between persons) and selfless (desiring the best for others). Christians see God's love in sending his Son to die on the cross to save sinners (Romans 5:8; John 3:16; 1 John 4:10). Christians are to be known by the fact that they love God and others (John 13:34-35). Their love is not to be like the love the world has (Luke 6:32, 35). Love is best seen in actions and in most cases is to be identified with what we do—in our compassion and commitment to those around us, regardless of the object's virtue (1 John 4:19). Our loving attitudes and behavior are to reflect God's love. Jesus said that only two commands are needed to govern our lives: love of God and love of neighbor. If such love is demonstrated, all the law and prophets are fulfilled.

Messiah See *Christ.*

Predestination God's sovereign working out of his purposes in the affairs of nations and in individual lives. God predestines those who are saved (Romans 8:28-29; Ephesians 1:4-5). He does not stand on the sidelines, a helpless spectator (so to speak) until we, with our repentance and conversion, give him permission to do something. Unless our names were written "in the book of life from the creation of the world" (Revelation 17:8) we would not even make the motion of turning from sin. Predestination means that our salvation, from first to last, is God's work. See also *Election*.

Propitiation/Expiation Offering whatever will turn away anger; paying the penalty.

IMPORTANT BIBLE WORDS cont.

Propitiation has to do with persons, expiation with things. Sin arouses the wrath of God; if people are to be forgiven, something must be done about his anger. Jesus' death on the cross brought about a process of propitiation; it was the means by which divine anger was averted from sinners.

Redemption Originally, the payment of a price to secure the release of a prisoner of war. The word came to be used also of the release of a slave, and sometimes of a person under sentence of death (Exodus 21:28-30). Redemption always means the payment of a price to secure release. People who sin become slaves of sin (John 8:34); they cannot free themselves from that slavery. Christ's death on the cross was the payment of a ransom price (Mark 10:45) by which sinners are set free. Now that they are redeemed they must live as free people (1 Corinthians 6:19-20; Galatians 5:1).

Regeneration Being reborn; the subject of Jesus' discourse with Nicodemus in John 3 (cf. Titus 3:5). This word is not found often in Scripture, but the idea is important. Regeneration is seen to be the work of the Holy Spirit (John 3:5-8). The "natural man" always thinks of salvation (however understood) as resting in one's own hands, but Jesus taught that it is necessary for a divine work to take place if anyone is to be saved. Sinners must be reborn spiritually.

Remnant Something remaining. In the Old Testament some passages refer to total destruction of a nation (e.g., the Babylonians in Jeremiah 50:26). When God brings judgment on his people, however, he does not destroy the faithful with the wicked, but leaves a remnant (Ezekiel 6:8; Micah 2:12). The concept of a remnant stood for that part of the nation who were faithful even though most people rejected the ways of God (Isaiah 4:2-4. The fact of the existence of a remnant is said to be due to God himself (Isaiah 1:9; Zephaniah 3:12). The remnant, then, is the real people of God, a concept we also find in the New Testament, "a remnant chosen by grace" (Romans 11:5).

Repentance Sorrowing over and forsaking sin, a wholehearted turning away from all that is evil. This is more than regret or remorse, attitudes that point to sorrow over sin but no more. Repentance was looked for in Old Testament times (Ezekiel 14:6; 18:30). It was the first item in the preaching of John the Baptist (Matthew 3:1-2), Jesus (Matthew 4:17), and the apostles (Mark 6:12; cf. Acts 2:38). Beyond repentance, faith is needed. But repentance is indispensable. Sin must be forsaken decisively.

Resurrection The raising and transformation of a person who has died. Resuscitation means the bringing back of people to this life after they have left it, for example, the raising of the son of the widow of Nain (Luke 7:11-15) or of Lazarus (John 11). Resurrection is more than that. Jesus rose on the third day after he died, but his new body was transformed. It was not subject to the limitations of his former early life (Luke 24:16, 31; John 20:19). Jesus' resurrection, following his atoning death, is central to the Christian faith (1 Corinthians 15:14-19). Believers, too, will be resurrected (1 Thessalonians 4:16; 1 Corinthians 15:42-57).

Revelation Uncovering, making plain what was not known before. The word may be used of something God makes known during a church service (1 Corinthians 14:26), but more usually it has to do with something on a larger scale, like God's righteousness, wrath (Romans 1:17-18), or righteous judgment (Romans 2:5). It may be used to describe a book (Revelation 1:1). God reveals things through the Spirit (1 Corinthians 2:10). The gospel is not something people have made up but has been revealed by Christ (Galatians 1:11-12). The fullness of revelation awaits the return of Christ (2 Thessalonians 1:7; 1 Peter 1:13).

Righteousness Right standing, specifically before God. Among the Greeks, righteousness was an ethical virtue. Among the Hebrews it was a legal concept; the righteous man was the one who got the verdict of acceptability when tried at the bar of God's justice. Christ's death took away our sins and made it possible for sinners to have "the righteousness of God," i.e., right standing before God (Romans 1:16-17; 3:22; 5:17). That gift of righteousness is to be followed by upright living (Romans 6:13-14).

Salvation Deliverance of various kinds, for example, deliverance from the enemy (Exodus 14:13). In the Bible it is God who brings salvation from temporal as well as spiritual ills. Thus in the Gospels, referring to his miraculous healings, Jesus sometimes says, "Your faith has saved you," meaning "healed you" (Luke 18:42 KJV). Characteristically, the term refers to salvation from sin (Romans 1:16; 1 Thessalonians 5:9). Salvation means the decisive defeat of sin on the cross, but also victory over evil in a believer's daily life. Its full content will be realized only in the life to come (Hebrews 9:28; 1 Peter 1:5).

Sanctification The process of developing holiness. God said to Israel, "Be holy, because I am holy" (Leviticus 11:44-45). Because God wants us to become like him, it is necessary that his people be a special kind of people, holy men and women. The basic idea in sanctification is "being set apart for God; those thus set apart live in a way that is pleasing to God. They have no power of their own to do that, but God enables them (2 Corinthians 3:17-18). Sanctification is not an option. God requires it of all his people (1 Thessalonians 4:3).

Second Coming Christ's return at the end of the world to establish God's kingdom (1 Corinthians 15:23-25). The New Testament does not use this expression; it refers simply to "the coming" (*parousia*), also called a "reveal(ing)" of Jesus (1 Corinthians 1:7), or an "appearing" (Titus 2:13). There is dispute about the relationship of Christ's second coming to the thousand years, or millennium (Revelation 20:4), but none as to the fact that it will be God's decisive and indispensable intervention. Christ's coming to destroy all evil will be the culmination of his redemptive work.

Sin Anything that fails to conform to the law of God. Evil is a complex phenomenon in the Scriptures. The idea of sin is conveyed by a variety of expressions with meanings like missing the mark, rebelling, going astray, transgressing, stumbling, etc. Basically "sin is lawlessness" (1 John 3:4), referring to an inward attitude as well as to the breaking of written commandments. All people commit sin (1 Kings 8:46; Romans 3:23). To deny that we have sinned is to make God a liar (1 John 1:10); all his dealings with humanity are on the basis that we are sinners. But the blood of Jesus cleanses from all sin (1 John 1:7).

Sovereignty Term used to describe the fact that God is the supreme ruler of everything. God created the world and all that is in it. He sustains the entire created order in existence. He guides the affairs of human beings and nations. He providentially interacts with all that takes place. He works for the good of the world and finally will bring all things to a satisfactory conclusion. Because he is God, he has the absolute right to work his will. Sometimes sovereignty is misunderstood to mean that God forces his will on people and that we are not free to choose. That is false. God's sovereignty includes the free choices of human beings. What makes God's sovereignty effective is that his will is ultimately done—sometimes along with, sometimes in spite of, our free choices.

Spiritual Gifts Special gifts of the Spirit (*charismata*; e.g., Romans 12:6-8; 1 Corinthians 12:4-11, 28-31). There is some dispute as to whether these gifts were all meant as permanent endowments of the Christian church or as gifts only for its early days. In modern times, charismatics claim to exercise particular gifts, especially "tongues," "healing," and "prophecy." Other believers emphasize the fruit

IMPORTANT BIBLE WORDS cont.

of the Spirit more than spiritual gifts (Galatians 5:22-23).

Tithe Word meaning "tenth," used of the offering of a tenth for religious purposes. Abraham gave a tenth to Melchizedek, the priest-king (Genesis 14:18-20). The Israelites were required to give a tithe to the Levites (Numbers 18:21, 24), and the Levites in turn were to give a tithe of the tithe to the priests (Numbers 18:25-28). The tithe was taken from things like grain, fruits, and animals (Leviticus 27:30-32). There is no command to tithe in the New Testament (cf. 1 Corinthians 16:2), but many Christians believe that the concept is a useful guide in their giving.

Tongues Speaking in a language one has not learned. Luke wrote of a gift of tongues on the day of Pentecost (Acts 2:4-6), when everybody understood what was being said. Elsewhere we read of the Spirit's enabling people to speak in words that neither they nor anyone else understood unless they had another gift, that of interpretation (1 Corinthians 12:10, 28). The possessor of the gift of tongues used it to speak about God, but edified nobody but himself, Paul said (1 Corinthians 14:2-4). His mind was not active (1 Corinthians 14:14). Paul did not forbid the use of the gift, however; he spoke in tongues himself (1 Corinthians 14:18). But he regulated its use (1 Corinthians 14:27-28) and saw edification as a more important consideration (1 Corinthians 14:4-5).

Wrath of God In Scripture, God's strong and vigorous opposition to everything evil. There is a Greek verb that can be used both of anger and of the swelling of buds as the sap rises. It points to the kind of anger that results from a settled and consistent disposition, and not to a losing of one's temper. God's wrath is like that, rather than like human anger on a grand scale. With us, wrath always has elements of passion, lack of self-control, and irrationality. The wrath of God does not.

"" FOCUS QUOTE

The New Testament holds up a strong light by which a man can read even the small print of his soul. —John A. Hutton

EVERYDAY PHRASES IN THE BIBLE

Identify the book and, if possible, the chapter and verse where these commonly used phrases originated.

1. The skin of my teeth.
2. Wolf in sheep's clothing.
3. Salt of the earth.
4. Holier than thou.
5. Woe is me!
6. Can a leopard change his spots?
7. A drop in a bucket.
8. Eat, drink, and be merry.
9. Pride goeth before a fall.
10. Give up the ghost.
11. Spare the rod and spoil the child.
12. My brother's keeper.
13. Fat of the land.
14. A lamb for the slaughter.
15. The blind leading the blind.

ANSWERS

1. "I am escaped with the skin of my teeth" (Job 19:20).
2. "Beware of false prophets, which come to you in

sheep's clothing, but inwardly they are ravening wolves" (Matthew 7:15).
3. "Ye are the salt of the earth" (Matthew 5:13).
4. "I am holier than thou" (Isaiah 65:5).
5. "Woe is me! for I am undone" (Isaiah 6:5).
6. "Can the Ethiopian change his skin, or the leopard his spots?" (Jeremiah 13:23).
7. "Behold, the nations are as a drop of a bucket, and are counted as the small dust of the balance" (Isaiah 40:15).
8. "A man hath no better thing under the sun, than to eat, and to drink and to be merry" (Ecclesiastes 8:15).
9. "Pride goeth before destruction, and an haughty spirit before a fall" (Proverbs 16:18).
10. "But man dieth, and wasteth away; yea, man giveth up the ghost, and where is he?" (Job 14:10).
11. "He that spareth the rod hateth his son" (Proverbs 13:24).
12. "Am I my brother's keeper?" (Genesis 4:9).
13. "And he shall eat the fat of the land" (Genesis 45:18).
14. "He is brought as a lamb to the slaughter" (Isaiah 53:7).
15. "If a blind man leads a blind man, both will fall into a pit" (Matthew 15:14).

WHO DID WHAT FIRST?

1. Who had the first birthday party in the Bible?
2. Where was the first beauty contest in the Bible, and who won?
3. Who was the first Christian martyr?
4. What is the first dream mentioned in the Bible?
5. What is the first war mentioned in the Bible?
6. Who was the first drunk?
7. Where was the first piggy bank?
8. Who was the first person to fall asleep during a sermon?
9. What is the first commandment in the Bible?
10. What is the first purchase of land in the Bible?
11. What was the first instance of book burning?
12. What was the first military coup in Israel?
13. Who used the first pseudonym?
14. Who built the first city?
15. Who was the first hunter?
16. Who was the first murderer?
17. What is the first book of the Bible named after a woman?
18. Who is the first prophet mentioned in the Bible?
19. Where did Jesus work his first miracle?
20. What was the first of the ten plagues of Egypt?
21. Who was the first king of Israel?
22. Who were the first foreign missionaries?
23. Who was the first shepherdess?
24. Who was the first single man to be exiled?
25. Who was the first judge of Israel?
26. Who was the first disciple chosen by Jesus?
27. Who wore the first bridal veil?
28. Who told the first lie?
29. Who was the first priest mentioned in Scripture?
30. Who wore the first ring?
31. What was the first city called?
32. What was the first animal out of the ark?
33. Where were the disciples first called Christians?
34. Who took the first census of the Hebrews?
35. Who was the first shepherd?
36. Who were the first exiles?
37. Who were the first twins?
38. Who constructed the first altar?
39. Who built the first Jerusalem temple?
40. Who planted the first garden?
41. Who was the first metal craftsman?
42. Who was the first farmer?
43. Who was the first polygamist?
44. What is the first commandment with a promise attached to it?
45. Who was the first apostle to be martyred?
46. Who was the first child mentioned in the Bible?
47. Who was the first daughter mentioned by name?
48. What is the first color mentioned in the Bible?
49. Who planted the first vineyard?

ANSWERS

1. Pharaoh, at the time Joseph was in Egypt (Genesis 40:20)

2. The one at the court of Persian ruler Ahasuerus. The winner was Esther (Esther 2).
3. Stephen (Acts 6:7—8:2)
4. The dream of Abimelech, in which he was told to return Sarah to Abraham (Genesis 20:3-8)
5. The war of the kings of the north, led by Chedorlaomer, king of Elam (Genesis 14)
6. Noah, who planted a vineyard after leaving the ark (Genesis 9:21)
7. In the temple at Jerusalem. It was a chest, ordered by King Joash, who had a hole bored in the lid to keep priests from stealing funds (2 Kings 12)
8. Eutychus, who dozed off and fell out of a window during Paul's sermon (Acts 20:9)
9. "Be fruitful and multiply" (Genesis 1:28)
10. Abraham bought the Cave of Machpelah as a tomb for Sarah (Genesis 23:3-20)
11. Jeremiah's scroll, sent to King Jehoiakim, was burnt piece by piece as it was being read to the king (Jeremiah 36:21-23)
12. Absalom led an attempt to overthrow his father, David (2 Samuel 15–18)
13. Esther, whose real name was Hadassah (Esther 2:7)
14. Cain (Genesis 4:17)
15. Nimrod (Genesis 10:9)
16. Cain (Genesis 4:8)
17. Ruth.
18. Abraham (Genesis 20:7)
19. Cana (John 2:1-11)
20. The river turns to blood (Exodus 7:14-24)
21. Saul (1 Samuel 10:1)
22. Paul and Barnabas (Acts 13)
23. Rachel (Genesis 29:9)
24. Cain (Genesis 4:12)
25. Othniel (Judges 3:9)
26. Simon Peter (John 1:42)
27. Rebekah (Genesis 24:65)
28. The serpent (Genesis 3:4)
29. Melchizedek (Genesis 14:18)
30. Pharaoh (Genesis 41:42)
31. Enoch, named after Cain's son (Genesis 4:17)
32. The raven (Genesis 8:7)
33. The raven (Genesis 8:7)
34. The priest Eleazar (Numbers 26:1-2)
35. Abel (Genesis 4:2)
36. Adam and Eve, driven from the garden (Genesis 3:24)
37. Jacob and Esau (Genesis 25:23-26)
38. Noah (Genesis 8:20)
39. Solomon (1 Kings 6)
40. God (Genesis 2:8)
41. Tubal-cain (Genesis 4:22)
42. Cain (Genesis 4:2)
43. Lamech (Genesis 4:19)
44. "Honor your father and mother" (Deuteronomy 5:16; Ephesians 6:2-3) The promise is that the person will have a long life if he honors his parents.
45. James (Acts 12:1,2)
46. Cain (Genesis 4:1)
47. Naamah, daughter of Lamech (Genesis 4:22)
48. Green—"I have given every green herb" (Genesis 1:30)
49. Noah (Genesis 9:20)

The Holy Scriptures tell us what we could never learn any other way: they tell us what we are, who we are, how we got here, why we are here and what we are required to do while we remain here. —A. W. Tozer

WHAT JONAH FELT LIKE

They picked up Jonah and threw him overboard into the raging sea—and the storm stopped! . . . Now the Lord had arranged for a great fish to swallow Jonah. And Jonah was inside the fish three days and three nights. Jonah 1:15, 17 TLB

In February 1891, the ship *Star of the East* was off the Falkland Islands when the crew spotted an 80-foot sperm whale. Two rowboats filled with crewmen were launched to capture the monster. Closing in, one harpooner let go his weapon and shafted the whale, which lashed out, almost overturning the boats. Returning to the ship with their dead whale, the crewmen realized one sailor, James Bartley, was missing. It was decided he had been tossed overboard in the fight and had drowned.

Six hours later the crewmen began removing the blubber from the dead beast. By midnight the task was still unfinished, and the sailors went to bed. In the morning, they resumed their job. Then the unexpected happened. According to M. de Parville, editor of the *Journal des Debats,* writing in Paris in 1914, "Suddenly the sailors were started by something in the stomach which gave spasmodic signs of life. Inside was found the missing sailor, James Bartley, doubled up and unconscious. He was placed on deck and treated to a bath of seawater which soon revived him, but his mind was not clear and he was placed in the captain's quarters." Recovering, Bartley recalled being hit by the whale's tail and that he had been "encompassed by great darkness, and he felt he was slipping along a smooth passage that seemed to move and carry him forward. His hands came in contact with a yielding, slimy substance, which seemed to shrink from his touch. He could easily breathe, but the heat was terrible. It seemed to open the pores of his skin and draw out his vitality. The next he remembered he was in the captain's cabin."

Except for the fact that his face, neck, and hands had been bleached white, Bartley—like Jonah—survived the belly of the monster.

DISTINCTIVE BIBLE PERSONALITIES

1. Earliest:	**Adam**	world's first human being	Gen. 2:7
2. Oldest:	**Methuselah**	son of Enoch, who lived to be 969	Gen. 5:27
3. Strongest:	**Samson**	carnal Nazarite whom God used to deliver Israel from the Philistines	Judg. 14:6; 15:5
4. Wisest:	**Solomon**	king of Israel and son of David	1 Kings 3:12
5. Richest:	**Solomon**		1 Kings 10:23
6. Tallest:	**Goliath**	over nine feet tall, killed in battle by David	1 Sam. 17:4
7. Shortest:	**Zacchaeus**	who climbed a sycamore tree to see Jesus	Luke 19:3-4
8. Fattest:	**Eglon**	Moabite king killed by the judge Ehud	Judg. 3:17
9. Meekest:	**Moses**	Israel's great lawgiver and author of Scripture's first five books	Num. 12:3
10. Cruelest:	**Manasseh**	who shed blood from one end of Judah to the other but later repented	2 Chr. 33:1-13
11. Fastest:	**Asahel**	described in Scripture as "light of foot as a wild roe"	2 Sam. 2:18
12. Greatest of the prophets:	**John the Baptist**	forerunner of Christ	Matt. 11:11
13. Guiltiest:	**Judas**	who betrayed the Savior for 30 pieces of silver	Matt. 27:3-5
14. Proudest:	**Nebuchadnezzar**	Babylonian king who destroyed Jerusalem and was later humbled by God himself	Dan. 4
15. Most Beautiful:	**Esther**	Jewish queen who saved her people from the first holocaust attempt in history	Esther 2:7
16. Most Traveled:	**Paul**	the great theologian and missionary	Acts 13:4; 15:36; 18:23
17. Most Sorrowful:	**Jeremiah**	persecuted by his own countrymen for preaching on sin and who saw his beloved Jerusalem destroyed	Jer. 9:1; Lam. 1:12

18. Most Persecuted:	**Job**	attacked by Satan, totally misunderstood by his wife, and criticized by his friends	Job 1–2
19. Most Lovestruck:	**Jacob**	who agreed to work seven years for the hand of Rachel	Gen. 29:18-20
20. Most Frightened:	**Belshazzar**	whose knees knocked as the handwriting on the wall appeared	Dan. 5:6
21. Most Rash:	**Jephthah**	who vowed to offer a special sacrifice if God would allow him to win a battle. The sacrifice turned out to be his daughter	Judg. 11:30
22. Most Doubtful:	**Thomas**	who said he could not believe in Christ's resurrection until he saw and touched the Savior	John 11:16; 20:24-29

FOCUS QUOTE

It ain't those parts of the Bible that I can't understand that bother me; it is the parts that I do understand. —Mark Twain

WHAT IS GOD LIKE?

23 Facts about God

1. God is self-existent . . . . . Exod. 3:13-14
2. God is self-sufficient . . . . . Ps. 50:10-12
3. God is eternal . . . . . Deut. 33:27; Ps. 90:2
4. God is infinite . . . . . 1 Kings 8:22-27; Jer. 23:24
5. God is omnipresent . . . . . Ps. 139:7-12
6. God is omnipotent . . . . . Gen. 18:14; Rev. 19:6
7. God is omniscient . . . . . Ps. 139:2-6; Isa. 40:13-14
8. God is wise . . . . . Prov. 3:19; 1 Tim. 1:17
9. God is immutable . . . . . Heb. 1:10-12; 13:8
10. God is sovereign . . . . . Isa. 46:9-11
11. God is incomprehensible . . . . . Job 11:7-19; Rom. 11:33
12. God is holy . . . . . Lev. 19:2; 1 Pet. 1:15
13. God is righteous and just . . . . . Ps. 119:137
14. God is true . . . . . John 17:3; Titus 1:1-2
15. God is faithful . . . . . Deut. 7:9; Ps. 89:1-2
16. God is light . . . . . James 1:17; 1 John 1:5
17. God is good . . . . . Ps. 107:8
18. God is merciful . . . . . Ps. 103:8-17
19. God is gracious . . . . . Ps. 111:4; 1 Pet. 5:10
20. God is love . . . . . John 3:16; Rom. 5:8
21. God is spirit . . . . . John 4:24
22. God is one . . . . . Deut. 6:4-5; Isa. 44:6-8
23. God is a Trinity . . . . . Matt. 28:19; 2 Cor. 13:14

QUESTIONS PEOPLE WOULD LIKE TO ASK GOD

Suppose you could ask God any *three* questions on this list. What would they be?

	National %
Will there ever be lasting world peace?	37
How can I be a better person?	33
What does the future hold for me and my family?	31
Will there ever be a cure for all diseases?	28
Why is there suffering in the world?	28
Is there life after death?	26
What is heaven like?	22
Will man ever love his fellow man?	21
Why is there evil in the world?	16
When will the world end?	16
Why was man created?	10
Don't know/Don't believe in God	8

Note: Percentages add to more than 100% due to multiple responses.

Gallup Survey for the Christian Broadcasting Network, Inc. Taken from *100 Questions and Answers.* Published by Princeton Religion Research Center. © 1989 by George Gallup, Jr., and Sarah Jones. Used by permission.

QUESTIONS GOD ASKS PEOPLE

Whom did God ask:

1. "How long will this people provoke me?" (Hint: a leader.)
2. "Whom shall I send, and who will go for us?" (Hint: a prophet.)
3. "Have I any pleasure at all that the wicked should die?" (Hint: a prophet.)
4. "Doest thou well to be angry?" (Hint: a reluctant prophet.)
5. "Who told thee that thou wast naked?"
6. "Why is thy countenance fallen? If thou doest well, shalt thou not be accepted?" (Hint: a farmer.)
7. "How long wilt thou mourn for Saul, seeing I have rejected him from reigning over Israel?" (Hint: a judge and prophet.)
8. "I am the Lord, the God of all flesh; is there anything too hard for me?" (Hint: a prophet.)
9. "Son of man, can these bones live?" (Hint: a prophet.)
10. "Who is this that darkeneth counsel by words without knowledge?" (Hint: a righteous man.)
11. "Who hath made man's mouth?" (Hint: a leader.)
12. "What is this that thou hast done?" (Hint: a woman.)
13. "Shall the clay say to him that fashioneth it, What makest thou?" (Hint: a foreign king.)
14. "Shall seven years of famine come unto thee in thy land? Or wilt thou flee three months before thine enemies?" (Hint: a king.)
15. "Shall I not spare Nineveh, that great city?" (Hint: a prophet.)
16. "Hast thou an arm like God? Or canst thou thunder with a voice like him?" (Hint: a righteous man.)
17. "Why is this people of Jerusalem slidden back by a perpetual backsliding?" (Hint: a prophet.)
18. "Have I not commanded thee? Be strong and of good courage; be not afraid." (Hint: a conqueror.)
19. "Is anything too hard for the Lord?" (Hint: a patriarch.)
20. "Hast thou killed, and also taken possession?" (Hint: a king.)

ANSWERS

1. Moses (Numbers 14:11)
2. Isaiah (6:8)
3. Ezekiel (18:23)
4. Jonah (4:9)
5. Adam (Genesis 3:11)
6. Cain (Genesis 4:6-7)
7. Samuel (1 Samuel 16:1)
8. Jeremiah (32:26-27)
9. Ezekiel (37:3)
10. Job (38:2)
11. Moses (Exodus 4:11)
12. Eve (Genesis 3:13)
13. Cyrus (Isaiah 45:1-9)
14. David (2 Samuel 24:13)
15. Jonah (4:11)
16. Job (40:9)
17. Jeremiah (8:4-12)
18. Joshua (1:1, 9)
19. Abraham (Genesis 18:13)
20. Ahab (1 Kings 21:19)

Taken from *The Complete Book of Bible Trivia.* Copyright © 1988 by J.Stephen Lang. Published by Tyndale House Publishers. Used by permission.

100 BEST-SELLING REFERENCE BOOKS

This list was compiled from information supplied by publishers. The first sales figure shown for each entry is the number of copies sold from June 1988 through May 1989; the second figure is the total number sold in the title's history with the publisher.

Although the books are ranked according to the total sold in the past year, not all publishers granted permission for sales totals to be published. Unreleased or unavailable figures are designated by "n.a.," but the books are ranked in their proper position.

A "c" preceding the ISBN number indicates a cloth edition; a "p" indicates a paperback edition.

1. **Halley's Bible Handbook** H. H. Halley. Zondervan ISBN: c 0-310-25720-4 © 1979 n.a. This book provides a concise Bible commentary, archaeological facts, maps, and a record of church history.
2. **Harper's Bible Commentary** James Mays, editor. Harper & Row ISBN: c 0-06-065541-0 © 1988. 52,000 / 52,000. This fully illustrated volume helps readers understand the Old and New Testaments and Apocrypha.
3. **The Practical Bible Dictionary and Concordance** Barbour ISBN: p 0-916441-28-8 © 1985. 51,516 / 340,998. This volume includes a concise Bible dictionary, a concordance, a section of Bible facts and figures, and a course on how to begin regular Bible study.
4. **Strong's Exhaustive Concordance of the Bible** James Strong. World Bible Publishers ISBN: c 0-529-06679-3 © 1980, 1986. 42,607 / n.a. This edition of the century-old reference offers larger type, Christ's words in red, and Hebrew-Greek keying.
5. **Cruden's Complete Concordance** Alexander Cruden. Zondervan ISBN: p 0-310-22921-9, c -22920-0, 22910-3 © 1949 n.a. This reference includes more than 200,000 entries for both KJV and RSV texts.
6. **The New Strong's Concordance of the Bible, Popular Edition** James Strong. Thomas Nelson ISBN: c 0-8407-4951-1 © 1985. 42,000 / 263,642. Designed for laypeople, this concordance lists words not included in the popular edition but featured in the exhaustive edition.
7. **The New Compact Bible Dictionary** T. Alton Bryant, editor. Zondervan ISBN: p 0-310-22082-3, c -22080-7 © 1967 n.a. This volume provides concise definitions of people, places, objects, and events.
8. **Matthew Henry's Commentary on the Whole Bible** Matthew Henry. Zondervan ISBN: c 0-310-26010-8 © 1961 n.a. Henry's classic devotional commentary has been condensed here to one volume.
9. **Serendipity Bible Study Book** Lyman Coleman. Zondervan ISBN: p 0-310-25081-1 © 1986 n.a. This NIV study companion helps group leaders prepare to teach New Testament material.
10. **What the Bible Is All About** Henrietta Mears. Regal Books/Gospel Light ISBN: c 0-8307-6902-9, p 0-8307-0862-2 © 1953. 32,773 / 379,000. Emphasizing themes, this book gives an overview of the Bible.
11. **Smith's Bible Dictionary** William Smith. Barbour ISBN: p 1-55748-017-6 © 1987. 25,547 / 38,135. This volume defines and explains thousands of significant biblical words.
12. **Bible Knowledge Commentary—New Testament** John Walvoord and Roy Zuck. Victor Books ISBN: c 0-88207-812-7 © 1983 n.a. This verse-by-verse exposition is based on the New International Version.
13. **Expository Dictionary of Bible Words** Lawrence Richards. Zondervan ISBN: c 0-310-39000-1 © 1985 n.a. Richards defines 1,500 English Bible words in their biblical language context.
14. **Vine's Expository Dictionary of Biblical Words, Revised** W. E. Vine, et al.

Thomas Nelson ISBN: c 0-8407-7559-8 © 1985. 22,000 / 117,910. This edition includes a modern typeface and two-column format. It's keyed to *Strong's Exhaustive Concordance* and other references.

15. **Nelson's Illustrated Bible Dictionary** Herbert Lockyer Sr., editor. Thomas Nelson ISBN: c 0-8407-4955-4 © 1986. 21,000 / 50,388. With 5,500 entries based on the New King James text, this volume also offers maps, charts, photos, and tables of information.
16. **The New Strong's Concordance of the Bible, Popular Edition** James Strong. Thomas Nelson ISBN: c 0-8407-4951-1 © 1985. 20,000 / 80,000. This conveniently sized commentary offers many features of the *New Strong's Exhaustive Concordance.*
17. **Christianity Through the Centuries** Earle Cairns. Zondervan ISBN: c 0-310-38360-9 © 1954, 1981 n.a. This church history covers the Western church from 5 B.C. to the present, with text, charts, maps, and illustrations.
18. **The New Unger's Bible Dictionary** Merrill Unger, et al. Moody ISBN: c 0-8024-9037-9 © 1988 n.a. With almost 6,800 articles and 500 photos, this volume defines unfamiliar biblical terms and names.
19. **Bible Questions and Answers** Thomas Nelson ISBN: c 0-8407-2879-4 © 1987. 18,000 / 90,253. The 6,000 questions and answers in this book are organized under the following subjects: history, poetry, prophecy, Gospels, acts of the apostles, and Epistles.
20. **Nelson's New Compact Illustrated Bible Dictionary** Lawrence Urdang, editor. Thomas Nelson ISBN: p 0-8407-5636-4 © 1978. 18,000 / 136,777. This book contains descriptions of biblical places, names, events, and books.
21. **The Compact Survey of the Bible** John Balchin, editor. Bethany House ISBN: p 0-87123-964-7 © 1987. 17,907 / 41,342. This concise overview of the Bible offers insight on key themes and primary messages and points to applications.
22. **Cruden's Concordance** Alexander Cruden. Barbour ISBN: p 1-55748-015-X © 1987. 17,615 / 29,513. This title includes more than 200,000 entries.
23. **How to Read the Bible for All Its Worth** Gordon Fee and Douglas Stuart. Zondervan ISBN: p 0-310-3736-1 © 1982 n.a. This book helps readers understand the Bible's messages and purposes.
24. **The Teacher's Commentary** Lawrence Richards. Victor Books ISBN: c 0-89693-810-7 © 1987 n.a. Including maps and charts, this volume helps teachers explain and apply every portion of the Bible.
25. **Willmington's Book of Bible Lists** Harold Willmington. Tyndale ISBN: p 0-8423-8803-6 © 1987 n.a. This reference offers biblical information in readily accessible groups, categories, and lists.
26. **The New Manners and Customs of Bible Times** Ralph Gower. Moody ISBN: c 0-8024-5954-4 © 1987 n.a. This book discusses the lifestyle and customs of the Bible's writers and characters.
27. **The Bible Almanac** James Packer, et al., editors. Thomas Nelson ISBN: c 0-8407-5162-1 © 1980. 17,000 / 314,759. This is a layperson's guide to the people and cultures of Bible times.
28. **The Hard Sayings of the Old Testament** Walter Kaiser. InterVarsity ISBN: p 0-8308-1221-0 © 1988. 16,739 / 16,739. Kaiser clarifies 70 of the Old Testament's enigmatic statements.
29. **Lewis Sperry Chafer Systematic Theology, Abridged** Lewis Sperry Chafer and John Walvoord, editor. Victor Books ISBN: c 0-89693-567-1 © 1988. 16,257/ 16,925. This two-volume work discusses systematic soteriology, ecclesiology, eschatology, and more.
30. **Expository Dictionary of New Testament Words** W. E. Vine. Zondervan ISBN: p 0-310-33781-X © 1937, 1981 n.a. Combining the original four volumes into one, this classic provides precise meanings of New Testament words and phrases.

100 BEST-SELLING REFERENCE BOOKS cont.

31. **New Bible Dictionary** J. D. Douglas, editor. Tyndale ISBN: c 0-8423-4667-8 © 1982 n.a. More than 2,000 entries discuss all the books, people, key words, and major doctrines of the Bible and provide background historical information.
32. **Bible Knowledge Commentary—Old Testament** John Walvoord and Roy Zuck. Victor Books ISBN: c 0-88207-813-5 © 1985 n.a. This verse-by-verse exposition is based on the New International Version.
33. **Smith's Bible Dictionary** William Smith. Thomas Nelson ISBN: p 0-8407-3085-8, c -5542-2 © 1986. 14,400 / 81,577. These editions contain special articles of biblical topics, illustrations, and maps.
34. **Zondervan Pictorial Bible Dictionary** Merrill. Tenney, editor. Zondervan ISBN: c 0-310-33160-9 © 1963 n.a. With more than 5,000 entries and 700 illustrations, this volume includes monographs on biblical topics.
35. **Harper's Bible Dictionary** Paul Achtemeier. Harper &. Row ISBN: c 0-06-069862-4, -069863-2 © 1985. 13,830 / 102,000. Prepared by 179 members of the Society of Biblical Literature, this volume contains 3,700 entries, outlines of all the books of the Bible, and color maps and photographs.
36. **Gospel Parallels, Fourth Edition** Burton Throckmorton. Thomas Nelson ISBN: c 0-8407-5150-8 © 1979. 13,000 / 349,522. This book provides a thorough study of the first three Gospels by comparing corresponding passages in adjacent columns.
37. **Willmington's Guide to the Bible** Harold Willmington. Tyndale ISBN: c 0-8423-8804-4 © 1981 n.a. Written in lay language, this volume includes an archaeological handbook, theological manual, and an illustrated Bible encyclopedia.
38. **The International Bible Commentary** F. F. Bruce, editor. Zondervan ISBN: c 0-310-22020-3 © 1986 n.a. This volume offers an analytical look at the NIV Bible by 43 contemporary scholars.
39. **Romans (Tyndale New Testament Commentary)** F. F. Bruce. Eerdmans ISBN: p 0-8028-0062-9 © 1985. 11,526 / 40,478. Exegetical in nature, this commentary provides readers an inexpensive resource that is neither too technical nor too brief.
40. **The NIV Complete Concordance** Edward Goodrick and John Kohlenberger III. Zondervan ISBN: c 0-310-43650-8 © 1981 n.a. This book lists more than 250,000 references covering 12,800 key NIV words.
41. **Meredith's Book of Bible Lists** Joel Meredith. Bethany House ISBN: p 0-87123-023-2 © 1980. 11,076 / 139,506. This collection of Bible facts is presented in list form.
42. **Bible Index Pocketbook** Shaw ISBN: p 087788-077-8 © 1981. 10,484 / 167,808 This small title contains more than 1,000 subjects and related Bible references.
43. **1 Peter (Tyndale New Testament Commentary)** Wayne Grudem. Eerdmans ISBN: p 0-8028-0407-1 © 1988. 10,450 / 10,450. Exegetical in nature, this commentary provides readers an inexpensive resource that is neither too technical nor too brief.
44. **The Hard Sayings of Jesus** F. F. Bruce. InterVarsity ISBN: p 0-87784-927-7 © 1983. 10,354 / 54,413. Bruce clarifies 70 of Jesus' hard-to-understand or hard-to-apply statements.
45. **The Mother's Topical Bible** Honor Books ISBN: c 0-89274-545-2 © 1988. 10,320 / 10,320. This volume offers prayers and Scriptures for situations that mothers encounter.
46. **The Canon of Scripture** F. F. Bruce. InterVarsity ISBN: c 0-8308-1258-X © 1988. 10,221 / 10,221. Bruce investigates the Bible's nature and historical development.
47. **Basic Theology** Charles Ryrie. Victor Books ISBN: c 0-89693-814-X © 1986 n.a. This study of systematic theology is written for laypeople.

48. **People and Places in the Bible** John Farrar. Barbour ISBN: p 1-55748-030-3 © 1987. 9,857 / 21,204. Short definitions are given for names of biblical characters and locations.

49. **Expositor's Bible Commentary, Vol. 4** Frank Gaebelein, editor. Zondervan ISBN: c 0-310-36460-4 © 1988 n.a. This volume surveys 1 and 2 Kings, 1 and 2 Chronicles, Ezra, Nehemiah, Esther, and Job in the New International Version.

50. **New International Dictionary of the Bible, Pictorial Edition** Merrill Tenney and J. D. Douglas, editors. Zondervan ISBN: c 0-310-33190-0 © 1987 n.a. More than 5,000 entries and 700 pictures and maps are included in this updated version of the *Zondervan Pictorial Dictionary.*

51. **The Book of New Testament Word Studies** Eric Partridge. Barbour ISBN: p 1-55748-031-1 © 1987. 9,507 / 21,520. This book defines difficult Bible words in modern terms, provides Scripture cross-references, and discusses Greek terms.

52. **Unger's Bible Handbook** Merrill Unger. Moody ISBN: c 0-8024-9039-5 © 1966 n.a. This volume offers concise commentary on the Bible, including archaeology, historical background, the intertestamental period, church history, and more.

53. **Luke (Tyndale New Testament Commentary)** Leon Morris. Eerdmans ISBN: p 0-8028-0419-5 © 1988. 9,396 / 9,396. Exegetical in nature, this commentary provides readers an inexpensive resource that is neither too technical nor too brief.

54. **Boyd's Bible Handbook** Robert Boyd. Harvest House ISBN: c 0-89081-3523 © 1983 n.a. More than 100 maps and illustrations help readers better understand and apply biblical principles.

55. **The Compact Dictionary of Doctrinal Words** Terry Miethe. Bethany House ISBN: p 0-87123-678-8 © 1988. 8,443 / 8,443. Definitions in this book help readers understand Christian doctrines and truths.

56. **Handbook of Life in Bible Times** J. A. Thompson. InterVarsity ISBN: c 0-87784-949-8 © 1986. 8,395 / 28,695. Illustrated with full-color photographs, this book is keyed to specific Bible passages.

57. **Unger's Bible Dictionary** Merrill Unger. Moody ISBN: c 0-8024-9035-2 © 1957 n.a. This volume offers current information on archaeology, geography, chronology, and other topics.

58. **Encyclopedia of Bible Difficulties** Gleason Archer. Zondervan ISBN: c 0-310-43570-6 © 1982 n.a. This book addresses problems and questions in the biblical text that are raised against the position of inerrancy.

59. **Eerdmans Handbook to the Bible, Revised** David & Pat Alexander. Eerdmans ISBN: c 0-8028-3486-8 © 1983. 8,176 / 89,981. Prepared by biblical scholars, this illustrated book answers Bible questions with text, maps, charts, and photos.

“” FOCUS QUOTE **The most learned, acute, and diligent student cannot, in the longest life, obtain an entire knowledge of the Bible. The more deeply he works the mind, the richer he finds the ore.**
—Sir Walter Scott

---

60. **Expositor's Bible Commentary, Vol. 10** Frank Gaebelein, editor. Zondervan ISBN: c 0-310-36520-1 © 1976 n.a. This NIV commentary covers Romans through Galatians.

61. **Matthew (Tyndale New Testament Commentary)** Richard France. Eerdmans ISBN: p 0-8028-0063-7 © 1987. 7,979 / 14,235. Exegetical in nature, this commentary provides readers an inexpensive resource that is neither too technical nor too brief.

62. **Acts (Tyndale New Testament Commentary)** I. Howard Marshall. Eerdmans ISBN: p 0-8028-1423-9 © 1980. 7,928 / 101,357. Exegetical in nature, this commentary provides readers an inexpensive resource that is neither too technical nor too brief.

100 BEST-SELLING REFERENCE BOOKS cont.

63. **The Message of II Corinthians** Paul Barnett. InterVarsity ISBN: p 0-8308-1228-8 © 1988. 7,905 / 7,905. Barnett discusses each passage in light of Paul's conflict with the Corinthian church, presenting implications for today's Christian.
64. **Acts (New International Commentary on the New Testament)** F. F. Bruce. Eerdmans ISBN: c 0-8028-2418-8 © 1988. 7,856 / 16,037. For serious Bible students, this commentary reflects modern archaeological and linguistic scholarship in its discussion of the text.
65. **The International Standard Bible Encyclopedia, Vol. 4** G. W. Bromiley, editor. Eerdmans ISBN: c 0-8028-8164-5 © 1988. 7,832 / 22,3120. This volume covers Q through Z.
66. **John (Tyndale New Testament Commentary)** R. V. G. Tasker. Eerdmans ISBN: p 0-8028-1403-4 © 1960. 7,817 / 165,532. Exegetical in nature, this commentary provides readers an inexpensive resource that is neither too technical nor too brief.
67. **Revelation (Tyndale New Testament Commentary)** Leon Morris. Eerdmans ISBN: p 0-8028-0273-7 © 1987. 7,655 / 12,762. Exegetical in nature, this commentary provides readers an inexpensive resource that is neither too technical nor too brief.
68. **Galatians (Tyndale New Testament Commentary)** R. Alan Cole. Eerdmans ISBN: p 0-8028-1408-5 © 1965. 7,286 / 160,749. Exegetical in nature, this commentary provides readers an inexpensive resource that is neither too technical nor too brief.
69. **Young's Analytical Concordance to the Bible** Robert Young. Eerdmans ISBN: c 0-8028-8084-3 © 1960. 7,273 / 454,034. This exhaustive concordance contains 311,000 references, 30,000 readings, and 70,000 Greek and Hebrew words.
70. **A Survey of the New Testament, Revised** Robert Gundry. Zondervan ISBN: c 0-310-25410-8 © 1982 n.a. This book is designed to acquaint readers with the Bible through articles that introduce and analyze the material.
71. **New Topical Textbook** Barbour ISBN: p 1-55748-066-4 © 1988. 7,083 / 7,083. This book offers thousands of topically arranged Scripture passages and R. A. Torrey's "Methods of Bible Study."
72. **Mark (Tyndale New Testament Commentary)** R. Alan Cole. Eerdmans ISBN: p 0-8028-1401-8 © 1962. 6,926 / 131,340. Exegetical in nature, this commentary provides readers an inexpensive resource that is neither too technical nor too brief.
73. **Things to Come** J. Dwight Pentecost. Zondervan ISBN: c 0-310-30890-9 © 1958 n.a. This encyclopedic reference covers eschatology and biblical prophecy, including methods of interpretation.
74. **Expositor's Bible Commentary, Vol. 11** Frank. Gaebelein, editor. Zondervan ISBN: c 0-310-36530-9 © 1978 n.a. This NIV commentary covers Ephesians through Philemon.
75. **New Testament Fulfillment of Old Testament Prophecies** Barbour ISBN: p 1-55748-056-7 © 1988. 6,765 / 6,765. This book offers many proofs that Jesus is the Messiah.
76. **1 Corinthians (Tyndale New Testament Commentary)** Leon Morris. Eerdmans ISBN: p 0-8028-0064-5 © 1987. 6,513 / 12,096. Exegetical in nature, this commentary provides readers an inexpensive resource that is neither too technical nor too brief.
77. **The International Standard Bible Encyclopedia, Vol. 3** G. W. Bromiley, editor. Eerdmans ISBN: c 0-8028-8163-7 © 1986. 6,481 / 21,942. This volume covers K through P.
78. **The International Standard Bible Encyclopedia, Vol. 1** G. W. Bromiley, editor. Eerdmans ISBN: c 0-8028-8161-0 © 1979. 6,465 / 26,456. Based on the RSV text, this series includes articles on every biblical person or place name, as well as other terms. It's cross-referenced to the KJV and NEB. This volume covers A through D.

79. **Expositor's Bible Commentary, Vol. 12** Frank Gaebelein, editor. Zondervan ISBN: c 0-310-36540-6 © 1982 n.a. This NIV commentary covers Hebrews through Revelation.
80. **Colossians & Philippians (Tyndale New Testament Commentary)** N. T. Wright. Eerdmans ISBN: p 0-8028-0309-1 © 1988. 6,339 / 6,339. Exegetical in nature, this commentary provides readers an inexpensive resource that is neither too technical nor too brief.
81. **Richards' Complete Bible Handbook** Lawrence Richards. Word ISBN: p 084-9930-979 © 1987. 6,314 / 16,485. Formerly titled *The Word Bible Handbook,* this volume offers information about Scripture and how to apply it.
82. **Expositor's Bible Commentary, Vol. 9** Frank Gaebelein, editor. Zondervan ISBN: c 0-310-36510-4 © 1984 n.a. This NIV commentary covers John and Acts.

FOCUS FACT

500 million of 822 million Europeans have never opened, let alone read, the Bible.

83. **The NIV Harmony of the Gospels** Stanley Gundry and Robert Thomas. Harper & Row ISBN: c 0-06-063523-1 © 1988. 6,305 / 6,305. This classic has been revised for NIV students.
84. **Pastoral Epistles (Tyndale New Testament Commentary)** Donald Guthrie. Eerdmans ISBN: p 0-8028-1413-1 © 1958. 6,287 / 146,792. Exegetical in nature, this commentary provides readers an inexpensive resource that is neither too technical nor too brief.
85. **Chronological Charts of the New Testament** H. Wayne House. Zondervan ISBN: p 0-310-41641-8 © 1981 n.a. This book discusses the New Testament milieu, including history, weights and measures, social structures, and more.
86. **The International Standard Bible Encyclopedia, Vol. 2** G. W. Bromiley, editor. Eerdmans ISBN: c 0-8028-8162-9 © 1982. 6,167 / 24,813. This volume covers E through J.
87. **Chronological Charts of the Old Testament** John Walton. Zondervan ISBN: p 0-310-36291-1 © 1978 n.a. This book compares various parts of the Old Testament to achieve a chronological harmony of the text.
88. **The Expanded Vine's Expository Dictionary of New Testament Words** W. E. Vine and John Kohlenberger III, editor. Bethany House ISBN: p 0-87123-619-2 © 1984. 6,070 / 40,140. This edition is keyed to *Strong's Concordance, Brown's New International Dictionary,* and *Arndt/Gingrich's Greek Lexicon.*
89. **James (Tyndale New Testament Commentary)** Douglas Moo. Eerdmans ISBN: p 0-8028-0079-3 © 1987. 6,053 / 12,682. Exegetical in nature, this commentary provides readers an inexpensive resource that is neither too technical nor too brief.
90. **The Old Testament Speaks, Third Edition** Samuel Schultz. Harper & Row ISBN: c 0-06-067134-3 © 1980. 6,020 / 54,468. Using modern scholarship to place the Scriptures in their Middle East setting, this book introduces readers to the Old Testament's history and literature.
91. **Philippians (Tyndale New Testament Commentary)** Ralph Martin. Eerdmans ISBN: p 0-8028-0310-5 © 1988. 5,991 / 13,106. Exegetical in nature, this commentary provides readers an inexpensive resource that is neither too technical nor too brief.
92. **Handy Dictionary of the Bible** Merrill Tenney. Zondervan ISBN: p 0-310-33151-X © 1965 n.a. This compact volume covers persons, places, and things in the Bible, arranged alphabetically.
93. **Expositor's Bible Commentary, Vol. 1** Frank Gaebelein, editor. Zondervan ISBN: c 0-310-36430-2 © 1979 n.a. Based on the NIV text, this commentary includes current research and scholarship.
94. **Manners and Customs of Bible Lands** Fred Wight. Moody ISBN: c 0-8024-5175-6 © 1953 n.a. This book gives Bible students an understanding of the

100 BEST-SELLING REFERENCE BOOKS cont.

Scriptures' background.

95. **Chronological and Background Charts of Church History** Robert Walton. Zondervan ISBN: p 0-310-36281-4 © 1986 n.a. This set of 81 charts discusses key persons, events, dates, and ideas in church history.
96. **The Cross of Christ** John Stott. InterVarsity ISBN: c 0-87784-998-6 © 1986. 5,777 / 43,198. This study examines the role of the cross in Christian theology, life, and mission.
97. **2 Peter & Jude (Tyndale New Testament Commentary)** Michael Green. Eerdmans ISBN: p 0-8028-0078-5 © 1987. 5,775 / 11,883. Exegetical in nature, this commentary provides readers an inexpensive resource that is neither too technical nor too brief.
98. **Romans, Part 1 (Word Biblical Commentary)** James Dunn. Word ISBN: c 084-9902-371 © 1988. 5,769 / 5,769. This study is designed for serious Bible students and members of the academic community.
99. **The Eerdmans Bible Dictionary** Alan Myers, editor. Eerdmans ISBN: c 0-8028-2402-1 © 1987. 5,753 / 30,054. With more than 1,000 pages, this volume offers 5,000 entries on virtually all Bible topics.
100. **How to Read the Bible Everyday** Carmen Rojas. Servant ISBN: p 0-89283-399-8 © 1988. 5,666 / 5,666. This guide helps Catholics make Scripture a regular part of their daily devotions.

Bookstore Journal, Official Trade Publication of the Christian Booksellers Association. Copyright © 1990. Reprinted by permission.

THE GOLDEN RULE

Do not that to thy neighbor that thou wouldst not suffer from him. *Pittacus of Lesbos* (650–570 B.C.)

Never do to others what you would not like them to do to you. *Confucius* (550–478 B.C.)

We should behave to friends as we would wish friends to behave to us. *Aristotle* (384–322 B.C.)

What is hateful to you, do not to your fellowmen. That is the entire law; all the rest is commentary. *Talmud* (Judaism)

Do for others what you want them to do for you. *Jesus Christ in Matthew 7:12* (Christianity)

Hurt not others in ways that you yourself would find hurtful. *Dana-Varga* (Buddhism)

This is the sum of duty; do naught unto others which would cause you pain if done to you. *Mahabharata* (Brahmanism)

Regard your neighbor's gain as your own gain and your neighbor's loss as your own loss. *T'ai Shang Kan Ying P'ien* (Taoism)

That nature alone is good which refains from doing unto another whatsoever is not good for itself. *Dadistan-i-dinik* (Zoroastrianism)

No one of you is a believer until he desires for his brother that which he desires for himself. *Sunnah* (Islam)

Do not do unto others as you would that they should do unto you. Their tastes may not be the same. *George Bernard Shaw*

When we and ours have it in our power to do for you and yours what you and yours have done for us and ours, then we and ours will do for you and yours what you and yours have done for us and ours. *Old English Toast*

Every man takes care that his neighbor does not cheat him. But a day comes when he begins to care that he does not cheat his neighbor. Then all goes well. *Ralph Waldo Emerson*

We have committed the Golden Rule to memory; let us now commit it to life. *Edwin Markham*

Church History

100 MOST IMPORTANT EVENTS IN CHURCH HISTORY

Rank	Event	Year
1	Council of Nicea	325
2	Luther posts "Ninety-five Theses"	1517
3	East-West split	1054
4	Vatican II opens	1962
5	Augustine converted	386
6	Bible printed by Gutenberg	1455
7	Council of Trent begins	1545
8	Chalcedon and Leo the Great	451
9	Thomas Aquinas completes *Summa Theologica*	1272
10	Calvin's *Institutes,* 1st edition published	1536
11	Edict of Milan	313
12	Jerome completes Vulgate	406
13	King James Bible published	1611
14	Diet of Worms	1521
15	The Great Schism	1378
16	Henry VIII and Act of Supremacy	1534
17	Benedict's monastic *Rule*	540
18	Athanasius letter establishes 27 books of NT canon	367
19	Great Awakening begins	1735
20	Destruction of Jerusalem by Titus	70
21	Crusades launched by Pope Urban II's speech	1095
22	Anabaptist movement begun	1525
23	Martin Luther King, Jr., leads march on Washington	1963
24	Christianization of Russia	988
25	John and Charles Wesley converted	1738
26	Paris and Oxford founded	c.1150
27	Charlemagne crowned Holy Roman Emperor	800
28	Westminster Confession	1647
29	Passage of Bill of Rights	1789
30	Gregory the Great elected Pope	590
31	Gorbachev becomes General Secretary of Communist Party of USSR	1985
32	Augsburg Confession	1530
33	First Vatican Council meets	1869
34	Wycliffe supervises English Bible translation	c.1380
35	Karl Barth writes *Epistle to the Romans*	1919
36	*Book of Common Prayer* released	1549
37	World Council of Churches organized	1948
38	Zwingli called as people's priest at Zurich Minster	1518
39	Fourth Lateran Council held under Innocent III	1215

Rank	*Event*	*Year*
40	Wilberforce leads abolition of slave trade	1807
41	Origen begins writing	c.215-220
42	Treaties of Westphalia	1648
43	Edict of Nantes	1598
44	Tyndale's New Testament published	1525
45	Monastery at Cluny founded	910
46	Hus burned at the stake	1415
47	Peter and Paul executed	c.65
48	Francis renounces wealth	1208
49	Cyril and Methodius' mission to Slavs	864
50	Colloquy at Marburg	1529
51	Donatist Schism begins	312
52	Patrick begins mission to Ireland	432
53	Bernard founds monastery at Clairvaux	1115
54	Athanasius becomes bishop of Alexandria	328
55	Syllabus of Errors issued by Pope Pius IX	1864
56	Tertullian begins writing	196
57	International Missionary Conference, Edinburgh	1910
58	Anthony takes up life of solitude	269
59	Establishment of Spanish Inquisition	1478
60	William Carey sails for India	1793
61	Battle of Tours	732
62	Waldensian movement begins	1175
63	British and Foreign Bible Society formed	1804
64	Chinese church grows despite Cultural Revolution	1965
65	Bultmann calls for demythologization of NT	1941
66	Justin Martyr's *First Apology* dedicated	c.150-155
67	*Fundamentals* published	1929
68	Synod of Dort	1618
69	Public churches begin to be built	c.230
70	Kierkegaard writes *Attack on Christendom*	1854
71	Boniface sets out as missionary	716
72	Bede's *Ecclesiastical History* published	731
73	John Knox's final return to Scotland	1559
74	St. Bartholomew's Day Massacre	1572
75	Bunyan writes *The Pilgrim's Progress*	1678
76	Anselm becomes Archbishop of Canterbury	1093
77	Chrysostom consecrated bishop of Constantinople	398
78	First trial of Galileo	1616
79	John Keble's Sermon initiates Oxford Movement	1833
80	Columba establishes mission community on Iona	563
81	Xavier begins mission to Japan	1549
82	Mayflower Covenant drafted	1620
83	Bonhoeffer executed	1945
84	Synod of Whitby	664
85	Roger Williams establishes Providence, RI	1636
86	Francis Asbury assumes leadership of USA Methodist congregations	1772
87	Azusa Street revival breaks out	1906
88	Whitefield converted	1735

Rank	Event	Year
89	Richard Allen elected bishop of the new AME church	1816
90	John Smyth baptizes self and other Christians	1609
91	Charismatic renewal advances in USA	1960
92	William & Catherine Booth found Salvation Army	1878
93	Los Angeles Crusade catapults Billy Graham	1949
94	Irenaeus appointed bishop of Lyons	177
95	Ambrose prevails in "sit in" confrontation	385
96	D.L. Moody's conversion	1855
97	Finney leads revival in Rochester	1830
98	Student Volunteer Movement begins	1886
99	Niebuhr's *Nature and Destiny of Man,* Volume 1	1941
100	Medellin Conference	1968

Source: *Christian History Magazine,* Fall 1990. Copyright 1990. Christianity Today, Inc. Used by permission.

CHRONOLOGY OF WORLD EVANGELIZATION FROM AD 30 TO 1990

1st Century

AD 30 Jesus begins public ministry, starts on his immediate plan to win the world.

31 Jesus chooses Twelve Apostles, unfolds his master plan of personal evangelism, gives them power and authority, commissions them to go initially only to Israelites (Matthew 10:1-6); later commissions Mission of the 70 disciples to evangelize the 70 Gentile nations (Luke 10:1).

33 Jesus' Great Commission given by the Risen Lord as his final plan and as spiritual counterpart of Genesis 1:28 with 2 components of evangelizing and discipling: "Go forth to every part of the world (in Greek, *cosmos*), and proclaim the Good News to the whole creation" (Mark 16:15, NEB); "Go to all peoples everywhere and make them my disciples" (Matthew 28:19, GNB).

Jesus as Risen Lord and later Ascended King gives Great Commission in a number of different forms at different times during the 40 days to different groups, including individuals, emphasizing the 7 mandates: Receive! Go! Witness! Proclaim! Disciple! Baptize! Train!

34 Apostles (the Twelve plus others) begin evangelizing Jews widely: several remain in Jerusalem for a decade or two, several travel outside, but most continue to evangelize only Jews until AD 38 (Peter), 43 (Paul), and after AD 50 (others).

35 Proliferation of "signs and wonders" among early believers (listed 9 times in Acts); miracles and healings at this time an everyday occurrence and an essential part of proclamation of the gospel; "power evangelism" thus one of the normal kinds of evangelism in the Early Church.

36 Martyrdom of Stephen the protomartyr; Jewish persecution of Early Church, especially of Hellenistic Christians; gospel spreads rapidly through persecution and martyrdom.

38 After 5-year period of hesitation and partial obedience to Christ's Great Commission, first Gentiles are deliberately evangelized by the Twelve Apostles.

Commission to evangelize pagan Gentiles as Gentiles first forced on consciousness of Jewish church, through baptism by Peter of Cornelius, a God-fearer but not a Jewish proselyte (Acts 10:1-48).

c.38 Twelve Apostles, after 5 years' uncertainty, scatter across globe spreading the gospel, from Ethiopia (Matthew), to Armenia (Bartholomew) to India (Thomas); all martyred over subsequent 60 years.

CHRONOLOGY OF WORLD EVANGELIZATION FROM AD 30 TO 1990 cont.

46	Paul's 1st missionary journey (45-48), with Barnabas: Antioch, Cyprus, Pamphilia, Pisidia, Lycaonia; develops strategy of urban evangelization and urban ministry, moving from city to city or town to town.
61	Paul writes: "The Good News which has reached you is spreading all over the world" (Colossians 1:6, Jerusalem Bible); "The Good News, which you have heard, has been preached to the whole human race" (Colossians 1:23; Greek "to all creation under the sky").
65	Prophecies of John the Divine: "I saw another angel flying high in the air, with an eternal message of Good News to announce to the peoples of the earth, to every race, tribe, language and nation" (Revelation 14:6-11, GNB).
66	Evangelist Luke concludes his 2-volume narrative (Luke-Acts): The worlds of empire and Judaism have now been evangelized, the gospel is now known to all peoples throughout them, and the Great Commission there largely completed.

2nd Century

c.100	Christianity predominantly urban, based in Roman cities, spreading from city to city along trade routes; later missions to Armenia, Ethiopia, China (under Nestorians) all center on capital cities.
c.130	Christianity spreads principally and normally, though not exclusively, through (as prevailing strategy) the planting of churches which then serve as missionary communities to evangelize their areas by continuing to attract and enlist converts; most converts are reached through casual contacts, witnessing a martyrdom, hospitality and care of strangers, et alia.
c.140	Hermas writes: "The Son of God . . . has been preached to the ends of the earth" (*Shepherd of Hermas).*
c.150	Justin Martyr (c100-165) founds disciple-training school over a house in Rome, documents current "signs and wonders"(exorcisms, healings, and prophesyings), and writes: "The first Apostles, twelve in number, in the power of God went out and proclaimed Christ to every race of men"; and "There is not one single race of men, whether barbarians, or Greeks, or whatever they may be called, nomads, or vagrants, or herdsmen dwelling in tents, among whom prayers and giving of thanks are not offered through the name of the Crucified Jesus"; teaches that all orthodox Christians believe in a resurrection of the flesh and in a millennial reign in the New Jerusalem; martyred at Rome.
156	Phrygia: rise of Montanism under new convert Montanus (c120-c175), a puritanical, prophetic, charismatic, millennial, apocalyptic movement claiming to be a new age of the Holy Spirit; 206, Tertullian joins; 230, movement excommunicated by Synod of Iconium; continues underground until c880.
c.180	Irenaeus bishop of Lyons (c120-203) documents recent charismata (exorcisms, visions, prophecies), and teaches that Antichrist will be a Jew of the tribe of Dan, also Christ will inaugurate a literal millennium of 1,000 years.
197	Tertullian (c160-222) documents recent healings and exorcisms, also writes: "Christ commanded them to go and teach all nations. Immediately, therefore, so did the apostles"; "The blood of the martyrs is seed"; and "There is no nation indeed which is not Christian"; 206, joins Montanist movement.

3rd Century

c.205	First known Christian scholar and apologist Clement of Alexandria (c155-215) deals with problem of how to relate Christian faith to Greek philosophy and culture, writes: "The whole world, with Athens and Greece, has already become the domain of the Word."

c.220 Origen (c185-254) writes: "The gospel of Jesus Christ has been preached in all creation under heaven, to Greeks and barbarians, to wise and foolish. . . . It is impossible to see any race of men which has avoided accepting the teaching of Jesus"; "The divine goodness of Our Lord and Saviour is equally diffused among the Britons, the Africans, and other nations of the world"; and "The preaching of the gospel through the whole Oikumene (whole inhabited earth) shows that the church is receiving divine support"; but also "Many people, not only barbarians, but even in the Empire, have not yet heard the word of Christ"; and "The gospel has not yet been preached to all nations, since it has not reached the Chinese or the Ethiopians beyond the river, and only small parts of the more remote and barbarous tribes"; 248, in *Contra Celsum* foresees possibility of conversion of entire world.

249 Seven missionary bishops sent to peoples of Gaul by Cornelius of Rome: Gatien (Tours), Trophime (Arles), Paul (Narbonne), Saturnin (Toulouse), Denis (Paris), Martial (Limoges), Austremoine (Clermont); many others also strategically located and sent in all directions.

c.270 Rise of monasticism in Egypt, as direct challenge to lifestyle of the rich: (1) eremitical (Anthony of Egypt, c251-356), (2) cenobitic (Pachomius, c287-346); widespread over next 2 centuries, with many documented healings, exorcisms, miracles, signs and wonders; Egyptian monks travel widely, evangelizing in Europe, Britain, Ireland, et alia.

4th Century

303 10th and last imperial Roman persecution, under Diocletian; aimed at clergy and bishops, with substantial defections; destruction of all church buildings and Scriptures ordered; 500,000 Christians killed or executed in witness under total persecution.

308 Church of the Martyrs with 29 bishops in Egypt organized by bishop Meletius (died 325) of Lycopolis, in opposition to leniency towards lapsi favored by Peter I Ieromartyros (Seal of Martyrs) patriarch of Alexandria who is himself martyred in 311; ideal of martyrdom as major factor in evangelizing the world spreads; Meletian sect is approved by Arians, lasts until c520.

c.310 Eusebius of Caesarea (c265-339) writes apologetic works: "Praeparatio evangelica" (refuting paganism), "Demonstratio evangelica" (fulfilment of Hebrew prophecy in Christ); 314, completes his *Ecclesiastical History,* and *Martyrs of Palestine*; writes "The doctrine of the Saviour has irradiated the whole Oikumene (whole inhabited earth)"; 325, at Council of Nicea expounds Matthew 28:19.

313 Constantine at Milan issues *Edict of Toleration* legalizing Christianity throughout Roman empire; 323, becomes sole emperor, attempts to spread gospel by law and authority.

325 Council of Nicea I (1st Ecumenical Council): council makes political province the basic unit for church's larger divisions, brings church's jurisdictional areas into line with secular dioceses and provinces of Roman empire, in order better to witness.

347 Cyril bishop of Jerusalem (310-386) teaches that Antichrist will be a magician who takes over Roman empire, claims to be Christ, deceives Jews by rebuilding Temple, persecutes Christians, then is slain at Second Advent by the Son of God.

c.360 8-volume *Apostolic Constitutions,* a Syrian collection of ecclesiastical law, makes frequent allusions to Great Commission of Jesus in Matthew 28:19-20.

374 A layman, Ambrose of Milan (c339-397), acclaimed bishop by crowds; in his writings, documents current healings and glossolalia; later teaches Second Coming of Christ will be preceded by destruction of Rome and appearance of Antichrist on Earth.

CHRONOLOGY OF WORLD EVANGELIZATION FROM AD 30 TO 1990 cont.

378 Jerome (c345-419) writes: "From India to Britain, all nations resound with the death and resurrection of Christ"; estimates 1.9 million Christians to have been martyred since AD 33 (out of 120 million Christians, i.e. 1.6% or 1 in 60); documents numerous current "signs and wonders" (healings, exorcisms, miracles).

392 Ascetic writer John Cassian (c360-435) enters Bethlehem monastery; 415, founds monastery in Marseilles; promotes spread of monasticism in West; much evangelization due to these itinerant evangelistic monks.

398 John Chrysostom (c344-407) appointed patriarch of Constantinople, founds training school for native Gothic evangelists; writes, "'Go and make disciples of all nations' was not said for the Apostles only, but for us also"; teaches that final Antichrist under direct inspiration of Satan will appear immediately before Second Advent of Christ in AD 430.

5th Century

c.410 Episcopate in Proconsular Africa, Numidia and Mauretania expands to 768 bishops; total episcopate across North Africa, including Egypt and Donatists, numbers 1,200 bishops; Honoratus at Lerins monastery trains succession of notable missionary bishops, sent across world for Christ.

426 Augustine (354-430) bishop of Hippo completes in 13 years his treatise *The City of God* (De Civitate Dei), against background of Visigoth invasion of Rome; propounds allegorical millennialism, but also teaches that future final Antichrist will arise as Nero Redivivus; opposes emerging theory of cessation of charismatic gifts, as overreaction to excesses of Montanism, et alia, with the teaching that miracles and charismata ended with the Apostolic age; documents numerous recent miracles, exorcisms, healings, and resuscitations.

428 French apologist Prosper Tiro (c390-463) defends Augustine of Hippo, writes treatise *De Vocatione Omnium Gentium* envisaging conversion of all barbarians to Christ, whose grace extends everywhere: "Nulla pars mundi ab Evangelio vacat Christi."

499 Task of translating Jesus' message into Greek and Latin cultures virtually completed, after 16 generations.

6th Century

c.510 Irish Peregrini or Exultantes Christi (unorganized wandering hermits and preachers using pugilatores scotorum [Irish writing-tablets] as their major piece of equipment) embark on peregrinatio pro Christi amore as missionary pilgrims for Christ, begin to migrate across Europe for next 400 years, to the Alps, Germany, Danube, Italy, also to Orkneys, Faeroes, Iceland, converting much of Europe in one of great missionary feats of all time.

535 Cosmas Indicopleustes, Nestorian merchant missionary over most of world, retires to monastery and in 547 completes his global survey *Topographia Christiana* in 12 books.

c.550 Nestorian monasticism organized and reformed by Abraham of Kashkar (501-586); numerous monasteries and missions begun, with special concern for physical and spiritual needs of people; through persecution, spreads across Asia to Yemen, South India, Ceylon, Samarkand, China.

594 Roman Pope Gregory the Great (540-604) publishes *Dialogues* describing contemporary Christian miracles, visions, prophecies, supernatural awareness, and other spiritual gifts; places detailed planning of organized missions to all heathen among his major objectives, in view of imminence of Last Judgment.

7th Century

635 China (then richest and most civilized nation on Earth): first missionary (Alopen, a Nestorian bishop from Syria) reaches Thailand and then Tang Chinese capital Ch'ang-an (Hsian), translates Scriptures for emperor Tai-tsung; Nestorianism influential till suppressed for a time in 845.

8th Century

c.700 End of Patristic Age, during which Greek Fathers and Latin Fathers have all expounded the words *euangelizo, euangelizesthai, euangelismos, evangelizare, evangelizatio, evangelizator,* et alia.

720 Anglo-Saxon translations of John's Gospel by historian and theologian Bede (Baeda, c673-735), monk at Jarrow on Tyne; Bede predicts fall of Colosseum will be followed by that of Rome and then also of the whole world.

c.780 Forced baptism of Saxon race by Charlemagne; 4,500 executed in one day for resisting, thousands more deported.

10th Century

962 Holy Roman Empire founded by Otto I (912-973), king of Germany, crowned by Pope John XII; seen as embodiment of rule of Christ on Earth; 10 million by AD 1000, 16 million by AD 1200, 29 million by 1800; finally abolished in 1806.

11th Century

1000 Millennial year preceded by widespread terrors; followed by 150 years of vast increase in pilgrimages to Holy Land, with widespread continuing belief in imminent end of world with final king of the Franks leading all faithful to Jerusalem to await Second Coming of Christ.

Catholic Apostolic Church of the East (East Syrian or Nestorian church) is by now the most extensive in world, with 250 dioceses across Asia and 12 million adherents; expansion of Nestorianism in Tenduc, country of Keraits with Karakorum as capital, home of legendary ruler Prester John.

1090 College of Cardinals established in Rome by reforms of Pope Urban II (c1042-1099), to expand rule of Christ across the Earth.

1095 Military expeditions by Western Christians against Muslim powers to liberate Holy Land, launched by Pope Urban II, known as Crusades: 1st 1095-99 (People's Crusade); 2nd 1147-49; 3rd 1189-93 (Richard the Lion-Heart); 4th 1202-04; 5th 1212-21 (Children's Crusade); 6th 1228-29; 7th 1248-54; 8th 1270-72 (Prince Edward of England).

12th Century

c.1180 Joachim of Fiore (c1130-1202), Italian Cistercian abbot and mystic, divides all history into three 40-generation ages or periods (Old Testament, New Testament, future age), writes *Vaticini del Vangelo Eterno* (Prophecies of the Eternal Gospel) and *Expositio in Apocalypsim* describing imminent crisis of evil, apocalyptic symbols of Antichrist, and his 3rd or Final Age of the Spirit (Love) coming by 1260 after Age of the Father (Law), and Age of the Son (Grace), for spiritual men through pilgrimage and great tribulation in a spiritualized Johannine Church replacing carnal Petrine Church; Joachimism spreads widely over next 3 centuries.

CHRONOLOGY OF WORLD EVANGELIZATION FROM AD 30 TO 1990 cont.

c.1190 Rise of demand for vernacular versions of Scriptures, illustrated by *Historia Scholastica*, a narrative of biblical history, by 12th-century scholar Petrus Comestor (c1100-1180); poetical and prose versions now available in Old French (Provençal, Vaudois), Italian, Spanish.

13th Century

1209 Francis of Assisi (1182-1226) founds traveling preachers (Franciscans), largest of the mendicant orders (OFM); widespread healings, signs and miracles reported; 1270, missionaries in almost every part of the known world; by 1400, missions from Lapland to Congo and Azores to China; soon reaches a medieval peak of 60,000 Franciscans by 1400, 77,000 by 1768, falling to 14,000 by 1900, rising to 40,000 by 1970.

1215 Dominic (1170-1221) founds Order of Preachers (OP, Dominicans) in southern France for "Propagation of the Faith through Preaching," "accepting our Lord's command, Go ye into all the world"; soon reaches a peak of 12,000 Dominicans, falling to 7,055 by 1983; other orders of mendicant friars arise including in 1256 Augustinians (OSA).

1221 First of many papal mission encyclicals on foreign missionary affairs: Bull of Honorius III, "Ne si secus" to the 13 metropolitans of the Catholic church, asking them to send out missionaries.

c.1250 Height of the Catholic church's political power in Europe, taken for granted by most Christians as God's instrument for spreading the rule of Christ around the world.

c.1260 Italy and Europe: greatest period of religious art begins, and lasts 400 years, with as central theme Christ's passion and crucifixion; all art—paintings, drawings, tapestries, stained-glass windows, sculpture, architecture—now regarded as major method of teaching and evangelizing illiterate populations.

1266 Mongol ruler Kublai Khan (1215-1294) requests Roman pope: "Send me 100 men skilled in your religion . . . and so I shall be baptized, and then all my barons and great men, and then their subjects. And so there will be more Christians here than there are in your parts"; 2 Dominicans sent, but turn back; then 1278, pope sends 5 Franciscans; greatest missed opportunity in Christian history.

14th Century

1349 Apogee of East Syrian or Nestorian expansion across Asia, geographically more extensive and more prosperous than ever before or since; 25 metropolitans (each with 6-12 suffragan bishops) in 250 dioceses in China, India, Kashgar, Samarkand, Turkestan, et alia, with total of over 15 million Christians; a mighty organization with missionary enterprise unsurpassed in Christian history.

1399 Catalan Dominican wandering preacher Vincent Ferrer (c1350-1419) reevangelizes and transforms Christendom throughout Europe; brings Jews to dialogues, converts 25,000 across Europe; preaches 6,000 apocalyptic sermons each 3 hours long, with glossolalia, healings, miracles widely reported; writes of future coming of Antichrist, predicts world will end after 2537 more years in AD 3936 (based on number of verses in Book of Psalms).

15th Century

c.1400 Societas Peregrinantium pro Christo founded by Franciscans.

1420 Taborites, extreme militant wing of Bohemian Hussites at Tabor south of Prague, founded as strict biblicists under their bishop Nicholas of Pelhrimov, seek to establish Kingdom of God by force of arms and military campaigns including destruction of churches; finally defeated at Lipany in 1434, Tabor captured 1452.

1431 Council of Basle (17th Ecumenical Council): question of papal supremacy, and the Hussite heresy; edict orders all Jews to attend Christian sermons.

1450 Invention of printing (typography and the printing press) by Johannes Gutenberg (c1395-1468) at Mainz, Germany, in order to disseminate the Holy Scriptures across the world; 1455, inventor ruined financially by lawsuit; in 6 languages by 1478; by 1500, more than 100 printed editions of the Bible produced.

1455 German mystic Thomas à Kempis (c1380-1471) writes *The Imitation of Christ;* a major influence on evangelization.

1493 Pope issues Demarcation Bull "Inter Caetera," giving Portugal authority over Africa, much of Asia and later Brazil; Spain given authority over rest of world west of a north-south line 345 miles west of the Azores.

16th Century

1500 Total of saints and martyrs who are known by name, formally recognized or canonized by the churches, now numbers over 10,000; from 1500-1903, Rome recognizes 113 further canonizations and 547 beatifications; total by 1985, known by name, for all confessions: 50,000 (0.1% of grand total all martyrs by 1985, known and unknown); total effect on world evangelization has been incalculable.

1517 Leonardo da Vinci (1452-1519), greatest genius ever, artist, scientist, engineer, inventor (submarine, tanks, aircraft, parachute, helicopter, anatomy, "Last Supper," etc.), produces "Visions of the End of the World" or "Deluge," depicting with overpowering pictorial imagination the primal forces that rule nature.

c.1520 Martin Luther (1483-1546) writes: "The gospel will always be preached. . . . It has gone out throughout the length and the breadth of the world. . . . It is made known farther and farther, to those who have not heard it before," and "The gospel preached by the Apostles in various languages, sounds forth even now till the end of time"; teaches that institution of papacy, and hence every pope (without singling individuals out), is Antichrist; expects Advent of Christ in 1558.

1523 Spanish monarch orders Cortes to enforce mass conversion of Amerindians across New World; in Mexico, Franciscans baptize over a million in 7 years, with at times 14,000 a day; by 1536, 6 million Amerindians baptized in 17 years in Mexico alone; c1550, 800,000 Peruvian Amerindians confirmed by one archbishop of Lima.

Ignatius Loyola (1491-1556) works in Palestine for conversion of Muslims; 1534, founds Society of Jesus, with missions around world (Japan by 1549); 1556, Society becomes leading missionary order with 1,000 Jesuits; peaks at 36,038 by 1965, falls to 25,550 in 1983 in 200 countries; official scope "Defense and Propagation of the Faith through Preaching."

1528 Berne Disputation, with its *10 Theses,* brings Reformation to city of Berne; Anabaptists insist that Great Commission applies to everyone who confesses Christ's name.

1530 Luther and Calvin teach that Great Commission (Mark 16:15) was work of 1st-century Apostles only and expired with them.

1534 Anabaptist refugees from persecution seize city of Munster, found Kingdom of a Thousand Years, eject unbelievers, establish New Jerusalem; 1534 city captured, King John of Leiden executed; the major 16th-century millenarian outburst.

1536 Sculptor and painter Michelangelo Buonarroti (1475-1564) completes vast painting "The Last Judgment" in Sistine Chapel, Vatican, a powerful fresco of the Day of Wrath inspired by Dante and medieval hymn "Dies irae."

CHRONOLOGY OF WORLD EVANGELIZATION FROM AD 30 TO 1990 cont.

1547 Nostradamus (Michel de Notredame, 1503-1566), astrologer and physician, makes extensive prophecies from 1547, first published as *The Centuries* in 1555; condemned by Roman Index in 1781; the most widely read seer of the Renaissance, in print continuously ever since, with vast literature of commentaries; end of world predicted for 1666, or 1734, 1886, 1943, 2000, 2038, or 3797.

c.1547 Anabaptists view Great Commission as binding on all church members.

1559 Anabaptists the only Reformed grouping to deliberately work for and obey Jesus' Great Commission, especially through Hutterian Brethren's itinerant evangelism.

1568 Commission of cardinals instituted in Rome by Pius V for foreign missions in East Indies, for Italo-Greeks, and for Protestant lands of Europe; 1573, congregation for conversion of infidels formed.

1580 Discalced (Reformed) Carmelite Sisters become a separate order; by 1983, 11,649 cloistered contemplative nuns in 727 monasteries; serving evangelization of the world in name of Christ by prayer and works of charity.

1584 Jesuit priest Alonso Sanchez drafts evangelistic scheme for invasion and military conquest of China; others plan for forcible baptism of all peoples of the world.

1588 Anglican parish priest Hadrian Saravia (1531-1613) becomes one of first non-Roman advocates of foreign missions, stressing binding validity of Matthew 28:19: "The command to preach the gospel to the Gentiles pertained not only to the age of the apostles, but to all future times to the end of the world."

Consistorial Congregation erected in Rome, responsible for all matters concerning all Catholic bishops and dioceses across world except Eastern-rite and missionary jurisdictions; includes Pontifical Commission for Migration and Tourism; 1967, renamed Sacred Congregation for Bishops.

1589 Russian Orthodox patriarchate instituted ('The Third Rome'); 1700, Peter the Great orders christianization of Siberia, 1721 abolishes patriarchate, rules church directly; as state church, its missions expand across Europe, Central Asia, Persia, Siberia, 1685 China, 1743 Kamchatka, 1784 Alaska, 1861 Mongolia, 1861 Japan, 1898 Korea, by means of traders, merchants, colonists, soldiers, diplomats, exiles, settlers (1 million Russians in Siberia from 1700-1783), monks, bishops, missionaries; 1826, best epoch of Russian Orthodox missions begins; 1870, Orthodox Missionary Society founded by metropolitan of Moscow, I. Veniaminov (1797-1879), in 55 Russian dioceses; whole mission enterprise destroyed in 1917 Revolution.

17th Century

c.1600 Episcopi Vagantes (Wandering Bishops, or Bishops-at-Large, in 15 disputed or contested lines of apostolic succession) begin to multiply across Europe; 1866, Julius Ferrette as bishop of Iona begins their modern era; by 1975, 760 bishops-at-large lead 280 distinct autocephalous Catholic churches/denominations with 10,285,000 adherents in 80 countries; each proposes grandiose plan for reunion of Christendom and conversion of world, calling on Rome, Constantinople, Canterbury, and Geneva to abandon their global pretensions and join each's new ecclesiastical body.

c.1610 Dominican historian Tomas Malvenda (1566-1628) translates Hebrew Old Testament into Latin, writes treatise on coming of Antichrist.

1613 Major missionary work by Discalced Carmelite monk of Spain, Thomas a Jesu (1564-1627), *De procuranda salute omnium gentium,* urges and envisages conversion of entire world to Christ.

1622 Sacred Congregation for the Propagation of the Faith (Propaganda, meaning dissemination or progressive plantation) founded by Pope Gregory XV (1554-1623); 1967, renamed by Pope Paul VI as SC for the Evangelization of Peoples.

1627 English biblical scholar Joseph Mede (1586-1638), a premillennialist, writes *Apocalyptica: Key of the Revelation;* formulates theory of progressive millennialism (later termed postmillennialism): Christ will only return at close of man-made millennium on Earth.

1648 Spanish Jesuit Ildefonso de Flores (1590-1660) calculates total Christian martyrs of all epochs to date at 11 million; major impact of martyrdom on world evangelization recognized; his estimate agrees closely with later survey done in 1980-1990.

1656 Calvinist and Puritan statesman Oliver Cromwell (1599-1658), protector of Commonwealth of England, Scotland and Ireland from 1653-1658, allows Jews prohibited since 1290 to return to England, in order to hasten Christ's Second Coming.

1657 Quint (Fifth) Monarchy Men (named from Daniel 2:44; after empires of Assyria, Persia, Greece, Rome, the Fifth is at hand as the Millennium), a Puritan sect, propose abolishing established church in England to bring about Parousia; 1657 and 1661, rise in armed revolt against Cromwell, but crushed.

1667 English poet John Milton (1608-1674) in his *Paradise Lost* draws attention to the Christian goal "To Evangelize the Nations."

1680 Founding in Rheims of Christian Brothers (FSC) to teach Christian doctrine to the poor and working classes across the world; by 1976, 12,641 lay brothers; by 1983, declines to 9,348.

1698 First 2 non-Roman missionary societies formed, by Church of England: Society for Promoting Christian Knowledge (SPCK), and (1701) Society for the Propagation of the Gospel in Foreign Parts (SPG); goal of world evangelization claimed, but in practice they work largely in British sphere of influence.

18th Century

1700 Evangelistic campaigns in Germany of Ernst Christoph Hochmann von Hochenau (1670-1721), major separatist Pietist/Lutheran mystic of his time, converted 1693. Regarding the conversion of the Jews as the sign of Christ's impending return, he engaged briefly in Jewish missionary work.

1703 Spiritans (CSSp, Holy Ghost Fathers) founded for "Evangelizzazione degli infedeli"; by 1983, 857 houses with 3,671 missionaries.

1705 Origin of Danish-Halle Mission (Lutheran), forerunner of Protestant missionary societies; first workers include Protestant pioneers to Tranquebar (India): Bartholomew Ziegenbalg (1682-1719), Heinrich Plutschau (1677-1747) and Christian Schwartz (1726-1798).

1710 Canstein House printing press, Halle (Germany) with first Bible society (Cansteinische Bibelanstalt) founded by Count Karl von Canstein: 3 million Bibles and NTs printed in 80 years.

1725 The Great Awakening, revival in New England (USA) spreading throughout the Thirteen Colonies; begun under T.J. Frelinghuysen in New Jersey; mass conversions of dechristianized European populations in North America, led by revivalist Jonathan Edwards (1703-1758), who expounds progressive millennialism (later called postmillennialism), envisaging establishment of Christ's millennial kingdom on Earth around year 1990, with Second Advent at close of millennium; Edwards calls for "concerts of prayer" for world revival; Awakening lasts until 1770.

CHRONOLOGY OF WORLD EVANGELIZATION FROM AD 30 TO 1990 cont.

1732 Moravian missions land in St Thomas, West Indies; 1733, Greenland; 1736, among Samoyeds of Archangelsk; 1787, Society of the United Brethren for Propagating the Gospel among the Heathen, formed in Pennsylvania, USA; 1732-1862, Moravians send abroad 2,000 missionaries.

1774 United Society of Believers in Christ's Second Appearing (Shakers) founded in Niskeyuna, NY (USA) by Ann Lee and pilgrims from England as millennial messianic sect in New World, based on celibacy.

1780 Deutsche Christentumsgesellschaft (Christendom Society)begun in Germany to build kingdom of God on an ecumenical basis; 1815, members found Evangelische Missionsgesellschaft in Basel (Basel Mission).

1782 Concerts of Prayer (for revival and world mission), as envisaged by Jonathan Edwards, begin and spread in Britain, then from 1790 in USA; basis for subsequent worldwide missionary advance.

1783 Native Baptist Church, first Jamaican Afro-Christian movement, begun by ex-slave, George Lisle; plays a significant political role 80 years later; precursor of later End-time pentecostal renewal across world.

1785 Evangelical awakenings (revivals) throughout Wales under Howel Harris (1714-1773) and others: 1785 Brynengan, 1786 Trecastle, 1791 Bala, 1805 Aberystwyth, 1810 Llangeitho, 1817 Beddgelert, 1821 Denbighshire, 1822 Anglesey, 1828 Carmarthenshire, 1832 Caernarvonshire, 1840 Merionethshire, 1849 South Wales, et alia.

1787 English Baptist minister Andrew Fuller (1754-1815) writes *The Gospel of Christ Worthy of All Acceptation* and over 128 other titles, urges obedience to the Great Commission.

1792 William Carey (1761-1834) publishes first statistical global survey of Christian world mission: *An Enquiry Into the Obligations of Christians, to Use Means for the Conversion of the Heathens,* accurately enumerating populations and Christians on all continents in world's first statistical survey (world population 731 million: 57% pagan/Hindu/Buddhist, 18% Muslim, 14% RC, 6% Protestant, 4% Orthodox, 1% Jewish); 1793, sails for India under Particular Baptist Society for Propagating the Gospel Among the Heathen (formed 1792); at Serampore, initiates modern era of Protestant world missions, serves without home leave for 41 years in Bengal, translates and prints Bible in 35 languages.

1795 London Missionary Society begun; founders' "vision of a world covered by missionary centres that would reach out and link up until there was no place where the gospel was not preached."

19th Century

1800 Widespread evangelistic camp meetings begin in USA; Kentucky Revival awakening, with crowds of up to 25,000, sweeps over Kentucky, Tennessee, and the Carolinas.

1802 Massachusetts Baptist Mission Society formed "for the evangelization of frontier communities."

1804 British & Foreign Bible Society (BFBS) founded, in London, with vision of providing Scriptures to whole world.

1806 USA: Haystack Prayer Meeting at Williams College, MA, launches North America foreign missions, to preach the gospel to all nations; 1810, these students form Society of Inquiry on the Subject of Missions; soon after, ABCFM is formed.

1810 W. Carey conceives idea of regional ecumenical missionary conferences around globe; nothing results until 1825 Bombay and 1854 New York.

Congregationalists in Massachusetts, USA, organize American Board of Commissioners for Foreign Missions (ABCFM) "to devise, adopt and prosecute ways and means for propagating the gospel among those who are destitute of the knowledge of Christianity"; by 1880, 1,200 missionaries overseas; 1961, renamed United Church Board for World Ministries, "to serve Christ in the world"; 1985, 229 foreign missionaries in 54 countries.

1814 Society of Jesus reestablished by Pope Pius VII (1742-1823) after 40 years' ban, with renewed interest in global mission and evangelization.

1815 Italian priest Caspar Del Bufalo (1786-1837) founds Missioners of the Most Precious Blood, with "his goal for his missioners the evangelization of the world" through charitable works.

1818 *The Conversion of the World: or the Claims of 600 Millions, and the Ability and Duty of the Churches Respecting Them:* book by G. Hall & S. Newell (ABCFM, India); proposal to convert heathen millions across world by sending 30,000 Protestant missionaries from USA and Europe in 21 years, at cost of US$4 from each Protestant and Anglican communicant in Christendom.

1819 Missionary Society of Methodist Episcopal Church organized; 1939 constitution states "The supreme aim of missions is to make the Lord Jesus Christ known to all peoples in all lands as their divine Saviour"; 1940, 1964, reorganized as Board of Global Ministries, United Methodist Church; 1974, 839 foreign missionaries (9.5% non-USA); 1985, 516 foreign missionaries in 50 countries.

1824 USA: beginnings of interdenominational city-wide cooperative evangelism; spreads to cities across world.

1825 Bombay Missionary Union (Anglicans, Congregationalists, Presbyterians, et alii) formed; first interdenominational regional conferences of missionaries 1855 in India, 1872 Japan, 1873 first all-India decennial conference, 1877 China, c1885 Mexico, et alia.

1826 Glasgow City Mission founded by David Nasmiths, secretary of 23 Christian societies, first of 50 city missions begun in Britain's largest cities (Bristol, Chester, Edinburgh, Glasgow, Leeds, Liverpool, 1832 London, York, et alia); also 1833 New York City Mission, Boston, Brooklyn, etc.; also 1848 Hamburg, 1874 Berlin, and 70 other German cities by 1899.

1827 J.N. Darby (1800-1882), Anglican clergyman, joins Christian Brethren movement in Dublin; propounds dogma of total premillennial apostasy and ruin of Christendom (the major churches); later develops "dispensationalism," a new variety of futurist premillennialism, dividing biblical and later history into 7 eras or dispensations.

1828 Karl Gutzlaff (1803-1851), a Lutheran, begins work in Indonesia, Siam, southern China, Hong Kong; 1844, attempts to evangelize China in one generation through 300 evangelists.

1829 Christian Brethren begin foreign missions as A.N. Groves and party go out to Baghdad, then later to India; much later, loosely organized as Christian Missions in Many Lands; by 1965, 1,200 foreign missionaries in 55 countries.

1830 USA: widespread campaigns through professional evangelists Andrew, Barnes, Burchard, Baker, Caughey, Griffith, Inskip, Knapp, Maffit, Swan.

Joseph Smith (1805-1844) at Fayette, NY (USA), has visions of incurable corruption of Christendom, and of divine restoration of Christ's church, which lead to establishment of Church of Jesus Christ of Latter-day Saints (Mormons); 1844, murdered by mob; movement migrates to Utah as headquarters of the coming millennial kingdom; subsequently evolves into massive heterodox organization unrelated to the rest of global Christianity, governed since 1844 by a Council of the Twelve Apostles; by 1988, its world mission includes 34,750 foreign missionaries (1- or 2-year termers) working in over 82 countries with annual mission budget of over US$550 million.

CHRONOLOGY OF WORLD EVANGELIZATION FROM AD 30 TO 1990 cont.

1831 Seminary president J.H. Rice calls Presbyterian Church in the US "a Missionary Society, the object of which is to aid in the conversion of the world."

1837 Board of Foreign Missions, Presbyterian Church in the USA established "to aid in the conversion of the world . . . every member of this church is a member for life of said society and bound to do all in his power for the accomplishment of this object"; 1958, becomes Commission on Ecumenical Mission and Relations, for which "The supreme and controlling aim of the Christian Mission to the world is to make the Lord Jesus Christ known to all men . . . in which Christians of all lands share in evangelizing the world and permeating all of life with the spirit and truth of Christ." ABCFM mission strategist Rufus Anderson (1796-1880) restores apostolic model for mission; in essay "The Time for the World's Conversion Come," first published in 1837 journal, argues that the churches are now, for the first time ever in history (as a result of rise of voluntary mission societies), adequately organized to complete the conversion of the world.

1841 CMS general secretary Henry Venn (1796-1873) requires all missionaries to complete annual questionnaires recording church growth statistics, as a means of monitoring progress in world evangelization; propounds "three-self" goal of mission that local churches must become self-supporting, self-governing, self-propagating.

1844 First Young Men's Christian Association (YMCA) founded, by Evangelicals in London; 1855, World Alliance of YMCAs founded in Paris (France), with headquarters in Geneva, emphasizing "extension of His Kingdom"; world vision, lay witness to Christ, global missionary thrust; 1894, World YWCA for women; subsequently, concerns broaden; 1988, 6.5 million men members in 74 National YMCA Movements and in 16 other countries; and 5 million women members.

1845 Southern Baptist Convention, largest USA Baptist denomination, comes into being in reaction against ABFMS refusing to accept slave-owners as missionaries; based from its origin on global mission, it founds Board of Domestic Missions (later, Home Mission Board) and Foreign Mission Board, beginning work in China, then 1846 Liberia and 1850 Nigeria; by 1988, has 7,000 full-time professional missionaries at home and abroad.

1846 Beginnings of world conciliarism: Evangelical Alliance formed in London by 800 Christians representing 52 confessions, to further unity among Evangelicals worldwide; national alliances then formed in Britain and Canada (1846), Sweden and Germany (1847), India (1849), Turkey (1855), USA (1867); and international conferences held in London 1851, Paris 1855, Berlin 1857, Geneva 1861, Amsterdam 1867, New York 1873, Basel 1879, Copenhagen 1884, Florence 1891, London 1896 and the final one in 1907; 1912, title officially changed to World's Evangelical Alliance (WEA).

1850 British Quaker millionaire and missions philanthropist Robert Arthington (1823-1900) donates millions to missionary societies and accumulates vast store of information on frontier evangelization of all peoples in world; 1900, his will expounds global strategy of (a) do a world survey of unreached peoples, (b) supply these peoples with translations of Luke, John and Acts, (c) teach 10 people in each tribe to read the gospel, (d) visit each tribe until a church emerges, (e) that tribe evangelizes the next, while (f) missionaries move on to regions beyond; Arthington is later followed by long series of eccentric millionaire philanthropist-strategists in Europe and USA.

1854 First Union Missionary Convention, in New York, USA, guided by Alexander Duff (1806-1878): "To what extent are we authorized by the Word of God to expect the conversion of the world to Christ?"; similar conference held in London, England; 1867, Duff appointed to first chair of evangelism and evangelical theology at New College, Edinburgh.

Foreign Mission Committee, Canada Presbyterian Synod, inaugurated; 1962, becomes Board of World Mission, United Church of Canada, "committed by its very nature to a global mission."

c.1855 Russian surge of world mission: Orthodox missiologist N.I. Ilminsky (1821-1891) works out scientific basis for missionary work; vast missionary expansion; 1870-1917, Orthodox Missionary Society organized (St Petersburg, Russia); 1917, its world mission is destroyed by Bolshevik Revolution.

1857 USA: evangelist D.L. Moody (1837-1899), a Congregationalist, evolves organized mass evangelism in Chicago; during his lifetime estimated to have had individual evangelistic personal dealings with 750,000 persons; perfects methods of preparation and publicity in cooperative city campaigns, use of theaters and tents, finance committees; other evangelists R.A. Torrey (1856-1928), Billy Sunday (1862-1925), Robert P. Wilder (1863-1938); beginnings of large-scale lay-centered evangelism.

1858 Sermons on evangelization increase: 1858 J. Parker publishes "The duty of the present generation of Christians to evangelize the world," New York; 1866 C. Dickson publishes "The duty of the Church to evangelize the World," Presbyterian Church of the USA, New York.

1859 Founding of Society of St Francis de Sales (Salesians of Don Bosco, SDB), a religious congregation dedicated to Christian education of youth across world; by 1975, 18,426 men in 1,524 houses; by 1983, 16,982 in 1,466 houses; also 17,269 Salesian Sisters (FMA).

1860 Earl of Shaftesbury, British evangelical social reformer (A.A. Cooper, 1801-1885), states: "Those who hold the truth have the means enough, knowledge enough, and opportunity enough, to evangelize the globe fifty times over."

1861 USA: Woman's Union Missionary Society of America for Heathen Lands (WUMSA) formed in New York as pioneer women's sending society, with 40 other women's societies arising later.

1862 Founding of Congregation of Immaculate Heart of Mary (Scheutists, CICM) with as goal "Evangelizzazione dei popoli"; by 1983, 1,507 members in 53 houses; over the years many Scheutist missionaries have been martyred.

1863 Universal Catholic Church (later renamed New Apostolic Church) founded in Germany by excommunicated German prophet H. Geyer of Catholic Apostolic Church (UK), emphasizing a successional apostolate subject to a chief apostle with quasi-papal powers, and the gifts of the Holy Spirit including prophecy, tongues, miraculous healing, sacraments, hierarchy of 48 living Apostles; by 1988, has 1.7 million members worldwide (mainly Germans) in 45 countries; cooperates with no other church.

1865 Christian Revival Association (1878, renamed Salvation Army) founded by Methodist evangelist William Booth in England for urban social outreach and street evangelism; 1985, 4,226,900 Salvationists in 75 countries, with vast social service and evangelistic activities and institutions; overriding first agenda defined in 1987 by SA general as "To emphasize the supremacy of evangelism in fulfilling of the Lord's great commission. . . . To work to the end that every man and woman and child has the opportunity to hear the good news of the gospel."

1867 Beginnings of confessional conciliarism: Archbishop of Canterbury C.T. Longley (1794-1868) convenes first decennial Lambeth Conference of all bishops of Anglican Communion (London), with 76 bishops present; 1875, origin of World Alliance of Reformed Churches and 1876 World Methodist Council; by 1983, grand total of 45 world confessional councils are in existence, representing all major Christian traditions, and all with own approaches to world mission.

Founding of Combonians (MCCI/FSCI/MFSC) with as goal "Evangelizzazione dei popoli, non ancora o non sufficientemente evangelizzati"; by 1983, 1,938 missionaries.

CHRONOLOGY OF WORLD EVANGELIZATION FROM AD 30 TO 1990 cont.

1869 Anglican Broad Church Evangelical, F.W. Farrar, later dean of Canterbury, describes Europeans as God's chosen evangelizers: "The Aryan should advance farther and farther to . . . the evangelization of the whole habitable globe."

1870 Rise of first megaministry (reaching over 1% of world per annum, i.e. 14 million people a year): BFBS, ABS and other Bible societies' distribution reaches 38,000 scriptures a day.

Pan-Orthodox world missions emerge: Orthodox Missionary Society organized in Russia by metropolitan of Moscow, I.Veniaminov (1797-1879); branches in 55 Russian dioceses; rapid missionary expansion; by 1900, Russians form largest single Christian ethnolinguistic people in whole world; 1917, Bolsheviks destroy Russian world missions; 1959, Pan-Orthodox world mission reorganized based on Athens (Greece).

Churches of Christ (Non-Instrumental), schism from Disciples of Christ, organize in USA; by 1985, they sent out 982 foreign missionaries in 74 countries, with related churches in total of 141 countries.

1872 Salesian Sisters (FMA) founded, in Italy, for world mission by prayer and works of charity; by 1983, 17,269 nuns, in 60 countries.

1873 East London Institute for Home and Foreign Missions formed (UK); 1900, renamed Regions Beyond Missionary Union invoking Apostle Paul's world vision (2 Corinthians 10:16); by 1985, 103 North American missionaries in 5 countries, 58 British in 5 countries, with total 200 missionaries of all nationalities.

1877 Shanghai, China: 1st General Foreign Missions conference, with 473 missionaries from 20 Protestant societies; states, "We want China emancipated from the thraldom of sin in this generation"; probable origin, among field missionaries, of Watchword "The Evangelization of the World in This Generation"; similar conferences in 1890 and 1907.

1880 Circulation of Watchcry (Watchword) on various Protestant mission fields becomes crystallized in 1885 article by A.T. Pierson entitled "A plan to evangelize the world," published in his journal *The Missionary Review of the World after 20 Years of Reflection*; Pierson calls for "an ecumenical council solely to plan a world-wide campaign and proclaim the good tidings to every living soul in the shortest time."

1881 United Society of Christian Endeavor formed in USA; 1895, World's Christian Endeavor Union organized (38,000 societies across world, with 2,225,000 members); 1927, International Society of Christian Endeavor; by 1965, 3 million members in 85 Protestant denominations in 80 countries; by 1987, 2 million in 78 nations.

1884 A.O. Van Lennep publishes statistical survey *The Growth of Christianity during Nineteen Centuries* (New York), blaming inadequate growth on lack of giving (in USA, annual per capita expenditure on alcohol is $49.70 but on foreign missions only $0.05); concludes, "When Christ's Church shall be as lavish in its outlay of men and money as the world is, the conversion of Nations will not long be postponed."

1885 At D.L. Moody's Northfield Convention for lay workers, A.T. Pierson chairs committee to "divide the world according to a comity agreement" and then pursue "the immediate occupation and evangelization of every destitute district of the earth's population," so that "the entire current population of the earth would hear the gospel by the year 1900"; Moody prepares in 3 days "An Appeal to Disciples Everywhere," claiming task could be completed even if only 10 million active Christians participated.

1886 1st International Christian Student Conference, Mount Hermon, MA, USA addressed by D.L. Moody, A.T. Pierson, et alii; 251 attenders.

1887 Christian and Missionary Alliance organized in USA; 1975, Alliance World Fellowship founded, in 51 nations; by 1985, 874 USA foreign missionaries in 50 countries.

1888 Student Volunteer Movement for Foreign Missions organized with 2,200 initial volunteers, based on Watchword "The Evangelization of the World in This Generation"; 1892, Student Volunteer Missionary Union (SVMU) begun in Britain; by 1945, as a result of SVM, a total of 25,000 university graduates have gone overseas as foreign missionaries.

One By One Band started in London by T. Hogben as "a worldwide fellowship devoted wholly to winning men to Christ," based on Hogben's book *God's Plan for Soul Winning.*

1889 Japan: 500 Japanese students at Student Conference send telegram to SVM Conference, Northfield (USA), urging "Make Jesus King."

SVM chairman John R. Mott writes to sister Hattie that the task of world evangelization will be accomplished by the dawn of the 20th century.

1890 Scandinavian Alliance Mission of North America founded for worldwide evangelism and church planting; 1949, renamed TEAM (The Evangelical Alliance Mission); 1985, 929 USA missionaries in 25 countries.

1893 Sudan Interior Mission begun as Africa Industrial Mission in order to evangelize the world's largest single totally unevangelized area with no resident missionary among 90 million people (Africa's 4,000-mile Sahel and Sudan); 1982, renamed SIM International, expands to Latin America; 1985, 654 missionaries in 15 countries.

1895 Association of Pentecostal Churches in America (1919, renamed Church of the Nazarene) formed, 1897 begins foreign missions; by 1987, World Mission Division has 617 foreign missionaries in 84 countries, with two AD 2000 programs: Thrust to the Cities ("maximizing holiness evangelism in key cities") and Two Million Adherents by 1995.

World Student Christian Association/Federation (WSCF) emerges from Vadstena Castle meeting, Sweden, begun by SCMs around world whose "aim was to claim students—the future leaders of their nations—for Christ and for the evangelization of the world"; after 1914, non-evangelistic interests predominate (leadership, social issues, universities, Christian presence, etc.); 1987, over 3 million members and participants.

1897 4th Lambeth Conference; 194 Anglican bishops present; first of 14 resolutions on foreign missions passed: "We recommend that prompt and continuous efforts be made to arouse the Church to . . . the fulfilment of our Lord's great commission to evangelize all nations."

House of Laymen, Province of Canterbury (Church of England) resolves: "In view of the Great Commission to evangelize the world, its long and serious neglect . . . the whole Church needs rousing on this question."

Encyclical letter "On the Holy Spirit" issued by Pope Leo XIII, directing attention to the 7-fold gifts of the Spirit (Isaiah 11) and promoting universal novena (9-day cycle of prayer) to Holy Spirit before Pentecost Sunday each year; millions influenced.

Arabia, and the world, "could easily be evangelized within the next 30 years if it were not for the wicked selfishness of Christians"—Samuel Zwemer, Apostle to Islam (1867-1952).

1899 Gideons International begun, for free distribution of Bibles; by 1965, active in 75 countries rising to 133 by 1985 and 137 by 1988, with 30,000 overseas members; 1987, 24 million Bibles distributed, with grand total 400 million placed over 89 years.

At end of "Golden Age of Jewish Missions" (19th century), over 200,000 Jews have been baptized as Protestants, and similar numbers as Roman Catholics; 650 Protestant missionaries minister to Jews at 213 mission stations across world; many believe future conversion of the Jews could ensure completion of world evangelization.

20th Century

1900 New York Ecumenical Missionary Conference: 2,500 members, 200,000 attenders; delegates from 162 mission boards; 500 speakers, huge public meetings; formation of an international missionary committee (to complete world missionary task) canvassed, urged, then unanimously adopted only to fizzle out soon after.

CHRONOLOGY OF WORLD EVANGELIZATION FROM AD 30 TO 1990 cont.

Methodist layman John R. Mott publishes classic, *The Evangelization of the World in This Generation;* many Christian strategists envisage winning of entire world to Christ during 20th century, then seen as certain to be "the Christian century."

Origins of Pentecostalism in USA: British-Israelite holiness preacher Charles F. Parham (1873-1929, Methodist) opens Bethel Bible School near Topeka, Kansas, with 40 students; 1901, they receive baptism of Holy Spirit; 1903 revival spreads through Kansas, 1905 Houston, 1906 to Los Angeles and thence across world (1906 Norway, 1907 Chile, 1908 China, 1909 Korea, 1910 Brazil, and so on).

Total of all Christian denominations begins to rise steeply as Christianity spreads across world, from only 92 in AD 1000, to 150 in AD 1500, to 510 in AD 1800, to 1,900 by AD 1900; then by 1985 to 22,000; proliferation seen by many in 1900 as a sure guarantee that world will soon become evangelized.

1901 Latter-Rain teaching: after 1,800 years of apparent cessation of large-scale charismata and 100 years of expectancy and teaching in USA on gifts of the Spirit, "restoration of all things" begins with Spirit-baptism and glossolalia, as pentecostal power is restored to the church; thousands of seekers travel to revival centers in USA, Europe, Asia, South America; expounded in D.W. Myland, *The Latter Rain Pentecost* (1910).

Founding of Consolata Missionary Fathers (IMC), in Turin, specifically for "Evangelizzazione degli infedeli"; by 1983, 1,008 foreign missionaries in 248 houses.

1902 Young People's Missionary Education Movement (1911, title shortened to MEM) founded by 15 USA denominational boards, YMCA and SVMU, to enlist missionaries outside college world.

4th International Convention, Student Volunteer Movement for Foreign Missions, in Toronto, Canada, produces 691-page report World-wide Evangelization, the Urgent Business of the Church.

1903 All Nations Flag Church (Church of God of Prophecy) founded, 1911 begins work overseas (Bahamas); by 1985, links with 69 countries.

1904 Welsh revival through ministry of Evan Roberts (1878-1951) in Glamorganshire, Anglesey, Caernarvonshire, with 100,000 converts in Wales in 6 months; short-lived (1904-1906), but literally sweeps the world; worldwide publicity from the press; leads into worldwide Pentecostal movement including 1905 Switzerland and Germany, 1907 England.

1905 National conciliarism begins: 1905 Fédération Protestante de France, 1908 Federal Council of the Churches of Christ in North America (1950 NCCCUSA), 1922 National Christian Council of China, 1922 Aliança Evangélica de Angola, et alia, up to 550 nationwide councils by 1983, all in theory committed to world mission.

1906 Proliferation of world mission atlases, both Protestant (1906, 1910, 1925, 1938) and RC (1906, 1913, 1929), with statistics listed by mission societies or RC dioceses rather than by denominations and countries.

C.F. Parham teaches that missionaries need only to receive the baptism with the Holy Ghost and can then, through the gift of glossolalia, be immediately understood in native languages to the farthest corners of the world; but Pentecostal missionaries abroad try this only to report failure.

1st General Conference of Missionaries to the World of Islam, convened through Reformed missionary S.M. Zwemer, held in Cairo, Egypt.

Laymen's Missionary Movement (LMM) launched as foreign missions auxiliary agency via SVM and 17 major North American Protestant denominations; uses large city-wide conferences, crusade dinners, business methods, publicity etc; by 1916, one million men have attended its 3,000 conferences, quadrupling USA Protestant mission giving.

1907 Laymen's Missionary Movement of Southern Baptists formed by 200 laymen "for mobilized laymen to evangelize our world in our lifetime," asserting that "Southern Baptists are able financially and otherwise to conquer the world for Christ"; 1927, renamed Baptist Brotherhood of the South; 1938, goal of "A Million Men for Christ"; 1950, Brotherhood Commission of SBC; 1987, enrollment 572,987 including 235,687 boys under 18 years.

1910 World Missionary Conference, Edinburgh, Scotland (previously called 3rd Ecumenical Missionary Conference until 1908 change); 1,355 delegates; beginning of 20th-century ecumenical movement; report of Commission I is entitled Carrying the Gospel to All the Non-Christian World, stating, "The Church is confronted today with a literally worldwide opportunity to make Christ known," and including survey "Unoccupied sections of the world."

Reunion of Christendom through organic union of denominations set forth as goal by bishop C.H. Brent (1862-1929) of Protestant Episcopal Church in the USA, as essential stage to conversion of world.

Men and Religion Forward Movement (MRFM, 1910-12) advances LMM concerns into a global social gospel organization, but includes nationwide evangelism, social-evangelism crusades, home and foreign missions, business ethics, detailed research on 70 cities, and every kind of Christian endeavor; reaches 1,492,646 persons in 60 USA towns through 7,062 meetings; 1913, carried worldwide by touring party.

Church of God (Cleveland) "initiates efforts at world evangelism," begins World Missions in Bahamas, Egypt and Cuba; by 1985, 109 foreign missionaries with churches in 98 countries; 1987, elaborate plan Decade of Destiny announced for every year 1988-1999.

1912 First attempt by a mission body to reach systematically every home in an entire nation: 1912-17 in Japan, Oriental Missionary Society reaches its 10,300,000 homes; later extended to other countries, then to world.

1913 English missionary C.T. Studd (1862-1931), deeply impressed by report Carrying the Gospel, founds Christ's Etceteras (later renamed Worldwide Evangelization Crusade) to focus on evangelizing "the remaining unevangelized parts (peoples) of the world."

United Missionary Campaigns across USA under LMM, Foreign Missions Conference of North America, and Home Missions Council of USA; 695 Protestant interdenominational conferences held by 1916.

1915 Elim Foursquare Gospel Alliance and Revival Party begun in Britain by Pentecostal healer G. Jeffreys (1889-1962); 1935, founds World Revival Crusade.

1917 True Jesus Church (Chen Ye-Su Chiao Hui) begun in Peking, a charismatic schism ex Apostolic Faith Movement; by 1975, a Chinese world mission with missionaries serving in Hong Kong, India, Indonesia, Japan, Korea, Malaysia, Singapore and USA.

Interdenominational Foreign Mission Association of North America (IFMA) founded "to make possible a united testimony concerning the existing need for a speedy and complete evangelization of the world," organized by SAGM, CIM, CAM, AIM, SIM, SAIM, WUMSA and later other Protestant missions of fundamentalist stance: 1967, 44 member missions with 8,500 missionaries in over 100 countries; 1979, 49 agencies with over 9,000 in over 115 countries; 1985, 103 nondenominational agencies in USA and Canada with over 11,000 foreign missionaries (over 8,000 from North America).

1918 Worldwide Evangelism, a vision of Pentecostal evangelist Aimee S. McPherson (1890-1944), who then in 1922 broadcasts first radio sermon, and in 1923 founds Angelus Temple, Los Angeles, and the International Church of the Foursquare Gospel.

USA Methodists launch Christian Crusade for World Democracy, to further Protestant missionary expansion.

CHRONOLOGY OF WORLD EVANGELIZATION FROM AD 30 TO 1990 cont.

USA Presbyterian executives believe the War experience justifies "Protestant Christianity in launching a united drive for world evangelism."

Interchurch World Movement of North America (IWM) launched to seek "complete evangelization of all life" and "conquest of the world for Christ" in one massive "forward movement"; vast support from entire range of 34 major USA denominations and 85% all USA Protestant missions; 1919, motto "The giving of the whole Gospel to the whole world by the whole church"; aims to include virtually all church-related activity; 1920, World Survey Conference, Atlantic City (NJ) with 1,700 church leaders produces massive 2-volume *World Survey* books, with plan proposing evangelization of world within 3 years; 1920, member denominations raise its $336,777,572 budget but refuse to release it; in 7-day period, IWM collapses in financial fiasco and bankruptcy.

1919 International Missionary Council (IMC) launched (directly succeeding Continuation Committee of 1910 World Missionary Conference, Edinburgh) with preliminary conference in Crans, Switzerland, then in 1921 (1-6 October) formally constituted and founded at Lake Mohonk, NY (USA); 2nd meeting in Oxford, England, in 1923.

1920 Interchurch World Movement, before its own disintegration, proposes (1) a federal "United Churches of Christ in America," and (2) a global "League of Denominations" (parallel to League of Nations); both proposals fizzle out.

Ecumenical Patriarchate of Constantinople issues encyclical addressed to "all the Churches of Christ" calling for formation of a "League of Churches."

Catholic missiologist P. Charles (1883-1954) of Louvain identifies goal of mission as the founding or planting of the visible church in all lands and in all cultural groups (Charles, *Etudes missiologiques,* 1956).

Mennonite Central Committee begun in Akron, PA (USA); many varieties of development services; by 1985, 527 foreign missionaries in 50 countries, based on long Anabaptist/Mennonite centrality of the Great Commission.

General Council of Cooperating Baptist Missions of North America organized; first vision to evangelize Africa extended in 1924 to Venezuela, then to worldwide outreach; 1953, renamed Baptist Mid-Missions; 1965, 725 USA missionaries in 27 countries; 1985, 636 missionaries in 32 countries.

1921 Institute of Social and Religious Research, New York, organized under J.R. Mott to carry on IWM's socioreligious scientific surveys; lasts until 1934.

Oxford Group formed in Britain (1921-38), later renamed Moral Re-Armament (MRA); as evangelical renewal centering on personal devotion to Christ, the 4 Absolutes, personal evangelism, and "drawing-room evangelism," spreads rapidly through major denominations and across world; by 1950 no longer solely christocentric, embracing renewal among Buddhists, Hindus, et alii.

General Council of the Assemblies of God USA appoints committee on worldwide cooperation for "the calling of a conference for the formation of an ecumenical union of Pentecostal believers for the more perfect and rapid evangelization of the world"; committee proves unable to meet and the effort collapses by 1923.

Origins of global electronic church: first broadcast of a church worship service (Calvary Episcopal Church, Pittsburgh, USA), first Baptist broadcast, 1922 first Pentecostal broadcast (Aimee S. McPherson); by 1988, regular listeners/viewers for Christian programs number 1.2 billion (24% of the world).

1923 BBC (Britain) commences radio broadcasting, including daily Christian programs; in USA, 10 churches now operate radio stations; by 1928, 60 stations, falling by 1933 to 30; in 1936, BBC commences religious television.

c.1923 Million Testaments Campaigns founded in Philadelphia, USA, by journalist G.T.B. Davis, for scripture distribution in needy areas including China, Latin America, and the Jewish world.

1924 USA: White ministers all withdraw from interracial Pentecostal Assemblies of the World (Unitarian Pentecostals) to form a separate white denomination, explaining that "the mixture of races prevents the effective evangelization of the world"; becomes The Pentecostal Church, Incorporated.

United Pentecostal Church International begun in USA; by 1985, Foreign Missions Division has 212 foreign missionaries in 50 countries.

1926 Lighthouse of International Foursquare Evangelism (LIFE Bible College) begun by Aimee S. McPherson in Los Angeles, USA, for training in world mission and evangelism.

1927 1st World Conference on Faith and Order, Lausanne; over 400 delegates from 90 churches (Roman Catholics being forbidden by pope).

Association of Baptists for Evangelism in the Orient (ABEO) formed; 1939, name changed to ABWE (WE = World Evangelism); 1985, 462 missionaries in 21 countries.

1928 World Fundamental Baptist Missionary Fellowship (later, World Baptist Fellowship Mission) founded in Texas; its "purpose is to help to fulfill the Great Commission by the evangelization of the world" through indigenous Baptist churches; 1985, 126 missionaries in 23 countries.

1929 Congregationalist missionary Frank C. Laubach (1884-1970) begins "Each one teach one" method in Philippines, develops literacy primers for 300 languages worldwide; 1950, publishes *Literacy as Evangelism.*

1930 Movement for World Evangelization (Mildmay Movement) begun in London to generate converts worldwide as "God's key representatives" in the entire global range of secular worlds, leading to world evangelization within one generation; begins with world survey, with on-the-spot surveys of every mission field on Earth, publishes *World Dominion;* 1955, begins annual Christian Holiday Crusade at Filey (UK); gradually abandons original global plan in order to supply evangelists and ministerial conferences for Britain, later for Portugal, Spain, India, Australia, New Zealand, et alia.

Formation of World Council for Life and Work, replacing Continuation Committee of 1925 Stockholm Conference.

"The Lutheran Hour" broadcast over station WHK in Cleveland, Ohio, begun by LCMS; 1931, heard by 5 million a week, 1943 15 million, 1965 30 million in 120 countries over more than 1,000 radio stations; 1940, foreign broadcasting now named Bringing Christ to the Nations; 1945, worldwide to 20 million a week; 1975, broadcast in over 50 languages, heard by 22 million a week; 1987, 40 million regular listeners in 34 languages around world.

International Missions (originally The India Mission) founded in USA by B. Davidson, "dedicated to the propagation of the gospel in obedience to the Great Commission, the ultimate goal being the establishing of self-supporting and self-propagating New Testament churches in all fields"; 1985, 159 missionaries in 12 countries.

Foundation Farthest Out begun as "a world-belt of prayer around the world"; renamed Association of Camps Farthest Out (CFO International, USA) as "one of the vital instruments that God is using to establish the Kingdom of God on the Earth"; 1988, prayer camps in 85 countries.

1931 Unevangelized Fields Mission (UFM) founded in London, UK; 1980, renamed UFM International; 1985, 338 missionaries in 12 countries.

Radio Vatican inaugurated in Rome by Pius XI (1857-1939); entrusted to Jesuits; daily announcement motto "Laudetur Jesus Christus" (Praised be Jesus Christ); 1975, broadcasts to 157 countries in 32 languages for 16 hours a day; 1982, John Paul II inaugurates Vatican Television; 1987, in 35 languages.

World-Wide Prayer & Missionary Union founded (Chicago), serving 50 evangelical missions agencies.

CHRONOLOGY OF WORLD EVANGELIZATION FROM AD 30 TO 1990 cont.

1932 Conference of Bible Societies, London, discusses ways and means of international cooperation to bring the Scriptures to the whole world.

1933 Pentecostal preacher W.M. Branham (1909-1965) offends mainline Pentecostal denominations by prophesying that 1906-1977 is the Laodicean Church Age, followed immediately by mass apostasy, Second Advent of Christ, and the Millennium in 1977; Branhamites (followers) claim him as Last Prophet with messianic attributes.

Origin of the Navigators, a one-by-one disciple-making agency based on multiplication theory/process "to contribute to the fulfillment of the Great Commission"; 1985, 191 overseas personnel in 30 countries.

1934 W. Cameron Townsend begins Wycliffe Bible Translators for Scripture translation by professional linguists, with overseas work under name Summer Institute of Linguistics (SIL); 1959, slogan "Two Thousand Tongues To Go" coined; by 1985, 3,022 translators serving overseas in 55 countries, aiming to translate Scriptures into every remaining tribal language on Earth.

First Youth for Christ rally in Brantford, Ontario, under Paul Guiness; 1944, YFC International begun, first in USA cities, as a worldwide evangelistic movement "specializing in aggressive teen-age evangelism"; 1948, first of 12 annual world congresses of evangelism (Switzerland, Tokyo, Caracas, Mexico City, Sao Paulo, et alia); in 95 nations by 1987, now attempting to identify 600 Pacesetters to raise up a worldwide youth prayer movement.

1935 World Revival Crusade founded by Pentecostal leader G. Jeffreys.

World Intercessors (Prayer Circle Department of Oriental Missionary Society) begun as worldwide prayer movement for world evangelization; over 2,000 prayer groups by 1968; 1987, over 40,000 participants (600 groups in USA alone); World Intercession School of Prayer (6 lessons); prayer seminars; 90,000 receive magazine *Prayer and Praise Guide.*

1936 Student Foreign Missions Fellowship (SFMF) begun by IVCF (USA); 1946, begins triennial mass conventions with "Complete Christ's Commission" and 1948 Urbana series with over 17,000 attenders each time.

1937 Child Evangelism Fellowship founded, based on belief that "before Christ's return a mighty work among children will encircle the globe"; by 1985, 160 foreign missionaries in 60 countries.

1938 4th World Missionary Conference/Meeting of International Missionary Council, Tambaram, Madras, India; 471 delegates from 69 countries; report states: "We summon the Churches to unite in the supreme work of world evangelization until the kingdoms of this world become the Kingdom of our Lord."

Gospel Recordings (Language Recordings International) founded: "the aim of the work is to produce gospel records in every known language and dialect" in order to spread the gospel throughout the world; by 1967, recordings made in 3,400 languages and dialects, rising by 1988 to over 4,300.

World Home Bible League founded in Chicago with as objective "the placement of a Bible in every Bibleless home, so that people can be won for Jesus Christ"; 1965, in 30 countries with over 4 million Scriptures distributed; 1985, in over 70 countries.

1939 Conference of Bible Societies, Woudschoten (Netherlands), proposes a World Council of Bible Societies.

World-wide Signs Following Evangelism, Inc., begun under United Fundamentalist Church (Los Angeles, USA).

1941 Brazil: emergence, as a new theory of evangelization, of idea of grassroots or base ecclesial communities (comunidades eclesiais de base, BECs or CEBes); 1963 formally established, with the Catholic Church standing with the poor; fully developed after 1968 Medellin and 1979 Puebla conferences.

Origin of large-scale international multilingual Bible correspondence course organizations: Emmaus Bible School founded in Toronto, Canada; by 1966, courses mushroom worldwide, especially in closed countries (Morocco 110,000 enrollments).

1942 Ling Liang World-Wide Evangelistic Mission founded in Shanghai, China "to send Chinese missionaries to the uttermost part of the world"; 1965, in 10 countries.

New Tribes Mission begun in USA to evangelize unreached tribes across the world; by 1985, 1,438 USA missionaries in 18 countries; 1988, 2,500 missionaries working in 160 tribes, "with 2,500 tribes still to be reached."

Committee on World Literacy and Christian Literature (Lit-Lit) organized by F.C. Laubach's World Literacy Committee, and Committee for Christian Literature, Foreign Missions Conference of North America (25 major boards and agencies); work in over 60 countries.

1943 USA: National Religious Broadcasters of North America formed, as official broadcasting arm of National Association of Evangelicals, with 50 organizations growing by 1979 to over 800; by 1986, annual convention attracts 4,000.

Global Outreach Mission founded (Buffalo, NY); by 1985, 114 foreign missionaries in 13 countries.

Conservative Baptist Foreign Mission Society formed in Wheaton, IL (USA); by 1985, 525 missionaries in 25 countries, based on Great Commission imperative.

1944 Dutch East Indies sees rise of Third-World missionaries: Chinese evangelist John Sung trains 5,000 3-man evangelistic teams who make major impact across country; 1969, Japanese and Pakistani evangelistic teams; 1975, Asian Evangelists Commission (AEC)conducts crusades in Palembang, Medan and other cities.

1945 Evangelical Foreign Missions Association organized in USA: "We recognize our responsibility under the Great Commission to give all men everywhere the privilege of hearing and receiving the message of salvation . . . present an urgent call to more effectively evangelize the unreached of our generation"; by 1987, 83 member agencies sending out 13,343 missionaries (11,593 from North America, 1,726 being 1-2 year short-termers).

Massive surge of new Christian parachurch agencies or multinationals independent of the churches, increasing by 1980 to 17,500 distinct and separate agencies, with multifold ministries; great majority articulate commitment to Great Commission.

Norwegian missiologist O.G. Myklebust proposes creation of an International Institute of Scientific Missionary Research, with an association and conferences devoted to global mission; ignored until IAMS formed in 1970.

1946 Series of massive student conferences in North America: 1st IVSFM Conference, Toronto, on "Complete Christ's Commission" with 575 participants; 1948, 1st Urbana Conference, 1,400 students; steady rise in numbers to 17,112 by 1976 ("Declare His Glory among the Nations"), and 18,145 by 1984 ("Faithful in Christ Jesus").

Conference of Bible Societies, Haywards Heath (UK), creates United Bible Societies (UBS) as federation and fellowship of 13 autonomous Bible societies from Europe and North America; expands rapidly by 1986 to 70 member societies and 30 national offices, working in 180 countries; UBS becomes "a worldwide fellowship whose aim is to reach every person with the Bible or some part of it in a language he can understand and at a price he can afford."

World Literature Crusade (WLC) begins in Canada for radio outreach, then expands to systematic tract distribution through Every Home Crusades in 103 countries, with goal of reaching every home on Earth by 1970; results by 1985 in 1.42 billion gospel messages handed out producing 14.5 million documented written responses for Christ.

Egede Institute of Missionary Study & Research, in Oslo, founded to promote scholarly research in the world mission of the church.

CHRONOLOGY OF WORLD EVANGELIZATION FROM AD 30 TO 1990 cont.

Asociación Misionera Evangélica Nacional (AMEN, National Evangelical Missionary Association) begun as home mission in Peru; 1979, reorganized (with Methodist personnel) as a Third-World home and foreign missionary society with a global vision, renamed Asociación Misionera Evangélica a las Naciones; thousands of young Peruvians trained; missions in 20 countries including UK, France and Spanish North Africa (Melilla).

1947 5th Meeting of International Missionary Council, Whitby, Toronto, Canada; 112 delegates from 40 countries; upholds "the evangelization of the world in this generation," coins term "expectant evangelism."

Lutheran World Federation (LWF) founded, with first purpose stated as "To bear united witness before the world to the Gospel of Jesus Christ as the power of God for salvation"; 1st Assembly, at Lund, Sweden; 1949, LWF Commission on World Missions formed, meets at Oxford (UK).

Fuller Theological Seminary founded by C.E. Fuller in Pasadena, CA (USA), as part of his expressed desire "to see the world evangelized in this generation."

World Revival Prayer League (National Christian Women's Prayer League) founded, based on Tokyo, Japan.

Oral Roberts Evangelistic Association founded (Tulsa, OK, USA), with own foreign missions program: 1953, begins Pentecostal television preaching; becomes massive ministry with worldwide healing crusades, Oral Roberts University, City of Faith, Charismatic Bible Ministries.

1948 1st World Congress on World Evangelization (also termed 1st World Congress on Evangelism) convened by YFCI (with Billy Graham) in Beatenberg, Switzerland (August), first of long annual series: 1949, 2nd World Congress in Cannes, France; 1950, 3rd in Brussels; 1951, 4th in Winona Lake, IN (USA); 1952, 5th in Belfast; 1953, 6th in Tokyo (1,200 delegates from 24 countries: workshops, crusades, teams into 43 of Japan's 44 prefectures, 4,000 commitments to Christ); 1955 Sao Paulo (Brazil), 1956 Caracas (Venezuela), 1957 Copenhagen; 1959 Madras (India), also Tokyo, also Mexico City, 1960 Bristol (UK), then series discontinued; culminating in 1966 Berlin Congress.

World Council of Churches (WCC) inaugurated in 1st Assembly at Amsterdam by 147 churches from 44 countries; theme "Man's disorder and God's design"; 351 delegates and 238 alternates, but no RC observers; "We intend to stay together" (22 August–4 September); 7th function of WCC is stated as "To support the churches in their task of evangelization."

International Council of Christian Churches (ICCC) founded (anti-ecumenical, fundamentalist); 1st Congress at Amsterdam as rival to WCC; 150 persons from 29 countries (August); later plenary congresses every 3 or 4 years; 1948-1984, 98 major ICCC conferences held; 1983 plenary with 4,000 delegates from 93 nations and 399 denominations with (1988) 4.7 million members.

Christian Crusade (Christian Echoes National Ministry, USA) organized as anticommunist mission, moves to Tulsa, OK; heard over 400 radio stations, 10 TV stations; 1953, launches ICCC Bible Balloon project, sending over 1 million Scripture portions into communist Eastern Europe by means of hydrogen-filled balloons; also other missions across world.

Latter Rain Revival (New Order of the Latter Rain) erupts among classical Pentecostals in Saskatchewan, Canada, spreads rapidly to Europe, USA, and across world; emphasis on laying on of hands with prophecy, government by order of living apostles; begins Global Missions Broadcast; from 1965, merges into Charismatic Movement.

1949 T.L. Osborn Evangelistic Association established (also termed Association for Native Evangelism), for mass evangelism utilizing citizen Christian workers in overseas countries; 1965, in over 40 countries, having reached over 20,000 unevangelized areas.

World Gospel Crusades (Every Creature Crusade) founded with as its purpose "the evangelization of the world through the mass media of communication—literature distribution, Scripture distribution, correspondence courses, radio, TV, united evangelistic campaigns"; by 1965, in 60 nations; by 1986, only 4 overseas workers left, in 2 countries.

Survey Application Trust (London) produces 5-yearly survey, World Christian handbook (1949, 1952, 1957, 1962, 1968) edited by K.G. Grubb (1900-1980), with church membership statistics compiled and totaled for first time by denomination and country.

Cursillos de Cristianidad (short courses) movement begun in Spain by RC bishop J. Hervas; short 3-day retreats to renew personal faith of Catholics; 1950s spreads to Latin America, then to USA, 1961 Britain, then globally; many leaders later become first Catholic charismatics.

1950 USA: beginnings of evangelistic association evangelism (Billy Graham Evangelistic Association, et alia); by 1976 Billy Graham has preached face-to-face to 50,780,505 across world, in 229 crusades, with 1,526,729 inquirers (decisions or converts: 3.0% of attenders), and to 104,390,133 by end of 1984.

Help Open Paths to Evangelize (HOPE Bible Mission) founded in USA "to take the gospel to unevangelized areas"; bimonthly news sheet *His Millions.*

World Vision founded (Monrovia, CA, USA) for relief and development, emergency aid, pastors' conferences; emphasis on using research, new technology, new systems, new tools, new media, "using a computer to help evangelize the world . . . to reach the world for Christ in this generation" (vice president T.W. Engstrom, 1966 Berlin Congress on Evangelism); 1988, works in over 80 countries with over 4,400 staff (mainly nationals) on 4,254 projects.

USA: evangelistic broadcasting spreads: 1950, Billy Graham begins on ABC radio, and 1951 on TV; 1953, Rex Humbard telecasts weekly, 1958 opens 5,000-seat Cathedral of Tomorrow (Akron, OH).

"Hour of Decision" radio program with Billy Graham begins over 150 stations; 1951, 20 million listeners (200,000 letters received per year); by 1978, 900 radio/TV stations worldwide, and a million letters per year (with 70 million viewers in USA).

Full Gospel Business Men's Fellowship International (FGBMFI) founded in USA as an end-time ministry by dairy magnate D. Shakarian after a vision of the people of every continent; preachers and women excluded; grows rapidly by 1970 to 300,000 members in 700 chapters worldwide, and by 1986 to 700,000 regular attenders worldwide in 3,000 chapters (1,715 in USA) in 95 countries including USSR, Czechoslovakia, Saudi Arabia, and other closed countries.

Baptist Bible Fellowship International founded as fundamentalist mission, with (by 1985) 620 foreign missionaries in 58 countries.

Missionaries of Charity (1950 Sisters, 1963 Brothers) begun in Calcutta by Mother Teresa, one of world's greatest Catholic evangelists, to minister in the name of Jesus to the poor, destitute, sick, and dying; by 1986, 2,500 sisters, 600 novices, and 344 religious houses in 77 countries including Cuba, Nicaragua, and most closed countries, with attempts to open in China and USSR; global aim "worldwide evangelization bringing Jesus to the poorest of the poor."

World-Wide Missions International organized by 35 churches in Nigeria; 1965, 1,100 workers in over 70 nations, with magazine circulation (World-Wide Missions) of 800,000; 1985, decline to 15 USA missionaries in 31 countries.

1951 1st World Congress of the Lay Apostolate, in Rome, aiming to mobilize laity (99.8% of all Christians) for outreach to the world; subsequent congresses in Rome in 1957, 1967, 1975.

1952 Worldwide Revival Movement inaugurated in Ireland by W.E. Allen and Revival Publishing Company (Lisburn) to promote theme "Revival is the key to world evangelization."

CHRONOLOGY OF WORLD EVANGELIZATION FROM AD 30 TO 1990 cont.

World Wide Pictures established by BGEA; 1953, classic movie *Mr. Texas;* by 1984, over 100 films produced and distributed, with 28,000 showings a year; viewed by over 50 million persons with 1.5 million decisions for Christ; some dubbed in 17 languages (100 prints circulate in Japan in Japanese).

1953 Worldwide Evangelization Crusade begins work on Java, founds Batu Bible School, results in indigenous Indonesian Missionary Fellowship (organized 1961), with its own plan for world evangelization with 206 personnel by 1980.

World Committee for Christian Broadcasting (WCCB) constituted in Britain, then International Committee for Christian Broadcasting (ICCB); 1961, founds World Association for Christian Broadcasting (WACB), 1968 merges with Coordinating Committee for Christian Broadcasting (CCCB) to form World Association for Christian Communication (WACC).

Congress of Catholic Action, in Chimbote (Peru), one of roots of liberation theology; this new approach to man and God, primarily from Latin America, leads to mushrooming of BECs (base ecclesial communities), new ministries, and above all to new approaches to evangelization.

1954 2nd Assembly of World Council of Churches, in Evanston, IL, USA: "Christ the Hope of the World"; 502 delegates; report states, "To evangelize is to participate in Christ's life and ministry to the world."

WCC official survey, Evangelism: the Mission of the Church to Those outside Her Life, notes "an almost chaotic confusion as to the meaning and scope of evangelism"; surveys the future and suggests: "The drama of missions and evangelism may, indeed, under God's rule over time and history be only in its infancy."

MAP International begun as interdenominational evangelical service agency providing medical assistance to 82 countries by 1985.

World Missionary Evangelism begun as nondenominational service agency (Dallas, TX, USA) in 14 countries.

New Life League World Missionary Society begun (Waco, TX, USA), "winning the world for Christ through the published word"; Restoration Baptist; missionary printing presses, radio, mass media, literature, in 50 countries (including printing Bibles for China).

1955 World Conference on Missionary Radio (WCMR) begun in USA; 1963, joins with National Religious Broadcasters of North America (NRB) to form International Christian Broadcasters (ICB), which disbands in 1968.

Midnight Call Missionary Work (L'Appel de Minuit) founded in Zurich, Switzerland, "to extend the redemptive message of the gospel into unreached parts of the world."

1956 USA: charismatic (neo-pentecostal) renewal begins among Episcopal and Protestant churches, first being at Trinity Episcopal Church, Wheaton, IL; rapidly increases to 10% of all clergy and 1 million laity by 1970, and to 1.6 million active Spirit-baptized charismatics by 1980; over these decades, vast new proliferation of "signs, wonders and healings" arises worldwide accompanying expansion of charismatic movement.

DWME of WCC begins publication of regular series, *A Monthly ILtter about Evangelism*; in subsequent 33 years covers every conceivable aspect of evangelism and world evangelization.

Catholic bishop L.-J. Suenens publishes *The Gospel to Every Creature;* considerable influence on Vatican Council II.

1957 Global Conquest program (Assemblies of God USA) prepared as a "new strategy for world evangelization," for "the rapid evangelization of the world before the return of Christ," with detailed 3-year goals especially focusing on large cities; name changed in 1967 to Good News Crusades; 1968, Council on Evangelism with its Statement of Purpose makes major impact.

Nights of Prayer for World-Wide Revival (NPWR) launched in London by Anglican layman and CMS missionary to India, G.S. Ingram (c1881-1969); continues till his death.

Send the Light (later termed Operation Mobilization) incorporated in USA, Mexico, then in over 50 countries; an interdenominational youth agency sending short-term mission workers abroad for evangelism and literature distribution.

Conference of World Confessional Groups founded, in Geneva, supported by 7 WCFs: BWA, FWCC, ICC, LWF, WCCC, WMC, WPA (WARC); 1968, RCC joins; 1968, name changed to Conference of World Confessional Families; 1979, renamed Conference of Christian World Communions; 1985, 29th Conference meets in Windsor, UK, with 20 WCFs/CWCs; now meeting annually; agreed positions on world mission emerge.

1958 Bibles For The World (BFTW) begun by Hmar believer from Northwest India in order "to mail a Bible to every telephone subscriber in the world by 1985"; BFTW is "committed to mail one billion Bibles to one billion families on planet earth"; by 1986 "It is the stated goal of BFTW to mail a book-size copy of the New Testament, in the language of the people, to a billion homes" using telephone directories; NTs mailed 1971-1982 total to 6,444,628; 1987, averages 1,500,000 a year.

1959 Southern Baptists in USA develop long-term emphasis on "Sharing Christ around the World"/"Sharing Christ with the Whole World" (Baptist Jubilee Advance, 1959-1964, jointly with 20 other USA Baptist groups); 1970 SB Convention approves concept and phrase "Bold Mission," and Home Mission Board develops it in 1974 "Sharing Christ's Bold Mission"; 1974 SB Convention in Dallas authorizes Foreign Mission Board and Home Mission Board to plan "Bold new strategies" for last 25 years of century; 1976 FMB develops "Total Missions Thrust: Global Discipleship: Foreign Missions looks toward AD 2000" and 1976 "Bold New Thrusts in Foreign Missions 1976-2000"; 1976 "Bold Mission Thrust—Acts 1.8," 1977 "by the year 2000" added; 1977 BMT adopted by many state conventions and associations.

First nationwide Evangelism-in-Depth campaign organized, in Nicaragua (125 local churches, 65,000 homes visited, 126,000 attenders in 14 local crusades, 2,604 professions of faith, 500 prayer cells formed); on successful conclusion, Latin America Mission sponsors similar campaigns in 11 other Latin American countries by 1971 (1961 Costa Rica, 1962 Guatemala, 1964 Venezuela, 1965 Bolivia and Dominican Republic, 1967 Peru, 1968 Colombia, 1970 Ecuador and Haiti, 1971 Mexico and Paraguay); spreads to other parts of world, including Tokyo 1980 and Mexico 1986 (Evangelismo a Fondo); but after 1975 fades out as a movement because largely accepted and incorporated into church programs.

Worldwide Missionary Society (Sekai Senkyo Kyokai) founded in Yokohama, Japan, to send Japanese missionaries to all foreign countries; mainly in India.

1960 IFMA Congress on World Missions, Chicago, USA; closing statement reads: "We declare the need for a total mobilization of all the resources . . . so that the total evangelization of the world may be achieved in this generation"; resurgence among Conservative Evangelicals of the Watchword "The Evangelization of the World in this Generation"; congress report by J.O. Percy entitled *Facing the unfinished task.*

Baptist International Missions founded as fundamentalist missions body, with (by 1985) 593 foreign missionaries in 53 countries.

World Missionary Assistance Plan (World MAP) founded (California, USA) as interdenominational, evangelical, charismatic service agency; inaugurates Leadership Spiritual Renewal Seminars "to create spiritual renewal among all the world's church leadership to bring change within all nations, hence worldwide evangelization, to be completed by the year 2000"; by 1987, claims 60% of that goal has been completed.

CHRONOLOGY OF WORLD EVANGELIZATION FROM AD 30 TO 1990 cont.

IVP editor/director J.T. Bayly writes satirical novel *The Gospel Blimp,* about an agency, International Gospel Blimps, Inc., who operate an airship towing sign "One Billion Unreached"; ends in disaster; archetype of attempts to evangelize by depersonalized technology without personal contact with unevangelized populations.

Youth With A Mission (YWAM) begins as evangelical-charismatic sending agency, expanding as outgrowth of the Jesus Movement in USA; at first, little church consciousness; 1977, outfits 10,000-ton evangelistic ship m.v. *Anastasis* for discipleship and mercy ministries; by 1983, the world's largest evangelistic agency with 14,000 short-term young people sent overseas each year, in 56 countries; by 1987, 50,000; goal to field 100,000 a year by AD 2000.

1961 World Missionary Press begun (New Paris, IN, USA) as nondenominational agency distributing Scripture booklets in 214 languages in 179 countries.

2nd World Survey of Unreached Areas (Areas of the World Unreached by the Gospel): L.G. Brierley publishes section 4, The challenge of the unachieved, and other WEC survey volumes describing "The 19 Point Programme to Reach the Unreached"; also survey articles in WEC's magazine *World Wide*; in introduction quoting WEC founder C.T. Studd, Brierley states: "Unless some new heroic effort is made by God's people entailing great sacrifices, great faith and desperate courage, the evangelization of the whole world in this and several future generations is a patent impossibility."

1st Pan-Orthodox Conference, Rhodes (Greece); agreement to move towards a future Great & Holy Council of the Orthodox Church; subsequent conferences 1963, 1964, 1968, 1976.

World Evangelism founded in USA by Pentecostal evangelist Morris Cerullo; 1967, World Evangelism Society of Great Britain.

3rd Assembly of WCC, in New Delhi, India; Russian and other Orthodox Churches join WCC; integration of WCC and IMC, latter emerging as Division of World Mission and Evangelism (DWME and CWME) whose report states, "Two-thirds of the human race are without the knowledge of Christ as the light of the world"; report on "Christian witness" states "All disciples stand under the Great Commission of the One Lord."

Joint Action for Mission (JAM) promulgated by International Missionary Council, then by DWME/WCC as "a plan of ecumenical mission," local or global, "recommended by CWME to be followed in all six continents"; but meets resistance from confessional and institutional structures of churches and missionary agencies, and soon peters out.

First religious TV station opened, in USA: WYAH (M.G. Robertson, in Tidewater, VA), later Christian Broadcasting Network; by 1980, almost every major metropolitan center in USA has its own religious TV station; by 1987, CBN World Outreach involves "sharing the love of Jesus in more than 85 nations."

6th International Student Missionary Convention, Urbana, IL, USA; 5,027 attenders; "The world must be evangelized in one decade" (Billy Graham); "We can evangelize the world in this decade. It is possible" (Clyde Taylor, NAE).

World Association for Christian Broadcasting (WACB) founded, becoming by 1968 the WACC.

World Radio Missionary Fellowship inaugurates HCJB-TV (Quito, Ecuador) as pioneer missionary telecaster; 1985, 218 overseas personnel in 8 countries.

Swiss Protestant scholar Karl Barth (1886-1968) writes: "The Great Commission is truly the most genuine utterance of the risen Jesus"; widespread resurgence of interest by theologians in Commission's significance and interpretation.

African/Independent Lutheran Church (Loyalist Religion) founded in Maragoli (Kenya) as Luhya indigenous body; 1980, renamed Third World Missions Federation, with aim to promote world evangelization by Third-Worlders.

1962 Haggai Institute for Advanced Leadership Training begins courses in Singapore as a service agency training Christian leaders in national and world evangelization, with 5,100 Third-World alumni in 99 nations by 1987, and a goal of 10,000 by AD 2000.

1963 International Christian Broadcasters (ICB) formed by USA Evangelicals; 1967, meets in Concordia, Milwaukee; but fades out by 1968, displaced by NRB (USA).

7th UBS Council Meeting, Hakone (Japan), with 27 member societies, launches plan "God's Word for a New Age," agrees to publish Bible selections, sets global goal of Scripture distribution: a Bible in every literate Christian home, an NT for every literate Christian, a portion for every literate adult, Scripture outreach to every nonliterate, and a selection for every soul on earth.

New Life For All (NLFA) begins as 10-year campaign in Nigeria, spreads across African countries.

Methodist professor of evangelism R.E. Coleman writes a classic, *The Master Plan of Evangelism,* expounding evangelistic message and methodology of Jesus, God's strategy of world conquest, long-range goals, based on training Twelve Apostles "to go with the Gospel to the whole world," "to win the world for Christ."

1964 Missiologist D.A. McGavran begins *Church growth bulletin;* 1979, renamed *Global church growth*, stated to be "the only worldwide missiological magazine dedicated exclusively to the Great Commission Mission," whose purpose "is to report from the Church Growth perspective, what God is doing in world evangelization and to share effective strategies, insights and resources."

Evangelical missions quarterly (EMQ) founded by IFMA/EFMA, operated by EMIS, "dedicated in obedience to the command of Jesus Christ to the proclamation of the gospel of the Son of God to the whole world"; over next 25 years, all material relates directly or indirectly to world evangelization.

1965 Oriental Orthodox Churches Conference, in Addis Ababa: first conference of heads of Armenian, Coptic, Ethiopian, Syrian, and Malabar churches; "The Church's role is to convey the message of salvation to the world . . . Christ's command 'Go into all the world and preach the Gospel' . . . should be its central concern, its main preoccupation."

World Evangelization Research Centre begun in Nairobi, Kenya, by CMS missionary D.B. Barrett for ecumenical-interdenominational-scholarly research; also termed CSWE (Centre for the Study of World Evangelization).

Emphasis on evangelizing tribes and peoples leads to 7-year DWME/AACC Unreached Peoples research project throughout Africa sponsored by 1965 consultation on "The Evangelisation of West Africa Today" at Yaoundé, Cameroon.

1966 Evangelical Congress on "The Church's Worldwide Mission," Wheaton, IL, USA, sponsored by both IFMA and EFMA; 938 delegates from 71 countries agree to Wheaton Declaration, holding local church chiefly responsible for ongoing mission and evangelism: "We covenant together . . . for the evangelization of the world in this generation, so help us God!"

World Congress on Evangelism, Berlin: "One race, one gospel, one task"; 1,200 delegates from over 100 countries; from now on, strategic plans and conferences for countrywide and world evangelization proliferate; closing Statement states "Evangelism is the proclamation of the Gospel."

1st Assembly of Pacific Conference of Churches, in Lifou, Loyalty Islands (New Caledonia), on theme "Go Ye . . ."

Missions Advanced Research and Communication Center (MARC) founded by World Vision (E.R. Dayton) in Los Angeles with the express goal of "making available and understandable the tools of technology which can aid the Church in giving every man an opportunity to say yes to Jesus Christ."

Release the World for Christ begun as Greek Orthodox agency based in Houston, TX, USA, holding evangelistic crusades overseas (India, Thailand).

1967 International Correspondence Institute founded by Assemblies of God USA as Bible courses arm of Good News Crusades, with accumulative enrollment of 5,077,014 in 164 nations by 1987, with 280,810 recorded decisions for Christ (5.5%).

CHRONOLOGY OF WORLD EVANGELIZATION FROM AD 30 TO 1990 cont.

South Korea: massive evangelistic campaigns held: 1965, 17-denomination 80th anniversary of Protestantism (20,000 professions of faith); 1967, Crusade for World Revival (30,000 attenders a night), linked with organization CWR begun in 1965 in Britain; 1973, Seoul crusade (3,210,000 attenders, 275,000 enquirers); 1974, EXPLO 74 training conference on evangelism and discipleship (323,419 workers from 78 countries); 1977, National Evangelization Crusade; 1978 Here's Life Korea; 1980, 16.5 million attend 4-day World Evangelization Crusade, in Seoul; et alia.

1968 4th Assembly of WCC, in Uppsala, Sweden: "Behold, I make all things new"; 2,741 participants (704 delegates, 750 press); report states, "Our part in evangelism might be described as bringing about the occasions for men's response to Jesus Christ"; but also there is "widespread defeatism in the churches about the work of evangelism and world mission" (D.T. Niles).

World Association for Christian Communication (WACC) founded as merger of WCCB, WACB, and CCCB; works in 60 countries.

Association for World Evangelism (AWE) founded in Portland, Oregon (USA); nondenominational; 1985, 8 workers in France and Switzerland.

African Independent Churches Service (AICS) proposed by D.B. Barrett as service agency to assist Africa's 5,000 indigenous denominations in order to help them to mobilize the world's 85 million non-white indigenous Christians in 7,000 denominations in a global plan to evangelize the world; 1976, Egyptian Orthodox bishop A. Markos launches scheme (Organization of African Instituted [Indigenous] Churches, OAIC) based in Nairobi, Kenya, with vast activities, conferences, TEE, et alia; by 1987 a major force but with its global goal abandoned.

1969 Pentecostal evangelist Jimmy L. Swaggart begins USA radio ministry "Camp Meeting Hour," then in 1972 television ministry; by 1987, Jimmy Swaggart Ministries air telecasts over 3,200 TV stations in 15 languages viewed by 510 million in 145 countries weekly, raising donations of $150 million a year, and claim "the medium of television is the most expedient method of spreading the gospel the world has ever known. It is God's directive that the Great Commission be carried out by this means"; 1988, partial collapse due to sex scandal.

World Evangelism Foundation founded (Texas, USA) by Baptist missionaries to mobilize Southern Baptist laypersons to spread Partnership Evangelism; by 1988, over 7,000 persons from USA have held 200 major evangelistic campaigns in 40 countries, with 200,000 decisions for Christ.

1970 5th Assembly, Lutheran World Federation (LWF), Evian (France), on theme "Sent into the World"; new Commission on Church Cooperation (CCC) formed centered on evangelism, meets 1971 Tokyo, 1972 Kecskemet (Hungary), 1973 Santiago (Chile), 1974 Lund, 1975 Adelaide, 1976 Saskatoon, 1978 Montreux, 1979 Singapore, 1981 Chicago, 1982 Stavanger.

9th International Student Missionary Convention, Urbana, IL, USA, on theme "World Evangelism: Why? How? Who?"; 12,304 attenders.

Popular books on premillennial eschatology (an interpretation held by 41% of all Evangelicals, and countless others) sell 31 million copies over 15 years, especially H. Lindsay's 9-title series beginning with *The Late Great Planet Earth;* these however all dismiss human responsibility for global mission and world evangelization after only miniscule passing mention (less than 1% of text). "AD 2000: 350 million Christians in Africa" published in IRM by D.B. Barrett, on Third-World progress towards world evangelization.

Frankfurt Declaration on Mission, promulgated by 14 Conservative Evangelical Lutheran theologians in Germany.

12th Baptist World Congress, Tokyo, launches 5-year evangelistic program "World Mission of Reconciliation Through Jesus Christ"; officially gets under way in 1973, with campaigns across world.

OM purchases 2,500-ton evangelistic ship m.v. Logos for UK §80,000 to visit large-city ports in difficult countries around world, with literature evangelism, book sales, missionary conferences; 110 crew, total 1,500 crew from 1970-88; 20 million persons exposed to gospel through related shore teams, 7 million visitors aboard buying literature in 107 different countries; 1988, ship (now valued at §1 million) runs aground and is lost off Tierra del Fuego; 1977, sister ship m.v. *Doulos* (6,000 tons) begins travels, reaching 600 visitors per conference.

1971 Final Advance of Scripture Translation (FAST) launched with WBT/SIL cooperation as computerized closure vision to finally complete remaining task of translating Bible into every language; main purpose to galvanize denominational Bible translating agencies (Baptist, Pentecostal, Catholic, et alia), but finally terminates in 1983 despite over 5,000 languages still remaining untranslated.

International Crusades begun in Dallas, Texas, as agency coordinating Southern Baptist 2-week Partnership Crusades overseas; goal: "To see one million people pray to receive Christ by the turn of the century using partnership evangelism."

Conference on Church-Mission Relationships in Creative Tension, held at Green Lake, WI (USA), with 400 attenders, under aegis of EMIS and sponsored by IFMA/EFMA: "We affirm the continuing worldwide mandate upon the worldwide church to fulfill the Great Commission of Jesus Christ."

1972 International Catholic Charismatic Renewal Office (ICCRO) founded as International Communications Office in Ann Arbor, MI (USA); first 2 International Leaders Conferences (1973, 1975) held there; 1976, office transferred to Brussels; 1981 relocates as ICCRO in Rome, organizes 5 worldwide leaders' conferences (4 in Rome, 1 in Dublin), 1985 relocates in Vatican "moving to the heart of the Church," by 1988 representing 63.5 million Catholic pentecostals in over 160 countries.

Consultation on the Gospel and Frontier Peoples, Chicago (December), sponsored by NCCCUSA and North American boards; detailed survey presented by D.B. Barrett entitled "Frontier situations for evangelisation in Africa, 1972: a survey report," tabulating data, documenting and mapping situation of 213 Muslim peoples, 411 peoples responsive to Christianity, and 236 unevangelized peoples.

Great Commission Prayer Crusade launched by Campus Crusade for Christ International; leadership by women; a few conferences held (Dallas 1976, 1984 International Prayer Assembly, Seoul).

World Conference and Assembly of CWME/WCC, Bangkok, Thailand (3rd Meeting of CWME): "Salvation Today"; moratorium on foreign missions and missionaries proposed by younger churches, widely accepted 1972-80; report states, "Each generation must evangelize its own generation" (29 December 1972-8 January 1973).

1973 Mission to the World (agency of Presbyterian Church in America) launched; 1987, 500 missionaries in 40 countries, church planting in 12 countries; stress on taking its appropriate part in Great Commission; goals include evangelizing 25 world-class cities by 1993.

Korea: 1st Annual Summer Institute of World Mission (SIWM) in Seoul; by 14th Institute in 1986, some 1,000 students have been trained at East-West Center for overseas service, with goal of 10,000 Asian foreign missionaries by AD 2000.

Globe Missionary Evangelism begun (Pensacola, Florida), with 65 foreign missionaries in 15 countries (by 1985).

All-Asia Missions Consultation, Seoul, Korea; formation of Asia Missions Association (AMA); 1975 Inaugural Convention publishes "Seoul Declaration on Christian Mission."

Urbana 73: 10th Inter-Varsity Missionary Convention, Urbana, on theme "Jesus Christ: Lord of the Universe, Hope of the World"; 14,158 attend (December); similar number each successive year up to Urbana 87 and Urbana 90 in 1990.

CHRONOLOGY OF WORLD EVANGELIZATION FROM AD 30 TO 1990 cont.

Trinity Broadcasting Network launched, in southern California, as Pentecostal television station "to get the gospel to every living human being on planet Earth" before Jesus comes; by 1986, TBN owns 55 TV stations in USA with 26 affiliates, also stations in Guatemala, St Kitts-Nevis, Italy, Ciskei.

World Film Crusade founded in Florida, USA (later known as World Thrust Films, or World Mission Crusade); 1985, Brother John publishes *Winning the World: a proposal on how to win the world for Christ now . . . in our generation*; 1987; further plan announced under name World Mission Teams.

Pentecostal missions executive D.A. Womack writes *Breaking the stained-glass barrier* urging church "to abandon its sanctuaries of security and return to the evangelistic strategy of the Apostle Paul (the Ephesian Method of spontaneous lay evangelism)"; proposes mathematical formula measuring evangelization.

1974 Operation World, a prayer survey, published by P.J. Johnstone (Dorothea Mission, and WEC; subsequent editions 1978, 1980, 1986), emphasizing world evangelization through daily intercession, centrality of local churches, and the call to "mobilize the churches of the whole world to finish the task."

International Congress on World Evangelization (ICOWE), Lausanne, Switzerland, on "Let the Earth Hear His Voice"; 2,700 delegates, from 150 countries, 4,000 total (50% from Third World); produces Lausanne Covenant stating: "Evangelism itself is the proclamation of the historical, biblical Christ" (July); results by 1980 in vast, amorphous, network known as Lausanne Movement directed by LCWE (Lausanne Committee for World Evangelization).

EXPLO-74 in Seoul, Korea: 2nd Training Congress on Evangelism (Campus Crusade for Christ); 323,419 residents for one week, evening meetings 800,000 daily, with one rally drawing a new world record of 1.5 million (90% responding to invitation to commitment to Christ); biggest Christian conference in history to date (August).

"Sharing Christ's Bold Mission," theme developed by Southern Baptist Home Mission Board, extended to worldwide application.

Philippines: DAWN (Discipling A Whole Nation) conference; 75 leaders of 4,000 Evangelical churches plan to have 50,000 churches planted by AD 2000, one in every barrio in the country (November); 1985, National Church Growth Strategy Congress with 300 leaders of 12,000 Evangelical churches reaffirms this goal (19-22 February); after 1981 it becomes a world plan, with motto "389 People can change the World: you can be one of them," involving 25 countries by 1987, with goal to begin by AD 2000 a DAWN project in every country of the world, with slogan "7 Million More Churches by 2000 AD."

Presbyterian Order for World Evangelism begun (later under USCWM, Pasadena, CA), as denominational support agency.

1975 Full Gospel World Mission Association established (1 April) in Seoul, Korea, as sending body supporting 8 overseas churches and 22 Korean missionaries; by 1985, 143 missionaries in 21 countries.

5th Assembly of WCC, in Nairobi, Kenya: "Jesus Christ frees and unites," 2,085 participants (850 delegates, 600 press); report on "Confessing Christ today" states, "We are commissioned to proclaim the Gospel of Christ to the ends of the earth."

13th Baptist World Congress (BWA), Stockholm, on theme "New People for a New World—Through Christ"; 9,936 delegates from 92 countries.

Associates for World Evangelization (AWE) begun for students associated with USCWM.

New Life International begun as evangelical charismatic service agency involved in TEE, literature, research; 1984, renamed Total World Evangelization Vision (Fresno, CA, USA), in 8 countries.

Genesis Project is begun to produce whole Bible on film, word for word; 33-year project envisaged, covering OT/NT with 300 films as the New Media Bible, to be dubbed in 27 languages; by 1986, 33 films emerge, but only Genesis and Luke completed; major achievement the *Jesus* film with CCCI.

World Evangelical Fellowship Missions Commission inaugurated in Seoul, Korea, dedicated to development of the non-Western missionary movement (Third World missions), utilizing a network of agencies and Evangelical fellowships across the world.

1976 Southern Baptist Convention USA, meeting in Norfolk, VA, adopts resolution and plan for remainder of century to implement world evangelization through strategy Bold Mission Thrust: "To enable every person in the world to have opportunity to hear and to respond to the gospel of Christ by the year 2000"; at 1988 midpoint, Foreign Mission Board reaffirms this intention.

Gabriel Olasoji World Evangelism (GOWE) founded in Ibadan (Nigeria) with motto "Reaching the Unreached" based on Mark 16:15; by 1988, power evangelism and mass crusades in 25 nations.

Pasadena, CA, USA: founding of US Center for World Mission, restricted to Conservative Evangelicals.

LCWE Strategy Working Group (SWG) formed; meets every year or two, works on plural strategies and tactics rather than any single overall strategy.

Australia: Congress on World Missions and Evangelism (May).

AMEN (American Military Evangelizing Nations) formed, by USA denomination Churches of Christ, for lay evangelism by US armed forces around world.

Church Growth International Seminars begun in Seoul by P. Yonggi Cho; by 1986, 70,000 pastors and leaders from 30 countries have attended; at 10th Seminar in 1986, goal of world evangelization announced with specific plan to win 10 million Japanese to Christ by AD 2000.

1st Chinese Congress on World Evangelization (CCOWE), Hong Kong, on "Vision and Mission," with 1,600 participants from over 20 countries (August); CCCOWE (Chinese Coordination Centre of World Evangelism) set up in Hong Kong (October).

EFMA mission executives meet and tally the number of people groups in the unreached category which their agencies alone are in touch with, or are planning to reach by 1990; total estimated at 6,000 people groups.

Lausanne Intercession Advisory Group formed after ICOWE I; organizes conferences, annual day of prayer for world evangelization (Pentecost Sunday).

Habitat for Humanity International founded (USA) "to eliminate poverty housing throughout the world in the name of Jesus Christ, seeking to glorify Him and to spread His Gospel throughout the earth"; 1988, builds 2,000 houses in 300 cities; goal by 1996, to build in 2,000 North American cities and in 60 other countries.

Fellowship of World Christians (FOW) begun by USCWM for students (mostly ex-AWE) concerned for world evangelization; rallies; defunct by 1978; 1985, name taken over by different group (World Literature Crusade) offering 100 people a year two-week mission encounters in Mexico, Haiti, et alia.

1977 1st Conference on the Charismatic Renewal in the Christian Churches; ecumenical, at last embracing all pentecostal traditions; on theme "Jesus is Lord"; in Kansas City, USA; 59,000 present (July); but after this ecumenical climax, charismatic conferences revert to monodenominational or monoconfessional status (15,000 Lutheran charismatics each year in Minneapolis, 10,000 RCs in Notre Dame, et alii).

World Conference on Audio-Visuals and Evangelization, Munich (November).

Here's Life, World (saturation and total mobilization evangelization campaign), organized by Campus Crusade for Christ, bankrolled by History's Hundred (100 USA billionaires), launched in 100 countries, on every continent, with announced goal "to fulfil the Great Commission in the whole world by the end of 1980."

1978 World Mission 1978-1981 begun as World Methodist Council's 4-year plan of global evangelism.

International Conference on the Charismatic Renewal in the Catholic Church, in Dublin: "You shall be My Witnesses"; 15,000 participants, led by L.-J. Suenens cardinal primate of Belgium (June).

CHRONOLOGY OF WORLD EVANGELIZATION FROM AD 30 TO 1990 cont.

1st Norwegian Congress on World Evangelization (related to LCWE), followed about every 2 years by Danvik National Conferences on Evangelization, with 140 church leaders, held in Drammen (Norway) in 1980, 1981, 1982, 1984, 1986.

Attempt by MARC (USA) to set up an information network for world evangelization entitled SHARE (Systems, Hardware and Research for Evangelization); scheme founders by 1985 due to inability to obtain original field data.

Great Commission Strategy Resource Network (GCSRN) launched by CCCI "to finish the task of reaching by 1980 those who have not yet heard the gospel," based on 5 functions: (1) information gathering and distribution, (2) resource reference, (3) research, (4) vision rooms, (5) international communication system; but peters out until by 1987 is reduced to computer hardware maintenance.

1979 Anglican renewal agency SOMA (Sharing of Ministries Abroad) founded, "dedicated to fostering Renewal in the Holy Spirit world wide so as to enable and equip the Church to fulfil the Great Commission of Jesus Christ, to proclaim the Kingdom of God and minister in the power of the Holy Spirit"; holds international conferences 1981 Singapore, 1983 Nairobi, 1984 Fiji; by 1987, its work in 50 countries covers 26 of the 31 Anglican Provinces worldwide.

Foursquare Missions International announces plan to begin work among 100 unreached peoples; by 1985, has 83 foreign missionaries with related churches in 47 countries (International Church of the Foursquare Gospel).

Over 10,000 pilgrims attend International Charismatic Pilgrimage to Lourdes on shrine's 100th anniversary (July).

12th Pentecostal World Conference, in Vancouver, Canada: "The Holy Spirit in the Last Days" (October).

Canadian Congress on World Evangelization.

International Mission Congress (FABC and SC Propaganda), in Manila, on "Towards a New Age in Mission: the Good News of the Kingdom to the Peoples of Asia" (2-7 December).

Jesus film produced by The Jesus Project, Campus Crusade for Christ, filmed in Palestine in 1979; by 1986, is circulating dubbed in 106 languages; annual viewers then total 275 million, decisions for Christ reach 33 million (12%); 1988, goal announced for 5,000 teams with copies dubbed in 271 languages of over a million speakers each by 1993 plus 1,000 other strategic languages and dialects by 1998 with 5 million viewers a night; also that, by AD 2000, 6 billion people shall have seen it of whom 600 to 1,500 million pray to receive Christ.

Evangelist Billy Graham (at IVCF Urbana conference) and USA Evangelical foreign mission leaders issue call for "120,000 missionaries by the year 2000" in order to reach unreached peoples and establish "A church for every people by AD 2000."

USA: Angel-I/Angel-II/Angel-III Project to blanket Earth with gospel broadcasts proposed by NRB and WEF: 3 satellites in geostationary orbit filling roles of 3 angels of Revelation 14:6-11, each covering a third of Earth's surface, fulfilling Matthew 24:14 "for a witness unto all nations"; by 1983, author realizes project has been "committeed to death," so proposal passes into oblivion, though use of satellites for USA Christian TV grows.

TV evangelist J. Bakker of PTL Ministries announces plan to start PTL missions throughout the world; funds raised but plan fizzles out within a year; 1987, Ministries collapse in financial and sex scandal.

Lutherans for World Evangelization begun in Pasadena, CA (USA), as research and information service.

Caleb Project begun by USCWM to tap potential of students and young adults committed to world mission, undertaking field research among unreached peoples; 1986, merges with Joshua Projects.

1980 LCWE International Consultation on Simple Life-Style, Hoddesden, UK (March), on how adoption of biblical life-styles could accomplish world mission.

Stuttgart Congress on World Evangelization, Germany (April).

A large African indigenous charismatic church, World Evangelical Crusaders in Christ Ministries (Benin City, Nigeria), begins Operation World Begin From Here; other AIC denominations across Africa also advance similar global plans.

1st World Missionary Conference on Mission and Evangelism (4th Meeting of CWME/WCC), in Melbourne, Australia, with title "Your Kingdom come" and theme "Good News to the Poor"; 650 delegates representing 300 churches from 100 countries; "The proclamation of the Gospel to the whole world remains an urgent obligation of all Christians" (12-24 May).

LCWE Consultation on World Evangelization (COWE) in Pattaya, Bangkok: "How shall they hear?"; 875 delegates from 87 countries; 17 miniconsultations (16-27 June).

USA: 8th Annual Meeting, American Society of Missiology (ASM), in Wheaton, IL, on theme "World Evangelization Today: Convergence or Divergence?" (22-24 August).

10th United Bible Societies Council Meeting, Chiang Mai (Thailand), with 68 member societies, on theme "God's Word: open for all" (September); over last 80 years, annual circulation of complete Bibles in all languages has risen from 5.4 million in 1900 to 36.8 million by 1980; UBS plan for decade to provide by 1990 common Bible translations in every language with over 1 million literates.

World Evangelization Crusade (Here's Life, Korea), Seoul; 16,500,000 attendances, including largest single meeting in Christian history to date (2.7 million).

United States Festival of World Evangelization; 50,000 participants (September).

Third Wave of 20th-century Renewal in the Holy Spirit begins in 40 major Evangelical churches, emphasizing power evangelism, power encounters, power healing, et alia.

1981 Christian broadcasting expands from origin in 1921 to global force heard or seen regularly by 23% of world's population.

USA: new generation of charismatic TV evangelists arises, including Oral Roberts (who began Pentecostal TV preaching in 1953) and son Richard, Pat Robertson, Rex Humbard, Jimmy Swaggart, Kenneth Copeland, Paul Crouch, Jim Bakker, et alia.

Evangelize the World by Computer Dialing: a scheme, proposed by several agencies, involving continous automatic dialing through world's telephone directories and giving recorded messages to whoever replies.

2nd Chinese Congress on World Evangelization (CCOWE), on "Life and Ministry," with over 1,500 church leaders, Singapore (June).

World Evangelization Strategy Work Group begun, formed by Baptist World Alliance; numerous meetings, papers; publishes *World Evangelization Now!;* presses idea of a Baptist Fund for World Evangelization (to support Third-World missionaries); 1988, BWA General Council announces "Vision 2000: Jesus Christ for All People" as "a vision for encouraging world evangelization by the year 2000 AD."

14th World Methodist Conference meets in Hawaii, endorses WMC's World Evangelism Committee's Continuing Plan for the Mission to the 80s (Decade of Evangelism), also known since 1971 inception as World Evangelism.

Mission to Unreached Peoples (USA) begun under original name Gooddeeds.

Dominion Video Satellite (Dominion Network) incorporated in Florida (USA) to provide Christian radio/TV programs over DBS system (direct broadcast satellites), based on Great Commission, DBS as the angel of Revelation 14:6, 30-inch portable dish receivers, and bypassing of secular control over TV.

1982 Project 223 begun by YWAM, "to establish a vital permanent ministry in every country on Earth," in 2 stages: (1) trailblazing, sending teams on evangelistic trips, one team to each of the world's 223 countries, involving initially 15,000 short-termers (2 weeks to 1 year) each year; completed in 1988 with No. 222 (Pitcairn Islands) and No. 223 (Svalbard & Jan Mayen Islands); also Project 300 to reach the 300 world-class megacities, with YWAM presence in 69 by 1988; and (2) pioneering (permanent

CHRONOLOGY OF WORLD EVANGELIZATION FROM AD 30 TO 1990 cont.

residence) in 90 countries by 1988; with AD 2000 goal of 100,000 workers, aiming to fulfill the Great Commission in 25 years by AD 2011; 1988, among many new Projects introduced in Target 2000: Great Commission Torch Run, begun in Jerusalem on Easter Sunday, to involve 1 million runners.

1st ICFG Global Leadership Conference (Los Angeles) launches "Harvest Vision: 1990," a plan produced by Foursquare Missions International to reach 160 hidden people groups, enter 76 new countries, and total 2.1 million ICFG members, all by 1990.

5th Conference, International Association for Mission Studies (IAMS), Bangalore, India, on theme "Christ's Mission to the Multitudes: Salvation, Suffering and Struggle" (4-9 January); IAMS exists "for the scholarly study of Christian witness and its impact in the world."

Publication of World Christian encyclopedia: a comparative survey of churches and religions in the modern world, AD 1900-2000, designed deliberately as global survey to document world evangelization, the unfinished task, and rise of a global evangelization movement.

LCWE Chicago Consultation on Terminology concerning Unreached Peoples; subsequently, clear distinction drawn between (a) "ethnolinguistic peoples" (being legitimate targets of church-planting efforts to establish beachheads with as goal in each a viable organized church fellowship able to evangelize its own culture), and (b) "bridges" or "bridge people groups" (smaller social or functional groupings affording opportunities for evangelism without church planting) (25-26 March).

World Satellite Evangelism (motto "Using Mass Media to Reach the Unreached of the World for Christ") begun in Tulsa, OK, (USA) "mobilizing media to reach every person in every home with the gospel" especially in closed countries; forms a global media task force in 50 nations, starting Christian universities and other centers.

1st Korean World Mission Congress, in Pasadena, CA (USA), with 300 delegates from Korean churches on 5 continents, "to unite Koreans worldwide for the Great Commission of Christ" and "to establish a Korean World Mission Coordinating Center" (17-30 May).

Major document Mission and Evangelism: an Ecumenical Affirmation produced in Geneva by CWME and officially promulgated by Central Committee of WCC (July).

Institute for World Evangelism established in Atlanta, GA (USA), as major long-range achievement of World Evangelism Committee, World Methodist Council; its 1987 3rd biennial International Seminar, Atlanta, on theme "The Holy Spirit and World Evangelization" draws over 100 delegates from 33 countries; authentic Wesleyan evangelism, with 2-fold witness to personal salvation and social redemption, given a new credibility and acceptance in Methodism worldwide.

IFMA Frontier Peoples Committee formed; attempts to survey constituency of 96 IFMA member mission agencies in USA and Canada, but little substantial results; 1988, 71st IFMA Annual Meeting in Hamilton (Ontario) takes as its theme "Countdown 2000" (12-15 September).

EFMA Missions Consultation on "The Challenge of Our Task," in Colorado Springs, CO, USA (27-30 September), based on World Christian encyclopedia; 1989, EFMA Mission Executives Retreat on "Evangelizing the World by AD 2000," in Colorado Springs (25-28 September).

1983 World Baptist Congress on Urban Evangelism, in Niteroi, Brazil (26 June-3 July).

Lengthy document "A global strategy for world evangelization by AD 2000: list of 105 steps or stages or aspects" produced for Southern Baptist Foreign Mission Board by WERC (Nairobi).

1st International Conference for Itinerant Evangelists, Amsterdam; theme "Do the Work of an Evangelist"; 3,800 evangelists from 132 nations (July).

6th Assembly of WCC in Vancouver, Canada, on theme "Jesus Christ the Life of the World"; 900 delegates (300 being women) from 310 member denominations, 850 journalists, 15,000 attenders at opening service (24 July–10 August).

Global Mapping Project started on USCWM campus, to assist churches with data and maps, with as objective "Visualizing the Task of World Evangelization."

Lumen 2000 launched as Catholic global television evangelism agency, based in Dallas (USA) and Vatican City, "to preach the gospel of Jesus to the uttermost parts of the Earth, spreading the love of Jesus around the globe"; 1986, in 50 countries.

Committee on the Holy Spirit & Frontier Missions (CHSFM) begun in conjunction with USCWM to involve charismatics in frontier missions among hidden peoples; defunct by 1985.

L.E. Keyes writes *The last age of missions: a survey of Third World mission societies,* describing world evangelization by 5,000 missionaries in over 400 Third-World locally-supported societies and boards (especially from Brazil); since 1940, movement has mushroomed, with AD 2000 projection of 100,000 non-Western missionaries from 1,000 non-Western mission agencies.

New Focus Incorporated founded (San Bernardino, CA) as "a Great Commission ministry committed to sports media strategies to reach the whole world with the gospel by the year 2000"; geared especially to TV specials at Olympics in 1988 in Korea, 1992 in Barcelona (Spain), 1996, and 2000.

1984 LCWE International Prayer Assembly for World Evangelization, Seoul, Korea (June); title, "Seeking God's Face for a Movement of Prayer for the World"; 3,200 participants from 69 nations.

Ethnic Chinese Congress on World Evangelization (ECCOWE), in Honolulu, with 144 delegates (5-12 July).

Over 30 national and 8 regional LCWE conferences on world evangelization, plus intensive prayer, commitment and planning, are organized for 5-year period leading into 1989 ICOWE II.

7th Assembly, Lutheran World Federation (LWF) in Budapest, Hungary, on "In Christ—hope for the world"; 12,000 attenders (22 July-5 August).

STEP (Strategy to Every People) Programme introduced by WEC International, calling for "800 for the 80s" (800 new WEC workers for the 1980s), evangelizing 45 new peoples through resident teams; original name "Worldwide Evangelization Crusade" now changed to "Worldwide Evangelization for Christ" because 90% of new goals are among Muslim peoples.

Venezuelan Baptist Convention launches plan named Baptist World Discipleship Movement.

Costa Rica: interdenominational missions society begun by 14 denominations, 1986 formalized as Federación Misionera Evangélica Costarricense (FEDEMEC), launches campaign "Unidos en Cristo Evangelizando las Naciones" specifically "From Costa Rica to the Uttermost Parts of the Earth," aiming to mobilize 10,000 world prayer missionaries and to send out 500 missionaries to 25 unreached peoples by AD 2000.

1985 "Mission 2000" scheme proposed by missiologists D.A. McGavran and R.D. Winter, aiming to plant a church in each of world's unreached peoples by AD 2000 through formation of 100,000 local church mission fellowships in Western countries.

Korea: massive increase in number of Protestant and Catholic Korean missionaries sent abroad since first Protestant in 1912; by 1973, 620 serving abroad in 30 countries (270 Protestants, 250 Korean indigenous, 90 Roman Catholics), rising by 1987 to 511 Protestants in 89 Korean mission agencies (increased from 47 agencies in 1982) in 47 nations; 1985, Protestant churches announce world evangelization plans calling for 10,000 Korean missionaries abroad by AD 2000 with at least one working in every country of the world.

Youth Congress on World Evangelization, Stuttgart, Germany (February).

Interchurch Consultation on Future Trends in Christian World Mission, Maryknoll, NY, on research methodology, sociopolitical issues, and unfinished tasks of world evangelization (15-17 February).

CHRONOLOGY OF WORLD EVANGELIZATION FROM AD 30 TO 1990 cont.

LCWE/WEF Consultation on the Work of the Holy Spirit and Evangelization, in Oslo, Norway; over 70 participants from 30 countries (May); results in published book *God the Evangelist.*

1st Global Evangelization Strategy Consultation, Ridgecrest, NC (USA), with 70 participants from Baptist churches across world associated with Southern Baptist Convention; results inter alia in publication of "The AD 2000 Series" (25-28 June).

World Conference of Baptist Evangelists, Bolivar, MO (USA): "Strategies of evangelism to win world cities" (July).

6th All-Christian Peace Assembly (ACPA), convened by Christian Peace Conference (CPC), in Prague, on theme "God calls: choose life; the hour is late!"; 800 participants from 90 countries (2-9 July).

5th West Malaysia Chinese Congress on World Evangelization, sponsored by CCCOWE, in Port Dickson (5-9 August).

International Consultation on Missions (ICOM) convened in Jos, Nigeria, by NEMA (Nigeria Evangelical Missions Association) and WEF, on theme "Mobilizing Indigenous Missions for the Final Harvest"; 83 mission executives, mainly Nigerians (11 August).

Global Simultaneous Evangelistic Missions launched in Indonesia, Nigeria and other countries by World Methodist Council; thousands of local mission outreach campaigns planned across world.

Asia Committee for World Evangelization, Hong Kong (3-6 September).

God's Global Envoys—Nonresidential Missionaries for World Evangelization, an overall plan evolved by WERC/FMB, Richmond, VA, USA, envisaging cooperation of entire spectrum of all Christians of all traditions whether like-minded or not; based on 3 elements: (a) segmentization of unevangelized world into 3,000 distinct segments (peoples, cities, countries), (b) matching-up of segments with one professional missionary each, and (c) nonresidential mission and ministry through computerized research and networking; 1985, first descriptions published in print (May).

Project "The World by 2000" announced by 3 major Christian broadcasting agencies, FEBC, HCJB/World Radio Missionary Fellowship, TWR (and later ELWA-SIM): to complete by AD 2000 giving everyone on Earth the opportunity to hear the gospel of Christ by radio (September); 1987, target modified to be (1) all major trade languages with over 1 million speakers each by AD 2000, then (2) all minor trade languages, then later (3) the world's 6,500 "heart" languages.

World Ambassadors, a plan of Maranatha Christian Ministries to evangelize the world through conversions among the 200,000 international non-Christian students from 170 nations (65 closed to missionaries) who are resident in the USA; slogan "Reaching international students to reach the world" by returning home to plant churches; goal to train 15,000 such leaders each year.

World Consultation on Evangelism, Lake Junaluska (USA), sponsored by World Evangelism (World Methodist Council) (September); 5-year evangelism plan for 1987–1991 adopted.

1st Venezuelan Congress of World Missions, Maracay, aiming to appoint 500 missionaries by 1987 (15-19 October).

CWME Orthodox Advisory Group meets in Sofia (Bulgaria) on 1,100th anniversary of death of Methodius, issues call to rectify Orthodoxy's failure to fulfill Jesus' Great Commission and "to reach out to the unreached" (21-26 October).

Global Network of Centers for World Mission formed, based on 30 research and study centers; 1986, issues Singapore Statement (27 June); 1988, holds its 1st World Meeting, in Singapore (1-9 November).

Amsterdam Prayer Conference for World Evangelization, sponsored by LCWE, YWAM, et alia (November).

EXPLO-85 global Christian training teleconference organized in 95 locations in 55 countries simultaneously by Campus Crusade for Christ (CCCI), using satellite video relays (6 uplinks, several thousand downlinks), training 550,000 Christian workers from 100 countries worldwide in prayer, evangelism and discipleship, with 4 telecasts reaching 60 million (27-31 December).

Association of International Mission Services (AIMS) begun, to serve Charismatic Renewal, with slogan "Unity in the Spirit for World Evangelization"; 75 member agencies.

1986 "Reaching the World's Cities by AD 2000," a plan of Assemblies of God (USA), Division of Foreign Missions, with "declared objective to help evangelize every city on the face of the earth."

Consultation on Evangelizing World Class Cities, Moody Bible Institute, Chicago (14-17 March).

Worldwide Student NetWork launched by CCCI (USA) with goal of evangelizing by AD 2000 all the world's 30,000 tertiary-level universities and colleges (3,000 top universities, 8,000 university colleges, 19,000 vocational or professional colleges) with 60 million students, generating parallel surge from the campus to the entire world.

International Prophetic Ministry Convention, Mount Carmel (Israel) and Jerusalem; 30 modern prophets and 5,000 attenders, at Easter (Christians of all confessions).

1st General Assembly, Latin American Evangelical Confraternity (CONELA, founded 1982, with 225 member denominations, councils, associations and agencies), in Maracaibo, Venezuela; topic, challenge to evangelize Latin America and the world, with "millions of Latin American missionaries sent to the Muslim world and other regions where they are needed" (M. Ortiz, president); 95 delegates and over 1,000 attenders (22-25 April).

USA: International Conference for Equipping Evangelists (charismatic) in Sacramento, CA, "training thousands of evangelists to equip millions of Christians to reach billions of unbelievers" (5-9 May).

8th General Assembly, World Evangelical Fellowship, in Singapore, on "Renew the Church—Reach the World," with 250 delegates from 50 WEF member alliances and fellowships (22-27 June).

2nd International Conference for Itinerant Evangelists (ICIE), Amsterdam; 8,000 evangelists from 150 countries (12-21 July).

3rd Chinese Congress on World Evangelization (CCOWE '86) sponsored by CCCOWE, held in Taipei (Taiwan), on theme "Renewal, Breakthrough and Growth"; 1,900 Chinese church leaders from over 20 countries (6-13 August); CCCOWE produces 6-volume survey in Chinese (2 volumes in English) of whole Chinese diaspora across world.

4th Triennial Convention, Asia Missions Association (AMA), in Pasadena, CA, USA, on "Thy Will be done on Earth" (6-12 October); Asians abroad as foreign missionaries reported as 10,210, with AD 2000 total expected to be 67,000.

Good News World (Operation World/Mass Scripture Distribution), a global plan announced by Southern Baptist Sunday School Board, Nashville (TN), as: "Purpose: To place Scriptures in the hands of everyone in the world in 1994 to prepare for worldwide revival in 1995."

"Toward 2000," a program of Issachar Frontier Missions Research (Seattle, USA), specializing in witness in closed countries; publishes *Strategic Times journal.*

Mandate '86, 1st Annual Mid-West Student Missions Conference, "to reach the world's unreached," organized in Illinois (USA) with 800 students by IVCF-related students, supported by CCCI, AoG, SBC, IVCF et alia, with 9 related regional meetings; also Mission Advance 86 (Hamilton, Canada, 850 students); 1987, numerous student-run conferences—Mandate '87 (in Muncie, IN; 1,200 students, 23-25 January), Harvest (in Minneapolis, 6-8 February), Vision, Proclaim, Go (Global Outreach), GAP (Global Awareness Project).

USA: Presbyterian Church announces Decade of Evangelism for 1990–2000.

North American Leaders Congress on the Holy Spirit and World Evangelization (RC/Protestant charismatic renewal), New Orleans, with over 7,500 pastors and leaders, also 4,000 other attenders (October); vast numbers of regional and denominational conferences and seminars proliferate.

CHRONOLOGY OF WORLD EVANGELIZATION FROM AD 30 TO 1990 cont.

US Society for Frontier Missiology founded in Colorado Springs; 1987, 2nd Annual Meeting in Orlando, Florida (USA) discusses AD 2000 closure and countdown thinking; 86 mission leaders from 46 North American agencies (25-26 September).

Intercontinental Broadcasting Network (IBN) begun in Virginia Beach, USA, by independent charismatics linking up with European counterparts.

Global Strategy Group formed to coordinate planning for Southern Baptist Foreign Mission Board (December).

K.P. Yohannan (founder, Gospel For Asia) writes *The coming revolution in world missions,* describing a coming Third Wave of mission, namely a massive movement producing one million evangelists from thousands of native missionary movements in India, Asia, and across the world.

Missiologist J.H. Kane writes *Wanted: World Christians* (these being essential for world evangelization), holding as key "A World Christian is one who recognizes his own personal responsiblity for world missions."

Televised Evangelism for All, a project proposed by Christian Broadcasting Network vice-president N. Van Hamm: 6 million 10-inch flat liquid-screen printed-circuit solar-cell television units, costing $1 each, dumped out of aircraft across world, glide to Earth over unevangelized peoples, pretuned to 18-language transmissions over 3 or 4 geostationary satellites.

1987 John Paul II announces new Office in Rome, "Evangelization 2000," initially confined to Catholics, with news service New Evangelization 2000, and later to lead into ecumenical 1990-2000 Decade of Evangelization; comprising retreats, biggest public rally ever, 3-satellite global telecasts, global homilies, conscientization teams, mass video cassette distribution, with as aim to win 1.5 billion new Christians "as a present for Jesus on his 2,000th birthday."

44th Annual Convention & Exposition, National Religious Broadcasters (USA), Washington, with over 4,000 broadcasters, on theme "Communicating Christ to the Nations" (31 January-4 February).

Consultation on World Evangelization, Singapore, with 31 global charismatic renewal leaders (RC/Lutheran/SOMA-Anglican, et alii) (9-12 February).

International Conference of Evangelical Bible Societies (ICEBS) founded "to evangelize and disciple all nations through the placement of God's word," with 10 member agencies: ASGM, BLI, EHC, IBS, LBI, OD, PTL, WGC, WHBL, WMP.

National Charismatic Leaders' Conference (North American Renewal Service Committee, NARSC), related to global Charismatic Renewal in mainline denominations (300 million Christians, fielding 74,000 foreign missionaries), meets in Glencoe, MO (USA), appoints World Evangelization Strategy Committee with AD 2000 goal in mind (4-8 May).

World Literature Crusade changes name to Every Home for Christ, proclaims goal "to systematically place 2 gospel booklets in every home in the world, one country at a time, by AD 2000"; 40% of world's homes reached since 1946; 1986, 21,969,676 pieces of literature distributed, producing 178,509 written responses (0.8%); 1957–86, tracts distributed total 1,462,406,418, with 14,605,937 responses (1.0%).

Proposal "Countdown to the Year 2000" circulated by USCWM founder R.D. Winter, with statistics and graphics urging the engaging (entering) and reaching (discipling) by mission agencies of 1,500 new unreached peoples every year until 17,000 have been reached by AD 2000.

Global-Village Evangelism (based on Marshall McLuhan's description of the world as now a "global village") launched by Bibles For The World as "a revolutionary new concept in missions which places the local church in the center of the world mission program."

Singapore '87 LCWE International Younger Leaders' Conference on world evangelization; 300 younger Evangelical leaders from 67 countries (1-10 June).

North American General Congress on the Holy Spirit and World Evangelization, in New Orleans (successor to 1977 Kansas City ecumenical charismatic rally); over 50,000 participants (RC/Protestant charismatic renewal), 51% RCs; theme "Power Evangelism" (22-26 July); launches magazine *AD 2000 Together* with front page motto "To Bring the Majority of the Human Race to Jesus Christ by the End of the Century."

Dominion Network (satellites to homes) launched into orbit by Community Satellite Corporation, USA, utilizing DBS (direct broadcast satellites).

Global Share Network announced by Global Mapping International (USA) as a missions mapping database.

T. Yamamori writes *God's new envoys: a bold strategy for penetrating closed countries,* presenting a detailed plan describing the strategic work Christian lay tentmakers in secular work can perform in world evangelization; chapter 6 entitled "The Basic Battle Plan" calls for 100,000 such persons in 77 closed countries.

Research project "The Future of the Christian World Mission" begun under auspices of American Society of Missiology, majoring on scenarios for the future of world evangelization.

Mission World '89 (International Satellite Mission) announced by Billy Graham Evangelistic Association, to originate from a major global city (Seoul) and to be beamed by satellite to hundreds of other cities across the world; but whole plan suddenly cancelled 5 months later and replaced by scaled-down London crusade in 1989 with relays across England only.

Global Broadcasting System (GBS) launched for Christian radio and TV broadcasting to any place on Earth through "Top Hat" system of super-pressure platform network of 800 high-tech balloons at 120,000 feet altitude covering whole world.

Adopt-a-People, a proposal to link North American churches and mission agencies with specific unreached people groups, begun by USCWM.

Christian Communication Technology (CCT) formed to develop AVCAPI (computer/laser reading system for illiterates) with goal: "By the year 2000, CCT will teach every capable and willing man, woman and child on earth to read the Bible in their own language."

Worldwide Prayer Crusade launched from Vatican City by Evangelization 2000 office, geared to Decade of Universal Evangelization 1990-2000; sudden, unexpected, and massive enthusiastic response from contemplatives, convents, and monasteries worldwide.

Project 2000 begun by Partnership International, formerly Christian Nationals Evangelism Commission (CNEC, begun 1943), now in 50 countries; project pledges "to help establish an evangelistic growing church in each of the 17,000 unreached people groups of the world by the year 2000," "to help strengthen 400 ministries under 80 different indigenous national organizations."

Destiny '87 Conference (Here's Life, Black America); 1,700 Black Americans gather in Atlanta, GA, to affirm "a growing number of black Christians believe it is their destiny to play a major role in world evangelization."

New Life 2000 announced as closure project by Campus Crusade for Christ/Here's Life, World—"The comprehensive global strategy to take the gospel to every culture on every continent by the year 2000; to present the gospel message to 6.5 billion people; to see 1 billion people receive Jesus Christ as Lord and Savior; to establish 10,000 New Life Bible study groups; to establish 1 million new churches; to provide 5,000 teams showing the *Jesus* film 100 times a year to 1,000 people per night (yielding 10% to 25% salvation decisions a night); to establish 15,000 prayer movements by 1995, in every city over 50,000 and all university campuses."

Interdenominational Global Missions Conference (Dallas I) convened (17-18 September) by Southern Baptist FMB president R.K. Parks, with 20 mission agencies present; agreement on (1) prayer and fasting every Pentecost weekend up to AD 2000 as "focused intercession for global evangelization," and (2) sharing data, plans and strategies; 1988, Dallas II (February), followed by teleconferences.

CHRONOLOGY OF WORLD EVANGELIZATION FROM AD 30 TO 1990 cont.

Status Report on the Great Commission published by World Mission Teams (formerly World Mission Crusade), Florida, as open letter addressed "To All Pastors of All Christian Churches" setting out logistics and finances of how to evangelize the world by means of "the fourth dimension in evangelism" (1st = personal witness, 2nd = printing, 3rd = broadcasting, 4th = motion picture evangelism).

Decade of Harvest inaugurated by Assemblies of God (USA), as denominational program to reach all persons on Earth by AD 2000; coordination by Total Church Evangelism Strategy Committee, renamed in 1987 Harvest Task Force (for work within USA); 1988 (July), world conference of AoG-related churches overseas to plan strategy.

Ibadan, Nigeria: Consultation between All Africa Baptist Fellowship and Overseas Mission Bodies (October); produces Ibadan Declaration, on Great Commission and "mutual sharing in the holistic evangelisation of the world."

2nd Asia Leadership Congress on World Evangelization (ALCOWE or ALCOE II), under LCWE/ALCOWE auspices, in Singapore, on theme "Witnessing for Christ through the Local Church" (20-28 October).

1st Ibero-American Missions Congress (Congreso Misionero Ibero-Americano, COMIBAM '87), in Sao Paulo (Brazil), with 3,500 Evangelical representatives (70% pentecostal/charismatic) from across Latin America, and preceded by series of national missions consultations in 23 countries; goal of world evangelization, with 10,000 new Latin American foreign missionary vocations generated (23-28 November).

Church of God (Cleveland, TN), with work in 98 countries, launches "Decade of Destiny for Church of God World Missions," with a different continent targeted for each year from 1990 to 2000.

Advance Ministries: Reaching the Unreached, a mission-sending agency serving the USA's 60,000 independent charismatic churches, begun with Mennonite support.

World Evangelism World Plan 1987-1991 launched at Jamaica meeting after 15th World Methodist Conference (Nairobi, July 1986, 3,000 delegates) on theme "Christ Jesus: God's 'Yes' for the World": 1988 Aldersgate Year, Open-Air Preachings, 1989 World Conference on Physical & Spiritual Poverty, 1990 4th International Christian Youth Conference, 1991 Conference on World Evangelization followed by 16th World Methodist Conference in Singapore.

1988 Conferences on evangelization: since 1945, some 5,510 conferences on mission and evangelism (at international, continental, regional or national level) have been held, via 5 groupings: 1,050 by Roman Catholic agencies; 1,100 by Ecumenical Movement agencies; 2,100 by Protestant and Anglican mission agencies; 840 by Evangelical mission agencies; and 420 by Charismatic Renewal agencies.

2nd All-India Congress on Missions and Evangelism (AICOME '88), sponsored by indigenous-mission body India Missions Association, IMA (with 300 member agencies), in Pune, India; 350 participants (4-8 January); global total of organized Third-World mission agencies now 500.

World Evangelization Database (segmentizing world into 250 countries, 11,000 ethnolinguistic peoples, 15,000 languages, 3,300 metropolises, et alia), first begun in 1962 as computer knowledge base, is finally brought online globally by WERC/FMB to assist mission agencies to match up nonresidential missionaries with entire unevangelized world; operated by massive computerized AI network, the World Evangelization Expert System (WEES).

Literature on evangelization: on narrower definition, titles strictly on "evangelize," "evangelism" or "evangelization" total 400 new books and articles every year; on broader definition, titles on evangelization and synonyms total 10,000 a year.

World Prayer Force inaugurated in Saint Petersburg, FL (USA), aiming to enroll 165 million Christians (10% of world total) promising to pray daily for world evangelization.

Inter-Agency Consultation for Resources and Information on Reaching the Unreached (Dallas II), held in Irving, TX (USA), by 28 denominations and agencies (9-11 February); followed by sharing of online databases and a series of Great Commission electronic teleconferences, with all mission executives and leaders participating from own headquarters.

Evangelistic citywide mass campaigns: several hundred organized multidenominational campaigns (under Billy Graham, Luis Palau, et alii), and some 3,000 denominational campaigns, are held in 1,300 metropolises and cities across the world each year; also hundreds of megameetings (over 100,000 attenders) under Christ For All Nations and numerous other charismatic agencies, using slogan "The Great Commission to Each Generation."

Singapore II Consultation on World Evangelization, with 65 global charismatic renewal leaders organized as CUWE, Charismatics United for World Evangelization with the new watchword "The whole church, bringing a whole Christ, to the whole world!," "to consider the distinctive contribution that the charismatic renewal could make in spreading the Christian gospel in the years leading up to AD 2000" (February).

Consultation to inaugurate Third World Missions Advance (TWMA), convened by AMA/IMF/EMS/COMIBAM; 35 Third-World leaders meet in Portland, OR, USA (9-13 May); International Mutual Fund created; TWMA aims to represent the hundreds of new missions agencies, with potential of fielding 100,000 Third-World missionaries by AD 2000.

Explosive growth of charismatic, evangelical and fundamentalist "video churches," video denominations and video mission agencies; vast rash of house-church networks begins to spread in all countries with large denominations.

Leadership '88, an LCWE conference in Washington, DC, for 2,200 emerging leaders, to "equip them to take aggressive action to fulfill the Great Commission," to "strategize to join together for world evangelization" and "to form new networks for completing the task of world evangelization" (27 June-1 July).

North American African World Missions Congress (Initiative '88) to implement global evangelization, organized by Nigerians after 1986 formation of North American Commission of African Christians; theme "African Initiatives in World Missions: a Strategic Gathering for a New Decade"; 1,500 Africans from over 30 African countries, living in North America, present in Chicago (13-17 July).

7th General Congress, International Association for Mission Studies (IAMS), in Rome, on theme "Christian Mission towards the Third Millennium: the Gospel of Hope" (29 June-5 July).

International Evangelical Bible Consultation/Conference (sponsored by LCWE, BGEA et al), in Amman, Jordan, stressing biblical position on justice and human rights.

World Wesleyan Conference on Witness and Evangelism, sponsored by World Methodist Council, on 250th anniversary of John Wesley's conversion.

'88 World Evangelization Crusade, Korea, led by charismatics (Methodists, Presbyterians) and pentecostals.

1989 Global Consultation on World Evangelization by AD 2000 and Beyond, convened in Singapore by a group including LCWE/COMIBAM/FMB-SBC/YWAM, inviting 2 representatives of each of the 78 major current megaplans for world evangelization, "open to all leaders of Great Commission groups within the worldwide body of Christ" (5-8 January).

2nd World Consultation on Frontier Missions (WCFM).

2nd World Conference on Mission and Evangelism (5th Meeting of CWME/WCC, Commission on World Mission and Evangelism), San Antonio, TX (USA); 600 attenders, mostly church nominees; theme "Your Will be Done: Mission in Christ's Way"; distributes pan-Orthodox missionary icon widely (22 May-1 June).

World Evangelization Conference on Liberation Theology and Personal Salvation (sponsored by World Methodist Council), in Latin America.

CHRONOLOGY OF WORLD EVANGELIZATION FROM AD 30 TO 1990 cont.

Lausanne II, or 2nd International Congress on World Evangelization (ICOWE II) convened by Lausanne Committee (LCWE), in Manila; congress theme, "Proclaim Christ Until He Comes"; attended by 6,000 evangelizers (11-20 July).

15th Pentecostal World Conference, in Singapore, on theme "Behold the Glory of the Lord"; over 6,000 delegates from 100 countries, 30,000 attenders (27 September–1 October).

Consultation on Dimensions of Christian Martyrdom, dealing with effects of martyrdom on upbuilding and evangelistic growth of whole church; total martyrs since AD 33 estimated at 40,500,000 (0.5% of all Christians ever), with current rate of 320,000 each year.

Jerusalem Charismatic Leaders Meeting (Pentecost 89)convened for 120 Renewal leaders worldwide, dealing with power intercession, power evangelism, world evangelization; in Jerusalem over Pentecost weekend (7-14 May).

1990 Vast increases in all types of evangelization and of evangelistic activity: virtually all major Christian denominations and agencies announce programs leading up to AD 2000.

Decade of Universal Evangelization (also termed Worldwide Decade of Evangelization) inaugurated by John Paul II and other world Christian leaders, calling all Christians to a decade of mission, with as aims (a) to unite all Christians and all churches by AD 2000, and (b) to bring the total of Christ's disciples to over 50% of world (3.1 billion) by AD 2000.

Round the World Prayer Event, organized by World Evangelism (World Methodist Council), to inaugurate evangelism in decade of 1990s.

Peace Council/Convocation of Christians: World Convocation on Justice, Peace, and the Integrity of Creation (JPIC), a worldwide ecumenical event, convened by RCC, WCC et alia, to oppose injustice, war and environmental destruction.

USA: Joint IFMA/EFMA Conference convenes, after 1988 IFMA conference on "Countdown 2000" and 1989 EFMA conference on "Evangelizing the World by AD 2000"; approves specific allotments for 1995 schedule for reaching all peoples on Earth with gospel.

World Congress on the Holy Spirit and World Evangelization, in Indianapolis, on "Power Evangelism"; over 60,000 attenders (Catholic/Protestant charismatic renewal).

EXPLO '90 global Christian 5-day training teleconference organized in all major countries by Campus Crusade for Christ (expanded version of EXPLO-85); also their *Jesus* film becomes after 10 years translated into world's 280 languages each with over 1 million mother-tongue speakers, and is being shown to 10 million persons every night, of whom 2 million become converts or enquirers each night.

Asia Regional Missions Congress on AD 2000 and Beyond (LCWE/TWMA/AMA/et alia).

Africa Regional Missions Congress on AD 2000 and Beyond (LCWE/TWMA/EMS/et alia).

AD 2000 National Consultations proliferate, planned each for one country during the period 1990-1999 by LCWE/TWMA/et alia.

1991 Global Congress of Charismatic Leaders for World Evangelization, in Brighton (UK), to usher in decade of evangelization before AD 2000; 10,000 renewal leaders (8-14 July).

7th Assembly, World Council of Churches (WCC), in Canberra, Australia, with delegates from 350 member denominations; call to global commitment; ongoing programs include the Ecumenical Decade (1988-1998) for Churches in Solidarity with Women (launched at Easter 1988).

4th Chinese Congress on World Evangelization, CCOWE '91 (sponsored by CCCOWE/LCWE), in Hong Kong.

Sudden growth and mushrooming worldwide of youth churches completely outside control by denominations: loosely organized churches begun and run by charismatic under-25s, meeting at lunchtimes in hotels, theaters, cinemas, shops, warehouses, anywhere; huge growth of converts.

Conference on World Evangelization organized in Singapore by World Methodist Council.

AD 2000 Regional Consultations sponsored by LCWE/TWMA/et alia begin in earnest: 1991 North America; 1991 Europe; 1991 Middle East & North Africa; 1993 Asia; 1993 Latin America; 1993 Africa.

After 30 years' preparation since 1961 1st Pan-Orthodox Conference (on island of Rhodes), Great & Holy Council of the Orthodox Church convenes in Greece as first fully recognized ecumenical council of the entire church since 7th Ecumenical Council (Council of Nicaea II, last one recognized by Eastern Orthodox) in AD 787; statement promulgated on Orthodoxy's mission to the world; mission icon distributed.

Possible future scenarios with plans

1994 Final decade of 20th century proves to be greatest decade in Christian history for signs and wonders, miracles, conversions, evangelism and evangelization: greatest sign or wonder being Christians loving one another and gathering in unity everywhere.

1999 World-level conference convened by Evangelicals with a representative from every people group on Earth, in last-minute attempt to complete evangelization of panta ta ethne by AD 2000.

Catholics begin preparations to celebrate Jubilee Year of AD 2000, in the Holy Year series, with pope to telecast on 25 December 2000 to 6 billion viewers via network of satellites.

2000 Celebration 2000, a massive global event on the part of all Great Commission Christians, in myriads of locations; already by 1988 being planned in detail.

Respect for Christ: person of Christ now widely known and respected throughout world, by all world religions, even among atheists and agnostics; also his teachings and his gospel (but not his church) are understood and valued, though not accepted or implemented, almost universally.

Entire world finally reached with Christian gospel for first time in history, in the sense that everyone everywhere has heard or hears the gospel in depth with understanding and has access to Scripture, churches, missions, Christians, Christian broadcasting (with 4,000 Christian radio and TV stations worldwide), movies, literature, and other means of grace.

Global church-planting goal completed: at least one fellowship or church or congregation or nucleus of disciples has been planted as an ongoing indigenous witness in each of the world's 11,500 ethnolinguistic peoples and 4,000 metropolises of over 100,000 population.

2004 Massive pentecostal-charismatic latter-rain revival sweeps across whole of Asia due to power evangelism with signs and wonders, with 150 million converts in Korea, Japan, China, Viet Nam, Thailand, Malaysia, Indonesia, Burma, Cambodia, India, Sri Lanka and Pakistan.

2006 Declining Euroamerican denominations in Western world spark off itinerant tourist churches, groupings of believers ceaselessly travelling and witnessing around the Earth; Latin Americans independently form itinerant pilgrim churches which multiply phenomenally across world.

2008 Global church research project to determine which major events or situations in past history of evangelization should be changed by messages or messengers sent from today, as soon as science invents method of tachyonic time travel and alteration of the past; preference for rectifying the great missed opportunities of Christian history (as with China in 1266, 1644, 1843).

CHRONOLOGY OF WORLD EVANGELIZATION FROM AD 30 TO 1990 cont.

2009 Total global charismatic worship of Christ introduced, in which at a fixed time each Sunday one billion living believers across world are holographically present visibly at same location; the ultimate in inspiration and evangelistic converting power.

2011 Religious pilgrims become a major force in world, over 400 million religious zealots (50% being Christians) constantly on move from shrine to shrine and country to country, ignoring secular and state restrictions; Christian pilgrims form a vast unorganized network of continuously itinerant pilgrim churches.

2027 Christian broadcasting (overt and clandestine) utilizes vast range of 3,000 major languages, programs of every type; reputation for truth results in 90% of world as regular audience; but dangerously exposed to disinformation tactics and terrorism.

c.2030 Church of the future plays dynamic part in the evolution of mankind, bringing the world to final perfection in Point Omega (Teilhard de Chardin).

2030 Conversion of China to Christianity through multitude of Chinese house-church evangelists and witnesses, resulting in 1.5 billion zealous, charismatic, nondenominational Christians, who then launch their own global mission without reference to Western or Eastern churches and missions, or to historic Christianity, or to the 1,200 previously proposed world evangelization plans.

2045 Global Bible distribution reaches optimal maximum level of 10 billion Scriptures per year (whole Bibles, NTs, portions, selections), in languages understood by whole world's population; but highly susceptible both to antichristian terrorism and also to world government edicts.

2050 Christianity now dominated worldwide by Third-World indigenous pentecostal-charismatic bodies, spreading like wildfire through unorganized self-replicating media churches.

2080 Spread of Christianity throughout Chinese and Arab races generates vast missionary zeal to point where both launch independent schemes for total world evangelization and conversion.

2090 Church of the Martyrs: on one scenario, ruthless 80-year persecution by world government reaches climax, decimates global Christianity, reduces churches to a tiny minority, then liquidates all churches, which thus follow their Master to final execution and martyrdom.

Biblical end-time scenarios

(The remaining 10 schemas below represent biblical end-time visions often quoted or used as justification for world evangelization plans throughout history. No suggested future dates of any kind can be proposed for these visions.)

Revivals and rapid church growth with mass acceptance of gospel in some parts of the world, with mass rejection of gospel in others: millions converted in last great global spiritual revival; worldwide signs and wonders accompany proclamation of the gospel in every land.

Failure of the church to evangelize the world, part remaining still unevangelized until the Tribulation (Matthew 10:23b).

The Four Horsemen of the Apocalypse (opening of the first 4 Seals), white, red, black, pale: (1) war/conquest/deception/false religions/cults/pseudo-messiah/antichrist, (2) slaughter, (3) famine, (4) death [or (1) missionary preaching of the gospel, (2) civil war/bloodshed, (3) famine/hunger/disease/poverty, (4) terror/pestilence/death/destruction; 25% of world slaughtered] (Matthew 24:7, Revelation 6:1-8).

Sufferings of the church multiplied as it prophesies and witnesses to the world (Revelation 10:9-11).

Great Commission of Christ fulfilled in the sense that universal preaching of the gospel to all nations (world evangelization, discipling of the peoples) has been finally accomplished by the church militant on Earth, with disciples and witnesses found in every race and population and people and language (Matthew 24:14, 28:19-20).

Penultimate direct supernatural work of the Holy Spirit in proclamation, evangelization and conversions throughout world as Church Age draws to its close (Acts 2:16-17).

The 144,000 converted Israelites become End-time evangelists who reach world's last unreached people groups and so complete task of world evangelization (Revelation 7:4-8).

Last supernatural proclamation from heaven of Everlasting Gospel of love in all its fullness to every nation, and kindred, and tongue, and people, either to convert or to seal doom of mankind; last appeal and announcement of final chance for repentance and salvation, imminent end of Age of Grace with following judgment upon wicked in climax of Great Tribulation (Rev 14:6-7, being Revelation's 4th group of 7 visions; Lk 16:31).

Universal spread and acceptance of the Kingdom of God (as envisaged by Irenaeus in AD 180); gradual conversion of vast numbers to Christ.

The Two Witnesses (Olive Trees, Lampstands: Moses and Elijah, Law and Prophecy; Joshua and Zerubbabel the anointed religious and civil leaders; the witness-bearing two-sevenths of the universal church about to be martyred), after 42 months or 3½ years (literal or figurative) of preaching the gospel and opposing New Age philosophy, complete their task of world evangelization through bearing witness to claims of Christ, are slain by Antichrist symbolizing near-obliteration of the church, in 3rd Persecution; but then are raised from dead, symbolizing final global revival of faith in Christ with millions converted (Zecheriah 4:11-14, Revelation 11:3-14).

Seven Hundred Plans to Evangelize the World by David B. Barrett and James W. Reapsome. Published by New Hope, Birmingham, AL. Used by permission.

FOCUS FACT

From the time of Nero (A.D. 64) until the conversion of Emperor Constantine and the Edict of Milan (A.D. 313), whereby Christianity was made legal, the Christian faith was officially regarded as a *religio prava,* an evil or depraved religion.

Source: *Glimpses*, published by Christian History Instititute.

TWENTY SIGNIFICANT CHURCH HISTORY LEADERS

Selected by Dr. Earle E. Cairns, author and historian

Justin Martyr (c.100–165). Christian apologist. Born of pagan parents in Samaria, he was converted about 132. A few years later he went to Rome and stoutly declared his Christian faith to the highest in the land, trying to show how it went beyond even the noblest aspects of Greek philosophy. Finally, with some fellow believers, he was denounced as a Christian and subversive and was condemned to be beheaded. Justin is held to have been the first Christian apologist to bring together the claims of faith and reason. His *First Apology* (c.155) and *Dialogue with Trypho* (c.160) both emphasize that Christians are the inheritors, the heirs of Israel and its promises.

Constantine the Great (c.274/280–337). First Christian emperor of Rome. Brought up at the court of Diocletian, he became Western emperor after a military victory near Rome in 312, which he attributed to the God of the Christians. The Edict of Milan in 313 decreed full toleration and other advantages for Christians, including the restitution of confiscated property. In 325, by now

TWENTY SIGNIFICANT CHURCH HISTORY LEADERS cont.

sole emperor of East and West, Constantine summoned the Council of Nicea to settle the Arian controversy. He presided at the opening sessions. The result was a victory for orthodoxy, but Constantine had no theological discernment and was soon thereafter swayed by bishops of Arian tendencies. In 330 he established a new capital in the East, which he called Constantinople.

Athanasius (c.293–373). Bishop of Alexandria. Although only a deacon at the Council of Nicea, it was there he became the chief defender of orthodox Christianity against Arianism. Bishop of his native Alexandria from 328, his determination to uphold the true doctrine of God involved him in exhausting controversies with highly placed Arians in church and state. He was banished several times, returning finally only about six years before his death. By his faithful ministry, steadfast character, significant writings, and zeal for God's truth, he contributed much toward the triumph of orthodoxy at the Council of Constantinople eight years after his death.

"" FOCUS QUOTE

He became what we are that he might make us what he is.
—Athanasius

Augustine of Hippo (354–430). Bishop of Hippo (modern Annaba, Algeria). Born and educated in North Africa, he became a teacher of rhetoric, a profession continued when he went to Milan in 384. Influenced by that city's bishop, Ambrose, he forsook Manichaeism for Christianity. While visiting Hippo in 391 he was reluctantly ordained, and in 395 he was consecrated as successor to Bishop Valerius. He defended Christianity against attacks by Manichees, Donatists, pagans, and Pelagians, and showed himself a faithful pastor, preacher, administrator, and encourager of monasticism. Augustine is often called the greatest thinker in Christian antiquity. His writings include *The Confessions* (c.399) and *The City of God* (c.413–427). His *Confessions* is considered to be the first instance of Christian spiritual autobiography. His basic understanding of theology was that "I believe in order that I may understand"—*"credo ut intelligam."*

Innocent III (1160–1216). Pope from 1198. One of the greatest of medieval popes, he defended his office ably against the claims of emperors and other rulers. He supported the Fourth Crusade, encouraged the beginnings of the Franciscan and Dominican orders, summoned the Lateran Council of 1215, and launched a campaign in France against the Albigensians. He was a shrewd organizer and statesman, and under him the Papal States were expanded.

Francis of Assisi (1182–1226). Founder of the Franciscans. Son of a prosperous merchant, he turned in 1205 to a life of prayer and poverty, renouncing his worldly possessions. He began to preach in 1208, and in 1209 he received papal approval for the establishing of his order. Francis resigned the leadership in 1223, disliking internal disputes about administration. He spent his last three years in solitude and prayer and in occasional writing. He is the first known stigmatist; he received the stigmata in 1224 while praying on Monte La Verna. He composed the *Canticle of the Sun* and the very familiar prayer beginning, *"Make me an instrument of thy peace."*

John Wycliffe (c. 1329–1384). English Reformer. Priest and Oxford philosopher, he became widely known during his last ten years, when he was rector of Lutterworth in Leicestershire. Critical of the church's acquisitive attitude to property, he began to question other things publicly. Right thinking and right living were almost identical for Wycliffe. He instituted "simple" itinerant priests to supplement church services by religious instruction in the vernacular. They were helped by an English translation of the Bible and by Wycliffe's tracts and sermons.

His proclamation of a simple gospel, though unwelcomed in England until the 16th century, greatly influenced Jan Hus. Wycliffe has been called the "morning star of the Reformation."

FOCUS QUOTE **My conscience is captive to the Word of God. . . . Here I stand, I can do no other.** —Martin Luther at Worms

---

Martin Luther (1483–1546). Leader of the Reformation in Germany. Son of a Saxon miner, he graduated in arts at Erfurt, then in 1505 forsook further studies in law to become an Augustinian. He was ordained in 1507, and from 1508 taught theology at Wittenberg. There his lectures began to reflect his growing belief that justification by faith rather than by works expressed the church's true faith. He grew increasingly uneasy about the sale of papal indulgences as a means of boosting church revenue, but his demand for a theological examination of the practice brought only a trial for heresy. Others who saw the need for reforms in Roman Catholicism gathered around him and protested that the gospel of Jesus Christ had become obscured in the church by worldly accretions. Excommunicated by the pope and outlawed by the emperor, Luther nonetheless found powerful protectors and sympathizers, and soon the cause of the Reformation was irreversible. Luther rejected on one hand various kinds of religious extremists within protestantism, and on the other such humanists as Erasmus, who sought reform from within the old church. Luther's fear of anarchy led him to side with authority against the Peasants' Revolt in 1525, an action that alienated some of the common people. And he differed also with the Swiss Reformer Ulrich Zwingli over the meaning of the Lord's Supper. Luther was a prolific writer, issuing pamphlets to combat the evils of the time and doctrinal works that would set Protestantism on a sound theological foundation. His greatness can be seen, suggests one scholar, in that more books have been written about him than about anyone else in history except Jesus of Nazareth.

Ulrich Zwingli (1484–1531). Swiss Reformer. An admirer of Erasmus, he became chief preacher at Zurich's Great Munster (1518), where his New Testament lectures marked the beginning of the Swiss Reformation. He attacked Roman Catholic doctrine and practice; defeated its supporters in public debate; and supported by the civil authorities, suppressed the Mass, celebrated the Lord's Supper after a Reformed manner, and established ecclesiastical independence. Zwingli's view of the Eucharist as purely symbolic estranged him from Luther and made a united protestantism impossible. The Reformation divided Switzerland, and in the ensuing civil war, Zwingli was killed while serving as chaplain and standard-bearer with the Protestant forces.

FOCUS QUOTE **There is no work better than another to please God; to pour water, to wash dishes, to be a cobbler, or an apostle: all is one.** —William Tyndale

---

William Tyndale (c.1495–1536). English biblical translator and martyr. Educated at Oxford and Cambridge and ordained about 1521, he studied further under Luther at Wittenberg and completed his New Testament translation at Worms in 1526. Copies were smuggled into England, and his life was thereafter in danger. He continually revised that work, translated also parts of the Old Testament and wrote *Obedience of a Christian Man* (1528). Tyndale followed Luther on the authority of Scripture and on justification by faith but tended toward the sacramental views of Zwingli. Possibly at Henry VIII's instigation, he was betrayed to the imperial authorities and strangled and burned at the stake near Brussels. His translations formed the bases of the Authorized and Revised Versions of the Bible.

TWENTY SIGNIFICANT CHURCH HISTORY LEADERS cont.

Menno Simons (1496–1551). Early Mennonite leader. Ordained as a Roman Catholic priest in the Netherlands in 1524, he had misgivings about the church's teaching on infant baptism and the Eucharist and in 1536 he left the church and became prominent in the Anabaptist movement. Hunted and with a price on his head, he moved from place to place debating, encouraging, and writing extensively (he established a printing press). Each of his many works reflects his aim in the preface, quoting 1 Corinthians 3:11: "No other foundation can any one lay than that which is laid, which is Jesus Christ."

Conrad Grebel (c.1498–1526). Founder of the Swiss Brethren Movement, also called Anabaptist. Having broken with Zwingli in 1524, Grebel organized the Brethren as an independent Anabaptist church in Zurich. An able humanist and biblical scholar, he defied the city council's ban on his activities, and performed the first adult baptism in modern history. He served two prison terms, totaling six months, before his early death.

FOCUS QUOTE

God thrust me into the fray.
—John Calvin after the publication of *Institutes.*

John Calvin (1509–1564). French Protestant reformer. Born in Picardy, he studied theology in Paris and law at Orleans and Bourges, during which time he came under protestant influence. He broke with Roman Catholicism in 1533 after a conversion experience in which he felt called to restore the church to its original purity. Forced to leave Paris because of rising feelings against protestantism, he settled in Basel and in 1536 published the *Institutes of the Christian Religion* in Latin. His studious inclinations were disrupted when, on a visit to Geneva in 1536, he unwillingly agreed to become William Farel's colleague in organizing the Reformation there. Appointed preacher and professor of theology, he excluded the unworthy from Communion and proposed other reforms. The result was the expulsion of Calvin and Farel from the city in 1538. In Strasbourg for the next three years he got to know Martin Bucer and Philip Melanchthon, and he published a commentary on Romans. Welcomed back to Geneva in 1541, he established a regime with a strong Old Testament emphasis that gave the supreme council under Calvin wide powers over the private lives of citizens. Adultery, blasphemy, and heresy were punishable by death. Calvin and Calvinism controlled church and state. Calvin preached regularly, introduced congregational singing into the Reformed church services, and gave lectures that brought students from near and far. His Bible commentaries are still hailed as classics. He was also a champion of the Huguenots, welcomed protestant refugees from Mary Tudor's England, trained John Knox for his leadership of the Scottish Reformation, and counseled protestants in other lands. Calvin believed that virtue should be practiced for its own sake, regardless of future rewards and punishments.

George Fox (1624–1691). Founder of the Society of Friends, or Quakers. Apprenticed to a shoemaker, he left his Leicestershire home in 1643 to seek religious enlightenment. After painful experiences he spoke of having found One who spoke to his condition, and in 1646 he came to reply on the "inner light of the living Christ." He forsook church attendance, rejected outward sacraments and paid clergy, and taught that truth is to be found primarily in God's voice speaking to the soul. So emerged the "Friends of Truth." Fox taught the priesthood of all believers and urged a simple lifestyle on his colleagues, who later included William Penn. He established a base at Swarthmore Hall in northwest England but traveled widely at home and abroad. Eight times he saw the inside of prisons, serving terms totaling six years. He fought prison conditions and other social evils and sought to establish religious toleration in an intolerant age. Fox could show a mean spirit on occasion toward opponents, but he was a true pacifist, whose use of group silence was a brake on impetuous conduct.

Philip Jacob Spener (1635–1705). German pastor and founder of Pietism. Influenced by Johann Arndt and Richard Baxter and distressed by the lack of personal content in the theology of his day, he set out to reform Lutheranism from within. For individuals, he stressed the local church and instituted small group sessions (*collegia pietatis*) that encouraged fellowship, Bible study, the priesthood of all believers, right behavior, piety, devotion, and love instead of argument. For the church in Germany, he called for spiritual preaching and for the reform of theological education, an emphasis that resulted in the founding of the University at Halle (1694), where dogmatics was deemphasized and personal piety was stressed. And for the church at large, Spener emphasized missions and evangelism. Spener's influence was enormous in the church, and some see the roots of the later romanticism here.

“” FOCUS QUOTE **God buries his workmen but carries on his work.** —Charles Wesley

Count von Nikolaus Ludwig Zinzendorf (1700–1760). Founder of the Moravian church. Born in Dresden and raised in Pietist circles, he studied law at Wittenberg and in 1721 entered Saxon government service. Herrnhut, the famous Christian community, emerged from his giving of refuge to a group of Bohemian refugees on his estate. He left government service in 1727 and was ordained as a Lutheran pastor in 1734 and as bishop of the Unitas Fratrum in 1737. From Herrnhut, Zinzendorf sent his missionaries to many countries; John Wesley was only one from other traditions who found his heart strangely warmed through contact with the Moravians. Zinzendorf himself traveled extensively, notably in America, and spent five years ministering in England. It is hard to overestimate his contribution to the modern missionary movement.

“” FOCUS QUOTE **Lord, let me not live to be useless.** —John Wesley

Charles Wesley (1707–1788). Methodist hymn writer. Eighteenth child of a Lincolnshire rector, he graduated from Oxford, where he was a member of the Holy Club and was ordained in 1735. Three years later he experienced an evangelical conversion and became a revivalist preacher, often in company with his brother John. He traveled little after 1756 but preached in Bristol and (from 1771) London. He produced several thousand hymns, many of which are still regularly sung. They include "Love Divine, All Loves Excelling," "Lo! He Comes, With Clouds Descending," "Jesus, Lover of My Soul," and "Hark! The Herald Angels Sing."

John Wesley (1703–1791). Founder of Methodism. Fifteenth child of Samuel and Susanna Wesley, he was educated at Oxford and ordained in the Church of England but did not experience conversion until 1738. Soon afterwards, he embarked on his great task: "To reform the nation, particularly the church, and to spread scriptural holiness over the land." Before he died he had preached more than 40,000 sermons and covered nearly 250,000 miles. He encountered opposition from hostile mobs, uncooperative clergy, and other Evangelicals who disliked his Arminian theology, and he unwillingly fathered a breakaway church. When he died, however, one secular magazine hailed him as "One of the few characters who outlived enmity and prejudice."

William Booth (1829–1912). Founder of the Salvation Army. Born in Nottingham and converted in 1844, he was a Methodist preacher; but chafing under denominational restrictions, he left in 1861 to pursue

TWENTY SIGNIFICANT CHURCH HISTORY LEADERS cont.

independent evangelistic work that led him to London's East End. Out of his "Christian Mission" there developed the Salvation Army (1878). Booth was a tireless fighter against such things as squalid slums, uncaring authority, abused children, drink, forced labor conditions, internal dissension, and unfounded charges, but chiefly against the devil and all his works. His book *In Darkest England—and the Way Out* (1890) became a best seller. He traveled 5 million miles and preached nearly 60,000 sermons. Forty thousand people attended his funeral in London.

Washington Gladden (1836–1918). American Congregational pastor. He served churches in Massachusetts, New York, and Ohio, and liked to speak of a practical gospel that had liberated him from "the bondage of an immoral theology." He wrote twelve books and was a leader in formulating and popularizing the so-called social gospel. He was also the author of the well-known hymn "O Master, Let Me Walk With Thee."

Source: Taken from *The Concise Dictionary of the Christian Tradition* by J. D. Douglas, Walter A. Elwell, and Peter Toon.

THE PENDULUM EFFECT IN CHURCH HISTORY

Montanism A 2nd-century Christian heresy. It originated in Montanus, a Christian who, in a Phrygian village about 156, fell into a trance and reportedly began to "prophesy under the influence of the Spirit." Two young women also prophesied, and the movement quickly spread through Asia Minor. Montanus claimed to have a new and final revelation, foretold the return of Christ and the establishment of the New Jerusalem on a Phrygian plain, encouraged fasting, and welcomed persecution. The Asia Minor bishops finally excommunicated the Montanists about 177, but the sect survived until the 6th century (remnants of it into the 9th century). Tertullian was its most famous adherent.

Gnosticism (Gk. *gnosis,* "knowledge") Salvation through special knowledge. The word covers a wide variety of 1st- and 2d-century teachings, some of which may be called Christian Gnosticism. All have the essential ingredient that salvation is by enlightenment and by possession of special knowledge. Famous teachers were Valentinus (2d century), Basilides (2d century), and Marcion (d. 160). Christian authors who attacked Gnosticism as being pagan in origin and for misusing the Bible were Irenaeus (d. 200), Tertullian (d. 225), and Hippolytus (d. 236). Modern knowledge of Gnosticism has been greatly supplemented by archaeological findings, notably at Nag-Hammadi in 1945.

Monasticism A way of Christian life involving asceticism, self-denial, and obedience to a superior, followed in whole or partial seclusion from the secular world. Usually it is according to a fixed rule of life and under lifelong vows of poverty, chastity, and obedience. The purpose is to seek God and to gain perfection; this pursuit may involve service to human beings or commitment to a life of prayer.

Christian monasticism began in Egypt and was introduced into the West in the 4th century. A rule was provided by St. Benedict (480–543) that was used as the basis of many communities of monks and nuns. In the East the great center of monasticism has been Mount Athos in Greece. Protestants have criticized monasticism on the basis that it encourages the idea of salvation by works and that it elevates the idea of celibacy over that of the married state.

Scholasticism (Lat. *schola,* "place of learning") The system and method of philosophy and theology developed in the academic centers of medieval Europe. It has a technical (scholastic) language and method. Much material was derived from the early fathers, especially Augustine of Hippo, and it made use of the philosophy of Aristotle. The most famous exponent of scholasticism was Thomas Aquinas (1225–1274). As protestant theologians of the late 16th and 17th centuries used a technical method and vocabulary to produce protestant doctrine, what they produced in their learned tomes is often called "Protestant scholasticism."

Mysticism The experience in which the believer arrives at a special union of love with God. It transcends knowledge of God achieved through the normal powers of mind

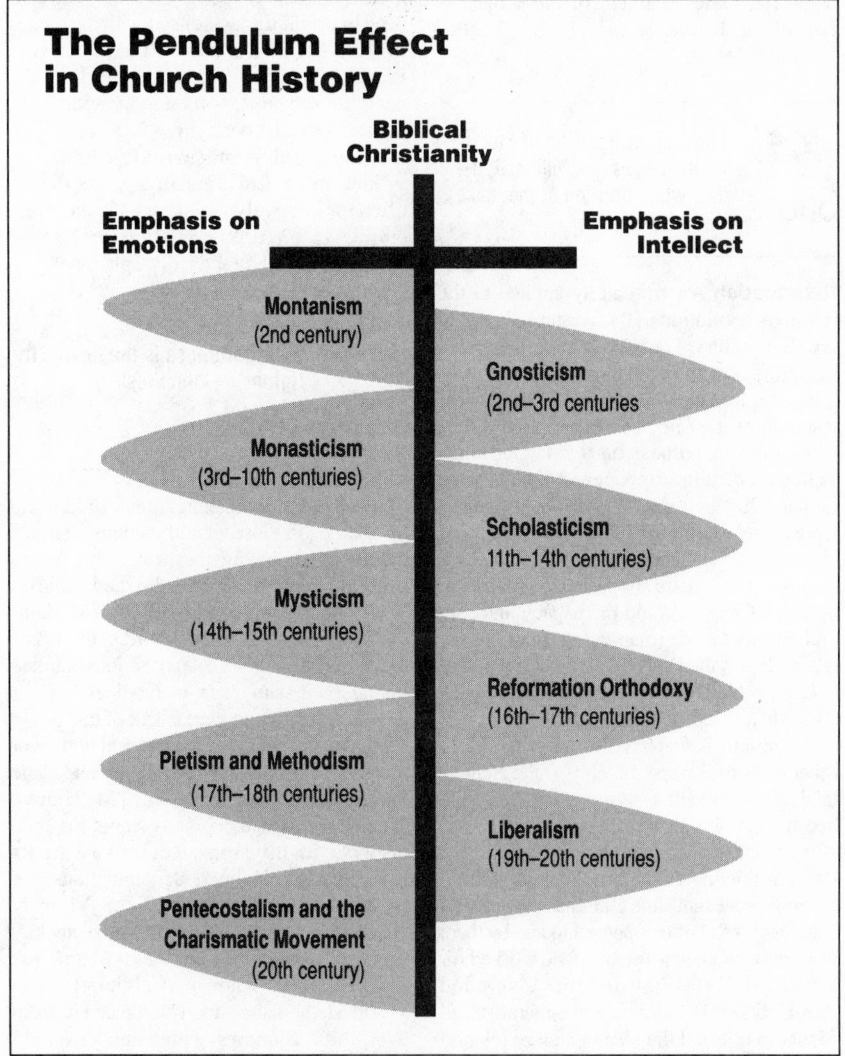

Source: Taken from *Chronological and Background Charts of Church History* by Robert Walton. Copyright 1986 by The Zondervan Corporation. Used by permission.

and reason. There is a loss of the sense of time with great feelings of joy and exultation. God is felt to be extremely near. It is fellowship with God known through the embrace of a unifying love. To know what mysticism is requires a personal knowledge of mystical experience or the reading of books by those known as mystics (e.g., Teresa of Avila, John of the Cross, Julian of Norwich, and Eckhart). A classic treatment of the subject is found in *Mysticism* (1911) by Evelyn Underhill.

“” FOCUS QUOTE **Lord, open the King of England's eyes.** —William Tyndale while burning at the stake

Reformation A term chiefly applied to the religious revolution in the Western church in the 16th century. The Reformation originated in Germany with the inability of Roman Catholicism to cope with Martin Luther's protest against the sale of indulgences in 1517. This shortsightedness on the part of long-entrenched authority opened the door to demand for the renewal of biblically based Christianity—primitive purity in doctrine, worship, and organization. Progress was helped in those early years by political squabbling between Charles V and the papacy and several influential German rulers throwing in their lot with the Protestants. The movement was introduced into Switzerland by Ulrich Zwingli and continued by John Calvin. It was Calvinism that spread more readily to other parts of Europe, notably to the Netherlands and Scotland. Calvinism fathered what became known as the Reformed churches. Alongside the two main groupings—respectively following Luther and Calvin and becoming protestant state churches (or national churches)—and often opposed to and by them were the extreme protestants who worked for a radical Reformation; they included Anabaptists, Mennonites, and Separatists, all of whom rejected the idea of a close relation between church and state and called for religious liberty. The two great doctrinal emphases of the Reformation as confessed by the protestants were the final authority of the Bible in matters of faith and conduct (the formal principle) and the doctrine of justification by faith (the material principle). The Counter-Reformation was Roman Catholicism's belated reaction to the Reformation.

Pietism A renewal movement among German Lutherans that began in the 17th century. In origin it is associated with the names of P.J. Spener (1635–1705) and A.H. Francke (1663–1727). It emphasized the need for genuine communion with God, pointed out that dead orthodoxy was of no use, and called for missions to the heathen.

Pietism is also used in a wider sense, often pejoratively, to designate an overemphasis on religious experience and claims to be led by the Holy Spirit.

“” FOCUS QUOTE **Sour godliness is the devil's religion.** —John Wesley

Methodism The teaching, organization, and discipline of those denominations that see themselves following the idea of Christianity originally supplied by John and Charles Wesley in the 18th century. The word "Methodists" came into use in Oxford in the 1720s as a description of a group of serious-minded young men who were methodical in their devotions and good works. Out of this group came the leaders of the evangelical revival of the 18th century, and out of the revival came the societies of the people called Methodists. They have spread to many countries and, because of divisions, comprise various Methodist and Holiness denominations—of which twenty are found in the U.S. Virtually all Methodist bodies are Arminian in doctrine (the exception is the Welsh Methodists [Presbyterians who are Calvinist]). The World Methodist Council has delegates from over forty countries representing over 45 million members, and this does not account for all Methodists. Modern Methodism worship varies from a strong liturgical emphasis on the one side to an emphasis on freedom on the other. This in turn reflects the origins of Methodism—converts from the Church of England made by Church of England priests (therefore liturgical) and the pursuit of "scriptural holiness" and the fullness of the Spirit by the membership of the societies (therefore freedom). In terms of church polity it is connectional.

Liberalism A form of theology that flourished in the Western church from the mid-19th to the early 20th century. Found primarily in Protestantism, it also had supporters in Roman Catholicism. The key themes were freedom and progress—freedom from old dogmas and freedom to investigate new ideas, progress in collaboration with the new confident sciences. Important thinkers who set the stage for this type of theology were F.D.E. Schleiermacher (1768–1834) and Albrecht Ritschl (1822–1889). The result was a theology that had few points of contact left with the traditional view of the Bible and Christian faith. Two world wars and the massive influence of Karl Barth caused the demise of the old liberal theology as a major movement. It still lives on in a new dress in modern forms of theology that deny the deity of Jesus Christ and allow belief only in what is said to be rational.

Pentecostalism Either a movement in which the gifts of the Holy Spirit are said to be experienced or several denominations that emphasize the possession and exercise of the gifts of the Spirit. The name arises since the Spirit (and thus the gifts of the Spirit) were first given to the church at the Feast of Pentecost (Acts 2). As a movement in modern times it began with the Topeka Revival of 1901 and the Azusa Street Revival of Los Angeles in 1906, with claims to certain gifts of the Spirit, especially speaking in tongues. Similar events took place in other places, and thus the movement to encourage prayer for and receipt of the gifts began. It occurred outside the mainline denominations and churches and led ultimately to the formation of various new groups—Assemblies of God, Pentecostal Assemblies of the World, Pentecostal Church of God, and United Pentecostal Church International. These denominations, with others, have continued; but since World War II a new form of the Pentecostal movement has arisen and has deeply affected most of the traditional churches and denominations. It is known as the Charismatic movement or Neo-Pentecostalism and is best described as a renewal movement in which the gifts of the Spirit are emphasized in the context of each church being seen as a body of Christ.

Charismatic Movement Contemporary religious phenomenon that embodies a renewed emphasis on the person and work of the Holy Spirit. Beginning in the late 1950s and early 1960s non-Pentecostal Christians, many from the mainline denominations, began experiencing Pentecostal visitations that included speaking in tongues, divine healings, prophecies, and various physical phenomena such as prostrations and fainting, in a way reminiscent of the great awakenings of the past. It created a vast unrest and rethinking on the part of traditional non-Pentecostal Christians, including the Roman Catholics, of what place such gifts and experiences ought to play in the Christian life. Voluminous literature and over one hundred official denominational documents have discussed its value pro and con with the general feeling (although not universally held) that one ought not to bridle the Holy Spirit, who "blows where he will," but still one must "test the spirits" to see if they are of God.

Church Life

100 LARGEST CHURCHES IN AMERICA

1989-1990 Worship Attendance

Att.	*Name*	*City, ST*	*Affil.*	*Pastor*
20000	First Baptist Church	Hammond, IN	IB	Dr. Jack Hyles
14605	Willow Creek Community	S. Barrington, IL	IND	Rev. Bill Hybels
12000	Calvary Chapel	Santa Ana, CA	CALC	Pastor Chuck Smith
11000	Thomas Rd Baptist Church	Lynchburg, VA	IB	Dr. Jerry Falwell
10000	First Assembly of God	Phoenix, AZ	AG	Dr. Tommy J. Barnett
9500	North Phoenix Baptist	Phoenix, AZ	SBC	Dr. Richard Jackson
8700	Chapel in University Pk	Akron, OH	IND	Rev. Knute Larson
8500	Second Baptist Church	Houston, TX	SBC	Dr. H. Edwin Young
8000	Grace Community Church	Sun Valley, CA	BIB	Dr. John MacArthur
7850	Mt. Paran Church of God	Atlanta, GA	COGC	Dr. Paul Walker
7700	Harvest Fellowship	Riverside, CA	CALC	Pastor Greg Laurie
7650	Chapel Hill Harvester	Decatur, GA	INDC	Bishop Earl Paulk
7500	Calvary Chapel	Downry, CA	CALC	Jeff Johnson
7327	Deliverance Evangelistic	Philadelphia, PA	INDC	Rev. Benjamin Smith
7000	Church on the Rock	Rockwall, TX	INDC	Dr. Larry Lea
7000	First Baptist Church	Jacksonville, FL	SBC	Drs. Lindsey Jr./Vines
6750	First Baptist Church	Dallas, TX	SBC	Dr. C. A. Criswell
6700	Orlando Christian Center	Orlando, FL	INDC	Rev. Benny Hinn
6500	Bellevue Baptist Church	Cordova, TN	SBC	Dr. Adrian Rogers
6500	Faith Flshp Outreach	Edison, NJ	INDC	Dr. David DeMola
6500	Victory Christian Center	Tulsa, OK	INDC	Rev. Billy Joe Daugherty
6250	Akron Baptist Temple	Akron, OH	IB	Dr. Charles Billington
6000	Beaverton Foursquare	Beaverton, OR	FSQ	Rev. Ron Mehl
6000	Calvary Church	Santa Ana, CA	IND	Dr. David Hocking
6000	Capital Christian Center	Sacramento, CA	AG	Dr. Glen D. Cole
6000	Crenshaw Christian Center	Los Angeles, CA	INDC	Dr. Fred K. C. Price
6000	Elmbrook Church	Waukesha, WI	IND	Dr. Stuart Briscoe
6000	First Evangelical Free	Fullerton, CA	EFC	Dr. Charles Swindoll
6000	Highland Park Baptist	Chattanooga, TN	IB	Dr. J. Don Jennings
6000	Lakewood Church	Houston, TX	INDC	Dr. John Osteen
6000	Mt. Olivet Lutheran	Minneapolis, MN	ELCA	Dr. Paul M. Youngdahl
6000	Overlake Christian	Kirkland, WA	ICC	Dr. Bob Moorehead
5438	Crystal Cathedral	Garden Grove, CA	RCA	Dr. Robert Schuller
5347	Church on the Way	Van Nuys, CA	FSQ	Dr. Jack Hayford
5300	First Baptist Church	Orlando, FL	SBC	Dr. Jim Henry
5200	Crossroads Cathedral	Oklahoma City, OK	AG	Dr. Daniel T. Sheaffer
5150	Horizon Fellowship	San Diego, CA	CALC	Pastor Mike McIntosh
5127	1st Assembly of God	Tacoma, WA	AG	Dr. Fulton W. Buntain
5100	New Hope Community	Portland, OR	INDC	Rev. Dale E. Galloway
5035	First Baptist Church	Houston, TX	SBC	Dr. John Bisagno
5030	Southeast Christian	Louisville, KY	ICC	Dr. Robert L. Russell
5000	Bethany World Prayer Ctr.	Baker, LA	INDC	Rev. Larry Stockstill

Att.	*Name*	*City, ST*	*Affil.*	*Pastor*
5000	Calvary Chapel	W. Covina, CA	CALC	Pastor Paul Ries
5000	First Baptist Church	Atlanta, GA	SBC	Dr. Charles Stanley
5000	Hartford Mem Baptist	Detroit, MI	PNB	Dr. Charles Adams
5000	Melodyland Christian Ctr	Anaheim, CA	INDC	Dr. Ralph Wilkerson
5000	Peachtree Presbyterian	Atlanta, GA	PCUSA	Dr. Frank Harrington
5000	West Angeles Ch of God	Los Angeles, CA	COGIC	Dr. Charles E. Blake
5000	World Harvest	Columbus, OH	INDC	Dr. Rod Parsley
4943	Vineyard Fellowship	Anaheim, CA	INDC	Pastor John Wimber
4861	Young Nak Presbyterian	Los Angeles, CA	KPCA	Rev. Hee Min Park
4845	Full Gospel Tabernacle	Orchard Park, NY	AG	Dr. Tommy Reid
4600	South Coast Community	Irvine, CA	IND	Dr. Tim Timmons
4600	Vineyard Christian Fellowship	Wheatridge, CO	INDC	Pastor Tom Stipe
4500	Coral Ridge Presbyterian	Ft. Lauderdale, FL	PCA	Dr. James Kennedy
4500	Trinity Baptist Church	San Antonio, TX	SBC	Dr. Buckner Fanning
4331	Central Church	Memphis, TN	IND	Dr. James Latimer
4300	Family Worship Center	Baton Rouge, LA	INDC	Rev. Jimmy Swaggart
4200	Calvary Chapel	Albuquerque, NM	CALC	Pastor Skip Heitzig
4200	People's Church	Fresno, CA	AG	Dr. George L. Johnson
4038	Prestonwood Baptist	Dallas, TX	SBC	Dr. Jack Graham
4000	Applegate Christian Center	Jacksonville, OR	CALC	Pastor John Courson
4000	Bethel AME Church	Baltimore, MD	AME	Rev. Frank M. Reid III
4000	Cherry Hills Community	Englewood, CO	EP	Dr. J.M. Dixon
4000	Church of Christ	Boston, MA	CC	Rev. Al Baird
4000	First Baptist Church	Euless, TX	SBC	Dr. Jimmy Draper
4000	First Baptist Church	Jackson, MS	SBC	Dr. Frank Pollard
4000	Highland Park Presbyterian	Dallas, TX	PCUSA	Dr. B. Clayton Bell
4000	Mt. Ephraim Baptist	Atlanta, GA	NBC	Rev. R.L. White
4000	Pleasant Grove M. Bapt	Houston, TX	NBC/USA	Dr. Charles Jackson
4000	Saddleback Community	Mission Viejo, CA	SBC	Rev. Rick Warren
4000	Trinity Baptist Church	Jacksonville, FL	IB	Dr. Bob Gray
4000	Valley Cathedral	Phoenix, AZ	INDC	Dr. Donald Price
3850	First Baptist Church	Gonzales, TX	SBC	Rev. Harvey W. Hoffman
3850	Oriental Mission Church	Los Angeles, CA	IND	Dr. Dong Sun Lim
3836	First Assembly of God	Grand Rapids, MI	AG	Rev. Wayne M. Benson Sr.
3800	Menlo Park Presbyterian	Menlo Park, CA	PCUSA	Rev. Walt Gerber
3750	Champion Forest Baptist	Houston, TX	SBC	Dr. O. Damon Shook
3700	McGregor Baptist Church	Ft. Myers, FL	SBC	Rev. Jim Holbrook
3692	University Presbyterian	Seattle, WA	PCUSA	Dr. Bruce Larson
3626	Bryn Mawr Presbyterian	Bryn Mawr, PA	PCUSA	Dr. Eugene C. Bay
3615	Calvary Church	Charlotte, NC	IND	Rev. Ross Rhoads
3600	Christian Faith Center	Seattle, WA	IND	Pastor Casey Treat
3600	Christian Life Center	Stockton, CA	UP	Dr. Kenneth F. Haney
3600	Faith Tabernacle	Chicago, IL	INDC	Rev. Al Smith
3587	First Baptist Church	Modesto, CA	IB	Dr. William Yeager
3550	First Baptist Church	W. Palm Beach, FL	SBC	Dr. Keith Thomas
3500	Bible Way Temple	Washington, DC	BWCW	Bishop Smallwood Williams
3500	Bountiful Blessings	Memphis, TN	INDC	Bishop G.E. Patterson
3500	Chapel on N Forrest Rd	Williamsville, NY	INDC	Dr. James W. Andrews
3500	Concord Baptist Church	Dallas, TX	NBCA	Rev. E.K. Bailey
3500	Full Faith Ch of Love	Shawnee, KS	INDC	Rev. Ernie Gruen
3500	Higher Dimensions Center	Tulsa, OK	INDC	Dr. Carlton Pearson
3492	Cornerstone Church	San Antonio, TX	INDC	Dr. John C. Hagee
3400	Loveland M. Baptist	Fontana, CA	SBC	Dr. Charles Singleton
3374	Frazer Memorial UMC	Montgomery, AL	UMC	Rev. John Mathison
3339	First Presbyterian	Greenville, SC	PCUSA	Rev. Randolph Kowalski

Att.	Name	City, ST	Affil.	Pastor
3300	Madison Church of Christ	Madison, TN	CC	Steve Flatt
3297	Lake Ave Congregational	Pasadena, CA	CCCC	Dr. Paul Cedar
3200	Evangel Christian Ctr	Louisville, KY	AG	Rev. Bob Rodgers
3200	Roswell Street Baptist	Marietta, GA	SBC	Dr. Nelson Price
3200	Sunshine Reformed Church	Grand Rapids, MI	CRC	Rev. Lewis VanderMeer
3200	Washington National COG	Ft. Washington, MD	COGC	Dr. T.L. Lowery

100 LARGEST SUNDAY SCHOOLS IN AMERICA

1989-1990 Sunday School Attendance

Att.	Name	City, ST	Affil.	Pastor
20000	First Baptist Church	Hammond, IN	IB	Dr. Jack Hyles
11743	Willow Creek Community Ch.	S. Barrington, IL	IND	Rev. Bill Hybels
10000	Thomas Road Baptist Church	Lynchburg, VA	IB	Dr. Jerry Falwell
9685	First Assembly of God	Phoenix, AZ	AG	Dr. Tommy J. Barnett
8057	Metro Assembly of God	Brooklyn, NY	AG	Rev. Bill Wilson
7615	First Baptist Church	Dallas, TX	SBC	Dr. W. A. Criswell
6272	First Baptist Church	Jacksonville, FL	SBC	Drs. Lindsey Jr./Jerry Vines
6004	University Presbyterian	Seattle, WA	PCUSA	Dr. Bruce Larson
5200	Bellevue Baptist Church	Cordova, TN	SBC	Dr. Adrian Rogers
5181	Second Baptist Church	Houston, TX	SBC	Dr. H. Edwin Young
4898	Akron Baptist Temple	Akron, OH	IB	Dr. Charles Billington
4735	First Baptist Church	Houston, TX	SBC	Dr. John Bisagno
4666	First Assembly of God	Tacoma, WA	AG	Dr. Fulton W. Buntain
4500	Crossroads Cathedral	Oklahoma Cty, OK	AG	Dr. Daniel T. Sheaffer
4476	North Phoenix Baptist	Phoenix, AZ	SBC	Dr. Richard Jackson
4400	New Life Church	Philadelphia, PA	AG	Rev. Tony McCreary
4179	First Assembly of God	Grand Rapids, MI	AG	Rev. Wayne M. Benson Sr.
3854	Prestonwood Baptist	Dallas, TX	SBC	Dr. Jack Graham
3800	Trinity Baptist Church	Jacksonville, FL	IB	Dr. Bob Gray
3700	Grace Community Church	Sun Valley, CA	BIB	Dr. John MacArthur
3533	First Baptist Church	Orlando, FL	SBC	Dr. Jim Henry
3500	Calvary Church	Santa Ana, CA	IND	Dr. David Hocking
3300	Capital Christian Center	Sacramento, CA	AG	Dr. Glen D. Cole
3270	First Baptist Church	Atlanta, GA	SBC	Dr. Charles Stanley
3009	Hyde Park Baptist Church	Austin, TX	SBC	Dr. Ralph M. Smith
3000	Calvary Church	Charlotte, NC	IND	Rev. Ross S. Rhoads
3000	Highland Park Presbyterian	Dallas, TX	PCUSA	Dr. B. Clayton Bell
2801	Ward Evangelical Presb	Livonia, MI	EP	Dr. Bartlett L. Hess
2800	Happy Church	Denver, CO	AG	Rev. Wallace R. Hickey
2703	First Baptist Church	Euless, TX	SBC	Dr. Jimmy Draper
2606	Central Church	Memphis, TN	IND	Dr. James Latimer
2588	Grace Presbyterian	Peoria, IL	PCUSA	Rev. David G. Williams
2574	Lake Ave Congregational	Pasadena, CA	CCCC	Dr. Paul Cedar
2558	Skyline Wesleyan Church	Lemon Grove, CA	WES	Dr. John Maxwell
2500	Chapel in University Park	Akron, OH	IND	Rev. Knute Larson
2500	Trinity Church	Cedar Hill, TX	AG	Rev. David L. Smith
2500	First Baptist Church	Lubbock, TX	SBC	Dr. Hayes Wicker
2470	Braeswood Assembly	Houston, TX	AG	Pastor Earl J. Banning
2452	First Baptist Church	Jackson, MS	SBC	Dr. Frank Pollard
2444	Eastside Baptist Church	Marietta, GA	SBC	Dr. Clark Hutchinson
2437	Graceland Baptist Church	New Albany, IN	SBC	Rev. Steve Marcum
2435	Peachtree Presbyterian	Atlanta, GA	PCUSA	Dr. Frank Harrington

Att.	Name	City, ST	Affil.	Pastor
2421	First Baptist Church	Arlington, TX	SBC	Dr. Charles R. Wade
2420	Champion Forest Baptist	Houston, TX	SBC	Dr. O. Damon Shook
2416	First Presbyterian	Greensboro, NC	PCUSA	Dr. Jerold Shetler
2400	Green Acres Baptist	Tyler, TX	SBC	Dr. Dennis Parrott
2389	First Southern Baptist	Del City, OK	SBC	Dr. Tom Elliff
2376	Dawson Memorial Baptist	Birmingham, AL	SBC	Dr. Titus Aldridge
2347	Southeast Christian	Louisville, KY	ICC	Dr. Robert L. Russell
2347	Calvary Temple	Irving, TX	AG	Rev. J. Don George
2329	First Baptist Church	Amarillo, TX	SBC	Dr. W. Winfred Moore
2300	First Evangelical Free	Fullerton, CA	EFC	Dr. Charles Swindoll
2300	Park Cities Baptist	Dallas, TX	SBC	Dr. James L. Pleitz
2300	Washington National COG	Ft. Washington, MD	COGC	Dr. T.L. Lowery
2264	Shades Mt. Baptist	Birmingham, AL	SBC	Dr. Charles Carter
2248	Roswell Street Baptist	Marietta, GA	SBC	Dr. Nelson Price
2238	Travis Avenue Baptist	Fort Worth, TX	SBC	Dr. Joel C. Gregory
2235	Grace Community Church	Tempe, AZ	BIB	Dr. Larry Finch
2225	First Presbyterian	Flint, MI	PCUSA	Dr. William N. Jackson
2225	Lakeview Temple	Indianapolis, IN	AG	Rev. Thomas Paino
2203	Sagemont Baptist Church	Houston, TX	SBC	Dr. John Morgan
2200	Los Gatos Christian	Los Gatos, CA	ICC	Dr. Daniel Henderson
2190	Young Nak Presbyterian	Los Angeles, CA	KPCA	Rev. Hee Min Park
2200	First Baptist Church	Ft. Lauderdale, FL	SBC	Dr. O.S. Hawkins
2182	Highview Baptist Church	Louisville, KY	SBC	Rev. William Hancock
2163	Assembly of God	Pace, FL	AG	Rev. Glyn Lowery Jr.
2162	First Baptist Church	Springdale, AR	SBC	Dr. Ronnie Floyd
2140	First Baptist Church	Midland, TX	SBC	Dr. James C. Denison
2114	Hoffmantown Baptist	Albuquerque, NM	SBC	Rev. Gerald Farley
2109	Frazer Memorial UMC	Montgomery, AL	UMC	Rev. John Mathison
2076	Wheaton Bible Church	Wheaton, IL	BIB	Dr. David Krentel
2065	First Baptist Church	Pasadena, TX	SBC	Dr. Barry Landrum III
2059	Cottage Hill Baptist	Mobile, AL	SBC	Dr. Fred Wolfe
2057	First Baptist Church	Norfolk, VA	SBC	Dr. Kenneth S. Hemphill
2050	Madison Church of Christ	Madison, TN	CC	Steve Flatt
2047	San Jacinto Baptist	Amarillo, TX	SBC	Dr. Stan Coffey
2040	First Baptist Church	Jonesboro, GA	SBC	Dr. Charles Carter
2005	First Presbyterian	Jackson, MS	PCUSA	Dr. James Baird
2000	Briarwood Presbyterian	Birmingham, AL	PCUSA	Dr. Frank Barker
2000	Harvest Fellowship	Riverside, CA	CALC	Pastor Greg Laurie
1996	Myers Park Presbyterian	Charlotte, NC	PCUSA	Rev. Timothy Croft
1992	Casas Adobes Baptist	Tucson, AZ	SBC	Rev. Roger Barrier Jr.
1976	Rehoboth Baptist Church	Tucker, GA	SBC	Dr. Richard G. Lee
1972	Calvary Temple	Irving, TX	AG	Rev. Don J. George
1972	Dauphin Way Baptist	Mobile, AL	SBC	Dr. Darrell Robinson
1960	Trinity U. Presbyterian	Santa Ana, CA	PCUSA	Rev. George Munzing
1938	Whitesburg Baptist	Huntsville, AL	SBC	Rev. Jimmy E. Jackson
1934	First Baptist Church	Carrollton, TX	SBC	Dr. Wayen Allen
1906	Mt. Paran Church of God	Atlanta, GA	COGC	Dr. Paul Walker
1870	Coral Ridge Presbyterian	Ft. Lauderdale, FL	PCA	Dr. James Kennedy
1863	People's Church	Fresno, CA	AG	Dr. George L. Johnson
1852	Templo Calvario Assembly	Santa Ana, CA	AG	Rev. Daniel De Leon
1818	First Presbyterian	Colorado Springs, CO	PCUSA	Dr. John H. Stevens
1813	Germantown Baptist	Germantown, TN	SBC	Dr. Ken Story
1800	First Presbyterian	Orlando, FL	PCUSA	Dr. J. Howard Edington
1783	First Baptist Church	Roanoke, VA	SBC	Dr. Charles Fuller
1783	Summer Grove Baptist	Shreveport, LA	SBC	Rev. Wayne DuBose

Att.	Name	City, ST	Affil.	Pastor
1780	Calvary Baptist Church	Winston-Salem, NC	SBC	Dr. Mark Corts
1776	Grace Presbyterian	Houston, TX	PCUSA	Dr. David G. McKechnie
1754	Colonial Presbyterian	Kansas City, MO	PCUSA	Rev. Ted Nissen
1754	First Baptist Church	W. Palm Beach, FL	SBC	Dr. Keith Thomas
1745	Castle Hills Baptist	San Antonio, TX	SBC	Dr. George H. Harris
1739	First Church - Nazarene	Bethany, OK	NAZ	Dr. Melvin McCullough
1734	Tallowood Baptist Church	Houston, TX	SBC	Rev. Lester B. Collins

100 FASTEST-GROWING CHURCHES IN AMERICA

1989-1990 Fastest-Growing Churches

No.	89-90 Gain	'89 Wor.	'90 Wor.	Church	City	State	Affil.	Pastor
1	2600	3100	5700	Calvary Chapel	Albuquerque	NM	CALC	Pastor Skip Heltzig
2	2000	1000	3000	Mt. Ephriam Baptist	Atlanta	GA	NBC	Rev. R. L. White
3	1690	8656	10356	Willow Creek Comm.	So. Barrington	IL	IND	Dr. Bill Hybels
4	1345	1710	3055	Saddleback Valley Comm.	Mission Viejo	CA	SBC	Rev. Rick Warren
5	1213	5761	6974	First Baptist Church	Jacksonville	FL	SBC	Drs. Lindsey Jr./Jerry Vine
6	1005	1095	2100	Windsor Village UMC	Houston	TX	UMC	Dr. Kirbyjon Caldwell
7	1000	1000	2000	Family Worship Center	Lakeland	FL	INDC	Rev. Reggie Scarborough
*	1000	4000	5000	Bethany World Prayer Ctr	Baker	LA	INDC	Rev. Larry Stockstill
8	940	1400	2340	East Brent Baptist Church	Pensacola	FL	SBC	Dr. Dale Patterson
9	905	4232	5137	Overlake Christian Church	Kirkland	WA	ICC	Dr. Bob Moorehead
10	900	2900	3800	West Angeles (COGIC)	Los Angeles	CA	COGIC	Bishop Charles E. Blake
11	893	7200	8093	Mt. Paran Church of God	Atlanta	GA	COG-C	Dr. Paul Walker
12	860	3100	3960	Boston Church of Christ	Boston	MA	CC	Kip McKean
13	850	3650	4500	Southeast Christn Church	Louisville	KY	ICC	Robert L. Russell
14	819	6337	7158	Deliverance Evangelistic	Philadelphia	PA	INDC	Rev. Benjamin Smith
15	700	500	1200	Heritage Christian Center	Denver	CO	INDC	Rev. Dennis Leonard
*	700	1100	1800	Church of the Open Door	Crystal	MN	CMA	Rev. David Johnson
*	700	700	1400	Sunnycrest Bapt Church	Marion	IN	SBC	Rev. Garland A. Morrison
16	692	4308	5000	Beaverton Foursquare Ch.	Beaverton	OR	FSQ	Dr. Ron Mehl
17	680	1170	1850	New York Church of Christ	New York	NY	CC	Steve Johnson
18	635	7336	7971	Second Baptist Church	Houston	TX	SBC	Dr. Edwin Young
19	624	1283	1907	Central Community COG	Wichita	KS	COG-A	Rev. Raymond E. Cotton
20	600	4000	4600	So. Coast Comm. Church	Irvine	CA	IND	Dr. Tim Timmons
*	600	1800	2400	San Jacinto Bapt Church	Amarillo	TX	SBC	Dr. Stan Coffey
*	600	3200	3800	Hyde Park Baptist Church	Austin	TX	SBC	Dr. Ralph M. Smith
*	600	1400	2000	Calvary Fellowship	Seattle	WA	INDC	Wayne Taylor
21	570	3660	4230	Full Gospel Tabernacle	Orchard Park	NY	AG	Dr. Tommy Reid
22	550	2150	2700	Briarwood Presby. Church	Birmingham	AL	PCA	Dr. Frank Barker
23	550	250	800	Mt. Zion Baptist Church	Seattle	WA	ABC	Rev. Samuel McKinney
24	543	177	720	Hosanna First Assembly	Baton Rouge	LA	AG	Rev. Glen J. Berteau
25	510	190	700	EV Free Ch. of the Canyons	Canyon Country	CA	EFC	Rev. Jim Harris
26	504	9164	3668	University Presby. Church	Seattle	WA	PCUSA	Dr. Bruce Larson
27	500	3000	3500	Full Faith Church of Love	Shawnee	KS	INDC	Rev. Ernie Gruen
*	500	1000	1500	Agape Church	Little Rock	AR	INDC	Rev. Happy Caldwell
*	500	1200	1700	Bountiful Blessings	Memphis	TN	COGIC	Bishop G. E. Patterson
*	500	6500	7000	Church on the Rock	Rockwall	TX	INDC	Dr. Larry Lee
*	500	3000	3500	Temple Calvario Assembly	Santa Ana	CA	AG	Rev. Daniel DeLeon
*	500	600	1100	First Baptist Church	Woodstock	GA	SBC	Rev. Johnny Hunt
*	500	5000	5500	Capital Christian Center	Sacramento	CA	AG	Dr. Glen D. Cole
*	500	1600	2100	First Baptist Church	Merritt Island	FL	SBC	Dr. Larry Thompson
*	500	1500	2000	New Covenant Church	Philadelphia	PA	COGA	Dr. C. Milton Grannum
*	500	3500	4000	Peachtree Presby. Church	Atlanta	GA	PCUSA	Dr. Frank Harrington
*	500	1500	2000	Belmont Church	Nashville	TN	CC	Dr. Don Finto
*	500	900	1400	Woodland Pk Bapt Church	Chattanooga	TN	SBC	Rev. Wayne Barber
*	500	6000	6500	Chapel Hill Harvester Ch.	Decatur	GA	INDC	Bishop Earl Paulk
*	500	2000	2500	Higher Dimens. Evang. Ctr	Tulsa	OK	INDC	Rev. Carlton Pearson

No.	89-90 Gain	'89 Wor.	'90 Wor.	Church	City	State	Affil.	Pastor
28	460	90	550	Denver Church of Christ	Denver	CO	CC	Rev. Preston Shepard
29	457	2543	3000	Hoffmantown Bapt Church	Albuquerque	NM	SBC	Rev. Norm Boshoff
30	450	2650	3100	First Presbyterian Church	Marietta	GA	PCUSA	Dr. Jim Speed
*	450	2650	3100	First Baptist Church	Ft. Lauderdale	FL	SBC	Dr. O. S. Hawkins
31	438	2332	2770	First Baptist Church	Midland	TX	SBC	Dr. Daniel Vestal
32	432	1876	2308	Ben Hill U. Meth. Church	Atlanta	GA	UMC	Rev. Walter L. Kimbrough
33	427	919	1346	Kentwd Comm. Wesleyan	Kentwood	MI	WES	Rev. Wayne Schimdt, Jr.
34	400	1100	1500	Northway Chr. Comm. Ch.	Wexford	PA	INDC	Rev. Jay Passavant
*	400	3800	4200	Trinity Baptist Church	San Antonio	TX	SBC	Dr. Buckner Fanning
*	400	4500	4900	Pleasant Grove M. Bapt Ch.	Houston	TX	NBC-USA	Dr. Charles Jackson
*	400	1940	2340	Casas Adobes Bapt Church	Tuscon	AZ	SBC	Rev. Rober Barrier, Jr.
*	400	1600	2000	Faith Bible Chapel	Arvada	CO	IND	Rev. George Morrison
*	400	2100	2500	Hickory Grove Bapt Ch.	Charlotte	NC	SBC	Dr. Joe B. Brown
*	400	3300	3700	McGregor Baptist Church	Fort Myers	FL	SBC	Rev. Jim Holbrook
*	400	3200	3600	Cherry Hills Comm. Ch.	Englewood	CA	EP	Dr. Jim Dixon
*	400	1100	1500	Word of Grace	Mesa	AZ	INDC	Rev. Gary Kinnaman
35	399	1131	1530	First Nazarene of Long Bch	Long Beach	CA	NAZ	Rev. John Calhoun
36	376	750	1125	Bible Center Cathedral	Evansville	IN	INDC	Rev. Rick Van Hoose
37	364	1016	1380	Atlanta Shores Bapt Ch.	Virginia Beach	VA	IB	Pastor George Sweet
38	360	510	870	First Assembly of God	Brooksville	FL	AG	Rev. David A. Garcia
39	350	2250	2600	Concord Baptist Church	Dallas	TX	NBCA	Rev. E. K. Bailey
*	350	2750	3100	Rehobeth Baptist Church	Tucker	GA	SBC	Dr. Richard G. Lee
*	350	1050	1400	First Baptist Church	Moore	OK	SBC	Rev. Bobby Boyles
*	350	4350	4700	Horizon Christn Fellowship	San Diego	CA	CALC	Rev. Mike McIntosh
40	348	127	475	Eastwood Presby. Church	Montgomery	AL	PCA	Rev. Aaron Fleming
41	346	963	1309	Lake Pointe Bapt Church	Rowlett	TX	SBC	Rev. Steve Stroope
42	335	2566	2901	Skyline Wesleyan Church	Lemon Grove	CA	WES	Dr. John Maxwell
43	328	439	767	Faith Evang. Free Church	Milford	OH	EFC	Pastor Raymond F. Dupont, Jr.
44	325	325	650	No. Coast EV Free Church	Oceanside	CA	EFC	Rev. Larry W. Osborne
46	306	1044	1350	San Diego Ch. of Christ	San Diego	CA	CC	Bruce Williams
47	300	3700	4000	Christ Church	Oakbrook	IL	IND	Dr. Arthur K. Dekruyter
*	300	2000	2300	First Baptist Church	Broken Arrow	OK	SBC	Rev. Nick Garland, Jr.
*	300	400	700	Greenwood CME Church	Memphis	TN	CME	Rev. Benjamin Smith
*	300	2200	2500	Cathedral of Praise	South Bend	IN	INDC	Rev. Lester Sumrall
*	300	1800	2100	Grace Chapel	Lexington	MA	IND	Dr. Howard Clark
*	300	600	900	World Changers	College Park	GA	INDC	Rev. Creflo Dollar
*	300	2000	2300	Kansas City Fellowship	Kansas City	MO	INDC	Pastor Mike Sullivan
*	300	1400	1700	Smokerise Baptist Church	Stone Mountain	GA	SBC	Rev. Truett Gannon
*	300	7700	8000	Harvest Christn Fellowship	Riverside	CA	CALC	Pastor Greg Laurie
*	300	1900	1600	First Baptist Church	Snellville	GA	SBC	Dr. James Merritt
*	300	2900	3200	Roswell Street Bapt Ch.	Marietta	GA	SBC	Dr. Nelson Price
*	300	1650	1950	Metropolitan Bapt. Church	Houston	TX	SBC	Dr. Curtis Dodd
*	300	400	700	North Park Baptist Church	Humble	TX	IB	Rev. John Gross
*	300	2200	2500	Allen Temple Bapt. Church	Oakland	CA	SBC	Dr. J. Alfred Smith, Jr.
*	300	800	1100	New Earth M. Bapt. Ch.	Decatur	GA	ABC	Rev. Eddie L. Long
*	300	1600	1900	Friendship M. Bapt. Ch.	Charlotte	NC	NBC-USA	Rev. Clifford A. Jones, Sr.
*	300	3550	3850	The Oriental Mission Ch.	Los Angeles	CA	INDC	Rev. Dong Sun Lim
*	300	1800	2100	Homewood Full Gospel	Homewood	IL	INDC	Rev. Walter Pederson
*	300	3750	4050	Trinity Baptist Church	Jacksonville	FL	IB	Dr. Bob Gray
*	300	750	1050	First Assembly of God	Victorville	CA	AG	Rev. Tommy C. Anderson
*	300	2000	2300	Victory Temple As. of God	Metairie	LA	AG	Frank A. Bailey II
*	300	1700	2000	First Assembly of God	Shreveport	LA	AG	Rev. Rodney Duron
*	300	350	650	Lakewood Assem. of God	Dallas	TX	AG	Rev. Ronald W. Crawford
*	300	800	1100	Assembly of God	Manasas	VA	AG	Rev. Charles B. Nestor
*	300	750	1050	Christ Cov. Presby. Church	Matthews	NC	PCA	Harry Reader III
*	300	5900	6200	Faith Fellowship World Outreach	Edison	NJ	INDC	Dr. David T. Demola
*	300	350	650	EV Free Ch. of Laguna Hills	Laguna Hills	CA	EFC	Rev. Donald R. Smith
*	300	350	650	EV Free Ch. of Coneja Val.	Newbury Park	CA	EFC	Rev. Steve Larson
*	300	450	750	Grace Community Church	Houston	TX	CEA	Rev. Steve Riggler

Church Growth Today, Dr. John N. Vaughan, editor.

50 LARGEST CHURCHES IN THE WORLD

1989-1990 worship attendance.

Worship	*Church*	*City, State, Country*	*Pastor*
180,000	Yoida Full Gospel Church	Seoul, KOREA	Dr. Cho, Paul Yonggi
80,000	Vision de Futuro	Santa Fe, ARGENTINA	Omar Cabrero
70,000	Deeper Christian Life Ministry	Akoka, Yaba: LAGOS, NIGERIA	William Kumuyi
70,000	Waves of Love and Peace	Buenos Aires, ARGENTINA	Hector Jimenez
50,000	Jotabeche M. Pentecostal Church	Santiago, CHILE	Jose Javier Vasquez
50,000	Kum Ran Methodist Church	Seoul, KOREA	Dr. Kim, Hong Do
47,000	Nambu Full Gospel Church	Seoul, KOREA	Cho, Yong Mok
40,000	Soong Eui Methodist Church	Incheon, KOREA	Dr. Lee, Ho Moon
35,000	Jesus Is Lord Fellowship	Manila, PHILIPPINES	Eddie Villanueva
30,000	Madureira Assembly of God	Rio de Janeiro, BRASIL	Louis Francisco Fonte
28,000	Sung Rak Baptist Church	Seoul, KOREA	Dr. Kim, Dong Ki
26,000	Young Nak Presbyterian Church	Seoul, KOREA	Dr. Lim, Young Soo
25,000	Kwang Lim Methodist Church	Seoul, KOREA	Dr. Kim, Sun Do
20,000	Miracle Center	Benin City, NIGERIA	Dr. Benson Idahosa
20,000	First Baptist Church *	Hammond, IN, USA	Dr. Jack Hyles
20,000	Church of the Miracles of Jesus	Buenos Aires, ARGENTINA	———
20,000	Centro Evangelical	San Salvador, EL SALVADOR	Hector Bojorquez
20,000	Hyesung Presbyterian Church	Seoul, KOREA	Yoo, Bok Jong
20,000	Suwon Joong Ang Baptist Church	Suwon, KOREA	
18,000	The So-Mang Presby. Church	Seoul, KOREA	Kwak, Sun Hee
17,000	Elam Church	San Salvador, EL SALVADOR	Sergio Solorzano
15,000	Cathedral of Praise	Manila, PHILIPPINES	David Sumral
15,000	Kam Nam Full Gospel Church	Seoul, KOREA	Kim, Sung Kwang
15,000	Dae Sung Presbyterian Church	Seoul, KOREA	Yoon, Sung Taek
15,000	Myungseong Presby. Church	Seoul, KOREA	Kim, Sam Hwan
15,000	Assembly of God	Campo de Sao Custovos, BRASIL	Notulu Barro Ferreira
14,605	Willow Creek Community Church	So. Barrington, IL, USA	Dr. Bill Hybels
14,000	Choong Hyeon Presby. Church	Seoul, KOREA	Dr. Lee, Jong Yun
14,000	Primeira Iglreja Baptista	Niteroi, BRASIL	Dr. Nilson Fanini
12,600	Seobu Presbyterian Church	Pusan, KOREA	Lee, Jae Soon
12,000	Calvary Chapel of Costa Mesa	Santa Ana, CA, USA	Chuck Smith
12,000	Dues E Amor	Sao Paulo, BRASIL	———
12,000	Incheon Full Gospel Church	Incheon, KOREA	Choi, Sung Kyu
11,000	Ju-An Presbyterian Church	Inchon, KOREA	Pastor Kyum Il Na
11,000	Thomas Road Baptist Church	Lynchburg, VA, USA	Dr. Jerry Falwell
10,500	Bible Baptist Church	Cebu City, PHILIPPINES	Dr. Armie F. Jesilva
10,500	Deeper Christian Life Ministry	Ibadan, NIGERIA	Isaiah Lawson
10,000	Kang Nam Joong Ang Bapt. Ch.	Seoul, KOREA	Dr. Kim, Choong Ki
10,000	Calvary Church	Seoul, KOREA	Dr. Park, Jo Jun
10,000	First Assembly of God	Phoenix, AZ, USA	Dr. Tommy Barnett
9,500	North Phoenix Baptist Church	Phoenix, AZ, USA	Dr. Richard Jackson
8,800	Deeper Christian Life Ministry	Kaduna, NIGERIA	Christopher Anasado
8,700	The Chapel in University Park	Akron, OH, USA	Knute Larson
8,600	Suyoung Ro Presbyterian Church	Pusan, KOREA	Jung, Pil Do
8,500	Deeper Christian Life Ministry	Kano, NIGERIA	Ransome Bello
8,500	Ku-Ro Joong Ang Meth. Church	Seoul, KOREA	Kwak, Jeon Tae
8,500	Second Baptist Church	Houston, TX, USA	Dr. Edwin Young
8,000	Sa-Rang Presbyterian Church	Seoul, KOREA	Han, Heum Ok

Worship	*Church*	*City, State, Country*	*Pastor*
8,000	Grace Community Church	Sun Valley, CA, USA	Dr. John MacArthur
7,850	Mt. Paran Church of God	Atlanta, GA, USA	Dr. Paul Walker

(*)Estimated attendance based on latest available information. Note: Most of the Latin America churches reflect both main church and satellite centers attendance. For information, additions, or corrections, contact: Dr. John Vaughan, International Megachurch Research Center, Southwest Baptist University, 1601 S. Springfield, Bolivar, MO. 65613, USA. Telephone (417) 326-1773. FAX (417) 326-1783. Appreciation is expressed to U.S. denominations and churches and to the following people whose research assisted in portions of this research: Korea: Rev. Sang-sik Ham, Dr. Han, Yo Lee; USA: Dr. Peter Wagner; West Germany: Dr. Jörg Knoblauch.

24 MEGAREASONS FOR THE MEGACHURCH PHENOMENON

1. Gradual disappearance of denominationally loyal churchgoers born before 1930 who preferred the intimacy and spontaneity of life in a small congregation.
2. Growing number of people who commute 3 to 40 miles to work and find it easy to commute 5 to 20 miles to church.
3. Improvement in the quality and safety of highways.
4. Convenient off-street parking.
5. Higher-quality physical facilities, preaching, music, nurseries, teaching, and youth ministries.
6. Freedom to ignore denominational labels and shop for a church that meets needs.
7. Rapid increase in exodus of people born since 1945 from Roman Catholic churches into evangelical and charismatic Protestant congregations.
8. Most Americans born after 1940 grew up in a world of big institutions.
9. Capability to design and staff range of specialized ministries.
10. The power of the critical mass—the 26-year-old looking for a spouse is more likely to be successful in a singles ministry that includes 1,200 people than in a group of 9 singles.
11. Shift in priorities in many denominations from people and needs to institutions and tradition.
12. Focus on attendance in megachurches contrasted with emphasis on membership in long-established congegations.
13. More persuasive public relations and advertising program in megachurches.
14. Sensitivity and responsiveness to "the market" as opposed to smaller congregations driven by tradition.
15. Refusal by municipalities to grant permission to long-established congregations to increase off-street parking or physical facilities because of complaints from the neighbors.
16. Decision by a growing proportion of the 3 to 7 million Americans who attend two churches every week in order to have their religious needs met to switch to "one-stop shopping" at a megachurch.
17. Search by millions of people born in the 1942-67 era for a Christ-centered church that offers Bible-centered preaching and teaching.
18. Capability of the larger churches to offer a broad range of choices for worship and ministry.
19. Inability of the vast majority of Protestant churches in the late 1960s to welcome the Jesus People.
20. Greater preference for a faster pace for corporate worship.
21. Shift toward the theological Left by many pastors, while most of the churchgoers born since 1955 are theologically more conservative than their parents.
22. Satisfaction by members to learn that 20 to 35 percent of their contributions are allocated to missions, benevolences, and community outreach compared to the 10 to 16 percent typical of smaller congregations.
23. Inability or unwillingness of majority of long-established churches to accommodate that growing number of self-identified charismatic Christians who seek a church with a prayer-and-praise service.
24. Trend in American society toward larger institutions.

Source: Lyle E. Schaller in *Christianity Today* magazine, March 5, 1990 issue. Used by permission.

MAJOR DENOMINATIONAL GROUPS, TABLE 1

by Robert Charles Walton
Chairman, Bible Department
The Christian Academy, Media, PA

Group	*Origins*	*Form of Government*	*Major Creedal Documents*	*Sacraments or Ordinances*
Roman Catholic	Trace origins to Peter as first Pope; 451—primacy of Bishop of Rome formally recognized	Episcopal	Ecumenical creeds such as Nicea (325), Constantinople (381), and Chalcedon (451)	Infant baptism, penance, confirmation, eucharist, marriage, ordination, extreme unction; (convey grace)
Orthodox	1054—Leo IX & Michael Cerularius finalized split developed over centuries; 1970—Orthodox Church of America	Episcopal	Ecumenical creeds of seven ecumenical councils prior to 787	Baptism by trine immersion, confirmation, eucharist, penance, ordination, marriage, anointing of sick; (convey grace)
Lutheran	1517—Martin Luther posts 95 Theses in Wittenberg, Germany; break complete by 1520; 1748—Mohlenberg forms ministerium of PA	Incorporates both Episcopal and Congregational elements	1530—Augsburg Confession; 1577— Formula of Concord	Infant baptism, Lord's Supper (consubstantiation); (convey grace)
Reformed	16th century in Switzerland (Zwingli, Calvin), France (Huguenots), Germany, Hungary, Netherlands	Modified Presbyterian	1558— Gallican Confession; 1561—Belgic Confession; 1563—Heidelberg Catechism; 1566—2nd Helvetic Confession; 1619—Canons of Synod of Dordt	Infant baptism, Lord's Supper; (symbolic)

Continued on next page

FOCUS FACT

From June 26 to July 1, 1983, Rev. Ronald Gallagher at the Baptist Temple, Appomattox, VA, preached for 120 hours—the longest sermon on record according to the 1989 ***Guinness Book of World Records.***

Group	*Origins*	*Form of Government*	*Major Creedal Documents*	*Sacraments or Ordinances*
Anabaptist	1525—Conrad Grebel, Felix Manz in Zurich; later in Germany and Netherlands (Menno Simons); 1683— First Mennonites in PA	Congregational	1527—Schleitheim Confession; generally anti-creedal	Believer's baptism (often by effusion), Lord's Supper (symbolic)
Episcopal	1534—Henry VIII repudiates papal authority; 1789—Protestant Episcopal Church formed in Philadelphia, PA	Episcopal	Thirty-nine Articles (1563)	Infant baptism, holy communion, others; (convey grace)
Presbyterian	1560—John Knox in Scotland; 1706—Francis Makemie forms Philadelphia Presbytery	Presbyterian	1648—Westminster Confession of Faith	Infant baptism, Lord's Supper (spiritual presence)
Baptist	16th Century Anabaptist; 1609—John Smyth, England, General Baptists; 1638—Eng. Particular Baptists; 1638—Roger Williams, Providence, RI	Congregational	1689—London Confession; 1742—Philadelphia Confession; 1832— New Hampshire Confession; generally non-creedal	Believer's baptism by immersion, Lord's Supper (symbolic)
Methodist	John Wesley in England; 1784—Asbury & Coke, Baltimore, MD—Methodist Episcopal Church; 1795—Methodist Church in England	Episcopal	1739—Articles of Religion; generally non-creedal	Infant or believer's baptism by sprinkling, pouring, or immersion, Lord's Supper
Christian Church Disciples of Christ	Barton Stone, KY; Thomas & Alexander Campbell, PA; organized 1832	Congregational	Anti-creedal	Believer's baptism by immersion, Lord's Supper (weekly)
Pentecostal	1901—Charles F. Parham, Topeka, KS; 1906—William J. Seymour, Azusa Street Revival	Mostly Congregational (some groups Episcopal)	Generally non-creedal	Believer's baptism by immersion, Lord's Supper

MAJOR DENOMINATIONAL GROUPS, TABLE 2

Group	*Relationship to State*	*Other Emphases and Distinctives*	*Major Representatives in the United States (over 250,000 members)*
Roman Catholic	Vatican City is a sovereign state, and church is established by concordates with many nations	Pope as Vicar of Christ, apostolic succession, transubstantiation, authority of tradition (Popes, Councils, Church Fathers, Canon Laws) elaborate ritual, clerical celibacy, veneration of Mary & saints	Roman Catholic Church
Orthodox	Affiliated with state in various nations of Eastern Europe and Middle East	Celibacy of monks and bishops only; Holy Spirit proceeds only from God the Father; elaborate ritual; veneration of icons	Orthodox Church in America; Greek Archdiocese of North and South America
Lutheran	Close ties at one time in Germany and Scandinavia	Justification by faith; liturgical worship	Evangelical Lutheran Church of America; Lutheran Church, Missouri Synod; Wisconsin Evangelical Lutheran Synod
Reformed	Close ties at one time in Switzerland, Netherlands	Calvinistic; simple worship emphasizing sermon	Reformed Church in America; Christian Reformed Church; United Church of Christ (merger of various Congregational, Reformed, and Lutheran bodies)
Anabaptist	Oppose all church-state ties	Strict church discipline; simple lifestyle; pacifism; often practice footwashing; separation from world	None over 250,000 (American Anabaptists include Mennonites, Amish, and Hutterites)
Episcopal	Established in England	*Book of Common Prayer* used in worship; Archbishop of Canterbury recognized as head of Anglican communion; "Middle Way" between Catholics and Protestants	Episcopal Church; Christian Reformed Church; United Church of Christ (merger of various Congregational, Reformed, and Lutheran bodies)
Presbyterian	Established in Scotland	Calvinistic; plurality of elders; simple worship emphasizing sermon	Presbyterian Church, U.S.A.
Baptist	Emphasize separation of church and state	Autonomy of local church; freedom of conscience; simple worship emphasizing sermon	Southern Baptist Convention; American Baptist Convention; American Baptist Association; National Baptist Convention, U.S.A.; National Baptist Convention of America; National Primitive Baptist Association, U.S.A.; Conservative Baptist Association; General Association of Regular Baptists
Methodist	No church-state ties	Arminian; perfectionist; organization grew from Wesley's Methodist Societies; emphasize social action	United Methodist Church; African Methodist Episcopal Church; Christian Methodist Episcopal Church; Church of the Nazarene

Group	*Relationship to State*	*Other Emphases and Distinctives*	*Major Representatives in the United States (over 250,000 members)*
Christian Church Disciples of Christ	No church-state ties	Baptism necessary for salvation; return to New Testament Christianity; freedom of biblical interpretation; autonomy of local church; some groups reject instrumental music	Christian Church (Disciples of Christ)
Pentecostal	No church-state ties	Holy Spirit baptism; speaking in tongues; divine healing; Arminian; perfectionist	Assemblies of God; Pentecostal Church of God in America; United Pentecostal Church International; Church of God (Cleveland, TN); Church of God in Christ

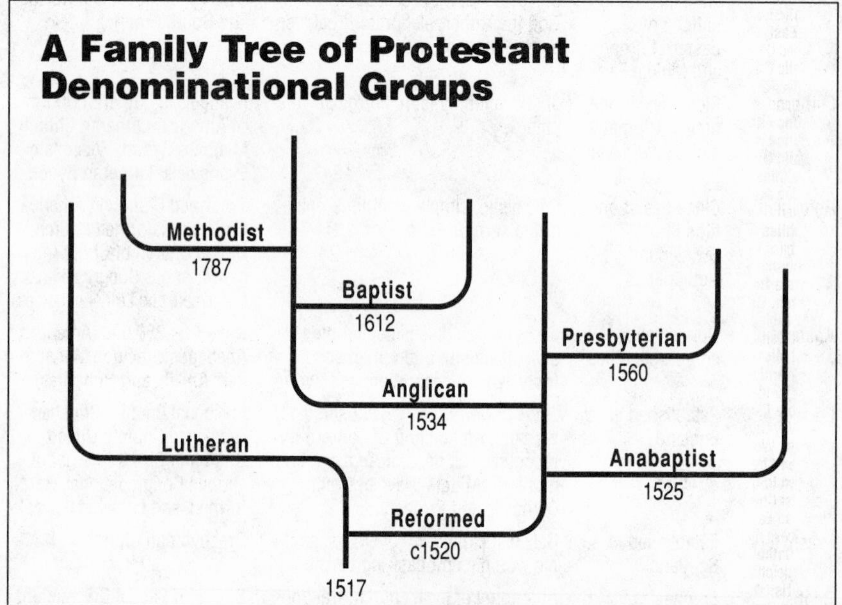

UNITED STATES DENOMINATIONAL STATISTICS

The following table provides current and non-current statistics for United States religious bodies, listed alphabetically. Current statistics are defined as those gathered and reported for 1989 and 1988. Those bodies having current statistics, and the statistics themselves, are shown in boldface type. Non-current statistics are those for 1987 or earlier. They appear in lightface type. No statistics for "Full, Communicant, or Confirmed members," "Number of Sunday or Sabbath Schools," and "Total Enrollment" are reported for bodies having non-current statistics.

Religious Body	*Year Reported*	*No. of Churches*	*Inclusive Membership*	*Full, Communicant or Confirmed Members*	*No. of Pastors Serving Parishes*	*Total No. of Clergy*	*No. of Sunday or Sabbath Schools*	*Total Enrollment*
Advent Christian Church	**1988**	**251**	**19,900**	**19,900**	**300**	**560**	**300**	**18,472**
African Methodist Episcopal Church	1981	6,200	2,210,000	6,050	6,550			
African Methodist Episcopal Zion Ch.	1987	6,060	1,220,260	6,300	6,698			
Alaska Moravian Church	1987	23	5,159	11	15			
Albanian Orthodox Archdiocese in Am.	1978	16	40,000	18	25			
Albanian Orthodox Diocese of Am.	**1989**	**2**	**586**	**586**	**1**	**3**	**2**	**31**
Allegheny Wesleyan Meth. Connection (Original Allegheny Conference)	1987	122	2,434	102	199			
Amana Church Society	1987	7	810	12	13			
American Baptist Association	1986	1,705	250,000	1,740	1,760			
American Bapt. Churches in the U.S.A.	**1988**	**5,839**	**1,549,563**	**1,549,563**	**5,250**	**8,276**	**N.R.**	**361,265**
American Carpatho-Russian Orthodox Greek Greek Catholic Church	1976	70	100,000	61	66			
American Rescue Workers	1984	20	2,700	35	53			
The Anglican Orthodox Church	1983	40	6,000	6	6			
The Antiochian Orthodox Christian Archdiocese of North America	**1988**	**150**	**300,000**	**300,000**	**138**	**172**	**150**	**21,500**
Apostolic Catholic Assyrian Church of the East, North American Diocese	**1989**	**22**	**120,000**	**120,000**	**92**	**109**	**22**	**1,050**
Apostolic Christian Church (Nazarene)	1985	48	2,799		176	176		
Apostolic Christian Churches of Am.	**1988**	**80**	**11,300**	**11,240**	**290**	**329**	**80**	**7,000**
Apostolic Faith Mission of Portland Oregon	1987	45	4,100		74	64		
Apostolic Faith Mission Church of God	**1989**	**18**	**6,200**	**4,700**	**27**	**32**	**18**	**1,570**
Apostolic Lutheran Church of America	**1988**	**57**	**7,707**	**2,995**	**25**	**34**	**44**	**2,010**
Apostolic Overcoming Holy Church of God	**1988**	**177**	**12,479**	**12,479**	**127**	**130**	**N.R.**	**N.R.**
Armenian Apostolic Church of America	1986	18	29,070		16	19		
Armenian Church of Am., Diocese of	1979	66	450,000		45	61		
Assemblies of God	**1988**	**11,123**	**2,147,041**	**1,275,148**	**15,617**	**30,552**	**10,692**	**1,363,881**
Assemblies of God, International Fellowship (Independent/Not Affiliated)	1962	136	N.R.		136	367		
Associate Reformed Presbyterian Church, General Synod	**1988**	**181**	**36,949**	**31,922**	**157**	**237**	**164**	**16,042**
Baptist Bible Fellowship, International	1966	3,449	1,405,900		3,400	4,500		
Baptist General Conference	**1989**	**789**	**135,125**	**135,125**	**1,200**	**1,700**	**789**	**67,030**
Baptist Missionary Association of Am.	**1988**	**1,347**	**227,897**	**227,879**	**1,500**	**2,650**		**95,406**
Beachy Amish Mennonite Church	**1989**	**100**	**6,800**	**6,800**	**86**	**325**	**N.R.**	**N.R.**
Berean Fundamental Church	1981	49	3,350		51	53		
The Bible Church of Christ	**1988**	**6**	**6,405**	**4,800**	**8**	**47**	**6**	**684**
Bible Way Church of Our Lord Jesus Christ, World Wide, Inc.	1970	350	30,000		350	350		
Brethren Church (Ashland, Ohio)	**1988**	**124**	**14,753**	**14,753**	**97**	**173**	**124**	**6,893**
Brethren In Christ Church	**1988**	**193**	**17,081**	**16,580**	**185**	**233**	**185**	**9,365**
Buddhist Churches of America	1964	100	100,000		70	115		
Bulgarian Eastern Orthodox Church (Diocese of N. & S. Am. and Australia)	1971	13	86,000		N.R.	11		
Christ Catholic Church	**1988**	**13**	**1,382**	**1,137**	**12**	**12**	**0**	**0**
Christadelphians	1964	850	15,800		None	None		
The Christian and Missionary Alliance	**1988**	**1,793**	**259,612**	**133,575**	**1,669**	**2,261**	**1,606**	**189,424**
Christian Brethren (a.k.a. Plymouth Brethren)	1984	1,150	98,000		N.R.	500		
Christian Catholic Church (Evangelical Protestant)	**1988**	**6**	**2,500**	**2,500**	**10**	**19**	**6**	**1,000**
Christian Church (Disciples of Christ)	**1988**	**4,159**	**1,073,119**	**707,985**	**3,963**	**6,849**	**4,159**	**327,354**
Christian Church of No. Am., Gen. Cncl	1985	104	13,500		107	169		
Christian Churches and Churches of Christ	**1988**	**5,579**	**1,070,616**	**1,070,616**	**5,525**	**6,596**	**N.R.**	**N.R.**
The Christian Congregation	**1988**	**1,456**	**107,902**	**107,902**	**1,454**	**1,460**	**1,310**	**79,187**
Christian Methodist Episcopal Church	1983	2,340	718,922		2,340	2,650		
Christian Nation Church, U.S.A.	1986	5	200		5	23		
Christian Reformed Church in No. Am.	**1988**	**699**	**222,408**	**143,424**	**609**	**1,075**	**N.R.**	**N.R.**
Christian Union	1984	114	6,000		80	114		
Church of Christ	1972	32	2,400		169	188		
Church of Daniel's Band	1951	4	200		4	10		
The Church of God	1978	2,035	75,890		1,910	2,737		
Church of God (Anderson, Ind.)	**1988**	**2,336**	**198,842**	**198,842**	**1,989**	**3,315**	**2,226**	**181,667**
Church of God by Faith	1973	106	4,500		125	150		
Church of God (Cleveland, Tenn.)	**1989**	**5,763**	**582,203**	**582,203**	**6,207**	**7,544**	**5,436**	**509,250**

Religious Body	Year Reported	No. of Churches	Inclusive Membership	Full, Communicant or Confirmed Members	No. of Pastors Serving Parishes	Total No. of Clergy	No. of Sunday or Sabbath Schools	Total Enrollment
Church of God General Conference (Oregon, Ill.)	**1989**	**88**	**5,767**	**4,415**	**67**	**87**	**88**	**3,357**
The Church of God in Christ	1982	9,982	3,709,661		9,204	10,426		
The Church of God in Christ, Internatnl	1982	300	200,000		700	1,600		
Church of God in Christ (Mennonite)	**1989**	**70**	**9,256**	**9,256**	**347**	**347**	**N.R.**	**N.R.**
The Church of God of Prophecy	**1989**	**2,111**	**73,977**	**73,977**	**N.R.**	**N.R.**	**2,308**	**88,432**
The Church of God of the Mountain Assembly	1977	105	3,125		162	162		
Church of God (Seventh Day) Denver, CO	1987	135	6,498		73	100		
Church of God (Which He Purchased with His Own Blood)	1986	7	800		10	10		
Church of Illumination	1983	4	9,000		60	60		
The Church of Jesus Christ (Bickertonites)	**1988**	**70**	**2,986**	**2,657**	**272**	**282**	**68**	**1,816**
The Church of Jesus Christ of Latter-Day Saints	1987	8,682	4,000,000		26,046	29,714		
Church of Our Lord Jesus Christ of the Apostolic Faith	1954	155	45,000		150	185		
Church of the Brethren	**1988**	**1,079**	**151,169**	**151,169**	**975**	**1,553**	**N.R.**	**N.R.**
Church of the Living God (C.W.F.F.)	1985	170	42,000		N.R.	170		
Church of the Lutheran Brethren of Am.	**1988**	**128**	**13,695**	**7,827**	**115**	**202**	**124**	**10,884**
Church of the Lutheran Confession	**1988**	**67**	**8,655**	**6,304**	**52**	**72**	**64**	**1,379**
Church of the Nazarene	**1988**	**5,129**	**552,264**	**550,711**	**4,171**	**8,988**	**5,054**	**861,761**
Churches of Christ	**1989**	**13,375**	**1,626,000**	**1,278,000**	**N.R.**	**N.R.**	**N.R.**	**N.R.**
Churches of Christ in Christian Union	**1988**	**260**	**10,418**	**10,418**	**167**	**360**	**260**	**18,200**
Churches of God, General Conference	**1988**	**343**	**33,778**	**33,778**	**237**	**327**	**343**	**27,623**
Community Churches, International Council of	**1989**	**200**	**250,000**	**250,000**	**N.R.**	**350**	**N.R.**	**N.R.**
Congregational Christian Churches, National Association of	1989	400	90,000	90,000	375	575	N.R.	N.R.
Congregational Holiness Church	1981	174	8,347		176	488		
Conservative Baptist Assoc. of Am.	**1988**	**1,121**	**204,496**	**204,496**	**N.R.**	**N.R.**	**N.R.**	**N.R.**
Conservative Congregational Christian Conference	**1988**	**176**	**29,015**	**29,015**	**271**	**457**	**157**	**11,692**
Coptic Orthodox Church	**1989**	**40**	**160,000**	**160,000**	**44**	**44**	**N.R.**	**N.R.**
Cumberland Presbyterian Church	**1988**	**752**	**91,491**	**85,304**	**440**	**725**	**752**	**42,536**
Duck River (and Kindred) Assoc. of Baptists	1975	85	8,632		148	148		
Elim Fellowship	1983	36	N.R.		144	185		
The Episcopal Church	**1988**	**7,360**	**2,455,422**	**1,725,581**	**8,131**	**14,694**	**N.R.**	**556,168**
The Estonian Evang. Lutheran Church	**1988**	**24**	**7,399**	**N.R.**	**19**	**N.R.**	**N.R.**	**N.R.**
Ethical Culture Movement	**1988**	**21**	**3,212**	**3,212**	**19**	**43**	**12**	**357**
Evangelical Church	1987	155	17,417		160	288		
Evangelical Congregational Church	**1988**	**156**	**33,318**	**24,980**	**113**	**197**	**153**	**17,510**
The Evangelical Covenant Church	**1988**	**584**	**87,750**	**87,750**	**836**	**1,260**	**532**	**74,922**
Evangelical Free Church of America	1986	880	95,722		N.R.	1,484		
Evangelical Friends Alliance	1982	217	24,095		192	483		
Evangelical Lutheran Church In Am.	**1988**	**11,120**	**5,251,534**	**3,931,878**	**10,083**	**16,083**	**10,125**	**1,166,059**
Evangelical Lutheran Synod	**1989**	**123**	**21,378**	**15,518**	**98**	**141**	**110**	**3,900**
Evangelical Mennonite Church	**1989**	**26**	**3,888**	**3,888**	**43**	**62**	**25**	**4,018**
Evangelical Methodist Church	1987	130	8,282		151	238		
Evangelical Presbyterian Church	**1989**	**155**	**50,300**	**48,500**	**181**	**225**	**155**	**25,000**
Fellowship of Evang. Bible Churches	**1988**	**14**	**1,925**	**1,450**	**18**	**47**	**14**	**1,680**
Fellowship of Fundamental Bible Churches	1984	31	1,840		31	52		
The Fire Baptized Holiness Church (Wesleyan)	1958	53	988		N.R.	N.R.		
Free Christian Zion Church of Christ	1956	742	22,260		321	420		
Free Lutheran Congregations, The Association of	**1987**	**193**	**26,870**	**20,485**	**114**	**139**	**180**	**8,100**
Free Methodist Church of North Am.	**1988**	**1,071**	**73,647**	**54,432**	**1,133**	**1,802**	**1,088**	**107,723**
Free Will Baptists, National Assoc. of	**1988**	**2,496**	**204,382**	**204,382**	**2,800**	**2,895**	**2,496**	**155,666**
Friends General Conference	1987	505	31,690		None	None		
Friends United Meeting	**1988**	**545**	**54,501**	**48,325**	**341**	**601**	**463**	**24,000**
Full Gospel Assemblies, International	1984	150	3,800		122	399		
Full Gospel Fellowship of Churches and Ministers, International	1985	450	65,000		850	850		
Fundamental Methodist Church, Inc.	1987	13	733		14	21		
General Association of Regular Baptist Churches	**1989**	**1,585**	**260,000**	**260,000**	**2,000**	**2,050**	**1,585**	**310,000**

Religious Body	*Year Reported*	*No. of Churches*	*Inclusive Membership*	*Full, Communicant or Confirmed Members*	*No. of Pastors Serving Parishes*	*Total No. of Clergy*	*No. of Sunday or Sabbath Schools*	*Total Enrollment*
General Baptists (General Assoc. of)	**1988**	**868**	**74,086**	**74,086**	**N.R.**	**1,483**	**N.R.**	**N.R.**
General Church of the New Jerusalem	1971	33	2,143		17	31		
General Conference of Mennonite Brethren Churches	1988	128	17,065		N.R.	N.R.		
General Conference of the Evangelical Baptist Church, Inc.	1952	31	2,200		22	37		
General Convention, The Swedenborgian Church	**1988**	**50**	**2,423**	**2,423**	**45**	**54**	**N.R.**	**N.R.**
General Six Principle Baptists	1970	7	174		4	7		
Grace Brethren Churches, Fellowship of	1985	312	41,767		424	519		
Grace Gospel Fellowship	**1988**	**52**	**4,500**	**2,500**	**68**	**125**	**N.R.**	**N.R.**
Greek Orthodox Archdiocese of North and South America	1977	535	1,950,000		610	655		
The Holiness Church of God, Inc.	1968	28	927		25	36		
Holy Ukrainian Autocephalic Church in Exile	1965	10	4,800		15	24		
House of God, Which Is the Church of the Living God, the Pillar and Ground of the Truth, Inc.	1956	107	2,350		80	120		
Hungarian Reformed Church in Am.	**1988**	**31**	**12,500**	**10,500**	**24**	**26**	**20**	**600**
Hutterian Brethren	1987	77	3,988		N.R.	N.R.		
Independent Fundamental Churches of America	1980	1,019	120,446		782	1,366		
International Church of the Foursquare Gospel	**1988**	**1,363**	**198,715**	**193,619**	**N.R.**	**5,076**	**1,014**	**46,624**
Internatnl Pentecostal Church of Christ	**1989**	**75**	**2,628**	**2,628**	**123**	**123**	**75**	**3,884**
Jehovah's Witnesses	**1989**	**8,851**	**804,639**	**804,639**	**None**	**None**	**None**	**None**
Jews*	**1988**	**3,416**	**5,935,700**	**3,750,000**	**N.R.**	**6,500**	**N.R.**	**N.R.**
Kodesh Church of Immanuel	1980	5	326		2	28		
Korean Presbyterian Church In America, General Assembly of the	1986	180	24,000		200	225		
Latvian Evangelical Lutheran Church in America, The	**1988**	**56**	**13,211**	**11,914**	**29**	**45**	**N.R.**	**N.R.**
Liberal Catholic Church-Province of the United States of America	1987	34	2,800		64	127		
Liberty Baptist Fellowship	1987	510	200,000		150	N.R.		
The Lutheran Church-Missouri Synod	**1988**	**5,939**	**2,604,278**	**1,962,674**	**5,238**	**8,193**	**5,737**	**652,332**
Lutheran Churches, The Am. Assoc. of	**1988**	**78**	**15,150**	**11,210**	**63**	**80**	**N.R.**	**N.R.**
Mennonite Church	**1988**	**1,023**	**92,682**	**92,682**	**1,448**	**2,469**	**N.R.**	**N.R.**
Mennonite Church, The Gen. Conf.	**1988**	**224**	**34,693**	**34,693**	**212**	**379**	**224**	**16,179**
Metropolitan Church Association, Inc.	1958	15	443		13	62		
Metropolitan Community Churches, Universal Fellowship of 1985	230	34,000			240	266		
The Missionary Church	**1988**	**290**	**26,332**	**26,332**	**317**	**615**	**N.R.**	**N.R.**
Moravian Church-Northern Province	**1988**	**100**	**31,468**	**24,092**	**92**	**169**	**99**	**7,071**
Moravian Church-Southern Province	**1988**	**54**	**21,467**	**17,518**	**53**	**87**	**54**	**8,968**
National Baptist Convention of America	1956	11,398	2,668,799		7,598	28,574		
National Baptist Convention, U.S.A., Inc.	1958	26,000	5,500,000		26,000	27,500		
National Primitive Bapt. Convention, Inc.	1975	616	250,000		460	636		
National Spiritualist Assoc. of Churches	1984	142	5,558		128	142		
Netherlands Reformed Congregations	1984	14	5,520		3	4		
New Apostolic Church of North Am.	**1988**	**491**	**36,972**	**36,972**	**734**	**823**	**N.R.**	**2,203**
North American Baptist Conference	**1988**	**259**	**42,629**	**42,269**	**286**	**445**	**259**	**23,485**
North Am. Old Roman Catholic Church	1986	133	62,611		109	150		
North American Old Roman Catholic Church (Archdiocese of New York)	**1988**	**5**	**615**	**615**	**6**	**9**	**3**	**39**
Old German Baptist Brethren	**1988**	**55**	**5,497**	**5,497**	**288**	**288**	**N.R.**	**N.R.**
Old Order Amish Church	**1988**	**756**	**68,040**	**68,040**	**3,024**	**3,049**	**N.R.**	**N.R.**
Old Order (Wisler) Mennonite Church	1980	36	9,731		N.R.	N.R.		
Open Bible Standard Churches, Inc.	**1989**	**325**	**46,000**	**42,000**	**587**	**937**	**285**	**25,000**
The (Original) Church of God	1971	70	20,000		50	124		
Orthodox Church in America	1978	440	1,000,000		457	531		
The Orthodox Presbyterian Church	1987	188	19,094		160	334		
Pentecstl Assemblies of the World, Inc.	1960	550	4,500		450	600		
Pentecostal Church of God, Inc.	**1988**	**1,157**	**86,000**	**40,000**	**N.R.**	**1,584**	**N.R.**	**N.R.**
Pentecostal Fire-Baptized Holiness Ch.	1969	41	545		80	80		

*Inclusive membership represents estimates of the total number of Jews seen as an ethnic, social, and religious community. Full membership is the number of Jews estimated to be associated with synagogues and temples of the Orthodox, Conservative, and Reform branches by officials of the congregational organizations of these three groups.

Religious Body	Year Reported	No. of Churches	Inclusive Membership	Full, Communicant or Confirmed Members	No. of Pastors Serving Parishes	Total No. of Clergy	No. of Sunday or Sabbath Schools	Total Enrollment
The Pentecostal Free Will Baptist Church, Inc.	1985	130	10,700		118	171		
Pentecostal Holiness Ch., Internatnl	**1988**	**1,472**	**116,764**	**116,764**	**2,046**	**3,314**	**1,472**	**146,776**
Pillar of Fire	1949	61	5,100		N.R.	N.R.		
Polish National Catholic Church of Am.	1960	162	282,411		141	141		
Presbyterian Church in America	**1988**	**1,067**	**208,394**	**169,846**	**1,139**	**1,905**	**N.R.**	**101,543**
Presbyterian Church (U.S.A.)	**1988**	**11,505**	**2,929,608**	**2,929,608**	**10,549**	**19,746**	**N.R.**	**1,097,095**
Primitive Advent Christian Church	1984	10	546		11	11		
Primitive Baptists	1960	1,000	72,000		N.R.	N.R.		
Primitive Methodist Church, U.S.A.	**1989**	**85**	**8,244**	**5,779**	**54**	**84**	**85**	**4,896**
Progressive Natl Bapt. Convention, Inc.	1967	655	521,692		N.R.	863		
The Protestant Conference (Lutheran)	**1988**	**7**	**1,035**	**768**	**7**	**7**	**6**	**136**
Protestant Reformed Churches in Am.	1980	21	4,544		19	31		
Reformed Church in America	**1988**	**925**	**333,798**	**200,631**	**853**	**1,698**	**900**	**100,489**
Reformed Church in the United States	1985	34	3,778		28	34		
Reformed Episcopal Church	**1988**	**78**	**6,274**	**6,274**	**66**	**122**	**73**	**3,877**
Reformed Mennonite Church	1970	12	500		18	21		
Reformed Meth. Union Episcopal Ch.	1983	18	3,800		24	33		
Reformed Presbyt. Church of No. Am.	**1988**	**68**	**5,174**	**3,737**	**59**	**127**	**68**	**2,925**
Reformed Zion Union Apostolic Church	1965	50	16,000		28	N.R.		
Relig. Society of Friends (Conservative)	1984	28	1,744		N.R.	17		
Religious Society of Friends (Unaffiliated Meetings)	1980	112	6,386		N.R.	N.R.		
Reorganized Church of Jesus Christ of Latter Day Saints	**1988**	**1,137**	**190,950**	**190,950**	**17,048**	**170,489**	**N.R.**	**N.R.**
The Roman Catholic Church	**1988**	**23,091**	**54,918,949**	**N.R.**	**34,390**	**52,948**	**N.R.**	**7,025,181**
The Romanian Orthodox Episcopate of America	**1988**	**34**	**60,000**	**60,000**	**28**	**67**	**30**	**1,800**
Russian Orthodox Church in the U.S.A., Patriarchal Parishes	1985	38	9,780		37	45		
The Russian Orthodox Church Outside of Russia	1955	81	55,000		92	168		
The Salvation Army	**1988**	**1,097**	**433,448**	**129,165**	**2,630**	**5,198**	**1,121**	**112,941**
The Schwenkfelder Church	**1988**	**5**	**2,516**	**2,516**	**7**	**9**	**5**	**848**
Second Cumberland Presbyterian Church in the U.S.	1959	121	30,000		121	125		
Separate Baptists in Christ	**1988**	**101**	**10,000**	**10,000**	**101**	**165**	**N.R.**	**N.R.**
Serbian Eastern Orthodox Church in the U.S.A. and Canada	1986	68	67,000			60	82	
Seventh-Day Adventist Church	**1988**	**4,145**	**687,200**	**687,200**	**2,265**	**4,537**	**4,193**	**480,457**
Seventh Day Baptist Gen. Conference	1987	81	5,149		39	92		
Social Brethren	1975	40	1,784		47	47		
Southern Baptist Convention	**1988**	**37,517**	**14,812,844**	**14,812,844**	**37,300**	**63,625**	**36,211**	**7,905,239**
The Southern Methodist Church	1985	150	7,231		80	94		
Sovereign Grace Baptists	**1988**	**275**	**2,600**	**2,600**	**260**	**275**	**250**	**1,900**
Syrian Orthodox Church of Antioch (Archdiocese of the U.S.A. and Canada)	1988	28	30,000	N.R.	20	25	N.R.	N.R.
Triumph The Church and Kingdom of God in Christ (International)	1972	475	54,307		860	1,375		
True (Old Calendar) Orthodox Church of Greece (Synod of Metropolitan Cyprian), American Exarchate	**1989**	**7**	**1,100**	**1,100**	**5**	**13**	**N.R.**	**N.R.**
Ukrainian Orthodox Church in the U.S.A.	1966	107	87,745		107	131		
Ukrainian Orthodox Church of America (Ecumenical Patriarchate)	1986	27	5,500		36	37		
Unitarian Universalist Association	**1988**	**958**	**178,623**	**N.R.**	**600**	**1,140**	**830**	**46,242**
United Brethren in Christ	1982	256	26,869		320	382		
United Christian Church	1987	12	420		8	11		
United Church of Christ	**1988**	**6,362**	**1,644,787**	**1,644,787**	**5,096**	**10,145**	**6,395**	**437,836**
United Holy Church of America	1960	470	28,890		379	400		
The United Methodist Church	1987	37,641	9,055,575	20,	927	38,177		
United Pentecostal Church, Internatnl	**1989**	**3,592**	**500,000**	**500,000**	**N.R.**	**7,279**	**N.R.**	**N.R.**
United Zion Church	**1987**	**13**	**850**		**19**	**20**		
Unity of the Brethren	1988	26	2,873	2,873	19	22	22	1,465
Vedanta Society	1988	13	2,500	2,500	14	14	N.R.	N.R.
Volunteers of America	1978	607	36,634		704	704		
The Wesleyan Church	1987	3,217	185,861	2,	662	3,783		
Wisconsin Evang. Lutheran Synod	**1988**	**1,191**	**418,691**	**316,987**	**1,111**	**1,538**	**1,161**	**49,713**
World Confessional Lutheran Assoc.	1987	12	1,530		18	27		

GROWTH OF WOMEN CLERGY IN 21 USA DENOMINATIONS: 1977-1986

	No. in 1977	*Rank Order*	*No. in 1986*	*Rank Order*	*Gain or Loss*	*1977-86 % Increase or Decrease*
American Baptist Churches	157	(11)	429	(10)	+272	173%
American Lutheran Church	18	(16)	306	(12)	+288	1,600
Assemblies of God	1,572	(2)	3,718	(1)	+2,146	136
Christian Ch. (Disciples of Christ)	388	(6)	743	(7)	+355	91
Christian Congregation	125	(12)	290	(13)	+165	132
Church of God (Anderson, Ind.)	272	(10)	275	(14)	+3	1
Church of the Brethren	27	(15)	120	(16)	+93	344
Church of the Nazarene	426	(4)	355	(11)	-71	-17
Episcopal Church	94	(13)	796	(6)	+702	747
Free Methodist Church	11	(17)	69	(17)	+58	527
International Church of the Foursquare Gospel	804	(3)	666	(8)	-138	-17
Lutheran Church in America	55	(14)	484	(9)	+429	780
Mennonite Church	4	(18)	48	(18)	+44	1,100
Mennonite Church, Gen. Conference	4	(18)	33	(20)	+29	725
Moravian Church (Unitas Fratrum)	3	(20)	16	(21)	+13	433
Presbyterian Church (U.S.A.)	(370)	(8)	1,519	(4)	+1,149	310
Reformed Church in America	1	(21)	42	(19)	+41	+4,100
Salvation Army	3,037	(1)	3,220	(2)	+183	6
United Church of Christ	400	(5)	1,460	(5)	+1,060	265
United Methodist Church	319	(9)	1,891	(3)	+1,572	493
Wesleyan Church	384	(7)	255	(15)	-129	-33
	8,471		16,735		+8,264	+98

From *Yearbook of American and Canadian Churches,* 1989 edited by Constant H. Jacquet.

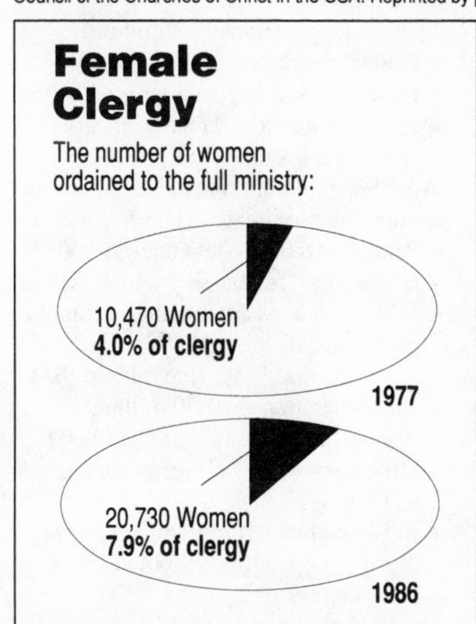

Source: *1989 Yearbook of American & Canadian Churches*

BABY BOOMERS

Increasingly, baby boomers are attending church. Research shows that 42.8 percent of older baby boomers (those born 1946-1958) regularly attend. Predictions are that the church of the 1990s will see a boom in church attendance as baby boomers mature, settle down, and raise their families.

Christianity Today reports in the October 6, 1989, issue that David A. Roozen, William McKinney, and Wayne Thompson, a research team at Hartford Seminary, found that the number of older baby boomers who go to church regularly has risen from 33.5% in the early seventies to 42.8% in the early eighties—an increase of more than 9%. High-income baby boomers (those making more than $30,000 a year) have returned in the greatest numbers.

WHAT PEOPLE ARE SAYING

Adults of the baby boom cohort have apparently burned out on popular culture to the extent that religion is now assuming a more important place in their lives. —*George Barna,* Barna Research Group, Glendale, CA

The minute they have kids, their relativistic worldview collapses. They want to raise children with moral bearings. —*Roy Carlisle,* West Coast literary agent and father of two, speaking of his San Francisco friends

People who just a few years ago couldn't wait to get to work at 7 a.m. are sliding in at 9, taking weekends off. The same career-driven souls once ready to drag their families to smogsville for the almighty job are no longer willing to tax their hearts for a higher tax bracket.

They're not dropping out, they're dropping back, working for a living—with the accent on living. Replacing money as the carrot at the end of the stick: a sense of personal fulfillment and time—for family, friends, for kicking back.—*Anita Manning* in *USA Today,* December 13, 1989

We have always followed the foibles and the adventures of the baby boomers. In the 50s, it was *Leave It to Beaver*; in the 60s, it was the youth movement and protesting, and then, in the 70s, boomers were getting older, getting jobs. In the 80s, it was yuppies. Now, in the 90s, they're going into their 40s, and we're going to follow them into middle age. I believe in the 90s the great status symbol, the thing we're going to yearn after, is experience.

A growing sense that there's more to life than material things is raising consciousness about moral issues. We already see an increased awareness of ethics in business and personal life, an interest in the environment and social problems, yet without the great protest of the 1960s.—*Joe Cappo* in *Future Scope: Success Strategies for the 1990s & Beyond.* Longman Financial Services Publishing

Church leadership is falling into the hands of baby boomers, who look for significance and satisfaction in their activities outside of work. —*Peter Drucker,* at Gospel Light Publications' Third Annual Denominational Conference, Ventura, CA

You can't hug a BMW, after all. We have a better appreciation for balance in our lives. . . . We'll go through a period of looking deeper into our lives, moving inward rather than upward. —*Psychologist Marilyn Ruman,* Encino, CA

There's a strong desire for people to live long, happy and healthy lives, and they realize this is not attainable under present conditions. We're going to see a redirection of priorities. —*Gerald Celente,* trend analyst, Socio-Economic Research Institute of America, Rhinebeck, NY

WHO ARE THE BABY BOOMERS?

1. Elite Workers (approximately 2.3 million)
   - Annual earnings—$30,000 plus
   - Education—high school and/or trade school only
   - Jobs—foremen, plumbers, electricians, other trades
2. Yuppies (approximately 4 million)
   - Annual earnings—$40,000 plus
   - Education—college and/or grad. school
   - Jobs—professional, management/executive, doctors, etc.
3. Would-be's (would like to be Yuppies but are not—approximately 11.8 million)
   - Annual earnings—less than $30,000
   - Education—college or graduate school
   - Jobs—teachers, administrators, middle management, etc.
4. The New Collar Class (the middle class of this generation—30-50 million)
   - Annual earnings—$25,000-$30,000
   - Education—both college graduates and non-graduates
   - Jobs—computer programmers, word processor operators, school teachers, truck drivers, etc.

Baby Boomers and the Future of World Missions by Dr. James F. Engel and Jerry D. Jones.

FOCUS QUOTE **In the physical universe, energy does not perish but is transformed. In like manner, religious values are lifted into a higher case or degenerate into a lower one. When the nuns gave up their long habits, the girls put on maxi-coats; when the rosary as a devotion was dropped, the hippies put beads around their necks; when mysticism evaporated into an irrelevant ideal, youths sought the ecstasy not through the long haul of asceticism, but the short trip through pharmaceuticals; when seminaries, schools and convents dropped discipline, which is an inner violence against our vices, the street mobs picked up violence but directed it this time against neighbor, race and state. When the pulpits no longer resounded with that Name "above every name," the young began calling themselves "Jesus People."** —Fulton J. Sheen

WHERE HAVE THEY COME FROM?

	Born around 1946	*Born around 1958*
TV series	"Father Knows Best"	"The Partridge Family"
Kiddie Show	"Howdy Doody"	"Romper Room"
Toy	Mr. Potato Head (with a real potato)	Mr. Potato Head (the all-plastic version)
Runner-up Toy	The Hula Hoop	G.I. Joe
Goopy stuff	Garden-variety mud	Play-Doh
Singing Family	The Everly Brothers	The Jackson Five
Teen dance step	The Mashed Potato	The Bump
Transportation	Scooters	Skateboards
Monsters	Godzilla, King Kong	"The Munsters"
Cartoon	"Mighty Mouse"	"The Flintstones"
Comic-book heroes	Superman	Batman
Sports heroes	Jackie Robinson	Hank Aaron
Female role model	Annette Funicello of the Mouseketeers	Stefanie Powers as April Dancer in "The Girl from U.N.C.L.E."
Most significant childhood memory	Air raid drills	No cartoons after JFK was shot
Adult activity	Choosing a commune	Choosing a personal financial planner

USA Weekend, 19-21 August 1988 and *Baby Boomers and the Future of World Missions* by Dr. James F. Engel and Jerry D. Jones. Copyright © 1989. Used by permission.

FOCUS QUOTE **Some churches train their greeters and ushers to smile, showing as many teeth as possible. But I can sense that kind of display—and when I am greeted by a man who is smiling because he has been trained to smile, I know I am shaking the flipper of a trained seal.** —A.W. Tozer in *Tragedy in the Church*

BABY BOOMER CHURCH ATTENDANCE BY MARITAL AND FAMILY STATUS

Single	33.7%
Divorced/Widowed	33.5%
Married with	
no children	38.2%
children under 6	42.5%
children 6 and over	48.3%

Roozen and McKinney, *The Big Chill Generation Warms to Worship.*

What Are Their Interests?

In 1988, 281 Chicago area evangelical baby boomers were asked to make a choice between a series of ministry opportunities. The specific question presented to them was:

Below are seven pairs of ministry opportunities. Imagine that you had the resources to financially support any of them. Which one in each pair would you rather support on a monthly basis?

Here is how they answered.

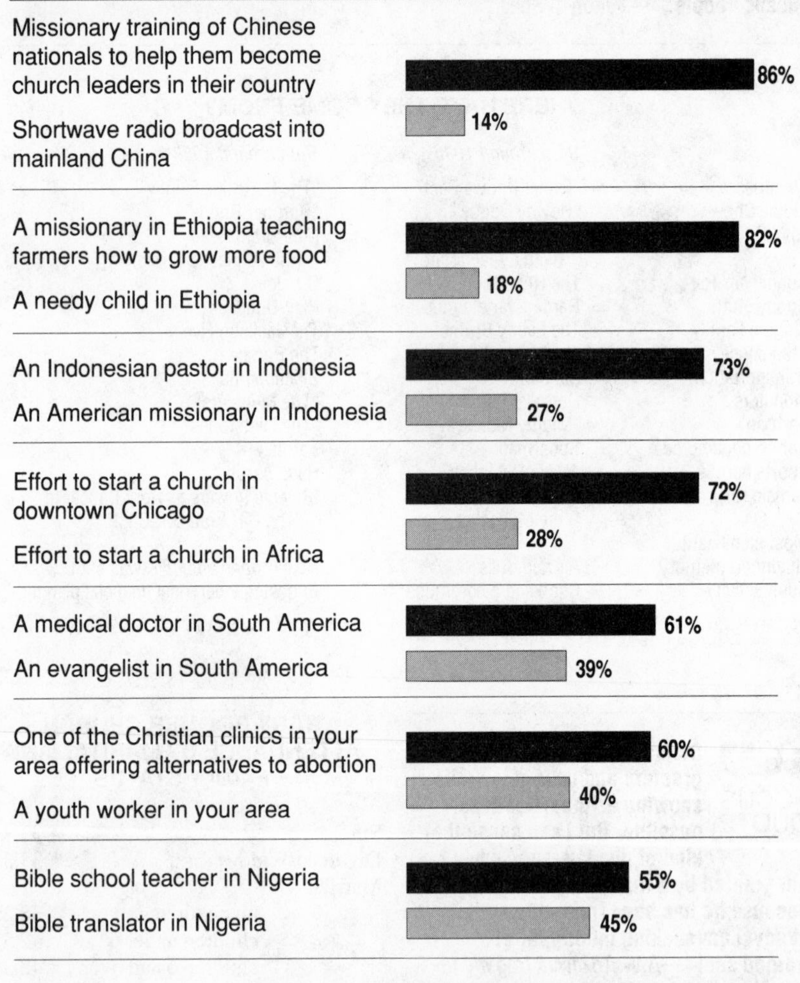

Baby Boomers and the Future of World Missions by Dr. James F. Engle and Jerry D. Jones. Copyright © 1989. Used by permission.

Frequency of Church Attendance

2 or 3 Times a Month
14%
9%
Once a Month
Every Week
38%
6%
Don't Attend
32%
Less Than Monthly

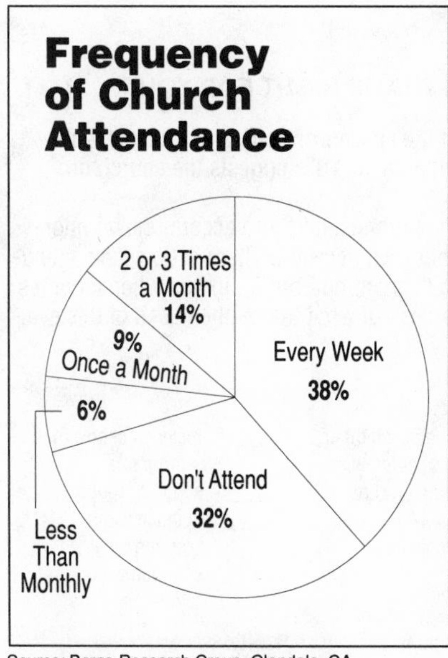

Source: Barna Research Group, Glendale, CA.

FIVE MOST CO[...] REASONS PEOPL[...] ATTEND CHURCH

1. Churches are always asking for money (yet nothing significant seems to be happening through the use of the money).
2. Church services are boring and lifeless.
3. Church services are predictable and repetitive.
4. Sermons are irrelevant to daily life as it is lived in the real world.
5. The pastor makes people feel guilty and ignorant, so they leave church feeling worse than when they entered the doors.

Results of community survey taken by leaders of Willow Creek Community Church, Barrington, IL. Willow Creek Community Church is the second largest church in the U.S. and the 26th largest church in the world.

Church Attendance by Generations

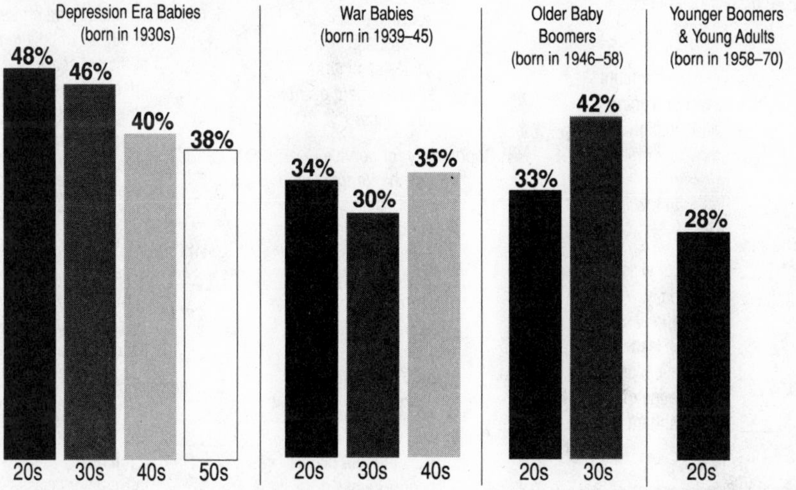

Depression Era Babies (born in 1930s)
48%
46%
40%
38%
20s
30s
40s
50s
War Babies (born in 1939–45)
34%
30%
35%
20s
30s
40s
Older Baby Boomers (born in 1946–58)
33%
42%
20s
30s
Younger Boomers & Young Adults (born in 1958–70)
28%
20s

Each generation's church attendance, at various ages, is represented.

Sources: The Gallup Poll and National Research Council

HOW TO FIND THE CHURCH THAT'S RIGHT FOR YOU

For each element enter a number from 1 to 10 in the space provided. A "1" indicates the church is totally inadequate for your needs in that area; a "10" suggests the church provides exactly what you are looking for.

When you are evaluating the relative appeal of churches, take into account how important each of the measured characteristics is in your own decision. There is no sense attending a church that is great in all the areas you don't care about, but flounders when it comes to the things you feel are most important—regardless of what the mathematics of this evaluation system indicate.

Evaluation Criteria

A. Spiritual beliefs about:
- ____ God
- ____ Jesus Christ
- ____ the Holy Spirit
- ____ communion
- ____ the Bible
- ____ sin, Satan
- ____ salvation
- ____ sacraments
- ____ purpose of life
- ____ the role of women
- ____ baptism
- ____ spiritual gifts
- ____ social issues

B. Worship experience:
- ____ sermons
- ____ music
- ____ service contents
- ____ style of worship
- ____ participation
- ____ tone of worship
- ____ prayer
- ____ attitude toward worship

C. Leadership:
- ____ sense of vision
- ____ active laity
- ____ opportunities to lead
- ____ enough leaders
- ____ discernible priorities
- ____ knowledge of the Bible
- ____ commitment to the Bible

D. People:
- ____ friendly
- ____ people your age
- ____ committed
- ____ involved with each other
- ____ accepting of differences
- ____ people you know are there
- ____ congregational unity

E. Special programs:
- ____ adult Sunday school
- ____ youth program
- ____ missions activity
- ____ Bible study groups
- ____ women's programs
- ____ sports program
- ____ community outreach
- ____ evangelism
- ____ prayer
- ____ social events
- ____ discipleship
- ____ issues seminars
- ____ entertainment events
- ____ counseling

F. Opportunity for service:
- ____ match members' gifts with needs
- ____ multiple opportunities
- ____ appealing opportunities
- ____ laity ownership or programs
- ____ express gratitude for service
- ____ time commitments expected

G. Structure:
- ____ easy to meet people
- ____ people involved
- ____ ministers accessible
- ____ well-organized
- ____ method of government
- ____ focus on people, not programs
- ____ support groups
- ____ in touch with community
- ____ communications tools

H. Size:
- ____ membership
- ____ youth program

I. Location:
- ____ security of area
- ____ distance from home
- ____ part of community

J. Facilities and equipment:
- ____ condition of buildings
- ____ sufficient space
- ____ adequate parking
- ____ athletic facilities
- ____ classroom space
- ____ library
- ____ sound equipment
- ____ video equipment

K. Affiliations:
- ____ denomination
- ____ community associations
- ____ national coalitions

L. Follow-up by church:
- ____ contacted
- ____ reasons for their interest
- ____ introductory class

George Barna in *How to Find* Your *Church*. Published by World Wide Publications.

10 QUESTIONS CHRISTIANS ASK

1. Should Christians pay closer attention to the Lord's Day?
2. Should Christians be involved in politics?
3. How can I know God's will for my life?
4. Is the charismatic renewal, seen in many churches today, from God?
5. Should we expect miracles today?
6. Should Christians seek the gift of prophecy still today?
7. Should women be ordained to Christian ministry?
8. Can I really trust the Bible?
9. Will a loving God really condemn people to hell? Is Christ the only way?
10. What will heaven be like?

Tough Questions Christians Ask. Edited by David Neff. Published by Victor Books/Scripture Press Publications.

CHRISTIAN EDUCATION PERIODICALS

Christian Education Today
P.O. Box 15337, Denver, CO 80215

Christian Education Journal
P.O. Box 650, Glen Ellyn, IL 60138

Current Christian Abstracts Periodical
P.O. Box 7596, Columbia, MO 65205

CHRISTIAN EDUCATION ASSOCIATIONS

Association of Professors and Researchers in Religious Education 1100 E. 55th Street, Chicago, IL 60615

Christian Education Association P.O. Box 4532, Huntsville, AL 35802

Evangelical Teacher Training Association P.O. Box 327, Wheaton, IL 60189

Fellowship of Christian Educators 0N345 Willow Road, Wheaton, IL 60187

International Christian Education Association 24200 Woodward Ave., Pleasant Ridge, MI 48069

National Christian Education Association 302 Lake Street, Huntington, IN 46750

Professional Association of Christian Education (PACE) 8405 N. Rockwell, Suite 222, Oklahoma City, OK 73162

Religious Education Association 409 Prospect Street, New Haven, CT 06511-2177

“” FOCUS QUOTE **The holiest moment of the church service is the moment when God's people—strengthened by preaching and sacrament—go out of the church door into the world to be the church.**—Ernest Southcott

WHAT CHRISTIANS BELIEVE: THE APOSTLES' CREED

The Apostles' Creed is a concise statement of faith that has been adopted or used over the centuries by virtually every branch of Christendom. Quite possibly this creed came into being in Rome about 150 AD. Although it was believed to state correctly the apostles faith, the possibility that any apostle had any part in composing it is unlikely. We use it here as a summary of Christian doctrine, explaining it clause by clause, so that readers will be able to see what believers of every description have believed from the beginning of the church.

The Apostles' Creed
In the words of this creed Christians confess: *I believe in God the Father almighty, maker of heaven and earth, and in Jesus Christ, his only Son, our Lord, who was conceived by the Holy Ghost, born of the virgin Mary, suffered under Pontius Pilate, was crucified, dead, and buried; he descended into hell. The third day he rose again from the dead. He ascended into heaven, and sitteth on the right hand of God the Father almighty. From thence he shall come to judge the*

WHAT CHRISTIANS BELIEVE: THE APOSTLES' CREED cont.

quick and the dead. I believe in the Holy Ghost, the holy catholic church, the communion of saints, the forgiveness of sins, the resurrection of the body, and the life everlasting.

I believe in God the Father almighty, maker of heaven and earth

That statement describes God as Christians know him. The word *Father* summarizes all that Christ had said about God's loving, providing, caring, forgiving, and answering of prayer. In his inmost nature, God is like a good father toward all people, though not all live as his children (Luke 15:11-32; John 1:12).

Almighty means that God is supreme over all, acting in total freedom within the limits he sets for himself—his own character—and the responsible freedom he has given to humankind. That means that God is supreme in history and will in the end outwit evil and get his own way. Because God is fatherly love, love is the ultimate power in the world.

The phrase *maker of heaven and earth* points to God as originator, fashioner, and sustainer of all that is. To him belong all things and all creatures. To believe in God is to worship, trust, pray, obey him, enjoy his world, and esteem everything in it with a sense of responsibility and care (Matthew 6:25-33; Romans 11:33-36; 1 Timothy 1:17).

And in Jesus Christ, his only Son, our Lord

Here the foundations of Christian faith are laid in history—not in experiences or vision or emotion, but in Jesus of Nazareth, a first-century Jew, the Jesus of the Gospels. *Jesus* is the Greek form of *Joshua*, meaning "God saves," or "Savior" (Matthew 1:21).

The title *Christ,* meaning "anointed," signifies one sent on divine mission (John 17:18; 20:21; 1 John 4:14), but especially the expected king who was to restore the Davidic monarchy, rule in God's name, and establish God's kingdom. That hope was nourished by numerous prophecies (Deuteronomy 18:15; 2 Samuel 7:16; Psalms 2; 110; Isaiah 9:2-7; Micah 5:2; Zechariah 9:9; Malachi 3:1-4) and was in part fulfilled by Jesus (Matthew 20:29-21:11; 22:41-45). But Jesus adopted from Ezekiel (2:1, etc.) and Daniel (7:13) the ambiguous title *Son of man* and reinterpreted Messiahship by other prophecies: those of the Servant of God who would suffer to achieve God's will (Isaiah 42:1-4; 52:13-53:12; Matthew 12:17-21; Luke 4:16-21; Acts 8:30-35; 1 Peter 2:21-25).

In calling Jesus God's *only Son* the church underlines Christ's uniqueness in history. Others are children of God by divine favor, through Christ, by rebirth (John 1:12-13; 3:3, 5) and adoption (Galatians 4:4-5). Jesus is Son of God, in likeness and in essential nature, originally, eternally, and by right (Matthew 21:37; John 3:16-18; Romans 1:4; Hebrews 1:1-3). He is, among all the religious heroes of humanity, the only divine Savior (Acts 4:12).

He is *our Lord,* Lord of mind (Philippians 2:5), of conscience (Romans 13:14), of will (2 Corinthians 10:5), of relationships (Romans 14:3-4; 1 Corinthians 7:39), of Scripture (Matthew 5:21-22), of the church (Colossians 1:18), of life and death (Romans 14:7-9). To believe in Jesus is to trust only and completely in him as Savior, to serve and follow him as Lord out of gratitude, admiration, and love.

Who was conceived by the Holy Ghost, born of the virgin Mary

In these words the creed asserts the central miracle of Christianity, the incarnation of God in Christ (Luke 1:35). Jesus was not produced by time and circumstances (though he was divinely prepared for). He came (John 13:3), intervening in human affairs by God's initiative, as one given (John 3:16) and sent (John 6:57). His origin and nature were divine (John 1:1). Yet he was born of a woman (Galatians 4:4), was truly human, grew, was tempted, asked questions, prayed, and was weary, hungry, sorrowful, suffering, rejected, and mortal (John 1:14; Philippians 2:6-7; Hebrews 2:5-18; 1 John 4:2).

In the words *born of the virgin,* Christ's divine origin is again stressed. He was born "not of the will of man" (see Matthew 1:18-25). (To many early Christians who were convinced that the original sin was transmitted through human fathers, Christ's virgin birth also resolved the problem of how Christ could be truly human and sinless.) The name of Mary in the creed reminds Christians of the true place of this pious Jewess as mother of the Lord. To believe these things about Jesus is to wonder at his perfect humanity and strive to be conformed to his likeness.

Suffered under Pontius Pilate, was crucified, dead, and buried; he descended into hell
Here we have a five-fold insistence that Jesus really died. Here are listed the date, judicial circumstances, cruel manner, obvious physical consequence, and inescapable spiritual consequence that he descended, not into the place of fire and torment popularly understood as hell, but into hades, the abode of departed spirits (Luke 23:43; and the puzzling 1 Peter 3:18-20; see Acts 2:27, 31). So the creed answered charges that Christ did not truly die, but swooned, was rescued, escaped because, some asserted, a son of God could never die.

It need not surprise us that nothing is said about why Jesus died. The creed was recited at baptism, where the convert accepted Christ's death on his or her behalf and died with Christ to sin, self, and the world (Romans 6:1-23; Galatians 2:20; 6:14). It was also recited at the Lord's Supper, where Christ's blood of the new covenant between God and humankind was clearly and repeatedly set forth. Jesus died as the Lamb of God bearing away the sins of the world, the righteous for the unrighteous to bring us to God. He offered expiation for sin, redeeming humankind (John 1:29; 1 Peter 3:18; 1 John 4:10; Romans 3:24-25; 2 Corinthians 5:18-21). In so doing, he demonstrated God's love for sinful men and women (1 John 4:9-10). To believe that is to live gratefully, pardoned, and at peace.

The third day he rose again from the dead
That assertion offers another dated historical fact. Jesus did not merely survive or pass through death; he rose (or, as Scripture often insists, God raised him "out from among the dead" (Acts 2:32; 1 Corinthians 15:15; 1 Peter 1:21). The central facts are that Christ conquered death and is alive forevermore, a living, present Savior. Here we have a second reason for Christ's uniqueness: he has risen from the dead. He returned from death as the same Christ, yet different, glorified. Far from the disciples' expecting the event, their hopes creating the conviction that it had happened, they were astonished, unbelieving, and afraid. At first they did not recognize him. Paul recited the evidence (1 Corinthians 15). Later the Gospels record the remembered details with much of the wonder and confusion of the experience still in their stories.

The risen Christ is the focus of the Christian's daily faith. His resurrection confirms who he is (Romans 1:4), that God accepted his sacrifice (Romans 4:25), and that all who are in Christ will also someday rise (1 Corinthians 15:20-23). Those holding such a faith live in Christ's company, sure of everlasting life, unafraid of death.

He ascended into heaven, and sitteth on the right hand of God the Father almighty
Here we have the church's declaration that Jesus was at last fully vindicated, crowned, in the sense of sharing God's throne, and victorious. The Jewish messianic prophecies of kingship were fulfilled beyond anything the prophets foresaw. The ascension of Christ is beautifully described in Luke 24:50-51, more fully in Acts 1:9-11 and dramatically (as the homecoming of a victorious Roman general) in Ephesians 4:7-10. Arguments about the meaning of *up and down* are somewhat childish. Christ passed into the eternal sphere of God's immediate presence in victory and glory. Remembering that these are human words for divine realities, how else can human language express such ideas except in three-dimensional terms?

To believe in Christ's ascension is to know that we have a friend at court interceding for us (Romans 8:34). It is to be drawn upward in aspiration and hope to things above (Colossians 3:1-3). It is to be reminded that the author and perfecter of our faith has himself gone all the way before us, through struggle and suffering to glory (Hebrews 12:1-3).

WHAT CHRISTIANS BELIEVE: THE APOSTLES' CREED cont.

From thence he shall come to judge the quick and the dead

Christian faith has a forward look, too. Christ's story is not ended. Just as Jesus promised to be with us always (Matthew 28:20), so he promised to return (Matthew 24:30; 25:31; John 14:3), thus consummating our spiritual fellowship with him in his manifestation in power and glory. The early church eagerly expected his return (Acts 1:10-11; Philippians 3:20, 21; 1 Thessalonians 1:10; 2:19; 2 Timothy 4:8). 1 Thessalonians 4:16 attempts to describe his coming. Usually that truth is expressed in metaphors, such as lightning (Matthew 24:27), the secret thief (Matthew 24:43; 1 Thessalonians 5:2), the arriving bridegroom (Matthew 25:6), the returning master (Matthew 24:46; 25:19). The time has been fixed by God but is unknown to us (Matthew 24:36, 42, 44; Acts 1:7), and even to Christ himself (Matthew 24:36). That point is emphatically made.

At Christ's coming, Christians will be changed into his likeness, bodily (1 Corinthians 15:51-52; Philippians 3:20-21) and spiritually (1 John 3:2). To believe this is to be vigilant, faithful in service, lest he should come suddenly and find us asleep (Mark 13:35-37).

A second purpose of Christ's coming is for judgment of the living (*quick*) and the dead (John 5:22; Acts 17:31). Jesus himself said he will judge accordingly as people have served him in serving others (Matthew 25:31-46), that is, by the supreme law of love for God and neighbor. Such judgment will be universal (Romans 2:5-11, 16; 14:10). But Christians need fear no condemnation, for they have passed from death to life (Romans 8:1, 38-39; John 5:24). Yet we Christians must all appear before the judgment seat of Christ for assessment of our service (2 Corinthians 5:10; Romans 14:10-12).

Christian belief in divine judgment is therefore not self-righteous nor vengeful, but is instead a deep confidence in the moral constitution of the world—that truth and right are eternal and will triumph. In the end, God is king. To believe that fact is to live humbly and reverently, with enduring certainty that our struggle and sacrifice will prove worthwhile.

Completing its statement about Jesus, the creed seems to take a fresh breath before drawing very large conclusions from what God has done in Christ.

I believe in the Holy Ghost

Ghost is the old word for "disembodied spirit." In the Old Testament the invisible power of God at work in the world is called his *breath*. The same word also means spirit: God's personal activity, manifest only by its effects. Jesus was conceived by God's Spirit (Luke 1:35), anointed by the Spirit in baptism (Luke 3:22), and endowed by the Spirit for his ministry (Luke 4:18). At the end he promised the same spirit to the disciples (Luke 24:49; John 14:16-17, 26; 16:7-15; Acts 1:8).

Pentecost is the record of the Spirit's coming on the church (Acts 2). At first, the spectacular effects—equipping and empowering Christians especially for communication and for healing—impressed onlookers (Acts 2:1-4; 3:1-10; 1 Corinthians 12:4-11). Later, as the Spirit was recognized more clearly as the Spirit of Jesus (Acts 16:7; 2 Corinthians 3:17), the deeper effects in Christian character were more highly valued. That especially meant love (Galatians 5:22-23; 1 Corinthians 13; 2 Corinthians 3:18). The Spirit teaches, leads into truth, convicts, shows things to come. One might say that the Spirit replaces Jesus.

The church experiences the Spirit as the Spirit of truth, purity (holiness), power, and progress. All Christians are born of the spirit (John 3:5) and possessed of the Spirit (Romans 8:9; 1 Corinthians 12:13). Regrettably, not all live in full enjoyment of his ministry and gifts. To believe in the Spirit is to open all the windows of one's soul in surrender and trust to his coming in.

The holy catholic church, the communion of saints

The Spirit of Jesus is not an abstract idea but is embodied in the living church, the body of Christ (1 Corinthians 12:12-27), which Christ purchased (Acts 20:28), loves and cherishes

(Ephesians 5:22-30), and indwells (1 Corinthians 3:16; Ephesians 3:16-17). Despite its faults the church is rightly called holy, a people set apart for Christ. Because there is only one body of Christ through the whole world and all time it is rightly called *catholic*, although several sections of the church have adopted that title as meaning orthodox or true. Christianity is corporate as well as individual. It creates a kingdom, a family of God, a band of disciples bound together by a law of love.

Differences of tradition, government, and culture do not destroy our essential oneness in Christ. The communion of saints extends from the church militant on earth to include the church triumphant in heaven. When we believe in Christ, we identify with some convenient local outcropping of the church. We love it, are loyal to it, serve it, yet we cherish fellowship with all who acknowledge Christ as Lord. We emphasize things that unite us; we are honest and tolerant about things that divide us.

The forgiveness of sins

Fatalists, some psychologists, and remorseful, guilt-ridden souls find it hard to believe that forgiveness is possible. What's done is done, they say. Physical and social consequences of wrongdoing are indeed sometimes permanent. Restitution for wrongdoing is part of penitence; the Christian convert should never expect to be let off from doing what can be made right, or from receiving what is deserved from wrongdoing. At times it happens that we do escape the consequences of our sin. Other times we must receive help from God to bear whatever the undesirable results.

Forgiveness is essentially a changed relationship with God. It is being accepted, reconciled (2 Corinthians 5:18-21), loved, trusted—with all concealment ended, sin confessed and put away. God forgives, initially, for Jesus' sake (Ephesians 4:32), then cleanses (1 John 1:7) and strengthens (Ephesians 3:16), enabling us to overcome temptation (Romans 6:6-7, 12-14). The catalyst of forgiveness is penitence, confession, and faith (Acts 2:37-38; 1 John 1:9). The fruit of forgiveness is a healing peace (Romans 5:1) and a spirit of forgiving toward others (Matthew 6:12, 14-15; 18:23-35).

The resurrection of the body, and the life everlasting

Christian belief in eternal life rests in part on humankind's almost universal intuition of the indestructible nature of the human spirit. It rests on the promises and resurrection of Christ. It rests on our present experience of fellowship with the eternal God, who will not allow the soul he made, loves, and has redeemed, to be extinguished. (Psalms 16:10-11 and 73:23-26 lay a foundation for Matthew 22:31-32; Romans 8:38-39; Philippians 1:21, 23; John 10:27-29).

As an unborn child cannot imagine the world that awaits it after birth, so our imagination now fails to picture the life to come. Our personality will endure. "Because I live," Jesus said, "you also will live." "I will raise him [the one who believes in Christ] at the last day" (John 14:19; 6:39-40, 44, 54).

Hebrew thought resisted the widespread dividing-up of the human being into body and spirit. Each person is an embodied spirit. Disembodied we are naked (2 Corinthians 5:1-4), less than human. Immortality, therefore, involves a resurrection body. But the Gospel resurrection-stories and the writings of the apostle Paul insist on our continuing identity amid that change (1 Corinthians 15:36-53; Philippians 3:20-21). The immortal soul inherits a body transformed to be appropriate for its new life, imperishable, glorious, powerful, spiritual (1 Corinthians 15:42-44). To believe this adds realism to our thoughts of eternal life and profound sacredness to our present body (1 Corinthians 6:13-14; Romans 8:10-11, 23).

MAJOR THEOLOGICAL SCHOOLS OF THOUGHT

Orthodoxy (Gk. *orthos,* right; *doksa,* opinion). Used in several ways: (1) of the teaching of the ecumenical councils from Nicea to Chalcedon on the doctrines of the Trinity and Person of Christ; (2) of the worship, doctrine, and organization of the so-called Orthodox churches that submit to the teaching of the seven ecumenical councils; (3) by North American Evangelicals to describe basic evangelical doctrine, which adds to the Trinity and Person of Christ views about the Atonement, the Bible, and personal faith.

Calvinism The teaching of John Calvin (1509-1564) or of one of his successors or followers. Calvin's own theology is summarized in his *Institutes of the Christian Religion.* It represents an attempt to expound the meaning of Scripture in the light of the experience of the church before and during the Reformation. Thus aspects of traditional theology are retained (e.g., the doctrine of the Trinity and the person of Christ) and other aspects are renewed and restated (i.e., the new emphasis on justification by faith). Calvinism was developed by his successors as they were in debate with Roman Catholics, Lutherans, and among themselves. Classic expositions of developed Calvinism are found in the Canons of the Synod of Dort (1618) and the Westminster Confession of Faith (1647). This may be described as Reformed orthodoxy, High Calvinism, or simply Calvinism.

Arminianism The approach to the doctrines of God and his salvation that had its origin with Jacobus Arminius (1560-1609), a Dutch theologian. The doctrines of Arminius were articulated in the conviction that the teaching of the successors of John Calvin (1509-1564) in the Calvinist churches was developing in an unsatisfying and unbiblical way. The doctrines were set forth in the Remonstrance (1610). This document taught that God eternally elected in Christ all who will believe in Christ, that Christ died for every person, that each believer must be regenerated by the Holy Spirit, that it is possible to resist the grace of God, and therefore that the possibility of falling completely from grace must be seriously entertained. The orthodox Calvinists responded to these articles by their own five articles produced at the Synod of Dort (1618-1619). Arminianism is used also of two English theological movements. First, that associated with Archbishop Laud in the 1620s and 1630s; and second, that taught by John Wesley, the founder of the Methodist church. Methodist teaching is often called Arminianism.

Evangelical A word with several meanings. (1) When used in Germany, it usually refers to the Lutheran state church. (2) In the Church of England it refers to a party, or school (often called "Low Church"), who trace their origins to the "Evangelical Revival" of the 18th century. (3) In a general context it refers to a particular conservative Protestant form of Christianity that especially emphasizes the inspiration and authority of the Bible and the need for personal conversion to God.

Liberalism A form of theology that flourished in the Western church from the mid-19th to the early 20th century. Found primarily in Protestantism, it also had supporters in Roman Catholicism. The key themes were freedom and progress—freedom from old dogmas and freedom to investigate new ideas, progress in collaboration with the new confident sciences. Important thinkers who set the stage for this type of theology were F. D. E. Schleiermacher (1768-1834) and Albrecht Ritschl (1822-1889). The result was a theology that had few points of contact left with the traditional view of the Bible and Christian faith. Two world wars and the massive influence of Karl Barth caused the demise of the old liberal theology as a major movement. It still lives on in a new dress in modern forms of theology that deny the deity of Jesus Christ and allow belief only in what is said to be rational.

Pentecostalism Either a movement in which the gifts of the Holy Spirit are said to be experienced or several denominations that emphasize the possession and exercise of the gifts of the Spirit. The name arises since the Spirit (and thus the gifts of the Spirit) were first given to the church at the Feast of Pentecost (Acts 2). As a movement in modern times it began with the Topeka Revival of 1901 and the Azusa Street Revival of Los Angeles in 1906, with claims to certain gifts of the Spirit, especially speaking in tongues. Similar events took place in other places, and thus the movement to encourage prayer for and receipt of the gifts began. It occurred outside the mainline denominations and churches and led ultimately to the formation of various new groups—Assemblies of God, Pentecostal Assemblies of the World, Pentecostal Church of God, and United Pentecostal Church International. These denominations, with others, have continued; but since World War II a new form of the Pentecostal movement has arisen and has deeply affected most of the traditional churches and denominations. It is known as the Charismatic movement or Neo-Pentecostalism and is best described as a renewal movement in which the gifts of the Spirit are emphasized in the context of each church being seen as a body of Christ.

Ecumenism (Gk. *oikumene,* "the whole inhabited world"). With the modern concern for Christian unity, ecumenical has the meaning of "working for unity and reunification." Ecumenism is everything involved in this process—ethos, methods, and activities. The origin of the ecumenical movement is usually taken as the 1910 Edinburgh Missionary Conference. The World Council of Churches was formed in 1948 and is now the focal point of this work for unity. Since much of the evangelical Christianity in the world remained outside the movement, it is not as yet truly ecumenical (covering all the world).

Fundamentalism A term coined around 1920 to describe conservative Evangelicalism, found particularly in the U.S. Taking its name from a series of booklets entitled *The Fundamentals* (1910-1915), it is an attempt to preserve traditional Protestant doctrines and values—especially the belief in the inerrancy and literal interpretation of Scripture—from the eroding effects of rationalism and modernism.

Neoorthodoxy A type of Protestant and Reformed theology of the 20th century, the name of Karl Barth (Barthianism) is especially associated with it. It is neo (new) in that it opposes the dominant Liberalism of the day; it is orthodox in that it attempts to recover the major theological themes of the Reformation and the Patristic period. This approach involves the use of higher critical methods in the interpretation of the Bible. They do not regard the Scripture to be inerrant but believe that God speaks through Scripture and his Son to obligate humankind to obedience and faithfulness to God.

Charismatic/Neo-Pentecostalism Contemporary religious phenomenon that embodies a renewed emphasis on the person and work of the Holy Spirit. Beginning in the late 1950s and early 1960s non-Pentecostal Christians, many from the mainline denominations, began experiencing Pentecostal visitations that included speaking in tongues, divine healings, prophecies, and various physical phenomena such as prostrations and fainting, in a way reminiscent of the great awakenings of the past. It created a vast unrest and rethinking on the part of traditional non-Pentecostal Christians, including the Roman Catholics, of what place such gifts and experiences ought to play in the Christian life. Voluminous literature and over one hundred official denominational documents have discussed its value pro and con with the general feeling (although not universally held) that one ought not to bridle the Holy Spirit, who "blows where he will," but still one must "test the spirits" to see if they are of God.

New Evangelicalism Term used in the U.S. to describe the modified form of traditional, conservative Evangelicalism (or Fundamentalism) that manifests a greater emphasis on social concern and responsibility. Basic doctrines are not changed, but they are related to concern for the external as well as internal lives of human beings. The idea of holistic salvation represents a further development.

WHAT WE SING, WHAT WE MEAN

Duane Shinn

What We Sing	*What We Mean*
I Surrender All	I Surrender Some
There Shall Be Showers of Blessing	There Shall Be Sprinkles of Blessings
Fill My Cup, Lord	Fill My Spoon, Lord
Oh, How I Love Jesus	Oh, How I Like Jesus
He's Everything to Me	He's Quite a Bit to Me
I Love to Tell the Story	I Love to Talk about Telling the Story
Take My Life and Let It Be	Take My Life Then Let Me Be
It Is No Secret What God Can Do	It Is My Secret What God Can Do
There Is Sunshine in My Soul Today	There Is Scattered Cloudiness in My Soul Today
We Are One in the Spirit	We Are One in the Bond of Our Denomination
Onward Christian Soldiers	Onward Christian Reserves
Where He Leads Me I Will Follow	Where He Leads Me I Will Consider Following
Just As I Am	Just As I Pretend to Be
Stand Up, Stand Up for Jesus	Stand Up, Stand Up (but Keep Your Arms Down) for Jesus
When the Saints Go Marching In	When the Saints Go Sneaking In

STRANGE CHURCH NAMES

- Country Club Christian Church/from Michael Smith, Liberty, MO
- Ralph Lutheran
- Looney Valley Lutheran
- Big Canoe Lutheran/from Rev. Anthony G. Boder (and the *1988 Yearbook of the Evangelical Lutheran Church in America*), Brooklyn Center, MN
- Happy Church/from Mike LaTorra, Arvada, CA
- Dolly Pond Church of God in Grasshopper Settlement
- Mitchell Chapel Church of the Fire Baptized Holiness Church of God of the Americas
- African Casteroil Dead Church
- Catholic Church of South Africa King George Win the War/from Craig Meyer (from A.C. Griders book *Reminiscences*), Madison, WI
- First United Church of Kane/from Peter deVries, Templeton, PA
- Light Pink Baptist Church/from Bob Korth, Cincinnati, OH
- The Church of the Big Hole [Note: Important to watch your step!]/from Kurt Boyum, Fairmont, MN

LAUGHABLE LAWS CONCERNING THE CHURCH AND THE SABBATH

In Gilman, Connecticut, it's strictly against the law to slurp your soup on Sunday. Anyone caught slurping soup in public on the Sabbath is subject to arrest and a fine of $5.00.

Young girls are never allowed to walk a tightrope in Wheeler, Mississippi, with one exception: they may walk a tightrope if it's inside a church.

It's against the law in Blackwater, Kentucky, to tickle a woman under her chin with a feather duster while she is attending a church service. To do so can bring a $10.00 fine and one day in the local jail.

Lingerie cannot be hung on a back yard clothesline on Sunday in Toomsboro, Georgia, unless the undies are carefully hidden from view by a screen or fence.

A woman weighing over two hundred pounds cannot ride a horse anywhere in public on Sunday in Opal, Wyoming.

Logandale, Nevada, won't allow anyone to fly over a large body of water on the Sabbath unless they carry food in the plane. In addition, eating snake meat on Sunday is prohibited.

No one can eat unshelled, roasted peanuts while attending church in Idanha, Oregon; nor can churchgoing Christians eat watermelon on the Sabbath.

In Colebrook, Pennsylvania, a city ordinance makes it illegal to give a cigarette to a female at any time while church services are being held.

Within the city limits of Studley, Virginia, there is a local law which prohibits swinging a yo-yo anywhere in public on the Sabbath, and especially in church or during Sunday School.

In Slaughter, Louisiana, no turtle races are allowed on the Sabbath, nor are turtle races allowed within 100 yards of a local church at any time.

No citizen is allowed to dress up in any red-colored garment and then attend a church service in Leecreek, Arkansas.

A local ordinance in Snowhill, Alabama, prohibits fishermen from chewing tobacco on Sunday without the written permission of a local physician.

All citizens of Bagdad, Florida are outlawed from dipping snuff while on the grounds of any local church. Neither are they allowed to smoke a pipe or a cigar on the Sabbath. (Nothing is mentioned about cigarettes in this law.)

In Leona, Kansas, no female wearing a nightgown—sheer or otherwise—can be rescued by a fireman on the Sabbath. This law specifically states that a woman of any age must always get fully dressed before she can be legally assisted by firemen during a Sunday fire.

A local ordinance in Honey Creek, Iowa, prohibits anyone other than a policeman from carrying a slingshot to church on the Sabbath.

The law in the community of Garysburg, North Carolina, allows the shooting of whales from an airplane on the Sabbath. However, no other animals, including birds, can be hunted in this manner, nor can fish be shot while church is in progress.

It's against the law in Maizie, Kentucky, to drive a car down a public street on Sunday while a dog or cat sits between the driver and the passenger. This law mentions nothing about having the pet on either party's lap.

Robert W. Pelton. Reprinted with permission from The Door, issue #89, 1224 Greenfield Dr., El Cajon, CA 92021.

SERMONS ACTUALLY PREACHED

- Do I Have to Wear a Bun in My Hair? (Matthew 5:28)/from Rev. San Warfield, Cincinnati, OH
- Groan! Groan! That's Okay: God Is Molding You Today/Joel Osborn, Madison, WI
- Up To Your Neck in Whale Puke/Rev. Paul "Bud" D. Pratt, Flint, MI
- The Sermon I Won't Preach/Pastor Michael Loomis, Buffalo, NY
- God's Word: Why Hell Is Like Heaven (Luke 16:19-31)/Brad Whitlock, Raleigh, NC
- The Problem of Denial: Do You Really Love God or Are There Roosters in Your Life?/Marcia Hirst, Bakersfield, CA
- You Won't Get Quaker Oats By Sowing Wild Oats/Dean McIntyre, Clovis, NM
- We Didn't Know Who You Was/Kay Freyer, Mequon, WI
- Hypotasso/Pastor Michael Loomis, Buffalo, NY
- Peanut and the Purdy Girl/Donna Hildebrand, Medford, OR

Reprinted with permission from *The Door*, issue #91, 1224 Greenfield Dr., El Cajon, CA 92021

A BENCH? A PEW? AREN'T THEY ALL BENCHES?

In Colonial America, benches in the front of the church were purchased by upper class members for their exclusive use. To these, were given a distinctive name to set them apart: pew.

Gradually, the practice faded out giving way to the assertion of some church leaders that "all the church is for all the people." Rather than downgrade the pew to the bench, the bench was upgraded to the pew. And so we have our present day pew.

SEEN ON CHURCH BULLETIN BOARDS

- The competition is fierce, but we're still open for business.
- Last chance to pray before entering the freeway.
- God so loved the world that he didn't send a committee.
- Keep off the grass. This means thou.
- Come to church Sunday. If you have no sins, bring someone who has.
- Join our sit-in demonstration every Sunday.
- Come in and pray today. Beat the Christmas rush.
- If you have troubles, come in and tell us about them. If you have none, come in and tell us how you do it.
- The Lord loves a cheerful giver. He also accepts from a grouch.
- Everyone occupies some kind of pulpit and preaches some kind of sermon every day.
- All new sermons, no reruns.

QUESTIONS NOT TO ASK!

Before, during, or after church:

- You asleep?
- Now what's the matter?
- Have I kept you waiting?
- You don't remember me, do you?
- Will you promise not to get mad if I ask you something?

Jane Goodsell, Press Associates in the February 1990 issue of *Reader's Digest*.

DO YOU KNOW THE DIFFERENCE?

Reverend: From the Latin "reverendus" meaning "worthy of respect." The British began the custom of calling their minister "Reverend"—an indicator of respect for him and his leadership.

Pastor: Comes from the Latin word for shepherd and "pascere" which means "to feed." The Bible speaks of Christ as the Shepherd feeding his flock and ministers as "shepherds of the flock."

Parson: In the demanding hardships of Colonial American life, few had time for educational pursuits. And so the local minister often became the resource person for information. Before long, people began to refer to him as the "town person." Spoken with the heavy New England accent, the phrase was sometimes misunderstood and gradually turned into the "town parson" as it made its way across the country.

Vicar: From the Latin "vicarius" meaning substitute. Ministers are referred to as substitutes or representatives of Christ on earth.

Evangelist: From the Greek "euangelion" and Latin "evangelium," meaning good news. Traveling ministers brought good news to the people to whom they ministered, and so became known as evangelists.

NATIONAL ASSOCIATION OF EVANGELICALS AWARDS

LAYPERSON-OF-THE-YEAR AWARD

The Layperson-of-the-Year is chosen based on: Christian character and commitment; tangible relationship with NAE, including agreement with the NAE Statement of faith; lay leadership in evangelical activity and thought; strategic support of evangelical work in general; public recognition of his/her work in a leadership capacity.

1961 Kenneth Keyes, Highlands, NC
1962 Carl Gundersen, Des Plaines, IL
1963 Herbert Taylor, Chicago, IL
1964 John Anderson, Rockford, IL
1965 Stephen Paine, Houghton, NY
1966 Robert VanKampen, Santa Barbara, CA
1967 Bill Jones, Los Angeles, CA
1968 John Broger, Falls Church, VA
1969 George Wilson, Minneapolis, MN
1970 Ted Engstrom, Monrovia, CA
1971 Seth Rohrer, Elkhart, IN
1972 Frank D. Nicodem, Mt. Prospect, IL
1973 George Willms, Newton, KS
1974 Everett Graffam, King of Prussia, PA
1975 Lester Gerig, Ft. Wayne, IN
1976 Jack Frizen, Wheaton, IL
1977 Paul Steiner, Ft. Wayne, IN
1978 Floyd Robertson, Annandale, VA
1979 Walter Meloon, Orlando, FL
1980 Abner Haldeman, Upland, CA
1981 Everett Koop, Philadelphia, PA
1982 James Dobson, Arcadia, CA
1983 Charles Colson, Washington, D.C.
1984 William Armstrong (R-CO), Washington, D.C.
1985 Joni Eareckson Tada, Woodland Hills, CA
1986 Stanley Tam, Lima, OH
1987 Daniel Coats (R-IN), Ft. Wayne, IN
1988 Orville & Ruth Merillat, Adrian, MI
1989 Tony Hall, Dayton, OH
1990 Donald Duff, Ft. Wayne, IN

J. ELWIN WRIGHT AWARD

The J. Elwin Wright award is chosen based on: faithfulness in advancing evangelical cooperation on both a national and international level throughout a productive career; initiated and been instrumental in implementing plans of action which have contributed to the cause of increasing evangelical cooperation; contributed, through speaking and/or writing, ideas and strategies that have strengthened the evangelical movement; inspired and motivated others to join in the cause of evangelical unity.

1989 Dr. Oswald Hoffman
1990 Dr. Carl F. H. Henry

JAMES DeFOREST MURCH AWARD

The James DeForest Murch award is chosen based on: performance of editorial functions for a denominational magazine or other evangelical publication throughout a productive career; attained and maintained a high degree of excellence of editorial skills as evidenced by the quality of the periodicals produced; provided leadership and promoted integrity in evangelical publishing; stimulated and motivated readers through personal and editorial writing.

1989 Dr. O. W. Polen

1990 Forrest J. Boyd

MUSTARD SEED AWARD

Sponsored by LOVE INC., a division of World Vision. Recognizes the church with the most enterprising outreach to the poor. Criteria for the award are based on the program's innovativeness, use of volunteers, demonstrated results, long-term focus, sound management and capacity to be duplicated or adapted by other churches.

1989 First Annual Noon Day Ministry, First Baptist Church, Albuquerque, NM

Education

CHURCH-RELATED ELEMENTARY AND HIGH SCHOOLS

Accredited schools with an enrollment of 100 or more.
Boarding facilities indicated by !. Special education indicated by &.

State/School	*City*	*Affiliation*	*Grades/ Enrollment*
Alabama			
Kingwood Christian Schl	Alabaster	Assembly of God	P-12 / 380
Faith Christian Schl	Anniston	Presbyterian	K-8 / 105
Central Park Christian Schls	Birmingham	Baptist	P-12 / 336
Parkway Christian Academy	Birmingham		P-12 / 606
Shades Mountain Christian Schls	Birmingham	Independent	P-12 / 592&
Tuscaloosa Christian Schl	Cottondale	Baptist	K-12 / 241
Grace Baptist Church Schls	Decatur	Baptist	P-12 / 223
Northside Methodist Academy	Dothan	Methodist	P-12 / 486
Florence Christian Academy	Florence	Free Will Baptist	K-12 / 160
Tabernacle Christian Schl	Gardendale	Baptist	P-12 / 243
Liberty Christian Academy	Guin	Free Will Baptist	P-12 / 176
Bethel Baptist Schl	Hartselle	Baptist	P-12 / 179
Brooklane Baptist Academy	Hueytown	Baptist	K-12 / 236
Triana Village Baptist Schl	Huntsville	Baptist	P-12 / 223
Chilton Christian Academy	Jemison	Baptist	K-12 / 113
Faith Academy	Mobile	Life Church of Mobile	P-12 / 444&
Greystone Christian Schl	Mobile	Greystone Bible Church	P-12 / 247
Calvary Christian Academy	Montgomery	Baptist	K-12 / 250
Trinity Christian Schl	Opelika	Presbyterian	K-8 / 173
Trinity Christian Academy	Oxford	Baptist	P-12 / 411
Dale County Christian Schl	Ozark	Baptist	K-12 / 126
Shelby Christian Schl	Pelham	Baptist	1-12 / 116
Bible Methodist Schl	Pell City	Methodist	K-12 / 166
Grace Baptist Schl	Prattville	Baptist	K-12 / 212
Magnolia Springs Christian Schl	Theodore	Baptist	P-12 / 231
West End Christian Schl	Tuscaloosa	Baptist	P-12 / 392
Alaska			
Abbott Loop Christian Schl	Anchorage	Abbott Loop Christian Cntr	K-12 / 284&
Anchorage Christian Schl	Anchorage	Baptist	K-12 / 468
Grace Christian Schl	Anchorage	Brethren	K-12 / 296
Muldoon Christian Schl	Anchorage	Muldoon Community Assembly	K-12 / 134
Far North Christian Schl	Fairbanks	Far North Missionary Fellowship	K-12 / 116
Juneau Christian Schl	Juneau	Bethel Christian Cntr	P-8 / 158
Valley Baptist Academy	Juneau	Baptist	P-8 / 103
Kodiak Christian Schl	Kodiak		P-8 / 100
North Pole Christian Schl	North Pole		P-12 / 148
Valley Christian Schl	Palmer	Baptist	P-12 / 102
Arizona			
Glendale Baptist Schls	Glendale	Glendale Bible Church	K-12 / 100
Northwest Christian Academy	Glendale	Sweetwater Church	P-12 / 486
Eastside Christian Schls, Inc.	Mesa		P-8 / 170
Redeemer Christian Schl	Mesa	Church of The Redeemer	K-8 / 207
Southwest Indian Schl	Peoria	World Gospel Mission	7-12 / 103!

State/School	City	Affiliation	Grades/ Enrollment
Christian Challenge Academy	Phoenix	Phoenix Christian Assembly	P-8 / 123
Fountainhead Christian Academy	Phoenix	Fountainhead Christian Comm Chrch	P-12 / 140
Grace Christian Schl	Phoenix	Brethren	K-10 / 403
Light & Life Christian Schl	Phoenix	Free Methodist	P-8 / 220
Mexican Gospel Mission Evangelical Schl	Phoenix	The Evangelical Church	K-12 / 157
Northwest Community Christian Schl	Phoenix		P-12 / 776
Paradise Valley Christian	Phoenix		P-8 / 192
Phoenix Christian Grade Schl	Phoenix	Reformed	K-8 / 171
Phoenix Christian High Schl	Phoenix	Independent	9-12 / 260
Scottsdale Christian Academy	Phoenix		P-12 / 587
Valley Cathedral Christian Schl	Phoenix	The Valley Cathedral	P-8 / 291
Western Christian Schl	Phoenix	Evangelical	K-8 / 161
Christian Academy of Prescott	Prescott	Baptist	P-8 / 145
Twin Wells Indian Schl	Sun Valley	Native American Ministries	1-9 / 148!&
Immanuel Mission Schl	Teec Nos Pos		K-12 / 103
Grace Community Christian Schl	Tempe	Grace Comm Church of the Valley	K-8 / 458
Tri-City Christian Academy	Tempe	Baptist	K-12 / 419
Valley Christian High Schl	Tempe		9-12 / 196
Grace Christian Schls	Tucson	Grace Chapel	P-8 / 408
Palo Verde Christian Schl	Tucson	Baptist	K-12 / 280
Tucson Christian Schl	Tucson	Baptist	P-12 / 197
Hilltop Christian Schl	Window Rock	Western Indian Ministries	P-8 / 171
Arkansas			
Westside Christian Learning Cntr	El Dorado	Baptist	P-11 / 294
Calvary Christian Schl	Forest City		P-12 / 200
Fort Smith Christian Schl	Fort Smith	Baptist	K-12 / 247
Arkansas Baptist High Schl	Little Rock	Baptist	9-12 / 150&
Cloverdale Christian Academy	Little Rock	Assembly of God	K-8 / 178
Heritage Christian Schl	Little Rock	Baptist	K-12 / 148
Southwest Christian Academy	Little Rock		P-8 / 140
Walnut Valley Christian Academy	Little Rock	Bible Church of Little Rock	K-8 / 334&
Abundant Life Schls	North Little Rock	Baptist	P-12 / 390
New Life Christian Schl	Pine Bluff	Baptist	P-11 / 188
Shiloh Christian Schl	Springdale	Baptist	K-12 / 450
California			
Sahag-Mesrob Armenian Christian Schl	Altadena		1-8 / 152
Discovery Christian Schls	Anaheim	Independent	P-8 / 353
Trinity Lutheran Christian Schl	Anaheim	Lutheran	P-8 / 186
Apple Valley Christian Schl	Apple Valley	Baptist	P-12 / 372&
Arcadia Christian Schl	Arcadia		P-8 / 371
Christian Schl of Arcata	Arcata	Baptist	K-8 / 140
Coastal Christian Schl	Arroyo Grande		K-12 / 255
North County Christian Schl	Atascadero	Independent	K-12 / 282
Forest Lake Christian Schl	Auburn		P-12 / 381
Light & Life Christian Schl	Azusa	Free Methodist	P-8 / 300&
Heritage Academy	Bakersfield	Heritage Bible Church	P-8 / 590
Stockdale Christian Schls	Bakersfield	Assembly of God	P-8 / 586&
Baldwin Park Christian Schl	Baldwin Park	Baptist	P-10 / 287
Barstow Christian Schl	Barstow	Free Methodist	P-8 / 223&
Cherry Valley Brethren Schls	Beaumont	Brethren	P-8 / 193
Bell Gardens Christian Schl	Bell Gardens	Full Gospel	K-8 / 178
Christian Schl of the Desert	Bermuda Dunes		K-12 / 329
Bloomington Christian Schl	Bloomington	Nazarene	P-12 / 418
Christian Church Schl	Camarillo	Camarillo Christian Church	P-12 / 509&
West Valley Christian Schl	Canoga Park	West Valley Christian Church	K-12 / 309&
Santa Clarita Christian Schl	Canyon Country	Baptist	K-9 / 238&
Dana Point Christian Schl	Capistrano Beach	Calvary Chapel	K-8 / 210
Peninsula Christian Schl	Carson		K-8 / 137

State/School	City	Affiliation	Grades/ Enrollment
Redwood Christian Schl	Castro Valley		K-12 / 904&
Covenant Christian Schl	Chula Vista		K-10 / 110
Western Christian Schl	Claremont		K-8 / 180
Colton Christian Schl	Colton	Assembly of God	P-12 / 221
Calvary Christian Academy	Compton	Calvary Immanuel COGIC	K-9 / 109
Tower of Faith Christian Academy	Compton	Tower of Faith Evangelistic Chrch	P-8 / 136
Concord Christian Schl	Concord	Full Gospel	P-8 / 340
Kings Valley Grade Schl	Concord	Concord Christian Cntr	K-8 / 275
Tabernacle Baptist Schl	Concord	Baptist	P-8 / 402
Ygnacio Valley Christian Schl	Concord	Independent	K-8 / 171
Corona Christian Schl	Corona	Corona Christian Cntr	P-12 / 138
Crossroads Christian Schl	Corona	Crossroads Christian Church	K-9 / 320
Newport Christian Schls	Corona Del Mar	Covenant Community Church	P-12 / 198
Western Christian Schl	Covina		7-12 / 447
San Francisco Christian Schl	Daly City	Baptist	K-12 / 258
San Ramon Valley Christian Academy	Danville	Presbyterian	K-8 / 201
Calvary Chapel Christian Schl	Downey	Calvary Chapel of Downey	P-9 / 453
Valley Christian Cntr Schl	Dublin	Valley Christian Cntr	P-12 / 758
Christian Unified Schls of San Diego	El Cajon	Baptist	P-12 / 1132&
El Monte Christian Schl	El Monte	Wesleyan	P-8 / 210
El Sobrante Christian Schl	El Sobrante	Assembly of God	K-8 / 341
Encinitas Christian Schl	Encinitas	North County Fellowship	K-8 / 100
Escondido Christian Schl	Escondido	Foursquare	P-8 / 531
Light & Life Christian Schl	Escondido	Free Methodist	P-8 / 400
Freedom Christian Schl	Fair Oaks	Open Bible Church	K-12 / 103
Ambassador Baptist Schls	Fontana	Baptist	P-12 / 500
First Southern Baptist Christian Schl	Fountain Valley	Baptist	P-8 / 516
Christian Community Schls	Fremont	Fremont Community	P-8 / 507
Fremont Christian Schl	Fremont	Assembly of God	K-12 / 867
Fresno Christian Schls	Fresno		K-12 / 685&
Eastside Christian Elementary Schl	Fullerton	Eastside Christian	P-8 / 429
Calvary Baptist Elementary Schl	Gardena		K-8 / 421
Gardena Valley Christian Schl	Gardena	Assembly of God	K-8 / 375
Foothill Christian Schls	Glendora	Foothill Christian Cntr	P-8 / 536
Hillcrest Christian Schl	Granada Hills		K-9 / 411&
Hacienda Christian Schl	Hacienda Heights	Nazarene	P-8 / 165
Harbor Christian Schls	Harbor City	Foursquare	P-12 / 250&
Acacia Baptist Schl	Hawthorne	Baptist	K-8 / 197
American Heritage Christian Schl	Hayward	Baptist	K-12 / 148
Hayward Christian Schl	Hayward	Assembly of God	K-8 / 140
Baptist Christian Schl	Hemet	Baptist	P-12 / 437
Hesperia Christian Schl	Hesperia	Hesperia Community	P-12 / 566
New Life Christian Schl	Hesperia	Foursquare	P-8 / 341
Liberty Christian Schl	Huntington Beach	Baptist	1-12 / 428
Faith Academy	Imperial	Assembly of God	P-9 / 136
Celeste Scott Christian Schl	Inglewood	Ladies of Song	P-10 / 300
Christ-Centered Childrens University	Inglewood	Apostolic	K-9 / 175
Inglewood Christian Schl	Inglewood	First Christian Church	K-8 / 335
Liberty Christian Academy	Irvine	Baptist	P-8 / 157
Whittier Christian High Schl	La Habra		9-12 / 750
La Mesa Christian Schl	La Mesa	Baptist	K-8 / 128
Brethren Elementary & Junior High Schls	La Mirada	Brethren	K-8 / 309
Lindsey Schls	La Mirada		P-8 / 154
Calvary Baptist Schl	La Verne	Baptist	P-12 / 263
Mission Hills Christian Schls	Laguna Hills	Mission Hills Christian Cntr	K-8 / 190
Christian Cntr Schl	Lakeport	Lakeport Christian Cntr	P-9 / 109
Antelope Valley Christian Schl	Lancaster	Independent	P-12 / 250
Bethel Christian Academy	Lancaster	Baptist	P-12 / 584
Lancaster Christian Schl	Lancaster	Nazarene	K-8 / 169
Landmark Christian Schl	Lancaster	Baptist	P-12 / 131
Kings Christian Schl	Lemoore	Nondenominational	K-12 / 209

State/School	*City*	*Affiliation*	*Grades/ Enrollment*
Mokelumne River Schl	Lodi		K-8 / 161
At The Cross Christian Schl	Long Beach	Calvary Chapel Paramount	K-12 / 158
Bethany Baptist Schl	Long Beach	Baptist	K-9 / 304
East L A Light & Life Christian Schl	Los Angeles	Free Methodist	K-9 / 166
First Church of God Christian Schl	Los Angeles	Church of God	K-8 / 347
Miracle Baptist Christian Schl	Los Angeles	Baptist	K-9 / 244
Pacific Christian High Schl	Los Angeles		7-12 / 123
Sycamore Grove Schl	Los Angeles	Pillar of Fire Church	K-8 / 144
West Angeles Christian Academy	Los Angeles	Church of God	K-8 / 240
Westminster Academy	Los Angeles	Independent	K-8 / 214
Los Gatos Christian Schl	Los Gatos	Los Gatos Christian Church	K-8 / 425&
Manteca Christian Schl	Manteca	Assembly of God	P-8 / 228
Merced Christian Schl	Merced	Baptist	K-8 / 140
Bethany Christian Academy	Midway City	Bethany Bible Fellowship	K-8 / 269&
Milpitas Christian Schl	Milpitas		P-8 / 665
Calvary Temple Christian Schl	Modesto		P-8 / 181
Modesto Christian Schl	Modesto	Neighborhood Church	K-12 / 549&
Orangeburg Christian Schl	Modesto	Baptist	P-8 / 130
Montebello Baptist Schl	Montebello	Baptist	K-8 / 284&
Southbay Christian Schl	Mountain View	Southbay Christian Cntr	P-12 / 468
Southport Christian Academy	National City	Southport Christian Cntr	K-12 / 145
Baptist Christian Schls	Norwalk	Baptist	K-12 / 132
Grace Christian Schl	Norwalk	Evangelical Free	P-12 / 281
Nazarene Christian Schl	Norwalk	Nazarene	P-9 / 413
Norwalk Christian Schl	Norwalk	Norwalk Assembly	P-8 / 295
Trinity Lutheran Schl	Norwalk	Lutheran	P-8 / 238
Christian Life Schl	Novato	Assembly of God	P-10 / 327
Calvary Christian Schl	Ontario	Calvary Church	P-9 / 324
Crystal Cathedral Academy	Orange	Crystal Cathedral	K-8 / 160
Independence Christian Schl	Orange	Orange Villa Bible Church	K-8 / 181&
Southern California Christian Schl	Orange		7-12 / 303&
Valley Christian Academy	Orcutt	Baptist	K-12 / 363
Alma Heights Christian Academy	Pacifica	Pillar of Fire Church	K-11 / 205
Country Christian Schl	Palo Cedro	Little Country Church	P-8 / 296
Paradise Christian Schl	Paradise	Baptist	K-10 / 114
Brethren Jr/Sr High Schl	Paramount	Greater Lng Bch Chrstn Schls, Inc.	7-12 / 490
Gethsemane Baptist Schl	Paramount	Baptist	K-12 / 259
Pasadena Christian Schl	Pasadena		K-8 / 525
Temple Christian Schls	Perris	Baptist	P-12 / 410
Community Christian Schls	Pine Grove	Community Church of Pine Grove	P-9 / 223
Christian Cntr Schl	Pittsburg	Assembly of God	P-12 / 403
Hueneme Christian Schl	Port Hueneme	Baptist	P-8 / 390
Cornerstone Christian Schl	Poway	Grace Trinity Church	K-8 / 150
Grace Baptist Schls	Redding	Baptist	K-12 / 361
North Valley Christian Schl	Redding	Baptist	P-12 / 295
Calvary Chapel Christian Schl of Redlands	Redlands	Calvary Chapel	K-10 / 203
Coast Christian Schl	Redondo Beach	Calvary Church	P-12 / 750
Deep Valley Christian Schl	Redwood Valley		P-8 / 108
Immanuel High Schl	Reedley	Mennonite Brethren	9-12 / 235
Immanuel Christian Schl	Ridgecrest	Southern Baptist	K-12 / 194
Riverside Christian High Schl	Riverside	Interdenominational	P-12 / 408
Capital Christian Schl	Sacramento		P-12 / 977
Citadel Baptist Schl	Sacramento	Baptist	K-12 / 107
Colonial Christian Academy	Sacramento	Baptist	P-12 / 204
Liberty Towers Christian Schl	Sacramento	Nazarene	K-8 / 213
Southpointe Christian Schl	Sacramento		K-8 / 105
Trinity Christian Schls	Sacramento	Trinity Church	P-8 / 435
Salinas Christian Schls	Salinas	Assembly of God	P-8 / 337
Winham Street Christian Academy	Salinas		K-12 / 123
Arrowhead Christian Academy	San Bernardino		7-12 / 130

State/School	*City*	*Affiliation*	*Grades/ Enrollment*
New Life Christian Academy	San Bernardino	New Life Fellowship	K-12 / 125
Valley Christian Schl	San Bernardino	Nazarene	P-8 / 295
Highland Christian Schls	San Bruno	Church of The Highlands	P-8 / 727
Alpha Beacon Christian Schl	San Carlos	Independent	P-12 / 255
Clairemont Christian Schl	San Diego	Clairemont First Assembly	K-12 / 249&
Horizon Christian Schl	San Diego	Horizon Christian Fellowship	K-8 / 270&
Midway Baptist Schls	San Diego	Baptist	K-12 / 395
Mira Mesa Christian Schl	San Diego	Chapel of The Rock	K-8 / 104
Voice of Pentecost Christian Schl	San Francisco		K-12 / 113
San Gabriel Christian Schl	San Gabriel	San Gabriel Union Church	K-8 / 631&
Christian Community Academy	San Jose	Christian Community Church	K-12 / 270
Liberty Baptist Schl	San Jose	Baptist	K-12 / 471
Valley Christian Schls	San Jose		K-12 / 867&
Capistrano Valley Christian Schls	San Juan Capistrano	Baptist	P-12 / 900&
Calvary Church Christian Schl	Santa Ana		K-8 / 495
Santa Barbara Christian Schl	Santa Barbara		K-8 / 275
North Valley Baptist Schls	Santa Clara	Baptist	K-12 / 131
John H. Jenkins Christian Academy/ Preschool	Santa Paula	Baptist	P-12 / 200
Rincon Valley Christian Schl	Santa Rosa	Santa Rosa Bible Church	P-12 / 314
Santa Rosa Christian Schl	Santa Rosa		K-9 / 271
Bible Missionary Fellowship Christian Schl	Santee	Baptist	K-12 / 151
Carlton Hills Christian Elementary Schl	Santee	Lutheran	K-8 / 149
Baymonte Christian Schls	Scotts Valley		K-12 / 188&
Maranatha High Schl	Sierra Madre		9-12 / 452
Grace Brethren Schl	Simi Valley	Brethren	P-9 / 492&
Santa Fe Christian Community Schl	Solana Beach		K-12 / 478
Santa Ynez Valley Christian Academy	Solvang		K-8 / 120
Brookside Christian High Schl	Stockton		7-12 / 180
Calvary Christian Academy	Stockton	Baptist	K-12 / 136
Northside Christian Academy	Stockton	Free Will Baptist	K-8 / 135
Sierra Christian Schl	Stockton		K-8 / 124
Stockton Christian Schls	Stockton	Christian Life Cntr	K-12 / 250
Grace Community Church Schls	Sun Valley		K-12 / 495&
Village Christian Schls	Sun Valley	Village Church	K-12 / 1821
Calvary Academy	Susanville	Baptist	1-12 / 116
The Linfield Schl	Temecula	Independent	K-12 / 401
First Baptist Academy	Thousand Oaks	Baptist	P-8 / 264
Hillcrest Christian Schl	Thousand Oaks	Hillcrest Christian Cntr	P-12 / 309
Mother Lode Christian Schl	Tuolumne		K-12 / 228
Turlock Christian Schls	Turlock		K-12 / 362
Colonial Bible Church Schl	Tustin	Colonial Bible Church	P-8 / 241
Vacaville Christian Academy	Vacaville	Independent	P-8 / 226
North Hills Christian Schl	Vallejo	Baptist	P-12 / 471
College Heights Christian Schl	Ventura	Baptist	K-8 / 250
Temple Christian Schl	Ventura	Baptist	K-8 / 140
Victor Valley Christian Schls	Victorville	Assembly of God	P-12 / 428
Tri-City Christian Schl	Vista	Baptist	P-12 / 713&
Christian Chapel Schls	Walnut	Christian Chapel	P-8 / 635
Berean Christian High Schl	Walnut Creek	Regular Baptist	9-12 / 300
Walnut Creek Christian Academy	Walnut Creek	Baptist	K-8 / 250
Woodlands Chr Schl/Contra Costa Chr High	Walnut Creek		P-12 / 304
North Kern Christian	Wasco	Wasco Bible Church	P-8 / 104&
Monte Vista Christian Schl	Watsonville		6-12 / 615!&
South Hills Academy	West Covina	Baptist	K-8 / 640
West Covina Christian Schl	West Covina	Baptist	K-8 / 500&
Westminster Christian Schl	Westminster	Christ Church	P-8 / 301
Bethany Christian Schl	Whittier	Baptist	K-8 / 414
Whittier Christian Schls	Whittier	Calvary Baptist Church	P-8 / 1052&
Pacific Harbor Christian Schl	Wilmington		P-9 / 369

State/School	City	Affiliation	Grades/ Enrollment
Wilmington Christian Schl	Wilmington	Assembly of God	K-12 / 381
Woodland Christian Schls	Woodland	Baptist	K-9 / 450&
Friends Christian Schl	Yorba Linda	Friends	P-8 / 1252
Faith Christian Schls	Yuba City	Independent	K-12 / 331
Grace Christian Academy	Yuba City	Baptist	P-8 / 107
Colorado			
Maranatha Christian Cntr	Arvada		P-12 / 643
Colorado Springs Christian Schl	Colorado Springs		P-12 / 813&
Evangelical Christian Academy	Colorado Springs	Presbyterian	P-10 / 340
Springs of Life Christian Schl	Colorado Springs	Full Gospel	K-8 / 130
Beth Eden Baptist Schl	Denver	Baptist	K-12 / 254
Colorado Christian Schl	Denver	Calvary Temple	P-8 / 248&
Silver State Baptist Schl	Denver	Baptist	K-12 / 451
Heritage Christian Schl	Fort Collins		P-12 / 198&
Faith Baptist Schl	Longmont	Baptist	K-12 / 337
Colorado West Christian Schl	Montrose	Reformed Presbyterian	P-12 / 142
Connecticut			
West Woods Christian Academy	Hamden	West Woods Bible Chapel	K-12 / 149
Cornerstone Christian Schl	Manchester	Nazarene	K-11 / 179
Fellowship Baptist Schls	Middlestown	Baptist	P-12 / 129
Emmanuel Christian Academy	Newington	Baptist	K-12 / 245
North Stonington Christian Academy	North Stonington	Baptist	P-12 / 187
Wildwood Christian Schl	Norwich	C&MA	P-8 / 158
Central Christian Academy	Southington	Baptist	K-12 / 187
Christian Heritage Schl	Trumbull		K-12 / 355
Heritage Christian Academy	Wallingford	Baptist	K-12 / 147
Baptist Bible Academy	Waterford	Baptist	K-12 / 126
Hartford Christian Academy	West Hartford	Baptist	K-12 / 186
Delaware			
Capitol Baptist Schl	Dover	Baptist	P-12 / 166
Christian Tabernacle Academy	Lincoln		K-12 / 141
New Castle Baptist Academy	New Castle	Baptist	P-12 / 671
Concord Christian Academy	Wilmington	Baptist	K-12 / 153
Florida			
Altamonte Christian Schl	Altamonte Springs	Baptist	P-12 / 304
Christian Day Schl	Belle Glade	Baptist	K-12 / 331
Boca Raton Christian Schl	Boca Raton	Bibletown Community Church	K-8 / 209
Brandon Heights Christian Schl	Brandon	Baptist	K-10 / 213
Grace Christian Schl	Brandon	Grace Community Church	P-12 / 301
Tampa Bay Christian Schl	Brandon		P-12 / 129
Brunswick Christian Academy	Brunswick	Baptist	K-12 / 311
Lakeside Christian Schl	Clearwater		P-12 / 288&
Skycrest Christian Schl	Clearwater	Baptist	P-8 / 412
DeLand Christian Schl	DeLand	Nazarene	K-12 / 104
Deltona Christian Schl	Deltona	Baptist	P-12 / 129
Heritage Christian Academy	Englewood	Baptist	K-12 / 138
New Testament Christian Schl	Floral City	Baptist	P-12 / 146
Grace Brethren Christian Schl	Fort Lauderale	Brethren	K-8 / 166
Evangelical Christian Schl	Fort Myers	Baptist	P-12 / 505
Riverside Christian Schl	Fort Myers	Baptist	K-12 / 110
Sonshine Christian Academy	Fort Myers	Evangelistic Cntr	P-12 / 130
Fort Walton Christian Schl	Fort Walton Beach	Baptist	P-12 / 113
Countryside Christian Schl	Gainesville	Baptist	K-12 / 108
Heritage Christian Schl	Gainesville	Baptist	P-12 / 240
Landmark Christian Schl	Haines City	Baptist	P-12 / 358
Gadsden Christian Academy	Havana	Baptist	P-12 / 352
Dade Christian Schl	Hialeah	Baptist	P-12 / 1375
First Baptist Schl	Hialeah	Baptist	P-12 / 316

State/School	City	Affiliation	Grades/ Enrollment
Hobe Sound Bible Academy	Hobe	Florida Evangelistic Association	K-12 / 227
Hollywood Christian Schl	Hollywood	Baptist	K-12 / 1042
Sheridan Hills Christian Schl	Hollywood	Baptist	K-12 / 385
South Dade Baptist Church Schl	Homestead	Baptist	K-10 / 159
Grace Christian Schls of Pasco	Hudson	Grace Bible Church	P-12 / 215
Glendale Christian Schl	Indian River	Baptist	K-8 / 113
Island Christian Schl	Islamorada	Island Community Church	P-12 / 293
First Coast Christian Schl	Jacksonville	Baptist	K-12 / 157
Grace Christian Academy	Jacksonville	Grace Bible Church	K-9 / 284
Harvest Christian Academy	Jacksonville	Baptist	P-12 / 136
San Pablo Christian Learning Cntr & Schl	Jacksonville	Baptist	P-12 / 158
Southern Baptist Academy	Jacksonville	Baptist	P-11 / 541
Trinity Christian Academy	Jacksonville	Baptist	P-12 / 1544
University Christian Schl	Jacksonville	Baptist	P-12 / 738
Victory Christian Academy	Jacksonville	Baptist	P-12 / 602
Word of Life Schls	Jacksonville		P-12 / 139
Jupiter Christian Schl	Jupiter	Baptist	K-12 / 295
Heritage Christian Schl	Kissimmee	Baptist	K-12 / 185
Lake Park Baptist Schl	Lake Park	Baptist	P-8 / 320
Evangel Christian Schl	Lakeland	Carpenters Home Church	P-12 / 440
Lakeland Christian Schl	Lakeland		K-12 / 722&
Temple Christian Schl	Lakeland	Baptist	P-12 / 307
Central Pinellas Christian Schl	Largo	Baptist	K-12 / 198
Harvest Temple Christian Schl	Largo		P-12 / 221
Merritt Island Christian Schl	Merritt Island	Baptist	P-12 / 304
Cutler Ridge Christian Academy	Miami	Baptist	K-12 / 259
Florida Christian Schl	Miami	Baptist	P-12 / 561
King's Christian Schl	Miami	Southwest Community Church	K-9 / 217
Miami Christian Schl	Miami	Independent	P-12 / 365
Northwest Christian Academy	Miami	Baptist	P-12 / 549
Westwood Christian Schl	Miami	Baptist	P-12 / 1041
Santa Rosa Christian Schl	Milton	Grace Fellowship Church	P-12 / 183
Florida Bible Christian Schl	Miramar	Florida Bible Church	K-12 / 338
Grace Community Day Care and Schl	Naples	Grace Community Church	K-12 / 134
Rocky Bayou Christian Schl	Niceville	Baptist	P-12 / 309
Oak Griner Christian Schl	Ocala	Baptist	K-8 / 175
Ocala Christian Academy	Ocala	Baptist	K-12 / 640
Grace Christian Schls	Okeechobee	Brethren	P-12 / 175
Community Christian Schl	Oneco	Baptist	P-12 / 380
Azalea Park Baptist Church	Orlando	Baptist	P-8 / 146
Downey Christian Schl	Orlando	Downey Memorial Church	P-12 / 274
Eastland Christian Schl	Orlando	Baptist	K-12 / 189
Edgewood Ranch Academy	Orlando	Edgewood Ranch Foundation, Inc.	7-12 / 105
Faith Christian Academy	Orlando	Assembly of God	K-8 / 151
Orlando Christian Schl	Orlando	Baptist	K-12 / 213
Pine Hills Christian Academy	Orlando	Baptist	P-12 / 409
The Master's Academy	Orlando	Baptist	K-12 / 400
Calvary Christian Academy	Ormond Beach	Assembly of God	K-12 / 250
Panama City Christian Schl	Panama City	Baptist	P-12 / 486
East Hill Christian Schl	Pensacola		P-10 / 382
Pensacola Christian Schl	Pensacola	Baptist	P-12 / 1937
First Baptist Christian Schl	Pinellas Park	Baptist	P-12 / 173
Pinellas Park Christian Schl	Pinellas Park	Baptist	P-12 / 195
Ambassador Christian Academy	Plantation	Baptist	P-12 / 117
Highlands Christian Academy	Pompano Beach	Baptist	K-12 / 486
Community Christian Schl	Port Charlotte	Baptist	P-8 / 288
Port Charlotte Christian Schl	Port Charlotte	Assembly of God	P-12 / 115
Faith Christian Schl	Port Saint Joe	Faith Bible Church	P-9 / 114
Princeton Christian Schl	Princeton	Nazarene	K-12 / 283
Providence Christian Schl	Riverview	Baptist	P-12 / 414
Greater Bethel Christian Schl	Riviera Beach	Primitive Baptist	P-12 / 189

State/School	City	Affiliation	Grades/ Enrollment
Ruskin Christian Schl	Ruskin	Baptist	P-12 / 162
Trinity Chapel Christian Schl	Saint Augustine		P-12 / 148&
Keswick Christian Schl	Saint Petersburg	Moody Bible Institute	P-12 / 679
Northside Christian Schl	Saint Petersburg	Baptist	P-12 / 766
Faith Christian Schl	Sarasota	Assembly of God	P-8 / 261
West Florida Christian Schl	Sarasota	Baptist	P-12 / 137
Community Christian Schl	Seminole	Community Bible Church	K-11 / 236
Warner Christian Academy	South Daytona	Church of God	P-12 / 581
First Baptist Christian Schl	Stuart	Baptist	P-8 / 205
North Florida Christian Schl	Tallahassee	Baptist	P-12 / 1286
Citrus Park Christian Schl	Tampa	Baptist	K-9 / 298
Faith Outreach Christian Schl	Tampa		K-12 / 108
Tampa Baptist Academy	Tampa	Baptist	P-12 / 465
Tampa Christian Academy	Tampa	Northwest Christian Church	K-9 / 351
Temple Heights Christian Schl	Tampa	Baptist	P-12 / 713
West Gate Christian Schl	Tampa	Baptist	P-12 / 143
Park Avenue Baptist Schl	Titusville	Baptist	P-8 / 278
Berean Christian Schl	West Palm Beach	Baptist	K-12 / 345
First Baptist Christian Schl	West Palm Beach	Baptist	P-8 / 260
Summit Christian Schl	West Palm Beach	Baptist	P-12 / 415
The King's Academy	West Palm Beach	Baptist	K-12 / 1163
Calvary Baptist Christian Schl	Winter Garden	Baptist	K-12 / 272
First Baptist Church Schl	Winter Garden	Baptist	K-12 / 232
Haven Christian Academy	Winter Haven	Baptist	P-12 / 148
Nassau Christian Academy	Yulee	Baptist	P-12 / 147
Georgia			
Byne Memorial Baptist Schl	Albany	Baptist	K-12 / 513
Athens Christian Schl	Athens	Baptist	K-12 / 681
Prince Avenue Baptist Christian Schl	Athens	Baptist	K-12 / 170
De Kalb Christian Academy	Atlanta	C&MA	K-12 / 529
Curtis Baptist Schl	Augusta	Baptist	7-12 / 121
Southgate Christian Schl	Augusta	Baptist	K-12 / 319
Forrest Hills Christian Schl	Avondale Estates	Baptist	K-12 / 299
Old Suwanee Christian Schl	Buford	Baptist	K-9 / 117
Mt. Pisgah Christian Schl	College Park	Baptist	K-12 / 159
Calvary Christian Schl	Columbus	Baptist	K-8 / 201
Christian Heritage Academy	Columbus	Baptist	1-12 / 256
Grace Christian Schl	Columbus	Baptist	K-12 / 251
Philadelphia Christian Schl	Conyers	Baptist	K-12 / 239
Tabernacle Christian Schl	Covington	Baptist	K-12 / 117
Green Pastures Christian Academy	Decatur		P-12 / 244
Buford Highway Christian Schl	Doraville	Baptist	K-8 / 109
King's Way Christian Schl	Douglasville	Baptist	K-12 / 194
Chalecdon Christian Schl	Dunwoody	Reformed Presbyterian	P-12 / 115
Colonial Hills Christian Schl	East Point	Baptist	K-12 / 310
Fayette Christian Schl	Fayetteville	Baptist	K-12 / 410
Forest Park Christian Schl	Forest Park	Baptist	K-12 / 161
Lake City Christian Schl	Forest Park	Baptist	K-12 / 282
Glennville Christian Academy	Glennville	Free Will Baptist	K-12 / 173
Calvary Baptist Schl	Hampton	Baptist	K-12 / 111
North Cobb Christian Schl	Kennesaw	Nondenominational	K-8 / 240
Shiloh Hills Christian Schl	Kennesaw	Baptist	K-12 / 521
Northeast Atlanta Christian Schl	Lawrenceville	Baptist	K-12 / 240
Lithia Christian Academy	Lithia Springs		P-12 / 134
Central Fellowship Christian Academy	Macon	Baptist	K-12 / 492
Gilead Christian Academy	Macon	Baptist	K-12 / 454
Progressive Christian Academy	Macon	Baptist	P-8 / 494
Eastside Baptist Christian Schl	Marietta	Baptist	K-9 / 296
Augusta Christian Schls	Martinez		P-12 / 641
Clayton Christian Schl	Morrow		P-8 / 401

State/School	*City*	*Affiliation*	*Grades/ Enrollment*
Maranatha Christian Academy	Oakwood	Baptist	K-12 / 264
Bible Baptist Christian Schl	Riverdale	Baptist	K-10 / 172
Pineland Christian Academy	Savannah	Baptist	K-12 / 169
Smyrna Christian Academy	Smyrna	Baptist	K-12 / 240
New Hope Christian Academy	St. Marys	Baptist	K-12 / 182
Mt. Vernon Christian Schl	Stockbridge	Baptist	K-12 / 319
Stone Mountain Christian Schl	Stone Mountain	Baptist	K-12 / 447
Lowndes Christian Academy	Valdosta	Baptist	K-12 / 170
Open Bible Christian Schl	Valdosta	Baptist	K-12 / 233
Warner Robins Christian Academy	Warner Robins	Baptist	K-12 / 177
Southside Christian Schl	Waycross	Baptist	K-1 / 222
Hope Christian Academy	Winder	Baptist	K-12 / 174
Hawaii			
Kaahumanuhou Christian Schl	Kahului	Assembly of God	P-12 / 104
Kailua Church Christian Schl	Kailua		P-12 / 137&
Koolau Baptist Church Academy	Kaneohe	Baptist	K-12 / 134
Windward Nazarene Academy	Kaneohe	Nazarene	P-8 / 197
Hanalani Schls	Mililani	Baptist	K-12 / 492
Doris Todd Memorial Christian Schls	Paia	Berean Mission, Inc.	P-8 / 143
Lanakila Baptist Schls	Waipahu	Baptist	K-12 / 324
Idaho			
Cole Christian Schl	Boise	Cole Community Church	P-9 / 321
Valley Christian Schl	Lewiston	Valley Christian Cntr	P-12 / 127
Nampa Christian Schls	Nampa	Interdenominational	K-12 / 265&
Twin Falls Christian Academy	Twin Falls	Baptist	P-12 / 118
Illinois			
Mississippi Valley Christian Schl	Alton	Baptist	K-12 / 214
Aurora Christian Schl	Aurora		P-12 / 900
Covenant Christian Schl	Aurora	Living Waters Fellowship	K-8 / 114
Beardstown Christian Academy	Beardstown	First Christian Church	P-8 / 105
Calvary Baptist Christian Schl	Belvidere	Baptist	K-12 / 109
Bethany Christian Schl	Berwyn	Bethany Tabernacle	P-12 / 330
East Park Baptist Academy	Boody	Baptist	K-12 / 135
Judah Christian Schl	Champaign		K-12 / 254
Midwestern Christian Academy	Chicago	Midwest Bible Church	P-8 / 200
Northwest Christian Schl	Chicago	Independent	K-8 / 132
Ravenswood Baptist Schl	Chicago	Baptist	P-12 / 224
Decatur Christian Schl	Decatur	Baptist	1-10 / 142
Brentwood Baptist Academy	Des Plaines	Baptist	P-12 / 153
Marquette Manor Baptist Academy	Downers Grove	Baptist	P-12 / 372
Christian Fellowship Schl	Duquoin	Christian Fellowship Church	P-12 / 181
Bethany Christian Academy	Galesburg	Baptist	K-12 / 124
Faith Baptist Christian Schl	Groveland	Baptist	K-12 / 197
Quentin Road Christian Schl	Hawthorn Woods	Quentin Road Bible Church	P-12 / 268
Homewood Christian Academy	Homewood	Full Gospel	K-12 / 242
Ridgewood Baptist Academy	Joliet	Baptist	K-11 / 225
Grace Baptist Academy	Kankakee	Baptist	P-12 / 208
La Salle - Peru Christian Schl	La Salle	Baptist	K-12 / 157
Medinah Christian Schl	Medinah	Baptist	P-8 / 245
Calvary Christian Schl	Naperville	Calvary Temple Church	K-8 / 212
Calvary Baptist Academy	Normal	Baptist	K-12 / 366
Christian Heritage Academy	Northbrook		P-8 / 128
South Side Baptist Schl	Oak Lawn	Baptist	P-12 / 218
Stone Church Christian Academy	Palos Heights	Stone Church	K-8 / 173
Peoria Christian Schl	Peoria		P-12 / 475
Bible Baptist Schl	Quincy	Baptist	P-12 / 143
Berean Baptist Christian	Rockford	Baptist	P-12 / 264
Family Christian Fellowship Academy	Rockford		K-12 / 130
North Love Christian Schl	Rockford	Baptist	K-12 / 175

State/School	*City*	*Affiliation*	*Grades/ Enrollment*
Rockford Baptist Schls	Rockford	Baptist	K-12 / 196
Rockford Christian Elementary	Rockford		P-8 / 445
Bible Baptist Christian Academy	Romeoville	Baptist	K-12 / 163
Schaumburg Christian Schl	Schaumburg	Baptist	P-12 / 653
Somonauk Baptist Schls	Somonauk	Baptist	K-12 / 102
Calvary Academy	South Holland		K-12 / 234
Christian Elementary Schl	Springfield	West Side Christian Church	K-8 / 275
Twin City Nazarene Schl	Sterling	Nazarene	K-12 / 159
Lake County Baptist Schl	Waukegan	Baptist	K-12 / 168
Wheaton Christian High Schl	West Chicago		9-12 / 215
Wheaton Christian Grammar Schl	Wheaton	Wheaton Soc for Chrstn Instr	K-8 / 450
Waukegan Christian Schl	Zion		K-12 / 252
Indiana			
Indiana Christian Academy	Anderson	Baptist	P-12 / 290
Liberty Christian Schl	Anderson	Independent	P-12 / 323
Faith Christian Academy	Auburn	Baptist	K-12 / 134
Faith Christian Academy	Berne	Baptist	P-12 / 116
Bethesda Christian Schls	Brownsburg	Baptist	K-12 / 297
Temple Christian Schl	Connersville	Baptist	K-12 / 143
Faith Heritage Christian Schl	Evansville	Baptist	K-12 / 128
Blackhawk Christian Schl	Fort Wayne	Baptist	K-12 / 365
Calumet Baptist Schls, Inc.	Griffith	Regular Baptist	P-12 / 289
Heritage Christian Schls	Hammond	Assembly of God	P-12 / 189
Baptist Academy	Indianapolis	Baptist	P-12 / 200
Colonial Christian Schl	Indianapolis	Baptist	K-12 / 329
Eagledale Christian Schl	Indianapolis	Baptist	K-12 / 196
Heritage Christian Schl	Indianapolis		K-12 / 844&
Suburban Baptist Schls	Indianapolis	Baptist	P-12 / 287
Kokomo Christian Schl	Kokomo	Baptist	P-12 / 247
Lowell Baptist Schl	Lowell	Baptist	K-12 / 154
Chapel Heights Academy	Marion	Baptist	K-12 / 142
Lakeview Christian Schl	Marion	Wesleyan	P-12 / 330
Tabernacle Christian Schl	Martinsville	Baptist	K-12 / 155
First Baptist Christian	Mishawaka	Baptist	P-8 / 161
Heritage Hall Christian Schl	Muncie	Baptist	P-12 / 339
United Christian Schl	Nappanee		1-12 / 108
Grace Baptist Christian Schl	Plymouth	Baptist	K-12 / 110
Portage Christian Schls	Portage	Dunes Christian Educators, Inc.	P-12 / 170
Bethel Christian Schl	Princeton	Bethel Memorial Church	K-8 / 103
Christian Cntr Schl	South Bend	Christian Cntr Cathedral of Praise	K-12 / 242
Terre Haute Baptist Schl	Terre Haute	Baptist	K-12 / 169
South Haven Christian Schl	Valparaiso	South Haven Christian Church	K-12 / 126
Emmanuel Christian Schl	Wabash	Free Will Baptist	P-8 / 122
Iowa			
Cedar Rapids Christian Schl	Cedar Rapids	Baptist	P-12 / 122
Cedar Valley Christian Schl	Cedar Rapids	Cedar Valley Bible Church	P-9 / 162
Quint City Baptist Schl	Davenport	Baptist	K-12 / 107
Des Moines Christian Schl	Des Moines		P-12 / 765&
Community Christian Schls	Fort Dodge	Evangelical Free	P-12 / 129
Morningside Christian Schl	Sioux City	Billy Sunday Memorial Tabernacle	K-12 / 233
Walnut Ridge Baptist Academy	Waterloo	Baptist	K-12 / 321
Kansas			
Central Christian Schl	Hutchinson		P-12 / 308
Muncie Christian Schl	Kansas City		P-12 / 167
Oak Grove Baptist Schl	Kansas City	Baptist	K-12 / 199
Newton Bible Christian Schl	Newton	Newton Bible Church	K-8 / 141
Berean Christian Schl	Olathe	Berean Fundamental Church	K-12 / 145
Kansas City Christian Schl	Prairie Village		K-12 / 495
Maranatha Academy-West Campus	Shawnee		K-12 / 412

State/School	City	Affiliation	Grades/ Enrollment
Shawnee Mission Christian Schl	Shawnee Mission	Baptist	K-12 / 114
Cair Paravel Latin Schl	Topeka		K-12 / 225
Kentucky			
Christian Fellowship Schl	Benton	Christian Fellowship Church	K-12 / 175
Anchored Christian Schl	Bowling Green	Baptist	K-12 / 135
Calvary Christian Schl	Covington	Baptist	K-12 / 388
Assembly Christian Schl	Lexington	Assembly of God	K-12 / 131&
Lexington Christian Schl	Lexington		P-12 / 286
Riverside Christian Schl	Lost Creek	Brethren	K-12 / 122
Alliance Christian Academy	Louisville	C&MA	P-8 / 163
Evangel Schls	Louisville	Evangel Tabernacle	K-12 / 243
Highview Baptist Schl	Louisville	Baptist	P-12 / 770
Northside Christian Schl	Louisville	Baptist	K-12 / 139
Louisiana			
Mt. Olive Christian Schl	Athens	Baptist	K-12 / 115
Family Christian Academy	Baton Rouge		P-12 / 519&
Parkview Baptist Schl	Baton Rouge		K-12 / 1147
Northlake Christian Schls	Covington		K-12 / 423
Northside Christian Schl	Crowley	Assembly of God	P-12 / 186
Family Life Christian Academy	Lafayette		K-8 / 107
Westbank Cathedral Academy	Marrero		K-8 / 208
Word of Faith Academy	New Orleans		K-12 / 245
Riverside Christian Academy	River Ridge	Baptist	P-12 / 229&
Claiborne Christian Schl	West Monroe	Family Worship Cntr	P-12 / 227
Maine			
Bangor Baptist Schls	Bangor	Baptist	K-12 / 136
Kennebunk Christian Academy	Kennebunk	Advent Christian Church	K-12 / 130
Eastgate Christian Schl	New Gloucester	Eastgate Christian Fellowship	K-9 / 111
Temple Academy	Waterville	Calvary Temple	K-12 / 145
Windham Assembly Christian Academy	Windham	Assembly of God	P-12 / 122
Maryland			
Annapolis Area Christian Schl	Annapolis		K-12 / 625&
Arlington Baptist Schl	Baltimore	Baptist	P-12 / 743
Baltimore Christian Academy	Baltimore	Assembly of God	P-12 / 275
Faith Bible Church Academy	Baltimore	Faith Bible Church	K-12 / 103
Grace Christian Schl	Bowie	Baptist	K-8 / 219
Camp Springs Christian Schl	Camp Springs	Camp Springs Community Church	P-12 / 392
Victory Christian Schl	Charlotte Hall	Baptist	1-12 / 120
Independent Baptist Academy	Clinton	Independent Baptist	K-12 / 153
Wesleyan Christian Schl	Denton	Wesleyan Methodist	K-11 / 119
Elkton Christian Schl	Elkton	Baptist	K-12 / 250
Maranatha Baptist Church Academy	Elkton	Baptist	K-12 / 103
Frederick Christian Academy	Frederick	Baptist	K-12 / 278
Granite Baptist Church Schl	Glen Burnie	Baptist	K-12 / 244
Heritage Academy	Hagerstown	Baptist	K-12 / 282
Lanham Christian Schl	Lanham	Brethren	P-12 / 324
Puritan Christian Schl	Laytonsville	Orthodox Presbyterian	K-12 / 123
Lexington Park Christian Schl	Lexington Park		1-8 / 151
Mount Airy Full Gospel Christian Schl	Mount Airy	Full Gospel Church	P-12 / 160
Odenton Christian Schl	Odenton	Baptist	K-12 / 307
Liberty Christian Schl	Owings Mills	Reformed Presbyterian	P-8 / 208&
Harford Christian Schl	Street	Evangelical Methodist	K-12 / 597
Bethel Christian Schl	Suitland	Baptist	P-8 / 314
Capitol Christian Academy	Upper Marlboro	Baptist	K-12 / 483
Clinton Christian Schl	Upper Marlboro	Baptist	N-12 / 563
Riverdale Baptist Schl	Upper Marlboro	Baptist	K-12 / 1019
Carroll Christian Academy	Westminster	Church of the Open Door	K-12 / 389
Holly Grove Christian Schl	Westover	Mennonite	P-8 / 135

State/School	City	Affiliation	Grades/ Enrollment
Massachusetts			
Brockton Christian Elementary	Brockton	Baptist	K-8 / 168
First Baptist Christian Academy	East Longmeadow	Baptist	P-8 / 110
Christian Schl of Greater Fall River	Fall River	Independent	P-8 / 196
Lexington Christian Academy	Lexington	Independent	7-12 / 213&
Twin City Christian Schls	Lunenburg	Baptist	K-12 / 313
North Shore Christian Schl	Lynn		P-8 / 210&
New Testament Christian Schl	Norton	Baptist	K-12 / 183
Faith Baptist Christian Academy	Palmer	Baptist	K-12 / 111
Parkway Christian Academy	Revere	Parkway Christian Cntr	P-8 / 230
Dayspring Christian Academy	South Attleboro	Assembly of God	P-8 / 228&
Fair Haven Christian Schl	South Hamilton	Fair Haven Chapel, Essex	K-8 / 115
Trinity Schl of Cape Cod	South Yarmouth		P-8 / 192
Pioneer Valley Christian Schl	Springfield		P-12 / 272&
Springfield Christian Schl	Springfield	Glorious Gospel Church	P-12 / 217
New England Baptist Academy	West Bridgewater	Baptist	K-12 / 200
Michigan			
Berean Baptist Academy	Adrian	Baptist	K-12 / 128
Lenawee Christian Schl	Adrian	Independent	P-12 / 633&
Oakland Christian Schl	Auburn Hills		K-12 / 618
Metro Baptist Schls	Belleville	Baptist	K-12 / 147
Northern Michigan Christian Academy	Burt Lake	Northern Michigan Bible Church	K-12 / 142
Heritage Christian Schl	Cadillac		P-12 / 113
Plymouth Christian Academy	Canton	Baptist	P-12 / 448
Springfield Christian Academy	Clarkston	Baptist	K-12 / 419
Faith Baptist Schls	Davison	Baptist	K-12 / 335
Faith Christian Schl	Fruitport	Baptist	K-12 / 126
Harbor Light Christian Schl	Harbor Springs	Harbor Light Chapel	K-12 / 118
Saint Matthew Lutheran Schl	Holt	Lutheran	P-12 / 146&
Hidden Springs Christian Schl	Howell	Hidden Springs Retreat Cntr	K-12 / 125&
Freedom Baptist Academy	Hudsonville		K-12 / 350
Jackson Baptist Elementary Schls	Jackson	Baptist	K-12 / 392
Howardsville Christian Schl	Marcellus	Howardsville Gospel Chapel	K-12 / 147
Mount Pleasant Baptist Academy	Mount Pleasant	Baptist	P-12 / 146
Calvary Baptist Academy	Muskegon	Baptist	K-10 / 150
North Branch Wesleyan Academy	North Branch	Wesleyan	P-12 / 296
Oxford Christian Academy	Oxford	Baptist	K-12 / 220
North Hills Christian Schl	Port Huron	Nazarene	P-12 / 128
Rochester Hills Christian Schl	Rochester	Baptist	K-12 / 264
Oakfield Baptist Academy	Rockford	Baptist	P-12 / 143
Calvary Christian Schl	Roseville	Baptist	K-12 / 276
Community Baptist Christian Schl	Saginaw	Baptist	K-12 / 200
Zoe Christian Academy	Saint Clair Shores	New Life Fellowship of Believers	K-8 / 194
Saline Christian Schl	Saline	Assembly of God	P-12 / 271
Sturgis Christian Schl	Sturgis	Nazarene	K-12 / 115
Light And Life Christian Schl	Taylor	Free Methodist	K-8 / 164
State Line Christian Schl	Temperance	Baptist	K-12 / 353
Bethany Christian Schl	Troy	Baptist	K-12 / 450
Juniata Christian Schl	Vassar	Baptist	K-12 / 287
Macomb Christian Schl	Warren	Baptist	P-11 / 333
Grace Christian Schl	Watervliet	Grace Christian Education Assoc	K-12 / 247
Tri-Unity Christian Schls	Wyoming		K-12 / 628
Calvary Christian Academy	Ypsilanti	Baptist	K-12 / 360
Minnesota			
Meadow Creek Christian Schl	Andover	Meadow Creek Church	P-12 / 520
Lake Region Christian Schl	Baxter	Baptist	K-12 / 160
Bethany Academy	Bloomington	Bethany Missionary Church	K-12 / 155&
Chisago Lakes Baptist Academy	Chisago City	Baptist	K-12 / 176
Chapel Hill Academy	Deephaven		K-10 / 135

State/School	City	Affiliation	Grades/ Enrollment
Beaver River Christian Schl	Duluth	Fredenberg Chrstn Ed Assoc	K-12 / 155
Maranatha Christian Academy	Edina	Cathedral of Praise	K-12 / 286
Christian Life Church Schls	Farmington	Christian Life Church	K-12 / 170
Hillcrest Lutheran Academy	Fergus Falls	Lutheran Brethren	9-12 / 116
Woodcrest Baptist Academy	Fridley	Baptist	K-12 / 209
Fourth Baptist Christian Schl	Minneapolis	Baptist	K-12 / 594
Northside Christian Schl	Minneapolis		K-9 / 203
Powderhorn Christian Schl	Minneapolis	Nondenominational	K-8 / 120&
Park Christian Schl	Moorhead		K-8 / 200
Owatonna Christian Schl	Owatonna	Baptist	K-12 / 283
Victory Christian Academy	Rochester	Baptist	K-12 / 128
First Baptist Church Schls	Rosemount	Baptist	K-12 / 269
Faith Baptist Christian Schl	St. Paul	Baptist	K-8 / 182
Temple Baptist Schls	St. Paul	Baptist	K-12 / 104
New Life Christian Schl	Woodbury	Baptist	P-12 / 355&
Mississippi			
Amory Christian Academy	Amory	Free Will Baptist	K-12 / 131
Temple Christian Academy	Gulfport	Baptist	1-12 / 112
C M & I High Schl	Jackson	Holiness	P-12 / 326
Southern Baptist Educational Cntr	Olive Branch	Baptist	P-12 / 703&
Missouri			
Eagle Heights Christian Schl	Avondale	Baptist	K-11 / 196
First Baptist Academy	Belton	Baptist	P-12 / 163
Pisgah Christian Schl	Excelsior Springs	Baptist	P-12 / 158
Twin City Christian Academy	Festus	Baptist	K-12 / 293
Faith Christian Schl	Florissant	Baptist	K-12 / 187
Gray Summit Christian Schl	Gray Summit	Baptist	K-12 / 108
Harrisonville Church Schl	Harrisonville	Mennonite	K-8 / 134
Englewood Christian Schl	Independence	Assembly of God	P-12 / 423
New Hope Christian Schl	Independence	Baptist	K-12 / 140
Blue Ridge Christian Schl	Kansas City	Blue Ridge Bible Church	K-12 / 458&
Northland Cathedral Academy	Kansas City	Assembly of God	K-8 / 112
Tri-City Christian Schl	Kansas City	Baptist	P-12 / 625
Southern Missouri Christian Schls, Inc.	Poplar Bluffs	Assembly of God	K-12 / 123
Kingdom Christian Academy	Saint Ann	Independent	P-10 / 192
Saint Joseph Christian Schl	Saint Joseph		K-12 / 111
Christian Schls of Springfield	Springfield	Baptist	P-12 / 298
New Covenant Academy	Springfield	Independent	K-11 / 153
Cornerstone Christian Academy	St. Clair	Baptist	K-12 / 165
Wesleyan Christian Schl	Warrenton	Wesleyan	K-12 / 140
Montana			
Emmanuel Christian Schl	Great Falls	Emmanuel Church	K-12 / 102
Nebraska			
Nebraska Christian Schls	Central City		K-12 / 157!
Lincoln Christian Schls	Lincoln		K-12 / 346
Parkview Christian Schl	Lincoln	Baptist	K-12 / 117
Bellevue Christian Academy & High Schl	Omaha	Assembly of God	1-12 / 428
Omaha Christian Academy	Omaha	Nondenominational	K-9 / 130
New Hampshire			
Good Shepherd Schl	Barrington		P-8 / 124
Faith Christian Cntr	Bedford		K-12 / 174
Concord Christian Schl	Concord	Baptist	K-12 / 253
Dublin Christian Academy	Dublin	Baptist	K-12 / 169
Faith Christian Academy	Gilford	Baptist	P-8 / 180
Bethel Christian Schl	Hudson	Baptist	K-8 / 132
Tabernacle Christian Schls	Hudson	Baptist	P-12 / 168

State/School	City	Affiliation	Grades/ Enrollment
Laconia Christian Schl	Laconia	Laconia Christian Fellowship	K-12 / 183
Southeastern N.H. Christian Academy	Somersworth	Baptist	K-12 / 218
New Jersey			
Central Jersey Christian Schls	Asbury Park		K-12 / 178
Brookdale Christian Schl	Bloomfield	Baptist	P-8 / 240
Cape May County Christian Schl	Cape May Court Hse	Faith Fellowship Chapel	K-12 / 178
Bethel Baptist Christian Schl	Cherry Hill	Baptist	K-8 / 239
Crossroads Christian Academy	Clinton	Baptist	P-8 / 222
American Christian Schl	Flanders	Baptist	P-8 / 107
Heritage Christian Schls	Garfield	Baptist	P-12 / 130
Hackensack Christian Schl	Hackensack	Baptist	P-12 / 314
Baptist High Schl	Haddon Heights	Baptist	6-12 / 154
The Kings Christian Schl	Haddon Heights		K-12 / 812&
Faith Christian Schl	Hamilton Square	Baptist	P-8 / 377
Hawthorne Christian Academy	Hawthorne	Hawthorne Gospel	K-12 / 368&
North Jersey Christian Academy	Linden	Calvary Tabernacle	K-12 / 114&
Lighthouse Christian Academy	Manahawkin	Baptist	K-8 / 143
Maranatha Baptist Schl Ministry	Millville	Baptist	K-12 / 100
Bethel Christian Academy	Newark	Assembly of God	K-8 / 184
Parsippany Christian Schl	Parsippany	Baptist	P-12 / 257
Madison Avenue Baptist Academy	Paterson	Baptist	K-12 / 156
Park Bible Academy	Pennsville	Baptist	K-12 / 110
Phillipsburg Christian Academy	Phillipsburg	The Fellowship Church	P-8 / 117
Timothy Christian Schl	Piscataway		K-12 / 465
Gloucester Christian Schl	Pitman	Bethel Community Church	K-12 / 272
Bethel Christian Schl	Port Republic		P-12 / 182
Ringwood Christian Schl	Ringwood	Baptist	P-8 / 183
New Life Christian Schl	South Plainfield	New Life Gospel Church	K-10 / 409
Ambassador Christian Academy	Tom River	Baptist	P-12 / 266
Mercer Christian Academy	Trenton		K-12 / 171
Victory Christian Schl	Williamstown	Baptist	P-12 / 368
Zarephath Christian Schl	Zarephath	Pillar of Fire	K-12 / 107
New Mexico			
Community Christian Schl	Alamogordo	Christ Community Church	P-10 / 170&
Evangel Temple Academy	Albuquerque	Evangel Temple	P-12 / 218
Victory Christian Schl	Albuquerque	Alameda Bible Church	K-12 / 115
Brethren Navajo Missionry & Brding Schl	Counselor	Brethren	K-12 / 117!
Mesilla Valley Christian Schls	Las Cruces	Independent	K-12 / 304
Gateway Christian Schl	Roswell	Baptist	P-12 / 142
Temple Baptist Christian Schl	Santa Fe	Baptist	P-12 / 102
Nevada			
Christian Cntr Schls	Boulder City	Foursquare	P-8 / 100
Trinity Christian Schl	Las Vegas	Trinity Temple	P-12 / 443
New York			
Perth Bible Christian Academy	Amsterdam	Perth Bible Church	P-12 / 212
Glad Tidings Academy	Bronx		P-8 / 288
Bethel Christian Learning Cntr	Cambria Heights	New Greater Bethel Church	1-10 / 101
Upton Lake Christian Schl	Clinton Corners	Evangelical Free	K-12 / 111
Upper Room Christian Schl	Dix Hills		P-12 / 314
Elmira Christian Academy	Elmira		K-12 / 107
Levant Christian Schl	Falconer	Wesleyan	P-12 / 205
Good Shepherd Schl	Kingston	Morning Star Christian Fellowship	P-8 / 122&
Latham Christian Academy	Latham	Baptist	P-12 / 225
Lima Christian Schl	Lima	Baptist	K-12 / 174&
Loudonville Christian Schl	Loudonville	Loudonville Community Church	P-8 / 223
Harmony Christian Schl	Middletown	Baptist	P-9 / 175
Manhattan Christian Academy	New York	Manhattan Bible Church	K-12 / 250
Valley Heights Christian Academy	Norwich	Baptist	P-12 / 111

State/School	City	Affiliation	Grades/ Enrollment
Christian Learning Cntr	Painted Post		P-11 / 110
Lakeshore Christian Schl	Plattsburgh	Baptist	K-12 / 100
Tabernacle Christian Academy	Poughkeepsie	Baptist	1-12 / 106
Northern Dutchess Christian Schl	Rhinebeck	Baptist	P-8 / 116
Living Water Christian Schl	Riverhead		P-12 / 131
Northstar Christian Academy	Rochester	Baptist	K-12 / 490
Mountainside Christian Academy	Schroon Lake	Mountainside Bible Chapel	K-12 / 134
Schenectady Christian Schl	Scotia	Presbyterian	K-12 / 357
Faith Heritage	Syracuse	Interdenominational	K-12 / 600
Tioga Cntr Christian Schl	Tioga Cntr	Baptist	P-12 / 105
West Seneca Christian Schl	West Seneca	Baptist	K-12 / 343
Yonkers Christian Academy	Yonkers		P-8 / 114
North Carolina			
Asheville Christian Academy	Asheville		K-12 / 208
Rhema Christian Schl	Asheville	Assembly of God	K-9 / 120
Charlotte Christian Schl	Charlotte		K-12 / 630
Hilltop Christian Schl	Fuquay-Varina	Baptist	K-12 / 124
Vandalia Christian Schl	Greensboro	Baptist	K-12 / 442
Greenville Christian Academy	Greenville	Baptist	K-12 / 398
Wesleyan Education Cntr	High Point	Wesleyan	P-12 / 811&
Sheets Memorial Christian Schl	Lexington	Baptist	P-12 / 285
Bible Baptist Christian Schl	Matthews	Baptist	K-12 / 335
The Gramercy Schl	Newport	Faith Evangelical Bible Church	K-8 / 124
Friendship Christian Schls	Raleigh	Baptist	P-12 / 457
Wake Christian Academy	Raleigh	Baptist	K-12 / 621
Community Baptist Schls	Reidsville	Baptist	P-8 / 175
Rockwell Christian Schl	Rockwell	Baptist	K-8 / 154
Roxboro Christian Academy	Roxboro	Independent	P-12 / 164
North Hills Christian Schl	Salisbury	North Hills Church	P-12 / 254
Calvary Christian Schl	Southern Pines	Calvary Memorial Church	K-12 / 117
Carolina Christian Academy	Thomasville		K-12 / 154
Columbus Christian Academy	Whiteville	Missionary Alliance Church	K-12 / 105
Wilmington Christian Academy	Wilmington	Baptist	K-12 / 560
Salem Baptist Christian Schl	Winston Salem	Baptist	1-8 / 198
North Dakota			
Shema Christian Schl	Grand Forks	Shema Christian Schl / Inc.	K-8 / 103
Shiloh Christian Schl	Mandan	Independent	K-12 / 251
Our Redeemers Christian Schl	Minot	Lutheran Brethren	P-8 / 106
Ohio			
Ashland Christian Schl	Ashland	Brethren	P-8 / 300
Ashtabula Christian Life Academy	Ashtabula	Assembly of God	K-12 / 173
Heritage Christian Schl	Brooklyn	Baptist	K-12 / 343
Wayside Christian Schl	Bucyrus	Wayside Chapel	K-12 / 132
Geauga Christian Schl	Burton	Assembly of God	K-12 / 145
World Harvest Christian Academy	Canal Winchester	World Harvest Church	P-10 / 258
Heritage Christian Schl	Canton		P-12 / 442
Central Baptist Schls	Cincinnati	Baptist	K-12 / 243
Norwood Baptist Christian Schl	Cincinnati	Baptist	K-12 / 225&
Baptist Christian Schl	Cleveland	Baptist	7-12 / 102
Westside Baptist Christian Schl	Cleveland		K-8 / 120
Columbus Christian Schl	Columbus	The Redeemers Church	K-12 / 146&
Liberty Christian Academy	Columbus	Independent	1-12 / 302
Maranatha Christian Schl	Columbus	Baptist	K-12 / 341
Sonshine Christian Academy	Columbus		P-12 / 202
Cuyahoga Valley Christian Academy	Cuyahoga Falls		7-12 / 450
Dayton Christian Schls, Inc.	Dayton	Independent	K-12 / 1860&
Temple Christian Schl	Dayton	Baptist	K-12 / 156
Delaware Christian Schl	Delaware	Delaware Bible	K-12 / 228
East Liverpool Christian Schl	East Liverpool	Independent	P-12 / 185

State/School	City	Affiliation	Grades/ Enrollment
Open Door Christian Schl, Inc.	Elyria	Church of the Open Door	P-12 / 625&
The Kings Academy-Upper Schl	Elyria	Christ The King Community	4-12 / 180
Tri-County Christian Schls	Fairfield	Assembly of God	K-12 / 543&
Heritage Christian Schl	Findlay	Baptist	K-12 / 250
Evangel Christian Academy	Gahanna	Assembly of God	P-8 / 255&
Ohio Valley Christian Schl	Gallipolis	Baptist	K-12 / 202
Faith Christian Schl	Greenville	Baptist	P-12 / 151
Hamilton Christian Schl	Hamilton	Baptist	P-12 / 185
Lake Cntr Christian Schl	Hartville	Mennonite	K-8 / 210&
Licking County Christian Academy	Heath	Baptist	K-12 / 279
Valley Christian Schls	Kettering	Christ Life Sanctuary	P-8 / 155
Lima Christian Academy	Lima	Calvary Bible Church	K-12 / 102
Temple Christian Schl	Lima	Baptist	K-12 / 375
North Coast Christian Academy	Lorain	Church On The North Coast	1-8 / 106
Mansfield Christian Schl	Mansfield	Independent	K-12 / 638
Temple Christian Schl	Mansfield	Baptist	K-12 / 259
Marietta Christian Schl	Marietta	Marietta Bible Cntr Church	K-12 / 123
First Baptist Christian Schl	Medina	Baptist	P-12 / 322
Middletown Christian Schl	Middletown	Baptist	K-12 / 388
Christian Cntr Schls	Parma	Foursquare	K-12 / 240
Parma Heights Christian Academy	Parma Heights	Baptist	K-8 / 159
Ridgeville Christian Schls, Inc.	Springboro	Ridgeville Community Church	P-12 / 355
Cathedral Christian Schl	Sylvania	Cathedral of Praise	K-12 / 105
Toledo Christian Schls	Toledo	Nondenominational	K-12 / 706
Troy Christian Schls	Troy	Baptist	K-8 / 226
Warren Christian Schl	Warren	Assembly of God	K-12 / 169
Dailyville Christian Schl	Waverly	Baptist	P-10 / 117
Christ The King Christian Schl	Westerville	Lutheran	K-10 / 191
Northside Christian Schl	Westerville	Calvary Bible Church	K-12 / 242
Willo Hill Christian Schl	Willoughby	Baptist	K-12 / 329
Grace Brethren Christian Schl	Worthington		P-12 / 1071
Xenia Christian Day Schl	Xenia	Baptist	K-12 / 169
Xenia Nazarene Christian Schl	Xenia	Nazarene	P-8 / 260
Calvary Christian Academy	Youngstown	Pentecostal	K-12 / 216
Youngstown Christian Schl	Youngstown	Assembly of God	P-12 / 300
Zanesville Christian Schl	Zanesville	Maranatha Bible Church	K-12 / 173
Oklahoma			
Tulsa Emmanuel Christian Schl	Broken Arrow		K-12 / 108
Christian Heritage Academy	Del City	Baptist	P-12 / 536
Mid-Del Christian Schl	Del City	Assembly of God	P-12 / 334
Oklahoma Christian Schls	Edmond	Independent	P-12 / 459
Oklahoma Bible Academy	Enid		7-12 / 124
Cookson Hills Christian Schl	Kansas	Christian & Church of Christ	1-12 / 120!&
Star Christian Schl of Fine Arts	Moore	Independent	K-10 / 105
Community Christian Schl	Norman	Independent	P-11 / 211
The Master's Schl	Norman	Baptist	P-8 / 117
Britton Christian Academy	Oklahoma City	Independent	P-12 / 142
Grace Christian Academy	Oklahoma City	Assembly of God	K-12 / 347
Life Christian Schl	Oklahoma City	Life Christian Cntr	P-12 / 484
Liberty Academy	Shawnee	Baptist	P-12 / 396
Evangelistic Temple Schl	Tulsa		P-8 / 180
Tulsa Christian Schls	Tulsa	Baptist	K-12 / 650
Oregon			
Faith Bible Christian Schl	Aloha	Faith Bible Church	P-12 / 286
Hope Christian Schl	Aloha	Living Hope Fellowship	K-9 / 179
Morning Star Christian Schl	Bend	Neighborhood Church	K-10 / 145
Damascus Christian Schl	Boring		K-12 / 222
Canyonville Bible Academy	Canyonville		K-12 / 105!
Santiam Christian Schls, Inc.	Corvallis		6-12 / 137

State/School	*City*	*Affiliation*	*Grades/ Enrollment*
Eugene Christian Schls	Eugene	Nondenominational	P-12 / 202
Willamette Christian Schl	Eugene	Willamette Christian Cntr	P-8 / 290
Grace Christian Schl	Gladstone	Assembly of God	K-9 / 189
Pleasant Valley Christian Schl	Grants Pass	Pleasant Valley Vineyard	P-8 / 110
Bethlehem Christian Schl	Lake Oswego	Baptist	P-8 / 244
East Linn Christian Academy	Lebanon	Nondenominational	K-12 / 290
Grace Christian Schl	Medford	Baptist	P-8 / 416
Kingsview Christian Schl	North Bend	Nazarene	K-8 / 182
Portland Christian Schls	Portland		K-12 / 717
Temple Christian Schl	Portland	Bible Temple	K-12 / 359&
West Hills Christian Schl	Portland	Nondenominational	K-8 / 230
Douglas County Christian Schls	Roseburg		P-11 / 215
Umpqua Valley Christian Schls	Roseburg	Foursquare	K-12 / 121
Pennsylvania			
Lehigh Christian Academy	Allentown		P-8 / 160
Eden Christian Academy	Allison Park	Independent	P-10 / 337&
Centre County Christian Academy	Bellefonte	Baptist	P-12 / 176
Belleville Mennonite Schl	Belleville		P-12 / 252&
Bethlehem Christian Day Schl	Bethlehem		K-8 / 170
Bloomsburg Christian Schl	Bloomsburg	Baptist	K-12 / 251
Cumberland Valley Christian Schl	Chambersburg	The Open Door Church	K-12 / 317
Shalom Christian Academy	Chambersburg		K-12 / 372
Calvary Baptist Academy	Clymer	Baptist	K-12 / 102
Blair City Christian Schl	Duncansville	Foot of Ten Indpndnt Bible Chrch	K-12 / 301
Mt. Calvary Christian Schl	Elizabethtown	Mt. Calvary Church	K-12 / 313
Bethel Christian Schl of Erie	Eria	Baptist	K-12 / 236
South Hills Christian Schl	Finleyville	Baptist	K-12 / 225
Open Door Christian Academy	Fort Washington	Church of The Open Door	P-8 / 196
High Point Baptist Academy	Geigertown	Baptist	K-12 / 436
Johnstown Christian Schl	Hollsopple		K-12 / 268&
Mt. View Christian Schl	Hummelstown	Mt. View Bible Church	K-12 / 212
Canaan Christian Academy	Lake Ariel	Canaan Bible Chapel	K-12 / 188
Lancaster Christian Schl	Lancaster		P-12 / 396
Living Word Academy	Lancaster	The Worship Cntr	K-12 / 411
New Danville Mennonite Schl	Lancaster	Mennonite	K-8 / 221
Chapel Christian Academy	Limerick	Limerick Chapel	K-12 / 384
Lititz Christian Schl	Lititz	Brethren	P-8 / 259
Wilson Christian Academy	McKeesport	Wilson Foundation	P-12 / 137
Calvary Baptist Christian Academy	Meadville	Baptist	P-12 / 178
The Christian Academy	Media		P-12 / 830
Conestoga Christian Schl	Morgantown		K-12 / 250
Twin Valley Bible Academy	Morgantown	Twin Valley Bible Chapel	K-12 / 161
Mt. Carmel Christian Schl	Mt. Pleasant	Mt. Carmel Community Church	K-12 / 194
Grace Christian Schl	Myerstown	Brethren	P-12 / 193
Delaware County Christian Schl	Newton Square	Independent	K-12 / 835&
Penn Christian Academy	Norristown	Nondenominational	1-8 / 194
Calvary Temple Christian Academy	Philadelphia		P-8 / 259
Cedar Grove Academy	Philadelphia		P-12 / 735&
Christ Independent Baptist Academy	Philadelphia	Baptist	K-12 / 111
Timothy Academy	Philadelphia	Baptist	P-8 / 301
North Hills Christian Schl	Pittsburgh	Baptist	K-12 / 173
Plumstead Christian Schl	Plumsteadville		6-12 / 336
Ebenezer Faith Christian Schl	Plymouth	Baptist	K-12 / 127
Portersville Christian Schl	Portersville	C&MA	P-12 / 227
Red Lion Christian Schl	Red Lion	Red Lion Bible Church	P-12 / 199
Beaver Valley Christian Academy	Rochester		K-12 / 116&
Faith Christian Schl	Roseto		P-12 / 319
Faith Christian Schl	Roslyn	Faith Community Church	P-9 / 173
Upper Bucks Christian Schl	Sellersville	Baptist	P-12 / 641
Sharon Christian Academy	Sharon	Baptist	P-12 / 143

State/School	*City*	*Affiliation*	*Grades/ Enrollment*
Locust Grove Mennonite Schl	Smoketown		K-8 / 457
Somerset Alliance Comm Christian Schl	Somerset	C&MA	K-8 / 105
Watsontown Christian Academy	Watsontown	C&MA	/ 152
Canyon Christian Academy	Wellsboro	Baptist	K-12 / 117
West Chester Christian Schl	West Chester	Baptist	K-12 / 371
Christian Schl of York	York		K-12 / 670&
West Side Christian Schl	York	Baptist	K-12 / 127
Rhode Island			
Barrington Christian Academy	Barrington	Baptist	K-8 / 148
West Bay Christian Academy	North Kingstown		K-8 / 143
First Baptist Christian Schl	Warwick	Baptist	K-12 / 315
South Carolina			
Oakwood Christian Schl	Anderson	Baptist	K-12 / 512
Calvary Christian Schl	Belton	Baptist	K-12 / 135
Beaufort Christian Schl	Burton	Baptist	K-12 / 126
Northside Christian Schl	Charleston Heights	Baptist	K-12 / 642
Grace Christian Schl	Columbia	Baptist	K-12 / 512
Easley Christian Schl	Easley	Baptist	K-12 / 174
Landmark Christian Academy	Easley	Baptist	K-12 / 105
Florence Christian Schls	Florence	Baptist	K-12 / 615
Maranatha Christian Schl	Florence	Free Will Baptist	1-12 / 212
Heritage Christian Schl	Gaffney	Baptist	K-12 / 199
Hampton Park Christian Schl	Greenville	Baptist	K-12 / 510
Mitchell Road Christian Academy	Greenville	Presbyterian	P-8 / 284&
Southside Christian Schl	Greenville	Baptist	K-12 / 741
Emmanuel Baptist Schl	Hartsville	Baptist	K-12 / 241
Hilton Head Christian Academy	Hilton Head Island	Baptist	K-12 / 142
Faith Christian Schl	Laurens	Baptist	P-12 / 120
St. Paul's Christian Schl	Leesville	Methodist	K-12 / 174
Calvary Christian Schl	Myrtle Beach	Calvary Bible Church	K-12 / 398
Ferndale Baptist Schl	North Charleston	Baptist	K-12 / 436
Garden City Christian Schl	Orangeburg	Baptist	K-12 / 328
Orangeburg Christian Schl	Orangeburg	Baptist	K-12 / 188
New Covenant Christian Schl	Pageland	Baptist	K-11 / 172
Trinity Christian Schl	Rock Hill	Trinity Bible Church	K-12 / 361
Westgate Christian Schl	Spartanburg	Baptist	K-12 / 215
Sumter Christian Schl	Sumter	Sumter Bible Church	K-12 / 475
Temple Baptist Christian Schl	Sumter	Baptist	P-12 / 189
The Academy of Arts	Taylors	Baptist	K-12 / 152
South Dakota			
James Valley Christian Schl	Huron	Interdenominational	K-12 / 132
Sunshine Bible Academy	Miller		K-12 / 122!
Tennessee			
Lighthouse Christian Schl	Antioch	Baptist	K-12 / 380
Fairview Christian Academy	Athens	Baptist	K-12 / 108
Tri-Cities Christian Schl	Blountville	Baptist	P-12 / 878
Calvary Christian Schl	Chattanooga	Baptist	P-12 / 179
Grace Baptist Academy	Chattanooga	Baptist	K-11 / 629
Tennessee Temple Academy	Chattanooga	Baptist	K-12 / 631
Bible Baptist Academy	Clarksville	Baptist	K-12 / 122
College Heights Christian Academy	Gallatin	Baptist	K-9 / 204
Hendersonville Christian Academy	Hendersonville	Baptist	K-12 / 198
Berean Academy	Hixson	Baptist	K-12 / 191
Hamill Road Christian Schl	Hixson	Baptist	K-8 / 160
Trinity Christian Academy	Jackson		K-9 / 146
Cedar View Christian Schl	Kingsport	Methodist	K-12 / 188
Kingsport Christian Schls	Kingsport	Baptist	K-12 / 241
Calvary Baptist Schl	Kingston	Baptist	K-12 / 252

State/School	City	Affiliation	Grades/ Enrollment
Christian Academy of Knoxville	Knoxville	Independent	K-12 / 381
Knoxville Baptist Christian Schls	Knoxville	Baptist	K-12 / 305
Madison Nazarene Christian Academy	Madison	Nazarene	K-12 / 148
Metropolitan Baptist Schl	Madison	Baptist	K-12 / 248
Central Baptist Schl	Memphis	Baptist	K-12 / 227
Evangelical Christian Schls	Memphis	Interdenominational	K-12 / 1426
Macon Road Baptist Schl	Memphis	Baptist	K-12 / 252
Randall Christian Academy	Memphis	Free Will Baptist	K-12 / 186
Thrifthaven Baptist Schls	Memphis	Baptist	K-12 / 296
Word of Faith Christian Academy	Memphis		P-10 / 154
Mount Juliet Christian Academy	Mount Juliet	Baptist	1-12 / 217&
Franklin Road Christian Schl	Murfreesboro	Baptist	K-12 / 306
Christ Presbyterian Academy	Nashville	Presbyterian	K-9 / 364&
Woodbine Christian Academy	Nashville	Free Will Baptist	K-12 / 202
Faith Christian Academy	Oliver Springs		K-12 / 100
Pleasant View Christian Schl	Pleasant View	Baptist	K-12 / 345
Temple Baptist Schl	Powell	Baptist	K-12 / 261
Harrison Chilhowee Baptist Academy	Seymour	Baptist	8-12 / 122!
Volunteer Christian Academy	Sparta	Baptist	K-12 / 105
South Haven Christian Academy	Springfield	Baptist	K-12 / 107
Texas			
Trinity Christian Academy	Addison		K-12 / 902
Living Stones Christian Schl	Alvin		K-12 / 260
Amarillo Christian Cntr Academy	Amarillo		K-12 / 100
Bible Heritage Schl	Amarillo		P-12 / 144
San Jacinto Christian Academy	Amarillo	Baptist	P-10 / 220
West Texas Christian Schl	Amarillo	Baptist	K-9 / 125
Bethel Christian Schl	Arlington	Assembly of God	P-12 / 175
Pantego Christian Academy	Arlington	Pantego Bible Church	P-9 / 374&
Texas Christian Academy	Arlington	Baptist	K-12 / 321
Central Christian Schl	Austin	Assembly of God	K-12 / 159&
Nazarene Christian Schl	Austin	Nazarene	K-8 / 100
Baytown Christian Academy	Baytown	Alliance Bible Church	P-12 / 199
Cathedral In The Pines Christian Schl	Beaumont		K-8 / 350
Bellaire Christian Academy	Bellaire	Baptist	K-11 / 208
First Baptist Schl	Brownsville	Southern Baptist	P-8 / 287
Bracken Christian Schl	Bulverde	Independent	P-8 / 112
Trinity Christian Schl	Cedar Hill		P-12 / 524
Cornerstone Christian Schl	Cedar Park	Baptist	P-8 / 118
Hilltop Baptist Academy	Cedar Park	Baptist	P-12 / 182
Covenant Christian Academy	Colleyville	Presbyterian	P-9 / 109
Covenant Christian Schl	Conroe	Conroe Bible Church	P-8 / 157&
Lifestyle Christian Schl	Conroe	Assembly of God	K-12 / 199
People's Baptist Church Schl	Corpus Christi	Baptist	K-12 / 130
Corsicana Christian Academy	Corsicana	Independent	K-12 / 102
Brandon Street Christian Academy	Dallas	Foursquare	P-12 / 151
First Baptist Academy	Dallas	Baptist	K-12 / 682
First Baptist Academy East Campus	Dallas	Baptist	K-8 / 157
Life Christian Schl of Dallas	Dallas	Assembly of God	P-12 / 183
Metropolitan Christian Schl	Dallas	Metropolitan Tabernacle	P-8 / 278
Tyler Street Christian Academy	Dallas	United Methodist	P-12 / 470
Liberty Christian Schl	Denton		K-12 / 299&
Brook Hollow Christian Schl	DeSoto	Baptist	K-12 / 198
Christway Academy	Duncanville		K-12 / 194
Northeast Christian Academy	El Paso	Baptist	K-12 / 212
The Oaks	Euless	Covenant	1-8 / 112
Lexington Academy	Farmers Branch	Word of Faith World Outreach Cntr	P-12 / 225
Castleberry Baptist Christian Schl	Fort Worth	Baptist	K-12 / 131
Christian Temple Schl	Fort Worth		K-12 / 135
Lake Country Christian Schl	Fort Worth	Baptist	K-12 / 315

State/School	City	Affiliation	Grades/ Enrollment
Meadowbrook Christian Schl	Fort Worth	Bethel Temple	P-10 / 291
Seminary South Assembly Day Schl	Fort Worth		P-8 / 174
Temple Christian Schl	Fort Worth	Baptist	K-12 / 524
Westridge Christian Schl	Fort Worth	Baptist	K-8 / 211
Garland Christian Academy	Garland	Baptist	K-12 / 668
Evangel Temple Christian	Grand Prairie	Assembly of God	P-12 / 323
Shady Grove Christian Academy	Grand Prairie	Shady Grove Church	K-12 / 233
Greenville Christian Schl	Greenville		K-12 / 242
Central Christian Academy	Houston	Independent	K-12 / 101
Greenwood Village Christian Schl	Houston	Baptist	K-12 / 232
North Houston Christian Schls	Houston	Baptist	K-12 / 186
San Jacinto Christian Schl	Houston	Baptist	P-12 / 185
Sweetwater Christian Schl	Houston	Assembly of God	K-12 / 410
Berean Christian Schl of Humble	Humble	Baptist	P-9 / 168
Irving Christian Academy	Irving	Baptist	K-12 / 237
Vineyard Christian Schl	Jacksonville	The Vineyard Church	P-8 / 109
Grace Christian Academy	Killeen	Grace Christian Cntr	K-10 / 134
Brazosport Christian Schl	Lake Jackson		P-9 / 185
Eaglemount Christian Schl	Lewisville	Eaglemount Family Ministries	P-10 / 107
Grace Christian Schls	Longview	Brethren	K-8 / 190
Trinity Christian Schls	Lubbock	Trinity Church	P-10 / 523&
Angelina Christian Schl	Lufkin	Assembly of God	P-9 / 208
Community Christian Schl	Orange	Community Church	K-12 / 306
Fountain Gate Christian Schls	Plano	Fountain Gate Ministries	P-8 / 145
Canyon Creek Christian Academy	Richardson	Baptist	K-12 / 230
Church On The Rock Christian Schl	Rockwall	Church On The Rock	P-9 / 456
Castle Hills First Baptist Schl	San Antonio	Baptist	P-12 / 520
New Covenant Faith Academy	San Antonio	New Covenant Fellowship Church	P-8 / 109
Rainbow Hills Baptist Schl	San Antonio	Baptist	P-11 / 198
San Antonio Christian Schls	San Antonio	Independent	K-12 / 630&
Sunnybrook Christian Academy	San Antonio	Temple of Praise	P-12 / 197
Trinity Church Education	San Antonio	Trinity Church	K-8 / 170
Glad Tidings Christian Schl	Sherman	Assembly of God	K-12 / 164
Faith Lutheran Church Schl	Sugar Land	Lutheran	P-8 / 205
Northside Assembly, Inc.	Texarkana	Northside Assembly	K-12 / 256
Concordia Lutheran High Schl	Tomball	Lutheran	9-12 / 125
Christian Heritage Schl	Tyler	Youth With A Mission	P-12 / 183
Utah			
Intermountain Christian Schl	Salt Lake City	Evangelical Free	P-12 / 253
Vermont			
Websterville Baptist Christian Schl	Websterville	Baptist	K-12 / 142
Trinity Baptist Schls	Williston	Baptist	K-12 / 112
Virginia			
Engleside Christian Schl	Alexandria	Baptist	K-12 / 210
Dayspring Christian Fellowship	Blacksburg		P-12 / 109
Gateway Christian Academy	Blacksburg	Baptist	K-12 / 112
Great Hope Baptist Schl	Chesapeake	Baptist	K-12 / 142
Greenbrier Christian Academy	Chesapeake		K-12 / 610
Stonebridge Schl	Chesapeake		P-8 / 182
Richmond Christian Schl	Chesterfield	Baptist	K-12 / 400&
Culpeper Christian Schl	Culpeper	Independent	K-8 / 115
Evangel Christian Schl	Dale City	Baptist	K-12 / 225
Southall Christian Schl	Danville	Baptist	K-12 / 168
Valley Baptist Christian Schl	Edinburg	Baptist	K-12 / 133
Bethlehem Baptist Christian Academy	Fairfax	Baptist	P-12 / 463
Fairfax Baptist Temple Academy	Fairfax	Baptist	K-12 / 278
Timberlake Christian Schl	Forest	Baptist	K-12 / 399
Faith Baptist Schls	Fredericksburg	Baptist	K-12 / 220
Fredericksburg Christian Schl	Fredericksburg		P-10 / 468

State/School	*City*	*Affiliation*	*Grades/ Enrollment*
Gloucester Christian Academy	Gloucester	Lighthouse Worship Cntr	P-11 / 101
Bethel Christian Schl	Hampton	Baptist	P-12 / 269
Hampton Christian High Schl	Hampton	Covenant	7-12 / 162&
West End Christian Schl	Hopewell	Presbyterian	P-12 / 234
Mt. Carmel Christian Academy	Luray	Baptist	K-12 / 187
Lynchburg Christian Academy	Lynchburg	Baptist	P-12 / 961&
Emmanuel Christian Schl	Manassas	Baptist	P-12 / 491
Fresta Valley Christian Schl	Marshall		P-12 / 170
Martinsville Christian Schl	Martinsville	Baptist	K-12 / 126
Denbigh Baptist Christian Schl	Newport News	Baptist	K-12 / 234
Bayview Christian Schl	Norfolk	Baptist	P-9 / 109
Norfolk Christian Schls	Norfolk	Tabernacle Church of Norfolk	P-12 / 861&
Alliance Christian Schls	Portsmouth	C&MA	K-12 / 263
Central Baptist Church Schl	Portsmouth	Baptist	K-12 / 171
Commonwealth Christian Schl	Richmond	Baptist	K-12 / 200
Landmark Christian Schl	Richmond	Baptist	K-12 / 347
Roanoke Valley Christian Schls	Roanoke	Baptist	K-12 / 539&
Christian Heritage Academy	Rocky Mount	Independent	K-12 / 106
Berean Christian Academy	Salem	Baptist	K-12 / 210
Immanuel Christian Schl	Springfield	Immanuel Bible Church	K-8 / 212
Word of Life Christian Academy	Springfield	Assembly of God	P-12 / 299
Stanleytown Baptist Academy	Stanleytown	Baptist	K-12 / 105
Grace Christian Schl	Staunton	Community Fellowship Church	K-9 / 108
Shenandoah Valley Christian Academy	Stephens City	Baptist	K-12 / 160
Faith Christian Schl	Sterling	Faith Bible Church	P-8 / 216&
Atlantic Shores Christian Schl	Virginia Beach	Baptist	P-12 / 495
Tabernacle Baptist Schls	Virginia Beach	Baptist	K-12 / 285
Williamsburg Christian Academy	Williamsburg	Williamsburg New Testament Church	P-12 / 145
Rosedale Christian Academy	Winchester	Baptist	K-12 / 145
Heritage Christian Schl	Woodbridge	Baptist	K-11 / 158
Woodbridge Christian Schl	Woodbridge		K-10 / 148
Washington			
Arlington Christian Schl	Arlington	Independent	K-12 / 194
El-Shaddai High Schl	Auburn	Christian Enterprises	7-12 / 160
Neighborhood Christian Schl	Bellevue	Assembly of God	P-8 / 175
Heritage Christian Schl	Bothell	Baptist	P-9 / 461
Bremerton Christian Schl	Bremerton		K-12 / 222
Centralia Christian Schl	Centralia	First Christian Church	P-8 / 246
Silver Lake Christian Schl	Everett	Silver Lake Chapel	P-8 / 140
Columbia Heights Christian Academy	Longview	Assembly of God	K-12 / 183
Snohomish County Christian Schl	Lynwood	Independent	P-12 / 482
Grace Academy	Marysville	Baptist	P-12 / 234
Viewcrest Christian Schl	Mount Vernon	Assembly of God	P-12 / 129
Mountlake Christian Schl	Mountlake Terrace		P-12 / 133&
Evergreen Christian Schl	Olympia	Evergreen Christian Church	P-10 / 269
Christ the King Academy	Poulsbo	Christ Memorial Church	K-8 / 150
Redmond Christian Schl	Redmond		P-11 / 175
Crista Schls	Seattle	Crista Ministries	P-12 / 1166
Seattle Christian Schl	Seattle		K-12 / 567
Valley Christian Schl	Spokane	Valley Fourth Memorial	K-12 / 176
Kings Way Christian Schl	Vancouver	Church of God	K-8 / 163
Valley Assembly Schl	Veradale	Assembly of God	P-12 / 116
Liberty Christian Schl	Walla Walla		K-8 / 106
West Side Christian Schl	Yakima	Baptist	K-12 / 240
West Virginia			
Cross Lanes Christian Schl	Charleston	Cross Lanes Bible Church	K-12 / 267
Fair Haven Christian Schl	Charleston	Baptist	K-12 / 120
Emmanuel Christian Schl	Clarksburg	Baptist	K-12 / 129

State/School	City	Affiliation	Grades/ Enrollment
Elk Valley Christian Schl	Elkview	Baptist	K-12 / 139
Calvary Christian Schl	Fairmont	Baptist	K-12 / 100
Grace Christian Schl	Huntington	Grace Gospel Church	K-12 / 234
Mid-America Christian Schl	Huntington	Baptist	K-9 / 108
Mingo Christian Schl	Lenore	Baptist	K-12 / 197
Faith Christian Academy, Inc.	Martinsburg	Independent	P-12 / 164
Martinsburg Christian Academy	Martinsburg	Baptist	K-12 / 147
Alliance Christian Schl	Morgantown	Alliance Ministries, Inc.	P-9 / 181
Mercer Christian Academy	Princeton	Baptist	K-12 / 284
Greater Beckley Christian Schls	Prosperity	Baptist	K-12 / 173
Rainelle Christian Academy	Rainelle	Baptist	K-12 / 173
Teays Valley Christian	Scott Depot	Scott Depot Christ Fellowship	K-12 / 236
New Life Christian Academy	Summersville		P-12 / 105
Wisconsin			
Green Bay Christian Schl	Green Bay	Interdenominational	K-8 / 221
Christian Life Schl	Kenosha	Assembly of God	K-12 / 304&
Faith Christian Schl	La Crosse	Baptist	P-12 / 110&
Calvary Baptist Schl	Menomonee Falls	Baptist	K-12 / 163
Falls Baptist Academy	Menomonee Falls	Baptist	K-8 / 107
Heritage Christian Schls, Inc.	Milwaukee	Independent	K-12 / 853
Oshkosh Community Christian Schl	Oshkosh	Independent	P-9 / 127
Good Shepherd Christian Academy	River Falls	Communion of Saints	K-12 / 111
Maranatha Academy, Inc.	Superior	Interdenominational	K-12 / 109
Union Grove Christian Schl	Union Grove	Baptist	P-12 / 138
Waukesha Christian Academy	Waukesha	Baptist	K-10 / 126
Calvary Life Academy	West Bend	Assembly of God	P-12 / 130
Faith Christian Schl	Williams Bay		K-12 / 185
Wyoming			
Heritage Christian Schl	Gillette		P-12 / 118
Puerto Rico			
Colegio Bautista De Levittown	Levittown	Baptist	P-12 / 435
Alberta, Canada			
Glenmore Christian Academy	Calgary	C&MA	P-9 / 413
Heritage Christian Schls	Calgary		K-12 / 520
Covenant Community Training Cntr	Edmonton	Peoples Church	P-12 / 135
Meadowlark Christian Schl	Edmonton	Baptist	K-9 / 103
Millwoods Christian Schl	Edmonton	Calvary Community Church	K-12 / 243
Fort Saskatchewan Christian Schl	Fort Saskatchewan	C&MA	K-9 / 100
Grande Prairie Christian Schl	Grande Prairie		K-9 / 145&
Cornerstone Christian Schl	Medicine Hat		K-12 / 132
Olds Koinonia Christian Schl	Olds		K-12 / 115
Strathcona Christian Academy	Sherwood Park	C&MA	P-12 / 629
Prairie General Education Schls	Three Hills	Prarie Bible Institute	K-12 / 608!
Ontario, Canada			
KRT Christian Schl	Brampton	Kennedy Road Tabernacle	P-10 / 472
Park Avenue Academy	Burlington	Park Avenue Church	P-8 / 171
Stouffville Christian	Claremont		P-10 / 180&
Niagara Christian College	Fort Erie	Brethren in Christ	7-12 / 190!
Crestwicke Christian Academy	Guelph	Baptist	P-8 / 163
Scarborough Christian Schl	Miliken		K-12 / 217
Newmarket & District Christian Academy	Newmarket	Grace Church	K-8 / 229
Oakville Christian Schl	Oakville		P-11 / 203&
Grace Christian Academy	Peterborough	Grace Christian Ministries, Inc.	K-8 / 121
Pickering Christian Schl	Pickering		P-8 / 120
Faith Christian Academy	Saint Thomas	Baptist	P-8 / 118&
Peoples Christian Schls	Willowdale		K-12 / 685

Source: Association of Christian Schools International, LaHabra, CA and American Association of Christian Schools, Fairfax, VA. Used by permission.

What Kids Want to Be When They Grow Up

What kids want	%
Happily married	38%
Rich	24%
Physically fit, healthy	19%
Surrounded by friends	14%
Other	5%

Source: Sesame Place Kids' Poll of 450 kids, ages 5-12

FOCUS QUOTE

Who among the evangelicals can stand up to the great secular or naturalistic or atheistic scholars on their own terms of scholarship and research? Who among the evangelical scholars is quoted as a normative source by the greatest secular authorities on history or philosophy or psychology or sociology or politics?—Charles Malik

FOCUS QUOTE

So far as the university is concerned, I have no patience with piety alone—I want the most rigorous intellectual training, I want the perfection of the mind; equally, I have no patience with reason alone—I want the salvation of the soul, I want the fear of the Lord, I want at least neutrality with respect to the knowledge of Jesus Christ.—Charles Malik

FOCUS FACT

The largest Christian elementary/high school in the world? Liceo Cristiano in San Salvador, El Salvador, founded in 1963 by the Assemblies of God, has an enrollment of more than 19,000 students through grade 12.

RELIGIOUS TRAINING FOR CHILDREN STRONGLY FAVORED

Question: Would you want a child of yours to receive any religious instruction?

	Yes / %	*No / %*	*No opinion / %*
NATIONAL	86	7	7
Men	83	9	6
Women	88	6	6
Whites	86	8	6
Blacks	87	7	6
Hispanics	80	10	10
Protestants	90	5	5
Catholics	91	4	5
Churched	96	2	2
Unchurched	73	14	13
Respondents with children 4-18	90	6	4

Source: *100 Questions and Answers: Religion in America* by George Gallup, Jr. and Sarah Jones. Published by Princeton Religion Research Center. Copyright 1989. Used by permission.

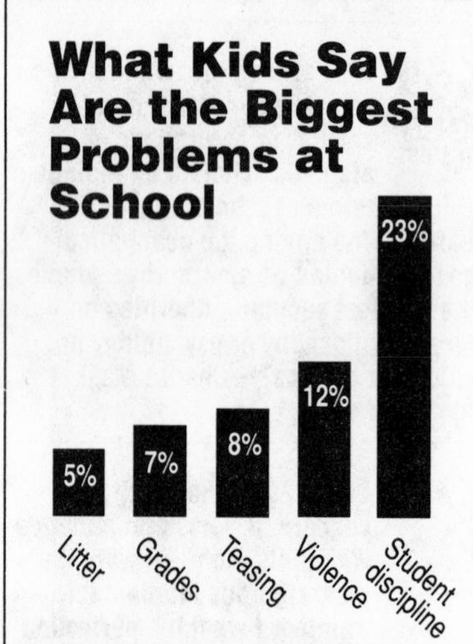

Source: Waldenbooks, survey of 5,000 kids

FOCUS QUOTE

Many great leaders of the past were home-schooled, including John Quincy Adams, William Penn, Abraham Lincoln, Thomas Edison, Woodrow Wilson, Franklin D. Roosevelt, General George Patton, and General Douglas MacArthur.

Historical evidence indicates that prior to the introduction of public education and compulsory school attendance laws, Americans were probably the most literate people in the world.

Source: *Home Education: Is It Working?* Published by Home Oriented Private Education for Texas

INTERNATIONAL SCHOOLS

AUSTRALIA

Address: Australian Christian Academy
319 S. Pine Rd., P.O. Box 10,
Strathpine 4500 QLD
Australia
Affiliation: Australian Christian Academy
Type: National
Grades: 1-12
Enrollment: 756

Address: Fountain Centre Christian School
Box 101, Booleroo Centre
SA 5482
Australia
Affiliation: Booleroo Ministry Centre
Type: National
Grades: 1-12
Enrollment: 25

Address: Pacific Hills Christian School
Locked Bag No. 3, Round
Corner 2158, NSW
Australia
Affiliation: Christian Brethren Schools Ltd.
Type: National

AUSTRIA

Address: Vienna Christian School
Postfach 277, A-1050 Vienna
Austria
Affiliation: Mult-Mission
Type: Missionary
Grades: 1-10
Enrollment: 50

BAHAMAS

Address: Kingsway Academy
N4378, Nassau
Bahamas
Affiliation: Independent
Type: National
Grades: K-12
Enrollment: 654

Address: Windermere High School
Box 63, Governor's Harbour, Eleuthera
Bahamas
Affiliation: Gospel Missionary Union
Type: National
Grades: 9-12
Enrollment: 93
Notes: Boarding Facilities

BELGIUM

Address: International Christian Academy
Chaussee de Waterloo 36,
1640 Rhode St., Genese
Belgium
Affiliation: Assemblies of God
Type: Missionary
Grades: K-6
Enrollment: 16

BOLIVIA

Address: Carachipampa Christian School
Cajon 736, Cochabamba
Bolivia

Affiliation: SIM International
Type: Missionary
Grades: K-12
Enrollment: 146

Address: Santa Cruz Christian Learning Center
Cajon 4049, Santa Cruz
Bolivia
Affiliation: Multi-Mission
Type: Missionary
Grades: P-12
Enrollment: 127
Notes: Special Education

BRAZIL

Address: Academia Crista de Boa Viagem
Rua Ribeiro de Brito, 700 Boa Viagem, 50,000 Recife, PE
Brazil
Affiliation: Boa Viagem Presbyterian
Type: National
Grades: P-4
Enrollment: 90

Address: Amazon Valley Academy
CP 3030 Agencia Independencia, Belem Para 66,041
Brazil
Affiliation: UFM International, Inc.
Type: Missionary
Grades: 1-12
Enrollment: 110
Notes: Boarding Facilities/Special Education

Address: Fortaleza Academy
Caixa Postal 1691, Fortaleza CE 60,151
Brazil
Affiliation: Baptist Mid-Missions
Type: Missionary
Grades: 1-12
Enrollment: 68
Notes: Boarding Facilities

Address: New Tribes Mission School
Caixa Postal 1421, Manaus 69,062, Amazonas
Brazil
Affiliation: New Tribes Mission
Type: Missionary
Grades: K-12
Enrollment: 86

Address: Pan American Christian Academy
Caixa Postal 12,491, 04798 Sao Paulo
Brazil
Affiliation: Missionary
Type: Special Education
Grades: K-12
Enrollment: 276

BRITISH WEST INDIES

Address: Grand Turk Christian Academy
P.O. Box 14, Grand Turk, Turks & Caicos
British West Indies
Affiliation: Bible Baptist Church
Type: National
Grades: K-6
Enrollment: 195

Address: Triple C School
P.O. Box 498 Grand Cayman
British West Indies
Affiliation: Church of God
Type: National
Grades: K-12
Enrollment: 253
Notes: Special Education

COLOMBIA

Address: El Camino Academy
Apartado Aereo 101241, Bogota 10
Colombia
Affiliation: Independent
Type: Missionary
Grades: K-12
Enrollment: 71

Address: New Tribes Mission School
A.A. 23-53, Villavicencio Meta
Colombia
Affiliation: New Tribes Mission
Type: Missionary
Grades: 1-12
Enrollment: 48
Notes: Boarding Facilities

DOMINICAN REPUBLIC

Address: Caribe-Vista School
c/o 1000 South 350 East, Marion, IN 46953
USA
Affiliation: New Horizons Youth Ministries
Type: Missionary
Grades: 7-12
Enrollment: 36
Notes: Boarding Facilities/Special Education

Address: Colegio Cristiano Logos
Apartado 2647, Santo Domingo
Dominican Republic
Affiliation: Iglesia Biblica Del Senor Jesucristo
Type: National
Grades: P-7
Enrollment: 197

Address: Santiago Christian School
Apartado 62, Santiago
Dominican Republic
Affiliation: Missionary
Type: P-12
Grades: 309
Enrollment: Special Education

INTERNATIONAL SCHOOLS cont.

ECUADOR

Address: Alliance Academy
Casilla 6186, Quito
Ecuador
Affiliation: C&MA
Type: Missionary
Grades: K-12
Enrollment: 485
Notes: Boarding Facilities/Special Education

Address: Nate Saint Memorial School
Shell, Pastaza
Ecuador
Affiliation: HCJB
Type: Missionary
Grades: K-8
Enrollment: 24

EL SALVADOR

Address: Liceo Cristiano
Apartado 989, San Salvador
El Salvador
Affiliation: Assemblies of God
Type: National
Grades: P-12
Enrollment: 19,017

ETHIOPIA

Address: Bingham Academy
Box 4937, Addis Ababa
Ethiopia
Affiliation: SIM International
Type: Missionary
Grades: 1-8
Enrollment: 141
Notes: Boarding Facilities

FED REPUBLIC OF GERMANY

Address: Black Forest Academy
Postfach 1109, 7842 Kandern 1
Fed Republic of Germany
Affiliation: Janz Team Ministries
Type: Missionary
Grades: 1-12
Enrollment: 200
Notes: Boarding Facilities/Special Education

Address: Trinity Christian School
Neckarplatt 3, 6800 Mannheim 51
Fed Republic of Germany
Affiliation: Overseas Christian Servicemen's Center
Type: Missionary
Grades: K-12
Enrollment: 46

FED STATES OF MICRONESIA

Address: Berea Christian School
P.O. Box 9, Moen, Truk 96942
Fed States of Micronesia
Affiliation: Independent
Type: National
Grades: K-12
Enrollment: 588

Address: Nukuno Christian Elementary
P.O. Box 174, Moen, Truk 96942
Fed States of Micronesia
Affiliation: Nukuno Protestant Church
Type: National
Grades: K-8
Enrollment: 179

GUAM

Address: Evangelical Christian Academy
P.O. Box 23998, GMF 96921
Guam
Affiliation: Chalan Pago Evangelical Church
Type: National
Grades: P-12
Enrollment: 124

Address: Harvest Christian Academy
P.O. Box 23189, GMF 96921
Guam
Affiliation: Harvest Baptist Church
Type: National
Grades: P-12
Enrollment: 770

Address: Trinity Christian School
P.O. Box 11343, Yigo 96929
Guam
Affiliation: First Assembly of God
Type: National
Grades: K-8
Enrollment: 281

GUATEMALA

Address: Christian Academy of Guatemala
Apartado 25-B, 01903 Guatemala City
Guatemala
Type: Missionary
Grades: K-12
Enrollment: 157

Address: Inter-American School
Apartado 24, Quexaltenango 09902
Guatemala
Affiliation: Assn. of North Am. Missionary Parents
Type: Missionary
Grades: P-12
Enrollment: 134

HAITI

Address: Cowman School
M.F.I.-Haiti, Box 15665,
West Palm Beach, FL 33406 USA

Affiliation: OMS International
Type: Missionary
Grades: K-8
Enrollment: 30

Address: Quisqueya Christian School
M.F.I.-Haiti, Box 15665,
West Palm Beach, FL 33406
USA
Affiliation: Independent
Type: Missionary
Grades: P-12
Enrollment: 281
Notes: Special Education

HONDURAS

Address: Academia Los Pinares
Apartado 143-C, Tegucigalpa DC
Honduras
Affiliation: Multi-Mission
Type: Missionary
Grades: P-12
Enrollment: 454

INDONESIA

Address: Bandung Alliance School
J1 Gunung Agung 14,
Bandung 40141, Java
Indonesia
Affiliation: C&MA
Type: Missionary
Grades: 1-6
Enrollment: 40

Address: Hillcrest International School
Tromol Pos 4, Sentani 99000,
Irian Jaya
Indonesia
Affiliation: Multi-Mission
Type: Missionary
Grades: 9-12
Enrollment: 25
Notes: Boarding Facilities

Address: Sentani International School
Kotak Pos 239, Sentani, Irian Jaya
99352
Indonesia
Affiliation: C&MA
Type: Missionary
Grades: 1-8
Enrollment: 100
Notes: Boarding Facilities

Address: Wesley International School
Kotak Pos 88, Malang 65101 East Java
Indonesia
Affiliation: OMS International
Type: Missionary
Grades: K-7
Enrollment: 32

JAPAN

Address: Christian Academy in Japan
1-2-14 Shinkawa Cho, Higashi
Kurume Shi, Tokyo 203
Japan
Affiliation: Multi-Mission
Type: Missionary
Grades: K-12
Enrollment: 285
Notes: Boarding Facilities

Address: Kansai Christian School
951 Tawaraguchi Cho, Ikoma Shi,
Nara Ken 630-02
Japan
Affiliation: Multi-Mission
Type: Missionary
Grades: 1-12
Enrollment: 40

Address: Neighborhood School
P.O. Box 4, Okinawa City 904, Okinawa
Japan
Affiliation: Assemblies of God
Type: National
Grades: P-12
Enrollment: 260

Address: Okinawa Christian School
P.O. Box 42, Urasoe City,
Okinawa 901-21
Japan
Affiliation: Okinawa Christian School Assoc.
Type: Missionary
Grades: P-12
Enrollment: 308

KENYA

Address: Hannah Hunter Cole Memorial School
Box 53435, Nairobi
Kenya
Affiliation: Conservative Bapt. Foreign Mission
Type: Missionary
Grades: K-8
Enrollment: 13

Address: Rift Valley Academy
P.O. Box 80, Kijabe
Kenya
Affiliation: Africa Inland Mission
Type: Missionary
Grades: K-12
Enrollment: 480
Notes: Boarding Facilities

Address: Rosslyn Academy
P.O. Box 14146, Nairobi
Kenya
Affiliation: Assemblies of God, Baptist, Mennonites
Type: Missionary
Grades: K-10
Enrollment: 218
Notes: Special Education

INTERNATIONAL SCHOOLS cont.

KOREA

Address: Korea Christian Academy
O-Jung Dong, Taejon 300-210
Korea
Affiliation: Southern Baptist, Southern Presbyterian
Type: Missionary
Grades: K-12
Enrollment: 75

Address: Liberty Christian School
P.O. Box 23, Uijongbu 480-600
Korea
Affiliation: Liberty Mission of Korea
Type: Missionary
Grades: P-12
Enrollment: 271

LIBERIA

Address: Barnes Foundation School
P.O. Box 2029, Monrovia
Liberia
Affiliation:
Type: National
Grades: P-9
Enrollment: 119

Address: ELWA Academy
P.O. Box 192, Monrovia
Liberia
Affiliation: SIM International
Type: Missionary
Grades: P-8
Enrollment: 170

Address: West Africa Christian High School
P.O. Box 37, Monrovia
Liberia
Affiliation: SIM Intl & Assemblies of God
Type: Missionary
Grades: 9-11
Enrollment: 25

MALAYSIA

Address: Dalat School
Tanjong Bungah, 11200 Penang
Malaysia
Affiliation: C&MA
Type: Missionary
Grades: 1-12
Enrollment: 194
Notes: Boarding Facilities

MEXICO

Address: Colegio Emaus
Apartado Postal 991, Hermosillo, Sonora
Mexico
Affiliation: Emmaus Evangelical Fellowship
Type: National
Grades: K-12
Enrollment: 165

Address: Puebla Christian School
Apartado 511, 72000 Puebla, Puebla
Mexico
Affiliation: CAM Intl & UFM Intl
Type: Missionary
Grades: 1-9
Enrollment: 36
Notes: Special Education

NEW ZEALAND

Address: Hebron Christian College
P.O. Box 77-105, Mt. Albert, Auckland 3
New Zealand
Affiliation: Auckland Christian Fellowship
Type: National
Grades: K-12
Enrollment: 166

NIGER

Address: Sahel Academy
B.P. 10065, Niamey
Niger
Affiliation: SIM Francophone
Type: Missionary
Grades: 1-9
Enrollment: 29
Notes: Boarding Facilities

NIGERIA

Address: Good Shepherd Christian Academy
P.M.B. 100 Akot Anta P.A., Ukanafun,
Akwa Ibom State
Nigeria
Affiliation: Independent
Type: National
Grades: P-5
Enrollment: 60
Notes: Boarding Facilities/Special Education

NORTHERN MARIANA ISLANDS

Address: Grace Christian Academy
Navy Hill 643 C.K., Saipan, MP 96950
Northern Mariana Islands
Affiliation: Saipan First Assemblies of God
Type: National
Grades: K-12
Enrollment: 154

PAKISTAN

Address: Murree Christian School
P.O. Jhika Gali, Murree Hills
Pakistan

Affiliation: Multi-Mission
Type: Missionary
Grades: K-12
Enrollment: 170
Notes: Boarding Facilities

PALAU, REPUBLIC OF

Address: Bethania High School
Koror, W. Caroline Islands 96940
Republic of Palau
Affiliation: Palau Evang. Church & Liebenzell Mission
Type: National
Grades: 0-12
Enrollment: 89
Notes: Boarding Facilities

PANAMA

Address: Hogar Misionero
Chame
Panama
Affiliation: New Tribes Mission
Type: Missionary
Grades: 1-12
Enrollment: 27
Notes: Boarding Facilities

PAPUA NEW GUINEA

Address: Aiyura International Primary School
Box 407, Ukarumpa Via Lae
Papua New Guinea
Affiliation: Summer Inst. of Linguistics
Type: Missionary
Grades: K-6
Enrollment: 290

Address: New Tribes Mission School
P.O. Box 1079, Goroka
Papua New Guinea
Affiliation: New Tribes Mission
Type: Missionary
Grades: K-12
Enrollment: 144
Notes: Boarding Facilities

PARAGUAY

Address: Asuncion Christian Academy
Casilla 1562, Asuncion
Paraguay
Affiliation: Multi-Mission
Type: Missionary
Grades: P-12
Enrollment: 191

PHILIPPINES

Address: Faith Academy
P.O. Box 820, 1299 Makati
Philippines
Affiliation: Multi-Mission
Type: Missionary
Grades: K-12
Enrollment: 638
Notes: Boarding Facilities/Special Education

Address: Grace Christian High School
P.O. Box 2712, Manila
Philippines
Type: National
Grades: P-12
Enrollment: 5001

PORTUGAL

Address: Greater Lisbon Christian Academy
Rua Marechal Carmona, 27,
Loures 2670
Portugal
Affiliation: Assn of Baptist for World Evangelism
Type: Missionary
Grades: K-12
Enrollment: 35

Address: InterNational
Avenida de Sintra Lote #1, Cascais 2750
Portugal
Affiliation: Independent
Type: Missionary
Grades: P-7
Enrollment: 37

PUERTO RICO

Address: Academia Menonita
Collins Esq Asomante, Caparra Heights
00920
Puerto Rico
Affiliation: Mennonite Church
Type: National
Grades: P-12
Enrollment: 695

Address: Carib Christian School
P.O. Box 470, Ramey Stn., Aguadilla
00604
Puerto Rico
Affiliation: Borinquen Baptist Church
Type: National
Grades: P-9
Enrollment: 470

Address: Wesleyan Academy
Box 1489, Guaynabo 00657
Puerto Rico
Affiliation: Wesleyan Church Corp.
Type: National
Grades: P-12
Enrollment: 800

SENEGAL

Address: Dakar Academy
B.P. 3189, Dakar
Senegal
Affiliation: Multi-Mission
Type: Missionary

INTERNATIONAL SCHOOLS cont.

Grades: K-10
Enrollment: 95
Notes: Boarding Facilities

SIERRA LEONE

Address: Kabala Rupp Memorial School
Box 28, Kabala Via Freetown
Sierra Leone
Affiliation: Multi-Mission
Type: Missionary
Grades: 1-9
Enrollment: 23
Notes: Boarding Facilities

SPAIN

Address: Evangelical Christian Academy
Calle Talia 26, 28022 Madrid
Spain
Affiliation: Multi-Mission
Type: Missionary
Grades: K-12
Enrollment: 45

TAIWAN R.O.C.

Address: Morrison Academy - Taipei
Ting Chou Lu 705, P.O. Box 30-134, Taipei 10098
Taiwan R.O.C.
Affiliation: Morrison Christian Assn.
Type: Missionary
Grades: K-8

Address: Morrison Academy - Kaohsiung
400 Hsin Hsing Lane, Kao Tan, Jen Wu District, Kaohsiung 81405
Taiwan R.O.C.
Affiliation: Morrison Christian Assn.
Type: Missionary
Grades: K-8

Address: Morrison Academy - Taichung
Box 27-24, Taichung 40098
Taiwan R.O.C.
Affiliation: Morrison Christian Assn.
Type: Missionary
Grades: K-12
Notes: Boarding Facilities/Special Education

Address: Morrison Academy - Taitung
P.O. Box 90, Taitung 95099
Taiwan R.O.C.
Affiliation: Morrison Christian Assn.
Type: Missionary
Grades: K-8

TONGA

Address: Lavengamalie Christian School
P.O. Box 367, Nuku'alofa
Tonga
Affiliation: Tokaikolo Christian Fellowship
Type: National
Grades: P-12
Enrollment: 1300

VENEZUELA

Address: Christiansen Academy
Apartado 75, San Cristobal, Tachira
Venezuela
Affiliation: Evangelical Alliance Mission
Type: Missionary
Grades: 1-12
Enrollment: 85
Notes: Boarding Facilities/Special Education

Address: Colegio American de Aragua
Apartado 530, Maracay, Aragua 2101A
Venezuela
Affiliation: Evangelical Free Church of America
Type: Missionary
Grades: K-8
Enrollment: 27

VIRGIN ISLANDS

Address: School of the Good Shepherd
P.O. Box 1069, Kingshill Saint Croix 00851
Virgin Islands
Affiliation:
Type: National
Grades: P-8
Enrollment: 151

Address: St. Croix Christian Academy
P.O. Box 712, Christiansted 00821
Virgin Islands
Affiliation: First Assembly of God
Type: National
Grades: P-5
Enrollment: 195

WEST AFRICA

Address: International Christian Academy
BP 1171, Bouake 01, Cote d'Ivoire
West Africa
Affiliation: Multi-Mission
Type: Missionary
Grades: 1-12
Enrollment: 202
Notes: Boarding Facilities

Address:	Vavoua International School BP 131, Vavoua, Cote d'Ivoire West Africa
Affiliation:	WEC International
Type:	Missionary
Grades:	1-12
Enrollment:	47
Notes:	Boarding Facilities

ZAMBIA

Address:	Sakeji School P.O. Box 20, Ikelenge, Via Kitwe Zambia
Affiliation:	Brethren Missions
Type:	Missionary
Grades:	1-9
Enrollment:	99
Notes:	Boarding Facilities

Source: Association of Christian Schools International, LaHabra, CA. Used by permission.

FOCUS FACT

Only one book survived a 1764 fire that totally destroyed the original Harvard library. The title: *Christian Warfare Against the Devil, World, and Flesh.*

HOW TO FIND MORE SCHOOL INFORMATION

For information regarding additional Christian schools write:

- Christian Schools International, 3350 E. Paris Ave, S.E., P.O. Box 8709, Grand Rapids, MI 49518-8709
- American Association of Christian Schools, Box 1088, Fairfax, VA 22030
- Association of Christian Schools International, P.O. Box 4097, Whittier, CA 90607

For information regarding schools affiliated with Lutheran churches write:

- Wisconsin Evangelical Lutheran Synod, 2929 Mayfair Road, Milwaukee, WI 53222 (386 schools)
- The Lutheran Church—Missouri Synod, 1333 S. Kirkwood Road, St. Louis, MO 63122-7295 (1099 schools)
- Evangelical Lutheran Church in America, 8765 W. Higgins Road, Chicago, IL 60631-4194 (154 schools)

THE TEN LARGEST CHURCH-RELATED ELEMENTARY/HIGH SCHOOLS IN THE U.S.

School	*Address*	*Affiliation*	*Grades*	*Enroll*
1. Pensacola Christian School	Pensacola FL	Baptist	P-12	1937
2. Dayton Christian Schools Inc.	Dayton OH	Independent	K-12	1860
3. Village Christian Schools	Sun Valley CA	Village Church	K-12	1821
4. Trinity Christian Academy	Jacksonville FL	Baptist	P-12	1544
5. Evangelical Christian Schools	Memphis TN	Interdenominational	K-12	1426
6. Dade Christian School	Hialeah FL	Baptist	P-12	1375
7. North Florida Christian School	Tallahassee FL	Baptist	P-12	1286
8. Friends Christian School	Yorba Linda CA	Friends	P-8	1252
9. Crista Schools	Seattle WA	Crista Ministries	P-12	1166
10. The King's Academy	West Palm Beach FL	Baptist	K-12	1163

The Voices of Tomorrow

At the annual meeting of the National Association of Student Councils in Prairie View, Illinois, in July 1989, USA TODAY asked the high school student leaders about their attitudes and their hopes for the future. Among their replies:

When looking for a college, cost is uppermost in students' minds:

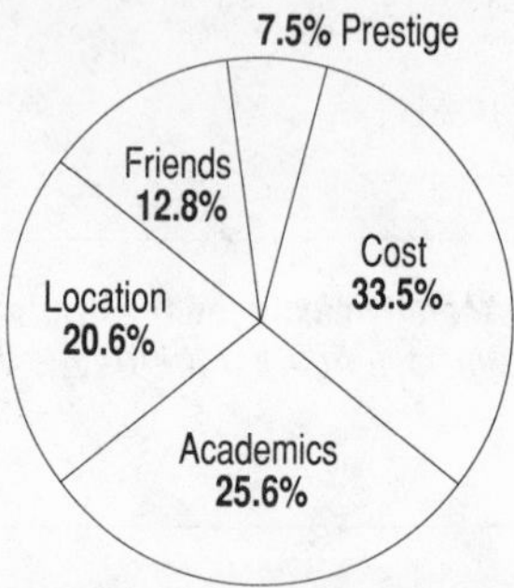

Looking to the future, marriage is slightly more important than career:

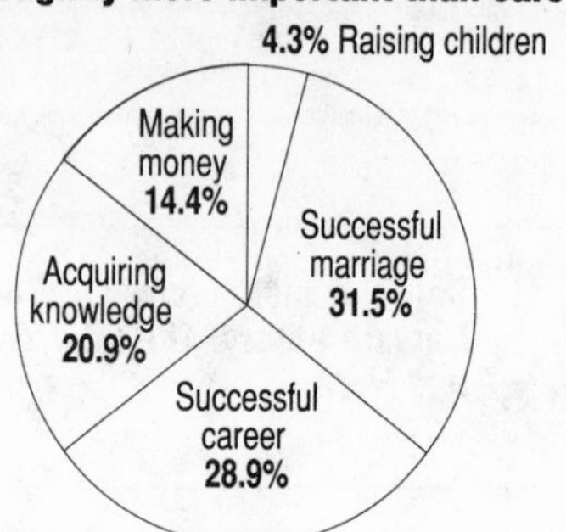

The biggest influence on their lives?

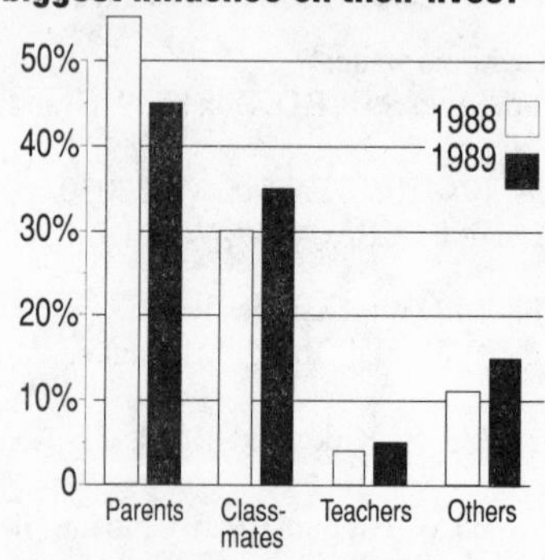

What's most important in a job?

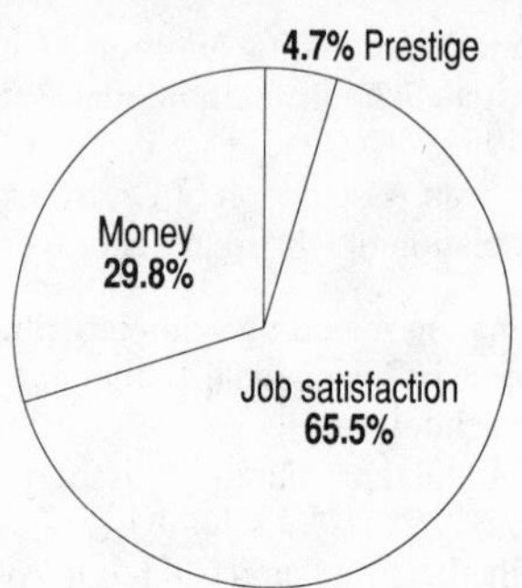

Personality is the most important attribute in a spouse:

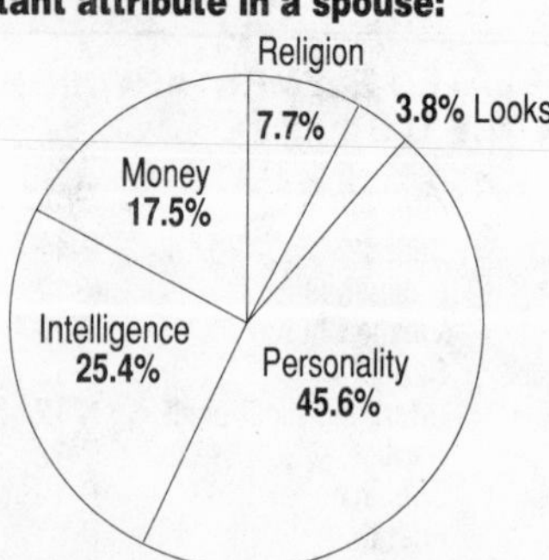

Main concern for the world's future is the environment:

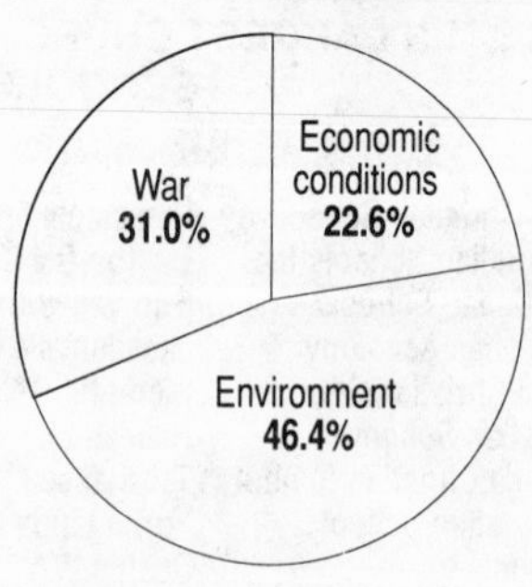

Source: USA TODAY poll of 703 high school student leaders

AMERICANS WANT RELIGION IN SCHOOLS

Question: Here are some sample questions about the Bible, including both Old and New Testaments. Please tell me whether you would or would not object to the public schools. . . .

	Would not object %	*Would object* %	*No opinion* %
Teaching about the major religions of the world	79	16	5
Using the Bible in literature, history, and social studies classes	75	20	5
Making facilities available after school hours for use by student organizations	74	21	5
Offering elective courses in Bible studies	75	20	5

Source: *100 Questions and Answers: Religion in America* by George Gallup, Jr. and Sarah Jones. Published by Princeton Religion Research Center. Copyright 1989. Used by permission.

HOW MANY TEENS CAN NAME THE TEN COMMANDMENTS?

Commandments Named:	*All teenagers* %	*Regular churchgoers* %	*Non-regular* %
Don't steal	68	73	63
Don't commit adultery	61	69	54
Don't murder	59	67	52
Don't covet	37	45	30
Honor father and mother	34	45	24
Don't bear false witness	29	36	22
Don't take God's name in vain	28	33	24
Don't have other gods	25	35	15
Keep Sabbath Day	16	24	9
Don't worship idols	10	13	7

Source: Gallup Poll, *Emerging Trends.*

CHURCH-RELATED COLLEGES AND UNIVERSITIES

Entrance difficulty rating, as determined by the schools themselves: 1—30% acceptance rate; 2—60% acceptance rate; 3—85% acceptance rate; 4—95% acceptance rate; 5—100% acceptance rate.

School	*City, ST*	*Affiliation*	*Enroll*	*Tuition / Board*	*Diff./Type*
United States					
Adrian College	Adrian, MI	United Methodist	1207	$8096 / $2545	3 / LA
Agnes Scott College	Decatur, GA	Presbyterian—Women's college	591	$10450 / $4180	2 / LA

School	*City, ST*	*Affiliation*	*Enroll*	*Tuition / Board*	*Diff./Type*
Alaska Bible College	Glennallen, AK	Nondenominational	70	$2060 / $3200	5 / BC
Alaska Pacific University	Anchorage, AK	United Methodist	809	$6330 / $3870	3 / LA
Albion College	Albion, MI	Methodist	1700	$9222 / $3682	3 / LA
Albright College	Reading, PA	United Methodist	1306	$11956 / $3620	2 / LA
Alderson-Broaddus College	Philippi, WV	Baptist	759	$7336 / $2490	3 / LA
Allegheny College	Meadville, PA	United Methodist	1956	$14000 / $3890	3 / LA
Alma College	Alma, MI	Presbyterian	1241	$9852 / $3626	3 / LA
American Baptist College	Nashville, TN	Baptist	167	$1805 / $1884	/ BC
American Indian Bible College	Phoenix, AZ	Assemblies of God	99	$2530 / $2340	5 / BC
American University	Washington, DC	Methodist	10153	$12100 / $5100	3 / LA
Anderson University	Anderson, IN	Church of God	2115	$7330 / $2610	3 / LA
Appalachian Bible College	Bradley, WV	Baptist	186	$3390 / $2600	4 / BC
Arizona College of the Bible	Phoenix, AZ	Independent	130	$3790 / $1420 (Room)	4 / BC
Arkansas Baptist College	Little Rock, AR	Baptist	268	$1670 / $2200	5 / BC
Arkansas College	Batesville, AR	Presbyterian	831	$5330 / $2660	3 / LA
Arlington Baptist College	Arlington, TX	Baptist	182	$2350 / $2350	5 / BC
Asbury College	Wilmore, KY	Nondenominational	1082	$6734 / $2271	3 / LA
Ashland University	Ashland, OH	Brethren	4391	$8632 / $3568	3 / LA
Atlanta Christian College	East Point, GA	Independent	180	$3208 / $2200	4 / LA
Atlantic Christian College	Wilson, NC	Christian Church (Dscpls of Christ)	1434	$5700 / $2570	3 / LA
Augsburg College	Minneapolis, MN	Lutheran	2702	$8835 / $3328	3 / LA
Augustana College	Rock Island, IL	Lutheran	2267	$10308 / $3492	3 / LA
Augustana College	Sioux Falls, SD	Evangelical Lutheran Church in Amer	2004	$8640 / $2650	3 / LA
Austin College	Sherman, TX	Presbyterian	1227	$8735 / $3498	3 / LA
Averett College	Danville, VA	Baptist	1216	$7900 / $4100	3 / LA
Azusa Pacific University	Azusa, CA	Interdenominational	2933	$7740 / $3400	3 / LA
Baker University	Baldwin City, KS	United Methodist	1,121	$5995 / $2990	3 / LA
Baldwin-Wallace College	Berea, OH	Methodist	4713	$9225 / $3675	3 / LA
Baptist Bible College	Springfield, MO	Baptist	815	$1490 / $2190	5 / BC
Baptist Bible College of Pennsylvania	Clarks Summit, PA	Baptist	620	$4979 / $2971	4 / BC
Baptist College at Charleston	Charleston, SC	Baptist	2051	$5832 / $2902	3 / LA
Barber-Scotia College	Concord, SC	Presbyterian Church (USA)	383	$3000 / $2487	5 / LA
Bartlesville Wesleyan College	Bartlesville, OK	Wesleyan	465	$4495 / $3600	4 / LA
Bay Ridge Christian College*	Kendleton, TX	Church of God	45	N/A / N/A	N/A / BC
Baylor University	Waco, TX	Baptist	11774	$5620 / $3485	3 / LA
Beaver College	Glenside, PA	Presbyterian Church (USA)	2294	$9210 / $4225	3 / LA
Belhaven College	Jackson, MS	Presbyterian	721	$5850 / $2100	3 / LA
Belmont College	Nashville, TN	Baptist	2706	$5250 / $2650	3 / LA
Benedict College	Columbia, SC	Baptist	1616	$4571 / $2280	5 / LA
Bennett College	Greensboro, NC	United Methodist	572	$5230 / $2250	3 / LA
Berean College	Springfield, MO	Assemblies of God	685	(cred)$59 / N/A	5 / LA
Bethany Bible College	Scotts Valley, CA	Assemblies of God	465	$5725 / $3000	4 / LA
Bethany College	Bethany, WV	Christian Church (Dscpls of Christ)	825	$9700 / $3630	3 / LA
Bethany College	Lindsborg, KS	Lutheran	736	$6067 / $2912	3 / LA
Bethel College	McKenzie, TN	Cumberland Presbyterian	536	$4100 / $2350	4 / LA
Bethel College	Mishawaka, IN	Missionary Church	585	$6410 / $2500	4 / LA
Bethel College	North Newton, KS	General Conference Mennonite	605	$6182 / $2800	3 / LA
Bethel College	St. Paul, MN	Baptist General Conference	1832	$9250 / $3380	3 / LA
Bethune-Cookman College	Daytona Beach, FL	Methodist	2145	$4134 / $2545	4 / LA
Biola University	La Mirada, CA	Nondenominational	2566	$9172 / $3820	3 / LA
Birmingham-Southern College	Birmingham, AL	Methodist	1937	$8435 / $3280	3 / LA

School	City, ST	Affiliation	Enroll	Tuition / Board	Diff./Type
Blackburn College	Carlinville, IL	Presbyterian	486	$7420 / $3300	3 / LA
Bloomfield College	Bloomfield, NJ	Presbyterian	1605	$7050 / $3500	4 / LA
Blue Mountain College	Blue Mountain, MS	Southern Baptist	355	$3120 / $1940	4 / LA
Bluefield College	Bluefield, VA	Baptist	435	$5020 / $3320	3 / LA
Bluffton College	Bluffton, OH	Mennonite	625	$7065 / $2901	3 / LA
Bob Jones University	Greenville, SC	Independent	4367	$3340 / $3060	2 / LA
Boise Bible College	Boise, ID	Nondenominational	65	$2826 / $2450	5 / BC
Brewton-Parker College	Mt. Vernon, GA	Southern Baptist	1804	$3150 / $2130	5 / LA
Bridgewater College	Bridgewater, VA	Church of the Brethren	985	$8520 / $3960	3 / LA
Bryan College	Dayton, TN	Interdenominational	551	$5270 / $3200	3 / LA
Buena Vista College	Storm Lake, IA	Presbyterian	1045	$8953 / $2794	3 / LA
California Baptist College	Riverside, CA	Southern Baptist	673	$5410 / $3130	4 / LA
California Lutheran University	Thousand Oaks, CA	Lutheran	2853	$8730 / $4000	3 / LA
Calvary Bible College	Kansas City, MO	Independent	317	$3500 / $2440	5 / BC
Calvin College	Grand Rapids, MI	Christian Reformed	4325	$6790 / $2860	3 / LA
Campbell University	Buies Creek, NC	Baptist	4820	$6386 / $2515	3 / LA
Campbellsville College	Campbellsville, KY	Baptist	642	$4500 / $2760	3 / LA
Capital University	Columbus, OH	Evangelical Lutheran Church in Amer	3008	$9530 / $3330	3 / LA
Carroll College	Waukesha, WI	Presbyterian	1478	$9360 / $3070	3 / LA
Carson-Newman College	Jefferson City, TN	Southern Baptist	2017	$6100 / $2580	3 / LA
Carthage College	Kenosha, WI	Lutheran Church in America	2002	$9400 / $3350	3 / LA
Catawba College	Salisbury, NC	United Church of Christ	1044	$7300 / $3500	3 / LA
Cedar Crest College	Allentown, PA	United Church of Christ	962	$9680 / $4180	3 / LA
Cedarville College	Cedarville, OH	Baptist	1942	$5238 / $3255	3 / LA
Centenary College	Hackettstown, NJ	Methodist	820	$9550 / $4575	3 / LA
Centenary College of Louisiana	Shreveport, LA	Methodist	1033	$6180 / $2910	3 / LA
Central Baptist College	Conway, AR	Baptist	183	$2040 / $1700	4 / BC
Central Bible College	Springfield, MO	Assemblies of God	972	$3120 / $2600	4 / BC
Central Christian College of the Bible	Moberly, MO	Christian Churches/ Churches of Christ	73	$2280 / $2000	5 / BC
Central College*	McPherson, KS	Free Methodist	275	$5200 / $2700	N/A / LA
Central Indian Bible College*	Mobridge, SD	Assemblies of God	55	N/A / N/A	N/A / BC
Central Methodist College	Fayette, MO	Methodist	754	$6160 / $2950	3 / LA
Central University of Iowa	Pella, IA	Reformed Church in America	1751	$8725 / $3172	3 / LA
Central Wesleyan College	Central, SC	Wesleyan	439	$6500 / $2820	4 / LA
Centre College	Danville, KY	Presbyterian	855	$8568 / $3355	2 / LA
Chapman College	Orange, CA	Christian Church (Dscpls of Christ)	2221	$11910 / $4640	3 / LA
Christ College Irvine	Irvine, CA	Lutheran Church—Missouri Synod	569	$7995 / $2310	3 / LA
Christian Heritage College	El Cajon, CA	Baptist	340	$6240 / $3100	3 / LA
Cincinnati Bible College	Cincinnati, OH	Church of Christ	614	$3366 / $2826	5 / LA
Circleville Bible College	Circleville, OH	Churches of Christ	148	$2960 / $2580	4 / BC
Claflin College	Orangeburg, SC	United Methodist	850	$4118 / $1890	4 / LA
Clear Creek Baptist Bible College	Pineville, KY	Southern Baptist	153	$1780 / $2000	5 / BC
Clearwater Christian College	Clearwater, FL	Nondenominational	310	$3600 / $3000	4 / LA
Coe College	Cedar Rapids, IA	Presbyterian	1217	$9430 / $3600	3 / LA
College of Idaho	Caldwell, ID	Presbyterian	1189	$8550 / $2300	3 / LA
College of Wooster	Wooster, OH	Presbyterian	1787	$11,570/3660	3 / LA
Colorado Christian University	Lakewood, CO	Interdenominational	781	$4380 / $1980	3 / LA
Columbia Bible College	Columbia, SC	Independent	938	$4265 / $2445	3 / BC
Columbia College	Columbia, MO	Christian Church (Dscpls of Christ)	704	$6498 / $2935	4 / LA
Columbia College	Columbia, SC	United Methodist	1173	$7600 / $2890	3 / LA
Concordia College	Ann Arbor, MI	Lutheran Church—Missouri Synod	416	$6326 / $3290	3 / LA
Concordia College	Moorhead, MN	Lutheran	2884	$8125 / $2525	3 / LA
Concordia University	River Forest, IL	Lutheran Church—Missouri Synod	1275	$6896 / $3363	3 / LA

School	City, ST	Affiliation	Enroll	Tuition / Board	Diff./Type
Concordia College	St. Paul, MN	Lutheran Church—Missouri Synod	1128	$7800 / $2850	4 / LA
Concordia College	Bronxville, NY	Lutheran	416	$7540 / $3900	3 / LA
Concordia College	Portland, OR	Lutheran Church—Missouri Synod	555	$7050 / $2800	4 / LA
Concordia Lutheran College	Austin, TX	Lutheran Church	607	$5960 / $3000	4 / LA
Concordia Univ., Wisconsin	Mequon, WI	Wisconsin Synod	1480	$6700 / 3100	3 / LA
Concordia Lutheran Theological Seminary	St. Catharines, ON	Lutheran Church—Missouri Synod	42	N/A / N/A	N/A / LA
Concordia Teachers College	Seward, NE	Lutheran Church—Missouri Synod	810	$5750 / $2500	3 / LA
Cornell College	Mount Vernon, IA	Methodist	1147	$9980 / $3510	3 / LA
Covenant College	Lookout Mountain, GA	Presbyterian Church in America	580	$7550 / $3250	3 / LA
Crichton College	Memphis, TN	Independent	348	$3900 / $1350	4 / LA
Criswell College Studies	Dallas, TX	Southern Baptist	379	$2680 / N/A	5 / BC
Culver-Stockton College	Canton, MO	Christian Church (Dscpls of Christ)	1067	$6160 / $2340	3 / LA
Cumberland College	Williamsburg, KY	Southern Baptist	1881	$3980 / $2476	4 / LA
Dakota Wesleyan University	Mitchell, SD	United Methodist	640	$5700 / $2500	3 / LA
Dallas Baptist University	Dallas, TX	Southern Baptist	2269	$4620 / $2923	3 / LA
Dallas Christian College	Dallas, TX	Christian Churches/ Churches of Christ	92	$2203 / $2590	4 / LA
Dana College	Blair, NE	Evangelical Lutheran Church in Amer	486	$6420 / $2520	3 / LA
Davidson College	Davidson, NC	Presbyterian	1400	$11327 / $3567	2 / LA
Davis & Elkins College	Elkins, WV	Presbyterian	856	$6853 / $3512	4 / LA
Deaconess College of Nursing	St. Louis, MO	United Church of Christ	197	$5000 / $2000	3 / LA
Defiance College, The	Defiance, OH	United Church of Christ	1006	$7184 / $3040	3 / LA
Depauw University	Greencastle, IN	United Methodist	2415	$10550 / $3860	3 / LA
Doane College	Crete, NE	United Church of Christ	671	$7250 / $2325	3 / LA
Dordt College	Sioux Center, IA	Christian Reformed	1038	$6400 / $2240	3 / LA
Dr. Martin Luther College	New Ulm, MN	Wisconsin Evangelical Lutheran Synod	443	$3132 / $1650	5 / LA
Drew University	Madison, NJ	United Methodist	2289	$13992 / $4376	2 / LA
Drury College	Springfield, MO	Christian Church (Dscpls of Christ)	1395	$6950 / $2740	3 / LA
Duke University	Durham, NC	United Methodist	10376	$14123 / $5066	1 / LA
Earlham College	Richmond, IN	Friends	1267	$11610 / $3393	3 / LA
East Coast Bible College	Charlotte, NC	Church of God	273	$2790 / $1850	4 / BC
East Texas Baptist University	Marshall, TX	Baptist	811	$4050 / $2752	3 / LA
Eastern College	St. Davids, PA	American Baptist	1282	$8720 / $3470	3 / LA
Eastern Mennonite College	Harrisonburg, VA	Mennonite	969	$6895 / $3080	3 / LA
Eastern Nazarene College	Quincy, MA	Nazarene	912	$7020 / $3100	3 / LA
Eckerd College	St. Petersburg, FL	Presbyterian	1351	$10895 / $3030	3 / LA
Edward Waters College	Jacksonville, FL	African Methodist Episcopal	686	$3000 / $3540	N/A / LA
Elizabethtown College	Elizabeth, PA	Church of the Brethren	1878	$10700 / $3750	2 / LA
Elmhurst College	Elmhurst, IL	United Church of Christ	3007	$7276 / $2850	3 / LA
Elon College	Elon, NC	United Church of Christ	3368	$6170 / $3150	3 / LA
Emmanuel Coll Schl of Christian Minist	Franklin Springs, GA	Pentecostal Holiness	38	$3360 / $2490	5 / BC
Emmaus Bible College	Dubuque, IA	Nondenominational	178	$1700 / $3580	5 / BC
Emory & Henry College	Emory, VA	United Methodist	853	$6800 / $3700	3 / LA
Emory University	Atlanta, GA	Methodist	9398	$13700 / $4300	2 / LA
Erskine College	Due West, SC	Associate Reformed Presbyterian	514	$8760 / $3105	3 / LA
Eugene Bible College	Eugene, OR	Open Bible Standard Church	118	$3192 / $2250	4 / BC
Eureka College	Eureka, IL	Christian Church (Dscpls of Christ)	438	$7775 / $2920	3 / LA

School	*City, ST*	*Affiliation*	*Enroll*	*Tuition / Board*	*Diff./Type*
Evangel College	Springfield, MO	Assemblies of God	1525	$5278 / $2730	3 / LA
Faith Baptist Bible College	Ankeny, IA	Regular Baptist	299	$3514 / $2494	5 / BC
Ferrum College	Ferrum, VA	Methodist	1238	$6500 / $3000	3 / LA
Fisk University	Nashville, TN	United Church of Christ	891	$4665 / $2285	3 / LA
Fla. Bapt. Theological College	Graceville, FL	Southern Baptist	386	$1254 / (rm only)$900	5 / BC
Florida Bible College	Kissimmee, FL	Independent	131	$2740 / $1700	5 / BC
Florida Christian College	Kissimmee, FL	Christian Churches/ Churches of Christ	127	$3140 / $1466	4 / BC
Florida Southern College	Lakeland, FL	United Methodist	1955	$6080 / $3870	3 / LA
Fort Wayne Bible College*	Fort Wayne, IN	Missionary Church	385	N/A / N/A	N/A / BC
Franklin College of Indiana	Franklin, IN	American Baptist	801	$7700 / $2825	3 / LA
Free Will Baptist Bible College	Nashville, TN	Free Will Baptist	269	$2770 / $2560	5 / LA
Fresno Pacific College	Fresno, CA	Mennonite Brethren	1364	$6780 / $3010	3 / LA
Friends Bible College	Haviland, KS	Friends	104	$5975 / $2500	5 / BC
Friends University	Wichita, KS	Friends	1287	$6575 / $2400	3 / LA
Furman University	Greenville, SC	Baptist	2794	$9874 / $3632	2 / LA
Gardner-Webb College	Boiling Springs, NC	Baptist	2189	$5770 / $3200	3 / LA
Geneva College	Beaver Falls, PA	Reformed Presbyterian	1308	$6670 / $3250	3 / LA
George Fox College	Newberg, OR	Friends	944	$8135 / $3400	3 / LA
Georgetown College	Georgetown, KY	Baptist	1562	$5266 / $3150	3 / LA
Gettysburg College	Gettysburg, PA	Evangelical Lutheran Church in Amer	1950	$13625 / $3160	2 / LA
God's Bible School & College	Cincinnati, OH	Interdenominational	210	$2525 / $2090	4 / BC
Gordon College	Wenham, MA	Interdenominational	1216	$10700 / $3406	3 / LA
Goshen College	Goshen, IN	Mennonite	1152	$7205 / $3105	3 / LA
Grace Bible College	Grand Rapids, MI	Grace Gospel Fellowship	113	$3355 / $2400	4 / BC
Grace College	Winona Lake, IN	Brethren	738	$6550 / $3200	3 / LA
Grace College of the Bible	Omaha, NE	Independent	312	$3392 / $2140	3 / BC
Grand Canyon University	Phoenix, AZ	Southern Baptist	1842	$4928 / $2280	3 / LA
Grand Rapids Baptist College	Grand Rapids, MI	Baptist	902	$4846 / $3330	4 / LA
Grand Rapids Schl of the Bible and Music*	Grand Rapids, MI	Independent	185	N/A / N/A	N/A / BC
Grand View College	Des Moines, IA	Evangelical Lutheran Church in Amer	1407	$6740 / $2720	4 / LA
Great Lakes Bible College	Lansing, MI	Independent	132	$3390 / $2460	4 / BC
Greensboro College	Greensboro, NC	United Methodist	1078	$6000 / $3000	3 / LA
Greenville College	Greenville, IL	Free Methodist	743	$7761 / $3300	3 / LA
Grove City College	Grove City, PA	Presbyterian	2125	$4390 / $2390	3 / LA
Guilford College	Greensboro, NC	Friends	1155	$9540 / $3922	3 / LA
Gustavus Adolphus College	St. Peter, MN	Evangelical Lutheran Church in Amer	2349	$11000 / $2750	2 / LA
Hamline University	St. Paul, MN	United Methodist	2235	$10865 / $3809	3 / LA
Hampden-Sydney College	Hampden-Sydney, VA	Presbyterian	944	$11117 / $3741	2 / LA
Hannibal-LaGrange College	Hannibal, MO	Southern Baptist	995	$4300 / $1900	5 / LA
Hanover College	Hanover, IN	Presbyterian	1072	$5750 / $2540	3 / LA
Hardin-Simmons University	Abilene, TX	Baptist	1863	$4930 / $2410	3 / LA
Hastings College	Hastings, NE	Presbyterian	953	$6990 / $2610	3 / LA
Heidelberg College	Tiffin, OH	United Church of Christ	1303	$10100 / $3220	3 / LA
Hendrix College	Conway, AR	United Methodist	1029	$6653 / $2595	3 / LA
Hesston College*	Hesston, KS	Mennonite	550	$5200 / $3000	N/A / LA
High Point College	High Point, NC	United Methodist	2023	$6085 / $2985	3 / LA
Hillsdale Free Will Baptist College	Moore, OK	Free Will Baptist	135	$2355 / $2540	5 / LA
Hiram College	Hiram, OH	Christian Church (Dscpls of Christ)	930	$11116 / $3531	3 / LA
Hobart College	Geneva, NY	Episcopal	1105	$15346 / $4899	2 / LA
Hobe Sound Bible College	Hobe Sound, FL	Nondenominational	182	$3100 / $2215	5 / BC
Hood College	Frederick, MD	United Church of Christ	1976	$10780 / $5345	3 / LA
Hope College	Holland, MI	Reformed Church in America	2770	$9426 / $3610	3 / LA

School	*City, ST*	*Affiliation*	*Enroll*	*Tuition / Board*	*Diff./Type*
Houghton College	Houghton, NY	Wesleyan	1164	$8123 / $3044	3 / LA
Houston Baptist University	Houston, TX	Baptist	2243	$4720 / $2595	3 / LA
Howard Payne University	Brownwood, TX	Southern Baptist	1283	$3950 / $2420	4 / LA
Huntingdon College	Montgomery, AL	United Methodist	838	$5160 / $2900	3 / LA
Huntington College	Huntington, IN	United Brethren in Christ	611	$7370 / $3010	3 / LA
Illinois College	Jacksonville, IL	Interdenominational	813	$5000 / $2900	3 / LA
Illinois Wesleyan University	Bloomington, IL	United Methodist	1749	$10085 / $3475	2 / LA
Independent Baptist College*	Dallas, TX	Baptist	35	N/A / N/A	N/A / BC
Indiana Wesleyan University	Marion, IN	Wesleyan	1068	$6420 / $2930	3 / LA
International Bible College	Florence, AL	Churches of Christ	131	$1889 / $700 (Room)	5 / BC
Iowa Wesleyan College	Mt. Pleasant, IA	United Methodist	803	$6500 / $2750	3 / LA
Jamestown College	Jamestown, ND	Presbyterian	841	$6420 / $2980	3 / LA
Jarvis Christian College	Hawkins, TX	Christian Church (Dscpls of Christ)	543	$3631 / $2712	4 / LA
John Brown University	Siloam Springs, AR	Nondenominational	930	$4980 / $2860	3 / LA
John Wesley College	High Point, NC	Interdenominational	60	$3740 / $1200	4 / BC
Johnson Bible College	Knoxville, TN	Christian Churches/ Churches of Christ	434	$3050 / $3275	4 / BC
Jordan College*	Cedar Springs, MI	Nondenominational	2280	$4165 / N/A	4 / LA
Judson College	Elgin, IL	Baptist	522	$7040 / $3590	3 / LA
Judson College	Marion, AL	Baptist	420	$3930 / $2390	3 / LA
Kansas City College & Bible School	Overland Park, KS	Church of God	81	$2495 / $2353	4 / BC
Kansas Wesleyan University	Salina, KS	United Methodist	761	$6220 / $2900	3 / LA
Kendall College	Evanston, IL	United Methodist	400	$6051 / $3777	3 / LA
Kentucky Christian College	Grayson, KY	Christian Churches/ Churches of Christ	479	$3028 / $2760	4 / BC
Kentucky Mountain Bible* Institute	Vancleve, KY	Holiness	45	N/A / N/A	5 / BC
Kentucky Wesleyan College	Owensboro, KY	Methodist	850	$5600 / $3100	3 / LA
King College	Bristol, TN	Presbyterian Church (USA)	588	$5900 / $3050	3 / LA
King's College	Briarcliff Manor, NY	Nondenominational	513	$7515 / $3520	3 / LA
Knoxville College	Knoxville, TN	Presbyterian	1225	$4890 / $3400	5 / LA
Lafayette College	Easton, PA	Presbyterian Church (USA)	1993	$14000 / $4600	2 / LA
LaGrange College	LaGrange, GA	United Methodist	964	$4975 / $3315	3 / LA
Lakeland College	Sheboygan, WI	United Church of Christ	1766	$7445 / $3100	3 / LA
Lambuth College	Jackson, TN	United Methodist	804	$4200 / $2800	3 / LA
Lancaster Bible College	Lancaster, PA	Nondenominational	289	$5720 / $2690	4 / BC
Lane College	Jackson, TN	Christian Methodist Episcopal	525	$4000 / $2242	4 / LA
Lebanon Valley College	Annville, PA	United Methodist	1303	$10650 / $4240	3 / LA
Lee College	Cleveland, TN	Church of God	1535	$4013 / $2700	4 / LA
Lees-McRae College	Banner Elk, NC	Presbyterian Church (USA)	833	$5000 / $2700	4 / LA
Lemoyne-Owen College	Memphis, TN	Independent	1130	$3600 / N/A	5 / LA
Lenoir-Rhyne College	Hickory, NC	Lutheran	1853	$8060 / $3300	3 / LA
LeTourneau University	Longview, TX	Nondenominational	773	$6802 / $3680	3 / LA
Liberty University	Lynchburg, VA	Baptist	16605	$4750 / $3400	4 / LA
LIFE Bible College	Los Angeles, CA	Church of Foursquare Gospel	370	$3670 / $2325	5 / LA
Lincoln Christian College	Lincoln, IL	Christian Churches/ Churches of Christ	357	$3610 / $2410	4 / BC
Lindenwood College	St. Charles, MO	Presbyterian	2105	$7680 / $3900	3 / LA
Lindsey Wilson College	Columbia, KY	United Methodist	1153	$4832 / $2980	5 / LA
Linfield College	McMinnville, OR	American Baptist	1312	$9490 / $3050	3 / LA
Livingstone College	Salisbury, NC	African Methodist Episcopal Zion	558	$3774 / $2468	4 / LA
Louisiana College	Pineville, LA	Southern Baptist	1242	$3860 / $2532	3 / LA

School	*City, ST*	*Affiliation*	*Enroll*	*Tuition / Board*	*Diff./Type*
Lubbock Christian University	Lubbock, TX	Church of Christ	1075	$5180 / $2330	5 / LA
Luther College	Decorah, IA	Evangelical Lutheran Church in Amer	2299	$9750 / $3100	3 / LA
Lutheran Bible Institute of Seattle	Issaquah, WA	Lutheran	138	$2410 / $3085	4 / BC
Lycoming College	Williamsport, PA	United Methodist	1204	$10200 / $3650	3 / LA
Lynchburg College	Lynchburg, VA	Christian Church (Dscpls of Christ)	2559	$8800 / $4300	3 / LA
Macalester College	St. Paul, MN	Presbyterian	1855	$11542 / $3500	2 / LA
MacMurray College	Jacksonville, IL	United Methodist	620	$7650 / $3170	3 / LA
Magnolia Bible College	Kosciusko, MS	Churches of Christ	53	$2400 / $1100	5 / BC
Malone College	Canton, OH	Evangelical Friends	1457	$6744 / $2800	3 / LA
Manchester College	North Manchester, IN	Church of the Brethren	1100	$7260 / $2810	3 / LA
Manhattan Christian College	Manhattan, KS	Christian Churches/ Churches of Christ	206	$3010 / $2320	5 / BC
Manna Bible Institute*	Philadelphia, PA	Independent	50	N/A / N/A	N/A / BC
Maranatha Baptist Bible College	Watertown, WI	Baptist	477	$3150 / $2470	5 / BC
Mars Hill College	Mars Hill, NC	Baptist	1344	$5650 / $2700	4 / LA
Mary Baldwin College	Staunton, VA	Presb Church (USA)/ Women's College	684	$8050 / $5550	3 / LA
Maryville College	Maryville, TN	Presbyterian	787	$7750 / $3550	3 / LA
Master's College	Newhall, CA	Nondenominational	1008	$6450 / $3690	3 / LA
McKendree College	Lebanon, IL	United Methodist	1098	$6331 / $2980	3 / LA
McMurry University	Abilene, TX	United Methodist	1720	$4950 / $2270	3 / LA
McPherson College	McPherson, KS	Church of the Brethren	462	$5930 / $2960	3 / LA
Mercer University	Macon, GA	Baptist	3985	$5895 / $3375	3 / LA
Mercer University Atlanta	Atlanta, GA	Baptist	1300	$5895 / N/A	3 / LA
Meredith College	Raleigh, NC	Baptist	2212	$4910 / $2470	3 / LA
Messiah College	Grantham, PA	Brethren in Christ	2280	$8070 / $3990	3 / LA
Methodist College	Fayetteville, NC	United Methodist	1447	$6650 / $2850	4 / LA
Miami Christian College	Miami, FL	Nondenominational	180	$4480 / $2880	3 / BC
Mid-America Bible College	Oklahoma City, OK	Church of God	236	$4118 / $2440	4 / BC
Mid-Continent Baptist Bible College	Mayfield, KY	Baptist	109	$1550 / $1312	5 / BC
MidAmerica Nazarene College	Olathe, KS	Nazarene	1189	$5090 / $2990	5 / LA
Midland Lutheran College	Fremont, NE	Lutheran	935	$7590 / $2400	3 / LA
Midway College	Midway, KY	Christian Church (Dscpls of Christ)	522	$4700 / $3250	4 / LA
Miles College	Birmingham, AL	Christian Methodist Episcopal	620	$3700 / $2300	N/A / LA
Milligan College	Milligan College, TN	Independent	760	$5742 / $2606	3 / LA
Millikin University	Decatur, IL	Presbyterian (USA)	1805	$9256 / $3544	3 / LA
Millsaps College	Jackson, MS	United Methodist	1443	$8196 / $3080	3 / LA
Minnesota Bible College	Rochester, MN	Christian Churches/ Churches of Christ	100	$2910 / $1050 (Room)	4 / BC
Mississippi College	Clinton, MS	Southern Baptist	4221	$4432 / $2260	3 / LA
Missouri Baptist College	St. Louis, MO	Southern Baptist	1032	$5030 / $2300	4 / LA
Missouri Valley College	Marshall, MO	Presbyterian	1177	$7479 / $4356	3 / LA
Mobile College	Mobile, AL	Baptist	1190	$4350 / $2892	4 / LA
Monmouth College	Monmouth, IL	Presbyterian	672	$10635 / $3000	3 / LA
Montreat-Anderson College	Montreat, NC	Presbyterian	414	$5250 / $3000	4 / LA
Moody Bible Institute	Chicago, IL	Independent	1507	$650 / $3600	3 / BC
Moravian College	Bethlehem, PA	Moravian	1785	$11660 / $3780	3 / LA
Morningside College	Sioux City, IA	United Methodist	1240	$8466 / $2830	3 / LA
Morris Brown College	Atlanta, GA	African Methodist Episcopal	1805	$6040 / $3250	3 / LA
Morris College	Sumter, SC	Baptist	796	$3540 / $2255	5 / LA
Mount Olive College	Mount Olive, NC	Free Will Baptist	996	$5500 / $2550	4 / LA
Mount Union College	Alliance, OH	United Methodist	1359	$10680 / $3100	3 / LA

School	City, ST	Affiliation	Enroll	Tuition / Board	Diff./Type
Mount Vernon Nazarene College	Mount Vernon, OH	Nazarene	1061	$5490 / $2840	3 / LA
Muhlenberg College	Allentown, PA	Lutheran	1630	$14100 / $3935	2 / LA
Multnomah School of the Bible	Portland, OR	Interdenominational	659	$4650 / $2600	4 / BC
Muskingum College	New Concord, OH	Presbyterian Church (USA)	1122	$10325 / $3080	3 / LA
Nazarene Bible College*	Colorado Springs, CO	Nazarene	520	N/A / N/A	N/A / BC
Nebraska Christian College	Norfolk, NE	Christian Churches/ Churches of Christ	129	$2290 / $3010	4 / BC
Nebraska Wesleyan University	Lincoln, NE	United Methodist	1607	$7188 / $2570	3 / LA
Newberry College	Newberry, SC	Lutheran	701	$6600 / $2600	3 / LA
North Carolina Wesleyan College	Rocky Mount, NC	United Methodist	1475	$6400 / $3100	3 / LA
North Central Bible College	Minneapolis, MN	Assemblies of God	1174	$4420 / $2810	5 / BC
North Central College	Naperville, IL	United Methodist	2555	$9186 / $3528	3 / LA
North Park College	Chicago, IL	Evangelical Covenant	1098	$9930 / $3765	3 / LA
Northeastern Bible College*	Essex Fells, NJ	Nondenominational	200	$5400 / $2800	3 / BC
Northland College	Ashland, WI	United Church of Christ	721	$7510 / $3240	3 / LA
Northwest Christian College	Eugene, OR	Interdenominational	216	$5270 / $3072	4 / LA
Northwest College of the Assemblies of God	Kirkland, WA	Assemblies of God	695	$5150 / $2300	4 / LA
Northwest Nazarene College	Nampa, ID	Nazarene	1133	$6510 / $2490	3 / LA
Northwestern College	Orange City, IA	Reformed Church in America	1064	$7400 / $2700	3 / LA
Northwestern College	St. Paul, MN	Interdenominational	1036	$7575 / $2520	3 / LA
Northwestern College	Watertown, WI	Wisconsin Evangelical Lutheran (Men's College)	218	$2915 / $1580	3 / LA
Nyack College	Nyack, NY	C&MA	814	$6380 / $3080	4 / BC
Oak Hills Bible College	Bemidji, MN	Independent	112	$3330 / $2280	4 / BC
Oakland City College	Oakland City, IN	General Baptist	648	$6146 / $2480	5 / LA
Ohio Northern University	Ada, OH	United Methodist	2595	$10845 / $3195	3 / LA
Ohio Wesleyan University	Delaware, OH	United Methodist	1966	$12328 / $4526	2 / LA
Oklahoma Baptist University	Shawnee, OK	Baptist	2173	$3826 / $2450	3 / LA
Oklahoma City University	Oklahoma City, OK	Methodist	3778	$4558 / $3060	3 / LA
Olivet College	Olivet, MI	Congregational Christian Church	766	$6860 / $2715	3 / LA
Olivet Nazarene University	Kankakee, IL	Nazarene	1875	$5548 / $3078	4 / LA
Oral Roberts University	Tulsa, OK	Nondenominational	4170	$5595 / $3660	3 / LA
Ottawa University	Ottawa, KS	American Baptist	525	$5600 / $2760	3 / LA
Otterbein College	Westerville, OH	United Methodist	2315	$9261 / $3414	3 / LA
Ouachita Baptist University	Arkadelphia, AR	Baptist	1316	$4410 / $2000	3 / LA
Ozark Christian College	Joplin, MO	Christian Church (Dscpls of Christ)	535	$2080 / $1990	5 / BC
Pacific Christian College	Fullerton, CA	Nondenominational	535	$4350 / $3000	3 / LA
Pacific Coast Bapt. Bible College	San Dimas, CA	Baptist	N/A	N/A / N/A	N/A / BC
Pacific Lutheran University	Tacoma, WN	Evangelical Lutheran	3855	$10449 / $3780	3 / LA
Paine College	Augusta, GA	Methodist	580	$4950 / $2585	4 / LA
Palm Beach Atlantic College	West Palm Beach, FL	Southern Baptist	1375	$4960 / $2650	3 / LA
Patten College	Oakland, CA	Interdenominational	333	$3310 / $3508	4 / LA
Paul Quinn College	Waco, TX	African Methodist Episcopal	517	$2900 / $2750	5 / LA
Pfeiffer College	Misenheimer, NC	United Methodist	905	$6620 / $2960	3 / LA
Philadelphia College of Bible	Langhorne, PA	Nondenominational	578	$5870 / $3400	3 / BC
Philander Smith College	Little Rock, AR	United Methodist	620	$2150 / $1150	5 / LA
Phillips University	Enid, OK	Christian Church (Dscpls of Christ)	1005	$7627 / $2462	3 / LA
Piedmont Bible College	Winston-Salem, NC	Baptist	276	$2890 / $2100	5 / BC
Piedmont College	Demorest, GA	Congregational Christian Church	529	$2736 / $2680	4 / LA

School	*City, ST*	*Affiliation*	*Enroll*	*Tuition / Board*	*Diff./Type*
Pikeville College	Pikeville, KY	Presbyterian Church (USA)	915	$3900 / $2350	5 / LA
Pillsbury Baptist Bible College	Owatonna, MN	Baptist	411	$3250 / $2296	5 / LA
Point Loma Nazarene College	San Diego, CA	Nazarene	2221	$7221 / $3390	4 / LA
Practical Bible Training School*	Johnson City, NY	Independent	160	N/A / N/A	N/A / BC
Presbyterian College	Clinton, SC	Presbyterian	1146	$9458 / $3024	3 / LA
Puget Sound Christian College	Edmonds, WA	Christian Church/ Churches of Christ	82	$3915 / $2700	5 / LA
Queens College	Charlotte, NC	Presbyterian	1573	$8300 / $4200	3 / LA
Randolph-Macon College	Ashland, VA	United Methodist	1120	$9280 / $3945	3 / LA
Randolph-Macon Woman's College	Lynchburg, VA	Methodist	750	$10860 / $4750	3 / LA
Reformed Bible College	Grand Rapids, MI	Independent	193	$4320 / $2500	5 / BC
Regent University*	Virginia Beach, VA	Interdenominational	850	$2900 / N/A	N/A / LA
Rhodes College	Memphis, TN	Presbyterian	1386	$11628 / $4282	2 / LA
Roanoke Bible College	Elizabeth City, NC	Independent Christian	112	$2000 / $2060	4 / BC
Roanoke College	Salem, VA	Evangelical Lutheran Church in Amer	1696	$9400 / $3600	3 / LA
Roberts Wesleyan College	Rochester, NY	Free Methodist	824	$8082 / $2826	3 / LA
Rocky Mountain College	Billings, MT	Interdenominational	705	$5800 / $2883	3 / LA
Rust College	Holly Springs, MS	United Methodist	925	$3000 / $1500	3 / LA
Saint Augustine's College	Raleigh, NC	Episcopal	1885	$4150 / $2950	4 / LA
Saint Paul's College	Lawrenceville, VA	Episcopal	736	$4288 / $2855	4 / LA
Salem College	Winston-Salem, NC	Moravian	886	$9075 / $5600	3 / LA
Samford University	Birmingham, AL	Baptist	4159	$5500 / $2754	3 / LA
San Jose Christian College	San Jose, CA	Independent	184	$4806 / $2460	5 / BC
Schreiner College	Kerrville, TX	Presbyterian	618	$6700 / $4300	3 / LA
Seattle Pacific University	Seattle, WA	Free Methodist	3435	$9000 / $3432	3 / LA
Sheldon Jackson College	Sitka, AK	Presbyterian	290	$5390 / $4100	5 / LA
Shenandoah College and Conservatory	Winchester, VA	United Methodist	1016	$7400 / $3500	3 / LA
Shorter College	Rome, GA	Baptist	883	$5000 / $3070	3 / LA
Simpson College	Indianola, IA	Methodist	1737	$8985 / $3100	3 / LA
Simpson College	Redding, CA	C&MA	206	$5672 / $3300	4 / BC
Sioux Falls College	Sioux Falls, SD	American Baptist	962	$6210 / $2575	3 / LA
Southeastern Baptist College	Laurel, MS	Baptist	62	$2220 / $1700	5 / BC
Southeastern Bible College	Birmingham, AL	Nondenominational	141	$3470 / $2576	3 / BC
Southeastern Coll of the Assemblies of God	Lakeland, FL	Assemblies of God	1130	$2805 / $2360	5 / BC
Southern Baptist College	Walnut Ridge, AR	Southern Baptist	517	$2706 / $1812	4 / LA
Southern California College	Costa Mesa, CA	Assemblies of God	898	$6360 / $3100	3 / LA
Southern Methodist University	Dallas, TX	United Methodist	8924	$9880 / $4498	3 / LA
Southern Nazarene University	Bethany, OK	Nazarene	1402	$3696 / $2822	5 / LA
Southwest Baptist University	Bolivar, MO	Southern Baptist	2920	$5785 / $2210	5 / LA
Southwestern Assemblies of God College	Waxahachie, TX	Assemblies of God	701	$3390 / $2512	5 / BC
Southwestern Coll of Christian Ministr	Bethany, OK	Pentecostal Holiness	97	$3139 / $2270	4 / BC
Southwestern College	Phoenix, AZ	Conservative Baptist	126	$4320 / $1960	4 / BC
Southwestern College	Winfield, KS	United Methodist	649	$4152 / $2484	3 / LA
Southwestern University	Georgetown, TX	Methodist	1219	$7600 / $3994	2 / LA
Spring Arbor College	Spring Arbor, MI	Free Methodist	807	$7246 / $2783	4 / LA
St. Andrews Presbyterian College	Laurinburg, NC	Presbyterian	794	$7650 / $3445	3 / LA
St. Louis Christian College	Florissant, MO	Independent Christian	143	$2870 / $1915	4 / LA
St. Olaf College	Northfield, MN	Lutheran	3132	$11200 / $3100	2 / LA
St. Paul Bible College	St. Bonifacius, MN	C&MA	560	$5850 / $3016	4 / BC
Sterling College	Sterling, KS	Presbyterian	457	$6250 / $2800	4 / LA
Stetson University	DeLand, FL	Baptist	3090	$9285 / $3670	3 / LA
Stillman College*	Tuscaloosa, AL	Presbyterian	750	$3550 / $2440	3 / LA
Summit Christian College	Fort Wayne, IN	Missionary Church	371	$5420 / $2610	4 / LA
Susquehanna University	Selinsgrove, PA	Lutheran	1529	$13120 / $3850	3 / LA

School	*City, ST*	*Affiliation*	*Enroll*	*Tuition / Board*	*Diff./Type*
Tabor College	Hillsboro, KS	Mennonite Brethren	436	$5590 / $2750	3 / LA
Tarkio College	Tarkio, MO	Presbyterian	553	$6760 / $3200	3 / LA
Taylor University	Upland, IN	Independent	1708	$8183 / $3142	3 / LA
Teikyo Westmar University	LeMars, IA	Methodist	566	$7493 / $2948	4 / LA
Tennessee Temple University	Chattanooga, TN	Baptist	1130	$3870 / $3064	4 / LA
Tennessee Wesleyan College	Athens, TN	United Methodist	605	$4614 / $2876	4 / LA
Texas Christian University	Fort Worth, TX	Christian Church (Dscpls of Christ)	6725	$7096 / $2580	3 / LA
Texas College	Tyler, TX	Methodist Episcopal	441	$3150 / $2430	5 / LA
Texas Lutheran College	Seguin, TX	Evangelical Lutheran Church in Amer	1015	$5300 / $2940	3 / LA
Texas Wesleyan University	Fort Worth, TX	United Methodist	1561	$5200 / $3180	3 / LA
Thiel College	Greenville, PA	Evangelical Lutheran Church in Amer	918	$7830 / $3800	3 / LA
Toccoa Falls College	Toccoa Falls, GA	C&MA	795	$4130 / $2750	3 / BC
Transylvania University	Lexington, KY	Christian Church (Dscpls of Christ)	1076	$8906 / $3748	3 / LA
Trevecca Nazarene College	Nashville, TN	Nazarene	1436	$4775 / $2450	5 / LA
Trinity Bible College	Ellendale, ND	Assemblies of God	410	$3848 / $2988	5 / BC
Trinity Christian College	Palos Heights, IL	Christian Reformed	534	$6890 / $2910	3 / LA
Trinity College	Deerfield, IL	Evangelical Free	849	$8130 / $3690	3 / LA
Trinity College of Florida*	Holiday, FL	Independent	125	N/A / N/A	N/A / BC
Trinity University	San Antonio, TX	Presbyterian	2573	$9676 / $4050	2 / LA
Tusculum College	Greenville, TN	Presbyterian	642	$5544 / $3000	3 / LA
Union College	Barbourville, KY	United Methodist	1050	$5020 / $2320	3 / LA
Union University	Jackson, TN	Southern Baptist	1730	$3900 / $2030	3 / LA
United Wesleyan College*	Allentown, PA	Wesleyan	165	$5200 / $2700	5 / BC
University of Dubuque	Dubuque, IA	Presbyterian	1126	$7945 / $2850	3 / LA
University of Evansville	Evansville, IN	United Methodist	3290	$8600 / $3320	3 / LA
University of Findlay	Findlay, OH	Church of God	1799	$7375 / $3186	3 / LA
University of Indianapolis	Indianapolis, IN	United Methodist	3119	$7590 / $3050	3 / LA
University of Mary Hardin-Baylor	Belton, TX	Southern Baptist	1762	$4380 / $2600	4 / LA
University of Puget Sound	Tacoma, WA	Methodist	3303	$11420 / $3800	2 / LA
University of Richmond	Richmond, VA	Baptist	4909	$10850 / $2765	2 / LA
University of the Nations*	Kailu-Kona, HI	Interdenominational	1450	$5800 / $2850	N/A / LA
University of The Ozarks	Clarksville, AR	Presbyterian	796	$3010 / $2160	3 / LA
University of the South	Sewanee, TN	Episcopal	1075	$12720 / $3010	2 / LA
University of Tulsa	Tulsa, OK	Presbyterian	4318	$7450 / $3100	3 / LA
Upsala College	East Orange, NJ	Evangelical Lutheran Church in Amer	990	$8850 / $3940	3 / LA
Ursinus College	Collegeville, PA	United Church of Christ	1100	$11520 / $4250	2 / LA
Valley Forge Christian College	Phoenixville, PA	Assemblies of God	529	$3076 / $2524	4 / BC
Valparaiso University	Valparaiso, IN	Lutheran Church—Missouri Synod	3858	$9070 / $2700	3 / LA
Vennard College	University Park, IA	Interdenominational	153	$3869 / $2050	4 / BC
Virginia Intermont College	Bristol, VA	Baptist	521	$5980 / $3620	4 / LA
Virginia Union University	Richmond, VA	Baptist	1200	$5840 / $3010	4 / LA
Virginia Wesleyan College	Norfolk, VA	United Methodist	1280	$7400 / $3900	3 / LA
Voorhees College	Denmark, SC	Episcopal	590	$5672 / $2522	4 / LA
Wake Forest University	Winston-Salem, NC	Baptist	5337	$9700 / $2470	2 / LA
Warner Pacific College	Portland, OR	Church of God	450	$7044 / $3188	3 / LA
Warner Southern College	Lake Wales, FL	Church of God	423	$4850 / $2740	4 / LA
Warren Wilson College	Swannanoa, NC.	Presbyterian Church (USA)	523	$7550 / $812	3 / LA
Wartburg College	Waverly, IA	Lutheran	1456	$8860 / $2960	3 / LA
Washington Bible College	Lanham, MD	Nondenominational	315	$4978 / $3070	3 / BC
Wayland Baptist University	Plainview, TX	Baptist	2052	$3670 / $2390	4 / LA
Waynesburg College	Waynesburg, PA	Presbyterian Church (USA)	1155	$6706 / $2860	3 / LA
Wesley College	Dover, DE	United Methodist	1200	$6475 / $3675	3 / LA
Wesley College	Florence , MS	Independent	50	$1600 / $2000	5 / LA

School	*City, ST*	*Affiliation*	*Enroll*	*Tuition / Board*	*Diff./Type*
Wesleyan College	Macon, GA	Methodist Women's College	522	$7490 / $3850	3 / LA
West Coast Christian College	Fresno, CA	Church of God	160	N/A / N/A	N/A / LA
W. Virginia Wesleyan College	Buckhannon, WV	United Methodist	1571	$10930 / $3000	3 / LA
Western Baptist College	Salem, OR	Baptist	358	$6225 / $2943	4 / BC
Westminster College	Fulton, MO	Presbyterian	734	$7700 / $3300	3 / LA
Westminster College	New Wilmington, PA	Presbyterian Church (USA)	1554	$9550 / $2730	3 / LA
Westmont College	Santa Barbara, CA	Independent	1256	$11530 / $4650	3 / LA
Wheaton College	Wheaton, IL	Nondenominational	2548	$8836 / $3640	2 / LA
Whitworth College	Spokane, WA	Presbyterian	1788	$9090 / $3425	3 / LA
Wilberforce University	Wilberforce, OH	African Meth. Episcopal	779	$6092 / $3170	4 / LA
Wiley College	Marshall, TX	United Methodist	406	$3946 / $2544	5 / LA
Willamette University	Salem, OR	United Methodist	2223	$9980 / $3550	2 / LA
William Carey College	Hattiesburg, MS	Southern Baptist	1600	$4352 / $2120	4 / LA
William Jewell College	Liberty, MO	Baptist	1400	$7450 / $2530	3 / LA
William Penn College	Oskaloosa, IA	Friends	671	$7800 / $2320	3 / LA
William Tyndale College	Farmington Hills, MI	Independent	383	$4410 / $3060	4 / LA
William Woods College	Fulton, MO	Christian Church (Dscpls of Christ)	750	$7400 / $3200	3 / LA
Wilmington College	Wilmington, OH	Friends	890	$7660 / $2900	3 / LA
Wilson College	Chambersburg, PA	Presbyterian	792	$10076 / $4530	3 / LA
Wingate College	Wingate, NC	Baptist	1690	$5070 / $2550	3 / LA
Wisconsin Lutheran College	Milwaukee, WI	Wisconsin Evangelical Lutheran	273	$6360 / $3000	3 / LA
Wittenberg University	Springfield, OH	Evangelical Lutheran Church in Amer	2340	$12,747 / $3843	3 / LA
Wofford College	Spartanburg, SC	United Methodist	1121	$8085 / $3700	3 / LA
Canadian					
Aldersgate College	Moose Jaw, SK	Free Methodist	47	$3150 / $2290	5 / LA
Bethany Bible College	Sussex, NB	Wesleyan	165	$2750 / $2650	4 / BC
Briercrest Bible College	Caronport, SK	Interdenominational	870	$2519 / $2270	3 / BC
Canadian Bible College	Regina, SK	C&MA	415	$3191 / $3000	5 / BC
Catherine Booth Bible College*	Winnipeg, MB	Salvation Army	60	N/A / N/A	N/A / BC
Central Baptist Bible College*	Toronto, ON	Baptist	65	N/A / N/A	N/A / BC
Central Pentecostal College	Saskatoon, SK	Pentecostal	75	$1880 / $2600	5 / BC
College of Emmanuel and St. Chad	Saskatoon, SK	Episcopal	46	$1220 / $3045	5 / LA
Columbia Bible College*	Clearbrook, BC	Mennonite	220	N/A / N/A	N/A /
Eastern Pentecostal Bible College*	Peterborough, ON	Pentecostal	500	N/A / N/A	N/A / BC
Emmanuel Bible College	Kitchener, ON	Missionary Church	211	2596 / 2600	3 / BC
Hillcrest Christian College	Medicine Hat, AB	Congregational	75	$2420 / $2200	4 / BC
King's College*	Edmonton, AB	Nondenominational	295	$2785 / $1155	3 / LA
London Baptist Bible College*	London, ON	Baptist	160	N/A / N/A	N/A / BC
Mennonite Brethren Bible College	Winnipeg, MB	Mennonite Brethren	85	$1800 / $2550	5 / BC
North American Baptist College*	Edmonton, AB	North American Baptist	220	$1900 / $2800	3 / BC
Northwest Baptist Theological College*	Vancouver, BC	Baptist	160	N/A / N/A	N/A / BC
Northwest Bible College*	Edmonton, AB	Pentecostal	140	N/A / N/A	N/A / BC
Ontario Bible College	Willowdale, ON	Independent	343	$2786 / $3124	3 / BC
Redeemer College	Ancaster, ON	Interdenominational	373	$6043 / $2958	N/A / LA
Steinbach Bible College*	Steinbach, MB	Mennonite	80	N/A / N/A	N/A / BC
Trinity Western University	Langley, BC	Evangelical Free	1300	$5525 / $3760	3 / LA
Western Pentecostal Bible College	Clayburn, BC	Pentecostal Assemblies	224	$2297 / $2760	4 / BC
Winnipeg Bible College	Otterburne, MB	Nondenominational	307	$3240 / $2710	5 / BC

Source: *Peterson's Guide to Four-Year Colleges, 1991* © 1990 Peterson's Guides Inc. Used by permission. * indicates college not listed in *Peterson's Guide to Four-Year Colleges.*

COLLEGES AND UNIVERSITIES THAT OFFER CORRESPONDENCE AND/OR VIDEO COURSES

Baptist Bible College
628 E. Kearney
Springfield, MO 65803

Briercrest Bible College
Caronport, SK
S0H 0S0

Central Bible College
3000 N. Grant
Springfield, MO 65803

Cincinnati Bible College
2700 Glenway Avenue
Cincinnati, OH 45204

Columbia Bible College
P.O. Box 3122
Columbia, SC 29230

Emmaus Bible College
2570 Asbury Road
Dubuque, IA 52001

Eugene Bible College
2155 Bailey Hill Road
Eugene, OR 97405

Evangel College
Springfield, MO 65802

Fort Wayne Bible College
1025 W. Rudisill Blvd.
Ft. Wayne, IN 46807

Johnson Bible College
7900 Johnson Drive
Knoxville, TN 37998

Kentucky Christian College
617 N. Carol Malone Blvd.
Grayson, KY 41143

LIFE Bible College
1100 Glendale Blvd.
Los Angeles, CA 90026

Mid-America Bible College
3500 S.W. 119th Street
Oklahoma City, OK 73170

Moody Bible Institute
820 N. LaSalle Drive
Chicago, IL 60610

North Central Bible College
910 Elliot Avenue South
Minneapolis, MN 55404

Ontario Bible College
25 Ballyconnor Ct.
Willowdale, ON M2M 4B3

Philadelphia College of Bible
Langhorne Manor
Langhorne, PA 19047

Reformed Bible College
1869 Robinson Road
Grand Rapids, MI 49506

Regent University
3765 Candlers Mountain Road
Box 20000
Lynchburg, VA 24506

Seattle Pacific University
W 3307 Third Avenue
Seattle, WA 98119

Southeastern Bible College
2901 Pawnee Avenue
Birmingham, AL 35256

Southeastern College of Assemblies of God
1000 Longfellow Blvd.
Lakeland, FL 33801

Southwestern Assemblies of God College
1200 Sycamore
Waxahachie, TX 75156

Tennessee Temple University
1815 Union Avenue
Chattanooga, TN 37404

Trinity Bible College
50 South Sixth Avenue
Ellendale, ND 58436

Valley Forge Christian College
Charlestown Road
Phoenixville, PA 19460

Washington Bible College
6511 Princess Garden Pkwy
Lanham, MD 20706

Westminster Theological Seminary
Box 27009
Philadelphia, PA 19118

FOCUS FACT

The practice of awarding honorary degrees dates back to 1692 when Harvard bestowed a doctorate on Professor Increase Mather. By giving him this more distinguished title, Harvard tried to ensure that Mather would be successful when he was sent to England to raise money for the college.
—From *Alma Mater* by Don Betterton, published by Peterson's Guides.

MOST SELECTIVE CHURCH-RELATED COLLEGES

With the exception of Duke, the following schools have been listed by *Peterson's Guide* with an entrance difficulty of 2, which indicates a 60 percent acceptance rate. Duke is the only religious-based school that carries a rating of 1, which indicates a 30 percent acceptance rate.

School	*City ST*	*Affiliation*
Duke University	Durham, NC	United Methodist
Agnes Scott College	Decatur, GA	Presbyterian—Women's
Albright College	Reading, PA	United Methodist
Bob Jones University	Greenville, SC	Independent
Centre College	Danville, KY	Presbyterian
Davidson College	Davidson, NC	Presbyterian
Drew University	Madison, NJ	United Methodist
Elizabethtown College	Elizabeth, PA	Church of the Brethren
Emory University	Atlanta, GA	Methodist
Furman University	Greenville, SC	Baptist
Gettysburg College	Gettysburg, PA	Evang. Lutheran Church in Am.
Gustavus Adolphus College	St. Peter, MN	Evang. Lutheran Church in Am.
Hampden-Sydney College	Hampden-Sydney, VA	Presbyterian
Hobart College	Geneva, NY	Episcopal
Illinois Wesleyan University	Bloomington, IL	United Methodist
Lafayette College	Easton, PA	Presbyterian Church (USA)
Macalester College	St. Paul, MN	Presbyterian
Muhlenberg College	Allentown, PA	Lutheran
Ohio Wesleyan University	Delaware, OH	United Methodist
Rhodes College	Memphis, TN	Presbyterian
Southwestern University	Georgetown, TX	Methodist
St. Olaf College	Northfield, MN	Lutheran
Trinity University	San Antonio, TX	Presbyterian
University of Puget Sound	Tacoma, WA	Methodist
University of Richmond	Richmond, VA	Baptist
University of the South	Sewanee, TN	Episcopal
Ursinus College	Collegeville, PA	United Church of Christ
Wake Forest University	Winston-Salem, NC	Baptist
Wheaton College	Wheaton, IL	Nondenominational

FIFTEEN LARGEST CHURCH-RELATED COLLEGES/UNIVERSITIES

School	*City ST*	*Affiliation*	*Enrollment*
Liberty University	Lynchburg, VA	Baptist	16605
Baylor University	Waco, TX	Baptist	11774
Duke University	Durham, NC	United Methodist	10376
American University	Washington, DC	Methodist	10153
Emory University	Atlanta, GA	Methodist	9398
Southern Methodist University	Dallas, TX	United Methodist	8924
Texas Christian University	Fort Worth, TX	Christian Church	6725
Wake Forest University	Winston-Salem, NC	Baptist	5337
University of Richmond	Richmond, VA	Baptist	4909
Campbell University	Buies Creek, NC	Baptist	4820
Baldwin-Wallace College	Berea, OH	Methodist	4713

Ashland University	Ashland, OH	Brethren	4391
Bob Jones University	Greenville, SC	Independent	4367
Calvin College	Grand Rapids, MI	Christian Reformed	4325
University of Tulsa	Tulsa, OK	Presbyterian	4318

FOCUS FACT

Five of the nine colonial colleges in America were established as a result of the First Great Awakening: Dartmouth College; Princeton University; Rutgers University; University of Pennsylvania; and Brown University.

TWENTY MOST EXPENSIVE CHURCH-RELATED COLLEGES

	Tuition	*School*	*City ST*	*Affiliation*
1.	$15346	Hobart College	Geneva, NY	Episcopal
2.	$14123	Duke University	Durham, NC	United Methodist
3.	$14100	Muhlenberg College	Allentown, PA	Lutheran
4.	$14000	Allegheny College	Meadville, PA	United Methodist
5.	$14000	Lafayette College	Easton, PA	Presbyterian
6.	$13992	Drew University	Madison, NJ	United Methodist
7.	$13700	Emory University	Atlanta, GA	Methodist
8.	$13625	Gettysburg College	Gettysburg, PA	Evangelical Lutheran
9.	$13120	Susquehanna University	Selinsgrove, PA	Lutheran
10.	$12747	Wittenberg University	Springfield, OH	Evangelical Lutheran
11.	$12720	University of the South	Sewanee, TN	Episcopal
12.	$12328	Ohio Wesleyan University	Delaware, OH	United Methodist
13.	$12100	American University	Washington, DC	Methodist
14.	$11956	Albright College	Reading, PA	United Methodist
15.	$11910	Chapman College	Orange, CA	Christian Church
16.	$11660	Moravian College	Bethlehem, PA	Moravian
17.	$11628	Rhodes College	Memphis, TN	Presbyterian
18.	$11610	Earlham College	Richmond, IN	Friends
19.	$11570	College of Wooster	Wooster, OH	Presbyterian
20.	$11542	Macalester College	St. Paul, MN	Presbyterian

BELIEFS AND BEHAVIOR OF COLLEGE STUDENTS

Believe in God	89%
Believe in divinity of Jesus Christ	77%
Member of a church or synagogue	67%
Religious beliefs very important	55%
Denominational preference:	
Protestant	49%
Roman Catholic	29%
Jewish	4%
Other	9%
Attend religious services weekly	34%
Religious commitment stronger since entering college	27%
Religious commitment weaker since entering college	23%
Read the Bible at least weekly	24%
Describe as born-again or evangelical Christian	23%
Member of campus religious group	12%
Favorably impressed by New Age movement	6%
Professed agnostic or atheist	6%
Some chance of joining religious cult group	2%

Source: The Gallup Organization Poll of 1,227 adults, age 18 and older, conducted October 12–15, 1989.

COLLEGE NICKNAMES

Deacons . . . . . Bloomfield College, Bloomfield, NJ (Presbyterian)

Preachers . . . . Concordia Seminary, St. Louis, MO (Lutheran—Missouri Synod)

Fighting Christians . . Elon College, Elon, NC (United Church of Christ)

Battling Bishops . . . . North Carolina Wesleyan College, Rocky Mount, NC (United Methodist)

Fighting Parsons . . . . Nyack College, Nyack, NY (Christian and Missionary Alliance)

Prophets . . . . . Oklahoma Baptist University, Shawnee, OK

—From *Alma Mater* by John Betterton, published by Peterson's Guides.

MOST COMMON NAMES FOR CHURCH-RELATED COLLEGES

Central . . . . 13 schools
Trinity . . . . 10 schools
Concordia . . . . 8 schools
Columbia . . . . 7 schools
Southwestern . . . . 6 schools
Eastern . . . . 6 schools
Lutheran . . . . 6 schools

"Honorable mention" names with five schools each: American, Bethany, Bethel, Emmanuel, Florida, Northwest, Pacific, Reformed

FOCUS FACT

Average annual tuition in 1968 at a public four-year institution was $1,566; at a private four-year college tuition was $7,693. If tuition continues to increase 8 percent each year as it has every year year since 1981, by the year 2005 the total cost for a year of college will be $19,000 at a public college and $42,000 at a private college. These numbers factor in cost increases for books, room, and board. —The College Board

SEMINARIES AND GRADUATE SCHOOLS

School	*City, ST*	*Affiliation*	*Enroll*
United States			
Acadia Divinity School	Wolfville, NS	Baptist	120
Alliance Theological Seminary	Nyack, NY	C&MA	280
American Baptist Seminary of the West	Berkeley, CA	American Baptist	93
American Baptist Theological Seminary	Nashville, TN	Baptist	170
Anderson University School of Theology	Anderson, IN	Church of God	
Andover Newton Theological School	Newton Centre, MA	United Church of Christ/Amer Baptist	395
Asbury Theological Seminary	Wilmore, KY	Interdenominational	794
Ashland Theological Seminary	Ashland, OH	Brethren	423
Assemblies of God Theological Seminary	Springfield, MO	Assemblies of God	285
Atlantic School of Theology	Halifax, NS	Interdenominational	123
Austin Presbyterian Theological Seminary	Austin, TX	Presbyterian Church (USA)	255
Azusa Pacific University Graduate School of Theology	Azusa, CA	Wesleyan	108
Bangor Theological Seminary	Bangor, ME	United Church of Christ	102
Baptist Missionary Association Theological Seminary	Jacksonville, TX	Baptist Missionary Association	76
Beeson Divinity School	Birmingham, AL	Southern Baptist	90

School	*City, ST*	*Affiliation*	*Enroll*
Berkeley Divinity School	New Haven, CT	Episcopal	N/A
Bethany Theological Seminary	Oak Brook, IL	Church of the Brethren	130
Bethel Theological Seminary	St. Paul, MN	Baptist General Conference	514
Biblical Theological Seminary	Hatfield, PA	Nondenominational	190
Boston University School of Theology	Boston, MA	United Methodist	513
Brite Divinity School	Fort Worth, TX	Christian Church (Disciples of Christ)	206
Calvin Theological Seminary	Grand Rapids, MI	Christian Reformed	230
Candler School of Theology	Atlanta, GA	United Methodist	769
Capital Bible Seminary	Lantham, MD	Interdenominational	185
Central Baptist Theological Seminary	Kansas City, KS	American Baptist	140
Chicago Theological Seminary	Chicago, IL	United Church of Christ	176
Christian Theological Seminary	Indianapolis, IN	Christian Church (Disciples of Christ)	338
Church Divinity School of the Pacific	Berkeley, CA	Episcopal	108
Church of God School of Theology	Cleveland, TN	Church of God	177
Cincinnati Bible Seminary	Cincinnati, OH	Christian Churches & Churches of Christ	289
Claremont School of Theology	Claremont, CA	United Methodist	265
Colgate Rochester Div Schl/Crozer Theol Seminary	Rochester, NY	American Baptist	208
Columbia Biblical Seminary & Grad School of Missions	Columbia, SC	Nondenominational	420
Columbia Theological Seminary	Decatur, GA	Presbyterian Church (USA)	547
Concordia Seminary	St. Louis, MO	Lutheran—Missouri Synod	555
Concordia Theological Seminary	Fort Wayne, IN	Lutheran Church—Missouri Synod	530
Covenant Theological Seminary	St. Louis, MO	Presbyterian	158
Dallas Theological Seminary	Dallas, TX	Nondenominational	1350
Denver Conservative Baptist Seminary	Denver, CO	Conservative Baptist	489
Denver Seminary	Denver, CO	Conservative Baptist	
Drew University Theological School	Madison, NJ	United Methodist	600
Duke University Divinity School	Durham, NC	United Methodist	443
Eastern Baptist Theological Seminary	Philadelphia, PA	American Baptist	382
Eastern Mennonite Seminary	Harrisonburg, VA	Mennonite	101
Eden Theological Seminary	St. Louis, MO	United Church of Christ	172
Emmanuel School of Religion	Johnson City, TN	Christian Churches & Churches of Christ	139
Episcopal Divinity School	Cambridge, MA	Episcopal	117
Episcopal Theological Seminary of the Southwest	Austin, TX	Episcopal	67
Erskine Theological Seminary	Due West, SC	Presbyterian	189
Evangelical School of Theology	Myerstown, PA	Evangelical Congregational	72
Faith Baptist Seminary	Ankeny, IA	Baptist	
Fuller Theological Seminary	Pasadena, CA	Interdenominational	2670
Garrett-Evangelical Theological Seminary	Evanston, IL	United Methodist	351
General Theological Seminary	New York, NY	Episcopal	161
Golden Gate Baptist Theological Seminary	Mill Valley, CA	Southern Baptist	910
Gordon-Conwell Theological Seminary	South Hamilton, MA	Interdenominational	721
Graduate Theological Union	Berkeley, CA	Interdenominational	374
Grand Rapids Baptist Seminary	Grand Rapids, MI	Baptist	
Harding Graduate School of Religion	Memphis, TN	Churches of Christ	183
Hartford Seminary	Hartford, CT	Interdenominational	161
Harvard University Divinity School	Cambridge, MA	Nondenominational	470
Hood Theological Seminary	Salisbury, NC	A.M.E. Zion	35
Houston Graduate School of Theology	Houston, TX	Friends	122
Howard University Divinity School	Washington, DC	Nondenominational	191
Iliff School of Theology	Denver, CO	United Methodist	332
Interdenominational Theological Center	Atlanta, GA	Interdenominational	264
Lancaster Theological Seminary	Lancaster, PA	United Church of Christ	233
Lexington Theological Seminary	Lexington, KY	Christian Church (Disciples of Christ)	167
Liberty Baptist Theological Seminary	Lynchburg, VA	Baptist	253
Lincoln Christian Seminary	Lincoln, IL	Christian Churches & Churches of Christ	178
Louisville Presbyterian Theological Seminary	Louisville, KY	Presbyterian Church (USA)	187
Luther Northwestern Theological Seminary	St. Paul, MN	Lutheran-ELCA	723
Luther Rice Seminary	Jacksonville, FL	Baptist	3100
Lutheran School of Theology at Chicago	Chicago, IL	Lutheran-ELCA	309
Lutheran Theological Seminary at Gettysburg	Gettysburg, PA	Lutheran-ELCA	282

School	City, ST	Affiliation	Enroll
Lutheran Theological Seminary at Philadelphia	Philadelphia, PA	Lutheran-ELCA	262
Lutheran Theological Southern Seminary	Columbia, SC	Lutheran-ELCA	159
Master's Seminary	Sun Valley, CA	Interdenominational	677
McCormick Theological Seminary	Chicago, IL	Presbyterian Church (USA)	556
Memphis Theological Seminary	Memphis, TN	Presbyterian	135
Mennonite Biblical Seminary	Elkhart, IN	Mennonite	122
Mennonite Brethren Biblical Seminary	Fresno, CA	Mennonite Brethren	122
Methodist Theological School in Ohio	Delaware, OH	United Methodist	239
Midwestern Baptist Theological Seminary	Kansas City, MO	Southern Baptist	513
Moody Graduate School	Chicago, IL	Interdenominational	400
Moravian Theological Seminary	Bethlehem, PA	Moravian	58
Multnomah Graduate School	Portland, OR	Interdenominational	170
Nashotah House	Nashotah, WI	Episcopal	69
Nazarene Theological Seminary	Kansas City, MO	Nazarene	444
New Brunswick Theological Seminary	New Brunswick, NJ	Reformed Church in America	139
New Orleans Baptist Theological Seminary	New Orleans, LA	Southern Baptist	2113
New York Theological Seminary	New York, NY	Interdenominational	280
North American Baptist Seminary	Sioux Falls, SD	North American Baptist	134
North Park Theological Seminary	Chicago, IL	Evangelical Covenant	138
Northern Baptist Theological Seminary	Lombard, IL	American Baptist	181
Oral Roberts University School of Theology	Tulsa, OK	Interdenominational	413
Pacific Lutheran Theological Seminary	Berkeley, CA	Lutheran-ELCA	129
Pacific School of Religion	Berkeley, CA	Interdenominational	206
Payne Theological Seminary	Wilberforce, OH	A.M.E.	15
Perkins School of Theol of Southern Methodist Univ	Dallas, TX	United Methodist	444
Phillips Graduate Seminary	Enid, OK	Christian Church (Disciples of Christ)	131
Pittsburgh Theological Seminary	Pittsburgh, PA	Presbyterian Church (USA)	450
Presbyterian School of Christian Education	Richmond, VA	Presbyterian Church (USA)	113
Princeton Theological Seminary	Princeton, NJ	Presbyterian Church (USA)	798
Protestant Episcopal Theological Seminary in Virginia	Alexandria, VA	Episcopal	222
Reformed Episcopal Seminary	Philadelphia, PA	Reformed Episcopal	45
Reformed Presbyterian Theological Seminary	Pittsburgh, PA	Reformed Presbyterian	80
Reformed Theological Seminary	Jackson, MS	Reformed	336
Reformed Theological Seminary	Orland, FL	Reformed	120
Saint Paul School of Theology	Kansas City, MO	United Methodist	258
San Francisco Theological Seminary	San Anselmo, CA	Presbyterian Church (USA)	791
Seabury-Western Theological Seminary	Evanston, IL	Episcopal	87
Shaw Divinity School	Raleigh, NC	Baptist	102
Southeastern Baptist Theological Seminary	Wake Forest, NC	Southern Baptist	1003
Southern Baptist Theological Seminary	Louisville, KY	Southern Baptist	2232
Southwestern Baptist Theological Seminary	Fort Worth, TX	Southern Baptist	4001
Talbot School of Theology	La Mirada, CA	Interdenominational	511
Trinity Episcopal School for Ministry	Ambridge, PA	Episcopal	108
Trinity Evangelical Divinity School	Deerfield, IL	Evangelical Free	1094
Trinity Lutheran Seminary	Columbus, OH	Lutheran-ELCA	249
Union Theological Seminary	New York, NY	Interdenominational	403
Union Theological Seminary in Virginia	Richmond, VA	Presbyterian Church (USA)	225
United Theological Seminary	Dayton, OH	United Methodist	338
United Theological Seminary of the Twin Cities	New Brighton, MN	United Church of Christ	204
University of Chicago Divinity School	Chicago, IL	Interdenominational	273
University of Dubuque Theological Seminary	Dubuque, IA	Presbyterian Church (USA)	194
University of the South School of Theology	Sewanee, TN	Episcopal	157
Vanderbilt University Divinity School	Nashville, TN	Interdenominational	271
Virginia Union University School of Theology	Richmond, VA	Baptist	124
Wartburg Theological Seminary	Dubuque, IA	Lutheran-ELCA	230
Wesley Biblical Seminary	Jackson, MS	Interdenominational	95
Wesley Theological Seminary	Washington, DC	United Methodist	363
Western Conservative Baptist Seminary	Portland, OR	Baptist	480
Western Evangelical Seminary	Portland, OR	Interdenominational	157
Western Theological Seminary	Holland, MI	Reformed Church in America	166
Westminster Theological Seminary	Philadelphia, PA	Independent	538
Wheaton College Graduate School	Wheaton, IL	Interdenominational	300

School	*City, ST*	*Affiliation*	*Enroll*
Winebrenner Theological Seminary	Findlay, OH	Churches of God	43
Yale University Divinity School	New Haven, CT	Interdenominational	455

Canadian

School	*City, ST*	*Affiliation*	*Enroll*
Canadian Theological Seminary	Regina, SK	C&MA	153
Concordia Lutheran Seminary	St. Catharines, ON	Lutheran/Missouri Synod	
Edmonton Baptist Seminary	Edmonton, AB	North American Baptist	60
Emmanuel College of Victoria University	Toronto, ON	United Church of Canada	241
Huron College Faculty of Theology	London, ON	Anglican	56
Joint Board of Theological Colleges	Montreal, PQ	Interdenominational	18
Knox College	Toronto, ON	Presbyterian	137
Lutheran Theological Seminary	Saskatoon, SK	Lutheran-ELCIC	111
McGill University Faculty of Religious Studies	Montreal, PQ	Interdenominational	145
McMaster Divinity College	Hamilton, ON	Baptist	145
Ontario Theological Seminary	Willowdale, ON	Interdenominational	371
Queen's Theological College	Kingston, ON	United Church	88
Regent College	Vancouver, BC	Interdenominational	362
St. Andrew's College	Saskatoon, SK	United Church of Canada	54
St. Stephen's College	Edmonton, AB	United Church of Canada	82
Toronto School of Theology	Toronto, ON	Interdenominational	
Trinity College Faculty of Divinity	Toronto, ON	Anglican	135
University of Winnipeg Faculty of Theology	Winnipeg, MB	United	116
Vancouver School of Theology	Vancouver, BC	Interdenominational	111
Waterloo Lutheran Seminary	Waterloo, ON	Lutheran-ELCIC	133
Winnipeg Theological Seminary	Otterburne, MB	Interdenominational	208
Wycliffe College	Toronto, ON	Anglican	141

INFORMATIVE BOOKS TO HELP YOU FIND THE RIGHT EDUCATIONAL INSTITUTION

Peterson's Four Year Colleges In addition to profiles on over 1,900 institutions, a complete majors directory, an entrance difficulty directory, and a full listing of cost level, this 2,700-page book contains nearly 800 in-depth descriptions written by admissions directors about their own colleges.

Consider a Christian College Answers questions that students and their families ask when they are interested in pursuing postsecondary education at a Christian college. Provides information on the 78 member schools of the Christian College Coalition.

Peterson's College Money Handbook Full account of costs and details on financial aid packages and merit scholarships at more than 1,700 accredited U.S. four-year colleges. Features an overview of the financial aid process, a financial aid glossary, and a worksheet for calculating the expected family contribution, plus over 90 directories of non-need scholarships by type, athletic scholarships by sport, and money-saving options.

The ISS Directory of Overseas Schools Guide to 500 overseas schools. Profiles include tuition and fees, description of facilities and programs, and breakdown of nationalities of staff and students and accreditation source.

Financial Resources for International Study Listing of financial aid awards for U.S. citizens who study abroad. Covers over 600 grants of at least $500.

Peterson's Guide to Independent Secondary Schools Guide to nearly 1,400 accredited day schools, boarding schools, and schools serving students with special needs. Contains directories that identify schools by type, religious affiliation, financial aid offerings.

The Independent Study Catalog The National University Continuing Education Association's guide to independent study through correspondence instruction for people who want to study without the restriction of regular class attendance. Lists 10,000 correspondence courses at the high school, college, and graduate levels.

1991 Summer Employment Directory of the United States Lists 50,000 summer jobs for students and teachers with businesses, expeditions, resorts, summer camps, theaters, and the government. Includes a job category index to help users locate specific types of positions.

For more information on these books write to Peterson's Guides, P.O. Box 2123, Princeton, NJ 08543-2123 or call 1-800-EDU-DATA.

HOME SCHOOL SUPPORT ORGANIZATIONS

Alabama

Alabama Home Educators, Inc., PO Box 160091, Mobile, 36616, 1984

Alaska

Alaska Private & Home Educators Association, PO Box 70, Talkeetna, 99676, 907-733-2482, 1987

Arizona

Arizona Families for Home Education, PO Box 4661, Scottsdale, 85261, 602-948-7310, 1982

Christian Home Educators of Arizona, 3015 S. Evergreen Road, Tempe, 85282, 602-897-7688, 1990

Arkansas

Arkansas Christian Home Education Association, PO Box 501, Little Rock, 72203, 501-834-7729, 1981

California

Christian Home Educators Association of California, PO Box 28644, Santa Ana, 92799-8644, 715-537-5121, 1982

Colorado

Colorado Home Schooling Network, 7490 W. Apache, Sedalia, 80135, 303-688-4136, 1981

Homes Offering Meaningful Education (HOME), 1015 S. Gaylord, #226, Denver, 80209, 303-777-1082, 1985

Connecticut

Connecticut Home Schoolers Association, Box 464, Chester, 06412, 203-526-5005, 1983

Education Association of Christian Homeschoolers, Box 446, Broad Brook, 06106

Emanuel Homestead Home Education Resource Center, PO Box 355, S. Woodstock, 06267, 203-974-2416

Delaware

Tri-State Home School Network, Box 7193, Newark, 19714, 303-368-4217, 1987

Florida

Florida at Home, 7615 Clubhouse Estates Drive, Orlando, 32819, 407-422-5357, 1986

Florida Parent-Educators Association, 9245 Woodrun Road, Pensacola, 32514, 904-477-9642, 1984

Georgia

Georgians for Freedom in Education, 5986 Randy Lane, Ellenwood, 30049, 404-832-1910, 1983

Hawaii

Christian Homeschoolers of Hawaii, 91-824 Oama Street, Ewa Beach, 96706, 808-689-6398, 1986

Hilo Home School Association, PO Box 469, Mt. View, 96771, 808-968-8434, 1989

Idaho

Idaho Home Educators, Box 4022, Boise, 83711-4022, 1982

Illinois

Illinois Christian Home Educators, PO Box 261, Zion, 60099,1984

Indiana

Indiana Association of Home Educators, PO Box 17135, Indianapolis, 46217, 317-782-3397, 1983

Iowa

Iowa Home Educators' Association, PO Box 213, Des Moines, 50301, 1983

Kansas

Kansas for Alternative Education, 19985 Renner Road, Spring Hill, 66083, 913-686-2310, 1984

Kansas Home Educators, 3201 Berry Road, Kansas City, 66106, 913-722-2386

Teaching Parents Association, 100 E. 109th Street North, Valley Center, 67147, 316-755-2159, 1980

Kentucky

Kentucky Christian Home Schooling Association, 1301 Bridget Drive, Fairdale, 40118, 502-363-5104, 1985

Kentucky Home Education Association, 580 Ruckerville Road, Winchester, 40391, 606-744-6404, 1989

Louisiana

Christian Home Educator's Fellowship, PO Box 14421, Baton Rouge, 70898-4421, 504-642-2059, 1985

Louisiana Citizens for Home Education, 3403 Van Buren, Baker, 70714, 504-755-5472, 1982

Maine

Christian Homeschool Association of Maine, PO Box 5496, Augusta, 04332, 207-872-2015, 1985

Guardians of Education for Maine, HC Route 68, Box 124, Cushing, 04563, 207-254-6336, 1978

Maine Homeschool Association, PO Box 3283, Auburn, 04240, 207-777-1700, 1988

Maryland

Maryland Association of Christian Home Education Organizations, PO Box 1041, Emmitsburg, 21727, 301-662-0022, 1984

Maryland Home Education Association, 9085 Flamepool Way, Columbia, 21045, 301-730-0073, 1980

Massachusetts

Massachusetts Home Learning Association, PO Box 1976, Lenox, 01240, 413-637-2169, 1987

Massachusetts Home Schooling Association of Parent Educators, 15 Ohio Street, Wilmington, 01887, 508-658-8970

Michigan

Christians United to Reclaim Education, PO Box 71050, Madison Heights, 48071-0050, 1985,

Information Network for Christian Homes, 4150 Ambrose N.E., Grand Rapids, 49505, 616-364-4438, 1984

Minnesota

Minnesota Association of Christian Home Educators, Box 188, Anoka, 55303, 612-753-2370, 1984

TEACH Institute and Accrediting Association, 4350 Lakeland Avenue North, Robbinsdale, 55422, 612-535-5514, 1983

Mississippi

Mississippi Home Schoolers, Box 2067, Starkville, 39759, 601-324-2668, 1983

Missouri

Families for Home Education, 21709 E. Old Atherton Road, Independence, 64058, 816-796-0978

Montana

Grapevine, 1702 Highway 83 North, Seeley Lake, 59868, 406-754-2481, 1986

Home Schoolers of Montana, Box 40, Billings, 59101, 406-248-6762, 1982

Montana Coalition of Home Educators, PO Box 654, Helena, 59624, 406-357-2893, 1988

Nebraska

Nebraska Home Educators Association, 5000 Grand View Lane, Lincoln, 68521, 402-476-9925, 1986

Nevada

Home Schools United—Vegas Valley, PO Box 26811, Las Vegas, 89126, 702-870-9566, 1983

Nevada Home Schools—Northern Division, Box 21323, Reno, 89515, 702-323-0566, 1985

Silver State Education Advocates, 2516 Janelle Drive, Sparks, 89431, 702-356-7058, 1989

New Hampshire

Christian Home Educators of New Hampshire, Box 1653, Hillsboro, 03244

New Hampshire Home Educators Association, 9 Mizoras Drive, Nashua, 03062, 1983

New Jersey

Education Network of Christian Home Schoolers of New Jersey, 65 Middlesex Road, Matawan, 07747, 201-583-7128, 1989

New Jersey Unschoolers Network, 2 Smith Street, Farmingdale, 07727, 201-938-2473, 1977

New Mexico

National Association for the Legal Support of Alternative Schools, PO Box 28223, Santa Fe, 87501, 505-471-6938

New Mexico Christian Home Educators, 5749 Paradise N.W., Albuquerque, 87114, 505-897-1772, 1984

New Mexico Family Educators, PO Box 13383, Albuquerque, 87192, 505-892-5783, 1982

New York

Home Schoolers Exchange, RD 1, Box 172E, East Chatham, 12060, 518-392-4277, 1984

Loving Education at Home, PO Box 332, Syracuse, 13205, 518-377-6019, 1983

North Carolina

North Carolinians for Home Education, 204 N. Person Street, Raleigh, 27601, 919-834-6243, 1983

North Dakota Home School Association, PO Box 539, Turtle Lake, 52575, 701-448-9193, 1984

Ohio

Christian Home Educators of Ohio, PO Box 9083, Canton, 44711, 216-673-7272, 1983

Oklahoma

Coalition of Christian Home Educators of Oklahoma, PO Box 471032, Tulsa, 74147-1032, 918-455-6284, 1984

Oregon

Oregon Christian Home Educators' Association Network, 2515 NE 37th, Portland, 97212, 503-288-1285, 1986

Parents' Education Association, PO Box 1482, Beaverton, 97075, 1983

Pennsylvania

Parent Educators of Pennsylvania, RD 2, Box 141, Wrightsville, 17368, 717-252-0286, 1985

Pennsylvania Homeschoolers, RD 2, Box 11, Kittanning, 16201, 412-783-6512, 1981

Rhode Island

Parent Educators of Rhode Island, PO Box 782, Glendale, 02826, 1984

Rhode Island Guild of Home Teachers, 272 Pequot Avenue, Warwick, 02886, 401-737-2264

South Carolina

South Carolina Home Educators Association, PO Box 33, Goose Creek, 29445, 803-761-3076, 1989

South Dakota

South Dakota Home School Association, 1606 South 4th Avenue, Sioux Falls, 57105, 605-334-2213, 1983

Western Dakota Christian Home Schools, Box 528, Black Hawk, 55718-0528, 605-787-5928, 1983

Tennessee

National Coalition of Alternative Community Schools, 58 Schoolhouse Road, Summertown, 38483, 615-964-3670, 1976

Tennessee Home Education Association, 3677 Richbriar Court, Nashville, 37211, 615-834-3529, 1984

Texas

Family Educators Alliance of South Texas, 1400 N. Flores, San Antonio, 78212, 1989

Hearth & Home Ministries, Inc., PO Box 835105, Richardson, 75083, 214-231-9838, 1984

Home Oriented Private Education for Texas, PO Box 43887, Austin, 78745, 512-280-4673, 1986

Southeast Texas Home School Association, 5620 FM 1960 W. Box 354, Houston, 77069-4202, 713-586-8897, 1984

Utah

Utah Christian Home Schooling, 3190 South 4140 West, West Valley City, 84120, 1985

Vermont

Vermont Home Schoolers Association, Spruce Knob Road, Middletown Springs, 05757, 802-235-2620, 1985

Vermont Homeschoolers Association, RFD, Wells, 05774, 198

Virginia

Home Educators Association of Virginia, PO Box 1810, Front Royal, 22630-1810, 703-635-9322, 1984

Home School Legal Defense Association, Paeonian Springs, 22129, 703-882-3838, 1983

National Center for Home Education, PO Box 125, Hwy 9 at Route 781, Paeonian Springs, 22129, 703-882-4770, 1990

Washington

Family Learning Organization of Washington, PO Box 7256, Spokane, 99207-0256, 509-467-2552, 1983

Homeschooler's Support Association, 23335 269th Avenue SE, Maple Valley, 98038

National Homeschool Association, PO Box 58746, Seattle, 98138-1746, 206-1544, 1988

Washington Association of Teaching Christian Homes (WATCH), PO Box 554, Colville, 99114, 509-684-3270, 1989

Washington Homeschool Organization (WHO), PO Box 938, Maple Valley, 98038, 206-432-3935, 1986

West Virginia

West Virginia Home Education Association, PO Box 266, Glenville, 26351, 304-462-8296, 1986

West Virginians for Religious Training, PO Box 7504, Charleston, 25356, 304-776-1948, 1982

Wisconsin

Wisconsin Parents' Association, Inc., PO Box 2502, Madison, 53701, 1983

Wyoming

Homeschoolers of Wyoming, PO Box 2197, Mills, 82644, 307-235-4928, 1988

Source: *The Big Book of Home Learning, Volume 1, Getting Started* by Mary Pride. Published by Crossway Books. Copyright © 1990. Used by permission of Good News Publishers/Crossway Books, Westchester, IL 60154

FOCUS FACT

Statistical analysis of more than 80 studies indicates that a pupil taught individually achieves on the average 30 percentile points higher on norm-referenced standard achievement tests than a pupil taught in a conventional classroom of 25 or more students.

Source: *Home Education: Is It Working?* Published by Home Oriented Private Education for Texas

HOME SCHOOL GOVERNMENT INFORMATION

Alabama Private Schools Unit, Room 348, State Office Bldg., Montgomery, 36103, 205-261-2910

Alaska Centralized Correspondence Study, Department of Education, PO Box GA, Juneau, 99811-0544, 907-789-2835

Arizona Department of Ed., 1535 W. Jefferson St., Phoenix, 85007, 602-542-3759

Arkansas Dept. of Education, Room 404-B, #4 State Capitol Mall, Little Rock, 72201, 501-682-4252

California Alternative Education Unit, Dept. of Education, PO Box 944272, Sacramento, 94244-2720, 916-322-1048

Colorado State Office of Education, 201 E. Colfax Avenue, Denver, 80203, 303-866-6678

Connecticut State Department of Education, PO Box 2219, Hartford, 06145, 203-566-5458

Delaware Dept. of Public Instruction, PO Box 1402, Dover, 19903, 302-736-4629

Florida Dept. of Education, Administrator of Student Services, Tallahassee, 32301, 904-488-8974

Georgia State Dept. of Education, 1661 Twin Towers East, Atlanta, 30334, 404-656-2446

Hawaii Dept. of Education, PO Box 2360, Honolulu, 96804, 808-548-6095

Idaho Dept. of Education, Len B. Jordan Office Bldg., Boise, 83720, 208-334-2165

Illinois Board of Ed., S-284, 100 N. First Street, Springfield, 62777, 217-782-3950

Indiana Dept. of Education, Room 229, State House, Indianapolis, 46204-2798, 317-232-6614

Iowa Dept. of Education, Grimes State Office Bldg., Des Moines, 50319-0146, 515-281-5295

Kansas Board of Education, Topeka, 66603, 913-296-3142

Kentucky Dept. of Ed., Capital Plaza Tower, Frankfort, 40601, 502-564-2116

Louisiana Dept. of Education, PO Box 94064, Baton Rouge, 70804, 504-342-3473

Maine Dept. of Educational and Cultural Services, Augusta, 04333, 207-784-2094

Maryland State Dept. of Education, 200 W. Baltimore Street, Baltimore, 21201-2595, 301-333-2433

Massachusetts Dept. of Education, 1385 Hancock Street, Quincy, 02169,

Michigan Dept. of Education, PO Box 30008, Lansing, 48909, 517-373-3324

Minnesota Dept. of Education, Room 710, Capitol Square Bldg., 550 Cedar Street, St. Paul, 55101, 612-296-6595

Mississippi State Dept. of Education, PO Box 771, Suite 301, Jackson, 39205, 601-359-3598

Missouri Dept. of Elementary & Secondary Education, PO Box 480, Jefferson City, 65102, 314-751-7602

Montana Office of Public Instruction, Room 106, Capitol Station,, Helena, 59620, 406-444-4402

Nebraska State Dept. of Ed., 301 Centennial Mall South, Lincoln, 68509, 402-471-2783

Nevada State Dept. of Education, Basic Education Branch, 400 West King Street, Carson City, 89710, 702-687-3136

New Hampshire Division of Standards and Certification, 101 Pleasant Street, Concord, 03301, 603-271-3453

New Jersey Non-Public School Services, 225 West State Street, CN 500, Trenton, 08625, 609-292-5161

New Mexico Dept. of Education, Instructional Support, Education Building, Santa Fe, 87501-2786, 505-827-6515

New York State Education Dept., Room 475 BBA, Albany, 12234, 518-474-4948

North Carolina Division of Non-Public Education, 116 Wet Jones Street, Raleigh, 27603-8001, 919-733-4276

FOCUS FACT

Estimates range from 250,000 students to 1,000,000 students who are being taught at home. Even at the minimum estimate of 250,000 students there are more home schoolers nationally than there are public school students in 16 states! The maximum estimate of one million home schoolers living in one area would represent the 12th largest state in student enrollment.

The Home School Court Report Spring 1990 issue.

North Dakota Dept. of Public Instruction, State Capitol, 600 East Blvd., Bismark, 58505, 701-224-2295

Ohio Dept. of Education, Columbus, 43215, 614-466-2761

Oklahoma State Dept. of Education, Oklahoma City, 73105, 405-521-3333

Oregon State Dept. of Ed., 700 Pringle Parkway SE, Salem, 97310, 503-378-3702

Pennsylvania Dept. of Education, Advisory Services, 333 Market Street, Harrisburg, 17126, 717-783-3750

Rhode Island Dept. of Ed., 22 Hayes Street, Providence, 02908, 401-277-2031

South Carolina Dept. of Education, Columbia, 29201, 803-734-8500

South Dakota State Division of Education, Kneip Office Bldg., 700 Governors Drive, Pierre, 57501-2293, 605-773-4662

Tennessee Home Schools, Dept. of Education, 542 Cordell Hull Building, Nashville, 37219, 615-741-2963

Texas Education Agency, 1701 N. Congress, Austin, 78701, 512-463-9734

Utah State Ofc. of Education, 250 E. 500 S., Salt Lake City, 84111, 801-533-6040

Vermont Home Study, Independent School Consultant, State Office Building, 120 State Street, Montpelier, 05602, 802-828-3124

Virginia Dept. of Education, PO Box 6A, Richmond, 23216,

Washington Office of Private Education, Old Capitol Building, FG-11, Olympia, 98504, 206-753-256

West Virginia Office of Accreditation, Capitol Complex, B-346, Charleston, 25305, 304-348-3788

Wisconsin Dept. of Public Instruction, 125 S. Webster Street, PO Box 7841, Madison, 53707, 606-266-5761

Wyoming State Dept. of Ed., Hathaway Building, Cheyenne, 82002, 307-777-6213

Source: *The Home School Manual* by Theodore E. Wade, Jr. Copyright © 1988 and 1990. Published by Gazelle Publications, 5580 Stanley Drive, Auburn, CA 95603. Used by permission.

HOME SCHOOL EDUCATIONAL ORGANIZATIONS

A Beka Correspondence School/A Beka Video Home School
PO Box 18000, Pensacola, FL, 32523-9160, 800-874-2352

Advanced Training Institute of America
Box One, Oak Brook, IL, 60521, 708-323-9800

Alpha Omega Publications
PO Box 3153, Tempe, AZ, 85281, 800-821-4443

Alta Vista Home School Curriculum
PO Box 222, Medina, WA, 98039, 206-454-7691

Associated Christian Schools Curriculum
PO Box 27115, Indianapolis, IN, 46227, 317-881-7132

Bob Jones University Press
Greenville, SC, 29614, 800-845-5731

Christian Liberty Academy Satellite Schools
502 Euclid Avenue, Arlington Heights, IL, 60004, 708-259-8736

Christian Light Education
PO Box 1126, Harrisonburg, VA, 22801, 703-424-0750

Christian Schools International
3350 E. Paris Avenue SE, Grand Rapids, MI, 49508, 800-635-8288

Creative Christian Education
PO Box K, Angwin, CA, 94508, 707-695-3004

Hewitt Research Foundation
PO Box 9, Washougal, WA, 98671, 206-835-8708

Home Study International
6940 Carroll Avenue, Takoma Park, MD, 20913, 202-722-6570

International Institute
PO Box 99, Park Ridge, IL, 60068

Lindenwood Academy
PO Box 3405, Fort Smith, AR, 72913-3405, 501-782-6277

McGuffey Academy
1000 E. Huron, Milford, MI, 48042, 800-521-4350

Rod and Staff Publishers
Crockett, KY, 41413, 606-522-4348

Summit Christian Academy
PO Box 802041, Dallas, TX, 75380, 214-991-2096

Sycamore Tree
2179 Meyer Place, Costa Mesa, CA, 92627, 714-650-4466

SECONDARY CORRESPONDENCE SCHOOLS

American School
850 E. 58th Street, Chicago, IL 60637, 312-947-3300

Arizona, University of
Correspondence/Independent Study, 1955 East Sixth Street, Tucson AZ 85719, 602-621-1896

Arkansas, University of
Department of Independent Study, #2 University Center, Fayetteville AR 72701, 501-575-3647

Citizens' High School
5575 Peachtree Road, Atlanta, GA 30341, 404-455-8258

Colorado at Boulder, University of,
Division of Continuing Education, Box 178, Boulder CO 80309-0178, 303-331-2801

Florida, University of
Dept. of Independent Study, 1223 NW 22nd Avenue, Gainesville FL 32611, 904-392-1711

Granton Institute of Technology
263 Adelaide Street West, Toronto, ON M5H 1Y3, 416-977-3929

Hadley School for the Blind
700 Elm Street, Winnetka, IL 60093, 708-446-8111

Home Study International
6940 Carroll Avenue, Takoma Park, MD 20912, 202-722-6570

ICS Newport/Pacific High School
Oak Street and Pawnee Avenue, Scranton, PA 18509, 717-342-7701

Idaho, University of
Correspondence Study in Idaho, CEB-116, Moscow ID 83843-4171, 208-885-6641

Indiana University
Independent Study Program, School of Continuing Studies, Owen Hall, Bloomington IN 47405, 812-855-3693

Kansas, University of
Lawrence, KS 66045, 913-864-4440

Kentucky, University, Eastern
Division of Extended Programs, Coates 27A, Richmond KY 40475-0931, 606-622-2003

Learning and Evaluation Center
479 Drinker Street, PO Box 616, Bloomsburg, PA 17815, 717-784-5220

Massachusetts Dept. of Education
Correspondence Instruction, 1385 Hancock Street, Quincy MA 02169, 617-770-7582

Minnesota, University of
Department of Independent Study, 45 Westbrook Hall, 77 Pleasant Street SE, Minneapolis MN 55455, 612-624-0000

Mississippi State University
Continuing Education, PO Drawer 5245, Mississippi State MS 39762, 601-325-2649

Missouri, University of
Center for Independent Study, 136 Clark Hall, Columbia MO 65211, 314-882-2491

Nebraska, University of
Independent Study, 269 Nebraska Center, Lincoln NE 68583-0900, 402-472-1926

North Dakota State University
Division of Independent Study, State University Station, Box 5036, Fargo ND 58104-5036, 701-237-7182

Oklahoma, University of
Independent Study Department, 1700 Asp, Norman OK 73037, 405-325-1921

Oregon State System of Higher Education
Independent Study, PO Box 1633, Portland OR 97207, 503-464-4865

South Dakota, University of
Independent Study Division, 414 E. Clark, Vermillion SD 57069, 605-677-6108

Tennessee, University of
Dept. of Independent Study, 420 Communications Bldg., Knoxville TN 37996-0300, 615-974-5134

Texas Tech University
Division of Continuing Education, PO Box 4110, Lubbock TX 79409, 806-828-6392

Texas, University of, at Austin
EIMC Independent Learning, PO Box 7700, Austin TX 78713-7700, 512-471-7716

Utah State University
Independent Study, UMC 5000, Logan UT 84322-5000, 801-750-2328

Washington State University
Independent Study Program, 202 Van Doren Hall, Pullman WA 99164-5220, 509-335-3557

Wisconsin, University of
Extension, Independent Study, 432 North Lake Street, Madison WI 53706, 608-263-2055

Wyoming, University of
Correspondence Study Department, PO Box 3294, University Station, Laramie WY 82071, 307-742-5631

Source: *The Home School Manual* by Theodore E. Wade, Jr. Copyright © 1988 and 1990. Published by Gazelle Publications, 5580 Stanley Drive, Auburn, CA 95603. Used by permission.

HOME SCHOOL MAGAZINES

Christian Educator, The Christian Liberty Academy Satellite Schools, 203 E. McDonald Road, Prospect Heights, IL 60070 708-259-8736.

Creative Learning Magazine PO Box 37568, San Antonio, TX 78237. Learning activities around a monthly theme.

Home Education Magazine PO Box 1083, Tonasket, WA 98855 509-684-9855. Articles and "kids' pages" with a wide variety of interests. $24 for 6 issues.

Home Free CBN Publishing, CBN Center, Virginia Beach, VA 23463 804-424-7777. Sent to Home Free Club members. The $29.95 yearly membership fee includes discounts on other home school materials.

Home School Digest Wisdom Publications, PO Box 3154, LaVale, MD 21502 301-759-3218. $10 for four quarterly issues.

Home School Gazette PO Box 359, Burtonsville, MD 20866 301-421-1473. Features articles submitted by children.

Hostex News PO Box 2241, Santa Fe, NM 87504-2241. Stories, poems, drawings, pen pals, for and by home study students. Provides opportunity for kids to get into print. $10 for 8 issues.

KidsArt News PO Box 274, Mt. Shasta, CA 96067 916-926-5076. A 16-page quarterly magazine with art activities for children. $8 per year.

Parent Scene PO Box 2222, Redlands, CA 92373 714-792-2412. Newsletter sent without charge by Dr. Kay Kuzma, seminar speaker, mother and founder of the family ministry and radio program, "Parent Scene."

Teaching Home, The PO Box 20219, Portland, OR 97220-0219 502-253-9633. Magazine for Christian home school families. Affiliated support organizations in 22 states consider TTH their official journal and furnish material to include in center inserts for copies for their territories.

Source: *The Home School Manual* by Theodore E. Wade, Jr. Copyright © 1988 and 1990. Published by Gazelle Publications, 5580 Stanley Drive, Auburn, CA 95603. Used by permission.

BOOKLIST: HOME SCHOOLING

The Big Book of Home Learning, Volume 1, Getting Started By Mary Pride. Puts you in touch with the books, catalogs, magazines, supplies and organizations that can help your child's educational success. Published by Crossway Books, 9825 W. Roosevelt Road, Westchester, IL 60153 $15.

The Christian Home School By Gregg Harris. Beginner's book on home schooling. Answers commonly asked questions, defuses common objections, provides tips on how to make home schooling work. Published by Christian Life Workshops, 182 SE Kane, Gresham, OR 97080 $13.95.

For the Children's Sake By Susan Schaeffer Macaulay. Explains how to make education a "wonderful, life-enriching, joyous" experience. Draws heavily on the philosophy of 19th century British educator Charlotte Mason. Published by Crossway Books, 9825 W. Roosevelt Rd., Westchester, IL 60153 $7.95.

Home School Burnout By Raymond S. Moore and Dorothy N. Moore. Addresses home schooling burnout: what it is, what causes it and how to cure it. Includes encouraging examples of successful home school parents. Published by Wolgemuth & Hyatt, Publishers, Inc., 1749 Mallory Lane, Suite 110, Brentwood, TN 37027 $14.95.

Home School Manual, The By Theodore E. Wade. Guide dealing with all aspects of home schooling. Published by Gazelle Publications, 5580 Stanley Drive, Auburn, CA 95603

Survivor's Guide to Home Schooling by Luanne Shackelford and Susan White. Amusing book answers all the questions other books avoid, like how in the world you're going to get the laundry done while home schooling six kids. Published by Crossway Books, 9825 W. Roosevelt Road, Westchester, IL 60153 $8.95.

Evangelism

SIGNIFICANT EVANGELISTS THROUGHOUT HISTORY

Daniel Moul

Gilbert Tennent (1703-1764). The First Great Awakening began in the 1720s, largely through the efforts of the Presbyterian Minister Gilbert Tennent and the Dutch Reformed Minister Theodorous Jabobus Frelinghuysen. Both encouraged personal experiences of redemption, calling people to repentance through pastoral counseling and sermons.

Tennent trained for the ministry in a simple "log college" run by his father and located next to his home. His ministry began in New Brunswick, New Jersey, where he met Frelinghuysen. Revivals began in both churches by 1729, and by 1740 the Great Awakening was at its zenith. George Whitefield considered Tennent "a son of thunder." He said of Tennent, "Hypocrites must either soon be converted or enraged at his preaching," and "He is deeply sensible of the deadness and formality of the Christian church in these parts, and has given noble testimonies against it."

Tennent travelled through Massachusetts and Connecticut on a preaching tour, enjoying great success. In Boston, one pastor reported that in the course of three months, 600 people visited him "concerned for their souls."

Jonathan Edwards (1703-1758). One of the greatest theologians America has produced, Jonathan Edwards played a prominent role in the Great Awakening. His famous sermon, "Sinners in the Hands of an Angry God," helped spark revival in his town of Northampton, Massachusetts. As people witnessed the changes in church-goers' lives, revival spread to the surrounding communities. Edwards described and defended the awakening in his book, *A Faithful Narrative of the Surprising Work of God in the Conversion of Many Hundred Souls in Northampton and the Neighboring Towns.*

Thousands were converted through his sermons, which he would read without emotional hype. His strength in preaching centered in his careful exposition of the Scriptures, intellectual rigor, focus on Christ, and call to personal piety and holy affection.

A graduate of Yale and a Presbyterian minister for twenty-two years of one of the largest and wealthiest churches in Massachusetts, he also served as a missionary to the Mohican Indians before assuming the presidency of the College of New Jersey (now Princeton University). He died from a smallpox vaccine shortly after taking office.

FOCUS FACT

George Whitefield's voice was so loud and clear he could be heard by 20,000 people.

George Whitefield (1714-1770). While studying at Oxford, George Whitefield received a book from Charles Wesley. Through it, he explained, "God showed me that I must be born again, or be damned." Ordained in the Anglican church, Whitefield drew large crowds

SIGNIFICANT EVANGELISTS THROUGHOUT HISTORY cont.

wherever he spoke. His "vulgar style" of preaching in the everyday language of his audience drew criticism from some fellow ministers. After he was denied the pulpits in some churches, he, along with the Wesleys, pioneered evangelistic preaching in fields and marketplaces.

Originally coming to Georgia to establish the first orphanage in America, Whitefield traveled throughout the colonies. He was well-known for his dramatic style and strong voice, which satisfied audiences of more than 20,000 at one time. His energy and enthusiasm were contagious, and he became one of driving forces of the Great Awakening.

During his tours he preached an average of forty hours each week. Over the thirty-three years of his ministry, he preached around 18,000 sermons and established schools, orphanages, and religious societies. His goal in ministry was "to awaken a drowsy world, to rouse them out of their formality, as well as profaneness, to put them upon seeking a present and great salvation." He died during a preaching tour in Rhode Island.

Francis Asbury (1745-1816). America's greatest Methodist leader, Francis Asbury oversaw the tremendous growth of the Methodist church from less than 3000 in 1775 to around 60,000 by 1790. As the first bishop of the American Methodist Church, he was instrumental in forming the church into a mature organization whose influence extended throughout the frontier.

"" FOCUS QUOTE

Go into every kitchen and shop; address all, aged and young, on the salvation of their souls. —Francis Asbury on his conviction that preachers should be "out and about"

Asbury promoted revival camp meetings and circuit-riding preachers as key strategies for evangelizing the young nation. He wrote, "I pray God that there may be twenty camp meetings in a week, and wonderful seasons of the Lord in every direction." His preachers were known for their diligence; in bad weather people would say, "There is nothing out today but crows and Methodist preachers."

Asbury modeled the commitment of the Methodist preachers. Although often ill, he rode 4000 to 6000 miles each year. In all, he traveled over 300,000 miles by horseback, wrote 50,000 letters, and ordained 4000 preachers.

Richard Allen (1760-1831). Born into slavery, Richard Allen was converted through the ministry of a Methodist circuit rider in Delaware at age seventeen. Allen's change of character and genuine faith prompted his master, Mr. Stokeley, to open his house for meetings of prayer and preaching. After Stokeley became a Christian he made it possible for his slaves to purchase their freedom. For the next five years Allen worked odd jobs to save money and became an itinerant preacher, traveling with leading Methodist preachers of the day.

He visited Philadelphia to preach in 1786 and decided to stay, becoming a member of St. George's Methodist and working among the blacks of the city. He wrote, "I soon saw a large field open in seeking and instructing my African brethren, who had been a long forgotten people, and few of them attended public worship."

As the number of black worshipers increased at St. George's, segregated seating was enforced. Allen determined that a separate church for blacks was necessary, and finally one Sunday after especially humiliating treatment, a group of blacks left St. George's Church, promising never to go back.

Bishop Francis Asbury dedicated Bethel, the first black Methodist church, in 1799, and ordained Allen as the pastor. In 1816, after years of tension over matters of jurisdiction, black pastors met in Philadelphia to organize the African Methodist Episcopal Church. Allen was elected as the first bishop and continued serving as pastor of Bethel A.M.E. Church. His organizing abilities enabled the young denomination to grow, increasing sevenfold during his years of oversight.

A man of action and energy, Allen was committed to improving the lot for Africans in America. Along with overseeing a successful series of businesses, he was heavily involved in civic affairs. In his ministry he called people to repentance and eternal life, but also to physical liberation through self-help, education, moral reform, and through attacking the vices of dishonesty and drunkenness.

Charles Grandison Finney (1792-1875). Charles Finney left his promising law career in 1821 after receiving "a retainer from the Lord to plead his cause," and in so doing initiated a new era of revivalism. While Jonathan Edwards and George Whitefield had focussed on God's work in converting sinners, Finney focussed on the role of the evangelist and the sinners in securing their salvation. He wrote, "A revival of religion is not a miracle. It is not a miracle, or dependent on a miracle, in any sense . . . a revival is the result of the right use of the appropriate means."

These means, or "New Measures," included praying for sinners by name, permitting women to pray in the meetings, holding meetings for weeks at a time, establishing the anxious bench for those wanting to repent, and reasoning with the audience like a lawyer with a jury.

Finney was criticized by eminent church leaders including Lyman Beecher and Asahel Nettleton. He responded with published arguments and repeated success in his evangelistic meetings.

He expected that a changed heart would be reflected in a changed life, and he repeatedly spoke out against alcohol and slavery. After pastoring the Broadway Tabernacle (built especially for him), Finney taught theology at the newly-formed Oberlin College. Later he became president of the college, opening its doors to blacks and women.

He continued to hold evangelistic meetings throughout the midwest and northeast. He spoke at Whitefield's Tabernacle in London; the inquiry room filled with 1600 people. Literally hundreds of thousands of people converted to Christ as a result of his ministry, including many who were highly educated and who appreciated his lawyerly arguments and conversational sermons.

"" FOCUS QUOTE

I look upon this world as a wrecked vessel. God has given me a lifeboat and said to me, "Moody, save all you can." —D. L. Moody

---

Dwight Lyman Moody (1837-1899). D. L. Moody was the leading evangelist of his day. Born in Massachusetts, he moved to Boston before finishing school and found a job as a shoe clerk. While there, his Sunday school teacher led him to Christ. After he moved to Chicago and established a successful shoe business, he established a Sunday school in North Market Hall which grew to a weekly attendance of 1500.

When he was 23, Moody left his shoe business, began working with the Young Men's Christian Association, and developed his evangelistic, fund-raising, and organizational skills.

In 1873 he and soloist Ira Sankey traveled to England to hold evangelistic meetings. Though poorly educated, Moody preached sincere, simple sermons that drew large crowds. When the pair returned to America they were national sensations and quickly became the most influential evangelists in the nation.

SIGNIFICANT EVANGELISTS THROUGHOUT HISTORY cont.

Moody carefully organized and publicized his meetings in major cities throughout America. Stressing the importance of the local church, he devised a new strategy. He divided the city into sections, and held meetings in a centrally-located church in each section. Volunteers from each section publicized the meetings and assisted in them. Moody wrote, "The plan of holding meetings in the tabernacle centralizes the interest and possibly draws out larger crowds, but the churches are the places to do effective work." In the course of his ministry Moody traveled at least 1 million miles and preached to more than 100 million people.

Moody established a number of educational institutions, including Northfield Seminary for girls, Mount Hermon School for boys, and the Chicago Bible Institute (now Moody Bible Institute). In addition, Moody was actively involved in a number of rescue missions and other expressions of Christian social compassion.

Summer student conferences held near his home in Massachusetts grew into the Student Volunteer Movement, through which thousands of students dedicated their lives to missions. SVM's motto reflected Moody's own desire: "the evangelization of the world in this generation."

Moody's message addressed the "Three R's:" Ruin by Sin, Redemption by Christ, and Regeneration by the Holy Ghost. Instead of employing the sensationalism of Finney, Moody won his audiences with sentimental stories that focused on a loving, father God who wishes to bring lost people back into relationship with himself.

Sam Jones (1847-1906). Called the "Moody of the South," Sam Jones was born into a family of Methodist circuit riders in Alabama. Jones began drinking to blunt the pain of recurrent ulcers; as a result he ruined his law practice and drove away his wife. He finally quit drinking after his dying father asked Jones to meet him in heaven. One week later he became a Christian and soon began preaching.

Jones became a Methodist circuit rider in North Carolina and became known for his logical sermons and exceptional speaking ability. Through the early 1880s he preached in urban centers throughout the South, and, following a campaign in Brooklyn in 1885, he preached in every major city in America.

Nashville became the center for his ministry. In 1885 he began preaching in a tent holding 3000, and by 1892 10,000 converts had joined churches in the area. A wealthy businessman converted through his ministry wanted a permanent building for Jones and built the Union Gospel Tabernacle, later home to the Grand Ole Opry.

Jones spoke bluntly in simple language using wit and stories in a style similar to Will Rogers. His message was aimed first to rouse church members to a dynamic faith and then to call the unsaved to commitment. He spoke out against gambling, evolution, and liquor, and insisted that Christians lead a life of moral excellence.

J. Wilbur Chapman (1859-1918). Chapman assisted D. L. Moody during the 1893 World's Fair in Chicago, and worked a year with B. Fay Mills, a classmate and friend. Mills pioneered Simultaneous Evangelistic Campaigns in which simultaneous evangelistic meetings occurred throughout a whole city.

Chapman refined Mill's approach, and soloist Charles Alexander joined him between 1908 and 1918. Special attention was given to share the gospel with shut-ins, the elderly, men on skid row, and others who would not come to the main meetings.

A long Philadelphia campaign in 1908 recorded 1.4 million attenders. In Boston in 1909, more than 30 assistant evangelists and 1000 personal workers reaped 7,000 decisions among the 720,000 attenders. After the Boston meetings the success of the simultaneous meetings waned, and the Chapman–Alexander team returned to more traditional evangelistic meetings both in the U.S. and around the world.

Amanda Berry Smith (1837-1915). Born a slave, Amanda Smith became an internationally-known evangelist. She gave her life to Christ at thirteen at a Methodist Episcopal church in Pennsylvania and dedicated her life to God's service at eighteen. After her husband and youngest child died, she gave herself to evangelistic work among blacks in New York.

Her gift for speaking was recognized by her friends, who encouraged her to speak at a holiness camp meeting attended primarily by whites. A warm reception there led to more invitations, and she became a regular speaker at holiness meetings.

She spoke at a Keswick conference and a number of evangelistic meetings throughout England, traveled to India to work as a visiting evangelist, then to Liberia in West Africa for seven years. She returned to America and preached throughout the east.

In addition to her evangelist work, she organized women's temperance groups and groups for children. She retired near Chicago and poured herself and her savings into an orphanage for black children.

Billy Sunday (1862-1935). Billy Sunday captured America's mood during the pre-World War I era and was probably America's most flamboyant evangelist. Born in a log cabin and raised in Iowa, Sunday first reached national prominence as a professional baseball player. Known for his speed, he stole 96 bases in 100 games. He played for Chicago, Pittsburgh, and Philadelphia.

While in Chicago he was converted at Pacific Garden Mission, attended a Presbyterian church, and married Helen A. Thompson, who attended there. In 1891 he left Philadelphia and a salary of $500.00 per month to work with the YMCA in Chicago at $83.33 per month. With the YMCA, Sunday held prayer meetings, distributed tracts in bars, and led meetings on the street.

From 1893 to 1895 he worked as an advance man for J. Wilbur Chapman, from whom Sunday learned the art of holding evangelistic meetings. When Chapman settled into a pastorate in 1895, Sunday was asked to hold evangelistic campaigns. Chapman lent Sunday his sermons to get him started.

Ordained in the Presbyterian Church in 1903, even though his theological education was weak, Sunday continued his evangelistic campaigns in small towns. As the reputation of the "Baseball Evangelist" grew, Sunday received national media attention and moved his meetings to larger cities. From 1912 to 1918, Sunday was one of the most popular preachers in America. Magazines and newspapers printed transcripts of his sermons and "box scores" recording the number of converts.

For each city campaign, Sunday and his team arrived weeks in advance to build support, develop local volunteer committees, and build a wooden tabernacle for the meetings. Sawdust covered the wooden floors to keep down the noise, and those who converted to Christ during the meetings were said to have "hit the sawdust trail."

Sunday was known for his wild gestures and one-line zingers. He raised chairs over his head and imitated drunkards when preaching against liquor. His one-liners include, "Going to church don't make a man a Christian any more than going to a stable makes a man a horse," and "the bars of the Church are so low that any old hog with two or three suits of clothes and a bank roll can crawl through." Sunday became a chief spokesman for national morality and decency. He preached hard and often against alcohol, saying "I'm trying to make America so dry that a man must be primed before he can spit."

His popularity declined quickly after the war. A change in the national mood, questions of impropriety in the publishing of a book, and an unwillingness to submit to financial accountability all contributed to his decline from public prominence. His ministry continued, however, and he died while preaching in Mishawaka, Indiana, in 1935.

W. J. Seymour (d. 1923). Charles F. Parham, a non-denominational evangelist originally from Iowa, opened Bible schools first in Topeka, Kansas, and then in Houston, Texas. His students

SIGNIFICANT EVANGELISTS THROUGHOUT HISTORY cont.

studied the Scriptures in late 1900 and determined that speaking in tongues was the biblical evidence for the baptism of the Holy Spirit, an event separate from conversion or sanctification. Mrs. N. O. LaBerge first spoke in tongues in early 1901 and the Pentecostal movement was born.

W. J. Seymour, a black hotel waiter in Houston, carried the message to Los Angeles as an associate pastor. After being locked out of the church for his views, a small group moved their meeting to an old building on Azusa Street.

Word of the Azusa Street revival spread widely; people came from all across the country. Often speaking in tongues for the first time, visitors returned home with their hearts on fire, bringing Pentecostalism with them.

Seymour presided over the Azusa Street meetings and three years of continuous revival. Pentecostal revival spread around the world, and by 1960 10 million people held Pentecostal convictions. Today, Pentecostal denominations are among the fastest-growing churches in the world.

Mel Trotter (1870-1960). Wounded by his dysfunctional family, Mel Trotter, then an alcoholic, visited the Pacific Garden Mission in Chicago the night he had planned to commit suicide. He gave his life to Christ, and his new faith transformed his life.

In a short time Trotter moved to Grand Rapids to establish a new rescue mission, then helped start sixty more. These missions provided basic food and shelter along with evangelistic activities.

Speaking in tough street slang and familiar with the pain of the slums, Trotter communicated the love of Christ in a powerful way. He wrote, "The only way you can get men to Christ is by love, and you have got to love them into the kingdom of God. A rescue mission without love wouldn't amount to anything."

During World War I Trotter preached to soldiers at bases around America. He recorded 15,000 conversions during a year and a half of ministry. He assisted Billy Sunday after the war and held his own evangelistic campaigns as well.

Evangeline Booth (1865-1950). Eva's family life centered around the Salvation Army, a young organization started by her father, William. Her parents modeled compassion for the less fortunate, piety, and personal religious commitment. She often played at preaching with her brothers and sisters while growing up, and at fifteen she began her work with the Army, selling the *War Cry* on the streets of London. At seventeen she received her own Salvation Army post.

She preached, sang, and played guitar in public houses and run-down halls, gaining the nickname, "White Angel of the Slums." Her natural peacemaking abilities and common sense were often employed in the service of the Army. When hot spots arose, General Booth said, "Send Eva."

For this reason Eva first came to America. Now calling herself Evangeline, she patched up a potential defection of the American branch of the Salvation Army and later became commander of the quickly growing U.S. forces. Under her able leadership the Salvation Army developed rescue homes for "fallen women," help for unwed mothers, convicts, and the unemployed. After the San Francisco earthquake of 1906, Evangeline established the disaster relief arm of the Army.

She spoke in support of the prohibition movement and her public lectures were well attended. She was a good speaker and musician. Some of her hymns are still in the Salvation Army songbook.

For the Salvation Army's service to American soldiers in World War I, Evangeline was awarded the Distinguished Service Medal in 1919. She demonstrated her commitment to the United States by becoming a citizen in 1923.

Eleven years later she left America with "a pang," returning to England in order to take the leadership of the worldwide Salvation Army. A hard worker, Evangeline drove herself at a crushing pace for weeks on end, then retreated for periods of complete rest. After her retirement in 1939 she returned to her home in the U.S. and died at age eighty-five.

Billy Graham (b. 1918). Billy Graham's early years included milking chores on his parents dairy farm in Charlotte, North Carolina, and a love for baseball. At sixteen Graham was converted at the Charlotte revival meetings of Mordecai Ham. He studied at a small Florida Bible college (now Trinity College), and began preaching with the encouragement of the college's dean. Graham had prepared four sermon outlines in advance, but when he preached for the first time, he sped through all four outlines in just eight minutes.

V. Raymond Edman, president of Wheaton College (Illinois), encouraged young Graham to complete his studies at Wheaton. There he met his future wife, Ruth Bell, and took the pastorate of the Gospel Tabernacle, located only a few blocks from campus.

After pastoring the First Baptist Church of Western Springs, Illinois, 1943-1945, Graham accepted Torrey Johnson's invitation to become a Youth for Christ evangelist. During the following two years he traveled 200,000 miles to participate in meetings in 47 states.

From 1947 to 1952 Graham served as president of Northwestern Schools in Minneapolis and continued his evangelistic ministry.

He was catapulted into national prominence during the Los Angeles meetings of 1949. Originally planned for three weeks, the public response to the gospel was so great that the meetings were extended first one week, then another, then another—lasting eight weeks in all. The Hearst newspapers covered the meetings and brought Graham national attention.

The Hour of Decision radio broadcast began in 1950 and by 1984 had a listening audience estimated at 20 million. Schools of Evangelism were established to train pastors in evangelism, starting in 1962. In 1967 Graham used closed circuit television for the first time.

In the course of his ministry Billy Graham has traveled to 84 countries and every state in the U.S. He has preached the gospel in person to more than 100 million people around the world. His characteristic humility has remained unchanged through the years, as has his message: lasting peace and the solutions to the problems of the world today can be found only in the personal transformation which comes through turning to Christ and being born again.

Prayer and extensive preparations mark each city-wide crusade. Churches work together in common purpose; local lay people learn to share their faith through Christian Life and Witness classes, and Schools of Evangelism train pastors; thousands of counselors receive training; choirs of several thousand voices are organized. Extensive use of the media and invitations by thousands of believers bring the unconverted to the meetings, which often set attendance records wherever the meetings are held.

Graham's ministry has played a significant role in shaping the modern ethos of evangelicalism. In 1966 he helped found *Christianity Today*, a national magazine designed to help pastors and educated lay persons. The Billy Graham Evangelistic Association helped sponsor the World Congress on Evangelism in Berlin and the Lausanne Conference in 1974. This second conference brought together over 2,400 people from 150 countries. The Lausanne Covenant, which emerged from the meetings, has become the basis for Christian cooperative evangelism around the world. Two special international conferences for evangelists were held in Amsterdam in 1983 and 1986.

Billy Graham has played a unique role as the major figure in Protestant Christianity worldwide. His integrity and commitment to evangelism have enabled Christians of various theological traditions to work in unprecedented cooperation, and converts from the ministry of the BGEA are serving Christ and his church around the world.

About the author: Daniel Moul is Research and Technical Resources Coordinator, Institute of Evangelism, Billy Graham Center.

788 PLANS TO EVANGELIZE THE WORLD AD 30–1991

A table of 788 plans, proposals, visions, goals, programs, organizations, slogans, mottoes, publications, events, statements or attempts, all related specifically to implementing world evangelization. Titles in italics refer to published books or to journals. In a sense, this listing is only symbolic. Other plans exist, unknown and unheralded. New plans are surfacing weekly.

Most of the global plans listed are described in further detail, in historical context in "Worldwide Evangelization Movements from AD 30–1990" under Church History.

The meanings of the 16 columns are as follows. Evaluations shown by code values chosen for particular plans are not evaluations of the sponsoring bodies or events themselves, but are evaluations of the relevance and significance of the plans vis-a-vis world evangelization.

Column

1. No: Reference number in this listing.
2. Year of origin.
3. Brief name for plan.
4. Author: Name of author, sponsor or most prominent individual.
5. Init: Initials or acronym for plan or for its originating church, agency, or organization (parentheses give alternative or additional names; hyphens elaborate entities within wide organizations; slashes separate cooperating agencies or organizations).
6. Type: Code indicates level from absence of human plans to massively-detailed master plans.
   0. a vision or view or scenario of the end-time with God's plan for world evangelization
   1. a one-time challenge to Christians to evangelize the world
   2. published sermon or letter
   3. printed document, book, survey, publication
   4. pledge, declaration
   5. unorganized movement or campaign
   6. statement of purpose by an organization or board
   7. announcement of plan with no details worked out
   8. serious plan with some details, procedures
   9. well worked-out scheme with considerable detail and strategy
   10. massively-detailed plan detailing logistics, personnel, finances, schedules
7. Min: Main type of outreach ministry proposed by the sponsor of the plan.
   0. no human activity proposed or required, God will do it by supernatural means
   1. no human activity proposed except repentance and nurture of one's personal life
   2. prayer, worship, monastic life, revivals
   3. survey, research, communication
   4. relief, liberation, dialogue, apologetics
   5. presence, lifestyle, martyrdom, lay apostolate
   6. broadcasting, film, video, audio, hi-tech
   7. preaching, evangelism
   8. power evangelism with sings and wonders, healing, miracles
   9. converting, discipling
   10. church planting, baptizing
   11. forcible baptism and church rule
   12. military conquest with forcible baptism and church rule
   13. training, leadership, networking, administration
   14. literature, Scripture distribution, literacy, art
8. Origin: Where this plan originated. The name given is that of the country at the time of origin, which in several early cases differs from its current name in 1991.
9. Tradition: Affiliation. Note a distinction between two often-confused terms: "Nondenominational" refers to plans developed independently of existing major denominations; whereas "Interdenominational" is reserved for those plans in whose evolution a number of denominations have been involved, exercise control and receive a degree of accountability. By contrast a denominational label (Methodist, Baptist, Lutheran, etc.) usually implies a firmer degree of control and accountability.
10. Coop: Degree of cooperation with other agencies.
    0. none
    1. minimal
    2. partial; other like-minded traditions may participate if they wish
    3. general; cooperation of all like-minded traditions needed, wanted and assumed
    4. essential; cooperation of like-minded traditions indispensable
    5. total; plan envisages cooperation of entire
       spectrum of Christians of all traditions, like-minded and otherwise
11. P: Literature about the plan.
    0. nothing written except incidental reference
    1. briefly written up in published form
    2. published article, encyclical, message
    3. published book, books
    4. printed publicity materials
    5. detailed plans printed for private use
    6. detailed plans published as a book or books
12. Dline: Year of closure or date when end-time envisaged. Dash means no date proposed.
13. Reso: Total resources of mission-related personnel and finances employed for implementing this plan. The term "worker-year" is similar to "man-hour" or "man-year" and gives a rough estimate of the scale of work and resources involved, assuming on average a plan lasts 10 years.
    0. negligible; less than 1 worker-year (one individual's work only)
    1. minimal; 1-10 worker-years (a few individuals)
    2. limited; 10-100 worker-years (a small team, under $10,000 year)
    3. modest; 100-1,000 worker-years (from 10-100 workers, $10,000-100,000 a year)
    4. sizeable; 1,000-10,000 worker-years (from 100-1,000 workers, $100,000 to $10 million a year)
    5. massive; over 10,000 worker-years (over 1,000 workers, $10 million to $100 million a year)
    6. gigantic; over 50,000 worker-years (over 5,000 workers, $100 million a year or $1 billion over one decade)
14. Unev: Percentage of the world's population at year of plan's origin that was unaware of Christianity.
15. Ratio: Ratio of total unevangelized persons in world divided by total Christians in world when plan originated. This ratio is a measure of the relative difficulty of the unfinished task.
16. Status: Status as a global plan to implement world evangelization as of 1988. This variable refers to the current status of the plan, not necessarily the same as the current status of its sponsor.
    0. fizzled out, abandoned without reaching stated goal
    1. defunct, little or insufficient interest shown
    2. defunct, completion of task claimed
    3. implemented but goal not, or not yet, achieved
    4. still alive, but plan clearly fizzling out
    5. still alive, but plan in decline
    6. still alive, but static
    7. still alive, but with original goals abandoned, scaled down, redefined or otherwise igored
    8. alive and making progress toward goals
    9. alive and being massively implemented

No. 1	Year 2	Brief name for plan 3	Author 4	Init 5	Type 6	Min 7	Origin 8	Tradition 9	Coop 10	P 11	Dline 12	Reso 13	Unev 14	Ratio 15	Status 16
1	AD 30	"The Kingdom of God has arrived"	Jesus of Nazareth	-	1	8	Palestine	-	5	3	-	4	99.9	-	9
2	31	The Twelve Apostles as personal evangelists	Jesus the Rabbi	-	8	8	Palestine	-	5	3	-	2	99.9	-	3
3	31	Mission to Israel	Jesus the Messiah	-	8	8	Palestine	-	5	3	-	2	99.9	-	1
4	31	Mission of the Seventy	Jesus the Son of Man	-	8	8	Palestine	-	5	3	-	3	99.9	-	1
5	32	Lightning spread to all nations	Jesus the Returning Judge	-	0	8	Palestine	-	5	3	-	3	99.9	-	1
6	33	Great Commission–1	The Risen Lord	-	1	8	Palestine	Apostolic	5	3	-	4	99.8	42550.0	9
7	33	Great Commission–2	The Ascended King	-	1	8	Palestine	Apostolic	5	3	-	4	99.8	42550.0	9
8	34	Mission of the Twelve to the Jewish Diaspora	The Twelve Apostles	-	5	8	Palestine	Apostolic	5	3	70	3	99.4	17020.0	1
9	35	Power Evangelism, with Signs and Wonders	The Twelve Apostles	-	7	8	Palestine	Apostolic	5	3	-	2	99.0	6481.0	3
10	36	Martyrdom: witness unto death	Stephen the Protomartyr	-	0	5	Palestine	Apostolic	5	3	-	1	98.6	5594.0	3
11	38	Evangelization of the first Gentiles	The Twelve Apostles	-	5	8	Palestine	Apostolic	5	3	-	2	97.7	4157.0	3
12	38	Peter's mission to the Gentiles	Apostle Peter	-	5	8	Palestine	Apostolic	5	3	-	1	97.7	4157.0	3
13	c38	Worldwide witness of the Twelve	The Twelve Apostles	-	5	5	Palestine	Apostolic	5	3	-	2	97.7	4157.0	1
14	46	Paul's urban mission from city to city	Apostle Paul	-	8	8	Syria	Apostolic	5	3	-	1	94.4	944.0	3
15	61	Preaching to all Creation	Apostle Paul	-	6	8	Greece	Apostolic	5	3	-	2	88.2	294.0	2
16	65	Worldwide Proclamation by Three Angels	John the Divine	-	0	0	Asia Minor	Apostolic	5	3	-	0	86.5	288.3	9
17	66	A History of the Great Commission (Luke–Acts)	Luke the Physician	-	3	8	Italy	Apostolic	5	3	-	3	86.1	287.0	2
18	c85	*Epistle of Barnabas*	Barnabas	-	3	1	Cyprus	Apostolic	3	2	2000	0	78.2	156.4	0
19	94	"Entire Roman Empire has been evangelized"	Clement of Rome	-	3	8	Italy	Catholic	3	2	-	1	74.5	149.0	2
20	96	Foreordained martyrdom	John the Divine	-	0	5	Asia Minor	Apostolic	5	3	-	3	73.7	122.8	9
21	c100	Evangelization via cities and trade routes	Ignatius of Antioch	-	5	9	Syria	Catholic	3	1	-	3	72.0	120.0	8
22	c130	Church-planting and conversions through casual contacts	Telesphorus	-	5	10	Italy	Catholic	3	1	-	2	70.8	47.2	8
23	c140	*Shepherd of Hermas*	Hermas	-	3	7	Italy	Catholic	3	2	-	3	70.4	39.1	2
24	c150	Disciple-training school proclaiming Christ to every race	Justin Martyr	-	7	13	Italy	Catholic	3	3	-	3	70.0	35.0	2
25	156	New Age of the Holy Spirit	Montanus	-	0	1	Asia Minor	Montanist	0	2	-	0	69.8	31.7	0
26	c180	Antichrist, Christ, and Millennium	Irenaeus of Lyons	-	0	0	France	Catholic	0	2	-	0	68.8	23.7	0
27	197	"The blood of the martyrs is seed"	Tertullian	-	0	5	Tunisia	Montanist	1	3	-	1	68.1	20.0	2
28	c205	Apologetics relating gospel to pagan philosophy and culture	Clement of Alexandria	-	7	3	Egypt	Orthodox	3	3	-	1	67.9	17.9	2
29	c220	Reaching unreached populations throughout the Oikumene	Origen	-	2	7	Egypt	Orthodox	3	3	-	3	67.4	13.8	9
30	249	Missionary bishops strategically located across world	Cornelius of Rome	-	9	10	France	Catholic	0	3	-	5	66.5	9.6	0
31	c270	Eremitical monasticism challenging lifestyle of the rich	Anthony	-	5	2	Egypt	Orthodox	2	3	-	4	65.9	7.9	8
32	303	Witness under total persecution	Peter I Seal of Martyrs	-	0	5	Egypt	Orthodox	5	3	-	5	64.9	6.1	8
33	308	Church of the Martyrs	Meletius of Lycopolis	-	0	5	Egypt	Orthodox	0	3	-	5	64.7	5.8	0
34	c310	*Demonstratio Evangelica*	Eusebius of Caesarea	-	3	1	Palestine	Orthodox	3	3	-	2	64.6	5.8	2
35	313	State establishment of Christianity as outreach plan	Constantine	-	10	12	Byzantium	Orthodox	0	3	-	5	64.5	5.6	0
36	c320	Itinerant evangelization by Cenobitic monasticism	Pachomius	-	8	2	Egypt	Orthodox	2	3	-	5	64.2	5.4	8
37	325	Ecumenical councils plan Christian presence	Eusebius of Caesarea	-	10	13	Palestine	Orthodox	5	3	-	5	64.0	5.1	0
38	347	"Antichrist will persecute Christians"	Cyril of Jerusalem	-	0	5	Palestine	Orthodox	0	2	-	0	63.1	4.4	0
39	c360	*Apostolic Constitutions*	Dionysius Exiguus	-	3	7	Syria	Orthodox	2	3	-	1	62.6	4.1	0
40	374	Signs, Healings, and Glossolalia	Ambrose of Milan	-	2	8	Italy	Catholic	1	2	-	1	62.0	3.8	0
41	378	Signs, Wonders, and Martyrs	Jerome	-	0	5	Palestine	Catholic	1	3	-	5	61.9	3.7	2
42	378	"Antichrist has been born"	Martin of Tours	-	0	1	France	Catholic	0	2	-	0	61.9	3.7	0
43	392	Western monasticism with itinerant evangelization	John Cassian	-	5	2	Palestine	Catholic	2	3	-	5	61.3	3.4	8
44	398	Constantinople Schl of Evangelists for Great Commission	John Chrysostom	-	8	13	Byzantium	Orthodox	3	3	430	3	61.1	3.3	0

No. 1	Year 2	Brief name for plan 3	Author 4	Init 5	Type 6	Min 7	Origin 8	Tradition 9	Coop 10	P 11	Dline 12	Reso 13	Unev 14	Ratio 15	Status 16
45	c410	Universal episcopate as plan for world mission	Innocent I	-	10	10	Algeria	Catholic	0	5	-	5	60.7	3.2	8
46	417	*Historia Adversus Paganos*	Paulus Orosius	-	0	1	Spain	Catholic	3	3	-	0	60.5	3.2	0
47	426	*The City of God*	Augustine of Hippo	-	3	8	Tunisia	Catholic	4	3	-	1	60.2	3.1	0
48	428	*De Vocatione Omnium Gentium*	Prosper Tiro	-	0	7	France	Catholic	3	3	-	0	60.2	3.1	0
49	499	Cultural translation of Jesus' message	Symmachus	-	5	14	Greece	Orthodox	3	3	-	4	58.0	2.6	3
50	c510	Irish Peregrini: Missionary Pilgrims for Christ	Columbanus	-	5	8	Ireland	Celtic	2	1	-	4	58.3	2.6	0
51	535	*Topographia Christiana*	Cosmas Indicopleustes	-	3	3	Egypt	Nestorian	1	3	-	2	59.0	2.6	0
52	c550	Nestorian monasticism sends mission across Asia	Abraham of Kashkar	-	5	2	Persia	Nestorian	0	1	-	5	59.5	2.6	0
53	594	"The Last Judgment demands missions to all heathen"	Gregory the Great	-	2	7	Italy	Catholic	0	3	-	1	60.8	2.5	0
54	635	Nestorian world missions	Alopen	-	9	7	Syria	Nestorian	0	1	-	5	62.4	2.6	0
55	c700	Patristic Age: Greek and Latin Fathers expound *evangelizo*	Theodotus of Ancyra	-	3	3	Greece	Orthodox	2	3	-	4	65.0	2.7	0
56	720	Fall of Colosseum, Rome, and the World	Bede	-	0	0	England	Anglican	2	3	-	0	65.8	2.8	0
57	780	Nestorian strategy of metropolitan sees worldwide	Timothy I	-	10	10	Persia	Nestorian	0	3	-	5	68.2	3.0	0
58	c780	Forcible baptism of whole races begun	Charlemagne	-	8	11	France	Catholic	0	1	-	5	68.2	3.0	0
59	960	Imminent End of the World	Bernard of Thuringia	-	0	0	Germany	Catholic	0	2	992	0	74.2	3.7	0
60	962	Holy Roman Empire as Rule of Christ on Earth	John XII	-	10	11	Germany	Catholic	0	3	-	5	74.2	3.7	0
61	992	Coming of Antichrist into World	Adso of Montier-en-Der	-	0	0	France	Catholic	0	3	1000	0	74.8	4.0	0
62	999	Advent travel to Jerusalem	Gregory V	-	5	5	Palestine	Catholic	0	1	1000	2	75.0	4.0	0
63	1000	Mass millennial pilgrimage to await Advent	Sylvester II	-	5	5	Palestine	Catholic	1	1	1000	3	75.0	4.0	0
64	1000	Global spread of Catholic Apostolic Church of the East	Ishoyabh IV	-	10	10	Syria	Nestorian	0	3	-	5	75.0	4.0	0
65	1090	College of Cardinals to expand Rule of Christ	Urban II	-	6	13	Vatican	Roman Catholic	0	5	-	2	74.6	4.0	8
66	1095	Crusades for the Defense of Christianity	Urban II	-	10	12	Italy	Roman Catholic	0	5	-	5	74.5	4.0	0
67	1139	*Prophecy of the Popes*	Malachy O'Morgain	-	0	0	Ireland	Roman Catholic	0	3	2000	1	74.3	3.9	8
68	1179	Imminent major catastrophe in AD 1186	John of Toledo	-	0	0	Spain	Roman Catholic	0	1	1186	0	74.1	3.8	0
69	c1180	Final Age of the Spirit	Joachim of Fiore	-	0	0	Italy	Roman Catholic	0	3	1260	0	74.1	3.8	0
70	c1190	Vernacular scriptures: *Historia Scholastica*	Petrus Comestor	-	5	14	France	Roman Catholic	1	3	-	2	74.1	3.8	9
71	1209	Order of Friars: mendicant orders of travelling preachers	Francis of Assisi	OFM	10	8	Italy	Roman Catholic	1	5	-	6	73.9	3.7	9
72	1215	Order of Preachers: "Propagation of the Faith through Preaching"	Dominic	OP	10	7	France	Roman Catholic	0	5	-	6	73.9	3.7	9
73	1221	Bull "Ne Si Secus" to the 13 Catholic Metropolitans	Honorius III	-	2	13	Vatican	Roman Catholic	0	2	-	2	73.8	3.6	3
74	c1250	Church's temporal power as God's instrument for mission	Innocent IV	-	10	11	Italy	Roman Catholic	0	3	-	5	73.5	3.4	5
75	c1250	Popular preachers warn of Coming of Antichrist	Berthold von Regensburg	OFM	0	0	Germany	Roman Catholic	1	1	-	2	73.5	3.4	0
76	1254	Imminent Third Age of the Holy Spirit	Gerard of Borgo San Donnino	-	0	1	Italy	Roman Catholic	1	3	1260	0	73.5	3.4	0
77	c1260	Religious art: painting, stained glass, sculpture	Duccio de Buoninsegna	-	0	14	Italy	Roman Catholic	1	3	-	5	73.4	3.3	8
78	1266	"Send me 100 men"	Kublai Khan	-	1	9	Mongolia	Roman Catholic	0	1	-	2	73.3	3.3	0
79	c1280	Congregation of Friars Pilgrims for Christ Among the Gentiles	William of Tripoli	OP	8	7	France	Roman Catholic	0	2	-	4	73.2	3.2	0
80	1288	*Notitia Seculi*	Alexander of Roes	-	0	1	Germany	Roman Catholic	0	2	1500	0	73.1	3.1	0
81	1290	*The Coming of Antichrist*	Arnold of Villanova	-	0	0	Spain	Roman Catholic	0	3	-	0	73.1	3.1	0
82	1315	*Liber de Fine:* Preaching plus Military Force	Ramon Lull	OFM	1	12	Algeria	Roman Catholic	0	3	-	1	72.7	3.0	0
83	1315	The Final Coming of Antichrist	Hugh of Newcastle	OFM	0	0	France	Roman Catholic	0	2	-	0	72.7	3.0	0
84	1349	East Syrian/Nestorian apogee	Yabalaha III	-	10	10	Syria	Nestorian	0	3	-	5	72.0	3.0	0
85	c1350	Revelation of Antichrist in AD 2000	St John of the Cleft Rock	-	0	1	Italy	Roman Catholic	0	0	2000	0	72.0	3.0	0
86	1399	Wandering preachers proliferate across world	Vincent Ferrer	OP	2	8	Spain	Roman Catholic	0	1	3936	3	73.0	3.0	9

No. 1	Year 2	Brief name for plan 3	Author 4	Init 5	Type 6	Min 7	Origin 8	Tradition 9	Coop 10	P 11	Dline 12	Reso 13	Unev 14	Ratio 15	Status 16
87	c1400	Societas Peregrinantium pro Christo	William of Casale	OFM	8	7	Italy	Roman Catholic	0	2	-	4	73.0	3.0	0
88	1420	Taborite Kingdom of God	Nicholas of Pelhrimov	-	9	12	Bohemia	Hussite	0	1	-	5	74.2	3.2	0
89	1431	Council of Basle orders non-Christians to attend sermons	Eugenius IV	-	2	11	Switzerland	Roman Catholic	1	3	-	3	74.9	3.3	0
90	1450	Dissemination of Scriptures by typography and printing	Johannes Gutenberg	-	9	14	Germany	Roman Catholic	1	5	-	5	76.0	3.5	8
91	1455	*The Imitation of Christ*	Thomas à Kempis	-	3	5	Germany	Roman Catholic	1	3	-	1	76.3	3.6	6
92	1490	Reforming beggar-monks itinerate evangelizing	Wolfgang Capito	-	5	7	Germany	Roman Catholic	0	1	-	3	78.4	4.0	0
93	1493	"Inter Caetera"	Alexander VI	-	2	11	Vatican	Roman Catholic	0	3	-	1	78.6	4.1	0
94	1499	3-story Rhine ark	Johannes Stoeffler	-	0	1	Germany	Roman Catholic	0	1	1524	0	78.9	4.1	0
95	1500	World missions via Spanish/Portuguese imperialism	Alexander VI	-	10	11	Vatican	Roman Catholic	0	5	-	5	79.0	4.2	0
96	1500	End-time predictions	Bartolomeo di Saluzzo	-	0	0	Italy	Roman Catholic	0	1	-	1	79.0	4.2	0
97	1500	Saints and martyrs as evangelizing witnesses	George Novi of Sophia	-	5	5	Italy	Roman Catholic	1	3	-	5	79.0	4.2	8
98	1517	"Visions of the End of the World"	Leonardo da Vinci	-	0	14	Italy	Roman Catholic	2	3	-	1	78.7	4.1	6
99	c1520	Completion of the Task by the Twelve Apostles	Martin Luther	-	0	0	Germany	Lutheran	2	3	1558	0	78.6	4.1	2
100	1523	Conquistadores enforce mass baptism across New World	Charles V	-	10	12	Mexico	Roman Catholic	0	3	-	5	78.5	4.1	0
101	1523	Conversion of Islam and the Whole World to Christ (Jesuits)	Ignatius Loyola	SJ	10	9	Palestine	Roman Catholic	0	6	-	6	78.5	4.1	9
102	1523	Astrologers' prediction of End of World in 1524	Paracelsus (von Hohenheim)	-	0	1	Switzerland	Roman Catholic	0	1	1524	1	78.5	4.1	0
103	1528	Berne Disputation and its Ten Theses	Ulrich Zwingli	-	2	7	Switzerland	Reformed	2	1	-	4	78.4	4.1	0
104	1530	Melchiorites and the New Jerusalem	Melchior Hofmann	-	9	12	Netherlands	Anabaptist	0	1	1533	5	78.4	4.1	0
105	1530	Cessation of Apostolic Commission	John Calvin	-	0	0	Switzerland	Reformed	2	1	-	0	78.4	4.1	2
106	1534	New Zion and the Kingdom of a Thousand Years	John of Leiden	-	9	12	Germany	Anabaptist	0	1	-	5	78.3	4.1	0
107	1536	"The Last Judgment" inspired by hymn "Dies Irae"	Michelangelo Buonarroti	-	0	14	Italy	Roman Catholic	2	3	-	2	78.3	4.1	6
108	1547	*The Centuries* with detailed future prophecies	Michel de Nostradamus	-	0	1	France	Roman Catholic	0	3	2000	4	78.1	4.1	9
109	c1547	Anabaptist view of the Great Commission	Michael Sattler	-	1	7	Germany	Anabaptist	0	1	-	3	78.1	4.1	9
110	c1550	Numerology of Apocalypse and End of World in 1666	J.H. Bullinger	-	0	0	Switzerland	Reformed	2	1	1666	1	78.0	4.1	0
111	1559	Hutterian Brethren's itinerant evangelism	Jakob Hutter	-	5	8	Moravia	Anabaptist	0	1	-	3	77.8	4.1	9
112	1568	Commission of Cardinals begun for foreign missions	Pius V	-	6	13	Vatican	Roman Catholic	0	5	-	2	77.6	4.1	0
113	1573	Congregation for Conversion of Infidels	Gregory XIII	-	6	13	Vatican	Roman Catholic	0	3	-	2	77.5	4.1	0
114	1580	Discalced Carmelite Sisters: evangelization by prayer	Theresa of Avila	-	10	2	Spain	Roman Catholic	0	5	-	5	77.4	4.1	9
115	1584	Evangelistic military conquest	Alonso Sanchez	SJ	9	12	Spain	Roman Catholic	0	3	-	0	77.3	4.1	0
116	1588	Binding validity of Great Commission	Hadrian Saravia	-	2	7	England	Anglican	3	2	-	1	77.2	4.1	0
117	1588	Consistorial Congregation (Sacred Congregtn for Bishops)	Sixtus V	-	10	13	Vatican	Roman Catholic	0	5	-	6	77.2	4.1	9
118	1589	Russian Orthodox state-supported missions	Peter the Great	ROC	10	10	Russia	Eastern Orthodox	0	5	-	4	77.2	4.1	0
119	1594	Logarithms and the Apocalypse, and Number of the Beast	John Napier	-	0	0	Scotland	Presbyterian	1	3	-	1	77.1	4.1	0
120	1600	Bruno's Magico-Religious System	Giordano Bruno	-	0	1	Italy	Roman Catholic	0	3	-	1	77.0	4.1	0
121	c1600	Episcopi Vagantes with plans for Reunion of Christendom	Julius Ferrette	-	5	2	Italy	Old Catholic	0	3	-	4	77.0	4.1	5
122	1610	The Coming of Antichrist	Tomas Malvenda	OP	0	0	Italy	Roman Catholic	0	1	-	1	76.7	4.0	0
123	1613	*De Procuranda Salute Omnium Gentium*	Thomas a Jesu	-	3	9	Spain	Roman Catholic	0	3	-	1	76.6	3.9	0
124	1620	Mission preaching restricted to Twelve Apostles	Johann Gerhard	-	0	1	Germany	Lutheran	0	3	-	0	76.3	3.9	2
125	1622	Propaganda Fide: Spreading the Faith to the World	Gregory XV	-	10	7	Vatican	Roman Catholic	0	6	-	6	76.3	3.8	9
126	1627	Progressive Millennialism before Return of Christ	Joseph Mede	-	0	1	England	Anglican	2	3	-	1	76.1	3.8	4
127	1648	Eleven Million Martyrs	Ildefonso de Flores	SJ	0	5	Spain	Roman Catholic	1	3	-	5	75.4	3.6	8
128	1656	Return of the Jews	Oliver Cromwell	-	0	1	England	Anglican	0	1	-	0	75.2	3.5	0
129	1657	Fifth Monarchy Men	Thomas Venner	-	0	0	England	Anglican	0	1	c1660	2	75.2	3.5	0
130	1658	Antichrist as Parody of Christ	Bartholomaus Holtzhauser	-	0	0	Germany	Roman Catholic	0	0	-	0	75.2	3.5	0

No. 1	Year 2	Brief name for plan 3	Author 4	Init 5	Type 6	Min 7	Origin 8	Tradition 9	Coop 10	P 11	Dline 12	Reso 13	Unev 14	Ratio 15	Status 16
131	c1660	Millennium centered on church in Peru	G. Tenorio	OFM	0	1	Peru	Roman Catholic	0	3	-	0	75.2	3.5	0
132	1663	Missionary Work among Unevangelized Peoples	Justinian von Welz	-	3	7	Germany	Lutheran	2	3	-	2	75.2	3.5	1
133	1667	"To Evangelize the Nations" *(Paradise Lost)*	John Milton	-	2	7	Britain	Anglican	3	3	-	1	75.1	3.5	5
134	1680	Christian Brothers: evangelization by schools	J.-B. de La Salle	FSC	10	13	France	Roman Catholic	0	5	-	5	75.0	3.4	9
135	1693	Knights of the Apocalypse	Innocent XII	-	7	12	Italy	Roman Catholic	0	1	-	2	74.9	3.4	0
136	1698	Society for Promoting Christian Knowledge	Thomas Bray	SPCK/SPG	9	9	Britain	Anglican	2	5	-	4	74.8	3.4	7
137	1700	Missions to Jews	E.C.H. von Hochenau	-	7	7	Germany	Lutheran	0	0	-	1	74.8	3.4	1
138	1703	Spiritans: "Evangelizzazione degli infedeli"	C.F. Poullart des Places	CSSp	10	7	France	Roman Catholic	0	5	-	5	74.8	3.4	9
139	1705	Danish-Halle Mission	B. Ziegenbalg	-	10	7	Denmark	Lutheran	2	5	-	4	74.7	3.3	7
140	1710	Canstein Bible Society	K.H. von Canstein	-	9	14	Germany	Lutheran	2	3	-	4	74.7	3.3	3
141	1725	Great Awakening and Progressive Millennialism	Jonathan Edwards	-	8	1	NorthAm	Congregationalist	2	3	1990	3	74.5	3.4	0
142	1730	End of the World by Deluge	William Whiston	-	0	0	Britain	Anglican	0	1	1736	0	74.4	3.4	0
143	1732	Society for Propagating the Gospel among the Heathen	N.L. von Zinzendorf	-	9	8	Germany	Moravian	2	5	-	4	74.4	3.4	8
144	1770	Tribulation and Antichrist in AD 2000	Jeanne Le Rocher	-	0	0	France	Roman Catholic	0	0	2000	0	73.6	3.3	0
145	1774	United Society of Believers in Christ's Second Appearing	Ann Lee	-	0	0	Britain	Quaker	0	1	-	2	73.5	3.3	0
146	1780	Christendom Society and Basel Mission	C.G. Blumhardt	DCG/EMB	9	7	Germany	Evangelical	2	5	-	4	73.4	3.2	7
147	1782	Concerts of Prayer (for revival and world mission)	Jonathan Edwards	-	9	2	Britain	Evangelical	2	5	-	3	73.3	3.2	3
148	1783	Revival pentecostalism among Black slaves	George Lisle	-	5	8	Jamaica	Baptist	0	1	-	3	73.3	3.2	9
149	1785	Evangelical awakenings throughout Wales	Howel Harris	-	5	8	Wales	Anglican	2	1	-	3	73.2	3.2	9
150	1787	*The Gospel of Christ Worthy of All Acceptation*	Andrew Fuller	-	3	7	Britain	Baptist	2	3	-	0	73.2	3.2	1
151	1792	*Obligations of Christians for Conversion of the Heathens*	William Carey	BMS	3	3	Britain	Baptist	2	3	-	0	73.0	3.2	5
152	1795	London Missionary Society	William Ellis	LMS	9	9	Britain	Congregationalist	2	2	-	4	72.9	3.2	7
153	1800	Revival camp meetings sweep across large populations	James McGready	-	5	8	USA	Methodist	1	1	-	4	72.8	3.2	4
154	1802	Massachusetts Baptist Mission Society	Hezekiah Smith	MBMS	7	7	USA	Baptist	1	1	-	2	72.4	3.1	1
155	1804	Foreign-language Bible Societies: BFBS, ABS, et alia	Thomas Charles	BFBS	10	14	Britain	Interdenominational	2	5	-	5	72.0	3.1	9
156	1805	*Le Dernier Homme:* first modern End-of-the-World novel	J.-B. Cousin de Grainville	-	0	1	France	Roman Catholic	0	3	-	1	71.8	3.1	0
157	1806	Society of Inquiry on the Subject of Missions	Adoniram Judson	-	1	2	USA	Baptist	2	2	-	2	71.6	3.1	0
158	1810	Ecumenical missionary conferences	William Carey	BMS	8	13	India	Baptist	3	1	-	0	70.7	3.0	1
159	1810	American Board of Commissioners for Foreign Missions	S. Newell	ABCFM(UCBWM)	10	9	USA	Congregationalist	2	5	-	5	70.7	3.0	7
160	1811	*Dissertation on Antichrist*	Ethan Smith	-	0	0	USA	Evangelical	0	2	1866	1	70.5	3.0	0
161	1814	Reestablished Jesuit missions	Pius VII	SJ	10	4	Italy	Roman Catholic	0	5	-	4	69.9	3.0	9
162	1815	"The Duty and Reward of Evangelizing the Heathen"	H. Bardwell	-	2	7	USA	Evangelical	1	3	-	0	69.7	3.0	0
163	1815	Missions of the Most Precious Blood	Caspar Del Bufalo	-	9	4	Italy	Roman Catholic	0	5	-	4	69.7	3.0	8
164	1815	*The Spirit of British Missions*	Josiah Pratt	CMS	2	7	Britain	Anglican	2	3	-	0	69.7	3.0	1
165	1818	*The Conversion of the World: or the Claims of 600 Millions*	G. Hall & S. Newell	ABCFM	3	9	India	Congregationalist	2	3	-	1	69.0	2.9	0
166	1819	Missionary Society of the Methodist Episcopal Church	N. Bangs	BGM	10	7	USA	Methodist	1	5	-	6	68.8	2.9	9
167	c1820	Lucifer Unchained by 1940	Catherine Emmerich	-	0	0	Germany	Roman Catholic	0	1	c1980	0	68.6	2.9	0
168	1823	"The Conversion of the World"	Josiah Pratt	CMS	2	9	Britain	Anglican	2	2	-	0	67.9	2.8	0
169	1824	Interdenominational citywide cooperative evangelism	A.F. Schauffler	-	10	7	USA	Interdenominational	2	3	-	5	67.7	2.8	8
170	1825	Bombay Missionary Union	William Carey	BMU	6	7	India	Interdenominational	3	1	-	3	67.5	2.8	0
171	1826	Glasgow City Mission and 200 other city missions	David Nasmiths	LCM/NYCM/&c	9	7	Britain	Nondenominational	2	3	-	4	67.3	2.6	5
172	1827	Premillennial apostasy of Christendom: Dispensationalism	J.N. Darby	-	0	0	Ireland	Brethren	0	3	-	1	67.0	2.7	0
173	1828	Evangelizing in One Generation through Native Evangelists	Karl F.A. Gutzlaff	-	8	7	China	Lutheran	2	1	-	4	66.8	2.7	0
174	1829	Christian Brethren (Christian Missions in Many Lands)	A.N. Groves	CMML	5	5	Britain	Brethren	0	3	-	4	66.6	2.7	8
175	1830	Evangelistic campaigns through professional evangelists	Evangelist Andrew	-	9	7	USA	Interdenominational	1	1	-	5	66.4	2.7	3

No. 1	Year 2	Brief name for plan 3	Author 4	Init 5	Type 6	Min 7	Origin 8	Tradition 9	Coop 10	P 11	Dline 12	Reso 13	Unev 14	Ratio 15	Status 16
176	1830	Church of Jesus Christ of Latter-day Saints	Joseph Smith	CJCLdS	10	5	USA	Mormon	0	5	-	6	66.4	2.7	9
177	1831	Presbyterian Church in the United States	J.H. Rice	PCUS	10	7	USA	Presbyterian	1	5	-	5	66.1	2.6	7
178	1832	Catholic Apostolic Church	Edward Irving	CAC	0	0	Britain	Catholic Apostolic	0	2	c1840	4	65.9	2.6	4
179	1836	Appeal from Missionaries at the Sandwich Islands	William Richards	ABCFM	2	7	Hawaii	Congregationalist	2	2	-	1	65.0	2.5	0
180	1836	*Thoughts on Evangelizing the World*	T.S. Skinner	-	3	7	USA	Evangelical	2	3	-	0	65.0	2.5	0
181	1837	Board of Foreign Missions, Presbytrn Church in the USA	J.C. Lowrie	BFM(COEMAR)	10	7	USA	Presbyterian	1	5	-	5	64.8	2.5	7
182	1837	*The Time for the World's Conversion Come*	Rufus Anderson	ABCFM	2	9	USA	Congregationalist	3	3	-	1	64.8	2.5	0
183	1841	Church growth statistics: monitoring world evangelization	Henry Venn	CMS	8	10	Britain	Anglican	2	5	-	3	63.9	2.4	8
184	1842	Predictions of the End of the World	John Dee	-	0	0	Britain	Anglican	0	1	1842	0	63.7	2.4	0
185	1844	Seventh-day Adventists	William Miller	SDA	0	1	USA	Adventist	0	5	1844	6	63.2	2.4	9
186	1844	Christadelphians (Brothers of Christ)	John Thomas	-	0	0	USA	Christadelphian	0	3	-	2	63.2	2.4	4
187	1844	World Alliance of YMCAs/World YWCA	George Williams	YMCA/YWCA	6	13	Switzerland	Evangelical	3	3	-	5	63.2	2.4	7
188	1845	Southern Baptist Convention	James B. Taylor	SBC-FMB	10	7	USA	Baptist	1	5	-	6	63.0	2.4	9
189	1846	Evangelical Alliance and world conciliarism	P. Schaff	EA	9	13	Germany	Reformed	2	3	-	5	62.8	2.3	8
190	1850	Pyramidology and the future of Christianity	John Taylor	-	0	0	Britain	Anglican	0	3	2001	2	61.9	2.3	1
191	1850	"Antichrist will not delay his coming"	Bertine Bouquillon	-	0	1	France	Roman Catholic	0	0	-	0	61.9	2.3	0
192	1850	Millionaire philanthropist-strategists	Robert Arthington	-	9	7	Britain	Quaker	0	3	-	4	61.9	2.3	3
193	1854	First Union Missionary Convention	Alexander Duff	-	4	13	Britain	Presbyterian	2	2	-	2	60.8	2.2	0
194	1854	Foreign Mission Committee, Canada Presbyterian Synod	J. Geddie	CPS/BWM-UCC	9	7	Canada	Presbyterian	1	5	-	4	60.8	2.2	7
195	c1855	Russian Orthodox scientific basis for missions	N.I. Ilminsky	ROC	3	10	Russia	Eastern Orthodox	0	3	-	0	60.6	2.2	0
196	1857	Organized large-scale lay-centered mass evangelism	D.L. Moody	-	10	7	USA	Congregationalist	2	4	-	5	60.1	2.1	8
197	1858	"The Duty of the present generation to evangelize the World"	J. Parker	-	2	7	USA	Evangelical	3	1	-	0	59.8	2.1	0
198	1859	Salesians: Christian education of youth across world	John Bosco	SDB	10	13	Italy	Roman Catholic	0	5	-	5	59.5	2.1	9
199	1860	Liverpool Conference on Missions	Earl of Shaftesbury	-	4	7	Britain	Anglican	3	3	-	0	59.3	2.1	0
200	1860	Reorganized Church of Jesus Christ of Latter Day Saints	Joseph Smith II	RCJCLDS	6	7	USA	Mormon	0	3	-	4	59.3	2.1	8
201	1861	Women's mission societies	Francis Mason	WUMSA	9	7	USA	Congregationalist	2	5	-	5	59.0	2.0	4
202	1862	Scheutists: "Evangelizzazione dei popoli"	Theophile Verbist	CICM	10	7	Belgium	Roman Catholic	0	5	-	5	58.7	2.0	9
203	1863	New Apostolic Church	H. Geyer	NAK(NAC)	0	1	Germany	Catholic Apostolic	0	5	-	6	58.5	2.0	9
204	1865	Christian Revival Association	William Booth	SA	9	8	Britain	Salvationist	0	3	-	5	57.9	2.0	9
205	1866	"The Duty of the Church to evangelize the World"	C. Dickson	PCUSA	2	7	USA	Presbyterian	3	1	-	0	57.7	1.9	0
206	1867	Confessional conciliarism: Lambeth Conference of Bishops	C.T. Longley	CofE	9	13	Britain	Anglican	3	3	-	5	57.4	1.9	8
207	1867	Combonians: "Evangelizzazione dei popoli"	Daniele Comboni	MCCI/FSCI/MFSC	10	7	Italy	Roman Catholic	0	5	-	5	57.4	1.9	8
208	1869	Aryan Race as God's Chosen Evangelizers	F.W. Farrar	-	2	7	Britain	Anglican	1	0	-	0	56.9	1.9	0
209	1870	Megaministries (each reaching 1% of the world per year)	Charles Jackson	BFBS/ABS/NBS	10	14	Britain	Interdenominational	3	6	-	5	56.6	1.9	8
210	1870	Pan-Orthodox world missions	I. Veniaminov	ROC/OMS	9	10	Russia	Eastern Orthodox	1	3	-	5	56.6	1.9	7
211	1870	Churches of Christ (Non-Instrumental)	A. Campbell	CC	10	9	USA	Disciples	1	3	-	5	56.6	1.9	7
212	1870	Watch Tower Bible & Tract Society	Charles T. Russell	WTBTS-IBSA	10	5	USA	Witnesses	0	6	1874	6	56.6	1.9	9
213	1871	"Apostolic Missions: the Gospel for Every Creature"	Joseph Angus	BMS	2	7	Britain	Baptist	1	2	-	0	56.4	1.9	0
214	1872	Salesian Sisters: evangelization by works of charity	John Bosco	FMA	10	4	Italy	Roman Catholic	0	5	-	5	56.1	1.8	9
215	1873	Regions Beyond Missionary Union	H.G. Guinness	RBMU	8	7	Britain	Nondenominational	0	5	-	4	55.8	1.8	8
216	1874	*Signs of the Times*	James White	SDA	8	1	USA	Adventist	0	3	-	4	55.6	1.8	8
217	1875	Verbites: "Evangelizzazione dei Popoli"	Arnold Janssen	SVD	10	7	Netherlands	Roman Catholic	0	5	-	5	55.3	1.8	9
218	1876	Watchcry	A.T. Pierson	PCUSA	1	3	USA	Presbyterian	3	3	-	1	55.0	1.8	0
219	1877	Shanghai Watchword	A.T. Pierson	-	4	7	China	Interdenominational	3	2	-	2	54.8	1.8	0
220	1880	"A plan to evangelize the World," *The Missionary Review*	A.T. Pierson	-	3	3	USA	Presbyterian	3	2	-	1	54.0	1.7	0
221	1881	World's Christian Endeavor Union	Francis E. Clark	USCE	9	13	USA	Interdenominational	2	3	-	5	53.7	1.7	5

No. 1	Year 2	Brief name for plan 3	Author 4	Init 5	Type 6	Min 7	Origin 8	Tradition 9	Coop 10	P 11	Dline 12	Reso 13	Unev 14	Ratio 15	Status 16
222	1884	*The Christian Century*	C.C. Morrison	-	3	14	USA	Nondenominational	3	3	2000	3	52.9	1.6	5
223	1884	"No conversion of Nations without adequate outlay"	A.O. Van Lennep	-	3	3	USA	Ecumenical	3	3	-	1	52.9	1.6	0
224	1885	Ecumenical Council: "An Appeal to Disciples Everywhere"	D.L. Moody	-	2	3	USA	Congregationalist	3	2	1900	2	52.7	1.6	0
225	1886	1st International Christian Student Conference	D.L. Moody	-	4	13	USA	Interdenominational	3	3	1900	2	52.4	1.6	0
226	1887	Christian & Missionary Alliance	A.B. Simpson	C&MA	9	7	USA	Holiness	2	3	-	5	52.1	1.6	9
227	1888	Student Volunteer Movement for Foreign Missions	R.P. Wilder	SVMFM/SVMU	9	13	USA	Interdenominational	3	5	1900	5	51.9	1.6	0
228	1888	The Great Controversy	Ellen G. White	SDA	3	1	USA	Adventist	0	3	-	0	51.9	1.6	9
229	1888	One By One Band: God's Plan for Soul Winning	T. Hogben	-	8	5	Britain	Nondenominational	1	3	-	3	51.9	1.6	0
230	1889	Make Jesus King	R.P. Wilder	-	1	7	Japan	Interdenominational	3	1	1900	2	51.6	1.6	0
231	1889	SVMFM closure prediction: World Evangelization by 1900	John R. Mott	SVMFM	0	7	USA	Methodist	3	1	1900	0	51.6	1.6	1
232	1890	Scandinavian/Evangelical Alliance Mission	F. Franson	TEAM	9	9	USA	Nondenominational	2	4	-	5	51.3	1.6	9
233	1891	*The Encyclopedia of Missions: Historical, Statistical*	H.O. Dwight	-	3	3	USA	Ecumenical	3	3	-	3	51.0	1.6	3
234	1893	Africa Industrial Mission/SIM International	Walter Gowans	SIM	8	7	Canada	Nondenominational	2	5	-	5	50.6	1.5	9
235	1894	*Methods of the Evangelization of the Non-Christian World*	R.N. Cust	BFBS	3	3	Britain	Anglican	3	3	-	1	50.3	1.5	0
236	1895	*Make Colleges In All Lands Centers of Evangelization*	L.D. Wishard	-	3	13	USA	Ecumenical	3	3	-	1	50.0	1.5	0
237	1895	Assoc of Pentecostal Churches in America (Nazarene)	P.F. Bresee	APCA-CoN	6	8	USA	Holiness	1	3	-	5	50.0	1.5	9
238	1895	World Student Christian Federation	John R. Mott	WSCF	8	13	Sweden	Ecumenical	3	6	-	5	50.0	1.5	7
239	1896	Liverpool Students Conference	R.P. Wilder	-	4	13	Britain	Interdenominational	3	3	-	2	49.8	1.5	0
240	1897	4th Lambeth Conference: resolution on Great Commission	Frederick Temple	-	4	13	Britain	Anglican	3	3	-	3	49.5	1.5	0
241	1897	Canterbury House of Laymen: resolution on Great Commission	Eugene Stock	CMS	4	13	Britain	Anglican	3	3	-	3	49.5	1.5	0
242	1897	"Selfishness of Christians is the only hindrance"	S.M. Zwemer	RCA	1	5	Arabia	Reformed	3	1	-	0	49.5	1.5	0
243	1897	Encyclical "On the Holy Spirit"	Leo XIII	-	2	2	Vatican	Roman Catholic	0	2	-	1	49.5	1.5	3
244	1899	Gideons International	J. Nicholson	-	9	14	USA	Nondenominational	1	5	-	5	49.0	1.4	9
245	1899	Golden Age of Jewish Missions	Leopold Cohn	-	5	7	Germany	Interdenominational	2	3	-	4	49.0	1.4	8
246	1900	New York Ecumenical Missionary Conference	J.S. Dennis	-	4	7	USA	Ecumenical	3	3	-	4	48.7	1.4	0
247	1900	*The Evangelization of the World in This Generation*	John R. Mott	SVMFM	3	3	USA	Ecumenical	4	3	1925	1	48.7	1.4	0
248	1900	Pentecostalism (First Wave, Renewal in the Holy Spirit)	C.F. Parham	-	5	8	USA	Pentecostal	0	3	-	5	48.7	1.4	8
249	1900	Spread of denominationalism across world	Cosmo Gordon Lang	-	5	10	USA	Interdenominational	1	3	-	5	48.7	1.4	3
250	1901	Latter Rain restoration	D.W. Myland	-	7	8	USA	Pentecostal	0	1	-	5	48.6	1.4	8
251	1901	Consolata Fathers: "Evangelizzazione degli infedeli"	G. Allamano	IMC	10	7	Italy	Roman Catholic	0	5	-	5	48.6	1.4	8
252	1902	Missionary Education Movement	C.G. Trumbull	MEM	10	13	USA	Interdenominational	3	4	-	5	48.5	1.4	0
253	1902	*Centennial Survey of Foreign Missions*	J.S. Dennis	APM	3	3	USA	Presbyterian	3	6	-	3	48.5	1.4	0
254	1902	*World-wide Evangelization the Urgent Business of the Church*	T. Jays	SVMFM	4	7	Canada	Interdenominational	4	3	-	4	48.5	1.4	0
255	1903	All Nations Flag Church/Church of God of Prophecy	A.J. Tomlinson	CGP	9	8	USA	Pentecostal	0	3	-	4	48.3	1.4	8
256	1904	Welsh Revival	Evan Roberts	-	5	8	Wales	Methodist	2	3	-	4	48.2	1.4	0
257	1904	Premillennialism's theory that world is already evangelized	W.E. Blackstone	-	0	1	USA	Fundamentalist	0	3	-	2	48.2	1.4	2
258	1905	National conciliarism as basis for world mission	John R. Mott	-	6	13	France	Reformed	3	3	-	5	48.1	1.4	8
259	1906	World mission atlases and surveys	H.P. Beach	-	3	3	USA	Ecumenical	4	3	-	2	48.0	1.4	6
260	1906	Glossolalia to accomplish world evangelization	C.F. Parham	-	0	1	USA	Pentecostal	0	1	-	2	48.0	1.4	0
261	1906	1st Gen. Conference of Missionaries to the World of Islam	S.M. Zwemer	RCA	4	7	Egypt	Reformed	3	3	-	3	48.0	1.4	0
262	1906	Laymen's Missionary Movement	J.B. Sleman	LMM	10	5	USA	Interdenominational	3	4	-	5	48.0	1.4	0
263	1907	*Lord of the World*	R.H. Benson	-	3	1	Britain	Roman Catholic	0	3	c2020	1	47.9	1.4	0
264	1907	Laymen's Missionary Movement of Southern Baptists	Joshua Levering	LMMSB/SBC	8	13	USA	Baptist	1	5	-	4	47.9	1.4	8
265	1908	*The Unfinished Task of the Christian Church*	J.L. Barton	-	3	3	Britain	Ecumenical	4	3	-	1	47.7	1.4	0

No. 1	Year 2	Brief name for plan 3	Author 4	Init 5	Type 6	Min 7	Origin 8	Tradition 9	Coop 10	P 11	Dline 12	Reso 13	Unev 14	Ratio 15	Status 16
266	1910	"Unoccupied sections of the world"/World Missionary Conference	John R. Mott	WMC	3	3	Britain	Ecumenical	4	3	-	3	47.5	1.3	3
267	1910	Reunion of Christendom (Episcopal Church in the USA)	C.H. Brent	-	8	13	USA	Anglican	4	3	-	4	47.5	1.3	4
268	1910	Vision of coming of Antichrist	Pius X	OFM	0	1	Vatican	Roman Catholic	0	2	-	1	47.5	1.3	0
269	1910	*Can the World Be Won For Christ?*	N. Maclean	-	3	9	Britain	Ecumenical	4	3	-	1	47.5	1.3	0
270	1910	Men and Religion Forward Movement	John R. Mott	MRFM	10	13	USA	Interdenominational	3	4	-	5	47.5	1.3	0
271	1910	Church of God (Cleveland) World Missions	R.M. Evans	CoGWM	10	8	USA	Pentecostal	0	5	-	5	47.5	1.3	9
272	1910	*God's Missionary Plan for the World*	J.W. Bashford	-	3	3	Britain	Ecumenical	3	3	-	1	47.5	1.3	0
273	1911	*Unoccupied Mission Fields*	S.M. Zwemer	RCA	3	3	USA	Reformed	3	3	-	1	47.4	1.3	0
274	1912	*International Review of Missions*	J.H. Oldham	IRM	3	3	Britain	Ecumenical	4	3	-	3	47.2	1.3	7
275	1912	Reaching Every Home	C.E. Cowman	OMS	8	7	Japan	Holiness	2	2	-	3	47.2	1.3	3
276	1913	Christ's Etceteras (Worldwide Evangelization Crusade)	C.T. Studd	WEC	9	7	Britain	Nondenominational	0	5	-	5	47.1	1.3	9
277	1913	United Missionary Campaigns	John R. Mott	LMM/FMCNA/ HMC	10	7	USA	Ecumenical	3	4	-	4	47.1	1.3	0
278	1914	Encyclical concerning the Last Age	Benedict XV	-	0	2	Vatican	Roman Catholic	0	2	1914	1	47.0	1.3	0
279	1914	Church Peace Union	John R. Mott	CPU/WAIF	7	4	USA	Ecumenical	2	2	-	2	47.0	1.3	0
280	1914	Inauguration of Kingdom of God on Earth	Charles T. Russell	WTBTS-IBSA	10	5	USA	Witnesses	0	6	1914	5	47.0	1.3	0
281	1915	Elim Foursquare Gospel Alliance	G. Jeffreys	-	8	8	Britain	Pentecostal	0	2	-	3	46.9	1.3	5
282	1916	World Dominion Movement: surveys of unevangelized regions	S.J.W. Clark	SAT(WDM)	9	3	Britain	Ecumenical	3	5	-	3	46.7	1.3	0
283	1916	*The World and the Gospel*	J.H. Oldham	IRM/IMC	3	4	Britain	Ecumenical	4	3	-	1	46.7	1.3	0
284	1917	True Jesus Church	Paul Wei	TJC	9	8	China	Pentecostal	0	5	-	4	46.6	1.3	9
285	1917	Interdenominational Foreign Mission Association	H.W. Frost	IFMA	10	13	USA	Fundamentalist	2	5	-	6	46.6	1.3	9
286	1918	Worldwide Evangelism	Aimee S. McPherson	ICFG	10	8	USA	Pentecostal	0	3	-	5	46.4	1.3	9
287	1918	Christian Crusade for World Democracy	John R. Mott	CCWD	9	4	USA	Methodist	1	3	-	2	46.4	1.3	0
288	1918	United Drive for World Evangelism	R.E. Speer	-	7	7	USA	Presbyterian	1	0	-	0	46.4	1.3	1
289	1918	Interchurch World Movement of North Am., *World Survey*	S.E. Taylor	IWM(IWMNA)	10	13	USA	Ecumenical	3	6	1922	5	46.4	1.3	0
290	1919	International Missionary Council	A.L. Warnshuis	IMC	9	13	Switzerland	Ecumenical	3	3	-	4	46.3	1.3	0
291	1920	League of Denominations	S.E. Taylor	IWM (IWMNA)	7	13	USA	Ecumenical	4	2	-	0	46.2	1.3	1
292	1920	League of Churches of Christ	Meletios IV Metaxakis	-	7	13	Turkey	Eastern Orthodox	4	2	-	0	46.2	1.3	1
293	1920	Planting of church in all cultures	P. Charles	-	8	10	Belgium	Roman Catholic	1	3	-	5	46.2	1.3	3
294	1920	Mennonite Central Committee	J.A. Lapp	MCC	8	4	USA	Mennonite	1	2	-	4	46.2	1.3	8
295	1920	General Council of Co-operating Baptist Missions	W.C. Haas	BMM	8	7	USA	Baptist	0	5	-	5	46.2	1.3	6
296	1921	Institute of Social and Religious Research	John R. Mott	-	8	3	USA	Ecumenical	3	3	-	3	46.0	1.3	0
297	1921	Oxford Group (Moral Re-Armament)	F.N.D. Buchman	MRA	5	5	Britain	Interdenominational	2	3	-	5	46.0	1.3	4
298	1921	Ecumenical Union of Pentecostal Believers	F.A. Hale	AoG-USA	7	13	USA	Pentecostal	2	0	-	0	46.0	1.3	1
299	1921	Electric or electronic church	Aimee S. McPherson	ICFG	10	6	USA	Pentecostal	1	6	-	5	46.0	1.3	8
300	1922	1st International Missionary Congress	Benedict XV	IMC	4	7	Netherlands	Roman Catholic	1	3	-	3	45.9	1.3	0
301	1922	"Miserimus Redemptor"	Pius XI	-	2	1	Vatican	Roman Catholic	0	2	c1930	1	45.9	1.3	0
302	1922	Catholic Action: "Ubi arcano"	Pius XI	-	2	5	Italy	Roman Catholic	0	5	-	5	45.9	1.3	5
303	1923	Daily radio and television church services	George V	BBC(UK)	10	6	Britain	Nondenominational	2	6	-	5	45.8	1.3	6
304	1923	*Evangelism in the Modern World*	E.A. French	-	3	7	Britain	Methodist	2	3	-	2	45.8	1.3	0
305	c1923	Million Testaments Campaigns	G.T.B. Davis	-	8	14	USA	Nondenominational	1	3	-	3	45.8	1.3	0
306	1924	Global White leadership in world evangelization	R.E. McAlister	PAW/PCI	7	13	USA	Pentecostal	0	0	-	3	45.6	1.3	0
307	1924	United Pentecostal Church International	J.G. Scheppe	UPCI-FMD	10	8	USA	Pentecostal	0	5	-	5	45.6	1.3	9
308	1925	Universal Christian Conference on Life and Work	N. Soderblom	-	4	4	Sweden	Ecumenical	4	3	-	4	45.5	1.3	0

No. 1	Year 2	Brief name for plan 3	Author 4	Init 5	Type 6	Min 7	Origin 8	Tradition 9	Coop 10	P 11	Dline 12	Reso 13	Unev 14	Ratio 15	Status 16
309	1925	*World Missionary Atlas*	H.P. Beach	ISRR/IMC	3	3	USA	Ecumenical	3	3	-	3	45.5	1.3	0
310	1926	*The Unfinished Task of Foreign Missions*	R.E. Speer	-	3	3	USA	Presbyterian	4	3	-	1	45.3	1.3	0
311	1926	Lighthouse of International Foursquare Evangelism	Aimee S. McPherson	LIFE-ICFG	8	13	USA	Pentecostal	0	3	-	4	45.3	1.3	8
312	1927	1st World Conference on Faith and Order	V.S. Azariah	-	4	4	Switzerland	Ecumenical	4	3	-	4	45.2	1.3	0
313	1927	Association of Baptists for World Evangelism	R.C. Thomas	ABWE	9	7	USA	Baptist	0	3	-	4	45.2	1.3	8
314	1927	*The Future of Christianity*	G.H. Williams	-	3	3	Britain	Anglican	3	2	-	1	45.2	1.3	0
315	1928	*The Unfinished Evangelistic Task*	C.H. Fahs	IMC	3	3	Britain	Ecumenical	4	3	-	1	45.1	1.3	0
316	1928	World Fundamental Baptist Missionary Fellowship	J.F. Norris	WFBMF(WBFM)	8	10	USA	Fundamentalist	0	4	-	4	45.1	1.3	9
317	1929	Each One Teach One	F.C. Laubach	-	9	14	Philippines	Congregationalist	4	3	-	5	44.9	1.3	0
318	1930	Movemt for World Evangeliztn/Christian Holiday Crusade	Thomas Cochrane	MWE-CHC	8	7	Britain	Nondenominational	1	4	-	3	44.8	1.3	5
319	1930	World Council for Life and Work	William Temple	-	4	4	Britain	Ecumenical	4	3	-	4	44.8	1.3	0
320	1930	Voice of Prophecy	H.M.S. Richards	SDA	0	6	USA	Adventist	0	5	-	5	44.8	1.3	9
321	1930	Bringing Christ to the Nations (The Lutheran Hour)	W.A. Maier	LCMS	10	6	USA	Lutheran	2	5	-	5	44.8	1.3	9
322	1930	International Missions	B. Davidson	IM	9	10	USA	Nondenominational	0	5	-	4	44.8	1.3	8
323	1930	Association of Camps Farthest Out	Glenn Clark	CFO	8	2	USA	Charismatic	2	4	-	4	44.8	1.3	8
324	1931	Unevangelized Fields Mission	E.J. Pudney	UFM	9	7	Britain	Interdenominational	0	5	-	4	44.6	1.3	9
325	1931	Laudetur Jesus Christus (Radio Vatican)	Pius XI	SJ	10	6	Vatican	Roman Catholic	0	5	-	5	44.6	1.3	9
326	1931	World-Wide Prayer & Missionary Union	D. Dimlich	WWPMU	8	2	USA	Interdenominational	2	4	-	4	44.6	1.3	5
327	1932	Conference of Bible Societies	Eric M. North	ABS/BFBS	4	14	Britain	Ecumenical	4	3	-	4	44.5	1.3	3
328	1933	Laodicean Church Age with Millennium in 1977	W.M. Branham	-	0	0	USA	Pentecostal	0	4	1977	4	44.4	1.3	0
329	1933	The Navigators	Dawson Trotman	-	9	9	USA	Nondenominational	2	4	-	4	44.4	1.3	8
330	1934	*Jesus Christ and World Evangelization*	Alexander McLeish	WDM	3	3	Britain	Ecumenical	3	3	-	1	44.2	1.3	0
331	1934	Evangelize to a Finish to Bring Back the King	A.B. Buxton	IVMF-IVF	4	7	Britain	Interdenominational	2	3	-	3	44.2	1.3	0
332	1934	Biblical Research Society	D.L. Cooper	BRS	0	14	USA	Messianic Jewish	0	3	-	2	44.2	1.3	0
333	1934	Two Thousand Tongues To Go	W.C. Townsend	WBT-SIL	10	14	USA	Interdenominational	1	5	-	5	44.2	1.3	9
334	1934	Youth for Christ International	Torrey Johnson	YFCI	9	7	Canada	Interdenominational	0	5	-	5	44.2	1.3	9
335	1935	World Revival Crusade	G. Jeffreys	WRC	5	8	Britain	Pentecostal	0	3	-	3	44.1	1.3	5
336	c1935	World Intercessors	Alice Huff	OMS(IAMS)	8	2	USA	Holiness	1	2	-	4	44.1	1.3	8
337	1936	Student Foreign Missions Fellowship	R.C. McQuilkin	SFMF-IVCF	9	13	USA	Interdenominational	2	3	-	5	43.9	1.3	0
338	1936	*Awaiting the Light: Unevangelized Areas of the World*	J.G.K. Harman	IVMF	3	3	Britain	Interdenominational	2	3	-	1	43.9	1.3	0
339	1936	Holy Spirit Assoc for Unification of World Christianity	Sun Myung Moon	HSAUWC	10	13	Korea	Presbyterian	0	5	-	5	43.9	1.3	7
340	1937	Child Evangelism Fellowship	J.I. Overholtzer	CEF	9	7	USA	Nondenominational	1	4	-	4	43.8	1.3	8
341	1938	*Evangelism for the World Today (125 opinions)*	John R. Mott	IMC	3	3	USA	Ecumenical	3	3	-	3	43.7	1.3	3
342	1938	"Unoccupied fields," *Interpretative Statistical Survey*	J.I. Parker	IMC	3	3	Britain	Ecumenical	3	2	-	1	43.7	1.3	0
343	1938	4th World Missionary Conference	William Paton	IMC	4	7	India	Ecumenical	3	3	-	3	43.7	1.3	0
344	1938	Gospel Recordings International	Joy Ridderhof	GRI	9	6	USA	Nondenominational	0	5	-	3	43.7	1.3	8
345	1938	World Home Bible League	W.A. Chapman	WHBL	8	14	USA	Nondenominational	2	4	-	4	43.7	1.3	8
346	1939	World Council of Bible Societies	Hendrik Kraemer	BFBS/ABS/NBS	4	14	Netherlands	Ecumenical	4	3	-	4	43.5	1.3	0
347	1939	"The Unfinished Evangelistic Task"	Alexander McLeish	IMC/WDM	3	3	India	Ecumenical	3	2	-	1	43.5	1.3	0
348	1939	"Sunday schools and world evangelism"	A. Black	IRM	3	14	Britain	Ecumenical	3	2	-	0	43.5	1.3	0
349	1939	World-Wide Signs Following Evangelism	L.R.M. Kopp	UFC	7	8	USA	Messianic Jewish	0	2	-	2	43.5	1.3	0
350	1941	Base ecclesial communities	Helder Camara	CEBEs(BECs)	8	4	Brazil	Roman Catholic	1	5	-	4	43.2	1.3	9
351	1941	*The Battle of World Evangelization*	A.T. Houghton	IVF/BCMS	3	7	Burma	Anglican	2	3	-	1	43.2	1.3	0
352	1941	International multilingual Bible correspondence courses	Oswald J. Smith	EBS-BCC	9	14	Canada	Nondenominational	2	5	-	4	43.2	1.3	9
353	1942	1st World Survey of Unreached Areas: "The Black Spots Survey"	L.G. Brierley	WEC	3	3	Britain	Nondenominational	0	5	-	2	43.2	1.3	1

No. 1	Year 2	Brief name for plan 3	Author 4	Init 5	Type 6	Min 7	Origin 8	Tradition 9	Coop 10	P 11	Dline 12	Reso 13	Unev 14	Ratio 15	Status 16
354	1942	Ling Liang World-Wide Evangelistic Mission	T.S.K. Dzao	-	8	7	China	Nondenominational	0	3	-	3	43.1	1.3	5
355	1942	New Tribes Mission	P.W. Fleming	NTM	9	7	USA	Fundamentalist	1	4	-	5	43.1	1.3	9
356	1942	Committee on World Literacy & Christn Literature (Lit-Lit)	F.C. Laubach	FMCNA	8	14	USA	Ecumenical	3	3	-	2	43.1	1.3	0
357	1943	National Religious Broadcasters	W.W. Ayer	NRB	10	6	USA	Nondenominational	2	5	-	5	43.0	1.2	7
358	1943	*"Into All the World ": the Great Commission*	S.M. Zwemer	-	3	3	USA	Reformed	2	3	-	1	43.0	1.2	0
359	1943	Global Outreach Mission	J.O. Blackwood	GOM	8	7	USA	Nondenominational	1	3	-	4	43.0	1.2	8
360	1943	Conservative Baptist Foreign Mission Society	Vincent Brushwyler	CBFMS	7	10	USA	Baptist	1	4	-	5	43.0	1.2	9
361	1944	Third-World missionaries begin international evangelizing	John Sung	AEC	5	8	Indonesia	Interdenominational	2	1	-	5	42.8	1.2	8
362	1945	Evangelical Foreign Missions Association	Clyde W. Taylor	EFMA/NAE	8	13	USA	Interdenominational	2	4	-	6	42.7	1.2	9
363	1945	Parachurch agencies support Great Commission ministries	Herman C. Rutgers	NBS/ABS	10	13	Netherlands	Interdenominational	2	5	-	5	42.7	1.2	8
364	1945	International Institute of Scientific Missionary Research	O.G. Myklebust	IISMR	8	3	Norway	Lutheran	4	1	-	0	42.7	1.2	1
365	1946	"Complete Christ's Commission" and IVSFM conferences	Clyde W. Taylor	IVSFM/SFMF	9	13	USA	Interdenominational	2	3	-	4	42.6	1.2	0
366	1946	United Bible Societies	J.R. Temple	UBS/BFBS	10	14	Britain	Ecumenical	4	5	-	6	42.6	1.2	9
367	1946	World Literature Crusade	J. McAlister	WLC-EHC	10	14	Canada	Nondenominational	2	5	1970	4	42.6	1.2	8
368	1946	*Into All the World: a Statement on Evangelism*	V.C. Alexander	-	3	7	Scotland	Presbyterian	1	3	-	2	42.6	1.2	0
369	1946	Egede Institute of Missionary Study and Research	O.G. Myklebust	EIMSR	8	3	Norway	Lutheran	3	3	-	2	42.6	1.2	5
370	1946	Asociación Misionera Evangélica a las Naciones	Obed Alvarez	AMEN	8	7	Peru	Methodist	2	3	-	4	42.6	1.2	8
371	1947	Whitby IMC Meeting: "Expectant Evangelism"	C.W. Ranson	IMC	4	7	Britain	Ecumenical	4	3	-	2	42.4	1.2	0
372	1947	Commission on World Missions, Lutheran World Federatn	Hanns Lilje	CWM-LWF	4	7	Sweden	Lutheran	2	3	-	4	42.4	1.2	7
373	1947	*Euntes Docete*	J. Saraiva Martins	PUU	3	14	Vatican	Roman Catholic	1	2	-	2	42.4	1.2	6
374	1947	*We Can If We Will: The Challenge of World Evangelism*	R.V. DeLong	-	3	14	USA	Holiness	2	3	-	1	42.4	1.2	0
375	1947	Fuller Theological Seminary	C.E. Fuller	-	1	13	USA	Conservative Evang	2	5	-	4	42.4	1.2	8
376	1947	World Revival Prayer League	Margaret K. Ross	-	6	2	Japan	Nondenominational	2	1	-	1	42.4	1.2	0
377	1947	Oral Roberts Evangelistic Association	Oral Roberts	OREA/ORU/CBM	9	8	USA	Pentecostal	1	4	-	6	42.4	1.2	9
378	1948	10 World Congresses on World Evangelization	Torrey Johnson	YFCI	4	7	Switzerland	Nondenominational	2	3	-	4	42.3	1.2	0
379	1948	World Council of Churches, 7th Function	W.A. Visser t' Hooft	WCC	6	4	Netherlands	Ecumenical	3	6	-	5	42.3	1.2	9
380	1948	International Council of Christian Churches	C. McIntire	ICCC	6	13	USA	Fundamentalist	0	5	-	5	42.3	1.2	5
381	1948	Christian Crusade/ICCC Bible Balloon Project	B.J. Hargis	CENM/ICCC	7	7	USA	Fundamentalist	0	4	-	3	42.3	1.2	0
382	1948	*Set a Watchman: a World Survey*	F.C. Maddox	IVF	3	3	China	Interdenominational	2	3	-	1	42.3	1.2	0
383	1948	New Order of the Latter Rain: Global Missions Broadcast	George Hawtin	NOLR	5	8	Canada	Pentecostal	0	3	-	4	42.3	1.2	3
384	1949	WCC Study "The Evangelization of Man in Modern Mass Society"	J.C. Hoekendijk	WCC	3	3	Switzerland	Ecumenical	4	3	-	2	42.1	1.2	0
385	1949	Association for Native Evangelism	T.L. Osborn	-	8	8	USA	Pentecostal	0	4	-	4	42.1	1.2	8
386	1949	World Gospel Crusades/Every Creature Crusade	C.E. Cowman	WGC/OMS	9	14	USA	Holiness	1	3	-	3	42.1	1.2	4
387	1949	*World Christian Handbk (1949, 1952, 1957, 1962, 1968)*	K.G. Grubb	WCH/WDM	3	3	Britain	Ecumenical	4	3	-	2	42.1	1.2	0
388	1949	Cursillos de Cristianidad	J. Hervas	-	8	13	Spain	Roman Catholic	1	5	-	4	42.1	1.2	7
389	1950	Billy Graham Evangelistic Association	Billy Graham	BGEA	10	7	USA	Nondenominational	2	6	-	5	42.0	1.2	9
390	1950	Help Open Paths to Evangelize (HOPE)	G.F. Gudladt	HOPE	7	7	USA	Fundamentalist	0	2	-	2	42.0	1.2	0
391	1950	World Vision International	Bob Pierce	WV-WVI	8	4	USA	Nondenominational	1	4	-	6	42.0	1.2	9
392	1950	*Literacy as Evangelism/World Literacy Evangelism*	F.C. Laubach	WLE	3	14	Philippines	Ecumenical	4	3	-	3	42.0	1.2	3
393	1950	Evangelistic broadcasting/Cathedral of Tomorrow	Rex Humbard	-	1	6	USA	Pentecostal	0	4	-	5	42.0	1.2	8
394	1950	Hour of Decision	Billy Graham	BGEA	7	6	USA	Baptist	1	5	-	4	42.0	1.2	8
395	1950	Full Gospel Businessmen's Fellowship International	D. Shakarian	FGBFI	1	13	USA	Pentecostal	2	5	-	5	42.0	1.2	9
396	1950	Baptist Bible Fellowship International	F. Donnelson	BBFI	6	7	USA	Baptist	0	3	-	5	42.0	1.2	8
397	1950	Missionaries of Charity	Mother Teresa	MC	6	4	India	Roman Catholic	2	3	-	5	42.0	1.2	9
398	1950	World-Wide Missions International	Basil Miller	WWM	6	7	Nigeria	Fundamentalist	0	1	-	4	42.0	1.2	5

No. 1	Year 2	Brief name for plan 3	Author 4	Init 5	Type 6	Min 7	Origin 8	Tradition 9	Coop 10	P 11	Dline 12	Reso 13	Unev 14	Ratio 15	Status 16
399	1951	1st World Congress of the Lay Apostolate	Pius XII	-	1	5	Italy	Roman Catholic	0	3	-	3	41.8	1.2	3
400	1952	*Christ's Hope of the Kingdom*	Alexander McLeish	WDM	3	3	Britain	Ecumenical	3	3	-	1	41.7	1.2	0
401	1952	"Trends in world evangelism"	E.J. Homrighausen	WCH-SAT	3	3	Britain	Ecumenical	3	2	-	0	41.7	1.2	0
402	1952	"The Great Commission for Anabaptists"	F.H. Littell	-	3	7	USA	Methodist	3	3	-	1	41.7	1.2	0
403	1952	Worldwide Revival Movement	W.E. Allen	-	3	2	Ireland	Nondenominational	0	3	-	2	41.7	1.2	0
404	1952	World Wide Pictures	Billy Graham	WWP-BGEA	10	6	USA	Evangelical	3	5	-	4	41.7	1.2	9
405	1953	Indonesian Missionary Fellowship	Petrus Octavianus	WEC/IMF	8	7	Indonesia	Nondenominational	0	5	-	4	41.7	1.2	8
406	1953	World Committee for Christian Broadcasting	Edwin Robertson	WCCB/BBC/ICCB	1	6	Britain	Ecumenical	2	1	-	2	41.5	1.2	0
407	1953	"World Evangelization in Our Time"	D.B. Barrett	CMS/BFBS	3	3	Britain	Anglican	5	2	-	0	41.5	1.2	1
408	1953	Congress of Catholic Action: Liberation Theology	G. Gutierrez	CA/CEBes	4	4	Peru	Roman Catholic	1	5	-	5	41.5	1.2	8
409	1954	"Christ the Hope of the World"	W.A. Visser t' Hooft	WCC	4	13	USA	Ecumenical	4	6	-	4	41.3	1.2	3
410	1954	WCC Survey "Evangelism: the mission of the Church"	J.C. Hoekendijk	WCC	3	3	Switzerland	Ecumenical	4	3	-	3	41.3	1.2	0
411	1954	MAP International	L.E. Dixon	MAP	6	4	USA	Nondenominational	2	2	-	5	41.3	1.2	6
412	1954	Schemes for future evangelization	J.E. Rattenbury	MCGB	3	3	Britain	Methodist	1	3	-	0	41.3	1.2	0
413	1954	*The Bible in World Evangelism*	A.M. Chirgwin	UBS/BFBS	3	14	Britain	Ecumenical	4	3	-	1	41.3	1.2	0
414	1954	World Missionary Evangelism	J.E. Douglas	WME	6	7	USA	Nondenominational	1	1	-	3	41.3	1.2	5
415	1954	New Life League World Missionary Society	F.D. Jarvis	NLL	6	14	USA	Baptist	0	4	-	4	41.3	1.2	8
416	1955	World Conference on Missionary Radio	C.W. Jones	WCMR	4	6	USA	Nondenominational	1	1	-	2	41.1	1.2	0
417	1955	Midnight Call Missionary Work	W. Malgo	-	7	7	Switzerland	Evangelical	1	2	-	3	41.1	1.2	0
418	1955	*A Survey of World Missions*	J.C. Thiessen	-	3	3	USA	Conservative Evang	2	3	-	2	41.1	1.2	0
419	1956	Charismatic Movement (Second Wave, Renewal in the Holy Spirit)	R. Winkler	-	5	2	USA	Charismatic	3	5	-	5	41.0	1.2	8
420	1956	*A Monthly Letter About Evangelism*	D.T. Niles	DWME-WCC	3	14	Switzerland	Ecumenical	4	2	-	3	41.0	1.2	7
421	1956	*The Gospel to Every Creature*	L.-J. Suenens	-	3	14	Belgium	Roman Catholic	4	3	-	1	41.0	1.2	0
422	1956	*Mission Fields Today: A Brief World Survey*	A.J. Dain	IVF	3	3	Britain	Anglican	3	3	-	2	41.0	1.2	0
423	1957	*World Evangelism Today*	D.T. Niles	WCC	3	3	Switzerland	Ecumenical	4	3	-	2	40.8	1.2	0
424	1957	Global Conquest	J.P. Hogan	AoG(USA)	8	8	USA	Pentecostal	0	3	1960	4	40.8	1.2	0
425	1957	Nights of Prayer for World-wide Revival	George S. Ingram	CMS	7	2	India	Anglican	2	0	-	1	40.8	1.2	0
426	1957	Easter Day Encyclical	Pius XII	-	0	1	Vatican	Roman Catholic	1	2	c1965	1	40.8	1.2	0
427	1957	*The Unfinished Task*	S.C. Neill	WCC/CMS	3	3	Ireland	Anglican	4	3	-	1	40.8	1.2	0
428	1957	Operation Mobilization/Send The Light	George Verwer	OM-STL	10	5	USA	Nondenominational	2	5	-	5	40.8	1.2	9
429	1957	Conference of World Confessional Groups	B.B. Beach	WCFs/CWCs	6	13	Switzerland	Ecumenical	4	1	-	1	40.8	1.2	5
430	1958	Ecumenical Mission to the World	Alan Walker	ACC	2	7	Australia	Methodist	3	0	-	1	40.6	1.2	0
431	1958	*Porefthendes* (Go Ye)	A. Yannoulatos	SYNDESMOS	4	14	Greece	Eastern Orthodox	1	4	-	2	40.6	1.2	0
432	1958	Bibles For The World	Rochunga Pudaite	BFTW	8	14	India	Conservative Evang	2	4	-	3	40.6	1.2	6
433	1958	*Bilan du Monde: Encyclopédie Catholique du Monde Chrétien*	Jean Frisque	FERES	3	3	Belgium	Roman Catholic	2	3	-	2	40.6	1.2	0
434	1959	Sharing Christ with the Whole World	Baker J. Cauthen	SBC	6	7	USA	Baptist	0	1	-	5	40.5	1.2	3
435	1959	Evangelism-in-Depth	R.K. Strachan	EiD	10	5	Nicaragua	Interdenominational	3	3	-	5	40.5	1.2	6
436	1959	Prophecies of the final Antichrist	P.I. Rissaut	-	0	0	Palestine	Roman Catholic	0	1	2004	0	40.5	1.2	0
437	1959	Worldwide Missionary Society	David Tsutada	-	7	7	Japan	Nondenominational	1	1	-	2	40.5	1.2	0
438	1960	*Facing the Unfinished Task*	J.O. Percy	IFMA	4	7	USA	Fundamentalist	0	4	-	2	40.3	1.2	0
439	1960	Baptist International Missions	D. Sisk	BIM	6	7	USA	Baptist	0	4	-	5	40.3	1.2	8
440	1960	World MAP (World Missionary Assistance Plan)	R. Mahoney	WMAP	8	13	USA	Pentecostal	3	4	2000	3	40.3	1.2	5
441	1960	*The Gospel Blimp*: "One Billion Unreached"	Joseph T. Bayly	IVCF-IVP	3	14	USA	Nondenominational	2	3	-	1	40.3	1.2	0
442	1960	Youth With A Mission	Loren Cunningham	YWAM/AoG	10	8	USA	Pentecostal	3	5	-	6	40.3	1.2	9

No. 1	Year 2	Brief name for plan 3	Author 4	Init 5	Type 6	Min 7	Origin 8	Tradition 9	Coop 10	P 11	Dline 12	Reso 13	Unev 14	Ratio 15	Status 16
443	1961	World Missionary Press	W. Goodman	WMP	8	14	USA	Nondenominational	1	1	-	3	40.1	1.2	0
444	1961	2nd World Survey: "19 Point Programme to Reach the Unreached"	L.G. Brierley	WEC	9	7	Britain	Nondenominational	0	5	-	2	40.1	1.2	1
445	1961	1st Pan-Orthodox Conference	Athenagoras I	-	6	5	Greece	Eastern Orthodox	2	3	-	3	40.1	1.2	8
446	1961	World Evangelism	Morris Cerullo	WE(MCWE)	7	8	USA	Pentecostal	1	1	-	3	40.1	1.2	5
447	1961	Commission on World Mission and Evangelism	D.T. Niles	DWME-CWME	7	7	India	Ecumenical	3	3	-	5	40.1	1.2	9
448	1961	Joint Action for Mission	Lesslie Newbigin	JAM-WCC	7	4	Switzerland	Ecumenical	3	2	-	2	40.1	1.2	0
449	1961	Christian Broadcasting Network/CBN World Outreach	M.G. Robertson	WYAH(CBN)	6	6	USA	Charismatic	1	5	-	6	40.1	1.2	9
450	1961	6th International Student Missionary Convention	Clyde W. Taylor	IVCF-SFMF	4	13	USA	Interdenominational	2	3	1971	2	40.1	1.2	0
451	1961	World Association for Christian Broadcasting	Edwin Robertson	WACB/WCCB/BBC	6	6	Kenya	Ecumenical	2	1	-	2	40.1	1.2	0
452	1961	World Radio Missionary Fellowship: HCJB-TV	C.W. Jones	HCJB-TV/WRMF	9	6	Ecuador	Nondenominational	1	4	-	4	40.1	1.2	8
453	1961	Theological centrality of the Great Commission	Karl Barth	-	1	3	Switzerland	Reformed	3	1	-	0	40.1	1.2	1
454	1961	Third World Missions Federation	Elam Angali	TWMF	7	7	Kenya	Lutheran	2	0	-	1	40.1	1.2	4
455	1962	Vatican Council II (21st Ecumenical Council)	John XXIII	-	10	7	Vatican	Roman Catholic	2	6	-	5	40.0	1.2	3
456	1962	Presence evangelizatn: *The Missionary Nature of the Church*	J. Blauw	NMC	3	5	Netherlands	Ecumenical	3	3	-	0	40.0	1.2	0
457	1962	Haggai Institute for Advanced Leadership Training	John Haggai	HIALT	8	13	Singapore	Nondenominational	3	4	-	4	40.0	1.2	6
458	1962	Catholic prophecies of Antichrist	G. Barberin	-	0	0	Palestine	Roman Catholic	0	3	-	3	40.0	1.2	0
459	1963	Witness in Six Continents	Lesslie Newbigin	CWME-WCC	7	5	Mexico	Ecumenical	3	3	-	4	39.8	1.2	0
460	1963	International Christian Broadcasters	C.W. Jones	ICB	7	6	USA	Nondenominational	2	1	-	2	39.8	1.2	0
461	1963	"Pacem in Terris"	John XXIII	-	3	14	Vatican	Roman Catholic	1	2	-	2	39.8	1.2	0
462	1963	"God's Word for a New Age"	Olivier Beguin	UBS	9	14	Japan	Ecumenical	3	2	-	5	39.8	1.2	0
463	1963	New Life For All	W. Bellamy	NLFA	9	9	Nigeria	Interdenominational	3	3	-	5	39.8	1.2	4
464	1963	Jesus' strategy for the world: *The Master Plan of Evangelism*	Robert E. Coleman	-	9	5	USA	Methodist	3	3	-	2	39.8	1.2	3
465	1964	"Lumen Gentium" and "Ad Gentes"	Paul VI	-	3	7	Vatican	Roman Catholic	2	3	-	4	39.6	1.2	7
466	1964	Each One Teach and Win One	F.C. Laubach	-	8	14	USA	Congregationalist	3	3	-	3	39.6	1.2	4
467	1964	*Global Church Growth*	D.A. McGavran	ICG-SWM	8	10	USA	Interdenominational	2	2	-	2	39.6	1.2	5
468	1964	Secretariat for Non-Christians	Sergio Pignedoli	-	6	4	Vatican	Roman Catholic	1	3	-	3	39.6	1.2	6
469	1964	*Evangelical Missions Quarterly*	James W. Reapsome	EMQ/EMIS	3	3	USA	Evangelical	3	2	-	3	39.6	1.2	8
470	1965	Oriental Orthodox Churches Conference	Kyrillos VI	OOCC	6	5	Ethiopia	Oriental Orthodox	2	3	-	3	39.5	1.2	7
471	1965	World Evangelization Research Centre	D.B. Barrett	WERC/CSWE	8	3	Kenya	Anglican	3	2	-	1	39.5	1.2	6
472	1965	Unreached Peoples emphasis	V.E.W. Hayward	IRM/AACC/WERC	8	3	Cameroon	Ecumenical	3	3	-	2	39.5	1.2	8
473	1965	Secretariat for Non-Believers	Franz König	-	6	4	Vatican	Roman Catholic	1	3	-	3	39.5	1.2	6
474	1965	"Decree on the Apostolate of the Laity"	Paul VI	-	3	5	Vatican	Roman Catholic	5	3	-	4	39.5	1.2	8
475	1966	Wheaton Declaration: "The Church's Worldwide Mission"	Clyde W. Taylor	EFMA/IFMA	4	7	USA	Conservative Evang	3	3	-	2	39.3	1.2	0
476	1966	World Congress on Evangelism	Billy Graham	BGEA/CT	7	7	Germany	Interdenominational	3	3	-	3	39.3	1.2	0
477	1966	Pacific Conference of Churches: "Go Ye . . ."	Baiteke Nabetari	PCC	7	7	New Caledonia	Ecumenical	3	1	-	2	39.3	1.2	0
478	1966	Missions Advanced Research and Communication Center	E.R. Dayton	MARC-WVI	8	3	USA	Nondenominational	2	4	2000	4	39.3	1.2	5
479	1966	Release the World for Christ	C. Panos	GOC	1	7	Greece	Eastern Orthodox	1	1	-	2	39.3	1.2	4
480	1967	Sacred Congregation for the Evangelization of Peoples	Sergio Pignedoli	SCEP-RCC	10	7	Vatican	Roman Catholic	2	6	-	6	39.1	1.2	9
481	1967	International Correspondence Institute	G. Flattery	AoG(USA)-ICI	9	14	Belgium	Pentecostal	1	6	-	4	39.1	1.2	8
482	1967	Crusade for World Revival	P. Yonggi Cho	CWR	1	7	Korea	Pentecostal	2	1	-	3	39.1	1.2	0
483	1967	Council of the Laity (Pontificium Consilium pro Laicis)	Maurice Roy	-	6	5	Vatican	Roman Catholic	1	4	-	5	39.1	1.2	6
484	1967	*Encyclopedia of Modern Christian Missions*	B.L. Goddard	-	3	3	USA	Nondenominational	4	3	-	2	39.1	1.2	2
485	1968	"Behold I make all things new"	N. Goodall	WCC	5	7	Sweden	Ecumenical	3	3	-	3	38.9	1.2	0

No. 1	Year 2	Brief name for plan 3	Author 4	Init 5	Type 6	Min 7	Origin 8	Tradition 9	Coop 10	P 11	Dline 12	Reso 13	Unev 14	Ratio 15	Status 16
486	1968	Total World Evangelization	J.F. Shepherd	-	3	7	USA	Evangelical	2	2	-	0	38.9	1.2	0
487	1968	World Association for Christian Communication	Edwin Robertson	WACC/WACB	6	6	Britain	Ecumenical	3	6	-	4	38.9	1.2	3
488	1968	Anglican Consultative Council	J.W.A. Howe	ACC	6	13	Britain	Anglican	2	3	-	4	38.9	1.2	7
489	1968	"A strategy for world evangelism"	E.L. Copeland	SBC-FMB	3	3	USA	Baptist	2	2	-	0	38.9	1.2	0
490	1968	Association for World Evangelism	F. Reddington	AWE	7	7	USA	Nondenominational	2	0	-	1	38.9	1.2	0
491	1968	African Independent Churches Service	D.B. Barrett	AICS/CMS/COC	9	13	Kenya	Ecumenical	5	5	-	5	38.9	1.2	7
492	1969	Jimmy Swaggart Ministries	Jimmy L. Swaggart	JSM-AoG	10	6	USA	Pentecostal	0	4	-	6	38.8	1.2	9
493	1969	"Peace on Earth" International Assemblies	Nathan H. Knorr	IBSA-JWs	10	5	Denmark	Witnesses	0	6	1975	5	38.8	1.2	8
494	1969	World Evangelism Foundation	W.H. Jackson	WEF/FMB-SBC	9	7	USA	Baptist	0	4	-	4	38.8	1.2	8
495	1970	Commission on Church Cooperation	J.A. Scherer	CCC-LWF	6	4	France	Lutheran	2	2	-	3	38.6	1.2	6
496	1970	9th International Student Missionary Convention	Clyde W. Taylor	-	1	13	USA	Interdenominational	2	4	-	3	38.6	1.2	0
497	1970	*The Late Great Planet Earth*	H. Lindsay	-	0	1	USA	Fundamentalist	0	3	-	2	38.6	1.2	8
498	1970	"AD 2000: 350 million Christians in Africa"	D.B. Barrett	IRM/CMS/SWM	8	3	Kenya	Anglican	5	5	2000	0	38.6	1.2	7
499	1970	Frankfurt Declaration on Mission	P. Beyerhaus	-	4	7	Germany	Conservative Evang	2	1	-	1	38.6	1.2	0
500	1970	World Mission of Reconciliation through Jesus Christ	Robert S. Denny	BWA	8	7	USA	Baptist	1	3	-	2	38.6	1.2	0
501	1970	"Strategy for world evangelism: are we too late?"	C.F.H. Henry	CT/WVI	3	3	USA	Conservative Evang	3	2	-	0	38.6	1.2	0
502	1970	Missionary Message to the World	Paul VI	-	1	7	Samoa	Roman Catholic	2	2	-	2	38.6	1.2	0
503	1970	*Saturation Evangelism*	G.W. Peters	-	3	7	USA	Conservative Evang	3	3	-	1	38.6	1.2	0
504	1970	m.v. Logos and literature evangelism	George Miley	OM	9	14	Britain	Nondenominational	0	5	-	4	38.6	1.2	4
505	1971	"Issues in World Evangelism"	J.R.W. Stott	IVP	3	7	Britain	Anglican	3	3	-	0	37.9	1.2	0
506	1971	Final Advance of Scripture Translation	A. Bergstedt	FAST/SIL	8	14	USA	Nondenominational	1	1	-	2	37.9	1.2	0
507	1971	International Crusades	B.W. Mieth	IC	7	7	USA	Baptist	1	4	2000	4	37.9	1.2	5
508	1971	Conference on Church-Mission Relationships	James W. Reapsome	EMIS	4	7	USA	Conservative Evang	3	3	-	2	37.9	1.2	0
509	1971	World Evangelization Strategy Consultation	P. Rees	-	4	3	USA	Nondenominational	2	0	-	1	37.9	1.2	0
510	1971	Evangelical Alliance Commission on World Mission	A.M. Derham	EAGB	3	7	Britain	Evangelical	3	3	-	2	37.9	1.2	0
511	1972	International Catholic Charismatic Renewal	Ralph Martin	ICCRO	5	2	USA	Roman Catholic	2	3	-	6	37.2	1.1	9
512	1972	"World evangelisation"/*World Pentecost*	Donald Gee	WPC	2	8	Britain	Pentecostal	1	2	-	1	37.2	1.1	0
513	1972	Consultation on the Gospel and Frontier Peoples	R. Pierce Beaver	-	4	3	USA	Interdenominational	3	3	-	3	37.2	1.1	0
514	1972	*The Explo Story: a Plan to Change the World*	P. Eshleman	CCCI	3	7	USA	Nondenominational	2	3	-	1	37.2	1.1	0
515	1972	MIAMSI (Rome)	G. Benelli	MIAMSI	6	5	Italy	Roman Catholic	1	1	-	2	37.2	1.1	0
516	1972	*Koinonia/Look/The Frontiersman*	L.G. Brierley	WEC-IRO	3	14	Brazil	Nondenominational	2	2	-	2	37.2	1.1	8
517	1972	Great Commission Prayer Crusade	Vonette Bright	GCPC-CCCI	4	2	USA	Nondenominational	3	4	1980	3	37.2	1.1	5
518	1972	Salvation Today	John G. Gatu	CWME-WCC	4	4	Thailand	Ecumenical	3	2	-	1	37.2	1.1	0
519	1973	Mission to The World	Paul E. McKaughan	PCA-MTW	9	10	USA	Presbyterian	2	4	-	4	36.5	1.1	8
520	1973	Summer Institute of World Mission	P. Yonggi Cho	SIWM	8	7	Korea	Presbyterian	2	3	-	4	36.5	1.1	8
521	1973	Globe Missionary Evangelism	K. Sumrall	GME	8	8	USA	Charismatic	1	1	-	4	36.5	1.1	6
522	1973	Seoul Declaration on Christian Mission	David J. Cho	AMA	4	7	Korea	Evangelical	3	4	-	2	36.5	1.1	0
523	1973	10th Inter-Varsity Missionary Convention	J.E. Kyle	IVCF-SFMF	1	7	USA	Interdenominational	3	3	-	2	36.5	1.1	0
524	1973	Trinity Broadcasting Network	Paul F. Crouch	TBN	7	6	USA	Pentecostal	1	4	-	6	36.5	1.1	9
525	1973	World Film Crusade/Winning the World for Christ	Brother John	WFC-WTF-WMC	7	6	USA	Nondenominational	3	4	-	2	36.5	1.1	4
526	1973	Ephesian Method: *Breaking the Stained-glass Barrier*	David A. Womack	AoG	9	8	USA	Pentecostal	2	3	-	2	36.5	1.1	3
527	1974	Confessing Christ Today	A. Yannoulatos	-	6	7	Romania	Eastern Orthodox	1	3	-	5	35.8	1.1	0
528	1974	*Operation World: a Guide to Praying for the World*	Patrick J. Johnstone	DM/STL/OM	3	2	Zimbabwe	Conservative Evang	2	3	-	2	35.8	1.1	3
529	1974	Lausanne Committee for World Evangelization	G. Osei-Mensah	ICOWE-LCWE	6	13	Switzerland	Conservative Evang	3	5	-	5	35.8	1.1	9
530	1974	EXPLO-74 (2nd Training Conference on Evangelism)	Joon Gon Kim	CCCI	8	13	Korea	Nondenominational	2	3	-	4	35.8	1.1	0
531	1974	Holy Year Jubilee	Paul VI	-	1	7	Vatican	Roman Catholic	0	3	-	5	35.8	1.1	0

No. 1	Year 2	Brief name for plan 3	Author 4	Init 5	Type 6	Min 7	Origin 8	Tradition 9	Coop 10	P 11	Dline 12	Reso 13	Unev 14	Ratio 15	Status 16
532	1974	Sharing Christ's Bold Mission	Baker J. Cauthen	FMB-SBC	8	7	USA	Baptist	0	3	-	5	35.8	1.1	0
533	1974	3rd Synod of Bishops: "The Evangelization of the Modern World"	Wladyslaw Rubin	SB-RCC	4	4	Vatican	Roman Catholic	1	3	-	6	35.8	1.1	9
534	1974	World Mission 1975 (World Methodist Mission)	Alan Walker	WMC	8	7	Israel	Methodist	1	1	-	4	35.8	1.1	0
535	1974	Mission Renewal Teams	B. Goheen	IVCF	7	7	USA	Nondenominational	2	0	-	3	35.8	1.1	0
536	1974	*Reaching the Unreached*	E.C. Pentecost	MARC-WVI	7	3	USA	Conservative Evang	2	3	-	1	35.8	1.1	0
537	1974	Discipling A Whole Nation	J. Montgomery	DAWN	9	9	Philippines	Nondenominational	3	4	-	3	35.8	1.1	8
538	1974	*Religious and the Evangelization of the World*	J. Cloutier	CRC-CCC	7	2	Canada	Roman Catholic	1	3	-	2	35.8	1.1	0
539	1974	*World Evangelism and the Word of God*	A.P. Johnston	-	3	7	USA	Fundamentalist	2	3	-	1	35.8	1.1	0
540	1974	Presbyterian Order for World Evangelism	Roberta Winter	POWE	6	3	USA	Presbyterian	2	2	-	1	35.8	1.1	4
541	c1974	Missão Antioquia	Jonatan Santos	MA/WEC	8	7	Brazil	Nondenominational	0	1	-	3	35.8	1.1	8
542	1975	Full Gospel World Mission Association	P. Yonggi Cho	FGWMA/AoG	8	8	Korea	Pentecostal	0	3	-	4	35.1	1.1	9
543	1975	World Conference on the Holy Spirit	M. Benhayim	-	1	2	Israel	Pentecostal	1	4	-	2	35.1	1.1	0
544	1975	"Jesus Christ Frees and Unites"	Philip Potter	WCC	4	4	Kenya	Ecumenical	3	4	-	5	35.1	1.1	3
545	1975	"New People for a New World—Through Christ"	Robert S. Denny	BWA	1	7	Sweden	Baptist	1	3	-	5	35.1	1.1	0
546	1975	World evangelization communication strategy	J.F. Engel	-	3	3	USA	Anglican	2	3	-	2	35.1	1.1	0
547	1975	Total Missions Thrust: Global Discipleship	Baker J. Cauthen	FMB-SBC	9	9	USA	Baptist	0	6	-	5	35.1	1.1	0
548	1975	Project Look Up	J. Wiebe	PLU/ICB	8	6	USA	Evangelical	1	4	-	3	35.1	1.1	0
549	1975	Associates for World Evangelization	Bruce Graham	AWE	4	7	USA	Evangelical	2	0	-	1	35.1	1.1	0
550	1975	International Missionary Congress	Agnelo Rossi	IMC-RCC	4	3	Italy	Roman Catholic	1	3	-	3	35.1	1.1	0
551	1975	*Evangelii Nuntiandi*	Paul VI	-	3	7	Vatican	Roman Catholic	3	3	-	3	35.1	1.1	3
552	1975	Total World Evangelization Vision	L. Southwick	NLI-TWEV	6	14	USA	Charismatic	1	4	-	2	35.1	1.1	5
553	1975	Genesis Project: New Media Bible	J. Heyman	NMB-GP/CCCI	8	6	USA	Nondenominational	1	4	-	4	35.1	1.1	5
554	1975	World Evangelical Fellowship Missions Commission	Theodore Williams	MC-WEF	8	13	Korea	Conservative Evang	2	3	-	5	35.1	1.1	9
555	1976	Bold Mission Thrust	W. Hultgren	BMT-SBC	10	7	USA	Baptist	1	6	2000	6	34.4	1.1	9
556	1976	Gabriel Olasoji World Evangelism	Gabriel K. Olasoji	GOWE	8	8	Nigeria	Pentecostal	3	4	-	3	34.4	1.1	8
557	1976	US Center for World Mission	R.D. Winter	USCWM	10	7	USA	Conservative Evang	2	4	-	4	34.4	1.1	9
558	1976	Lausanne Strategy Working Group	C.P. Wagner	SWG-LCWE	8	3	USA	Conservative Evang	3	4	-	3	34.4	1.1	4
559	1976	Congress on World Missions and Evangelism	A.J. Dain	-	1	7	Australia	Evangelical	3	4	-	1	34.4	1.1	0
560	1976	American Military Evangelizing Nations	Ira North	AMEN-CCCC	7	7	USA	Disciples	1	1	-	3	34.4	1.1	4
561	1976	Church Growth International Seminars	P. Yonggi Cho	AoG	5	10	Korea	Pentecostal	2	4	2000	4	34.4	1.1	9
562	1976	1st Chinese Congress on World Evangelization	Thomas Wang	CCOWE	4	7	Hong Kong	Evangelical	3	4	-	2	34.4	1.1	8
563	1976	EFMA People Groups Tally	Wade Coggins	EFMA	3	3	USA	Conservative Evang	3	1	1990	2	34.4	1.1	0
564	1976	Lausanne Intercession Advisory Group	Vonette Bright	LCWE/CCCI	7	2	USA	Nondenominational	3	4	-	3	34.4	1.1	5
565	1976	Habitat for Humanity International	M.D. Fuller	HHI	8	4	USA	Evangelical	1	4	-	3	34.4	1.1	6
566	1976	Fellowship of World Christians	Bruce Graham	FOW/AWE/ USCWM	1	7	USA	Evangelical	2	1	-	2	34.4	1.1	0
567	1977	Charismatic Renewal in the Christian Churches	K. Ranaghan	-	1	7	USA	Pentecostal/Charismtc	3	3	-	3	33.7	1.0	9
568	1977	"Catechetics in our time"	Paul VI	-	3	13	Vatican	Roman Catholic	1	3	-	3	33.7	1.0	3
569	1977	World Conference on Audio-Visuals and Evangelization	C. Hemelink	-	4	6	Germany	Ecumenical	3	2	-	3	33.7	1.0	0
570	1977	Here's Life, World	Bill Bright	CCCI-HLW	10	7	USA	Nondenominational	2	5	1980	5	33.7	1.0	8
571	1978	World Mission 1978-1981	Alan Walker	WMC	9	7	Australia	Methodist	1	2	1981	5	33.0	1.0	0
572	1978	Internatnl Conference on the Catholic Charismatic Renewal	L.-J. Suenens	ICCRO	4	2	Ireland	Roman Catholic	2	2	-	3	33.0	1.0	0
573	1978	Danvik National Conferences on World Evangelization	Sigurd Aske	-	1	7	Norway	Evangelical	3	3	-	2	33.0	1.0	0
574	1978	Maryknoll "Statement of Mission Vision"	Raymond A. Hill	MM	4	4	USA	Roman Catholic	1	5	-	2	33.0	1.0	3
575	1978	*The Battle for World Evangelism*	A.P. Johnston	-	3	7	USA	Fundamentalist	2	3	-	1	33.0	1.0	0

No. 1	Year 2	Brief name for plan 3	Author 4	Init 5	Type 6	Min 7	Origin 8	Tradition 9	Coop 10	P 11	Dline 12	Reso 13	Unev 14	Ratio 15	Status 16
576	1978	Systems, Hardware & Research for Evangelizatn (SHARE)	S. Wilson	SHARE-MARC-WVI	9	3	USA	Nondenominational	3	4	-	3	33.0	1.0	0
577	1978	Great Commission Strategy Resource Network	Larry Poland	GCSRN-CCCI	9	3	USA	Nondenominational	2	5	1980	3	33.0	1.0	0
578	1979	"The unfinished task of world mission"	J. Verkuyl	-	3	3	Costa Rica	Reformed	3	2	-	1	32.3	1.0	0
579	1979	Sharing of Ministries Abroad (SOMA)	Michael C. Harper	SOMA	9	8	Britain	Anglican	3	4	-	4	32.3	1.0	8
580	1979	Conference on Unreached Peoples	H. Marquardt	WEF	4	3	Germany	Conservative Evang	3	1	-	2	32.3	1.0	0
581	1979	National Missionary Congress: "A New Missionary Era"	Dermot J. Ryan	IMU	1	4	Ireland	Roman Catholic	1	2	-	3	32.3	1.0	0
582	1979	Pan-Orthodox Consultation on Monastic Life & Witness	Shenouda III	GOC/ROC/COC/&c	4	2	Egypt	Orthodox	1	2	-	3	32.3	1.0	8
583	1979	Foursquare Missions International	L. Edwards	ICFG-FMI	8	8	USA	Pentecostal	1	5	-	3	32.3	1.0	9
584	1979	International Charismatic Pilgrimage to Lourdes	L.-J. Suenens	ICCRO	5	2	France	Roman Catholic	1	3	-	4	32.3	1.0	0
585	1979	12th Pentecostal World Conference	E. Dando	PWC	1	8	Canada	Pentecostal	2	3	-	2	32.3	1.0	0
586	1979	Canadian Congress on World Evangelization	L.F.S. Ford	CCWE	1	7	Canada	Evangelical	3	2	-	2	32.3	1.0	0
587	1979	"Towards a New Age in Mission"	Jaime L. Sin	FABC	1	4	Philippines	Roman Catholic	1	4	-	3	32.3	1.0	0
588	1979	The Jesus Project ("Jesus" Film)	P. Eshleman	CCCI	10	6	Israel	Nondenominational	3	5	2000	6	32.3	1.0	9
589	1979	"120,000 Missionaries by the Year 2000"	Billy Graham	BGEA/IVCF	1	7	USA	Evangelical	3	2	2000	1	32.3	1.0	0
590	1979	Angel-I/Angel-II/Angel-III Project	B. Armstrong	NRB/WEF	8	6	USA	Nondenominational	3	3	-	1	32.3	1.0	0
591	1979	PTL Ministries	J. Bakker	PTL/AoG	4	6	USA	Pentecostal	1	4	-	5	32.3	1.0	0
592	1979	*World Christian Magazine*	G. Aeschliman	ISLCFM	6	14	USA	Evangelical	3	2	-	2	32.3	1.0	4
593	1979	Lutherans for World Evangelization	B. Day	LWE	6	3	USA	Lutheran	1	4	-	1	32.3	1.0	4
594	1979	Caleb Project/Joshua Project teams	S. Hawthorne	USCWM	9	3	USA	Evangelical	2	4	-	3	32.3	1.0	6
595	1979	*Unreached Peoples* series	C.P. Wagner	LCWE/MARC	5	3	USA	Evangelical	3	3	-	3	32.3	1.0	6
596	1979	"World evangelism by 2000 AD: can it be done?"	R.D. Winter	USCWM	3	10	USA	Conservative Evang	2	2	2000	0	32.3	1.0	1
597	1980	Global papal apostolic travels	John Paul II	-	10	7	Vatican	Roman Catholic	2	5	-	5	31.6	1.0	7
598	1980	International Consultation on Simple Life-Style	Harvie Conn	LCWE	1	5	Britain	Evangelical	3	3	-	3	31.6	1.0	1
599	1980	Stuttgart Congress on World Evangelization	P. Beyerhaus	-	1	7	Germany	Evangelical	3	4	-	2	31.6	1.0	0
600	1980	Operation World Begin From Here	Peter P.O. Alliu	WECCM	6	8	Nigeria	Charismatic	1	0	-	1	31.6	1.0	4
601	1980	"Your Kingdom Come"	Emilio Castro	CWME-WCC	4	4	Australia	Ecumenical	3	4	-	4	31.6	1.0	3
602	1980	Consultation on World Evangelization	G. Osei-Mensah	COWE-LCWE	4	7	Thailand	Conservative Evang	3	4	-	3	31.6	1.0	0
603	1980	"World Evangelization Today"	G.H. Anderson	ASM	3	3	USA	Nondenominational	2	2	-	1	31.6	1.0	0
604	1980	10th United Bible Societies Council Meeting	Ulrich Fick	UBS	10	14	Thailand	Ecumenical	4	3	1990	3	31.6	1.0	8
605	1980	World Evangelization Crusade	P. Yonggi Cho	CCCI	1	8	Korea	Evang/Charismatic	2	4	-	5	31.6	1.0	0
606	1980	US Festival of World Evangelization	Billy Graham	-	1	7	USA	Interdenominational	3	4	-	4	31.6	1.0	0
607	1980	Pan-Orthodox Consultation on Preaching & Teachg Today	A. Yannoulatos	GOC/ROC/COC/&c	4	7	Yugoslavia	Orthodox	1	2	-	5	31.6	1.0	8
608	1980	International Congress on Evangelization and Atheism	Karl Rahner	PUU/SJ	4	4	Italy	Roman Catholic	1	3	-	4	31.6	1.0	0
609	1980	"A Church for Every People by the Year 2000" (Edinburgh 1980)	R.D. Winter	USCWM	1	10	Britain	Conservative Evang	3	5	2000	4	31.6	1.0	5
610	1980	Third-Wave Renewal in the Holy Spirit: Power Evangelism	C.P. Wagner	-	5	8	USA	Evang/Charismatic	2	3	-	5	31.6	1.0	8
611	1980	*Planning Strategies for World Evangelization*	D.A. Fraser	MARC-WVI	8	3	USA	Conservative Evang	3	3	-	1	31.6	1.0	0
612	1981	Christian broadcasting worldwide	Paul Freed	-	10	6	Netherlands	Nondenominational	2	5	-	5	31.6	1.0	8
613	1981	Charismatic TV evangelists	Oral Roberts	CBN/PTL/&c	1	6	USA	Pentecostl/Charismtc	1	5	-	5	31.6	1.0	5
614	1981	*It Is Harvest Time*	P. Beyerhaus	-	3	3	Germany	Conservative Evang	3	3	-	1	31.6	1.0	0
615	1981	Evangelize the World by Computer Dialing	Bill Bright	CCCI	7	6	USA	Nondenominational	0	0	-	0	31.6	1.0	0
616	1981	2nd Chinese Congress on World Evangelization	Thomas Wang	CCCOWE	4	7	Singapore	Evangelical	3	3	-	2	30.9	1.0	8
617	1981	World Evangelization Strategy Work Group	Imotemjen Aier	BWA	6	3	USA	Baptist	1	2	-	2	30.9	1.0	4
618	1981	Decade of Evangelism, World Evangelism Committee	Alan Walker	WE-WMC	10	7	USA	Methodist	1	2	1990	5	30.9	1.0	8
619	1981	*World Evangelization and the Simple Life-style*	Harvie Conn	-	3	5	USA	Presbyterian	3	3	-	2	30.9	1.0	1
620	1981	"Reaching Unreached Peoples"	Patrick J. Johnstone	EMA/WEC	4	3	Britain	Evangelical	3	2	-	2	30.9	1.0	0

No. 1	Year 2	Brief name for plan 3	Author 4	Init 5	Type 6	Min 7	Origin 8	Tradition 9	Coop 10	P 11	Dline 12	Reso 13	Unev 14	Ratio 15	Status 16
621	1981	Mission to Unreached Peoples (Gooddeeds)	D.D. Martin	MUP	6	9	USA	Nondenominational	1	4	-	2	30.9	1.0	5
622	1981	Dominion Network/Video Satellite	R.W. Johnson	DVS-DBS	10	6	USA	Charismatic	3	5	-	4	30.9	1.0	8
623	1982	Project 223	Floyd McClung	YWAM	10	8	USA	Charismatic	2	5	2011	6	30.1	0.9	9
624	1982	Harvest Vision: 1990	L. Edwards	ICFG-FMI	9	8	USA	Pentecostal	1	5	1990	4	30.1	0.9	5
625	1982	International Association for Mission Studies	F. Verstraelen	IAMS	6	13	India	Nondenominational	2	3	-	4	30.1	0.9	1
626	1982	"The Unevangelized," *World Christian Encyclopedia, AD 1900-2000*	D.B. Barrett	WERC/CMS	3	3	Kenya	Ecumenical	5	5	2000	2	30.1	0.9	8
627	1982	Beachhead Peoples and Bridge People Groups	R.D. Winter	LCWE/USCWM	8	3	USA	Conservative Evang	3	2	2000	3	30.1	0.9	5
628	1982	World Satellite Evangelism	P.I. McClendon	WSE/WSC/ORU	8	6	USA	Charismatic	2	5	-	4	30.1	0.9	8
629	1982	1st Korean World Mission Congress	Yong Chik Han	-	8	8	Korea	Evangelical	2	4	-	4	30.1	0.9	8
630	1982	*Mission and Evangelism: An Ecumenical Affirmation*	Emilio Castro	CWME-WCC	3	7	Switzerland	Ecumenical	3	3	-	4	30.1	0.9	6
631	1982	Institute for World Evangelism	George Morris	IWE-WMC	9	7	USA	Methodist	1	3	1991	4	30.1	0.9	9
632	1982	*Panta ta ethni* (To All Peoples)	A. Yannoulatos	GOC-AD	3	14	Greece	Eastern Orthodox	1	2	-	2	30.1	0.9	4
633	1982	Frontier Peoples Committee	Larry Allman	IFMA-FPC	7	3	USA	Fundamentalist	2	1	-	2	30.1	0.9	4
634	1982	"The Challenge of Our Task"	Wade Coggins	EFMA	4	3	USA	Conservative Evang	4	3	2000	2	30.1	0.9	1
635	1983	World Baptist Congress on Urban Evangelism	Nilson Fanini	BWA	4	7	Brazil	Baptist	1	3	-	2	29.4	0.9	0
636	1983	"A global strategy for world evangelization: 105 steps"	D.B. Barrett	WERC-CSWE	9	3	Kenya	Anglican	5	5	2000	1	29.4	0.9	0
637	1983	1st International Conference for Itinerant Evangelists	Werner Burklin	BGEA	3	7	Netherlands	Conservative Evang	3	4	-	4	29.4	0.9	3
638	1983	"Jesus Christ the Life of the World"	Ted Scott	WCC	10	4	Canada	Ecumenical	4	3	-	5	29.4	0.9	3
639	1983	Global Mapping Project	R.H. Waymire	GMP	6	3	USA	Conservative Evang	2	4	-	2	29.4	0.9	4
640	1983	Lumen 2000	Bobby Cavnar	L-2000/CTV	9	6	USA	Roman Catholic	1	5	2000	4	29.4	0.9	8
641	1983	Committee on the Holy Spirit and Frontier Missions	G. Adkins	CHSFM/USCWM	7	3	USA	Charismatic	2	2	-	1	29.4	0.9	1
642	1983	Third World mission societies: *The Last Age of Missions*	Larry D. Pate	OCM/TWMA	5	8	Brazil	Evangelical	3	3	2000	5	29.4	0.9	9
643	1983	New Focus	R.K. Drollinger	-	7	6	USA	Nondenominational	3	5	2000	4	29.4	0.9	8
644	1984	Worldwide Priests Retreat	Tom Forrest	ICCRO	4	2	Vatican	Roman Catholic	2	4	2000	4	28.6	0.9	3
645	1984	International Prayer Assembly for World Evangelization	Vonette Bright	LCWE/CCCI	8	2	Korea	Evangelical	3	3	-	4	28.6	0.9	0
646	1984	Ethnic Chinese Congress on World Evangelization	Thomas Wang	ECCOWE	4	7	USA	Evangelical	3	4	-	2	28.6	0.9	3
647	1984	*International Journal of Frontier Missions*	Darrell Dorr	IJFM	3	3	USA	Conservative Evang	3	2	2000	2	28.6	0.9	5
648	1984	National and Regional LCWE Conferences	L.F.S. Ford	ICOWE-2	8	13	USA	Conservative Evang	3	1	-	4	28.6	0.9	6
649	1984	"In Christ—Hope for the World"	Zoltan Kaldy	LWF	1	4	Hungary	Lutheran	2	3	-	3	28.6	0.9	1
650	1984	STEP Programme (Strategy to Every People)	Patrick J. Johnstone	STEP-WEC	10	9	Britain	Nondenominational	1	5	1990	4	28.6	0.9	9
651	1984	World Catholic Federation for the Biblical Apostolate	Alberto Ablondi	WCFBA	1	14	India	Roman Catholic	2	3	-	3	28.6	0.9	9
652	1984	Baptist World Discipleship Movement	F. Aular	-	7	9	Venezuela	Baptist	1	1	-	2	28.6	0.9	1
653	1984	*The Unfinished Task*	J.E. Kyle	IVCF	3	3	USA	Nondenominational	3	3	-	1	28.6	0.9	1
654	1984	Twenty-one Strategies for Lausanne	Bradford Smith	SWG-LCWE	8	13	USA	Conservative Evang	2	0	-	2	28.6	0.9	1
655	1984	"Unidos en Cristo Evangelizando las Naciones"	R.H. Sperger	FEDEMEC/WEGO	8	9	Costa Rica	Evangelical	2	1	-	3	28.6	0.9	6
656	1985	Mission 2000	D.A. McGavran	SWM/USCWM	7	10	USA	Conservative Evang	3	4	2000	3	27.9	0.9	0
657	1985	Internatnl Missionary Congress: "Bringing Christ to Man"	R. Pellegrino	PUU	1	4	Italy	Roman Catholic	1	3	-	4	27.9	0.9	0
658	1985	Korean Churches' Plan for Entering Every Country	Han Ki Man	-	10	8	Korea	Interdenominational	3	1	2000	5	27.9	0.9	9
659	1985	Youth Congress on World Evangelization	H. Marquardt	-	1	5	Germany	Evangelical	3	1	-	3	27.9	0.9	0
660	1985	Future Trends in Christian World Mission	W. Knipe	MM(CFMSA)/ASM	3	3	USA	Roman Catholic	2	4	-	2	27.9	0.9	0
661	1985	*God the Evangelist*	David F. Wells	LCWE/WEF	4	8	Norway	Evang/Charismatic	2	3	-	1	27.9	0.9	3
662	1985	Integrity Keepers Conventions	F.W. Franz	IBSA-JWs	10	5	USA	Witnesses	0	6	1995	6	27.9	0.8	9
663	1985	Global Evangelization Strategy Consultation	R.K. Parks	FMB-SBC	6	3	USA	Baptist	1	3	2000	3	27.9	0.9	4
664	1985	World Conference of Baptist Evangelists	Perry Ellis	BWA/SBC	1	7	USA	Baptist	1	1	-	2	27.9	0.9	0
665	1985	"God calls: choose life: the hour is late!"	Pimen I	ACPA/CPC	1	13	Czechoslov	Ecumenical	4	2	-	2	27.9	0.9	5

No. 1	Year 2	Brief name for plan 3	Author 4	Init 5	Type 6	Min 7	Origin 8	Tradition 9	Coop 10	P 11	Dline 12	Reso 13	Unev 14	Ratio 15	Status 16
666	1985	5th West Malaysia Chinese Congress on World Evanglzn	Gideon Chong	CCCOWE	1	7	Malaysia	Evangelical	3	3	-	3	27.9	0.9	0
667	1985	"Mobilizing Indigenous Missions for the Final Harvest"/ICOM	Panya Baba	NEMA/ECWA/SIM	7	7	Nigeria	Evangelical	2	2	2000	4	27.9	0.9	8
668	1985	Global Simultaneous Evangelistic Missions	Alan Walker	WMC	10	7	Indonesia	Methodist	2	1	-	5	27.9	0.9	4
669	1985	Asia Committee for World Evangelization	Fred Magbanua	LCWE	4	13	Hong Kong	Evangelical	3	1	-	2	27.9	0.9	8
670	1985	Global Strategy Committee, Seventh-day Adventists	Neal C. Wilson	GSC-SDA	10	7	USA	Adventist	1	5	2000	6	27.9	0.9	9
671	1985	God's Global Envoys: Nonresidential Missionaries	D.B. Barrett	WERC/FMB	8	3	USA	Interdenominational	5	6	2000	5	27.9	0.9	8
672	1985	International Catholic Programme of Evangelization	Mario Capello	ICPE	8	7	Malta	Roman Catholic	0	2	-	5	27.9	0.9	5
673	1985	The World by 2000	Paul E. Freed	TWR/FEBC/HCJB	9	6	USA	Nondenominational	1	5	2000	5	27.9	0.9	9
674	1985	World Ambassadors	Mark A. Kyle	MCMI	7	8	USA	Charismatic	1	4	-	3	27.9	0.9	6
675	1985	World Consultation on Evangelism	Dwight Loder	WE-WMC	4	7	USA	Methodist	1	5	1991	2	27.9	0.9	0
676	1985	1st Venezuelan Congress of World Missions	Calixto Patricio	-	7	7	Venezuela	Evangelical	3	1	2000	3	27.9	0.9	4
677	1985	CWME Orthodox Advisory Group	A. Yannoulatos	CWME-WCC	4	7	Bulgaria	Orthodox	1	3	-	4	27.9	0.9	9
678	1985	Global Network of Centers for World Mission	Darrell Dorr	USCWM	9	7	USA	Nondenominational	3	5	2000	3	27.9	0.9	6
679	1985	Amsterdam Prayer Conference for World Evangelization	David Bryant	LCWE/YWAM	8	2	Netherlands	Evang/Charismatic	3	4	-	4	27.9	0.9	3
680	1985	EXPLO-85 Global Christian Training Teleconference	Bailey Marks	CCCI	10	13	USA	Evang/Charismatic	3	5	-	5	27.9	0.9	3
681	1985	Association of International Mission Services	Howard Foltz	AIMS	8	13	USA	Charismatic	3	4	2000	3	27.9	0.9	6
682	1985	"Emergency call for United Global Evangelism"	D.A. McGavran	SWM/CGI	1	10	Korea	Interdenominational	3	2	-	0	27.9	0.9	1
683	1985	*Power Evangelism, Power Healing, and Power Encounters*	John Wimber	-	7	8	USA	Charismatic	2	3	-	2	27.9	0.9	8
684	1986	Reaching the World's Cities by AD 2000	J.P. Hogan	AoG(USA)-DFM	9	8	USA	Pentecostal	1	4	2000	5	27.1	0.8	9
685	1986	Consultation on Evangelizing World-Class Cities	R. Bakke	MBI	4	7	USA	Conservative Evang	1	3	-	2	27.1	0.8	4
686	1986	*Touch the World Through Prayer*	W.L. Duewel	OMS	8	2	USA	Holiness	2	3	-	1	27.1	0.8	6
687	1986	Worldwide Student NetWork	David English	WSNW/CCCI	9	7	USA	Evangelical	2	5	2000	2	27.1	0.8	6
688	1986	International Prophetic Ministry Convention	B. Maoz	-	4	1	Israel	Pentecstl/Charismatic	1	4	-	2	27.1	0.8	1
689	1986	Latin American Evangelical Confraternity	M. Ortiz	CONELA	7	7	Venezuela	Conservative Evang	1	4	-	3	27.1	0.8	1
690	1986	International Conference for Equipping Evangelists	Terry Edwards	CEI	7	13	USA	Charismatic	2	4	-	3	27.1	0.8	5
691	1986	"Renew the Church—Reach the World"	David M. Howard	WEF	6	13	Singapore	Conservative Evang	3	5	2000	5	27.1	0.8	9
692	1986	2nd International Conference for Itinerant Evangelists	Werner Burklin	ICIE/BGEA	4	7	Netherlands	Evangelical	3	4	-	5	27.1	0.8	8
693	1986	3rd Chinese Congress on World Evangelization	Thomas Wang	CCCOWE	4	13	Taiwan	Evangelical	3	5	-	2	27.1	0.8	3
694	1986	24th International Old Catholic Congress	G.A. van Kleef	IOCBC	6	13	Germany	Old Catholic	1	2	-	4	27.1	0.8	0
695	1986	Asia Missions Association: "Thy Will be Done on Earth"	David J. Cho	AMA/KIM	6	13	Korea	Evangelical	3	4	-	3	27.1	0.8	0
696	1986	Good News World/Mass Scripture Distribution	J. Godwin	BSSB-SBC	7	14	USA	Baptist	0	0	1995	1	27.1	0.8	1
697	1986	"Toward 2000" (Issachar Frontier Missions Research)	G.K. Otis III	IFMR	8	7	USA	Conservative Evang	1	5	2000	3	27.1	0.8	8
698	1986	*To the Ends of the Earth*	Joseph L. Bernadin	NCCB/USCMA	7	7	USA	Roman Catholic	2	3	-	3	27.1	0.8	9
699	1986	Mandate '86	J.E. Kyle	IVCF	7	13	USA	Evangelical	3	4	-	3	27.1	0.8	9
700	1986	Presbyterian Decade of Evangelism	C. Kirkpatrick	PC(USA)	7	7	USA	Presbyterian	1	4	2000	4	27.1	0.8	9
701	1986	Leaders' Congress on the Holy Spirit & World Evangelizn	H. Vinson Synan	NARSC	7	8	USA	Pentecstl/Charismatic	3	4	-	4	27.1	0.8	3
702	1986	Society for Frontier Missiology	R.D. Winter	USSFM-SFM	6	3	USA	Conservative Evang	2	2	2000	2	27.1	0.8	4
703	1986	Intercontinental Broadcasting Network	J. Martin	IBN	7	6	Norway	Charismatic	1	4	-	2	27.1	0.8	4
704	1986	Global Strategy Group	R.K. Parks	FMB-GSG	6	9	USA	Baptist	2	1	2000	3	27.1	0.8	7
705	1986	One Million Native Missionaries	K.P. Yohannan	GFA	9	7	India	Nondenominational	1	3	-	4	27.1	0.8	8
706	1986	*Wanted: World Christians*	J.H. Kane	-	3	3	USA	Conservative Evang	2	3	-	1	27.1	0.8	6
707	1986	Televised Evangelism for All	N. Van Hamm	CBN	9	6	USA	Charismatic	0	0	-	3	27.1	0.8	6
708	1987	Evangelization 2000/*New Evangelization 2000*	Tom Forrest	E-2000	10	9	Vatican	Roman Catholic	3	4	2000	6	26.4	0.8	9
709	1987	"Communicating Christ to the Nations"	Robert A. Cook	NRB	1	6	USA	Conservative Evang	1	1	-	1	26.4	0.8	1

No. 1	Year 2	Brief name for plan 3	Author 4	Init 5	Type 6	Min 7	Origin 8	Tradition 9	Coop 10	P 11	Dline 12	Reso 13	Unev 14	Ratio 15	Status 16
710	1987	Consultation on World Evangelization	Larry Christenson	CCC/NARSC/ SOMA	6	8	Singapore	Pentecstl/Charismatic	4	1	2000	3	26.4	0.8	6
711	1987	International Conference of Evangelical Bible Societies	J.R. Powell	ICEBS/IBS	8	14	USA	Nondenominational	2	4	-	4	26.4	0.8	8
712	1987	"By the Year 2000: Is God telling us something?"	Thomas Wang	LCWE	3	13	Singapore	Interdenominational	4	2	2000	1	26.4	0.8	8
713	1987	World Evangelization Strategy Committee	Gary Clark	WESC-NARSC	9	3	Britain	Pentecstl/Charismatic	5	3	2000	1	26.4	0.8	6
714	1987	Every Nation by 2000—Every Home for Christ	D.W. Kietzman	WLC-EHC	8	14	USA	Conservative Evang	1	4	2000	4	26.4	0.8	8
715	1987	"Countdown to the Year 2000"	R.D. Winter	USCWM	7	9	USA	Conservative Evang	3	1	2000	1	26.4	0.8	6
716	1987	Global-Village Evangelism	Rochunga Pudaite	BFTW-GVE	7	14	India	Conservative Evang	0	4	-	3	26.4	0.8	3
717	1987	LCWE Younger Leaders' Conference/Singapore '87	B. Stiller	LCWE	4	13	Singapore	Evangelical	3	4	-	3	26.4	0.8	3
718	1987	Global Rosary for World Peace	John Paul II	L-2000/CTV	8	2	Vatican	Roman Catholic	1	1	-	4	26.4	0.8	9
719	1987	*AD 2000 Together*	H. Vinson Synan	NARSC	8	8	USA	Pentecstl/Charismatic	4	4	2000	5	26.4	0.8	9
720	1987	Community Satellite Corporation	R.W. Johnson	CSC/DBS	9	6	USA	Charismatic	1	4	-	4	26.4	0.8	8
721	1987	Global Share Network	R.H. Waymire	GMI	4	6	USA	Nondenominational	3	4	-	1	26.4	0.8	1
722	1987	God's 100,000 New Envoys	T. Yamamori	FFH	3	5	USA	Evangelical	3	3	-	2	26.4	0.8	5
723	1987	The Future of the Christian World Mission	D.B. Barrett	FCWM/ASM	0	3	Britain	Anglican	5	2	-	1	26.4	0.8	6
724	1987	Mission World '89 (International Satellite Mission)	Billy Graham	BGEA	7	7	USA	Evangelical	3	4	-	4	26.4	0.8	0
725	1987	Global Broadcasting System (Top Hat platform network)	Paul F. Crouch	GBS	8	6	USA	Evang/Charismatic	0	5	-	3	26.4	0.8	1
726	1987	Adopt-a-People	W. Tullis	USCWM	9	13	USA	Conservative Evang	2	4	-	3	26.4	0.8	6
727	1987	Christian Communication Technology	J.O. Crawford	CCT-AVCAPI	8	14	USA	Evangelical	2	4	2000	3	26.4	0.8	8
728	1987	Worldwide Prayer Crusade	Sheila Beatty	E-2000/CTV	7	2	Vatican	Roman Catholic	4	4	2000	2	26.4	0.8	8
729	1987	Project 2000: Helping Nationals focus on the Unreached	A. Finley	CNEC-PI	8	7	USA	Conservative Evang	2	4	2000	4	26.4	0.8	6
730	1987	Destiny '87: Here's Life, Black America	Crawford Loritts	CCCI/IVCF	6	7	USA	Evangelical	1	4	-	2	26.4	0.8	1
731	1987	New Life 2000: A Revolutionary Plan (Here's Life World)	C. Osterberg	CCCI	10	7	USA	Nondenominational	2	5	2000	6	26.4	0.8	9
732	1987	*Towards 2000: Reaching the World's Billions*	Benjamin George	CFC/YFC	3	5	Malaysia	Conservative Evang	3	3	2000	0	26.4	0.8	8
733	1987	Interdenominational Global Missions Conferences	R.K. Parks	-	4	13	USA	Interdenominational	3	1	-	3	26.4	0.8	5
734	1987	*Status Report on the Great Commission*	C.D. Hutchins	WMT(WMC)	9	6	USA	Nondenominational	5	6	2000	2	26.4	0.8	8
735	1987	Decade of Harvest	J.P. Hogan	AoG(USA)	10	8	USA	Pentecostal	1	4	2000	6	26.4	0.8	9
736	1987	Ibadan Declaratn on Holistic Evangelization of the World	S. Akande	AABF/BWA	4	13	Nigeria	Baptist	1	2	-	2	26.4	0.8	1
737	1987	2nd Asia Leadership Congress on World Evangelization	John Cho	ALCOWE II	4	13	Singapore	Evangelical	3	4	-	3	26.4	0.8	8
738	1987	COMIBAM '87/Ibero-American Missions Congress	Luis Bush	COMIBAM	4	8	Brazil	Evang/Charismatic	3	4	2000	5	26.4	0.8	9
739	1987	Decade of Destiny for Church of God World Missions	C. Moree	CoGWM	8	8	USA	Pentecostal	0	4	2000	4	26.4	0.8	8
740	1987	Advance Ministries: Reaching the Unreached	Steve Shank	-	6	8	USA	Charismatic	3	1	-	3	26.4	0.8	8
741	1987	"The Missing Key to World Evangelization"	D. Shibley	-	3	2	USA	Charismatic	2	3	-	2	26.4	0.8	8
742	1987	World Evangelism World Plan 1987-1991	Maxie D. Dunnam	WE-WMC	10	7	Jamaica	Methodist	1	3	1991	5	26.4	0.8	9
743	1988	5,300 conferences on evangelization	G.H. Anderson	OMSC/WCC/&c	4	13	Switzerland	Interdenominational	3	2	-	5	25.6	0.8	4
744	1988	"Great Commission Deadline: the Year 2000"	James W. Reapsome	CT/EMIS/EMQ	3	3	USA	Evangelical	3	2	2000	1	25.6	0.8	8
745	1988	*The Church Triumphant at the End of the Age*	Nate Krupp	-	3	3	USA	Nondenominational	2	3	c2000	1	25.6	0.8	6
746	1988	Churches of the Poor	Julio de Santo Ano	-	5	5	Mexico	Interdenominational	1	1	-	5	25.6	0.8	8
747	1988	2nd All-India Congress on Missions & Evangelism	Ebenezer Sunder Raj	AICOME/IMA/EFI	8	7	India	Nondenominational	3	5	-	3	25.6	0.8	8
748	1988	World Evangelization Expert System/Database	D.B. Barrett	WEES/WED/WERC	9	3	USA	Interdenominational	5	5	2000	3	25.6	0.8	8
749	1988	10,000 new books/articles a yr. on mission & evangeliztn	W. Henkel	BM	3	3	Germany	Nondenominational	2	2	-	5	25.6	0.8	8
750	1988	World Prayer Force (to enroll 165 million Christians)	John Gibson	WPF-WMT(WTF)	7	2	USA	Nondenominational	5	4	2000	2	25.6	0.8	8
751	1988	Inter-Agency Consultation on Reaching the Unreached	E.R. Dayton	FMB/WVI/&c	8	3	USA	Interdenominational	3	1	2000	1	25.6	0.8	6
752	1988	Evangelistic mass campaigns: Christ For All Nations	Reinhard Bonnke	CFAN/LPEA/&c	10	7	Argentina	Interdenominational	2	4	-	5	25.6	0.8	8
753	1988	Charismatics United for World Evangelization	Larry Christenson	CUWE/CCC/ NARSC	8	8	Singapore	Pentecstl/Charismatic	4	5	2000	5	25.6	0.8	9

No. 1	Year 2	Brief name for plan 3	Author 4	Init 5	Type 6	Min 7	Origin 8	Tradition 9	Coop 10	P 11	Dline 12	Reso 13	Unev 14	Ratio 15	Status 16
754	1988	Christian prophetic utterances	A. Woldben	-	1	1	Israel	Interdenominational	0	3	-	0	25.6	0.8	6
755	1988	Third World Missions Advance	David J. Cho	TWMA/AMA/PI	4	7	Brazil	Conservative Evang	4	1	2000	5	25.6	0.8	9
756	1988	Video churches and missions	K. Chareonwongsak	CSM	5	6	Thailand	Charismatic	2	1	2000	5	25.6	0.8	8
757	1988	Leadership '88: LCWE emerging leaders conference	Glandion Carney	LCWE	4	13	USA	Evangelical	3	4	-	3	25.6	0.8	8
758	1988	North American African World Missions Congress	Ekpo Ekpo	NACAC	4	7	Nigeria	Conservative Evang	3	4	-	3	25.6	0.8	8
759	1988	International Association for Mission Studies	J. Wietzke	IAMS	4	3	Italy	Nondenominational	2	3	2000	4	25.6	0.8	3
760	1988	International Evangelical Bible Consultation	Billy Graham	BGEA/LCWE	1	13	Jordan	Conservative Evang	2	1	-	2	25.6	0.8	3
761	1988	World Wesleyan Conference on Witness & Evangelism	Maxie D. Dunnam	WMC	4	7	Britain	Methodist	1	4	1991	3	25.6	0.8	3
762	1988	'88 World Evangelization Crusade	P. Yonggi Cho	-	7	8	Korea	Charismatic	3	4	2000	3	25.6	0.8	8
763	1989	Global Consultation on AD 2000 and Beyond	Thomas Wang	LCWE/TWMA/FMB	9	13	Singapore	Evang/Ecumenical	5	5	2000	3	25.6	0.8	9
764	1989	2nd World Consultation on Frontier Missions	L. Chen	WCFM	4	7	USA	Conservative Evang	2	2	2000	2	24.9	0.8	8
765	1989	2nd World Conference on Mission & Evangelism	Eugene Stockwell	CWME-WCC	4	7	Switzerland	Ecumenical	3	4	-	4	24.9	0.8	8
766	1989	International Bishops' Retreat 2000	Tom Forrest	E-2000	4	2	Vatican	Roman Catholic	1	5	2000	5	24.9	0.8	9
767	1989	World Evangelization Conference on Liberation Theology	Maxie D. Dunnam	WMC	4	4	Brazil	Methodist	1	4	-	3	24.9	0.8	8
768	1989	2nd International Congress on World Evangelization	Thomas Wang	ICOWE II	9	8	Singapore	Interdenominational	3	4	2000	4	24.9	0.8	8
769	1989	15th Pentecostal World Conference	Jakob Zopfi	PWC/AoG	4	8	Singapore	Pentecostal	2	4	2000	4	24.9	0.8	9
770	1989	Consultation on Dimensions of Christian Martyrdom	K.H. Ting	-	4	5	Korea	Nondenominational	3	5	-	1	24.9	0.8	8
771	1989	Jerusalem Charismatic Leaders Meeting	Michael C. Harper	-	7	8	Israel	Charismatic	4	1	-	2	24.9	0.8	8
772	1990	Proliferation of denominational/agency AD 2000 plans	Paul E. McKaughan	GEM/LCWE	7	7	USA	Interdenominational	2	4	2000	4	24.1	0.7	9
773	1990	Decade of Universal Evangelization	John Paul II	E-2000	10	7	Vatican	Roman Catholic	2	5	2000	6	24.1	0.7	9
774	1990	Round the World Prayer Event	Maxie D. Dunnam	WE-WMC	8	2	Britain	Methodist	2	4	-	2	24.1	0.7	8
775	1990	Peace Council/Convocation of Christians	Emilio Castro	JPIC-WCC/RCC	6	4	Australia	Ecumenical	3	4	-	4	24.1	0.7	8
776	1990	Joint IFMA/EFMA Conference on Countdown Thinking	Wade Coggins	IFMA/EFMA	4	7	USA	Conservative Evang	3	4	2000	3	24.1	0.7	8
777	1990	World Congress on the Holy Spirit & World Evangelization	H. Vinson Synan	-	6	8	USA	Pentecstl/Charismatic	4	5	2000	5	24.1	0.7	8
778	1990	EXPLO '90 Worldwide Satellite Strategy	Bill Bright	CCCI-HLW	9	6	USA	Nondenominational	1	5	2000	5	24.1	0.7	9
779	1990	Asia Regional Missions Congress on AD 2000	David J. Cho	AMA/TWMA	4	7	Korea	Evangelical	3	4	2000	4	24.1	0.7	9
780	1990	Africa Regional Missions Congress on AD 2000	Panya Baba	LCWE/EMS/&c	4	7	Nigeria	Evangelical	3	4	2000	4	24.1	0.7	9
781	1990	AD 2000 National Consultations	Luis Bush	LCWE/TWMA	4	7	Argentina	Evangelical	3	2	2000	4	24.1	0.7	9
782	1991	Global Congress of Charismatic Leaders for World Evangelization	Michael C. Harper	CUWE/ICCRO	6	8	Britain	Pentecstl/Charismatic	4	4	2000	6	23.3	0.7	9
783	1991	7th Assembly, World Council of Churches	Emilio Castro	WCC	4	4	Australia	Ecumenical	3	4	-	5	23.3	0.7	8
784	1991	4th Chinese Congress on World Evangelization	Hay-Him Chan	CCCOWE	4	7	Hong Kong	Evangelical	3	4	-	3	23.3	0.7	8
785	1991	Charismatic youth churches	Benson Idahosa	-	5	5	Nigeria	Charismatic	2	1	-	4	23.3	0.7	9
786	1991	WMC Conference on World Evangelization	Joe Hale	WE-WMC	4	7	Singapore	Methodist	1	3	-	3	23.3	0.7	8
787	1991	AD 2000 Regional Consultations	Luis Bush	LCWE/TWMA	8	7	Philippines	Evangelical	4	5	2000	4	23.3	0.7	9
788	1991	Great & Holy Council of the Orthodox Church	Demetrios I	EPC	6	5	Greece	Eastern Orthodox	2	5	-	4	23.3	0.7	8
Possible future scenarios with plans															
789	1994	Signs, Wonders, Miracles, and Evangelization	-	-	5	8	-	Pentecstl/Charismatic	-	-	2000	5	21.1	0.6	9
790	1995	World Christian Congress on AD 2000 and Beyond	-	LCWE/TWMA/&c	9	8	-	Evang/Ecumenical	-	-	2000	5	20.3	0.6	9
791	1995	3rd World Consultation on Frontier Missions	-	-	4	7	-	Conservative Evang	-	-	2000	2	20.3	0.6	9
792	1996	Armageddonist Millennium	-	-	0	1	-	Fundamentalist	-	-	-	0	19.6	0.6	9
793	1997	Conversion of Jewish race	-	-	5	7	Israel	Messianic Jewish	-	-	-	5	19.6	0.6	9
794	1999	Eve of Millennium Conference	-	-	4	7	-	Interdenominational	-	-	2000	5	17.3	0.5	9
795	1999	AD 2000 Jubilee Year	-	RCC	10	13	Vatican	Roman Catholic	-	-	2000	5	17.3	0.5	9
796	2000	Celebration 2000	-	-	9	13	-	Pan-Christian	-	-	2000	5	16.6	0.5	9

No. 1	Year 2	Brief name for plan 3	Author 4	Init 5	Type 6	Min 7	Origin 8	Tradition 9	Coop 10	P 11	Dline 12	Reso 13	Unev 14	Ratio 15	Status 16
797	2000	Respect for Christ	-	-	1	1	-	-	-	-	-	5	16.6	0.5	9
798	2000	Entire World finally reached for Christ	-	-	0	13	-	-	-	-	2000	6	16.6	0.5	9
799	2000	Global church-planting	-	-	10	10	-	-	-	-	2000	6	16.6	0.5	-
800	2004	Pentecostal-charismatic Latter-Rain revival	-	-	0	8	-	Pentecstl/Charismatic	-	-	-	5	15.1	0.4	-
801	2006	Itinerant tourist churches	-	-	10	10	-	-	-	-	-	4	14.3	0.4	-
802	2008	Global church research project "The Past"	-	-	9	3	-	-	-	-	-	1	13.5	0.4	-
803	2009	Global holographic worship	-	-	10	2	-	-	-	-	-	6	13.1	0.4	-
804	2011	Itinerant pilgrim churches	-	-	9	10	-	-	-	-	-	4	12.4	0.4	-
805	2027	Broadcasting in 3,000 languages	-	-	10	6	-	-	-	-	2050	6	6.5	0.2	-
806	2030	Church of Point Omega	-	-	0	0	-	-	-	-	-	5	5.8	0.2	-
807	2030	Chinese global evangelization	-	-	10	8	China	-	-	-	2030	5	5.8	0.2	-
808	2045	Global scripture distribution	-	-	10	14	-	-	-	-	2050	5	2.2	0.1	-
809	2050	Self-replicating media churches	-	-	10	10	-	-	-	-	-	5	1.0	0.0	-
810	2080	Chinese/Arab global conversion mission	-	-	10	9	China	-	-	-	2080	5	0.7	0.0	-
811	2090	Church of the Martyrs	-	-	0	5	-	-	-	-	2090	5	0.6	0.0	-

Seven Hundred Plans to Evangelize the World by David B. Barrett and James W. Reapsome. ©1988 by Foreign Mission Board of the Southern Baptist Convention. Published by New Hope, Birmingham, AL. Used by permission.

788 GLOBAL PLANS ARRANGED BY CURRENT STATUS

Code	*Status*	*Plans*	*%*	*Sub-totals*
0	Fizzled out, dead, forgotten	297	37.7	
1	Defunct because no interest	41	5.2	51% fizzled
2	Defunct because completion claimed	14	1.8	out,dead
3	Implemented but not achieved	49	6.2	
4	Alive but fizzling out	31	3.9	17% fizzling
5	Alive but in decline	38	4.8	out, dying
6	Alive but static	39	4.9	
7	Alive but redefined	25	3.2	32% alive
8	Alive and making progress	134	17.0	and making
9	Alive and being massively implemented	120	15.2	progress
	Total Plans	788	100.0	

FOCUS FACT

America needs to be re-evangelized. In 1900 there were 27 churches for every 10,000 people. Now there are only 12 churches for every 10,000 people.

Twenty-five percent of America's churches have fewer than 35 in attendance for worship Sunday mornings, 50 percent have fewer than 75, and 80 percent have fewer than 100. Eighty-three percent of evangelical churches have plateaued or are declining in attendance.—Robert S. Ricker, president, Baptist General Conference, in the May 1990 issue of *The Standard*.

FOCUS FACT

Not more than 10 percent of evangelical churches in North America are involved significantly in world evangelization.

FOCUS QUOTE

One day a lady criticized D. L. Moody for his methods of evangelism in attempting to win people to the Lord.

Moody's reply was, "I agree with you. I don't like the way I do it either. Tell me, how do you do it?"

The lady replied, "I don't do it."

Moody retorted, "Then I like my way of doing it better than your way of not doing it."

FOCUS QUOTE

While women weep, as they do now, I'll fight; while little children go hungry, I'll fight; while men go to prison, in and out, in and out, as they do now, I'll fight; while there is a drunkard left, while there is a poor, lost girl upon the streets, where there remains one dark soul without the light of God—I'll fight! I'll fight to the very end!—William Booth, the founding general of the Salvation Army.

FOCUS FACT

25% of Americans say they have had a powerful religious experience
77% pray to God at least occasionally
72% say they believe Jesus is God or the Son of God

Source: *The Unchurched American—10 Years Later.* Published by The Princeton Religious Research Center, 1988.

WHO WATCHES TV EVANGELISTS?

20 Cities with the Highest Viewing Levels

1. Washington, DC
2. Dallas, TX
3. Atlanta, GA
4. Houston, TX
5. Sioux Falls, SD
6. Birmingham, AL
7. Nashville, TN
8. Chattanooga, TN
9. Jackson, MS
10. Detroit, MI
11. Philadelphia, PA
12. Johnstown–Altoona, PA
13. Greensboro, NC
14. Indianapolis, IN
15. Charleston–Huntington, WV
16. Charlotte, NC
17. Greenville–New Bern, NC
18. South Bend, IN
19. Columbia, SC
20. Richmond, VA

20 Cities with the Lowest Viewing Levels

1. Salt Lake City, UT
2. Albuquerque–Santa Fe, NM
3. El Paso, TX
4. Flint–Bay City, MI
5. San Diego, CA
6. Pittsburgh, PA
7. Phoenix, AZ
8. Las Vegas, NV
9. Waco, TX
10. Hartford–New Haven, CT
11. Austin, TX
12. Providence–New Bedford, RI
13. Raleigh–Durham, NC
14. Milwaukee, WI
15. West Palm Beach–Ft. Pierce, FL
16. Cleveland, OH
17. Omaha, NE
18. San Antonio, TX
19. Tampa, FL
20. Albany, NY

Source: Stephen Winzenburg, Grand View College, Des Moines, IA.

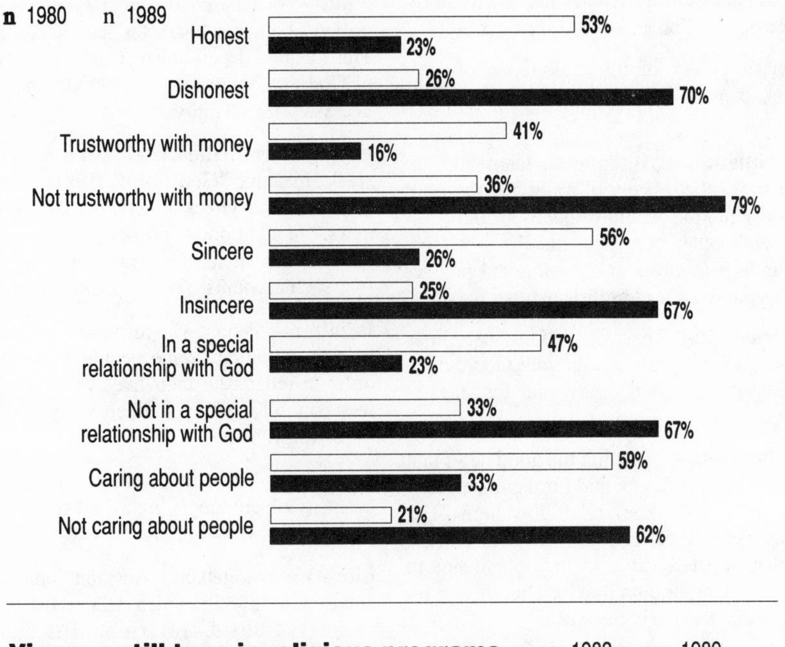

Source: Gallup poll of 1,238 adults taken between Sept. 7-10, 1989.

EVANGELISM FOCUSWORDS

Altar call—A request issued during an evangelistic sermon that people move to the front of the meeting hall if they want to inquire about Christianity or express a commitment to follow Christ. Used informally to refer to any direct invitation for people to become Christians.

Commitment—Becoming a Christian requires more than mental assent that God exists. "Making a commitment" to Christ means one is willing to change as he or she learns what it means to follow him.

Contact evangelism—Meeting people for the specific purpose of talking with them about the gospel.

Conversion—A popular expression marking the beginning of the Christian life describing both a person's response to the gospel and God's regenerating work in him or her. A person responds in faith and repentance to the grace of God and the activity of the Holy Spirit in his or her life.

Conviction—The act of the Holy Spirit in which a person recognizes his or her sinfulness before God and need for salvation.

Decision—A commitment to repent of one's sins, especially self-love, and to follow Christ.

Discipleship—A disciple is a learner. Discipleship is the process of following the Lord Jesus Christ in relationships of accountability with other believers, ideally in a local church. It involves discovering and practicing what it means to follow Christ.

Eternal Life—The quality of life that comes from living in relationship with God, which Christians experience now and for all eternity.

Evangelism—Spreading the good news that Jesus Christ is Savior and Lord and persuading people to come and follow him. "The results of evangelism," as summarized in the Lausanne Covenant, "include obedience to Christ, incorporation into his church, and responsible service in the world."

Evangelist—While all Christians are to share their faith, evangelists are especially gifted and active in doing evangelism.

Evangelistic talk—A sermon or lecture presented with the specific intent to explain the gospel and invite people to become Christians. It usually includes an invitation first to make a commitment and second to express that commitment, often in the form of an altar call.

Evangelization—Direct or indirect activity that contributes to people coming to a saving knowledge of Christ. This term is sometimes used as a synonym for evangelism, but it usually has a wider focus, as in "world evangelization."

Evangelized—People who have an intellectual and emotional understanding of the gospel along with some understanding of its personal application, and who have chosen to accept or reject Christ's claim on their life. Mission strategists also use this term to refer to a population segment which has a viable church.

Faith—Trust based on what God has revealed about his character and intentions. This includes depending on Christ as the Son of God and Savior of humankind, which is necessary for salvation.

Gospel—From the Anglo-Saxon "godspell," meaning "God-story." This is a translation for the Greek *euangelion* or "good news." In addition, a "gospel" is an account of Jesus' life and teaching; the Bible contains four such accounts. See also *evangelism.*

Inquirers—People who respond to an evangelistic invitation. Some people respond in order to rededicate their lives to God or to seek counsel and prayer; others wish to begin following Christ.

Invitation—The climax of an evangelistic event in which people are asked to make a decision to follow Christ.

Life-style evangelism—An intentional orientation to life in which Christians consciously build relationships with non-Christians in order to develop true friendships and share the most important part of their lives, that is, their relationship with God through Christ. Sometimes called relational or friendship evangelism.

Lost, the—Non-Christians, who face eternity apart from God in hell.

Plan of Salvation—A summary of the basic truths of the gospel and steps necessary to become a Christian, which includes turning from sin and turning to Christ. Popular plans include the Four Spiritual Laws, the Bridge Illustration, the Romans Road, and the Evangelism Explosion presentation. See also Salvation.

Pre-evangelism—Efforts to cultivate a positive attitude toward Christianity in non-believers or communicate the basics of a Christian world view. In today's secular world, this can mean simply cultivating a willingness to believe there is a spiritual dimension to life.

Relevancy—The gospel is relevant to all people in all ages because we are all sinners. The challenge in evangelism is to communicate the relevance of the gospel to non-Christians in word and deed.

Revival—A work of God in a particular time and place in which an unusually large number of people turn to Christ and Christians are renewed in their commitment, holiness, and evangelistic zeal.

Salvation—God's work in saving people from the power and effects of sin. This is possible through the sacrificial life and death of Jesus Christ. God saves people when they come to him in faith, saving them from eternal death and slavery to sin and its habits and adopting them as his people.

Saved—The condition of every Christian: free from slavery to sin and eternal death, and living in relationship with God.

Seekers—People who are interested in learning more about Christ and Christianity but who have not yet become Christians.

Sinner—A person who sins; a person who lives in a state of sin; a person who still lives under the curse of original sin and is alienated from God.

Tract—A small pamphlet that instructs or challenges its readers to change. Evangelistic tracts, the most common kind of Christian tract, challenge readers to become Christians.

Witnessing—Sharing the content of the gospel and one's faith experience with non-Christians.

Source: Daniel Moul, Research and Technical Resources Coordinator, Institute of Evangelism, Billy Graham Center.

FOCUS FACT

Eighty-five percent of the people who make a commitment to Christ do so by the time they are eighteen.

Source: *The Unchurched American—10 Years Later.* Published by The Princeton Religious Research Center, 1988.

BOOKLIST: SIGNIFICANT BOOKS ON EVANGELISM

Abraham, William J. *The Logic of Evangelism.* Grand Rapids: Eerdmans, 1989.

The author argues that evangelism should focus on initiation into the kingdom of God, not on proclamation or church growth, and he examines the implications of this change of focus.

Aldrich, Joseph C. *Life-Style Evangelism: Crossing Traditional Boundaries to Reach the Unbelieving World.* Portland, OR: Multnomah Press, 1983.

Excellent practical guide for developing a natural Christian witness.

Bayly, Joseph. *The Gospel Blimp.* Elgin, IL: David C. Cook Publishing Company, 1960.

A satire of misdirected evangelism in story form. Entertains while addressing problems we face in doing evangelism.

Bright, Bill. *Witnessing Without Fear.* Here's Life Publishers, Inc., 1987.

The founder of Campus Crusade for Christ shares how personal evangelism has become a way of life.

The Calling of an Evangelist. J. D. Douglas, Ed. Minneapolis: World Wide Publications, 1987.

A compendium of addresses from the Second International Congress for Itinerant Evangelists held in Amsterdam, the Netherlands, in 1986. An international array of contributors provide theological and practical guidance in evangelism for pastors and evangelists.

Calver, Clive, Derek Copley, Bob Moffett, and Jim Smith. *A Guide to Evangelism.* Basingstoke, Hanks, UK: Marshall Morgan & Scott, 1984. Available through Zondervan in the United States.

This book covers theory and practice in evangelism, highlighting evangelistic insights for a whole range of societal groupings, from the retired to work colleagues to the P.T.A. Written for Great Britain, but applicable almost everywhere.

Cocoris, G. Michael. *Evangelism: A Biblical Approach.* Chicago: Moody Press, 1984.

A sensible look at evangelism through the words and practices recorded in Scripture.

Coleman, Robert E. *The Master Plan of Evangelism.* Old Tappan, NJ: Fleming H. Revell Company, 1963.

The author examines the Scriptures to uncover Jesus' plan for making disciples. Popular around the world.

Engel, James F., and H. Wilbert Norton. *What's Gone Wrong with the Harvest? A Communications Strategy for the Church and World Evangelism.* Grand Rapids: Zondervan Publishing House, 1975.

A good introduction to ways that communication and persuasion strategy can make our evangelism more effective.

Fish, Roy. *Every Member Evangelism for Today.* San Francisco: Harper Religious Books, 1976.

An update of J. E. Connant's classic *Every Member Evangelism.* A strong challenge for every Christian to witness for Christ.

Ford, Leighton. *Good News Is for Sharing.* Elgin, IL: David C. Cook Publishing, 1977.

Good introduction to what evangelism is and how every Christian can do it.

Graham, Billy. *How to be Born Again.* Waco, TX: Word Books, 1977.

This book, along with *World Aflame* and *Peace with God,* presents Jesus Christ as the only way to God and only hope of the world.

Green, Michael. *Evangelism in the Early Church.* Grand Rapids: Eerdmans, 1970.

Well-researched look at the principles of evangelism as practiced by the early church. These principles are applied in *Evangelism: Now and Then* (Inter-Varsity Press, 1979).

Kennedy, James. *Evangelism Explosion.* Rev. ed. Wheaton, IL: Tyndale House Publishers, 1983.

Popular manual for practical training in evangelism. Good presentation of principles and methods for reproducing disciples in the local church.

Kunz, Marilyn, and Catherine Schell. *How to Start a Neighborhood Bible Study.* Revised ed. Dobbs Ferry, New York: Neighborhood Bible Studies, 1981.

This little booklet offers helpful advice on how to use investigative Bible studies as an evangelistic tool with the non-Christians in your everyday life.

Let the Earth Hear His Voice. Edited by J. D. Douglas. Minneapolis: World Wide Publications, 1975.

A compendium of addresses from the historic International Conference on World Evangelism, Lausanne, Switzerland, in 1974. Provides a widely comprehensive and representative look at evangelism from leaders around the world.

Little, Paul. *How to Give Away Your Faith.* Downers Grove, IL: Inter-Varsity, 1966.

Helpful guide in learning to share your faith.

Packer, James I. *Evangelism and the Sovereignty of God.* Downers Grove, IL: Inter-Varsity Press, 1961.

A concise, readable argument for Christians to energize their evangelistic witness with a proper understanding of God's role in the evangelistic process.

Pippert, Rebecca M. *Out of the Saltshaker and into the World: Evangelism as a Way of Life.* Downers Grove, IL: Inter-Varsity Press, 1979.

Popular down-to-earth look at lifestyle evangelism.

Veerman, David R. *Youth Evangelism: When They're in Your Neighborhood but Not in the Fold*. Wheaton, IL: Victor Books, 1988.

Helpful for adults who want to build relationships and share the gospel with junior and senior high young people.

Wimber, John, and Kevin Springer. *Power Evangelism*. San Francisco: Harper & Row, 1986.

Examines the role of "signs and wonders" in evangelism.

Source: Compiled and annotated by Daniel Moul, Research and Technical Resources Coordinator, Institute of Evangelism, Billy Graham Center.

JESUS: THE MOST TRANSLATED FILM IN HISTORY

Released in the U.S. in 1979 by Warner Brothers, *Jesus* has been dubbed into more than 130 languages and viewed in 155 countries by more than 355 million people. More than 200 mission agencies and denominations have used the film. It has been shown on national television; portable generators and projectors have been used to show the film in remote areas. By 1993 Campus Crusade, the catalyst for the translation effort, hopes to translate the film into all of the 271 languages spoken by more than one million people. Other organizations are interested in translating it into still more languages.

Campus Crusade estimates that more than 30 million people have indicated decisions to follow Christ as a result of watching the film.

Source: *Christianity Today*, October 20, 1989 issue.

HOW BIG IS THE USA EVANGELICAL WORLD?

More than 12 million Americans are evangelical, if evangelical means a person (1) has had a "born again experience"; (2) believes in the literal truth of the Bible; and (3) attempts to evangelize others.

Source: *Religion in America:* The Gallup Report, 1987.

BILLY GRAHAM CENTER

The Billy Graham Center is a division of Wheaton College dedicated to the study and promotion of world evangelization. The Center exists to work with Christian leaders around the world in developing strategies and skills for communicating the gospel.

The Institute of Evangelism equips pastors and laity to more effectively communicate the gospel. Other Institutes at the Center include the Institute of Prison Ministries and the Institute of Chinese Studies. A library, archive, and museum offer unsurpassed resources for the study of evangelism; they are open to scholars and the public. Other institutes of Wheaton College include the Institute for the Study of Christianity and Marxism, the Institute for the Study of American Evangelicals, and the Institute for Muslim Studies.

Persons interested in obtaining information about the Institutes and conferences may contact Billy Graham Center, Wheaton College, Wheaton, Illinois 60187. Tel: (708) 260-5157.

A CHRONOLOGY OF MODERN REVIVAL MOVEMENTS

Richard Owen Roberts

1517ff The Great Protestant Reformation under John Calvin, John Knox, Martin Luther, Ulrich Zwingli, and a hosts of others marks the beginning of a marvelous series of modern revival movements.

1560ff The Puritan age, continuing for more than a century following the first years of the reign of Elizabeth I, was one of the most blessed seasons of revival in all the history of the church. Men like Richard Baxter in England and Vavasor Powell

A CHRONOLOGY OF MODERN REVIVAL MOVEMENTS cont.

	and Walter Craddock in Wales were used extensively by God at this time.
1596	The Revival of the General Assembly of the Church of Scotland. This began in a Solemn Assembly in Edinburgh during the General Assembly of the church. John Davidson of Prestonpans was a chief leader.
1620-1630	An awakening occurred in Wales in connection with the publication of the first popular edition of the Welsh Bible by Vicar Prichard.
1623-1641	Revival in Ulster, North Ireland, principally among the Presbyterians.
1625	Revival at Stewarton, Scotland.
1630	The Revival of the Kirk of Shotts, Scotland. John Livingstone was greatly used of God in this movement.
1639ff	The spirit of revival affecting New England was so general at this time that a son born to Richard and Catharine Mather was named Increase in appreciation for what God was doing. Among those ministering during this season of awakening were John Cotton, Richard Mather, and John Wilson.
1647-1670	John Eliot, Apostle to the American Indians, was one of the first evangelists in America. Although pastor of the Church in Roxbury, Massachusetts, from 1631 until his death in 1690, Eliot spent a great portion of his time itinerating among the tribes in Massachusetts and Plymouth Colonies. In this work he met with those extraordinary results which must be described as revival.
1669-1729	During the nearly sixty years of his pastoral ministry at Northampton, Massachusetts, Solomon Stoddard saw four or five distinct seasons of revival.
1720ff	Under the ministry of Theodorus Jacobus Frelinghuysen, a Dutch Reformed minister at New Brunswick, New Jersey, the Great Awakening had its beginnings. A fearless preacher, Frelinghuysen did not restrict his ministry to the Raritan Valley but itinerated in New York, New Jersey, and Pennsylvania. Gilbert Tennent was among the later revival leaders greatly affected by him.

FOCUS FACT

Most of the great denominations in America grew to strength because of the 19th-century awakenings.

1721	A remarkable revival of religion occurred at Windham, Connecticut, under the pastoral leadership of Samuel Whiting, pastor of the First Congregational Church.
1727ff	A powerful movement began in Germany under the leadership of Count Nicholas Ludwig-Graf von Zinzendorf that resulted in a major missionary thrust and powerfully influenced the Wesleys in the early years of their labors. The movement was variously known as the Unitas Fratrum or the Moravian Church. Peter Boehler and August Gottlieb Spangenberg were among the leaders who worked with Zinzendorf.
1727	A major earthquake shook New England and one of the results was a series of brief but potent revivals in widely scattered places. Among those whom God used at this time were James Allen, John Brown, William Cooper, John Cotton III, Thomas Foxcroft, and Thomas Prince.

1734-1735 The Congregational Church at Northampton, Massachusetts, had experienced revival under Solomon Stoddard's ministry but things were at a rather low ebb spiritually for the first several years of Jonathan Edwards's labors there. The major quickening that began in 1734 was one of the streams that contributed to the Great Awakening that followed.

1734 The First Congregational Church at Washington, Connecticut, experienced the first of several awakenings.

1735-1770 George Whitefield was converted in 1735 and very soon thereafter was preaching with great power and effectiveness. In the United Kingdom, the quickening that began under his ministry is generally referred to as the Evangelical Revival. Whitefield was the dominant figure in the movement that lasted, with several ebbs and flows, until his death in 1770. Charles Wesley was converted in 1738 and itinerated widely until his marriage in 1749. His older brother John was converted in the same year as Charles and was soon the major figure in the non-Calvinistic branch of the work. Other major participants in the English movement included John Berridge, John Cennick, Risdom Darracott, John William Fletcher, John Gambold, William Grimshaw, James Hervey, Martin Madan, and William Romaine. In addition to the well-known Methodist Church that emerged out of the awakening, the Countess of Huntingdon's Connexion was, for many years, a beneficial influence in Britain.

1735-1770 Howell Harris of Wales was brought to a vital relationship with Christ at approximately the same time as Whitefield. He too began itinerating almost immediately thereafter and quickly the beginnings of a mighty awakening were felt in various parts of the principality. Griffith Jones had started the Welsh Circulating Charity School Movement in 1730 and this became a contributory to the revival. Other principle figures in the Welsh awakening include Howell Davies, Daniel Rowland, and William Williams. The Welsh Calvinistic Methodist Church became the principle vehicle through which this movement expanded.

1738-1770 The powerful movement in America, led principally by Whitefield, became known as the Great Awakening. Whitefield's first ministry in the United States was in Georgia where profound effects were felt as the result of a three- to four-month ministry. By 1740 a significant portion of the colonies was ablaze with revival fires. God chose to use dozens of men in this awakening, including Isaac Backus, Joseph Bellamy, John Blair, Samuel Blair, David Brainerd, Samuel Buell, James Davenport, Samuel Davies, Jonathan Dickinson, Jonathan Edwards, Samuel Finley, Samuel Hopkins, Daniel Marshall, Jonathan Parsons, Ebenezer Pemberton, Benjamin Pomeroy, John Rowland, Shubal Stearns, Gilbert Tennent, John Tennent, William Tennent, Sr., William Tennent, Jr., and Eleazer Wheelock.

1742ff Whitefield's ministry at Cambuslang and Kilsyth was especially powerful and led to major revivals in these centers as well as widely scattered parts of Scotland.

1749-1752 Revival in Holland.

1774 Revival in the Church in Somers, Connecticut, under the pastoral leadership of Charles Backus, at Brown University in Providence, Rhode Island, and in several other places in America.

1776-1809 Under the leadership of Henry Alline, an extensive movement of the Spirit affected Nova Scotia.

A CHRONOLOGY OF MODERN REVIVAL MOVEMENTS cont.

1779-1789 Revival at Hampden-Sidney College and in numerous places in Virginia and North Carolina.

1781 Revival at Dartmouth College in Hanover, New Hampshire, the institution founded by Eleazer Wheelock.

1783 Revivals at both Princeton College in New Jersey and Yale College in Connecticut.

1784 Franklin, Massachusetts, experienced a revival under the ministry of Nathaniel Emmons. The First Presbyterian Church in Newark, New Jersey, was also stirred at this time.

1786 The revival at Trecastle, Wales.

1788 The Allgauer revival among the Bavarian Catholics led by Martin Boos, Michael Feneberg, Johannes Goszner, Ignatius Lund, and Johann Sailer.

1788 Revival at Dartmouth, Massachusetts, under Daniel Hix.

1789-1790 Revival in several parts of America.

1791 Revival at Bala, Wales, under the ministry of Thomas Charles who became the founder of the British and Foreign Bible Society.

1792ff A powerful series of revivals gripped the Congregational Church in Lee, Massachusetts, in 1792, 1800, 1806, 1813, 1821, 1827, and 1831.

1792-1820? The Second Great Awakening in America. This was a wide scale movement affecting nearly every section of the nation. For instance, extensive revivals affected New Salem, Connecticut, 1793; Boston, 1803-1805; Freeport, Maine, 1811; Concord, New Hampshire, 1816, etc.

1795ff Several extensive revivals gripped and altered Yale College under the Presidency of Timothy Dwight, including the revivals of 1801, 1808, 1810.

1796ff An awakening in Norway persisted for some time under the ministry of Hans Nielsen Hauge.

1797 Revival at Walthem Abbey School, Essex, England.

1798 Revival at Auburn Theological Seminary, Auburn, New York.

1798-1800 Revival at Moulin, Scotland.

1798-1799 Typical of the period, the Congregational Church of West Simsbury, Connecticut, experienced revival under the leadership of its pastor, Jeremiah Hallock in 1798-1799, 1805, 1812-1813, 1816, and 1821.

1799-1848 Revival was occurring in some part of western New York state every year during this long period.

1800 The southern Camp-Meeting Revival deeply affected Kentucky, Tennessee, and the Carolinas. Alexander and Thomas Campbell, Peter Cartwright, James McGready, Richard McNemar, David Purviance, David Rice, and Barton Warren Stone were among the leaders. Both the Cumberland Presbyterian Church and some branches of the Churches of Christ and Disciples of Christ Churches grew out of this awakening. This movement probably had its origins in touches of the Holy Spirit on the area as early as 1787.

1800 Movements in Scotland including Harris, Lewis, and Perthshire.

1800ff Revival in several places in Canada.

1804 Revival on the Island of Arran, Scotland.

1804-1806 Revival at Williams College, Williamstown, Massachusetts.

1805 Revival at Aberystwyth, Wales.

1806 Revival at Darwen in the County of Lancaster, England.

1806-1814 A powerful movement largely under the leadership of John Elias profoundly affected the children of Wales and its Sunday schools.

1807 In England, there were movements particularly among the Independent and Primitive Methodists with a strong focus on Camp-Meetings and revivals. Hugh Bourne, William Clowes, and Lorenzo Dow were among the leaders.

1807-1827 Almost continuous revival occurred in Portland, Maine, under the pastoral ministry of Edward Payson.

1810-1815 Llangeitho and many other places in Wales were affected in a movement similar to the southern revival of 1800 in America. Both Christmas Evans and John Elias were much used of God during this period.

1810 A Revival in the Russian Orthodox Church led to the formation of the Russian Bible Society in 1813. There were also revivals in Switzerland, parts of Germany, and other places on the continent that were partially under the leadership of the Haldane brothers.

1810 Revivals at Andover Seminary and Williams College in Massachusetts.

1812-1814 Revival occurred at Arran and in Skye, Scotland.

1814 Revival in Cornwall, England.

1814 Revival at Yale College in Connecticut.

1815 Revival at Princeton University in New Jersey. Numerous areas of Vermont also experienced revival including Chazy and Montpelier.

1815-1848 Several revivals touched parts of Germany during this period.

1816 Under the leadership of James Patterson, a revival moved the First Presbyterian Church of Philadelphia toward Christ.

1817 The Town of Northeast, Dutchess County, New York, experienced a gracious movement of the Spirit.

1817-1822 The Beddgelert revival was mostly restricted to the Mt. Snowden area of North Wales. William Williams [Williams of Wern] was the principal human agent.

1818 A second wave of revival affected the Auburn Theological Seminary.

1818ff Revival in Chillicothe, Ohio, under John Collins.

1819 Revival at Hamilton College in New York state.

1820 Revival in Pomerania, Germany.

1820ff Revival at St. Helena during the last years of Napoleon's exile.

1820 Revival in Homer, New York, as well as other places in the western regions of the state. The Albany Presbytery also experienced a great work of the Holy Spirit at this time. Union College in Schenectady was wonderfully affected under the ministry of Asahel Nettleton.

1821-1843 A remarkable series of revivals took place at Williams College in Williamstown, Massachusetts, during the time Edward Dorr Griffin was President

A CHRONOLOGY OF MODERN REVIVAL MOVEMENTS cont.

	[1821-1836] and thereafter under the leadership of Prof. Albert Hopkins who was the major tool God used in 1832 and at least every four years for the rest of his time at the College.
1823-1833	Revivals at Park Street Church, Boston, under the leadership of Edward Dorr Griffin.
1824-1835	The revival on the Island of Lewis in the north of Scotland.
1826	Revival at the Female Seminary in Beverly, Massachusetts.
1826-1827	Revival in Troy, New York, under the leadership of Charles G. Finney. Also in Oneida and Ithaca, New York.
1827	Revivals at Yale College, New Haven, Connecticut, and Dartmouth College, Hanover, New Hampshire.
1828-1830	The revival at Carmarthenshire, Wales, sometimes described as The Great Rejoicing Revival.
1830ff	Widespread movements of revival affected many parts of the United States from 1830 onward until the powerful prayer meeting revival of 1857-1858. Especially active during the thirties were Jedediah Burchard, Daniel Baker, James Caughey, Charles G. Finney, Emerson Andrews, Edward Dorr Griffin, James Inskip, Jacob Knapp, John Newland Maffitt, Asahel Nettleton, and Jabez Swan.
1830	Another wave of revival under the Haldane brothers touched Switzerland. Louis Gaussen, Ceasar Malan, and J. H. Merle D'Aubigne were among the leaders.
1830	A gracious movement of the Spirit under the Monods touched France.
1831	A major movement of revival affected much of the American east coast as well as such far reaching places as Iowa where God used the ministry of Reuben Gaylord.
1831	Revival in Ceylon.
1831-1832	Another revival under the leadership of John Elias occurred principally in Caernarvonshire, Wales. It was both very sudden and wonderfully deep.
1833-1836	Revivals at Albany, Hamilton, Homer, Saratoga, Schenectady, Utica, and many other places in New York state and adjacent regions.
1834-1835	A season of general revival touched numerous places in Canada.
1837-1838	Another general season of revival affected America at this time, affecting many communities and institutions including Cazenovia Seminary in upper New York state, Rutgers University in New Jersey, and the Portland area in Oregon.
1837-1843	A very powerful movement, led by the missionaries under the American Board of Commissioners, brought large numbers of Hawaiians to Christ. Records indicate that as much as 20 percent of the population was converted. Titus Coan was among the most largely used at this time.
1838-1843	Revival in Columbus, Ohio.
1839-1842	A fairly widespread movement under John Jones of Talsarn affected Wales.
1839-1843	A general season of revival touched Scotland and was especially powerful in the highlands. Included in the many places visited were Aberdeen, Dundee,

	Glasgow, Kilsyth, Perth, and Strathay. William Chalmers Burns and Robert Murray McCheyne were among the choice instruments.
1841	The revival in Cardiganshire, Wales, that powerfully impacted David Morgan of 1858-1859 fame.
1841-1842	Revival in the Channel Islands of Britain.
1842	Revival at Charlinch, Somersetshire, England.
1842	The revival in Richmond, Virginia, in which Cornelius Walker was a participant.
1842	The Boston Revival under Jacob Knapp, Charles G. Finney, and Edward Norris Kirk.
1842	Norwegian revival.
1843	The Hermannsburg revival in western Germany.
1844-1846	Revivals in Canada under the powerful preaching of William Chalmers Burns.
1844-1850	Another movement, in which missionaries of the American Board of Commissioners were vitally used, occurred among the Nestorians in Persia.
c.1845ff	Revival in Denmark under such men as Soren Kierkegaard and Nikolai Grundtvig.
1847ff	Extensive revivals began in China under William Chalmers Burns and continued under J. Hudson Taylor.
1849-1850	A movement spoken of as the Cholera Revival gripped Wales, especially in the South.
1857-1858	The Third Great Awakening, sometimes called the Prayer-Meeting Revival, began at the Old Dutch Reformed Church, Fulton Street, in New York City. Before many months had passed, almost every major population center in America was deeply touched as well as many small town and rural areas. A city missionary, Jeremiah Lanphier, was the initial agent God used in this revival. Upwards of a million converts were reported in two years in America and another million in the movement that followed in the United Kingdom.
1858-1862	The gracious movement that began in New York the previous year reached the United Kingdom soon thereafter and had an especially powerful impact upon Wales (under the leadership of David Morgan and Humphrey Jones) and Ireland (under many leaders including William Arthur, Andrew and Horatius Bonar, H. Grattan Guinness, Edward Payson Hammond, etc.) and affected to a lesser extent both England (Brownlow North and Charles Spurgeon were active participants) and Scotland (Reginald Radcliffe and Brownlow North were chief instruments). Sweden and Canada were among the other nations touched at this time.
1860	Revival in the Tinnavelly District of South India.
1860	Revival in the Ukraine.
1860	A major move of the Holy Spirit swept the churches of South Africa. Andrew Murray was a chief instrument.
1860	The Netherlands experienced the hand of God at work with G. Van Prinsterer and Abraham Kuyper as the human agents.
1861	The movement that began in America in 1857 touched Jamaica and resulted in a major spread of Christianity among the natives.

A CHRONOLOGY OF MODERN REVIVAL MOVEMENTS cont.

1861-1862 Cornish revivals in England.

1861-1865 A very powerful revival occurred in the southern army during the Civil War conflict. Large numbers of fighting men were converted on the front lines. Such Christian generals as Robert E. Lee and Stonewall Jackson played a very significant part in this amazing movement of the Spirit.

1866 Revival at Lafayette Avenue Church in New York City. This movement reappeared in 1872.

1869ff Several revivals affected the Clarendon Street Church in Boston under the ministry of Adoniram Judson Gordon.

1870 Revival at Newport, Monmouthshire, England.

1870-1912 Under the Presbyterian mission, a large scale movement greatly affected the Hindu Chuhras in the Punjab. At the same time a work among Baptists, Lutherans, and Methodists brought in almost a million converts among the Telugu.

1871 The revival in South Wales.

1872 A wide spread movement affected Japan.

1873-1875 Dwight L. Moody's campaigns in England and Scotland were powerfully used of the Holy Spirit in revival.

1875-1877 A somewhat localized movement under Richard Owen and John Richard Hughes blessed Wales.

1876 A movement under the leadership of Skogsbergh and Paul Peter Waldenstrom affected the state church in Sweden.

1879 Revival at Banza, Manteke.

1880-1910 Scattered seasons of revival touched many in Germany and resulted in 100,000 conversions in the state churches.

1881 Revival in Cincinnati, Ohio, during under the leadership of Thomas Harrison.

1882-1884 A second movement under the leadership of Richard Owen reached many hearts in Wales.

1884 Another wave of revival moved Norway toward Christ.

1883-1890 Revivals blazed in several parts of Japan.

1887-1894ff A long lasting revival occurred among Lutheran and London Missionary Society churches in Madagascar.

1889 The revival at Rothesay in the Island of Bute.

1892 An evangelistic crusade in Cincinnati and Covington, Ohio, resulted in clear evidences of genuine revival.

1893 A revival was experienced in St. Paul, Minnesota, under the ministry of B. Fay Mills.

1895 The Revival in Lisbon, New Hampshire.

1896 The Uganda revival.

1902-1904 Reuben A. Torrey and Charles M. Alexander made a worldwide tour during part of this period and saw revival in several places including Australia.

1903-1905 A deep spiritual movement began quietly in several places in Wales in 1903 and then became very public under the leadership of Evan Roberts in 1904. 100,000 converts were reported within six months. The movement spread rapidly to other parts of the world including America, China, Denmark, Finland, Germany, India, Korea, Madagascar, Russia, and Sweden. Pandita Ramabai became an outstanding leader in India as did "Praying" John Hyde.

1904 While ministering in Pittsburgh, Pennsylvania, J. Wilbur Chapman saw a deep stirring of the Holy Spirit throughout Allegheny County.

1905 An awakening took place in St. Paul, Minnesota, also under the preaching of J. Wilbur Chapman.

1906-1909 The Azusa Street meeting in Los Angeles marked the beginnings of the modern Pentecostal movement.

1907-1990 The Korean revival began and continues to some extent even to this day.

1908 Largely under the ministry of Jonathan Goforth, a marvelous revival began in Manchuria.

1909 Under the leadership of J. Wilbur Chapman, an extensive movement of the Spirit affected the City of Boston during the simultaneous crusade.

1921 A very considerable movement, affecting large portions of the Lower Congo, began under the preaching of Simon Kimbangu.

1925 A charismatic movement within the Anglican Churches of Nigeria led to many conversions and the establishment of several indigenous churches.

1927-1937 Revival in China.

1927-1935 The East African Revival movement appears to have started in Ruanda and quickly affected vast numbers of people. It spread rapidly across Uganda, Zaire, Malawi, and numerous other places. Revival conventions drew as many as 50,000 persons.

1930-1933 The Shantung revival in China was principally among those under the leadership of the Southern Baptist Convention. C. L. Culpepper was one of the leaders.

1932 A Charismatic revival in the American Methodist churches of Southern Rhodesia under the leadership of Johane Maranke led to the formation of the massive African Apostolic Church that has spread across much of Africa.

1936 Powerful revival at Wheaton College, Wheaton, Illinois.

1936-1948 Revival in Ethiopia, especially among the Wallamo tribe.

1938ff Revival in South Africa under Nicholas Bhekinkosi Bhengu.

1941 Revivals touched many of the Orthodox Churches in German-occupied Russia.

1943 Another revival at Wheaton College, Wheaton, Illinois.

1949-1953 Revival in the Highlands and Islands of Scotland under the leadership of Duncan Campbell.

1950 Revivals at Wheaton College, Wheaton, Illinois; Asbury College, Wilmore, Kentucky; and other Christian schools.

1953 Revival in the Congo.

1953-1971 Revival in Indonesia and in the Solomon Islands.

1954 Revival in Buenos Aries, Argentina under Tommy Hicks.

A CHRONOLOGY OF MODERN REVIVAL MOVEMENTS cont.

1955-1957	The Palavan revival.
1958	Revival at Asbury College.
1970	Another brief but potent revival affected Asbury College and Seminary in Wilmore, Kentucky, and spread swiftly to numerous other campuses.
1970-1972	The Jesus People revival among American young people affected principally the hippies on the West Coast.
1971ff	Revival in Viet Nam.
1971-1972	The Canadian revival centered in Saskatchewan and affected principally the western parts of the nation. Ralph and Lou Sutera were among the chief instruments.

For extensive bibliographic details on the revivals listed see "Revival Literature: An Annotated Bibliography with Biographical and Historical Notices," Wheaton, Illinois, 1987, and "Whitefield in Print: A Bibliographic Record of Works by, for and against George Whitefield. With Annotations, Biographical and Historical Notices and Bibliographies of his Associates and Contemporaries," Wheaton, Illinois, 1988. Available from Richard Owen Roberts, Publishers, Box 21, Wheaton, Illinois 60189.

FOCUS FACT

There have been more martyrs produced in the 20th century than in all the other centuries combined since the time of Christ. Many have come out of Russia. In the 1930s and the 1940s tens of thousands of Christians lost their lives to the state authorities. Out of 47,000 Russian Orthodox churches which existed in 1917, by 1939 there may have been as few as 100 left open.—Kent Hill, executive director, The Institute on Religion and Democracy in Wasington, DC.

FOCUS FACT

American missionary work started in a haystack during a thunderstorm! In 1860, during an awakening at Williams College in western Massachusetts, Samuel Mills and four other students hid themselves in a haystack to avoid a summer thunderstorm. While there they united in prayer and pledged themselves to go as missionaries wherever God might lead them. Out of this group went the first American missionaries.

Source: *Christian History* Magazine, Issue 23. Copyright © 1989, Christianity Today, Inc. Used by permission.

BOOKLIST: SIGNIFICANT BOOKS ON REVIVAL

The Spiritual Awakeners: American Revivalists from Solomon Stoddard to Dwight L. Moody by Keith Hardman. Moody Press, 1983.

Charles Grandison Finney 1792-1875, Revivalist and Reformer by Keith Hardman. Syracuse University Press, 1987.

An Endless Line of Splendor by Earle E. Cairns. Tyndale House Publishers, 1988.

Memoirs of C. G. Finney by Garth Rosell and A. G. Dupuis. Zondervan Publ. House, 1989.

The Sense of His Presence: Experiencing Spiritual Regenesis by David R. Mains. Word, Inc., 1988.

Dynamics of Spiritual Life: An Evangelical Theology of Renewal by Richard Lovelace. Inter-Varsity Press, 1979.

The Journal of George Whitefield. Banner of Truth, 1960.

Jonathan Edwards, A New Biography by Iain Murray. Banner of Truth, 1987.

Revivals, Awakenings, and Reform by William G. McLoughlin. Univ. of Chicago, 1978.

Source: Compiled by Dr. Keith J. Hardman for *Christian History* Magazine, Issue 23. Copyright © 1989 Christianity Today, Inc. Used by permission.

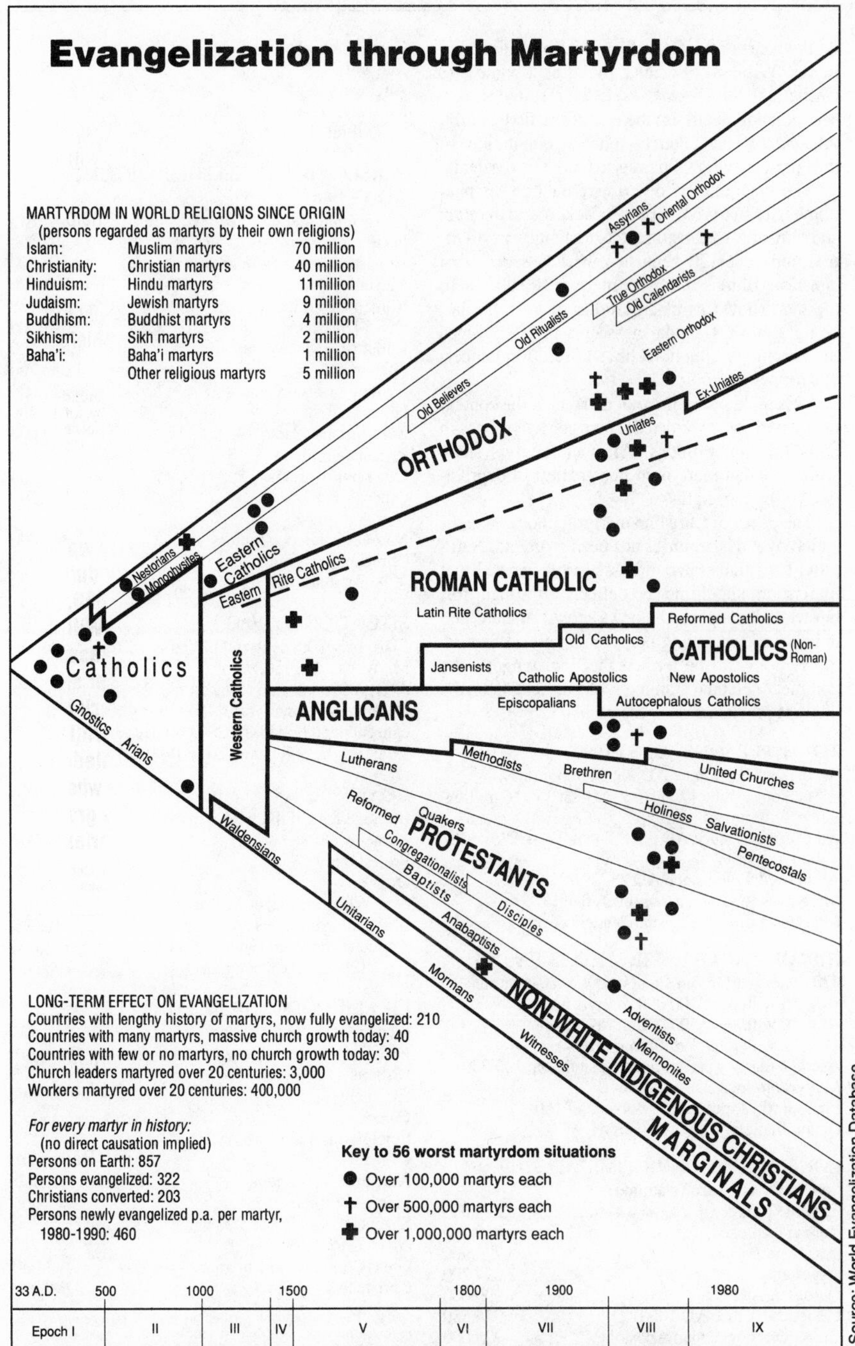

40 MILLION CHRISTIANS KILLED FOR THEIR FAITH IN 220 COUNTRIES ACROSS 20 CENTURIES

At the heart of the Great Commission is the command "Witness!" Because living as a witness to Christ (NT Greek *martyrs*) often resulted in persecution and death, by the end of the first century AD, *martyrs* had taken on today's connotations of the "martyr" who witnesses to Christ by his death.

The diagram sets descriptive data on the phenomena of martyrdom onto a background diagram showing the expansion of Christianity in all its traditions over 20 centuries. History's 56 worst situations of mass martyrdom (over 100,000 each) are then shown as black crosses or dots, the last being Amin's Uganda massacres in 1971. Since then no major situations have arisen (too dangerous for persecutors).

This table puts Christian martyrs in the context of all persons regarded as martyrs by their own non-Christian religions. All such martyrs share with Christian martyrs in this greatest of deprivations of human rights.

The effect of Christian martyrdom on evangelization over the centuries has been profound. Naturally, Christians have almost always insisted that martyrdom should not be deliberately sought for; but when it happens, the news spreads widely, and unbelievers, including persecutors, are converted. Martyrdom can be termed the final witness, the complete personal statement of faith in Christ, the ultimate proclamation of the gospel.

TOTAL PERSONS, AD 33-1990

All persons born since AD 33: 34,903 million
All persons evangelized since AD 33: 13,116 million (38% of human race)
All Christians since AD 33: 8,286 million (24% of human race)
All martyrs killed since AD 33: 40,725,000
Martyrs as % all Christians ever: 0.49%
Martyrs among all Christian leaders ever: 2.0%

HISTORICAL OVERVIEW, AD 33-1990

420 major martyrdom situations over 20 centuries
- 56 with over 100,000 martyrs each
- 20 with over 500,000 martyrs each
- 12 with over 1 million martyrs each

Average martyrs per martyrdom situation: 100,000
Martyrdom loci: 220 countries
Ecclesiastical traditions involved: all 160
Denominations with own martyrs: 4,000

CONFESSIONS OF VICTIMS, AD 33-1990
(total martyrs of each tradition)

Eastern Orthodox	8,524,000
Roman Catholics	6,850,700
East Syrians (Nestorians)	3,723,900
Protestants	2,694,700
Quasi-Christians	1,000,000
Catholics (before AD 1000)	926,550
Gregorians (Armenian Apostolic)	925,000
Ethiopian Orthodox	625,000
West Syrians (Jacobites)	425,700
Coptic Orthodox	406,900
Masonites	128,200
Anglicans	124,000
Non-White Indigenous Christians	117,000
Total all martyrs	40,725,000

PERSECUTORS AND THEIR VICTIMS, AD 33-1990

Persecutors responsible	*Martyrs*
Secular governments	24,402,200
Atheists (overlap with above)	12,400,800
Muslims	5,821,200
Roman Catholics	4,534,100
Quasi-Christians	2,591,000
Buddhists (Mahayana)	1,608,100
Shamanists	1,083,700
Eastern Orthodox	527,000
Hindus	411,400
Zoroastrians (Parsis)	397,000
Pagans (animists)	225,600
Other non-Christians	202,100
Other Christians	165,500
Subtotals:	
Non-Christian persecutors	32,900,000
Christian persecutors	7,825,000
Total all martyrs	40,725,000

SITUATION BY 1990

Martyrs in 20th century (1900-1990): 26,625,000
Martyrs since 1950: 9,965,000
Average annual martyrs since 1950: 249,100 per year
Recent annual martyrs: 300,000 per year
Current annual martyrs: 290,000 per year
Countries heavily involved in 1990: 50

CONFESSIONS OF VICTIMS, 1990
(average annual martydom rates)

Roman Catholics	180,000
Protestants	60,000
Orthodox	25,000
Non-White Indigenous Christians	14,000
Marginal Protestants	10,000
Anglicans and Old Catholics	1,000
Total martyrs per year	290,000

LIKELIHOOD OF BEING MARTYRED
(at current rates)

Full-time workers	%	*per year*
Bishops	5.0	15
Evangelists	4.0	133
Catechists	3.5	175
Foreign missionaries	3.0	131
Clergy	2.0	303
All Christian workers	2.0	1,700
Monks, brothers	1.9	63
Sisters, nuns	1.8	300
Other Christians		
Great Commission Christians	1.6	133,000
Christians (all kinds)	1.0	290,000

Source: Reproduced with permission from *Our Globe and How to Reach It* by David B. Barrett and Todd M. Johnson. Published by New Hope, Birmingham, AL. Data source: World Evangelization Database

Family

VALUES IN THE HOME

Dr. James C. Dobson

In a Focus on the Family radio interview with Bob Biehl, president of Masterplanning Associates, a creative suggestion was offered to parents that I now strongly endorse. It related to the process by which values can be transmitted from one generation to the next. All mothers and fathers know it is their responsibility to teach their beliefs and concepts to their children, but this task is usually approached in a haphazard and casual manner. Mr. Biehl designed a procedure by which parents can instill their most highly valued principles and then reinforce them by the technique of repetition.

The first step in this system is to list the values which parents consider most critical. They should be designed and written for a particular child at his current age and level of understanding. Children are then offered money for memorizing the concepts in sets of five, paying them what they could earn for physical labor. When the entire list has been learned, approximately 75 percent of the original payment could be earned for memorizing it again. The reward would drop to 50 percent the third time through, and 25 the fourth. By this repetitive process, the individual items begin to "live" in the mind of the child, being recalled when a violation of the principle is observed in everyday life.

While each parent should create his own list of values and concepts, I am providing herewith the set we are using in our home. Please feel free to modify it, adapt it to a younger or older age child, or eliminate the statements with which you disagree. (If you would be willing to share your list with me, I would enjoy reading and perhaps adopting some of the items you have created.)

Appreciation is expressed to Mr. Biehl for his suggestion of this creative approach to parental instruction. He would agree that we are most likely to "shoot straight" when we have clear, well-defined targets at which we aim. His system identifies the targets—the values—which we hope to hit on behalf of our children.

1. "Seek ye first the Kingdom of God, and his righteousness, and all these things shall be added unto you" (Matthew 6:33). This is the fundamental principle of life on which all others rest.
2. Overcommitment and time pressure are the greatest destroyers of marriages and families. It takes time to develop any friendship . . . whether with a loved one or with God himself.
3. The overwhelming feeling of being "in love" is not a very reliable emotion during the early years (or at any age!). This intense affection can evaporate in a matter of days, leaving the person confused (and perhaps unhappily married). The only way to know you are in love with another person is to give yourselves plenty of time to get acquainted. Once the decision is made and marriage occurs, then your *commitment* to one another will be much more important than the feelings, which come and go.
4. The universe and everything in it will someday pass away and be made new by the Creator. Therefore, the events of *today* that seem so important are not really very

significant, except for those matters that will survive the end of the universe (such as securing your own salvation and doing the work of the Lord).

5. God is like a Father to his children. He loves them more than they can understand, but he also expects them to be obedient to his will. And he has said, "The wages of sin is death" (Romans 6:23). It is still true.
6. This is the way to be successful in life: Treat every person as you want to be treated; look for ways to meet the physical, emotional and spiritual needs of those around you. Suppress your desire to be selfish and to seek unfair advantage over others. Try to turn *every* encounter with another person into a new or stronger friendship. Then when this confidence with people is combined with hard work, your future success is assured.
7. Human worth does not depend on beauty or intelligence or accomplishments. We are all more valuable than the possessions of the entire world, simply because God gave us that value. This fact remains true, even if every other person on earth treats us like losers.
8. Strong desire is like a river. As long as it flows within the banks of God's will—be the current strong or weak—all is well. But when it floods over those boundaries and seeks its own channels, then disaster lurks in the rampage below (James Dobson, Sr.).
9. The killing of unborn children through medical abortions is one of the most evil occurrences of our time, with 1.5 million babies sacrificed in America each year and 55 million worldwide.
10. Comparison is the root of all feelings of inferiority. The moment you begin examining other people's strengths against your most obvious weaknesses, your self-esteem starts to crumble!
11. Never risk that which you can't afford to lose.
12. There will come a day, much quicker than we as your parents would wish, when you will no longer be comfortable living at home. You will want to move out and establish a home of your own. After that time, we will be more like your friends than your parents. Although we have enjoyed every phase of your life to this moment, we also look forward to the time when you will be an adult and assume responsibility for your own life.
13. If you're going through difficult times today, hold steady. It will change soon. If you are experiencing smooth sailing and easy times now, brace yourself. It will change soon. The only thing you can be certain of is change.
14. God created *two* sexes, male and female. They are equal in worth, although each is unique and different. It is not only impossible to blend maleness and femaleness into a single sex (unisex), it is dangerous to even attempt it.
15. The *love* of money is the root of all evil (1 Timothy 6:10). That's why Jesus issues more warnings about materialism and wealth than any other sin. It takes a steady hand to hold a full cup.
16. Christians should never consult astrologers, psychics or those who practice witchcraft (Isaiah 47:13, 14). They are usually phonies who only pretend to have extrasensory powers. But in some cases, they are working in cooperation with Satan. Rather than tamper with this evil world, the one true God wants us to bring our needs and problems and decisions to him. He has promised to lead us into all truth (John 8:32).
17. One of the secrets of successful living is found in the word *balance,* referring to the avoidance of harmful extremes. We need food, but we should not overeat. We should work, but not make work our only activity. We should play, but not let play rule us. Throughout life, it will be important to find the safety of the middle ground, rather than the imbalance of the extremes.
18. Your life is before you. Be careful of the choices you make now that you could regret later. This regret is the subject of an old poem whose author has been forgotten. I hope you'll never have reason to apply it to yourself.

Across the fields of yesterday,
He sometimes comes to me
A little lad just back from play—
the boy I used to be
He looks at me so wistfully
When once he's crept within
It is as if he hoped to see
the man I might have been.

19. Those who are the happiest are not necessarily those for whom life has been easiest. Emotional stability is an *attitude*. It is refusing to yield to depression and fear, even when black clouds float overhead. It is improving that which can be improved and accepting that which is inevitable.
20. Communism and socialism are economic systems whereby the government assumes responsibility to see that each person's needs are met and that no one individual earns more than the state feels is fair. Capitalism, such as we have in America, is based on free enterprise, whereby a person can achieve a better income for himself and his family by working and sweating and saving and investing. To compare these systems, think of yourself about to take a history test. Suppose you studied very hard and earned an "A" grade, but the teacher gave you a "C" so he could share some of your correct answers with a failing student who didn't study at all. Obviously this would destroy your motivation to study in the future. This need for personal incentives explains why capitalism produces more energetic people than communism and socialism, and why America is the richest nation on earth.
21. Take in a great breath of air and then blow it out. Contained in that single breath were at least three nitrogen atoms that were breathed by every human being who ever lived, including Jesus Christ, William Shakespeare, Winston Churchill and every president of the United States. This illustrates the fact that *everything* we do affects other people, positively or negatively. That's why it is foolish to say, "Do your own thing if it doesn't hurt anybody else."
22. Faith in God is like believing a man can walk over Niagara Falls on a tightrope while pushing a wheelbarrow. Trust in God is like getting in the wheelbarrow! To believe God can do something miraculous is one thing; to risk his willingness to do it in your life is another.
23. With God, even when nothing is happening . . . something is happening.
24. The first five minutes are vitally important, especially to:

    A new friendship
    A pastor's sermon
    A family during the early morning hours
    A dad who has just come home from work
    A television program
    A salesman's presentation
    A visit to the doctor

    Those first few moments of any human activity set the stage for everything that follows. If we accomplish our purpose quickly, we will probably be successful over the long haul. Therefore, spend more time preparing the first five minutes than any comparable period of time.
25. Whenever two human beings spend time together, sooner or later they will probably irritate one another. This is true of best friends, married couples, parents and children, or teachers and students. The question is: How do they respond when friction occurs?

There are four basic ways they can react:

a. They can internalize the anger and send it downward into a memory bank that never forgets. This creates great pressure within and can even result in disease and other problems.

b. They can pout and be rude without discussing the issues. This further irritates the other person and leaves him to draw his own conclusions about what the problem may be.

c. They can blow up and try to hurt the other person. This causes the death of friendships, marriages, homes and businesses.

d. Or, they can talk to one another about their feelings, being very careful not to attack the dignity and worth of the other person. This approach leads to permanent and healthy human relationships.

26. Don't marry someone with intolerable characteristics in the hope of changing him or her. If you can't live with someone who drinks, or someone who isn't a Christian, or someone who isn't clean, then don't marry that kind of person. The chances for miraculous improvements are slim. What you see is what you get!
27. "Except the Lord build a house, they labor in vain which build it" (Psalms 127:1).
28. Feelings are neither right nor wrong. It's what you do with them that causes the problems.
29. Most loneliness results from *insulation* rather than *isolation*. In other words, we are lonely because we insulate ourselves, not because others isolate us.
30. Some men watch so many sporting events on television that they wouldn't even know of their wives' decision to divorce them unless it was announced on Wide World of Sports! Remember, balance and moderation are needed in television watching, too.
31. The human body seems indestructible when we are young. However, it is incredibly fragile and must be cared for if it is to serve us for a lifetime. Too often, the abuse it takes during early years (from drugs, improper nutrition, sporting injuries, etc.) becomes painful handicaps during later years. One eighty-year-old man said it best: "If I'd known I was gonna live so long, I'd have taken better care of myself."
32. Before you criticize your parents for their failures and mistakes, ask yourself: "Will I *really* do that much better with my own children?" The job is tougher than it looks, and mistakes are *inevitable!*
33. Remember this about bragging and self-centeredness: Conceit is a weird disease—it makes everybody sick except the guy who has it. Or like the mother whale told her baby, "When you get to the surface and start to blow, that's when you get harpooned!"
34. Satan will attempt to offer you *whatever* you hunger for, whether it be money, power, sex or prestige. But Jesus said, "Blessed are those who hunger and thirst after righteousness" (Matthew 5:6).
35. Sexual contact between a boy and a girl is a progressive thing. In other words, the amount of touching and caressing and kissing that occurs in the early days tends to increase as they become more familiar and at ease with one another. Likewise, the amount of contact necessary to excite one another increases day by day, leading in many cases to an ultimate act of sin and its inevitable consequences. This progression must be consciously resisted by Christian young people who want to serve God and live by his standards. They can resist this trend by placing deliberate controls on the physical aspect of their relationship, right from the first date.
36. God is entitled to a portion of our income. Not because he needs it, but because we need to give it.
37. "For what shall it profit a man if he shall gain the whole world and lose his own soul?" (Jesus Christ, Mark 8:36).
38. It is better to be single and unhappy than unhappily married.

39. In order to find a satisfactory life's work, it is necessary to answer five vitally important questions:
What do I like to do?
What do I have an opportunity to do?
What do I have an ability to do?
What can I earn a living doing?
What can I do that will bring respect from society?
Unfortunately, all five of these questions must lead to the same answer if job satisfaction is to be found. Any one that is missing will create a certain degree of frustration. This explains why so many people have trouble getting started in adult life. It also makes clear why divine assistance is needed in choosing a profession or occupation.
40. "A wet bird never flies at night." (My grandfather said that to me when I was a child, and warned me not to forget it. I remember his words but never did figure out what he meant!)

Source: *Values in the Home* by Dr. James C. Dobson.

FAMILY ACTIVITIES FOR EACH SEASON OF THE YEAR

Winter

CHRISTMAS TRADITIONS

Yuletide Family Fun. Start a tradition of viewing family photographs, slides, and movies at Christmastime. It's fun to see how everyone has changed and to reminisce about past holidays together.

On December 1, set up a jigsaw puzzle with a winter or Christmas scene on a card table. As guests visit your home throughout the holidays, encourage them to work on the puzzle. Challenge your family to complete it by Christmas Day, perhaps saving the final piece for then.

Go caroling with another family and invite them over for refreshments.

Cover a large Styrofoam ball with sprigs of mistletoe, and hang it in a doorway as a reason for family hugs and kisses. (Be sure to pick up any berries that fall from this ornament, since they are poisonous and may be swallowed by small children.)

Make large letters out of newspaper or construction paper to spell the words "Happy Birthday, Jesus" on a large, front window of your home.

Growing Christmas Collections. Every year, give each child an ornament of his or her own. As the children grow up, they will have their own ornaments to cherish and eventually take with them into their families' homes. Give a different kind each year. Here are some suggestions: crystal; straw; wood; metal; cloth.

These ornaments should be collections of special memories, to be treasured throughout the years.

WINTER ACTIVITIES

Family Fun for the New Year. Materials needed: decorated coffee can; colored construction paper; 3″x3″ cardboard patterns, one for each family member; scissors; pencils.

During the first week of the New Year, place a colorfully decorated coffee can near the kitchen table. Label it "Family Fun Throughout the Year."

Give each member of the family a different colored piece of construction paper, scissors, a pencil and a 3″x3″ cardboard pattern.

Have each person trace the square pattern five times on his construction paper, and cut out the shapes.

Everyone should then write on each of their squares a family activity which they would like to do on "Family Fun" night, and drop the slips of paper into the container.

Each week, draw one activity from the can. The person whose color was selected one week does not get another turn until all other colors have been chosen. This gives each family member a fair chance to choose an activity.

FAMILY ACTIVITIES FOR EACH SEASON OF THE YEAR cont.

Replenish the coffee can with new cards as needed.

Celebration of the First Snow. Make up a simple song or cheer for the sight of the first snowflake.

Decorate your home with paper snowflakes. Make them by folding a piece of white paper in half, then half again three more times. Cut snips randomly from the corners and edges. Use your imagination, so no two will be alike. Unfold the papers and hang the snowflakes by black thread in doorways and from ceiling fixtures.

Build "snowmen" and "snow forts" from marshmallows and toothpicks. Set them on a mirror, and use the display for a table centerpiece!

Birdseed Pretzels. Birdseed pretzels are sure to draw a winter crowd of feathered guests. Explain to your children how difficult it is for birds to find food during these months, and how they can help by providing attractive nourishment for the birds in your neighborhood:

Lay a 12-inch piece of waxed paper on a protected surface. (The corners may have to be taped down to keep the paper from curling.)

Squirt wide lines of Elmer's Glue on the waxed paper to form a pretzel-like design in which all lines meet another.

Sprinkle birdseed or sunflower seeds onto the glue, and allow the project to dry overnight.

Turn the designs upside down on a flat surface. Carefully peel away the waxed paper.

Hang the "pretzels" from tree limbs or fences using strands of thread.

A VALENTINE'S DAY TREAT

How Mom and Dad Met. With the family gathered around, Mom and Dad can tell the story of their first date and courtship. They may want to include: How and where they met; activities and places they enjoyed while dating; when they "fell in love"; what qualities attracted them to one another; humorous stories about their courtship and engagement.

Everyone will enjoy pictures of Dad and Mom when they were young. And, as a nice touch, they can show the family how they kissed the very first time!

Winter Gardens. While nothing is growing outside, you can start a garden inside your home by planting vegetables and placing them in your kitchen window:

a. Beans. Fill small paper cups or sections of an egg carton with potting soil. Soak bean seeds or dried beans such as navy, pinto or butter beans in water overnight. Push two beans into the soil in each cup until they are just below the surface, and cover them. Water daily.

b. Carrots. Cut off the tops of several carrots, leaving about one inch of carrot attached to each top. Place the carrot tops in a saucer or pie pan and add enough water to keep the bottom of each piece in water. Do not allow them to dry out. Before long, roots will form and new tops will grow.

c. Sweet potatoes. Cut sweet potatoes in the same way as carrots, and use the same method to grow green tops. Toothpicks can be used to suspend the potato from the rim of a small glass. Keep enough water in the glass so that the bottom of the vegetable cutting stays totally submerged.

d. Alfalfa or bean sprouts. Fold several paper towels and place them in the bottom of a flat bowl or large saucer. Soak the towels with water and sprinkle alfalfa seeds or beans on them. Keep the towels wet. In a few days the seeds will sprout, and can be used in salads or on sandwiches. (Sprouts can also be grown in a sealed jar. Put just enough water in a jar to partially cover the seeds. As the water inside the jar evaporates, moisture eventually condenses on the underside of the lid and "rains" down on the seeds. You will have sprouts within a few days.)

Spring

SIGNS OF SPRING

Spring First. Use a bulletin board or chalkboard in your home to record special signs of spring. Print the title "Spring Firsts" at the top of the board.

As a family, discuss things that remind each person of a typical spring sight. Then decide which things everyone should notice, and list them on the board. The first person to spot a sign of spring can put his or her name on the board beside the "Spring First," and paste on a picture of what was observed.

First Robin Contest After a cold winter, welcome spring by having a "first robin" contest. The first member of the family to see and report a robin is the winner. This contest can continue even after children are grown. No matter where they live, they can call home with "first robin" and claim victory. This tradition celebrates the triumphant return of spring.

SPRINGTIME FUN

The following activity is especially good for elementary and preschool-age children. But be prepared for their older brothers and sisters to participate as well!

Spring Penny Walk. When the flowers and trees begin to bloom, take a "Spring Penny Walk" and enjoy the beautiful sights of spring. Toss a penny at each intersection to determine what path will be taken. ("Heads" indicates a right turn and "tails" specifies a left turn.) After returning home, have each member of the family color a picture of what he or she liked best about the springtime walk. Share the results after dinner.

FAMILY EASTER SUNRISE SERVICE

Ahead of time . . . Choose a special, quiet place from which the sunrise can be seen.

Prepare a simple, carry-along breakfast of boiled eggs, rolls, juice, etc. (Each person's breakfast can be packed in a colorful Easter basket, with surprises hidden in the bottom.)

The week before Easter, read from the Bible or a Bible storybook about the events leading up to the Resurrection, and discuss them together.

The night before Easter Sunday, talk about how the disciples must have felt on the Saturday night before the Resurrection; how Jesus' mother must have felt; what Mary Magdalene and those who had known Jesus might have felt.

On Easter morning. . . . Rise early enough to get to your special place before the sun does!

Wear casual clothes (you can get ready for church later), and take warm jackets and blankets.

Sit together on a blanket, and read the Easter story from the Bible.

As the sun comes peeping over the horizon, sing a victorious song about our risen Lord. Then, with your eyes wide open, thank God for the Resurrection and what it means to your family.

Celebrate by sharing the simple breakfast you prepared.

FRUIT BLOSSOM FESTIVAL

Decorate windows and bulletin boards with pictures cut from magazines or seed catalogs of the fruit most commonly grown in your area.

Bring dead limbs into the house and decorate them with mock blossoms made from tissue or crepe paper. Make ice cream using frozen fruit from last year's crop.

Celebrate the bees. Explain how without them, there would be no fruit. Ask one of your children to find out why and report on the subject at supper.

Tie "welcome ribbons" around each budding tree. Match the ribbons to the colors of the fruit that each tree will bear.

Plant a seedling. If your yard is small, a dwarf tree is best. You may want to use this idea in the fall, so the seedling can develop a root system during the dormant winter months.

MAY DAY SURPRISE

On May 1, rise early in the morning and pick a bouquet of spring flowers. Place the flowers in a pretty basket that can hang on a doorknob. (You can make your own basket from construction paper.)

Hang the May basket on the knob of the front door at a friend's house. Ring the doorbell, and hide. When someone comes to the door, jump out and shout, "May Day!"

Summer

SUMMER MEMORY BOOK

At the beginning of summer, record dates and descriptions of special outings, family activities and unusual events. Paste or tape ticket stubs, programs, place cards and other

FAMILY ACTIVITIES FOR EACH SEASON OF THE YEAR cont.

souvenirs into a "summer memory book" for your family.

Review the notebook with family members at the end of the summer, and enjoy the memories you have created!

SUMMER LOLLIPOP COOKIES

Use a favorite crispy cookie recipe:

Roll out the dough (not too thin) and cut into round shapes with a cookie cutter or a glass.

Place the cookies on a baking sheet, insert a wooden Popsicle stick one or two inches into the base of each one, and bake.

After cookies have cooled, frost them with a sunshine-yellow icing.

Candies or raisins can be used to decorate the "suns" with faces!

JULY 4TH PATRIOT PARADE

Ahead of time . . . Invite family and friends to join in the parade.

Decorate bikes, trikes, wagons, "Big Wheels," and doll buggies with red, white or blue paper stars, crepe-paper streamers and ribbons.

Have each participant choose a patriot to represent. Make suitable costumes from crepe paper, construction paper and old clothes. (Some possible characters: George Washington, Betsy Ross, Uncle Sam, Abraham Lincoln, Daniel Boone, Davy Crockett, Paul Revere, Martha Washington, a bugler, a drummer.)

Get family pets into the act. Tie bright ribbons, bows or strips of paper to leashes, collars, cages or pet boxes. (Be careful to separate pets who don't like each other.)

At the scheduled time . . . Have observers sit in lawn chairs where they can see the "parade route."

Announce the beginning of the parade with a bugle call, and signal the drummer(s) to lead the procession.

Have an announcer introduce each patriot or parade entry as that "act" passes by.

After the parade, have the announcer invite everyone to sing "America the Beautiful" together. Serve cold slices of watermelon.

PATRIOTIC GIFTS

A Present for Our Land. Give a living and growing present to our land by planting a tree or bush. Determine what kind of plant should be selected and where it would grow best.

Talk with your children about the environmental reasons for giving such a gift. (It releases oxygen into the atmosphere, gives shelter to birds, provides shade, etc.) Plant the tree or bush in your yard, or ask the city or park service to select an appropriate spot for it in the community.

July 4th "We Love You, America" Dinner. Plan an all-American dinner:

Include traditional foods such as hot dogs, hamburgers, apple pie and ice cream.

Decorate the table with a patriotic theme, using red, white and blue napkins, tablecloths and flowers.

If a globe is available, show young children where the United States is located in relation to other countries. Talk about the customs of peoples in other countries and our own, and reasons why people love their native lands.

Look in an encyclopedia for further information concerning Independence Day, and share it with everyone. After you have discussed the article, ask each child to remember one important fact or idea he or she learned from it.

NEIGHBORHOOD ART SHOW

Ahead of time . . . With other families in the neighborhood, agree on a place, time and date for the art show. Give two or three weeks' notice.

Make colorful signs about the event and post them in places where they will attract attention.

While the children make art pieces for the show, mothers and fathers can plan simple refreshments.

On the day of the show . . . Collect all entries at an early hour (which should be announced in advance) such as 9 a.m.

Make sure each item is clearly marked with the name of the artist and the price.

Separate entries into categories, such as paintings, sculptures and drawings.

Set up displays, keeping categories together and arranging entries so they may be easily seen.

At show time . . . Serve refreshments while parents and friends browse.

Provide a cashier's table where art may be purchased. If the money is to return to the individual artists, have the cashier keep track of the items sold.

After the event . . . Make each artist responsible for picking up unsold items and taking them home.

Have a clean-up committee put away tables and chairs, pick up trash and take care of leftover refreshments.

Autumn

LEAF CRAFTS

Crayon-Leaf Transfers. Materials needed: white or light-colored construction paper; crayons; an iron and an ironing board.

Collect strong leaves without holes or flaws. (Green leaves are usually strong and not easily torn.)

With bright crayons, carefully color the outer side of each leaf.

Lay the construction paper on an ironing board. Arrange the leaves on top of it, with the colored sides face down on the paper.

Iron the leaves with a medium-to-hot iron. (You can iron through a sheet of waxed paper if you prefer not to iron directly onto the leaves.)

Peel the waxed paper (if you used any) and the leaves from the paper. A crayoned print will be left on the construction paper.

Have fun decorating a wall, bulletin board or bedroom door with these natural art pieces—or turn them into note paper or attractive gift wrap!

Stained-Glass Leaves. Materials needed: waxed paper, construction paper, glue, scissors, an iron and an ironing board.

Collect brightly colored leaves of different sizes or shapes.

Make identical picture frames from two sheets of construction paper. Cut a rectangle, square, oval, circle or more ornate design from the center of each sheet. Trim the outer edges to whatever shape you desire.

Cut a piece of waxed paper large enough so that, when folded double, it is larger than the cut-out center of the construction paper frame.

Place one or two leaves inside the folded waxed paper.

Iron with a medium-to-hot iron until the waxed paper layers are sealed to each other around the leaves.

Insert the sealed sheet between the two paper frames, and glue the edges of the frames together.

Tape the completed "stained-glass leaves" to your windows, or hang them in a selected place in your home.

HALLOWEEN FUN

The Night before Halloween. Place a candle and a small amount of dry ice inside a carved-out pumpkin. (The ice will release a spooky vapor.) An adult should handle these to avoid the danger of a child burning himself from the ice or the candle. Also, set an eerie atmosphere with decorations and lighting effects. Let the children dress up in their Halloween costumes and masks. Discuss the characters they are pretending to be. Also, talk about the different kinds of invisible "masks" we sometimes wear, and why people wear them.

In addition, encourage each member of the family to share some of their fears—real and imaginary. Discuss how these might be diminished or dispelled.

For refreshments, serve Halloween cupcakes and orange soda.

THANKSGIVING TRADITIONS

Invite a few guests to dinner who otherwise would spend Thanksgiving Day alone. A few days before the dinner, ask each guest to recall several of his or her favorite dishes from previous Thanksgivings or other holidays. Serve one of each guest's favorite dishes with your turkey dinner. They will be delighted by your thoughtfulness!

Create a Centerpiece. As a family project, create a traditional centerpiece to be used each year on your Thanksgiving table.

FAMILY ACTIVITIES FOR EACH SEASON OF THE YEAR cont.

It can be as simple or as complex as you choose, but family participation is important. Be creative!

Some suggestions: Pilgrim salt and pepper shakers, a *papier-maché* turkey, a horn o' plenty filled with fresh fruits and vegetables, or a dried flower arrangement.

"Thank You" Place Cards. Fold 3″x5″ cards in half to make place cards for every person at the Thanksgiving table.

Decorate the cards in a Thanksgiving theme, writing each person's name on the front of a card.

On the inside, write a thank-you message. Make each message personal, honest and specific.

Larger cards may be used so that every member of the family can write a message to each person. That way, all receive an expression of gratitude from several people.

"I'm Thankful For . . ." Play the "20 Questions" game, and base it on things for which each person is thankful. The person who is "it" thinks of one thing for which he or she is thankful, and the others try to guess what it is by asking questions which can only be answered yes or no. If the group cannot guess the answer in 20 questions or less, the person who is "it" is the winner.

Any Season

THE FIRST TO SHARE

Celebrate the arrival of nature's first fruits by sharing as a family:

a. The first rosebud. Place it in a prominent place and enjoy its beauty together.

b. The first apple from the tree. Divide it and make every bite count!

c. The first cider. Buy it as a family. Make a tradition by always serving it in a special way; with popcorn, hot with cinnamon sticks and honey, or straight from the jug.

d. The first pumpkin pie. Make a tradition of inviting the same guest(s) to share it—such as a grandparent, friend, neighbor or relative.

THE GIFT OF WORK

To help your children appreciate the gift of work, make arrangements to take them to your place of employment on a regular workday. If that is impossible, share pictures and materials with them that demonstrate the work you do.

Talk about how work is a gift to us and about the joy we find in contributing to other person's lives through the use of our skills.

Take an outing to your place of employment. (If both parents work, include both jobs.) Help the children learn about the end result of your specific job.

Show them the entire facility, especially your work area, and introduce them to some of your coworkers.

Eat together in the plant cafeteria, an office snack shop or a nearby restaurant where you often go for lunch. If you usually take your lunch, pack one for each member of the family.

At the end of the day, discuss how each person in your family does specific jobs to make your home run smoothly. Thank God together for the health, strength and intelligence to work.

THE GIFT OF WHO YOU ARE

This gift is very special for a family member away at college or in the service, and makes a thoughtful birthday present. It is great medicine for counteracting discouragement all year long!

Buy large, empty capsules from a drugstore or pharmacy.

On strips of bright-colored paper, have each member of the family write, "I love you because. . ." and sign his or her name on the back. Each person may contribute many words of encouragement!

Roll the strips tightly and insert one in each capsule.

Put the capsules into a small box, and wrap or decorate the package. Then send it to the person you are honoring. He or she can read the slips of paper now, or save them as bolsters for their self-esteem in the future!

Source: Gloria Gaither and Shirley Dobson in *Let's Make A Memory.* Published by Word, Incorporated, Dallas, TX. Copyright © 1983. Used by permission.

CHRISTIAN LEADERS TELL HOW THEY LIKE TO SPEND LEISURE TIME

"What do you most like to do in your leisure moments?"

Steve Green, soloist: I like to read, work in the yard, and play games with my children.

Josh McDowell, president of Josh McDowell Ministries, author, speaker, and promoter of "Why Wait" campaign: One of the greatest privileges in the world is to be married to my wife and to be father of our four children. In spite of my heavy traveling schedule, one of my favorite things to do is to have creative and intimate dates with each of my children and wife. Every moment I invest with them will reap temporal fulfillment and eternal dividends.

Lloyd Ogilvie, pastor, First Presbyterian Church of Hollywood: I enjoy golf, fishing and my grandchildren. I enjoy traveling and studying Scottish history and customs. Each summer I spend my study leave at the University of Edinburgh in Scotland.

Anne Ortlund, author, speaker: I like to be with my husband . . . running on the beach . . . walking around Balboa Island . . . watching clean movies while sharing popcorn and Diet Coke.

R. C. Sproul, president of Ligonier Ministries, author, speaker: I read, golf, play jazz piano, and play Nintendo with my grandchildren.

Kenneth N. Taylor, chairman of the board, Tyndale House Publishers, author, translator of *The Living Bible*: My leisure time is spent writing, with grandchildren, reading, and worrying.

THIRTY IDEAS FOR HUSBANDS AND FATHERS

1. Old sayings. After dinner tonight, quiz your children on how many old sayings they know and understand. Write out the first half of the adage and ask them to fill in the rest. Sayings such as: "Don't put all your eggs in . . . ," "All is fair in love and . . . ," and "Children should be seen and. . . ." You'll be amazed at what answers turn up and the discussion that follows. Then try giving the first half of Bible proverbs, such as: "The getting of treasures by a lying tongue is . . ." (Proverbs 21:6). Let them look up the answers, then talk about them.

2. How teachable are you? Surprise your children tonight by asking them to tell you about something they're currently studying in school—some new mathematical or chemical formula, a new psychological or sociological study, a current trend in English literature, etc. Select a topic you know little about, and really get into it.

3. Instant motorcycle. Remember how you used to turn your bike into a motorcycle by fastening cardboard squares to the frame with clothespins so that they rapped against the spokes? Maybe it's time your child discovered the trick.

4. Motivation plus. To spark interest, let your kids choose and lead the family devotions for a week. Tell them they can be as creative and imaginative as they want, as long as you approve their plan. Motivation and responsibility grow through this experience. Use it frequently.

5. Call your wife at 10:30 A.M. sometime this week and say in these words, or others more natural to you, "I was just thinking of you and wanted to say that I'm immensely pleased that you are my wife. . . . You're wonderful!"

6. Chores, children, and character. The chores we did as a child are a fond memory for most of us. Sadly, children today are missing the valuable character qualities that regular chores build. They've become lost in our quest for leisure and labor-saving devices. But assigning chores is a most productive way of teaching responsibility and accountability to your children.

a. Start early. Even 3-year-olds can set tables, though it may take three times as long.

b. Don't discourage volunteers. Between the ages of 8 and 12, children go through an especially helpful age when they want to model their parents.

c. When possible, cooperate with the interests and abilities of the child in assigning chores. Children take a lot of pride in getting good at something they want to do.

d. Divide and rotate both the less desirable and the most popular tasks equally among all the family members.

e. Spell out each task in writing and make clear what the standard of performance is for a job well done. Leaving this up to individual interpretation creates problems.

f. Create and display a chart where assignments and performance are logged.

g. Don't spare the praise. If you spend more time criticizing a poorly done job than praising a good one, you're actually rewarding the negative behavior more than the positive performance. Lavish compliments are fun to give and never hurt anyone.

7. Picture memories. Tonight after dinner, haul out the family photo albums or slides for an hour of reminiscing. It's lots of fun, great for reinforcing family unity and recognizing growth. Follow it up with a short planning session for your next outing. Add a little popcorn and make an evening of it. (By the way, is your youngest child getting shortchanged in the photo department? It happens in most every family, so keep working at it!)

8. Take a moment to jot a note to your child's schoolteacher. Thank him or her for the interest poured into your child and express your appreciation. A similar note to a Sunday school teacher, scout leader, or anyone else involved regularly with your child can really make his or her day. Everyone needs sincere praise and encouragement.

9. The observation game. This is excellent for teaching children of any age to observe details (yourself, too). After you've been to a place or event together, test each other on memory of details that were there, i.e. "Did you see the man wearing tennis shoes and a suit?" With older children, test for things like inner qualities, personality traits, and nationalities. "Did you see the married couple that wasn't happy?" "Did you see the German, the Italian, and the Englishman?"

10. Library search. If you haven't been to the library with your kids recently, go for an hour this Saturday. Help them find one good historical fiction and one hobby or craft resource they can absorb in the next four weeks. If the library has a recording, filmstrip, video, or film department, check one out for your next family night at home. (The library, your church, club, or business may have a projector or VCR you can borrow.)

11. The story factory. Try some "add on" stories with your family after dinner or when you're driving somewhere. One person begins ("Once upon a time. . ." will do), and the next person adds a phrase, character, or action. Keep on going till it draws to a natural close or you're all on the floor with laughter.

12. Magnified fun. If you don't already have one, pick up a large, high-powered magnifying glass at a stationery store on the way home from work tonight. Spend a half-hour with your children, rediscovering your backyard, their hair and skin, food and clothing, insects . . . just about everything.

13. To better love her. If your wife hasn't said it recently, certainly a book or marriage counselor has: "It's the little things that count!" And it's true. One *Dads Only* reader put it this way: "Your wife doesn't really want a dozen roses every day. Just one rose a month will do." It's the small but consistent remembrances—the little touches—that fan the flame of romance in marriage, that say as nothing else can: "I love you," "You're beautiful!" "You're the only one in the world for me." Surveys indicate that the absence of romance and love ranks high as a source of depression in women. First Peter

3:7 instructs us, "Husbands . . . live with your wives in an understanding way. . . ." Certainly part of such "understanding" is to know her so well that you sense just what special expressions, gifts or touches will be the "little things" she'll cherish and thrive on. Become a student of your wife. Watch and listen for the important clues.

For starters, consider some "little things" like these:

a. Send her a Mailgram in which you express your love and invite her out to dinner with you.

b. Drop by a bookstore, library, or newsstand and bring her a book or magazine on home decorating, cooking, sewing, tennis, or anything that may be a special hobby or interest of hers.

c. Leave a note for her on the bathroom mirror, in the cupboard, in the dresser drawer, on her pillow . . . anywhere!

d. Turn off the TV in the middle of a program just because you'd rather visit with her and know about her day.

e. Buy her a gift she wouldn't buy for herself, like a music box or a special teacup and give it to her on an "unspecial" day.

14. Frisbee golf. Grab a frisbee or two, some bath towels, your family, and head for the backyard or your local park. Lay out a golf course as large as space will allow, using the towels spread on the ground as "holes." (The frisbee scores upon landing if any part is touching the towel.) The person with the fewest throws in completing the course wins. You can team little folks with older ones to make the competition more even.

15. A sense of specialness is one of the great gifts we can give our children. In Psalms 139:13-18 God describes how special we are to him. Use the passage as a springboard for some family sharing about each other. Ask each member to think of two special qualities about each of the others and then share them. Watch out; it could be an emotional evening.

16. Love letters shouldn't be the sole domain of the young. If you haven't written one to your wife recently, take 20 minutes and do it right now. Talk about her most endearing quality and thank her for being your wife.

17. Imagination. Get inside your child's imagination with a "Pretend that you're a . . ." game. Select an object and ask your son or daughter to tell you how it feels to be that object. For starters try: a swimming pool, a tall building, a car, a tree, a bus, a church building, or a doormat. Concentrate on feelings and emotions.

18. Bedtimes. Maybe you've never thought of yourself as a bedtime storyteller. But it's one of the best and most entertaining ways to pass along values to your children. The tales you spin become treasured memories to both you and your child.

Storytelling is quite easy if you keep these simple concepts and ideas in mind:

a. Nature stories are a natural. They can be about animals, trees, or phenomena such as brooks, volcanoes, even thunder and lightning. For example, an "I met a frog . . ." story could be approached this way: (1) Look up frogs in an encyclopedia and discover some facts—things like size, unique features, kinds of noises they make, how they are hatched, misconceptions about them and special abilities. (2) Decide what facts to use and give at least one of them personal significance to your child. (3) Make up the story by imagining that a frog you met is talking to you. Try it out. The more you tell it, the more interesting it will get. Then write it down for your children to read or illustrate with drawings.

b. "Look at that over there" stories can be about man-made things like bridges, paintings, pianos, airplanes, clocks, or medicine.

c. "Give me three words" stories begin by letting the children pick three words like "little girl, grandma, vacations," then you weave a story from them.

d. "Do you remember the story of . . . " stories take the characters from a familiar children's tale and give them a new adventure of your own making.

As you launch into your story, concentrate on describing the people, places and objects in detail (color, movement, size, and shape), include some humor, choose a moral that the child can apply and let it come to a natural conclusion.

So, suppress your fears and give storytelling a try. You'll look forward to bedtimes as much as your children will.

19. Exploring. Remember that side street or back road you always wondered about . . . that quaint shop you've never checked out? Your wife and children probably have such places too. So, set some limits (such as mileage, time, and expense) and let each family member choose where he or she wants to take the family "exploring." Go each Saturday morning until everyone has led an adventure.

20. Instead of TV tonight, invest an hour after dinner "reminiscing" about when each family member: 1) had the most fun; 2) felt the most embarrassed; 3) cried the hardest; 4) was so tired that; 5) never worked harder; and 6) felt the closest to God. The family scrapbook or photo albums can embellish the sharing or jog your memories. And close by thanking God for the privileges and protection he has given each family member.

21. Last thoughts of the day. Remain active in your child's subconscious all night—certainly a prime reason for resolving any tensions in your relationship before your child falls asleep. Turn the "last thoughts" principle to your advantage each evening this week by expressing to your child (1) one specific character strength he or she has, and (2) recalling an action your child did that day that made you proud. Bedtimes are not the moment for punishment or criticism.

22. Ping-Pong baseball. Grab a Ping-Pong ball, roll up a newspaper for a bat, and try a little game of "Work-up" in the living room. There are no strikes, and the ball must be hit or you're out. Adjust rules to fit your children's ages and skills.

23. Meals are a great learning environment for younger children. They can practice the alphabet, multiplication tables, or spelling words. Vocabulary can be increased by naming animals, historical dates, famous people . . . even places and geography. If you have a teenager who is studying a foreign language, let him lead a meal devoted only to speaking that language. The possibilities are endless.

24. Table sentences. One person starts and each person around the table adds a word till the sentence is finished. There's no penalty for completing the sentence. The next person starts a new one.

25. A little squeeze can communicate a lot of love. When you bow to say the blessing, join hands and give the person on your right a little "love" squeeze. The important point is clear: A little love given brings some in return.

26. Creative analogies can sharpen verbal skills and bring out thoughts and feelings sometimes hard to express. Start with everyone stating the relationship between a personal characteristic or feeling and some other familiar phenomenon. For example: "I'm as thin as a stick" or "I'm as happy as a lark."

27. The return. After dinner tonight, suggest that your family go again on a favorite vacation or outing—this time by memory. With everybody contributing, try to recall all the steps and events that happened, beginning with packing suitcases and the car, incidents en route, and the chronology of each day's events until you returned. Get out your photos taken on the trip. You'll discover this "walk through" will trigger lots of warm memories, and this time the trip won't cost a cent.

28. Grace at meals can easily lapse into a lifeless routine. You can enliven these important prayers by adding variety: 1) Slow down the prayer so each thought is emphasized. 2) Discuss the prayer's key ideas during the first moments of the meal. 3) Pray at the end of the meal. 4) Have each family member offer a short portion of the prayer. 5) Start eating without prayer and when someone notices, lead a discussion about why a prayer of thanksgiving is important, what should be included in the prayer, how specific it can or should be and what causes grace at mealtime to lose its significance. 6) Try singing grace and holding hands for variety.

29. Precede breakfast with some physical exercise together. Have each member of the family lead one "waker-upper."

30. Practical prayers. It's difficult for children, even adults, to see prayer as a direct course of action in meeting needs and solving problems. Concentrate this month on guiding your child to pray for specific circumstances in his life and the lives of others in your family and his circle of friends. Keep a simple log next to the bed, with requests and God's answers. Watch their enthusiasm about prayer grow!

Source: Paul Lewis in *Dads Only.* Published by Corporate Family Resources, Julian, CA.

Dads Only, edited by Paul Lewis, is a bimonthly newsletter with tips, research, and ideas for fathers. For subscription information write P.O. Box 340, Julian, CA 92036 or call 1-800-HELP-DAD. Additional resources are available from National Center for Fathering, 217 Southwind Place, Manhattan, KS 66502.

FOCUS FACT

In 1965 the average parent spent 30 hours a week with a child. Today the average parent spends only 17 hours.

Source: Focus on the Family Bulletin

CHECKLIST FOR SPIRITUAL TRAINING

Dr. James C. Dobson

Listed below is a checklist for parents—a set of targets at which to aim. Many of the items require maturity that children lack, and we should not try to make adult Christians out of our immature youngsters. But we can gently urge them toward these goals—these targets—during the impressionable years of childhood.

Essentially, the six scriptural concepts that follow should be consciously taught, providing the foundation on which all future doctrine and faith will rest. I encourage every Christian parent to evaluate his child's understanding of these six areas:

Concept I— "And thou shalt love the Lord thy God will all thy heart" (Mark 12:30).

1. Is your child learning of the love of God through the love, tenderness and mercy of his parents? (most important)
2. Is he learning to talk about the Lord, and to include him in his thoughts and plans?
3. Is he learning to turn to Jesus for help whenever he is frightened or anxious or lonely?
4. Is he learning to read the Bible?
5. Is he learning to pray?
6. Is he learning the meaning of faith and trust?
7. Is he learning the joy of the Christian way of life?
8. Is he learning the beauty of Jesus' birth and death?

Concept II— "Thou shalt love thy neighbor as thyself" (Mark 12:31).

1. Is he learning to understand and empathize with the feelings of others?
2. Is he learning not to be selfish and demanding?
3. Is he learning to share?
4. Is he learning not to gossip and criticize others?
5. Is he learning to accept himself?

Concept III— "Teach me to do thy will; for thou art my God" (Psalm 143:10).

1. Is he learning to obey his parents as preparation for later obedience to God? (most important)
2. Is he learning to behave properly in church—God's house?

3. Is he learning a healthy appreciation for both aspects of God's nature: love and justice?
4. Is he learning that there are many forms of benevolent authority outside himself to which he must submit?
5. Is he learning the meaning of sin and its inevitable consequences?

Concept IV— "Fear God, and keep his commandments: for this is the whole duty of man" (Ecclesiastes 12:13).
1. Is he learning to be truthful and honest?
2. Is he learning to keep the Sabbath day holy?
3. Is he learning the relative insignificance of materialism?
4. Is he learning the meaning of the Christian family and the faithfulness to it which God intends?
5. Is he learning to follow the dictates of his own conscience?

Concept V— "But the fruit of the Spirit is . . . self-control" (Galatians 5:22, 23, RSV).
1. Is he learning to give a portion of his allowance (and other money) to God?
2. Is he learning to control his impulses?
3. Is he learning to work and carry responsibility?
4. Is he learning to tolerate minor frustration?
5. Is he learning to memorize and quote Scripture?

Concept VI— " . . . he that humbleth himself shall be exalted" (Luke 14:11).
1. Is he learning a sense of appreciation?
2. Is he learning to thank God for the good things in life?
3. Is he learning to forgive and forget?
4. Is he learning the vast difference between self-worth and egotistical pride?
5. Is he learning to bow in reverence before the God of the universe?

Source: James C. Dobson in *Straight Talk to Men and Their Wives.* Published by Word, Incorporated, Dallas, TX. Copyright © 1980. Used by permission.

SEVEN REASONS FAMILY DEVOTIONS ARE IMPORTANT

1. It unifies the home life, and puts faith in the place of friction.

2. It brings to the family group a sense of God's presence.

3. It shows the children that God is relevant to everyday living, and not just a Being to be worshiped on Sunday.

4. It gives members of the family an opportunity for self-examination and confession of sin.

5. It strengthens the members of the household for the tasks and responsibilities they are to face during the day.

6. It insulates us against the hurts and misunderstandings which come our way.

7. It supplements the work of the church, and makes of our homes a sanctuary where Christ is honored.

Source: Billy Graham in *My Answer.* Published by Doubleday and Company. Copyright © 1960.

THE POWER OF POSITIVE KISSING

A German group of psychologists, physicians and insurance companies who cooperated on a research project, designed to find the secret to long life and success, made a surprising discovery. The secret? Kiss your wife each morning when you leave for work!

The meticulous German researchers discovered that men who kiss their wives every morning have fewer automobile accidents on their way to work than men who omit the morning kiss. The good-morning kissers miss less work because of sickness and earn 20 to 30 percent more money than non-kissers. How do they explain their findings? According to West Germany's Dr. Arthur Szabo, "A husband who kisses his wife every morning begins the day with a positive attitude."

Source: *Servant Magazine* published by Prairie Bible Institute. January 1990 issue.

A YEAR'S READING PROGRAM FOR AGES 0–3

January	**My Book of Bible Rhymes* by John Knapp II, Illustrated by Dianne Turner Deckart, David C. Cook Publishing Company
February	*Good Night Moon* by Margaret Wise Brown, Illustrated by Clement Hurd, Harper & Row, Publishers
March	**Read Aloud Bible Stories, Volumes 1 and 2* by Ella K. Lindvall, Moody Press
April	*A to Z Picture Book* by Gyo Fujikawa, Grosset & Dunlap
May	**God Made It All* by Mary Thornton Blanton, Scripture Press, SonFlower Books
June	*Colors* by John J. Reiss, Bradbury Press
July	*Animals on the Farm* by Feodor Rojankovsky, Alfred A. Knopf
August	*Mother Goose* by Michael Hauge, Holt, Rinehart & Winston
September	*Pat The Bunny* by Dorothy Kunhardt, Golden Books
October	**God Made All the Colors* by Linden Evans, Lion Publishing Corporation
November	*Brown Bear, Brown Bear, What Do You See?* by Bill Martin, Jr., Holt, Rinehart & Winston
December	*Poems to Read to the Very Young* by Josette Frank, illustrated by Eloise Wilkins, Random House

Source: All books selected by Elaine K. McEwan. Further information about these and other books are included in *How to Raise a Reader* by Elaine K. McEwan, available at your local Christian bookstore.

* Books from Christian publishers are indicated with an asterisk.

FOCUS FACT

When Mother Teresa received her Nobel Prize she was asked, "What can we do to help promote world peace?" "Go home and love your family," she replied.

A YEAR'S READING PROGRAM FOR AGES 4–7

January	**A Child's Book of Prayers* by Christine Harder Tangvald, David C. Cook Publishing Company
February	*The Very Hungry Caterpillar* by Eric Carle, Puffin
March	**Big Thoughts for Little People* by Kenneth Taylor, Tyndale House Publishers
April	**Who's a Friend of the Water Spurting Whale?* by Sanna Anderson Baker, Illustrated by Tomie dePaola, David C. Cook Publishing Company
May	*Bread and Jam for Frances* by Russell Hoban, Illustrated by Lillian Hoban, Harper & Row, Publishers
June	*Mike Mulligan and His Steam Shovel* by Virginia Lee Burton, Houghton Mifflin Company
July	*The Five Hundred Hats of Bartholomew Cubbins* by Dr. Seuss, Vanguard Press
August	*Animal Alphabet* by Bert Kitchen, Dial
September	*The Helen Oxenbury Nursery Story Book* by Helen Oxenbury, Alfred A. Knopf

October *Now You Can Read Stories from the Bible by Elaine Ife and Rosalind Sutton, Thomas Nelson, Inc., Publishers
November *The Mitten* by Alvin Tresselt, Lothrop, Lee & Shepard
December *The Christmas Pageant* by Tomie DePaola, Winston Press

A book your child will enjoy year-round: *Egermeier's Bible Story Book* by Elsie Egermeier, Warner Press

Source: All books selected by Elaine K. McEwan. Further information about these and other books are included in *How to Raise a Reader* by Elaine K. McEwan, available at your local Christian bookstore. Copyright © 1987. Published by David C. Cook Publishing Company. Used by permission.

* Books from Christian publishers are indicated with an asterisk.

A YEAR'S READING PROGRAM FOR AGES 8–10

January *Homer Price* by Robert McCloskey, Viking
February *The Lion, the Witch, and the Wardrobe* by C.S. Lewis, The Macmillan Company
March *Charlotte's Web* by E.B. White, Harper & Row, Publishers
April *Little House in the Big Woods* by Laura Ingalls Wilder, Harper & Row, Publishers
May *A Wrinkle in Time* by Madeleine L'Engle, Farrar, Straus & Giroux
June *The Secret Garden* by Frances Hodgson Burnett, Illustrated by Tasha Tudor, J.B. Lippincott
July *Tales of the Kingdom by David and Karen Mains, Illustrated by Jack Stockman, David C. Cook Publishing Company
August *The Princess and the Goblin by George MacDonald, Illustrated by Linda Hill Griffith, David C. Cook Publishing Company
September *The Great Brain* by John D. Fitzgerald, Dial
October *The Incredible Journey* by Shelia Burnford, Little Brown
November *Where the Red Fern Grows* by Wilson Rawls, Bantam Books
December *The Best Christmas Pageant Ever* by Barbara Robinson, Avon

A book your child will enjoy year-round: *The Children's Bible In 365 Stories* by Mary Batchelor, Lion Publishing Corporation

Source: All books selected by Elaine K. McEwan. Further information about these and other books are included in *How to Raise a Reader* by Elaine K. McEwan, available at your local Christian bookstore. Copyright © 1987. Published by David C. Cook Publishing Company. Used by permission.

* Books from Christian publishers are indicated with an asterisk.

A YEAR'S READING PROGRAM FOR AGES 10–12

January *The Book of Three* by Lloyd Alexander, Holt, Rinehart & Winston
February *The Wind in the Door* by Madeleine L'Engle, Farrar, Straus, and Giroux
March *Tales of the Resistance by David & Karen Mains, David C. Cook Publishing Co.
April *Island of the Blue Dolphins* by Scott O'Dell, Houghton
May *Sarah, Plain and Tall* by Patricia MacLachlan, Harper & Row, Publishers
June *Dangerous Journey: The Story of Pilgrim's Progress by Oliver Hunkin, editor. Illustrated by Alan Parry, Wm. B. Eerdmans Publishing Company
July *Bridge to Terabithia* by Katherine Paterson, Thomas Y. Crowell
August *In Search of Perlas Grandes by Timothy C. Davis, Accent Books

September *Potter by Walter Wangerin, Jr., David C. Cook Publishing Company
October *The Yearling* by Marjorie Kinnan Rawlings, Illustrated by N.C. Wyeth, Charles Scribner's Sons
November *Treasure Island* by Robert Louis Stevenson, Illustrated by N.C. Wyeth, Charles Scribner's Sons
December *Classics to Read Aloud to Your Children* by William F. Russell, Crown Publishers

A book your child will enjoy year-round: *The Illustrated Bible,* Living Values Edition, David C. Cook Publishing Company

Source: All books selected by Elaine K. McEwan. Further information about these and other books are included in *How to Raise a Reader* by Elaine K. McEwan, available at your local Christian bookstore. Copyright © 1987. Published by David C. Cook Publishing Company. Used by permission.

* Books from Christian publishers are indicated with an asterisk.

FOCUS FACT

The most influential book cited by 223 corporate CEOs and college presidents is the Bible. 25% say the Bible is the book they'd recommend first to young people.

Source: National College of Education, Evanston, IL, survey.

A YEAR'S READING PROGRAM FOR PARENTS WITH CHILDREN 0–3

January *The First Three Years of Life* by Burton L. White, Prentice-Hall, Inc.
February *Infants and Mothers: Differences in Development* by T. Berry Brazelton, Delacorte Press
March *The Complete Book of Baby and Child Care for Christian Parents* by Grace H. and Hebert L. Ketterman, Fleming H. Revell
April *A Hug and a Kiss and a Kick in the Pants* by Kay Kuzma, David C. Cook Publishing Company
May *Heart and Home: A Reaffirmation of Traditional Mothering* by Debra Evans, Crossway Books
June *The Christian Family* by Larry Christenson, Bethany House Publishers
July *Seven Things Children Need* by John M. Drescher, Herald Press
August *Dare to Discipline* by James Dobson, Tyndale House Publishers
September *The Encyclopedia of Christian Parenting* by Leslie Keylock, editor, Fleming H. Revell
October *What Happens When Your Children Grow* by Margaret Bailey Jacobsen, Victor Books/Scripture Press
November *Building Your Child's Faith* by Alice Chapin, Here's Life Publishers
December *How to Play with Your Children* by Brian and Shirley Sutton-Smith, Hawthorn Books

Source: All books selected by Elaine K. McEwan. Further information about these and other books are included in *Super Kid? Raising Balanced Children in a Super Kid World* by Elaine McEwan, available at your local Christian bookstore. Copyright © 1988. Published by David C. Cook Publishing Company. Used by permission.

* Books from Christian publishers are indicated with an asterisk.

A YEAR'S READING PROGRAM FOR PARENTS WITH CHILDREN 4–7

January **Christian Child-Rearing and Personality Development* by Paul D. Meier, Baker Book House

February **Hide or Seek* by James Dobson, Fleming H. Revell

March **How to Talk with Your Children about God* by Frances Loftiss Carroll, Prentice-Hall, Inc.

April *Traits of a Healthy Family* by Dolores Curran, Ballantine/Epiphany Books

May *How to Make Your Child a Winner* by Victor Cline, Walker and Company

June *The Quality Time Almanac: A Source Book of Ideas and Activities for Parents and Kids* by S. Adams Sullivan, Doubleday Company

July **Dr. Dobson Answers Your Questions* by James Dobson, Tyndale House

August **From the Inside Out* by Kay Kuzma, David C. Cook Publishing Company

September *Self-Esteem: The Key to Your Child's Well Being* by Harris Clemes and Reynold Beam, G. Putnam's Sons

October *The Parents Book of Physical Fitness for Children* by Martin I. Lorin, Atheneum

November *Kids and Play* by Joanne F. Oppenheim, Ballantine Books

December *Bringing Up a Moral Child* by Michael Shulman and Eva Mekler, Addison-Wesley Publishing Company, Inc.

Source: All books selected by Elaine K. McEwan. Further information about these and other books are included in *Super Kid? Raising Balanced Children in a Super Kid World* by Elaine McEwan, available at your local Christian bookstore. Copyright © 1988. Published by David C. Cook Publishing Company. Used by permission.

* Books from Christian publishers are indicated with an asterisk.

“” FOCUS QUOTE **If parents took the responsibility that should rightfully be theirs, we wouldn't have 99% of the problems we have in the schools in America.** —Guy Doud, from his recent Focus on the Family film, *Molder of Dreams.*

A YEAR'S READING PROGRAM FOR PARENTS WITH CHILDREN 8–10

January *The Challenge of Friendship: Helping Your Child Become a Friend* by Shirley Gould, Dutton Publishing

February **Discovering Your Child's Design* by Ralph Matson and Thom Black, David C. Cook Publishing Company

March **Rights, Wrongs, and In-Betweens* by Jim Larson, Augsburg Publishing House

April *Raising Good Children* by Thomas Lickona, Bantam Books

May **Parents, Take Charge!* by Perry L. Draper, Tyndale House Publishers

June **Parenting Isn't for Cowards* by James Dobson, Word Inc.

July *Working and Caring* by T. Berry Brazelton, Addison-Wesley
August **Should You Be the Working Mom?* by Bee-Lan C. Wang and Richard J. Stellway, David C. Cook Publishing Company
September **The Intimate Family* by Marlee Alex, Questar Publishers, Inc.
October **Preparing Your Child for Success at School* by Cheri Fuller, Honor Books/Harrison House
November **Parents' Most-Asked Questions about Kids and Schools* by Cliff Schimmels, Victor Books/Scripture Press
December *The Difficult Child* by Stanley Turecki and Leslie Tonner, Bantam Books

Source: All books selected by Elaine K. McEwan. Further information about these and other books are included in *Super Kid? Raising Balanced Children in a Super Kid World* by Elaine McEwan, available at your local Christian bookstore. Copyright © 1988. Published by David C. Cook Publishing Company. Used by permission.

* Books from Christian publishers are indicated with an asterisk.

“” FOCUS QUOTE **Sometimes we're so concerned about giving our children what we never had growing up, we neglect to give them what we *did* have growing up.** —Dr. James Dobson

---

A YEAR'S READING PROGRAM FOR PARENTS WITH CHILDREN 10–12

January **Why Wait? What You Need to Know about the Teen Sexuality Crisis* by Josh McDowell and Dick Day, Here's Life Publishers
February **Keeping Your Teen in Touch with God* by Robert Laurent, David C. Cook Publishing Company
March **How to Keep Your Kids on Your Team* by Charles Stanley, Oliver Nelson Books
April **Raising Positive Kids in a Negative World* by Zig Ziglar, Oliver Nelson Books
May *Growing with Sports: A Parents' Guide to the Young Athlete* by Ernest M. Vandeweghe and George L. Flynn, Prentice-Hall, Inc.
June **How to Motivate Your Child toward Success* by William Steuart McBirnie, Tyndale House Publishers
July **Home: Where Life Makes Up Its Mind* by Charles R. Swindoll, Multnomah Press
August **How to Enjoy a Family Fight* by Will Cunningham, Questar Publishers, Inc.
September **Kids Who Have Too Much* by Ralph E. Minear and William Proctor, Thomas Nelson, Inc., Publishers
October **40 Ways to Teach Your Child Values* by Paul Lewis, Tyndale House Publishers
November *The Birth Order Book* by Kevin Leman, Dell Publishing Company
December **Parents and Teenagers* by Jay Kesler, Victor Books/Scripture Press

Source: All books selected by Elaine K. McEwan. Further information about these and other books are included in *Super Kid? Raising Balanced Children in a Super Kid World* by Elaine McEwan, available at your local Christian bookstore. Copyright © 1988. Published by David C. Cook Publishing Company. Used by permission.

* Books from Christian publishers are indicated with an asterisk.

100 BEST-SELLING CHILDREN'S BOOKS

This list was compiled from information supplied by publishers. The first sales figure shown for each entry represents the number of copies sold during that period; the second figure is the total number sold in that book's history with that publisher.

Although books are ranked according to the total sold in the past year, not all publishers granted permission to release these figures. Unreleased or unavailable figures are designated by "n.a.," but the books are ranked in their correct order.

Of the top 100 books, category totals (according to publishers' grading) are: preschool, 8; primary, 13; junior, 12; young teen, 3; preschool and primary, 37; and primary and junior, 27.

1. **The Lion, the Witch and the Wardrobe,** C.S. Lewis, Macmillan Copyright © 1950. (Junior / 167,648 / n.a.) This book in "The Chronicles of Narnia" series tells how Aslan, the noble lion, frees Narnia from the spell of the White Witch.
2. **The Chronicles of Narnia (boxed set),** C.S. Lewis, Macmillan Copyright © 1956. (Junior / 141,373 / n.a.) Each boxed set comprises the seven titles in the "Narnia" series.
3. **The Picture Bible,** Iva Hoth, illus. by Andre LeBlanc, and Bible editing by Elvan Olmstead, Cook Copyright © 1979. (Young Teen / 97,985 / n.a.) This full-color, picture-strip version of the Bible includes brief captions.
4. **God's Greatest Day,** Cook Copyright © 1986. (Preschool and Primary / 68,685 / 157,172.) This 3″x4″ title in the "My Jesus Pocketbook" series focuses on Easter.
5. **A Very Special Birthday,** Cook Copyright © 1986. (Preschool and Primary / 84,926 / 193,734.) This 3″x4″ title in the "My Jesus Pocketbook" series focuses on Christ's birth.
6. **Bedtime Hugs for Little Ones,** Debby Boone, Harvest House Copyright © 1988. (Preschool and Primary / 72,948 / 72,948.) This book provides children and parents an opportunity to discuss growing up, the dark, dreams, shooting stars, and being loved.
7. **Nursery Rhymes,** Cook Copyright © 1986. (Preschool and Primary / 56,794 / 141,173.) This 3″x4″ title in the "My Jesus Pocketbook" series discusses discipleship.
8. **ABC's,** Cook Copyright © 1986. (Preschool and Primary / 54,687 / 129,483.) This 3″x4″ title in the "My Jesus Pocketbook" series teaches youngsters about praise.
9. **Lord's Prayer,** Cook Copyright © 1986. (Preschool and Primary / 53,280 / 125,903.) This 3″x4″ title in the "My Jesus Pocketbook" series focuses on prayer.
10. **Twenty-Third Psalm,** Cook Copyright © 1986. (Preschool and Primary / 52,501 / 124,199.) This 3″x4″ title in the "My Jesus Pocketbook" series teaches kids about trust.
11. **The Story of Christmas for Children,** Beverly Wiersum and illus. by Lorriane Wells, Ideals Copyright © 1979. (Preschool and Primary 2,500 / n.a.) This book tells the story of Christ's birth in easy-to-read rhyme.
12. **Manners,** Cook Copyright © 1983. (Preschool and Primary / 50,116 / 119,560.) This 3″x4″ title in the "My Jesus Pocketbook" series discusses relationships.
13. **Scripture Pictures,** Cook Copyright © 1986. (Preschool and Primary / 48,656 / 117,303.) This 3″x4″ title in the "My Jesus Pocketbook" series teaches readers Bible skills.
14. **Prince Caspian,** C.S. Lewis, Macmillan

Copyright © 1951. (Junior / 48,414 / n.a.) This book in "The Chronicles of Narnia" series tells how Prince Caspian and his army of Talking Beasts conquer the Telemarines.

15. **The Ten Commandments,** Cook Copyright © 1987. (Preschool and Primary / 47,228 / 66,704.) This 3″x4″ title in the "My Jesus Pocketbook" series teaches obedience.
16. **The Story of Easter for Children,** Beverly Wiersum and illus. by Lorrianne Wells, Ideals Copyright © 1987. (Preschool / 44,900 / n.a.) This book tells the story of Easter in easy-to-read rhyme.
17. **Noah and the Floating Zoo,** Cook Copyright © 1986. (Preschool and Primary / 42,554 / 85,123.) This 3″x4″ title in the "My Jesus Pocketbook" series teaches trust.
18. **Mandie and the Secret Tunnel,** Lois Gladys Leppard, Bethany House Copyright © 1983. (Primary and Junior / 42,372 / 168,001.) Almost a teenager, Mandie is certain God no longer loves her. She watches her father being buried and her mother remarry. It seems Uncle Ned is her only friend.
19. **Mandie and the Holiday Surprise,** Lois Gladys Leppard, Bethany House Copyright © 1988. (Primary and Junior / 41,992 / 41,992.) Mandie can't wait to see family and friends. Will she have a special present waiting when she arrives home for Christmas?
20. **Anybody Can Be Cool, but Awesome Takes Practice,** Lorraine Peterson, Bethany House Copyright © 1988. (Young Teen / 40,797 / 40,797.) Teens discover the truth of a person's value in Christ through 13 weeks of inspiring and challenging devotional readings.
21. **The Voyage of the "Dawn Treader,"** C.S. Lewis, Macmillan Copyright © 1952. (Junior / 40,101 / n.a.) This book in "The Chronicles of Narnia" series tells how King Caspian sails through magic waters to the end of the world.
22. **Little Visits With Jesus,** Mary Manz Simon, Concordia Copyright © 1987. (Preschool and Primary / 40,000 / n.a.) This family devotional continues the tradition of the *Little Visits With God* and *More Little Visits With God* volumes.
23. **Learning to Count,** Cook Copyright © 1986. (Preschool and Primary / 39,836 / 96,648.) This 3″x4″ title in the "My Jesus Pocketbook" series teaches kids to trust God.
24. **Li'l Critters,** Cook Copyright © 1986. (Preschool and Primary / 39,678 / 92,668.) This 3″x4″ title in the "My Jesus Pocketbook" series focuses on faith.
25. **Meet Kirsten: An American Girl,** Janet Shaw, Pleasant Copyright © 1987. (Primary and Junior / 39,383 / 108,154.) After a dangerous journey and loss of a friend, Kirsten Larson finds New York different from the Swedish village her family left behind.
26. **Meet Samantha: An American Girl,** Susan Adler, Pleasant Copyright © 1987. (Primary and Junior / 39,051 / 105,976.) Samantha Parkington befriends Nellie, a servant girl who works next to Samantha's wealthy grandmother. Samantha and Nellie try to find out why Jessie, who became Samantha's second mother, leaves one day.
27. **The Bible in Pictures for Little Eyes,** Kenneth Taylor, Moody Copyright © 1956. (Preschool / n.a.) This classic makes Bible stories understandable to young children through simple words and pictures.
28. **The Beginning,** Cook Copyright © 1986. (Preschool and Primary / 37,937 / 80,710.) This 3″x4″ title in the "My Jesus Pocketbook" series teaches about Creation.
29. **Praise,** Cook Copyright © 1987. (Preschool and Primary / 37,569 / 71,677.) This 3″x4″ title in the "My Jesus Pocketbook" series discusses how to praise God.
30. **God's Fruit,** Cook Copyright © 1986. (Preschool and Primary / 37,323 / 91,105.) This 3″x4″ title in the "My

100 BEST-SELLING CHILDREN'S BOOKS cont.

Jesus Pocketbook" series teaches kids about love.

31. **Mandie and the Mysterious Bells,** Lois Gladys Leppard, Bethany House Copyright © 1988. (Primary and Junior / 36,798 / 54,309.) This title is part of the "Mandie Books" series of mystery adventures set in the North Carolina backwoods at the turn of the century.
32. **Kirsten Saves the Day: A Summer Story,** Janet Shaw, Pleasant Copyright © 1988. (Primary and Junior / 35,924 / 72,270.) Kirsten finds honeycombs with which she decides to surprise Papa. Unknown to Kirsten and her brother, Peter, bears are after the treasure, too.
33. **Daniel in the Lion's Den,** Cook Copyright © 1986. (Preschool and Primary / 35,810 / 78,858.) This 3″x4″ title in the "My Jesus Pocketbook" series focuses on trust.
34. **Samantha Saves the Day: A Summer Story,** Valerie Tripp, Pleasant Copyright © 1988. (Primary and Junior / 35,604 / 71,693.) Samantha, Agnes, and Agatha find a sketchbook showing a waterfall at Teardrop Island. The three set out for the island and find themselves in the middle of a dangerous storm.
35. **Changes for Samantha: A Winter Story,** Valerie Tripp, Pleasant Copyright © 1988. (Primary and Junior / 34,719 / 68,216.) Samantha moves to New York City to live with Uncle Gard and Aunt Cornelia. After Nellie disappears, Samantha finds her in a New York orphanage, and the girls plan to escape.
36. **Jonah and the Big Fish,** John and Kim Walton, Cook Copyright © 1986. (Preschool and Primary / 34,667 / 75,376.)This 3″x4″ title in the "My Jesus Pocketbook" series teaches obedience to God.
37. **Noah's Ark,** Peter Spier, Doubleday Copyright © 1981. (Preschool / 34,584 / 210,000.) Winner of a Caldecott Medal, this book tells Noah's story through full-color illustrations and a translation of a 17th-century Dutch poem.
38. **Changes for Kirsten: A Winter Story,** Janet Shaw, Pleasant Copyright © 1988. (Primary and Junior / 34,206 / 67,173.) The family home is destroyed by a fire started by a raccoon. The future seems bleak until Kirsten and her brother, Lars, make an important discovery in the woods.
39. **Molly Saves the Day: A Summer Story,** Valerie Tripp, Pleasant Copyright © 1988. (Primary and Junior / 33,932 / 68,191.) Molly and her friends, Linda and Susan, love Camp Gowonagin until the camp's Color Wars begin. Susan is on the red team; Molly and Linda are on the blue team. Will Molly save the day?
40. **Big Little Person,** Cook Copyright © 1986. (Preschool and Primary / 33,102 / 67,675.) This 3″x4″ title in the "My Jesus Pocketbook" series teaches forgiveness.
41. **If God Loves Me, Why Can't I Get My Locker Open?** Lorraine Peterson, Bethany House Copyright © 1980. (Young Teen / 32,029 / 519,102.)Ninety-one short readings are tailored to teen problems with searching questions and appropriate scriptures.
42. **Changes for Molly: A Winter Story,** Valerie Tripp, Pleasant Copyright © 1988. (Primary and Junior / 32,012 / 62,760.) Molly's dad returns home in time for the Red Cross show. Molly wants the starring role to show him how grown up she is. Will the wrong hairstyle and sickness keep her from stardom?
43. **My Little Bible Picture Book,** Cook Copyright © 1988. (Preschool / 31,963 / 31,963.) This collection of Bible stories includes short prayers and Bible verses.
44. **Bird Alphabet,** Llewellyn Teresa McKernan and illus. by Heidi Petach, Standard Copyright © 1988. (Preschool and Primary / 31,944 / 59,844.) Birds illustrate each letter of the alphabet. *A* is for albatross and *Z* is for the zebra finch.
45. **My Loving Family,** Cook Copyright © 1987. (Preschool and Primary / 31,555 / 49,989.) This 3″x4″ title in the "My

Jesus Pocketbook" series teaches kids about the love God provides through families.

46. **Meet Molly: An American Girl,** Valerie Tripp, Pleasant Copyright © 1987. (Primary and Junior / 31,518 / 87,416.) It's World War II. Because of shortages, Molly must use a hula skirt as a Halloween costume—until brother Ricky plays a mean trick. War may break out on the homefront.
47. **The Little Lost Sheep,** Mary Lee Lindsey and illus. by Ruth O'Connell, Standard Copyright © 1988. (Primary / 31,344 / 56,144.) Through the eyes of a lamb, this book tells what it is like to be lost.
48. **Samuel, God's Helper,** Cook Copyright © 1987. (Preschool and Primary / 30,399 / 54,742.) This 3″x4″ title in the "My Jesus Pocketbook" series teaches obedience.
49. **Bear, Your Manners Are Showing,** Kathleen Meyer and illus. by Creative Studios, Standard Copyright © 1987. (Preschool / 30,144 / 88,944.) A little bear learns the meaning of thank you, please, excuse me and I'm sorry when his mother stamps these words on his paws.
50. **Mandie and the Cherokee Legend,** Lois Gladys Leppard, Bethany House Copyright © 1983. (Primary and Junior / 29,348 / 126,596.) In this "Mandie Book," Mandie discovers her ancestry and learns of a mysterious Indian legend.
51. **Kirsten's Surprise: A Christmas Story,** Janet Shaw, Pleasant Copyright © 1987. (Primary and Junior / 29,068 / 75,164.) Kirsten wants to keep Swedish traditions alive for the family's first Christmas in America. A blizzard comes up and a journey to town becomes a brush with disaster.
52. **Kirsten Learns a Lesson: A School Story,** Janet Shaw, Pleasant Copyright © 1987. (Primary and Junior / 28,207 / 72,567.) Kirsten has trouble in school because she doesn't speak English well. She must decide if running away solves the problem.
53. **Samantha's Surprise: A Christmas Story,** Maxine Schur, Pleasant Copyright © 1987. (Primary and Junior / 28,200 / 71,362.) No one pays attention to Samantha and her wish for a doll. She blames Uncle Gard's friend, Cornelia. When Christmas morning comes, Samantha is in for more than one surprise.
54. **Happy Birthday, Kirsten: A Springtime Story,** Janet Shaw, Pleasant Copyright © 1988. (Primary and Junior / 27,415 / 67,756.) Kirsten must care for the new baby and misses playing with friends and going to school. But her hard work is rewarded as her 10th birthday becomes a celebration with family and friends.
55. **Big Thoughts for Little People,** Kenneth Taylor, Tyndale Copyright © 1983. (Preschool and Primary / 27,372 / 420,285.) First in the "Little People" series, this illustrated ABC book is designed to teach children Christian values.
56. **Mandie and the Forbidden Attic,** Lois Gladys Leppard, Bethany House Copyright © 1985.) (Primary and Junior / 27,239 / 108,493.) In this "Mandie Book," Mandie and her friend investigate noises in their boarding school's attic and break school rules in the process.
57. **Bible Promises,** Cook Copyright © 1988. (Preschool and Primary / 27,236 / 27,236.) This 3″x4″ title in the "My Jesus Pocketbook" series teaches faith and trust.
58. **Samantha Learns a Lesson,** Susan Adler, Pleasant Copyright © 1987. (Primary and Junior / 27,087 / 70,474.) Samantha wants to teach her friend Nellie how to read so the other children will not call her names. In the process, Samantha learns an important lesson from Nellie.
59. **At Home in North Branch,** Arleta Richardson, Cook Copyright © 1988. (Primary and Junior / 27,052 / 27,052.) This title in the "Grandma's Attic" series finds Mabel happily married to Len. Despite

100 BEST-SELLING CHILDREN'S BOOKS cont.

unexpected trials, Mabel and Sarah Jane remain friends.

60. **One Minute Christmas Story,** Shari Lewis, Doubleday Copyright © 1988. (Primary / 27,000 / 64,000.) This book presents timeless tales, such as the *Gift of the Magi,* as well as new stories condensed for busy parents.
61. **Happy Birthday, Samantha,** Valerie Tripp, Pleasant Copyright © 1988. (Primary and Junior / 26,838 / 65,893.) Samantha's 10th birthday is nearly ruined until she receives an invitation to visit New York City. Samantha and twins, Agnes and Agatha, make some surprising discoveries.
62. **Thank You, God, for Christmas,** Henrietta Gambill and illus. by Kathryn Hutton, Standard Copyright © 1988. (Preschool and Primary / 26,000 / 26,000.) Children learn to give thanks for the events surrounding Jesus' birth.
63. **New Girl in Town,** Judy Baer, Bethany House Copyright © 1988. (Junior / 25,985 / 25,985.) Book 1 in the Cedar River Daydream series. Lexi Leighton decides whether to compromise her Christian values to gain new friends.
64. **Lent Is for Children,** Julie Kelemen, Liguori Copyright © 1987. (Junior / 25,983 / 53,583.) Discover the why as well as the how-to of Lenten basics: prayer, fasting, and sacrifice.
65. **In Grandma's Attic,** Arleta Richardson, Cook Copyright © 1984. (Preschool and Primary / 25,919 / 137,121.) This title in the "Grandma's Attic" series shows Mabel as an adventurous girl who encounters a generous Indian.
66. **Mandie and the Hidden Treasure** Lois Gladys Leppard, Bethany House Copyright © 1987. (Primary and Junior / 24,612 / 60,491.) Mandie and her friends search for an elusive treasure. All-forgotten names and threats from an angry man threaten their search.
67. **Molly's Surprise: A Christmas Story,** Valerie Tripp, Pleasant Copyright © 1987. (Primary and Junior / 24,576 / 62,848.) Dad is off to war. The grandparents can't come for the holidays. Thanks to Molly, the best surprise arrives on Christmas morning.
68. **Mandie and the Ghost Bandits,** Lois Gladys Leppard, Bethany House Copyright © 1984. (Primary and Junior / 24,379 / 100,999.) In this "Mandie Book," Mandie and her friends discover the value of their Christian faith while solving a mystery involving a missing gold shipment and a train wreck.
69. **A Child's Story of Jesus,** Barbara Kanaar and illus. by Kathryn Hutton, Standard Copyright © 1986. (Preschool and Primary / 24,200 / 64,900.) This "Happy Day Book" involves young readers in the story of Jesus' life by asking them to point to items in the illustrations.
70. **Great Bible Stories for Children,** Lane Easterly editor, Thomas Nelson Copyright © 1974. (Primary / 24,000 / 1,005,548.) Eighty-two stories from the Old and New Testaments are included in this large-print book.
71. **Happy Birthday, Molly** Valerie Tripp, Pleasant Copyright © 1988. (Primary and Junior / 23,986 / 59,550.) Molly and her English friend, Emily, worry about their Dads in war-torn London. It takes a special surprise to turn Molly's 10th birthday into a real English tea.
72. **Molly Learns a Lesson: A School Story,** Valerie Tripp, Pleasant Copyright © 1987. (Primary and Junior / 23,737 / 61,590.) Molly and two friends plan their own lend-a-hand contest. Molly learns some important lessons when they are caught spying on the other third-grade girls.
73. **It's Fun to Choose,** Dru Cunningham and illus. by Richard Hackney, Standard Copyright © 1988. (Preschool and Primary / 23,700 / 23,700.) Children learn they must make choices everyday.
74. **Mandie and the Trunk's Secret,** Lois Gladys Leppard, Bethany House Copyright © 1985. (Primary and Junior / 23,664 / 95,293.) In this "Mandie Book," Mandie and her friend find old letters in a

trunk that lead to a mystery involving hidden diamonds, an enemy, and a secret cabin.

75. **The First Noel,** Illus. by Patrick McRae, Ideals Copyright © 1988. (Preschool / 23,500 / 23,500.) This book tells the Christmas story in large print with music and lyrics included.
76. **My First Book of Prayers,** Illus. by Margaret Tarrant, Ideals Copyright © 1988. (Preschool / 23,500 / 23,500.) This title is part of the "My First Book of . . ." series in which children gain a sense of accomplishment in various subjects.
77. **Advent Is for Children,** Julie Kelemen, Liguori Copyright © 1988. (Junior / 23,460 / 23,460.) This book is designed to help youngsters prepare for Christmas and see past the glitter to the gift of Christmas.
78. **Trouble With a Capital "T"** Judy Baer, Bethany House Copyright © 1988. (Junior / 22,755 / 22,755.) This is book 2 in the "Cedar River Daydream" series. Lexi becomes the target of Minda's anger. Will Lexi be able to respond with love?
79. **Noah's Ark and the Lost World,** John Morris, Master Books Copyright © 1988. (Primary / 22,618 / 22,618.) Dinosaurs, the Flood, and the ark are considered from a biblical perspective along with a glimpse of the world before the Flood.
80. **"The Littlest Angel" Set,** Charles Tazewell and illus. by Sergio Leone, Ideals Copyright © 1988. (Preschool / 22,500 / 22,500.) Six mini-board books, 10 pages each, are based on the Littlest Angel.
81. **I'm Glad I'm Your Grandma,** Bill and Kathy Horlacher and illus. by Kathryn Hutton, Standard Copyright © 1987. (Preschool and Primary / 22,000 / 48,000.) In this "Happy Day Book," Grandma enjoys being involved in the lives of her grandchildren.
82. **Joy, Joy the Mass: Our Family Celebration,** Jeannine Timko Leichner, Our Sunday Visitor Copyright © 1978. (Primary / n.a.) An activity-oriented presentation of the Mass with prayers and liturgical responses included.
83. **A New Blanket for Josh,** Phyllis Martin and illus. by Gwen Connelly, Standard Copyright © 1988. (Preschool and Primary / 21,644 / 21,644.) Mom discovers a solution for Josh, who finds that giving up an old blanket is like losing a dear friend.
84. **Making Things Right: The Sacrament of Reconciliation,** Jeannine Timko Leichner, Our Sunday Visitor Copyright © 1983. (Primary / n.a.) This book provides children an understanding of the sacrament of penance.
85. **More Stories From Grandma's Attic,** Arleta Richardson, Cook Copyright © 1979. (Junior / 21,283 / 110,876.) More adventures provided in the "Grandma's Attic" series as Mabel O'Dell grows up on a farm in Michigan 100 years ago.
86. **Dinosaur ABC's Activity Book,** Master Books Copyright © 1986. (Primary / 21,229 / n.a.) This book serves as a curriculum supplement for science education. The fun pack includes dinosaur toys and a pencil.
87. **What the Bible Is All About for Young Explorers,** Francis Blankenbaker, editor, Regal Books / Gospel Light Copyright © 1986. (Primary and Junior / 20,629 / 157,500.) This book, based on Henrietta Mears's classic *What the Bible Is All About,* is a Bible handbook for children.
88. **Sam's Christmas Joy.** Rebekah Stion and illus. by Lorraine Arthur, Standard Copyright © 1988. (Preschool and Primary / 20,500 / 20,544.) With the help of his dog Sam, Dean learns the joy of giving.
89. **Family Fun,** Al Hartley, Barbour Copyright © 1988. (Primary / 20,357 / 20,357.) This title is part of the "Barney Bear Christian Activity" series.
90. **Lightning Bugs and Lullabies,** Margaret Hillert and illus. by Judy Hand, Standard Copyright © 1988. (Preschool and Primary / 20,244 / 20,244.) This book of children's poetry discusses the intricacies concerning God's world.
91. **Rock-a-Bye Bible,** Marjorie Decker, World Bible Copyright © 1987. (Preschool and Primary / 20,240 / 32,300.) Themes are

100 BEST-SELLING CHILDREN'S BOOKS cont.

based on Christian Mother Goose rhymes with a related Scripture verse.

92. **The Great Dinosaur Mystery,** Paul Taylor, Master Books Copyright © 1987. (Junior / 20,225 / n.a.) Did people and dinosaurs live together? Are dinosaurs alive today? This book discusses these biblical and historical puzzles.
93. **Happy Home,** Al Hartley, Barbour Copyright © 1988. (Primary / 20,140 / 20,140.) This title is part of the "Barney Bear Christian Activity" series.
94. **Fun in the Car,** Al Hartley, Barbour Copyright © 1988. (Primary / 19,659 / 19,659.) This title is part of the "Barney Bear Christian Activity" series.
95. **God, I've Gotta Talk to You,** Anne Jennings and Walter Wengarin Jr. and illus. by Jim Roberts, Concordia Copyright © 1974. (Primary / 19,607 / 881,983.) This title is part of the "Arch Book" series, which tells a familiar Bible story with text and illustrations.
96. **Flying Colors,** Al Hartley, Barbour Copyright © 1988. (Primary / 19,399 / 19,399.) This title is part of the "Barney Bear Christian Activity" series.
97. **Mandie and the Charleston Phantom,** Lois Gladys Leppard, Bethany Copyright © 1986. (Primary and Junior / 19,268 / 70,103.) Mandie's adventures with the Charleston phantom are part of the thirteen titles in the "Mandie" series set in North Carolina at the turn of the century.
98. **School Fun,** Al Hartley, Barbour Copyright © 1988. (Primary / 19,039 / 19,039.} This title is part of the "Barney Bear Christian Activity" series.
99. **The Secret Baseball Challenge,** Jerry Jenkins, Moody Copyright © 1986. (Junior / n.a. / 18,895.) This title is first in the "Dallas O'Neil" series.
100. **Sharing Makes Me Happy,** Dot Cachiaras and illus. by Lorraine Arthur, Standard Copyright © 1982. (Preschool and Primary / 18,800 / 139,000.)In sharing a secret or sharing a task, we can also share love.

“” FOCUS QUOTE

The family circle is the supreme conductor of Christianity.
—Henry Drummond

ADOPTION AGENCIES

Most of the agencies listed provide intercountry adoption placements. Religious organizations are noted with an asterisk. Service areas and requirements will differ with agency. Some agencies are more efficient than others so check with other clients who have adopted from the agency before applying.

Agency Name	*Address/City/Zip*
Alabama	
*Wales Goebel Ministry	2908 Pump House Road, Birmingham 35243
Adoptions International of Alabama, Inc.	1538 Wellington View Road, Birmingham 35209
Arizona	
*Globe International Adoption, Inc.	6334 West Villa Theresa Drive, Glendale 85308
Dillon Southwest	P.O. Box 3535, Scottsdale 85257
California	
*Catholic Charities San Francisco	2045 Lawton Street, San Francisco 94122
AASK America/Aid to Adoption of Special Kids	1540 Market, San Francisco 94102

Agency Name	*Address/City/Zip*
Adoption Horizons	P.O. Box 247, Arcata 95521
Adoption Services International	4737 Ortega Drive, Ventura 93003
Bal Jagat—Children's World, Inc.	9311 Farralone Avenue, Chatsworth 91311
Bay Area Adoption Services	P.O. Box 2617, Sunnyvale 94087
Family Connections	1528 Oakdale Road, Modesto 95355
Life Adoption Services	440 West Main Street, Tustin 92680

Colorado

*Hand in Hand International	4695 Barnes Road, Colorado Springs 80917
Friends of Children of Various Nations, Inc.	600 Gilpin Street, Denver 80218
Universal Family	315 South Clay, Denver 80219

Connecticut

Family Service, Inc.	92 Vine Street, New Britain 06052
Heal the Children Northeast, Inc.	Box 129, New Milford 06776
International Alliance for Children	23 South Main Street, New Milford 06776

District of Columbia

ASIA	7720 Alaska Avenue N.W., Washington 20012
The American Adoption Agency	1228 M Street N.W., Washington 20005
The Barker Foundation	4114 River Road N.W., Washington 20016
World Child	5121 Colorado Avenue N.W., Washington 20011

Florida

*Shepherd Care Ministries, Inc.	5935 Taft Street. Suite B, Hollywood 33021
Adoption Center, Inc.	500 N. Maitland Avenue, Maitland 32751
Suncoast International Adoptions	P.O. Box 332, Indian Rocks Beach 34635
Universal Aid for Children	P.O. Box 610246, North Miami 33162

Georgia

Children's Services International	1819 Peachtree Road #318, Atlanta 30309
Homes for Children International	1655 Peachtree Street NE, #1109, Atlanta 30309
Illien Adoptions, International	1254 Piedmont Avenue NE, Atlanta 30309
Open Door Adoption Agency	P.O. Box 4, Thomasville 31799

Idaho

Adoptions In Idaho	P.O. Box 729, Post Falls 83854

Illinois

*Bensenville Home Society	331 South York Road, Bensenville 60106
*Evangelical Child and Family Agency	1530 N. Main Street, Wheaton 60187
*Sunny Ridge Family Center	2S426 Orchard Road, Wheaton 60187
Adoption World	One E. Erie, #235, Chicago 60611
Children's Home and Aid Society of Illinois	730 N. Main street, Rockford 61103
Travelers and Immigrants Aid of Chicago	327 LaSalle Street, Chicago 60604

Iowa

Hillcrest Family Services	1727 1st Avenue SE, Cedar Rapids 52402

Kansas

*Gentle Shepherd Child Placement Services	P.O. Box 1172, Olathe 66061

Maine

*International Christian Adoption Agency	60 W. River Road, Waterville 04901
Growing thru Adoption	P.O. Box 7082, Lewiston 04240

Maryland

*Associated Catholic Charities of Baltimore, Inc.	320 Cathedral Street, Baltimore 21201
ACORN	10784A Hickory Ridge Road, Columbia 21043

Massachusetts

Aliance for Children, Inc.	110 Cedar Street, Wellesley 02181
Cambridge Adoption and Counseling Associates, Inc.	Box 190, Cambridge 02142
International Adoptions, Inc.	282 Moody Street, Waltham 02154
World Adoption Services, Inc.	161 Auburn Street, Newton 02166

Michigan

*Bethany Christian Services	901 Eastern Avenue NE, Grand Rapids 49503
Americans for International Aid and Adoption	877 S. Adams, Birmingham 48011

Agency Name	*Address/City/Zip*
Children's Hope Adoption Services	7823 South Whiteville Road, Shepherd 48883
Foreign Adoption Consultants	P.O. Box 489, Kalamazoo 49005
Minnesota	
*Catholic Charities Archdiocese, St. Paul/Minneapolis	215 Old 6th Street, St. Paul 55102
*Lutheran Social Services	2414 Park Avenue South, Minneapolis 55404
Building Families Through Adoption	Box 550, Dawson 56232
Children's Home Society of Minnesota	2230 Como Avenue, St. Paul 55108
Crossroads, Inc.	4940 Viking Drive, #388, Edina 55435
HOPE International Family Services Inc.	421 Main Street, Stillwater 55082
Missouri	
*Highlands Child Placement Services	1445 Boonville Avenue, Springfield 65802
*Love Basket, Inc.	8965 Old Lemay Ferry Road, Hillsboro 63050
Adoption Resource Center, R&R Health Services	2207 Park Avenue, St. Louis 63104
Family Adoption and Counseling Services, Inc.	9378 Olive Street Road, #320, St. Louis 63132
Worldwide Love for Children	1221 E. Republic Road, Springfield 65807
Montana	
Adoptions in Montana	554 W. Broadway, #557A, Missoula 59802
Montana Intercountry Adoption, Inc.	109 S. 8th Avenue, Bozeman 59715
New Jersey	
Children of the World	855 Bloomfield Avenue, Glen Ridge 07028
Children's Services International, Inc.	P.O. Box 688, Long Valley 07853
Golden Cradle Adoption Agency	2201 Route 38, Cherry Hill 08002
New Mexico	
Rainbow House International	19676 Highway 85, Belen 87002
New York	
*Evangelical Adoption and Family Service, Inc.	119 Church Street, North Syracuse 13212
Adoption and Counseling Service, Inc.	1 Fayette Park, Syracuse 13202
Family Focus Adoption Agency	P.O. Box 388, Glen Oaks 11004
Family Resources	226 N. Highland Avenue, Ossining 10562
Family Service of Westchester, Inc.	470 Mamaroneck Avenue, White Plains 10605
Parsons Child and Family Center	845 Central Avenue, Albany 12206
North Dakota	
*Covenant Children	P.O. Box 2344, Bismark 58502
New Horizons Foreign Adoption Services, Inc.	2876 Woodland Place, Bismark 58501
Ohio	
*Lutheran Social Services of Central Ohio	57 E. Main Street, Columbus 43215
Spaulding for Children—Beech Brook	3737 Lander Road, Cleveland 44124
Oklahoma	
*Deaconess Home	5401 N. Portland Avenue, Oklahoma City 73112
*Dillon's Children's Services, Inc.	7615 E. 63rd Place South #215, Tulsa 74133
Project Adopt	1613 N. Broadway, Oklahoma City 73103
Small Miracles International, Inc.	7430 SE 15th, #220, Midwest City 73110
Oregon	
*Give Us This Day, Inc.	2207B Portland Road, P.O. Box 796, Newberg 97132
*Holt International Children's Services	P.O. Box 2880, Eugene 97402
Plan Loving Adoptions Now, Inc.	P.O. Box 667, McMinnville 97128
Pennsylvania	
*Catholic Social Services	222 N. 17th Street, Room 329, Philadelphia 19103
*Tressler Lutheran Service Associates	25 W. Springettsbury avenue, York 17403
Adoptions International Inc.	Benson Manor, #101, Jenkintown 19046
Children and Home Study Associates	31 E. Franklin Street, Media 19063
Love the Children	221 W. Broad Street, Quakertown 18951
The Adoption Agency	63 W. Lancaster Avenue, Ardmore 19003
Welcome House	P.O. Box 836, Doylestown 18901
South Carolina	
*Love Life Adoption Agency	P.O. Box 247, Florence 29503

Agency Name	*Address/City/Zip*
Tennessee	
*Catholic Charities of Tennessee, Inc.	30 White Bridge Road, Nashville 37205
*Holston United Methodist Home for Children	P.O. Box 188, Greenville 37744
Texas	
*Agape Social Services, Inc.	3200 Maple, #400, Dallas 75201
Adoption Resource Consultants of North Texas	P.O. Box 1224, Richardson 75083
Child Placement of Texas	615 N. 2nd Street, Killeen 76541
The Care Connection, Inc.	400 Harvey Street, San Marcos 78666
Vermont	
Rootwings Ministries, Inc.	P.O. Box 614, Barre 05641
Virginia	
*Catholic Family Services	4206 Chamberlayne Avenue, Richmond 23227
*Family Life Services, Inc.	520 Eldon Street, Lynchburg 24501
Family Services of Tidewater, Inc.	222 19th Street, West Norfolk 23517
Pan American Adoption Agency, Inc.	12604 Kahns Road, Manassas 22111
Washington	
*Catholic Community Services	1715 E. Cherry, P.O. Box 22608, Seattle 98122
*New Hope of Washington	1100 Lake City Way NE, Seattle 98125
*Open Arms	16429 NE 133rd Court, Redmond 98052
*Regular Baptist Child Placement Agency	Box 16353, Seattle 98116
Adoption Advocates International	658 Black Diamond Road, Port Angeles 98362
Western Assoc of Concerned Adoptive Parents (WACAP)	P.O. Box 88948, Seattle 98138
Wisconsin	
*Evangelical Child and Family Agency	2401 N. Mayfair Road, Milwaukee 53226
*Lutheran Soc Services, Wisconsin and Upper Michigan	3200 W. Highland Boulevard, Milwaukee 53208
Adoption Option, Inc.	1804 Chapman Drive, Waukesha 53186
Pauquette Children's Service	325 W. Connant, P.O. Box 162, Portage 53901

Source: *The Adoption Option* by Angela Elwell Hunt. Published by Victor Books. Copyright © 1989 by SP Publications, Inc. Used by permission.

10 MISTAKES PARENTS MAKE WITH TEENAGERS

1. Do as I say, not as I do
2. I'm the adult. I'm right
3. Because I said so, that's why
4. You want to be what?
5. This room's a pig sty
6. Can't you do anything right?
7. Where did you find him?
8. You did what?
9. Do you mind if we talk about something else?
10. I'm kind of busy right now. Could you come back later?

Source: Jay Kesler in *Ten Mistakes Parents Make with Teenagers (And How To Avoid Them).* Published by Wolgemuth & Hyatt Publishers, Inc. Copyright © 1988. Used by permission.

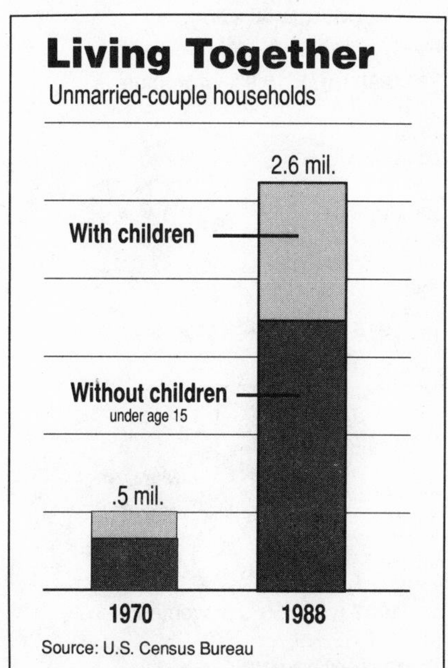

20 LIES WE BELIEVE

1. I must be perfect
2. I must have everyone's love and approval
3. It is easier to avoid problems than to face them
4. It's somebody else's fault
5. You can have it all
6. You are only as good as what you do
7. Life should be easy
8. Life should be fair
9. People are basically good
10. It's all your fault
11. You can and should meet all my needs
12. You owe me
13. I shouldn't have to change
14. You should be like me
15. God's love must be earned
16. Because I'm a Christian, God will protect me from pain and suffering
17. All my problems are caused by my sins
18. It is my Christian duty to meet all the needs of others
19. A good Christian doesn't feel angry, anxious or depressed
20. God can't use me unless I'm spiritually strong

Source: Chris Thurman in *The Lies We Believe*. Published by Thomas Nelson Inc., Publishers. Copyright © 1989. Used by permission.

More Married Women Work

Now more women work than don't, and of those women who do work, most are married.

Women in the work force

Widowed or divorced 17.9%
Married 13.9%
Single 68.2%

1890 total: 18.9% of women

15.1%
Married 36.4%
Single 48.5%

1940 total: 27.4% of women

19.4%
Married 54.7%
Single 25.9%

1987 total: 56% of women

Source: U.S. Census Bureau

Divorce and Kids

MILLIONS
1.2
Under age 18
1.0
.8
.6
.4
More than 1 million kids affected: recent dip due to declining birth and divorce rates
.2

Source: U.S. Census Bureau, National Center for Health Statistics

BABIES, KITTENS, AND PUPPIES BORN EVERY HOUR IN USA

Babies 415
Kittens 3,500
Puppies 2,000

Source: American Humane Society

Vows Pledged, Vows Broken

Marriage Rates
per 1000 people

16
15
14
13
12
11
10
9
8
7
6
5
4
3

End of WW II

Excluding the war, marriage rates have kept constant, while divorce rates have almost tripled.

1920 1940 1960 1980

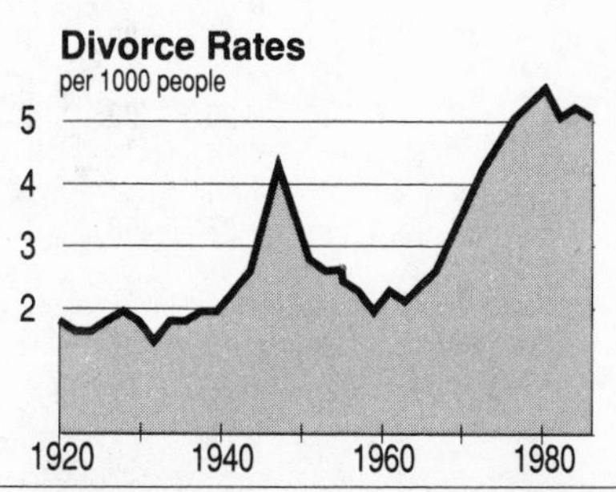

Source: U.S. Census Bureau, National Center for Health Statistics

HOW KIDS SEE THE FUTURE

People will work in space 80%
People will live in space 63%
Average lifespan of people will be 100 years 60%
People will communicate with extra-terrestrial beings 51%
We will buy artificial human body parts off the shelf 51%
Solar power will provide energy 50%

Source: *Science World* magazine survey of 12,300 junior and senior high school students.

FOCUS QUOTE

We have careful thought
for the stranger
And smiles for the sometime
guest
But oft for our own the bitter
tone
Though we love our own
the best.

—Margaret E. Sangster in *Our Own*

SINGLES

From March 1987 to March 1988 there was an increase of nearly 1.3 million single adults in the USA. This includes all never-marrieds, widowed, and divorced Americans over the age of 18.

According to the US Census Bureau, as of March 1988 there were 66.3 million single adults, approximately 37 percent of the total US adult population. If you were to take the entire populations of New York, Pennsylvania, Ohio, Michigan, New Jersey, Massachusetts, and Connecticut, it would be approximately equal to the total number of single adults in the US.

Source: *Single Adult Ministries Journal,* January 1990 issue

REASONS SINGLES DO NOT ATTEND CHURCH

Reason	*Describes Very Well*	*Not a Reason*
• Your family is not interested in church, so you do not get involved	12%	65%
• You or another household member have to work on the day of worship	18	65
• You don't know of any church that you would like to try	10	67
• It's your only day off, and you prefer to spend it doing other things	21	54
• Your lifestyle is not compatible with what would be expected by a church	13	51
• You have visited some churches, but have not found one that you like	17	58
• You have not found a church that teaches the same things you believe	16	61
• Your health does not permit you to get involved	5	87
• The church really does not have anything to offer you	12	55
• You have had bad experiences with churches in the past	15	66
• You moved to a new area and never got around to finding a new church	19	63
• You are just not interested in religion	12	60
• You just don't have the time to attend or get involved in a church	18	49
• No one has invited you to attend a service with them, and you would feel uncomfortable going by yourself	7	75

Source: *Single Adults in America. Published by The Barna Research Group, Glendale, CA. Copyright © 1987. Used by permission.*

PROMOTING INTEREST AMONG THE UNCHURCHED IN ATTENDING A CHURCH

Statement	*Singles*			*Marrieds*		
	Yes	*No*	*DK*	*Yes*	*No*	*DK*
• A church called you on the telephone to invite you to one of their worship services	38%	54%	8%	36%	56%	8%
• A church sent you a brochure about the church and invited you to attend one of their services	42	52	6	47	47	6
• A church sponsored seminars on community and family problems that were open to the general public	48	46	6	60	38	2
• A church sent you a cassette tape of a typical service so that you could hear what the services are like	61	33	6	36	62	2
• A church minister or church leader visited you at home to introduce you to the church and invite you to attend	40	56	4	37	58	5
• A church was recommended by a respected community leader	42	53	5	40	58	2
• A church sponsored a musical concert for the community	45	52	3	37	58	4

Source: *Single Adults in America. Published by The Barna Research Group, Glendale, CA. Copyright © 1987. Used by permission.*

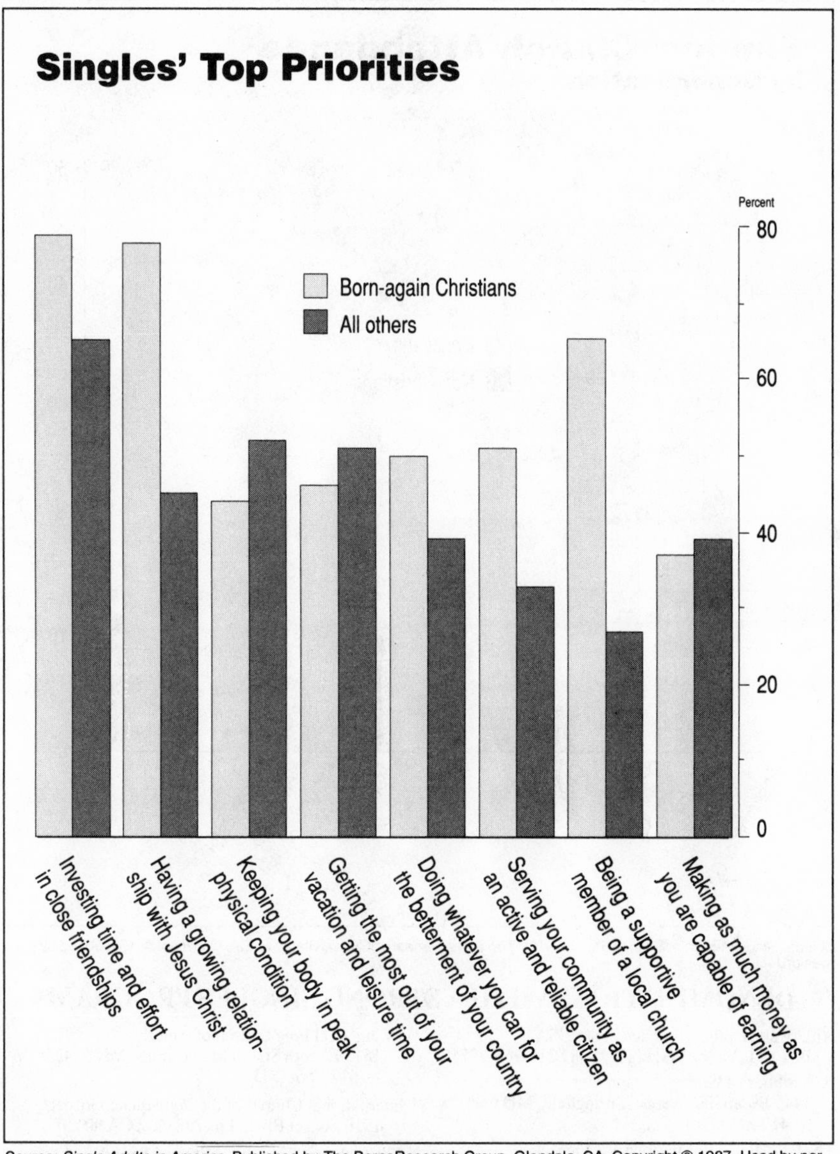

Source: *Single Adults in America.* Published by The BarnaResearch Group, Glendale, CA. Copyright © 1987. Used by permission.

MAGAZINES FOR SINGLES

Christian Activities Calendar, P.O. Box 730, Ojai, CA 93023, $14.95, bi-monthly

Christian Single, 127 Ninth Avenue North, Nashville, TN 37234, $17.75, monthly

In Search, P.O. Box 370, Elkhart, IN 46515, free, quarterly

Singles Scene, P.O. Box 454, Crossville, TN 38557, $20.00, monthly

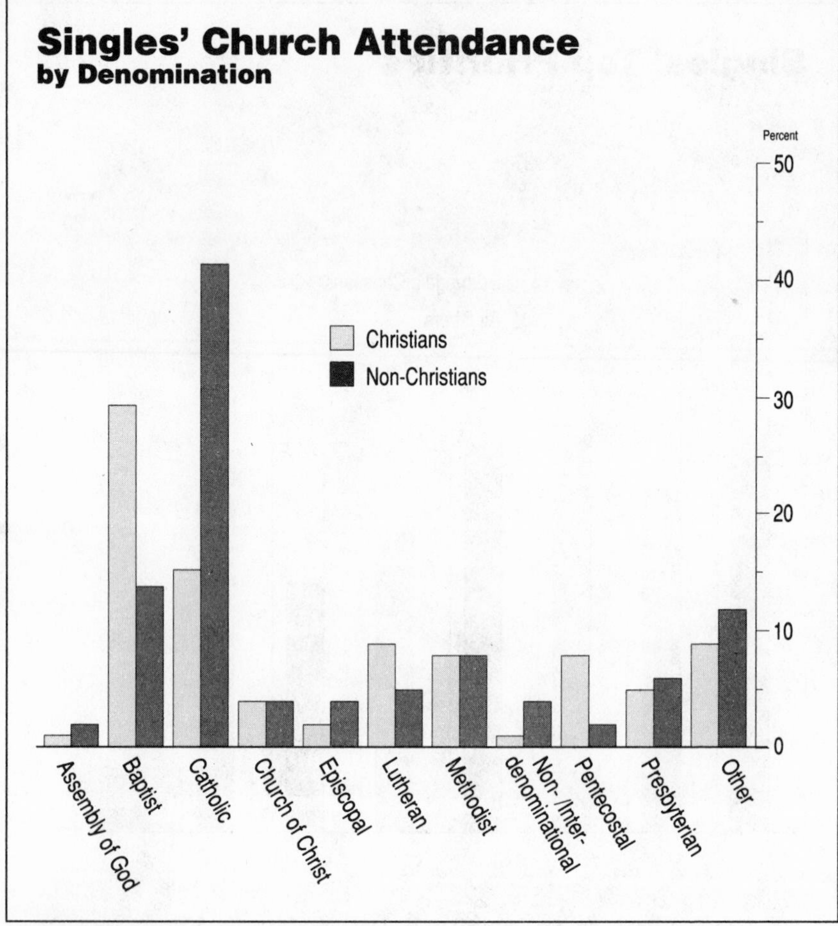

Source: *Single Adults in America.* Published by The Barna Research Group, Glendale, CA. Copyright © 1987. Used by permission.

DENOMINATIONS WITH A STRONG SINGLES PROGRAM

American Baptist Churches in the USA
Box 851, Valley Forge, PA 19482 215-768-2271

Assemblies of God
1445 Boonville Avenue, Springfield, MO 65807 417-862-2781

The Christian and Missionary Alliance
P.O. Box 35000, Colorado Springs, CO 80935-3500 719-599-5999

Church of God
P.O. Box 2430, Cleveland, TN 37311 615-478-7229

Church of the Nazarene
6401 The Paseo, Kansas City, MO 64131 816-333-7000

Episcopal Church
P.O. Box 12385, Dallas, TX 214-363-5471

Evangelical Free Church of America
1515 E. 66th Street, Minneapolis, MN 55423 612-866-3343

International Church of the Foursquare Gospel
1910 Sunset Blvd., Los Angeles, CA 90026

The Lutheran Church—Missouri Synod
1333 S. Kirkwood Road, St. Louis, MO 63122 314-965-9000

Presbyterian Church (USA)
100 Witherspoon Street, Louisville, KY 40202 502-569-5487

Southern Baptist Convention
127 9th Avenue North, Nashville, TN 37234 615-251-2575

Source: *National Single Adults Resource Directory*

Importance of Church Characteristics

To Churched Singles

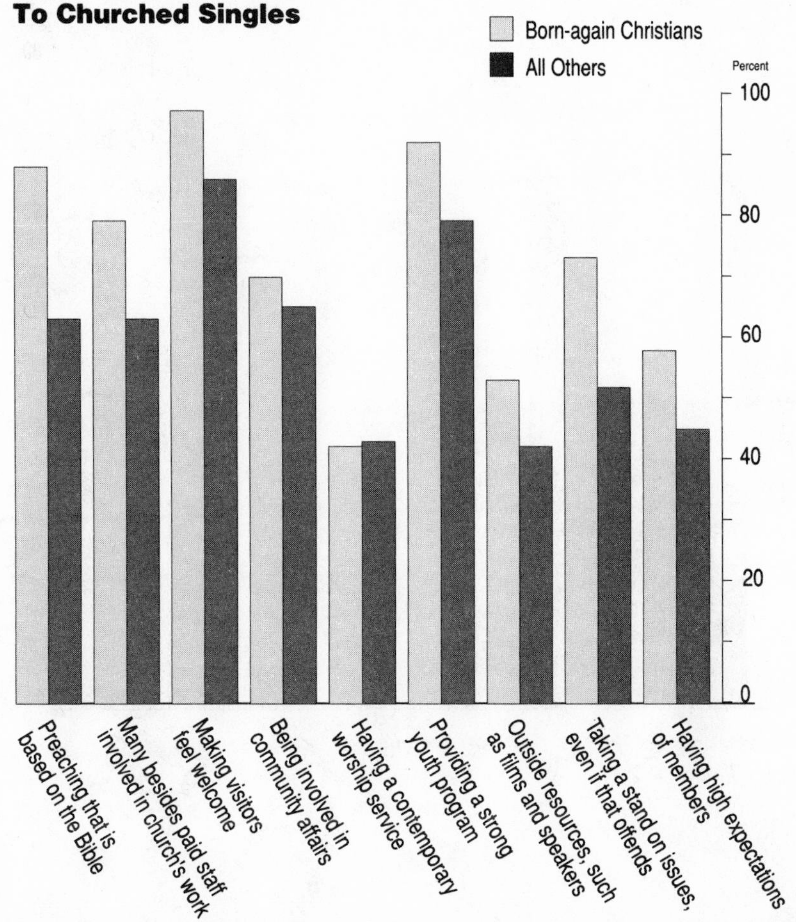

Source: *Single Adults in America*. Published by The Barna Research Group, Glendale, CA. Copyright © 1987. Used by permission.

FOCUS FACT

Thirty-four percent of American men over the age of 18 are bachelors: the never-married, the divorced, and the widowed—an increase of 21 percent since 1980.

Source: *American Demographics* Magazine

Music Purchases among Single Adults

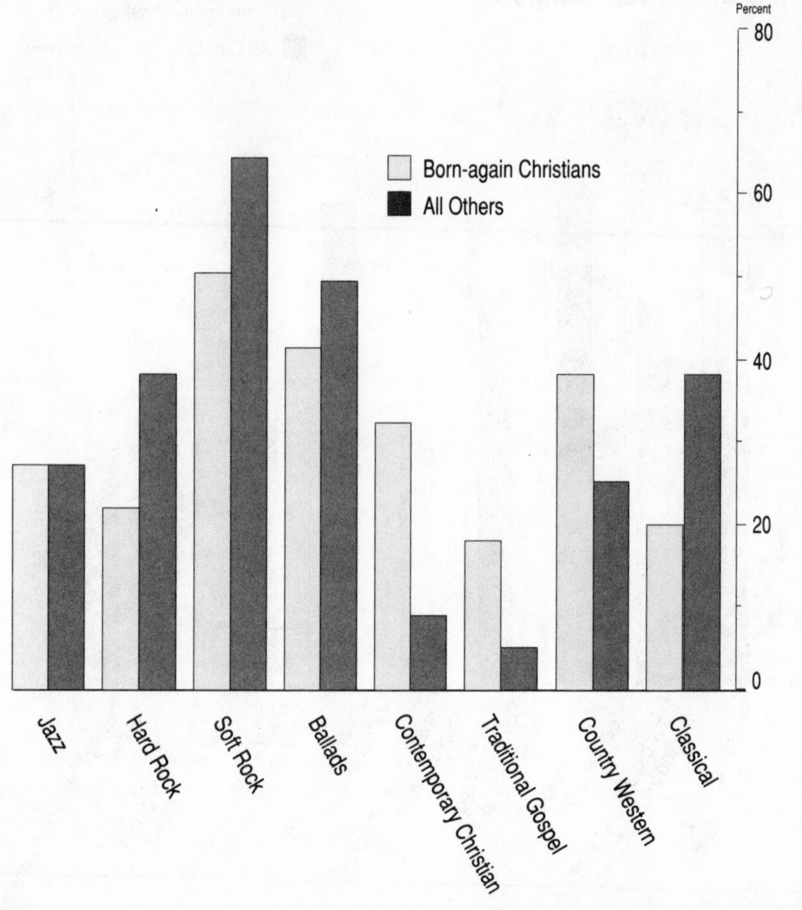

Percent

80

60

40

20

0

Born-again Christians

All Others

Jazz

Hard Rock

Soft Rock

Ballads

Contemporary Christian

Traditional Gospel

Country Western

Classical

Source: *Single Adults in America.* Published by The Barna Research Group, Glendale, CA. Copyright © 1987. Used by permission.

FOCUS FACT

Single adults are one of the most likely groups to get involved in short-term missions—more than 67 percent are open to this form of service, compared to 36 percent for marrieds.

Source: *Baby Boomers and The Future of World Missions* by Jim Engel and Jerry D. Jones

HOW SINGLES VIEW THE MEDIA

Most Entertaining:		Most Time-Consuming:	
VCR	52%	Book	51%
Book	13%	VCR	37%
Record	13%	Magazine	4%
Radio	12%	Record	3%
Magazine	4%	Radio	3%
Most Informative:		**Most Convenient:**	
Book	35%	VCR	44%
Magazine	30%	Radio	20%
Radio	16%	Record	12%
VCR	13%	Book	11%
Record	1%	Magazine	8%
Most Boring:		**Most Relaxing:**	
Radio	28%	Book	29%
Book	26%	VCR	27%
Magazine	16%	Record	20%
Record	10%	Radio	20%
VCR	9%	Magazine	3%

Source: *Single Adults in America.* Published by The Barna Research Group, Glendale, CA. Copyright © 1987. Used by permission.

Source: U.S. Census Bureau

WILDERNESS VACATION IDEAS FOR SINGLES

See leisure time section for other vacation ideas.

Backcountry and Beyond, Box 1181, McCall, ID 83638. Three- to fourteen-day wilderness adventure courses throughout the year. Activities include backpacking, canoeing, whitewater rafting, rock-climbing, high ropes, and challenge course.

Canonicus Camp and Conference Center, Box 299, Exeter Road, Exeter, RI 02822, 401-294-6318. Backpacking, canoeing, bicycling, and fitness.

Christian Adventures, 25 East 8th Street, Holland, MI 49423, 616-459-3952. Biking, hiking, or mountain climbing in the United States and Canada.

Discovery Expeditions, P.O. Box 1022, Grass Valley, CA 95945, 916-268-0877. Wilderness adventures.

Discovery Ministries, Rt. 3, Box 32, Eminence, MO 65466, 314-226-3213. Backpacking, canoeing, spelunking, cycling, and rock climbing.

Eagle Lake Camps, P.O. Box 6000, Colorado Springs, CO 80934, 719-472-1260. Resident camps and wilderness adventures.

Honey Rock High Road, Three Lakes, WI 54562, 715-479-7474 or 708-260-5124. Challenging adult wilderness program sponsored by Wheaton College.

South Dakota United Methodist Camps, P.O. Box 460, Mitchell, SD 57301. Backpacking, rock climbing and rappelling, canoeing and whitewater rafting.

Source: *National Single Adult Ministries Resource Directory.*

“” FOCUS QUOTE **The dark, uneasy world of family life—where the greatest can fail and the humblest succeed.** —Anonymous

A YEAR'S READING PROGRAM FOR SINGLES

January *The Road Less Traveled* by M. Scott Peck, Simon and Schuster
February *Remarriage and God's Renewing Grace: A Positive, Biblical Ethic for Divorced Christians* by Dwight Hervey Small, Baker Books or *The Blessing* by Gary Smalley and John Trent, Thomas Nelson, Inc.
March *Intimacy* by Terry Hershey, Harvest House
April *Singles Ask* by Harold Ivan Smith, Augsburg
May *Money, Sex and Power* by Richard Foster, Harper and Row
June *Healing for Damaged Emotions* by David Seamands, Victor Books
July *Too Close Too Soon* by Jim Talley and Bobbie Reed, Thomas Nelson
August *Growing Through Divorce* by Jim Smoke, Harvest House or *Wide My World, Narrow My Bed* by Luci Swindoll, Multnomah Press
September *Positively Single* by Harold Ivan Smith, Victor Books
October *Ordering Your Private World* by Gordon McDonald, Thomas Nelson
November *Becoming a Friend and Lover* by Dick Purnell, Here's Life
December *Inside Out* by Larry Crabb, NavPress

WHAT TO SAVE FOR RETIREMENT

To live a comfortable, nonworking life, you'll need at least 75 percent of your pre-retirement income. Part of that money will come from social security and maybe a pension. For the rest, you'll have to save. Here's what a typical working couple should be putting aside each year, assuming 5 percent wage inflation and retirement at the age of 65.

		Needed to invest annually*:	
Current salary	Current age	With a company pension	With a double IRA but no pension+
$35,000	30	$ 3,660	$ 4,000
	40	$ 4,360	$ 5,990
	50	$ 6,000	$ 9,970
$50,000	30	$ 7,590	$ 8,350
	40	$ 8,940	$11,790
	50	$12,280	$17,950
$75,000	30	$15,270	$18,050
	40	$17,890	$23,220
	50	$24,730	$33,700

*At 6 percent, taxed in a state and federal bracket of 30 percent. +Including $6,000 for the IRAs. Source: Ernst & Young.

CHURCH-RELATED RETIREMENT CENTERS

Retirement centers listed below have a population of 100 or more and offer independent living units.

Name	*Address/Phone*	*Affiliation*
Alabama		
Episcopal Place	1112 South 26th Street, Birmingham 35205/205-939-0085	Episcopal
Fair Haven Retirement Comm	1424 Montclair Road, Birmingham 35210/205-956-4150	Methodist
John Knox Manor Ret Tower	4401 Narrow Lane Road, Montgomery 36116/205-288-6462	Presbyterian

Name	*Address/Phone*	*Affiliation*
New Pilgrim Towers	3416 7th Avenue South, Birmingham 35222/205-323-3940	Baptist
Princeton Towers	909 Princeton Avenue, SW, Birmingham 35211/205-326-9197	Baptist
Wesley Acres	700 Cedar Lake Road, Decatur 35603/205-355-8281	Methodist
Wesley Manor	210 Honeysuckle Road, Dothan 36301/205-792-0921	Methodist
Wesley Terrace	1365 Gatewood Drive, Auburn 36830/205-826-7200	Methodist
Westminster Village	500 Spanish Fort Boulevard, Spanish Fort 36527/205-626-7007	Presbyterian
Arizona		
Baptist Village	11315 West Peoria Avenue, Youngtown 85363/602-972-2371	Baptist
Beatitudes Campus of Care	1616 West Glendale Avenue, Phoenix 85021/602-995-2611	United Church of Christ
Christian Care	11812 North 19th Avenue, Phoenix 85029/602-861-3241	Christian Churches
Glencroft Retirement Comm	8611 North 67th Avenue, Glendale 85302/602-939-9475	Mennonite, Apostolic, Christian, Friends
Good Shepherd Ret Center	10323 West Olive Avenue, Peoria 85345/602-974-2555	Lutheran
Orangewood	7550 North 16th Street, Phoenix 85020/602-944-4455	American Baptist
Paradise Valley Estates	11645 North 25th Place, Phoenix 85028/602-482-7100	Baptist
Tanner Gardens Apartments	4420 South 18th Place, Phoenix 85040/602-268-8866	African Methodist/ Episcopal
Waymark Gardens	5325 West Butler Drive, Glendale 85302/602-931-7002	Christian Church
Wooddale Retirement Comm	18616 North 99th Avenue, Sun City 85373/602-933-0022	Lutheran Brethren
Arkansas		
Good Samaritan Cedar Lodge	5 Cortez Road, Hot Springs Village 71909/501-922-2000	Lutheran
Good Shepherd Ecumenical Retirement Center	2701 Aldersgate Road, Little Rock 72205/501-224-7200	Ecumenical Ret Board
Parkway Village	14300 Rock Creek Parkway, Little Rock 72211/501-227-2036	Baptist
California		
Alhambra	2400 South Fremont Avenue, Alhambra 91803/213-289-6211	Lutheran
Atherton Baptist Homes	214 South Atlantic Boulevard, Alhambra 91801/818-289-4178	Baptist
Auburn Ravine Terrace	750 Auburn Ravine Road, Auburn 95603/916-823-6131	Congregational
Baptist Gardens	1011 Pine Avenue, Long Beach 90813/213-432-4454	Baptist
Bellflower Friendship Manor	9550 East Oak Street, Bellflower 90706/213-867-9550	Baptist
Bethany Center	580 Capp Street, San Francisco 94110/415-821-4515	United Methodist
Bethany Towers	1745 North Gramercy Place, Hollywood 90028/213-467-3121	Christian Church/DCC
Bethlehem Towers, Inc.	801 Tupper Street, Santa Rosa 95404/707-544-5560	Lutheran
Brethren Hillcrest Homes	2705 Mountain View Drive, La Verne 91750/714-593-4917	Church of the Brethren
Buttes Christian Manor	223 F Street, Marysville 95901/916-742-2421	Christian Church/DCC
California Christian Home	8417 East Mission Drive, Rosemead 91770/818-287-0438	Christian Church/DCC
Canterbury Woods	651 Sinex Avenue, Pacific Grove 93950/408-373-3111	Episcopal
Carlotta	41505 Carlotta Drive, Palm Desert 92260/619-346-5420	Lutheran
Carlsbad by the Sea	2855 Carlsbad Boulevard, Carlsbad 92008/619-729-2377	Lutheran
Carmel Valley Manor	8545 Carmel Valley Road, Carmel 93923/408-624-1281	Congregational
Casa de la Paloma	133 South Kenwood Street, Glendale 91205/818-243-0337	Presbyterian
Casa De Verdugo (Verdugo Home, Inc.)	155 0 175 N. Girard Street, Hemet 92344/714-658-2274	Baptist
Covenant Village of Turlock	2125 North Olive Avenue, Turlock 95380/209-632-9976	Evangelical Covenant
El Bethel Arms	1234 McAllister Street, San Francisco 94115/415-567-3950	Christian Church
El Bethel Terrace	1099 Fillmore Street, San Francisco 94115/415-931-4496	Baptist
Fairhaven Retirement Center	4360 63rd Street, Sacramento 95820/916-452-2100	World Gospel Mission
Fellowship Manor	1201 Golden Gate Avenue, San Francisco 94115/415-922-0154	Bethel AME Church
Fickett Towers	14801 Sherman Way, Van Nuys 91405/818-988-8628	Baptist
Forest Hill Manor	551 Gibson, Pacific Grove 93950/408-375-5125	Methodist
Good Shepherd Manor	4411-11th Avenue, Los Angeles 90043/213-299-5735	Episcopal
Grand Lake Garden	401 Santa Clara Avenue, Oakland 94610/415-893-8897	Baptist
Inland Christian Home	1950 S. Mountain Avenue, Ontario 91761/714-983-0084	Christian Reformed
Judson Terrace Homes	3000 Augusta Street, San Luis Obispo 93401/805-544-1600	Baptist
Kern Crest Manor	250 E. Tulare Street, Shafter 93263/805-746-6521	Mennonite Brethren
Lake Park Ret Residence	1850 Alice Street, Oakland 94612/415-835-5511	United Methodist
Life's Garden	450 Old San Francisco Road, Sunnyvale 94086/408-245-5433	Presbyterian
Lincoln Glen Manor	2671 Plummer Avenue, San Jose 95125/408-265-3222	Mennonite Brethren
Long Beach Brethren Manor	3333 Pacific Place, Long Beach 90806/213-426-6547	Church of the Brethren
Los Gatos Meadows	110 Wood Road, Los Gatos 95030/408-354-0211	Episcopal
Luther Tower	1455 Second Avenue, San Diego 92101/619-234-1271	Lutheran

Name	*Address/Phone*	*Affiliation*
Lytton Gardens and Health Care Center	656 Lytton Avenue, Palo Alto 94301/415-328-3300	Presbyterian/Methodist
Martin Luther Tower, Inc.	1001 Franklin Street, San Francisco 94109/415-771-9931	Lutheran
Mennonite Brethren Homes, Inc.	856 S. Reed Avenue, Reedley 93654/209-638-3615	Brethren
Monte Vista Grove Homes	2889 San Pasqual Street, Pasadena 91107/818-796-6135	Presbyterian
Mount Miguel Covenant Vil	325 Kempton Street, Spring Valley 92077/619-479-4790	Evangelical Covenant
Mount Rubidoux Manor	3993 Tenth Street, Riverside 92501/714-684-3154	Baptist
Mount San Antonio Gardens	900 East Harrison Avenue, Pomona 91767/714-624-5061	United Church of Christ
Neighborhood Manor, Inc.	1200 Woodrow Avenue, Modesto 95350/209-526-0308	Assembly of God
Oak Center Towers	1515 Market Street, Oakland 94607/415-465-1166	Episcopal
Piedmont Gardens	110-41st Street, Oakland 94611/415-654-7172	Baptist
Pilgrim Haven	373 Pine Lane, Los Altos 94022/415-948-8291	Baptist
Pilgrim Tower for the Deaf	1207 South Vermont Avenue, Los Angeles 90006/213-387-6541	Lutheran
Plymouth Square	1319 North Madison Street, Stockton 95202/209-466-4341	Congregational
Plymouth Tower	3401 Lemon Street, Riverside 92501/714-686-8202	Congregational
Plymouth Village of Redlands	900 Salem Drive, Redlands 92373/714-793-1233	Baptist
Presidio Gate Apartments	2770 Lombard Street, San Francisco 94123/415-567-1050	Episcopal
Quaker Gardens	12151 Dale Street, Stanton 90680/714-530-9100	Friends
Redwoods	40 Camino Alto, Mill Valley 94941/415-383-2741	Community Church
Regents Point	19191 Harvard Avenue, Irvine 82715/714-854-9500	Presbyterian
Rohlff's Memorial Manor, Inc.	2400 Fair Drive, Napa 94558/707-255-9555	Lutheran
Rosewood Retirement Comm	1301 New Stine Road, Bakersfield 93309/805-834-0620	Baptist
Royal Oaks Manor	1763 Royal Oaks Drive, Duarte 91010/818-359-9371	Presbyterian
Saint John's Retirement Vil	135 Woodland Avenue, Woodland 95695/916-662-1290	United Church of Christ
Salem Lutheran Home	2361 East 29th Street, Oakland 94606/415-534-3637	Lutheran
Samarkand of Santa Barbara	2550 Treasure Drive, Santa Barbara 93105/805-687-0701	Covenant
San Joaquin Gardens	5555 North Fresno Street, Fresno 93710/209-439-4770	Baptist
Seaview Lutheran Plaza	2800 Pacific View Drive, Corona Del Mar 92112/714-720-0888	Lutheran
Sequoias-Portola Valley	501 Portola Road, Portola Valley 94028/415-851-1501	Presbyterian
Sequoias-San Francisco	1400 Geary Boulevard, San Francisco 94109/415-922-9700	Presbyterian
Solheim Lutheran Home	2236 Merton Avenue, Los Angeles 90041/213-257-7518	Lutheran
Spring Lake Village	5555 Montgomery Drive, Santa Rosa 95405/707-538-8400	Episcopal
St. Paul's Manor and Health Care Center	P.O. Box 128048, San Diego 92112/619-239-2097	Episcopal
St. Paul's Towers	100 Bay Place, Oakland 94610/415-835-4700	Episcopal
Summerfield Plaza East & West	2624 Traction Avenue, Sacramento 95815/916-924-0961	National Church Residences
Sunny View Lutheran Home	22445 Cupertino Road, Cupertino 95014/408-253-4300	Lutheran
Town and Country Manor	555 East Memory Lane, Santa Ana 92706/714-547-7581	Christian and Missionary Alliance
Town Park Towers	60 North Third Street, San Jose 95112/408-288-8750	Presbyterian
Upland Manor	1125 W. Arrow Highway, Upland 91786/714-985-1215	Brethren
Valle Verde Ret Center	900 Calle De Los Amigos, Santa Barbara 93105/805-687-1571	Baptist
Valley Village	390 North Winchester Blvd, Santa Clara 95050/408-241-7750	United Church of Christ
Vista Towers	3000 Leeward Avenue, Los Angeles 90005/213-386-2786	Baptist
Walnut Manor	891 South Walnut Street, Anaheim 92802/714-776-7150	Lutheran
Wesley Manor	1655 S. Winchester Blvd, Campbell 95008/408-374-9511	Methodist
Western Park Apartments	1280 Laguna Street, San Francisco 94115/415-922-5436	Presbyterian
Westlake Christian Terrace	275-28th Street, Oakland 94611/415-893-2998	Christian Church
White Sands of La Jolla	7450 Olivetas Avenue, La Jolla 92037/619-454-4201	Presbyterian
Windsor Manor	1230 East Windsor Road, Glendale 91205/818-244-7219	Presbyterian
Wysong Plaza	111 North Chapel Avenue, Alhambra 91801/818-284-3956	National Church Residences

Colorado

Name	*Address/Phone*	*Affiliation*
Bonell Good Samaritan Ctr	708-22nd Street, Greeley 80631/303-352-6082	Lutheran
Christian Living Center at University Hills	2479 South Clermont Street, Denver 80222/303-758-3682	Christian Reformed
Eaton Terrace Residences	333 South Eaton Street, Lakewood 80226/303-937-3000	Baptist
First Christian Manor/dba Golden West Manor	1055 Adams Circle, Boulder 80303/303-444-3967	Christian Church
Frasier Meadows Manor	350 Ponca Place, Boulder 80303/303-499-4888	United Methodist
Liggins Tower	5150 East 34th Avenue, Denver 80207/303-321-3891	Baptist

Name	*Address/Phone*	*Affiliation*
Loveland Good Samaritan	2101 South Garfield, Loveland 80537/303-669-3100	Lutheran
Rocky Mountain Residences	1535 Franklin Street, Denver 80218/303-832-4859	Baptist
Senior Homes of Colorado	4901 East Kentucky Circle, Denver 80222/303-756-5218	Congregational, Presbyterian, American Baptist

Connecticut

Covenant Village and Pilgrim Manor	Missionary Road, Cromwell 06416/203-635-5511	Evangelical Covenant
Elim Park Baptist Home, Inc.	140 Cook Hill Road, Cheshire 06410/203-272-3547	Baptist
Immanuel House	15 Woodland Street, Hartford 06195/203-525-4228	Immanuel Church Housing Corp.
Noble Horizons	Lower Cobble Road, Salisbury 06068/203-435-9851	Church Homes, Inc.
Pierce Memorial Baptist Home	44 Canterbury Road, Brooklyn 06234/203-774-9050	Baptist
United Methodist Home of Connecticut, Inc.	584 Long Hill Avenue, Shelton 06484/203-929-5321	United Methodist

Delaware

Cokesbury Village	Lancaster Pike & Loveville Rd, Hockessin 19707/302-239-2371	United Methodist
Lutheran Senior Services	1201 North Harrison Street, Wilmington 19806/302-652-3737	Lutheran
Lutheran Senior Services of Dover, Inc.	430 Kings Highway, Dover 19901/302-674-1408	Lutheran
Methodist Country House	4830 Kennett Pike, Wilmington 19807/302-654-5101	Methodist
Methodist Manor House	1001 Middleford Road, Seaford 19973/302-629-4593	Methodist

District of Columbia

Friendship Terrace	4201 Butterworth Place, Washington 20016/202-244-7400	Episcopal
Presbyterian Home of the Distr. of Columbia	3050 Military Road, NW, Washington 20015/202-363-8310	Presbyterian
Thomas House	1330 Massachusetts Avenue, NW, Washington 20005/ 202-628-3844	Baptist

Florida

Alliance Retirement Center of Deland, Inc.	600 South Florida Avenue, Deland 32720/904-734-3481	Christian & Missionary Alliance
Asbury Arms, Inc.	1430 Dixon Boulevard, Cocoa 32922/305-632-4943	Methodist
Asbury Towers	1533 Fourth Avenue West, Bradenton 33505/813-747-1881	Methodist
Baptist Towers of Jacksonville	1400 La Baron, Jacksonville 32207/904-398-3406	Baptist
Bay Village of Sarasota	8400 Vamo Road, Sarasota 33581/813-966-5611	Presbyterian
Bradenton Manor	1700-21st Avenue West, Bradenton 34205/813-748-4161	Presbyterian
Central Manor	136 Fairview Avenue, Daytona Beach 32014/904-255-2622	Baptist
Christian Manor, Inc.	325 Executive Ctr Drive, West Palm Beach 32014/904-255-2622	Baptist
Covenant Village of Florida	9201 West Broward Boulevard, Plantation 33324/305-472-2860	Evangelical Covenant
Epworth Village West, Inc.	5300 West 16th Avenue, Hialeah 33012/305-556-3500	Methodist
Florida Christian Center Residential Center	1071 South Edgewood Avenue, Jacksonville 32205/904-389-3123	Christian Church
Florida Lutheran Ret Ctr, Inc.	431 North Kansas Avenue, Deland 32724/904-734-0603	Lutheran
Florida Presbyterian Homes, Inc.	16 Lake Hunter Drive, Lakeland 33803/813-688-5521	Presbyterian
Heritage Apartments	10200-122nd Avenue North, Largo 34643/813-393-3477	Presbyterian
Kissimmee Good Samaritan Vil	1550 Aldersgate Drive, Kissimmee 32741/407-933-3200	Lutheran
Lake Worth Towers, Inc.	1500 Lucerne Avenue, Lake Worth 33460/305-585-7591	Nazarene
Morris Manor	9050 Norfolk Boulevard, Jacksonville 32208/904-764-3252	Episcopal
Orlando Lutheran Towers	300 East Church Street, Orlando 32801/407-425-1033	Lutheran
Palm Shores of St. Petersburg	830 North Shore Drive, St. Petersburg 33701/813-894-2102	Baptist
Plymouth Harbor, Inc.	700 John Ringling Boulevard, Sarasota 34236/813-365-2600	United Church of Christ
Riverside Presbyterian Apartments, Inc.	1045 Oak Street, Jacksonville 32204/904-353-6111	Presbyterian
Riverside Presbyterian House, Inc.	2020 Park Street, Jacksonville 32204/904-388-9376	Presbyterian
Saint James' Residence of the Palm Beaches	208 Fern Street, West Palm Beach 33401/305-655-1504	Episcopal
Shell Point Village	15000 Shell Point Boulevard, Fort Myers 33908/813-454-2155	Christian and Missionary Alliance

Name	*Address/Phone*	*Affiliation*
Southwest Florida Ret Center	950 Tamiami Trail South, Venice 34285/813-484-9753	Lutheran
St. Mark Village	2655 Nebraska Avenue, Palm Harbor 34684/813-785-2577	Lutheran
Sunnyside Village	5201 Bahia Vista Street, Sarasota 34232/813-371-2729	Mennonite
Tampa Baptist Manor, Inc.	214 West Grand Central Avenue, Tampa 33606/813-253-2868	Baptist
Wesleyan Village	8225 Wesley Drive, Brooksville 34601/904-799-1644	Methodist
Westminster Oaks	4449 Meandering Way, Tallahassee 32308/904-878-1136	Presbyterian
Westminster Towers	70 West Lucerne Circle, Orlando 32801/407-841-1310	Presbyterian
William Booth Towers	633 Lake Dot Circle, Orlando 32801/407-843-5533	Salvation Army
Winter Park Towers and Vil	1111 South Lakemont Avenue, Winter Park 32792/407-647-4083	Presbyterian

Georgia

Name	Address/Phone	Affiliation
Asbury Harris Epworth Towers/ Wesley Homes	3033 Continential Colony, Parkway Southwest, Atlanta 30331/ 404-344-9400	Methodist
Branan Lodge/Wesley Homes, Inc.	Box 140, Clairsville 30512/404-745-5565	Methodist
Branan Towers/Wesley Homes, Inc.	1200 Glenwood Avenue, SE, Atlanta 30316/404-622-5471	Methodist
Briarcliff Oaks	2982 Briarcliff Road, NE, Atlanta 30329/404-634-3263	Baptist
Calvin Court Apartments	479 East Paces Ferry Road, Atlanta 30305/404-261-1223	Presbyterian
Campbell-Stone Apts, Inc.	2911 Pharr Court South, NW, Atlanta 30305/404-261-4132	Christian Church/DCC
Campbell-Stone North Apts	350 Carpenter Drive, NE, Atlanta 30328/404-256-2612	Christian Church
Canterbury Court	3750 Peachtree Road, NE, Atlanta 30319/404-261-6611	Episcopal
Christian City Ret Homes	7340 Lester Road, Atlanta 30349/404-964-3301	Christian Churches/ Churches of Christ
Clairmont Oaks	441 Clairmont Avenue, Decatur 30030/404-378-8887	Baptist
Gwinnett Christian Terrace	414 Berkmar Way, Lilburn 30247/404-925-3300	Church of Christ
Lanier Gardens/Wesley Homes, Inc.	801 Riverhill Drive, Athens 30610/404-546-1480	Methodist
Lutheran Towers	717 Juniper Street, Atlanta 30308/404-873-6087	Lutheran
Magnolia Manor Methodist Retirement Home	South Lee Street, Americus 31709/912-924-9352	Methodist
Philips Presbyterian Tower	218 East Trinity Place, Decatur 30030/404-373-4361	Presbyterian
Saint Anne's Terrace,Inc.	3100 Northside Parkway, NW, Atlanta 30327/404-238-9200	Episcopal
St. George's Court, Inc.	110 North Tenth Street, Griffin 30223/404-229-5405	Episcopal
St. John Towers/Wesley Homes, Inc.	724 Greene Street, Augusta 30901/404-722-2096	Methodist
St. Mark's Towers	One Towers Plaza, Brunswick 31520/912-267-7125	Episcopal
St. Paul Apartments	1330 Forsyth Street, Macon 31201/912-745-0829	Episcopal
Trinity Towers	2611 Springdale Road, SW, Atlanta 30315/404-763-4044	Episcopal
Vineville Christian Towers, Inc.	2394 Vineville Avenue, Macon 31204/912-743-4661	Christian Church
Wesley Woods Towers/ Wesley Homes, Inc.	1825 Clifton Road, NE, Atlanta 30329/404-728-6683	Methodist

Illinois

Name	Address/Phone	Affiliation
Brementowne Manor of Tinley Park	16130 South Oak Park Ave, Tinley Park 60477/708-429-4088	Mennonite
Carefree Village	P.O. Box 508, Woodstock 60098/815-338-2110	Woodstock Christian Care, Inc.
Christian Life Retirement Ctr	2750 North Mulford Road, Rockford 61111/815-633-5544	Assembly of God
Covenant Vil of Northbrook	2625 Technology Road, Northbrook 60062/708-480-6380	Evangelical Covenant
Englewood Cooperative/ aka Bethel Terrace	900 West 63rd Parkway, Chicago 60621/312-873-8703	Lutheran
Fairhaven Christian Home, Inc.	3470 N. Alpine Road, Rockford 61111/815-877-1441	Evangelical Free
Fairview Baptist Home	7 South 241 Fairview Avenue, Downers Grove 60516/ 708-852-4350	Baptist
Faith Countryside Homes	P.O. Box 220, Highland 62249/618-654-2393	Evangelical United Church of Christ
Friendship Village of Schaumburg	350 West Schaumburg Road, Schaumburg 60194/708-844-5000	Evangelical Ret Homes
Holmstad	700 West Fabyan Parkway, Batavia 60510/708-879-4000	Evangelical Covenant
Maple Lawn Homes	700 North Main, Eureka 61530/309-467-2337	Mennonite
Moorings	811 East Central Rd, Arlington Heights 60005/708-437-6700	Lutheran
Plymouth Place	315 N. La Grange Rd, La Grange Park 60525/708-354-0340	United Church of Christ

Name	*Address/Phone*	*Affiliation*
Presbyterian Home	3200 Grant Street, Evanston 60201/708-492-2900	Presbyterian
Rest Haven Christian Services	13259 S. Central Avenue, Palos Heights 60463/708-597-1000	Christian Reformed
Salem Village	1314 Rowell Avenue, Joliet 60433/815-727-5451	Lutheran
Spoon River Towers	401 North Illinois Street, Lewistown 61542/309-547-7274	Christian Church
Sunset Home	418 Washington Street, Quincy 62301/217-223-2636	Methodist
Sunset Manor	920 North Seminary Road, P.O. Box 508, Woodstock 60098/ 815-338-1749	Woodstock Christian Care, Inc.
United Methodist Village, Inc.	1616 Cedar Street, Lawrenceville 62439/618-943-3347	United Methodist
Wesley Village Retirement/ Health Care Center	1200 East Grant, Macomb 61455/309-833-2123	Methodist
Windsor Park Manor	124 Windsor Park Drive, Carol Stream 60188/708-682-4377	Interdenominational
Indiana		
Brethren Care (St. Paul's Retirement Comm)	Inwood Road, South Bend 46614/219-291-8205	Brethren
Brethren's Home of Indiana, Inc.	Route 2, P.O. Box 97, Flora 46929/219-967-4571	Brethren
Colonial Oaks Retirement Ctr	4725 Colonial Oaks Drive, Marion 46953/317-674-9791	Methodist
Concord Village	6723 South Anthony Blvd., Fort Wayne 46816/219-447-1591	Lutheran
Crawford Manor	5340 West 96th Street, Indianapolis 46268/317-873-6510	Baptist
Friendship Haven Ret Comm	2600 West Jefferson Street, Kokomo 46901/317-459-9343	Mennonite
Golden Years Homestead	8300 Maysville Road, Fort Wayne 46815/219-749-9655	Churches of Christ/ Christian Churches
Grace Village	Wooster Rd, P.O. Box 337, Winona Lake 46590/219-372-6100	Brethren
Greencroft Court Apts, Inc.	1820 Greencroft Boulevard, P.O. Box 819, Goshen 46526/ 219-534-1546	Mennonite
Hubbard Hill Estates Ret Comm	28070 C.R. 24 W., Elkhart 46517/219-295-6260	Missionary Church
Ken-Mar Apartments	210 West Pike Street, P.O. Box 1412, Martinsville 46151/ 317-342-5671	Christian Church
Peabody Retirement Comm	400 West 7th Street, North Manchester 46962/219-982-8616	Presbyterian
Swiss Village, Inc.	Berne 46711/219-589-3173	Mennonite
Timbercrest-Church of the Brethren Home	P.O. Box 501, North Manchester 46962/219-982-2118	Brethren
Village Christian Parke	675 South Ford Road, Zionsville 46077/317-873-5205	Christian Homes
Yellowood Terrace	2100 Greentree North, Clarksville 47130/812-282-7761	United Church of Christ
Iowa		
Calvin Manor	4210 Hickman Road, Des Moines 50310/515-277-6141	Presbyterian
Elsie Mason Manor	430 Grand Avenue, Des Moines 503209/515-243-8759	Baptist
Evangelical Free Church Home	112 W. 4th Street, Boone 50036/515-432-1393	Evangelical Free
Eventide Lutheran Home for the Aged	20th Street & 1st Ave. South, Denison 51442/712-263-3114	Lutheran
Friendship Haven,Inc.	South Kenyon Road, Fort Dodge 50501/515-573-2121	Methodist
Halcyon House	1015 South Iowa Avenue, Washington 52353/319-653-7264	Methodist
Heritage House	1200 Brookridge Circle, Atlantic 50022/712-243-1850	Methodist
Luther Park Apartments	2824 East 16th Street, Des Moines 50316/515-262-1153	Lutheran
Mayflower Homes, Inc.	616 Broad Street, Grinnell 50112/515-236-6151	United Church of Christ
Meth-Wick Retirement Comm	1224-13th Street, NW, Cedar Rapids 52405/319-365-9171	Methodist
Oaknoll Retirement Residence	701 Oaknoll Drive, Iowa City 52246/319-351-1720	Christian Ret Services
Ridgecrest Village	4130 Northwest Boulevard, Davenport 52806/319-391-3430	Christian Ret Homes, Inc.
Stone Crest Apartments	3330 East 25th Street, Des Moines 50317/515-265-2172	Christian Church
United Presbyterian Home	1203 East Washington Street, Washington 52353/319-653-5473	Presbyterian
Valley View Village	2571 Guthrie Avenue, Des Moines 50317/515-265-2571	Interdenominational
Wesley Acres Ret Community	3520 Grand Avenue, Des Moines 50312/515-271-6500	Methodist
Kansas		
Aldersgate Village	7220 Asbury Drive, Topeka 66614/913-478-9440	Methodist
Arkansas City Presbyterian Manor	1711 North Fourth Street, Arkansas City 67005/316-442-8700	Presbyterian
Brewster Place	1205 West 29th Street, Topeka 66611/913-267-1666	United Church of Christ Congregational
Buhler Sunshine Home	412 W. C Street, Buhler 67522/316-543-2251	Mennonite Brethren
Emporia Presbyterian Manor	2300 Industrial Road, Emporia 66801/316-343-2613	Presbyterian
First Christian Church Apts	3805 West 18th Street, Topeka 66604/913-272-6700	Christian Church

Name	Address/Phone	Affiliation
Friends Village	628 S. Hiram, Wichita 67213/316-267-8811	Evangelical Friends Alliance
Garden Valley Ret Village Inc.	1505 E. Spruce, Garden City 67846/316-276-7879	Mennonite Brethren
Lakeview Village, Inc.	9100 Park Street, Lenexa 66215/913-888-1900	Interdenominational
Lawrence Presbyterian Manor	1429 Kasold Drive, Lawrence 66049/913-841-4262	Presbyterian
Memorial Home for the Aged	P.O. Box 29, Moundridge 67107/316-345-2901	Mennonite, Methodist
Newton Presbyterian Manor	1200 East Seventh Street, Newton 67114/316-283-5400	Presbyterian
Parkside Homes, Inc.	200 Willow Road, Hillsboro 67063/316-947-2301	N/A
Pleasant View Home	108 N. Walnut, Inman 67546/316-585-6411	N/A
Salem Home	701 S. Main, Hillsboro 67063/316-947-2272	N/A
Salina Presbyterian Manor	2601 East Crawford, Salina 67401/913-825-1366	Presbyterian
Schowalter Villa	200 West Cedar, P.O. Box 5000, Hesston 67062/316-327-4261	Mennonite
Sunset Home	620 Second Avenue, Concordia 66901/913-243-2720	Baptist
Topeka Presbyterian Manor	4712 West 6th Street, Topeka 66606/913-272-6510	Presbyterian
United Methodist Homes	1135 College, Topeka 66607/913-234-0421	Methodist
Wesley Towers, Inc.	700 Monterey Place, Hutchinson 67502/316-663-9175	Methodist
Wichita Presbyterian Manor	4700 West 13th Street, Wichita 67212/316-942-7456	Presbyterian
Kentucky		
Baptist Towers, Inc.	1014 South Second, Louisville 40203/502-587-6632	Baptist
Chapel House	945 South Fifth Street, Louisville 40203/502-584-5178	Christian Church
Florence Christian Center	100 Christian Drive, Florence 41042/606-525-9233	Christian Church
Friendship House	960 South 4th Street, Louisville 40203/502-589-5747	Christian Church
Helmwood Village Ret Comm	106 Diecks Drive, Elizabethtown 42701/502-737-2738	Presbyterian
Wesley Manor Ret Comm	5012 East Manslick Road, P.O. Box 19258, Louisville 40219/502-969-3277	Methodist
Westminster Terrace	2116 Buechel Bank Road, Louisville 40218/502-499-9383	Presbyterian
Louisiana		
Cedar Hill Apartments	7401 Saint Vincent, Shreveport 71106/318-861-6915	Baptist
St. James Place of Baton Rouge, Inc.	333 Lee Drive, Baton Rouge 70808/504-769-1407	Episcopal
Maryland		
Asbury Methodist Village	201 Russell Avenue, Gaithersburg 20877/301-330-3000	Methodist
Carroll Lutheran Village	205 Saint Mark Way, Westminster 21157/301-848-0090	Lutheran
Collington Episcopal Life Care Community	10450 Lottsford Road, Mitchellville 20716/301-925-9610	Episcopal
Fahrney-Keedy Memorial Home, Inc.	Boonesboro 21713/301-733-6284	Brethren
Fairhaven	7200 Third Avenue, Sykesville 21784/301-795-8800	Episcopal
Friends House Ret Comm	17340 Quaker Lane, Sandy Spring 20860/301-924-5100	Quaker
Homewood Retirement Ctr	2750 Virginia Avenue, Williamsport 21795/301-582-1750	United Church of Christ
National Lutheran Home for the Aged	9701 Viers Drive, Rockville 20850/301-424-9560	Lutheran
New Towne Village	RR 2, Box 1, Leonardtown 20650/301-475-3161	Natl Church Residences
Ravenwood Lutheran Village	1183 Luther Drive, Hagerstown 21740/301-790-1000	Lutheran
Springvale Terrace	8505 Springvale Road, Silver Spring 20910/301-587-0190	United Church of Christ
Wesley Home, Inc.	2211 West Rogers Avenue, Baltimore 21209/301-664-4006	Methodist
Massachusetts		
Turtle Creek Residential Comm	401 Essex Street, Beverly 01915/617-922-1112	Baptist
Michigan		
Au Sable Valley Apartments	1441 Maple Drive, Fairview 48621/517-848-5630	Mennonite
Boulevard Temple United Methodist Ret Home	2567 West Grand Boulevard, Detroit 48208/313-895-5340	United Methodist
Canton Place	44505 Ford Road, Canton 48187/313-981-6420	Natl Church Residences
Cathedral Terrace	80 East Hancock, Detroit 48201/313-832-1020	Episcopal
Chelsea United Methodist Retirement Home	805 West Middle Street, Chelsea 48118/313-475-8633	United Methodist
Clawson Manor-New Life, Inc.	255 West Fourteen-Mile Road, Clawson 48017/313-435-5650	Methodist
Columbia Court	275 West Columbia Avenue, Belleville 48111/313-697-8200	Natl Church Residences
Danish Village	2566 Walton Boulevard, Rochester Hills 48309/313-375-1810	Lutheran
Detroit Baptist Manor	30301 W. 13 Mile Rd., Farmington Hills 48018/313-626-6100	Baptist

Name	*Address/Phone*	*Affiliation*
Evangelical Homes of Mich	6700 West Outer Drive, Detroit 48235/313-836-1700	United Church of Christ
Grand Ravine Apartments	725 Grand Street, Allegan 49010/616-673-7155	Lutheran
Lakeside Towers	15000 Shoreline Drive, Sterling Heights 48078/313-247-7411	Natl Church Residences
Luther Haven	464 East Grand Boulevard, Detroit 48207/313-579-2255	Lutheran
Luther Village Community	2000-32nd Street, SE, Grand Rapids 49508/616-452-6084	Lutheran
M J Clark Memorial Home	1546 Sherman, SE, Grand Rapids 49506/616-452-1568	Methodist
Park Place of Harper Woods	19460 Park Drive, Harper Woods 48225/313-884-2122	Natl Church Residences
Park Village Pines	2920 Crystal Lane, Kalamazoo 49009/616-372-1928	Christian Retirement Associates, Inc.
Pilgrim Manor, Inc.	2000 Leonard, NE, Grand Rapids 49505/616-458-1133	United Church of Christ
Porter Hills Presbyterian Vil, Inc.	3600 East Fulton, Grand Rapids 49546/616-949-4971	Presbyterian
Presbyterian Village East	33875 Kiely Drive, New Baltimore 48047/313-725-6030	Presbyterian
Presbyterian Village North	420 South Opdyke Road, Pontiac 48057/313-334-4379	Presbyterian
Presbyterian Vil of Detroit, Inc.	17383 Garfield Avenue, Redford 48240/313-531-6874	Presbyterian

Minnesota

Name	*Address/Phone*	*Affiliation*
Augustana Home of Minneapolis	1007 East 14th Street, Minneapolis 55404/612-333-1551	Lutheran
Augustana Lutheran Homes, Inc.	600 South Davis, Litchfield 55355/612-693-2430	Lutheran
Bethesda Lutheran Care Ctr	558 Capitol Boulevard, St. Paul 55103/612-221-2347	Lutheran
Chapel View Care Center	615 Minnetonka Mills Road, Hopkins 55343/612-938-2761	Methodist
Covenant Manor	5800 Saint Croix Avenue, Minneapolis 55422/612-546-6125	Evangelical Covenant
Crest View Lutheran Home	4444 Reservoir Blvd, Columbia Heights 55421/612-788-1678	Lutheran
Elim Home	101 S. 7th Avenue, Princeton 55371/612-389-1171	Evangelical Free
Elim Home	409 Jefferson Avenue, S.W., Watertown 55388/612-955-2691	Evangelical free
Elim Home	730-2nd Street, SE, Milaca 56353/612-983-2185	Evangelical Free
Glenwood Retirement Homes	719 SE Second Street, Glenwood 56334/612-634-5131	Lutheran
Grandview Christian Home	800 Second Avenue, NW, Cambridge 55008/612-689-1474	Baptist
Lutheran Retirement Home of Southern Minnesota	400 North 4th Avenue, East, Truman 56088/507-776-2031	Lutheran
Lynblomsten Center	1415 Almond Avenue, St. Paul 55108/612-646-2941	Lutheran
Mankato Lutheran Home	718 Mound Avenue, Mankato 56001/507-345-4576	Lutheran
Margaret S. Parmly Residence	28210 Old Towne Road, Chisago City 55013/612-257-5620	Lutheran
Martin Luther Manor	1401 East 100th Street, Bloomington 55425/612-888-7751	Lutheran
Mount Olivet-Careview Homes	5517 Lyndale Avenue S., Minneapolis 55419/612-827-5677	Lutheran
Presbyterian Homes of Minnesota, Inc.	3220 Lake Johanna Boulevard, St. Paul 55112/612-631-6100	Presbyterian
Seminary Memorial Home	906 College Avenue, Red Wing 55066/612-388-1591	Lutheran
Thorne Crest Retirement Ctr	1201 Garfield Avenue, Albert Lea 56007/507-373-2311	Baptist
Walker Methodist Residences/ Health Services	3737 Bryant Avenue South, Minneapolis 55409/612-827-8301	Methodist

Mississippi

Name	*Address/Phone*	*Affiliation*
Aldersgate Retirement Center	P.O. Box 3846, Meridian 39303/601-482-5561	Methodist
Boardtown Village	905 N. Montgomery Street, Starkville 39759/601-323-3461	Natl Church Residences
Methodist Retirement Comm	1450 Beach Boulevard, Biloxi 39530/601-435-3861	Methodist
Traceway Manor	2800 West Main Street, Tupelo 38801/601-844-1441	Methodist
Trinity Place	300 Airline Road, Columbus 39702/601-327-6716	Methodist
Wesley Manor Ret Comm	P.O. Box 16298, Hattiesburg 39402/601-264-8847	Methodist

Missouri

Name	*Address/Phone*	*Affiliation*
Armour Home	8100 Wornall Road, Kansas City 64114/816-363-1510	Women's Christian Association
Beautiful Savior Home	Route 2, Box 306, Belton 64012/816-331-0781	Lutheran
Foxwood Springs Living Ctr	P.O. Box 1400, Raymore 64083/816-331-3111	Christian Church
Friendship Village of West County	15201 Olive Street, Chesterfield 63017/314-532-1515	Evangelical Ret Homes
Gambrill Gardens, Inc.	One Strecker Road, Ellisville 63011/314-394-2992	Methodist
Good Samaritan Home	5200 South Broadway, St. Louis 63111/314-352-2400	Church of Christ
Jaycee Fairgrounds Village	1355 Fairgrounds Road, St. Charles 63301/314-947-1324	Natl Church Residences
Kingswood Manor	10000 Wornall Road, Kansas City 64114/816-942-0994	Methodist
Laclede Oaks Manor	701 S. Laclede Station Rd., St. Louis 63119/314-968-9200	Lutheran
Lenoir Health Care Center	3300 New Haven Road, Columbia 65201/314-443-2478	Christian Church
Lenoir Retirement Center	3612 Lenoir Street, Columbia 65201/314-876-5800	Christian Church

Name	Address/Phone	Affiliation
Maranatha Village	233 E. Norton Road, Springfield 65803/417-833-0016	N/A
Ozarks Methodist Manor	205 South College Street, P.O. Box C, Marionville 65705/ 417-463-2573	Methodist
Presbyterian Manor at Farmington	Manor Court, Farmington 63640/314-756-6768	Presbyterian
Tower Grove Manor	2710 South Grand Boulevard, St. Louis 63118/314-773-2800	Episcopal, Presbyterian
Montana		
Downtowner	100 Central Avenue, Great Falls 59401/406-761-1444	Methodist
Saint John's Lutheran Home	3940 Rimrock Road, Billings 59102/406-656-2710	Lutheran
Nebraska		
Christian Homes, Inc.	Holdrege 68949/308-995-4493	Evangelical Free
Maple Crest Retirement Ctr	2824 North 66th Avenue, Omaha 68104/402-551-2110	Baptist
Methodist Memorial Homes, Inc. Retirement Center	1320-11th Avenue, Holdrege 68949/308-995-8631	Methodist
Skyline Manor, Inc.	7300 Graceland Drive, Omaha 68134/402-572-5750	Nondenominational
New Hampshire		
Havenwood Ret Community	33 Christian Avenue, Concord 03301/603-225-5363	United Church of Christ
Heritage Heights	149 East Side Drive, Concord 03301/603-225-6999	United Church of Christ
New Jersey		
Asbury Tower	1701 Ocean Avenue, Asbury Park 07712/201-988-9090	Presbyterian
Cadbury	2150 Route 38, Cherry Hill 08002/609-667-4550	Quaker
Clymer Village	211 Red School Lane, Phillipsburg 08865/201-454-4661	Natl Church Residences
Evergreens	309 Bridgeboro Road, Moorestown 08057/609-235-2503	Episcopal
Francis Asbury Manor	70 Stockton Avenue, Ocean Grove 07756/201-774-1316	Methodist
Friends Home at Woodstown, Inc.	Friends Drive, P.O. Box 457, Woodstown 08098/609-769-1500	Friends
Harvest Village	114 Hayes Mill Road, Atco 08004/609-753-2000	Presbyterian
Heath Village	Schooleys Mountain Rd., Hackettstown 07840/201-852-4801	Episcopal
Kinder Towers	400 Hoover Road, Bloomfield 07003/201-748-0982	Natl Church Residences
Luther Arms	323 South Broad Street, Trenton 08618/609-392-5628	Lutheran
Luther Towers	489 West State Street, Trenton 08618/609-695-7755	Lutheran
Medford Leas Continuing Care Retirement Center	Route 70, Medford 08055/609-654-3000	Friends
Monroe Village	117 Hale Acre Road, Jamesburg 08831/201-521-6400	Presbyterian
Muhlenberg Gardens	1065 Summit Avenue, Jersey City 07307/201-792-4475	Lutheran
Navesink House	40 Riverside Avenue, Red Bank 07701/201-842-3400	Baptist
Pitman Manor	535 North Oak Avenue, Pitman 08071/609-589-7800	Methodist
Plainfield Tower West	601 West 7th Street, Plainfield 07060/201-668-1963	Presbyterian
Presbyterian Home at Meadow Lakes	Etra Road, P.O. Box 70, Hightstown 08520/609-426-6805	Presbyterian
Wesley Homestead	805 East 8th Street, Ocean City 08226/609-394-1608	Methodist
Wiley Christian Ret Comm	99 East Main Street, Marlton 08053/609-983-0411	Wiley Mission Society
Woodmere Senior Citizens Housing Corporation	250 Crescent Avenue, Spotswood 08884/201-251-3242	Reformed Church
New Mexico		
Encino House Midtown	609 Encino Place, NE, Albuquerque 87102/505-247-4185	New Mexico Conference of Churches
Landsun Homes, Inc.	2002 Westridge Road, Carlsbad 88220/505-887-2894	Methodist
University Terrace Good Samaritan Village	3025 Terrace Drive, Las Cruces Drive 88001/505-526-1362	Lutheran
New York		
Bethel Springvale Inn	500 Albany Post Road, Croton-on-Hudson 10520/914-739-4404	Methodist
Clinton Manor Apts, Inc.	50 Franklin Avenue, P.O. Box 100, Clinton 13323/315-853-3698	Lutheran
Embury Apartments, Inc.	Lawrence Street, Saratoga Springs 12866/518-587-3300	Methodist
Episcopal Church Home	24 Rhode Island Street, Buffalo 14213/716-884-6500	Episcopal
Fairport Baptist Home	4646 Nine Mile Point Road, Fairport 14450/716-377-0350	Baptist
Flushing House	38-20 Bowne Street, Flushing 11354/718-762-3198	Presbyterian
Fort Schuyler House, Inc.	3077 Cross Bronx Expressway, Bronx 10465/212-597-4100	Presbyterian
Good Shepherd-Fairview Home, Inc.	80 Fairview Avenue, Binghamton 13904/607-724-2477	Episcopal, Presbyterian

Name	*Address/Phone*	*Affiliation*
Heritage Village	Route 60, Gerry 14740/716-985-4612	Free Methodist
Hilltop Retirement Center	285 Deyo Hill Road, Johnson City 13790/607-798-7818	Methodist
Saint Margaret's House	49 Fulton Street, New York 10038/212-766-8122	Episcopal
Valley Manor	1570 East Avenue, Rochester 14610/716-442-6450	Presbyterian
Village of Saint John	2000 Bishop's Road, Smithtown 11787/516-724-2226	Episcopal
Wheatfield Tower	6849 Plaza Drive, Niagara Falls 14304/716-731-4600	Natl Church Residences
North Carolina		
Albemarle	200 Trade Street, Tarboro 27886/919-823-2799	Presbyterian
Brookridge Retirement Comm	1199 Hayes Forest Dr., P.O. Box 11024, Winston-Salem 27116/ 919-759-1044	Baptist
Brooks-Howell Home	29 Spears Avenue, Asheville 28801/704-253-6712	Methodist
Capital Towers	4812 Six Forks Road, Raleigh 27609/919-787-1231	Presbyterian
Cypress Glen	100 Hickory Street, Greenville 27858/919-830-0036	Methodist
Deerfield Episcopal Ret Comm	1617 Hendersonville Road, Asheville 28803/704-274-1531	Episcopal
Episcopal Home for Aging	East Thode Island Ave Exten, P.O. Box 2001, Sthrn Pines 28387/ 919-692-0300	Episcopal
Epworth Place	3420 Shamrock Drive, Charlotte 28215/704-532-7000	Methodist
Friends Homes, Inc.	925 New Garden Road, Greensboro 27410/919-292-8187	Friends
Givens Estates United Methodist Ret Comm	Sweeten Creek Road, Asheville 28803/704-274-4800	Methodist
Golden Years Home	P.O. Box 39, Falcon 28342/919-892-6048	Pentecostal Holiness
J.W. Abernathy Center United Church Homes	100 Leonard Avenue, Newton 28658/704-464-8260	United Church of Christ
Methodist Retirement Comm	2616 Durham Road, Durham 27705/919-383-2567	Methodist
Moravian Home, Inc.	5401 Indiana Avenue, Winston-Salem 27106/919-767-8130	Moravian Church
Presbyterian Home at Charlotte, Inc.	5100 Sharon Road, Charlotte 28210/704-553-1670	Presbyterian
Presbyterian Home of High Point	2001 Greensboro Road, P.O. Box 2007, High Point 27261/ 919-883-9111	Presbyterian
Scotia Village Ret Comm	2200 Elm Avenue, Laurinburg 28352/919-277-2000	Presbyterian
Triad United Methodist Home	1240 Arbor Road, Winston-Salem 27104/919-724-7921	Methodist
Twin Lakes Center	100 Wade Coble Drive, Burlington 27215/919-538-1400	Lutheran
Wesley Pines	100 Wesley Pines Road, Lumberton 28358/919-738-9691	Methodist
Wesleyan Arms Ret Center	1901 N. Centennial Street, High Point 27260/919-884-2222	Methodist
North Dakota		
Bethany Homes, Inc.	201 South University Drive, Fargo 58103/701-237-0720	Lutheran
Elim Home	3534 S. University Drive, Fargo 58103/701-237-4392	Evangelical Free
Ohio		
Bethany Lutheran Village	6451 Far Hills Avenue, Dayton 45459/513-433-2110	Lutheran
Booth Residence, c/o The Salvation Army	6000 Townevista Drive, Cincinnati 45224/513-242-4482	The Salvation Army
Breckenridge Village	36855 Rodge Road, Willoughby 44094/216-942-4342	Presbyterian
Brethren Care, Inc.	2000 Center Street, Ashland 44805/419-289-1585	Brethren
Brethren's Home	750 Chestnut Street, Greenville 45331/513-547-8000	Brethren
Bristol Village	111 Wendy Lane, Waverly 45690/614-947-2118	Natl Church Residences
Canterbury Court	450 North Elm Street, West Carrollton 45449/513-859-1106	Episcopal
Canton Christian Home	2550 Cleveland Avenue, NW, Canton 44709/216-456-0004	Christian and Churches of Christ
Copeland Oaks	800 South 15th Street, Sebring 44672/216-938-6126	Methodist
Covenant House, Inc.	702 North Erie Street, Toledo 43604/419-243-2334	Lutheran
Dorothy Love Ret Community	3003 West Cisco Road, Sidney 45365/513-498-2391	Presbyterian
Elyria United Methodist Home	807 West Avenue, Elyria 44035/216-323-3395	United Methodist
Fairlawn Haven	407 East Lutz Road, Archbold 43502/419-445-3075	Mennonite
First Community Village	1800 Riverside Drive, Columbus 43212/614-486-9511	First Community Church
Hilty Memorial Home	P.O. Box 265, Pandora 45877/419-384-3218	Missionary Church
Hopeton Village	153 University Drive, Chillicothe 45601/614-773-5220	Natl Church Residences
Lincoln Garden	98 Sturbridge Road, Columbus 43228/614-878-4394	Natl Church Residences
Llanfair Retirement Comm	1701 Llanfair Avenue, Cincinnati 45224/513-681-4230	Presbyterian
Luther Pines	805 Mumaugh Road, Lima 45804/419-225-9045	Lutheran
Lutheran Senior City	935 North Cassady Avenue, Columbus 43219/614-252-4987	Lutheran
Marjorie P. Lee Ret Comm	3550 Shaw Avenue, Cincinnati 45208/513-871-2090	Episcopal

Name	Address/Phone	Affiliation
Mount Pleasant Village	225 Britton Lane, Monroe 45050/513-539-7391	Presbyterian
Otterbein-Lebanon	585 North State Route 741, Lebanon 45036/513-932-2020	Methodist
Park Vista Retirement Comm	1216 Fifth Avenue, Youngstown 44504/216-746-2944	Presbyterian
Portage Trail Village	45 Cathedral Lane, Cuyahoga Falls 44223/216-929-4227	Natl Church Residences
Rockynol Retirement Comm	1150 West Market Street, Akron 44313/216-867-2150	Presbyterian
Stygler Village	140 Imperial Drive, Gahanna 43230/614-475-2255	Natl Church Residences
Twin Towers	5343 Hamilton Avenue, Cincinnati 45224/513-853-2000	Methodist
Wesley Glen, Inc.	5155 North High Street, Columbus 43214/614-888-7492	Methodist
West View Manor Ret Center	1715 Mechanicsburg Road, Wooster 44691/216-264-8640	Brethren
Worthington Christian Vil, Inc.	165 Highbluffs Boulevard, Worthington 43085/614-846-6076	Church of Christ
Oklahoma		
Carmen Home	P.O. Box 10, Carmen 73726/405-987-2577	Pentecostal Holiness
Corn Heritage Village	Corn 73024/405-343-2295	Mennonite Brethren
Fairview Fellowship Home	605 E. State Street, Fairview 73737/405-227-3784	Mennonite Brethren
Oklahoma Christian Apts, Inc.	325 Enz Drive, Edmond 73034/405-340-0311	Christian Church
Oregon		
Cascade Manor, Inc.	65 West 30th Street, Eugene 97405/503-342-5901	Methodist, Congregational, Presbyterian
Fairlawn Towne	1280 NE Kane Road, Gresham 97030/503-667-1965	Lutheran
Friendsview Manor	1301 East Fulton Street, Newberg 97132/503-538-3144	Quaker
Holladay Park Plaza	1300 NE 16th Avenue, Portland 97232/503-288-6671	Presbyterian
Mennonite Home	5353 Southeast Columbus, Albany 97321/503-928-7232	Mennonite
Olive Plaza	1133 Olive Street, Eugene 97401/503-683-3247	Christian Church
Oregon Baptist Ret Home	2545 NE Flanders Street, Portland 97232/503-232-5055	Baptist
Presbyterian Comm Care Ctr	1085 North Oregon Street, Ontario 97914/503-889-9133	Presbyterian
Rogue Valley Manor	1200 Mira Mar Avenue, Medford 97504/503-776-5212	Episcopal, Presbyterian, Methodist
Village Retirement Ctr, The	310 W. Ellendale Avenue, Dallas 97338/503-623-9211	Brethren
Weidler Retirement Center	1825 NE 108th Avenue, Portland 97220/503-255-7160	Baptist
Willamette Lutheran Homes, Inc.	7693 Wheatland Rd. N, P.O. Box 169, Salem 97308/503-371-2696	Lutheran
Pennsylvania		
Alliance Home, The,	770 S. Hanover Street, Carlisle 17013/717-249-1363	Christian and Missionary Alliance
Asbury Heights	700 Bower Hill Road, Pittsburgh 15243/412-341-1030	Methodist
Bethany Towers	335 Wesley Drive, Mechanicsburg 17055/717-766-7698	Bethany Development Corporation
Bethany Village Ret Center	325 Wesley Drive, Mechanicsburg 17055/417-766-0279	Methodist
Brethren Home	2990 Carlisle Pike, P.O. Box 128, New Oxford 17350/717-624-2161	Brethren
Brethren Village	3001 Lititz Pike, P.O. Box 5093, Lancaster 17601/717-569-2657	Brethren
Calvary Fellowship Homes, Inc.	502 Elizabeth Drive, Lancaster 17601/717-393-0711	Nondenominational
Cathedral Village	600 East Cathedral Road, Philadelphia 19128/215-487-1300	Episcopal
Cornwall Manor	P.O. Box 125, Cornwall 17016/717-273-2647	Methodist
Dock Woods Community, Inc.	275 Dock Drive, Lansdale 19446/215-368-4438	Mennonite
Elm Terrace Gardens, Inc.	660 North Broad Street, Lansdale 19446/215-362-6087	Baptist
Evangelical Congregational Church Retirement Village	S. Railroad Street, Myerstown 17067/717-866-6541	Congregational
Evangelical Manor	8401 Roosevelt Boulevard, Philadelphia 19152/215-624-5800	Methodist
Foulkeways at Gwynedd	Meeting House Road, Gwynedd 19436/215-643-2200	Friends
Frederick Mennonite Comm	Route 73, Frederick 19435/215-754-7878	Mennonite
G.D.L. Manor Corporation	570 Welsh Road, Huntingdon Valley 19006/215-947-7362	Lutheran
Germantown Home	6950 Germantown Avenue, Philadelphia 19119/215-848-3306	Lutheran
Gettysburg Lutheran Retirement Village	1075 Old Harrisburg Road, Gettysburg 17325/717-334-6204	Lutheran
Green Ridge Village	Big Spring Road, Newville 17241/717-776-3192	Presbyterian
Jefferson Apartments/ Christian Concern, Inc.	1514 West Marshall Street, Norristown 19403/215-539-4844	United Church of Christ
Kendal At Longwood	P.O. Box 100, Kennett Square 19348/215-388-7001	Friends
Landis Homes Ret Comm	1001 East Oregon Road, Lititz 17543/717-569-3271	Mennonite
Lebanon Valley Brethren Home	1200 Grubb Street, Palmyra 17078/717-838-5406	Brethren

Name	Address/Phone	Affiliation
Lewisburg United Methodist Homes	Lewisburg 17837/717-524-2271	United Methodist
Luther Crest	800 Hausman Road, Allentown 18103/215-398-8011	Lutheran
Lutheran Home at Topton	Home Avenue, Topton 19562/215-682-1225	Lutheran
Lutheran Manor Apartments	2085 Westgate Drive, Bethlehem 18018/215-866-6010	Lutheran
Menno-Haven, Inc.	2075 Scotland Avenue, Chambersburg 17201/717-263-8545	Mennonite
Messiah Village	100 Mount Allen Drive, Mechanicsburg 17055/717-697-4666	Brethren
Moravian Hall Square Retirement Community	175 West North Street, Nazareth 18064/215-746-1000	Moravian Church
Moravian Manor	300 West Lemon Street, Lititz 17543/717-626-0214	Moravian Church
Parkview Towers	111 Caroline Street, Munhall 15120/412-461-2993	Methodist
Passavant Retirement and Health Center	401 South Main Street, Zelienople 16063/412-452-5400	Lutheran
Paul's Run Retirement Comm	9896 Bustleton Avenue, Philadelphia 19115/215-934-3000	Lutheran
Penn Lutheran Village	800 Broad Street, Selinsgrove 17870/717-374-8181	Lutheran
Pennswood Village	Route 413, Newtown 18940/215-968-9110	Quaker
Peter Becker Community	Maple Avenue and Yoder Road, Harleysville 19438/215-256-9501	Brethren
Phoebe Home, Inc.	1925 Turner Street, Allentown 18104/215-435-9037	United Church of Christ
Phoebe Terrace, Inc.	1940 Turner Street, Allentown 18104/215-820-9081	United Church of Christ
Presbyterian Apartments, Inc.	322 North 2nd Street, Harrisburg 17101/717-233-5114	Presbyterian
Presbyterian Medical Center, Westminster Pl	1215 Hulton Road, Oakmont 15139/412-828-5600	Presbyterian
Presbyterian Senior Care	825 S. Main St., P.O. Box 677, Washington 15301/412-222-4300	Presbyterian
Quincy United Methodist Home	P.O. Box 217, Quincy 17247/717-749-3151	United Methodist
Riverside Presbyterian Tower	158 North 23rd Street, Philadelphia 19103/215-563-6200	Presbyterian
Rockhill Mennonite Comm	Box 21, Route 152, Sellersville 18960/215-257-2751	Mennonite
Rosemont Presbyterian Vil	404 Cheswick Place, Rosemont 19010/215-527-6500	Presbyterian
Rydal Park	1515 On The Fairway, Rydal 19046/215-885-6800	Presbyterian
Saint Andrew's Village	1155 Indian Springs Road, Indiana 15701/412-349-4870	Presbyterian
Sharpsburg Tower	601 Main Street, Sharpsburg 15215/412-784-0600	Natl Church Residences
Shrewsbury Lutheran Retirement Village	200 Luther Road, Shrewsbury 17361/717-235-6895	Lutheran
Simpson House	Belmont and Monument Avenues, Philadelphia 19131/ 215-878-3600	Methodist
Souderton Mennonite Homes	207 West Summit Street, Souderton 18964/215-723-9881	Mennonite
Tel Hai Retirement Comm	P.O. Box 190, Honey Brook 19344/215-273-3149	Mennonite
Thomas Campbell Christian Ctr	850 Beech Street, Washington 15301/412-225-2290	Christian Church
Wesbury United Methodist Community	31 North Park Avenue, Meadville 16335/814-724-8000	United Methodist
Wesley Village	Laflin Road, Pittston 18640/717-655-2891	Methodist

Rhode Island

Name	Address/Phone	Affiliation
Beneficent House	One Chestnut Street, Providence 02903/401-331-4755	Congregational
United Methodist Ret Center	40 Irving Avenue, East Providence 02914/401-438-4456	United Methodist

South Carolina

Name	Address/Phone	Affiliation
Greenwood Methodist Home	1110 Marshall Road, Greenwood 29646/803-227-1220	Methodist
Martha Franks Baptist Ret Ctr	1 Martha Franks Drive, Laurens 29360/803-984-4541	Baptist
Methodist Home	1000 Live Oaks Drive, SW, P.O. Drawer 327, Orangeburg 29116/ 803-534-1212	Methodist
Presbyterian Home of South Carolina	C M R Box 140, Summerville 29483/803-873-2550	Presbyterian
Westminster Towers	P.O. Box 2894, Rock Hill 29731/803-329-5121	Presbyterian

South Dakota

Name	Address/Phone	Affiliation
Dow-Rummel Village	1000 North Lake Avenue, Sioux Falls 57104/605-336-1490	United Church of Christ, Episcopal

Tennessee

Name	Address/Phone	Affiliation
Appalachian Christian Village	2021 Sherwood Drive, Johnson City 37601/615-928-3168	Christian Churches and Churches of Christ
Ascension Towers	3910 Stuart Road, Memphis 38111/901-454-1108	Lutheran
Christian Towers of Gallatin	138 East Franklin Street, Gallatin 37066/615-452-9363	Church of Christ
Luther Towers	274 South Highland, Memphis 38111/901-323-3639	Lutheran
McKendree Village, Inc.	4347 Lebanon Road, Hermitage 37076/615-889-6990	Methodist

Name	Address/Phone	Affiliation
Park Manor	115 Woodmont Boulevard, Nashville 37205/615-383-7303	Presbyterian
Parkview	1914 Poplar Avenue, Memphis 38104/901-725-4606	Presbyterian
Trezevant Manor and Allen Morgan Nrsng Cntr	177 North Highland at Waynoka, Memphis 38111/901-325-4000	Episcopal
Texas		
Amarillo Good Samaritan Retirement Center	2200 West Seventh, Amarillo 79106/806-374-6896	Lutheran
Bayou Manor	4141 South Braeswood Blvd, Houston 77025/713-666-2651	Presbyterian
Buckner Baptist Village	4800 Samuell Boulevard, Dallas 75228/214-381-2171	Baptist
Crestview Methodist Retirement Community	2501 Villa Maria Rd., P.O. Box 4008, Bryan 77805/409-776-4778	Methodist
Denton Good Samaritan Vil	2500 Hinkle Drive, Denton 76201/817-383-2651	Evangelical Good Samaritan Society
Edgewater Methodist Retirement Community	2228 Seawall Boulevard, Galveston 77550/409-763-6437	Methodist
Golden Palms Retirement and Health Center	2101 Treasure Hills Blvd, Harlingen 78550/512-421-4653	Baptist
Grace Presbyterian Village Ministries	550 East Ann Arbor, Dallas 75216/214-376-1701	Presbyterian
Lake Forest Good Samaritan Vil	3901 Montecito Drive, Denton 76205/817-383-1541	Lutheran
Lakewood Village Ret Center	5100 Randol Mill Road, Fort Worth 76112/817-451-8001	Christian Care Centers
Meadows	730 Babcock Street, San Antonio 78201/512-734-1155	Morningside Ministries
Park Place Towers	1300 South Harrison, Amarillo 79101/806-376-1177	Baptist
Presbyterian Manor, Inc.	4600 Taft Boulevard, Wichita Falls 76308/817-691-1710	Presbyterian
Presbyterian Village North	8600 Skyline Drive, Dallas 75243/214-349-3960	Presbyterian
Trinity Towers Manor Park	2208 North Loop 250 West, Midland 79707/915-689-9898	Presbyterian
Trinity Towers Retirement Ctr	2800 West Illinois, Midland 79701/915-694-1691	Presbyterian
Village Christian Apartments	7925 Rockwood Lane, Austin 78758/512-459-9550	Christian Services, Inc.
White Acres Good Samaritan Retirement Village	7304 Good Samaritan Court, El Paso 79912/915-581-4683	Lutheran
Virginia		
Burke Lake Gardens	9608 Old Keene Mill Road, Burke 22015/703-644-0061	Assembly of God
Culpeper Baptist Ret Comm	P.O. Box 191, Culpeper 22701/703-825-2411	Baptist
Goodwin House, Inc.	4800 Fillmore Avenue, Alexandria 22311/703-824-1185	Episcopal
Heritage Haven Ret Housing	1501 Virginia Avenue, Harrisonburg 22801/703-433-8900	Mennonite
Hermitage	1600 Westwood Avenue, Richmond 23227/804-355-5721	United Methodist
Hermitage in Northern Virginia	5000 Fairbanks Avenue, Alexandria 22311/703-820-2434	Methodist
Hermitage on the Eastern Shore	North Street Extended, Onancock 23417/804-787-4343	Methodist
Hunters Woods Fellowship House	2231 Colts Neck Road, Reston 22091/703-620-4450	Fellowship Square Fndn
Lake Anne Fellowship House	11450 North Shore Drive, Reston 22090/703-471-6474	Fellowship Square Fndn
Lake Ridge Fellowship House	12800 Harbor Drive, Woodbridge 22192/703-494-4455	Fellowship Square Fndn
Lakewood Manor Baptist Retirement Community	1900 Lauderdale Drive, Richmond 23233/804-740-2900	Baptist
Luther Manor	350 Malibu Drive, Virginia Beach 23452/804-463-3510	Lutheran
Newport News Baptist Retirement Community	955 Harpersville Road, P.O. Box 6010, Newport News 23606/804-599-4376	Baptist
Rappahannock Westminster—Canterbury	10 Lancaster Drive, Irvington 22480/804-438-4000	Episcopal, Presbyterian
Retirement Village Ltd.	315 North Second Street, Bridgewater 22812/703-828-3223	Brethren
Sunnyside Presbyterian Retirement Community	P.O. Box 928, Harrisonburg 22801/703-568-8200	Presbyterian
Westminster-Canterbury House	1600 Westbrook Avenue, Richmond 23227/804-264-6000	Episcopal, Presbyterian
Westminster-Canterbury of Lynchburg, Inc.	501 V.E.S. Road, Lynchburg 24503/804-386-3500	Episcopal, Presbyterian
Westminster-Canterbury of Winchester, Inc.	956 Westminster-Canterbury Drive, Winchester 22601/703-665-0156	Episcopal, Presbyterian
Washington		
Bayview Manor	11 West Aloha Street, Seattle 98119/206-284-7330	Methodist
Campus Towers Ret Residence	1767-20th Avenue, Longview 98632/206-423-6200	Baptist

Name	*Address/Phone*	*Affiliation*
Covenant Shores	9150 North Mercer Way, Mercer Island 98040/206-236-0600	Evangelical Covenant
Exeter House	720 Seneca Street, Seattle 98101/206-622-1300	Presbyterian
Fred Lind Manor	1802-17th Avenue, Seattle 98122/206-324-1632	Baptist
Hearthstone	6720 East Green Lake Way N., Seattle 98103/206-525-9666	Lutheran
Hilltop House	1005 Terrace Street, Seattle 98104/206-624-5704	Baptist
Horizon House	900 University Street, Seattle 98101/206-624-3700	United Church of Christ
Judson Park Ret Residence	23600 Marine View Dr. S., Des Moines 98198/206-824-4000	Baptist
Life Manor	1601 South Puget Sound, Tacoma 98405/206-383-3363	Assembly of God
Lilac Plaza	North 7007 Wiscomb Street, Spokane 99208/509-489-7612	Baptist
Northaven, Inc.	11045 Eighth Avenue, NE, Seattle 98125/206-365-3020	Olympic View Community Church
Rockwood Retirement Comm	2903 East 25th Avenue, Spokane 99223/509-536-6650	Methodist
Tacoma Lutheran Home and Retirement Comm	1301 Highland Parkway, Tacoma 98406/206-752-7112	Lutheran
Warm Beach Senior Comm	20420 Marine Drive N.W., Stanwood 98292/206-652-7585	Methodist
Wesley Homes	815 South 216th Street, Des Moines 98198/206-824-5000	Methodist
Yakima First Baptist Homes	6 North Sixth Street, Yakima 98901/509-248-3191	Baptist
West Virginia		
Ceredo Manor	P.O. Box 608, Ceredo 25507/304-453-4544	Natl Church Residences
Wisconsin		
Cedar Crest, Inc.	1700 South River Road, Janesville 53546/608-756-0344	United Methodist
Cedar Lake Home Campus of the Benevolent Corp	5595 Highway Z, West Bend 53095/414-334-9487	United Church of Christ
Evergreen Retirement Community, Inc.	1130 North Westfield Street, P.O. Box 1720, Oshkosh 54902/414-233-2340	United Methodist
Fairhaven Corporation	435 Starin Road, Whitewater 53190/414-473-2140	United Church of Christ
Grace Lutheran Foundation, Inc.	816 Porter Avenue, Eau Claire 54701/715-832-3003	Lutheran
Luther Manor	4545 North 92nd Street, Wauwatosa 53225/414-464-3880	Lutheran
Marquardt Memorial Manor, Inc.	1020 Hill Street, Watertown 53094/414-261-0400	Moravian Church
Northland Lutheran Retirement Community, Inc.	831 Pine Beach Road, Marinette 54143/715-732-0155	Lutheran
Oakwood Village	6201-09 Mineral Point Road, Madison 53705/608-231-3451	Lutheran
Tudor Oaks Retirement Comm	S77, W12929 McShane Rd., P.O. Box 901, Hales Corners 53130/414-529-0100	Baptist
Wyoming		
Heritage Towers	428 North Jefferson Street, Sheridan 82801/307-674-8825	Christian Church

Source: Selected from *1990 American Association of Homes for the Aging Directory of Members.*

65 AND GROWING

Year	*Population*	*Percent*
1900	3,100,000	4.0
1955	9,000,000	6.8
1985	28,500,000	12.0
2030	64,600,000	21.0

Source: US Bureau of the Census

“” FOCUS QUOTE **The family was established long before the church. My duty is to my family first.** —D. L. Moody

85 AND STILL GROWING

Year	*Population*	*Percent*
1900	125,000	4.0
1985	2,700,000	9.5
2030	8,600,000	13.0

Source: US Bureau of the Census

LIVING GOES ON: LIFE EXPECTANCY

Year	*Men*	*Women*
1900	46.3	48.3
1985	71.2	78.2
2030	81.8	87.1

Source: US Bureau of the Census

ORGANIZATIONS OFFERING RETIREMENT PLANNING SERVICES

Write for retirement planning packet:

American Association of Retired Persons
215 Long Beach Blvd., Long Beach, CA 90801

U.S. Government Printing Office
Washington, DC 20402

American Council on Life Insurance
1850 K Street NW, Washington, DC 20006

Action for Independent Maturity
1909 K Street NW, Washington DC 20049

Coming Soon: Age of the Aged

As the old get older, the percentage of young gets dramatically smaller.

Age distribution of total U.S. population

1960	1990	2030	Age:
9.3 %	12.7 %	20.7 %	65 and older
8.6	8.4	8.4	55–64
11.4	10.2	12.1	45–54
13.4	15.2	13.0	35–44
12.7	17.4	12.3	25–34
8.9	10.3	11.6	18–24
35.7	25.8	21.9	Under 18

Source: U.S. Census Bureau

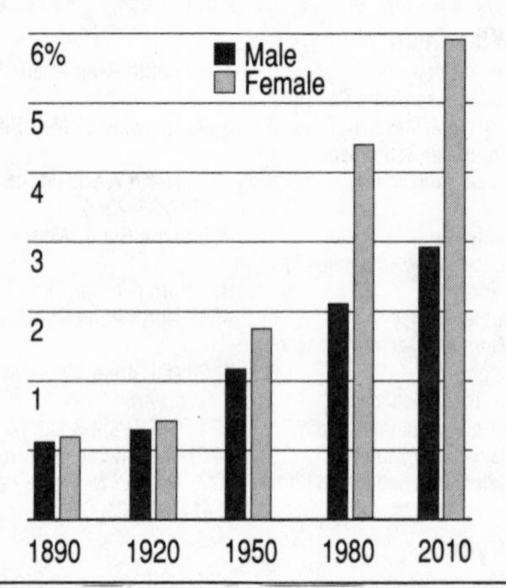

Source: U.S. Census Bureau

GOING ON 75 . . . IT'S TIME TO BE CAREFUL

In 1900, there were about 8,000 cars in the United States, only ten miles of concrete pavement, few spray cans to destroy the ozone layer. Everyone ate natural foods. The air was relatively unpolluted, and the ground was free of aluminum cans. There were no sugar substitutes and no artificial coloring. We had no atomic waste or PCBs, and our average life expectancy was 47 years.

Today we are doing everything wrong, and the life expectancy is up to 75 years, and if we are not careful, it could hit 90.

—William J. McIlrath in *Reader's Digest,* November 1989

A CHILD'S VIEW OF A RETIREMENT PARK

After Christmas break, the teacher asked her small pupils how they spent their holidays. One small boy's reply went like this:

We always spent Christmas with Grandma and Grandpa in their big brick home, but Grandpa got retarded and they moved to Florida.

They live in a place with lots of retarded people; they live in tin huts; they ride three-wheeled tricycles.

They go to a big building called a wrecked hall, but if it was wrecked, it is fixed up now. They play games there and do exercises but they don't do them very well.

There is a swimming pool and they go to it and just stand there in the water with their hats on. I guess they don't know how to swim.

My Grandma used to make cookies and stuff, but I guess she forgot how; nobody cooks there—they all go to the fast food restaurants.

As you come into the Park, there is a doll house with a man sitting in it. He watches all day, so they can't get out without him seeing them.

They all wear badges with their names on them. I guess they don't know who they are.

My Grandma said Grandpa worked hard all his life and earned his retardment. I wish they would move back home, but I guess the man in the doll house won't let them out.

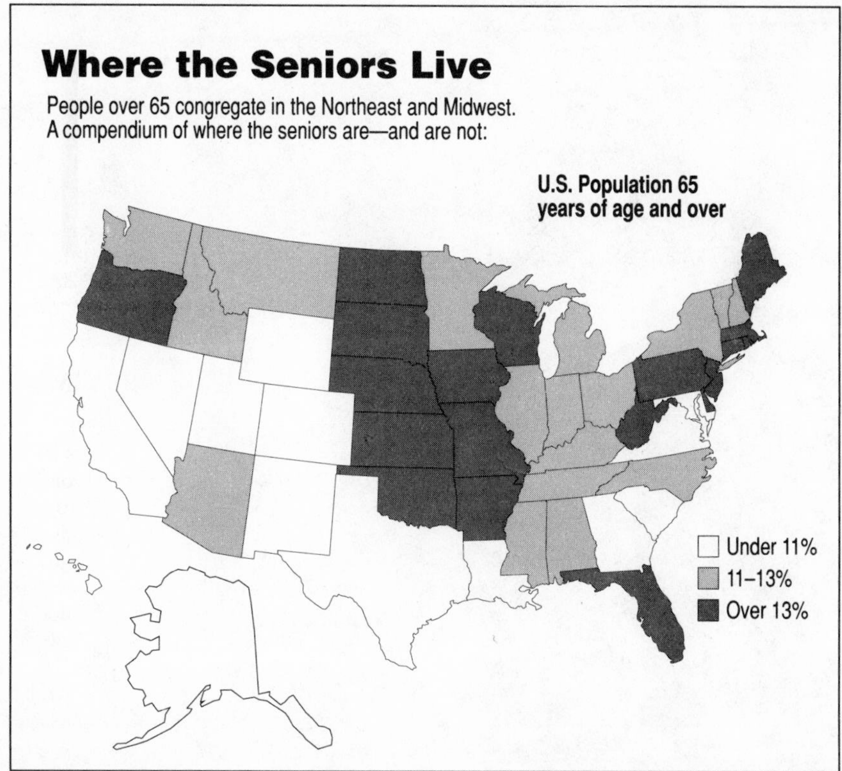

Source: U.S. Census Bureau

Leisure Time

1991 CHRISTIAN TOURS

Location, Travel Agency, Dates and Cost

Bible Study Cruise[a]
Templeton Tours
P.O. Box 2630, Boone NC 28607
(800-334-2630)

Jan 7-11 .... $735 to $895 from FL

Caribbean Capitals
New Creation Cruises & Vacations
Box 574837, Orlando FL 32857-4837
(800-554-5454)

Jan 12-19 .... $1240-$1670
Jan 26-Feb 1 .... $1240-$1670
Feb 9-16 .... $1240-$1670
Feb 23-30 .... $1240-$1670
Mar 9-14 .... $1240-$1670
Mar 23-30 .... $1240-$1670
Apr 6-13 .... $1240-$1670
Apr 20-27 .... $1240-$1670
May 4-9 .... $1240-$1670
May 18-25 .... $1240-$1670
Jun 1-8 .... $1240-$1670
Jun 8-15 .... $1240-$1670
Jun 15-22 .... $1240-$1670
Jun 29-Jul 5 .... $1240-$1670
Jul 13-20 .... $1240-$1670
Jul 27-Aug 2 .... $1240-$1670
Aug 10-17 .... $1240-$1670
Aug 24-31 .... $1240-$1670
Sep 21-28 .... $1240-$1670
Oct 5-12 .... $1240-$1670
Oct 19-26 .... $1240-$1670
Nov 2-9 .... $1240-$1670
Nov 16-23 .... $1240-$1670
Nov 30-Dec 6 .... $1240-$1670
Dec 14-21 .... $1240-$1670
Dec 28-Jan 3 .... $1240-$1670

Coral Ridge Ministries[a,e]
Templeton Tours
105 Meadowview Drive, Boone NC 28607
(800-334-2630)

Feb 11-15 .... $735-$895

Good News Bible Cruise[a,f]
Templeton Tours
105 Meadowview Drive, Boone NC 28607
(800-334-2630)

Mar 4-8 .... $735-$895

Intimate Caribbean
New Creation Cruises & Vacations
Box 574837, Orlando FL 32857-4837
(800-554-5454)

Feb 16-23 .... $1240-$1670
Mar 16-23 .... $1240-$1670
Jun 22-29 .... $1240-$1670
Jul 20-27 .... $1240-$1670
Aug 17-24 .... $1240-$1670
Oct 12-19 .... $1240-$1670
Nov 23-30 .... $1240-$1670
Dec 21-26 .... $1240-$1670

Jubilee at Sea[b,g]
Templeton Tours
105 Meadowview Drive, Boone NC 28607
(800-334-2630)

Feb 3-7 .... $739-$869

Mexican Riviera[c]
Found Free Travel
P.O. Box 17998, Nashville TN 37217
(615-399-1214)

Jan 12-19 .... $795-$1095

Mexico[d,h]
Specialty Travel & Tours
1407 Del Prado Blvd. Suite 13, Cape Coral FL
33990 (800-458-8281)

Jan 13-18 .... $799-$899

Sailabration[a,i]
Templeton Tours
105 Meadowview Drive, Boone NC 28607
(800-334-2630)

Jan 14-18 .... $735-$895

Western Caribbean
New Creation Cruises & Vacations
Box 574837, Orlando FL 32857-4837
(800-554-5454)

Jan 20-25	$755-$1055
Feb 3-8	$755-$1055
Feb 17-22	$755-$1055
Mar 3-8	$755-$1055
Mar 17-22	$755-$1055
Mar 31-Apr 4	$755-$1055
Apr 14-19	$755-$1055
May 12-17	$755-$1055
Jun 9-14	$755-$1055
Jun 23-28	$755-$1055
Jul 7-12	$755-$1055
Jul 21-26	$755-$1055
Aug 4-9	$755-$1055
Aug 18-23	$755-$1055
Sep 1-6	$755-$1055
Nov 3-8	$755-$1055
Dec 8-13	$755-$1055
Dec 22-27	$755-$1055

[a] Star Ship Atlantic
[b] Star Ship Majestic
[c] Star Ship Bermuda
[d] MV Crown Del Mar
[e] with D. James Kennedy
[f] with Dr. Charles Stanley
[g] Steve Roberson and Ralph Sexton, Jr.
[h] with Dr. & Mrs James Merritt
[i] with Adrian Rogers and Jerry Vines

VACATION SPOTS WORTH SEEING

Arizona

Flagstaff, *Oak Creek Canyon*
Scenic route. Spectacular 3,000 foot drop from rim. U.S. 89A between Flagstaff and Sedona 602-774-4505

Grand Canyon National Park
Sheer cliffs drop more than a mile to the floor of the Canyon and the Colorado River; width varies from one to 18 miles. Look for plaques with inscriptions from Mother Basilea Schlink at the Watch Tower at Desert View, at the head of Bright-Angel Trail, and outside Hermit's Rest Gift Ship. Admission fee. North rim (closed during winter) is off AZ Hwy. 67; South rim is off AZ Hwy. 64/U.S. 180 602-638-7888

Phoenix, *Desert Botanical Gardens*
10,000 varieties of desert plants from all over the world. Admission fee. 1201 N. Galvin Pkwy., Papago Park 602-252-8848

Arkansas

Eureka Springs, *The Bible Museum*
Collection of Bibles include handwritten volumes from pre-printing press days. Contains 7,000 volumes of old Bibles and 3,000 primitive manuscripts. Dr. Fred McGraw, Library of Congress, considers this the greatest collection anywhere. Admission fee. Daily May through October 9 A.M. to 8 P.M. except Monday and Thursday, 9 A.M. to 5 P.M. P.O. Box 471, Eureka Springs, AR 72632 501-253-8781

Eureka Springs, *Christ of the Ozarks*
Seven-story concrete sculpture of Christ. Span of the outstretched arms is 65 feet, weight is more than one million pounds. Magnetic Mountain.

Eureka Springs, *Eureka Springs Passion Play*
The drama portrays the story of Jesus, using a cast of more than 200 people. Stage effects include a replica of the street of Jerusalem. Admission fee. Daily May through October, except Monday and Thursday, at 8:30 P.M.; 7:30 P.M. after Labor Day. Off U.S. 62, three miles east of Eureka Springs 501-253-9200

Eureka Springs, *Walls of Jerusalem*
Life-size replica of Old Jerusalem.

California

Anaheim, *Disneyland*
Main Street U.S.A. fantasy. Experience the land of yesterday and the land of tomorrow. Admission fee. 1313 S. Harbor Blvd. 714-999-4000

Garden Grove, *The Crystal Cathedral*
The 120-feet-high, $18 million glass church houses the congregation of televangelist Dr. Robert Schuller. "Hour of Power" telecasts originate here. South of Disneyland off the Santa Ana Frwy.

12141 Lewis St. 714-971-4000

Glendale, *Forest Lawn Memorial Park*

Outstanding trilogy of huge paintings portraying the three most dramatic moments in the life of Christ: The Crucifixion, the Resurrection, and the Ascension. Forest Lawn also contains reproductions of Michelangelo's greatest sculptural works. Brief program of narration, special lighting and sound effects. 1712 S. Glendale Ave. 213-241-4151

Monrovia, *World Vision*

International network of Asian orphanages. Also actively involved in disaster relief and community development projects overseas. Two tours a day at 9:30 A.M. and 1:30 P.M. Tours last about two hours and include an audiovisual presentation. Off U.S. 210. 919 W. Huntington Dr. 818-357-7979

Rancho Palos Verdes, *Marineland*

More than 1,000 fish. The only swim-through coral reef in U.S. Admission fee. 6610 Palos Verdes Dr. South 213-377-1571

San Bernardino, *Arrowhead Springs Christian Conference Center*

Home of Campus Crusade. Spacious grounds. Group tours can be arranged. From Interstate 15E take state highway 18 to Waterman Canyon. Watch for entrance sign into the Conference complex. Campus Crusade, Arrowhead Springs, San Bernardino, CA 92414 714-886-5224

San Bernardino, *Missionary Aviation Fellowship*

Air support agency serving missionaries around the world. Tours are available during work hours. If possible, call in advance. Off I-10, southeast of San Bernardino. 1849 N. Wabash, Redlands Municipal Airport 714-794-1151

San Diego, *Museum of Creation and Earth History*

Opened in 1977 by the Institute of Creation Research, the museum presents evidence that refutes evolution. Associated with Christian Heritage College. Guides are on hand from 1-4 P.M. weekdays. Group tours conducted by appointment. In El Cajon, off U.S. Hwy. 8, east of San Diego 714-440-2443

San Diego, *Sea World*

Killer whales, sharks, great variety of fish, daily marine-life shows. Admission fee. 1720 S. Shores Rd. 619-226-3845

Universal City, *Universal Studios*

Here you can see (and experience) the parting of the Red Sea! An "electronic miracle" creates the illusion. A tour tram waits for the waters to part, then drives through. Five-hour tours through movie/television studios available. Admission fee. Junction Hollywood and Ventura Frwys. 818-508-5444

Victorville, *Roy Rogers/Dale Evans Museum*

Souvenirs of their personal and professional lives. You will see, Roy's famous horse, Trigger, in stuffed form, his gun collection and other displays. Dale's books are on sale in the museum gift ship. On the edge of the Mohave Desert at Victorville on I-15. Near Apple Valley Ranch.

Yosemite Village, *Yosemite National Park*

Half Dome and El Capitan tower above Yosemite Valley. Admission fee. 200 miles northwest of San Francisco off CA Hwy. 140 209-372-0264

Colorado

Colorado Springs, *Air Force Academy Chapel*

The chapel with 150 feet high spires is visible for miles. An aeronautical motif is prominent—the end of each pew in the Protestant chapel is sculptured to resemble an airplane propeller. Open 9 A.M. to 5 P.M. Monday through Saturday and 1 to 5 P.M. Sundays. Worship services at 9 and 11 A.M. are open to the public. 4.5 miles north of Colorado Springs, off I-25 719-472-2555

Colorado Springs, *Garden of the Gods*

1500 acres of towering red sandstone formations. Off I-25 or U.S. 24. 3500 Ridge Rd. 719-578-6933

Colorado Springs, *The Navigators' Glen Eyrie*

Conference center, although visitors are welcome to stop in for a visit. A 67-room sandstone tudor-style castle is the focal

VACATION SPOTS WORTH SEEING cont.

point of the 750-acre scenic grounds. The castle's red tiled roof was shipped, each tile individually wrapped, from England. Exit 146 off I-25. P.O. Box 20, Colorado Springs, CO 80901 303-598-1212

Colorado Springs, *Pike's Peak*
Drive, walk or take cog railway to summit. N. off CO 67 719-635-7506

Golden, *Golden Gate Canyon State Park*
Panorama views of Continental Divide. 2 miles north on CO 93, 14 miles west 303-592-1502

Connecticut

Hartford, *Harriet Beecher Stowe Home*
Harriet Beecher Stowe is author of Uncle Tom's Cabin, a powerful anti-slavery novel that rocked the nation. Next door is the home where Mark Twain once lived. Admission fee. 351 Farmington Ave. 203-527-6984

New Haven, *Yale University*
Concerned Christians launched this Ivy League school in 1701 as an alternative to Harvard. Jonathan Edwards was one of Yale's early graduates.

West Hartford, *Noah Webster House and Museum*
Birthplace of Noah Webster who spent 36 years developing his American Dictionary. Converted at age 40, he studied the Scriptures as diligently as the information which made up his enduring work. 18th century furnishings. Admission fee. North of Rt. 84. 227 S. Main St. 203-521-5262

Woodbury, *Glebe House*
Birthplace of American Episcopacy. Site of Samuel Seabury's election as the first bishop of the Episcopal Church in America. The first floor is an authentically restored home; the second floor is a church museum. Saturday through Wednesday, 1-5 P.M.

D.C.

Washington, *Library of Congress*
340 miles of bookshelves. Exhibits a three-volume, 1455 edition of the Gutenberg Bible. You will see a number of Bible quotations inside this library of libraries. Open daily except on Christmas and New Year's Day. Certain exhibit areas are open from 8:30 A.M. to 9:30 P.M. Monday through Friday; to 6:00 P.M. Saturdays. Closed Sundays and holidays. At the Thomas Jefferson Building, free 45-minute tours begin Monday through Friday, 9 A.M. through 4 P.M., and the 15-minute multi-media show before every hour starts at 8:45 A.M. Southeast of the Capitol. First St. and Independence Ave. 202-287-5000; James Madison Memorial Bldg. is 287-5111

Washington, *Lincoln Memorial*
Daniel Chester French marble statue of Lincoln. Erected in honor of Lincoln's greatness. Some of his more memorable words are inscribed in the walls, including his second inaugural address. West Potomac Park at 23rd St. NW 202-426-6895

Washington, *National Archives*
On view are the three foundational documents that underlie our national government: The Declaration of Independence, the United States Constitution, the Bill of Rights. Open daily. Constitution Ave. between 7th and 9th Streets, NW 202-523-3000

Washington, *National Presbyterian Church and Center*
Contains The Chapel of the Presidents, dedicated to Dwight D. Eisenhower, whose pew is marked. Seventeen presidents have worshiped here.

Washington, *National Shrine of the Immaculate Conception*
Largest Roman Catholic church in the United States. Headquarters for the Roman Catholic church in the United States. Michigan Ave. and Fourth St. NW.

Washington, *St. John's Church*
Built in 1816, it is often called the "Church of the Presidents." Every president since James Madison has attended it. Lower Manhattan's Lafayette Square.

Washington, *Thomas Jefferson Memorial*
19-foot bronze statue of Jefferson. Quotes inscribed in the walls will remind you of basic truths on which our country was founded. South bank of Washington's Tidal Basin, SW 202-426-6822

Washington, *United States Capitol*
A gallery pass from your Congressman will allow you to watch proceedings if Congress is in session. Each session opens in prayer, a tradition that began in 1774 when Rev. Jacob Duche offered the first prayer in the Continental Congress. Open 9 A.M. to 4:30 P.M. daily from November through April; until 10 P.M. the rest of the year. Capitol Hill, lst St.

Washington, *United States Supreme Court*
Classical building built in 1935. A tableau of the Ten Commandments is one of the emblems above the Bench. Moses is included among the great lawgivers in Herman A. MacNeil's marble sculpture group on the east front. Open 9 A.M. to 4:30 P.M. Monday through Friday; closed on Saturday, Sunday and holidays. 1st St. and Maryland Ave. NE 202-479-3000

Washington, *Vietnam Veteran Memorial*
Black granite wall. Names of those who gave their lives for freedom in Vietnam inscribed on wall. West end of the Mall 202-357-2700

Washington, *Washington Bible College*
Offers a limited number of guest accommodations during the school year. Is a 20-minute drive into the heart of the Capitol. Special rates for people in full-time Christian work. 6511 Princess Garden Pkwy, Lanham, MD 20801 301-552-1400

Washington, *Washington Monument*
Towering 555 feet into the air, the Washington Monument is Washington D.C.'s most prominent landmark. Elevator takes visitors to top. Admission fee. On the Mall near 15th St. NW 202-426-6839

Washington, *Washington National Cathedral*
Situated on the highest point of land in D.C.—Mount St. Alban. Famous men are buried here. Every year, more than 500,000 visit—to mourn a leader, to tour the Cathedral, to worship.

Washington, *The White House*
Tours of public rooms available 10 A.M. to noon, Tuesday through Saturday. During summer Saturday hours extended to 2 P.M. Closed Sunday, Monday and some holidays. No admission fee. E. Executive Ave. and 15th St. 202-456-2200

Delaware

Wilmington, *Old Swedes Church*
Oldest church in the United States standing as originally built and regularly used for church services. Built and dedicated in 1698 as Helga Trefaldighet Kyrcka (Holy Trinity Church) by Swedish settlers. Heart of Wilmington's industrial district.

Florida

Boca Raton, *Bibletown*
Winter Bible conference and sacred concert complex. Winter concerts run January through March. 2,000-seat auditorium. P.O. Box A, Boca Raton, FL 33432 305-391-7800

Florida City, *Everglades National Park*
Largest subtropical wilderness in U.S. Admission fee. 10 miles SW on FL 997 305-247-6211

Ft. Myers, *Shell Point Village*
Christian and Missionary Alliance retirement community. 75-acre village with more than 1,000 residents. McGregor Blvd., 15 miles south of Ft. Myers on Rt. 867, Ft. Myers, FL 33901 813-481-3737

Ft. Myers, *Thomas A. Edison Winter Home*
Home, gardens, laboratory. Admission fee. 2350 McGregor Blvd. 813-334-3614

Lake Buena Vista, *Walt Disney World*
Magic Kingdom, Epcot Center, MGM Studios Theme Park. Admission fee. 22 miles SW of Orlando, north on I-4. 305-824-2222

Orlando, *Sea World*
Marine shows, water-ski shows, fish. Admission fee. 7007 Sea World Dr. 305-351-0021

St. Petersburg, *Moody Keswick Bible Conference*
Largest winter Christian conference grounds on Florida's west coast. Sacred music concerts on Saturday nights from January to April. 7500 100th Way North, St. Petersburg, FL 33708 813-391-2998

Tampa, *Busch Gardens*
African theme; 3,000 animals. Allow a full day for this one. Admission fee. 3000

VACATION SPOTS WORTH SEEING cont.

Busch Blvd. 813-971-8282

West Palm Beach, *Lion Country Safari*
Experience jungle life. Drive through this 320-acre preserve to see animals in their natural environment. 18 miles west of I-95 on FL 80 305-793-1084

Winter Haven, *Cypress Gardens*
Boat trips through the Gardens. Daily water-skiing shows. Admission fee. SE off U.S. 27 on FL 540 813-324-2111

Georgia

Atlanta, *Jimmy Carter Library*
Exhibits on the Carter presidency. 1 Copen Hill, east of State Capitol 404-331-0296

Atlanta, *Martin Luther King, Jr., District*
Includes tomb and birthplace of Martin Luther King, Jr., as well as the Ebenezer Baptist Church where he was pastor. Open daily 9:30 A.M. to 5:30 P.M. Tours: Monday–Saturday at 10 A.M. to 4 P.M. 522 Auburn Ave. NE 404-331-3919

Columbus, *Callaway Gardens*
Resort, sports, and leisure education facilities on acres of gorgeously landscaped scenery. Approximately 15 miles north of Columbus off I-185.

St. Simons Island, *Christ Church*
Founded by Wesley Brothers in 1736. Island is setting of Eugenia Price best-selling novels.

Savannah, *Christ Episcopal Church*
John Wesley founded what is believed to be the world's first Sunday school at Christ Episcopal Church. 28 Bull St.

Savannah, *First African Baptist Church*
Organized in 1788, the first black church in the United States. 403 W. Bryan St.

Toccoa Falls, *Toccoa Falls Park*
At 186 feet the falls are 17 feet higher than Niagara Falls. Toccoa Falls College is nearby. Open daily until sundown.

Hawaii

Honolulu, Oahu, *Kawaiahao Church*
Honolulu's oldest church, the Westminster Abbey of Hawaii. The setting for royal inaugurations, weddings, funerals and other pageantry. Sunday services at 10:30 A.M. are in both Hawaiian and English. Open daily. 957 Punchbowl St. 808-538-6267

Honolulu, Oahu, *Pearl Harbor*
National historic landmark. The USS *Arizona* Memorial of the December 7, 1941 Japanese attack. Free tour of the USS *Arizona*. Daily except Mondays from Halawa Landing. 1 Arizona Memorial Place 808-422-2771

Lahaina, Maui, *Historic Lahaina Experience*
Begins at the onetime home of medical missionary Dr. Dwight Baldwin. Largest Banyan tree in the islands was planted in 1873 to commemorate the 50th anniversary of the first missionaries to arrive on the island. The tree spreads over two-thirds acre. Daily 10 A.M. to 4 P.M.

Illinois

Carbondale, *Bald Knob Cross*
Lighted white marble cross, visible day and night; Bald Knob Mountain, Illinois' second highest peak. Shawnee National Forest.

Charleston, *Lincoln Log Cabin State Park*
Final Illinois home of the Lincolns.

Chicago, *Moody Bible Institute*
Half-hour multimedia show. Moodyana Museum houses D.L. Moody's old artifacts. Tours begin at 10 A.M. and 1 P.M. 820 N. LaSalle St.

Chicago, *Moody Church*
Founded by D.L. Moody. Sunday services at 10:45 A.M. and 7 P.M. Across from Lincoln Park, at North Ave. and Clark St.

Chicago, *Pacific Garden Mission*
Granddaddy of U.S. rescue missions. The site was once an old-time beer garden. Evening services at 7 P.M. Open daily, 24 hours. Late afternoon and early evening visits recommended. 646 S. State St. 312-922-1462

Chicago, *Rockefeller Chapel*
One of the outstanding examples of Gothic architecture in the United States. Completed in 1928 at a cost of nearly $2,000,000. University of Chicago campus, 57th and Woodlawn Sts.

Decatur, *Lincoln Trail Homestead State Park*
First log cabin built by the Lincolns.

Salem, *William Jennings Bryan Birthplace*
White frame house of his birth contains

many of his personal possessions—family pictures, Bibles, law books, walking cane. Open daily from 1 to 5 P.M., except Thursdays. 618-548-1236

Springfield, *Lincoln Depot*
Here Lincoln's Springfield days ended with a farewell speech: "I now leave, not knowing when or whether ever I may return, with a task before me greater than that which rested upon Washington." On Monroe between 9th and 10th Sts.

Springfield, *Lincoln's Springfield Home*
It was in this modest clapboard home that Lincoln received the announcement of his nomination for the presidency in 1860. 426 S. 7th St. 217-492-4150

Springfield, *Lincoln's Tomb*
178 feet high granite spire marks the tomb of Lincoln and his family. Monument Ave. 217-782-2717

Wheaton, *Wheaton College*
Houses the Marion E. Wade Collection of books and papers by C.S. Lewis, J.R.R. Tolkien, Dorothy Sayers, and other writers of faith. Tours conducted three times daily at 11:15 A.M., 1:30 and 3:00 P.M. 25 miles east of Chicago.

Wheaton, *Billy Graham Center*
Panorama view of American evangelism from early church leaders to the present-day Billy Graham Evangelistic Association. Open 9:30 A.M. to 5:30 P.M. Tuesday, Wednesday, Thursday and Saturday; 1 to 9 P.M. Friday; 1 to 5 P.M. Sunday. 25 miles west of Chicago 708-260-5909

Indiana

Hammond, *First Baptist Church*
One of the largest Sunday schools/churches in the United States. Sunday school hour on Sundays at 9:30 A.M. 523 Sibley Blvd.

Nappanee, *Amish Acres*
Complex depicts the religious beliefs and customs of a people who still hold to the life-style of 17th century Europe. Outstanding Amish family style restaurant. Open daily 9 A.M. to 8 P.M. May through October; weekends only from November through April. 1 mile west of Nappanee on U.S. 6.

Valparaiso, *Chapel of the Resurrection*
Seating 3,000, one of the largest houses of worship on a college chapel. Valparaiso University campus, off U.S. 30.

Iowa

Amana, *Amana Colonies*
Iowa's most popular tourist attraction, the seven colonies blend the Old World with the new. Shops, factories and restaurants. Six museums within the 27,000-acre grounds. Take exit 225 between Des Moines and Davenport off I-80. Amana Colonies Travel Council, Amana, IA 52203 319-622-3828

Dubuque, *Mississippi River*
Mississippi River boat rides. Woodward Riverboat Museum—exhibits cover 300 years of riverboat history. Admission fee. 2nd St. Harbor 319-557-9545

Nashua, *Little Brown Church in the Vale*
Draws nearly 150,000 visitors a year. A popular wedding chapel. Couples come from all over the world. About forty miles northeast of Waterloo. Two miles northeast of Nashua on U.S. Hwy. 218.

West Branch, *Herbert Hoover's National Historical Site*
Birthplace and gravesite of former U.S. President Herbert Hoover. Schoolhouse Hoover attended, his father's blacksmith shop, and the Herbert Hoover Presidential Library-Museum. Admission fee. One-half mile north of Exit 254, off I-80 319-643-2541

Kansas

Abilene, *Eisenhower Center*
Family home, museum and library, chapel, and gravesites. Open 9 A.M. to 5 P.M. daily, year-round. 201 SE 4th St. 913-263-4751

Cedar Vale, *Wee Kirk of the Valley*
Perhaps the smallest church in U.S. The six pews seat two persons each—symbolic of the twelve disciples. In south central Kansas, 6 miles south of Cedar Vale.

Medicine Lodge, *Carry Nation Home*
Carry Nation, temperance crusader during the late 1800's and early 1900's, made use of her hatchet, Bible and loud-voiced

VACATION SPOTS WORTH SEEING cont.

prayers to break up or put out of business many liquor establishments. Today her home is a museum. U.S. Hwys. 160 and 281.

Kentucky

Bardstown, *My Old Kentucky Home State Park*

Stephen Foster outdoor drama. Mansion built 1793-1818 by Judge J. Rowan. Admission fee. 502-348-5971

Harrodsburg, *Shakertown*

The Shaker Village of Pleasant Hill, situated on more than two thousand acres, has been restored as a rural Shaker community in the early nineteenth century. Pleasant Hill Shakertown, Rt. 4, Harrodsburg, KY 40330 606-734-5411

Park City, *Mammoth Cave National Park*

Kentucky cave area. 300 miles of caverns. The Diamond Caverns are the gem of Kentucky caves with flowstone formations. Take Park City exit 48 off I-65 502-749-2891

Park City, *Mammoth Cave Wax Museum*

129 lifelike figures of famous Americans. Includes Leonardo da Vinci's "Last Supper," Moses receiving the Ten Commandments, and Billy Graham. Take Park City exit 48 off I-65.

Park City, *Wondering Woods*

Reconstructed 1900s town. Crafts and other skills are demonstrated. Sunday morning worship services in Old Community Meeting House. Take Park City exit 48 off I-65 to the junction of Hwys. 70 and 255. Chamber of Commerce, Rt. 1, Box 149, Wondering Woods, KY 42160 502-749-5221

Louisiana

Monroe, *Bible Research Center*

Very old and rare manuscripts, Bibles, engravings, maps, portraits and musical instruments are on display. Open Monday through Thursday. Closed in August. 2004 Riverside Dr.

Maryland

Annapolis, *U.S. Naval Academy*

Impressive ceremony of noon formation on Tecumseh Court at 12:05 P.M. weekdays, at 12:10 on Saturdays, and 12:30 on Sundays and holidays, weather permitting. The museum has one of the world's finest displays of sailing ship models. Open daily. Visitors Center, Ricketts Hall 301-263-6933

Baltimore, *Fort McHenry*

It was here on September 14, 1814 that lawyer Francis Scott Key jotted down the words to the Star Spangled Banner on the back of an old letter. Key was one of the founders of the American Sunday School Union. Admission fee. Three miles from Baltimore on East Fort Ave. Open 9 A.M. to 5 P.M. seven days a week 301-962-4290

Baltimore, *Lovely Lane Methodist Church*

Collection of Methodist historical materials. Contains John Wesley's personal copy of *Imitation of Christ*, a fragment from the diary of Susanna Wesley, possibly the first pulpit used by a Methodist preacher in America. Open weekdays 9 A.M. to 4 P.M. and Sundays after church. St. Paul and 22nd Sts. 301-889-1512

Massachusetts

Boston, *The Boston Tea Party Ship and Museum*

From Boston Harbor on the Freedom Trail a courtesy bus will take you there for a tour of a full-scale replica of the brig Beaver, one of the invaded British vessels. Tea-tossing. Congress St. Bridge 617-338-1773

Boston, *Freedom Trail*

The three-mile long trail is a walking tour of 16 sites and structures in downtown Boston and Charlestown. A red line on the sidewalk directs you from site to site. Originates at Information Center, Boston Common 800-858-0200

Boston, *Park Street Church*

An evangelical bastion, the church stands on Boston Common. In 1831 "America" was first sung here. In 1942 the National Association of Evangelicals was organized in this church. Sunday services at 10:30 A.M. and 7:30 P.M. Boston Common.

Pittsfield, *Hancock Shaker Village*
The third Shaker settlement, Hancock, "the City of Peace" was established in 1790. The Village recaptures the Shaker legacy of fine craftsmanship, love and simplicity. Admission fee. Open daily, June 1 to October 31. 5 miles west of Pittsfield at Rts. U.S. 20 and MA 41 413-443-0188

Plymouth, *Burial Hill*
Up a stone stairway where the first Pilgrim Fort was located and where Governor William Bradford is believed to be buried near his son. In back of the First Church in Town Square.

Plymouth, *The Mayflower Experience*
Three electronic theaters allow you to experience the voyage on the Mayflower during its historic crossing. Next to the Governor Bradford Motel. 114 Water St.

Plymouth, *Mayflower II*
Replica of the original Mayflower. "Crewman and passengers" will tell you about their experiences on the 1620 voyage. Anchored at the State Pier next to Plymouth Rock 508-746-1622

Plymouth, *Pilgrim Hall Museum*
The oldest historical museum in America. Contains the most complete collection of Pilgrim possessions and lore. Open daily. 75 Court St. at Chilton St. 508-746-1620

Plymouth, *Plimoth Plantation*
A re-creation of life in Plymouth Colony as it was in the early 1800's. 3 miles south of Plymouth Rock on Rt. 3A 508-746-1622

Plymouth, *Plymouth Rock*
The rock is small and under cover, yet it is symbolic of the inscription on the Plymouth Rock monument which reads: "They laid the foundation wherein every man through countless ages should have liberty." On the waterfront overlooking Plymouth Harbor.

Provincetown, *The Pilgrim Monument*
It is here on November 21, 1620 that the Pilgrims first touched shore. The tallest granite structure in the USA, the 255-foot monument dominates the town and is a landmark for fishermen, sailors and tourists. Daily throughout the summer. Town Hill, off Bradford St. 508-487-1310

Stockbridge, *Mission House*
In Stockton, Jonathan Edwards spent the final 8 years of his life among the Indians, while writing his famous theological treatises. Main and Sergeant Sts.

Stockbridge, *Norman Rockwell Museum*
18th century Georgian House. Exhibits many of Norman Rockwell's paintings. The famous Americana painter spent the final years of his life in Stockbridge. Admission fee. Main St. 413-298-3822

Williamstown, *Haystack Monument*
The Monument commemorates the historic haystack prayer meeting which resulted in the beginning of the foreign missions movement.

Michigan

Albion, *Birthplace of "The Old Rugged Cross"*
A bronze marker indicates where the Rev. George Bennard wrote what has become one of the most beloved hymns of all time. He once served in the Salvation Army but later became an itinerant evangelist. He died in 1958, relatively unknown. College Ct. and Michigan Ave.

Dearborn, *Greenfield Village/Henry Ford Museum*
300 years of Americana. Colonial homes and Motor House. Admission fee. 20900 Oakwood Blvd. 313-271-1620

Frankenmuth, *Christmas Village*
It's Christmas any time of the year in this Bavarian town where you can always shop for Christmas decorations and ornaments. A German missionary, August Craemer, led 15 immigrants from Bavaria to Frankemuth in 1845 to establish a home base for mission outposts. 517-652-6106

Holland, *Holland Tulip Festival*
Here you can see one of the largest tulip plantings in the country, visit a wooden shoe factory, tour a Netherlands museum, enjoy folk dances and a "Festival Musicale," a mix of hymns, anthems and spirituals. Write Tulip Time Office, Civic Center, 8th and Pine, Holland, MI 49423 616-396-4221

VACATION SPOTS WORTH SEEING cont.

Minnesota

Minneapolis, *Bethany Fellowship*

The complex has a Christian school, factory, church, mission society and publishing house. Tours available upon request on weekdays at 10 A.M. and 3 P.M. Write 6820 Auto Club Rd., Minneapolis, MN 55438 612-944-2121

St. Cloud, *Shakinah Bible Gardens*

This $3.8 million project includes gardens and waterfalls, re-creations of the Garden Tomb and Golgotha, and a 400-seat amphitheater. The exhibit center includes walk-in replicas of the Temple, Solomon's House, & Herod's Palace. Adjacent to St. Cloud off I-94. P.O. Box 823, St. Cloud, MN 56301 612-253-2811

Mississippi

Lucedale, *Palestinian Gardens*

Authentic scale model of the Holy Land at the time of Christ. Twenty acres scaled one yard to a mile. A walk through the gardens will acquaint you with Holy Land geography. Excellent preparation for a trip to Israel. 12 miles north of Lucedale, 6.5 miles east of U.S. Hwy 98. Rt. 9, Box 792, Lucedale, MS 39492

Missouri

Diamond, *George Washington Carver Monument*

Birthplace of a slave who rose to fame as a godly educator and agriculturalist. The Visitor Center traces Carver's career and achievements. Carver once said, "I love to think of nature as an unlimited broadcasting system through which God speaks to us." From Neosho or Carthage, take U.S. 71 Alternate to Diamond, then go west 2 miles on County Hwy V and south 1 mile.

Kansas City, *Hallmark Visitor's Center*

Presents history of Hallmark's growth. Crown Center Complex 816-274-3613

Independence, *Harry S. Truman Library and Museum*

Presidential Library of America's 33rd president and gravesite. Admission fee. U.S. 24 and Delaware St. 816-833-1400

Montana

West Glacier, *Glacier National Park*

Glacier adjoins Waterton Lakes National Park in Canada and the two parks comprise the Waterton/Glacier International Peace Park. 10,000 foot peaks, more than 50 glaciers. Worship services can be found on Sundays at more than a dozen locations. Admission fee. On U.S. Hwy 2 406-888-5441

Nebraska

Omaha, *Boys Town*

Now internationally known, Father Edward J. Flanagan in 1917 opened a facility for homeless boys. Tours of the 400-acre facility include the dairy farm and the Music Hall where the world-famous Boys Town Choir rehearses. Open daily from 8 A.M. to 4:30 P.M. 134th and W. Dodge Rds. 402-498-1111

New Hampshire

Hanover, *Dartmouth College*

Like other famous Ivy League schools, Dartmouth College was one of the results of the First Great Awakening. Its royal charter, signed by King George III, specified the school's intent to reach the Indian tribes and to educate English youth.

New Jersey

Princeton, *Princeton University*

Originally called "The College of New Jersey," Princeton was another outcome of the First Great Awakening. Jonathan Edwards and John Witherspoon, signer of the Declaration of Independence, were among Princeton's first presidents. Off Rts. 1 and 206 609-921-6748

New Mexico

Santa Fe, *The capital city of New Mexico*

The nation's most unusual capital. A full decade before the Pilgrims landed at Plymouth Rock, Don Pedro de Peralta established it. The Indians still hold open-air markets as they have for centuries. It is the nation's oldest city (1610) and its highest (7,000 feet). 800-777-CITY

Santa Fe, *Old Mission Churches*

The ancient city has several historic

mission churches including St. Francis Cathedral, Loretto Chapel—with its mysterious spiral staircase— and San Miguel Mission, the oldest mission church in the United States.

Taos, *Mission of St. Francis of Assisi*

One of the most beautiful Spanish churches in the southwest. Contains the mysterious painting, "The Shadow of the Cross" by Henri Ault. In daylight it portrays the barefoot Christ. In darkness, the portrait becomes luminescent, outlining the figure while clouds over Jesus' left shoulder form into a cross.

New York

New York City, *Historic New York City churches*

Visit: Trinity Church on Wall St., St. Paul's Chapel at Broadway and Fulton Sts., St. Patrick's Cathedral at 5th Ave. and 50th St., Cathedral of St. John the Divine at Amsterdam Ave. and 112th St., Riverside Church at Riverside Dr. and 122nd St., and Marble Collegiate Church at 29th St. and 5th Ave. Tours available. Check with each church for details.

New York City, *Salvation Army Headquarters*

Most Friday evenings from October through May the Salvation Army presents an inspirational program at its Centennial Memorial Temple. Tours of the territorial headquarters on the same site may be arranged in advance. 120 W. 14th St., between 6th and 7th Aves. 212-620-4968

New York City, *Statue of Liberty*

For more than a century the Statue of Liberty has been holding high the torch of freedom. The Statue of Liberty was given by the people of France to the people of the United States in recognition of ties forged during the American revolution. Open daily from 9 A.M. to 5 P.M. Extended hours in effect on weekends during the spring season; seven days a week during the summer. The Statue of Liberty Ferry leaves every hour on the hour from Battery Park, in lower Manhattan, to take you to Liberty Island where you follow the broad mall to the statue. 212-363-3200

West Point, *Cadet Chapel*

The Chapel dominates the entire Academy. This classic edifice of Gothic architecture contains the world's largest church organ. Sunday morning services are open to the public. Sunday evening concerts by the Military Academy Band, July and August. NY Hwy. 218 at New South Post 914-938-2638

North Carolina

Blue Ridge Parkway

469 miles of magnificent scenery on the Blue Ridge crest. Many natural and historic attractions. Runs between Great Smoky National Park and Shenandoah National Park in Virginia.

Murphy, *The Ten Commandments, Large Print edition*

At Field of the Wood, the Ten Commandments can be read in letters five feet high and four feet wide, all carved in stone. One mile away stands a 2,210-foot All Nations Cross, largest of its kind in the world. Open daily. West of Murphy and east of Turtletown off Hwy. 294.

Ohio

Canton, *Christian Hall of Fame*

Canton Baptist Temple contains 100 original oil portraits of Christian leaders from New Testament times to the present day. The 260 feet of corridors include paintings of Tertullian, Luther, Calvin, Knox, Carey, Hudson Taylor, and Billy Sunday. Off U.S. Rt. 30. 515 Whipple NW.

Cincinnati, *Harriet Beecher Stowe House*

In this house, Harriet Beecher Stowe researched what would become a classic best-seller, *Uncle Tom's Cabin*. The book, released in 1852, soon sold more than 300,000 copies. Stowe memorabilia, exhibits on black history. Open Tuesdays through Sundays. 2950 Gilbert Ave. 513-632-5120

Mentor, *Home of President James A. Garfield*

Lawnfield, home of the 20th president of the USA and the only president who was also an ordained preacher, is furnished with Garfield's personal possessions. Garfield

VACATION SPOTS WORTH SEEING cont.

preached frequently and once baptized 40 converts during an evangelistic campaign. Open daily except Mondays from mid-April to November. On U.S. 20. 8095 Mentor Ave. 216-255-8722

Oklahoma

Tulsa, *Oral Roberts University*

The University which evangelist Oral Roberts founded in 1963 has become Tulsa's top tourist attraction drawing about 180,000 visitors a year. All visits begin in the Prayer Tower at the heart of the campus. Tours are usually self-guided. Media presentations available on a continuous basis from 8:30 A.M. to 5:30 P.M. 2-1/2 miles south of the Skelly Bypass (I-44 and U.S. 66) on Lewis Ave.

Pennsylvania

Bethlehem, *Historic Bethlehem*

In 1741 a small group of Moravians from Germany settled in Bethlehem to minister to the Indians and the German settlers of Pennsylvania. The original Bethlehem has been restored, and to visit is to step back into three centuries of history. 11 W. Market St., Bethlehem, PA 18018 215-867-3788

Fallsington, *Historic Fallsington*

Fallsington's first houses were built by friends and followers of William Penn. This untouched village mirrors 300 years of American architectural history, from a primitive log cabin to the Victorian extravaganzas of the 19th century. Admission fee. Open March 15 to November 15, Wednesday through Sunday, 1 to 5 P.M.

Gettysburg, *Prince of Peace Museum*

Artist Paul Cunningham has re-created the life of Christ in a series of colorful, life-like three-dimensional scenes. South of Gettysburg Sq. on Rt. 15.

Hershey, *Hershey Gardens*

Theme gardens. 25,000 rose plants. Spring flowers. Admission fee. Park Blvd. 717-534-3005

Kennett Square, *Longwood Gardens*

One of the most beautiful gardens in the east. 350 acres, 20 indoor gardens. Former estate of Pierre S. Du Pont. U.S. 1 215-388-6741

Lancaster, *Pennsylvania Dutch Country*

Ride an Amish buggy, tour an Amish kitchen, watch Swiss cheese being made, shop at farmers markets and factory outlets. Explore both antiques and boutiques. Live as guests in a private Amish home. Lancaster County. Pennsylvania Dutch Visitors Bureau provides a tour guide and map, and a 72-page booklet "Pennsylvania Dutch Country Sampler." 1799 Hempstead Rd., Lancaster, PA 17601 717-299-8901

Philadephia, *Freedoms Foundation at Valley Forge*

Patriots Hall of Fame, a walk-through exhibit honoring famous Americans. "Forge of Freedom" and a multimedia presentation in the visitor center theatre. Faith of Our Fathers Chapel features Washington at prayer. Open air concerts during summer. For concert schedule write Freedoms Foundation, Valley Forge, PA 19481 215-933-8825

Philadelphia, *Independence Hall*

"The most historic square mile in America" where delegates to the Second Continental Congress debated whether or not to declare independence from Great Britain. Visitors may view the chamber in which the Constitution was framed. Independence National Historical Park 215-597-8974

Philadelphia, *The Liberty Bell*

July 8, 1776, the Liberty Bell heralded the news of liberty to the land. By coincidence, Leviticus 25:10 was inscribed on the bell: "Proclaim liberty throughout the land unto all the inhabitants thereof." Now in a glass and steel pavilion. Behind Independence Hall.

Philadephia, *University of Pennsylvania*

When Philadelphia churches denied George Whitefield access to their pulpits, some of his supporters, including Benjamin Franklin, erected a building to accommodate the crowds that wanted to hear him. This became the University's first building.

Philadelphia, *Valley Forge*

This 2500-acre park includes Washington's winter camp 1777-78, an old house owned by Quaker preacher Isaac Potts, a collection of Revolutionary arms and the original tent Washington used in the field, and Washington Memorial Chapel. N. Gulph Rd. and PA Hwy. 23 215-783-7700

Scranton, *Steamtown, USA*

World's largest collection of steam locomotives and steam era rolling stock, including the massive Union Pacific "Big Boy," the largest steam locomotive ever built. Train excursions available. Open May through October. 700 Lackawanna Rd.

Rhode Island

Providence, *Brown University*

Brown was one of the five colonial universities organized as a result of the First Great Awakening. Art galleries, Rockefeller Library and the Annmary Brown Memorial housing rare Renaissance books. At edge of city on Prospect Ave. 401-863-1000

Providence, *The First Baptist Church in America*

The first Baptist church in America, First Baptist in Providence has maintained continuous services for more than 350 years. From this first group came the largest Protestant movement in America. The present church dates back to 1775. Tours available 10 A.M. to 3 P.M. weekdays and 10 A.M. to noon on Saturdays, April through October.

South Carolina

Greenville, *Bob Jones University*

Houses one of the most important art collections in the Southeast. Its gallery of Sacred Art and Bible Lands Museum contains 30 rooms displaying the art of Europe from the thirteenth through the nineteenth centuries also includes works of major artists. Open from 2 to 5 P.M. throughout the year except Mondays.

South Dakota

Keystone, *Mount Rushmore National Monument*

Black Hills. Heads of four American presidents carved from the face of granite: George Washington, Thomas Jefferson, Abraham Lincoln and Theodore Roosevelt. The project took 14 years to complete. Off U.S. Hwy. 16A 605-574-2523

Rapid City, *Norwegian Chapel-in-the-Hills*

Exact copy of the famous 800-year-old Borgund Church in Norway. More than a half million have visited the church with its intricate wood carvings, dragon heads and ingenious construction. Vesper services at 8 P.M. during summer months. Southest of Rapid City off Hwy. 44.

Spearfish, *Black Hills Passion Play*

More than 200 actors and actresses dramatize the World's Greatest Story three times a week. The play depicts the Roman domination over Palestine, the devotion of the disciples and friends, and the supreme sacrifice of Christ. Mid-June through late August, every Sunday, Tuesday and Thursday. For best choice of seats, order tickets in advance. Black Hills Passion Play, Box 469, Spearfish, SD 57783 605-642-2646

Tennessee

Gatlinburg, *Christus Gardens*

Of special interest to children, life-size beeswax scenes include the Nativity, the Sermon on the Mount, "Suffer Little Children to Come Unto Me," and the Last Supper. The rotunda houses the nation's most complete collection of coins of biblical times. A half block from the center of Gatlinburg on River Rd. 615-436-5155

Gatlinburg, *National Bible Museum*

300 rare volumes of the Bible in 120 languages are on display. Artifacts date back to 1500 B.C., including a lamp believed to be from the time of Abraham. Admission fee. Open most of the year except Sundays. Between Christus Gardens and Aerial Tramway.

Nashville, *Baptist Sunday School Board*

Huge complex in downtown Nashville covers several blocks and employs about 1500 people. Largest postal customer in Nashville and responsible for Nashville being second only to Washington, D.C. in volume of second class mail shipped. One hour tours with audiovisual presentations weekdays from 8 A.M. to 3 P.M. 127 Ninth Ave. N., Nashville, TN 615-251-2796

Nashville, *Grand Ole Opry*

Live radio program featuring country music. 1804 Opryland Dr. 615-889-7502

VACATION SPOTS WORTH SEEING cont.

Nashville, *Methodist Publishing House*
Presses roll out approximately 100 Abingdon book titles a year, church school material and millions of *The Upper Room* magazine each month. Tours daily Monday through Friday at 10 A.M. and 2 P.M. 201 Eighth Ave. S.

Nashville, *The Parthenon*
Replica of the Greek Parthenon. Exact size of the original although materials are different. 9 A.M. to 4:30 P.M. Tuesday through Saturday, 1 to 4:30 P.M. Sundays. Centennial Park, West End Ave. 615-259-6358

Texas

Dallas, *Biblical Arts Center*
Exhibit centers around a 124 feet long and 20 feet high painting depicting the Miracle at Pentecost. Dramatic 30-minute sound and light presentation every hour at half past the hour. Admission fee. Open Tuesday through Saturday, 10 A.M. to 5 P.M. 7500 Park Ln. at Boedeker 214-691-4661

San Marcos, *Aquarena Springs*
Features Ralph, the diving pig, who does a swine dive into 71-degree Spring Lake. Underwater aquatic show, alligator exhibit and an old West Texas town are other attractions. Admission fee. Open daily except Christmas from 9 A.M. to 5:30 P.M. Take Exit 30 off I-35 for half a mile.

Utah

Salt Lake City, *Temple Square*
Symbolic heart of Mormonism. The Square is dominated by the Mormon Temple on the east, the Tabernacle on the west and a visitor's center filled with Mormon history. Noon recitals and Thursday Tabernacle choir rehearsals are open to the public. N., S., and W. Temple Sts. and Main St. 801-531-2534

Virginia

Virginia Beach, *700 Club*
View the filming of the 700 Club and the total operation of the Christian Broadcasting Network. Weekday tours every half hour from 10:30 A.M. to 2:30 P.M. For tickets write 700 Club "Tickets," CBN Center, Virginia Beach, VA 23463 804-424-7777

Williamsburg, *Colonial Williamsburg*
Relive the 18th century in this mile-long colonial city, restored by John D. Rockefeller, Jr., "that the future may learn from the past." 100 original buildings. Admission fee. Take Colonial Williamsburg exit off I-64 804-229-1000

Wisconsin

New Glarus, *Little Switzerland*
Relive Swiss history—visit a reconstructed blacksmith shop, schoolhouse, store, cabin, cheese factory and a replica of the first Swiss log church built for worship in 1849. U.S. Rts. 39 and 69.

Wyoming

Grand Teton National Park, *Church of the Transfiguration*
One of Wyoming's most photographed scenes. A wall of glass behind the altar permits a broad view of the towering sawtooth Teton range. The park itself has more than 200 miles of trails. 4 miles west of Jackson on U.S. 26/89/191 307-733-2880

STATE TOURISM OFFICES

Write or phone for helpful information.

Alabama Bureau of Tourism & Travel, 532 S. Perry St., Montgomery, AL 36104 1-800-Alabama

Alaska Alaska Division of Tourism, P.O. Box E, Juneau, AK 99811 907-465-2010

Arizona Office of Tourism, 1100 W. Washington, Phoenix, AR 85007 602-542-Tour

Arkansas Department of Parks and Tourism, 1 Capitol Mall, Little Rock, AR 72201 1-800-482-8999 (within state), 1-800-643-8383 (outside state)

California Office of Tourism, 1121 L Street, Suite 103, Sacramento, CA 95814 1-800-862-2543; X 100 (outside state)

Colorado Tourism Board, 1625 Broadway,

Suite 1700, Denver, CO 80202 1-800-433-2656

Connecticut Tourism Promotion Service, 865 Brook St., Rocky Hill, CT 06067 203-566-3948 (within state), 1-800-CT BOUND (outside state)

Delaware Tourism Office, 99 Kings Highway, P.O. Box 1401, Dover, DE 19903 1-800-441-8846

District of Columbia Washington Convention and Visitors Association, 1212 New York Ave., NW Washington, D.C. 20005 202-789-7000

Florida Department of Commerce Visitors Inquiry, 126 Van Buren St., Tallahassee, FL 32399 904-487-1462

Georgia Tourist Division, P.O. Box 1776, Atlanta, GA 30301 404-656-3590

Hawaii Visitors Bureau, 2270 Kalakaua Ave., Suite 901, Honolulu, HI 96815 808-923-1811

Idaho Department of Commerce, 700 W. State St., Boise, ID 83720 1-800-635-7820

Illinois Bureau of Tourism, 620 East Adams St., Springfield, IL 62701 217-782-7139

Indiana Tourism Division, 1 North Capitol, Suite 700, Indianapolis, IN 46204 317-232-8860

Iowa Bureau of Tourism, 200 E. Grand Ave., Des Moines, IA 50309 515-281-3100

Kansas Travel & Tourism Development, 400 W. 8th St., 5th Floor, Topeka, KS 66603 913-296-2009

Kentucky Department of Travel Development, Capital Plaza Tower, Frankfort, KY 40601 1-800-225-TRIP

Louisiana Office of Tourism, P.O. Box 94291, Baton Rouge, LA 70804 1-800-334-8626

Maine Publicity Bureau, 97 Winthrop St., P.O. Box 2300, Hallowell, ME 04347 207-289-2423

Maryland Office of Tourism Development, 217 E. Redwood St., Baltimore, MD 21202 301-333-6611

Massachusetts Office of Travel and Tourism, 100 Cambridge St., 13th Floor, Boston, MA 02202 617-727-3201

Michigan Travel Bureau P.O. Box 30226, Lansing, MI 48909 1-800-543-2937

Minnesota Minnesota Office of Tourism, 375 Jackson St., 250 Skyway Level, St. Paul, MN 55101 1-800-652-9747 (within state), 1-800-328-1461 (outside state)

Mississippi Division of Tourism, P.O. Box 849, Jackson, MS 39205 1-800-647-2290

Missouri Division of Tourism, 301 W. High St., P.O. Box 1055, Jefferson City, MO 65102 314-751-4133

Montana Travel Montana, 1424 9th Ave., Helena, MT 59620 1-800-541-1447

Nebraska Division of Travel and Tourism, 301 Centennial Mall South, P.O. Box 94666, Lincoln, NE 68509 1-800-742-7595 (within state), 1-800-228-4307 (outside state)

Nevada Commission on Tourism, Capitol Complex, Carson City, NV 89710 1-800-NEVADA-8

New Hampshire Office of Vacation Travel, P.O.Box 856, Concord, NH 03301 603-271-2666

New Jersey Division of Travel and Tourism, CN-826, Trenton, NJ 08625 609-292-2470

New Mexico New Mexico Tourism & Travel Division, Room 119, 1100 St. Francis Dr., Santa Fe, NM 87503 1-800-545-2040

New York Division of Tourism, 1 Commerce Plaza, Albany, NY 12245 1-800-225-5697

North Carolina Travel and Tourism Division, 430 North Salisbury St., Raleigh, NC 27611 1-800-VISIT NC

North Dakota North Dakota Tourism, Liberty Memorial Building, Capitol Grounds, Bismarck, ND 58505 701-224-2525 (within state), 1-800-437-2077 (outside state)

Ohio Ohio Division of Travel and Tourism, P.O. Box 1001, Columbus, OH 43266 1-800-BUCKEYE

Oklahoma Oklahoma Tourism and Recreation Dept., P.O. Box 60000, Oklahoma City, OK 73146 1-800-652-6552

Oregon Tourism Division, 595 Cottage St., NE, Salem, OR 97310 1-800-543-8838 (within state), 1-800-547-7842 (outside state)

Pennsylvania Bureau of Travel Development, 453 Forum Building, Harrisburg,

PA 17120 1-800-VISIT PA, X 275

Rhode Island Rhode Island Tourism Division, 7 Jackson Walkway, Providence, RI 02903 401-277-2601

South Carolina South Carolina Division of Tourism, Box 71, Columbia, SC 29202 803-734-0235

South Dakota Department of Tourism, Capitol Lake Plaza, Pierre, SD 57501 1-800-952-2217 (within state), 1-800-843-1930 (outside state)

Tennessee Department of Tourist Development, P.O. Box 23170, Nashville, TN 37202 615-741-2158

Texas Travel Information Services, P.O. Box 5064, Austin, TX 78763 512-463-8971

Utah Utah Travel Council, Council Hall, Capitol Hill, Salt Lake City, UT 84114 801-538-1030

Vermont Travel Division, 134 State St., Montpelier, VT 05602 802-828-3236

Virginia Division of Tourism, 202 North Ninth St., Suite 500, Richmond, VA 23219 804-786-4484

Washington Washington State Dept. of Trade and Economic Development, 101 General Administration Bldg., Olympia, WA 98504 206-753-5630

West Virginia Department of Commerce, State Capitol Complex, Charleston, WV 25305 1-800-225-5981

Wisconsin Division of Tourism, Box 7606, Madison, WI 53707 1-800-432-TRIP

Wyoming Wyoming Travel Commission, 1-25 at College Drive, Cheyenne, WY 82002 1-800-225-5996

FAVORITE VACATION SPOTS

ACW asked: "What is your favorite vacation spot?" The replies:

Jim Dobson: Mammoth Lake, CA. This is where we have made our warmest memories for our family.

Bill and Gloria Gaither: We've celebrated the childhood of Suzanne, Amy and Benji on the Nantucket, Massachusetts, beaches. Each year we've watched their little footprints grow bigger. And now we make the island our welcome mat for grown-up days.

Tim Hansel: Elk Canyon Ranch, a few miles out of Bozeman, MT. It must be one of the most beautiful places on planet earth. "Exquisite " is almost an understatement. Nestled in the mountains of Montana's big sky country, it is a western resort that has everything—horseback riding, tennis, swimming and some of the finest fly-fishing in the country. The accommodations are elegant and the food is four-star. I asked my family recently what was the most fun place they had ever been. And in unison they all cried, "Elk Canyon Ranch."

Billy Melvin: Chesapeake Bay, VA, because the fishing is good and I like the peace and tranquility.

Norman Vincent Peale: Either St. Moritz or Interlaken, Switzerland. Mrs. Peale and I like to walk on high mountain paths—good for body, good for soul. You're among mountain peaks and deep valleys. Gives physical exercise and spiritual inspiration.

Eugenia Price: Almost anywhere IF the place is small or so large I'm not likely to be recognized. Vacation for me—at least my favorite times—are those when a novel is really rolling. My own home is my favorite spot! But, now and then, Joyce Blackburn, with whom I live and work, and I need to get away from the mailbox and the telephone, so we select either a tiny town with a comfortable motel and some history to explore or a huge city—New York, Atlanta, etc.—in which I can, if I keep my trip a secret, "get lost" in a good hotel with dependable room service! We often rent a condo at Fernandina Beach, FL, or on Sanibel Island, FL. I seek no tennis, no golf, NO fishing nor boating! What I seek is nothing to do but read someone else's books.

Chuck Swindoll: My favorite vacation spot is not limited to a particular place but is a setting where certain ingredients are present. First, my wife and all those in our family. Next, a broad mixture of pleasurable delights: early morning quietness and the solitude of uninterrupted silence, a variety of activites throughout the day that may include exercise, a boat ride, water-skiing, fishing for the ultimate wide-mouth bass, laughter, meals, conversation, a hot cup of coffee by a campfire, a great book, and watching the sun set in all its colorful splendor. Ideally, those days provide time to reflect on where I've been—the lessons learned, the goals accomplished, the struggles endured, the blessing enjoyed—and to entertain a few random thoughts on where I'm going. Making such settings complete includes the moving strains of magnificent music, refreshing and unguarded discussions with my grown children and my sister, walks in the woods or along a seashore, fun stuff, plus hugs and kisses from my grandkids, and certainly meaningful moments all alone with Cynthia as we deliberately give ourselves permission to take time to sift the essentials from the incidentals.

TIPS FOR HAPPY VACATIONS

1. **Have reasonable expectations** rather than impossible ones that invariably lead to disappointment. A vacation will not necessarily make you a new person or salvage a troubled marriage.
2. **Examine your past vacations**. Be objective, but be compassionate. Don't vilify yourself, no matter how your past trips have turned out. Think of ways they could be improved.
3. **Relax**. Don't hurry past the beauty. Joy is a gentle and delicate living thing. Let it happen.
4. **Don't take yourself too seriously**. Expect some obstacles. Embrace them. Laugh at them if you can. Convert them into part of your vacation. Make an adventure out of your inevitable mishaps. Murphy's Law—which says that if anything can possibly go wrong, it will not only do so, but at the worst possible time—still has a habit of inviting itself on a lot of vacations. Don't let it ruin yours.
5. **Be creative**. Put a little variety into your celebrations. Don't let someone from a travel agency plan your happiness. Let your imaginative juices flow. Make each vacation a once-in-a-lifetime experience.
6. **Take all of you on vacation**. Use all of your senses. This is a time when you can be whole, when you can use your smeller for something more than just to hang your glasses on, and those funny-looking contraptions on the side of your head for something more than just to keep your hat off your shoulders. Don't just eat; taste your food. Let your vacation be a five-sense event.
7. **Plan a strategy for vacation diet**. Enjoy your food, but don't make it the whole purpose of your vacation. Resistance is usually a little lower during vacations. Fatigue, frustration, or even boredom sometimes stimulate indulgence. Have a plan. Overeating can ruin a vacation. Take low-calorie snacks for those long rides in the car.
8. **Get regular exercise**. A good balance between rest and activity is best.
9. **Take short vacations if long ones make you homesick**, especially if you are taking one of those special getaways without the kids. But give yourself enough time to unwind fully.
10. **Forget such maxims as "Hard work deserves a rest."** Don't spend all your time justifying your vacation.
11. **Break your routine**. Get up at a different time than you usually do during the year. If you never get to read—read. If you read as part of your job—put down the books for a few weeks.
12. **Do something unusual**. Be an experimenter. Meet new people, try new experiences. Let people think you're loony. Wear a funny hat or put your shirt on backwards for a day. Roller-skate down a shopping mall. Climb a mountain, or a

tree. Don't wear a watch for a week. Hug a tree, fly a kite, wear a button, jog in triangles. Fool somebody. Fool two somebodies. Go for a long walk in your bare feet. Poke some holes in your rigidity. This is not a time to be timid. Take a chance. It's worth it.

13. **Do something a little extravagant**. Buy something you've always wanted. Let go a little bit. Don't be so reasonable all the time.
14. **Learn something new** on your vacation. Teach yourself to play chess, or learn to needlepoint. Learn calligraphy and send fancy postcards to all your friends.
15. **Learn to look for the best and laugh at the worst**. You will usually see what you are looking for. Choose to see the good, the best, the beautiful. Also choose to laugh at the crazy things that always want to go on vacation with you—flat tires, flat hair, flat spirits, flat experiences.
16. **Give yourself permission to be happy**. Practice it. Work hard to eliminate that free-floating guilt that says you should be working or doing something more useful, and that you shouldn't be having such a good time.
17. **Let the hero out in you**. Live each day and each vacation as if it were your last opportunity. Rejoice and crack the skies with laughter. Let your passion for being alive and being one of God's people encourage you to be the very best you can be.

Source: Tim Hansel in *When I Relax, I Feel Guilty*. Published by David C. Cook Publishing Company. Copyright © 1979. Used by permission.

VACATION IDEAS

1. **Health vacations**. If you're feeling a little sluggish, maybe you need to spend some time focusing on yourself and your health. Develop some solid health patterns. It may be a tennis vacation, a jogging vacation on the coast, a cycling vacation to some friends, or a hiking vacation in the mountains. Work on filling your lungs with a lot of oxygen, your mind with a lot of good thoughts, and your body with a lot of good food.
2. **Educational vacations**. Learn something new: how to fix a car, do woodwork, or rock-climb. Go somewhere to learn how to paint or cook, or set aside special time at home to take classes at a local college.
3. **Back-roads vacations**. Use only back roads. Enjoy all the serendipitous events that naturally happen on such a trip.
4. **Children's vacations**. Let your children plan and, as much as possible, implement a short vacation. It might be very exciting seeing the world from their eyes. Stay flexible, and plan on a lot of surprises.
5. **Cheap vacations**. Discover how much you can do with as little money as possible. How many things can you do for twenty-five cents? One dollar? What can your whole family do for five dollars? Look in the newspapers for all the free films and exhibits you can go to. List all the places you can explore for nothing. How creative are you at eating for a day on $1.12?
6. **Sunset Magazine vacations**. Many of us want our houses to look like Better Homes and Gardens. But we need time to develop ideas that will fit our particular home. Take the time! Leave the children home and go see different kinds of architecture, color patterns, fences, and porch designs. Take a sketch pad and talk of all the wild possibilities over dinner.
7. **Reinventory vacations**. Take time to remember what is special to you. Redefine your values. What are some of your lifetime dreams? Your priorities? How could you improve? Be specific. Take whatever resources along with you that you might need (Bible, writing material, tapes, other books, etc.), but don't forget that unhurried and uncrowded time will be your most important resource.
8. **Memory lane vacations**. Revisit some of those special places that have been hallmarks in your life. Take the time to see old

friends. Spend some evenings remembering, laughing, telling stories, and maybe even going through some of the old annuals. Relish the nostalgia for a while.

9. **Evangelistic vacations**. Make your distinct purpose to share your faith in Jesus Christ. Revitalize not only the lives of other people but your own as well.
10. **Just Being vacations**. Take off your watch for a while. Forget what time it is. Eat when you're hungry instead of at noon. Reestablish your relationship with God, with your lifetime companion, and with yourself on the basis of who you are rather than what you do. Travel very light, plan very little, lead with your heart, and let life surprise you around every corner.
11. **Vacations you train for**. It may be a bike trip. Select a purpose and make a vacation out of getting ready for it.
12. **Seeing vacations**. Deliberately spend some days (either at home or traveling) to discover the magic of seeing. See color, for example. Follow one color for the whole day. You will be amazed at how much you've been blind to. Sit quietly on the grass and allow your eyes to marvel at the world around you. A bush, a cloud, or a leaf might become an unforgettable experience. Take along a camera, and photograph the splendor you see. If you like, choose to focus on seeing and photographing faces for a day.
13. **A wonder trip**. Explore the magnificence of life with all your senses. There is so much more there than normally meets the eye. Take time to ask questions rather than seek answers. How does grass grow up through cement? How does a bird fly? How do grunion know to ride the high tide?
14. **Gourmet vacations**. Turn an evening into a mini vacation by immersing yourself without inhibition into the life of a gourmet. Dress in your fanciest. Eat very slowly, tasting every morsel. Feast on the candlelight atmosphere. Take a menu home for memories.
15. **Change of life-style or service vacations**. Take your family to the midwest to work on a farm, or to help friends build a house. What about arranging a long trip with a truck driver you know? Volunteering your services at a hospital or a convalescent home?
16. **Exploration vacations**. Your only limit here is creativity. Explore a friendship through traveling together on a vacation. Explore a book or an idea.
17. **Once-in-a-lifetime specials**. Design a day around going for a ride in a helicopter, or going to a horse race. Find a bookbinder and find out how books are bound. Go skydiving or shoot the rapids. Go to an umbrella factory or follow the whole process behind the making of toilet paper.
18. **One parent, one child occasions**. Spend quality time with one of your children. It can just be dinner together, or it can be a whole weekend trip. You might participate in an event together or explore an idea together.
19. **Rest vacations**. Go somewhere where no one can find you, take the phone off the hook, and spend most of the days horizontal. Give yourself permission to get recharged.

Source: Tim Hansel in *When I Relax I Feel Guilty*. Published by David C. Cook Publishing Company. Copyright © 1979. Used by permission.

SERVICE OPPORTUNITIES AT HOME AND ABROAD

This directory is designed to introduce you to a range of short-term mission opportunities you may not know about. The directory contains a wide selection of jobs, places and agencies. You can find a way to use a two-week vacation, a summer, or up to three years of your life.

ABMJ/Chosen People Ministries
1300 Cross Beam Drive
Charlotte, NC 28217
(704)257-9000
Galen Banashak
Program. Summer Training and Evangelism

SERVICE OPPORTUNITIES AT HOME AND ABROAD cont.

(STEP), 4 wks. training, 2 wks. outreach.

Agency Background. Founded 1894 by Rabbi Leopold Cohn. ABMJ/CPM pioneered the biblical evangelistic methods still used in Jewish missions around the world.

Requirements and Costs. 18 yrs. and older, desire to reach Jewish people with the gospel. $995 for training, outreach covered by participating churches.

Training Provided. Scripture study, understanding and handling Jewish objections to Jesus. Evangelism experience during outreach.

Work Description. Visitation and door-to-door evangelism. Also help conduct Jewish evangelism seminars at participating churches.

Countries Served. U.S. cities, Israel, Argentina, Canada

Action International

P.O. Box 490
Bothell, WA 98041
(206)485-1967
Pearl Kallio

Program. Summer of Service (SOS), 8 wks; misc. short-term projects, 2 wks.–2 yrs.

Agency Background. Founded 1974, Interdenom. agency doing evangelism, Bible distribution, church planting, social work, support of nationals.

Requirements and Costs. 19 yrs. and older; prof. skills useful for longer term commitments. Raise own funds. SOS: approx. $2300. Other short terms: vary according to location and commitment.

Training Provided. SOS: 1-wk. orientation. Other short terms: depends on length of commitment.

Work Description. Discipleship, evangelism, counseling, youth work, Bible studies, music, drama, administration, literature distribution, social work, prison work, church planting. With SOS, live in homes of nationals.

Countries Served. Philippines

Africa Inland Mission Int'l

P.O.Box 178
Pearl River, NY 10965
(914)735-4014
Mr. Warren H. Day, Short/Full Term Program (STP) (FTP)
Mr. Wade Ewing, Volunteer Program (VP)

Program. FTP: 4 yrs. STP: 1–3 yrs. VP: 10 wks.–12 mos.

Agency Background. Founded 1895. Interdenom. missions agency serving 14 countries.

Requirements and Costs. 19 yrs. and older. Agree with doctrinal statement, French required in Zaire and Comoro Islands. Raise own funds. STP: cost varies according to location. VP: approx. $2500–$2800 for 3 mos.

Training Provided. STP: required orientation offered twice yearly. VP: orientation materials sent through mail (incl. reading), pre-field orientation of 1–2 days; 3 days for those going to Kenya.

Work Description. STP: development work, evangelism, medical work, Bible teaching, church planting, education. VP: clerical, teaching, construction, youth work, evangelism, general support ministries.

Countries Served. Africa and the surrounding islands

AIMS: World Christian Expeditions

P.O. Box 64534
Virginia Beach, VA 33464
(804)424-6333
Pat Foltz

Program. World Christian Expeditions (WCE) Participants are linked with existing programs of other short-term agencies. Variety of opportunities offered. About 200/calendar year.

Agency Background. Project of Association of International Mission Service (AIMS), which networks with individuals, churches, agencies and training institutions.

Requirements and Costs. Vary according to the agency selected.

Training Provided. Training materials available for purchase.

Work Description. Construction, medical,

drama, evangelism, Bible distribution, musical, helps.

Countries Served. Varies according to the agency selected. Europe, USSR, Africa, South America, LA/Central America, Far East, South East Asia, Middle East

Baptist General Conference (BGC) World Mission

2002 S. Arlington Hts. Rd.
Arlington Hts., IL 60005
(800)323-4215
John Marrs

Program. 6 mos.–2 yrs. Special ministries may be less than 6 mos.

Agency Background. Founded 1850s. Multiethnic denom. with cross-cultural witness in North America and 11 foreign countries.

Requirements and Costs. Must be a member of a BGC church. Prefer a minimum of 2 yrs. of college or equivalent experience, and technical skill. Raise own funds: varies with position and country. Single: $7800–$14,000/yr.

Training Provided. Orientation on the field.

Work Description. English teaching, puppetry, medicine, youth ministry, famine relief, and agricultural extension. Short-termers also serve in theological and MK schools, as well as in a guest house and child care.

Countries Served. Eastern Europe, Mexico, Far East, Eastern & Western Africa, Middle East, Latin America, urban areas of United States.

Caleb Project

1605 E. Elizabeth Street
Pasadena, CA 91104
(818)794-1532
Shane Bennett

Program. Joshua Project, Fall and Spring (5–6 mos.)

Agency Background. Interdenom. service agency, seeking to encourage and equip Christians to commit themselves to world evangelization.

Requirements and Costs. Complete "Perspectives on the World Christian Movement" course. Basic spiritual maturity and relational fitness. Raise own funds: $4500–$5000.

Training Provided. Advance reading and counsel. 5-week pre-field training before departure. Follow-up of 3 weeks.

Work Description. Teams conduct relationally-based sociological research in large cities to identify unreached peoples and encourage Christian workers.

Countries Served. Asia, Middle East, North Africa

Camp-of-the-Woods

Gilmantown Road
Speculator, NY 12164
(518)548-4311
C. Robert Purdy

Program. Cross-cultural Exchange camps, 4–10 wks.

Agency Background. International camping ministry to families & youth; Non-denominational. Founded 1900.

Requirements and Costs. College-age and older. Serve whole/part summer in USA as part of project. Raise own funds. $1000–$2500 (incl. airfare)

Training Provided. Personal spiritual growth, development of leadership potential, living and learning in a cross-cultural environment.

Work Description. Christian education (ages 3–12); teen activity leaders; camp and staff counselors, small group leaders. General maintenance and service projects.

Countries Served. Hong Kong, South Africa

Campus Crusade for Christ

Dept. 36-50 Arrowhead Springs
San Bernardino, CA 92414
(714)886-5224 ext. 5273
Penny Poppinga

Program. U.S. Summer Projects, 10–13 wks.

Agency Background. Founded 1951. Campus Crusade helps to fulfill the Great Commission by actively communicating the message of Jesus Christ to college students throughout the world.

Requirements and Costs. College student; $600–$1500, depending on project. Job also required while on project.

SERVICE OPPORTUNITIES AT HOME AND ABROAD cont.

Training Provided. Training throughout the program.

Work Description. Train others in evangelism and discipleship.

Countries Served. United States, urban and other areas.

Campus Crusade for Christ Int'l
(U.S. Campus Ministries)
Dept. 36-50 Arrowhead Springs
San Bernardino, CA 92414
(714)886-5224 ext. 5560
Randy Pierfelice

Program. Worldwide Student Network (WSN), Overseas Summer Opportunities, 6–8 wks.

Agency Background. In addition to the emphasis of Campus Crusade, WSN helps students of the world reach the world.

Requirements and Costs. Christian with teachable attitude, willing to share his or her faith. $1500–$3300, varies with location.

Training Provided. 1-wk. orientation in cross-cultural sensitivity, personal evangelism and follow-up. Support development materials provided.

Work Description. Show *Jesus* film to unreached peoples, personal evangelism, train national Christians, use of some vocational skills (especially medical).

Countries Served. East Africa, Southeast Asia, South America, Western Europe, Far East

Christian Camping International/USA
P.O. Box 646
Wheaton, IL 60189
(708)462-0300

Program. Summer staff and year-round positions at more than 1000 camps in the USA and hundreds of camps overseas.

Agency Background. CCI/USA is an association of Christian camps and conference centers with 11 sister associations around the world.

Requirements and Costs. Each individual camp determines their own transportation, salary, and benefits package.

Training Provided. Varies with each camp.

Work Description. Counselors, lifeguards, wranglers, teachers, nurses, food service workers, maintenance workers, etc.

Countries Served. Worldwide

A Christian Ministry in the National Parks
222 1/2 E. 49th Street
New York, NY 10017
(212)758-3450
Warren Ost

Program. Program staff in parks, 3–15 mos., year-round.

Agency Background. Founded 1952. Interdenom. ministry started by student working at Yellowstone Nat'l Park.

Requirements and Costs. College-age, flexible, contagious faith, disciplined work habits. Raise own transportation costs to/from park. Pay own rm/brd.

Training Provided. 2-day orientation.

Work Description. Work at secular job in the park (i.e. desk clerks, bellhops, waitressing, etc.), friendship evangelism.

Countries Served. In 65 U.S. national parks.

Christian Missionary Fellowship (CMF)
P.O. Box 8537
Ft. Collins, CO 80524
(303)225-9949
Joe Varela

Program. 1–3 mos.

Agency Background. Founded 1969. Nondenom.

Requirements and Costs. Agree with doctrinal statement. Raise own funds: $300/mo. plus airfare.

Training Provided. 2-week class for linguistic and support raising assistance for those who can travel to Colorado.

Work Description. Construction, evangelism, discipleship or prison work.

Countries Served. West Africa

Christian Outreach Int'l
12480 Wayzata Boulevard
Minnetonka, MN 55343
(612)541-5344
Jack Isleib

Program. Evangelizing through the medium of music and sports. Trips are about 25 days or can be longer.

Agency Background. C.O.I. is an interdenom. sending agency, organizing teams and lay people for short/long term mission work overseas. Founded in 1984.

Requirements and Costs. Personal commitment to Christ. Good music/sports ability. Application procedure. Desire to win souls to the Lord. Cost: $1150–$3500—short-term.

Training Provided. Training and orientation camp is held in the U.S. prior to departure, emphasizing practical evangelism and skill development.

Work Description. Evangelism using music/sports as a tool, reaching out to a wide variety of people in and out of churches. Ministry takes place in public squares, schools, athletic events, concerts. Wonderful opportunity to travel and minister the Gospel, and experience great personal growth. Daily Bible studies and group meetings.

Countries Served. U.K., Sweden, Finland, Norway, Germany, Switzerland, Italy, France, Holland, Germany, Austria and the Soviet Union.

Conservative Baptist Foreign Mission Society
P.O. Box 5
Wheaton, IL 60189
(708) 665-1200
Raymond Buker, Jr.

Program. Missionary Assistant Corps (MAC), 10 wks.–2 yrs.

Agency Background. A denom. sending agency engaged in evangelism, establishing churches and serving national churches. Also involved in education, literature, linguistics, medicine, radio and national support.

Requirements and Costs. Good health, fully trained for the position, single or married, able to sign CBFMS evangelical doctrinal statement. Raise own funds: $400/mo–$1000/mo. plus airfare.

Training Provided. Brief pre-field orientation and on-site training.

Work Description. Evangelism, church planting, home Bible studies, literature distribution, camp counseling, teaching, house-parenting, maintenance, construction, secretarial work, bookkeeping, and farming.

Countries Served. South America, Africa, Asia, Europe, Far East

Destination SUMMIT
New Tribes Mission
Sanford, FL 32771
(407)321-6196

Program. Assist, Summer (8 wks.) and Winter (4 wks.)

Agency Background. Founded 1979. Nondenom. division of New Tribes Mission. Emphasis on work in tribal regions.

Requirements and Costs. 15 yrs. and older. Raise own funds, costs vary with location and program.

Training Provided. 4-day orientation, follow-up.

Work Description. Missionary support, maintenance, construction and other manual labor.

Countries Served. East Asia, West Africa, Latin America, Greenland.

Destination SUMMIT
New Tribes Mission
Sanford, FL 32771
(407)321-6196

Program. INTERFACE Summer (9 wks.)

Agency Background. Founded 1989. Nondenom. Division of New Tribes Mission. Emphasis on study in tribal regions.

Requirements and Costs. 17 yrs. thru retirement. Raise own funds: $2981.

Training Provided. Brief pre-field orientation continued on-site.

Work Description. On-site college-level missions course, includes language and culture study with tribal people for teachers!

Countries Served. Papua New Guinea—Highlands Province

Eastern European Bible Mission (EEBM)
P.O. Box 110
Colorado Springs, CO 80901
(303)577-4450
Bill Baker, Margaret Sims

Program. Summer Mission Program, 1 mo. min., 2 mos. aver.

Agency Background. Non-denom. agency

SERVICE OPPORTUNITIES AT HOME AND ABROAD cont.

working to strengthen the church in Eastern Europe.

Requirements and Costs. Age range: 22–70. Sometimes families, good health, agree with doctrinal statement. German is helpful. Raise own funds: $32/day (Eastern Europe), $16/day (Holland); plus airfare.

Training Provided. Pre-field training manual to study; support-raising ideas and materials; in Europe, 30 hrs. of classroom training.

Work Description. Serve as teachers and encouragers in camps and seminars; work with children, teens and adults.

Countries Served. Eastern Europe

Eastern Mennonite Board of Missions
Oak Lane and Brandt Blvd.
Salunga, PA 17538-0628
(717)898-2251
Dan Gehman

Program. Youth Evangelism Service (YES) 7–11 mos.

Agency Background. Founded 1914. Denom. agency of Mennonite tradition with emphasis on community development, evangelism, support of national churches.

Requirements and Costs. Personal commitment to Christ and desire to share faith through word and deed. Raise own funds: $4000–$5000.

Training Provided. 1-day orientation; 3 mos. training in discipleship, evangelism, and hands-on experience; 1 mo. on-location language study for most teams.

Work Description. The team lives together and is involved in street (drama/mime), youth and other evangelism ministries.

Countries Served. Latin America, Central/Northern Europe, Far East, United States, Caribbean

Eastern Mennonite Board of Missions
Oak Lane and Brandt Blvd.
Salunga, PA 17538-0628
Dan Hoellwarth

Program. Summer TRAINING ACTION Teams (STAT). 2 mos.

Agency Background. Founded 1914. Denom. agency of Mennonite tradition with emphasis on community development, evangelism, support of national churches.

Requirements and Costs. Personal commitment to Christ and desire to share faith through word and deed. Raise own funds: $2300.

Training Provided. 1-day orientation; 1 mo. training in discipleship.

Work Description. Team lives together and is involved in construction and other manual labor.

Countries Served. Latin America, Central/Northern Europe, Far East, United States, Caribbean

Emmaus Road International
7150 Tanner Court
San Diego, CA 92111
(619)292-7020
Neal Pirolo

Program. Team Orientation, 1 day; Acts Boot Camp, 1 wk.; Acts Training Course, 12 wks.

Agency Background. Founded 1983. ERI helps churches mobilize, train and network individuals in cross-cultural outreach ministry.

Requirements and Costs. Church: Team desiring to do cross-cultural outreach. Individual: Ministry experience, church or agency sponsor, Scripture study skills, call to ministry. Costs: Team Orientation—offering; Acts Boot Camp—$165; Acts Training Course—$1200.

Training Provided. 12-wk. course: cultural adaptation, language learning, spiritual warfare, interpersonal relationships, orientation, Bible study. Team and 1-wk. curriculum adapted from 12-wk. course.

Work Description. Classroom training and experience living and working with a Mexican family in Tijuana. Teams and individuals network with established ministries.

Countries Served. Network of agency opportunities available worldwide.

Evangelical Free Church of America
Board of Overseas Missions
1515 E. 66th St.
Minneapolis, MN 55423
(612)866-3343

Lloyd Childs

Program. Summer Overseas (SOS) 4–8 wks.; Apprentice in Missions (AIM) 3 yrs.; Mission Associate (MA) 2 wks. to 2 yrs.

Agency Background. Founded 1887. Evangelical Free Church denom. Main thrust is church planting.

Requirements and Costs. Denom. member, college/sem. students, 20 yrs. and older. Raise own funds. SOS: $400–$650/mo. plus airfare; AIM/MA: $1000–$2000/mo. per adult.

Training Provided. 2-wk. orientation and candidate school. Follow-up on field.

Work Description. SOS: maintenance, secretarial, literature distribution, camp ministry, evangelism, teaching. AIM: evangelism, church planting, discipling, teaching. MA: medical, secretarial, accounting, teaching, mechanics, maintenance, construction.

Countries Served. Southeast Asia, East Asia, Europe, Africa, South America

FACE (Fellowship of Artists for Cultural Evangelism)

1605 E. Elizabeth Street
Pasadena, CA 91104
(818)398-2445
Mary Lou Totten

Program. FACE Summer Institute, 8 wks. (4 wks. classroom training); China Interface, 3–4 wks.

Agency Background. Founded 1976. Evangelical, interdenom., emphasis on bringing creative expression and cross-cultural missions together.

Requirements and Costs. 21 yrs. and older. Professional artists for workshops and for performances. Raise own funds. FACE Summer Institute: approx. $1300. China Interface: approx. $3000.

Training Provided. FACE Summer Institute: 4 wks. classroom; China Interface: 6 wks. rehearsal and orientation. Follow-up on field; sponsors M.A. degree in Arts/Cross-cultural Communication, Wm. Carey University, Pasadena.

Work Description. Painting, music, mime, drama, dance, puppets, poetry, literature (work with all ages).

Countries Served. FACE Summer Inst.: Pasadena, CA, Arizona Navajo Indian Reserv. China Interface: China.

The Fold, Inc.

P.O. Box 1188
Lyndonville, VT 05851
(802)626-5620
Fred Tomaselli
Tim Whiting

Program. Summer program, 10–12 wks.; Internships, 3–6 mos.

Agency Background. Founded 1967. Nondenom., family-style living.

Requirements and Costs. 20 yrs. and older. Rm/brd provided. Raise personal and trans. money plus small salary.

Training Provided. 1-wk. orientation plus weekly meetings. Follow-up.

Work Description. Work with troubled youth, discipling, Bible studies, recreational activities.

Countries Served. United States, rural and inner-city areas

Food for the Hungry

P.O. Box E
Scottsdale, AZ 85252
(602)955-8438 or
(800)2-Hunger
Gary Womelsduff

Program. Hunger Corps Projects (HCP) 1–3 wks., geared for church/school teams; Hunger Corps Volunteer (HCV) 2-yr. min. commitment.

Agency Background. Founded 1971. Nondenom., evangelical, involved in relief/community development, development of human resources and self-help projects.

Requirements and Costs. HCP: Terms—15 yrs. and older. Individuals—19 yrs. and older. HCV: 21 yrs. and older. No families with children. Cost varies. HCP: approx. $800 and up. HCV: approx. $950/mo.

Training Provided. Orientation, on-field training. Follow-up.

Work Description. HCP: Building projects. HCV: development and refugee/relief work.

Countries Served. Caribbean, Africa, Southeast Asia, So. Asia, Europe, Latin America

SERVICE OPPORTUNITIES AT HOME AND ABROAD cont.

Foreign Mission Board, Southern Baptist Convention
P.O. Box 6767
Richmond, VA 23230
(804)353-0151
Mike Barnett
Glenn Prescott

Program. International Service Corps, 4 mos.–2 yrs.; Tentmakers & Baptists Living Abroad, open-ended terms.

Agency Background. A denom. sending agency. Establishes churches, engaged in aid and/ or relief, development of human resources, radio and TV broadcasting and medicine.

Requirements and Costs. Good health, member in good standing of an active SBC church. Cost varies. Both paid and support-raising positions.

Training Provided. Cross-cultural training, technical skills, evangelism, and many other orientation, learning situations provided.

Work Description. Engineer, TESL, agricultural; teachers at all levels and in many categories.

Countries Served. Opportunities throughout the world.

Forward Edge Int'l
P.O. Box 65238
Vancouver, WA 98665
(206)693-3343
Joseph Anfuso

Program. Forward Edge Teams (FET), 10 days–3 wks.; 1-yr. internship in Europe or Latin America.

Agency Background. A nondenom. church-planting ministry.

Requirements and Costs. 14 yrs. and older. Should not be opposed to charismatic orientation, though need not be charismatic. Raise own funds: $199–$1995.

Training Provided. Audio cassette tapes, reading materials, plus a 3-day intensive training session and 1-day re-entry session. Fund-raising kit provided.

Work Description. Evangelism, medical, construction, back-packing.

Countries Served. Far East, United States, Europe, Central America

Global Outreach Mission
P.O. Box 711
Buffalo, NY 14240
(716)842-2220
Bill James

Program. Prince of Peace Corps (POPC), Summer, 7–8 wks.; Encounter Assignment (EA), 1–3 yrs.

Agency Background. Founded 1943. Interdenom., involved primarily in church planting, radio, camps, evangelism, literature distribution.

Requirements and Costs. POPC: 1 yr. of college. EA: 18 yrs. and older. Raise own funds. POPC: approx. $2000, trans. inc. EA: varies with commitment and location.

Training Provided. 1-wk orientation for POPC and EA in New York.

Work Description. POPC: evangelism, music, drama, literature distribution, children's ministry, church planting, construction, pastoral internships. EA: evangelism, church planting, maintenance, construction.

Countries Served. Europe, Latin America, South Asia, Caribbean

Gospel Missionary Union
10000 N. Oak
Kansas City, MO 64155
(816)734-8500
Rex Sandiford

Program. Summer Programs, 2–10 wks.

Agency Background. Founded 1892. Nondenom., evangelical, involved in evangelism, church planting, educational ministries, radio, literature distribution.

Requirements and Costs. 1 yr. of college, (Bible college and foreign language beneficial). Raise own funds: costs vary with location and commitment.

Training Provided. On the field.

Work Description. Work with missionaries, youth, camp work, VBS, literature distribution, evangelism, maintenance.

Countries Served. Europe, Alaska, Caribbean, Africa, Latin America

Greater Europe Mission
P.O. Box 668
Wheaton, IL 60189

(708)462-8050
Personnel Dept.

Program. Eurocorps "91," 9 wks. and 4 wks.

Agency Background. Emphasis on training Europeans to reach their own in one of ten Bible institutes or three seminaries and in church planting locations.

Requirements and Costs. At least 1 yr. out of high school. Good health, language ability, couples with no children. Raise own funds: approx. $2600 for 9 wks. and $1800 for 4 wks.

Training Provided. Training manual provided. Orientation at Wheaton College before departure. Ongoing orientation after arrival on field.

Work Description. Open-air evangelism, door-to-door surveys, literature distribution, construction, and conference ministries.

Countries Served. Most of the Western European countries and expanding in the East.

Habitat for Humanity
Habitat and Church Streets
Americus, GA 31709
(912)924-6935
FAX(912)924-6541
Amy Parsons

Program. Domestic programs, (headquarters and worksites), 3 mos. or longer; Int'l programs, 3 yrs.

Agency Background. Founded 1976. Ecumenical Christian housing ministry which works together with the poor to build low-cost housing for their purchase at no profit and no interest.

Requirements and Costs. Domestic: 18 yrs. and older; housing, food, insurance available. Construction and office experience welcomed. Int'l: 23 yrs. and older; housing, food, insurance, and fund-raising help provided. Some administration, construction, or community organizing experience required; international experience and language ability preferred.

Training Provided. Domestic: on-site training. Int'l: 11-wk. training at HQ in construction, procedures, intercultural awareness, community organizing, and development issues. Language training overseas, debriefing upon return.

Work Description. Headquarters: work in accounting, administration, construction, computers, graphic arts, hospitality, personnel, child care, photography, printing, public relations, translation. North American sites: project supervision, construction, personnel, office work. Int'l: community organizing, construction, administration, training, sharing life in another culture.

Countries Served. Africa, Latin America, Caribbean, Asia, Pacific Islands, North America

Harvesting in Spanish (HIS)
245 S. Benton Street
Lakewood, CO 80226
(303)232-3030
FAX(303)232-3561
Don Benner

Program. Indefinite length of term.

Agency Background. Founded 1976. Interdenom. missionary agency working in 8 countries.

Requirements and Costs. Spanish helpful, doctrinally hold to Lausanne Convention. Raise own funds: singles, $600/month; couples, $1000/mo.

Training Provided. Training manual provided.

Work Description. Work in orphanage, construction, medical and dental work, street, school and market evangelism.

Countries Served. Guatemala, El Salvador, Mexico, Panama, Costa Rica, Argentina, Peru, Colombia

Helps International Ministries, Inc.
Rt. 1, Box 171D
Harlem, GA 30814-1071
(404)556-3408
David DeJong

Program. Short-term, 1 wk.–2 yrs.

Agency Background. Founded 1976. Interdenom. technical sending agency serving other mission agencies and churches.

Requirements and Costs. 16 yrs. and older, good health. Raise own funds for trans. to/from location. Rm/brd may be provided.

Training Provided. On-the-field training.

Work Description. Construction, architecture,

SERVICE OPPORTUNITIES AT HOME AND ABROAD cont.

engineering, accounting, computer.
Countries Served. Africa, United States, Southeast Asia, Europe

Inner City Impact (ICI)
2704 W. North Avenue
Chicago, IL 60647
(312)384-4200
Kerri Johnson
Program. Summer in Chicago (SIC), June 8–Aug. 17, 1991.
Agency Background. Primary goals are evangelism, discipleship and church planting.
Requirements and Costs. Post high school, a desire to share Christ with others, teachable spirit, good attitude, flexible. Raise own funds: Singles, $1400–$1800, plus trans. Couples, $2200–$3100, plus trans.
Training Provided. Orientation provided before the program, follow-up provided during support raising.
Work Description. One-on-one model involvement with team discipleship. Could also be a Bible, music or crafts teacher, drama team, block club or recreation leader.
Countries Served. United States (Chicago)

International Christian Assistance
P.O. Box 583
Neenah, WI 54956
(414)722-3731
Jean Hoppe
Program. 21–60 days.
Agency Background. Founded 1974. Involved in agriculture, medical, trade schools; train native pastors.
Requirements and Costs. Mature leader. Raise own funds: $2500.
Work Description. Construction, agriculture, teaching, nursing, health, evangelism, church planting.
Countries Served. Ghana, Kenya, Uganda, Liberia, Mexico, U.S.

International Messengers
1600 Oakhills Road S.W.
Bemidji, MN 56601
(218)751-0388
Robert Rasmusson
Program. Group Action Projects (GAP), 3–6 wks.; Mission Project Planning Service (MPPS), 1–4 wks.
Agency Background. Evangelical, interdenom. missions organization comprised of an international staff team. Committed to the evangelization and discipleship of people of all nations; and to the motivation and training of members of the body of Christ for active involvement in world missions.
Requirements and Costs. 18 yrs. and older, committed Christian with a desire to serve. Raise own funds: ranges from $1000–$2500.
Training Provided. 2–7 days.
Work Description. Evangelistic English camps (teach English), work projects, other camp work.
Countries Served. Varies. Mainly Austria, Poland, Hong Kong, Czechoslovakia, Yugoslavia, Romania

International STEP
P.O. Box 10305
Jacksonville, FL 32247-0305
(904)398-6559
Tony Portell
Program. Short-term Evangelistic Projects, 2–3 wks. (depending on location).
Agency Background. Founded 1985. Provides young people and adults an opportunity to see and experience firsthand ministry in a foreign country.
Requirements and Costs. 15 yrs. and older. Raise own funds: $650–$1500 (scholarships available).
Training Provided. Home training provided through correspondence and videos for individuals and church groups: 2-day orientation and debriefing.
Work Description. One-to-one evangelism, preaching in churches, street ministry, mime, drama, music, puppets, clown ministry, medical teams, relief work.
Countries Served. Jamaica, Haiti, Philippines, England, France, Kenya, South Africa, Ecuador, Costa Rica, Guatemala, South Korea, China, Eastern Europe, Russia

International Teams
P.O. Box 203
Prospect Heights, IL 60070
(708)870-3800 or
(800)323-0428
David Horton

Program. Two-Year Program (TYP); Summer Servants Program (SSP), 6 weeks.

Agency Background. Evangelical, nondenom. mission agency that trains and sends teams overseas for 2 yrs. or for a summer (since 1961).

Requirements and Costs. TYP: 20 yrs. and older. SSP: min. 18 yrs. old, foreign language helpful. Raise own funds. TYP: $975-$1200/mo., varies upon location. SSP: $2000-$2500 (Chicago to field and return).

Training Provided. TYP: 4 mos. training in language, culture, interpersonal relations, evangelism, discipleship, church planting, support raising and other. SSP: 4-day pre-field orientation.

Work Description. TYP: church planting and community development. SSP: evangelism, open-air meetings, drama, puppets, etc., work alongside two-year and career teams.

Countries Served. France, Italy, Spain, Philippines, Portugal, Austria, Poland, East Germany, Czechoslovakia, Romania, Hungary, Bulgaria, Yugoslavia, USSR

LIFE Ministries
P.O. Box 200
San Dimas, CA 91773
(714)599-8491
Todd McCollum

Program. Directions 1–3 yrs.; Scrum Dendo, 10 wks., summer; career

Agency Background. Interdenom., ministries in teaching English as an opportunity for evangelism, church planting, national leadership training, and music.

Requirements and Costs. Directions: at least 21 yrs., min. 2 yrs. college. Scrum Dendo: at least 19 yrs., 1 yr. college. Raise own funds; varies with program.

Training Provided. Orientation, conversational English training, introduction to Japanese language and culture. Re-entry.

Work Description. Teaching conversational English in conjunction with a Japanese church, friendship evangelism. Also opportunities in administration, church planting, music, and national leadership training.

Countries Served. Japan

Mennonite Board of Missions
P.O. Box 370
Elkhart, IN 46515-0370
(219)294-7523
Nancy Thiessen

Program. Mennonite Service Venture, 3 wks. in the summer for individuals; 2 days–2 wks. year-round for groups.

Agency Background. Founded 1882. Seeks to lead and enable the Mennonite Church to be involved in programs of Christian ministry in North America and overseas.

Requirements and Costs. 14–18 yrs. Exceptions for youth and young adult groups. Raise own funds; varies, depending on travel.

Training Provided. Pre-field orientation. Study and orientation materials available for groups before and after experience.

Work Description. Painting, home repair, clean-up, construction, children's recreation programs, VBS.

Countries Served. Israel, United States, Canada, Ireland

Mercy Ships
P.O. Box 2020
Lindale, TX 75771-2020
(214)963-8341
Cindy Ryan

Program. Volunteer program, 2 wks.–3 mos. year-round.

Agency Background. Interdenom., division of Youth With A Mission, started in 1978 on the YWAM ship, *Anastasis*. Now also on the *Good Samaritan*. Both ships aid in relief and development and medical needs to nationals.

Requirements and Costs. 18 yrs. and older, good health. Raise own funds: $150/mo. plus trans. to/from, and personal money.

Training Provided. Minimum orientation. Follow-up upon request.

Work Description. Varies. Carpentry,

SERVICE OPPORTUNITIES AT HOME AND ABROAD cont.

waitressing, electrical and plumbing work, etc., on ships. Also literature distribution, evangelism, hospitality, translation, medical/ dental work, construction, etc., on land.

Countries Served. *Anastasis* and *Good Samaritan* ships to United States, Canada, Mexico, Caribbean, Dominican Republic

NAIM Ministries
P.O. Box 151
Point Roberts, WA 98281
(604)946-1227
Jim Hamilton

Program. Summer Missionary Institute, 8 weeks

Agency Background. Founded 1949. Interdenom. mission agency reaching Native Indian and Sikh and Hindu people by personal evangelism and church planting in villages and urban centers.

Requirements and Costs. 1 yr. of college, English speaker. Raise own funds: $625 per individual or $1035 per couple, plus trans. cost to/from Vancouver, BC.

Training Provided. 5 days of intensive cross-cultural training. Regular supervision and mid-summer refresher course.

Work Description. Live in an Indian village or community. Engage in evangelism and personal relationships, organizing activities, and community services.

Countries Served. Primarily in British Columbia, Canada

MK Educational Center
(A branch of New Tribes Mission)
P.O. Box 1200
Camdenton, MO 65020
(314)346-6053
David A. Lotz

Program. Teachers for 1990–1991 school yr. (10 mos.)

Agency Background. Interdenom., with objective to reach tribal peoples through evangelism, translation, tutoring, church planting. Also help maintain schools for MKs.

Requirements and Costs. Qualified teacher, min. 1 yr. classroom experience, conservative lifestyle. Raise own funds: varies with location.

Training Provided. 10-day pre-field orientation.

Work Description. Teaching elementary/ secondary children.

Countries Served. 20 countries

OMS International
P.O. Box A
Greenwood, IN 46142
(317)881-6751
O. Kemp Edwards

Program. NOW Corps, 2–5 mos. (usually summer).

Agency Background. Nondenom., based on Wesleyan Armenian theological tradition.

Requirements and Costs. 19 yrs. and older, good health. Raise own funds: varies with location.

Training Provided. Orientation stateside and abroad, manual provided covering cross-cultural principles, logistics, etc.

Work Description. Administrative, youth work, maintenance, arts/crafts, sports, evangelism, teaching English, Sunday school, camp counseling, discipling, secretarial.

Countries Served. South America, Europe, Asia, Caribbean

Operation Mobilization
P.O. Box 2277
Peachtree City, GA 30269
(404)631-0432
Chip Kirk

Program. Summer Program: Mexico, 2 months; Quebec, 1–2 months; Europe, 1–2 months. Also 1- and 2-yr. programs.

Agency Background. Founded 1957. Also known as Send the Light. Interdenom., with emphasis on short-term youth training, evangelism, literature distribution, discipling.

Requirements and Costs. Belong to local church, willingness to learn. Europe: 2 mos., approx. $1900. Mexico: 2 mos., approx. $1200. Canada: 2 mos., approx. $900. 1–2 yr. programs: approx. $500/mo.

Training Provided. Attend a 1-wk. training conference, read books, listen to tapes;

additional 1-wk. conference if going to Europe. Follow-up.

Work Description. Evangelism, literature distribution, open-air meetings, drama, mime, puppets, local church work, concerts, administration, bookkeeping, accounting.

Countries Served. Europe, Middle East, *MV Logos II* and *Doulos* ships, South Asia, Canada

Outreach Canada
#16—12240 Horseshoe Way
Richmond, B.C. V7A4X9
Gerry Kraft

Program. STEP, 8 wks.

Agency Background. Nondenom. Equips people for ministry through research, motivational models, training and mobilization by direct involvement.

Requirements and Costs. 18 yrs., 2 yrs. born-again Christian, cross-cultural experience, service in and endorsement of home church. Spanish required for Mexico. Mexico, $1500; Philippines, $2400; Zimbabwe, $3200.

Training Provided. Pre-field manual with language tapes, 3-day orientation in United States; training on field with supervisory guidance.

Work Description. Training and mobilizing local Christians in evangelism, small group Bible studies, discipleship.

Countries Served. Canada, Mexico, Philippines

Outreach For Christ International
6585 Eden Vale Blvd.
Suite #110
Eden Prairie, MN 55346
(612)934-5651
(800)541-SONG

Program. The Reach Out Singers: 3- and 9-wk. tours.

Agency Background. Founded 1973. Sponsoring organization for Reach Out Singers, works in partnership with Northern and Eastern Europe.

Requirements and Costs. 16–30 yrs., good health. Raise own funds: $2249–$4686.

Training Provided. Orientation combines evangelism training and music coaching with nationally known vocal coaches.

Work Description. Evangelism through music.

Countries Served. USSR, Europe, Scandinavian countries, Eastern Europe, Canada, United States, Australia, Southeast Asia, Middle East, Tanzania, Zimbabwe, New Guinea

Overseas Christian Servicemen's Center
P.O. Box 1268
Englewood, CO 80150
(303)762-1400
Dotty Hash

Program. Summer Ministries, 6 wks.–3 mos. (could go to 2 yrs.); Hospitality House and Malachi youth programs; Internships during year or summer.

Agency Background. Founded 1954. Ministry to American military worldwide.

Requirements and Costs. College-age, Christian walk, flexible, local church recommendation, prefer 1 yr. Bible training and ability to teach. Raise own funds: varies with commitment.

Training Provided. Orientation, on-the-field supervision. Evaluation at end of term.

Work Description. Malachi: ministry to military youth. Also Bible teaching, maintenance, evangelism, discipleship.

Countries Served. United States, Panama, Philippines, Korea, Japan, Germany, England, Italy, Spain

OC International
(formerly Overseas Crusades)
25 Corning Avenue
Milpitas, CA 95035
(408)263-1101
Judy Shewy (STEP)
Robin Cook, Sports Ambassadors (SA)

Program. STEP (Summer Team Evang. Program), 2–6 mos.; SA, 2–6 wks. or 4–6 mos.

Agency Background. Founded 1950. Interdenom., assisting in discipling nations and equipping nationals.

Requirements and Costs. Good health, Christian, 18 yrs. old. STEP: Summer $1400–$3000 SA: $2000–$3400 depending on location.

Training Provided. STEP: Pre-field manual,

SERVICE OPPORTUNITIES AT HOME AND ABROAD cont.

5 day on-field orientation. SA: Pre-field manual, training camp on-field.

Work Description. STEP: Evangelism, Bible studies, discipleship. SA: Play games against national clubs, share testimony, distribute literature, evangelism.

Countries Served. Canada, Mexico, Philippines, Argentina, Taiwan, Zimbabwe, Kenya

Pioneers
P.O. Box 527
Sterling, VA 22170
(703)478-0004
Ruth Wright

Program. Pioneers Active in Cross-cultural Evangelism (PACE), 7–8 wks.; Pioneers short-term, 1–2 yrs.

Agency Background. Founded 1979. Concerned with reaching the unreached with the gospel.

Requirements and Cost. Out of high school, conservative evangelical doctrine. Raise own funds. PACE: $2000–$3000. Short-term 1–2 yrs: varies.

Training Provided. Orientation manual provided. PACE: 3 days spent at Pioneers annual Candidate School for Specialized Training.

Work Description. PACE: evangelism, tutoring English, language/culture learning, children's ministry, literature distribution. PA: language/culture learning, participate as a team member with career missionary.

Countries Served. PACE: China, Papua New Guinea, S. America, India, Indonesia, Thailand, Mali, Guyana, Egypt

Presbyterian Church in America
Mission to the World/SIMA
P.O. Box 29765
Atlanta, GA 30359
(404)320-3373
Dan Camp

Program. Servants in Missions Abroad (SIMA), 2 yrs.; Summer, 2 mo.; Two-week exposure trips.

Agency Background. Founded 1974. Conservative Evangelical Presbyterian Church.

Requirements and Costs. Should be familiar with Westminster Confession of Faith. Raise own funds. 2 yr.: $1500/mo. plus $6000 one time. Summer: $1500–$3000. Two-week trips: $500–$1500.

Training Provided. Support-raising and cross-cultural training for 2-mo. and 2-yr. candidates.

Work Description. Evangelism, discipling, church construction, conversational English, teaching MKs, children's ministry.

Countries Served. Europe, Africa, Latin America, Asia, Caribbean, Australia

RBMU International
8102 Elberon Avenue
Philadelphia, PA 19111
(215)745-0680

Program. Project Timothy, 4–8 wks.

Agency Background. Founded 1873. Devoted to church planting among unreached people groups.

Requirements and Costs. Conservative evangelical Raise own funds: $1500–$2500, depending on field.

Work Description. Evangelism, puppet shows, music, testimony giving, light labor.

Countries Served. Indonesia, Philippines, Chile, Peru, Cameroon, United States

Reciprocal Ministries Int'l
15930 S.W. 96th Ave.
Miami, FL 33157
(305)251-8308
Herb Shoemaker

Program. Short-term Overseas Assignment (SOA), 2 wks.–2 yrs.; Ministry Teams (MT), 8–10 days; Work Teams (WT), 8–10 days; Sister Church Program (SCP), ongoing.

Agency Background. Interdenom., emphasis on lay ministries. Unique cross-cultural Sister Church Program, 10 yrs.

Requirements and Costs. 18 yrs. and older, some exceptions. Raise own funds. SOA: approx. $1000–$1500 for 4–6 wks. WT: $200–$300, plus trans. MT: $200–$300, plus trans.

Training Provided. SCP and SOA: 10 wk. training by tape.

Work Description. SOA: local church, VBS,

administration, teaching, evangelism. MT: evangelism, music, drama, retreats. WT: construction, maintenance, local church work. SCP: adopt a church in Third World country.

Countries Served. Caribbean, Europe

The Rocky Mountain Center for World Mission
P.O. Box 458
Pasadena, CA 91102
(818)796-5425
Jim Proud

Program. Short term, 2–8 wks.

Agency Background. Begun 1988. A mission center on the pattern of and affiliated with the U.S. Center for World Mission.

Requirements and Cost. 18 yrs. and older. Under 18 must be accomp. by parent or guardian. Good health, a growing Christian for at least 1 year. Raise own funds. 2 weeks: plus airfare. 4 weeks: depends on trip. $600–$800.

Training Provided. Orientation in Europe. Training manual provided.

Work Description. Deliver Bibles, food, medical and relief supplies; fellowship with other believers; evangelism, construction work, teaching in youth camps, teaching English.

Countries Served. Poland, Hungary, USSR, Costa Rica, Middle East

Send International
P.O. Box 513
Farmington, MI 48332
(313)477-4210 ext. 110
Verona Dutton

Program. Summer program, 10 wks.; short terms of 6 mo.–2 yrs.

Agency Background. Founded 1947. Nondenom., evangelical with Baptist tradition. Formerly Far Eastern Gospel Crusade.

Requirements and Costs. College-age. Raise own funds. Summer prog.: $1200–$3300. Short term: approx. $1300/mo.

Training Provided. Mainly on-field orientation. Follow-up.

Work Description. Summer Prog.: evangelism, discipleship, teaching, camp, VBS, administration, radio, maintenance. Short-term: professional skills (e.g. teaching, medical, administration), TESL, construction, evangelism.

Countries Served. United States, Southeast Asia

S.I.M. USA
P.O. Box 7900
Charlotte, NC 28217
(704)529-5100
Les Unruh

Program. 8 wks.–2 yrs.

Agency Background. Founded 1893. Interdenom. Main goal is evangelism.

Requirements and Costs. Good health, solid character references. Raise own funds: $11–$17/ day. Varies with location.

Work Description. Logistical and support to pilot programs in church planting.

Countries Served. Liberia, Niger, Benin, Ethiopia, Kenya, Ghana, Nigeria, Bolivia

South America Mission, Inc.
P.O. Box 6560
Lake Worth, FL 33466
(407)965-1833
Evie Opitz

Program. Short-Term (ST), 3 mos.–3 yrs.; Summer Team Program (STP), 4–8 wks.

Agency Background. Founded 1914. Interdenom., with objective to reach the unreached people throughout Latin America.

Requirements and Costs. ST: 21 yrs. STP: 1 yr. of college. Good health. ST: $1400/mo., inc. travel depending on location and length of time. STP: $1590, 1 mo.; $2050, 2 mos.

Work Description. ST: teaching, work with handicapped. STP: films, street meetings, camps, music, literature distribution.

Countries Served. Bolivia, Brazil, Peru, Colombia

Special Projects in the Tribes (SPRINT)
c/o World Outreach Fellowship
P.O. Box 585603
Orlando, FL 32858
(407)425-5552
Howard Lisech

Program SPRINT Ministries, Summer (7–8 wks.) and Winter (1–3 wks.)

Agency Background. Nondenom. Assist

SERVICE OPPORTUNITIES AT HOME AND ABROAD cont.

missions and Third World churches with needed projects.

Requirements and Costs. 15 yrs. and older, good health. Raise own funds. Summer: $1300–$3000. Winter: $980–$1400.

Training Provided. 5 days of pre-field training, includes cross-cultural, language, building group skills.

Work Description. Balanced ministry and work projects that are realistic yet leave a visible reminder of our love in action.

Countries Served. Papua New Guinea, Indonesia, Peru, Ecuador, Belize, Nepal, Philippines, Argentina, Bolivia, Alaska, Liberia

Stem Ministries

P.O. Box 290066
Minneapolis, MN 55429
(612)535-2944
Jan, Pat or Kathy

Program. 15 days.

Agency Background. Founded 1984. Independ. Christian organization placing short-termers overseas in 3 different countries.

Requirements and Costs. All ages (parental approval for youth 16 and under). Raise own funds: $300 plus round-trip airfare.

Training Provided. 4–8 hrs., pre-field; 8 hrs. on location; preparation manual given.

Work Description. Evangelism, construction, mercy, service and creative ministries.

Countries Served. Haiti, Jamaica, Trinidad

The Evangelical Alliance Mission (TEAM)

P.O. Box 969
Wheaton, IL 60189-0969
(708)653-5300
(800)343-3144
Barry Hancock

Program. Summer Program, June 10–Aug. 15, 1991; SST Program, 3–12 mos.; Assoc. Program, 1–4 yrs.

Agency Background. Founded 1890. Nondenom. Principal focus on planting churches. Involved in education and health care on many fields.

Requirements and Costs. Summer: 20 yrs./2 yrs. college. SST: 20 yrs. up, skill to match a need. Assoc.: training appropriate to particular assignment. Summer: Raise own funds, $1900–$3200. SST: Costs vary.

Training Provided. Summer: 1-wk pre-field orientation. SST: On-field orientation only. Assoc.: 3-wk. Candidate School.

Work Description. Summer: Evangelism, music, children's work, construction, etc. SST: Teaching, clerical, health care, etc. Assoc.: 127 openings in various areas.

Countries Served. 30 world areas in Europe, Africa, Latin America, East and West Asia

Teen World Outreach

7245 College Street
Lima, NY 14485
(716)582-2790
Jim Porter

Program. Summer: 4 and 7 wk. Adult Fall Teams: 2 wks.

Agency Background. Founded 1982. Interdenom. charismatic tradition in service with other agencies with short-term programs.

Requirements and Costs. 13 yrs. and older. Raise own funds. Summer: $995–$2895. Adult Fall: 21 yrs. and older, $795–$1995.

Training Provided. Support-raising training, technical skills, minimal language, evangelism, and drama.

Work Description. Building projects, repair and renovation programs, evangelism through drama and mime.

Countries Served. Amsterdam, Brazil, Costa Rica, France, India, Kenya, Mexico, Miami FL, New Guinea, New York City, Peru, Scotland, Egypt, South Africa

United World Mission

P.O. Box 250
Union Mills, NC 28167
(704)287-8996
Betty Sadler

Program. Summer, 6–7 wks.; MK school, 1–2 yrs. (grades 1–12).

Agency Background. Founded 1946; nondenom.; engaged primarily in church planting, targeting urban centers and unreached peoples groups.

Requirements and Costs. Summer: 18 yrs. and older raise own funds, $1600 and up. MK school: certified, raise partial support.

Training Provided. Pre-field orientation; further orientation on field.

Work Description. Summer: evangelism, music, children's/youth work, sports, drama, camping, etc. MK school: teaching one's grade or subject, Bible, assist in activities.

Countries Served. Summer: Europe, other countries MK school: Senegal

WorldTeam, Inc.
P.O. Box 143038
Coral Gables, FL 33114
(305)446-0861
David Melick

Program. Summer Teams, 1–8 wks.; Ministry, camps, evangelism, Bible clubs.

Agency Background. Founded 1928. Interdenom., evangelical sending agency engaged primarily in church planting and evangelism.

Requirements and Costs. 20 yrs. and older. Raise own funds. YHM: $2000, inc. trans. STP: varies with location.

Training Provided. 1 week U.S. work with missionary or national pastors on the field.

Work Description. STP: VBS, evangelism, music, camp work, missionary support in church planting, seminars.

Countries Served. Caribbean, Europe, South America

Wycliffe Associates
202 S. Prospect St.
Orange, CA 92669
(714)639-9950

Program. Construction length varies with project. Generally 2–3 wks.

Agency Background. A support ministry of lay people to Wycliffe Bible Translators and The Summer Institute of Linguistics.

Requirements and Costs. Willingness to serve and learn in a cross-cultural setting. Raise own funds: $7-10/day rm/brd. Trans. and visas can be handled through WA.

Training Provided. Fact sheet on location, culture, currency, climate and what to bring provided. Orientation on work site. Follow-up provided.

Work Description. WA home ministry: hospitality for missionaries traveling through the U.S., prayer ministry, local chapters. Missions Alive: construction and helpers. Utilities: skilled people for well drilling, electrical, etc.

Countries Served. Wycliffe fields worldwide and U.S. facilities

Youth In Mission
6401 The Paseo
Kansas City, MO 64131
(816)333-7000
Dale Fallon

Program. Youth in Missions Prog. (YIM). Summer (8 wks.): Advance, 1–2 yrs.

Agency Background. Founded late '60s. Interdenom., part of Nazarene Youth Int'l Ministry: purpose to provide hands-on experience in evangelism/discipleship ministries.

Requirements and Costs. 18 yrs. and older. Raise own funds. YIM: approx. $750–$1500 (partial subsidy). Advance: varies.

Training Provided. Training camp for 10 days.

Work Description. Youth work, puppetry, Bible studies, teaching Sunday school, evangelism, mime, drama, music.

Countries Served. United States (mainly urban areas), Caribbean, Europe, Latin America, Southeast Asia

YUGO Ministries
P.O. Box 25
San Dimas, CA 91773
(714)592-6621
Dennis Mohler

Program. Week-long outreach trips to Mexico.

Agency Background. Founded 1964. Non-profit evangelical organization dedicated to ministry in Mexico.

Requirements and Costs. Most weeks are planned for high school/college age. Two weeks are for junior-highers. $130–$150.

SERVICE OPPORTUNITIES AT HOME AND ABROAD cont.

Training Provided. Training materials provided in culture preparation and personal spiritual growth.

Work Description. Children's VBS, films, sports, drama, puppets, women's Bible studies, evangelistic services.

Countries Served. Mexico

Source: *Stepping Out.* Published by Short-Term Missions Advocates, Inc. Copyright © 1987. Used by permission. Updated by ACW staff.

SHOULD I GO OR NOT?

Below is a list of reasons why many people go on a short-term mission. Read through the entire list and mark ten items which reflect most closely your hopes and desires. Then return to those ten items and assign each one a numerical value:

3: most powerful motivator
2: strong motivator
1: not so strong a motivator

I want to go on a short-term . . .

Personal

___ for the excitement and fun of travel.
___ to see if I want to be a missionary.
___ to experience another culture.
___ to get away from home.
___ to get experience in a certain skill.
___ to get training as a Christian worker.
___ to buy duty-free electronics.
___ to add to my list of countries visited.
___ to see and experience real poverty.
___ as a way to spend a summer growing.
___ to find a mate with interests like mine.
___ other: ________________________

Spiritual

___ to know God as never before.
___ to show God that I'm serious about following him.
___ because I have a missionary call.
___ because God has told me specifically to go.
___ to gain favor with God.
___ to use my gifts for God.
___ other: ________________________

External

___ to help finish the task of world evangelization.
___ to better mobilize my church.
___ to help establish God's kingdom.
___ because it's strategic to help nationals.
___ to help rebuild a world with God's justice.
___ because Jesus commands it of us all.
___ other: ________________________

Needs-related

___ to help hungry children.
___ to give overworked missionaries a break.
___ because people are going to hell without the gospel.
___ because I feel compassion for poverty-stricken people.
___ other: ________________________

Within each of the five categories, add up the numbers that you have assigned to the ten most important motivating factors you have selected. There are no "correct" answers. You may have 15 or 20 points in a category, or none at all. The important thing is to recognize your motives and to work on balancing your reasons for going. There really is no "ideal" or "correct" balance of motives.

Source: *Stepping Out.* Published by Short-Term Missions Advocates, Inc. Copyright © 1987. Used by permission.

WHAT TO ASK AN AGENCY

Every agency is different, and every opportunity that an agency offers is unique. Use the chart below to learn what you can about each agency or opportunity that interests you.

Name of Agency:__________________________

	What I want	*OK by me*	*Not what I want*
Length of stay:			
Type of work:			
Amount of work:			
Location:			
Training:			
in support-raising:			
in the culture:			
in teamwork:			
debriefing:			
Contact with other culture:			
Cost:			
Team atmosphere:			
Doctrine:			
Living environment:			
Leadership, authority structure:			
Potential for career:			
Others' counsel about it:			

Source: *Stepping Out.* Published by Short-Term Missions Advocates, Inc. Copyright © 1987. Used by permission.

VACATIONS YOU NEVER THOUGHT TO TAKE

1. **Vacation from words**. We speak more than five thousand words in a day. A quiet revolution might occur if we didn't speak for a day.

2. **Vacation from food**. It's commonly called a fast, rather than a vacation—but make it a celebration rather than an endurance contest. It will change not only your weight but also your life-style.

3. **Vacation from seeing or hearing**. Years ago I taped my eyes for a good part of a week so that I was totally blind. That time probably taught me more about my senses than any five books could have done. Since then I've intentionally limited other senses in order to isolate and experience them. They have been priceless life investments.

4. **Vacation from complaining**. Trying it is poignant, painful, and enlightening.

Source: Tim Hansel in *When I Relax, I Feel Guilty*. Published by David C. Cook Publishing Company. Copyright © 1979. Used by permission.

CAMPS, CONFERENCES, RESORTS

The following camps, conference centers, and resorts are members of Christian Camping International/USA (CCI/USA), an association of Christian camps and conference centers and their leaders. *The Official Guide to Christian Camps and Conference Centers,* which provides more information about each of these camps is available for $9.95 plus shipping and handling. Write to:

Christian Camping International/USA
P.O. Box 646
Wheaton, IL 60189
Phone 708-462-0300 FAX 708-462-0499

State/Camp	*Address*	*Phone*
Alabama		
Alpine Camp for Boys, Inc.	Route 1, Box 216, Mentone, AL 35984	205-634-4200
Birmingham Baptist Camp	P.O. Box 21, Cooks Springs, AL 35052	205-884-2425
Camp Alamisco	P.O. Box 17100, Montgomery, AL 36193	205-272-7493
Camp Ambassador	Route 1, Box 53-A, Billingsley, AL 36006	
Camp Chula Vista	RT 6 Box 1720, Pell City, AL 35125	205-338-2940
Camp DeSoto	P.O. Box 432, Mentone, AL 35984	205-634-3411
Camp Laney for Boys	P.O. Box 289, Mentone, AL 35984	205-634-3561
Camp Skyline Ranch for Girls	P.O. Box 287, Mentone, AL 35984	800-448-9279
Camp Victory	Route 3, Box 212, Samson, AL 36477	205-898-7948
Marannook, Inc.	P.O. Box 581, Lafayette, AL 36862	205-864-7504
Ponderosa Bible Camp	P.O. Box 285, Mentone, AL 35984	205-634-3795
Saddle Rock Camp For Girls Inc	P.O. Box 299, Mentone, AL 35984	205-634-4608
Shocco Springs	P.O. Box 886, Talladega, AL 35160	205-761-1100
The King's Vineyard	Route 1, Box 168A, Ariton, AL 36311	205-762-2256
Alaska		
Camp Challenge	P.O. Box 1833, Palmer, AK 99645	907-745-3731
Camp Li-Wa	P.O. Box 10434, Fairbanks, AK 99710	907-457-6059
Camp Maranatha	P.O. Box 521038, Big Lake, AK 99652	
Cottonwood Creek Chr. Camp	Little Beaver Camp Ground, Wasilla, AK 99516	907-337-2135
Covenant Bible Camp	Box 32186, Mountain Village, AK 99632	907-591-2015
Echo Ranch Bible Camp	Box 210608, Auke Bay, AK 99821	907-789-9463
LaVerne Griffin Baptist Assembly	HC 33, Box 2893-J, Wasilla, AK 99687	907-376-6887
North Star Bible Camp	Mile 36.5 Hatcher Pass, Willow, AK 99688	907-495-6378
Solid Rock Bible Camp	P.O. Box 489, Soldotna, AK 99669	907-262-4741
Victory Bible Camp	HCO3, Box 8392, Palmer, AK 99645	907-745-4203
Arizona		
Arizona Mennonite Children's Camp	4334 W. Vista Ave., Glendale, AZ 85301	602-931-9241
Camp Grace & Grace Lodge	Rt 3, Box 2568, Lakeside, AZ 85929	602-537-2080
Camp Pinerock	1400 Pine Drive, Prescott, AZ 86303	602-445-8357
Camp Yavapines	P.O. Box 5810, Scottsdale, AZ 85261	602-991-6777
Church Of God Camps - Az	P.O. Box 423, Buckeye, AZ 85326	602-386-4861
Emmanuel Pines Camp	5095 Iron Springs Road, Prescott, AZ 86301	602-445-1509
Friendly Pines Camp	Senator Rd., Hc32 Box 520, Prescott, AZ 86301	602-445-2128
Huachuca Oaks Baptist Camp	Route 1, Box 113, Hereford, AZ 85615	602-378-2200
Lutheran Outdoor Ministry of No. Az	601 E. Highway 260, Payson, AZ 85541	602-474-2552
Mountain Meadow Ranch	Mountain Meadow Ranch, Paxon, AZ 85541	602-478-4435
Mt. Elden Chr. Conf. Ctr.	4005 N. Kaspar, Flagstaff, AZ 86004	602-526-0864

State/Camp	Address	Phone
Pine Summit Bible Camp & Conf.	HC 32 Box 293, Prescott, AZ 86303	
Prescott Pines Baptist Camp and Conference Center	P.O. Box 1226, Prescott, AZ 86302	602-445-5225
Saguaro Camp Cherith	Shadow Rim Ranch, Payson, AZ 85541	602-474-2438
The Comm. of Living Water, Inc.	P.O. Box 443, Cornville, AZ 86325	602-634-4421
Tonto Rim American Baptist Camp	HCR Box 95-P, Payson, AZ 85541	602-478-4630
United Christian Youth Camp	1400 Paradise Valley Road, Prescott, AZ 86303	602-445-0391
Victory Heights Bible Camp	HC 31, Box 161, Show Low, AZ 85901	602-739-4451
Arkansas		
Camp Wyldewood	P.O. Box 1255, Searcy, AR 72143	501-268-6809
Iron Mountain Christian Camp	P.O. Box 1087, Cabot, AR 72023	501-843-2967
John Brown University	Box 3053, Siloam Springs, AR 72761	501-524-3131
N AR District Nazarene Camp	PO Box 188, Greenbrier, AR 72058	501-751-9108
Ozark Conferences, Inc.	1300 Westpark Dr., Suite 5A, Little Rock, AR 72204	501-666-3266
Ozark-Lithia Camp	Star Rt. 10, Box 97, Hot Springs, AR 71909	501-624-9243
Park Hill Baptist Church	P.O. Box 4064, North Little Rock, AR 72116	501-753-3412
California		
Agape Christian Retreat & Conf.	21651 Yucca Road, Perris, CA 92370	714-657-0849
Alliance Redwoods	6250 Bohemian Highway, Occidental, CA 95465	707-874-3507
Alpine Covenant Conference Center	P.O. Box 155, Blue Jay, CA 92317	714-337-6287
American Explorers, Inc.	P.O. Box 985, Brea, CA 92622-0985	213-697-1339
Angeles Crest Christian Camp	2500 E. Nutwood #120, Fullerton, CA 92631	714-870-9190
Buffalo Valley Camp	P.O. Box 2607, Hemet, CA 92343	714-658-7960
California Conference Free Meth.	504 Woodrow Ave., Modesto, CA 95350	000-000-0000
Camp Alandale	P.O. Box 35, Idyllwild, CA 92349	714-659-5253
Camp Alta	P.O. Box 628, Alta, CA 95701	916-389-2277
Camp Berea	21553 Cedar Springs Rd., Twain Harte, CA 95383	209-928-4676
Camp Cedar Crest	P.O. Box 179, Running Springs, CA 92382	714-867-2531
Camp Cherith	11228 Agnes St., Cerritos, CA 90701	714-828-7585
Camp Chinquapin	P.O. Box 4309, Modesto, CA 95352	209-521-0182
Camp Emmanuel	P.O. Box 309, 8346 O'Donovan Rd., Creston, CA 93432	805-238-3582
Camp Hammer	21401 Big Basin Hwy, Boulder Creek, CA 95006	408-338-3200
Camp Maranatha	P.O. Box CC, Idyllwild, CA 92349	714-659-2739
Camp Mattole	P.O. Box 86, Eureka, CA 95501	
Camp O-Ongo For Boys and Girls	P.O. Box 60-CC, Running Springs, CA 92382	714-867-7041
Camp Old Oak Ranch	15250 Old Oak Ranch Rd., Sonora, CA 95370	209-532-4295
Camp Redwood Glen/Salv. Army	3100 Bean Creek Rd., Scotts Valley, CA 95066	408-438-0640
Camp Sugar Pine	48478 Mill Canyon Road, Oakhurst, CA 93644	209-683-4938
Camp Verdugo Pines	P.O. Box 1989, Wrightwood, CA 92397	619-249-3532
Camp Wawona	P.O. Box 2055, Wawona, CA 95389	209-375-6231
Camp Yolijwa	13724 Fenton Ave., Sylmar, CA 91342	818-367-8784
Campus by the Sea	P.O. Box 466, Avalon, CA 90704	231-510-0015
Canyon Meadows Conf. Ctr	41600 Lake Hughes Rd., Lake Hughes, CA 93532	805-724-1225
Capital Christian Center	P.O. Box 89, Weimar, CA 95736	
Captain's Kids Daycamp	3590 Elm Avenue, Long Beach, CA 90807	213-595-6881
Cedar Grove Bible Camp	3456 Triangle Road, Mariposa, CA 95338	209-742-7369
Cedar Lake Christian Camp	P.O. Box 1568, Big Bear Lake, CA 92315	714-866-5714
Church Prayer Ministry Int'l.	35686 Mission Blvd., Fremont, CA 94536	
City Team Camp May-Mac	P.O. Box 357, Felton, CA 95018	408-335-3019
Corralitos Conf. Center	2013 Eureka Canyon Rd., Watsonville, CA 95076	408-724-4235
Diamond Arrow Conf. Grounds	15742 Bloomfield Rd., Nevada City, CA 95959	916-265-3295
Discovery Expeditions/Christian Encounter Ranch	P.O. Box 1022, Grass Valley, CA 95945	916-268-0877
Echo Mountain Ranch Retreat Ctr	19101 Bear Creek Road, Los Gatos, CA 95030	408-354-7703

State/Camp	Address	Phone
El Camino Pines	13724 Fenton Ave., Sylmar, CA 91342	818-367-8784
Emerald Cove Camp	P.O. Box 449-ECC, Bass Lake, CA 93604	209-642-3512
Esther Christian Conference Ctr	P.O. Box 457, Wrightwood, CA 92397	619-249-3615
Family Maintenance Centers, Inc.	9250 Fruitridge Road, Sacramento, CA 95826	916-381-4380
Featherstone Canyon	P.O. Box 301, Lakeside, CA 92040	619-561-8275
Forest Home Christian Conf. Ctr	Forest Home, Forest Falls, CA 92339	714-794-1127
Forward Bible Conference, Inc.	3363 Coon Hollow Road, Placerville, CA 95667	916-622-1892
Golden Valley Camp	P.O. Box 115, Volcano, CA 95689	209-296-4616
Green Oak Ranch	1237 Green Oak Road, Vista, CA 92083	619-727-0251
Harmony Pines Christian Center	P.O. Box 1363, Wrightwood, CA 92397	619-249-6102
Harstone Bible Conference, Inc.	17856 Van Arsdale Road, Potter Valley, CA 95469	707-743-1621
Hartland Christn Camp and Conf. Ctr	P.O. Box 25, Badger, CA 93603	209-337-2349
Heavenly Hills Christian Camp	P.O. Box 1628, Twain Harte, CA 95383	209-586-1306
Hidden Lakes Retreat	44340 Sioux Terr., Fremont, CA 94539	415-651-1126
Hume Lake Christian Camps	256 N. Maple, Fresno, CA 93702	209-251-6043
Idyllwild Pines Camp and Conf. Ctr	P.O. Box 425 (26375 Hwy 243), Idyllwild, CA 92349	714-659-2605
Indian Hills Camp	15763 Lyons Valley Road, Jamul, CA 92035	619-466-7716
J H Mountain Ranch	8525 Homestead Lane, Etna, CA 96027	916-467-3468
Kidder Creek Orchard Camps	P.O. Box 208, Greenview, CA 96037	916-467-3265
Know Your Bible Camp	3462 E. Vista Way, Vista, CA 92084	619-724-4867
Koinonia Conference Grounds	1473 Eureka Canyon Road, Watsonville, CA 95076	408-722-1472
Lake Ave. Congregation Ch.Camp	393 North Lake Ave., Pasadena, CA 91101	818-795-7221
Laurel Pines Camp and Conference Grounds	P.O. Box 75, Redlands, CA 92373	714-793-3994
Let's Go Fishing	22 Del Rio Ct., Moraga, CA 94556	415-376-8277
Meteor Ranch Bible Conference	2255 E. Highway 20, Upper Lake, CA 95485	707-275-2170
Mile High Pines Camp	12131 Harclave Drive, Moreno Valley, CA 92387	714-247-7577
Mission Springs Conference Ctr	1050 Lockhart Gulch Road, Scotts Valley, CA 95066	408-335-9133
Missionary Athletes, Int'l.	P.O. Box 945, La Habra, CA 90633	213-690-4934
Morning Star Outreach	29444 Mission Blvd., Hayward, CA 94544	415-886-8558
Mount Cross Lutheran Camp	P.O. Box 387, Felton, CA 95018	408-336-5179
Mount Hermon Association, Inc.	P.O. Box 413, Mount Hermon, CA 95041	408-335-4466
Mountain Meadows Conference	Long Hayflat Road, Shingletown, CA 96088	916-474-3143
Mt. Gilead Bible Conference Inc.	13485 Green Valley Road, Sebastopol, CA 95472	707-823-4508
Mt. Hope Bible Conference Center	P.O. Box 240, Forbestown, CA 95941	916-675-2022
New Life Chalet	P.O. Box 1554, Pinecrest, CA 95066	209-965-8957
Oak Glen Christian Conf. Center	39364 Oak Glen Road, Yucaipa, CA 92399	714-797-2570
Oakhurst Christian Conf. Center	36616 Mudge Ranch Road, Coarsegold, CA 93614	209-683-6563
Old Oak Ranch Conference Center	15250 Old Oak Ranch Road, Sonora, CA 95370	209-532-4295
Palomar Baptist Camp	Palomar Mountain, CA 92060	619-457-2065
Paradise Springs Conf. Retreat Ctr	Box 68, Valyermo, CA 93563	805-944-4500
Pine Springs Ranch	P.O. Box 37, Mt. Center, CA 92361	714-659-3173
Pine Summit	P.O. Box 2871, Big Bear Lake, CA 92315	714-866-5801
Pine Valley Bible Conf. Grounds	P.O Box 400, Pine Valley, CA 92062	619-473-8879
Pinecrest Conference Center	P.O. Box 409, 1140 Pinecrest Road, Twin Peaks, CA 92391	714-338-4243
Ponderosa Pines Christian Camp	P.O. Box 1247, Running Springs, CA 92382	714-867-7037
Quaker Meadow Camp	P.O. Box 1607, Whittier, CA 90609	213-947-2883
Rancho Agua Viva Ministries	P.O. Box 8495, Chula Vista, CA 92012	619-585-8783
Rancho Capistrano Renewal Center	29251 Camino Capistrano, San Juan Capistrano, CA 92675	714-364-3023
Rancho Del Cielo	14488 Mussey Grade Rd., Ramona, CA 92065	619-789-1322
Rancho Ybarra Christian Camp	3150 Big Tujunga Canyon Road, Tujunga, CA 91042	818-353-2423
Rancho del Rey	655 Burnham Road, Oak View, CA 93022	805-649-3356
Rawhide Ranch	P.O. Box 216, Bonsall, CA 92003	619-758-0083

State/Camp	*Address*	*Phone*
Redwood Christian Park	15000 Two Bar Road, Boulder Creek, CA 95006	408-338-2134
Redwood Glen Baptist Camp	1430 Wurr Road, Loma Mar, CA 94021	415-879-0320
Retreat Ministries, Inc.	P.O. Box 94, Orange, CA 92666	714-532-5241
Sequoia Brigade Camp - A Camp for Boys	2952 Euclid Avenue, Concord, CA 94519	405-689-7618
Shasta Camp Cherith	4942 Stamas Lane #7, Fair Oaks, CA 95628	916-966-6934
Sierra Chr. Conf. Assoc., Inc.	Hell's Hollow Road, Groveland, CA 95350	408-243-0178
Sierra Christian Camping/ Camp Pinebrook	P.O. Box 1147, Pinecrest, CA 95364	209-965-3224
Sierra Pines Baptist Camp	P.O. Box 7, Little Norway, CA 95721	916-659-7111
Silver Spur Christian Conference Ctr	P.O. Box 578, Tuolumne, CA 95379	209-928-4248
Sky Mountain Christian Camp	P.O. Box 79, Emigrant Gap, CA 95715	916-389-2118
Sonshine Camps	2599 Newport Blvd., Costa Mesa, CA 92627	714-966-0763
Springs Of Living Waters	P.O. Box 1, Richardson Springs, CA 95973	916-893-6750
Springs of Living Water Youth with a Mission	15850 Richardson Springs Rd, Richardson Springs, CA 95973	916-893-6750
Summit Adventure	P.O. Box 498, Bass Lake, CA 93604	
The Salvation Army, Camp Mtn Crags and Camp Gilmore	26801 Dorothy Drive, Calabasas, CA 91302	818-347-6327
Tahquitz Conf. Assoc., Inc.	55251 S. Circle Drive, Idyllwild, CA 92349	714-659-2934
The King's Retreat	Drawer V, Tahoe City, CA 95730	916-583-1065
The Neighborhood Church	20600 John Dr., Castro Valley, CA 94546	415-537-4690
Thousand Pines American Baptist Outdoor Center	P.O. Box 3288, Crestline, CA 92325	714-338-2705
Victory Ranch	18080 Gilman Springs Road, Moreno, CA 92360	714-654-7766
Westminster Woods	6510 Bohemian Way, Occidental, CA 95465-9106	707-874-2426
Wolf Mountain Conference Assoc.	16555 Jericho Road, Grass Valley, CA 95949	916-273-8709
Wynola Bible Conference	3565 Wynola Road, Julian, CA 92036	619-765-0288
Young Life's Oakbridge Camp	P.O. Box 1739, Ramona, CA 92065	619-789-6980
Young Life's Woodleaf	P.O. Box 397, Challenge, CA 95925	916-675-2252
Colorado		
Bear Trap Ranch	P.O. Box 1327, Colorado Springs, CO 80901	719-632-0740
Black Forest Camp and Conf. Ctr	780 East Baptist Road, Colorado Springs, CO 80921	719-488-3750
Camp Cedaredge	1998 Highway 65, Cedaredge, CO 81413	303-856-6343
Camp Chief Ouray/YMCA of the Rockies	P.O. Box 648, Granby, CO 80446	303-887-2152
Camp Christian	P.O. Box 932, Clifton, CO 81520	303-984-2211
Camp Eden	11583 Camp Eden Road, Golden, CO 80403	303-642-3683
Camp Elim	5567 County Road 78, Woodland Park, CO 80863	719-687-2030
Camp Id-Ra-Ha-Je	571 County Road 43, Bailey, CO 80421	303-674-8442
Camp Id-Ra-Ha-Je West	27862 Co. Rd. 12, Somerset, CO 81434	303-929-5221
Camp Redcloud Inc.	P.O. Box 130, Lake City, CO 81235	303-944-2625
Camp Santa Maria	P.O. Box 28003, Lakewood, CO 80228-0003	303-935-0035
Christian & Miss. Alliance	P.O. Box 35000, Colorado Springs, CO 80935-3500	914-353-0750
Christian Wilderness Encounters	P.O. Box 28147, El Jebel, CO 81628	303-963-3215
Colorado Camp Cherith	1622 14th Avenue, Greeley, CO 80631	303-353-3170
Colorado Christian Service Camp	2017 W. Kiowa, Colorado Springs, CO 80904	719-634-3318
Covenant Heights Bible Camp	Longs Peak Route, Estes Park, CO 80517	303-586-2900
Crested Butte Family Life	Box 5023, Mt. Crested Butte, CO 81225	303-349-6307
Cross Bar X Youth Ranch	2111 County Road 222, Durango, CO 81301	303-259-2716
Deer Creek Christian Camp	228 S. Pine Drive, Bailey, CO 80421	303-838-5647
Eagle Lake Camp	P.O. Box 6000, Colorado Springs, CO 80934	719-472-1260
Eagle Ranch	26916 Highway 146, Dolores, CO 81323	303-562-3816
Estes Park Center	PO Box 20800, Estes Park, CO 80511-2800	
Golden Bell Ranch	380 County Road 512, Divide, CO 80814	719-687-9561

State/Camp	*Address*	*Phone*
Hamilton's Glory Cabin	Breckenridge, CO 80210	
High Peak Camp (The Salv. Army)	1930 Sherman St., Denver, CO 80203	303-861-4833
Horn Creek Conference Grounds	Westcliffe, CO 81252	719-783-2279
K-Life Summer Kamps	3651 S. Colorado Blvd., Englewood, CO 80110	303-781-0091
Living Rock Christian Retreat	P.O. Box 209, South Fork, CO 81154	719-873-5215
Meadowdale Ranch Conf. Center	5532 U.S. Highway 36 - LPR, Estes Park, CO 80517	303-586-4359
Noah's Ark Whitewater Rafting Co.	P.O. Box 850, Buena Vista, CO 81211	719-395-2158
Presbyterian Highlands Camp	P.O. Box 66, Allenspark, CO 80510	303-747-2888
Quaker Ridge Camp & Stables	30150 N. Highway 67, Woodland Park, CO 80863	719-687-9012
Rainbow Falls Park	P.O. Box 9062, Woodland Park, CO 80866	719-687-9074
Rocky Mountain Brigade Camp	P.O. Box 36280, Denver, CO 80236	303-972-2518
Rocky Mountain Mennonite Camp	709 County Road 62, Divide, CO 80814	719-687-9506
Singing River Ranch	1619 County 480, Evergreen, CO 80439	
Snow Mountain Ranch	PO Box 169, Winter Park, CO 80482	
Sonlight Christian Camp	P.O. Box 536, Pagosa Springs, CO 81147	303-264-4379
Spring Canyon	26000 C.R. 344, Buena Vista, CO 81211	303-395-2328
Twin Peaks Bible Camp	3058 1/2 Hill Ave., Grand Junction, CO 81504	303-434-8308
Woodbine Ranch	2584 N. Highway 67, Sedalia, CO 80135	303-688-3422
Young Life's Frontier Ranch	22150 Co. Rd. 322 POB 2025, Buena Vista, CO 81211	719-395-8696
Young Life's Trail West Lodge	Route 1, Buena Vista, CO 81211	303-395-2477
Young Life's Wilderness Ranch	General Delivery, Creede, CO 81130	303-473-4262
Connecticut		
Camp Berea, Inc.	Box 1105 J., Groton, CT 06340	203-572-8563
Evangelical Baptist Camp	574 Ashford Center Road, Ashford, CT 06778	
Mountain Lake Bible Conference	64 Mountain Lake Road, New Preston, CT 06777	203-868-2048
Delaware		
Camp Cherith in Pennsylvania	26 Broadfield Drive, Newark, DE 19713	302-731-1453
Surf Sessions	Route 3, Box 275B, Fenwick Island, DE 19944	302-539-2126
District of Columbia		
Camp Dynamite	1100 Savannah Street SE, Washington, DC 20032	202-574-3053
Camp Lightfoot	1522 R Street, N.W., Washington, DC 20009	202-387-8233
Florida		
ACA Academy	36540 Via Marcia Street, Fruitland Park, FL 32731	
Boca Raton Comm. Church Bible Town Ministries	601 N.W. 4th Avenue, Boca Raton, FL 33432	407-367-6823
Camp Dovewood	P.O. Box 606, Branford, FL 32008	904-935-0863
Camp Gilead	P.O. Box 98, Polk City, FL 33868	813-984-1353
Camp Horizon	7369 Sunnyside Drive, Leesburg, FL 34748	904-728-5822
Camp Kuluqua	Rt. 2 Box 110, High Springs, FL 32643	904-454-1351
Camp Limp A Little	17 Tera Lane, Winter Haven, FL 33880	813-299-8612
Camp O' The Pines	Box 18000, Pensacola, FL 32523	904-478-8480
Camp Sonlight	P.O. Box 183, Summerfield, FL 32691	904-245-9568
Camp Suwannee Retreat Center	P.O. Box 4313, Dowling Park, FL 32060	904-658-3333
Canaveral Christian Retreat Center	885 East Hall Road, Merritt Island, FL 32953	407-453-0350
Church of God Youth and Retreat Ctr	P.O. Box 895100, Leesburg, FL 34789	904-742-2500
Fl. Sheriffs Youth Camp	P.O. Box 1000, Barberville, FL 32105	904-749-9999
Gold Coast Christian Camp Inc.	7495 Parklane Road, Lake Worth, FL 33467	407-968-3136
Lake Aurora Christian Assembly	237 Golden Bough Road, Lake Wales, FL 33853	813-696-1102
Lake Swan Camp	Rt. 1, Box 1294, Melrose, FL 32666	
Land o' Sunshine Camp Cherith	Advent Christian Village, Dowling Park, FL 32060	813-397-3430
Maranatha Ministries Inc.	2665 Placid View Dr., Lake Placid, FL 33852	813-465-2197
North Florida Christian Svc. Camp	6779 Camp Road, Keystone Heights, FL 32656	904-473-3281
Teen Missions International, Inc.	885 East Hall Road, Merritt Island, FL 32953	407-453-0350

State/Camp	*Address*	*Phone*
The Lord's Barn Christian Retreat	2500 S.W. 167th Avenue, Homestead, FL 33031	305-248-6890
The Salv. Army Camp Keystone	P.O. Box 270848, Tampa, FL 33688-0848	813-962-6611
Voice in the Wilderness	19255 Campground Road, Brookville, FL 34601	904-796-6589
Young Life's Southwind	P.O. Box 550, Oklawaha, FL 32679	904-288-2500
Georgia		
Bible Memory Assoc. Camp & Conference Center	Route 7, Box 7402, Cleveland, GA 30528	404-865-2084
Calvin Center	13550 Woolsey Road, Hampton, GA 30228	404-946-4191
Camp Agape	2601 Flat Shoals Road, College Park, GA 30349	404-996-0600
Camp Hope	Rt. 2 Pony Lake Rd., Dahlonega, GA 30533	404-536-4787
Camp J.O.Y.	P.O. Box 1232, Hamilton, GA 31902	404-322-8267
Camp Westminster	Westminster Presby. Church, Atlanta, GA 30324	404-636-1496
Camp Win Shape	9 Berry College, Mt. Berry, GA 30149	404-235-8407
Coastal Empire Christn Svc. Camp	Route 1, Box 371, Sylvania, GA 30467	912-829-3994
Cohutta Springs Adventist Center	Route 1, Box 17-A, Crandall, GA 30711	404-695-9093
Community Bible Church	Rt. 3 Box 346-A, Dahlonega, GA 30533	404-953-8882
Fellowship Valley Retreat	Route 3, Box 3298, Clarkesville, GA 30523	404-754-4804
Hi-Life Christian Camp, Inc.	403 West Cuyler Street, Dalton, GA 30720	404-278-9713
North Georgia Christian Camp	Rt. 4, Box 4257, Clarkesville, GA 30523	
Rockridge Baptist Assembly	P.O. Box 267, Franklin, GA 30217	404-675-3494
Toccoa Wilderness Ministries	P.O. Box 1266, Blue Ridge, GA 30513	404-632-3554
Woodland Christian Camp	90 Woodland Camp Road, Temple, GA 30179	404-562-3103
Hawaii		
Camp Homelani	68-581 Crozier Dr., Waialua, HI 96791	808-637-4131
Camp Mokuleia	68-729 Farrington Hwy., Waialua, HI 96791	808-637-6241
Idaho		
ALACCA Bible Conference	HCR 67, Box 40, Grangeville, ID 83550	208-983-1188
Cocolalla Lake Bible Camp	East 2750 Killdeer Lane, Post Falls, ID 83854	208-773-3223
Daystar Conference Center	P.O. Box 455, Donnelly, ID 83615	208-325-8210
Lake Pend Oreille Camp and Retreat Center	P.O. Box 1756, Coeurd'Alene, ID 83814	208-664-5129
Quaker Hill Conf., Inc.	P.O. Box 1181, Mc Call, ID 83638	208-634-2083
Ross Point Camp and Conf. Center	S. 600 Ross Point Road, Post Falls, ID 83854	208-773-1655
Team Adventures Serving the Community - T.A.S.C.	21 S. Owyher, Boise, ID 83705	208-385-9557
Victory Cove	P.O. Box 971, Mc Call, ID 83638	208-634-2072
Illinois		
Camp Awana	3859 N. Central, Chicago, IL 60634	312-736-2792
Camp Good News	R.R. #1, Liberty Lane, Washington, IL 61571	309-444-3255
Camp Hickory	P.O. Box 400, Round Lake, IL 60073	708-546-2855
Camp Hope	Route 1, Box 69, Ewing, IL 62836	618-629-2188
Camp Kearney	311 Olive, Peoria, IL 61602	309-676-4604
Camp Manitoqua	8122 West Sauk Trail, Frankfort, IL 60423	815-469-2319
Camp Maranatha	RR 1 Box 143, Ramsey, IL 62080	217-539-4583
Camp Moyoca	22925 W. Villa Rica Rd., Antioch, IL 60002	708-395-9890
Camp One Way	Route 1, Box 245C, Mt. Auburn, IL 62547	217-676-2533
Central Illinois Conf. - UMC	1211 N. Park St., Bloomington, IL 61702	309-828-5092
City Limits Urban Camp	5100 W. Diversey, Chicago, IL 60639	312-286-0767
Dickson Valley Camp & Conf.	17K420 Finnie Road, Newark, IL 60541	
Easter Seal Camp Heffernan	206 S. Linden, Suite 4A, Normal, IL 61761	309-452-8074
Great Oaks Camping Association	Great Oaks Camp, P.O. Box 236, Lacon, IL 61540	309-674-7848
Green Valley Camp	501 E. Poplett's Hollow, Peoria, IL 61615	309-691-3079
Inner City Impact	2704 W. North Avenue, Chicago, IL 60647	312-384-4200

State/Camp	*Address*	*Phone*
LaMoine Christian Service Camp	R.R. 1, Box 46, Tennessee, IL 62374	217-654-2238
Lake Helen Bible Camp	P.O. Box 942, Decatur, IL 62525	217-423-2022
Lake Williamson Christian Center	P.O. Box 225, Carlinville, IL 62626	217-854-9686
Land-O-Lincoln Camp Cherith	Route 1, Tiskilwa, IL 61368	815-646-4344
Little Galilee Christian Assembly	R.R. 2, Box 266, Clinton, IL 61727	217-935-3809
Manville Nazarene Camp	Route 1, Box 181, Cornell, IL 61319	815-358-2522
Menno Haven	R.R. 1, Box 94, Tiskilwa, IL 61368-9710	815-646-4344
Moody Bible Institute	820 N. LaSalle Dr., Chicago, IL 60610	312-329-4000
Reynoldswood Christian Camp and Retreat Center	621 Reynoldswood Road, Dixon, IL 61021	815-284-6979
Riverwoods Christian Center	35701 Riverwoods Lane, St. Charles, IL 60174	708-584-2222
Rock River Bible Camp	P.O. Box 422, Dixon, IL 61021	815-652-4410
Rock River Christian Camp	16482 IL Rt 64W, Polo, IL 61064	815-493-6622
The Wilderness Experience Camp	5208 W 22 Place, Cicero, IL 60650	
Trail Ridge Camp Cherith	Box 486, Wheaton, IL 60189	708-668-1115
Triple Creek Ranch	PO Box 348, Elizabeth, IL 61028	
Wilhaven Day Camps, Inc.	P.O. Box 442, Libertyville, IL 60048	708-367-2267
Indiana		
Bear Lake Camp	RR 4, Box 125, Albion, IN 46701	
Beechwood Lake Camp	Rt. 5 Box 99E, Bloomfield, IN 47424	812-825-7770
Bible Memory Program	Box 382, Goshen, IN 46526	219-533-5388
Brethren Retreat Center	Route 3, Box 162, Shipshewana, IN 46565	219-768-4519
Camp Alexander Mack Camp and Conference Center	P.O. Box 158, Milford, IN 46542	219-658-4831
Camp Allendale	Route 1, Box 72, Trafalgar, IN 46181	317-878-4400
Camp Brosend	7599 Brosend Rd., Newburgh, IN 47630	812 853-3466
Camp Challenge	Rt. #16, Box 530, Bedford, IN 47421	812-834-5159
Camp Crosley	500 South Mulberry Street, Muncie, IN 47305	
Camp Good News	P.O. Box 344, North Webster, IN 46555	219-834-2769
Camp Ray Bird	808 South Michigan, South Bend, IN 46618	219-232-8523
Camp Reveal	1040 E. Boonville, New Harmony Road, Evansville, IN 47711	812-867-2668
Camp Tecumseh YMCA	Route #2, Box 311, Brookstown, IN 47923	317-564-2898
Cedar Lake Bible Conference and Youth Camps	P.O. Box 665, Cedar Lake, IN 46303	219-374-5941
Crystal Lake Baptist Camp	205 N. County Road 700 W., Warsaw, IN 46580	219-858-2451
Epworth Forest Conference Center	P.O. Box 16, North Webster, IN 46555	219-834-2212
F.C.A. National Conf. Center	Rt. 1, Box 81A, Marshall, IN 47859	317-597-2323
Higher Ground Camping and Retreat Ctr	3915 St. Route 46, West Harrison, IN 47060	812-637-3777
Lake James Christian Assembly	Route 2, Box 581, Angola, IN 46703	219-833-2786
Lake Placid Conference Center	0397 S. 200 E., Hartford City, IN 47348	317-348-3641
Lake Region Chrst.Assbly.	7005 E. 117th Ave., Crown Point, IN 46307	219-769-3855
Outdoor Ministries	P.O. Box 5008, Bloomington, IN 47407-5008	812-336-0186
Prairie Camp	28042 C.R. 24 West, Elkhart, IN 46517	219-293-1332
Quaker Haven Camp	R.R. 5, Box 183, Syracuse, IN 46567	219-834-4193
Rainbow Christian Camp	3522 N 1000 W 27, Converse, IN 46919	
Salvation Army Camp	RR 16 Box 180-1089, Bedford, IN 47421-9806	812-279-2495
Walnut Hills Retreat Ministry, Inc.	10026 E. Northshore Drive, Unionville, IN 47468	812-988-4405
Iowa		
Camp Hantesa	RR 1, Boone, IA 50036	
Camp Pine Lake	Route 2, Box 393, Eldora, IA 50627	515-858-5334
Camp Quaker Heights	Route 3, Box 53, Pine Lake, Eldora, IA 50627	515-858-5977
Central Baptist Camp	R.R. #1, Box 191-A, Lansing, IA 52151	319-535-7320

State/Camp	*Address*	*Phone*
Clear Lake United Methodist Camp	R.R. #1, Box 210, Clear Lake, IA 50428	515-357-2085
Dayton Oaks Baptist Camp	R.R. 1, Dayton, IA 50530	515-547-2417
East Iowa Bible Camp	R.R. 2, Deep River, IA 52222	319-655-7693
Ewalu Camp & Retreat Center	Rt. 2, Strawberry Point, IA 52076	
Forest Lake Baptist Camp	R.R. 3, Box 284, Bloomfield, IA 52537	515-684-8908
Hidden Acres	R.R. 1, Dayton, IA 50530	515-547-2751
Inspiration Hills Midwest Reformed Church Camp	R.R. 1, Box 168, Inwood, IA 51240	712-986-5193
Pine Lake Christian Center	Box 535, Eldora, IA 50627	515-858-3284
The Episcopal Center of Camps & Conferences	RR #4, Box 276, Boone, IA 50036	515-432-4389
Twin Lakes Bible Camp	RR 1, Box 194, Manson, IA 50563	712-297-7714
Willowbrook Bible Camp	4375 N.E. 38th St., Des Moines, IA 50317	515-262-5026
Kansas		
Camp Daniel	Route 2, Box 64C, Bonner Springs, KS 66012	913-441-6030
Camp Hiawatha - Salvation Army	1701 W 51st N, Wichita, KS 67204	
Camp Quaker Haven	RR 4, Box 453, Arkansas City, KS 67005	316-442-9690
Kansas Bible Camp	4508 W. 56th St., Hutchinson, KS 67502	316-662-7791
The Shepherd's Staff Conference & Retreat Center	Main and Kansas, Box 66, Rexford, KS 67753	913-687-3335
Kentucky		
Bethel Mennonite Camp	Buckhorn Creek Rd., Clayhole, KY 41317	606-666-4911
Bluegrass Christian Camp	7463 Athens Boonesboro Rd, Lexington, KY 40509	606-263-5239
Camp Nathanael	P.O. Drawer 129, Emmalena, KY 41740	606-251-3231
Eagle Ridge Center	8744 Barren River Rd., Bowling Green, KY 42101	502-843-1899
Twin Rocks Bible Camp	RR #1, Box 26-H, Viper, KY 41774	606-436-6643
Louisiana		
BMA Camp & Conference Center	P.O. Box 12000, Ringgold, LA 71068	318-894-3424
Judson Baptist Retreat Center	Route 1, Box 9H, Jackson, LA 70748	504-634-7225
Okaloosa Baptist Encampment	1280 Okaloosa Road, Eros, LA 71238	318-249-4495
Tall Timbers Bapt. Conf.	Route 1, Box 134a, Forest Hill, LA 71430	318-445-6797
Maine		
Aroostook Bible Camp	RFD 1, Box 227, Allagash, ME 04774	207-398-3403
Camp Berea	North Turner, ME 04266	207-224-7730
Camp Good News of Maine	778 Forest Avenue, Portland, ME 04103	207-772-8642
Camp Lawroweld	RR #1, Box 27, Weld, ME 04285	207-585-9229
Camp NOMACCA	15 3rd Street, Presque Isle, ME 04769	207-764-5499
Fair Haven Camps	RR #2, Box 1180, Brooks, ME 04921	207-722-3456
New England Camp Cherith	P.O. Box 154, Alfred, ME 04002	207-247-5251
Maryland		
Beachmont Christian Camp	6433 Mt. Vista Rd., Kingsville, MD 21087	301-592-8768
Camp Sandy Hill	P.O. Box B, North East, MD 21901	301-287-5160
Cedar Ridge Ministries - Wilderness Challenge	P.O. Box 439, Williamsport, MD 21795	301-582-0282
Hilltop	1089 Nesbitt Rd., Colora, MD 21917	301-658-5799
Peach Orchard Retreat Center	15712 Peach Orchard Rd, Silver Spring, MD 20905	301-384-2883
SDA Youth Camp	Rt. #1, Box 283, Hagerstown, MD 21740	301-824-2729
Summit Lake Camp	7610 Hampton Valley Rd., Emmitsburg, MD 21727	301-770-5338
Massachusetts		
American Baptist Camp & Conf. Centers of Massachusetts	Prescott Street, Groton, MA 01450	508-448-5763
Bement Camp and Conf. Center	Drawer F, Charlton Depot, MA 01509	508-248-7811

State/Camp	Address	Phone
Camp Chilaven	P.O. Box 152, E. Douglas, MA 01516	508-476-7766
Camp Northfield	RR 1, Box 62, Northfield, MA 01360	413-498-5984
Focus Study Center	RFD Box 459, Vineyard Haven, MA 02568	617-693-1359
Horizons Educational Assoc.	23 Pickering St., P.O. Box 98, Essex, MA 01929	508-468-6525
Lakeside Christian Camp	195 Cloverdale St., Pittsfield, MA 01201	413-447-8930
New England Keswick	P.O. Box 156, Chestnut Hill Rd, Monterey, MA 01245	413-528-3604
Salv. Army Camp Wonderland	147 Beverley St., Boston, MA 02116	617-542-5420
Michigan		
Bair Lake Bible Camp	12500 Prang St., Jones, MI 49061	616-244-5193
Bay Shore Camp	450 N. Miller, Sebewaing, MI 48759	517-883-2501
Brook Cherith Camp	4050 County Line Road, Pierson, MI 49339	616-937-5305
Camp Amigo	26455 Banker Road, Sturgis, MI 49091-9355	616-651-2811
Camp Ao-Wa-Kiya	8415 Glen Drive, Shelby, MI 49455	616-861-2466
Camp Arcadia	Arcadia, MI 49613	616-889-4361
Camp Au Sable	P.O. Box 546, Grayling, MI 49738	517-348-5491
Camp Barakel	P.O. Box 157, Fairview, MI 48621	517-848-2279
Camp Beechpoint	3212 125th Ave., Allegan, MI 49010	616-673-6155
Camp Friedenswald	15406 Watercress Drive, Cassopolis, MI 49031	616-476-2426
Camp Kaskitowa	4655 52nd, Holland, MI 49423	616-396-6460
Camp Lakeview, Inc.	5868 Tody Road, Goodrich, MI 48438	313-627-2530
Camp Living Waters	Route 1, Box 73, Luther, MI 49656	616-797-5107
Camp Mel Tro Mi	225 Commerce SW, Grand Rapids, MI 49503	616-691-7192
Camp Michawana	5800 Headlake, Hastings, MI 49058	616-623-5168
Camp Paradise	Box 657, Newberry, MI 49868	708-382-6200
Camp Selah	3600 Long Lake Road, Reading, MI 49274	517-283-2527
Camp Tall Turf	49 Bel-Air, Grand Rapids, MI 49503-3915	616-454-5308
Cedar Campus	P.O. Box 425, Cedarville, MI 49719	906-484-2294
Center Lake Bible Camp	4200 W. Twenty Mile Road, Tustin, MI 49688	616-829-3441
Christian Camping Ministries, Inc.	189-126th Avenue, Wayland, MI 49348	616-792-2081
Christie Lake Bible Camp	66713 Territorial Road, Lawrence, MI 49064	
Circle Y Ranch Inc.	65361 34th Ave., Bangor, MI 49013	616-427-7127
Cran-Hill Ranch	14444 17 Mile Road, Rodney, MI 49342	616-796-7669
Eagle Village Camps	R.R. #1, Box 300, Hersey, MI 49639	616-832-2234
Fa-Ho-Lo Park	3000 Mt. Hope Rd., Grass Lake, MI 49240	517-522-4510
Five Pines Christian Family Center	6597 Smith Road, Berrien Center, MI 49102	616-471-1396
Geneva Camp and Conference Ctr	3990 Lakeshore Drive, Holland, MI 49424	616-399-3150
Gitche Gumee Bible Camp	P.O. Box 30, Eagle River, MI 49924	906-337-0527
Good News Camp	3613 North M-30, Gladwin, MI 48624	517-426-9074
Grace Youth Camp	Box 392, Mears, MI 49436	616-873-3662
Gull Lake Bible Conference	1988 Midlake Drive, Hickory Corners, MI 49060	616-671-5155
Hiawatha Youth Camp	Box D, Southgate, MI 48195	313-284-0200
Honey Creek Christian Homes	11652 Grand River Avenue, Lowell, MI 49331	616-897-8461
Horizon Conferences	7176 Elm Drive, Manton, MI 49663	
Huron Forest Camp Cherith	1154 West River Road, Oscoda, MI 48750	517-739-3571
IDRAHAJE Youth Camp	214 N. Heisterman Street, Bad Axe, MI 48413	517-269-8904
Lael Baptist Camp	2062 Ferns Road, Lapeer, MI 48446	313-664-6795
Lake Ann Baptist Camp Inc.	P.O. Box 109, Lake Ann, MI 49650	616-275-7329
Lake Ellen Baptist Camp	212 Baptist Camp Road, Crystal Falls, MI 49920	906-542-3529
Lake Louise Baptist Camp	10750 Stafford Road, Boyne Falls, MI 49713	616-549-2889
Life Action Ranch	Clear Lake Road, Buchanan, MI 49107	616-695-2191
Little Pine Island Camp	6889 Little Pine Isl. Dr., Comstock Park, MI 49321	616-784-1404
Mahn-Go-Tah-See	P.O. Box 126, Hale, MI 48739	517-728-2495
Manton Youth Camp	9528 E. 16 mi. Rd., Manton, MI 49663	616-824-3200
Maranatha Bible and Mission. Conf.	4759 Lake Harbor Road, Muskegon, MI 49441	616-798-2161
Michiana Christian Service Camp	1619 Steinbauer Road, Niles, MI 49120	616-683-4403

State/Camp	Address	Phone
Michindoh Camp and Conf. Center	4545 E. Bacon Road, Hillsdale, MI 49242	517-523-3616
Miracle Camp	25281 80th Avenue, Lawton, MI 49065	616-624-6161
New Life Camp	701 E. Mayhew Road, Rose City, MI 48654	517-685-2949
Pine Ridge Bible Camp & Conf. Ctr	8415 17 Mile Rd, Cedar Springs, MI 49319-9566	616-866-1071
Pine Trail Camp	P.O. Box 35, Saugatuck, MI 49453	616-857-2564
Pioneers in Educational Prog.	1003 S. Oakland Street, St. Johns, MI 48879	517-224-5195
Portage Lake Cov. Bible Camp	Camp Delight Rd., Onekama, MI 49675	616-889-5911
Rock Lake Christian Assembly	7384 Vestaburg Road, Vestaburg, MI 48891	
Salvation Army Echo Grove Camp and Conference Center	1101 Camp Road, Leonard, MI 48038	313-628-3108
Simpson Park Camp	70199 Campground Road, Romeo, MI 48065	303-752-3202
Skyline Retreat Center and Summer Camp	5650 Sandhill Road, Almont, MI 48003	313-798-8240
Somerset Beach Campground	P.O. Box 307, Somerset Center, MI 49282	517-688-3783
Spring Hill Camps	Box 100, Evart, MI 49631	616-734-2616
Upper Peninsula Bible Camp	Box 377, Little Lake, MI 49833	906-346-6165
Warner Camp	P.O. Box 165, Grand Junction, MI 49056	616-434-6844
Wildwood Ranch	4909 Brophy, Howell, MI 48843	313-965-3224
Wisdom Valley Ranch & Camps	P.O. Box 3601, Grand Rapids, MI 49501-3601	616-243-6954
Youth Haven Ranch	3796 Perrine Rd., Bx 97, Rives Junction, MI 49277	517-569-3328
Minnesota		
Big Sandy Camp	HCR #3, Box 567, McGregor, MN 55760	218-426-3389
Big Stone Camp For Christ	RR 1, Ortonville, MN 56278	612-839-3001
Camp Good News	7000 -57th Ave., No., Ste #118, Crystal, MN 55428	612-536-0444
Camp Lebanon	Box 370, Upsala, MN 56384	612-573-2125
Camp Shamineau	Route 1, Motley, MN 56466	218-575-2240
Covenant Park Bible Camp	1572 County Road 7, Mahtowa, MN 55762	218-389-6398
Covenant Pines Bible Camp	HCR 4, Box 440, McGregor, MN 55760	218-768-2610
Inspiration Point Bible Camp	Route 1, Box 156, Clitherall, MN 56524	218-864-5379
Lake Beauty Covenant Bible Camp	Route 1, Box 149, Long Prairie, MN 56347	612-732-3218
Lake Geneva Bible Camp	1315 Portland Ave., South, Minneapolis, MN 55404	612-332-2409
Lake Koronis Assembly Grounds	15752 Country Road 181, Paynesville, MN 56362	612-243-4544
Lost Timber Bible Camp	RR 1, Box 152, Chandler, MN 56122	507-677-2555
Mink Lake Wilderness Camp	1901 West County Road E-2, St. Paul, MN 55112	612-633-0560
Nathanael Brigade Camp	4230 Kings Drive, Minnetonka, MN 55345	612-935-3714
North Central Camp Cherith	11308 Quinn Street NW, Coon Rapids, MN 55433	612-754-1878
Pioneer Campsite	130 Pioneer Drive, Wabasha, MN 55981	612-565-2242
Plymouth Point Bible Camp	HC 74, Box 2460, Hackensack, MN 56452	218-682-2714
Shalom House	HCR 77, Box 145, Pine River, MN 56474	218-543-4565
Shetek Baptist Camp, Inc.	P.O. Box 141, Slayton, MN 56172	
Silver Lake Camp, The Salv. Army	2950 West County Road E, Minneapolis, MN 55421	612-788-9048
Strawberry Lakes Christian Retreat	Route 1, Box 59, Ogema, MN 56569	218-983-3217
Timber Bay Camp	HCR 67, Box 382, Onamia, MN 56359	612-532-3200
Trout Lake Camp	HCR #77, Box 145, Pine River, MN 56474	218-543-4565
Wilderness Outreach	P.O. Box 727, Grand Marais, MN 55604	218-387-1620
Young Life's Castaway Club	Route #5, Box 374, Detroit Lakes, MN 56501	218-532-2662
Mississippi		
Camp Garaywa	P.O. Box 530, Jackson, MS 39205	601-968-3800
Camp Hidden Lake	Rt. 2 Box 21-B, Lexington, MS 39095	601-834-2149
Camp Of The Rising Son	French Camp Academy, French Camp, MS 39745	601-547-6169
Camp Pioneer	P.O. Box 6182, Jackson, MS 39208	601-939-3659
Central Hills Baptist Retreat	P.O. Box 237, Kosciusko, MS 39090-0237	601-289-9730
Lake Forest Ranch	Route 4, Box 189, Macon, MS 39341	601-726-4388
Lifeline Ministries	P.O. Box 627, Louisville, MS 39339	800-726-8915

State/Camp	*Address*	*Phone*
Pine Lake Fellowship Camp	Route 14, Box 272, Meridian, MS 39307	601-483-2267
Salvation Army Camp Hidden Lake	Route 2, Box 21-B, Lexington, MS 39095	601-834-2149
Twin Lakes Conference Center	Route 2, Box 148B, Florence, MS 39073	601-845-6858
Missouri		
Camp Allen	RFD 1, Box 45, Greenville, MO 63944	314-224-3826
Camp Bended Knee	P.O. Box 250, Van Buren, MO 63965	314-323-4347
Camp Penuel	P.O. Box 367, Ironton, MO 63650	314-546-3020
Camp Soaring Hawk	Pioneer Trail, Purdy, MO 65734	417-476-2565
Christian Witness Center	P.O. Box 746, Warsaw, MO 65355	816-438-7710
Dayspring Bible Camp	9470 Eddie and Park Road, St. Louis, MO 63126	314-843-2189
Discovery Ministries	Route 3, Box 32, Eminence, MO 65466	314-226-3213
First Baptist Church	525 South Ave., Springfield, MO 65806	417-866-7205
Heritage Crossing Camp	Route 4, Box 208C, Sullivan, MO 63080	314-629-0607
Kanakuk Kanakomo Kamps	HCR 4, Box 2124, Branson, MO 65616	417-334-2432
Logan Valley Christian Retreat	Route 3, Box 255, Ellington, MO 63638	314-663-2735
MO State Free Will Bapt. Camp	HCR-83, Niangua, MO 65713	417-473-6444
Miracle Hills Ranch	P.O. Box 272, Bethany, MO 64424	816-425-2278
Ne-Ka-Mo- Camp Cherith	8621 E. 83rd Terrace, Raytown, MO 64138	816-356-9028
Pinecrest Camp	HCR 71, Box 576, Fredericktown, MO	314-783-3534
Stoney Point Camp	Route 1, Box 594, Mineral Point, MO 63660	
The Salvation Army Camp Mihaska	State Route 23, Bourbon, MO 65441	314-732-5239
Turkey Hill Ranch Bible Camp	Route 71, Box 190, Vienna, MO 65582	314-744-5843
Windermere Baptist Assembly	P.O. Box 458 State Road AA, Roach, MO 65787	314-346-2205
YMCA Camp Lakewood	Rt #2, Potosi, MO 63664	314-438-2154
Montana		
Big Sky Bible Camp	501 McCaffery Road, Bigfork, MT 59911	406-837-4864
C-Bar-N Camp	P.O. Box 366, Augusta, MT 59410	406-562-3608
Camp Bighorn	321 Highway 135 South, Plains, MT 59859	406-826-3144
Clydehurst Christian Ranch	802 N. 27th Street, Billings, MT 59101	406-252-3886
Eastern Montana Bible Camp	Rt. 2, Box 120, Savage, MT 59262	
Glacier Kids	1702 Colton Blvd., Billings, MT 59102	
Legendary Lodge	Box 405, Greenough, MT 59836	406-677-2211
Mizpah Christn Retreat & Conf. Ctr	2121 U.S. Highway 89N, White Sulfur Springs, MT 59645	406-547-3833
Pines Youth Camp	P.O. Box 167, Glasgow, MT 59230	406-367-5271
Trail's End Ranch	Box 271, Ekalaka, MT 59324	406-775-6401
North Carolina		
Advent Christian General Conf.	P.O. Box 23152, Charlotte, NC 28212	704-545-6161
Ambassador Camp	119 W. Lewis Street, Whiteville, NC 28472	919-642-2853
Appalachian Advent Christn Camp	Rt. 1, Box 399, Blowing Rock, NC 28605	704-295-3525
Camp Cherith in the Carolinas	2937 Welcome Drive, Durham, NC 27705	919-489-9300
Camp Dayspring (Formerly C.E. Youth Camp)	P.O. Box 150, 7545 Highway 29 S., Browns-Summit, NC 27214	919-656-7937
Camp Dixie Inc.	Route 7, Box 247, Fayetteville, NC 28306	919-865-5180
Camp Lurecrest	7700 Wallace Street, Charlotte, NC 28212	704-568-7704
Camp Maranatha	Route 1, Box 460, Siler City, NC 27334	919-742-5617
Camp Oak Hill and Retreat Center	P.O. Box 6176, Raleigh, NC 27628	919-782-2888
Camp Rockmont	Lake Eden Road, Black Mountain, NC 28711	704-686-3885
Camp Willow Run	Camp Willow Run, Mangum Ln, Littleton, NC 27850	919-586-4665
Crusader Youth Camp	P.O. Box 1568, Dunn, NC 28334	919-892-4161
Falcon Youth Camp	P.O. Box 60, Falcon, NC 28342	919-980-1162
Hickory Cove Bible Camp	Route 6, Box 313, Taylorsville, NC 28681	704-632-2987
Living Water Ministries	750 W. Deep Creek Road, Bryson City, NC 28713	704-488-6012

State/Camp	Address	Phone
Merriwood Christian Camp	9640 Ctr GroveChurch Rd, Clemmons, NC 27012	919-766-5151
Mountain Top Youth Camp	P.O. Box 4086, Winston Salem, NC 27105	919-674-0924
Mountain Top Youth Camp	Rt. 1, Box 258, Pinnacle, NC 27043	919-767-7158
New Life Camp	Route 7, Box 251, Raleigh, NC 27614	919-847-0764
NOSOCA Pines Ranch	P.O. Box 25848, Charlotte, NC 28229-5848	704-535-6720
Parson of the Hills Camp Joy for Needy Children	P.O. Box 41, Hickory, NC 28603	704-328-1541
Pinhook Valley Christian Camp	Rt. 1, Box 298, Tuckaseigee, NC 28783	
Quaker Lake Camp	1503 NC Hwy 62 E, Climax, NC 27233	919-674-2321
Quiet Reflections Retreat, Inc	500 Pond Road, Spruce Pine, NC 28777	
Ridgecrest Summer Camps	P.O. Box 278, Ridgecrest, NC 28770	704-669-8051
South Mountain Christian Camp	Route 2, Box 1014, Bostic, NC 28010	704-245-3322
Teen Valley Ranch Christn Camp and Conference Center	P.O. Box 10, Plumtree, NC 28664	704-765-7860
The Cove Camp	P.O. Box 19223, Asheville, NC 28815	704-298-2092
The Master's Mission, Inc.	P.O. Box 547, Robbinsville, NC 28771	704-479-3492
The Vineyard Camp & Retreat Ctr	Route 1, Box 131, Westfield, NC 27053	919-351-2070
Triple C Bible Camp	Route 2, Box 89-B, Ahoskie, NC 27910	919-332-5426
Tuck-A-Way Christian Retreat	186 McCracker Road, Bryson City, NC 28713	704-488-9723
Young Life's Windy Gap	120 Cole's Cove Rd., Weaverville, NC 28787	704-645-7187
North Dakota		
Cooperstown Bible Camp	RR 2, Box 59A, Cooperstown, ND 58425	701-797-2174
Crystal Springs Baptist Camp	RR 1, Box 141, Medina, ND 58467	701-486-3467
Nebraska		
Camp Moses Merrill	Rt. 1, Box 170 A, Linwood, NE 68036	
Camp Rivercrest	RR #2, Box 224, Fremont, NE 68025	402-628-6465
Covenant Cedars Bible Camp	Box 68, Hordville, NE 68846	402-757-3241
Manna Resort	RR 1, Box 32, Fairfield, NE 68938	402-262-2280
Maranatha Bible Camp	P.O. Box 549, North Platte, NE 69103-0549	308-582-4513
NE Dist.Assemblies Of God	Star Rt. Box 2, Lexington, NE 68850	308-324-2163
NE Youth Leadership Dev. Ctr.	RR 2 Box 9A, Aurora, NE 68818	402-694-3934
Nat'l Camps -Blind Chldrn	4444 South 52nd St., Lincoln, NE 68506	402-488-0981
The Salv. Army Gene Eppley Camp	511 N. 20th St., Omaha, NE 68102	402-346-5155
Timberlake Ranch Camp	Rt. 1, Box 86, Marquette, NE 68854	308-946-2148
Whispering Cedars Baptist Camp	Route 1, Box 131, Genoa, NE 68640	402-993-6014
New Hampshire		
Brookwoods/Deer Run	Chestnut Cove Rd., Alton, NH 03809	603-875-3600
Camp Advenchur	Rt. 11 Box 321, Alton Bay, NH 03810	603-875-6163
Camp Fireside	49 Pond Hill Road, Rochester, NH 03867	603-332-1701
Camp Monomonac	RR 2, Box 436, Rindge, NH 03461	603-899-5473
Camp Spofford	Route 9A, Spofford Lake, NH 03462	603-363-4788
Monadnock Bible Conference	78 Dublin Road, P.O. Box C, Jaffrey Ctr, NH 03454	603-532-8321
New England Frontier Camp	P.O. Box 1813, Rochester, NH 03867	603-332-5869
Pilgrim Pines Conference Center	Box 40, W. Swanzey, NH 03469	603-352-0443
Rumney Bible Conference	P.O. Box 99, Rumney, NH 03266	603-786-9504
Singing Hills Christn Fellowship Inc.	HCR #75, Box 206, Plainfield, NH 03781	603-469-3236
Toah Nipi Retreat Center	Old Ashburnham Road, Ringe, NH 03461	
Windsor Hills Nazarene Family Camping Center	R.R. 2, Box 157, Hillsboro, NH 03244	603-478-3363
New Jersey		
America's Keswick	Keswick Grove, Whiting, NJ 08759	201-350-1187
Baptist Camp and Conference Ctr	57 Blossom Hill Road, Lebanon, NJ 08833	201-236-2638
Camp Iroquoina	5 Snowball Lane, Trenton, NJ 08619	609-890-0450

State/Camp	Address	Phone
Fellowship Conference Center	Valley Rd., Liberty Corner, NJ 07938	201-647-1777
Haluwasa	R.D. 5, Hammonton, NJ 08037	609-561-3081
Harvey Cedars Bible Conference	P.O. Box 1000, Harvey Cedars, NJ 08008	609-494-5689
Liebenzell Retreat Ctr and Camp	6 Heath Lane, Schooley's Mountain, NJ 07870	201-852-6012
New Life Island	P.O. Box AC, Frenchtown, NJ 08825	215-294-9644
Tri-State Bible Conf.	River Rd., R.D. 5 Box 3, Montague, NJ 07827	201-293-3522
United Methodist Camps and Conf.	801 Mt. Misery Road, Browns Mills, NJ 08015	609-893-3354
Village Dock Chr. Min.	Rt. 47, P.O. Box 101, Franklinville, NJ 08322	609-694-0001
New Mexico		
Bonita Park Nazarene Camp	Alto Route, Capitan, NM 88316	
Camp Stoney	Route 7, Box 115, Santa Fe, NM 87505	505-983-5610
Camp Villa de Niza	P.O. Box 610, Thoreau, NM 87323	505-862-7465
Fellowship Bible Church	10110 Constitution NE, Albuquerque, NM 87112	505-294-0571
Glorieta Conference Center	P.O. Box 8, Glorieta, NM 87535	505-757-6161
Lone Tree Bible Ranch	Box 523, Capitan, NM 88316	505-354-2523
Sacramento Methodist Assembly	P.O. Box 188, Sacramento, NM 88347	505-687-3414
Southwest Bible Camp	P.O. Box 265, Glenwood, NM 88039	505-539-2551
New York		
Beaver Camp	Star Route, Box 221, Lowville, NY 13367	315-376-2640
Bethany Baptist Camp	R.D. 1, Box 312, Sinclairville, NY 14782	716-287-2848
Boys J.I.M. Club of America	Box 58, Bemus Point, NY 14712	716-386-3806
Camp Asbury	Box 218, Silver Lake, NY 14549	716-237-5262
Camp Cherith - Adirondacks	R.D. 2 Box 309, Corinth, NY 12822	518-654-6262
Camp Cherith - Western NY	Hunt, NY 14846	716-468-3850
Camp Comanche, Inc.	P.O. Box 185, Ferndale, NY 12734	914-292-9314
Camp Deerpark	Box 405, Brandt Rd., Westbrookville, NY 12785	914-754-8669
Camp Findley	RR #2 Box 212, Clymer, NY 14724	716-769-7146
Camp Hickory Hill	2970 Kohler Road, Varysburg, NY 14167	716-535-7832
Camp Ironbell	RD 1, Box 76, Gerry, NY 14740	
Camp Li-Lo-Li	P.O. Box 70, Salamanca, NY 14779	716-945-4900
Camp Mandaville	R.D. 3, Potsdam, NY 13676	315-328-4581
Camp Mission Meadows	Box 42, Dewittville, NY 14728	716-386-5932
Camp Pinnacle	RD 1, Box 200, Voorheesville, NY 12186	512-872-1053
Camp Shiloh, Inc.	Box 428, Woodridge, NY 12789	914-434-4033
Camp Taconic	R.D. 2, Box 255, Red Hook, NY 12571	914-758-8764
Camp Vick	Box 109, Sandusky, NY 14133	716-492-4494
Camp Victory	115-50 Merrick Blvd., Jamaica, NY 11434	
Camp-of-the-Woods	Speculator, NY 12164	518-548-4311
Catskill Christian Assembly, Inc.	Route 1, Box 265, Prattsville, NY 12468	518-299-3611
Chambers Wesleyan Camp	RD 2, Box 26A, Beaver Dams, NY 14812	607-936-9843
Christian Camping Services	5698A Nipher Road, Bath, NY 14810	607-776-6705
Christian Youth Aflame	7245 College Street, Lima, NY 14485	716-582-2790
Cortland Bible Club Camp	P.O. Box 100, Pitcher, NY 13136	607-863-4225
Covenant Acres Camp and Retreat Center	P.O. Box 207, Pike, NY 14130	716-493-2220
Deerfoot Lodge	Speculator, NY 12083	518-966-4115
Delta Lake Bible Conference Center	Route 26, Turin Road, Rome, NY 13440	315-336-7210
Emmanuel Ranch, Ltd.	2026 Dunkley Road, Leicester, NY 14481	716-382-3914
Good Tidings Bible Conference	Box 103, Sutton Road, Cornwallville, NY 12418	518-239-4178
High Braes Refuge, Inc.	RR #1, Box 45B Waterbury Rd, Redfield, NY 13437	315-599-7362
Kings' Campground	c/o Camp Pinnacle, Voorheesville, NY 12186	212-724-4005
Lakeside Bible Conference	P.O. Box 670, Carmel, NY 10512	914-225-2005
LeTourneau Christian Conf. Center	4950 County Road 11, Rushville, NY 14544	716-554-3400
Lewis M. Fowler Camp & Conf. Ctr	Box 131, Speculator, NY 12164	518-548-6524

State/Camp	*Address*	*Phone*
Lighthouse Christian Camp	9574 Somerset Drive, Barker, NY 14012	716-688-9195
Living Waters Circle C Ranch	R.R. #2, Box 2303, Delevan, NY 14042	716-492-3687
Moosehead Christian Camping Ctr	South Cook Road, Lafayette, NY 13084	315-677-9490
New Horizons Ministries	189 Allen St., Hempstead, NY 11550	516-481-5769
Northern Frontier Camp	83 Coach Lane, Newburgh, NY 12550	914-564-2567
Odosagih Bible Conference	Hazelmere Avenue, Machias, NY 14101	716-353-8555
Ontario Bible Camp and Conf.	RR #1, Box 24, Lot 1, Oswego, NY 13126	315-343-6111
Pathfinder Lodge	P.O. Box, Cooperstown, NY 13326	315-446-5601
Peniel Bible Conference	P.O. Box 369, Lake Luzerne, NY 12846	518-696-4038
Pine Bush Bible Camp	R.D. 1, Box 316, Bloomingburg, NY 12721	914-361-1871
Pine Grove Camp	41 Pine Road, Saratoga Springs, NY 12866	518-587-1727
Sacandaga Bible Conference	P.O. Box 247, Broadalbin, NY 12025	518-883-3713
Salvation Army Camp Long Point	200 Twin Oaks Drive, Syracuse, NY 13206	315-536-6301
Stony Brook Schl Summer Progs.	Route 25A, Stony Brook, NY 11790	516-751-1800
Sunshine Acres	P.O. Box 427, Napanoch, NY 12458	914-647-4230
Troy Conference Camping	P.O. Box 560, Saratoga Springs, NY 12866	518-584-8214
Watebrook Retreat Center	P.O. Box 126, Cornwall, NY 12518	914-534-8911
White Lake Covenanter Camp	Mattison Road, PO Box 208, White Lake, NY 12786	914-583-9768
Wildwood Christian Camp	210 Longmeadow Drive, Syracuse, NY 13205-3030	315-492-2932
Young Life Saranac Village	Star Route Box 88, Saranac Lake, NY 12983	518-891-3010
Young Life's Lake Champion	P.O. Box 207, Glen Spey, NY 12737	914-856-6871
Ohio		
4-H Camp Palmer, Inc.	Route 1, Fayette, OH 43521	
Beulah Beach Camp and Conf. Ctr	6101 West Lake Road, Vermilion, OH 44089	216-967-4861
Big Prairie Camp - Assemblies	P.O. Box 83, Holmes Co.Rd, Big Prairie, OH 44611	216-496-2381
Butler Springs Christian Assembly	3701 State RT 41, Hillsboro, OH 45133	513-588-2205
Camp Burton	14282 Butternut Rd., Burton, OH 44021	216-834-8984
Camp Carl	135 Fir Hill, Akron, OH 44304	216-376-6400
Camp Cotubic	2158 Road 25N, Bellefontaine, OH 43311	513-468-2519
Camp ECCO	5140 Pioneer Road, S.E., Carrollton, OH 44615	216-739-4200
Camp Guardian	73394 Freeport Road, Piedmont, OH 43983	614-658-3638
Camp McPherson	1410 N. Mulberry St., Mount Vernon, OH 43050	614-392-0516
Camp Mowana	2276 Fleming Falls, R. R. #11, Mansfield, OH 44903	419-589-7406
Camp Otyokwah	3380 Tugend Road, Butler, OH 44822	419-883-3854
Church Of God Youth Camp	2474 Lebanon Rd., Lebanon, OH 45036	513-932-3003
College Hill Pres. Church	5742 Hamilton Ave., Cincinnati, OH 45224	513-541-5676
Evangelical Friends Church	1201 30th St. NW, Canton, OH 44709	216-493-1660
Faith Ranch	Box 384, Jewett, OH 43986	614-946-2255
Grand Valley Christian Center	Route 1, Box 262, Rock Creek, OH 44084	216-563-3081
Greenwood Lake Camp	US Route 42, Delaware, OH 43015	
Judson Hills Camp	3298 Township Road 629, Loudonville, OH 44842	419-994-4657
King's Domain Retreat and Conf. Ctr	5778 St. Route 350, Oregonia, OH 45054	513-932-2223
King's Valley Ranch	Route 2, Lower Salem, OH 457459799	614-585-2325
Kirkwood Camp and Conf. Center	5719 SR 73 West, Wilmington, OH 45177	513-382-3535
Koinonia Camp and Conf. Center	6810 Cork-Cold Springs Road, Geneva, OH 44041	216-466-1278
Marmon Valley Farm Camp	5807 County Road 153, Zanesfield, OH 43360	513-593-8051
Nazarene Youth Camps-C.OH	2708 Morse Rd., Columbus, OH 43229	614-475-1728
Ohio Camp Cherith	5924 Dunham Road, Maple Heights, OH 44137	216-662-8329
Ohio District Council Christian Youth Camp	380 West Lincoln Street, Oberlin, OH 44074	216-774-8103
Pleasant Vineyard Ministries	1191 Swan Beatty Road, Camden, OH 45311	513-452-3347
Quaker Canyon Camp	P.O. Box 55, Damascus, OH 44619	216-537-2991
Round Lake Christian Camp	114 State Route 3, Lakeville, OH 44638	419-827-2017
Stony Glen Camp	5300 W. Loveland Road, Madison, OH 44057	216-298-3264

State/Camp	Address	Phone
Stony Glen Christian Svc. Brigade Camp	3455 Birch St., Grove City, OH 43123	614-871-9976
The Salv. Army - Camp NEOSA	5037 Edgewood Road, S.W., Carrollton, OH 44615	216-735-2671
Wildwood Christian Education Ctr	941 Barg Salt Run Road, Milford, OH 45150	513-831-3242
Woodland Lakes Christian Camp	3054 Lindale - Mt. Holly Rd., Amelia, OH 45102	513-797-5268
Oklahoma		
Big Cedars Campground	8112 Brownsville Lane, Bethany, OK 73008	405-685-4143
Camp Bristow	Route 3, Box 175, Bristow, OK 74010	918-367-6590
Camp Look-Away	Rt. 5, Box 157, Tahlequah, OK 74464	
Camp Seminole	Route 2, Box 378A, Wewoka, OK 74884	405-382-5469
Camp Takatoka	Route 1, Box 287, Chouteau, OK 74337	918-476-5191
New Life Ranch	Route 1, Box 274, Colcord, OK 74338	918-422-5506
Shepherd's Fold Ranch	P.O. Box 86, Avant, OK 74001	918-263-3622
Sunset Bible Camp	Route 2, Box 1032, Mannford, OK 74044	918-965-2246
Oregon		
Aldersgate Bible Camp and Conf. Ctr	P.O. Box 16, Turner, OR 97392	503-743-2494
Big Lake Youth Camp	Hwy 20, Box 13100, Sisters, OR 97759	503-652-2225
Camp Arrah Wanna	0245 SW Bancroft, Ste G, Portland, OR 97201-4270	503-228-8394
Camp Elkanah	P.O. Box 150, La Grande, OR 97850	503-963-5050
Camp Emerald Forest	26000 Pittsburg Road, St. Helens, OR 97051	503-397-4226
Camp Harlow	3850 County Farm Road, Eugene, OR 97401	503-683-5416
Camp Kuratli-Trestle Glen	24751 S.E. Hwy. 224, Boring, OR 97009	503-658-3122
Camp Morrow Bible Conference	Route 1, Box 31CM, Wamic, OR 97063	503-544-2971
Camp Tadmor	43943 McDowell Creek Drive, Lebanon, OR 97355	503-451-4270
Canby Grove Conference Center	7501 Knight's Bridge Road, Canby, OR 97013	503-266-5176
Cannon Beach Conference Center	Box 398, Cannon Beach, OR 97110	503-436-1501
Canyonview Camp	12730 Finlay Road N.E., Silverton, OR 97381	503-873-8296
Crestview Manor Conference Ctr	P.O. Box 132, Corbett, OR 97019	503-695-2227
Drift Creek Camp	P.O. Box 2186, Lincoln City, OR 97367	503-996-3978
Eagle Fern Camp	37680 S.E. Camp Rd., Estacada, OR 97023	503-630-4978
Evangelical Center Conf. Grounds	18121 S.E. River Road, Milwaukie, OR 97267	503-654-0436
Evans Crk Upward Bound Camps for Handicapped, Inc.	36155 N. Fork Road, Lyons, OR 97358	503-897-2447
Melody Mountain Camp	Box 35, Meacham, OR 97859	503-983-2233
Molalla Retreat	36208 S. Forest Road, Molalla, OR 97038	503-829-9653
Mountain Lakes Bible Camp	2244 Wiard Street, Klamath Falls, OR 97603	503-883-2289
Oregon Camp Cherith	421 S. River, Newberg, OR 97132	503-538-7698
Tilikum: Center for Retreats and Outdoor Ministries	15321 NE North Valley Road, Newberg, OR 97132	503-538-2763
Trout Creek Bible Camp	8815 N.E. Glisan, Portland, OR 97220	503-695-2948
Twin Rocks Friends Conf.	18705 Highway 101N, Rockaway Beach, OR 97136	503-355-2284
White Branch Youth Camp	61500 Old McKenz. Hwy, McKenzie Bridge, OR 97413	503-822-3511
Wilderness Trails, Inc.	P.O. Box 4655, Medford, OR 97501	503-779-7756
Pennsylvania		
Arrowhead Bible Camp	Arrowhead Rd., Brackney, PA 18812	717-663-2419
Black Rock Retreat	1345 Kirkwood Pike, Quarryville, PA 17566	717-786-1266
Blue Mountain Christian Retreat	R.D. 2, Box 118-A, New Ringgold, PA 17960	717-386-2154
Brush Valley Christian Retreat	RD #3, Box 956, Rt. 259, Homer City, PA 15748	412-479-3993
Camp Allegheny	RD #2, Box 212, Stoystown, PA 15563	814-754-5122
Camp Andrews	1226 Silver Spring Road, Holtwood, PA 17532	717-284-2624
Camp Conquest	RD 2 Forest Rd., Denver, PA 17517	215-267-2006
Camp Hebron	957 Camp Hebron Road, Halifax, PA 17032	717-896-3441
Camp Joy-El	3741 Joy-El Drive, Greencastle, PA 17225	717-369-4539
Camp Ladore-The Salvation Army	P.O. Box 99, Waymart, PA 18472	717-488-6121

State/Camp	*Address*	*Phone*
Camp Lambec	100 Venango St., Mercer, PA 16137	412-662-4481
Camp Mantowagan	P.O. Box 95, Saxton, PA 16678	814-658-3815
Camp Men-O-Lan	1415 Doerr Road, Quakertown, PA 18951	215-679-5144
Camp Nazareth	R.D. 2, Box 2616, Mercer, PA 16137	412-662-4840
Camp Orchard Hill	R. R. 3, Box 275, Dallas, PA 18612	717-333-4098
Camp Sankanac	68 Bertolet School Road, Spring City, PA 19475	215-469-6320
Camp Sunrise Mountain	RD 1,, Markleysburg, PA 15650	412-329-8880
Camp Susque	P.O. Box 65, Trout Run, PA 17771	717-998-2151
Camp Timberledge	Beach Lake, PA 18405	717-729-7230
Christian Retreat Center	Box 13A, RD #1, East Waterford, PA 17021	717-734-3627
Deep Valley Christian Svc. Camp	First Christn Ch., PO Bx 109, Ellwood City, PA 16117	412-758-3348
Doorkeepers Christian Outreach	Box 57, Spring Creek, PA 16436	814-664-8547
Doubling Gap Center, Inc.	R.D.#3, Box 2260, Newville, PA 17241	717-776-5281
Eastern PA U.M.C. Camps and Conf.	P.O. Box 820, Valley Forge, PA 19482	215-666-9092
First Presbyterian Church Camp	R.D. #1, Box 16, Ligonier, PA 15658	412-238-6428
Grace Brethren Retreat Center	480 Forest Rd., Denver, PA 17517	215-267-2541
Greenview Bible Camp	R.D. #1, Denver, PA 17517	215-445-6022
Greenwood Hills Bible Conference	7062 Lincoln Way East, Fayetteville, PA 17222	717-352-2150
Gretna Glen Program Center	87 Mine Road, Lebanon, PA 17042-8955	717-273-6525
Handi*Camp	237 Fairfield Ave., Upper Darby, PA 19082	215-352-7177
Harmony Heart Camp	Rural Route #2, Box 246, Jermyn, PA 18433	717-254-6272
Haycock Camping Ministries	3100 School Road, Kintnersville, PA 18930	215-346-7155
High Places Christian Ranch Camp	P.O. Box 97, Mt. Morris, PA 15349	412-324-2770
His Thousand Hills	RD #6, Box 22, Wellsboro, PA 16901	717-724-2366
Innabah Program Center (U.M.C.)	R.D. 1, Spring City, PA 19475	215-469-6111
Judson Baptist Camp & Retreat	398 Holliday Road, N. Springfield, PA 16430	
Jumonville	RR #2, Box 128, Hopwood, PA 15445	412-439-4912
Kenbrook Bible Camp	507 Pine Meadow Drive, Lebanon, PA 17042	717-865-4547
Laurel Highlands Bapt. Camp	1201 Vermont Avenue, Aliquippa, PA 15001	814-445-7216
Laurel Lake Family Camp	RD #1, Box 83A, Rossiter, PA 15772	215-814-9300
Laurelville Menn. Church Ctr.	Route 5, Box 145, Mt. Pleasant, PA 15666	412-423-2056
Miracle Mtn Ranch Missions Inc.	R.D. #1, Box 95, Spring Creek, PA 16436	814-664-7673
Mont Lawn Camp/Paradise Lake Retreat Center	Box 252, Bushkill, PA 18234	717-588-6067
Montrose Bible Conference	P.O. Box 159, Montrose, PA 18801-0159	717-278-1001
Mountain View Bible Camp	Box 124, Riverside Road, Snydertown, PA 17877	717-672-2296
Mt. Gilead Camp and Conf. Ctr	Box 15, Abington, PA 19001	215-857-3727
Mt. Lou San Bible Camp	2200 Blue Mountain Pkwy, Harrisburg, PA 17112	717-545-2841
Muncy Terraces	PO Box 334, Muncy, PA 17756	717-546-2391
New Life Bible Camp Inc.	R.D. 1, Box 202, Buffalo Mills, PA 15534	814-842-3325
Oil City Conference	P.O. Box 229, Pleasantville, PA 16341	814-589-7330
Penn-Jersey Wesleyan Youth	2142 Ridgelawn Avenue, Bethlehem, PA 18018	
Penn-York Camp	RD #1, Box 420, Ulysses, PA 16948	814-848-9811
Pennsylvania-Delaware Conf. Ctr	430 Union Hall Road, Carlisle, PA 17013	717-243-7381
Pennwood Bible Camp	R.D. #1, Ulysses, PA 16948	814-435-2961
Pine Springs Camp	Box 186, Jennerstown, PA 15547	814-629-9834
Pine Valley Bible Conference	R.D. #2, Box 3595, Ellwood City, PA 16117	412-752-1661
Pinebrook Bible Conference	P.O. Box 1, Stroudsburg, PA 18360	717-424-1212
Pocono Mountain Bible Conf.	Box 87 Star Route, Gouldsboro, PA 18424	717-842-9746
Pocono Plateau Program Center	R.R. 2, Box 1002, Route 191, Cresco, PA 18326	717-676-3665
Refreshing Mountain Camp Inc.	455 Camp Road, Stevens, PA 17578	717-738-1490
Rhodes Grove Camp	7693 Brown's Mille Road, Chambersburg, PA 17201	717-375-4162
Seneca Hills Bible Conference	P.O. Box 288, Franklin, PA 16323	814-432-3026
Sherman Acres Camp	R.D. #5 Box 220, New Castle, PA 16105	412-652-4300
Spruce Lake Retreat	RD #1, Box 605, Canadensis, PA 18325	717-595-7505

State/Camp	Address	Phone
Streamside Camp & Conf. Center	R.D. #3, Stroudsburg, PA 18360	717-629-1902
Summer's Best Two Weeks	R.D. 2, Box 299, Boswell, PA 15531	814-629-9744
Teen Quest "Super Charge"	Box 500, Mount Pleasant, PA 15666	800-288-8336
Tel Hai Camp	R.D. 2, Box 126-1, Beaver Dam Road, Honey Brook, PA 19344	215-273-3969
Tuscarora Inn	RD 1, Box 1704, Mt. Bethel, PA 18343	717-897-6000
Tuscarora Resource Center	RD #1, Bx 1830, Sunrise Blvd, Mt. Bethel, PA 18343	717-897-5115
Twin Pines Camp, Conf. & Retrt Ctr	3000 Twin Pine Road, Stroudsburg, PA 18360	717-629-2411
Victory Valley Camp	7472 Sigmund Road, Zionsville, PA 18092-9736	215-966-5880
WLD Memorial Ranch	7351 W. Woolsey Road, Girard, PA 16417	814-474-3414
Wesley Woods Christian Ed. Ctr	RD #1 Box 155-A, Grand Valley, PA 16420	814-436-7802
Westminster Highlands	100 Venango St., Mercer, PA 16137	412-662-4481
White Sulphur Springs	RD #1, Box 233, Manns Choice, PA 15550	814-623-5583
Whitehall Camp	RD 1, Box 31, Emlenton, PA 16373-9514	
Rhode Island		
Canonicus Camp and Conf. Ctr	54 Exeter Road, Exeter, RI 02822	401-294-6318
South Carolina		
Awanita Valley	125 Mountain View Road, Marietta, SC 29661	803-836-3956
Ben Lippen Camp	P.O. Box 3999, Columbia, SC 29230	803-786-0766
Berea Bible Camp, Inc.	P.O. Box 9614, Columbia, SC 29290	
Bethel Bible Camp	100 Bethel Camp Road, Columbia, SC 29223	803-788-1724
Longridge Camp and Retreat Ctr	P.O. Box 220, Ridgeway, SC 29130	803-337-2082
Look-Up Lodge Christian Retreat	100 Old Highway 11, Travelers Rest, SC 29690	803-836-6392
South Dakota		
Byron Bible Camp	P.O. Box 211, Huron, SD 57350	605-352-7267
Tennessee		
Appalachian Christian Svc. Camp	Route One, Box 323, Uincoi, TN 37692	
Bancroft Bible Camp	141 Bancroft Drive, Kingsport, TN 37660	615-288-4532
Camp Ambassador	Rt. 3, Box 508, Goodlettsville, TN 37072	615-859-5433
Camp BA YO CA	Rt 7, Bx 224, Happy Hollow Rd, Sevierville, TN 37862	615-453-6274
Camp Eagle's Nest	3722 Deer Forest, Memphis, TN 38115	901-725-8263
Camp Garner Creek	P.O. Box 100924, Nashville, TN 37224	615-254-8343
Camp Glen Leven	3906 Franklin Road, Nashville, TN 37204	615-298-5549
Camp Hickory Hills	P.O. Box 551, Madison, TN 37138	615-847-2316
Camp Joshua	Route 10, Box 318A, Greenville, TN 37743	615-639-2879
Camp Ridgedale	P.O. Box 10, Bear Creek Road, Vanleer, TN 37181	615-763-2200
Camp Ta-Pa-Win-Go	P.O. Box 446, Elizabethton, TN 37643	615-543-2201
Camp Tsungani	6655 Winchester, Memphis, TN 38115	901-365-4648
Cedar Lake Camp	Rt. 3, Box 53 F, Livingston, TN 38570	615-823-5656
Cedine Bible Camp and Conf. Ctr	Route 1, Box 2390, Spring City, TN 37381	615-365-9565
Coldstream Christian Camp	1820 J.M. Goodman Road, Adams, TN	615-696-2302
Confrontation Point Ministries	P.O. Box 50, Ozone, TN 37842	615-484-8483
Doe River Gorge Christian Camp and Conference Center	P.O. Box 791, Elizabethton, TN 37644	615-928-8936
Hillmont Camp and Retreat Center	Route 1, Box 303, White Bluff, TN 37187	615-797-3616
Horton Haven Christian Camp	P.O. Box 276, Chapel Hill, TN 37034	615-364-7656
International Youth Camp	P.O. Box 2910, Cleveland, TN 37320-2910	615-479-8511
Lighthouse Christian Camp	Route 4, Box 344, Smithville, TN 37166	615-597-1264
Mountain Lake Ranch	Route 5, Box 181, Dandridge, TN 37725	615-397-3853
Mountain T.O.P.	P.O. Box 128, Altamont, TN 37301	615-692-3999
Smoky Mountain Christian Camp	P.O. Box 116, Coker Creek, TN 37314	615-261-2197
Wears Valley Retreat	Route 7, Box 291, Sevierville, TN 37862	615-453-2382

State/Camp	*Address*	*Phone*
Texas		
Baylor Camp	BU Box 7187, Waco, TX 76798	817-755-3505
Blue Barn Christian Retreat	Route 2, Box 239 G, Alba, TX 75410	214-765-2354
Brookhaven Retreat	Route 2, Box 289, Hawkins, TX 75765	214-769-2811
Burns Youth Encampment	Reagan Wells Rt, Box 109, Uvalde, TX 78801	
Camp Arrowhead	Route 9, Box 480, Cleburne, TX 76031	817-897-2323
Camp Buckner	Rt. 2, Box 25, Burnet, TX 78611	
Camp Copass Bapt. Encampment	Route 2, Box 638, Denton, TX 76201	817-565-0050
Camp Cullen	Rt. 3, Box 135-D, Trinity, TX 75862	713-594-2274
Camp El Har	5218 Kiwanis, Dallas, TX 75236	214-298-3873
Camp Hoblitzelle - S.Army	587 Singleton Road, Midlothian, TX 76065	214-775-2387
Camp Peniel, Inc.	HCO 4 Box 135, Marble Falls, TX 78654	512-693-2182
Camp Stewart For Boys/ Heart O' the Hills	Guadalupe River, Hunt, TX 78024	512-238-4670
Camp Ta-Ku-La, Inc.	P.O. Box 7, Chester, TX 75936	409-969-2455
Camp Tejas	Route 2, Box 102A, Giddings, TX 78942	409-366-2422
Center for Christian Growth/ T Bar M Sports Camp	P.O. Box 310600, New Braunfels, TX 78131-0600	512-625-2164
Christian Camp - Living Word	Rt. 1 Box 107, Point, TX 75472	214-598-2497
Circle 6 Ranch Baptist Camp	P.O. Box 976, Stanton, TX 79782	915-458-3467
Country Camp	P.O. Box 100, Columbus, TX 78934	409-732-6218
Daniel Springs Bapt. Camp	P.O. Box 310, Gary, TX 75643	214-685-2433
Don Anderson Ministries	Station A, Box 6611, Tyler, TX 75711	214-597-3018
El Shaddai Ranch	Route 2, Box 232, Yorktown, TX 78164	512-564-3552
Evangelical Brethren Camps	Rt. 1 Box 78B, Mt. Calm, TX 76673	817-533-2387
Forest Glen Christian Camp	P.O. Box 38062, Houston, TX 77238	713-847-0300
Frontier Camp	Route 1, Box 138, Grapeland, TX 75844	409-544-3206
H.E. Butt Foundation Camp	719 Earl Garrett St, P.O. Box 670, Kerrville, TX 78029-0670	512-896-2505
Harambe Oaks Ranch	P.O. Box 645, Fischer, TX 78623	512-935-2557
Heart O'the Hills/Camp Stewart	Route 1, Box 110C, Hunt, TX 78024	512-238-4670
Heart of Texas Bapt. Encampment	Route 1, Box 280A, Brownwood, TX 76801	915-784-5821
Hidden Acres Camp and Conf. Ctr	8501 Bruton Road, Dallas, TX 75217	214-388-1964
Hidden Falls Ranch, Inc.	P.O. Box 136, Wayside, TX 79094	806-764-3466
His Hill Ranch Camp and Conf. Ctr	Torchbearers, P.O. Box 9, Comfort, TX 78013	800-869-7967
Hus School Encampment	Route 2, Caldwell, TX 77836	713-272-8176
Iron Springs Christian Camp	Route 2, Box 148K, Whitney, TX 76692	817-694-2719
Jan-Kay Ranch, Incorporated	Route 1, Box 21, Detroit, TX 75436	214-674-3159
Mountain View Camp	P.O. Box 2097, Jacksonville, TX 75766	214-586-5361
Outdoor Discipleship Ministries	5112 Berridge Lane, Dallas, TX 75227	214-388-0131
Pantego Bible Church Day Camp	2203 W. Park Row, Arlington, TX 76013	817-274-1315
Pine Cove Conference Center	P.O. Box 9055, Tyler, TX 75711	214-561-0231
Piney Woods Camp Cherith	7307 Cornwall Bridge, Houston, TX 77041	713-937-9717
Pineywoods Baptist Encampment	POB 133, Woodlake, TX 75865	409-642-1723
Quest Unlimited Inc.	P.O. Box 160134, Austin, TX 78749	512-280-3743
S.A. Christadelphian Church	P.O. Box 39181, San Antonio, TX 78232	512-494-2370
Sandy Creek Bible Camp	Route 1, Box 803, Washington, TX 77880	713-836-6817
Sky Ranch Camp and Conf. Ctr	9330 LBJ Freeway, Suite 850, Dallas, TX 75243	214-437-9505
Texas Baptist Encampment	Drawer M, Palacios, TX 77465	512-972-2717
The Pines Cath. Camp and Conf. Ctr	P.O. Box 260391, Plano, TX 75026-0391	214-867-4684
Timberline Bapt. Camp & Conf.	Rt. 1, Box 151, Lindale, TX 75771	214-882-3183
Twin Oaks Ranch	P.O. Box 457, Buda, TX 78610	512-295-6151
Wilderness Ridge	10115 Kerrwood, Houston, TX 77080	713-827-8018
Woodland Hills Chr. Retreat	Rt. 3 Box 119F, Whitesboro, TX 76273	817-665-8979
YMCA Camp Cullen	Route 3, Box 135-D, Trinity, TX 75862	713-659-2733

State/Camp	Address	Phone
Zephyr Baptist Encampment	HCR #2, Box 7200, Sandia, TX 78383	512-547-2448
Utah		
Camp Utaba	7005 N Fork Road, Liberty, UT 84310	
Evangelical Camping Assoc.	4330 W. 3500 South #D, Salt Lake City, UT 84120	801-966-1242
Virginia		
Camp Bethel	P.O. Box 390, Wise, VA 24293	703-328-6876
Camp Blue Ridge	P.O. Box 120, Montebello, VA 24464	703-377-2413
Camp Eagle	P.O. Box 7010, Roanoke, VA 24019	703-366-2431
Camp Happyland	P.O. Box 14, Richardsville, VA 22736	703-399-1031
Camp Rudolph	P.O. Box 33, Yale, VA 23897	804-535-8147
Camp Shenandoah Springs	HC-6, Box 122, Madison, VA 22727	703-923-4300
Camp Tuk-A-Way	344 Day Avenue, Roanoke, VA 24016	
Camp Wikitoje	7511 N. Spring Run Road, Midlothian, VA 23112	804-739-3001
Covenant Vlg Christian Conf. Ctr	1510 Snughill Court, Vienna, VA 22182	703-821-8844
Dogwood Lake Conference Center	1317 Pleasant Valley Road, Winchester, VA 22601	703-667-9400
Eastern Mennonite College Prog. in Camping & Recreation	Park Road, Harrisonburg, VA 22801	703-433-2771
Grace Bible Camp and Retreat Ctr	Route 1, Box 74, Goshen, VA 24439	703-997-9316
Highland Retreat	Route 1, Box 121, Bergton, VA 22811	703-852-3226
Oak Hill Christian Service Camp	Route 1, Box 521, Mechanicsville, VA 23111	804-779-3050
Skyanchor Ministries	Box 7, Spring Grove, VA 23881	804-866-8791
The Master's Inn	Route 2, Box 94A, Altavista, VA 24517	804-369-5053
Triple-R Ranch, Inc.	3531 Bunch Walnut Road, Chesapeake, VA 23322	804-421-4177
Williamsburg Christian Retreat Ctr	9275 Barnes Road, Toano, VA 23168	804-566-2256
Washington		
ALPS	22122 35th Place South #H301, Kent, WA 98032	206-878-7839
Black Lake Bible Camp & Conf. Ctr	P.O. Box 2466, Olympia, WA 98507	206-357-8425
CRISTA Camps & Conferences (Island Lk Camp/Miracle Ranch)	12500 Camp Court N.W., Poulsbo, WA 98370	206-697-1212
Camas Meadows Bible Camp	POB 304, Cashmere, WA 98815	509-663-2171
Camp Arnold at Timberlake	33712 Webster Rd. E, Eatonville, WA 98328	206-847-2511
Camp Berachah	19830 S.E. 328th Place, Auburn, WA 98002	206-854-3765
Camp Casey Conference Center	1276 S. Fort Casey Road, Coupeville, WA 98239	206-678-5050
Camp Ghormley	HC 62, Box 190, Naches, WA 98937	509-672-4311
Camp Gilead	30919 NE Carnation Farm Rd, Carnation, WA 98014	206-333-4311
Camp Harmony	P.O. Box 698, Stanwood, WA 98292	206-629-4536
Camp McCullough	4010 N. 36th, Tacoma, WA 98407	206-759-4451
Camp Nooksack	Box 22256, Nooksack, WA 87276	206-322-6228
Camp of the Cascades	22825 Piessner Road S.E., Yelm, WA 98597	206-894-3838
Cascade Camp Cherith	2214 Bedal Lane, Everett, WA 98208	206-337-5930
Cedar Springs Camp and Conf. Ctr	4820 State Road 92, Lake Stevens, WA 98258	206-334-6215
Clear Lake Grace Brethren Camp	P.O. Box 257, Harrah, WA 98933	509-848-2746
Double-K Ranch	P.O. Box 98, Easton, WA 98925	509-656-2304
Fourth Memorial Church	Rt. #2, Box 80, Usk, WA 99180	509-445-1193
Lake Retreat Baptist Camp	27850 Retreat-Kanaskat Rd, Ravensdale, WA 98051	206-365-9890
Lakeside Bible Camp	S. 6443 W. Deerlake Road, Clinton, WA 98236	206-221-3936
Mt. Baker Baptist Conference Ctr	8444 Mt. Baker Highway, Deming, WA 98244	206-599-2921
North Pacific Trails	912 South 294th Place, Federal Way, WA 98003	206-839-1243
Reachout Expeditions	P.O. Box 464, Anacortes, WA 98221	206-293-3788
Royal Ridges Retreat	P.O. Box 778, Battle Ground, WA 98604	206-686-3737
Sambica Camp & Conference Ctr.	17700 W. Sammamish Rd. SE, Bellevue, WA 98008	216-746-9110
Shiloh Bible Camp	Box 524, Cosmopolis, WA 98537	206-532-5179
Sunset Lake Camp	P.O. Box D, Wilkeson, WA 98396	206-829-0311
Tall Timber Ranch	White River Road, Leavenworth, WA 98826	509-763-3127

State/Camp	*Address*	*Phone*
The Dunes Bible Camp	Route 1, Box 332, Ocean Park, WA 98640	206-665-4055
The Firs Bible and Missionary Conf.	4605 Cable Street, Bellingham, WA 98226	206-733-6840
The Salv. Army - Camp Gifford	P.O. Box 32, Spokane, WA 99210	509-325-6810
Union Gospel Mission	P.O. Box 202, Seattle, WA 98111	206-725-2432
Volunteers of Am. - Camp Volasuca	P.O. Box 268, Sultan, WA 98294	206-259-3191
Warm Beach Christian Camps and Conference Center	20800 Marine Drive NW, Stanwood, WA 98292	206-652-7575
Wilderness Northwest	1903 Duckabush Road, Brinnon, WA 98320	206-796-4968
West Virginia		
Camp She-Ki-Nah	P.O. Box 207, Hwy 60 West, Culloden, WV 25510	304-743-6743
Camp Tomahawk - The Salv. Army	Route 2, Hedgesville, WV 25427	304-754-3849
Hemlock Wilderness Brigade Cmp	Gen. Deliv. Trout Run Rd., Wardensville, WV 26851	304-367-6769
Howell's Mill Christian Assembly	Route 2, Box 118, Ona, WV 25545	304-743-4332
Mission Farms	Route 6, Box 265, Fairmont, WV 26554	304-363-1790
Mt. Salem Revival Grounds	P.O. Box 186, West Union, WV 26456	304-873-2444
Potomac Park Camp and Conf. Ctr	P.O. Box 787, Falling Waters, WV 25419	304-274-2031
The Salvation Army Camp Joy	P.O. Box 818, Bluefield, WV 24701	304-327-7411
Valley Vista Camp	Route 1, Box 37A, Huttonsville, WV 26273	304-422-4581
Wisconsin		
Army Lake Camp	1449 Army Lake Rd., East Troy, WI 53120	414-642-5130
Arrowhead Bible Camp	Route 3, New Auburn, WI 54757	715-967-2140
C.B.A. of Wisconsin	733 Coleman Street, Chippewa Falls, WI 54729	715-723-0894
Camp Fairwood	Rt. 2 Box 245A, Westfield, WI 53964	608-296-2801
Camp Forest Springs	N8890 Forest Lane, Westboro, WI 54490	715-427-5241
Camp Phillip	Route 3, Box 190-4, Wautoma, WI 54982	414-787-3202
Camp Zion	12701 Door Bluff Road, Ellison Bay, WI 54210	414-854-2790
Church of God of Prophecy Campgd	6522 W. Fremont Place, Milwaukee, WI 53219	414-543-6227
Covenant Harbor Bible Camp and Retreat Center	1724 Main St., Lake Geneva, WI 53147	414-248-3600
Crescent Lake Bible Camp	2750 Bible Camp Drive, Rhinelander, WI 54501	715-282-5614
Dells Christn Camp, Dells Bapt, Inc.	2803-2 Century Harbor Road, Middleton, WI 53562	608-836-5078
Fort Wilderness	Bx 715, 6180 Wilderness Tr., McNaughton, WI 54543	800-338-3678
Honey Rock/High Road	8660 Honey Rock Road, Three Lakes, WI 54562	715-479-7474
Inspiration Center	P.O. Box 948, Walworth, WI 53184	414-275-5753
Lake Geneva Youth Camp/Conf. Ctr	650 South Street, Lake Geneva, WI 53147	414-248-5500
Lake Lundgren Bible Camp	North 18250 Lake Lane, Pembine, WI 54156	715-324-5457
Lake Waubesa Bible Camp	2851 Crescent Dr., Bx 382, McFarland, WI 53558	608-838-3335
Living Waters Bible Camp	Route 1, Box 86A, Westby, WI 54667	608-634-4373
Northern Grace Youth Camp	R. R. #1, Gillett, WI 54124	414-855-2759
Phantom Ranch Bible Camp	W309 S10910 Highway I, Mukwonago, WI 53149	414-363-7291
Riverside Bible Conference	6355 Highway DD, Amherst, WI 54406	715-824-3198
Silver Birch Ranch	N6120 Sawyer Lake Road, White Lake, WI 54491	715-484-2742
Sky Lodge Christian Camp	Route 3, Box 650, Montello, WI 53949	608-297-2566
Spencer Lake Bible Camp	Route 2, Box 104, Waupaca, WI 54981	715-258-5707
The Arc	Route 1, Box 92, Osceola, WI 54020	715-294-2877
The Salvation Army Wonderland Camp and Conf. Center	P.O. Box 222, Camp Lake, WI 53109	414-889-4305
Timber-lee Christian Center	2381 Scout Road, East Troy, WI 53120	414-642-7345
Wesley Woods Conference Center	200 Stam Street, Williams Bay, WI 53191	414-245-6631
Wood Lake Baptist Camp	Route 1, Box 451, Grantsburg, WI 54840	715-689-2411
Wyoming		
Camp Bethel	Dayton, WY 82836	307-655-2490
Lone Tree Bible Ranch	Box 378, Glendo, WY 82213	307-735-4517
Rocky Mountain Lodge	Star Route Box 373, Jackson Hole, WY 83001	307-733-4945

NATIONAL PARKS

Park	*ST*	*Features*
Acadia	ME	Rugged seashore, 41,409 acres
Arches	UT	Unusual stone arches, 73,379 acres
Badlands	SD	Fossils, 243,244 acres
Big Bend	TX	Bordering the Rio Grande, 802,541 acres
Biscayne	FL	Coral reef, 173,039 acres
Bryce Canyon	UT	Erosion effects, 35,835 acres
Canyonlands	UT	Red-rock canyons, 337,570 acres
Capitol Reef	UT	Rock formation, 241,904 acres
Carlsbad Caverns	NM	Largest known caves, 46,755 acres
Channel Islands	CA	Marine mammals, 249,354 acres
Crater Lake	OR	Deep blue lake, 183,224 acres
Denali	AK	Mt. McKinley, North America's highest mountain (20,320 ft), 4,716,726 acres
Everglades	FL	Subtropical area, 1,398,938 acres
Gates of the Arctic	AK	Wilderness, 7,523,888 acres
Glacier	MT	Glaciers, 1,013,572 acres
Glacier Bay	AK	Wildlife, 3,225,284 acres
Grand Canyon	AZ	Mile-deep gorge, 1,218,375 acres
Grand Teton	WY	Picturesque range of high mountain peaks, 309,994 acres
Great Basin	NV	Exceptional scenic, biologic, and geologic attractions, 77,109 acres
Great Smoky Mountains	NC-TN	Highest mountain range east of Black Hills; luxuriant plant life, 520,269 acres
Guadalupe Mountains	TX	Contains highest point in Texas: Guadalupe Peak (8,751 ft), 86,416 acres
Haleakala	HI	10,023 ft. Haleakala volcano, 28,655 acres
Hawaii Volcanoes	HI	Volcanic area, 229,177 acres
Hot Springs	AR	Mineral hot springs, 5,839 acres
Isle Royale	MI	Wilderness island, 571,790 acres
Katmai	AK	Brown bear, fishing, 3,716,000 acres
Kenai Fjords	AK	Seacoast park, 669,541 acres
Kings Canyon	CA	Giant sequoias, 461,901 acres
Kobuk Valley	AK	Native culture, 1,750,421 acres
Lake Clark	AK	Wilderness, 2,636,839 acres
Lassen Volcanic	CA	Volcanic phenomena, 106,372 acres
Mammoth Cave	KY	Limestone, 52,419 acres
Mesa Verde	CO	Prehistoric cliff dwellings, 52,085 acres
Mount Rainier	WA	Glacial system, 235,404 acres
North Cascades	WA	Alpine landscape, 504,781 acres
Olympic	WA	Rain forest, 921,942 acres
Petrified Forest	AZ	Petrified wood, 93,532 acres
Redwood	CA	World's tallest known tree (369.2 ft), 110,132 acres
Rocky Mountain	CO	More than a hundred peaks over 10,000 ft., 265,200 acres

Park	*ST*	*Features*
Sequoia	CA	Giant sequoias, 402,482 acres
Shenandoah	VA	Skyline Drive, 195,382 acres
Theodore Roosevelt	ND	Wildlife, 70,416 acres
Voyageurs	MN	Wildlife, 218,036 acres
Wind Cave	SD	Limestone caverns, 28,292 acres
Wrangell-St. Elias	AK	Largest park system, 8,331,604 acres
Yellowstone	WY-MT-ID	Geyser area, 2,219,791 acres
Yosemite	CA	Giant sequoias, 761,170 acres
Zion	UT	Multicolored gorge, 146,598 acres

A YEAR'S READING PROGRAM FOR YOUR LEISURE TIME

Selected by Dr. John F. Walvoord, Chancellor, Dallas Theological Seminary

January . . . .*Mere Christianity* by C.S. Lewis
February . . . .*Balancing the Christian Life* by Charles C. Ryrie
March . . . .*Growing Deep in the Christian Life* by Charles R. Swindoll
April . . . .*What We Believe: Discovering Biblical Truth* by John F. Walvoord
May . . . .*Failure: The Backdoor to Success* by Erwin Lutzer
June . . . .*Happiness Is a Choice* by Frank B. Minirth and Paul Meier
July . . . .*Emotions: Can You Trust Them?* by James Dobson
August . . . .*Little House on the Freeway* by Tim Kimmel
September . . . .*Hudson Taylor's Spiritual Secret* by Dr. and Mrs. Howard Taylor
October . . . .*The Knowledge of the Holy* by A.W. Tozer
November . . . .*Facing Death and the Life After* by Billy Graham
December . . . .*Sense and Nonsense about Prayer* by Lehman Strauss

FOCUS QUOTE

Words are things; and a small drop of ink
Falling like dew upon a thought, produces
That which makes thousands, perhaps millions, think.
—George Byron

Media

TOP 10 BEST-SELLING BOOKS OF 1989

CLOTHBOUND

1. *My Utmost for His Highest* by Oswald Chambers, Barbour & Co., Discovery House Publishers
2. *Love for a Lifetime* by James Dobson, Multnomah Press
3. *The Language of Love* by Gary Smalley and John Trent, Focus on the Family Publishing/Word, Inc.
4. *Inside Out* by Larry Crabb, NavPress
5. *Out of the Blue* by Orel Hershiser with Jerry B. Jenkins, Wolgemuth & Hyatt, Publishers
6. *Disappointment with God* by Philip Yancey, Zondervan Publishing Company
7. *Love Must Be Tough* by James Dobson, Word, Inc.
8. *Against the Night* by Charles Colson, Vine Books/Servant Publications
9. *The Blessing* by Gary Smalley and John Trent, Thomas Nelson Publishers
10. *Living Beyond the Daily Grind (Book I)* by Charles Swindoll, Word, Inc.

PAPERBACK

1. *This Present Darkness* by Frank Peretti, Crossway Books/Good News Publishers
2. *Piercing the Darkness* by Frank Peretti, Crossway Books/Good News Publishers
3. *Spring's Gentle Promise* by Janette Oke, Bethany House Publishers
4. *Love Finds a Home* by Janette Oke, Bethany House Publishers
5. *Joshua* by Joseph Girzone, Macmillan Publishing Co.
6. *Hinds' Feet on High Places* by Hannah Hurnard, Tyndale House Publishers/ Walker & Co.
7. *Love Takes Wing* by Janette Oke, Bethany House Publishers
8. *Becoming a Woman of Excellence* by Cynthia Heald, NavPress
9. *Love Life for Every Married Couple* by Ed Wheat with Gloria Okes Perkins, Zondervan Publishing House
10. *Mere Christianity* by C. S. Lewis, Macmillan Publishing Co./Walker & Co.

TOP 10 BEST-SELLING BOOKS OF THE '80s

CLOTHBOUND

1. *Growing Strong in the Seasons of Life* by Charles Swindoll, Multnomah Press/Walker and Company
2. *Love Must Be Tough* by James Dobson, Word, Inc.
3. *Improving Your Serve* by Charles Swindoll, Word, Inc.
4. *The Strong-Willed Child* by James Dobson, Tyndale House
5. *A Shepherd Looks at Psalm 23* by W. Phillip Keller, Zondervan Publishing House
6. *The Christian Mother Goose Book* (Volume 1 of Trilogy) by Marjorie Ainsborough Decker, World Bible Publishers Inc.
7. *Love for a Lifetime* by James Dobson, Multnomah Press
8. *Loving God* by Charles Colson, Zondervan Publishing House/Walker and Company

9. *Strengthening Your Grip* by Charles Swindoll, Word, Inc.
10. *Irregular People* by Joyce Landorf, Walker and Company / originally released by Word Publishing

PAPERBACK

1. *Hinds' Feet on High Places* by Hannah Hurnard, Tyndale House/Walker & Company/Barbour & Company
2. *Dare to Discipline* by James Dobson, Tyndale House/Bantam Books
3. *Free to Be Thin* by Marie Chapian and Neva Coyle, Bethany House
4. *Three Steps Forward, Two Steps Back* by Charles Swindoll, Thomas Nelson/ Bantam Books/Walker and Company
5. *The Seduction of Christianity* by Dave Hunt and T.A. McMahon, Harvest House Publishers
6. *The Late Great Planet Earth* by Hal Lindsey, Zondervan/Bantam Books
7. *The Act of Marriage* by Tim and Beverly LaHaye, Zondervan/Bantam Books
8. *Ordering Your Private World* by Gordon MacDonald, Oliver-Nelson
9. *Love Life for Every Married Couple* by Ed Wheat with Gloria Okes Perkins, Zondervan Publishing House
10. *The Pursuit of Holiness* by Jerry Bridges, NavPress/Walker and Company

These lists were compiled from *Bookstore Journal's* best-seller lists of the 1980s—not actual sales. Titles received 10 points for each No. 1 placement, nine points for each No. 2, etc. Thus, while the rankings reflect sales, they shouldn't be considered the last word on '80s super-sellers. Publishers listed are current publishers of *all* editions. Reprinted by permission from the March 1990 issue of *Bookstore Journal*, official trade publication of the Christian Booksellers Association.

100 BEST-SELLING CHRISTIAN ADULT BOOKS

This list was compiled from information supplied by publishers. The first sales figure shown for each entry is the number of copies sold from June 1988 through May 1989, and the second figure is the total number sold in the title's history with the publisher.

Although the books are ranked according to the total sold in the past year, not all publishers granted permission for sales totals to be published. Unreleased figures are designated by "n.a.," but the books are ranked in their proper position. Some publishers chose to not submit figures.

1. **This Present Darkness** Frank Peretti
Good News/Crossway, Fiction © 1986. 350,000 / 495,000. A small-town reporter and pastor find themselves fighting a New Age plot to subjugate the townspeople and, eventually, the entire human race.
2. **The Bible Promise Book** Toni Sortor
Barbour, Inspiration © 1985. 321,774 / 954,000. This collection of more than 1,000 Bible promises is arranged alphabetically by topic.
3. **Love Takes Wing** Janette Oke
Bethany House, Fiction © 1988. 257,134 / 257,134. This book is seventh in the "Love Comes Softly" series.
4. **My Utmost for His Highest**
Oswald Chambers
Barbour, Devotional © 1935. 230,649 / 503,000. This is a classic devotional volume.
5. **All You Can Do Is All You Can Do But All You Can Do Is Enough!**
A. L. Williams
Thomas Nelson, Inspiration © 1988. 226,000 / 289,645. The founder of the world's largest individual life insurance company details his six-step system of success.
6. **Living Beyond the Daily Grind (Book I)** Charles Swindoll
Word, Inspiration © 1988. 208,852 / 208,852. This year-long study of selected songs and Bible verses helps readers face everyday issues.
7. **Prison to Praise** Merlin Carothers
Merlin R. Carothers Co., Biography © 1970. 201,000 / 5,017,000. The autobiographer shares his life from his rebellious youth to finding the Lord and becoming a chaplain.

8. **Standard Lesson Commentary** Jim Fehl, editor Standard Publishing, Christian Education © 1988. 191,500 / 191,500. Designed for Uniform Lesson users, this volume makes teaching Sunday school easier.
9. **Growing Wise in Family Life** Charles Swindoll Multnomah, Parenting © 1988. 174,664 / 174,664. Swindoll issues a call for godly wisdom to counteract the dismembering of the American family.
10. **Joshua** Joseph Girzone Macmillan, Fiction © 1987. 150,000 / n.a. This book presents a fictional look at Christ's life and message.
11. **Handbook for Today's Catholic** Redemptorist Pastoral Publication Liguori, Christian Education © 1966. 145,170 / 2,720,041. This volume discusses Catholic beliefs, practices, and prayers.
12. **The Language of Love** Gary Smalley and John Trent Focus on the Family, Love/Marriage © 1988. 130,390 / 130,390. The authors show how to maximize one's communication through emotional word pictures.
13. **Living Beyond the Daily Grind (Book II)** Charles Swindoll Word, Inspiration © 1988. 124,593 / 124,593. This year-long study of selected songs and Bible verses helps readers face everyday issues.
14. **Inside Out** Larry Crabb NavPress, Christian Living © 1987. 121,126 / 162,096. The author helps readers gain confidence to unlock guarded inner chambers and to let God in to heal, restore, and fulfill.
15. **The Strong-Willed Child** James Dobson Tyndale, Parenting © 1985. n.a. Dobson shares how to discipline the strong-willed child without breaking his or her spirit.
16. **Your Baby's Baptism** Redemptorists Liguori, Parenting © 1985. 115,400 / 447,251. A gift book for parents, this title discusses aspects of infant baptism.
17. **The New Birth** Kenneth Hagin Kenneth Hagin Ministries, Christian Living © 1975. 111,618 / 2,168,600. This mini-book explains what being "born again" means.
18. **Preparing for Adolescence** James Dobson Regal Books (Gospel Light), Christian Living © 1978. 109,570 / 467,000. Dobson talks to teens about the challenges they are learning to face.
19. **Answers to Life's Problems** Billy Graham Word, Christian Living © 1988. 103,903 / 103,903. Graham discusses the Bible's answers to questions regarding relationships, issues, psychological problems, and the Bible itself.
20. **The Lord of Victory** LeRoy Lawson Standard Publishing, Christian Living © 1988. 101,207 / 101,207. Lawson emphasizes Jesus' power as the key to victory over problems.
21. **The Gospel According to Jesus** John MacArthur Zondervan, Christian Living © 1988. n.a. MacArthur writes that there is no eternal life without surrender to the Lordship of Christ and that faith without works is dead.
22. **Hinds' Feet on High Places** Hannah Hurnard Tyndale, Inspiration © 1979. n.a. This allegory dramatizes the desire of God's children to be led to new heights of love, joy, and victory.
23. **Love Life for Every Married Couple** Ed Wheat with Gloria Okes Perkins Zondervan, Love/Marriage © 1980. n.a. This book helps readers rediscover the joy of marriage through communication and understanding each other's sexual make-up.
24. **Healing for Damaged Emotions** David Seamands Victor Books, Self-Help © 1981. n.a. This book shows how to claim God's help in defeating emotional problems that keep Christians from reaching spiritual maturity.

100 BEST-SELLING CHRISTIAN ADULT BOOKS cont.

25. **Love for a Lifetime** James Dobson
Multnomah, Love/Marriage © 1987. 92,481 / 347,162. Dobson shares insight about courtship, fidelity, commitment, finances, the uniqueness of men and women, and ways to build solid marriages.
26. **Why Tongues?** Kenneth Hagin
Kenneth Hagin Ministries, Christian Living © 1975. 91,320 / 1,610,800. This book presents 10 scriptural benefits of being filled with the Holy Spirit and speaking in tongues.
27. **Mere Christianity** C. S. Lewis
Macmillan, Apologetics © 1964. 91,000 / n.a. Lewis presents the common faith that unites believers.
28. **Secret Strength** Joni Eareckson Tada
Multnomah Press, Inspiration © 1988. 87,005 / 87,005. Devotional insights present secrets of God's strength, character, and grace.
29. **Dr. Dobson Answers Your Questions**
James Dobson
Tyndale, Christian Living © 1988. n.a. Dobson addresses a variety of topics in this mass paper volume.
30. **In Him** Kenneth Hagin
Kenneth Hagin Ministries, Christian Living © 1975. 77,257 / 1,853,600. Hagin examines individuals' redemptive rights in Christ.
31. **Apples of Gold** Jo Petty
C. R. Gibson, Inspiration © 1962. 76,000 / 3,294,570. This gift book offers inspirational nuggets.
32. **Power in Praise** Merlin Carothers
Merlin R. Carothers Co., Christian Living © 1972. 76,000 / 2,460,000. This title explains how people can experience the "praise power" that transforms lives.
33. **Dare to Discipline** James Dobson
Tyndale, Parenting © 1970, 1987. n.a. This guide discusses discipline and asserts that good parent-child relationships are built on respect and loyalty to God.
34. **If Only He Knew**
Gary Smalley with Steve Scott
Zondervan, Love/Marriage © 1982, 1987. n.a. Smalley clarifies for men the differences between the sexes and how to build a stronger marital relationship.
35. **The Tongue—A Creative Force**
Charles Capps
Harrison House Subject: Christian Living © 1977. 71,136 / 528,959. This discussion of the importance of speaking God's Word shows how a creative spiritual force can be released within believers.
36. **A Shepherd Looks at Psalm 23**
W. Phillip Keller
Zondervan, Inspiration © 1970. n.a. Keller discusses this Psalm from the perspective of a shepherd.
37. **For Better or for Best**
Gary Smalley with Steve Scott
Zondervan, Love/Marriage © 1982, 1987. n.a. Smalley shows how wives can cultivate better relationships with their spouses.
38. **Becoming a Woman of Excellence**
Cynthia Heald
NavPress, Christian Living © 1986. 69,800 / 191,389. This study teaches readers how to become excellent in their daily lives.
39. **Love Must Be Tough** James Dobson
Word Publishing, Love/Marriage © 1983. 68,011 / 638,086. Dobson outlines steps and principles that can help a determined spouse save a marriage when the other partner seems unconcerned.
40. **Satan's Underground** Lauren Stratford
Harvest House, Cults © 1988. 66,971 / 114,491. Stratford reveals her experiences with Satanism.
41. **Why Am I Afraid to Tell You Who I Am?** John Powell
Tabor Publishing, Self-Help © 1969. 66,677 / 3,136,693. This book discusses communication, trust, and love and shows readers how to grow in self-esteem, confidence, and personal relationships.
42. **Mothers and Sons**
Jean Lush & Pam Vredevelt
Revell, Parenting © 1988. 66,327 / 66,327. The authors offer guidelines and

counsel for building emotional, spiritual, and sexual stability.

43. **Plans, Purposes & Pursuits**
Kenneth Hagin
Kenneth Hagin Ministries, Christian Living © 1988. 66,312 / 88,416. This exhortation urges readers to seek God's plans and purposes for their lives and pursue them.

44. **God Calling** A. J. Russell
Revell, Inspiration © 1972. 65,229 / 1,465,931. Two listeners receive messages from God.

45. **A Precious Moments™ Christmas**
Sam Butcher
Thomas Nelson, Gift © 1988. 65,000 / 268,054. The joy of the holiday season comes to life in delicate, full-color illustrations and rhyme.

46. **Kingdoms in Conflict** Charles Colson
Zondervan, Issues © 1987. n.a. This book looks at the role of the church in society, the role of government in the world, and the role of Christians in each.

47. **Prayers That Avail Much, Vol. 1**
Word Ministries
Harrison House, Inspiration © 1980. 63,945 / 617,135. Scriptures expressed as prayers allow readers to have confidence and faith that they are praying in God's will.

48. **Hide or Seek** James Dobson
Revell, Parenting © 1974, 1979. 63,176 / 559,445. This guide suggests ways to build children's self-esteem.

49. **More Than a Carpenter**
Josh McDowell
Tyndale, Apologetics © 1980. n.a.
McDowell offers answers to people who are skeptical about Jesus' deity, His resurrection, and His claims on their lives.

50. **Lessons on Assurance** The Navigators
NavPress, Bible Study © 1957, 1975, 1980. 62,700 / 771,587. This is a personal-response Bible study to affirm young Christians' trust in the Lord.

51. **How to Get Better Grades and Have More Fun** Steve Douglass
Here's Life, Self-Help © 1986. 62,632 / 112,962. Steps for achieving academic success are presented.

52. **Vietnam: The Other Side of Glory**
William Kimball
Ballantine/Epiphany, Issues © 1988. 62,000 / 62,000. Vietnam vets discuss their religious experience in war and after.

53. **Free to Be Thin**
Marie Chapian and Neva Coyle
Bethany House, Health © 1979. 61,399 / 936,010. This plan for losing weight permanently focuses on a change of mind rather than weight loss.

54. **Design for Discipleship 1: Your Life in Christ** The Navigators
NavPress, Bible Study © 1973, 1980. 61,317 / 881,814. Questions and answers with key Scripture verses direct readers through five one-hour lessons in this study.

55. **Handbook for Healing**
Charles and Frances Hunter
Hunter Books, Health © 1987. 60,000 / 136,517. This book shows readers how to pray for healing for various illnesses.

56. **How to Heal the Sick**
Charles and Frances Hunter
Hunter Books, Health © 1981. 60,000 / 300,000. This book shows how to claim Jesus' promise of healing the sick by laying hands on them.

57. **Good Grief** Granger Westberg
Fortress Press, Self-Help © 1979. 59,735 / 1,220,210. Subtitled "A Constructive Approach to the Problem of Loss," this title discusses many forms of grief and presents 10 stages of normal grieving.

58. **See You at the Top** Zig Ziglar
Pelican Publishing, Self-Help © 1975. 59,224 / 1,236,559. Ziglar presents a program of self-development based on the foundation of a winning self-image.

59. **Disappointment With God**
Philip Yancey
Zondervan, Christian Living © 1988. n.a. Yancey offers comfort to those who have suffered loss and explains why God allows such losses.

100 BEST-SELLING CHRISTIAN ADULT BOOKS cont.

60. **Survival for Busy Women**
Emilie Barnes
Harvest House, Self-Help © 1986. 57,385 / 104,093. Barnes describes a system for efficient home management.

61. **The Act of Marriage**
Tim and Beverly LaHaye
Zondervan, Love/Marriage © 1976. n.a. This book outlines principles, goals, and guidelines for achieving a mutually satisfying sexual relationship within marriage.

62. **The Pursuit of Holiness** Jerry Bridges
NavPress, Christian Living © 1978. 56,063 / 714,977. Bridges shows readers how to live to please God.

63. **The Blessing**
Gary Smalley and John Trent
Thomas Nelson, Parenting © 1986. 56,000 / 240,948. This book shows how to assure family members of security and approval.

64. **What's on Your Mind?**
Merlin Carothers
Merlin R. Carothers Co., Christian Living © 1984. 55,000 / 465,000. This book discusses the importance of thinking pure thoughts.

65. **The Key to Zion** Bodie Thoene
Bethany House, Fiction © 1988. 54,719 / 54,719. Fifth in the "Zion Chronicles," this novel begins with the British starting to evacuate from Palestine.

66. **He Came to Set the Captives Free**
Rebecca Brown
Chick Publications, Cults © 1986. 54,500 / 108,236. This account of Satan's activities shows readers how to recognize and combat his power.

67. **The Kingdom of the Cults, Revised**
Walter Martin
Bethany House, Cults © 1985. 54,444 / 486,209. A classic in its field, this book offers comprehensive analysis of all the current major cult systems.

68. **Wisdom From the Bible**
Dan and Nancy Dick
Barbour, Devotional © 1986. 54,004 / 156,882. Each page of this devotional contains a verse from Proverbs and an inspirational thought.

69. **Operation World** Patrick Johnstone
Send the Light, Missions © 1978. 54,000 / n.a. This daily prayer guide helps readers focus on the needs of the nations of the world.

70. **Personal Pocket Promise Book**
David Wilkerson
Regal Books (Gospel Light), Inspiration © 1987. 53,937 / n.a. Bound in burgundy bonded leather, this gift book contains more than 850 biblical promises.

71. **Faith Worketh by Love**
Kenneth Hagin Jr.
Kenneth Hagin Ministries, Christian Living © 1979. 53,302 / 662,946. This minibook discusses why many people's prayers remain unanswered.

72. **The Friendships of Women**
Dee Brestin
Victor Books, Christian Living © 1988. n.a. Brestin discusses the power and pain in female relationships through an examination of Ruth and Naomi's friendship.

73. **Wings of Silver** Jo Petty
C. R. Gibson, Inspiration © 1967. 53,000 / 1,639,500. This gift book includes short phrases that offer guidelines for living and loving.

74. **Love Comes Softly** Janette Oke
Bethany House, Fiction © 1979. 52,430 / 746,589. First in a series, this book tells how a marriage of convenience blossoms into one of love.

75. **Mystery Mark of the New Age**
Texe Marrs
Good News/Crossway, Cults © 1988. 52,000 / 83,000. Satan's deceptive New Age symbols and practices are exposed.

76. **The Screwtape Letters** C. S. Lewis
Macmillan, Fiction © 1982. 52,000 / n.a. Screwtape advises his young nephew, Tempter, in the fine art of tempting a human soul to hell.

77. **The Complete Book of Bible Trivia**
J. Stephen Lang
Tyndale, Misc. © 1988. n.a. This collection offers more than 4,500 Bible questions and answers.

78. **God's Medicine** Kenneth Hagin
Kenneth Hagin Ministries, Christian Living © 1977. 51,247 / 1,135,800. Hagin presents God's prescription for health and healing according to Proverbs 4:20-22.

79. **Winter Is Not Forever** Janette Oke
Bethany House, Fiction © 1988. 50,208 / 233,406. Josh must decide what he wants to do with his life in Book 3 of the "Seasons of the Heart" series.

80. **Dollars & Sense** Mervin Thompson
Prince of Peace, Christian Living © 1988. 50,094 / 50,094. This book is a guide to Christian financial planning.

81. **Dark Secrets of the New Age**
Texe Marrs
Good News/Crossway, Cults © 1987. 50,000 / 141,000. This book examines the secret plan of the New Age Movement and tells what Christians must do to combat it.

82. **No Wonder They Call Him the Savior**
Max Lucado
Multnomah, Devotional © 1986. 49,883 / 161,228. Focusing on Christ's crucifixion, this book discusses the sayings, people, and principles of the cross.

83. **A Path Through Scripture** Mark Link
Tabor, Christian Education © 1987. 49,643 / 95,907. This high school text presents an introductory tour of the Old and New Testaments.

84. **Catholic Answers to Fundamentalists' Questions** Philip St. Romain
Liguori, Christian Education © 1984. 48,832 / 177,984. This book is arranged in a question-and-answer format.

85. **Maximized Manhood**
Edwin Louis Cole
Whitaker House, Christian Living © 1982. 48,661 / 335,949. Cole challenges men to assume the responsibility, leadership, and moral character God expects of them.

86. **Telling Yourself the Truth**
William Backus with Marie Chapian
Bethany House, Self-Help © 1980. 47,849 / 385,806. This book shows how to deal with misbeliefs according to biblical guidelines.

87. **30 Days to Understanding the Bible**
Max Anders
Wolgemuth & Hyatt, Bible Study © 1988. 47,700 / 47,700. This title offers a concise yet thorough overview of the Scriptures.

88. **What Happens When Women Pray?**
Evelyn Christenson
Victor Books, Christian Living © 1975. n.a. This book shows what happens when prayer becomes a life-changing dynamic in the church.

89. **The Cost of Discipleship**
Dietrich Bonhoeffer
Macmillan, Christian Living © 1963. 47,000 / n.a. Bonhoeffer discusses grace and the life of discipleship in this classic.

90. **Rebuilding Your Broken World**
Gordon MacDonald
Thomas Nelson, Christian Living © 1988. 47,000 / 58,024. MacDonald encourages those whose personal world has disintegrated and points the way to restoration and hope.

91. **Design for Discipleship 2: The Spirit-Filled Christian** The Navigators
NavPress, Bible Study © 1973, 1980. 46,944 / 721,801. Questions and answers with key Scripture verses direct readers through five one-hour lessons in this study.

92. **Shadows Over Stonewycke**
Michael Phillips and Judith Pella
Bethany House, Fiction © 1988. 46,922 / 46,922. Book 2 of "The Stonewycke Legacy" series is set shortly before World War II.

93. **Love's Unfolding Dream** Janette Oke
Bethany House, Fiction © 1987. 46,015 / 292,432. This is the sequel to *Love's Unending Legacy.*

94. **Angelwalk** Roger Elwood
Good News/Crossway, Fiction © 1988. 46,000 / 66,000. An angel questions God's actions and is permitted to wander through history, observing.

95. **A Moment a Day**
Mary Beckwith and Kathi Mills
Regal Books (Gospel Light), Devotional © 1988. 45,788 / 67,000. Selected passages

100 BEST-SELLING CHRISTIAN ADULT BOOKS cont.

by Shirley Dobson, Gloria Gaither, and others speak to busy women.

96. **Another Spring** June Masters Bacher
Harvest House, Fiction © 1988. 45,658 / 46,461. Fourth in the "Love's Soft Whisper" series, this book relates Courtney and Clint's custody battle for Courtney's sister's twins.

97. **20 Hot Potatoes Christians Are Afraid to Touch** Tony Campolo
Word, Issues © 1988. 45,479 / 45,479. Campolo confronts today's tough questions and gives honest, direct, and biblical answers.

98. **Christian Counseling: A Comprehensive Guide, Revised** Gary Collins
Word, Counseling © 1980, 1988. 45,400 / 145,400. This course in pastoral counseling includes discussion of recent research and new developments, including AIDS and eating disorders.

99. **Growing Strong in the Seasons of Life** Charles Swindoll
Multnomah, Devotional © 1983. 45,140 / 900,000. This collection of brief devotionals offers readings for a year.

100. **Evidence That Demands a Verdict, Vol. 1** Josh McDowell
Here's Life, Apologetics © 1972, 1979. 44,088 / 966,818. This classic defense of Christianity gives readers historical evidence for the validity of Christ's claims and identity.

FOCUS FACT

While a small percentage of Christians shop at a Christian bookstore, those who do, shop regularly.

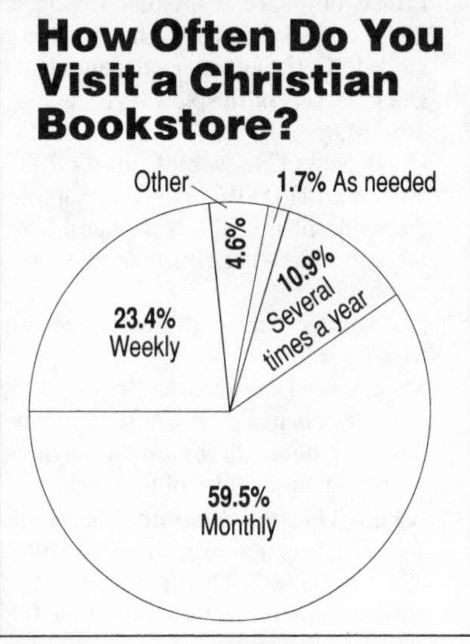

Source: *Bookstore Journal*, April 1990.

CHRISTIAN BOOK PUBLISHERS IN THE UNITED STATES

*Indicates Evangelical Christian Publishers Association membership.

Abbey Press		St. Meinrad IN 47577
Abbott Loop Publications	2626 Abbott Road	Anchorage AK 99507
Abingdon Press	201 - 8th Avenue S.	Nashville TN 37202
Accent Books	P.O. Bx 15337, 12100 W. 6th Ave.	Denver CO 80215
Agape Ministries	P.O. Box 2959	Titusville FL 32781
Augsburg Publishing House	Box 1209, 426 S. 5th Street	Minneapolis MN 55440
Ave Maria Press		Notre Dame IN 46556
B. B. Kirkbride Company, Inc.*	P.O. Box 606	Indianapolis IN 46206
Baker Book House*	P.O. Box 6287	Grand Rapids MI 49506
Ballantine/Epiphany Books	201 East 50 Street	New York NY 10022
Bantam Books	666 - 5th Avenue	New York NY 10103
Baptist Publishing House	1319 Magnolia Street	Texarkana TX 75501

Baptist Spanish Publishing House	P.O. Box 4255, 7000 Alabama St.	El Paso TX 79914
Barbour and Company, Inc.*	164 Mill Street	Westwood NJ 07675
Bethany House Publishers*	6820 Auto Club Road	Minneapolis MN 55438
Bethel Publishing	1819 S. Main	Elkhart IN 46516
Bob Jones University Press		Greenville SC 29614
Brethren Press	1451 Dundee Avenue	Elgin IL 60120
Bridge Publishing, Inc.	2500 Hamilton Blvd.	South Plainfield NJ 07080
Bristol Books*	P.O. Box 150	Wilmore KY 40390
Broadman Press*	127 - 9th Avenue N.	Nashville TN 37234
Brownlow Publishing Co., Inc.*	6309 Airport Freeway	Fort Worth TX 76117
C. R. Gibson Company*	32 Knight Street	Norwalk CT 06856
Casa Editorial Nueva Albanza	P.O. Box 9944	El Paso TX 79990
Casa Nazarene de Publicaciones	6401 The Paseo	Kansas City MO 64131
Charles Scribner's Sons	866 Third Avenue	New York NY 10022
Christian Books Publishing House	P.O. Box 3368	Auburn ME 04210
Christian Classics Inc.	P.O. Box 30	Westminster MD 21157
Christian Education Publishers*	P.O. Box 2789	La Jolla CA 92038
Christian Publications, Inc.	3825 Hartzdale Drive	Camp Hill PA 17011
Clarion Books	52 Vanderbilt Avenue	New York NY 10017
Collier Books/Macmillan Company	866 Third Avenue	New York NY 10022
Concordia Publishing House	3558 S. Jefferson	St. Louis MO 63118
Cornerstone Publishing Company	Suite 326-320 6336 N. Oracle Rd	Tucson AZ 85704
Creation House	190 N. Westmonte Drive	Altamonte Springs FL 32714
Creation Life Publishers, Inc./ Master Books Division*	P.O. Box 1606	El Cajon CA 92022
Dake Bible Sales, Inc	P.O. Box 1050	Lawrenceville GA 30246
David C. Cook Publishing Company*	850 N. Grove	Elgin IL 60120
Dayspring, Inc.	P.O. Box 201	Hazelwood MO 63042
Derek Prince Ministries	P.O. Box 300	Ft. Lauderdale FL 33302
Discovery House Publishers*	P.O. Box 3566	Grand Rapids MI 49501
Doubleday & Company*	666 Fifth Avenue	New York NY 10103
Editorial Betania	5541 N.W. 82nd Avenue	Miami FL 33166
Editorial Caribe	3934 S.W. 8th Street, Suite 303	Miami FL 33134
Editorial Unilit	1360 N.W. 88 Avenue	Miami FL 33172
Eerdmans Publishing Co., Wm. B.	255 Jefferson, S.E.	Grand Rapids MI 49503
Emmanuel Press	5451 Moongate Road	Spring Hill FL 33526
Faith and Life Press	P.O. Box 347, 724 Main	Newton KS 67114
Fleming H. Revell Company*	P.O. Box 150, 184 Central Ave.	Old Tappan NJ 07675
Focus on the Family Publishing*	801 Corporate Center Drive	Pomona CA 91768
Fortress Press	Box 1209, 426 South Fifth Street	Minneapolis MN 55440
Foundation Press*	1121 N. Kraemer Place	Anaheim CA 92806
Good Family Publishing*	P.O. Box 850	Sisters OR 97759
Good News Publ./Crossway Books*	9825 W. Roosevelt Road	Westchester IL 60153
Good Will Publishers*	229 N. Church Street, #400	Charlotte NC 28202
Gospel Light Publications/Regal Bks*	2300 Knoll Drive	Ventura CA 93003
Gospel Publishing House	1445 Boonville Avenue	Springfield MO 65802
Group Books*	2890 N. Monroe	Loveland CO 80539
Guideposts Associates, Inc.*	757 Third Avenue	New York NY 10017
Hannibal Books*	31 Holiday	Hannibal MO 63401
Harold Shaw Publishers	P.O. Box 567, 388 Gundersen Dr.	Wheaton IL 60189
Harper & Row, Publishers*	151 Union St., Icehouse One—401	San Francisco CA 94111
Harrison House	P.O. Box 35035	Tulsa OK 74153
Harvest House Publishers*	1075 Arrowsmith	Eugene OR 97402
Herald Press	616 Walnut Avenue	Scottdale PA 15683
Here's Life Publishers, Inc.*	P.O. Box 1576, 2700 Little Mountain Drive, Bldg. F.	San Bernardino CA 92405

CHRISTIAN BOOK PUBLISHERS IN THE UNITED STATES cont.

Holman Bible Publishers*	127 - 9th Avenue, N	Nashville TN 37234
Houghton Mifflin Company	2 Park Street	Boston MA 02108
Huntington House, Inc.	P.O. Box 53788	Lafayette LA 70505
Ideals Publishing Corporation	P.O. Box 140300	Nashville TN 37214
Ignatius Press	15 Oakland Avenue	Harrison NY 10528
Impact Books, Inc.	137 W. Jefferson	Kirkwood MO 63122
InterVarsity Press*	P.O. Box 1400, 5206 Main Street	Downers Grove IL 60515
John Knox Press	341 Ponce De Leon Avenue, NE	Atlanta GA 30308
Judson Press	P.O. Box 851	Valley Forge PA 19482
Keats Publishing, Inc.	P.O. Box 876	New Canaan CT 06840
Kregel Publications*	P.O. Bx 2607, 733 Wealthy St. SE	Grand Rapids MI 49501
Life Publishers Interntl/Vida Editorial	3360 N.W. 110th Street	Miami FL 33167
Light and Life Press	999 College Avenue	Winona Lake IN 46590
Lillenas Publishing Company	P.O. Box 419527	Kansas City MO 64141
Lion Publishing Corporation	1705 Hubbard Avenue	Batavia IL 60510
Loizeaux Brothers, Inc.*	P.O. Box 277, 1238 Corlies Ave.	Neptune NJ 07753
Lutheran Publishing House	3547 Indiana Ave.	St. Louis MO 63118
Macmillan Company	866 - 3rd Avenue	New York NY 10022
Maranatha Publications	P.O. Box 1799	Gainesville FL 32602
Master Books	P.O. Box 1606	El Cajon CA 92022
Moody Press	820 North LaSalle Drive	Chicago IL 60610
Mott Media*	1000 East Huron Street	Milford MI 48042
Multnomah Press*	10209 S.E. Division St.	Portland OR 97266
National Publishing Company*	P.O. Box 8386, 24th & Locust Sts.	Philadelphia PA 19101
NavPress*	P.O. Box 6000, 5015 N. 30th St.	Colorado Springs CO 80934
New Hope Publishing Company	9123 Lorene - 106	San Antonio TX 78216
New Leaf Press	P.O. Box 311	Green Forest AR 72638
Oliver-Nelson	Nelson Place at Elm Hill Pike	Nashville TN 37214
Omega Publications*	P.O. Box 4130	Medford OR 97501
Our Sunday Visitor, Inc.	200 Noll Plaza	Huntington IN 46750
Oxford University Press*	200 Madison Avenue	New York NY10016
Paulist Press	997 Macarthur Blvd.	Mahwah NJ 07430
Pocket Books - Washington Sq. Press	1230 Avenue of the Americas	New York NY 10020
Praise Publications	P.O. Box 710231	San Jose CA 95171
Presbyterian & Reformed Publishing	P.O. Box 817	Phillipsburg NJ 08865
Publishing Directions, Inc.*	1223 Potomac Street, NW	Washington DC 20007
Questar Publishers, Inc.*	P.O. Box 1720, 210 S. Elm Street	Sisters OR 97759
Roper Press*	915 Dragon Street	Dallas TX 75207
Scripture Press Publications	1825 College Avenue	Wheaton IL 60187
Scripture Press Publ./Victor Books*	1825 College Avenue	Wheaton IL 60187
Serendipity House, Inc.	2550 West Main Street	Littleton CO 80120
Servant Publications/Vine Books*	P.O. Box 8617, 840 Airport Blvd.	Ann Arbor MI 48107
Spire Books	184 Central Avenue	Old Tappan NJ 07675
Standard Publishing*	8121 Hamilton Avenue	Cincinnati OH 45231
STL Books	#2 Industrial Park Road	Waynesboro GA 30830
Strang Communications Company*	190 N. Westmonte Drive	Altamonte Springs FL 32714
Sweet Publishing Company*	3950 Fossil Creek Blvd., Suite 201	Fort Worth TX 76137
Sword of the Lord Publishers	224 Bridge Avenue	Murfreesboro TN 37130
Thomas Nelson, Inc. Publishers*	P.O. Box 141000, Nelson Place at Elm Hill Park	Nashville TN 37214
Tyndale House Publishers, Inc.	Box 80, 351 Executive Drive	Wheaton IL 60189
Upper Room	1908 Grand Avenue	Nashville TN 37202
V. Countryman Publishers	P.O. Box 90776	Houston TX 77290
Victory House, Inc.	P.O. Box 700238	Tulsa OK 74170
Warner Press, Inc.*	P.O. Box 2499, 1200 East 5th St.	Anderson IN 46018

Wellspring Books	Rt. 1, Box 27	Groton VT 05046
Wesley Press	8050 Castaway Drive	Indianapolis IN 46250
Western Publ. Co., Inc./Golden Books	1220 Mound Avenue	Racine WI 53404
Westminster Press	925 Chestnut Street	Philadelphia PA 19107
Whitaker House	580 Pittsburgh Street	Springdale PA 15144
William Carey Library Publishers	PO Bx 40129, 1705 N. Sierra Bonita	Pasadena CA 91104
Winston Seabury Press	151 Union Street	San Francisco CA 94111
Wolgemuth & Hyatt Publishers, Inc.*	1749 Mallory Lane, Suite 110	Brentwood TN 37027
Word, Inc.*	5221 N. O'Connor, Suite 1000	Irving TX 75039
World Bible Publishers, Inc.	P.O. Box 370, 11500 Riverside Dr.	Iowa Falls IA 50126
World Book and Bible House*	1500 Riverview Drive	Iowa Falls IA 50126
World Wide Publications*	1303 Hennepin Avenue	Minneapolis MN 55403
Worthy Publishing	3950 Fossil Creek Blvd., Suite 203	Fort Worth TX 76137
Youth Specialties, Inc.	1224 Greenfield Drive	El Cajon CA 92021
Zondervan Corporation*	1415 Lake Drive, SE	Grand Rapids MI 49506

CHRISTIAN BOOKS PUBLISHED WORLDWIDE

	1900	*1970*	*1980*	*1990*	*2000*
New commercial book titles per year	2,200	17,100	18,800	22,400	25,000
New titles including devotional	3,100	52,000	60,000	65,600	75,000
Christian periodicals	3,500	23,000	22,500	23,800	35,000
New books/articles on evangelization per year	300	3,100	7,500	11,000	16,000

Adapted from David B. Barrett, World Evangelization database.

CAMPUS LIFE BOOK OF THE YEAR AWARDS

Award of Excellence/Biography

1981	The Catch Me Killer	Bob Erler with John C. Souter	Tyndale House Publishers
1982	Lord of the Second Advent	Steve Kemperman	Regal Books/Gospel Light Publ.
1983	The Flames Shall Not Consume You	Mary Ellen Ton	David C. Cook Publishing Co.
1985	Empty Sleeves	Phillip Rushing	Zondervan Publishing House
1986	Sandy	Leighton Ford	InterVarsity Press
1987	Choices . . . Changes	Joni Eareckson Tada	Zondervan Publishing Company
1990	A Man Called Norman	Mike Adkins	Focus on the Family Publishing

Award of Excellence/Fiction

1986	Empyrion: The Search for Fierra	Stephen R. Lawhead	Crossway Books/Good News Publ.
1987	No Other Choice	Lissa Halls Johnson	Fleming H. Revell
1989	Two Worlds	Lorry Lutz	Tyndale House Publishers

Award of Excellence/General Interest

1981	Too Old to Cry, Too Young to Die	Edith Pendleton	Thomas Nelson, Inc., Publishers
1982	Abortion: The Silent Holocaust	John Powell	Argus Communications
1983	Irregular People	Joyce Landorf	Word, Inc.
1984	Choices	Stacy and Paula Rinehart	Navpress
1985	Beating the Break-up Habit	Dick Purnell with Jerry Jones	Here's Life Publishers
1986	Beyond Choice	Don Baker	Multnomah Press
1987	Doorposts	Timothy Botts	Tyndale House Publishers
1988	A View from the Zoo	Gary Richmond	Word, Inc.
1989	Being a Friend	Donald Bubna with Al Janssen	Tyndale House Publishers

CAMPUS LIFE BOOK OF THE YEAR AWARDS cont.

Year	Title	Author	Publisher
1990	If God Is So Good, Why Do I Hurt So Bad?	David B. Biebel	NavPress
Award of Excellence/Personal Growth			
1981	Living with Unfulfilled Desires	Walter Trobisch	InterVarsity Press
1983	How to Be Your Own Selfish Pig	Susan Schaeffer Macaulay	Chariot Bks/David C. Cook Publ. Co.
1984	Loving God	Charles Colson	Zondervan Publishing House
1985	When the Pieces Don't Fit—God Makes the Difference	Glaphre Gilliland	Zondervan Publishing House
1986	Dating, Sex & Friendship	Joyce Huggett	InterVarsity Press
1987	A Place to Stand When Life Throws You Off Balance	Mark R. Littleton	Multnomah Press
Award of Excellence/Poetry and Fiction			
1981	Alpha Centauri	Robert Siegel	Cornerstone Books
1982	Surprised by Light	Ulrich Schaffer	Harper & Row, Publishers
1983	The Valiant Papers	Calvin Miller	Zondervan Publishing House
1984	Dream Thief	Stephen R. Lawhead	Crossway Bks/Good News Publrs
1988	Heaven	Joseph Bayly	David C. Cook Publishing Co.
Award of Merit			
1981	Joseph	Joyce Landorf	Fleming H. Revell
1981	The Choice	Harold Myra	Tyndale House Publishers
1982	May's Boy	Shirlee Monty	Thomas Nelson, Inc., Publishers
1984	Dropping Your Guard	Charles R. Swindoll	Word, Inc.
1984	Finders Keepers	Dee Brestin	Harold Shaw Publishers
1984	Should I Keep My Baby?	Martha Zimmerman	Bethany House Publishers
1985	A House Divided	Katherine Edwards	Zondervan Publishing House
1985	Forgive and Forget	Lewis B. Smedes	Harper & Row, Publishers
1985	Growing into the Blue	Ulrich Schaffer	Harper & Row, Publishers
1985	Johnny Come Home	R.C. Sproul	Regal Books/Gospel Light Publtns
1985	The Sword and the Flame	Stephen R. Lawhead	Crossway Bks/Gospel Light Publtns
1986	Getting Along with Each Other	Richard Strauss	Here's Life Publishers
1986	Ordering Your Private World	Gordon MacDonald	Oliver-Nelson Books
1987	The Gates of Zion	Bodie Thoene	Zondervan Publishing House
Award of Merit/Biography			
1988	Cry Freedom	Lida Vaschenko with Cecil Murphy	Vine Books/Servant Publications
1988	I Never Sang You Happy Birthday	Judi Seifried	Chosen Books/Fleming H. Revell
1990	A Gift of Hope	Tony Melendez with Mel White	Harper and Row, Publishers
1990	One Step at a Time	Bob Wieland as told to Sarah Nichols	Zondervan Publishing House
Award of Merit/Fiction			
1983	In the Hall of the Dragon King	Stephen R. Lawhead	Crossway Bks/Good News Publrs
1987	Row This Boat Ashore	Nancy Rue	Crossway Bks/Good News Publrs
Award of Merit/General Interest			
1988	Will I Cry Tomorrow?	Susan M. Stanford	Fleming H. Revell
1990	Pregnant & Alone	Henrietta VanDerMolen	Harold Shaw Publishers
Award of Merit/Personal Growth			
1988	The Complete Campus Companion	Robert Kachur	InterVarsity Press
1989	No Answers	Bill Hybels	InterVarsity Press

Year	Title	Author	Publisher
1989	Sharing Your Faith Without Losing Your Friends	Joseph Aldrich	Multnomah Press
1990	Falling into the Big L	Karen J. Sandvig	Gospel Light/Regal Books
1990	Sex: It's Worth Waiting For	Greg Speck	Moody Press

Award of Merit/Poetry

Year	Title	Author	Publisher
1983	With Open Eyes	Ulrich Schaffer	Harper & Row, Publishers

Award of Merit/Poetry and Fiction

Year	Title	Author	Publisher
1990	A Requiem for Love	Calvin Miller	Word, Inc.
1990	Piercing the Darkness	Frank E. Peretti	Crossway Books
1990	Vienna Prelude	Bodie Thoene	Bethany House Publishers

Biography

Year	Title	Author	Publisher
1973	The Ghost in My Life	Susan B. Anthony II	Chosen Books
1979	Home Where I Belong	B.J. Thomas with Jerry B. Jenkins	Word, Inc.
1980	Kathy	Barbara Miller and Charles Paul Conn	Fleming H. Revell

Book of the Year

Year	Title	Author	Publisher
1973	The Hiding Place	Corrie ten Boom with John and Elizabeth Sherrill	Chosen Books
1974	Cry, the Beloved Country	Alan Paton	Charles Scribner's Sons
1976	If I Die at Thirty	Meg Woodson	Zondervan Publishing House

Book of the Year/General Interest

Year	Title	Author	Publisher
1977	Joni	Joni Eareckson and Joe Musser	Zondervan Publishing House

Editor's Choice

Year	Title	Author	Publisher
1981	Addicted to Mediocrity	Franky Schaeffer	Cornerstone Books
1981	Caring Enough to Forgive/ Caring Enough to Not Forgive	David Augsburger	Regal Books/Gospel Light Publ.
1981	Decision Making and the Will of God	Garry Friesen with J. Robin Maxson	Multnomah Press
1982	The Valiant Papers	Calvin Miller	Zondervan Publishing House
1982	With Wandering Steps and Slow	Joy Hoffman	InterVarsity Press
1987	Making Friends & Making Them Count	Em Griffin	InterVarsity Press
1987	Taliesin	Stephen R. Lawhead	Crossway Books/Good News Publ.
1987	The Amazing Body Human	Mark P. Cosgrove	Baker Book House

General Interest

Year	Title	Author	Publisher
1973	Tough Love	Bill Milliken	Fleming H. Revell
1974	How to Be a Christian Without Being Religious	Fritz Ridenour	Gospel Light Publications
1974	The End of Youngblood Johnson	Aaron Johnson and Jamie Buckingham	Chosen Books
1975	Tramp for the Lord	Corrie ten Boom and Jamie Buckingham	Fleming H. Revell
1978	The Acorn People	Ron Jones	Abingdon Press
1979	A Face for Me	Debbie Diane Fox with Jean Libman Block	Fleming H. Revell
1980	The Friendship Factor	Alan Loy McGinnis	Augsburg Publishing House

Mark of Excellence

Year	Title	Author	Publisher
1979	If You Haven't Got a Prayer	Stephen Crotts	InterVarsity Press
1979	Lust: the other Side of Love	Mel White	Fleming H. Revell
1979	Return from Tomorrow	George Ritchie	Chosen Books

CAMPUS LIFE BOOK OF THE YEAR AWARDS cont.

Personal Growth

1973	I Married You	Walter Trobisch	Harper & Row, Publishers
1975	Born To Grow	Larry Richards	Victor Books/Scripture Press
1976	How to Talk to God	Stephen Winward	Harold Shaw Publishers
1977	I Love The Word Impossible	Ann Kiemel	Tyndale House Publishers
1978	Winter Past	Nancy Smith	InterVarsity Press
1979	My Friend the Bible	John Sherrill	Chosen Books
1980	Out of the Salt Shaker and Into the World	Rebecca Manley Pippert	InterVarsity Press

Poetry/Fiction

1973	For Mature Adults Only	Norman C. Habel	Fortress Press
1974	Hope for the Flowers	Trina Paulus	Paulist Press
1975	I'm Out to Change My World	Ann Kiemel	Impact
1976	The Singer	Calvin Miller	InterVarsity Press
1977	The Secret Trees	Luci Shaw	Harold Shaw Publishers
1978	I Came to Love You Late	Joyce Landorf	Fleming H. Revell
1980	The Seven Last Years	Carol Balizet	Chosen Books

Special Category

1973	The Way		Tyndale House Publishers

1990 CRITICS' CHOICE AWARDS

Sponsored by *Christianity Today* magazine. Selected by professionals in each field.

Biography and History

First Place (tie) *Christian Doctrine and Modern Culture (Since 1700)* by Jaroslav Pelikan, University of Chicago
Altered Landscapes edited by David Lotz, Wm. B. Eerdmans Publishing Co.

Runner-Up *Great Leaders of the Christian Church* edited by John Woodbridge, Moody Press

Christian Living and Spirituality

First Place (tie) *Disappointment with God* by Philip Yancey, Zondervan Publishing House
In the Name of Jesus by Henri Nouwen, The Crossroad Publishing Co.

Runner-Up *Answering God* by Eugene Peterson, Harper & Row, Publishers

Commentaries

First Place *The Book of Ruth* by Robert Hubbard, Jr., Wm. B. Eerdmans Publishing Co.

Runners-Up *Romans 1–8* by James Dunn, Word, Inc.
1 & 2 Samuel by Joyce Baldwin, InterVarsity Press
Philippians by Moises Silva, Moody Press

Contemporary Issues

First Place *Battered into Submission* by James and Phyllis Alsdurf, InterVarsity Press

Runner-Up *Euthanasia* by Ed Larson and Beth Spring, Multnomah Press

Fiction

First Place *Piercing the Darkness* by Frank Peretti, Crossway

Runner-Up *The Furniture of Heaven* by Mike Mason, Harold Shaw Publishers

Reference and Textbooks

First Place *Dictionary of Pentecostal and Charismatic Movements* edited by Stanley Burgess and Gary McGee, Zondervan Publishing House

Runner-Up *Baker Encyclopedia of the Bible* edited by Walter Elwell, Baker Book House

Theology and Doctrine

First Place *The Canon of Scripture* by F. F. Bruce, InterVarsity Press

Runner-Up *Theology of the Reformers* by Timothy George, Broadman Press

GOLD MEDALLION BOOK AWARDS

Evangelical Christian Publishers Association Awards

Year	Title	Author	Publisher
Bible			
1988	Life Application Bible		Tyndale House Publishers
1989	Life Application Bible		Tyndale House Publishers
1990	Life Application Bible	King James Version	Tyndale House Publishers
Bible Study/Commentaries			
1982	Romans	William Hendriksen	Baker Book House
Bible Study/Theology			
1978	Eerdmans' Handbook to the History of Christianity	Edited by Tim Dowley	Wm. B. Eerdmans Publishing Co.
1979	Affliction	Edith Schaeffer	Fleming H. Revell
1980	International Standard Bible Encyclopedia, Volume I	Ed. by Geoffrey Bromiley	Wm. B. Eerdmans Publishing Co.
1981	The Bible Almanac	J. I. Packer, Merrill C. Tenney, William White, Jr.	Thomas Nelson, Inc., Publishers
Biography/Autobiography			
1978	A Severe Mercy	Sheldon Vanauken	Harper and Row, Publishers
1979	Paul: Apostle of the Heart Set Free	F. F. Bruce	Wm. B. Eerdmans Publishing Co.
1980	By Their Blood	James and Marti Hefley	Mott Media
1981	Faith Despite the KGB	Harmann Hartfeld	Diane Books Publishing, Inc.
1982	The Tapestry	Edith Schaeffer	Word, Inc.
1983	It's My Turn	Ruth Bell Graham	Fleming H. Revell
1984	Guest of The Revolution	Kathryn Koob	Thomas Nelson, Inc., Publishers
1985	A Time for Remembering	Patricia Daniels Cornwell	Harper and Row, Publishers
1986	Letters of Francis A. Schaeffer	Edited by Lane T. Dennis	Crossway Books/Good News Publ.
1987	C. S. Lewis Through the Shadowlands	Brian Sibley	Fleming H. Revell
1988	Heir to a Dream	Pete Maravich	Thomas Nelson, Inc., Publishers
1989	First Ladies of the Parish	Ruth A. Tucker	Zondervan Publishing House
1990	Dr. Dobson: Turning Hearts Toward Home	Rolf Zettersten	Word, Inc.
Children's Books			
1981	Who, What, When, Where Book About the Bible	William R. Coleman	David C. Cook Publishing Co.
1982	Leading Little Ones to God	Marian M. Schoolland, Illustrated by Paul Stoub	Wm. B. Eerdmans Publishing Co.
1982	What Happens When We Die?	Carolyn Nystrom, Illus. by Wayne A. Hanna	Moody Press
1983	Read-Aloud Bible Stories	Ella K. Lindvall and Kent Puckett	Moody Press
1984	Tales of The Kingdom	David and Karen Mains, Illustrated by Jack Stockman	David C. Cook Publishing Co.
1985	Marvelous Me	Anne Townsend, Illustrated by Saroj Vaghela	Lion Publishing Corp.
1986	Potter	Walter Wangerin, Jr.	David C. Cook Publishing Co.
1986	Talking Together About Love and Sexuality	Mildred Tengbom	Bethany House Publishers
1987	The International Children's Bible Handbook	Lawrence Richards	Sweet Publishing Co.

GOLD MEDALLION BOOK AWARDS cont.

1987	What The Bible Is All About for Young Explorers	Frances Blankenbaker	Regal Bks/Gospel Light Publ.

Christian Education

1982	Answers to the Cultist At Your Door	Robert and Gretchen Passantino and Raymond Schafer	Harvest House Publishers
1983	Early Childhood Kit	Pat Holt and Robyn Vander Weide	Fleming H. Revell
1984	Interntl Children's Vers., NT		Sweet Publishing Co.
1984	Youth Leader's Sourcebook	Edited by Gary Dausey	Zondervan Publishing House
1985	Sing to the Lord	Connie Fortunato	David C. Cook Publishing Co.
1986	Discipling the Young Person	Ed. by Paul Fleischmann	Here's Life Publishers
1987	Group Magazine's Best Youth Group Programs, Vol. 1	Cindy S. Hansen	Group Bks/Group Publishing, Inc.
1987	The Big Book of Home Learning	Mary Pride	Crossway Books/Good News Publ.
1988	It Couldn't Just Happen	Lawrence O. Richards	Worthy Publishing
1989	What'cha Gonna Do With What'cha Got: A Study in Christianomics	James W. Jackson	David C. Cook Publishing Co.
1990	Up Close & Personal	Wayne Rice	Zondervan Publishing House

Christian Living

1988	Living Above the Level of Mediocrity	Charles R. Swindoll	Word, Inc.
1988	Understanding People	Lawrence J. Crabb, Jr.	Zondervan Publishing House
1989	Inside Out	Larry Crabb	NavPress
1990	The Man in the Mirror	Patrick M. Morley	Wolgemuth & Hyatt, Publishers

Christian Ministry

1983	Between Two Worlds: The Art of Preaching in the 20th Century	John R. W. Stott	Wm. B. Eerdmans Publishing Co.
1984	Management: A Biblical Approach	Myron Rush	Victor Books/Scripture Press Publ.
1985	Counseling Teenagers	G. Keith Olson	Group Books
1986	Baker Encycl. of Psychology	Ed. by David G. Benner	Baker Book House
1987	Christian Countermoves In a Decadent Culture	Carl F. H. Henry	Multnomah Press
1988	Encyclopedia of Biblical and Christian Ethics	Edited by R. K. Harrison	Thomas Nelson, Inc., Publishers
1989	The Youth Builder	Jim Burns	Harvest House Publishers
1990	The Fine Art of Mentoring	Dr. Ted W. Engstrom with Norman B. Rohrer	Wolgemuth & Hyatt, Publishers

Christianity and Society

1983	The Mustard Seed Conspiracy	Tom Sine	Word, Inc.
1984	Approaching Hoofbeats: The Four Horsemen of the Apocalypse	Billy Graham	Word, Inc.
1985	The Least of These	Curt Young	Moody Press
1986	Involvement: Volume I & II	John R. W. Stott	Fleming H. Revell
1987	Crime and Its Victims	Daniel W. Van Ness	InterVarsity Press
1988	Kingdoms In Conflict	Charles W. Colson	Zondervan Publishing House
1989	Grand Illusions	George Grant	Wolgemuth & Hyatt, Publ., Inc.
1990	Against the Night	Charles Colson	Vine Books/Servant Publications

Classics

1983	Real Christianity	William Wilberforce and James Houston, editors	Multnomah Press
1984	Sermons of Martin Luther	Martin Luther	Baker Book House
1985	Religious Affections: How Man's Will Affects His Character Before God	James M. Houston, ed.	Multnomah Press
1986	The Princess and the Goblin	George MacDonald, Illus. by Linda Hill Griffith	David C. Cook Publishing Co.
1987	Spiritual Awakening	Ed. by Sherwood Eliot Wirt	Crossway Books/Good News Publ.
1987	The Works of Arminius: The London Edition	James Arminius	Baker Book House
1988	Oswald Chambers—The Best from All His Books	Oswald Chambers Harry Verploegh, compiler	Oliver Nelson Books
1989	Josephus: The Essential Writings	Paul L. Maier	Kregel Publications
1990	Oswald Chambers: The Best from All His Books Vol. II	Chosen & Edited by Harry Verploegh	Oliver Nelson Books

Commentaries

1983	Commentary on Galatians	F. F. Bruce	Wm. B. Eerdmans Publishing Co.
1983	The Expositor's Bible Commentary, Volume 12	Frank E. Gaebelein, Editor	Zondervan Publishing House
1984	Word Biblical Commentary, Jude, 2 Peter, Volume 50	Richard J. Bauckham	Word, Inc.
1985	The Epistles to the Colossians, to Philemon and to the Ephesians	F. F. Bruce	Wm. B. Eerdmans Publishing Co.
1986	NIV Study Bible		Zondervan Publishing House
1986	The Bible Knowledge Commentary OT	Ed. by John F. Walvoord and Roy B. Zuck	Victor Bks/Scripture Press Publ.
1987	The International Bible Commentary, NIV	Edited by F. F. Bruce	Marshall Pickering/Zondervan Publ.
1988	First Epistle to the Corinthians, New International Commentary on the NT	Gordon D. Fee	Wm. B. Eerdmans Publishing Co.
1989	The Epistle to the Romans	Leon Morris	Wm. B. Eerdmans Publishing Co.
1990	Mark 1	R. Kent Hughes	Good News Publ./Crossway Books
1990	Mark 2	R. Kent Hughes	Good News Publ./Crossway Books

Contemporary Issues

1980	Whatever Happened to The Human Race	Francis Schaeffer and C. Everett Koop	Fleming H. Revell
1981	Life Sentence	Charles Colson	Chosen Books
1982	Freedom of Simplicity	Richard J. Foster	Harper & Row, Publishers

Devotional

1988	With My Whole Heart	Karen Burton Mains	Multnomah Press
1989	A Musician Looks at the Psalms: A Journal of Daily Devotions	Don Wyrtzen	Zondervan Publishing House
1990	Glorious Intruder	Joni Eareckson Tada	Multnomah Press

Devotional/Christian Living

1984	Loving God	Charles Colson	Zondervan Publishing House
1985	In His Image	Paul Brand and Phillip Yancey	Zondervan Publishing House

GOLD MEDALLION BOOK AWARDS cont.

Year	Title	Author	Publisher
1986	Ordering Your Private World	Gordon MacDonald	Oliver Nelson Books
1987	A Closer Walk	Catherine Marshall, ed. by Leonard E. LeSourd	Chosen Books/Fleming H. Revell
Elementary Children			
1988	Catherine Marshall's Storybook for Children	Cath. Marshall LeSourd	Chosen Books
1989	Let's-Talk-About-It-Series	Lois Johnson	NavPress
1990	Destination: Moon	Astronaut James Irwin	Multnomah Press
Fiction			
1978	I Came to Love You Late	Joyce Landorf	Fleming H. Revell
1979	The Kiowa	Elgin Groseclose	David C. Cook Publishing Co.
1980	Caught in the Cross Fire	Levi Keidel	Herald Press
1981	Alpha Centuri	Robert Siegel	Crossway Books/Good News Publ.
1982	The Iron Sceptre	John White, Illustrated by Elmar Bell	InterVarsity Press
1983	Love's Long Journey	Janette Oke	Bethany House Publishers
1984	MacIntosh Mountain	Victor J. Kelly	Zondervan Publishing House
1985	Johnny Come Home	R. C. Sproul	Regal Bks/Gospel Light Publ.
1985	The Water Is Wide	Elizabeth Gibson	Zondervan Publishing House
1986	More Than Seven Watchmen	Helen Norris	Zondervan Publishing House
1987	The Gates of Zion	Bodie Thoene	Bethany House Publishers
1988	Taliesin	Stephen R. Lawhead	Crossway Books/Good News Publ.
1989	The Key to Zion	Bodie Thoene	Bethany House Publishers
1990	Piercing the Darkness	Frank E. Peretti	Good News Publ./Crossway Books
Gift Books/Poetry			
1984	A Prophetical Walk Through the Holy Land	Hal Lindsey	Harvest House Publishers
1985	The Miracles of Our Lord	Charles Caldwell Ryrie	Thomas Nelson, Inc., Publishers
1986	Come Before Winter . . . And Share My Hope	Charles R. Swindoll	Multnomah Press
1987	Doorposts	Timothy R. Botts	Tyndale House Publishers
1988	Love for a Lifetime	James C. Dobson	Multnomah Press
1988	Psalms of My Life	Joseph Bayly	David C. Cook Publishing Co.
1989	The American Character	Norman Vincent Peale	Fleming H. Revell
1990	Windsongs	Timothy R. Botts	Tyndale House Publishers
Insp/Dev/Christian Living			
1983	Giant Steps	Warren W. Wiersbe, ed.	Baker Book House
1983	Strengthening Your Grip	Charles Swindoll	Word, Inc.
Inspiration			
1978	Where Is God When It Hurts	Philip Yancy	Zondervan Publishing House
1979	A Step Further	Joni Eareckson	Zondervan Publishing House
1980	Love Has A Price Tag	Elisabeth Elliot	Servant Publications
1981	Fearfully and Wonderfully Made	Paul Brand and Philip Yancey	Zondervan Publishing House
Inspirational			
1988	The Quest for Character	Charles R. Swindoll	Multnomah Press
1989	Disappointment With God	Philip Yancey	Zondervan Publishing House
1990	Six Hours One Friday	Max Lucado	Multnomah Press
Inspirational/Devotional			
1982	Gaining Through Losing	Evelyn Christenson	Victor Books/Scripture Press Publ.
Juvenile			
1978	Jesus, Friend of Children		David C. Cook Publishing Co.

Year	Title	Author	Publisher
1979	Family Bible Encyclopedia	Berkeley and Alvera Mickelsen	David C. Cook Publishing Co.
1980	Our Family Got A Divorce	Carolyn E. Phillips	Gospel Light Publications
Marriage and Family			
1983	Seasons of a Marriage	H. Norman Wright	Regal Bks/Gospel Light Publ.
1984	Love Must Be Tough	James C. Dobson	Word, Inc.
1985	Parents and Teenagers	Edited by Jay Kesler	Victor Books/Scripture Press Publ.
1986	The Mystery of Marriage	Mike Mason	Multnomah Press
1987	The Blessing	Gary Smalley and John Trent	Thomas Nelson, Inc., Publishers
1988	As For Me and My House	Walter Wangerin, Jr.	Thomas Nelson, Inc., Publishers
1989	Growing Wise in Family Life	Charles R. Swindoll	Multnomah Press
1990	Lonely Husbands/Lonely Wives	Dennis Rainey	Word, Inc.
Missions/Evangelism			
1983	Eerdmans' Handbook to the World's Religions	R. Pierce Beaver, editor	Wm. B. Eerdmans Publishing Co.
1984	From Jerusalem To Irian Jaya	Ruth A. Tucker	Zondervan Publishing House
1985	Eternal Word and Changing Worlds	Harvie M. Conn	Zondervan Publishing House
1986	Beyond Hunger: A Biblical Mandate for Social Responsibility	Art Beals with Larry Libby	Multnomah Press
1986	The Church in China	Carl Lawrence	Bethany House Publishers
1987	Wanted: World Christians	J. Herbert Kane	Baker Book House
1988	Witnessing Without Fear	Bill Bright	Here's Life Publishers
1989	Youth Evangelism	David Veerman	Victor Books/Scripture Press Publ.
1990	Disarming the Secular Gods	Peter C. Moore	InterVarsity Press
Outreach			
1982	How to Really Love Your Teenager	Ross Campbell	Victor Books/Scripture Press Publ.
Personal/Group Bible Study			
1989	Living Beyond the Daily Grind	Charles R. Swindoll	Word, Inc.
1990	Life Application Bible Study Guide: Romans	Tyndale House Publishers	
Poetry			
1982	Surprised By Light	Ulrich Schaffer	Harper & Row, Publishers
1983	Eerdmans' Book of Christian Poetry	Pat Alexander, editor	Wm. B. Eerdmans Publishing Co.
Preschool Children			
1988	What Does God Do?	Illus. by Hans Wilhelm	Worthy Publishing
1989	Katie's Adventure at Blueberry Pond	Josh and Dottie McDowell	David C. Cook Publishing Co.
1990	Do You See Me, God?	Elspeth Campbell Murphy	David C. Cook Publishing Co.
Reference			
1983	International Standard Bible Encyclopedia, Volume 2	Ed. by Geoffrey W. Bromiley	Wm. B. Eerdmans Publishing Co.
Reference Works			
1982	New American Standard Exhaustive Concordance of the Bible	Robert L. Thomas, ed.	Holman Bible Publishers

GOLD MEDALLION BOOK AWARDS cont.

Reference/Text

Year	Title	Author	Publisher
1984	Eerdmans' Handbook to Christianity in America	Mark Noll, Nathan Hatch, George Marsden, David Wells, John Woodbridge	Wm. B. Eerdmans Publishing Co.
1985	Evangelical Dict. of Theology	Ed. by Walter A. Elwell	Baker Book House
1986	Theological Dict. of the NT Abridged in 1 Volume	Geoffrey W. Bromiley	Wm. B. Eerdmans Publishing Co.
1987	The International Standard Bible Encyclopedia, Vol. 3	Ed. by Geoffrey W. Bromiley	Wm. B. Eerdmans Publishing Co.
1988	The Eerdmans Bible Dict.	Allen C. Myers	Wm. B. Eerdmans Publishing Co.
1989	Great Leaders of the Christian Church	John D. Woodbridge, ed.	Moody Press
1990	The Zondervan NIV Atlas of the Bible	Carl Rasmussen	Zondervan Publishing House

Special Judge's Awards

Year	Title	Author	Publisher
1983	The Complete Works of Francis A. Schaeffer	Francis A. Schaeffer	Crossway Books/Good News Publ.

Texts

Year	Title	Author	Publisher
1983	General Revelation	Bruce Demarest	Zondervan Publishing House
1983	Old Testament Survey	William S. LaSor, David Allan Hubbard, Frederic W. Bush	Wm. B. Eerdmans Publishing Co.

Theology and Doctrine

Year	Title	Author	Publisher
1985	Miracles and the Critical Mind	Colin Brown	Wm. B. Eerdmans Publishing Co.
1986	Christian Theology, Three Vol.	Millard J. Erickson	Baker Book House
1987	Betrayal of the Church: Apostasy and Renewal in the Mainline Denom.	Edmund W. Robb and Julia Robb	Crossway Books/Good News Publ.

Theology/Doctrine

Year	Title	Author	Publisher
1982	Testaments of Love	Leon Morris	Wm. B. Eerdmans Publishing Co.
1983	The Case for Christianity	Colin Chapman	Wm. B. Eerdmans Publishing Co.
1984	God, Revelation, and Authority, Volume VI	Carl F. H. Henry	Word, Inc.
1988	The Cross of Christ	John R. W. Stott	InterVarsity Press
1989	The Canon of Scripture	F. F. Bruce	InterVarsity Press
1990	So Great Salvation	Charles C. Ryrie	Victor Books/Scripture Press

World Missions

Year	Title	Author	Publisher
1982	World of Difference	Thom Hopler	InterVarsity Press

Youth

Year	Title	Author	Publisher
1988	Am I The Only One Here with Faded Genes?	Marie Chapian	Bethany House Publishers
1989	Lifelines: Getting a Hold on Life Series	Fran and Jill Sciacca	World Wide Publications
1990	Lifelines Introductory Series (Booklets 1-4)	Fran & Jill Sciacca	World Wide Publications

Youth Books

Year	Title	Author	Publisher
1983	How to Be Your Own Selfish Pig	Susan Schaeffer Macauley	David C. Cook Publishing Co.
1984	Putting God First	Jim Burns, David Bundschuh, Illustrator	Harvest House Publishers

1984	The Christian Kids Almanac	Robert G. Flood, Illus. by Britt Taylor Collins	David C. Cook Publishing Co.
1984	Why Isn't God Giving Cash Prizes?	Lorraine Peterson	Bethany House Publishers
1985	You Can Make A Difference	Tony Campolo	Word, Inc.
1986	Judge For Yourself	Steve and Alice Lawhead	Victor Books/Scripture Press Publ.
1987	Handling Your Hormones	Jim Burns	Harvest House Publishers
1987	The Student Bible, NIV	Notes by Philip Yancey and Tim Stafford	Zondervan Publishing House

1990 READERS' CHOICE AWARDS

Selected by readers of *Christianity Today* magazine.

Book of the Year
First Place *Disappointment with God* by Philip Yancy, Zondervan Publishing House
Runner-Up *The Gospel According to Jesus* by John F. MacArthur, Jr., Zondervan Publishing House

Biography and History
First Place (tie) *Dr. Dobson* by Rolf Zettersten, Word, Inc.
Great Leaders of the Christian Church edited by John Woodbridge, Moody Press
Runner-Up *Guardians of the Great Commission* by Ruth Tucker, Zondervan Publishing House

Christian Living and Spirituality
First Place *Disappointment with God* by Philip Yancey, Zondervan Publishing House
Runner-Up *The Spirit of the Disciplines* by Dallas Willard, Harper & Row, Publishers

Commentaries
First Place *Hard Sayings of the Old Testament* by Walter Kaiser, InterVarsity Press
Runner-Up *The Bible Exposition Commentary* by Warren Wiersbe, Victor Books/Scripture Press

Contemporary Issues
First Place *Against the Night* by Charles Colson, Servant Publications
Runner-Up (tie) *Confronting the New Age* by Douglas Groothuis, InterVarsity Press
Understanding the New Age by Russell Chandler, Word, Inc.

Fiction
First Place *Piercing the Darkness* by Frank Peretti, Crossway
Runner-Up *A Requiem for Love* by Calvin Miller, Word, Inc.

Reference and Textbooks
First Place *Baker Encyclopedia of the Bible* edited by Walter Elwell, Baker Book House
Runner-Up *Dictionary of Pentecostal and Charismatic Movements* edited by Stanley Burgess and Gary McGee, Zondervan Publishing House

Theology and Doctrine
First Place *The Gospel According to Jesus* by John F. MacArthur, Jr., Zondervan Publishing House
Runner-Up *The Canon of Scripture* by F. F. Bruce, InterVarsity Press

CHRISTIAN BOOKSELLER ASSOCIATION AWARDS

Supplier of the Year
1976 Fleming H. Revell
1977 Fleming H. Revell
1978 Zondervan Publishing
1979 Fleming H. Revell
1980 Word, Inc.
1981 Word, Inc.
1982 Thomas Nelson Publishers
1983 Thomas Nelson Publishers
1984 Thomas Nelson Publishers
1985 Word, Inc.
1986 Thomas Nelson Publishers

1987 Word, Inc.
1988 Word, Inc.
1989 Spring Arbor, Inc.

Store of the Year

1980 Foothills Bible Book Store, La Mesa, CA
1981 Dightman's Bible Book Ctr, Tacoma, WA
1982 The Better Book Room, Wichita, KS
1983 Berean Christian Stores, Canton, OH
1984 The Christian Armory, Columbus, OH
1985 Better Books Christian Center, Tyler, TX
1986 Fresno Bible House, Fresno, CA
1987 Bender's Christn Sup., Williamsville, NY
1988 Christian Armory, Tucker, GA
1989 Berean Christian Bkstore, Phoenix, AZ

Salesman of the Year

1967 Bill Zondervan, Zondervan Publishing
1968 Sid Zullinger, Moody Press
1969 William Reynolds, Harper & Row
1970 Paul Van Duinen, Zondervan Publ.
1971 Jim Pletcher, Warner Press
1971 Lloyd Van Horn, Zondervan Publishing
1973 Gene Uber, Concordia
1974 Ernie Owen, Fleming H. Revell
1975 Lloyd Eshbach, Moody Press
1976 Milton Steinford, Harper & Row
1977 Bob Lossa, Fleming H. Revell
1978 Clarence Hageman, Thom. Nelson Publ.
1979 Lane Hostetter, Standard Publishing
1980 Dan Fetters, Warner Press
1981 Denny Bray
1982 Pat Burtch, Warner Press
1983 Jack Doyle, Dickson's
1984 Gordon Mohr, Thomas Nelson Publ.
1985 Judith White, Zondervan Publishing
1986 Vance Hooper, Thomas Nelson Publ.
1987 John Stoesz, Warner Press
1988 Wayne Adams, Word, Inc.
1989 David Lewis, Zondervan Publishing

Editor's Choice Award

1988 Moody Press
1989 Standard Publishing

Key Person Award

The Key Person Award is CBA's most prestigious individual recognition. This award is given to an individual whose unique contribution is so outstanding it is not feasible or likely to be duplicated by someone else.

1981 Paul Benson and Pat Zondervan
1985 Don Baughman and Paul Curry
1989 Peter Gunther and Lloyde Johnson

Hall of Honor

The Hall of Honor is an industry-wide honor, and recognizes exceptional service to the Christian bookselling/literature industry.

1986 John and Betty Bass
1989 Dr. Kenneth Taylor

CHRISTIAN MAGAZINE PUBLISHERS

Periodical, Address	*Category*	*Format*	*Circulation*	*Cost*
Action Magazine, PO Bx A, Greenwood, IN 46142	Missions	Quarterly	8500	Free
Actionline, PO Bx 203, Prospect Heights, IL 60070	Missions	Newsltr/6/yr	n/a	Free
AFA JOURNAL, PO Drawer 2440, Tupelo, MS 38803	Decency		375,000	15.00/yr
Again Magazine, PO Bx 106, Mt. Herman, CA 95041	Christian Living	n/a	2,500	10.00/yr
Aglow, PO Bx 1548, Lynnwood, WA 98046	Women	6/yr	36,000	10.97/yr
Around the World, PO Bx 553000, Miami, FL 33055	Missions	Quarterly	48,000	Free
Asbury Herald, The, 204 N. Lexington Ave., Wilmore, KY 40390	Christn Living	Quarterly	33,000	Free
Asian Report, PO Bx 9000, Mission Viejo, CA 92690	Missions			
Back to the Bible Today, Bx 82808, Lincoln, NE 68501	Christian Living	n/a	n/a	Free
Bethany Choice, The, 901 Eastern N.E., Grand Rapids, MI 49508	Pro-Life	3/yr	7,200	Free
Beyond, PO Bx 248, Waxhaw, NC 28173	Missions	6/yr	20,000	Free
Bible Review, 3000 Connecticut Ave. N.W., Suite 300, Washington, DC 20008	Bible	Bimonthly	40,000	14.95/yr
Bibles for the World News, Bx 805, Wheaton, IL 60189	Missions	Quarterly	35,000	Free
Biblical Archaeology Review, 3000 Connecticut Ave. N.W., Suite 300, Washington, DC 20008	Archaeology	Bimonthly	115,000	19.95/yr

Periodical, Address	*Category*	*Format*	*Circulation*	*Cost*
Bookstore Journal, 2620 Venetucci Blvd., Colorado Springs, CO 80906	Trade/Bookstore	12/yr	7087	43.00/yr
Bread Magazine, 6401 The Paseo, Kansas City, MO 64131	Youth	12/yr	27,000	7.50/yr
Breakthrough, PO Bx 1122, Wheaton, IL, 60189	Missions	6/yr	65,000	Donation
Bridgebuilder Magazine, 610 Rhode Island Ave., N.E., Washington, DC 20002	Racial Unity	6/yr	5,000	12.97/yr
Businessgram, 14305 N. Dale Mabry, PO Bx 273390, Tampa, FL 33618	Trade/Career	Nwsltr/11/yr	500	25.00 Sugg. donation
Call to Prayer, PO Bx WGM, Marion, IN 46952	Missions	6/yr	30,000	Donation
Campus Life Magazine, 465 Gundersen Dr., Carol Stream, IL 60188	Youth	10/yr	160,000	14.95/yr
CBMC Contact, PO Bx 3308, Chattanooga, TN 37404	Trade/Career	6/yr	14,000	12.95/yr
Central Texas Messenger, The, PO Bx 309, Del Valle, TX 78617		12/yr	5,000	8.00/yr
Charisma & Christian Life Mag., 190 N. Westmonte Dr., Altamonte Springs, FL 32714	Christian Living	12/yr	200,000	19.95/yr
Childlife Magazine, 919 W. Huntington Dr., Monrovia, CA 91016	Missions	Quarterly	550,000	Donation
Chosen People, The, 1300 Cross Beam Dr., Charlotte, NC 28217	Missions	11/yr	65,000	5.00/yr
Christ for the Nations, PO Bx 769000, Dallas, TX 75376	Evangelism	12/yr	35,000	Free
Christian Activities Calendar, PO Bx 730, Ojai, CA 93023	Singles	Mag./6/yr		14.95/2 yrs.
Christian Century, The, 407 S. Dearborn St., Chicago, IL 60605	Christn Thought	Weekly	35,000	28.00/yr
Christian Communicator, The, 26131 Av. Aeropuerto, San Juan Capistrano, CA 92675	Communictns	12/yr	N/A	14.97/yr
Christian Conjurer, 1705 Barbara Ln, Connersville, IN 47331	Digest	6/year		12.00 membshp
Christian Ed. Journal, PO Bx 650, Glen Ellyn, IL 60138	Christian Ed.	Journal/3/yr	2,700	9.00/yr
Christian Ed. Today, PO Bx 15337, Denver, CO 80215	Christian Ed.	Quarterly	9,000	3.00/copy
Christian Educators Journal, Dordt College English Dept., Sioux Center, IA 51250	Christian Ed.	Quarterly	4,000	7.50/yr
Christian Herald, 40 Overlook Dr., Chappaqua, NY 10514	Christian Living	11/yr	150,000	15.97/yr
Christian History Magazine, 465 Gundersen Dr., Carol Stream, IL 60188	Educational	Quarterly	15,000	16.00/yr
Christian Home and School, 3350 East Paris Ave., S.E., Grand Rapids, MI 49508	Parents	8/yr	9,500	10.95/yr
Christian Leadership Letter, 919 W. Huntington Dr., Monrovia, CA 91016	Leadership	Newsltr		Free
Christian Librarian, The, PO Bx 4, Cedarville, OH 45314	Trade/Career	Quarterly	400	16.00/yr
Christian Living for Senior Highs, 850 N. Grove Ave., Elgin, IL 60120	Youth	Quarterly	N/A	7.25/yr
Christian Management Report, PO Bx 4638, Diamond Bar, CA 91765	Trade/Career	6/yr	6,500	Free to mem.; 50.00/yr non-mem.
Christian Medical & Dental Society Journal, PO Bx 830689, Richardson, TX 75083	Trade/Career	Quarterly	8,300	16.00/yr
Christian Ministry, The, 407 S. Dearborn St., Chicago, IL 60605	Ministry	Bimonthly	9500	10.00/yr
Christian Mission, PO Bx 4488, Charlottesville, VA 22901	Missions	6/yr	24,000	Donation
Christian Newspaper, The, 2820 Linkhorne Dr., Ste. 231, Lynchburg, VA 24503	News	12/yr	20,000	Free
Christian Outdoorsman, The, PO Bx 18489, Fort Worth, TX 76118-9983	Recreation	6/yr	4,500	25.00/yr
Christian Parenting, PO Bx 3850, Sisters, OR 97759	Parents	6/yr	130,000	14.97/yr
Christian Psychology for Today, 2100 N. Collins Blvd., Richardson, TX 75080	Christian Living	Quarterly	7,477	10.00/yr
Christian Reader, The, PO Bx 80, 351 Executive Dr., Wheaton, IL 60189	Christian Living	Digest/6/yr	188,000	12.00/yr
Christian Research Journal, PO Bx 500, San Juan Capistrano, CA 92693	Christn Thought	Triannual	7,000	2.50/yr
Christian Retailing, 190 N. Westmonte Dr., Altamonte Springs, FL 32714	Trade/Bookstore	12/yr	9700	18.00/yr

Periodical, Address	Category	Format	Circulation	Cost
Christian School, 1308 Santa Rosa, Wheaton, IL 60187	Trade/Career	5/yr	3,000	10.00/yr
Christian Single, 127 Ninth Ave. N., Nashville, TN 37234	Singles	12/yr		
Christn Standard, 8121 Hamilton Ave., Cincinnati, OH 45231	Christian Living	Weekly	70,000	15.75/yr
Christian Writers Newsltr, PO Bx 8220, Knoxville, TN 37996	Communicatns	Newsltr/6/yr	400	10.00/yr
Christianity Today, 465 Gundersen Dr., Carol Stream, IL 60188	Christn Thought	18/yr	170,000	24.95/yr
Church and Society, 100 Witherspoon St., Louisville, KY 40202	Soc Respnsblty	Bimonthly	2350	7.50/yr
Church Herald, The, 6157 28th St., S.E., Grand Rapids, MI 49506	Christian Living	12/yr	48,000	11.25/yr
Citizen Magazine, 801 Corporate Ctr Dr., Pomona, CA 91799	Soc Respnsblty	12/yr	274,000	Donation: 15.00
Closer Walk, PO Bx 80587, Atlanta, GA 30366	Devotional	Digest/12/yr	16,987	17.00/yr
CLS Quarterly, PO Bx 1492, Merrifield, VA 22193	Trade/Career	4/yr	6,000	20.00/yr
Command Magazine, PO Bx 1177, Englewood, CO 80150	Trade/Career	Quarterly	6,500	12.00/yr
Commission, The, PO Bx 6767, Richmond, VA 23230	Missions			
Compassion Update, PO Bx 7000, Colorado Springs, CO 80933	Missions	6/yr	100,000	Free
Confident Living, PO Bx 82808, Lincoln, NE 68501	Christian Living	11/yr	93,000	10.95/yr
Connexions, 101 W. Ridgely Rd., Ste. 5-A, Lutherville, MD 21093	Christian Living	6/yr	3,300	Free
Contemporary Christian Music, 25231 Paseo De Alicia, Ste. 201, Laguna Hills, CA 92653	Youth	12/yr	40,000	18.00/yr
Cornerstone Magazine, 4747 N. Maiden, Chicago, IL 60640	Youth	6/yr	75,000	6.95/yr
Crusader, PO Bx 7259, Grand Rapids, MI 49510	Youth	7/yr	12,000	6.25/yr
Crux, 2130 Wesbrook Mall, Vancouver, B.C., V6T 1W6	Christn Thought	Quarterly	700	10.00/yr
Dads Only, PO Bx 340, Julian, CA 92036	Parenting	Newsltr/12/yr		24.00/yr
Daily Walk, PO Bx 80587, Atlanta, GA 30366	Devotional	12/yr	34,560	17.00/yr
Decision, 1300 Harmon Place, Minneapolis, MN 55403	Christian Living	11/yr	1,750,000	5.00/yr
Discipleship Journal, PO Bx 6000, Colorado Springs, CO 80934	Christian Living	6/yr	88,000	14.97/yr
Discovery Digest, PO Bx 22, Grand Rapids, MI 49555	Christian Living	Quarterly	400,000	Free
Door of Hope, PO Bx 303, Glendale, CA 91209	Missions	Quarterly	12,000	Free
Door, The, 1224 Greenfield Dr., El Cajon, CA 92021	Christian Living	6/yr	15,000	18.00/yr
Doorways, PO Bx C, Colorado Springs, CO 80901	Missions	4/yr	N/A	Free
Dreams and Visions, R.R. 1, Washago, ON, LOK-2B0	Fiction Writing			
East Asia's Millions, 404 S. Church St., Robesonia, PA 19551	Missions			
11 Chronicles Magazine, PO Bx 42, Medford, OR 97501		Semimonthly	5,000	10.00/2 yrs
Enterprise, The, 7185 Millcreek Dr., Mississauga, ON L5N 5R4	Missions			
Equipping the Saints, PO Bx 65004, Anaheim, CA 92815	Christian Living	Quarterly	100,000	Free
Europe Report, The, PO Bx 668, Wheaton, IL 60187	Missions	Tabloid/4/yr	35,000	Free
Eurovision Advance, PO Bx 1136, Claremont, CA 91711	Missions	Newsltr/4/yr	7,000	1.00/yr
Evangelical Beacon, The, 1515 E. 66th St., Minneapolis, MN 55423	Missions	17/yr	39,000	12.00/yr
Evang. Missions Quarterly, PO Bx 794, Wheaton, IL 60189	Missions	Bulletin/4/yr	9,500	14.95/yr
Evangelical World, PO Bx WEF, Wheaton, IL 60189	Missions	Newsltr/12/yr		Free
Evangelism, 12800 N. Lake Shore Dr., Mequon, WI 53092	Evangelism	Quarterly	2,000	10.00/yr
Family Walk, PO Bx 80587, Atlanta, GA 30366	Devotional	12/yr	18,933	17.00/yr
FEBC News, PO Bx 1, La Mirada, CA 90637	Missions	Quarterly	35,000	Free
Feed the Children, Bx 36, Oklahoma City, OK 73101	Missions	6/yr	115,000	Free
Focus on the Family Magazine, 801 Corporate Center Dr., Pomona, CA 91799	Family	12/yr	1,800,000	Free
Food for the Hungry, 7729 E. Greenway Rd., Scottsdale, AZ 85260	Missions	Newsltr/12/yr	40,000	Free
Footprints, PO Bx 700, San Diego, CA 92138	Evangelism	12/yr	100,000	Free
Forum, PO Bx 370, Elkhart, IN 46515	Singles	12/yr		
Fulness Magazine, PO Bx 79350, Fort Worth, TX 76179	Leadership	6/yr	15,000	14.95/yr
Global Prayer Digest, 1605 Elizabeth St., Pasadena, CA 91104	Missions	12/yr		8.00/yr
God's World Publicatns, PO Bx 2330, Asheville, NC 28802	College	30/yr	202,000	9.50/yr
Guideposts Mag., Seminary Hill Rd., Carmel, NY 10512	General	12/yr	4,239,396	8.95/yr

Periodical, Address	*Category*	*Format*	*Circulation*	*Cost*
Helping Hand, The, PO Bx 12609, Oklahoma City, OK 73157	Women	6/yr	3,000	3.00/yr
High Adventure, 1445 Boonville Ave., Springfield, MO 65802	Youth Boys	Quarterly	86,000	1.75/yr
Horizon International World Reporter, 17041 Ruffner St., San Diego, CA 92111	Missions	Quarterly	6,000	Free
Horizons, PO Bx 969, Wheaton, IL 60189	Missions	6/yr	48,957	2.00/yr
Ideals, Nelson Place at Elm Hill Pike, PO Box 148000, Nashville, TN	General	8/yr	240,0000	17.95/yr
Image Mag., 115 Warren Dr., Ste. D, W. Monroe, LA 71291	Christian Living	12/yr	8,000	15.00/yr
Image: A Journal of the Arts and Religion, 526 Ziela Ave., Front Royal, VA 22630				
In Other Words, PO Bx 2727, Huntington Beach, CA 92647	Missions	8/yr	220,000	Free
Increase Magazine, PO Bx 410, Hatfield, PA 19440	Missions	Quarterly	16,000	Free
Indian Life, PO Bx 3765 Station B, Winnipeg, MB, R2W 3R6	Missions	6/yr	65,000	5.00/yr
Internatl Bulletin of Missionary Research, PO Bx 1308E, Fort Lee, NJ 07024-9958	Missions	12/yr		12.00/yr
International Journal of Frontier Missions, PO Bx 40638, Pasadena, CA 91104	Missions	Quarterly	1,000	15.00/yr
Intervarsity Magazine, PO Bx 7895, Madison, WI 53707	College Evanglsm	Quarterly	95,000	Free
Journal of Christian Nursing, PO Bx 1650, Downers Grove, IL 60515	Trade/Career	Quarterly	12,000	14.95/yr
Journal of Christn Camping, PO Bx 646, Wheaton, IL 60189	Trade/Career	6/yr	6,000	19.95/yr
Journal of Pastoral Care, The, 1549 Clairmont Rd., Suite 103, Decatur, GA 30033	Pastoral	Quarterly	13,668	20.00/yr
Joyful Woman, The, 118 Shannon Lake Circle, Greenville, SC 29615	Women	6/yr	11,262	13.95/yr
Jubilee, PO Bx 17500, Washington, DC 20041	Christian Living, News	Newsltr/12/yr	175,000	Free
Jubilee International, PO Bx 17434, Washington, DC 20041	Evangelism	Quarterly	5,500	Free
Junior High Ministry Magazine, 2890 N. Monroe, PO Box 481, Loveland, CO 80539		5/yr	32,001	19.50/yr
Just Between Us, 1529 Cesery Blvd., Jacksonville, FL 32211		Bimonthly	6,500	14.95/yr
Kids!, 820 N. LaSalle, Chicago, IL 60610	Youth	9/yr	43,000	19.95/yr
Kindred Spirit, 3909 Swiss Ave., Dallas, TX 75204	Christn Thought	Quarterly	200,000	Free
Latin Am. Evangelist, PO Bx 52-7900, Miami, FL 33152	Missions	Quarterly	33,000	Free
Lausanne Communique, 2531 Nina St., Pasadena, CA 91107	Missions	Newsltr/6/yr		Free
Leadership, 465 Gundersen Dr., Carol Stream, IL 60188	Leadership	Journal/4/yr	70,000	22.00/yr
Librarians World, PO Bx 353, Glen Ellyn, IL 60138	Church Libraries	Quarterly	620	12.00/yr
Lifechangers, 50 Mitchell Blvd., Bx 13459, San Rafael, CA 94913	Christian Living	6/yr	5,500	Donation
Lighted Pathway, 1080 Montgomery Ave., Cleveland, TN 37311	Youth	12/yr	20,000	8.00/yr
LPEA Heartbeat, PO Bx 1173, Portland, OR 97207	Evangelism	Newsltr/10/yr	7,500	Free
Luke Society News, The, 1121 Grove St., Vicksburg, MS 39180	Missions	Organizatnl/2/yr	95,000	Free
Mag. for Christian Youth!, PO Bx 801, Nashville, TN 37202	Youth	12/yr	47,000	18.00/yr
Map Internatl Report, PO Bx 50, Brunswick, GA 31521	Missions	6/yr	15,000	Free
MARC News Letter, 919 W. Huntington Dr., Monrovia, CA 91016	Missions	Newsltr/6/yr		Free
Marketplace, The, 402-280 Smith St., Winnipeg, MB, R3C 1KC	Trade/Career	6/yr	5,000	10.00/yr
Marriage Partnership, 465 Gundersen Dr., Carol Stream, IL 60188	Marriage	Quarterly	65,000	19.95/yr
Mature Living, 127 Ninth Ave. N., Nashville, TN 37234	Seniors	12/yr	355,000	13.00/yr
Mature Years, 201 Eighth Ave. S., PO Box 801, Nashville, TN 37202	Seniors		99,940	9.50/yr
Media Update, PO Bx 969, Cardiff by the Sea, CA 92007	Music	6/yr	12,000	10.00/yr
Mennonite, The, Bx 347, 722 Main St., Newton, KS 67114	Christian Living	Biweekly	11,260	18.00/yr
Message of the Cross, The, 6820 Auto Club Rd., Minneapolis, MN 55438	Christian Living	6/yr	16,500	Free
Ministries Today, 190 N. Westmonte Dr., Altamonte Springs, FL 32714	Leadership	6/yr	30,000	19.95/yr
Mission Frontiers, 1605 Elizabeth St., Pasadena, CA 91104	Missions	12/yr	60,000	4.00/yr

Periodical, Address	Category	Format	Circulation	Cost
Missionary Monthly, 4517-A Broadmoor Ave., Grand Rapids, MI 49508	Missions	9/yr	4,000	10.00/yr
Missionary Tidings, The, 901 College, Winona Lake, IN 46590	Missions	9/yr	16,500	6.00/yr
Moments with God, 1 South 210 Summit Ave., Oakbrook Terrace, IL 60181	Devotional	Denom./4/yr	14,400	4.00/yr
Moody Monthly Magazine, 820 N. LaSalle Dr., Chicago, IL 60610	Christian Living	11/yr	175,000	19.95/yr
National and International Religion Report, PO Bx 21433, Roanoke, VA 24018	News	Newsltr/26/yr	4,800	78.00/yr
Native Reflections, Bx 891, Hot Springs, SD 57747	Missions	Quarterly	16,000	Free
Network, 627 South 34th St., Birmingham, AL 35222	Ecumenical	12/yr	15,000	12.00/yr
New England Church Life, 88 Tremont St., Suite 600, Boston, MA 02108	Church Life	12/yr	15,000	8.97/yr
News and Views, 1317 Weavers Way, Abilene, TX 79602	Singles			
Newswire, PO Bx 1122, Wheaton, IL 60189	Missions	Newsltr/6/yr	65,000	Donation
OC International, 25 Corning Ave., Milpitas, CA 95035	Missions	Quarterly	25,000	Donation
OMS Outreach, Bx A, Greenwood, IN 46142	Missions	6/yr	48,000	Donation
One-To-One, PO Bx 6000, Colorado Springs, CO 80934	Evangelism	Quarterly	49,000	Donation
Open Doors News Brief, PO Bx 27001, Santa Ana, CA 92799	Missions	12/yr	90,000	12.00/yr
Other Side, The, 300 W. Apsley, Philadelphia, PA 19144	Christian Living	6/yr	12,000	21.75/yr
Overcomer, The, 2020 Bell Ave., Des Moines, IA 50315	Youth	Quarterly	2,200	5.00/yr
Overseas Cncl Newsltr, PO Bx 751, Greenwood, IN 46142	Missions	5/yr	4,000	Free
Parents & Teenagers, 2890 N. Monroe, PO Box 481, Loveland, CO 80539	Parenting	Bimonthly	6,000	18.97/yr
Partnership Update, PO Bx WRC, Wheaton, IL 60189	Missions	12/yr	10,000	Free
Pastoral Renewal, PO Bx 8617, Ann Arbor, MI 48107	Leadership	Newsltr/6/yr	7,000	20.00 Donation
Pentecostal Minister, The, PO Bx 2430, Cleveland, TN 37320	Pastoral Ldrshp	Quarterly	5,500	15.00/yr
People of Destiny Magazine, 7881-B Beechcraft Ave., Gaithersburg, MD 20879	Christian Living	6/yr	12,000	12.95/yr
Perspectives on Science and Christian Faith, PO Bx 668, Ipswich, MA 01938	Trade/Career	Quarterly	3,600	20.00Ind, 30.00Inst
Plough, The, Hutterian Brethren, Ulster Park, NY 12487	Christian Living	Quarterly	14,000	7.00/yr
Plus Magazine, 66 E. Main St., Pawling, NY 12564	Christian Living	12/yr	888,000	8.00/yr
Possibilities, 1223 Potomac St. NW, Washington, DC 20007	Christian Living	6/yr	300,000	Free
Potential Magazine, 9135 Guilford Rd., #170, Columbia, MD 21046	Evangelism	6/yr	30,000	8.50/yr
Prayer Line, The, PO Bx 55146, Seattle, WA 98155	Prayer	Quarterly	3,800	Free
Preacher's Magazine, The, 6401 The Paseo, Kansas City, MO 64131	Leadership	4/yr	17,000	3.50/yr
Preaching Magazine, 1529 Cesery Blvd., Jacksonville, FL 32211	Pastoral	Bimonthly	7,000	22.95/yr
Psychology for Living, 1409 N. Walnut Grove Ave., Bx 5000, Rosemead, CA 91770	Psychology	12/yr	15,000	N/A
Pulpit Helps, 6815 Shallowford Rd., Chattanooga, TN 37422	Pastoral	12/yr	200,000	15.00/yr
Quiet Miracle, The, 625 E. North Broadway, Columbus, OH 43214	Missions	Organizatn/5/yr	17,000	Donation
Quiet Revolution, A, 1655 St. Charles St., Jackson, MS 39209	Evangelism	Quarterly	4,000	Donation
Railroad Evangelist Magazine, The, Route 4, Bx 97, Spencer, IN 47460	Trade/Career	6/yr	2,500	6.00/yr
Real Issue, The, 14679 Midway, Ste. 100, Dallas TX, 75244	Trade/Career	Quarterly	8,000	Free
Reformed Journal, The, 255 Jefferson Ave. S.E., Grand Rapids, MI 49503	Christn Thought, News	12/yr	2,800	15.00/yr
Religious Broadcasting Magazine, PO Bx 1926, Morristown, NJ 07962-1926	Trade/Career	12/yr	9,900	24.00/yr
Resource, 6401 The Paseo, Kansas City, MO 64131	Leadership	Quarterly	16,400	N/A
San Diego Christn Times, PO Bx 21009, El Cajon, CA 92021	News, commtary	12/yr	20,000	10.00/yr
Second Look Magazine, PO Box 3566, Grand Rapids, MI 49501-3566		Bimonthly	20,000	15.00/yr
Servant, Prairie Bible Institute, Three Hills, AB, TOM 2A0	Christian Living	6/yr	30,000	Free
Sharing the Victory, 8701 Leeds Rd., Kansas City, MO 64129	Youth	6/yr	45,000	9.00/yr

Periodical, Address	*Category*	*Format*	*Circulation*	*Cost*
SIM Now, 10 Huntingdale Blvd., Scarborough, ON, M1W 2S5	Missions	6/yr	136,000	Free
Singing News Magazine, PO Box 2810, Boone, NC 28607-2810	Music	12/yr	147,000	19.00/yr
Single Adult Ministries Journal, PO Bx 3010, Colorado Springs, CO 80934	Leadership	10/yr	4,500	21.00/yr
Single Minded, PO Bx 4933, Vancouver, BC, V6B 4A6	Singles	6/yr		
Singles Scene, PO Bx 454, Crossville, TN 38557	Singles	12/yr		
Singles/Young Adults Newsltr, 412 Sycamore St., Cincinnati, OH 45202	Singles			
Sojourners, Bx 29272, Washington, DC 20017	Political conscience movement	11/yr	46,000	24.00/yr
Soloing, Bx 15523, W. Palm Beach, FL 33416	Singles	Tabloid/6/yr		
Spiritual Counterfeits Project Newsltr, PO Bx 4308, Berkeley, CA 94704	Cults and Relig. Movements	Newsltr/4/yr	11,600	Free
Spiritual Fitness in Business, 1900 Firman Dr., Ste. 100, Richardson, TX 75081	Trade/Career	Newsltr/12/yr	1,400	36.95/yr
Student Venture, 17150 Via Del Campo, Ste. 200, San Diego, CA 92127	Youth	Quarterly	46,000	N/A
Sunday to Sunday, 465 Gundersen Dr., Carol Stream, IL 60188	Women/ Pastor's Wives	Quarterly	10,000	7.95/yr
Tabletalk, 270 So. North Lake Blvd., Ste. 1270, Altamonte Springs, FL 32701	Christn Thought	Newsltr/12/yr	50,000	Free
Teenage Magazine, 2890 N. Monroe, PO Box 481, Loveland, CO 80539	Teens	10/yr	32,111	17.97/yr
Teen Missions Control, 885 East Hall Rd., Merritt Island, FL 32953	Missions	N/A	60,000	Free
Teen Quest Magazine, Bx 82808, Lincoln, NE 68501	Youth/Teenagers	11/yr	65,000	10.95/yr
Today's Christian Woman, 465 Gundersen Dr., Carol Stream, IL 60188	Women	6/yr	200,000	14.95/yr
Today's Singles, 1933 Wisconsin Ave., Milwaukee, WI 53233	Singles	Tabloid/4/yr		Donation
Together, 919 W. Huntington Dr., Monrovia, CA 91019	Missions	Journal/4/yr		25.00/yr
Together Again, PO Bx 136130, Fort Worth, TX 76136	Evangelism	6/yr	57,000	Free
Touch, Bx 7259, Grand Rapids, MI 49510	Youth Girls	10/yr	15,000	7.50/yr
Trim Tab, The, 136 Providence Rd., Fayetteville, GA 30214	Trade/Career	6/yr	9,000	Free
U.S. Singles Today, PO Bx 927, Bedford, TX 76095	Singles	Tabloid		
United Evangelical Action, PO Bx 28, Wheaton, IL 60189	Christn Thought	6/yr	11,000	10.00/yr
Upper Room, The, 1908 Grand Ave., PO Box 189, Nashville, TN 37202-0189	Devotional	12/yr	2,175,000	4.50/yr
Urban Missions, PO Bx 27009, Philadelphia, PA 19118	Missions	5/yr	1,200	10.00/yr
Venture Magazine, PO Bx 150, Wheaton, IL 60189	Yth/Boys 10-15	6/yr	23,500	8.00/yr
Virtue Magazine, PO Bx 850, Sisters, OR 97759	Women	6/yr	120,000	14.95/yr
Vision Magazine, 3150 Bear St., Costa Mesa, CA 92626	Trade/Career	Quarterly	85,000	Free
Voice Magazine, 3150 Bear St., Costa Mesa, CA 92626	Evangelism to men	Digest/12/yr	600,000	4.95/yr
Voice of Prophecy News, PO Bx 2525, Newbury Park, CA 91320	Evangelism	6/yr	74,000	Free
War Cry, The, 799 Bloomfield Ave., Verona, NJ 07044	Christian Living	Biweekly	N/A	7.50/yr
Wesleyan Woman, The, PO Bx 50434, Indianapls, IN 46250	Women	Quarterly	3,400	5.00/yr
Wherever, PO Bx 969, Carol Stream, IL 60189	Missions	3/yr	19,000	Free
Wider Look, The, 68 Summerleaze Rd., Maidenhead, England, Sl6 8EP	Missions	Digest/4/yr		10.00/yr
Women Alive, PO Bx 4683, Overland Park, KS 66204	Women	6/yr	5,000	7.95/yr
Word of Faith, The, PO Bx 50126, Tulsa, OK 74150	Christian Living	12/yr	200,000	Free
World, Bx 2330, Asheville, NC 28802	News	Weekly	10,000	18.00/yr
World Christian Mag., PO Bx 40010, Pasadena, CA 91104	Missions	6/yr		13.00/yr
World Evangelization, 2531 Nina St., Pasadena, CA 91107	Missions	12/yr		Donation
World Harvest Mag., PO Bx 12, South Bend, IN 46624	Missions	6/yr	70,000	Free
World Vision Magazine, 919 W. Huntington Dr., Monrovia, CA 91016	Missions	6/yr	160,000	Free
Worldorama, PO Bx 12609, Oklahoma City, OK 73157	Missions	Quarterly	22,000	Free

Periodical, Address	Category	Format	Circulation	Cost
Worldwide News, PO Bx 800, Lititz, PA 17543	Evangelism	Newsltr/6/yr	15,000	Free
Worldwide Thrust, Bx 1707, Fort Washington, PA 19034	Missions	Quarterly	8,800	Free
Your Church Magazine, 1418 Lake St., Evanston, IL 60201	Leadership	6/yr	200,000	12.00/yr
Youth and Christn Ed. Leadrshp, 922 Montgomery Ave. NE, Cleveland, TN 37311	Christian Ed.	Quarterly	14,000	6.50/qtr
Youth Leader, The, 1445 Boonville Ave., Springfield, MO 65802	Christian Ed.	8/yr	4,000	13.50/yr
Youth Walk, PO Bx 80587, Atlanta, GA 30366	Devotional/Yth	12/yr	26,463	17.00/yr
Youthworker Jrnl, 1224 Greenfield Dr., El Cajon, CA 92021	Christian Ed.	Quarterly	11,000	24.00/yr

MEDIA AND CHRIST: 1900

What would happen if a big-city newspaper, instead of reporting the usual crime and violence, emphasized the good news and instituted a policy following the teachings of Jesus Christ? It happened once, with surprising results, when a Kansas daily took up a popular clergyman's challenge and appointed him editor in chief for one week in March 1900.

The clergyman was Dr. Charles M. Sheldon, a Congregational minister whose series of sermons was published in 1896 as a novel titled *In His Steps or What Would Jesus Do?* The book sold as many as 30 million copies making it one of history's leading best-sellers.

It was a news event in itself when Dr. Sheldon moved into the hard-boiled city room of the *Topeka Daily Capital* to run the newspaper according to the dictates of Christ. Reporters from across the United States converged on Topeka to cover the story, and thousands of additional subscriptions were sold. Dr. Sheldon made some notable changes in company policy. He banned smoking, drinking, and profanity from the editorial offices and eliminated the paper's advertisements for patent medicines, corsets, and sporting events.

The *Topeka Daily Capital* was transformed. Signed editorials became front-page items, while crime, society events, and theatrical notices were played down. A page one story about a famine in India included an appeal for contributions; the paper collected more than $1 million in aid to send to Bombay.

As a result of the experiment, daily circulation jumped from 15,000 to 367,000. Critics of the minister's policies credited the increase to novelty and publicity. But Sheldon's supporters maintained that it proved how much people crave the inspiration of good news.

Significa by Irving Wallace, David Wallechensky, Amy Wallace. © 1983. Published by E. P. Dutton, Inc.

MEDIA AND CHRIST: 1990

A two-year research project, The Religious News Service-Lilly Foundation Study of Religion Reporting and Readership in the Daily Press, confirms that church members want to see more evidence in the newspapers they read that religion is an important part of daily life for many Americans.

"They see much that could fit in the newspaper that does not. The idea that religion is not of interest to journalism seemed inferentially to indicate that it is not of interest to its readers. This turned out not to be true," says Judy Weidman, editor of Religious News Service.

USA Today columnist Barbara Reynolds quotes Peggy Say, sister of hostage Terry Anderson. Say, a Christian, comments, "I have often told reporters this, and I have almost given up on seeing it in print. They don't want to hear anything about faith."

Reynolds goes on to ask some pointed questions: "What does the press have against Jesus? Is there a bias against Christianity? Why are people who identify God . . . as responsible for changing world events not taken seriously by the media?"

RELIGIOUS MAGAZINES HAVE STAYING POWER

Of the 25 oldest magazines in the U.S., 12 are church-related.

		First Published
1	New England Journal of Medicine	1812
2	*American Bible Society Record*	1818
3	*Pittsburgh Catholic*	1844
4	Scientific American	1845
5	Town and Country	1846
6	*United Methodist Reporter*	1847
7	Journal of the Am. Medical Assoc.	1848
8	*Adventist Review*	1850
9	Harper's Magazine	1850
10	Atlantic	1857
11	*Lutheran*	1860
12	Ye Olde Bastards Bulletin	1863
13	Harper's Bazaar	1867
14	Medical Times	1872
15	Popular Science	1872
16	Signs of the Times	1874
17	McCall's	1876
18	American Salon	1877
19	*Baptist Record*	1877
20	*Christian Herald*	1878
21	*Presbyterian Survey*	1879
22	*Watchtower*	1879
23	Science	1880
24	*War Cry*	1880
25	Carpenter	1881
26	Farmer/The Dakota Farmer	1881
27	*Lutheran Witness*	1882
28	AAUW Outlook	1882
29	Grit	1882

Data refer to magazines that report a circulation of 100,000 or more and are published more than once a year. *U.S. News and World Report,* 16 October 1989, and Ulnch's International Periodicals Directory, R. R. Bowler Company.

FREQUENCY OF READING RELIGION NEWS

	Evangelicals %	*Non-Evangelicals* %
Whenever it appears	11.3	30.7
Frequently	8.3	19.0
Occasionally	20.1	23.3
Infrequently	25.5	13.9
Just about never	34.3	12.4
Don't know	0.4	0.7

RNS-Lilly Study of Religion Reporting and Readership in the Daily Press, October, 1989.

READER SATISFACTION WITH COVERAGE BY NEWSPAPER "MOST OFTEN READ"

Sports	5.74
Business	5.29
Entertainment	5.18
Education	5.00
Food	4.99
Health	4.76
The Arts	4.67
Personal Advice	4.39
Religion	4.32

RNS-Lilly Study of Religion Reporting and Readership in the Daily Press, October, 1989.

EVANGELICAL PRESS ASSOCIATION MAGAZINE AWARDS

Category/Publication		*Editor*	*Art Dir./Designer*	*Publisher*	*Award*
Christian Ministries					
1987	Jrnl of Christian Nursing	Ramona Cass	Kathy Lay Burrows	Nurses Christian Fellowship	Excellence
1987	Interlit	Tim Bascom	Joe Ragont	David C. Cook Foundation	Merit
1987	Leadership	Terry C. Muck	Jeff Carnehl	Christianity Today, Inc.	Merit
1987	Youth Worker	Noel Becchetti	Mark Rayburn	Wayne Rice and Mike Yaconelli	Merit
1988	Leadership	Terry C. Muck	Joan Nickerson	Christianity Today, Inc.	Excel.
1988	Interlit	Tim Bascom	Joe Ragont	David C. Cook Foundation	Merit
1988	Jrnl of Christian Nursing	Ramona Cass	Kathy Lay Burrows	InterVarsity Christian Fellowship	Merit
1988	Youthworker Journal	Noel Becchetti	Jack Rogers	Youth Specialties	Merit
1989	Jrnl of Christian Nursing	Ramona Cass	Kathy Lay Burrows	InterVarsity Christian Fellowship	Excel.

Category/Publication		Editor	Art Dir./Designer	Publisher	Award
1989	Interlit	Tim Bascom	Joe Ragont	David C. Cook Foundation	Merit
1989	Student Leadership	Robert M. Kachur	Krisy Maxey	InterVarsity Christian Fellowship	Merit
1989	Youthworker	Wayne Rice	Jack Rogers	Youth Specialties	Merit
Denominational					
1987	Good News	James V. Heidinger II	Mark Laurenson	Forum for Scriptural Christianity	Excel.
1987	Light and Life	Robert B. Haslam	Emiline Secaur	Free Meth. Church of North Am.	Merit
1987	Pentecostal Minister	Clyne W. Buxton	L. Travis Kirkland and Paul West	Church of God	Merit
1987	The Standard	Donald E. Anderson	Pamela Nelson	Baptist General Conference	Merit
1988	Pentecostal Evangel	Richard G. Champion	Randy Clute	Gospel Publishing House	Excel.
1988	Church of God Evangel	Hoyt E. Stone	L. Travis Kirkland	Church of God	Merit
1988	The Banner	Andrew Kuyvenhoven	R. Wayne De Jonge	CRC Publications	Merit
1988	The Standard	Donald E. Anderson	Pamela Nelsen	Baptist General Conference	Merit
1989	The Banner	Galen Meyer	R. Wayne DeJonge	Christian Reformed Church	Excel.
1989	Light and Life	Robert B. Haslam	Emiline Seaur	Free Meth. Church of North Am.	Merit
1989	The Christian Leader	Don Ratzlaff		U.S. Conference of Mennonite Brethren Churches	Merit
1989	The Church Herald	John Stapert	Carl Meinke	The Church Herald, Inc.	Merit
General					
1987	Moody Monthly	Robert Flood and Michael Umlandt	Kent Puckett Assoc.	Moody Bible Institute	Excel.
1987	Christian Reader	Dwight Hooten and Bonne Steffen	Tamara Burgh Norrgard	Kenneth N. Taylor	Merit
1987	Christianity Today	Terry C. Muck	Joan Nickerson	Christianity Today, Inc.	Merit
1987	Discipleship Journal	Susan Maycinik	Naomi Ann Trujillo	The Navigators	Merit
1988	Marriage Partnership	Harold L. Myra and Scott W. Bolinder	Gary Michael Gnidovic	Christianity Today, Inc.	Excel.
1988	Discipleship Journal	Susan Maycinik	Naomi Ann Trujillo	The Navigators	Merit
1988	The Christian Reader	Dwight Hooten	Rai Whitlock	Tyndale House Publishers, Inc.	Merit
1988	Today's Christian Woman	Dale Hanson Bourke	Gary Michael Gnidovic	Christianity Today, Inc.	Merit
1989	Today's Christian Woman	Dale Hanson Bourke	Gary Michael Gnidovic	Christianity Today, Inc.	Excel.
1989	Aglow	Gwen Weising	Kathy Boice	Women's Aglow Fellowship	Merit
1989	Christn Psychlgy for Today	Jane Mack	Graphic & Ed. Svcs.	Minirth-Meier Clinic	Merit
1989	Marriage Partnership	Ron R. Lee	Gary Michael Gnidovic	Christianity Today, Inc.	Merit
Missionary					
1987	Latin America Evangelist	John Maust and Paul E. Pretiz	Carlos Gordon	Clayton L. Berg, Jr.	Excel.
1987	In Other Words	Roger Garland	Ken Harris	Wycliffe Bible Translators	Merit
1987	The Chosen People	Jonathan Singer	Jonathan Singer	American Board of Missions to the Jews, Inc.	Merit
1987	World Vision	David Olson	Don Aylard	World Vision	Merit
1988	World Vision	Terry Madison	Don Aylard	World Vision	Excel.
1988	In Other Words	Roger Garland	Kathy McBride	Wycliffe Bible Translators	Merit
1988	Mountain Movers	Nick Henry	Mickey Flodin	Assemblies of God Division of Foreign Missions	Merit
1988	OMS Outreach	Eleanor Burr	Gene Bertolet	OMS International, Inc.	Merit
1989	World Vision	Terry Madison	Don Aylard	World Vision	Excel.
1989	Impact	Art Heerwagen		Conserv. Bapt. Foreign Missn Soc.	Merit
1989	In Other Words	Roger Garland	Kathy McBride	Wycliffe Bible Translators	Merit
1989	OMS Outreach	Eleanor Burr	Curt Buller and Dyann Brodie	OMS International	Merit
Newsletter					
1987	Bulletin	Clyne W. Buxton		Church of God	Excel.
1987	Jubilee	Megs Singer	Mike Harper	Prison Fellowship Ministries	Merit

Category/Publication		Editor	Art Dir./Designer	Publisher	Award
1987	Pastoral Renewal	John Blattner		Servant Ministries	Merit
1987	The Vineyard Newsletter	Suzanne N. Springer	Bob Payne	John Wimber	Merit
1988	Tabletalk	Ralph D. Veerman		Ligonier Ministries	Excel.
1988	Jubilee	Megs Singer	Brenda Young	Prison Fellowship Ministries	Merit
1988	Pastoral Renewal	John C. Blattner		Servant Ministries, Inc.	Merit
1988	Spiritual Fitness in Business	Steve Webb		Probe Ministries International	Merit
1989	Pastoral Renewal	John C. Blattner	Cynthia Parker	Servant Ministries	Excel.
1989	Breakthrough	Wil Triggs	Edward Tabb	Slavic Gospel Mission	Merit
1989	Brown Bulletin	Fred Lollar	David Andrus	John Brown University	Merit
1989	One-to-One	Judith Couchman	Richard Slaton	The Navigators	Merit
Organizational					
1987	Fundamentalist Journal	Deborah Wade Huff	Larry C. Bevins	Jerry Falwell	Excel.
1987	Decision	Roger Palms	Gary Carlson	The Billy Graham Evang. Assoc.	Merit
1987	Discovery Digest	Dave Branon and Kurt DeHaan	Brian Fowler	Radio Bible Class	Merit
1987	Possibilities	Jeanne A. Dunn	Publishing Directions	Dale Hanson Bourke	Merit
1988	Fundamentalist Journal	Deborah Wade Huff	Larry C. Bevins	Old-Time Gospel Hour	Excel.
1988	Equipping the Saints	Kevin Springer	Bob Payne	Vineyard Ministries International	Merit
1988	Possibilities	Jeanne Anne Dunn	Publishing Directions	Robert Schuller Ministries	Merit
1988	Response	Jennifer Johnson Gilnett	Dale Kegley	Seattle Pacific University	Merit
1989	Contact	Robaert J. Tamasy	Linda Peppers	Christian Business Men's Committee USA	Excel.
1989	Equipping the Saints	Kevin Springer	Bob Payne	Vineyard Ministries International	Merit
1989	Fundamentalist Journal	Deborah Wade Huff	Tracy Scrivener	Old-Time Gospel Hour	Merit
1989	Possibilities	Jeanne A. Dunn	Publishing Directions	Robert Schuller Ministries	Merit
Sunday School Take Home					
1987	Vista	Patsy Whittenberg		Wesley Press	Excel.
1987	Bible-in-Life Friends	Rita West	Gregory E. Clark	David C. Cook Publishing	Merit
1987	Christian Living	Anne E. Dinnan	Marilyn Duddles Earibon	David C. Cook Publishing	Merit
1987	In Touch	James Watkins		Wesley Press	Merit
1988	Sprint	Paul N. Woods		David C. Cook Publishing Co.	Excel.
1988	Bible-in-Life Friends	Nancy Raney	Donna Nelson	David C. Cook Publishing Co.	Merit
1988	Bible-in-Life Pix	Lois Keffer	Donna Nelson	David C. Cook Publishing Co.	Merit
1988	Sunday Digest	Janette L. Pearson		David C. Cook Publishing Co.	Merit
1989	Teens Today	Karen De Sollar		Beacon Hill Press	Excel.
1989	Bible-in-Life Pix	Charlene Hiebert		David C. Cook Publishing	Merit
1989	Sprint	Paul N. Woods	Kellie Richter	David C. Cook Publishing	Merit
1989	The Lookout	Mark A. Taylor		Standard Publishing	Merit
Youth					
1987	Venture	Steve P. Neideck	Lawrence Libby	Christian Service Brigade	Excel.
1987	Campus Life	James Long	Jeff Carnehl	Christianity Today, Inc.	Merit
1987	TQ	Roger S. Morrow and Nancy Brumbaugh	Victoria Valentine	Back To The Bible	Merit
1987	U	Verne Becker	Kathy Lay Burrows	InterVarsity Christn Fellowship	Merit
1988	Campus Life	Jim Long	Jeff Carnehl	Christianity Today, Inc.	Excel. (tie)
1988	The Mag. for Christn Youth!	Christopher B. Hughes	Susan J. Scrugg	The United Meth. Publ. House	Excel. (tie)
1988	Contemp. Christian Music	John W. Styll	Lynn Schrader	CCM Publications, Inc.	Merit
1988	TQ	Barbara K.Comito	Victoria Valentine	Good News Broadcasting Assoc.	Merit
1989	Kids!	Bonnie Burnett	Killion McCabe & Associates	Moody Bible Institute	Excel.
1989	Campus Life	James Long	Jeff Carmehl	Christianity Today	Merit
1989	Cornerstone	Dawn Herrin	Dick Randall	Jesus People USA	Merit
1989	TQ	Roger S. Morrow	Victoria Valentine	Good News Broadcasting Assoc.	Merit

CHRISTIAN RADIO AND TELEVISION STATIONS IN THE UNITED STATES

Radio stations listed here are all full-time Christian radio stations. TV stations are designated as Christian if religious programming is 150 hours or more per week; family if religious programming is 35-150 hours per week. Stations with religious programming below 35 hours per week are not included.

State / Channel / Frequency		*Address*	*City/Zip*
Radio			
AK	KATB 89.3 FM	PO Box 21089	Anchorage 99521
AL	WAGG 1320 AM	PO Box 697	Birmingham 35201
AL	WAPZ 1250 AM	PO Box 210339	Montgomery 36121
AL	WASG 1140 AM	1210 S. Main Street	Atmore 36502
AL	WAYD 1200 AM	PO Box 1331, Sam Lisenby Rd.	Ozark 36360
AL	WAYE 1220 AM	4650 Ave. W, Suite K, PO Box 3800-E	Birmingham 35208
AL	WBHY 840 AM	PO Bx 1328, 102 Dauphin St., #1103	Mobile 36602
AL	WBLX 550 AM	PO Box 1964	Mobile 36633
AL	WBTG 106.3 FM	PO Box 518, HH21 Countryboy Lane	Sheffield 35660
AL	WEBT 91.5 FM	PO Box 96	Valley 36864
AL	WFRC 90.5 FM	1010 7th Place	Phenix City 36867
AL	WJBU 930 AM Stereo	PO Box 930	Rainbow City 35902
AL	WKWL 1230 AM	PO Box 158	Florala 36442
AL	WLBF 89.1 FM	381 Mendel Parkway E., Box 17140	Montgomery 36117
AL	WLPH 1480 AM	561 12 Ct.	Pleasant Grove 35127
AL	WMBV 91.9 FM	PO Box 91.9	Dixon's Mills 36736
AL	WMGY 800 AM	2305 Upper Wetumpka Rd.	Montgomery 36107
AL	WMOB 1360 AM	Suite 206, 3943 Airport Blvd.	Mobile 36608
AL	WNDA 95.1 FM	2407 9th Ave.	Huntsville 35805
AL	WVRT 101.7 FM	RR 5, Box 70-A	Gordo 35466
AL	WVSM 1500 AM	Box 339	Rainsville 35986
AL	WWNT 1450 AM	226 N. Foster St., Ste. 24, PO Bx 1828	Dothan 36302
AL	WYDE 850 AM	90 Bagby Drive, Suite 310	Birmingham 35209
AR	KAAB 1130 AM	Box 2946	Batesville 72501
AR	KAAY 1090 AM	7123 I-30, Suite 1	Little Rock 72209
AR	KCGS 960 AM	PO Box 368	Marshall 72650
AR	KCMH 91.5 FM	PO Box 93	Mountain Home 72653
AR	KFDF 1580 AM	Suite 225, Central Mall	Fort Smith 72903
AR	KITA 1440 AM	723 W. 14th Street	Little Rock 72202
AR	KMTL 760 AM	PO Box 4360	North Little Rock 72116
AR	KPHN 94.5 FM	1311 Fort St., PO Box 98	Barling 72923
AR	KSBC 90.1 FM	PO Box 2771	Hot Springs 71914
AZ	KFLR 90.3 FM	2345 W. Buckeye Road	Phoenix 85009
AZ	KFLT 830 AM	PO Box 3025	Tucson 85702
AZ	KHAC 1110 AM	PO Box F	Window Rock 86515
AZ	KHEP 1280 AM	3883 N. 38th Ave.	Phoenix 85019
AZ	KMLE 107.9 FM	500 West Ray Road	Chandler 85224
AZ	KNLB 91.1 FM	PO Box V, 510 N. Acoma Blvd.	Lake Havasu City 86403
AZ	KVOI 690 AM	3425 E. Grant Road	Tucson 85716
AZ	KWFH 90.1 FM	PO Box 603, 401 15th Street	Parker 85344
AZ	KXEG 1010 AM	1817 N. 3rd St., Suite 202	Phoenix 85004
CA	KAMB 101.5 FM	90 E. 16th Street	Merced 95340
CA	KAVC 105.5 FM	PO Box 2069, 2997 Desert Street	Rosamond 93560
CA	KBIF 900 AM	261 N. Broadway	Fresno 93701
CA	KBRT 740 AM	3183 Airway Ave.	Costa Mesa 92626

State / Channel / Frequency	*Address*	*City/Zip*
CA KCJH 90.1 FM	PO Box 8744	Stockton 95208
CA KCLB 91.9 FM	50 Mark West Springs Road No. 3	Santa Rosa 95403
CA KDAR 98.3 FM	500 Esplanade Dr., Suite 1510	Oxnard 93030
CA KDNO 98.5 FM	1305 Glenwood	Delano 93215
CA KEAR 106.9 FM	1234 Mariposa Street	San Francisco 94107
CA KEBR 100.5 FM	3108 Fulton Avenue	Sacramento 95821
CA KECR 93.3 FM	312 W. Douglas	El Cajon 92020
CA KEFR 89.9 FM	PO Box 52	Le Grand 95333
CA KERI 1180 AM	Box 3189	Bakersfield 93385
CA KFAX 1100 AM	3106 Diablo Avenue	Hayward 94545
CA KFIA 710 AM	5705 Marconi Avenue	Carmichael 95608
CA KFRN 1280 AM	105 Linden Avenue	Long Beach 90802
CA KFSG 96.3 FM	1100 Glendale Blvd.	Los Angeles 90026
CA KGBA 100.1/98.3 FM	Box 133, 605 State Street	El Centro 92243
CA KGDP 660 AM Stereo	2634 Ocotillo Street	Santa Maria 93455
CA KGER 1390 AM	3759 Atlantic Ave., PO Box 7126	Long Beach 90807
CA KGFT 101.7 FM	5565 Carpinteria Ave., Suite 23	Carpinteria 93013
CA KHIS 800 AM 96.5 FM	521 H Street	Bakersfield 93304
CA KKLA 99.5 FM	4640 Lankershim Blvd.	North Hollywood 91602
CA KKMC 880 AM	SE Allisal Ste 501	Salinas 93901
CA KLFE 1240 AM	992 Inland Center Drive	San Bernardino 92408
CA KLRD 90.1 FM		Oak Glen 92399
CA KMJC 910 AM	500 Fesler Street, Suite 207	El Cajon 92020
CA KMRO 90.3 FM	2310 Ponderosa Dr., Suite 28	Camarillo 93010
CA KPRA 89.5 FM	25 Oak Knoll	Ukiah 95482
CA KPRO 1570 AM	7351 Lincoln Avenue	Riverside 92504
CA KPRZ 1210 AM	1635 South Rancho Santa Fe Road	San Marcos 92069
CA KPZE 1190 AM	1190 E. Ball Road	Anaheim 92805
CA KRDU 1130 AM	597 North Alta Avenue	Dinuba 93618
CA KSGN 89.7 FM	11498 Pierce Street	Riverside 92505
CA KSPD 790 AM	3636 N. First	Fresno 93726
CA KTSJ 1220 AM	1580 Clarmont Blvd. #202	Clarmont 91711
CA KTYM 1460 AM	6803 West Boulevard	Inglewood 90302
CA KVIP 540 AM 98.1 FM	PO Box 1359	Redding 96099
CA KWVE 107.9 FM	1644 North El Camino Real	San Clemente 92672
CA KYMS 106.3 FM	1748 W. Katella	Orange 92667
CA WGOR 650 AM	4610 Briarwood Drive	Sacramento 95821
CO KCIC 88.5 FM	3102 E Road	Grand Junction 81504
CO KLLV 550 AM	14780 State Hwy 140, Breen-Hesperus	Breen 81326
CO KRKS 990 AM	6535 West Jewell Avenue	Denver 80226
CO KWBI 91.1 FM	16075 West Belleview Avenue	Morrison 80465
CO KWYD 105.5 FM 1580 AM	PO Box 5668	Colorado Springs 80931
CT WCTF 1170 AM	13 Park Street, PO Box 1170	Vernon 06066
CT WFIF 1500 AM	90 Kay Avenue	Milford 06460
DC WYCB 1340 AM	Natl Press Bldg., 529 14th St. NW, #228	Washington 20045
FL WAFG 90.3 FM	5555 N. Federal Highway	Ft. Lauderdale 33308
FL WAPG 1480 AM	PO Box 632, 201 W. Asbury Street	Arcadia 33821
FL WAPN 91.5 FM	1508 State Avenue	Holly Hill 32017
FL WAYJ 88.7 FM	1860 Boyscout Drive	Fort Myers 33907
FL WAYR 550 AM	2500 Russell Road	Green Cove Spgs 32043
FL WCIE 91.1 FM	777 Carpenters Way	Lakeland 33809
FL WCIF 106.3 FM	PO Box 366, 702 E. New Haven Ave.	Melbourne 32902
FL WCVC 1330 AM	117 1/2 S. Henderson Road	Tallahassee 32312
FL WEGS 91.7 FM	703 N. Stewart Street	Milton 32570
FL WEXY 1520 AM	3411 NW 9th Avenue #701	Ft. Lauderdale 33309

State / Channel / Frequency	Address	City/Zip
FL WGNB 1520 AM,	Box 8888	St. Petersburg 33738
FL WGTO 540 AM	PO Box 123	Cypress Gardens 33884
FL WGTX 1280 AM	PO Box 627	DeFuniak Springs 32433
FL WHGS 90.3 FM	124 N. 10th Street, PO Box 1909	Haines City 33844
FL WHYM 610 AM	PO Box 17446	Pensacola 32522
FL WJLU 89.7 FM	2596 State Road 44	New Smyrna Bch 32069
FL WKES 101.5 FM	Box 8888	St. Petersburg 33738
FL WKZM 105.5 FM	PO Box 7627	Sarasota 34278
FL WLJP 91.5 FM	8410 US 19, Suite 107-A	New Port Richey 34668
FL WLTG 1430 AM	PO Box 15635	Panama City 32406
FL WLVF 930 AM	110 W. Scenic Highway	Haines City 33844
FL WLVS 1380 AM	1939 7th Avenue N	Lake Worth 33461
FL WMCU 89.7 FM	2300 N.W. 135th Street	Miami 33167
FL WMFJ 1450 AM	340 S. Beach Street	Daytona Beach 32014
FL WMIE 91.5 FM	1150 W. King Street	Cocoa 32922
FL WNCM 88.1 FM	2361 Cortez Road	Jacksonville 32216
FL WNLE 91.7 FM	Rt. 2, Box 705-A	Yulee 32097
FL WPCF 1290 AM 100.1 FM	1111 Laurie Avenue	Panama City Bch 32407
FL WPCS 89.3 FM	Box 18000	Pensacola 32523
FL WPFA 790 AM	4151 N. Pace Blvd.	Pensacola 32505
FL WPIO 89.3 FM	505 Josephine Street	Titusville 32796
FL WPLA 910 AM	PO Drawer J	Plant City 34289
FL WPSM 91.1 FM	13 Kelly Avenue	Fort Walton Bch 32548
FL WSEB 91.3 FM	Suite 110, 2800 Placida Road	Englewood 33533
FL WSOR 95.3 FM	940 Tarpon Street	Ft. Myers 33901
FL WTBH 91.5 FM	Rt. 2, Box 497	Chiefland 32626
FL WTIS 1110 AM	311 12th Avenue NE	St. Petersburg 33716
FL WTLN 1520 AM	PO Box 607000	Orlando 32860
FL WTWB 1570 AM	PO Box 7	Auburndale 33823
FL WVCF 1480 AM	Box 15550	Orlando 32858
FL WVIJ 91.7 FM	3279 Sherwood Road	Port Charlotte 33980
FL WWBC 1510 AM	1150 W. King Street	Cocoa 32922
FL WWOL 91.1 FM	124 N. 10th Street, PO Box 1909	Haines City 33844
FL WYFB 90.5 FM	Rt. 2, Box 1012	Keystone Heights 32656
GA WACL 570 AM	Box 858	Waycross 31502
GA WAEC 860 AM	1465 Northside Drive NW, Suite 14	Atlanta 30318
GA WBPS 89.5 FM	Box N, Highway 29	Winder 30680
GA WCCV 91.7 FM	PO Bx 708, #206 Cowan Bldg, E. Main St	Cartersville 30120
GA WCOP 1350 AM	PO Box 2127	Warner Robins 31099
GA WECC 1190 AM	2101 Highway 40 E., PO Box 1171	St. Marys 31558
GA WFAM 1050 AM	552 Laney-Walker Ext.	Augusta 30901
GA WFDR 1370 AM	PO Box 510	Manchester 31816
GA WGEC 103.9 FM	Box 15267	Springfield 31329
GA WGIA 1350 AM	PO Drawer 619, 245 Main Street	Blackshear 31516
GA WHYD 1270 AM	1825 Buena Vista Road	Columbus 31906
GA WJEP 1020 AM	PO Box 90	Thomasville 31799
GA WKZK 1600 AM	PO Box 1454	Augusta 30903
GA WMAC 1360 AM	Box 238	Metter 30439
GA WNIV 970 AM	805 Peachtree Street NE, Suite 633	Atlanta 30308
GA WRAF 90.9 FM	PO Box 128	Toccoa Falls 30598
GA WTPO 1050 AM	954 S. Main Street	Conyers 30207
GA WWEV 91.5 FM	889 Buford Road, Highway 20	Cumming 30143
GA WXLL 1310 AM	419 W. Ponce De Leon Avenue	Decatur 30030
GA WYFA 100.9 FM	T. 1, Box 305	Waynesboro 30830
GA WYFK 89.5 FM	Rt. 1, Box 109	Cataula 31804

State / Channel / Frequency	*Address*	*City/Zip*
GA WYFS 89.5 FM	Rt. 1, Box 358	Bloomingdale 31302
GA WYNX 1550 AM	2460 Atlanta Road	Smyrna 30080
GA WZOT 107.1 FM	PO Box 192	Rockmart 30153
HI KAIM 870 AM 95.5 FM	3555 Harding Avenue, PO Box 375	Honolulu 96816
IA KBQC 93.5 FM	4855 Forest Grove Drive	Bettendorf 52722
IA KFGQ 1260 AM	924 W. 2nd Street	Boone 50036
IA KNWS 102 FM 1090 AM	4880 Texas Street	Waterloo 50702
IA KTFC 103.3 FM	RFD #2	Sioux City 51106
IA KTFJ 1250 AM	RFD 2	Sioux City 51106
IA KTOF 104.5 FM	1957 Blairs Ferry Road, NE	Cedar Rapids 52402
IA KYFR 920 AM	618 1/2 W. Sheridan Avenue	Shenandoah 51601
ID KBGN 1060 AM	3303 E. Chicago	Caldwell 83605
ID KCIR 90.7 FM	1446 Filer Avenue E.	Twin Falls 83301
ID KFXD 580 AM	PO Box 107	Boise 83701
IL KJOR 550 AM	613 South La Grange Road	La Grange 60525
IL WCBW 104.9 FM	111 West Locust Street	Columbia 62236
IL WCRM 103.9 FM	PO Box 249, 651 S. 8th Street	Dundee 60118
IL WDLM 89.3 FM	Box 149	East Moline 61244
IL WGCA 88.5	PO Box 467	Quincy 62306
IL WGGH 1150 AM	Box 340, Old Rte. 13 E.	Marion 62959
IL WIBI 91.1 FM	Box 126	Carlinville 62626
IL WJCH 91.9 FM	13 Fairlane Drive	Joliet 60435
IL WLUJ 97.7 FM	PO Box 500	Petersburg 62675
IL WMBI 1110 AM 90.1 FM	820 N. LaSalle Drive	Chicago 60610
IL WPEO 1020 AM	1708 Highview Road E.	Peoria 61611
IL WVEL 1140 AM	28 S. 4th Street	Pekin 61554
IL WVLJ 105.5 FM	RR 1, Box 1231	Monticello 61856
IL WWRJ 1200 AM	613 South La Grange Road	La Grange 60525
IL WXAN 103.9 FM	Rt. 2, Box 213A	Ava 62907
IN WBRI 1500 AM	4802 E. 62nd Street	Indianapolis 46220
IN WFCV 1090 AM	909 Coliseum Blvd. N.	Fort Wayne 46805
IN WFRN 104.7 FM	25802 CR 26	Elkhart 46517
IN WMII AM	PO Box 1462	Jeffersonville 47131
IN WNTS 1590 AM	4800 E. Raymond Street	Indianapolis 46203
IN WRRD 940 AM	2711 Highway 62	Jeffersonville 47131
IN WVHI 1330 AM	PO Box 3636	Evansville 47735
IN WXIR 98.3 FM	4802 E. 62 Street	Indianapolis 46220
IN WXLW 950 AM	Box 22300, 3003 Kessler Blvd., N. Drive	Indianapolis 46222
IN WYCA 92.3 FM	6336 Calumet Avenue	Hammond 46324
KS KCNW 1380 AM	4535 Metropolitan	Kansas City 66106
KS KGCR 107.7 FM	Box 948	Goodland 67735
KS KJTY 88.3 FM	2519 N. Topeka Blvd.	Topeka 66617
KS KVCY 101.7 FM	PO Box 191	Ft. Scott 66701
KY WBCE 1200 AM	PO Box 128	Wickliffe 42087
KY WBFI 91.5 FM	Box 2, Highway 2595	McDaniels 40152
KY WCVK 90.7 FM	PO Box 539, 313 State Street	Bowling Green 42102
KY WDFB 1170 AM	PO Box 106, State Route 300	Danville 40422
KY WFIA 900 AM	410 S. Third Street	Louisville 40202
KY WFJT 1590 AM	Box 410, Spring Branch Road	Inze 41224
KY WLCK 1250 AM	PO Box 158, 104 1/2 Public Square	Scottsville 42164
KY WLJC 102.3 FM	North Rt. 11, Box 50	Beattyville 41311
KY WNKJ 89.3 FM	PO Box 1029	Hopkinsville 42240
KY WRSL 1520 AM	Box 237	Stanford 40484
KY WSOF 89.9 FM	PO Box 1246	Madisonville 42431
KY WVCT 91.5 FM	Rt. 11, Box 381	Keavy 40737

State / Channel / Frequency	Address	City/Zip
KY WWLK 900 AM	Box 90, Dale Avenue	Eddyville 42038
KY WWXL 103.5 FM 1450 AM	Route 5, Box 50	Manchester 40962
KY WXLN 103.9 FM	410 South Third Street	Louisville 40202
LA KAJN 102.9 FM	Box 1469	Crowley 70527
LA KCIJ 980 AM	Box 197	Shreveport 71161
LA KCKW 1480 AM	PO Box 1340	Jena 71342
LA KCTO 103.1 FM	Box 1319	Columbia 71418
LA KDBS 1410 AM	1515 Jackson Street	Alexandria 71301
LA KHAA 106.7 FM	650 Poydras St., Ste 1020	New Orleans 70130
LA KPAE 91.5 FM	13028 US Hwy., 190 W.	Port Allen 70767
LA KVDP 89.1 FM	Box 214	Dry Prong 71423
LA KXLA 990 AM Stereo	PO Box 990, Hwy. 80 West	Rayville 71269
LA WBIU 1210 AM	601 Hatchell Lane	Denham Springs 70726
LA WBSN 89.1 FM	3939 Gentilly Blvd.	New Orleans 70126
LA WQCK 92.7 FM	PO Box 7934	Clinton 70722
LA WSHO 800 AM	4900 Veterans Blvd.	Metairie 70006
MA WEZE 1260 AM	Milton PO Box 206	Boston 02186
MA WLVG 740 AM	1972 Massachusetts Avenue	Cambridge 02140
MD WBGR 860 AM	334 N. Charles Street	Baltimore 21201
MD WBZE 1030 AM Stereo	Box 3B, Montgomery Lane	Waldorf 20601
MD WCRH 90.5 FM	Route 2, Box 325	Williamsport 21795
MD WFSI 107.9 FM	918 Chesapeake Avenue	Annapolis 21403
MD WOEL 89.9 FM	PO Box 246	Elkton 21921
MD WOLC 102.5 FM	PO Box 130	Princess Anne 21853
MD WRBS 95.1 FM	3600 Georgetown Road	Baltimore 21227
ME WKTQ 1450 AM	PO Box 72	Norway 04268
ME WTME 1530 AM	PO Box 3128	Auburn 04210
MI WBCM 1440 AM	Davidson Bldg., Ste 301	Bay City 48708
MI WCLS 1500 AM	15704 Six and One-Half Mile Road	Battle Creek 49017
MI WCSG 91.3 FM	1159 Beltine, NE	Grand Rapids 49505
MI WFLT 1420 AM	317 S. Averill	Flint 48506
MI WGNR 88.9 FM	1331 Franklin SE	Grand Rapids 49506
MI WKJR 1520 AM	6803 Martin Road, PO Box 839	Muskegon 49443
MI WMAX 1480 AM	3250 28th Street SE	Grand Rapids 49508
MI WMIV 1550 AM	PO Box 190, 517 N. Beebe Street	Fremont 49412
MI WMPC 1230 AM	1800 North Lapeer Road	Lapeer 48446
MI WMUZ 103.5 FM	12300 Radio Place	Detroit 48228
MI WNLF 1390 AM	Box 338, 1613 W. Lawrence Highway	Charlotte 48813
MI WOLW 91.1 FM	PO Box 1066	Cadillac 49601
MI WPHN 90.5 FM	PO Box 1212, 1511 M-32 East	Gaylord 49735
MI WPRJ 1020 AM Stereo	8201 E. Chippewa Trail	Mt. Pleasant 48858
MI WUFL 1030 AM	42669 Garfield, Suite 328	Mt. Clemens 48043
MI WUFN 96.7 FM	2255 N. Concord Road	Albion 49224
MI WUGN 99.7 FM	510 Isabella Road, PO Box 366	Midland 48640
MI WUNN 1110 AM	1571 Tomlinson Road	Mason 48854
MI WWCM 990 AM Stereo	17 N. Huron Street	Ypsilanti 48197
MN KBHL 103.9	5l5 Pike Street E., Box 247	Osakis 56360
MN KBHW 99.5 FM	PO Box 433	International Falls 56649
MN KCFB 91.5 FM	Box 1683	St. Cloud 56302
MN KJLY 100.9 FM	PO Box 72, Faribault County Road 6	Blue Earth 56013
MN KKCM 1530 AM	Box 357, 421 E. 1st Street	Minneapolis 55379
MN KNOF 95.3 FM	1347 Selby Avenue	St. Paul 55104
MN KTIG 100.1 FM	PO Box 409	Pequot Lakes 56472
MN KTIS 900 AM 98.5 FM	3003 N. Snelling	St. Paul 55113
MN KYCR 1570 AM	5730 Duluth Street	Golden Valley 55422

State / Channel / Frequency	Address	City/Zip
MN WCTS 100.3 FM	2105 Fremont Avenue N.	Minneapolis 55411
MN WWJC 850 AM	1120 E. McCuen Street	Duluth 55808
MO KCCV 1510 AM	10841 E. 28th Street	Independence 64052
MO KJAB 90.1 FM	PO Box 336, 310 North Wade	Mexico 65256
MO KKLL 1100 AM	831 W. Daugherty, PO Box 1100	Webb City 64870
MO KLFJ 1550 AM	811 Boonville	Springfield 65802
MO KLJC 88.5 FM	15800 Calvary Road	Kansas City 64147
MO KMFC 92.1 FM	Box 998	Columbia 65205
MO KNEO 91.5 FM	PO Box 391	Neosho 64850
MO KSIV 1320 AM	1750 S. Brentwood Blvd., Suite 811	St. Louis 63144
MO KSTL 690 AM	814 N. Third Street	St. Louis 63102
MS WACR 1050 AM	1910 14th Avenue N., PO Box 1078	Columbus 39703
MS WCFB 1060 AM	PO Box 1626	Tupelo 38802
MS WFCA 107.8 FM	Rt. 1, Box 12	French Camp 39745
MS WJWF 1400 AM	702 2nd Avenue N., PO Box 707	Columbus 39703
MS WKCU 1350 AM	2192 Highway 72 E.	Corinth 38834
MS WMBC 103.1 FM	702 2nd Avenue N., PO Box 707	Columbus 39701
MS WMER 1390 AM	601 22 Avenue, 15th floor	Meridian 39301
MS WTWZ 1120 AM	PO Box 31	Clinton 39056
MT KGVW 640 AM	2050 Amsterdam Road	Belgrade 59714
MT KURL 730 AM	Box 31038	Billings 59107
MT KXEI 95.1 FM	Box 2426, 315 1st Street	Havre 59501
NC WAJA 1480 AM	251 Highlands Road	Franklin 28734
NC WBFJ 1550 AM	Suite A, 3066 Trenwest Drive	Winston-Salem 27103
NC WBZQ 1550 AM	918 Dickinson Avenue	Greenville 27834
NC WCIS 760 AM	PO Box 2798	Morgantown 28655
NC WEGG 710 AM	PO Box 608	Rose Hill 28458
NC WFGW 1010 AM	PO Box 158	Black Mountain 28711
NC WGAS 1420 AM	Box 250	Gastonia 28052
NC WGCR 720 AM	105 Mull Arcade	Brevard 28712
NC WGHB 1250 AM	Highway 121 North, PO Box 229	Farmville 27828
NC WHPE 95.5/238 FM	1714 Tower Avenue	High Point 27260
NC WHVN 1240 AM	5732 N. Tryon Street	Charlotte 28213
NC WMIT 106.9 FM	PO Box 158	Black Mountain 28711
NC WNOW 1030 AM	PO Box 23509	Charlotte 28212
NC WPET 950 AM	Box 16924	Greensboro 27415
NC WPGT 90.1 FM	515 Becker Drive	Roanoke Rapids 27870
NC WPJL 1240 AM Stereo	515 Bart Street, PO Box 27946	Raleigh 27611
NC WRTP 1530 AM	4411 Chapel Hill Blvd.	Durham 27707
NC WSGH 1040 AM	PO Box 25368	Winston Salem 27114
NC WSML 1200 AM	1040 Ivey Road, PO Box 900	Graham 27253
NC WSTS 96.5 FM	Box 529	Laurinburg 28352
NC WTSB 580 AM	PO Box 1123	Lumberton 28350
NC WVCB 1410 AM	Box 314	Shallotte 28459
NC WWGL 94.1 FM	PO Box 668	Lexington 27292
NC WWMO 830 AM	149 N. Fieldcrest Road	Eden 27288
NC WYCM 1080 AM	Drawer 38, Highway 158	Murfreesboro 27855
ND KFNW 1200 AM 97.9 FM	PO Box 6008	Fargo 58108
NE KGBI 100.7 FM	1515 S. 10th Street	Omaha 68108
NE KGRD 105.3 FM	Box 247	Orchard 68764
NE KJSK 900 AM	Box 99	Columbus 68601
NE KROA 95.7 FM	Box K	Doniphan 68832
NH WCRN 94.9 FM/67 KHZ	PO Box 6336	East Rochester 03867
NH WDER 1320 AM	8 Lawrence Road, Box 465	Derry 03038
NJ WAWZ 99.1 FM	Box 97	Zarephath 08890

State / Channel / Frequency	Address	City/Zip
NJ WFME 94.7 FM	289 Mt. Pleasant Avenue	West Orange 07052
NJ WKDN 106.9 FM	2906 Mt. Ephraim Avenue	Camden 08104
NJ WNNN 101.7 FM	Box 132	Salem 08079
NJ WSJL 102.3 FM	Box 258	Rio Grande 08242
NJ WWDJ 970 AM	167 Main Street, PO Box 970	Hackensack 07602
NM KDAZ 730 AM	Box 4338	Albuquerque 87106
NM KKIM 1000 AM	307 Los Ranchos Road, NW	Albuquerque 87107
NM KNMI 88.9 FM	PO Box 1230	Farmington 87499
NV KCRV 1340 AM	100 N. Arlington Avenue, Suite 240	Reno 89501
NV KILA 90.5 FM	2201 S. 6th Street	Las Vegas 89104
NV KNIS 94.7 FM	6363 Highway 50 E.	Carson City 89701
NY WCHP 760 AM	Rapid Road, PO Box 888	Champlain 12919
NY WCIK 103.1 FM	PO Box 506	Bath 14810
NY WDCX 99.5 FM	625 Delaware Avenue	Buffalo 14202
NY WFBR FM		West Seneca 14224
NY WFRS 88.5 FM	3200 Expressway Drive	Central Islip 11722
NY WFRW 90.7 FM	555 Canal Place	Palmyra 14522
NY WJIV 101.9 FM	Victory Mountain, PO Box 507	Cherry Valley 13320
NY WJSL 90.3 FM	Houghton College	Houghton 14744
NY WLIX 540 AM	138 West Main Street	Bay Shore 11706
NY WMHN 89.3	675 Holt Road	Webster 14580
NY WMHR 102.9 FM	4044 Makyes Road	Syracuse 13215
NY WNYM 1330 AM	60 West Castor Place, #2	Staten Island 10312
NY WOIV 105.1 FM	7095 Meyers Road East	Syracuse 13057
NY WRUN 1150 AM	Thomas Road	Oriskany 13424
NY WSIV 1540 AM	7095 Meyers Road East	Syracuse 13057
NY WTHE 1520 AM	266 Maple Place	Mineola 11501
NY WWWG 1460 AM	1850 S. Winton Road	Rochester 14618
NY WXIK 600 AM	Box 746	Watertown 13601
OH WAKW 93.3 FM	6275 Collegevue Place	Cincinnati 45224
OH WCRF 103.3 FM	9756 Barr Road	Cleveland 44141
OH WCUE 1150 AM	1675 State Road	Cuyahoga Falls 44223
OH WCVJ 90.9 FM	4422 Lenon New Lymer, PO Box 112	Jefferson 44047
OH WCVO 105 FM	4400 Reynoldsburg	New Albany 43054
OH WCVZ 93 FM	2477 East Pike	Zanesville 43701
OH WEEC 100.7 FM	2348 Troy Road	Springfield 45504
OH WFCJ 93.7 FM	PO Box 93.7	Dayton 45449
OH WGCF 830 AM	2909 Weymouth Road	Shaker Heights 44120
OH WGFT 1500 AM	131 West Boardman Street	Youngstown 44503
OH WGGN 97.7 FM	3809 Maple Avenue	Castalia 44824
OH WGOJ 105.5 FM	Box 725	Conneaut 44030
OH WHLO 640 AM	3535 S. Smith Road	Akron 44313
OH WHVT 90.5 FM	144 Lemon Street	Clyde 43410
OH WJYM 730 AM	8761 Fremont Pike	Perrysburg 43351
OH WMMX 1110 AM	16 S. Broad Street, Suite 5	Fairborn 45324
OH WPOS 102.3 FM	7112 Angola Road	Holland 43528
OH WQRP 88.1 FM	1514 W. Dorothy Lane	Dayton 45449
OH WRFD 880 AM	PO Box 802, N. High St. & Powell Rd.	Columbus 43985
OH WTGN 97.7 FM	1600 Elida Road	Lima 45805
OH WTOF 98.1 FM	120 Cleveland Avenue, NW	Canton 44702
OH WTSJ 1050 AM	800 Compton Road, Unit 33	Cincinnati 45231
OH WVMC 90.7 FM	500 Logan Road	Mansfield 44907
OH WZLE 104.9 FM	42851 North Ridge Road	Elyria 44035
OK KCFO 970 AM	3737 S 37 W Avenue	Tulsa 74107
OK KEOR 1590 AM	PO Box 608	Atoka 74525

State / Channel / Frequency	*Address*	*City/Zip*
OK KOKF 90.9 FM	Box 22000	Edmond 73123
OK KQCV 800 AM	1919 N. Broadway	Oklahoma City 73103
OK KTLV 1220 AM	3336 SE 67th Street	Oklahoma City 73135
OK KUTA 101.1 FM	Oral Roberts University	Tulsa 74171
OK KWJY 92.1 FM	PO Box 1600	Woodward 73802
OR KDOV 1230 AM	PO Box 520	Ashland 97520
OR KGRV 700 AM	PO Box 1598, 196 SE Main Street	Winston 97496
OR KLIQ 1290 AM	5410 SW Macadam, #240	Portland 97201
OR KLWJ 1090 AM	PO Box 1410	Umatilla 97882
OR KORE 1050 AM	2080 Laura Street	Springfield 97477
OR KPDQ 800 AM 93.7 FM	5110 SE Stark Street	Portland 97215
OR KYTT 98.7 FM	455 N. Broadway	Coos Bay 97420
PA WCHR 94.5 FM	Woodside Road	Yardley 19067
PA WCTL 106.3 FM	Old Lincolnville Road, R.D. 3	Union City 16438
PA WDAC 94.5 FM	Box 3022	Lancaster 17604
PA WFRJ 88.9 FM	PO Box 876	Johnstown 15907
PA WGCB 1440 AM 96.1 FM	Box 88, Windsor Road	Red Lion 17356
PA WGSI 103.1 FM	PO Box 434, Rt. 62 N.	Russell 16345
PA WJLY 1550 AM	1233 Braddock Avenue	Braddock 15104
PA WJSA 1600 AM 93.5 FM	262 Allegheny Street	Jersey Shore 17740
PA WJSM 1110 AM 92.7 FM	RD 2, Box 87	Martinsburg 16662
PA WJTL 90.3 FM	780 Eden Road	Lancaster 17601
PA WLIH 107.1 FM	Box 97	Wellsboro 16901
PA WNAP 1110 AM	2311 Old Arch Road	Norristown 19401
PA WQJU 107.1 FM	22 North Fourth Street	Mifflintown 17059
PA WRGN 88.1 FM	R.D. 3	Hunlock Creek 18621
PA WSCR 1320 AM	1520 N. Keyser Avenue	Scranton 18504
PA WTLR 89.9 FM	2020 Cato Avenue	State College 16801
PA WVCH 740 AM	Box A	Brookhaven 19015
PA WZZD 990 AM	PO Box 26098	Philadelphia 19128
PR WERR 104.1 FM	Box RR, 65 Infantry Station	Rio Piedras 00929
PR WIDA 1400 AM 90.5 FM	Box 188	Carolina 00628
PR WIVV 1370 AM	GPO Box A	San Juan 00936
PR WNRT 96.9 FM	PO Box 201	Manati 00701
PR WORO 92.5 FM	415 Carbonell Street	Hato Rey 00918
PR WRFE 105.5 FM	PO Box 847	Mayaquez 00709
PR WVID 90.3 FM	Box 3420, Marina Station	Mayaguez 00709
RI WARV 1590 AM	19 Luther Avenue	Warwick 92886
SC WAGP 88.7 FM	PO Box 119	Beaufort 29901
SC WBBR 1580 AM	PO Box 3886	Greenville 29608
SC WCKI 1300 AM	Box 709	Greer 29652
SC WFCH 88.5 FM	PO Box 1286	Mt. Pleasant 29464
SC WHPB 1390 AM	Box 490	Belton 29627
SC WLFJ 89.3 FM	2420 Wade Hampton Blvd.	Greenville 29614
SC WMCJ 950 AM	PO Box 67, 314 Remburt Dennis Blvd.	Moncks Corner 29461
SC WMHK 89.7 FM	PO Box 3122	Columbia 29230
SC WMUU 1260 AM	920 Wade Hampton Blvd.	Greenville 29609
SC WPSC 1510 AM	100 S. Arant Street, PO Box 305	Pageland 29728
SC WQXL 1470 AM	1303 Sunset Drive, Box 3277	Columbia 29230
SC WSSC 1340 AM	201 Oswego Road	Sumter 29151
SC WTGH 620 AM	1303 State Street	Columbia 29033
SC WXAX 1170 AM	PO Box 609	Lexington 29072
SC WYFG 91.1 FM	101 E. Overbrook Drive	Gaffney 29340
SC WYFH 90.7 FM	7796 Dorchester Road	North Charleston 29418
SC WZJY 1480 AM	PO Box 12039	Charleston 29412

State / Channel / Frequency		*Address*	*City/Zip*
SD	KCGN 101.5 FM	PO Box 101, East Hwy 12 and Airport Rd.	Milbank 57252
SD	KJIA 1520 AM	305 West 14th Street	Sioux Falls 57102
SD	KSLT 107.3 FM	PO Box 845, 745 5th Street	Spearfish 55783
SD	KVCX 101.5	PO Box 101	Gregory 57533
SD	KVSR 97.9 FM	4040 Tower Road	Rapid City 57702
TN	KSUD 730 AM	PO Box 3696	Memphis 38103
TN	KWAM 990 AM	80 N. Tillman Street	Memphis 38111
TN	WBCV 1550 AM	Box 68, 26 1/2 6th Street	Bristol 37621
TN	WBLC 1360 AM	PO Box 100	Lenoir City 37771
TN	WDYN 1070 FM	1815 Union Avenue	Chattanooga 37404
TN	WEAB 960 AM	106 Main Street, PO Box 559	Adamsville 38310
TN	WENR 1090 AM	PO Drawer 670, Highway 39 E.	Englewood 37329
TN	WGVT 980 AM	PO Box 989	Chattanooga 37401
TN	WHGG 88.3 FM	PO Box 2061	Bristol 37621
TN	WITA 1490 AM	7212 Kingston Pike	Knoxville 37919
TN	WMBW 89 FM	PO Box 11127	Chattanooga 37401
TN	WMCH 1260 AM	PO Box 128	Church Hill 37642
TN	WMOC 1450 AM	4707 12th Avenue	Chattanooga 37407
TN	WNAH 1360 AM	44 Music Square E.	Nashville 37203
TN	WNAZ 89.1 FM	333 Murfreesboro Road	Nashville 37210
TN	WNQM 1300 AM	3314 West End Avenue	Nashville 37203
TN	WOCV AM	Box 370	Oneida 37841
TN	WQKZ 96.7 FM	Box 191, 115 E. Jackson Street	Bolivar 38008
TN	WREA 1520 AM	Box 609	Dayton 37321
TN	WRJZ 620 AM	1515 E. Magnolia Avenue	Knoxville 37917
TN	WWGM 1560 AM	2003 Blair Blvd., PO Box 12040	Nashville 37212
TX	KAGC 1510 AM	PO Box 3420	Bryan 77805
TX	KAGN 91.3 FM	209 S. Danville, #132-A	Abilene 79605
TX	KBJS 90.3 FM	Box 193	Jacksonville 75766
TX	KCBI 90.9 FM	Box 1809	Dallas 75221
TX	KCTA 1030 AM	PO Box 898	Corpus Christi 78403
TX	KDFT 504 AM	PO Box 440	Ferris 75125
TX	KDLF 1150 AM	3185 Merriman Avenue, PO Box 545	Port Neches 77651
TX	KDRY 1100 AM	8100 Roughrider, Suite 202, Box 34478	San Antonio 78265
TX	KDVE 1510 AM	PO Box 1716, 117 Nederland Avenue	Nederland 77627
TX	KENT 920 AM	PO Box 3509	Odessa 79760
TX	KGLY 91.3 FM	PO Box 8525	Tyler 75711
TX	KHCB 105.7 FM	2424 South Blvd.	Houston 77098
TX	KHQS 98.3 FM	PO Box 918	Gatesville 76528
TX	KHVN 970 AM	1229 Corporate Drive W.	Arlington 76006
TX	KHYM 1060 AM	104 W. Cass Street	Gilmer 75644
TX	KIJN 1060 AM 92.3 FM	PO Box 458	Farwell 79325
TX	KIXL 970 AM	1018 W. 11th	Austin 78703
TX	KJAK 92.7 FM	Box 3890	Lubbock 79452
TX	KJIC 88.1 FM	2936 Oleander	Pasadena 77503
TX	KJOJ 106.9 FM	I-45 N	Spring 77381
TX	KKKK 99.1 FM	Box K	Midland 79711
TX	KLLF 1290 AM	PO Box 4647	Wichita Falls 76308
TX	KMOC 89.5	PO Box 41	Wichita Falls 76307
TX	KNBO 1530 AM	PO Box 848	New Boston 75570
TX	KNRB 1360 AM	3001 W. 5th Street	Fort Worth 76107
TX	KPAS 103.1 FM	PO Box 370982	El Paso 79937
TX	KPDR 90.5 FM	106 E. Texas Street, PO Box 469	Wheeler 79096
TX	KSBJ 88.1 FM	PO Box 187	Humble 77347
TX	KSKY 660 AM	2727 Inwood Road	Dallas 75235

State / Channel / Frequency	*Address*	*City/Zip*
TX KSLR 630 AM	5430 Fredericksburg Road, Suite 504	San Antonio 78229
TX KTDN 91.5 FM	PO Box 1518	Palestine 75802
TX KTFA 92.1 FM	PO Box 820, 200 Roundbunch	Bridge City 77611
TX KVNE 89.5 FM	PO Box 8525	Tyler 75711
TX KVOJ 1130 AM	Drawer HH	Edna 77957
TX KVTT 91.7 FM	11061 Shady Trail	Dallas 75229
TX KXOI 810 AM	PO Box 2344	Odessa 79760
UT KANN 1120 AM	2222 Washington Blvd.	Ogden 84401
UT KBBX 1600 AM	481 S. 400 E.	Bountiful 84010
UT KCGL 106 FM	481 S. 400 E.	Bountiful 84010
UT KEYY 1450 AM	PO Box KEYY	Provo 84603
VA WABS 780 AM	5545 Lee Highway	Arlington 22207
VA WBTX 1470 AM	PO Box 337	Broadway 22815
VA WDCT 1310 AM	PO Box 1310, 3909 Oak Street	Fairfax 22030
VA WDUF AM	Route 5, PO Box 391	Duffield 24244
VA WDYL 92.1 FM	10600 Jefferson Davis Highway	Richmond 23237
VA WFAX 1220 AM	161-B Hillwood Avenue	Falls Church 22046
VA WFTH 1590 AM	5021 Brook Road	Richmond 23227
VA WGGM 1410 AM	10600 Jefferson Davis Highway	Richmond 23237
VA WGTH 105.5 FM	PO Drawer 370	Richlands 24641
VA WIVE 1430 AM	PO Box 866	Ashland 23005
VA WJYJ 90.5 FM	PO Box 905, 830 Gunnery Hill Road	Spotsylvania 22553
VA WKBA 1550 AM	2043 10th Street, NE	Roanoke 24012
VA WKGK 1600 AM	Box 910	Saltville 24370
VA WKGM 940 AM	PO Box 339	Smithfield 23430
VA WMYT 1180 AM	2043 10 Street, NE	Roanoke 24012
VA WNLR 1150 AM	PO Box 400	Churchville 24482
VA WOKT 1040 AM	400 Alleghany Street	Blacksburg 24060
VA WPLZ 1240 AM	1012 North Avenue	Petersburg 23803
VA WPRZ 1250 AM	PO Box 3220	Warrenton 22186
VA WRIS 1410 AM	PO Box 6099	Roanoke 24017
VA WRVL 88.3 FM	Box 25000	Lynchburg 24506
VA WTJZ 1270 AM	553 Michigan Drive	Hampton 23669
VA WTRM 91.3 FM	PO Box 2627	Winchester 22601
VA WVZN 1170 AM	PO Box 11343	Lynchburg 24506
VA WXRI 105.3 FM	1318 Spratley Street, PO Box 1338	Portsmouth 23704
VA WYFI 99.7 FM	PO Box 1818	Chesapeake 23320
VA WYFJ 100.1 FM	407 S. Washington Highway	Ashland 23005
VA WYFT 103.9 FM	598 5th Street	Luray 22835
VA WZAM 1110 AM	5520 Greenwich Road	Virginia Beach 23462
VA WZAP 690 AM	180 Wallace Pike, PO Box 369	Bristol 24203
VT WGLY 103.1 FM	PO Box 150, Route 2	Waterbury 05676
WA KARI 550 AM	4840 Lincoln Road	Blaine 98230
WA KARR 1460 AM	220 Kirkland Avenue	Kirkland 98033
WA KBBO 1390 AM	Box 9188, 2120 Riverside Road	Yakima 98909
WA KBLE 1050 AM	114 Lakeside Avenue	Seattle 98122
WA KCIS 630 AM	19303 Fremont Avenue N.	Seattle 98133
WA KCMS 105.3 FM	19303 Fremont Avenue N.	Seattle 98133
WA KGNW 820 AM	2815 Second Avenue, Suite 100	Seattle 98121
WA KJVH 89.5 FM	1130 14th Avenue	Longview 98632
WA KLYN 106.5 FM	1843 Front Street	Lynden 98264
WA KMBI 107.9 FM 1330 AM	S 5408 Freya	Spokane 99223
WA KRSS 1230 AM	North 1306 Ash	Spokane 99201
WA KUDY 1280 AM	S 5106 Palouse Highway	Spokane 99203
WA KVSN 1500 AM	PO Box 4207	Tuymwater 98501

State / Channel / Frequency		Address	City/Zip
WI	WEMI 100.1 FM	360 Chute Street	Menasha 54952
WI	WGNV 88.5 FM	PO Box 88	Milladore 54454
WI	WNWC 102.5 FM	5606 Medical Circle	Madison 53719
WI	WRVM 102.7 FM	PO Box 212	Suring 54174
WI	WVCX 98.9 FM	PO Box 187	Tomah 54660
WI	WVCY 107.7 FM	2712 W. Vliet Street	Milwaukee 53208
WI	WWIB 103.7 FM	5558 Hallie Road	Chippewa Falls 54729
WV	WBKW 99.5 FM	PO Box AB, 102 N. Kanawha Street	Beckley 25801
WV	WEMM 107.9 FM	703 3rd Avenue	Huntington 25701
WV	WMEJ 91.9 FM	PO Box 7575	Huntington 25777
WV	WOAY 860 AM	PO Box 251	Oak Hill 25901
WV	WSCW 1410 AM	PO Box 8718, 605 D Street	South Charles 25303
WV	WVKV 1080 AM	PO Box 1080	Hurricane 25526
WV	WVVW 630 AM	Box 374, Greens Run Road	St. Marys 26170
WV	WXIT 1490 AM	136 High Street	Charleston 25311
WV	WYJP 100.9 FM	PO Box 8718, 605 D Street	South Charles 25303
WY	KUYO 830 AM	PO Box 90395	Casper 82905
Television			
AL	WHBR-TV Chan. 33 (F)	2080 County Road 63	Robertsdale 36567
AL	WMCF-TV Chan. 45 (F)	PO Box 45	Montgomery 36101
AL	WMPV-TV Chan. 21 (F)	120 Zeigler Circle E	Mobile 36608
AR	KVTN-TV Chan. 25 (C)	PO Box 22007	Little Rock 72221
AZ	K25AL Chan. 25 (C)	510 N. Acoma Blvd.	Lake Havasu City 86403
AZ	KPAZ-TV Chan. 21 (C)	3551 E. McDowell	Phoenix 85008
CA	Cable TV (C)	Redwood Chapel Community Church, 19300 Redwood Road	Castro Valley 94546
CA	K62BT-TV Chan. 62 (C)	PO Box 1606	Placerville 95667
CA	KAGL-TV Chan. 30 (C)	318 Mira Loma Avenue	Glendale 91204
CA	KCBA-TV Chan. 35 (F)	PO Box 3560	Salinas 93912
CA	KCSO-TV Chan. 19 (F)	PO Box 3689	Modesto 95352
CA	KFCB-TB Chan. 42 (C)	PO Box 4242, 5101 Port Chicago Hwy	Concord 94524
CA	KLXV-TV Chan. 65 (C)	PO Box 2B	San Jose 95109
CA	KMSG-TV Chan. 59 (F)	706 W. Herndon Avenue	Fresno 93650
CA	KNXT-TV Chan. 49 (F)	1550 N. Fresno Street	Fresno 93704
CA	KO7TA-TV Chan. 7 (F)	PO Box 172	Santa Marie 93456
CA	KO9UF-TV Chan. 9 (F)	PO Box 172	Santa Maria 93546
CA	KTBN-TV Chan. 40 (C)	2442 Michelle	Tustin 92680
CA	KVEA-TV Chan. 52, 57 (F)	3075 Cohasset Road	Chico 95926
CA	KWBB-TV Chan. 38 (F)	45 Franklin Street, Suite 205	San Francisco 94102
CA	VPN-TV Chan. 3, 6, 14, 26 (F)	3075 Cohasset Road	Chico 95926
CO	K47AQ-TV Chan. 47 (C)	455 S. Platte River Drive	Denver 80223
CO	KWBI-TV (F)	16075 W. Belleview Avenue	Morrison 80465
FL	Chan. 21 (C)	PO Box 6922	Clearwater 34618
FL	Chan. 59 (C)	PO Box 6922	Clearwater 34618
FL	Group W Cable (C)	1723 S. Bartow Highway	Lakeland 33801
FL	W15AG (C)	1305 E. Helvenston, PO Box 6922	Clearwater 34618
FL	W24AA (C)	2600 Pine Island Road	Cape Coral 33910
FL	W53 H I Chan. 53 (C)	PO Box 6922	Clearwater 34618
FL	W65BG-TV Chan. 65 (C)	300 N. Meridian Road	Tallahassee 32312
FL	WACX SUPER Chan. 55 (C)	4520 Parkbreeze Court	Orlando 32808
FL	WCLF-TV Chan. 22 (C)	PO Box 6922	Clearwater 34618
FL	WHFT-TV Chan. 45 (C)	3324 Pembroke Road	Pembroke Park 33021
FL	WPJX-TV Chan. 42 (F)	2104 SW 42nd Avenue	Ocala 32674
FL	WSWS-TV Chan. 66 (F)	1800 Pepperell Parkway, PO Box 870	Opelika 36801
FL	WTGL-TV Chan. 52 (C)	PO Box 1852	Cocoa 32923

State / Channel		*Address*	*City/Zip*
HI	K5OAP Chan. 50 (F)	1960 Kapiolani Blvd., Suite 113-327	Honolulu 96822
IA	Cable Chan. 13 (C)	217 N. High Street	Keokuk 52632
IA	Cable Team TV (C)	1000 E 41st Street	Sioux Falls 57105
IA	K60CL-TV Chan. 60 (C)	217 N. 4th Street	Keokuk 52632
IL	W51AF-TV Chan. 51 (C)	1 N. Wacker Drive	Chicago 60606
IL	W68BR-TV Chan. 68 (C)	1 N. Wacker Drive	Chicago 60606
IL	WCFC-TV Chan. 38 (C)	1 N. Wacker Drive	Chicago 60606
IL	WFHL-TV Chan. 23 (C)	2510 Parkway Court	Decatur 62526
IL	WTCT-TV Chan. 27 (C)	PO Box 1010, Route 37 N	Marion 62959
IL	WWTO-TV Chan. 35 (C)	E 1251 Road	Ottawa 61350
IN	WHMB-TV Chan. 40 (F)	Box 50250	Indianapolis 46250
IN	WHME-TV Chan. 46 (F)	61300 S. Ironwood Road	South Bend 46614
IN	WINM-TV Chan. 63 (F)	PO Box 11925	Ft. Wayne 46861
IN	WJRM-TV Chan. 17 (F)	Highway 56E	Salem 47167
IN	WKOI-TV Chan. 43 (C)	1702 S. 9th Street	Richmond 47374
IN	WO5BE-TV Chan. 5 (C)	PO Box 1462	Jeffersonville 47131
KS	KYFC-TV Chan. 50 (F)	4715 Rainbow	Shawnee Mission 66205
KY	WLCN-TV Chan. 19 (F)	Box 1087	Madisonville 42431
KY	WLJC-TV Chan. 65 (C)	Route 36, Box 50	Beattyville 41311
KY	WTSF-TV Chan. 61 (C)	3100 Bath Avenue	Ashland 41101
LA	KMCT-TV Chan. 39 (C)	PO Box 2957	West Monroe 71294
MI	Cable C.A.R.T.A. Chan. 29 (F)	PO Box 16296, 1441 E. Michigan Ave.	Lansing 48901
MI	WAQP-TV Chan. 49 (C)	PO Box 2215, 707 Federal Street	Saginaw 48605
MI	WGPR-TV Chan. 62 (F)	3140-6 E. Jefferson	Detroit 48207
MI	WLLA-TV Chan. 64 (F)	PO Box 431, 207 E. Water Street	Kalamazoo 49005
MI	WTLJ-TV Chan. 54 (C)	10290 48th Avenue	Allendale 49401
MN	K22AE-TV Chan. 22 (C)	303 N. Minnesota Street	New Ulm 56073
MN	K28AE-TV Chan. 28 (C)	64 Downtown Plaza	Fairmount 56031
MO	KNLC-TV Chan. 24 (C)	PO Box 924	St. Louis 63188
MO	KNLJ-TV Chan. 25 (C)	Rt. 2, Box 72	New Bloomfield 65063
MO	KTAJ-TV Chan. 16 (C)	RR 1, Box 403A	Agency 64401
MS	W56BH-TV Chan. 64 (C)	PO Box 786	Jackson 39205
NC	WEJC-TV Chan. 20 (F)	PO Box 2020	Lexington 27293
NC	WRDG-TV Chan. 16 (C)	PO Box 16	Burlington 27216
NM	K636D-TV Chan. 63 (F)	1017 N. Y. Avenue	Alamogordo 88310
NM	KCHF-TV Chan. 11 (C)	216 Frontage Road, Highway 14	Santa Fe 87505
NM	KNAT-TV Chan. 23 (C)	1510 Coors Road NW	Albuquerque 87105
NM	KRPV-TV Chan. 27 (C)	Box 967	Roswell 88201
NV	KREN-TV Chan. 27 (F)	PO Box 40127	Reno 89504
NY	WTBY-TV Chan. 54 (C)	PO Box 534, Route 9 & Merritt Road	Fishkill 12524
OH	WDLI-TV Chan. 17 (C)	6600 Atlantic Blvd. NE	Louisville 44641
OH	WGGN-TV Chan. 52 (C)	3809 Maple Avenue, PO Box 2397	Sandusky 44870
OH	WSFJ-TV Chan. 51 (C)	10077 Jacksontown Road, SE	Thomville 43076
OH	WTJC-TV Chan. 26 (C)	PO Box 26	Dayton 45401
OH	WTLW-TV Chan. 44 (F)	1844 Baty Road	Lima 45807
OK	KTBO-TV Chan. 14 (C)	3705 NW 63rd Street	Oklahoma City 73116
OK	KWHB-TV Chan. 47 (C)	PO Box 470047	Tulsa 74147
OR	K61CC-TV Chan. 61 (C)	838 Commercial NE	Salem 93701
PA	WFMZ-TV Chan. 69 (F)	East Rock Road	Allentown 18103
PA	WGCB-TV Chan. 49 (F)	Box 88, Windsor Road	Red Lion 17356
PA	WKBS-TV Chan. 47 (C)	Rt. 48, Signal Hill Drive	Wall 15148
PA	WPCB-TV Chan. 40 (C)	Rt. 48, Signal Hill Drive	Wall 15148
PA	WPHL-TV Chan. 17 (F)	5001 Wynnefield Avenue	Philadelphia 19131
PR	WECN-TV Chan. 64 (C)	Box 310, Road 167	Bayamon 00621
SC	WCCT-TV Chan. 57 (F)	PO Box 5757	West Columbia 29171

State / Channel	*Address*	*City/Zip*
SC WGGS-TV Chan. 16 (F)	PO Box 1616, 3409 Rutherford Road	Greenville 29602
SC WGSE-TV Chan. 43 (F)	PO Box 1616	Greenville 29602
SD Team TV (C)	1000 E. 41st Street	Sioux Falls 57105
TN Chan. 67 (C)	4707 12th Avenue	Chattanooga 37407
TN W61AR-TV Chan. 61 (C)	200 Hill Avenue	Nashville 37210
TN WHTN-TV Chan. 39 (F)	5202 Lebanon Road	Old Hickory 37138
TN WPMC-TV Chan. 54 (C)	PO Box 847	Jellico 37762
TX GETV Cable TV (C)	18755 Stone Oak Parkway	San Antonio 78258
TX K31A1 Chan. 31 (C)	PO Box 73313	Houston 77273
TX K66CA Chan. 66 (C)	PO Box 73313	Houston 77273
TX K67DU Chan. 67 (C)	PO Box 73313	Houston 77273
TX KIIRT-TV (F)	PO Box 1712	Jacksonville 75766
TX KLTJ-TV Chan. 57 (C)	3737 Red Bluff	Pasadena 77503
TX KO2MQ Chan. 2 (C)	PO Box 73313	Houston 77273
TX KO5HX-TV Chan. 5 (C)	PO Box 73313	Houston 77273
TX KO51A Chan. 5 (C)	PO Box 73313	Houston 77273
TX WUJA-TV Chan. 58 (C)	1386 N. Reagan Street	San Benito 78586
VA WAZT-TV Chan. 10 (F)	123 E. Court Street	Woodstock 22664
VA WEFC-TV Chan. 38 (C)	612 Bullitt Avenue SE	Roanoke 24013
VA WJCB-TV Chan. 49 (F)	1930 E. Pembroke Avenue	Hampton 23663
VA WLBU-TV Chan. 11 (F)		Lynchburg 24506
VA WTKK-TV Chan. 66 (F)	9008 Center Street	Manassas 22110
VA WZXK-TV Chan. 65 (C)	10211 Staples Mill Road	Glen Allen 23060
WA KTBW-TV Chan. 20 (C)	1909 South 341st Place	Federal Way 98003
WI WSCO-TV Chan. 14 (C)	3434 W. Kilbourn Avenue	Milwaukee 54174
WI WVCY-TV Chan. 30 (F)	2712 West Vliet Street	Milwaukee 53208
International		
6911-Switzerland Chan. 44/37/46	Via Per Pugerna, No. 3,	Campione, D'Italia
Guatemala Chan. 21	Audio Video de Guatemala, 20 Calle 7-71, Zona 14	La Canada
Netherlands	Evangelische Omroep, PO Box 565,	1200 AN Hilversum
South Africa Chan. 24	The Ciskei Government, PO Box 81	Bisho, Rep. of Ciskei
Taiwan	Overseas Radio & Television, Inc., PO Box 37-3	Taipei
USA, MET-TV Chan. 12	CBN Center	Virginia Beach, VA 23463
West Indies, Chan. 13	Bath Plain	Charlestown, Nevis

CHURCH ATTENDANCE UNCHANGED BY RELIGIOUS TV

Has watching religious TV changed your involvement in your local church or synagogue? Has your involvement increased or decreased? (Based on total viewers.)

Has not changed involvement	90%
Has changed involvement	8%
Increased	4
Decreased	2
Not sure	2
Not sure	2%
	100%

Gallup Poll, April 1987. From *100 Questions and Answers* by George Gallup, Jr., and Sarah Jones.

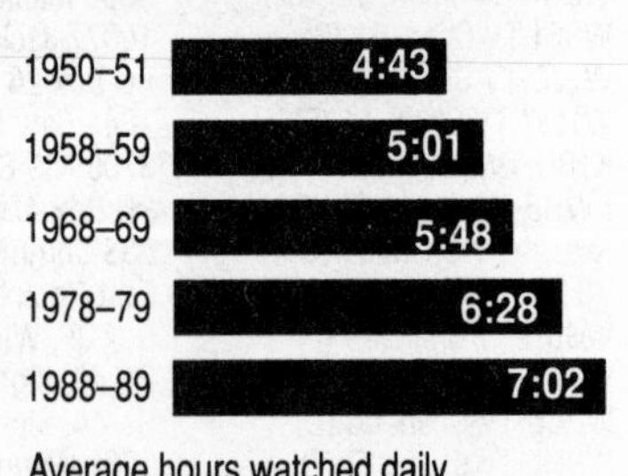

Source: Nielson Television Index

CHRONOLOGY OF CHRISTIAN RADIO AND TELEVISION

1865 English physicist James Clerk Maxwell assumes existence of electromagnetic waves.

1885-1888 German physicist Heinrich Hertz verifies Maxwell's theories.

1895 Italian physicist Guglielmo Marconi improves and applies Hertz's inventions.

1901 Marconi transmits messages across the Atlantic from England to Newfoundland.

1920 First radio broadcasts begin in the United States.

1921 U.S. Department of Commerce licenses 32 broadcasting stations.

1921 Origins of global electronic church: first broadcast of a church worship service—Calvary Episcopal Church, Pittsburgh, PA.
First Baptist radio broadcast.

1922 First Pentecostal broadcast by Aimee S. McPherson.

1923 Ten churches now operate radio stations. By 1928, 60 stations, falling by 1933 to 30.

1930 "The Lutheran Hour" broadcast over station WHK in Cleveland, Ohio, begun by the Lutheran Church—Missouri Synod; 1931, heard by five million a week, 1943 15 million, 1965 30 million in 120 countries over more than 1,000 radio stations; 1940, foreign broadcasting now named Bringing Christ to the Nations; 1945, worldwide to 20 million a week; 1975, broadcast in over 50 languages, heard by 22 million a week; 1987, 40 million regular listeners in 34 languages around world.

1930 Radio is now second only to newspapers as a major form of communciation.

1931 Radio Vatican inaugurated in Rome by Pius XI (1857-1939); entrusted to Jesuits; daily announcement motto "Laudetur Jesus Christus" (Praised be Jesus Christ); 1975, broadcasts to 157 countries in 32 languages for 16 hours a day; 1982, John Paul II inaugurates Vatican Television; 1987, in 35 languages.

1933 Experimental television transmission begins from Empire State Building, New York, NY.

1939 Public television programming in U.S. begins with the televising of the New York World's Fair opening.

1943 National Religious Broadcasters of North America formed as official broadcasting arm of National Association of Evangelicals, with 50 organizations growing by 1979 to over 800; by 1986, annual convention attracts 4,000.

1946 World Literature Crusade begins in Canada for radio outreach.

1949 Sales of television sets in U.S. reach 250,000 a month.

1950 Evangelistic broadcasting spreads: 1950, Billy Graham begins on ABC radio, and 1951 on TV; 1953, Rex Humbard telecasts weekly.

1950 Rise of television overshadows radio.
"Hour of Decision" radio program with Billy Graham begins over 150 stations; 1951, 20 million listeners (200,000 letters received per year); by 1978, 900 radio/TV stations worldwide, and a million letters per year (with 70 million viewers in US).

1953 World Committee for Christian Broadcasting constituted in Britain, then International Committee for Christian Broadcasting; 1961, founds World Association for Christian Broadcasting; 1968, merges with Coordinating Committee for Christian Broadcasting to form World Association for Christian Communication.

1955 World Conference on Missionary Radio begins in US; 1963, joins with National Religious Broadcasters of North America to form International Christian Broadcasters, which disbands in 1968.

1961 First religious TV station opens in US: WYAH (M. G. "Pat" Robertson, in Tidewater, Virginia), later Christian Broadcasting Network; by 1980, almost every major metropolitan center in US has its own religious TV stations; by 1987, CBN World Outreach involves "sharing the love of Jesus in more than 85 nations."
World Association for Christian Broadcasting founded, becoming by 1968 the World Association for Christian Communication.
World Radio Missionary Fellowship inaugurates HCJB-TV (Quito, Ecuador) as pioneer missionary telecaster; 1985, 218 overseas personnel in eight countries.

1963 US evangelicals form International Christian Broadcasters; 1967, meets in Concordia,

Milwaukee; fades out by 1968, displaced by National Religious Broadcasters.

1969 Pentecostal evangelist Jimmy L. Swaggart begins US radio ministry "Camp Meeting Hour," then in 1972 television ministry; by 1987, Jimmy Swaggart Ministries air telecasts over 3,200 TV stations in 15 languages viewed by 510 million in 145 countries weekly, raising donations of $150 million a year, and claim "The medium of television is the most expedient method of spreading the gospel the world has ever known. It is God's directive that the Great Commission be carried out by this means;" 1988, partial collapse due to sex scandal.

1973 Trinity Broadcasting Network, CA, launches Pentecostal television station "to get the gospel to every living human being on planet Earth" before Jesus comes; by 1986, TBN owns 55 TV stations in US with 26 affiliates, also stations in Guatemala, St. Kitts-Nevis, Italy, Ciskei.

1974 Number of radios worldwide reaches 922 million.

1975 International Christian Broadcasters begins Project Look Up. Plans to reach world via NASA's ATS-6 geostationary satellite to beam TV seminary teaching and lay institutes across world; 1977, begins broadcasts to Puerto Rico; satellite suddenly withdrawn by NASA; 1979, Project Look Up fizzles out due to inadequate funding, though committees go on meeting until after 1988.

1979 National Religious Broadcasters and World Evangelical Fellowship propose Angel-I/Angel-II/Angel-III Project to blanket earth with gospel broadcasts; three satellites in geostationary orbit filling roles of three angels of Revelation 14:6-11, each covering a third of earth's surface, fulfilling Matthew 24:14 "for a witness unto all nations"; by 1983, author realized project has been "committeed to death," so proposal passes into oblivion, though use of satellites for US Christian TV grows.

TV evangelist Jim Bakker of PTL Ministries announces plans to start PTL missions throughout the world; funds raised by plan fizzle out within a year; 1987, PTL Ministries collapses in financial and sex scandal.

1981 Christian broadcasting expands from origin in 1921 to global force heard or seen regularly by 23% of world's population.

New generation of charismatic TV evangelists arises, including Oral Roberts (who began Pentecostal TV preaching in 1953) and son Richard, Pat Robertson, Rex Humbard, Jimmy Swaggart, Kenneth Copeland, Paul Crouch, Jim Bakker, et al.

Dominion Video Satellite (Dominion Network), FL, to provide Christian radio/TV programs over direct broadcast satellite systems, based on Great Commission, direct broadcast satellites as the angel of Revelation 14:6, 30-inch portable dish receivers, and bypassing of secular control over TV.

1982 World Satellite Evangelism (motto: "Using Mass Media to Reach the Unreached of the World for Christ") begins in Tulsa, OK, "mobilizing media to reach every person in every home with the gospel" especially in closed countries; forms a global media task force in 50 nations, starting Christian universities and other centers.

1983 Catholic global television evangelism agency launches Lumen 2000, based in Dallas and Vatican City, "to preach the gospel of Jesus to the uttermost parts of the earth, spreading the love of Jesus around the globe"; 1986, in 50 countries.

1985 Three major Christian broadcasting agencies, FEBC, HCJB/World Radio Missionary Fellowship, TWR (and later ELWA-SIM) announce "Project: The World by 2000" to be completed by AD 2000, giving everyone on earth the opportunity to hear the gospel of Christ by radio (September); 1987, target modified to be: all major trade languages with over one million speakers each by AD 2000, then all minor trade languages, then later the world's 6,500 "heart" languages.

1986 Intercontinental Broadcasting Network begins in Virginia Beach, VA, by independent charismatics linking up with European counterparts.

Televised Evangelism for All, a project proposed by Christian Broadcasting Network vice-president N. Van Hamm: 6 million 10-inch flat liquid-screen printed-circuit solar-cell television units, costing $1 each, dumped out of aircraft across world, glide to earth over unevangelized peoples, pretuned to 18-language transmissions over three or four geostationary satellites.

1987 Global Rosary for World Peace and world evangelization prayed by John Paul II in St. Peter's basilica, Vatican, and by 16 Marian shrines across the world linked by 18 satellites and 75 TV cameras, with TV audience of 1.5 billion in over 30 countries in 35 languages; most complex and ambitious television program of all times.
Community Satellite Corporation, US, launches Dominion Network (satellites to homes) into orbit by utilizing direct broadcast satellites.
Global Broadcasting System launched for Christian radio and TV broadcasting to any place on earth through "Top Hat" system of super-pressure platform network of 800 high-tech balloons at 120,000 feet altitude covering the whole world.
1988 Regular listeners/viewers for Christian programs number 1.2 billion (14% of the world).

Possible Future Scenario

2000 Entire world finally reached with Christian gospel for first time in history, in the sense that everyone everywhere has heard or hears the gospel in depth with understanding and has access to Scripture, churches, missions, Christians, Christian broadcasting (with 4,000 Christian radio and TV stations worldwide), movies, literature and other means of grace.

Source: Extracted from "788 Global Plans" in *Seven Hundred Plans to Evangelize the World* by David B. Barrett and James W. Reapsome. Copyright © by Foreign Mission Board of the Southern Baptist Convention. Published by New Hope. Used by permission.

"" FOCUS QUOTE **The more children watch violent television, the more likely they are to be violent.** —Dr. William H. Deitz, pediatrician

FOCUS FACT **Intercollegiate Religious Broadcasters (IRB) introduces job applicants to employers and helps students keep in touch with what is happening in other schools.**

NATIONAL RELIGIOUS BROADCASTING AWARDS

Distinguished Service Award Presented to an individual or organization for outstanding contributions to the field of broadcasting
Milestone Award Presented to an individual or organization for 50 years of continuous service in the field of religious broadcasting
Broadcasting Hall of Fame Presented to a Christian broadcaster who has achieved wide recognition in religious media communication with the highest standards

Award of Merit	1959	Hour of Decision, Billy Graham
	1960	Old Fashioned Revival Hour, Charles E. Fuller
	1961	Lutheran Hour, Oswald C.J. Hoffmann
	1962	Light and Life Hour, Myron Boyd
	1963	Back to the Bible Broadcast, Theodore Epp
	1964	Revivaltime, C.M. Ward
	1964	The Far East Broadcasting Company, Robert Bowman
	1965	Radio Station HCJB, Clarence Jones
	1965	Showers of Blessing, T.W. Willingham
	1966	Christian Brotherhood Hour, W. Dale Oldham
	1966	TEAM, Tom Watson
	1967	Moody Radio Network, James E. Draper
	1967	Trans World Radio, Paul Freed
	1968	Radio Station ELWA, Raymond Davis
	1968	This Is the Life, Martin Neeb, Jr.

NATIONAL RELIGIOUS BROADCASTING AWARDS cont.

1969 Christian Broadcasting System, E. Otto DeCamp
1969 Morning Chapel Hour, Wilbur Nelson
1970 Bible Fellowship Hour, Celia Webb
1970 Chapel of the Air, John D. Jess
1971 Family Stations, Inc., Harold Camping
1971 Mennonite Broadcast, Inc. Kenneth Weaver
1972 Haven of Rest, Paul Evans
1973 Cornelius Keur, Paul Ramseyer
1973 Northwestern College Radio, KTIS AM-FM
1974 Christian Broadcasting Network, M.G. 'Pat' Robertson
1974 Radio Bible Class, Richard DeHaan
1975 John Brown University, John E. Brown, Jr.
1975 Southern Baptist Radio-TV Commission, Paul M. Stevens
1976 Grand Old Gospel Hour, B. Sam Hart
1976 KRDU, David Hofer
1976 Unshackled!, Harry G. Saulnier
1976 WRVM, Ken Hettinga
1977 Inspirational Broadcasting Corp., KPDQ, Robert W. Ball
1977 The Back to God Hour, Joel Nederhood
1979 Day of Discovery, Richard DeHaan
1979 KHEP, Jack Willis
1980 At Home with the Bible, Frank Pollard
1980 Hour of Freedom, Howard O. Jones
1980 WCFC-TV, Jerry Rose
1980 WKDH/WIVE, James Birkett
1981 Trinity Broadcasting Network, Paul Crouch
1981 WDAC, Paul Hollinger
1981 WFGW, Edna Edwards
1982 Focus on the Family
1982 Rex Humbard Television Ministry
1983 In Touch
1983 Insight for Living
1983 Le Sea Broadcasting Co., Lester Sumrall
1983 WRBS/Baltimore, Maryland
1984 100 Huntley Street
1984 Family Life Broadcasting
1984 Grace to You
1984 The First Estate, WNBC-TV
1984 Tips for Teens
1984 Wesleyan Hour
1984 WTLW-TV/Lima Ohio
1985 A Visit With Mrs. G.
1985 Afterglow
1985 KCFO/Tulsa, Oklahoma
1985 The Grace Worship Hour
1985 WPCB-TV 40/Wall, Pennsylvania
1986 Continente '85 Campaign—Luis Palau
1986 CTN Magazine—Glenn Plummer
1986 Explo '85—Bill Bright

Award	Year	Recipient
	1986	Inside Russia—Billy Graham
	1986	KFCB Chan. 42/Concord, California
	1986	KGNW/Seattle, Washington
	1986	KIRV/Fresno, California
	1986	Moody Presents
	1986	Point of View—Marlin Maddoux
	1986	The Pat Boone Show—Pat Boone
	1986	Un Mensaje a la Conciencia—Herman Pablo
	1986	WBCL/Fort Wayne, Indiana
	1986	WGCB/Red Lion, Pennsylvania
	1987	Al Sanders—Ambassador Advertising Agency
	1987	Ben Haden—Changed Lives
	1987	Dan Matthews—Christian Lifestyles Magazine
	1987	Jane Dickerson—The Filling Station
	1987	Jimmy and Joanne Thompson—Nite Line
	1987	John Helder—Coral Ridge Ministries
	1987	Juan Boonstra—La Hora de la Reforma
	1987	Nathan Travis Middleton—Sanctity of Human Life Week
	1987	Stephen Brown—Key Life
	1987	Lou Velker—WWCM
	1988	700 Club
	1988	Prime Time America
	1988	Salem Communications Corp.
Award of Merit for Management	1989	Jon Campbell, President, Ambassador Advertising Agency, Fullerton, CA
Award of Merit for Program Production	1989	Ron Hutchcraft, Saturday Night Alive, Moody Broadcasting Network, Chicago, IL
Black Ministry Award	1988	Anthony Evans
	1989	Clay Evans, What A Fellowship Hour, Chicago, IL
	1990	Dr. B. Sam Hart, Grand Old Gospel Fellowship, Philadelphia, PA
Board of Directors Award	1988	Richard E. Wiley
	1989	Senator Bill Armstrong, (R) Colorado
Broadcast Facility of the Year Award	1988	KFIA/Carmichael, CA
	1988	KJNP/North Pole, AK
	1988	KTBN, TBN/Santa Ana, CA
	1988	WCFC-TV/Chicago, IL
Broadcast Facility of the Year for Radio—Large Market	1989	KKLA-FM, Salem Communications Corp, Dennis Worden, General Mgr., Los Angeles
Broadcast Facility of the Year for Radio—Small Market	1989	KURL-AM, Enterprise Network, Billings, MT, Bruce Erickson
Broadcast Facility of the Year for Television	1989	WPCB-TV/Chan. 40, Russell and Norma Bixler, Pittsburgh, PA
Christian Broadcaster of the Year	1989	Pat Robertson, Christian Broadcasting Network, Virginia Beach, VA

NATIONAL RELIGIOUS BROADCASTING AWARDS cont.

Award	Year	Recipient
Direct Response and/ or Magazine Award	1988	Christian Management Review
	1989	Fund Raising Managament Magazine, Hoke Communications, Garden City, NY, William Olcott, Editor
Distinguished Service Award	1972	Stanley N. Whitcanack, Showers of Blessing
	1973	Thomas F. Zimmerman, Assemblies of God
	1974	Dean Burch, FCC Chairman
	1974	Eugene R. Bertermann, President of NRB
	1974	Pamela Ilott, CBS News
	1977	Richard E. Wiley, FCC Chairman
	1977	Sol Taishoff, Broadcasting Magazine
	1979	C. M. Ward, Revivaltime
	1980	Wendell Loveless
	1981	J. Vernon McGee, Thru the Bible
	1982	W. Dale Oldham, Christian Brotherhood Hour
	1983	Theodore Epp, Back to the Bible
	1984	Carl Smith, Consulting Engineer
	1984	Herrmann Braunlin, Hawthorne Gospel Church
	1984	Mary Dorr, Religion in Media
	1985	Clay Evans, What a Fellowship Hour
	1985	Mark Fowler, FCC Chairman
	1985	Neal Doty and Sherman Williams, Redwood Chapel
	1985	Orva Koenigsburg, Domain Communications
	1986	Bishop Samuel L. Green, Jr.
	1986	Patrick Buchanan
	1986	Paul Bearfield
	1987	John D. Jess
	1987	Joseph Barbera
	1987	Luis Palau
	1987	Paul Freed
	1987	Ralph Montanus, Sr.
	1987	Stephen Olford
	1987	Steve Allen
	1987	Ted Engstrom
	1988	George Sweeting, Moody Presents
	1988	Robert A. Cook, The Kings Hour
	1990	Dr. E. Brandt Gustavson, Trans World Radio, Chatham, NJ
	1990	Dr. Robert Cook, The King's Hour, Tannersville, PA
	1990	Tom Zimmerman, Lausanne Committee for World Evangelization, Springfield, MO
Headquarters and NRB Staff Award	1988	Esther DiGiovanni
	1989	Anne Dunlap, Administrative Assistant, National Religious Broadcasters, NJ
Hispanic Ministry Award	1988	Jose Reyes
	1989	Radio Vision Cristiana, Staten Island, NY
	1990	Alberto Mottesi, Alberto Mottesi Evangelistic Association, Midway City, CA
Milestone Award	1976	Moody Bible Institute
	1977	This Is the Life

	1978	Theodore Elsner
	1979	Dale Crowley
	1980	Glenn Tingley
	1981	Celia Webb, Bible Fellowship Hour
	1981	Charles Leaming, Faith Gospel Broadcast
	1981	Clarence Jones, HCJB
	1981	Dr. Oswald C.M. Hoffmann, The Lutheran Hour
	1981	Howard Ferrin, Mountaintop Hour
	1982	Gordon K. Powell, Radio Revival Hour
	1982	KFSG/Los Angeles, CA
	1982	Manford George Gutzke, The Bible for You
	1982	Pillar of Fire Radio Stations
	1983	David Webber, Southwest Radio Church of the Air
	1983	KPPC/Pasadena, CA
	1983	Quinton Everest, Your Worship Hour
	1983	Rev. Donald Baughey
	1983	Rex Humbard, Sr.
	1983	Russell Killman, Heaven and Home Hour
	1983	WMPC/Michigan
	1984	Berean Bible Society
	1984	Family Altar
	1984	KDRY/San Antonio, TX
	1984	Sunday Evening Club, Chicago, IL
	1984	Union Rescue Mission, Los Angeles, CA
	1985	Nation's Family Prayer Period
	1986	Celia Webb
	1986	Norman Vincent Peale
	1986	William and Anne Schafer, The Lifeline Hour
	1987	Ernest C. Manning
	1987	Noah Edward McCoy
	1987	Samuel Kelsey
	1987	Sunday School of the Air
	1987	The Biola Hour
	1987	The Calvary Hour
	1987	Wealthy Street Baptist Church
	1988	Park Street Church
	1989	Back to the Bible Broadcast, Lincoln, NE
	1989	Chapel of the Air, Wheaton, IL
	1989	Haven of Rest, Hollywood, CA
	1989	Radio Bible Class, Grand Rapids, MI
	1990	Chaplain Ray Hoekstra, International Prison, Dallas, TX
	1990	Dr. Jack MacArthur, Voice of Calvary, Seattle, WA
	1990	Dr. Jack Wyrtzen, Word of Life Fellowship, Schroon Lake, NY
	1990	Dr. James Boice, The Bible Study Hour, Philadelphia, PA
	1990	John D. Jess, Family Life Radio, Tucson, AZ
	1990	Mel Johnson, Northwestern College & Radio, Roseville, MN
	1990	Mrs. Robert Fraser, Fraser Gospel Hour, Philadelphia, PA
Ministry of the Year Award	1988	Focus On the Family
	1988	International Media Services
	1988	There's Hope

NATIONAL RELIGIOUS BROADCASTING AWARDS cont.

Award	Year	Recipient
New Ministry Award	1988	Minirth-Meier Clinic
NRB Chapter Award	1988	Caribbean Chapter
	1989	Midwest Chapter, Minneapolis, MN
President's Award	1988	Charles Colson
Radio Broadcast Facility of the Year	1989	Hope for the Heart, Dallas, TX
	1990	WIHS, Alfred C. Thyberg, Connecticut Radio Fellowship, Middletown, CT
Radio Program Producer	1990	Larry Burkett, Money Matters, Christian Financial Concepts, Dahlonega, GA
Religious Broadcasting Hall of Fame	1975	Clarence W. Jones, HCJB
	1975	John Zoller, Christ for Everyone
	1975	Walter A. Maier, The Lutheran Hour
	1976	George Palmer, Morning Cheer Broadcast
	1976	Paul Rader, Radio evangelist
	1976	R. R. Brown, Radio Chapel Service
	1977	'First Mate Bob' Paul Myers, Haven of Rest
	1977	Miss Lois Crawford, KFGQ
	1978	Donald Grey Barnhouse, Bible Study Hour
	1978	William Ward Ayer, First President of NRB
	1979	Herman Gockel, This Is the Life
	1980	Myron Boyd, Light and Life Hour
	1981	Billy Graham, Hour of Decision
	1982	Percy Crawford, Radio-TV Pioneer
	1983	Richard M. DeHaan, Radio Bible Class
	1984	Eugene R. Bertermann
	1985	Jerry Falwell, The Old Time Gospel Hour
	1986	M.G. (Pat) Robertson, Christian Broadcasting Network
	1986	Theodore H. Epp, Back to the Bible (posthumously)
	1987	Thomas F. Zimmerman
	1988	Charles Stanley, In Touch Ministry
	1989	J. Vernon McGee, Thru the Bible Broadcast, Pasadena, CA
Technical Achievement Award	1988	United Video (Tulsa, OK)
	1989	Joseph Flaherty, Chief Engineer, CBS
Technical Achievement in Program Production	1990	Adventures in Odyssey, Focus on the Family, Dr. James Dobson, Pomona, CA
Television Broadcast Facility of the Year	1989	Love Worth Finding, Bellevue Baptist Church, Memphis, TN
	1990	Super Channel 55, WACX-TV, Claud Bowers, Orlando, FL
Television Program Producer	1990	Dr. Billy Graham, Billy Graham Evangelistic Association, Minneapolis, MN
William Ward Ayer Distinguished Service Award	1989	Oswald C.J. Hoffmann, The Lutheran Hour, Lutheran Layman's League, St. Louis, MO
Youth Achievement Award	1988	Heidi Russell
	1989	Matthew Mighell, Northwestern College, Minneapolis, MN

Missions

MISSION AGENCIES

The following directory includes mission agencies with 25 or more full-time employees who are directly engaged in ministries outside of North America or who support those who are.

Action International Ministries. P.O. Box 490, Bothell, WA 98041. 206-485-1967 (1974). *Ministry:* Church planting, evangelism, literature distribution and support of national churches and workers. *Countries:* Philippines

Advent Christian World Missions. P.O. Box 23152, Charlotte, NC 28212. 704-545-6161 (1880). *Ministry:* Church planting, theological education, evangelism and support of national workers. *Countries:* India, Japan, Philippines

Africa Evangelical Fellowship. P.O. Box 2896, Boone, NC 28607. 704-264-6036 (1906). *Ministry:* Evangelism, church planting, theological education, correspondence courses, TEE and agricultural assistance. *Countries:* Angola, Botswana, Gabon, Malawi, Mauritius, Mozambique, Namibia, Reunion South Africa, Swaziland, United Kingdom, Zambia, Zimbabwe

Africa Inland Mission International, Inc. P.O. Box 178, Pearl River, NY 10965. 914-735-4014 (1895). *Ministry:* Evangelism, church planting, development and training of national leadership, theological education, TEE, literature production/distribution, medical work and support of national churches. *Countries:* Central Africa Rep, Chad, Comoros Islands, Kenya, Lesotho, Madagascar, Mozambique, Namibia, Seychelles, Sudan, Tanzania, Uganda, United Kingdom, Zaire

Africa Inter-Mennonite Mission, Inc. P.O. Box 518, Elkhart, IN 46515. 219-295-3711 (1911). *Ministry:* Agricultural assistance, church planting, theological education, evangelism, community development and medical work. *Countries:* Botswana, Burkina Faso, Lesotho, Transkei, Zaire

African Methodist Episcopal Church, Inc. 475 Riverside Drive, Room 926, New York, NY 10115. 212-870-2258 (1844). *Ministry:* Christian education, literature distribution and support of national workers. *Countries:* Lesotho, Liberia, Mozambique, Namibia, Nigeria, South Africa, Swaziland, Zambia

Allegheny Wesleyan Methodist Missions. P.O. Box 357, Salem, OH 44460. 216-332-0696 (1969). *Ministry:* Agricultural assistance,

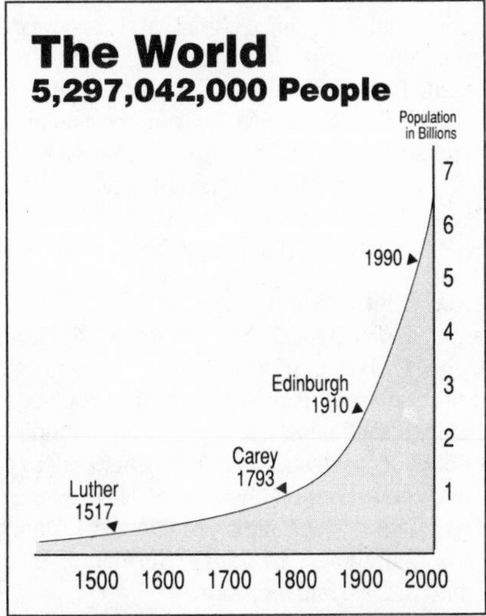

Source: *Perspectives on the World Christian Movement,* by Ralph D. Winter and Steven Hawthorne. Published by William Carey Library.

MISSION AGENCIES cont.

relief aid, church planting, Christian education, evangelism and self-help projects. *Countries:* Haiti, Peru

American Baptist Association Missionary Committee. P.O. Box 1050, Texarkana, TX 75504. 214-792-2783 (1924). *Ministry:* Church planting, evangelism, theological education and literature distribution. *Countries:* American Samoa, Australia, Colombia, Costa Rica, France, India, Israel, Japan, South Korea, Mexico, New Zealand, Nicaragua, Nigeria, Peru, Philippines, Solomon Islands

American Baptist Churches in the U.S.A. P.O. Box 851, Valley Forge, PA 19482. 215-768-2200 (1814). *Ministry:* Evangelism, church planting, human resource development, theological education, medical work and support of national churches. *Countries:* Burma, Costa Rica, Dominican Rep, El Salvador, Europe-General, Haiti, Hong Kong, India, Japan, Mexico, Nicaragua, Philippines, Thailand, Zaire

American Leprosy Missions, Inc. One Broadway, Elmwood Park, NJ 07407. 201-794-8650 (1906). *Ministry:* Medical, social rehabilitation and spiritual assistance to leprosy victims, public health, technical assistance and training programs. *Countries:* Angola, Benin, Brazil, Burma, Burundi, Cameroon, Central Africa Rep, China (PRC), Comoros Islands, Congo, Ethiopia, India, Indonesia, South Korea, Liberia, Malawi, Mozambique, Nepal, Paraguay, Philippines, Somalia, Taiwan (ROC), Tanzania, Thailand, Zaire

AMG International. P.O. Box 21000, Chattanooga, TN 37422. 615-894-6060 (1942). *Ministry:* Bible distribution, childcare, church planting, correspondence courses, theological education and support of national workers. *Countries:* Brazil, Burma, Colombia, Cyprus, Greece, Guatemala, Haiti, Hong Kong, India, Israel, Japan, Mexico, Pakistan, Peru, Philippines, Sri Lanka, Suriname, Taiwan (ROC), Thailand, Zaire

Arab World Ministries. P.O. Box 96, Upper Darby, Pa 19082. 215-352-2003 (1952). *Ministry:* Radio broadcasting, church planting, correspondence courses, evangelism and literature distribution/production. *Countries:* Algeria, Egypt, France, West Germany, Jordan, Mauritania, Morocco, Spain, Tunisia, United Kingdom, United Arab Emr

Assemblies of God. 1445 Boonville Avenue, Springfield, MO 65802. 417-862-2781 (1914). *Ministry:* Evangelism, church planting, relief aid, childcare programs, correspondence courses and support of national churches. *Countries:* Active in 109 countries

Associate Reformed Presbyterian Church. 1 Cleveland Street, Greenville, SC 29601. 803-233-5226 (1839). *Ministry:* Church planting, theological education, evangelism, literacy work, medical work and support of national churches. *Countries:* Asia-Mid East, Liberia, Mexico, Pakistan, Tanzania

Association of Baptists for World Evangelism, Inc. P.O. Box 5000, Cherry Hill, NJ 08034. 609-424-4606 (1927). *Ministry:* Church planting, theological education, evangelism, medical work and Bible translation. *Countries:* Argentina, Australia, Bangladesh, Brazil, Chile, Colombia, France, Gambia, Hong Kong, Italy, Japan, Kenya, Norway, Papua New Guinea, Paraguay, Peru, Philippines, Portugal, South Africa, Spain, Togo, United Kingdom

Baptist Bible Fellowship. P.O. Box 191, Springfield, MO 65801. 417-862-5001 (1950). *Ministry:* Evangelism, church planting, church construction and theological education. *Countries:* Active in 58 countries

Baptist Faith Missions. 1009 Balsam Drive, Lexington, KY 40504. 606-277-4947 (1923). *Ministry:* Church planting, Christian education, theological education, evangelism and furloughed missionary support. *Countries:* Brazil, Honduras, Peru, Philippines, South Korea

Baptist General Conference Board of World Missions. 2002 S. Arlington Heights Road, Arlington Heights, IL 60005. 312-228-0200 (1944). *Ministry:* Evangelism, church planting, development of human resources,

Major World Religions

	Where	Supreme Being	Founder/ Founded	Historical Leaders	Leadership	Sacred Writings	Holy Places	Typical Holy Days	Symbols
Christianity	Western Europe Western Hemisphere	God	Jesus A.D. 30	John the Baptist 12 disciples 4 Gospel writers Writers of Epistles	Varied Priests Ministers Lay people	Bible Old Testament New Testament	Bethlehem Jerusalem Rome Nazareth	Christmas Good Friday Easter	Protestant Catholic and Eastern Orthodox
Islam	Arabia Middle East Northern Africa	Allah	Muhammad A.D. 570–632	Muhammad Husein (grandson) Abu Bakr, Omar, Othman, Ali	None	Koran	Mecca Jerusalem	Ramadan (Sacred Month)	The crescent (New Moon)
Hinduism	India Sri Lanka (Ceylon)	Brahman All Reality	No founder 3200 B.C.	Mahatma Gandhi Ramakrishna	Sannyasis (holy men) Gurus (preachers)	Vedas Brahmanas Upanishads Great Epics	Benares Ganges River	The Mela Holi Festival Dasera Divuli	8-fold law cycle of birth and rebirth 8-spoked wheel
Confucianism	China Japan Korea	Confucius Shang-Ti	Confucius 557 B.C.	Yang Chu Moh Tih	None	NuChing Ssu Shu	None	None	None
Buddhism	China Japan India Burma	108 different names	Gautama 560–480 B.C.	Gautama Amitabha	Bhikkhus Monks Nuns Lamas	Dharma (Sutta) Vinaya Abhidhamma	Sarnath Lumbini Buddh-Gaya Kusinara	Perahera Festival in Ceylon Wesak (Kason) in May	Lotus blossom
Shintoism	Japan	Izanagi (Sky Father) Izanami (Earth Mother)	No founder A.D. 6th Cent.	None	None	Nihongi Kojiki	Mt. Fujiyama	New Year Bon (Festival of Dead) Tenri-Kyo (January)	Torii Mirror
Taoism	China	Jade emperor Many folk gods	Lao-Tzu (or Lao-Tse) 604 B.C.	Lao-Tse Chuang-Tse 350-275 B.C.	None	Tao-Te-Ching	Kiangsi and many holy mountains	Birthdays of Gods Festival of Souls Autumn Festival	Yin—female, dark Yang—male, light
Judaism	Israel Europe Western Hemisphere	Yahweh (Jehovah or God)	Abraham 1900 B.C.	Moses Amos Micah	Rabbis Laymen	Torah Talmud	Jerusalem	Rosh Hashanah Yom Kippur Hanukkah Purim Passover	Star of David Tablets of Law Menorah

MISSION AGENCIES cont.

theological education, TEE and medical work. Countries: Argentina, Asia-Mid East, Brazil, Cameroon, Cote d'Ivoire, Europe-Eastern, Ethiopia, France, India, Japan, Mexico, Philippines

Baptist International Missions, Inc. P.O. Box 9215, Chattanooga, TN 37412. 615-698-1523 (1960). *Ministry:* Radio/TV broadcasting, church planting, Christian education, evangelism, handicapped programs and armed services ministry. *Countries:* Active in 53 countries

Baptist Mid-Missions. P.O. Box 308011, Cleveland, OH 44130. 216-826-3930 (1920). *Ministry:* Evangelism, church planting, theological education, medical work and Bible translation. *Countries:* Argentina, Australia, Austria, Bangladesh, Brazil, Central Africa Rep, Chad, Cote d'Ivoire, Dominican Rep, Ecuador, Finland, France, Germany West, Ghana, Haiti, Honduras, Hong Kong, India, Ireland, Italy, Jamaica, Japan, Liberia, Mexico, Netherlands, New Zealand, Peru, Puerto Rico, Spain, St Lucia, St Vincent, Taiwan(ROC), United Kingdom, Venezuela

Baptist Missionary Association of America. 721 Main Street, Little Rock, AR 72201. 501-376-6788 (1950). *Ministry:* Planting churches, evangelism, Bible distribution and theological education. *Countries:* Australia, Bahamas, Bolivia, Brazil, Cape Verde Isls, Costa Rica, Honduras, India, Italy, Japan, South Korea, Mexico, Philippines, Taiwan (ROC), Uruguay

Baptist World Mission. P.O. Box 1463, Decatur, AL 35602. 205-353-2221 (1962). *Ministry:* Evangelism, church planting and Christian education. *Countries:* Argentina, Australia, Brazil, Colombia, Costa Rica, Dominican Rep, France, West Germany, Haiti, India, Israel, Italy, Japan, South Korea, Malaysia, Mexico, Papua New Guinea, Portugal, Puerto Rico, Singapore, South Africa, Spain, Thailand, United Kingdom, Uruguay

BCM International, Inc. 237 Fairfield Avenue, Upper Darby, PA 19028. 215-352-7177 (1936). *Ministry:* Camping programs, church planting, correspondence courses, evangelism, handicapped and youth ministry and literature production. *Countries:* Austria, Brazil, Cuba, France, West Germany, Ghana, Haiti, India, Ireland, Italy, Japan, Kenya, Mexico, Netherlands, Philippines, Spain, Sri Lanka, Suriname, Swaziland, Tanzania, United Kingdom, Zimbabwe

Berean Mission, Inc. 3536 Russell Blvd., St. Louis, MO 63104. 314-773-0110 (1937). *Ministry:* Church planting, theological education, TEE, evangelism, medical work and Bible translation. *Countries:* Barbados, Brazil, Dominica, Ecuador, Kenya, Liberia, Micronesia, New Zealand, Philippines, United Kingdom, Zaire

Bethany Fellowship Missions. 6820 Auto Club Rd., Minneapolis, MN 55438. 612-944-2121 (1945). *Ministry:* Church planting, evangelism, theological edcuation, literature distribution and missionary orientation. *Countries:* Brazil, Chile, Dominican Rep, France, West Germany, Indonesia, Japan, Mexico, Philippines, Puerto Rico, Singapore, Virgin Isls USA

Bible and Literacy League. 8955 Old LeMay Ferry Road, Hillsboro, MO 63050. 314-789-4368 (1973). *Ministry:* Childcare, church planting, Christian education, evangelism, support of national churches and support of national workers. *Countries:* Colombia, West Germany, Haiti, India, Kenya, Philippines, Tanzania, Uganda, Venezuela

Bible Christian Union, Inc. P.O. Box 410, Hatfield, PA 19440. 215-361-0500 (1904). *Ministry:* Church planting, radio/TV broadcasting, evangelism, missionary orientation and support of national churches. *Countries:* Austria, France, West Germany, Greece, Ireland, Italy, Netherlands, Portugal, Spain, Sweden, United Kingdom

The Bible League. 16801 Van Dam Road, South Holland, IL 60473. 708-331-2094 (1938). *Ministry:* Bible distribution, correspondence courses, evangelism, and literature distribution.

Bible Missionary Church, Foreign Missions Department. 4221 Richmond N.W., Grand Rapids, MI 49504. 616-453-8855 (1977). *Ministry:* Bible distribution, church planting, evangelism, literacy work, literature distribution and training. *Countries:* India

Biblical Ministries Worldwide. P.O. Box "L" 397, Langhorne, PA 19047. 215-752-1818 (1948). *Ministry:* Evangelism, church planting, correspondence courses, handicapped programs, literature production and armed services ministry. *Countries:* Antigua, Argentina, Australia, Austria, Belgium, Cyprus, West Germany, Guam, Honduras, Hong Kong, Ireland, Italy, Japan, Luxembourg, Mexico, Netherlands, New Zealand, Puerto Rico, Western Samoa, South Africa, Spain, United Kingdom, Uruguay

Billy Graham Evangelistic Association. P.O. Box 779, Minneapolis, MN 55440. 612-338-0500 (1950). *Ministry:* Evangelism, Christian education, radio/TV broadcasting, films and relief aid. *Countries:* France, West Germany, Hong Kong, Japan, United Kingdom

Brazil Gospel Fellowship Mission. P.O. Box 355, Springfield, IL 62702. 217-523-7176 (1939). *Ministry:* Radio broadcasting, church planting, correspondence courses, theological education and evangelism. *Countries:* Brazil

Bread for the World, Inc. 802 Rhode Island Avenue N.E., Washington, DC 20018. 202-269-0200 (1974). *Ministry:* Seeks to help shape U.S. public policies that affect hungry people, at home and overseas. Also provides educational resources on hunger.

Brethren Assemblies. P.O. Box 13, Spring Lake, NJ 07762. 201-449-8880 (1921). *Ministry:* Assists missionaries through funds transmission and other service agencies. *Countries:* Active in 51 countries

Calvary Commission, Inc. P.O. Box 100, Lindale, TX 75771. 214-882-5501 (1985). *Ministry:* Evangelism, church planting, Bible distribution, Christian education, literature distribution and support of national workers. *Countries:* Belize, West Germany, Mexico, Sweden, United Kingdom

Calvary Ministries International. P.O. Box 10305, Jacksonville, FL 32247. 904-398-6559 (1981). *Ministry:* Christian education, evangelism, funds transmission, missionary orientation, mobilization for mission and training. *Countries:* Bahamas, China (PRC), Costa Rica, Ecuador, France, Guatemala, Haiti, Israel, Jamaica, Kenya, Malawi, Netherlands, Nigeria, Philippines, Spain, Taiwan (ROC), United Kingdom

CAM International. 8625 La Prada Drive, Dallas, TX 75228. 214-327-8206 (1890). *Ministry:* Radio/TV broadcasting, church planting, theological education, evangelism and literature production/distribution. *Countries:* Costa Rica, El Salvador, Guatemala, Honduras, Mexico, Panama, Spain

Campus Crusade for Christ, International. Arrowhead Springs, San Bernardino, CA 92414. 714-886-5224 (1951). *Ministry:* Christian education, evangelism, support of national workers, training and small group dicipleship. *Countries:* Active in 95 countries

Child Evangelism Fellowship, Inc. P.O. Box 348, Warrenton, MO 63383. 314-456-4321 (1937). *Ministry:* Evangelism, camping programs, support of national workers, training and translation work. *Countries:* Active in 55 countries

China Ministries International. P.O. Box 40489, Pasadena, CA 91104. 818-398-0145 (1987). *Ministry:* Missionary and theological education, mission-related research and support of national workers. *Countries:* Hong Kong, Taiwan (ROC)

Chinese Christian Mission, Inc. P.O. Box 617, Petaluma, CA 94953. 707-762-1314 (1961). *Ministry:* Broadcasting, church planting, evangelism, literature distribution and production and training. *Countries:* Costa Rica, Hong Kong, Panama, Philippines, Singapore, Taiwan (ROC)

Chosen People Ministries, Inc. 1300 Cross Beam Drive, Charlotte, NC 28217. 704-523-

MISSION AGENCIES cont.

0523 (1894). *Ministry:* Church planting, evangelism, literature distribution, missionary orientation and video/film production. *Countries:* Argentina, France, Greece, Israel

Christ for India, Inc. P.O. Box 271086, Dallas, TX 75227. 214-388-7809 (1986). *Ministry:* Evangelism through support of national workers. *Countries:* India

Christian Aid Mission. Route 10, Box 1, Charlottesville, VA 22901. 804-977-5650 (1953). *Ministry:* Church planting, missionary education, funds transmission, mission-related research, serving other agencies and support of national workers. *Countries:* Active in 44 countries

Christian and Missionary Alliance. P.O. Box 35000, Colorado Springs, CO 80935. 719-599-5999 (1887). *Ministry:* Evangelism, church planting, radio/TV broadcasting, literature production/distribution, theological education and Bible translation. *Countries:* Active in 37 countries

Christian Blind Mission International (U.S.A.). P.O. Box 175, Wheaton, IL 60187. 708-690-0300 (1975). *Ministry:* Ministering to the blind through programs of medicine, community development, evangelism, literacy, education and other aid.

Christian Broadcasting Network. CBN Center, Virginia Beach, VA 23463. 804-424-7777 (1960). *Ministry:* Produces Christian programs for telecasting and radio broadcasting in the U.S. and parts of Asia, Europe, Middle East and Central America. *Countries:* Argentina, Chile, Colombia, Costa Rica, Cyprus, Dominican Rep, Ecuador, El Salvador, Guatemala, Israel, Lebanon, Panama, Peru, Philippines, Puerto Rico, Taiwan (ROC), Uruguay

Christian Catholic Church (Evangelical Protestant). Dowie Memorial Drive, Zion, IL 60099. 708-746-1411 (1896). *Ministry:* Church planting, evangelism, camping programs, literature production, support of national churches and youth ministry. *Countries:* Angola, Australia, Egypt, Guyana, Israel, Jamaica, Japan, Malawi, Philippines, South Africa, United Kingdom

Christian Church (Disciples of Christ). P.O. Box 1986, Indianapolis, IN 46206. 317-353-1491 (1920). *Ministry:* Church planting, support of national churches, agricultural assistance, community development, Christian education and medical work. *Countries:* Africa-General, Argentina, China (PRC), Cuba, Ecuador, Europe-General, Hong Kong, India, Indonesia, Jamaica, Japan, Kenya, South Korea, Lesotho, Mexico, Nepal, Nigeria, Paraguay, Philippines, Puerto Rico, Singapore, Swaziland, Taiwan (ROC), Thailand, Venezuela, Vietnam, Zaire, Zambia

Christian Church of North America Missions Department. P.O. Box 141-A, Transfer, PA 16154. 412-962-3501 (1927). *Ministry:* Radio/TV broadcasting, childcare, church planting, evangelism, literature distribution and support of national workers. *Countries:* Argentina, Australia, Barbados, Belgium, Chile, Colombia, France, West Germany, India, Italy, Luxembourg, Paraguay, Philippine, Switzerland, United Kingdom, Uruguay, Venezuela

Christian Churches/Churches of Christ. P.O. Box 2427, Knoxville, TN 37901. 615-577-9740 (1927). *Ministry:* Sends and supports missionaries directly from local congregations. *Countries:* Active in 74 countries

Christian Dynamics. 10878 N. 57th Avenue, Glendale, AZ 85304. 602-878-6892 (1976). *Ministry:* Agricultural assistance, childcare, church planting, literacy work, support of national workers and training. *Countries:* Bhutan, India, Nepal

Christian Literature Crusade, Inc. P.O. Box 1449, Fort Washington, PA 19034. 215-542-1242 (1941). *Ministry:* Literature production, Bible distribution and literature distribution. *Countries:* Colombia, France, West Germany, Hong Kong, Italy, Liberia, Philippines

Christian Medical Dental Society. P.O. Box 830689, Richardson, TX 75083. 214-783-8384

(1931). *Ministry:* Medical doctors, dentists and students serving in short-term medical projects in underdeveloped areas. *Countries:* Africa-General, Belize, Dominican Rep, Ecuador, Guatemala, Honduras, Jamaica, Mexico, Nicaragua, Philippines

Christian Missionary Fellowship (Indiana). P.O. Box 26306, Indianapolis, IN 46226. 317-542-9256 (1949). *Ministry:* Evangelism, church planting and medical work. *Countries:* Brazil, Ethiopia, Indonesia, Kenya, Mexico, Tanzania

Christian Reformed World Missions. 2850 Kalamazoo Avenue S.E., Grand Rapids, MI 49560. 616-246-0700 (1888). *Ministry:* Church planting, evangelism, theological education, TEE, literature distribution and extension education. *Countries:* Argentina, Bangladesh, Belize, Costa Rica, Dominican Rep, El Salvador, Guam, Guinea, Haiti, Honduras, Hong Kong, Japan, Kenya, Liberia, Mali, Mexico, New Zealand, Nigeria, Papua New Guinea, Philippines, Sierra Leona, Taiwan (ROC)

Christian Reformed World Relief Committee. 2850 Kalamazoo Avenue S.E., Grand Rapids, MI 49560. 616-241-1691 (1962). *Ministry:* Relief aid, agricultural assistance, literacy work, medical work and management consulting. *Countries:* Bangladesh, Belize, Costa Rica, Dominican Rep, Ecuador, El Salvador, Guatemala, Guinea, Haiti, Honduras, India, Indonesia, Kenyz, Liberia, Mali, Mexico, Nicaragua, Nigeria, Panama, Philippines, Sierra Leone, Sri Lanka, Uganda

Christians in Action, Inc. P.O. Box 728, Woodlake, CA 93286. 209-564-3762 (1958). *Ministry:* Church planting, evangelism, armed services ministry and misssionary orientation. *Countries:* Brazil, Ecuador, West Germany, Guatemala, Japan, Korea South, Macao, Mexico, Peru, Philippines, Sierra Leone, Switzerland, Taiwan (ROC), United Kingdom

Church of God (Anderson, Indiana) Missionary Board. P.O. Box 2498, Anderson, IN 46018. 317-642-0258 (1909). *Ministry:* Church planting, Christian education, evangelism, medical work, self-help projects and support of national workers. *Countries:* Bermuda, Bolivia, Brazil, Costa Rica, Egypt, Greece, Guam, Haiti, Hong Kong, Japan, Kenya, South Korea, Taiwan (ROC), Tanzania, Thailand, Uganda, Uruguay, Venezuela

Church of God in Christ, Mennonite General Mission. P.O. Box 230, Moundridge, KS 67107. 316-345-2533 (1933). *Ministry:* Evangelism, church planting, childcare programs, Christian education and medical work. *Countries:* Belize, Brazil, Dominican Rep, West Germany, Guatemala, Haiti, India, Mexico, Nigeria, Philippines

Church of God of Prophecy, World Mission Committee. P.O. Box 2910, Cleveland, TN 37320. 615-479-8511 (1903). *Ministry:* Evangelism, church planting, missionary orientation, training and orphanage work. *Countries:* Active in 74 countries

Church of God World Missions. P.O. Box 2430, Cleveland, TN 37320. 615-472-3361 (1910). *Ministry:* Church planting, church construction, Christian education and support of national churches. *Countries:* Active in 94 countries

Church of the Nazarene. 6401 The Paseo, Kansas City, MO 64131. 816-333-7000 (1900). *Ministry:* Church planting, theological education, medical work, support of national churches and self-help projects. *Countries:* Active in 83 countries

Church of the United Brethren in Christ. 302 Lake Street, Huntington, IN 46750. 219-356-2312 (1853). *Ministry:* Church planting, Christian education, theological education, medical work, support of national churches and workers. *Countries:* Honduras, Hong Kong, India, Jamaica, Macao, Mexico, Nicaragua, Sierra Leone

Churches of Christ. P.O. Box 814565, Dallas, TX 75381. (1961). *Ministry:* Sends and supports missionaries from local congregations. *Countries:* Active in 73 countries

Churches of Christ in Christian Union. P.O. Box 30, Circleville, OH 43113. 614-474-8856 (1909). *Ministry:* Church planting,

MISSION AGENCIES cont.

Christian education, theological education, furloughed missionary support, support of national churches and Bible translation. *Countries:* Antigua, Barbados, Bolivia, Dominica, Honduras, Kenya, Mexico, Papua New Guinea, Spain, Trinidad & Tobago

Churches of God General Conference, Commission on World Missions. P.O. Box 926, Findlay, OH 45839. 419-424-1961 (1898). *Ministry:* Church planting, community development, extension education, handicapped programs, medical work and support of national churches. *Countries:* Bangladesh, Haiti, India

Compassion International, Inc. P.O. Box 7000, Colorado Springs, CO 80933. 719-594-9900 (1952). *Ministry:* Childcare, community development, relief aid and self-help projects. *Countries:* Belize, Bolivia, Brazil, Burma, Burundi, Colombia, Dominican Rep, Ecuador, El Salvador, Fiji, Guatemala, Haiti, Honduras, Hong Kong, India, Indonesia, Jamaica, Kenya, South Korea, Malaysia, Mexico, Peru, Philippines, Rwanda, Singapore, Thailand, Tonga, Uganda, Zaire

Conservative Baptist Foreign Mission Society. P.O. Box 5, Wheaton, IL 60189. 708-665-1200 (1943). *Ministry:* Evangelism, church planting, theological education, TEE, medical work, literature production/distribution and Bible translation. *Countries:* Argentina, Austria, Brazil, Cote d'Ivoire, Europe-Western, France, West Germany, Hong Kong, India, Indonesia, Italy, Japan, Jordan, Kenya, Macao, Madagascar, Netherlands, Pakistan, Philippines, Portugal, Rwanda, Senegal, Singapore, Spain, Taiwan (ROC), Uganda, Venezuela, Zaire

Conservative Baptist Home Mission Society. P.O. Box 828, Wheaton, IL 60189. 708-653-4900 (1950). *Ministry:* Evangelism, church planting, church construction, TEE, armed services ministry and support of national churches. *Countries:* Belize, Dominican Rep, Guam, Honduras, Mexico, Puerto Rico

Conservative Mennonite Board of Missions and Charities. 9920 Rosedale Milford Center Road, Irwin, OH 43029. 614-857-1366 (1919). *Ministry:* Evangelism, church planting, relief aid, community development and medical work. *Countries:* Costa Rica, Ecuador, West Germany, Nicaragua

Dayspring International. 1062 Laskin Road, Suite 24A, Virginia Beach, VA 23451. 804-428-1092 (1979). *Ministry:* Evangelism, church planting, childcare programs, literacy work, support of national workers and video/film production. *Countries:* India

Derek Prince Ministries International. P.O. Box 300, Fort Lauderdale, FL 33302. 305-763-5202 (1963). *Ministry:* Audio recording/distribution, broadcasting, correspondence courses, literature distribution, translation work and video/film production

Eastern European Bible Mission. P.O. Box 110, Colorado Springs, CO 80901. 719-577-4450 (1972). *Ministry:* Bible distribution, camping programs, TEE, literature distribution, support of national churches and mission-related research. *Countries:* Bulgaria, Czechoslovakia, East Germany, Hungary, Poland, Romania, Soviet Union, Yugoslavia

Eastern Mennonite Board of Missions and Charities. P.O. Box 128, Salunga, PA 17538. 717-898-2251 (1914). *Ministry:* Evangelism, church planting, relief aid, community development, extension education and support of national churches. *Countries:* Australia, Belize, China (PRC), Dominican Rep, El Salvador, Ethiopia, France, West Germany, Guatemala, Haiti, Honduras, Hong Kong, Indonesia, Jamaica, Kenya, Luxembourg, Peru, Philippines, Somalia, Swaziland, Sweden, Tanzania, Venezuela, Virgin Islands U.S., Yugoslavia

Elim Fellowship. 7245 College Street, Lima, NY 14485. 716-582-2790 (1947). *Ministry:* Church planting, broadcasting, camping programs, TEE support of national churches and youth programs. *Countries:* Argentina, Brazil, Colombia, Costa Rica,

West Germany, Haiti, Hong Kong, Israel, Japan, Kenya, Malaysia, Mexico, Nigeria, Peru, South Africa, Spain, Tanzania, Uganda, United Kingdom, Zaire

EMC Missions (Evangelical Mennonite Church). 1420 Kerrway Court, Fort Wayne, IN 46805. 219-423-3649 (1943). *Ministry:* Evangelism, church planting, TEE, literature distribution, medical work and Bible translation. *Countries:* Asia-Southeast, Burkina Faso, Dominican Rep, West Germany, Indonesia, Japan, South Korea, Philippines, United Kingdom, Venezuela, Zaire, Zimbabwe

Episcopal Church, World Mission in Church and Society. 815 Second Avenue, New York, NY 10017. 212-867-8400 (1929). *Ministry:* Support of national churches, aid and relief, community development, medicine, training and support of national workers. *Countries:* Argentina, Brazil, China, Costa Rica, Dominican Rep, Ecuador, El Salvador, Guam, Guatemala, Haiti, Honduras, Israel, Japan, South Korea, Kenya, Lesotho, Malawi, Mexico, Namibia, Panama, Philippines, Puerto Rico, South Africa, Spain, Tanzania, Turks & Cai Iss, Uganda, United Kingdom, Vanuatu, Zaire, Zimbabwe

Evangelical Baptist Mission, Inc. P.O. Box 2225, Kokomo, IN 46904. 317-453-4488 (1928). *Ministry:* Evangelism, church planting, theological education, Bible translation and video/film production. *Countries:* Argentina, Australia, Benin, Cote d'Ivoire, France, French Guiana, West Germany, Italy, Japan, Mali, Martinique, Niger, Nigeria, South Africa, Sweden, United Kingdom

Evangelical Bible Mission, Inc. P.O. Drawer 189, Summerfield, FL 32691. 904-245-2560 (1939). *Ministry:* Church planting and construction, Christian education, literacy work, technical assistance and training. *Countries:* Belize, Dominican Rep, Ghana, Haiti, Nigeria, Papua New Guinea

Evangelical Congregational Church Division of Missions. P.O. Box 186, Myerstown, PA 17067. 717-866-7581 (1922). *Ministry:* Church planting, Christian education, support of national churches and workers, missionary education and Bible translation. *Countries:* India, Japan, Kenya, Liberia, Mexico

Evangelical Covenant Church. 5101 N. Francisco Avenue, Chicago, IL 60625. 312-784-3000 (1885). *Ministry:* Church planting, Christian education, TEE, medical work and support of national churches. *Countries:* Colombia, Ecuador, Japan, Mexico, Taiwan (ROC), Thailand, Zaire

Evangelical Free Church of America. 1515 E. 66th Street, Minneapolis, MN 55423. 612-866-3343 (1887). *Ministry:* Evangelism, church planting, extension education, theological education, TEE and medical work. *Countries:* Austria, Belgium, Brazil, France, West Germany, Hong Kong, Japan, Mexico, Peru, Philippines, Singapore, Venezuela, Zaire

Evangelical Friends Mission. P.O. Box 525, Arvada, CA 80001. 303-421-8100 (1978). *Ministry:* Evangelism, church planting, TEE, medical work, support of national churches and training. *Countries:* Bolivia, Burundi, Hong Kong, India, Mexico, Peru, Philippines, Rwanda, Taiwan (ROC)

Evangelical Lutheran Church in America. 8765 W. Higgins Road, Chicago, IL 60631. 312-380-2650 (1842). *Ministry:* Evangelism, church planting, theological education, human resource development, support of national churches and medical work. *Countries:* Active in 46 countries

Evangelism Explosion III International. P.O. Box 23820, Fort Lauderdale, FL 33307. 305-491-6100 (1970). *Ministry:* Training pastors and lay leaders to equip others for "lifestyle" evangelism. *Countries:* Australia, Belgium, Denmark, West Germany, Malawi, Netherlands, New Zealand, Norway, Portugal, South Africa, Spain, United Kingdom, Zambia, Zimbabwe

Evangelism Resources. P.O. Box 8263, Lexington, KY 40533. 603-858-3334 (1976). *Ministry:* Evangelism and training. *Countries:* Zaire

Every Home for Christ. P.O. Box 7139, Canoga Park, CA 91304. 818-341-7870 (1954). Ministry: Evangelism, correspondence

MISSION AGENCIES cont.

courses, literature production, literature distribution and support of national workers. *Countries:* Active in 43 countries

Faith Christian Fellowship International Church. P.O. Drawer 50370, Tulsa, OK 74150. 918-428-3861 (1978). *Ministry:* Evangelism, church planting, Christian education and funds transmission. *Countries:* Australia, Botswana, Costa Rica, Finland, West Germany, Guatemala, Hungary, India, Indonesia, Israel, Jamaica, Nigeria, Philippines, Poland, Sweden, United Kingdom, Zimbabwe

Far East Broadcasting Company, Inc. P.O. Box 1, La Mirada, CA 90637. 213-947-4651 (1945). *Ministry:* Radio broadcasting, correspondence courses and literature distribution. *Countries:* Burma, Hong Kong, Indonesia, Japan, South Korea, Neth Antilles, North Mariana Isls, Philippines, Singapore, Thailand

Fellowship of Evangelical Bible Churches. 5800 S. 14th Street, Omaha, NE 68107. 402-731-4780 (1936). *Ministry:* Church planting, Christian education, theological education, TEE, evangelism and medical work. *Countries:* Argentina, Bahamas, Belgium, Brazil, Colombia, Cuba, Ecuador, France, West Germany, Guadeloupe, India, Italy, Japan, Kenya, Latin Amer-Gen, Malawi, Mali, Mexico, Netherlands, Nigeria, Panama, Paraguay, Peru, Philippines, Taiwan (ROC), Togo, Uruguay, Zaire

Fellowship of Independent Missions. P.O. Box 72, Fairless Hills, PA 19030. 215-752-1170 (1950). *Ministry:* Evangelism, church planting, childcare programs, church construction, theological education and video/film production. *Countries:* Australia, Bahamas, Brazil, Ecuador, France, West Germany, Japan, Mexico, Morocco, Niger, Nigeria, Suriname, Sweden, United Kingdom, Uruguay, Venezuela

Food for the Hungry. P.O. Box E, Scottsdale, AZ 85252. 602-998-3100 (1971). *Ministry:* Relief aid, community development, human resource development and self-help projects. *Countries:* Bangladesh, Bolivia, Dominican Rep, Ethiopia, Guatemala, Haiti, Japan, Kenya, Mexico, Peru, Philippines, Switzerland, Thailand

Foundation for His Ministry. P.O. Box 9803, North Hollywood, CA 91609. 818-766-6923 (1967). *Ministry:* Relief aid, childcare, evangelism, medical work, support of national churches and training. *Countries:* United Kingdom, Kenya, Mexico

Foursquare Missions International. 1910 W. Sunset Blvd., Suite. 200, Los Angeles, CA 90026. 213-484-2400 (1923). *Ministry:* Church planting, theological education, literature production and training. *Countries:* Active in 57 countries

Free Gospel Church, Inc. P.O. Box 40159, Pasadena, CA 91104. 818-798-0807 (1982). *Ministry:* Evangelism and church planting with teams in the Muslim World

Free Methodist Church of North America. 901 College Avenue, Winona Lake, IN 46590. 219-267-7656 (1885). *Ministry:* Church planting, theological education, childcare programs, community development, Christian education and medical work. *Countries:* Brazil, Burundi, Chile, Dominican Rep, Ecuador, Egypt, Haiti, Hong Kong, India, Japan, Malawi, Mexico, Mozambique, Paraguay, Philippines, Puerto Rico, Rwanda, South Africa, Taiwan (ROC), Venezuela, Zaire, Zimbabwe

Frontiers. P.O. Box 40159, Pasadena, CA 91104. 818-798-0807 (1982). *Ministry:* Evangelism and church planting with teams in the Muslim World

Global Outreach Mission. P.O. Box 711, Buffalo, NY 14240. 716-842-2220 (1943). *Ministry:* Evangelism, church planting, relief aid, broadcasting, community development and support of national workers. *Countries:* Congo, Austria, Bangladesh, Bahamas, Brazil, Belgium, Guatemala, France, West Germany, Haiti, India, Ireland, Netherlands, Portugal, Spain, United Kingdom

Global Outreach, Ltd. P.O. Box 1, Tupelo, MS. 601-842-4615 (1970). *Ministry:* Community and human resource development, evangelism, medical work and self-help projects. *Countries:* Belize, Haiti, Honduras, India, Uganda

Globe Missionary Evangelism. P.O. Box 3138, Pensacola, FL 32516. 904-453-4318 (1973). *Ministry:* Evangelism, church planting, theological education, medical work and support of national churches. *Countries:* Austria, Cen Africa Rep, Costa Rica, Ecuador, France, West Germany, Greece, Guatemala, Haiti, Indonesia, Japan, Kenya, Mexico, Philippines, United Kingdom, Spain, Thailand

Go-Ye Fellowship. P.O. Box 26405, Los Angeles, CA 90026. 213-250-5347 (1944). *Ministry:* Church planting, broadcasting, correspondence courses, theological education, funds transmission and support of national churches. *Countries:* Argentina, Brazil, France, West Germany, Indonesia, Singapore, Taiwan (ROC), Thailand

Gospel for Asia, Inc. 1932 Walnut Plaza, Carrollton, TX 75006. 214-416-0340 (1979). *Ministry:* Evangelism, church planting, funds transmission, support of national churches and support of national workers in Asia.

Gospel Mission of South America, Inc. 1401 S.W. 21st Avenue, Ft. Lauderdale, FL 33312. 305-587-2975 (1923). *Ministry:* Evangelism, church planting, camping programs, correspondence courses, theological education and literature distribution. *Countries:* Argentina, Chile, Uruguay

Gospel Missionary Union. 10000 N. Oak, Kansas City, MO 64155. 816-734-8500 (1892). *Ministry:* Evangelism, church planting, Christian education, literature distribution, medical work and training. *Countries:* Argentina, Austria, Bahamas, Belgium, Belize, Bolivia, Brazil, Colombia, Ecuador, Europe-General, United Kingdom, France, West Germany, Greece, Italy, Mali, Mexico, Morocco, Panama, Spain

Grace Brethren Foreign Missions. P.O. Box 588, Winona Lake, IN 46590. 219-267-5164 (1900). *Ministry:* Evangelism, church planting, theological education, support of national churches and training. *Countries:* Argentina, Brazil, Cen Africa Rep, Chad, France, West Germany, Japan, Mexico, Philippines, Spain, United Kingdom

Grace Ministries International, Inc. P.O. Box 9405, Grand Rapids, MI 49509. 616-241-5666 (1939). *Ministry:* Church planting, theological education, literature production and medical supplies. *Countries:* Australia, Bolivia, Brazil, Neth Antilles, Puerto Rico, Philippines, Tanzania, Uruguay, India, Zaire

Greater Europe Mission. P.O. Box 668, Wheaton, IL 60189. 708-462-8050 (1949). *Ministry:* Evangelism, church planting, camping programs, theological education and TEE. *Countries:* Austria, Belgium, Eastern Europe, France, Greece, West Germany, Iceland, Ireland, Italy, Netherlands, Portugal, Spain, Sweden

Harvest Evangelism, Inc. P.O. Box 20310, San Jose, CA 95160. 408-248-5855 (1980). *Ministry:* Church planting, radio broadcasting, literature production, support of national churches and training. *Countries:* Argentina

Have Christ Will Travel Ministries, Inc. 528 E. Church Lane, Philadelphia, PA 19144. 215-438-6308 (1965). *Ministry:* Church planting, Bible distribution, broadcasting, camping programs, Christian education, mobilization for mission and training. *Countries:* Haiti, Liberia, Philippines

Helps International Ministries, Inc. P.O. Box 1209, Harlem, GA 30814. 404-556-3408 (1976). *Ministry:* Serves other agencies, church construction, computer services, financial accounting and other technical assistance. *Countries:* Kenya, Taiwan (ROC)

High Adventure Ministries, Inc. P.O. Box 7466, Van Nuys, CA 91409. 818-701-5133 (1972). *Ministry:* Radio broadcasting (short/medium wave) in 13 languages, evangelism, relief aid and literature distribution. *Countries:* Israel, Lebanon

MISSION AGENCIES cont.

Highland Christian Mission. P.O. Box 16528, Rochester, NY 14616. 716-227-0588 (1964). *Ministry:* Evangelism, church planting, Christian education, literacy work, technical assistance and youth programs. *Countries:* Papua New Guinea

Holt International Children's Services, Inc. P.O. Box 2880, Eugene, OR 97402. 503-687-2202 (1956). *Ministry:* Serves the needs of homeless children and families at risk through childcare programs, adoption, medical work, camping programs and self-help projects. *Countries:* Bolivia, Brazil, Costa Rica, Guatemala, India, South Korea, Philippines, Thailand

Holy Land Christian Mission. 2000 E. Red Bridge Road, Kansas City, MO 64131. 816-942-2000 (1936). *Ministry:* Childcare sponsorship, relief aid, community development, Christian education, medical work and self-help projects. *Countries:* Chile, Colombia, Dominican Rep, Gaza, Guatemala, Honduras, India, Israel, Philippines, Thailand, West Bank

Impact Ministries, Inc. P.O. Box 2500, Redmond, WA 98073. 206-882-0761 (1981). *Ministry:* Bible distribution, church construction, literature distribution, supplying equipment and support of national workers. *Countries:* Bulgaria, Czechoslovakia, East Germany, West Germany, Hungary, Poland, Romania, Soviet Union, Yugoslavia

Independent Board for Presbyterian Foreign Missions. 246 W. Walnut Lane, Philadelphia, PA 19144. 215-438-0511 (1933). *Ministry:* Evangelism, church planting, theological education, literature distribution and medical work. *Countries:* Australia, Brazil, Chile, Guatemala, Israel, Kenya, South Korea, Philippines, Taiwan (ROC), United Kingdom

Independent Faith Mission, Inc. P.O. Box 7791, Greensboro, NC 27407. 919-292-1255 (1950). *Ministry:* Serves local churches by servicing missionaries engaged in evangelism, church planting and theological education. *Countries:* Antigua, Italy, Kenya, Mexico, South Africa, Suriname, United Kingdom

India Evangelical Mission, Inc. P.O. Box 1633, Lakewood, CA 90716. 714-739-8068 (1966). *Ministry:* Evangelism, church planting, childcare programs, correspondence courses and literature distribution. *Countries:* India

India Gospel Outreach, Inc. P.O. Box 381, Alta Loma, CA 91701. 714-988-7165 (1984). *Ministry:* Church planting, theological education, medical work, church construction, support of national churches and missionary education. *Countries:* India

International Children's Care, Inc. P.O. Box 4406, Vancouver, WA 98662. 206-254-5061 (1978). *Ministry:* Childcare programs, Christian education and relief aid. *Countries:* Colombia, Costa Rica, Dominican Rep, Guatemala

International Christian Aid. 5189 Verdugo Way, Camarillo, CA 93010. 805-987-8888 (1960). *Ministry:* Relief aid, community development, literacy work, medical work, self-help projects and training

International Fellowship of Evangelical Students, USA. P.O. Box 7895, Madison, WI 53707. 608-274-9001 (1947). *Ministry:* Student evangelism, funds transmission, missions information service, mobilization for mission, serving other agencies and support of national workers. *Countries:* Africa-General, Austria, Belgium, Brazil, France, West Germany, India, Italy, Latin America-Central, Puerto Rico, Spain, Sri Lanka, Switzerland, United Kingdom

International Lutheran Laymen's League. 2185 Hampton Avenue, St. Louis, MO 63139. 314-647-4900 (1917). *Ministry:* Radio/TV broadcasting and correspondence courses. *Countries:* Argentina, Australia, Brazil, France, West Germany, Guatemala, Hong Kong, India, Indonesia, Japan, South Korea, Lebanon, New Zealand, Nigeria, Philippines, Portugal, South Africa, Taiwan (ROC), Venezuela

International Missions, Inc. P.O. Box 14866, Reading, PA 19612. 215-375-0300 (1930). *Ministry:* Evangelism, church planting and literature distribution. *Countries:* Hong Kong, India, Kenya, Pakistan, Philippines, Suriname, United Kingdom, Japan, Australia

International Pentecostal Church of Christ, Global Missions Department. P.O. Box 18145, Atlanta, GA 30316. 404-627-2681 (1917). *Ministry:* Church planting, Christian education, childcare, Bible distribution, literature distribution and providing medical supplies. *Countries:* India, Kenya, Mexico, United Kingdom

International Students, Inc. P.O. Box C, Colorado Springs, CO 80901. 719-576-2700 (1953). *Ministry:* Student evangelism, church planting, training and ministry among international student and trainees in the USA. *Countries:* Austria, France, Honduras, India, Japan, Jordan, Philippines, Portugal, Singapore, Sweden, Uganda, United Kingdom

International Teams. P.O. Box 203, Prospect Heights, IL 60070. 708-870-3800 (1960). *Ministry:* Evangelism, church planting, community development, literature distribution, missionary orientation and mobilization for mission. *Countries:* Austria, Europe-General, France, Italy, Philippines, United Kingdom

Interserve / USA (International Service Fellowship). P.O. Box 418, Upper Darby, PA 19082. 215-352-0581 (1964). *Ministry:* Extension education, medical work, theological education, agricultural assistance, technical assistance and serving other agencies. *Countries:* Asia-Mid East, Bangladesh, Bhutan, Egypt, India, Nepal, Pakistan

Japan-North American Commission on Cooperative Mission. 475 Riverside Drive, Room 618, New York, NY 10115. 212-870-2021 (1947). *Ministry:* Human resource development, Christian education, evangelism, support of national churches and serving other agencies. *Countries:* Japan

Jews for Jesus. 60 Haight Street, San Francisco, CA 94102. 415-864-2600 (1973). *Ministry:* Evangelism, literature production, literature distribution and missionary orientation. *Countries:* Argentina, Israel, United Kingdom

Korea International Mission, Inc. P.O. Box 40288, Pasadena, CA 91104. 818-797-1260 (1968). *Ministry:* Evangelism, church planting, Christian education, theological education, missionary orientation and video/film production. *Countries:* Hong Kong, Indonesia, South Korea, Philippines, Thailand

Larry Jones International Ministries, Inc. P.O. Box 36, Oklahoma City, OK 73101. 405-942-0228 (1964). *Ministry:* Relief aid, agricultural assistance, childcare programs, evangelism and medical work. *Countries:* Bangladesh, Belize, Chad, Costa Rica, Dominican Rep, El Salvador, Ethiopia, Ghana, Guatemala, Haiti, Honduras, Jamaica, Kenya, Mexico, Mozambique, Nigeria, Panama, Philippines, Poland, Sierra Leone, Sri Lanka, Thailand, Uganda

Latin America Mission, Inc. P.O. Box 52-7900, Miami, FL 33152. 305-884-8400 (1921). *Ministry:* Evangelism, church planting, camping programs, childcare programs, Christian education and theological education. *Countries:* Argentina, Brazil, Colombia, Costa Rica, Ecuador, Honduras, Mexico, Panama, Peru

Liberty Baptist Mission. P.O. Box 20000, Lynchburg, VA 24506. 804-239-2036 (1978). *Ministry:* Evangelism, church planting, community development, Christian education and theological education. *Countries:* Australia, France, West Germany, Kenya, South Korea, Mexico, Philippines, Trinidad & Tobago

Liebenzell Mission of U.S.A., Inc. P.O. Box 66, Schooley's Mountain, NJ 07870. 201-852-6012 (1941). *Ministry:* Evangelism, theological education, TEE, support of national churches, camping programs and youth programs. *Countries:* Guam, Japan, Micronesia, Papua New Guinea

MISSION AGENCIES cont.

Life Ministries. P.O. Box 200, San Dimas, CA 91773. 714-599-8491 (1965). *Ministry:* Evangelism, support of national churches and training. Teaches conversational English to Japanese students. *Countries:* Japan

Living Bibles International. 351 Main Place, Carol Stream, IL 60188. 708-369-0100 (1968). *Ministry:* Bible distribution, broadcasting, literature production and Bible translation. *Countries:* Botswana, Brazil, Burma, Denmark, Egypt, Ethiopia, Finland, France, West Germany, Ghana, Greece, Hong Kong, India, Indonesia, Italy, Kenya, Malawi, Malaysia, Mexico, Nepal, Netherlands, Nigeria, Norway, Philippines, Portugal, Sri Lanka, Sweden, Taiwan (ROC), Thailand, Uganda, United Kingdom, Yugoslavia, Zaire, Zambia, Zimbabwe

Living Water Teaching International. P.O. Box 3040, Broken Arrow, OK 74012. 918-455-8070 (1979). *Ministry:* Evangelism, correspondence courses, theological education, TEE, missionary orientation and youth programs. *Countries:* Australia, Colombia, El Salvador, Guatemala, Liberia, Nicaragua, Panama

Logo, Inc. 4100 W. Flagler, Suite B-3, Miami, FL 33134. 305-446-8297 (1965). *Ministry:* Church planting, TEE, literature production and distribution, supprt of national workers and video/film production. *Countries:* Argentina, Belize, Chile, Colombia, Ecuador, El Salvador, Guatemala, Honduras, Mexico, Paraguay, Uruguay

Luis Palau Evangelistic Association. P.O. Box 1173, Portland, OR 97207. 503-643-0777 (1978). *Ministry:* Evangelism, broadcasting, literature distribution and training. *Countries:* Argentina, Australia, Finland, Guatemala, Mexico, United Kingdom

Luke Society. P.O. Box 871, Vicksburg, MS 39180. 601-638-1629 (1964). *Ministry:* Evangelism, church planting, community development, medical work and support of national workers. *Countries:* Dominican Rep, Ecuador, Ghana, Honduras, India, Mexico, Peru, Philippines, Uganda

Lutheran Bible Translators, Inc. P.O. Box 2050, Aurora, IL 60507. 708-897-0660 (1964). *Ministry:* Bible translation, linguistics, literacy and literature production. *Countries:* Cameroon, Ecuador, Liberia, Papua New Guinea, Sierra Leone

Lutheran Brethren World Missions. P.O. Box 655, Fergus Falls, MN 56537. 218-739-3336 (1901). *Ministry:* Medical work, church planting, theological education, literature production and distribution, Bible translation and agricultural assistance. *Countries:* Cameroon, Chad, Japan, Taiwan (ROC)

Lutheran Church—Missouri Synod. 360 Park Avenue South, New York, NY 10010. 212-532-6350 (1945). Ministry: Relief aid, human resource development, providing medical supplies, medical work, self-help projects and technical assistance. Countries: Active in 45 countries

Maranatha Baptist Mission, Inc. P.O. Drawer 1425, Natchez, MS 39121. 601-442-0141 (1961). *Ministry:* Funds transmission and information service for missionaries. *Countries:* Antigua, Argentina, Australia, Austria, Bolivia, Brazil, Chile, Colombia, France, West Germany, Grenada, Haiti, Israel, Japan, Mexico, Norway, Papua New Guinea, Peru, Puerto Rico, Spain, United Kingdom, Venezuela

Maranatha Campus Ministries. P.O. Box 1799, Gainesville, FL 32602. 904-375-6000 (1975). *Ministry:* Evangelism, church planting, training and youth programs. *Countries:* Australia, Brazil, France, West Germany, Guatemala, Honduras, Indonesia, Ireland, Jamaica, Japan, South Korea, Mexico, New Zealand, Panama, Philippines, South Africa, Venezuela

Maranatha South Africa. 855 S. Newcombe Way, Denver, CO 80226. 303-980-9888 (1986). *Ministry:* Evangelism, church planting and construction, agricultural assistance, missionary education and support of national workers. *Countries:* South Africa

Medical Ambassadors International. P.O. Box 6645, Modesto, CA 95355. 209-524-

0600 (1973). *Ministry:* Medical work, evangelism, church planting, Bible distribution, human resource development and support of national workers. *Countries:* China (PRC), Dominican Rep, El Salvador, Guatemala, Haiti, Hong Kong, Honduras, India, Kenya, South Korea, Nepal, Nicaragua, Philippines, Tanzania, Zaire

Mennonite Board of Missions. P.O. Box 370, Elkhart, IN 46515. 219-294-7523 (1906). *Ministry:* Evangelism, church planting, theological education, literature production and support of national churches. *Countries:* Argentina, Belgium, Benin, Bolivia, Brazil, China(PRC), Cote d'Ivoire, France, Ghana, India, Ireland, Isarel, Japan, Nepal, Peru, Spain, Suriname, Sweden, United Kingdom, Uruguay, Zaire

Mennonite Brethren Missions/Services. 315 S. Lincoln, Hillsboro, KS 67063. 316-947-3151 (1878). *Ministry:* Church planting, agricultural assistance, community development, theological education and providing medical supplies. *Countries:* Afghanistan, Angola, Austria, Botswana, Brazil, Colombia, Ecuador, West Germany, India, Indonesia, Japan, Mexico, Nepal, Nigeria, Pakistan, Panama, Paraguay, Peru, Portugal, Spain, Uruguay, Zaire

Mennonite Central Committee. P.O. Box M, Akron, PA 17501. 717-859-1151 (1920). *Ministry:* Agricultural assistance, relief aid, community development, human resource development and self-help projects. *Countries:* Active in 51 countries

Mennonite Economic Development Associates. P.O. Box M, Akron, PA 17501. 717-738-3715 (1953). *Ministry:* Programs of economic development in less-developed areas of the world. *Countries:* Bolivia, Haiti, Jamaica, Paraguay, Tanzania, Uruguay

Mexican Mission Ministries, Inc. P.O. Box 636, Pharr, TX 78577. 512-787-3543 (1954). *Ministry:* Church planting, correspondence courses, theological education, TEE, literature distribution and youth programs. *Countries:* Mexico

Middle East Media. P.O. Box 359, Lynnwood, WA 98046. 206-778-0752 (1976). *Ministry:* Broadcasting, correspondence courses, literature production and distribution, evangelism and video/film production. *Countries:* Egypt

Ministries in Action, Inc. P.O. Box 140325, Coral Gables, FL 33114. 305-642-3113 (1961). *Ministry:* Evangelism, community development, extension education, support of national churches and training. *Countries:* Grenada, Haiti, Jamaica, St Lucia, St Vincent

Mission Aviation Fellowship (MAF). P.O. Box 3202, Redlands, CA 92373. 714-794-1151 (1945). *Ministry:* Aviation, community development, providing medical supplies, technical assistance, support of national workers and serving other agencies. *Countries:* Australia, Bangladesh, Botswana, Brazil, Ecuador, Ethiopia, Guatemala, Haiti, Honduras, Indonesia, Kenya, Lat A-Caribbean, Lesotho, Mali, Mexico, Suriname, Venezuela, Zaire, Zimbabwe

Mission Mailbag, Inc. P.O. Box 15237, Del City, OK 73155. 405-672-4989 (1962). *Ministry:* Broadcasting, evangelism, funds transmission and serving other agencies.

Mission Possible, Inc. P.O. Box 1596, Ft. Pierce, FL 34954. 305-465-0373 (1978). *Ministry:* Evangelism, relief aid, Christian education, medical work, missionary orientation and serving other agencies. *Countries:* Bahamas, Dominican Rep, Haiti, Honduras, Jamaica

Mission Society for United Methodists, The. P.O. Box 1103, Decatur, GA 30031. 404-378-8746 (1984). *Ministry:* Evangelism, church planting, training, support of national churches, medical work and education and agricultural assistance. *Countries:* Costa Rica, Ghana, Guatemala, Hong Kong, Indonesia, Philippines, Solomon Islands, Spain

Mission to Unreached Peoples. P.O. Box 66400, Seattle, WA 98116. 206-824-7550 (1981). *Ministry:* Evangelism, church planting, community development, missionary

MISSION AGENCIES cont.

orientation and mobilization for mission. *Countries:* Hong Kong, India, Indonesia, Nepal, Pakistan, Philippines, Taiwan (ROC), Thailand

Missionary Church—World Partners. 3901 S. Wayne Avenue, Fort Wayne, IN 46807. 219-456-4502 (1969). *Ministry:* Evangelism, church planting, theological education, TEE, medical work and support of national workers. *Countries:* Brazil, Dominican Rep, Ecuador, France, Haiti, India, Jamaica, Mexico, Nigeria, Sierra Leone, Spain

Missionary Revival Crusade. 102 E. Lyon Street, Laredo, TX 78040. 512-722-2646 (1959). *Ministry:* Broadcasting, church planting, correspondence courses, evangelism and literature distribution. *Countries:* Colombia, France, Guatemala, West Germany, Mexico, Spain, Sri Lanka, Yugoslavia

Moravian Church in North America, Board of World Missions. P.O. Box 1245, Bethlehem, PA 18016. 215-868-1732 (1949). *Ministry:* Support of national churches and workers, theological education, Bible translation, medical work and missions information services. *Countries:* Dominican Rep, Guyana, Honduras, Nicaragua, Tanzania, Virgin Islands USA

National Association of Free Will Baptists. P.O. Box 1088, Nashville, TN 37202. 615-361-1010 (1935). *Ministry:* Church planting, theological education, linguistics, literature production/distribution and medical work. *Countries:* Brazil, France, India, Cote d'Ivoire, Japan, Panama, Spain, Uruguay

National Council of the Churches of Christ in the U.S.A. 475 Riverside Drive, New York, NY 10115. 212-870-2257 (1946). *Ministry:* Agricultural and relief aid, community and human resource development, funds transmission, purchasing services, support of national churches and workers, mobilization for missions, self-help projects and technical assistance. *Countries:* Active in 57 countries

Navigators. P.O. Box 6000, Colorado Springs, CO 80934. 719-589-1212 (1933). *Ministry:* Evangelism, training and discipleship. *Countries:* Active in 41 countries

New England and World Missions. P.O. Box 1126, Worcester, MA 01613 (1983). *Ministry:* Evangelism, church planting, childcare programs, Christian education, medical work and self-help projects. *Countries:* Haiti

New Life League. P.O. Box 7623, Waco, TX 76714. (1954). *Ministry:* Church planting, broadcasting, childcare programs, theological education, literature production, medical work and support of national workers. *Countries:* Brazil, Costa Rica, Guatemala, Haiti, Hong Kong, India, Japan, Mexico, Nepal, Papua New Guinea, Sri Lanka, Norway, Thailand, United Kingdom

New Tribes Mission. 1000 E. First Street, Sanford, FL 32771. 407-323-3430 (1942). *Ministry:* Evangelism, church planting, Bible translation, linguistics, literacy work, missionary orientation and aviation. *Countries:* Australia, Bolivia, Brazil, Colombia, Cote d'Ivoire, Greenland, Guinea, Guinea-Bissau, India, Indonesia, Japan, South Korea, Liberia, Mexico, Panama, Papua New Guinea, Paraguay, Philippines, Senegal, Thailand, United Kingdom, Venezuela

North American Baptist Conference. 1 South 210 Summit Avenue, Oakbrook Terrace, IL 60181 (1883). *Ministry:* Church planting, theological education, relief aid, medical work and support of national churches. *Countries:* Brazil, Cameroon, Japan, Nigeria, Philippines

O.C. Ministries, Inc. 25 Corning Avenue, Milpitas, CA 95035. 408-263-1101 (1951). *Ministry:* Evangelism, church planting, support of national churches, mission-related research and training. *Countries:* Argentina, Brazil, Colombia, France, West Germany, Greece, Guatemala, India, Indonesia, Japan, Kenya, Mexico, Philippines, Singapore, Swaziland, Taiwan (ROC)

OMS International, Inc. P.O. Box A, Greenwood, IN 46142. 317-881-6751 (1901). *Min-*

istry: Evangelism, church planting, broadcasting, theological education, literature distribution and training. *Countries:* Brazil, Colombia, Ecuador, France, Greece, Haiti, Hong Kong, India, Indonesia, Japan, South Korea, Philippines, Spain, Taiwan (ROC)

Open Air Campaigners, U.S., Inc. P.O. Box 2440, Plainfield, NJ 07060. 201-757-8427 (1956). *Ministry:* Evangelism, literature distribution and training. *Countries:* Argentina, West Germany, India, Italy, Jamaica

Open Bible Standard Missions, Inc. 2020 Bell Avenue, Des Moines, IA 50315. 515-288-6761 (1935). *Ministry:* Evangelism, church planting, theological education, TEE, literature distribution and self-help projects. *Countries:* Argentina, Brazil, Chile, Cuba, Dominican Rep, El Salvador, Ghana, Grenada, Guatemala, Guinea, Jamaica, Japan, Kenya, Liberia, Mexico, Papua New Guinea, Peru, Philippines, Puerto Rico, Trinidad & Tobago, Uganda, Uruguay, Paraguay, Spain, St Vincent

Open Doors with Brother Andrew. P.O. Box 27001, Santa Ana, CA 92799. 714-531-6000 (1955). *Ministry:* Bible distribution in limited access or closed countries. *Countries:* Australia, Brazil, Europe-General, Hong Kong, Kenya, New Zealand, Netherlands, Philippines, Singapore

Operation Mobilization—U.S.A. P.O. Box 2277, Peachtree City, GA 30269. 404-631-0432 (1957). *Ministry:* Evangelism, church planting, literature distribution, missionary orientation and support of national workers. *Countries:* Argentina, Asia-Mid East, Austria, Bangladesh, Belgium, Brazil, Finland, France, West Germany, India, Ireland, Israel, Italy, Mexico, Nepal, Netherlands, Pakistan, Singapore, Spain, Sweden, Turkey, United Kingdom

Orthodox Presbyterian Church. 7401 Old York Road, Philadelphia, PA 19126. 215-635-0700 (1937). *Ministry:* Evangelism, church planting, theological education, literature distribution and support of national churches. *Countries:* Cyprus, Japan, Kenya, South Korea, Philippines, Suriname, Taiwan (ROC)

Overseas Christian Servicemen's Centers. P.O. Box 1268, Englewood, CO 80150. 303-762-1400 (1954). *Ministry:* Evangelism, literature distribution, armed forces ministry. *Countries:* West Germany, Italy, Japan, South Korea, Panama, Philippines, Spain, United Kingdom

Overseas Missionary Fellowship U.S.A. 404 South Church Street, Robesonia, PA 19551. 215-693-5881 (1865). *Ministry:* Evangelism, church planting, theological education, Christian education, support of national churches and training. *Countries:* Hong Kong, Indonesia, Japan, South Korea, Malaysia, Philippines, Singapore, Taiwan (ROC), Thailand

Partners International. P.O. Box 15025, San Jose, CA 95115. 408-298-0965 (1943). *Ministry:* Support of national workers involved in evangelism, church planting and theological education. *Countries:* Active in 37 countries

Pentecostal Church of God. P.O. Box 2248, Joplin, NO 64803. 417-624-7050 (1919). *Ministry:* Church planting, Bible distribution, agricultural assistance, relief aid, church construction, literature distribution and furloughed missionary support. *Countries:* Antigua, Belize, Brazil, Cote d'Ivoire, Cuba, Ghana, Guatemala, Haiti, Honduras, Hong Kong, India, Indonesia, Jamaica, Japan, Macao, Malawi, Mexico, Philippines, Portugal, Tanzania, Trinidad & Tobago, United Kingdom, Zaire, Zambia

Pentecostal Holiness Church. P.O. Box 12609, Oklahoma City, OK 73157. 405-787-7110 (1904). *Ministry:* Evangelism, church planting, TEE, missionary orientation, support of national churches and mobilization for mission. *Countries:* Argentina, Botswana, Chile, Costa Rica, France, West Germany, Haiti, Hong Kong, India, Israel, Italy, Jamaica, Kenya, Malawi, Mexico, Nigeria, Philippines, Singapore, South Africa, Spain, United Kingdom, Venezuela, Zambia, Zimbabwe

Pioneer Bible Translators. P.O. Box 381030, Duncanville, TX 75138. 214-296-4843

MISSION AGENCIES cont.

(1974). *Ministry:* Bible translation, linguistics, training, literacy work and support of national churches. *Countries:* Liberia, Papua New Guinea, Zaire

Pioneers. P.O. Box 527, Sterling, VA 22170. 703-478-0004 (1979). *Ministry:* Evangelism, church planting, linguistics, literacy work, support of national workers and Bible translation. *Countries:* China (PRC), France, Guyana, Indonesia, Japan, Kenya, Mongolia, Nepal, North Mariana I, Papua New Guinea, South Africa, Thailand

Pocket Testament League, Inc., The. P.O. Box 800, Lititz, PA 17543 (1908). *Ministry:* Scripture distribution, evangelism and discipleship. *Countries:* Austria, Belgium, Brazil, Czechoslovakia, France, West Germany, India, Indonesia, Italy, South Korea, Mexico, Philippines, Portugal, Spain, Taiwan (ROC), United Kingdom, Yugoslavia

Prakash Association, U.S.A. 99 Airport Blvd., Freedom, CA 95019. 408-722-2244 (1969). *Ministry:* Self-help projects, support of nationals and training. *Countries:* India

Presbyterian Church (U.S.A.). 100 Witherspoon Street, Louisville, KY 40202. 502-569-5000 (1837). *Ministry:* Relief aid, church planting, theological education, evangelism, support of national churches and workers. *Countries:* Active in 45 countries

Presbyterian Church in America Mission to the World. P.O. Box 29765, Atlanta, GA 30359. 404-320-3373 (1973). *Ministry:* Church planting, theological education, Bible translation, aviation, medical work and technical assistance. *Countries:* Active in 39 countries

PRM International. 760 Waverly Road, Holland, MI 49423. 616-396-5291 (1967). *Ministry:* Audio recording/distribution, cassette Bible distribution and evangelism, supplying equipment, technical assistance and training. *Countries:* Bangladesh, India, Kenya, Singapore, Sudan

RBMU International. 8102 Elberon Avenue, Philadelphia, PA 19111. 215-745-0680 (1948). *Ministry:* Evangelism, church planting, theological education, TEE and Bible translation. *Countries:* Cameroon, Chile, Indonesia, Peru, Philippines

R.E.A.P. (Reinforcing Evangelists and Aiding Pastors). P.O. Box 488, La Mirada, CA 90637. 213-802-2159 (1951). *Ministry:* Evangelism, church planting, literature production and support of national workers. *Countries:* Indonesia, Japan

Reformed Church in America. 475 Riverside Drive, New York, NY 10115. 212-870-2265 (1857). *Ministry:* Church planting, Christian education, agricultural assistance, medical work and serving other agencies. Countries: Bahrain, Egypt, Ethiopia, Honduras, India, Indonesia, Japan, Kenya, Kuwait, Mexico, Oman, Pakistan, Philippines, Singapore, Sudan, Taiwan (ROC) Zambia

Rio Grande Bible Institute, Inc. 4300 South Busines #281, Edinburg, TX 78539 (1946). *Ministry:* Theological education, broadcasting and training. *Countries:* Mexico

Salvation Army, U.S.A. 799 Bloomfield Avenue, Verona, NJ 07044. 201-239-0606 (1865). *Ministry:* Evangelism, literature distribution and production, medical work and support of national workers. *Countries:* Argentina, Bahamas, Brazil, Chile, Colombia, Congo, Costa Rica, West Germany, Guatemala, Guyana, Hong Kong, India, Indonesia, Jamaica, Japan, Kenya, South Korea, Mexico, Philippines, Singapore, South Africa, Spain, Sri Lanka, Suriname, Taiwan (ROC), Tanzania, Uganda, Uruguay, Venezuela, Zaire, Zambia, Zimbabwe

Samaritan's Purse. P.O. Box 3000, Boone, NC 28607. 704-262-1980 (1970). *Ministry:* Relief aid, evangelism and support of national workers.

Send International. P.O. Box 513, Farmington, MI 48332. 313-477-4210 (1947). *Ministry:* Evangelism, church planting, theological education, TEE, camping programs and support of national churches.

Countries: Hong Kong, Japan, Philippines, Spain, Taiwan (ROC)

Seventh Day Adventists. 6840 Eastern Avenue N.W., Washington, DC 20012. 202-722-6600 (1863). *Ministry:* Evangelism, church planting, mobilization for mission, missionary orientation, medical work, theological education, literature production and Christian education. *Countries:* Active in 67 countries

Shield of Faith Mission International. P.O. Box 144, Bend, OR 97709. 503-382-7081 (1953). *Ministry:* Evangelism, church planting, mssionary orientation and education, serving other agencies and training. *Countries:* Australia, Brazil, Mexico, Nigeria, Pakistan

Siloam International. P.O. Box 41910, Los Angeles, CA 90041. 213-255-2413 (1981). *Ministry:* Relief aid, community development, childcare projects, church planting, self-help projects and providing medical supplies. *Countries:* Haiti, India, Kenya, Peru

SIM International. P.O. Box 7900, Charlotte, NC 28241. 704-588-6100 (1893). *Ministry:* Church planting, community development, broadcasting, theological education, medical work and support of national workers. *Countries:* Benin, Bolivia, Burkina Faso, Cen Africa Rep, Cote d'Ivoire, Ethiopia, Ghana, Guinea, Haiti, Italy, Kenya, Liberia, Niger, Nigeria, Peru, Sudan

Slavic Gospel Association, Inc. P.O. Box 1122, Wheaton, IL 60189. 708-690-8900 (1934). *Ministry:* Radio broadcasting, literature production, Bible distribution, TEE and evangelism with a focus on Slavic peoples. *Countries:* Argentina, Ecuador, France, West Germany, Italy, Monaco, Soviet Union, Spain

Son Shine Ministries International, Inc. P.O. Box 456, Azle, TX 76020. 817-444-3777 (1977). *Ministry:* Evangelism, correspondence courses, missionary training and armed forces ministry. *Countries:* Australia, West Germany, Guam, United Kingdom

Source of Light Ministries International, Inc. 1011 Mission Road, Madison, GA 30650. 404-342-0397 (1953). *Ministry:* Church planting, correspondence courses, literature translation, production and distribution. *Countries:* Brazil, Chile, Guyana, India, Jamaica, South Korea, Liberia, Mexico, Peru, Philippines

South America Mission, Inc. P.O. Box 6560, Lake Worth, FL 33466. 305-965-1833 (1914). *Ministry:* Evangelism, church planting, theological education, TEE, aviation, programs for the handicapped. *Countries:* Bolivia, Brazil, Colombia, Peru

South American Missionary Society of the Episcopal Church. P.O. Box, 99 Ambridge, PA 15003. 412-266-0669 (1976). *Ministry:* Evangelism, church planting, Christian education, missionary education, theological education and medical work. *Countries:* Chile, Colombia, Costa Rica, Dominican Rep, Honduras, Peru

Southern Baptist Convention. P.O. Box 6767, Richmond, VA 23230. 804-353-0151 (1845). *Ministry:* Evangelism, church planting, relief aid, radio/TV broadcasting, theological education, literature production/ distribution. *Countries:* Active in 113 countries

Team Expansion, Inc. P.O. Box 4100, Cincinnati, OH 45204. 513-244-81 49 (1978). *Ministry:* Evangelism, church planting, missionary orientation, mobilization for mission, mission-related research and training. *Countries:* Argentina, Ireland, Senegal, Uruguay, Venezuela

Tele-Missions International, Inc. P.O. Box 563, Valley Cottage, NY 10989. 914-268-9222 (1954). *Ministry:* Broadcasting, evangelism and literature distribution. *Countries:* Africa-General, Ecuador, Kenya, Sierra Leone, Zaire

The Evangelical Alliance Mission (TEAM). P.O. Box 969, Wheaton, IL 60189. 708-653-5300 (1890). *Ministry:* Evangelism, church planting, linguistics, medical work, broadcasting. *Countries:* Austria, Brazil, Chad, Colombia, France, Hong Kong,

MISSION AGENCIES cont.

India, Indonesia, Italy, Japan, South Korea, Mexico, Mozambique, Nepal, Neth Antilles, Pakistan, Peru, Philippines, Portugal, South Africa, Spain, Sri Lanka, Taiwan (ROC), Trinidad & Tobago, Turkey, United Arab Emr, Venezuela, Zimbabwe

Things to Come Mission, Inc. P.O. Box 96, Cope, CO 80812. 303-357-4291 (1955). *Ministry:* Evangelism, church planting, broadcasting, theological education, literature production and support of national workers. *Countries:* Brazil, India, Indonesia, Kenya, Nigeria, Philippines, United Kingdom

Trans World Missions. P.O. Box 10, Glendale, CA 91209. 213-663-1176 (1949). *Ministry:* Evangelism, church planting, radio broadcasting, childcare programs, mobilization for mission and support of national workers. *Countries:* Brazil, Costa Rica, Guatemala, Mexico, Nicaragua

Trans World Radio. P.O. Box 98, Chatham, NJ 07928. 201-966-2700 (1952). *Ministry:* Medium and shortwave radio broadcasting from overseas facilities in over 70 languages, correspondence courses. *Countries:* Cyprus, Dominican Rep, Guam, Hong Kong, India, Malawi, Monaco, Netherlands, Neth Antilles, South Africa, Spain, Sri Lanka, Swaziland, United Kingdom, Uruguay, Venezuela

UFM Interntional. P.O. Box 306, Bala-Cynwyd, PA 19004. 215-667-7660 (1931). *Ministry:* Evangelism, church planting, theological education, TEE, literature production and distribution, medical work and Bible translation. *Countries:* Austria, Brazil, Dominican Rep, France, West Germany, Guyana, Haiti, Indonesia, Ireland, Italy, Mexico, Philippines, Puerto Rico, South Africa, Sweden

UIM International (United Indian Missions). P.O. Box 13614, Tucson, AZ 85732. 602-774-0651 (1956). *Ministry:* Evangelism, church planting, camping programs, aviation support, literature production and youth programs. *Countries:* Mexico

United Church Board for World Ministries. 475 Riverside Drive, New York, NY 10115. 212-870-2637 (1810). *Ministry:* Nurture of national churches and leaders, relief aid, community development, Christian education, theological education and medical work. *Countries:* Active in 58 countries

United Methodist Church. 475 Riverside Drive, 15th Floor, New York, NY 10115. 212-870-3720 (1940). *Ministry:* Evangelism, church planting, Christian education, theological education, support of national churches and training. *Countries:* Active in 66 countries

United Pentecostal Church International. 8855 Dunn Road, Hazelwood, MO. 314-837-7300 (1924). *Ministry:* Evangelism, church planting, relief aid, Bible distribution, theological education and training. *Countries:* Active in 64 countries

United States Center for World Mission. 1605 Elizabeth Street, Pasadena, CA 91104. 818-797-1111 (1976). *Ministry:* Missionary orientation and education, mission information services, mobilization for mission, mission-related research and serving other agencies

United World Mission. P.O. Box 250, Union Mills, NC 28167. 704-287-8996 (1946). *Ministry:* Church planting, Christian education, theological education, programs for the handicapped and support of national churches. *Countries:* Belgium, Bolivia, Brazil, Congo, Guatemala, South Korea, Mali, Philippines, Senegal, Venezuela, Spain, United Kingdom

Voice of China and Asia Missionary Society, Inc. P.O. Box 15-M, Pasadena, CA 91102. 818-796-3117 (1946). *Ministry:* Radio broadcasting, Christian education, missionary education, programs for the handicapped, support of national churches and workers. *Countries:* Hong Kong, India, South Korea, Philippines, Taiwan (ROC)

WEC International. P.O. Box 1707, Fort Washington, PA 19034. 215-646-2322 (1922). *Ministry:* Evangelism, church planting, theological education, literacy work, medical work and Bible translation. *Countries:* Asia-General, Asia-Mid East, Australia, Austria, Brazil,

Burkina Faso, Chad, Colombia, Cote d'Ivoire, Cyprus, France, Gambia, West Germany, Guinea-Bissau, Indonesia, Italy, Japan, Kenya, Liberia, Nepal, Pakistan, Philippines, Senegal, Spain, Sri Lanka, Taiwan (ROC), Thailand, United Kingdom, Venezuela, Zaire

WEGO, Inc. (World Encounter Gospel Organization). P.O. Box 763187, Dallas, TX 75376. 214-943-6365 (1974). *Ministry:* Evangelism, church planting, relief aid, theological education, support of national workers. *Countries:* Australia, Belgium, Belize, Chile, Colombia, West Germany, Ghana, India, Israel, Japan, Kenya, Lebanon, Mexico, New Zealand, Nigeria, Pakistan, Philippines, South Africa, Sri Lanka, United Kingdom, Zimbabwe

Wesleyan Church. P.O. Box 50434, Indianapolis, IN 46250. 317-576-8160 (1968). *Ministry:* Evangelism, church planting, theological education, TEE, medical work and Christian education. *Countries:* Australia, Brazil, Colombia, Guyana, Haiti, Honduras, India, Indonesia, Japan, South Korea, Liberia, Mexico, Nepal, Papua New Guinea, Peru, Philippines, Puerto Rico, Sierra Leone, South Africa, Sri Lanka, Suriname, Swaziland, Zambia, Zimbabwe

Wisconsin Evangelical Lutheran Synod. 2929 N. Mayfair Road, Milwaukee, WI 53222. 414-771-9357 (1955). *Ministry:* Church planting, broadcasting, theological education, literature production, support of national churches and workers. *Countries:* Brazil, Cameroon, Colombia, Hong Kong, Indonesia, Japan, Malawi, Mexico, Nigeria, Puerto Rico, Taiwan (ROC), Zambia

Word of Life Fellowship, Inc. P.O. Box 278, Schroon Lake, NY 12870. 518-532-7111 (1940). *Ministry:* Camping programs, broadcasting and youth programs. *Countries:* Argentina, Australia, Brazil, Chile, Ecuador, West Germany, Israel, Kenya, New Zealand, Portugal, Spain, United Kingdom

World Baptist Fellowship Mission Agency, Inc. P.O. Box 13459, Arlington, TX 76094. 817-274-7161 (1928). *Ministry:* Evangelism, church planting, TEE, funds transmission, literature distribution and missionary orientation. *Countries:* Brazil, Colombia, Ecuador, Fiji, France, Ghana, Guatemala, Honduras, Indonesia, Ireland, Mexico, New Zealand, Peru, Philippines, Portugal, Singapore, Spain, Sri Lanka, Thailand

World Concern. P.O. Box 33000, Seattle, WA 98133. 206-546-7201 (1973). *Ministry:* Community development, medical work, agricultural assistance, providing medical supplies and training. *Countries:* Afghanistan, Bangladesh, Bolivia, Burkina Faso, Chad, Costa Rica, El Salvador, Ehtiopia, Haiti, Kenya, Laos, Malaysia, Nepal, Pakistan, Philippines, Somalia, Sudan, Thailand, Uganda

World Gospel Mission. P.O. Box WGM, Marion, IN 46952. 317-664-7331 (1910). *Ministry:* Evangelism, church planting, Christian education, TEE and medical work. *Countries:* Argentina, Bangladesh, Barbados, Bolivia, Brazil, Burundi, Haiti, Honduras, India, Japan, Kenya, Mexico, Tanzania

World Indigenous Missions, Inc. P.O. Box 310627, New Braunfels, TX 78131. 512-629-0863 (1985). *Ministry:* Evangelism, church planting, Christian education and support of national workers. *Countries:* Dominican Rep, France, West Germany, Mexico, Philippines, Spain

World Mission Prayer League. 232 Clifton Avenue South, Minneapolis, MN 55403. 612-871-6843 (1937). *Ministry:* Evangelism, church planting, TEE, community development, medical work and support of national churches. *Countries:* Bangladesh, Bolivia, Ecuador, India, Kenya, Mexico, Nepal, Pakistan, Peru, Philippines

World Missions Far Corners, Inc. P.O. Box 2611, Long Beach, CA 90801. 213-427-9885 (1958). *Ministry:* Evangelism, church planting, radio broadcasting, correspondence courses, literature distribution and support of national workers. *Countries:* Bolivia, Ecuador, Ghana, Hong Kong, India, Jamaica, South Korea, Mexico, Peru, Philippines, South Africa, United Kingdom

World Neighbors, Inc. 5116 N. Portland Avenue, Oklahoma City, OK 73112. 405-946-3333

MISSION AGENCIES cont.

(1951). *Ministry:* Community development, agricultural assistance, self-help projects and training. *Countries:* Bolivia, Burkina Faso, Chad, Ghana, Haiti, Honduras, India, Indonesia, Kenya, Mali, Mexico, Nepal, Peru, Philippines, Tanzania, Togo, Uganda

World Outreach Fellowship. P.O. Box 585603, Orlando, FL 32858. 407-425-5552 (1981). *Ministry:* Missionary orientation and training, mobilization for mission, mission-related research and serving other agencies. *Countries:* Belize, Bolivia

World Radio Missionary Fellowship, Inc. P.O. Box 553000, Opa Locka, FL 33055. 305-624-4252 (1931). *Ministry:* Radio broadcasting, evangelism, technical assistance, community development, medical work and training. *Countries:* Ecuador, Panama

World Reach, Inc. P.O. Box 26155, Birmingham, AL 35226. 205-979-2400 (1982). *Ministry:* Evangelism, church planting, relief aid, Bible distribution, literature distribution and medical work. *Countries:* Guatemala, Honduras, Kenya, Somalia, Tanzania, Uganda, Zambia

World Relief Corporation. P.O. Box WRC, Wheaton, IL 60189. 708-665-0235 (1944). *Ministry:* Relief aid, community development, support of national churches, self-help projects, technical assistance and training. *Countries:* Afghanistan, Bangladesh, Burkina Faso, El Salvador, Ethiopia, Guatemala, Haiti, Honduras, Hong Kong, India, Indonesia, Kenya, Malawi, Mali, Morocco, Mozambique, Philippines, Senegal, Sri Lanka, Swaziland, Thailand, Zaire

World Salt Foundation, Inc. P.O. Box 1929, Newnan, GA 30264. 404-253-8451 (1978). *Ministry:* Evangelism, church planting and Bible distribution. *Countries:* Belize, Brazil, Cameroon, Chile, Costa Rica, Guatemala, Haiti, Hong Kong, India, Ireland, Israel, Mexico, Philippines, Puerto Rico, Thailand

World Servants. 8233 Gator Lane, #6, West Palm Beach, FL 33411. 407-790-0800 (1985). *Ministry:* Community development, childcare programs, mobilization for mission, medical work and missionary orientation.

World Vision. P.O. Box O, Pasadena, CA 91109. 818-357-7979 (1950). *Ministry:* Childcare programs, community development, relief aid, evangelism, leadership development and public health.

World Vision International. 919 W. Huntington Drive, Monrovia, CA 91016. 818-303-8811 (1978). *Ministry:* Childcare programs, relief aid, community development, evangelism, medical work and training. *Countries:* Active in 64 countries

Worldteam, Inc. P.O. Box 14308, Coral Gables, FL 33114. 305-446-0861 (1928). *Ministry:* Evangelism, church planting, TEE and training. *Countries:* Brazil, Cuba, Dominican Rep, France, Grenada, Guadeloupe, Haiti, Italy, Spain, St Lucia, St Vincent, Suriname, Trinidad & Tobago, United Kingdom

Worldwide Discipleship Association, Inc. 110 Carnegie Place, Suite 100, Fayetteville, GA 30214. 404-460-1337 (1974). *Ministry:* Evangelism, church planting, training national leaders, youth programs and TEE. *Countries:* Japan, Kenya, South Korea

Wycliffe Bible Translators, International. 7500 W. Camp Wisdom Road, Dallas, TX 75236. 214-709-2400 (1934). *Ministry:* Bible translation, linguistics, literacy and missionary training. *Countries:* Africa-General, Asia-South, Australia, Austria, Brazil, Cameroon, Colombia, Cote d'Ivoire, Ecuador, West Germany, Indonesia, Kenya, Latin America-Central, Malaysia, Mexico, Netherlands, Panama, Papua New Guinea, Peru, Philippines, Senegal, Singapore, Suriname, Sudan, Thailand, Togo, United Kingdom

Young Life, Inc. P.O. Box 520, Colorado Springs, CO 80901. 719-473-4262 (1941). *Ministry:* Evangelism—primarily to young people through youth and camping programs. *Countries:* Algeria, Australia, Austria, Belgium, Burma, Brazil, China (PRC), Costa Rica, Denmark, Dominican Rep, France, West Germany, India, Japan, Kenya, South Korea, Malawi, Mexico, Peru, Philippines, Singapore, South Africa, Switzerland, Uganda, United Kingdom, Virgin Islands USA, Zimbabwe

Youth Enterprises, Inc. P.O. Box 777, Chula Vista, CA 92012. 619-421-9828 (1960). *Ministry:* Evangelism and literature distribution through sports programs. *Countries:* Bolivia, Brazil, Costa Rica, France, Guatemala, South Korea, Mexico, New Zealand, United Kingdom

Youth for Christ/USA. P.O. Box 419, Wheaton, IL 60189. 708-668-6600 (1944). *Ministry:* Evangelism, mobilization for mission, youth ministries and camping programs. *Countries:* American Samoa, Austria, Brazil, Burma, Colombia, Ecuador, France, West Germany, Guatemala, Kenya, Lebanon, Liberia, Netherlands, Panama, Portugal, Singapore, South Africa, Spain, Sweden, Switzerland, United Kingdom

Youth with a Mission (YWAM). P.O. Box 55309, Seattle, WA 98155. 206-283-1071 (1960). *Ministry:* Evangelism, relief aid and training. *Countries:* Active in 75 countries.

Source: *Mission Handbook, 14th Edition.* W. Dayton Roberts and John A. Siewert, editors. Co-Published by MARC (Missions Advanced Research and Communications Center) and Zondervan Publishing House. Copyright © 1989. Used by permission.

FOCUS FACT

The average English cat costs about $225 per year to feed—which is more than the average income of the one billion people who live in the world's fifteen poorest nations. —Lloyd Timberlake in *Only One Earth*

USA MISSION AGENCY STATISTICS

Overseas personnel sent from the U.S.A.	*1985*	*1988*
Total personnel (career and short-term)	58,700	70,969
Person/year equivalent index	48,300	52,208
Career Personnel	37,500	40,221
Short-term Personnel	21,200	30,748
Percentage of total personnel that is career	64%	57%
Percentage of total personnel that is short-term	36%	43%
Number of "tentmakers" sponsored or supervised	NA	873
Mission agencies based in the U.S.A.		
Number of agencies with career personnel	371	395
Percentage of agencies with career personnel	56%	57%
Median number of career personnel for an agency	16	13
Average number of career personnel for an agency	101	101
Number of agencies with short-term personnel	209	208
Percentage of agencies with short-term personnel	32%	30%
Mission funding in millions of U.S.A. dollars		
Total income for overseas ministries	1,320	1,728.1
Median amount of income for overseas in an agency	NA	.33
Average amount of income for overseas in an agency	NA	2.50
Overseas missions activity from the U.S.A.		
Number of countries with U.S.A. personnel or projects	187	186
Number of countries with U.S.A. personnel	175	177

Source: *Mission Handbook, 14th Edition.* W. Dayton Roberts and John A. Siewert, editors. Co-Published by MARC (Missions Advanced Research and Communications Center) and Zondervan Publishing House. Copyright © 1989. Used by permission.

FIFTEEN LARGEST MISSION AGENCIES

Ranked according to overseas career personnel

Rank / Agency	*Career Personnel*	*Short-term 1 yr or more*	*2-11 months*
1. Southern Baptist Conv. Foreign Missions	3,839	200	7,350
2. Youth with a Mission (YWAM)	2,506	0	13,954
3. Wycliffe Bible Translators International	2,269	316	0
4. New Tribes Mission	1,807	0	250
5. Christian Churches/Churches of Christ	1,717	NA	NA
6. Assemblies of God Foreign Missions	1,530	0	402
7. Churches of Christ	982	NA	NA
8. Christian and Missionary Alliance	917	54	134
9. The Evangelical Alliance Mission (TEAM)	872	69	148
10. General Conference Seventh-Day Adventist	842	59	46
11. Baptist Bible Fellowship International	734	NA	NA
12. Baptist Mid-Missions	636	NA	NA
13. Church of the Nazarene World Missions	629	0	35
14. Baptist International Missions	620	0	9
15. Association of Baptists for World Evangelism	618	16	33

Source: *Mission Handbook, 14th Edition.* W. Dayton Roberts and John A. Siewert, editors. Co-published by MARC (Missions Advanced Research and Communications Center) and Zondervan Publishing House. Copyright © 1989. Used by permission.

HOPEFUL TRENDS / ONGOING CONCERNS

Hopeful Trends

1. *Mushrooming of Third-World missionary sending agencies*. There may be more than 1,000 of them, fielding at least 35,000 workers. They represent a whole new wave of evangelistic vitality in the Church.
2. *Renewal in the Roman Catholic Church.* In many places there are as many renewed Catholic Christians as there are Evangelicals. Despite Pope John Paul II's efforts to control the charismatic movement, it still carries much momentum.
3. *Multiplication of "tentmakers" among Evangelicals.* As "professional" missionaries find it increasingly difficult to gain access to inhospitable nations, the number and caliber of "intentional laypersons" in these areas is growing sharply.
4. *Christian responses to world hunger.* An acute shortage of food—particularly in Africa—has evoked massive waves of compassion and continues to force upon the Church a healthy, holistic agenda.
5. *Spectacular technological advances.* The strategic advantages of modern research and communications to speed up the acquisition of basic knowledge and to foster unity and cooperation are dramatic, to say the least.

Ongoing Concerns

1. *World hunger and environmental abuse.* Sin and poverty are leaving their tragic trail across the face of society. As Christians we need not only to respond with compassion, but also to grapple with the causes of famine.

2. *Barriers preventing access to the gospel.* By AD 2000, more than half the world will live in cities (with their social isolation) and 80 percent in countries that bar traditional missions.
3. *The rise of Muslim fanaticism.* The Shi'ite form of Islam in some places, as well as the Sunni activism in others, is militant in its attempts to control society. Strong anti-Christian sentiments may well require innovative—and no doubt costly—evangelism.
4. *Oppression of women, children, castes, and racial minorities.* Women are the key to Christian development, as well as evangelism, and children are always the most vulnerable to opposing forces. Discrimination and the gospel are in strong contradiction.
5. *Deep-rooted disunity in the Christian community.* Many feel that as per John 17:21, the world will not be able to believe until the followers of Christ can become one, "as the Father is in me, and I in Him."

Source: *Mission Handbook, 14th Edition.* W. Dayton Roberts and John A. Siewert, editors. Co-published by MARC (Missions Advanced Research and Communications Center) and Zondervan Publishing House.

Future Outlook: What Still Needs to Be Done

The Tools	The Goals	Progress as of August 1990	Still to Be Accomplished
Satellite, TV	7 "world" languages	One language now (English)	Six languages to be on satellite
Major missionary radio	307 major languages	130 languages now broadcast	177 languages to be broadcast
Film ministry (Campus Crusade *Jesus* Film)	271 language groups	160 sound tracks	111 sound tracks to go
Scripture in print (Wycliffe and others)	6,170 "visual" languages	2,950 (at least one portion in print)	3,220 (need Scripture in print)
Audio cassettes (Gospel Recordings and others)	12,398 "audio" languages	4,432 (now on cassettes)	7,966 (to be put on cassettes)
Church planting (in unreached peoples, 15% of missionaries directly involved)	24,000 "church lineages" needed	12,456 (now with church movements)	11,544 (need a church movement)

Source: *Mission Frontiers* magazine. Used by permission.

The Finishable Task

Year (A.D.)	Total World Population (Millions) 1	People Who Do Not Claim To Be Christians (Millions) 2	People Who Call Themselves Christians (Millions) 3	Great Commission Christians (Out of Col. 3) (Millions) 4	Ratio of Non-Christians to Great Commission Christians (Col. 2 : Col. 4) 5	Unreached People Groups 6	Ratio of Congregations to Unreached People Groups (Col. 4÷100 : Col. 6) 7
100	181	180	1	0.5	360:1	60,000	1:12
1000	270	220	50	1	220:1	50,000	1:5
1500	425	344	81	5	69:1	44,000	1:1
1900	1,620	1,062	558	40	27:1	40,000	10:1
1950	2,504	1,650	854	80	21:1	24,000	33:1
1980	4,458	3,025	1,433	275	11:1	17,000	162:1
1990	5,245	3,487	1,758	534	6.5:1	11,544	463:1
2000	6,260	?	?	?	?	?	?

Whence These Amazing Numbers?

The first three columns are published figures in the World Christian Encyclopedia, plus recent updates by the author, David Barrett. He and Ralph Winter have talked over the estimates in column four involving this new phrase, Great Commission Christians. These figures have been developed in consultation with the Lausanne Statistics Task Force.

Source: *Mission Frontiers* magazine. Used by permission.

THE STATISTICS ARE . . .

- 3,500 new churches are opening every week worldwide.
- 28,000 become believers every day in the People's Republic of China. In 1950, when China closed to foreign missionaries, there were one million Christians. Today, conservative estimates say there are 40 to 50 million.
- 20,000 become Christians every day in Africa; that continent was 3 percent Christian in 1900 and is now more than 40 percent Christian.
- 70,000 become Christians every day in the world.
- In 1900, Korea had no Protestant church; it was thought "impossible to penetrate." In 1991 Korea is 30 percent Christian with 4,000 churches in Seoul alone.
- In Indonesia, the percentage of Christians is so high the government won't print the statistic—which is probably nearing 25 percent of the population.
- After 70 years of oppression in the Soviet Union, Christians number about 100 million—five times the number in the Communist Party and 36 percent of the population.
- More Muslims in Iran have come to Christ since 1980 than in the previous 1000 years combined.
- In AD 100, there were 360 non-Christians per evangelical Christian. Today the ratio is seven to every evangelical Christian.
- In AD 100 there were 12 unreached people groups per church congregation. In 1991, with five million churches worldwide, there are 416 congregations for every unreached people group.
- Of the 70 million evangelicals in America, 17.5 million are age 18 to 35. The 100,000 new missionaries needed are only half of 1 percent of these young adults in the U.S.
- American evangelicals have a disposable annual income of about $850 billion. About one-fifth of 1 percent of that income—$1.5 billion—would support the needed 12,000 church-planting teams.
- According to survey results, the prayer necessary would take only 2 percent of the time evangelical Christians spend daily watching TV and shopping.

Source: *Frontiers* magazine. January/February 1990 issue. Used by permission.

BOOKLIST: A 1991 MISSIONS READING PROGRAM

Selected by Edwin L. (Jack) Frizen, Jr., Executive Director, IFMA

January *From Jerusalem to Irian Jaya* by Ruth A. Tucker, Zondervan Publ. House.
February *What in the World is God Doing?* by C. Gordon Olson, Global Gospel Publishers.
March *Escape at Dawn* by Carol T. Talbot and Virginia J. Muir, Tyndale House Publishers.
April *Touch the World Through Prayer* by Wesley L. Duewel, Zondervan Publishing House.
May *Gold Fears No Fire* by Ralph Toliver, OMF Books.
June *Priority One* by Norm Lewis, Promise Publishing.
July *J. Hudson Taylor: A Man in Christ* by Roger Steer, OMF Books.
August *Countdown to AD 2000,* Edited by Thomas Wang, The AD 2000 Movement.
September *Guardians of The Great Commission* by Ruth A. Tucker, Zondervan Publishing House.
October *Today's Choices for Tomorrow's Mission* by David J. Hesselgrave, Zondervan Publishing House.
November *My Persian Pilgrimage* by William M. Miller, William Carey Library.
December *Dawn 2000: 7 Million Churches to Go* by Jim Montgomery, William Carey Library.

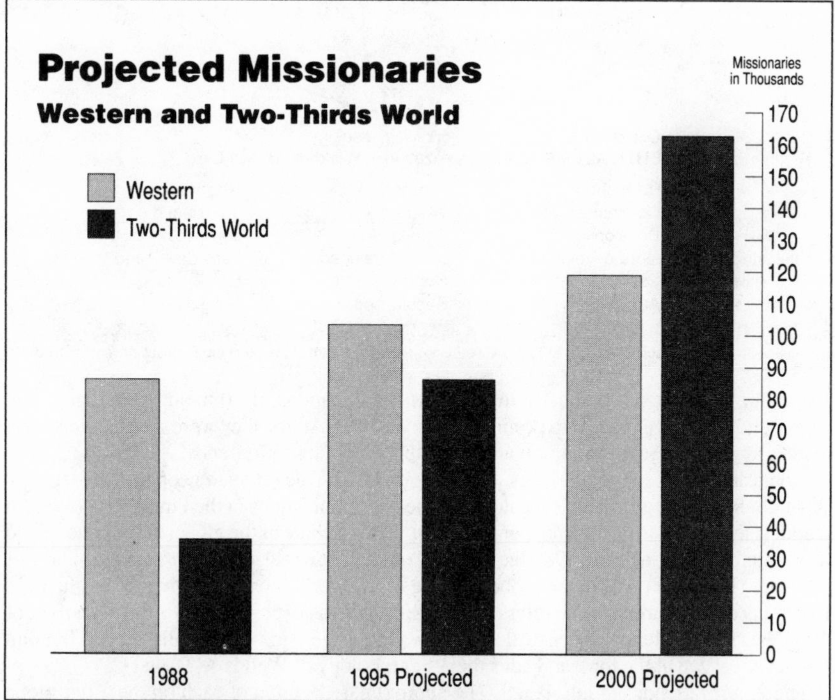

Today's Megatrends in Mission

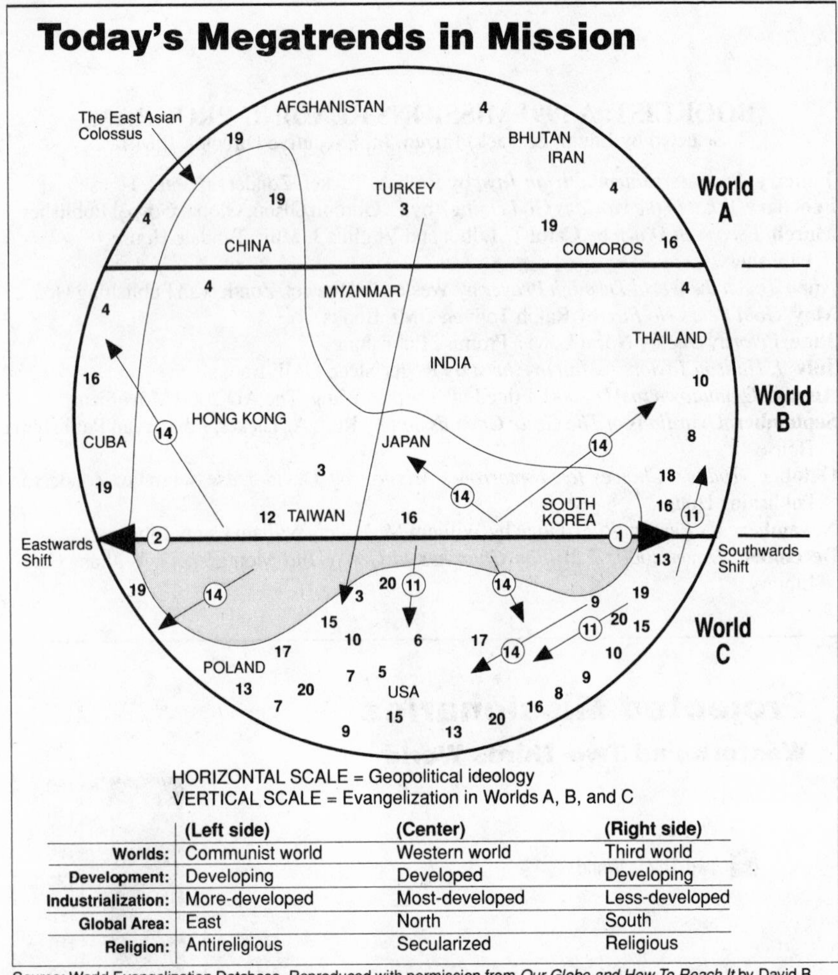

HORIZONTAL SCALE = Geopolitical ideology
VERTICAL SCALE = Evangelization in Worlds A, B, and C

	(Left side)	(Center)	(Right side)
Worlds:	Communist world	Western world	Third world
Development:	Developing	Developed	Developing
Industrialization:	More-developed	Most-developed	Less-developed
Global Area:	East	North	South
Religion:	Antireligious	Secularized	Religious

Source: World Evangelization Database. Reproduced with permission from *Our Globe and How To Reach It* by David B. Barrett and Todd M. Johnson. Copyright © 1990 by the Foreign Mission Board of the Southern Baptist Convention. Published by New Hope, Birmingham, AL.

The globe portrays schematically the approximate locations of 20 major Christian global megatrends that have come into prominence since 1980. At first they were seen as short-term trends; by 1990 they are taking on all the attributes of long-term trends.

Countries are located by 2 scales. (a) The horizontal scale refers to geopolitical ideology, as set out below the globe. This locates countries and populations in the First World (western world, also referred to as the West, or the North) in the middle of the globe, the Second World (Communist world, or since 1989 the former Communist world, or the Communist sphere of influence) on the left within the globe, and the Third World (nonaligned world) on the right within it. (b) The vertical scale refers to evangelization, as explained in words to the right of the globe. This locates countries by degree of evangelization (most-evangelized at the bottom, least-evangelized at the top), and adds the 3-tier typology of Worlds A, B, and C.

The 20 megatrends are numbered. The approximate location of each on the 3-tier globe is then shown by using the same numbers on the globe.

CHRISTIAN GLOBAL MEGATRENDS

1. Southward shift of Christian center of gravity from North to Third World (47%).
2. Eastward shift of Christian center of gravity from West to Communist world (21%).
3. Migrations of 1,000 Third-World peoples to Christian West.
4. Countries restricting access by foreign missions: 119 (43 closed countries).
5. Rise of 56 global ministry networks with 54 million computers.
6. Massive global growth of electronic radio/TV Christianity to 26% of world.
7. Mushrooming of literature on evangelization (11,000 items a year).
8. Proliferation of 400 conferences on evangelization each year.
9. 50 new global plans for world evangelization each year.
10. 2,500 evangelistic mass campaigns a year.
11. Emergence of 1,000 Third-World mission agencies.
12. Rise of the East Asian colossus with 80 million Christians.
13. 3 waves of worldwide pentecostal/charismatic renewal, to 372 million.
14. Power Christianity by osmosis across the world: signs and wonders.
15. Retrograde or negative Christian activities hindering world mission.
16. Pluralism: proliferation of 23,500 denominations and 30,000 religions across world.
17. Spread of Christian activism worldwide opposing injustice and human rights abuses.
18. New ministries to 1.3 billion urban poor in exploding "planet of slums."
19. Escalating martyrdoms reach 300,000 a year in 50 countries and in all Christian branches.
20. Emergence of the AD 2000 megamagnet throughout the world.

A. THE UNEVANGELIZED WORLD

133 million newly-evangelized each year, but offset by 142 million new births a year.

30 closed countries increasing by 2 a year.

Sizable numbers from 200 large unreached peoples migrate to Christian West.

B. THE EVANGELIZED NON-CHRISTIAN WORLD

Emergence of 1,000 Third-World mission agencies.

31 partially-closed countries increasing each year.

Reaction to social injustice and abuses in Third World.

Rapid spread of Christian activism in 30 World B countries (150 countries worldwide).

Escalating martyrdoms of Christian workers.

Vast numbers from 800 non-Christian peoples migrate to Christian West.

Numerous ministries escalate among 520 million slumdwellers.

C. THE CHRISTIAN WORLD

Eastward and southward shift of Christian center of gravity.

Christians now 32% in West, 21% in Communist world, 47% in Third World.

East Asian colossus: 80 million Christians (shaded gray) among 1.2 billion population.

Pluralism: over 10,000 new religions spread across West.

Retrograde Christian activities, with ecclesiastical crime $1.1 billion p.a., mainly in West.

Massive global growth of electronic radio/TV Christianity, used by 26% of world.

AD 2000 plans launched by most major churches and agencies.

> “” FOCUS QUOTE
> **There is not a home church and a foreign church. It is all one great work.**
> —Oswald Chambers

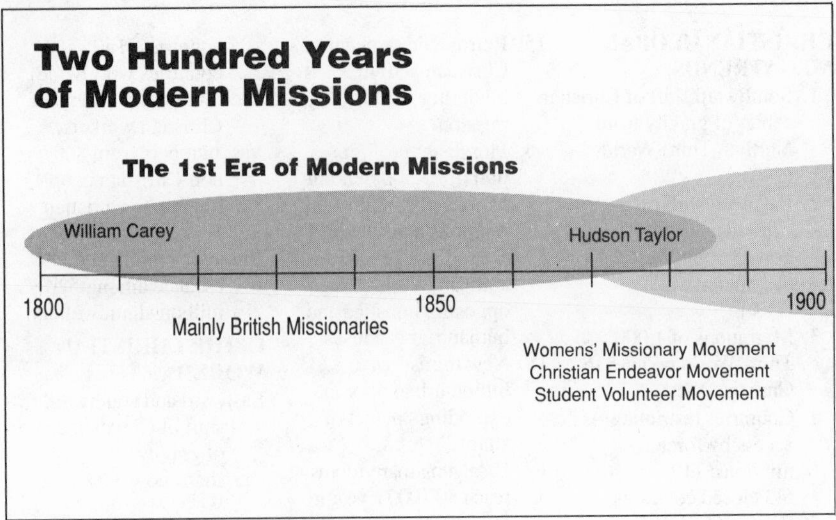

Source: *Mission Frontiers* Magazine. Used by permission.

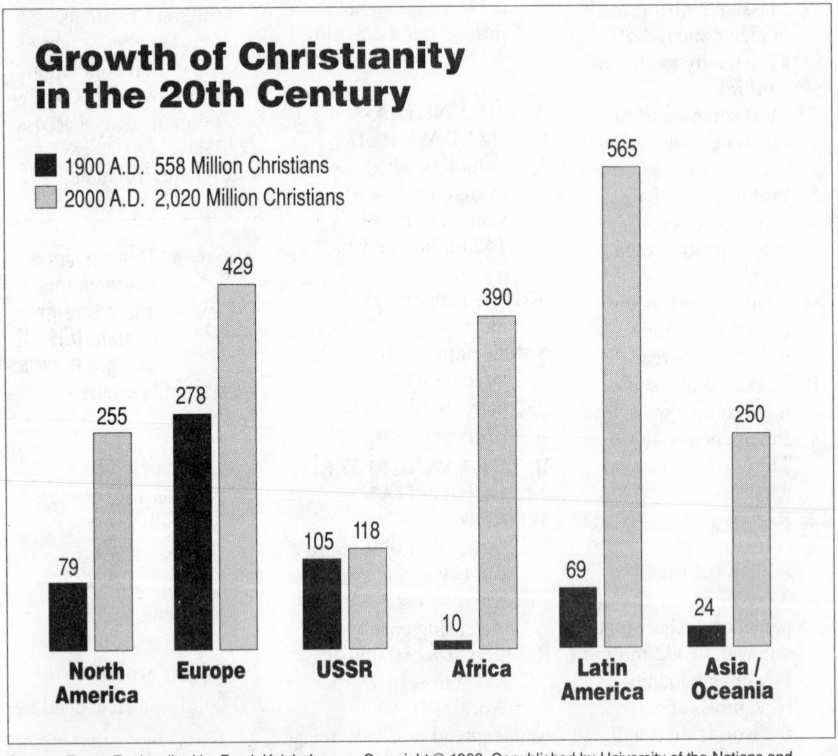

Growth of Christianity in the 20th Century

1900 A.D. 558 Million Christians
2000 A.D. 2,020 Million Christians

Region	1900 A.D.	2000 A.D.
North America	79	255
Europe	278	429
USSR	105	118
Africa	10	390
Latin America	69	565
Asia / Oceania	24	250

Source: *Target Earth*, edited by Frank Kaleb Jansen. Copyright © 1989. Copublished by University of the Nations and Global Mapping International. Used by permission.

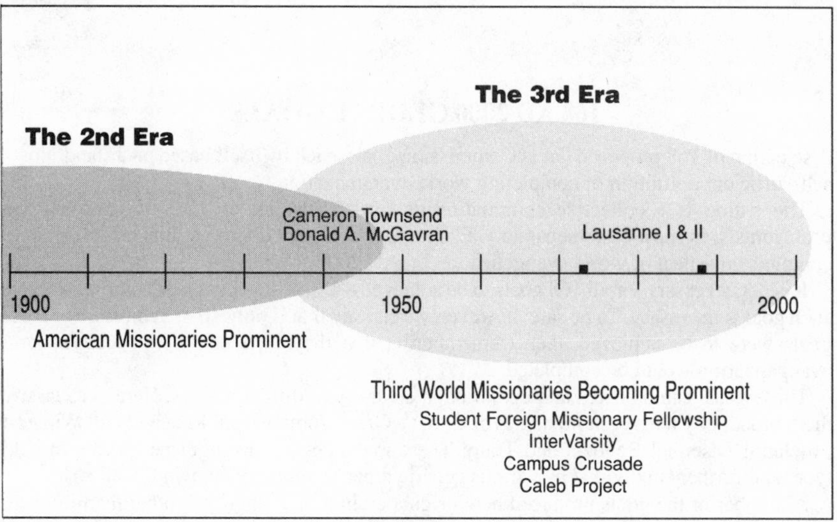

AD 2000 PLANS

- Throughout history, at least 788 global plans have emerged to evangelize the world.
- These plans have sprung from every continent and every major tradition of Christianity.
- More than one half of history's plans have emerged since 1948.
- By 1988, one new plan appeared each week, 31 percent of which were from the Two-Thirds world.
- About 254 global plans are active today and making progress, and one half have target dates for AD 2000.
- Of these, 89 spend more than $10 million a year.
- Of these, 33 spend more than $100 million a year.
- Between now and the year 2000, $40 billion will be spent on these plans.

Source: *Seven Hundred Plans to Evangelize the World*

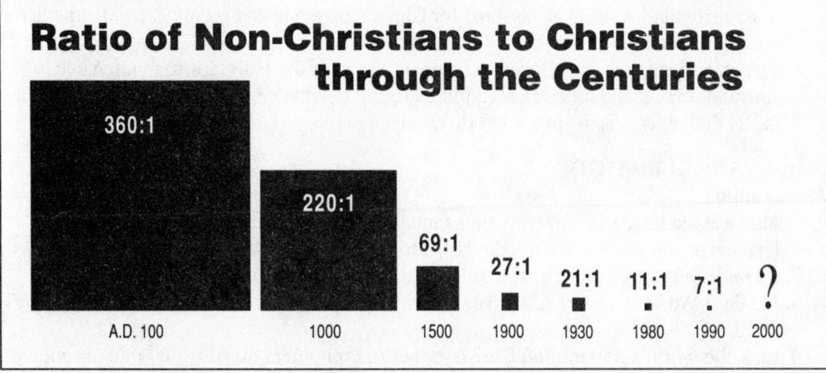

Source: *Mission Frontiers* Magazine. January/February 1990 issue. Used by permission.

168 AD 2000 GLOBAL GOALS

A selection of 168 proposed Great Commission goals, each by itself based on a stand-alone, self-sufficient definition of completing world evangelization.

The listing is a collective compilation of final goals put forward by agencies and protagonists, in most cases separately. Each one is considered to be a final closure goal to complete an aspect of world evangelization by AD 2000.

It is not necessary for all 168 goals to be achieved—by most people's definition, only one such goal is necessary. To be safe, however, we can say that if only 10 or at most 20 of these goals were to be achieved, then (remembering that they interact synergistically) world evangelization would be completed.

These goals can be listed and classified in a variety of different ways. Here, we classify them broadly by the Seven Mandates of Christ's Great Commission: Receive! Go! Witness! Proclaim! Disciple! Baptize! and Train! These mandates are distinguished below in bold type, and further subdivided by various generic types of ministry (shown in italics).

A number of the goals produced here originated in major languages other than English. Goals were sent in Bahasa Indonesian, Bengali, Chinese, French, German, Japanese, Korean, Malayalam, Portuguese, Sango, Spanish, Telugu, et al.

Individual Christians, groups, churches, organizations, or agencies are encouraged to select one or more of the goals to concentrate on implementing in collaboration with other Great Commission Christians and agencies which have similar goals.

PRAYER EVANGELISM (RECEIVE!)

1. Establish 15,000 prayer movements by 1995 in every city over 50,000 and on all 15,000 university campuses, evangelizing the urban and academic worlds by 2000.
2. Enlist by AD 2000, 30 million Christians to pray full-time every day for world evangelization through a globally-organized network of young pacesetter intercessors to cover all countries, cities, peoples, topics, needs, and persons.
3. Enroll 170 million Christians (10% of world total) in a world prayer force promising to pray daily for successful closure of world evangelization by 2000.
4. Enthuse all prayer-oriented or contemplative brothers and sister, monks and nuns, to regain past monastic enthusiasm for world evangelization and to rededicate monasteries and convents worldwide by 2000 to prayer support for the Great Commission task.
5. Prepare the entire global evangelization harvest force of Great Commission Christians to be ready and waiting at any time for Christ's parousia and second advent, whether today, or tomorrow, or in AD 2000, or beyond.
6. Preach and emphasize the need to receive the gift of the Holy Spirit, to intercede for spiritual revival and renewal of individuals and churches by 2000, and to promote the thesis that revival is the key to world evangelization.

PRE-EVANGELISM (GO!)

Preparation

7. Increase the proportion of Christian annual finance expended on World A, the Unevangelized World, from today's 1% to 4% by 2000.
8. Increase World A's share of Christian computers from today's 0% to 5% by 2000.
9. Increase World A's share of Christian computer specialists from today's 0% to 5% by 2000.
10. Link the world's 350 million Christian-owned computers by AD 2000 into one single global giganetwork to facilitate Great Commission Information exchange.

11. Circulate by AD 2000, as a service to apologetes and evangelists, a computerized Great Commission glossary-dictionary, listing (a) definitions of all the major English terms in use related to global mission and world evangelization, and (b) listings of the major wider Christian terms, words, and concepts (God, Christ, gospel, sin, disciple, etc.) with their equivalents in all languages of the world (2,500 languages with Scripture translation, 9,500 without).
12. Systematically place, by AD 2000, the best Christian apologetic and evangelistic literature and materials (including the Bible) in any language at all strategic points in all strata of the modern information/knowledge/computer/artificial intelligence explosion and revolution: in public-access databases, knowledge bases, OCLC (library retrieval), DIALOG (with 100 databases), Religion One, and all other similar secular services.
13. Translate by AD 2000 the most influential, effective, and persuasive works of Christian apologetics in any language into the top 20 non-Christian languages of the world, and publish and disseminate them widely through all varieties of print and electronic media.
14. Pursue systematic region-by-region dialogue with the world's organized atheists, agnostics, nonbelievers, and nonreligious, as well as with the great non-Christian world religions and newer cults and religious movements, so that all may genuinely understand each other's position and the full message of Christ may be fully understood in all these contexts by 2000.
15. Place into operation a Great Commission expert system to guide the prioritization of all proposed or suggested AD 2000 programs and ministries in any part of the world.
16. Have an electronic Great Commission global network and expert system to guide the actual accomplishment of all corporate and individual AD 2000 goals, both at intermediate years (1990, 1995) and also by the AD 2000 deadline.
17. Translate into 100 Christian megalanguages the major AD 2000 strategic planning documents and methods, including Great Commission expert systems, and the Kaleidoscopic Global Plan.
18. Encourage AD 2000 global and nonglobal plans to develop corporate plans and consequently achieve major collective goals for AD 2000.
19. Redistribute the great majority of Christian resources of manpower, money, and methods across the world's unevangelized peoples and cities strictly according to need, by 2000.

Development

20. Monitor and encourage a final massive attempt by AD 2000 at the promotion of human development in all its forms worldwide as an integral part of world evangelization.
21. Support FAO goal for eradication of human hunger by 2000, and then beyond.
22. Feed and nourish the world's 600 million persons on the verge of starvation during the year 2000, and see that they continue to live nourished lives thereafter.
23. Support WHO goal of safe drinking water for every soul on earth by 2000 and beyond.
24. Minister in the name of Jesus to all the world's poor, destitute, sick, and dying, bringing Jesus to the poorest of the poor in every country and city on earth by 2000.
25. Abolish the global state of absolute poverty (per capita daily income of under US $1) by AD 2000 through massive redistribution everywhere of national and international wealth, certainly by all Christian denominations and agencies, also by secular organizations persuaded by Christian activists.
26. Raise physical quality of life of all disadvantaged peoples of earth to a livable level by 2000, and even higher levels beyond.
27. Develop creative approaches for total ministry directed to the world's 2.4 billion children by AD 2000, through evangelism, education, aid and relief, in all languages and in all 15,000 population segments.

168 AD 2000 GLOBAL GOALS cont.

28. Support UNICEF goal to halve child deaths (38,000 a day in 1988) by 1997, then continuing to decrease by 2000 and beyond.
29. Support WHO goal to halt child diarrhea deaths by giving all parents of children under 5 access to ORT (oral rehydration therapy) and a trained health worker, the world proportion of children so covered to increase from 3% (1980) to 50% (1988) to 100% by AD 2000.
30. Support WHO goal of rise of worldwide immunization coverage from 9% (1980) to 50% (1987) to 100% by 1990, staying there through 2000, and beyond.
31. Increase annual medical consultations in Christian hospitals, dispensaries, centers, clinics, and mobile clinics, to 20 million a year worldwide by 2000.
32. Insist on a final negotiated settlement and end to the stateless or homeless status of 60 million refugees on earth, half of whom are children, by the symbolic 2,000th anniversary of the birth of the child Jesus, a refugee from political evil.
33. Eliminate poverty housing throughout the world in the name of Jesus Christ by AD 2000, and build adequate urban housing in its place in the cities of the world.
34. Extend adequate aid, assistance, care, and ministry to the world's entire 1.8 billion disabled persons (33% being children) in AD 2000.
35. Set in place by 2000, a network of fully trained, financed and prepared disaster-relief teams (and other Christian emergency structures) ready to minister anywhere in the world at an hour's notice.
36. Reduce the level of human suffering in 50 highly-disturbed countries to a minimum level by 2000, then eradicate it beyond.
37. Support UNESCO goal to increase adult literacy from the present 45% to 100% by 2000.
38. Increase pupils and students in all types of Christian schools and colleges to 30 million worldwide by 2000.
39. Monitor the status of human rights in every country and work with specializing agencies to see all abuses rectified by AD 2000.
40. Raise to an acceptable level by 2000 the level of human rights experienced by all populations who have been and still are severely discriminated against.
41. Monitor, with Amnesty International, the status of state-sanctified police/military torture in all countries, and see it abolished universally by 2000, and never recur beyond.
42. Monitor religious liberty or persecution in every country, have it reported regularly by Amnesty International, and see that action for liberty results by 2000.
43. Place into action by AD 2000 a massive worldwide Christian movement adamantly opposing and outlawing all war, warfare, mass-destruction weapons, militarization, paramilitarization, arms sales, arms traders, death squads, and all indiscriminate mass killings.
44. Curtail by AD 2000 the worst manifestations of the world's "structures of sin" through determined Christian publication and activism.
45. Support UTU goal of universal telephone access for every population on earth by 2000 and beyond.

PERSONAL EVANGELISM (WITNESS!)

Witness

46. Evangelize the Unevangelized World of 3,030 peoples, metropolises, and countries by 2000.
47. Establish a witness in every unreached people on earth by 2000.
48. Establish a witness in every unreached minipeople (people group) on earth by 2000.
49. Establish a witness in every unreached ethnos (micropeople) on earth by 2000.
50. Establish a witness in every unreached metropolis on earth by 2000.
51. Establish ongoing mission and ministry by 2000 in every one of the world's 120 closed

or closing countries, its 500 closed or closing metropolises, and its 2,000 closed or closing peoples.

52. Put in place by 2000 adequate ministry, witness, and diakonia, including structures, among the world's 10,000 urban slum populations.
53. See all 15,000 population segments on earth by AD 2000 either entered (with resident missionaries) or engaged (with other deliberate but nonresidential modes) by at least one denomination or agency but preferably several different yet cooperating denominations or agencies.
54. Engage, with foreign missionary presence and ministry, every closed country, unreached people, and unevangelized metropolis in the world by 2000.
55. Assign one worker or couple to work exclusively with each of the 3,030 unevangelized population segments by 2000.
56. Locate 100,000 bivocational Christian lay tentmakers in secular work in 120 closed or closing countries by 2000.
57. See at least 2 tentmakers become resident in every unevangelized people on earth by 2000.
58. See at least 2 tentmakers become resident in every unevangelized minipeople (people group) on earth by 2000.
59. See at least 2 tentmakers become resident in every unevangelized ethnos (micropeople) on earth by 2000.
60. See at least 2 tentmakers become resident in every unevangelized metropolis on earth by 2000.
61. Establish awareness of Christ and his gospel among all the world's populations by 2000.
62. Bring half the human race (50%, or 3.1 billion) face-to-face with Christ by AD 2000 by means of radio/TV, Scriptures, missions, personal witness, etc.
63. Direct evangelization by AD 2000 primarily to *panta ta ethne,* all nations and peoples and cities and populations, thus giving every individual in them adequate (but not necessarily a customized, personalized, individualized) opportunity to respond to Christ.
64. Visit every home on earth, leaving at least two gospel leaflets in each's language, by 2000.
65. Establish by AD 2000 a system for visiting each year the world's 30 million new homes (families) begun that year, leaving at least two gospel leaflets in each's languages.
66. Train and develop the world's 2.1 billion lay persons in the Mystical Body of Christ by AD 2000 in the apostolate of daily witness by word and deed, engaging non-Christians directly in conversation about Christ's message of redemption and liberation.
67. After a 10-year emphasis (1990-2000) on the perils of affluence, aim to see a majority of Great Commission Christians, leaders, churches, and agencies embracing and adopting the basic, simple, biblical, Christian life-style (including self-denial, fasting, tithing) and to see them implementing life-style evangelism worldwide by the beginning of the new Millennium.
68. Enable by AD 2000 one million youths as short-term missionaries every year to serve abroad for 2 weeks to a year as foreign missionaries especially witnessing in closed or closing territories and cities.
69. Emphasize to the entire Christian world by AD 2000 that martyrdom is a major form of evangelization, that the world's anticipated 500,000 annual Christian martyrs are major players in God's global plan, and that Christians suffering for their faith should realize they are playing a vital role in world evangelization.

Broadcasting

70. Record and make available a gospel message in every language on earth by 2000.
71. Expand broadcast Christian programs, now in 2,000 languages, to 3,000 languages by 2000.
72. Extend radiophonic schools (radio broadcasting plus local classes, phone-in, talk-back,

168 AD 2000 GLOBAL GOALS cont.

write-back, or other feedback) to every country in the world by 2000.

73. Ensure that regular television evangelism proceeds weekly in the world's 300 largest languages by 2000.
74. Ensure that regular radio evangelism proceeds weekly in the world's 1,000 largest languages by 2000.
75. Increase global audience listening regularly to Christian radio/TV from the present 25% to 50% (3.1 billion) by AD 2000.
76. Increase World A's (the Unevangelized World's) share of Christian broadcast hours from today's 0% to 20% by 2000.
77. Reach the entire world with the Christian gospel for the first time ever by AD 2000, in the sense that everyone everywhere has heard or hears the gospel in depth with understanding and has access to Holy Scripture, churches, mission, Christians, Christian broadcasting (through both secular stations and 4,000 Christian radio and TV stations worldwide), videos, movies, literature, and other means of grace.
78. Prepare or dub films on the Bible or life of Christ, specifically the *Jesus* film, in 500 languages and show to the world's entire population by 2000.
79. Produce and distribute by AD 2000 a thousand different Christian or biblical films, in 200 major languages, with 25,000 prints in circulation resulting in 500,000 showings a year, with 500 million viewers and 25 million decisions or converts.

PREACHING EVANGELISM (PROCLAIM!)

Proclamation

80. Present the gospel message to all 6.2 billion people by AD 2000.
81. Proclaim the gospel to every population segment on earth by 2000.
82. Proclaim the gospel to every culture on every continent by the year 2000.
83. Proclaim the gospel to every unevangelized people on earth by 2000.
84. Proclaim the gospel to every unevangelized minipeople (people group) on earth by 2000.
85. Proclaim the gospel to every unevangelized ethnos (micropeople) on earth by 2000.
86. Proclaim the gospel to every unevangelized metropolis on earth by 2000.
87. Provide every people and population on earth with a valid opportunity to hear the gospel in a language they can understand by 2000.
88. Establish by AD 2000 a system for directing evangelistic resources specifically towards the annual increase in the world's unevangelized population—new, first-time, unevangelized populations (children and youths reaching ages of decision, averaging 15 years old).
89. Send out one million native evangelists from among the thousands of native missionary movements in the Third World, to produce by 2000 a massive revolutionary Third Wave of missions across the world.
90. Have the 3 or 4 top leaders of the world's 2.1 billion Christians preach on live 30-satellite TV in 50 languages directly to the entire world of 6 billion souls on 25 December 2000, appealing to all to welcome and receive Jesus Christ as Lord and Savior on his 2,000th birthday.
91. Conduct by AD 2000 some 500 annual organized citywide multidenominational evangelistic campaigns, some 3,000 citywide denominational campaigns, and hundreds of evangelistic megameetings (each with over 100,000 attenders at once).
92. Conduct global citywide evangelistic campaigns simultaneously by AD 2000, in hundreds of metropolises worldwide, based on an originating campaign in a major Third-World city, beamed by satellite to participating cities.
93. Increase persons attending or reached by organized evangelistic campaigns to 100 million per year by 2000.

94. Increase World A's, the Unevangelized World's, share of citywide campaigns from today's nil to at least 100 (3% of total) by 2000.

Power Evangelism

95. See the decade of 1990-2000 close as greatest decade in Christian history for signs and wonders, miracles, conversion, evangelism and evangelization, with the greatest sign or wonder being Christians loving one another and gathering in unity everywhere.
96. Enable 300,000 itinerant charismatic evangelists to target unevangelized cities, countries, and peoples by 2000.
97. Train 50,000 three-man evangelistic teams of Third World evangelists by 2000, who will itinerate through unreached peoples and cities, evangelizing.
98. Deliberately exercise power evangelism in the world's least evangelized and most hostile environments so that by AD 2000 power Christianity (gifted ministries of signs and wonders) is not enjoyed solely in Christian lands.

PERSUASION EVANGELISM (DISCIPLE!)

Conversion

99. Bring the majority of the human race to Jesus Christ by the end of the century.
100. See at least half of humanity (51%) profess some form of allegiance to Christ by 2000.
101. See one billion people receive Christ as Savior and Lord or rededicate their lives to him and be incorporated into local congregations in the decade culminating in 2000.
102. See recorded inquirers or decisions for Christ (all types of campaigns, missions, correspondence course, decisions cards) reach 60 million a year by 2000.
103. See local church converts/baptisms/confirmation/receptions/new members reach 30 million a year for all churches by 2000.
104. Launch a movement on all 3,000 major university campuses in the world to help fulfill the Great Commission among the 60 million college students in the world's 30,000 tertiary-level universities and colleges by the year 2000.
105. Generate by AD 2000 thousands of converts worldwide as "God's key representatives" in key positions in the entire global range of secular worlds, which representatives will then bring about closure in world evangelization.
106. Make disciples of all nations by AD 2000 through the multiplication method "each one teach and reach one," in which one disciple wins one other within one month, both win one more each in the next month, these 4 win 4, then 8 win 8, etc., until the world is fully discipled after 32 months.
107. Finish the Worldwide Decade of Universal Evangelization (1990-2000) with all its major goals accomplished, with Christ and his gospel universally known and respected, with all Christians united as never before since the Apostolic era, and with over 50% of the world professing some sort of allegiance to Christ as Lord and Savior.

PLANTING EVANGELISM (BAPTIZE!)

Church Planting

108. Make at least a handful of disciples, and plant a beachhead church, within every unevangelized population segment on earth (country, people, metropolis) by 2000.
109. Establish a bridgehead church in every unreached ethnolinguistic people on earth by 2000.
110. Establish a bridgehead church in every unreached minipeople (people group) on earth by 2000.
111. Establish a bridgehead church in every unreached ethnos (micropeople) on earth by 2000.
112. Establish a bridgehead church in every unreached metropolis on earth by 2000.
113. Establish a church-planting movement in every people on earth by 2000.
114. See global church-planting goal completed, with at least one fellowship or church or congregation or nucleus of disciples planted as an ongoing indigenous witness in each

168 AD 2000 GLOBAL GOALS cont.

of the world's 11,500 ethnolinguistic peoples and 7,000 metropolises of over 50,000 population each in AD 2000.

115. See full emergence by AD 2000 of a vast worldwide rash of spontaneous house-church video networks spreading like wildfire across all countries with large denominations.
116. Have in place by AD 2000 a worldwide network of self-replicating media churches (self-propagating youth-led video/radio/TV house-church networks), with well-worked-out autospread procedures and optional low-key full logistical support from older churches and agencies.
117. Begin 3.5 million new churches or house worship centers over the period 1988-1999 resulting in a global total of 6 million churches and, on average, one church by AD 2000 for every 1,000 persons including peoples still unreached in 1988.
118. See 5 million small-group base ecclesial communities (comunidades de base, CEBes) mushroom among the world of the desperately poor by 2000, enabling the poor (46% of the world) to be world evangelizers in their own right.
119. See AD 2000 rapidly-multiplying self-replicating networks of (a) itinerant tourist churches ceaselessly circulating around the world, and (b) itinerant pilgrim churches circumambulating continually across the globe.
120. Mobilize the entire world's 6 million local churches and congregations to complete by AD 2000 the task of world evangelization in their localities and beyond.

PASTORAL EVANGELISM (TRAIN!)

Training

121. Increase World A's, the Unevangelized World's, share of full-time Christian workers from today's 0.7% to 5% by 2000.
122. Increase World A's share of foreign missionaries received from today's 0% to 40% by 2000.
123. Increase World A's share of foreign mission money received from today's 1.3% to 40% by 2000.
124. See that every one of the 7,000 metropolises on earth has several varieties of urban-industrial mission and ongoing ministry begun by AD 2000.
125. Have a system in place by AD 2000 to regularly extend family ministries, of at least rudimentary form, to all 30 million new families begun on earth each year, within one year of each family being begun.
126. Train 800,000 evangelists to equip 600,000,000 Christians to reach 4,000,000,000 unbelievers by the year 2000.
127. Have 600,000 career foreign missionaries of all nationalities serving abroad by 2000.
128. Have 200,000 Third-World citizens serving abroad as foreign missionaries by 2000.
129. Have the world's 22,000 denominations mobilized in such a way that by 2000 each is actively pursuing closure and contributing toward it.
130. See 20,000 foreign missionaries, at present working with Christians in Christian lands, redeployed to work with unevangelized non-Christian populations by 2000.
131. Have 10,000 trained pilgrim evangelizers in closed or closing populations by 2000, traveling around with all the largest religious pilgrimages and pilgrim movements.
132. Harness by AD 2000 the Christian world's one million professional theologians and 10,000 missiologists (including biblical scholars and teachers, church historians, etc.) so that they not only support the global evangelization movement but actively lead and guide it in all parts of the world.
133. Develop a foolproof, inexpensive, Christian communications network available to and usable by all Christians everywhere by 2000.
134. Get, by AD 2000, substantial Great-Commission-content messages (news stories about

Christianity, Christ, and the gospel) circulating every day in the world's 20 major languages of telecommunication, in 3 modes: (a) across the world's secular news services (wire services, teletype services, audio services, video services, film services, global telecommunication networks), (b) throughout the world's satellite networks (broadcasting, telephone, communication links), and (c) in the world's professional computer networks (academics, librarians, scholars, financiers, aid & relief, church executives, research & development, military/armed forces, police/INTERPOL, espionage, government, diplomacy, UN agencies, etc.).

135. Inaugurate numerous series of leadership spiritual renewal seminars to renew all the world's church leaders who will then bring fundamental change within all nations, and so bring about worldwide evangelization by 2000.
136. Plan an interactive series of local, national, regional, continental, confessional, and global consultations on world evangelization climaxing in AD 2000.
137. Celebrate the millennial year with Celebration 2000, a massive global event on the part of all Great Commission Christians, in myriads of locations across the world.

Literature

138. Increase World A's, the Unevangelized World's, share of annual Scripture distribution from today's 1% to 25% by 2000.
139. Increase World A's share of annual tract distribution from today's 4% to 20% by 2000.
140. Increase World A's share of Scripture languages from todays 3% to 10% by 2000.
141. Increase World A's share of annual Christian literature circulation from today's 0.2% to 10% by 2000.
142. Increase World A's share of Christian periodicals from today's 1% to 10% by 2000.
143. See annual distribution of Christian literature (tracts, leaflets, books, Scriptures) reach 2 billion pieces per year, evenly distributed worldwide by 2000.
144. Have adequate access to Holy Scripture by 2000 for every population segment on earth, through written or spoken translations either in its mother tongue, or a closely-related language or idiom, or a market language, or trade language, or lingua franca.
145. Publish a printed Gospel in every language on earth by 2000.
146. Translate and publish Scriptures (at least one Gospel) in 4,000 languages by AD 2000.
147. Complete media versions of the whole Bible (on audio cassette, tape, record, computer disk, hypertext, video, film) in the 6 major Christian languages by 2000.
148. Expand total languages possessing a basic list of printed essential Christian literature (Holy Scripture, commentaries, daily readings, daily living) from the present 500 to 3,000 by AD 2000.
149. Coordinate a whole series of megaministries (ministries each reaching over one million different people a day)—Scripture circulation, literature, broadcasting, tract distribution, house-to-house visiting, citywide evangelistic campaigns, nationwide crusades, etc.—to the point where cumulative evangelization far outstrips the birth rate and the whole world is reached by these methods by the end of this century.
150. Hand a tract with a gospel message or picture to every individual in the world by 2000.
151. Distribute a Scripture selection to every soul on earth, in his or her own language, by 2000.
152. Give a Gospel or portion to every literate person on earth by 2000.
153. Give a Gospel selection or leaflet, in pictorial or comic form with minimum words, to every preliterate soul on earth, in his or her own language, by 2000.
154. Help every literate Christian on earth to own his or her own copy of the New Testament by 2000.
155. Mail a New Testament to every telephone subscriber on earth by 2000.
156. Place a Bible in the hands of every family on earth by 2000.
157. Teach every capable man, woman, and child on earth, by the year 2000, to read the

168 AD 2000 GLOBAL GOALS cont.

Bible in their own language, using computer/laser technology.

158. Enroll 500 million non-Christians in Bible correspondence courses by 2000.
159. See Bible correspondence course graduates reach 50 million each year by 2000.

CLOSURE: SOME FUTURIST MEGAGOALS

160. Assist today's megacomplex of "2000 plans toward AD 2000" to achieve, collectively as well as individually, their AD 2000 goals.
161. Assist the Kaleidoscopic Global Plans view of today's 2,000 plans for AD 2000 to achieve their numerous goals.
162. See an enormous synergistic cross fertilizing effect evolve in which the "2,000 plans toward AD 2000" all interact and assist each other resulting in closure on most of their goals by 2000.
163. See individual goals of all 2,000 global and nonglobal AD 2000 plans fulfilled by the turn of the century.
164. Accomplish by AD 2000 definitive fulfillment of the 20 top global megapriorities as seen by Great Commission Christians.
165. See major features of future scenarios for world evangelization by 2000 actually take place.
166. Fulfill positive goals set out in alternate scenarios for world evangelization by AD 2000 and beyond.
167. See to it that all achievements by AD 2000, especially provision of concrete resources or totals, have provision for annual upgrading to take care of (a) attrition among human resources due to illnesses, resignation, retirements, departures, deaths, (b) replacement of concrete items due to wear and tear (15% of all Bibles, film prints, etc., disintegrate annually), and (c) the world's population explosion with 14 million new souls arriving on earth in the year 2000 itself; this overall provision then being extended for each successive year beyond.
168. Attain total world evangelization for first time ever by 31 December 2000 but regard that milestone date not primarily as the end of the 20th century but as the beginning of the 21st with its years beyond.

Source: *Countdown to AD 2000: The Official Compendium of the Global Consultation on World Evangelism by AD 2000 and Beyond.* Edited by Thomas Wang.

MISSION MAGAZINES

Action Magazine, P.O. Box A, Greenwood, IN 46142. Quarterly, free.

Actionline, P.O. Box 203, Prospect Heights, IL 60070. Organizational, bimonthly, free.

Around the World, P.O. Box 553000, Miami, FL 33055. Quarterly, free.

Asian Report, P.O. Box 9000, Mission Viejo, CA 92690.

Beyond, P.O. Box 248, Waxhaw, NC 28173. Organizational, bimonthly, free.

Bibles for the World News, Box 805, Wheaton, IL 60189. Organizational, quarterly, free.

Breakthrough, P.O. Box 1122, Wheaton, IL 60189. Soviet Union and Eastern Europe, bimonthly, donation.

Call to Prayer, P.O. Box WGM, Marion, IN 46952. Organizational, bimonthly, donation.

Childlife Magazine, 919 W. Huntington Drive, Monrovia, CA 91016. Organizational, quarterly, donation.

Chosen People, The, 1300 Cross Beam Drive, Charlotte, NC 28217. Jewish evangelism, 11/yr, $5.00/yr.

Christian Mission, P.O. Box 4488, Charlottesville, VA 22901. Support national workers, bimonthly, donation.

Compassion Update, P.O. Box 7000, Colorado Springs, CO 80933. Child aid, bimonthly, free.
Door of Hope, P.O. Box 303, Glendale, CA 91209. Quarterly, free.
Doorways, P.O. Box C, Colorado Springs, CO 80901. Organizational, 4/yr, free.
East Asia's Millions, 404 S. Church Street, Robesonia, PA 19551.
Europe Report, The, P.O. Box 668, Wheaton, IL 60187. Organizational, 4/yr, free.
Eurovision Advance, P.O. Box 1136, Claremont, CA 91711. Eastern bloc countries, quarterly, $1.00/yr.
Evangelical Missions Quarterly, P.O. Box 794, Wheaton, IL 60189. News, quarterly, $14.95/yr.
Evangelical World, P.O. Box WEF, Wheaton, IL 60189. Monthly, free.
FEBC News, P.O. Box 1, La Mirada, CA 90637. Organizational, quarterly, free.
Feed the Children, Box 36, Oklahoma City, OK 73101. Child aid, bimonthly, free.
Food for the Hungry, 7729 E. Greenway Road, Scottsdale, AZ 85260. Poverty, monthly, free.
Global Prayer Digest, 1605 Elizabeth Street, Pasadena, CA 91104. Monthly, $8.00/yr.
Horizon International World Reporter, 17041 Ruffner Street, San Diego, CA 92111. Organizational, quarterly, free.
Horizons, P.O. Box 969, Wheaton, IL 60189. Bimonthly, $2.00/yr.
In Other Words, P.O. Box 2727, Huntington Beach, CA 92647. Organizational, 8/yr, free.
Increase Magazine, P.O. Box 410, Hatfield, PA 19440. Organizational.
Indian Life, P.O. Box 3765 Station B, Winnipeg, MB, R2W 3R6. North American Indians, bimonthly, 5.00/yr.
International Bulletin of Missionary Research, P.O. Box 1308E, Fort Lee, NJ 07024-9958. Research/scholarly issues, monthly, $12.00/yr.
International Journal of Frontier Missions, P.O. Box 40638, Pasadena, CA 91104. Frontier missions, quarterly, $15.00/yr.
Latin America Evangelist, P.O. Box 52-7900, Miami, FL 33152. Latin America, quarterly, free.
Lausanne Communique, 2531 Nina Street, Pasadena, CA 91107. Bimonthly, free.
Luke Society News, The, 1121 Grove Street, Vicksburg, MS 39180. Biannual, free.
Map International Report, P.O. Box 50, Brunswick, GA 31521. Organizational, 6/yr, free.
MARC News Letter, 919 W Huntington Dr., Monrovia, CA 91016. Research, bimonthly, free.
Mission Frontiers, 1605 Elizabeth Street, Pasadena, CA 91104. Monthly, $4.00/yr.
Missionary Monthly, 4517-A Broadmoor Avenue, Grand Rapids, MI 49508. Reformed and Presbyterian churches, 9/yr, $10.00/yr.
Missionary Tidings, The, 901 College, Winona Lake, IN 46590. Women's missionary group news, 9/yr, $6.00/yr.
Native Reflections, Box 891, Hot Springs, SD 57747. Native Americans, quarterly, free.
Newswire, P.O. Box 1122, Wheaton, IL 60189. Eastern bloc countries, bimonthly, donation.
OC International, 25 Corning Ave., Milpitas, CA 95035. Organizational, quarterly, donation.
OMS Outreach, Box A, Greenwood, IN 46142. Organizational, bimonthly, donation.
Open Doors News Brief, P.O. Box 27001, Santa Ana, CA 92799. Eastern bloc, monthly, $12.00/yr.
Overseas Council Newsletter, P.O. Box 751, Greenwood, IN 46142. Training nationals, 5/yr, free.
Partnership Update, P.O. Box WRC, Wheaton, IL 60189. Organizational, monthly, free.
Quiet Miracle, The, 625 E. No. Broadway, Columbus, OH 43214. Missions, 5/yr, donation.
SIM Now, 10 Huntingdale Blvd., Scarborough, ON, M1W 2S5. Organizational, bimonthly, free.
Teen Missions Control, 885 East Hall Road, Merritt Island, FL 32953. Youth ministries, n/a, free.
The Commission, P.O. Box 6767, Richmond, VA 23230.
The Enterprise, 7185 Millcreek Drive, Mississauga, ON, L5N 5R4.
The Wider Look, 68 Summerleaze Road, Maidenhead, England, Sl6 8EP. World evangelization news, quarterly, $10.00/yr.

Together, 919 W. Huntington Drive, Monrovia, CA 91019. Ministry to two-thirds world poor, quarterly, $25.00/yr.
Urban Missions, P.O. Box 27009, Philadelphia, PA 19118. 5/yr, $10.00/yr.
Wherever, P.O. Box 969, Carol Stream, IL 60189. 3/yr, free.
World Christian Magazine, P.O. Box 40010, Padadena, CA 91104. *Time* magazine of world missions for world changers, bimonthly, $13.00/yr.
World Evangelization, 2531 Nina Street, Pasadena, CA 91107. News, monthly, donation.
World Harvest Magazine, P.O. Box 12, South Bend, IN 46624. Bimonthly, free.
World Vision Magazine, 919 W. Huntington Drive, Monrovia, CA 91016. Bimonthly, free.
Worldorama, P.O. Box 12609, Oklahoma City, OK 73157. Quarterly, free.
Worldwide Thrust, Box 1707, Fort Washington, PA 19034. Quarterly, free.

GUIDELINES FOR A MISSIONS CONFERENCE

The Planning

1. Set the date for the best time of the year—when the weather is good, few people will be away, and there are few conflicts with school activities and other events. Should be held at the same time every year.
2. Determine the duration of the conference; the eight-day conference is the most effective.
3. One year is needed to prepare adequately. Schedule speakers and musicians; other conference personnel.
4. Form subcommittees. Involvement of people is the key to interest and success.
5. Establish a work schedule.
6. Select a short, catchy conference theme; also a Scripture verse which expresses the theme.
7. Select a missionary display area.
8. Choose your conference participants: appointees, missionaries, main speakers, musicians, nationals.

EXPENSE REIMBURSEMENT AND HONORARIA

1. Pay travel, lodging, and meal expenses.
2. Determine honorarium. Range: from $50 to $200 per day.
3. Encourage volunteers to house and feed participants.

UTILIZATION

1. Appointees: one to two minutes.
2. Missionary report: five to six minutes.
3. Main speakers: 25 minutes.
4. Musicians: two or three numbers.
5. National report: five to seven minutes.

The Program

SUNDAY SCHOOL

1. Schedule missionaries in as many classes as possible.
2. Determine missionaries best suited for various age groups.
3. Print schedules two weeks in advance.

MAIN SERVICES

1. Determine number and times of services.
2. Print and distribute order of services to participants.
3. No dead spots or wasted time.
4. Keep introductions to a minimum.
5. Variety is an asset; interview a national or well-known missions leader for five to eight minutes; phone a missionary out on the field—install a phone in the sanctuary and amplify through the sound system; eight to ten minute skits; don't follow the same order of service every night; if your church has multiple choirs, have a combined choir leading the worship; utilize a small orchestra; schedule a "missionary choir" of 15 or more missionaries.

Special Events

1. Orientation dinner for participants on the Saturday evening prior to the conference.
2. A children's conference for children, grades one through five or six. A full-time children's worker should be brought in to conduct this conference.
3. Focus on the young people. Promote one night of the main conference as Youth Night. Plan an extravaganza after the service: the world's largest pizza; the world's

largest noodle; missionary scavenger hunt.

4. Flashes from the field—slide/tape or video presentation of your own missionaries 15 minutes prior to the evening service.
5. Ladies' luncheon midweek at an attractive restaurant. Keep cost low, provide missionaries with complimentary tickets.
6. Mens' breakfast Saturday morning before the closing Sunday of the conference. Select a speaker appealing to men (could be a woman). Schedule the conference musician to sing (doesn't matter if he's a she). Begin at 8 A.M. and finish by 9:30 A.M.
7. Missions banquet Saturday evening just before the final Sunday at 6:30 P.M. Make it a dress-up affair. Allow high school and college age young people to attend at half price. Ask the conference musician to do a 20–25 minute mini-concert.

The Promotion

INTERNAL PUBLICITY

1. Put promotional covers on hymnbooks.
2. Meet with Sunday school workers six weeks before the conference and ask them to promote it every Sunday in their classes.
3. Pulpit announcement: play a two-minute taped portion of a message by one of your speakers or play one minute of a song by your musician. Begin announcements eight weeks prior to the conference.
4. Begin prayer emphasis at mid-week services eight weeks prior to the conference. Each week devote increasing amount of prayer time; the week before opening day, devote the entire mid-week service to the conference.
5. Friday evening before the conference, schedule home prayer meetings.

DIRECT MAIL

1. Two mailings will be sufficient.
2. Letter one week prior with a brochure, faith-promise envelope, and prayer card.
3. Letter at mid-conference reminding people to pray for the conference, their faith-promise offering, and to attend the "Great Final Day."

PUBLIC ADVERTISING

1. Newspaper: regular, weekly ad for four weeks giving conference dates, speakers, and musicians.
2. Radio: both pay and free opportunities are frequently available. Send announcements to all stations, secular and Christian. Purchase spot announcements. Try for "drive times" (7 A.M. to 9 A.M. and 4 P.M. to 6 P.M.).
3. Television: try to get an interview the week before the conference; also try scheduling interviews for your conference guests. Many TV stations have a community calendar each week. Send the same information to them as you would to the radio stations.

Source: *The Big Event* by Dr. Kenneth Moon, minister at large, Greater Europe Mission. Used by permission. A more comprehensive treatment with sample exhibits and helpful sample promotional material is available for $5 from Greater Europe Mission, P.O. Box 668, Wheaton, IL 60189-0668. Send check with order and ask for *The Big Event: Planning Your Missions Conference.*

"" FOCUS QUOTE

The spirit of Christ is the spirit of missions, and the nearer we get to him the more intensely missionary we must become. —Henry Martyn

---

MISSIONARY CONFERENCE THEMES

A Church for Every People by AD 2000 • A Light to the Nations • Anywhere, provided it be forward (David Livingstone) • At the name of Jesus every knee shall bow (Philippians 2:10) • Beyond My World • Building Our World Vision • Challenge of the 90s • Countdown to the Year 2000 • Decade of Decision—Reaching Out for Christ in the 90s • Expect Great Things from God, Attempt Great Things for God (William Carey) • Faith Under Fire • God's Work in Today's World • God's People Uniting to Further His Kingdom • His Last Command—Our First Concern • His Plan—Our Purpose • If Not Me, Who? If Not Now, When? If Not Here, Where? • If Jesus Christ be God and died for me, then no sacrifice can be too great for me to make for him (C. T. Studd) • Information, Inspiration, Involvement • Jesus Christ: Lord of the Earth, Hope of the World • Let the Earth Hear His Voice • Light My Fire (with candles in all services) • Love This World Through Me • Mission on Line—'91 • Missions on the Move • Missions Means You! • Missions: Around the Community, Around the World • Missions: Lifework, Homework • Missions: God's Heart for the World • Missions: A Family Affair • Missions—A Mandate and a Privilege • Now let me burn out for Christ (Henry Martyn) • Oh for a hundred thousand lives to be spent in the service of Christ (George Whitfield) • Only as the church fulfills her missionary obligation does she justify her existence • Operation Opportunity • Our Church a Mission Station—Our Congregation a Missionary Team • Our Mission—(name of town) and the World for Christ • Our Best for Our Master • Partners in the Gospel—Partners in His Harvest • Pass It On—Across the Street; Reach Out—Across the Sea • People who change the world; will you be one of them? • People to People • Pushing Back the Darkness • Putting Wings to Missions (Isaiah 40:31) • Reach Out to the World • Reaching the World with God's Love • Reaching Out: Around the World, Across the Street • Tell the nations that the Lord reigns (Psalm 96:10) • Sharing the Good News • Should I Not Be Concerned? • So Send I You • The Unfinished Task—The Unchanging Task • The Time Is Now • The Word to a World in Revolution • The Word to the World in Chaos • The Servant God Uses • The Glory of the Impossible • The World Is Changing . . . the Need Remains • The World Is Waiting • The supreme task of the Church is the evangelization of the world • The light that shines farthest shines brightest nearest home • The prospects are as bright as the promises of God (Adoniram Judson) • The Mission of the Church Is Missions • To See As God Sees • Toward AD 2000 • Untold Millions Still Untold • Vision '91—God's Kingdom in Focus • We miss . . . They miss . . . Don't miss . . . Missions • What Will It Take? • Who Cares? • Why should anyone hear the Gospel twice before everyone has heard it once? (Oswald J. Smith) • Why Missions? • World Thrust '91 • World Evangelism Until Christ Returns • World Crisis—My Involvement • World Christians • World Changers • World in Review • You must go or send a substitute (Oswald J. Smith) • YOUnited in Mission • Your Waiting World

ADOPT-A-PEOPLE PROGRAM

The world is too big for any one church to tackle, and many pastors despair from the constant barrage of requests for funds and prayers. In this program, each church, depending on its size, adopts one or more 12,000 unreached people groups and its mission team. When a church adopts a people, it commits to pray for, financially support, and become acquainted with their adopted people. In this practical way a church can fulfill a part of its mission stewardship.

1. The adopt-a-people program provides a way for churches to become involved in reaching an unevangelized group.
2. Churches work through a chosen mission agency, providing informed, concerned, dedicated prayer and financial support.
3. It does not mean giving up current mission support, but taking on a new, more intimate commitment of responsibility for their unreached group.
4. It means hanging in there until a small, growing church is established which can begin evangelizing its own people.
5. It means the joy and excitement of being part of a worldwide cooperative effort involving thousands of churches and hundreds of mission agencies—each taking a small, bite-sized piece.

What can your church do?

1. Contact your denominational mission agency or select a mission agency from the list below. The "adoption list" of the groups not yet evangelized might look something like this:

Adopt-a-People

#9,320	☑	Teda	(Chad)	Adopted by First Presbyterian
#9,321	☐	Teimurtash	(Iran)	Not yet adopted
#9,322	☑	Tharu	(Nepal)	Adopted by Calvary Baptist
#9,323	☐	Totis	(India)	Not yet adopted
#9,324	☐	Tuareg	(Niger)	Not yet adopted
#9,325	☑	Turkomans	(Iran)	Adopted by Trinity Assembly

2. Determine which group to adopt.
3. Ask the agency you select to send you information on this group and to put you on the mailing list of the team working with them.
4. Begin to receive special offerings or save your loose change and send it to the agency supervising the efforts. Designate this money for outreach to your adopted people group.
5. Give reports and pray corporately during your church missionary activities.

Agencies Participating in the Adopt-A-People Program

(For addresses, refer to mission agencies list.)

Action International Ministries
Africa Inland Mission
AIMS, Operation Unreached
Church Planting International
Conservative Baptist Foreign Mission Soc.
Foursquare Missions International
Frontiers, Inc.
Gospel Recordings
Mission to Unreached Peoples
Overseas Missionary Fellowship
Partnership International
Pioneers
Presbyterian Frontier Fellowship
RBMU International
South America Mission, Inc.
Sudan Interior Mission International
The Evangelical Alliance Mission
WEC International
Youth With a Mission

For more information on the Adopt-A-People program write: U.S. Center for World Mission, Mobilization Division, 1605 Elizabeth Street, Pasadena, CA 91104.

FOCUSWORDS

Candidate: someone who has applied to a mission agency. The *candidate secretary* is the one who corresponds with people who apply to a mission. Some agencies gather candidates interested in career service at a week or two of *candidate school* to orient them to the agency and to evaluate each candidate for acceptance. Once accepted by the mission board, the candidate is called an *appointee*.

Church planting: means starting new churches, not landscaping the church lawn.

Contextualize: putting the truths of God into the context of the local culture. This involves seeing how one's own culture colors understanding of biblical truths, and then taking the unvarnished truth and applying it in another culture.

Deputation: commonly refers to the prayer and financial support rallying that career and short-term missionaries do before leaving for the field and during furloughs.

Development: a process enabling a community to provide for its own needs, beyond former levels, with dignity and justice.

Expatriate: someone who has left his or her home country to live and work in another country. When we visit another country, we don't see ourselves as internationals. We call ourselves "expatriates" or "expats" for short.

Field: short for the *mission field.* A field is anywhere that missionaries do their work. Regrettably, "field" sounds like it's out in the country or on a farm. Most mission situations are not farms and are usually urbanized to some extent. A *field director* is one who oversees those who are working together in a particular country, people group, or location.

Great Commission Christians: believers who take the Great Commission seriously.

Incarnational: living as much like and with the people to whom you're ministering as you are able. Just as Christ took on our flesh (incarnate means to en-flesh) and culture to serve us, so cross-cultural missionaries often aspire to enter the culture and struggles of the people they serve.

Indigenous: native; originating in and having characteristics of a certain place or country. "Indigenous music" is usually created by nationals in their local style.

International: what we call a national when he comes to our country.

Itinerant: refers to people or ministries that travel from place to place.

Mission agency: a Christian organization helping to further God's work in the world. There's an amazing variety of activities and emphases among the hundreds of mission agencies throughout the world. *Mission board* and *sending agency* are virtually the same thing. *Para-church* refers to a Christian organization independent of any church denominational structures. Many mission agencies are also para-church structures.

Missions committee: a specific group of people within some churches that oversees the missionary activity of the church. This committee often has responsibility to allocate money for mission purposes, as well as to equip and educate the entire church to support missionaries. Some churches have a *missions pastor* who oversees these missions endeavors.

National: any person who lives in another country. The *national leaders* are local people who are leading the church or mission. Many national leaders are also missionaries. A *national church* is one that is led by national leaders.

People group: a significantly large sociological grouping of individuals who perceive themselves to have a common affinity for one another because of their shared language, religion, ethnicity, residence, occupation, class or caste, situation, or combination of these.

Relief: the urgent provision of resources to reduce suffering resulting from a natural or man-made disaster.

Support: the finances and prayer missionaries need to ask others to give for their work. A *supporter* is one who gives money and prayers. A *support team* is the group of people who supports the missionary. They may or may not know each other.

Tentmaker: a cross-cultural witness who works at a paying, usually secular, job overseas. Often they are able to gain entry into *closed countries,* which severely restrict traditional mission efforts. Tentmakers rarely make tents for a living, like the apostle Paul did, but they all should have the intention to further God's work in the world.

Term: can refer to the length of a missionary's time commitment to a mission organization.

Many career missionaries serve successive "terms" of two to five years. Often they spend a period of months back in their home countries between terms, usually called a *furlough*. A *short term* can be as little as two weeks or as long as three years.

Third World: Years ago, the United States and "free" Europe came to be called "the West." Eastern bloc countries, such as the Soviet Union and other communist nations, formed a second world. A good chunk of the lands formerly colonized by European powers came to be dubbed as the "third world." Third-world countries are typically "underdeveloped" economically by western standards. Recently, someone from the third world, not realizing the history of the term, said, "Wait a minute, we're not even second. We don't want to be a 'third world.' We want to be called the 'two-thirds world' since two-thirds of the world's population lives in these countries." The third world is now sometimes referred to as the two-thirds world.

Unreached peoples: essentially "unchurched" peoples lacking an indigenous, evangelizing, church-planting movement. Without such a movement, the people within these groups will likely never hear and obey the gospel. An unreached people group is less than 20 percent practicing Christian.

Source: *Stepping Out* published by Short-Term Missions Advocate, Inc. Copyright © 1987. Used by permission.

"" FOCUS QUOTE

Do not weigh a risk by its probability of success but by the urgency and value of its possible achievement.

—Ralph D. Winter

20 SIGNIFICANT MISSIONARY LEADERS

Selected by Dr. Earle E. Cairns, author and historian.

Ulfilas (c.311–c.381). Apostle to the Goths, born perhaps in the region of the Lower Danube, which, according to some historians, had become the home of his Cappadocian parents, who in 246 had been taken captive by the Goths in one of their raids in Asia Minor. When about twenty he was taken by the king of the Goths on an embassage to Constantinople, where he remained for ten years. There became a Christian and received a good education. In Constantinople became acquainted with the Arian bishop, Eusebius of Nicomedia, who with other bishops consecrated him to the episcopate in 341. He then returned as a missionary to the Goths. It is said that the whole tribe of the Visigoths were won to the Christian faith. For the first seven years (341-348), he labored in his native land beyond the Danube, until persecution compelled him and his fellow Christians to seek refuge on Roman soil. From here he continued work among the Goths. By force of circumstances Ulfilas had been won to Arian Christianity. As an Arian, preached to the Goths and led them to the same doctrinal views of Christianity. Greatly enhanced missionary labors by inventing an alphabet for the Goths, and then by giving them most of the Bible in their own language.

Patrick or **Patricius** (c.389–c.461). Celtic missionary to Ireland. His father, Calpurnius, seems to have been a deacon in the local Celtic church, his grandfather a priest. When sixteen years old he was taken captive in one of the Irish pirate raids and was sold as a slave to a herdsman in North Ireland, where he was held for six years. He escaped and somehow found his way to Gaul, where he spent some time in a monastic school. After returning home he saw a vision and heard voices from the Irish coast, crying, "We beseech thee, child of God, come and walk again among us." Answering the call, he set out for Ireland. About 432 he gathered people about him in the open fields and preached Christ to them. His burning zeal, deep sincerity, and gentleness of manner won

20 SIGNIFICANT MISSIONARY LEADERS cont.

peasants and nobility alike. Planted scores of churches and baptized over 100,000 converts. At Armagh he founded a monastery which was to become important and historic in the annals of the Christian church. His preaching made a strong impact, not only upon the Ireland of his day, but upon all medieval missions and church life of Ireland, of Great Britain, and of Continental Europe. Both Catholics and Protestants like to claim Patrick, but he was neither. He was a Celtic missionary in the British Isles before the time of either Protestants or Roman Catholics. Chief writing and our chief source of information concerning his life is his *Confessions*.

Columba or **Columkille** (c.521–597). Irish Celtic missionary, "Apostle of Caledonia." Born of Royal stock at Gartan, a wild district in Donegal county, Ireland, son of an Ulster chief. Given an excellent education and in the Christian faith, early distinguishing himself for piety and zeal. Dedicated himself to monastic zeal. Ordained deacon and priest, about 551. In 563, at the age of forty-two, left Ireland with twelve companions, and landed on the small island of Iona, off the coast of Scotland. There founded his monastery from which center he and companions evangelized the Picts and more carefully taught the Scots who had already professed Christianity. He made Iona his chief abode and a great school and missionary training center. He made frequent visits to Scotland where he founded many churches. Also maintained a close connection with Ireland, making frequent visits there in behalf of his monasteries. Soon smaller societies had to be formed and other monasteries founded. Accounted one of the poets of Ireland, being the author of three hymns. Finished his missionary career dying beside the altar in the church while engaged in his midnight devotions. A product of the Celtic church of the Isles, whereas Augustine was from Rome and represented the Catholic church.

Augustine, Archbishop of Canterbury (d.c.604). Missionary to England and prior of St. Andrews monastery in Rome. In AD 596 Pope Gregory I sent him and several companions as missionaries from Rome to England. They were kindly received by King Ethelbert and permitted to worship in the Church of St. Martin where the Christian queen Bertha worshiped. In 597 the king was baptized. Later many of his subjects likewise were baptized. Augustine then went to Arles, France (597), to be consecrated as first archbishop of Canterbury. Gregory then made Augustine metropolitan bishop of England, which made England independent of the French see. He was successful in winning Kent and Essex to the Roman church.

Boniface or **Winfrid** or **Wilfrith** (680–755). English Benedictine missionary—"The Apostle to the Germans." An Anglo-Saxon, born in Devonshire, England. Early entered monastic life, and at thirty he was ordained. Seemingly had before him an assured place in his church in England; but preferred to be a missionary. About 716 with a few companions he sailed for Frisia, a group of small islands off the Dutch coast, to help Willibrord in his difficult task. Meeting strong opposition from the local Frisian king, he returned to England. Soon he was back on the continent, going first to Rome from 718 to 719, there receiving from Pope Gregory II a commission to Germany. Began work in Thuringia; but before many months, hearing of the death of the hostile Frisian king, went back to Frisia to help Willibrord establish the church in Frisia. From 719-722 worked with Willibrord; then went to Germany and entered upon the main work of his life. He first went to Hesse, and then later back to Thuringia. His ten years' work in these two provinces was highly successful. Great numbers of pagans were converted, the Irish or Celtic monks were brought largely into obedience to Rome. In 732 Pope Gregory III made Boniface an archbishop with authority to establish new sees in Germany. In 738, after third and last trip to Rome, organized the church in Bavaria, and later in Thuringia. About 744 helped to establish the important and influential monastery of Fulda. A year or two later was made archbishop of Mainz, also worked among the Franks, trying to reform the Frankish church. Everywhere Boniface went, it was with papal sanction and authority. In 739 the pope named him apostolic vicar or papal legate. His authority and influence were tremendous. In 742 assembled the first German council, organized churches, schools and monasteries according to the Roman pattern. He trained and sent missionaries from the German churches, and did more than any other to instill into the hearts of the bishops and clergy of Central Europe permanent obedience to the pope, and did much to lay the foundation for the medieval papacy. In 753 he went back to preach to the Frisians; with a company of monks and priests spent about two years traveling among them, preaching to them, baptizing thousands of converts, destroying pagan temples, and building churches. In 755, a body of hostile pagans fell upon the group, and Boniface was slain. He died with a copy of the Gospels in his hands.

Cyril or **Cyrillus,** original name **Constantinus** (c.826–869). Missionary to the Slavs, born in Thessalonica, studied at Constantinople. He and brother Methodius (c.815-885) both monks and priests in the Eastern Catholic church, in 860 went to the Khazars, a Tartar tribe on the northeast shore of the Black Sea, and planted a church. For a while they worked among the Bulgars whose king was Boris or Bogaris. About 862, in answer to an invitation from Duke Ratislav of Moravia, Emperor Michael III sent Cyril and his brother to Moravia, where they labored with great success. Cyril invented an alphabet and translated the Bible into the Slavic language. In 868 he and Methodius went to Rome and effected an agreement with Pope Adrian II for the use of the Slavic language; their work thus came under the supervision of the Roman church. In 869 Cyril died while in Rome. His brother returned to Moravia having been consecrated archbishop.

Methodius (d.885). "Apostle to the Slavs," born in Thessalonica, son of a military officer, educated in Constantinople. In 860 with his brother Cyril (d.869) began mission work on the northeast shore of the Black Sea. Later at the invitation of Duke Ratislav, they were sent to the Moravians. Great success attended their labors. In 868 the brothers, representatives of the Eastern church, went to Rome to effect an agreement with Pope Adrian II relative to their work. Cyril died in Rome the next year, and Methodius returned to Moravia. After the death of Ratislav of Moravia and of Pope Adrian II of Rome, the attitude of both Rome and the people of Moravia changed. In 879 again summoned to Rome, and though the independence of the Slavic church was confirmed, the status of the church became insecure. After the death of Methodius, Latin replaced the Slavic language and the church deteriorated and paganism again became dominant.

“” FOCUS QUOTE

Rewards God gives; reward God is.
—Ralph D. Winter

Lull, Raymond (c.1235–c.1315). Missionary to the Moslems. Born at Palma, capital of Majorca, one of the Baleric Islands. Lived a worldly life in the court of King James of Aragon until he was about thirty. Turned to the ascetic life and became a Franciscan tertiary. Began zealous preparation for missionary work among the Moslems, first learning the Arabic from a Moorish slave, then starting the College of Miramar to teach the Arabic and Chaldean tongues. For several years lectured in Paris and Montpellier. Wrote a book of diagrams and arguments to prove the truth and superiority of Christianity. In 1291, when about fifty-five, made first missionary trip to the Moslems. In Tunis, North Africa, challenged the fanatical Moslems to a public disputation, which resulted in banishment. Back home spent several years lecturing and writing. In 1305 or 1306 made a second attempt to convert the Moslems of Tunis, but was again banished. Back in Europe succeeded in securing a council decree to establish professorships of oriental languages at Avignon, Paris, Bologna, Oxford, and Salamanca. In 1315 at age 80

20 SIGNIFICANT MISSIONARY LEADERS cont.

made third attempt to penetrate the Moslem lines of North Africa. The Moslem population rose against him and drove him from the city with sticks and stones. The next day, on way back to Majorca, he died. Lull had introduced some new principles into the missionary enterprise by studying the Arabic language at home, writing and lecturing on missions, seeking to establish schools of oriental languages, and substituting love for force in missionary labors. His theologico-philosophical works were many, reaching perhaps the number of three hundred.

Las Casas, Bartolome de (1474–1566). Spanish priest and missionary to the American Indians of the West Indies. Born at Seville, Spain, studied the humanities and law at the universities of Seville and Salamanca, and entered the Dominican order in 1523. He and father were companions of Columbus in the latter's second voyage to America in 1498. Bartolome made his second trip to the New World when he came with Columbus to Haiti in 1502. As a planter owned Indian slaves as did the other colonists. In 1510 ordained priest, the first to be ordained in the New World. Soon saw the evil of enslaving the Indians, and released his slaves. Las Casas then returned to Spain to seek amelioration for the ill-treated Indians. Cardinal Ximenes appointed him Protector General of the Indians, and he returned with this commission to the New World. Spent most of his long life preaching to the American Indians and defending them against the cruelties of their conquerors. Nine times he traveled between America and Spain seeking respite for the horrible miseries which the Spaniards were inflicting upon the Indians. Efforts were in behalf of the Indians, not only in Haiti, but in Cuba, Peru, Guatemala, Nicaragua, St. Domingo, and Mexico. In 1544 at age seventy became bishop of Chiapa, Mexico. In 1547 returned to Spain and completed *Historia General de las Indias,* the source of much valuable information on the Spanish discoveries and conquests in the New World.

Xavier, Francis (1506–1552). Jesuit missionary, born in an aristocratic family in Navarre, Northern Spain. As a student in the University of Paris distinguished himself in philosophical studies. Came under the influence of Ignatius Loyola who persuaded him in 1534 to become a charter member of what was later to become the Society of Jesus, popularly known as the Jesuit Order. Ordained priest in 1537. In 1540, at the request of King John III of Portugal, Loyola appointed Xavier to go to India as papal legate. Sailing from Lisbon, Portugal, the next year, he landed in the Portuguese colony of Goa in West India in 1542. He had the Creed, the Lord's Prayer, the Ave Maria, and the Decalogue translated into the vernacular, and committed them to memory. Dissatisfied with the results he was achieving in India, in 1545 turned to the East Indies. Worked for three years, returning to India in 1548. During seven years in India and the Indies, he baptized people by the thousands, both adults and infants. Founded a missionary school at Goa. Having been made a missionary bishop of the entire East, felt he must go to other lands too. Left to others his work in southern Asia and proceeded to Japan in 1549. Spent two years preaching through interpreters and baptizing. Then leaving to others this mission also, proceeded toward China to build a church, making a visit to Goa on the way, in 1552. But he died of a fever off the coast of the mainland of South China, near Canton. Work was superficial, an exploration rather than a structure. He was canonized in 1622.

Carey, William (1761–1834). "The father of modern missions," born in the home of a poor Northamptonshire weaver and schoolmaster in Paulersbury, England. Elementary schooling received under father's teaching in the village school. At fourteen apprenticed to a shoemaker and cobbler. Applied himself so diligently to study while working that he early learned Latin, Greek, Hebrew, French, and Dutch, and in his teens could read the Bible in six languages. This bent toward language a great asset in his missionary life. In 1783 joined the Baptist church and shortly after began preaching. Along with his cobbling, teaching, and preaching, he continued his study of languages, he followed the missionary activities of John Eliot and David Brainerd, read with avidity the *Voyages* of Captain James Cook. As pastor at Moulton he preached missions and urged his neighboring ministers to do likewise. Wrote a treatise on "An Enquiry into the Obligations of Christians to Use Means for the Conversion of the Heathen." 1792, preached memorable sermon on "Expect Great Things from God; Attempt Great Things for God." In that year helped organize the English Baptist Missionary society, the next year went to India as one of its first missionaries. His first plan had been to go to Tahiti. First years on the field developed for him many hardships and disappointments. Financial reverses due to Dr. Thomas' mismanagement, illness and death among his children, and the serious mental illness of his wife until her death in 1807, made his work difficult. Soon after arriving in India became superintendent of an indigo factory from 1794 to 1799. In 1799, purchased a small indigo plantation and started a mission. Because of opposition from East India Company, 1800, he moved to Serampore in Danish territory a short distance from Calcutta. William Ward and Joshua Marshman joined him to form the famous Serampore Trio, where teaching, preaching, and printing provided the chief missionary activity and also provided much of the fund for carrying on the mission. In 1800 Carey baptized first converts, among them his oldest son, Felix. From 1831, professor of Oriental languages in the newly founded Fort William College in Calcutta, a position held for thirty years. He and Marsham did much translating of the Scriptures. The Bible or portions of it were issued by the Serampore press in about thirty-six languages and dialects. Besides preaching and translating the Scriptures, they translated Indian classics into English, prepared grammars and dictionaries in various languages, opened many mission stations in India, Burma and East Indies, and established schools out of which in 1818 came Serampore College. Did much for the advancement of horticulture and agriculture in India. He advocated two important missionary principles: (1) equality of missionaries and natives, and (2) self-sustaining missions. Forty-one years of missionary life in India were crowded full. He was an indefatigable worker, even to death at age seventy-three. The labors of few missionaries have been more fruitful. The Serampore Press under his direction rendered the Bible accessible to more than three hundred million people. Helped end the burning of child widows in 1829.

Morrison, Robert (1782–1834). First Protestant missionary to China, born in Morpeth, Northumbria, England, of Scottish father and English mother. In childhood an industrious student, as a man a learned scholar. In preparation for life work gave special attention to the study of theology, medicine, astronomy, and the Chinese language, the latter learned from a Chinese scholar who was living in London, and from some Chinese manuscripts in the British museum. In 1807 the London Missionary Society ordained and sent Morrison to Canton, China, first Protestant missionary to that land. The East India Company refused him passage; he went to Canton by way of New York. In China lived in a cellar and was rarely seen in public. He made such good progress in his mastery of the language that in 1809 he was employed by the British East India Company as an interpreter, a position held for the next twenty-five years. Worked assiduously for the mission, but labors were confined largely to literary activities, writing a Chinese grammar, preparing the standard Anglo-Chinese dictionary and encyclopedia, writing tracts and books, preparing a hymn book, translating morning and evening prayers from the *Book of Common Prayer*, and translating the entire Bible by 1823. Work was that of foundation laying, a very necessary part of the work of introducing missions in China. Number of converts as a result of twenty-seven years of labor perhaps did not exceed three or four, the first of which was not until after he had been seven years in China. Activities other than serving as interpreter for the East India Company, and translating and writing for the mission, consisted in treating the sick in his dispensary, and the founding of an

20 SIGNIFICANT MISSIONARY LEADERS cont.

Anglo-Chinese school at Malacca to train missionaries for the Far East. Made a trip to England in 1824, at which time he was made a fellow of the Royal Society. Promoted the cause of missions in China. In 1826 returned to China. As interpreter for the East India Company forced to become negotiator in the Anglo-Chinese War that had broken out about that time.

Mills, Samuel John (1783–1818). Promoter of foreign missions, born in Torringford, Connecticut. Graduated from Williams College and Andover Theological Seminary, and spent a short time at Yale. While in college a member of the famous haystack prayer group. During brief stay at Yale met and befriended young Henry Obookiah from the Sandwich Islands, who found a home and a genial fellowship with Samuel and his parents. In the seminary became a part of the prayer meeting and mission study group that resulted in the organization of the American Board of Commissioners for Foreign Missions in 1810, and in the sending of Judson, Rice, Nott, Hall, and Newell to India in 1812. He also helped start a mission to the Sandwich Islands. Licensed to preach in 1812, and made two missionary tours through the midwestern and southern states between 1812 and 1815, distributing Bibles and visiting sick soldiers. In 1815 ordained. The next year agent for the School for Educating Colored Men. Exerted some influence in the founding of the United Foreign Missionary Society for the Presbyterian and Reformed Churches, in the organization of the American Bible Society in 1816, and in the starting of an African school near Newark. In 1817 went as an agent of the colonization society to Western Africa, which led to the formulation of the Republic of Liberia.

Moffat, Robert (1795–1883). Pioneer translator and missionary, born at Ormiston, Scotland. At fourteen apprenticed as a gardener; formal education meager. Soon after conversion became interested in missions, and applied to the London Missionary Society. After some special instruction accepted and sent to Cape Town, South Africa, arriving there in 1817. Thrust into the center of several cannibalistic tribes in this colony which had just, three years before, come under the British. The next year, 1817, set out for Namaqualand, the home of the notorious outlaw, Afrikaner. To the surprise and marvel of everyone, won the dreaded outlaw to Christ. In 1817 brought him to Capetown. Moffat next went to Lattakoo in 1820. Mary Smith came from London to become Moffat's wife, and the couple settled at Kuruman in Bechuanaland in 1825, where a mission was soon established. Later, with much hard work and many obstacles, organized a mission station at Inyati among the Matabele. The Moffats spent the years 1839-1843 in England furthering the cause of missions in Africa. It was at this time that Livingstone was inspired by Moffat to go to Africa. After arriving on the field Livingstone married Moffat's daughter, Mary. In 1870 the aged missionaries returned to England. During last years in England labored untiringly for the cause to which he had devoted his earlier life and talents. While on the field translated the Bible into Sechvana by 1859, authored a hymn book, and wrote two missionary books on South Africa: *Labors and Scenes in South Africa* and *Rivers of Water in a Dry Place*.

“” FOCUS QUOTE **God had an only Son and he was a missionary and a physician.** —David Livingstone

---

Livingstone, David (1813–1873). Missionary and explorer. Born near Glasgow, Scotland, in poor family. With first wages bought a Latin grammar. By studying while at work and at home secured an early education. In 1830 at age seventeen entered the University of Glasgow, began the study of medicine and theology. Goal was to be missionary in China. In 1838 accepted by the London Missionary Society. The Opium War in China was on, and the society sent him to Africa in 1840.

Went to Robert Moffat's station in South Africa, but soon pushed on to the tribes farther north. In 1843 started a mission at Mabotsa, two hundred miles north of Moffat. In 1845 married Mary Moffat and built a home. The next year found it necessary to move forty miles farther north; built second home and established a station. Because of a long, continued drought soon had to move again. Went forty miles farther north to Kolebeng and built third and last house for himself and family. When Boers sacked this house he built no more. Began great work of missionary and colonial exploration, saying, "The end of the geographical feat is the beginning of the missionary enterprise." He discovered Lake N'gami in 1849 and the Victoria Falls in 1853. Sent his family to England; then made hazardous fourteen hundred mile trip to Loanda and back. In 1856 returned to England with high acclaim as a world-renowned explorer. Opened Africa both to missions and to civilization. In 1857 resigned from the London Missionary Society, returned to Africa under the British government with the three-fold goal: (1) to make Christ known to Africa; (2) to find the source of the Nile and open Africa to the west; and (3) to eradicate pernicious slave traffic. In 1858 discovered great lakes of East Africa. In 1864 he was back in England; but in 1865 returned to Africa to spend his last eight years. On this trip, 1871, Stanley found him when lost to the world. In 1873 his native helpers found him on his knees in the posture of prayer, his spirit having departed from the body. Body was taken to England and buried in Westminster Abbey.

Nevius, John Livingston (1829–1893). American Presbyterian missionary to China, born near Ovid, New York, educated at Ovid Academy, Union College, Schenectady, and Princeton Theological Seminary. In 1849 taught school in Georgia for a year and became a Christian. Upon conversion decided to prepare for the ministry; while in the seminary decided to be a missionary. In 1853 completed seminary course, ordained, married, appointed by the Presbyterian Mission Board, and assigned to Ningpo, China. They arrived in China when the Tai Ping Rebellion was in progress and found much difficulty in establishing work. Nevius was in Ningpo, Chekiang Province (1854-1859); in Japan (1859-1861), preparing a *Compendium of Theology.* for Chinese students; at Tungchow, Shantung Province (1861-1864); in America (1864-1868); and at Chefoo, Shantung (1871-1893), where he spent last days in Bible translation. Wrote *China and the Chinese* and *Demon Possession and Allied Themes.* Noted especially for the "Nevius Method," which places strong emphasis on the training of the Chinese Christians as much as possible to carry on their own work, with their own resources and from their own homes. Built churches in native style, and trained ablest nationals in Bible and prayer to be leaders. In 1890 Dr. Nevius met in conference with the Korean missionaries to explain the plan, following which time it was effectively applied in that country. Also introduced into China Western fruits and vegetables, Jersey cows for milk, and full tires for the wheels on their carts.

Taylor, James Hudson (1832–1905). Founder of China Inland Mission, born in Barnsley, Yorkshire, England. After spending time in the study of medicine and theology, went to China under the newly formed China Evangelization Society, arriving in Shanghai in 1854. He stressed prayer and faith only in money raising. Adopted Chinese dress. For six months lived in the home of Dr. Medhurst of the London Missionary Society, whose book *China* had helped stir him to go to China. Spent years 1854 to 1860 working in Shanghai, Swatow, and Ningpo. Before long retired from the society which had sent him out and continued as an independent worker. At Ningpo he had charge of a hospital, in 1858 married Maria Dyer, the daughter of a missionary in China. In 1860 returned home, spent the next five years translating the New Testament into the Ningpo dialect, writing a book on China, and praying for missionaries for inland China. His definite planning in 1865 at Brighton to establish a society for the evangelization of inland China and return to China in 1866

20 SIGNIFICANT MISSIONARY LEADERS cont.

with his wife and children and sixteen new missionaries was the beginning of the China Inland Mission. Became the director of the mission, traveled widely in China and Europe in its interest. Returned to China in 1872. At his death in 1905 at Changsha, there were 205 stations with 849 missionaries, and 125,000 Chinese Christians in the China Inland Mission.

Slessor, Mary (1848–1915). Scottish missionary to Africa. Born near Aberdeen, Scotland. Father died when she was a child and she became the main means of support for the family. The appeal of David Livingstone for missionaries to Africa intensified her desire to serve. With her mother's approval she sailed for Nigeria in 1876. For three years she labored so self-sacrificingly and strenuously that her health gave way. She had to return to Scotland and, when in 1880 she returned to Africa, she was assigned to Old Town and worked hard as before. In 1891 the British Government appointed her Vice-Consul for Okoyong. She knew the mind of the African well. In later years she chose to remain in Africa.

“” FOCUS QUOTE **Some wish to live within the sound of church and chapel bell. I wish to run a rescue mission within a yard of hell.**
—C.T. Studd

Studd, Charles T. (1862–1931). Missionary pioneer, born in England. C.T. Studd's father, Edward, had been converted in the Moody-Sankey campaign in 1877. Father then became deeply concerned about the spiritual welfare of his three sons. By the time C.T. was sixteen he had become an expert cricket player; when nineteen captain of his team at Eton. After finishing Eton College, attended Cambridge University (1880-1883), and here, too, was an outstanding cricketer. In 1883, while still at Cambridge, he heard Moody and Sankey and was converted, dedicating life and inherited wealth to Christ. He gave away about $150,000 while in China. He and six others, the famous "Cambridge Seven," offered themselves to Hudson Taylor for missionary service in the China Inland Mission and in 1885 sailed for China. They at once began the study of the language, donned Chinese garb, and ate with the Chinese, trying to substitute Chinese for Western ways, and to identify themselves with the natives. Three years later Studd married a young Irish missionary from Ulster. By 1894 the Studds were broken in health, and had to return to England. Unable to return to China they severed their connection with the China Inland Mission and turned their property over to the mission. In 1896-97 Mr. Studd toured the universities of America in behalf of the newly formed Student Volunteer Movement. In 1900 the family went to South India in search of a climate more conducive to Mr. Studd's health and for a place to serve. For six years C.T. Studd was pastor of the Union Church at Ootacamund, South India. After their return to England in 1906, he began to plan with Dr. Karl Kumm on a scheme of opening Africa from the Nile to the Niger for Christian missions. In 1910, leaving his wife and four daughters in England to care for the secretarial responsibilities for both the home base and the field, he started on his journey to penetrate the heart of Africa. On a part of the trip he was accompanied by Alfred Buxton, a young man who later became his son-in-law. The Heart of Africa Mission was organized in 1912. A mission was established at Niangara in 1913, in June 1915 twelve converts were baptized. Late in 1914 Studd returned to England for more missionaries, and in 1916 to Africa with a party of missionaries. In 1919 Gilbert Barclay, another son-in-law, joined the mission which was named the Worldwide Evangelization Crusade. Studd died in Africa two and a half years after Mrs. Studd, who had died in Malaga.

Zwemer, Samuel Marinus (1867–1952). American Dutch Reformed missionary to Moslems, born at Vriesland, Michigan, educated at Hope College, Holland, Michigan, and New Brunswick Theological Seminary in New Jersey. In college came under the influence of Robert Wilder, and became one of the first members of the Student Volunteer Movement, and one of its leaders. In 1888–1889 Zwemer and others formed a new missionary organization, The Arabian Mission. In 1889 James Cantine went to Arabia. The next year Zwemer was ordained and followed. In 1894 the regular board of the Dutch Reformed Church in America took over the mission. Between 1890 and 1905 Zwemer worked at Busrah, Bahrein Islands, and Muscat; later with headquarters at Cairo, Egypt, traveled over the most of the Islamic world, arousing in Europe and America interest in bringing the Christian faith to Moslems and in training missionaries. In spite of the firm hold of Islam on these lands a few converts were made. In 1906 organized and was chairman of the Conference on Islam at Cairo, but maintained his residence in the United States from 1905 to 1910 while promoting missions in his denomination. In 1910 returned to missionary field on the Arabian Gulf. Visited many missions over the Moslem world, making notable contributions to the cause in South Africa and the Netherlands Indies, where he preached in Dutch, English, and Arabic. Also visited India and China several times. In 1911 started the *Moslem World,* and was its editor for about forty years. For nearly a decade after returning from the mission field, professor of missions and comparative religions at Princeton Theological Seminary. Author of about fifty volumes in English, and a number in Arabic. A few of his works: *Arabia the Cradle of Islam, Moslem Doctrine of God, Islam a Challenge to Faith, The Unoccupied Mission Fields of Africa and Asia, The Moslem World,* and *Mohammed or Christ.*

Scudder, Ida (1870–1960). Medical missionary to south India. Born at Ranipet near Madras. Educated in Moody's girls' school at Northfield. Back in India to help her mother was "called" to be a medical missionary. Studied medicine at Women's Medical College in Philadelphia and Cornell University Medical School. Returned to India in 1900. Founded Schall Hospital at Vellore, a nursing school, school of pharmacy, and a medical college in 1915 for women and one for men in 1947.

Source: *Wycliffe Biographical Dictionary of the Church.* Elgin Moyer, revised and enlarged by Earle E. Cairns. Published by Moody Press. Copyright © 1982. Used by permission.

EXCUSES FOR NOT WANTING TO GO TO AFRICA

1. KENYA believe I don't want TOGO to Africa? I'm GHANA be afraid because all the BOTSWANA capsize, DAKAR will break down in the middle of the jungle, and ZAIRE plane might crash.
2. Monkey meat is high in cholesterol.
3. Preschoolers are as close to wildlife as I want to come.
4. Domino's Pizza can't deliver in 30 minutes or less.

Source: Word Records "Don't Send Me to Africa" by Scott Wesley Brown contest.

Used by permission of *Wherever* Magazine. © 1983, TEAM.

10 CITIES NEAREST HEAVEN

	Elevation feet	meters
1. Lhasa, Tibet, China	12,002	3658
2. La Paz, Bolivia	11,010	3630
3. Cuzco, Peru	11,152	3399
4. Sucre, Bolivia	9,331	2844
5. Quito, Ecuador	9,249	2819
6. Toluca, Mexico	8,793	2680
7. Bogotá, Colombia	8,675	2644
8. Cochabamba, Bolivia	8,390	2557
9. Addis Ababa, Ethiopia	7,900	2408
10. Asmara, Ethiopia	7,789	2374

THE BIGGER, THE BETTER?

Total number of children, grandchildren, and great-grandchildren born to the average:

West German woman 6
American woman 14
African woman 258

“” FOCUS QUOTE **My life, my reputation, my possessions, Lord, let me loose the tension of the grasping hand.** —Jim Elliot

QUESTIONNAIRE FOR WOULD-BE MISSIONARIES

Eating Habits

- Can you eat bony fish without choking?
- Can you drink lumpy, lukewarm, unknown beverages . . . and keep them down?
- Do you recognize hot pepper dishes without running for a bucket of water?
- Can you eat your bag lunch during a ten-minute flight in an MAF small plane with accompanying turbulence?

Personal Hygiene

- Shaving . . . cold water, no mirror, no shaving cream?
- Take a bath in 8 inches of water . . . with bucket and cup?
- Design, build, and use an outhouse. Can you manage if there is no outhouse?

Home Economics

- Can you shop for six weeks in advance?
- Or, wash dishes without running water?
- How about making toilet paper serve all your needs for paper products in the kitchen?
- Why sweep a dirt floor?
- Catch, eject, or eliminate unwanted reptiles, mammals, and large insects from the house?

Skills

- Do you know how to use hammer, chisel, plane, saw, ax, machete, hoe, or lasso?
- Can you fix radios, tape recorders, watches, cars, tractors, bicycles, houses, lawnmowers, plumbing, electrical wiring, generators?
- Can you plant a vegetable garden . . . or at least ask intelligent questions about someone else's?
- Can you ride a horse? If not, can you walk 20 miles?
- Have you had good experiences in off-road driving?
- Can you handle medical situations, with or without professional skills?
- Can you make complicated Bible truths clear and simple?
- Are you a skilled linguist?

Personal

- Are you willing to love and serve people who are demanding, ungrateful, or lie about you?
- Are you willing to trust God to supply your needs, protect you, and give you wisdom for situations beyond your experience or capabilities?

Source: *Lifeline Magazine*, published by Unevangelized Fields Mission.

ROBERT W. PIERCE AWARD FOR OUTSTANDING CHRISTIAN SERVICE

Sponsored by World Vision. Recipients are selected based on effectiveness of ministry, length of time devoted to ministry, number of people helped through the ministry, difficulty of situation, and quality of the ministry program.

Year	*Name*	*Job*	*Location*
1980	Dr. Kenneth A. Elliott	medical missionary	Upper Volta, West Africa
1981	Dr. Eleanor Soltau	World Presbyterian medical missionary	Middle East
1982	Fritz Urschitz	Liebenzell (Germany) missionary	Papua New Guinea
1983	Miriam Krantz	Mennonite missionary nutritionist	Nepal
1984	Molly Lou Holt	public health nurse	Korea
1985	Dr. Mary Varghese	doctor to the disabled	India
1986	Elfrieda Toews	C&MA missionary nurse	Irian Jaya, Indonesia
1987	Rev. Hedley J. Sleath	Methodist pastor	South Africa
1988	Dr. Bob Foster	Africa Evang. Fellowship med. missionary	Zambia
1989	Maria Das	lay pastor	Bangladesh

Next to going yourself comes the pleasure of getting someone else to go. Secure another person to enter foreign service and your life is doubled.
—Robert Wilder

Organizations & Foundations

EVANGELICAL COUNCIL FOR FINANCIAL ACCOUNTABILITY MEMBERS (as of April 1, 1990)

ECFA exists to increase the public's confidence in the business affairs of evangelical organizations by establishing standards, helping organizations meet the standards, certifying compliance, communicating with the public.

ACMC, Inc., P.O. Box ACMC, Wheaton, IL 60189 708-260-1660. Mobilizes local churches for world missions through consultation services, seminars, and communication ministries.

Advent Christian General Conference of America, P.O. Box 23152, Charlotte, NC 28212 704-545-6161. Serves denominational church by providing resources and training opportunities, legal entities, communications, funding plans, and becoming a catalyst for evangelism and edification.

Advent Christian Village, Inc., P.O. Box 4305, Dowling Park, FL 32060 904-658-3333. Services to children, individuals, retired adults, and families with special needs.

Africa Inland Mission International, Inc., P.O. Box 178, Pearl River, NY 10965 914-735-4014. Evangelizes unreached peoples, develops Christian leadership, encourages local evangelism and cross-cultural missionary outreach by churches.

African Bible Colleges, Inc., P.O. Box 103, Clinton, MS 39056 601-924-6842. Establishes and funds Bible colleges in Africa.

African Enterprise, Inc., P.O. Box 727, Monrovia, CA 91016 818-357-8811. Serves the church in Africa through African evangelists, leadership training, reconciliation ministry, and human need programs. Emphasis on urban complexes.

AGAPE Counseling Associates, Inc., 2530 Browncroft Blvd., Rochester, NY 14625 716-385-6030. Christian counseling, including support groups for pastors.

Agape Village–Church of the Exceptional, Inc., 3711 Agape Village Rd., Macon, GA 31210 912-471-3700. Provides homes and work for mentally retarded adults.

All Nations, Inc., 1605 Elizabeth Street, Pasadena, CA 91104 818-398-2473. Literacy program in ethnic languages, produces Christian literature in various languages and missions awareness materials for all age levels.

Alpha Center Inc., P.O. Box 604, Placentia, CA 92670-0604 714-993-4400. Professional counseling services, parenting program for barrio parents.

Ambassadors for Christ International, Inc., P.O. Box 48029, Atlanta, GA 30362 404-371-0404. National evangelistic teams.

Ambassadors For Christ, Inc., P.O. Box 0280, Paradise, PA 17562 717-687-8564. Ministers to Chinese students and professionals in the U.S.

America's Keswick, Keswick Grove, Whiting, NJ 08759 201-350-1187. Drug and alcohol rehabilitation program, Bible conference and retreat center.

American Association of Bible Colleges, P.O. Box 1523, Fayetteville, AR 72702 501-521-8164. Provides accreditation services, research, seminars, information services.

American Church of The Good Samaritan, Inc., 8323 Sand Lake Rd., Orlando, FL 32819-5099 407-351-0611. Distributes Scripture through Bible text greeting

ECFA MEMBERS cont.

cards. Chapel ministry and mission outreach program.

The American Council of the Ramabai Mukti Mission, P.O. Box 4912, Clinton, NJ 08809 201-735-8770. Ministries include orphanage, schools, medicine, homes for the blind, handicapped and destitute women, evangelism, agriculture, church planting in India.

American Family Association, P.O. Drawer 2440, Tupelo, MS 38803 601-844-5036. Promotes biblical ethic of decency.

American Leprosy Missions, Inc., One Broadway, Elmwood Park, NJ 07407 201-794-8650. Leprosy medical treatment, rehabilitation, research, public and patient education.

American Missionary Fellowship, P.O. Box 368, Villanova, PA 19085 215-527-4439. Plants and develops churches. Prison ministries, mailbox clubs in rural and urban America.

American Tract Society, P.O. Box 462008, Garland, TX 75046 214-276-9408. Prints and circulates religious tracts.

AMG International, P.O. Box 22000, Chattanooga, TN 37422 615-894-6060. Worldwide ministry through newspaper evangelism, support of national workers, radio and church planting. Supports orphanages, schools, day-care centers, hospitals, food and clothing centers, leprosariums, and clinic ministries. Publishes *Pulpit Helps,* maintains Expositors Microfilm library and AMG Publishers.

Appalachian Bible College, Box ABC, Bradley, WV 25818 304-877-6428. Collegiate-level biblical instruction.

The Art of Family Living, P.O. Box 2000, Dallas, TX 75221 214-669-1151. Teaches through radio broadcasts, audio cassette tapes, books.

Asbury Theological Seminary, 204 N. Lexington Ave., Wilmore, KY 40390 606-858-3581. Provides graduate, professional and continuing studies for ordained and lay ministries. Resource center for World Wesleyan Leadership.

Association of International Mission Services P.O. Box 64534, Virginia Beach, VA 23464 804-523-7979. Provides framework for unity and fellowship among churches, mission agencies, and training institutions. Involved in world evangelization.

Athletic Ministries International, Inc., P.O. Box 241076, Memphis, TN 38124 901-345-0258. Utilizes basketball to share the gospel.

Atlanta Care Center, Inc., P.O. Box 9629, Atlanta, GA 30319 404-261-2736. Helps women deal with unexpected pregnancy.

Atlanta Union Mission, P.O. Box 1807, Atlanta, GA 30301 404-588-4000. Provides shelter and care, activities, counseling, and religious instruction.

Atlantic City Rescue Mission, P.O. Box 5358, Atlantic City, NJ 08246 609-345-5517. Provides meals, shelter, food baskets, furniture, counseling. Residential rehabilitation/discipleship program.

Azusa Pacific University, P.O. Box A.P.U. Azusa, CA 91702-7000 818-969-3434. Fully accredited, coeducational, Christian university.

Bachman Memorial Home, Inc., P.O. Box 849, Cleveland, TN 37364-0849 615-479-4523. Provides emotional, spiritual, and developmental treatment to young men aged 13 to 19.

Back to God Hour of the Christian Reformed Church, 6555 W. College Dr., Palos Heights, IL 60463 708-371-8700. Radio and television ministry of the Christian Reformed Church. Produces radio and television programs.

Back to the Bible, P.O. Box 82808, Lincoln, NE 68501 402-474-4567. Teaches the Word of God through the media.

Bakersfield Rescue Mission, P.O. Box 2222, Bakersfield, CA 93303 805-325-0863. Evangelistic gospel services, meals, clothing, shelter. Live-in discipleship programs.

The Baptist Foundation of Oklahoma, 1141 N. Robinson, Oklahoma City, OK

73103 405-232-9677. Receives and administers endowment gifts for Baptist causes, offers estate planning services to individuals.

Baptist General Conference, 2002 S. Arlington Heights Rd., Arlington Heights, IL 60005, 708-228-0200. Fellowship of Baptist churches in the U.S. and Caribbean Islands.

Barry Moore Ministries, Inc., P.O. Box 611529, Port Huron, MI 48061-1529 519-681-3137. Conducts evangelistic crusades.

BCM International, Inc., 237 Fairfield Ave., Upper Darby, PA 19082 215-352-7177. Strengthens the local church, leading children, teenagers, and adults to faith in Jesus Christ, encouraging them to attend local Bible-believing churches.

Ben Haden Evangelical Association, Inc., 554 McCallie Ave., Chattanooga, TN 37402 615-267-7959. Produces a worldwide weekly TV and radio program.

The Berean League, 2875 Snelling Ave. North, St. Paul, MN 55113 612-633-0654. A coalition of Christians in Minnesota providing concise, credible information of current state, political, social, and moral issues, including relevant biblical principles.

Berean Mission, Inc., 3536 Russell Blvd., St. Louis, MO 63104 314-773-0110. Establishes and assists local churches in foreign countries and the U.S.

Berkeley Crisis Pregnancy Center, 2991 Shattuck Ave., #201, Berkeley, CA 94705 415-849-9916. Provides counseling and care for women and their families in the East Bay area who are experiencing pregnancy-related crises.

Bethany Bible Church, 6060 N. 7th Ave., Phoenix, AZ 85013 602-246-9788. Major emphasis is study of God's Word. Not affiliated with any denomination.

Bethany Christian Services, 901 Eastern Ave., N.E., Grand Rapids, MI 49503 616-459-6273. Private child welfare/child placement agency.

Bethel Bible Village, P.O. Box 5000, Hixson, TN 37343 615-842-5757. Family-style care for children from broken homes where one or both parents are in prison.

Bethel Ministries, P.O. Box 390, Wise, VA 24293 703-328-3161. Released time classes, Bible clubs, camping program, correspondence school, senior citizens, and jail ministry.

Bethel Temple of Evansville, Inc., 4400 Lincoln Ave., Evansville, IN 47715 812-477-8888. Interdenominational church, Christian school, television ministry, unwed mother's home, food and clothing bank.

Bible and Literacy League (BALL), 8955 Old Lemay Ferry Rd., Hillsboro, MO 63050 314-789-4368. Provides spiritual help, shelter and care; trains national leaders.

Bible Basics International, P.O. Box 340508, Tampa, FL 33694 813-920-2264. Teaching ministry to believers in third world and communist countries through literature and cassettes. Conducts seminars and conferences in churches, camps and retreats in the U.S.

Bible Christian Union, Inc., P.O. Box 410, Hatfield, PA 19440-0410 215-361-0500. Establishes and strengthens local churches with emphasis in Europe, evangelism, discipleship, and leadership training.

Bible Literature International, Inc., P.O. Box 477, Columbus, OH 43216 614-267-3116. Provides Bibles and literature through missions and national ministries worldwide.

Bible Study Fellowship, 19001 Blanco Rd., San Antonio, TX 78258 512-492-4676. Helps people better understand the Bible through a five-year course of study.

Bible Translations on Tape, Inc., P.O. Box 2500, Cedar Hill, TX 75104 214-291-1555. Records, programs, and distributes the Scriptures on cassettes predominately for people who are illiterate.

ECFA MEMBERS cont.

Bibles for the World, Inc., P.O. Box 805, Wheaton, IL 60189 708-668-7733. Prints and distributes Bibles worldwide, supports and trains national missionary workers, supports and educates needy children in India under the Partnership Parents program.

Bibletown Community Church, Inc., P.O. Box A, Boca Raton, FL 33429-9000 407-395-2400. Church services.

Bill Glass Evangelistic Association, P.O. Box 356, Dallas, TX 75221 214-291-7895. Interdenominational crusades, "Total Person Weekends" in prisons.

Billy Graham Evangelistic Association, 1300 Harmon Pl., Minneapolis, MN 55403 612-338-0500. Evangelistic crusades, Schools of Evangelism, "Hour of Decision," *Decision* magazine, literature distribution, and films.

Biola University, Inc., 13800 Biola Ave., La Mirada, CA 90639 213-944-0351. Offers undergraduate, masters, and doctoral programs.

Blessings International, Inc., 5881 S. Garnett Road, Tulsa, OK 74146 918-250-8101. Facilitates medical missions by being a source of pharmaceuticals and medical supplies for ministries primarily in developing nations.

Bob Cryder Team Ministries, Inc., P.O. Box 14845, Portland, OR 97214-0845 503-238-4728. Revival, discipleship, evangelistic crusades.

Body & Soul Ministries, 16004 Bonniebank Terrace, Germantown, MD 20874 301-258-1018. Promotes spiritual growth, physical discipline, and stewardship in nutrition and exercise.

Boise Bible College, Inc., 8695 Marigold Street, Boise, ID 83714-1220 208-376-7731. Biblical and general education programs.

Bowery Mission & Young Men's Home, 40 Overlook Drive, Chappaqua, NY 10514 914-769-9000. Gospel services, live-in discipleship program, soup kitchen, free clothing, bathing facilities, medical care, and overnight shelter. Christian Herald Children and *Christian Herald* Magazine.

Breakthrough, Inc., P.O. Box 121, Lincoln, VA 22078 703-338-4131. Intercessory prayer ministry, annual prayer conference.

Bryan College, P.O. Box 7000, Dayton, TN 37321 615-775-2041. Four-year, Christian liberal arts college.

Calcutta Mission of Mercy, P.O. Box 11108, Tacoma, WA 98411 206-756-2001. Provides Christian Bible school and Bible college training, day school, medical outreach ministries and training, feeding programs for the needy, church facilities, and other religious and charitable activities in any part of the world.

Caleb Project, P.O. Box 40455, Pasadena, CA 91114 818-398-2121. Mobilizes the church for involvement in missions.

Calvary Church, P.O. Box 470477, Charlotte, NC 28226 704-543-1200. Nondenominational, 4,000-member church.

CAM International, 8625 La Prada Drive, Dallas, TX 75228 214-327-8206. Establishes indigenous churches, assists existing churches in Spanish-speaking areas.

Campus Crusade for Christ International, Arrowhead Springs, San Bernardino, CA 92414 714-886-5224. Evangelistic and discipling ministry.

Cannon Beach Conference Center, P.O. Box 398, Cannon Beach, OR 97110 503-436-1501. Beach resort conference facility.

Carriage Town Mission, P.O. Box 214, Flint, MI 48506 313-233-8787. Gospel services, furnishes food, lodging, and assistance to the needy and unfortunate, youth program with inner city children.

Cedar Ridge Children's Home & School, Inc., Route 2, Box 325, Williamsport, MD 21795 301-582-0282. Boys' home and school, radio station, counseling services, and an outdoor adventure program.

Central Arkansas Christian Broadcasting, Inc., P.O. Box 2771, Hot Springs, AR 71914 501-623-3335. Educational radio FM station affiliated with Moody Bible Institute.

Central Church, Inc., P.O. Box 751950, Memphis, TN 38175-1950 901-365-4673. A New Testament church.

The Chapel, 895 N. Forest Rd., Buffalo, NY 14221 716-634-4440. Interdenominational church, daily radio broadcasts, television program, Christian Central Academy.

The Chapel of the Air, P.O. Box 30, Wheaton, IL 60189 708-668-7292. Radio broadcast ministry.

Chattanooga Bible Institute, 1001 McCallie Ave., Chattanooga, TN 37403 615-266-4574. Resource center for laity or clergy.

Chattanooga Prison Ministries, Inc., P.O. Box 3026, Chattanooga, TN 37404 615-622-5768. Ministers to inmates and their families within a 30-mile radius of Chattanooga.

Cherry Hills Community Church, 3651 S. Colorado Blvd., Englewood, CO 80110 303-781-0091. Seeks to help Christians in their knowledge of Scripture, Christlike character, skills for ministry; Christian school.

Chicago Bible Society, 104 S. Michigan Ave., #520, Chicago, IL 60603 312-236-2169. Promotes serious reading of the Scriptures and their distribution throughout the greater Chicago area. Provides Bible materials without charge to the disadvantaged, prisoners, the poor, the elderly, the blind, the handicapped, and those in shelters and rescue missions.

Child Evangelism Fellowship, Inc., P.O. Box 348, Warrenton, MO 63383 314-456-4321. Reaches the multitude of children with God's Word. Encourages them in daily devotions, witnessing, church attendance, missions.

Childcare International, P.O. Box W, Bellingham, WA 98225 206-647-2283. Meets the needs of the poor with emphasis on the children. Works in Haiti, Kenya, Uganda, Peru, India, Tonga, Mexico, and Southern California with clinics, schools, feeding programs, evangelism, food for work programs, nutrition centers, trade schools, agricultural projects, eye care and surgery, and child sponsorship.

Children's Ministries, Inc., 250 N. Highland Ave., Pittsburgh, PA 15206 412-363-0425. Aids the church through evangelism to children and young people. Encourages Bible reading. Offers services to churches and organizations.

China Ministries International, P.O. Box 40489, Pasadena, CA 91104-7489 818-398-0145. Evangelization of the Chinese people, particularly those living in Mainland China. Gathers and disseminates information on the church in China, trains Chinese evangelists via radio and literature. Provides seminary training in Hong Kong and Taiwan.

Chinese Christian Mission, Inc., P.O. Box 617, Petaluma, CA 94953 707-762-1314. Missionary-sending agency to the Chinese people.

Chinese Overseas Christian Mission, Inc., P.O. Box 310, Fairfax, VA 22030 703-273-3500. Seeks to reach the people of China by (1) sponsorship of daily broadcasts to China; (2) support of persons on campus contacting Chinese students; (3) tour-guided entertainment program; (4) recruitment and placing of campus workers; (5) missions conference and seminars.

Choices, Inc., 775 Second Street Pike, Southampton, PA 18966 215-322-8520. Ministry to women in crisis pregnancy situations; provides alternatives to women seeking abortions.

Chosen People Ministries, 1300 Cross Beam Drive, Charlotte, NC 28217-2800 704-357-9000. Arm of the local churches with specific emphasis on the Jews.

Christ for the Island World, P.O. Box 18962, Greensboro, NC 27410 919-855-0656. Supports national evangelists. Helps them purchase transportation, such as outboard motors and motorbikes.

Christ for the Nations, Inc., P.O. Box 769000, Dallas, TX 75376-9000 214-376-1711. Religious, educational, and missionary organization, two-year Bible school.

Christ Truth Radio Crusade, P.O. Box 610, Upland, CA 91786 714-981-2838. Prison ministry, distributing Bibles to

ECFA MEMBERS cont.

prisoners and offering them a correspondence course.

The Christian & Missionary Alliance, P.O. Box 35000, Colorado Springs, CO 80935-3500 719-599-5999. Church denomination committed to world missions.

Christian Action Council Education and Ministries Fund, 701 West Broad Street, #405, Falls Church, VA 22046 703-237-2100. Campaigns against abortion, infanticide, and euthanasia.

Christian Blind Mission International, P.O. Box 175, Wheaton, IL 60187 708-690-0300. Ministers to blind and handicapped people of the third world.

Christian Business Men's Committee International, P.O. Box 3239, Chattanooga, TN 37404 615-698-4444. Coordinates the CBMC ministry around the world.

Christian Business Men's Committee of U.S.A., P.O. Box 3308, Chattanooga, TN 37404 615-698-4444. Ministers to business and professional men.

Christian Camping International/USA, P.O. Box 646, Wheaton, IL 60189 708-462-0300. An association of Christian camps and conference centers.

Christian Challenge Northern California, Inc., P.O. Box 8100, Vallejo, CA 94590 408-272-8300. Communicates the gospel to the poor and oppressed in cities throughout the world.

Christian Chaplain Services, Inc., P.O. Box 860307, Los Angeles, CA 90086-0307 213-974-8085. Provides chaplains and chaplaincy services to jails, prisons, juvenile detention centers, homes for abused children, and drug and alcohol rehabilitation centers worldwide.

The Christian Church Extension Foundation, P.O. Box 260758, Lakewood, CO 80226 800-843-2233. Financial ministry to independent Christian Churches and Churches of Christ, offers interdenominational church data survey and consultant-guided analysis.

Christian College Coalition, 1776 Massachusetts Ave. N.W., Washington, DC 20036 202-293-6177. An association of approximately 80 liberal arts colleges in the U.S. and Canada. Sponsors professional development activities for faculty and administrators.

Christian Communications of Chicagoland, Inc., 1 N. Wacker Drive, Chicago, IL 60606 312-977-3838. Utilizes mass media as an arm of the church.

The Christian Community Foundation, 7617 Little River Tpk., #340, Annandale, VA 22003 703-362-7658. Services the tax, financial, and administrative needs of giving programs.

Christian Counseling & Enrichment, Inc., 14581 East Tufts Ave., Aurora, CO 80015 303-693-3954. Biblical counseling, consultation, and conferences to help leaders, boards, and staffs.

Christian Counseling Services, Inc., P.O. Box 60383, Nashville, TN 37206 615-254-8341. Marriage, family, and individual counseling, maternity, and adoption services. Individual and family counseling for homosexuality.

Christian Educators Association International, P.O. Box 50025, Pasadena, CA 91105 818-798-1124. Promotes Judeo-Christian values in our schools through magazine, newsletters, prayer groups, seminars, and national convention.

Christian Encounter Ministries, P.O. Box 1022, Grass Valley, CA 95945 916-268-0877. Residential and community counseling center; seminars, retreats, on-property camps, and wilderness camps.

Christian Eye Ministry, P.O. Box 3721, San Dimas, CA 91773 714-599-8955. Overseas medical mission organization to help eradicate blindness in less developed countries.

Christian Family Care Agency, 1121 East Missouri, Phoenix, AZ 85014 602-234-1935. Helps children and families in crisis: pregnancy assistance, foster care, adoption, and family counseling.

Christian Fellowship Church, 4100 Millersburg Rd., Evansville, IN 47711 812-867-6464. Nondenominational evangelical church, adult Bible Lay Institute.

Christian Financial Concepts, 601 Broad Street SE, Gainesville, GA 30501 404-534-1000. Teaches principles of finance and money management.

Christian Herald Association, 40 Overlook Drive, Chappaqua, NY 10514 914-769-9000. Publishes *Christian Herald* magazine. Related ministries: Family Bookshelf, The Bowery Mission of New York City, camping/counseling program for New York City youth.

Christian Herald Children, 40 Overlook Drive, Chappaqua, NY 10514 914-769-9000. Provides a donor-funded two-week camping experience each summer for 900 youngsters ages 6-12.

Christian Homes for Children, Inc., 275 State Street, Hackensack, NJ 07601-5512 201-342-4235. Adoption services, counseling, food and clothing, educational training, and foster care.

Christian Hope Indian Eskimo Fellowship (CHIEF), 1644 E. Campo Bello Drive, Phoenix, AZ 85022 602-482-0828. Ministers to the 36 million Native Americans in the 1,200 tribes of the western hemisphere.

Christian Lay Ministries, P.O. Box 68, Lake Junaluska, NC 28745 704-456-3960. Disciples laity. Sponsors developmental projects in Zaire, Africa.

Christian Laymen's Association of Will County, P.O. Box 2454, Joliet, IL 60434 815-723-6837. Summer day camp for ages 5-12. Youth activities.

Christian Leadership Concepts, Inc., P.O. Box 24274, Nashville, TN 37202 615-726-1717. Trains Christians to use their leadership abilities.

Christian League for the Handicapped, Inc., P.O. Box 948, Walworth, WI 53184 414-275-6131. Encourages disabled persons toward maximum independence.

Christian Legal Society, P.O. Box 1492, Merrifield, VA 22116 703-642-1070. Fellowship of lawyers, judges, law professors, and law students. Promotes the constitutional right of free exercise of religion, resolving conflicts among Christians.

Christian Life Missions, 388 East Gundersen Drive, Wheaton, IL 60188 708-653-4200. Works through other established missions. Operates the Christian Writers Institute; sponsors writing seminars.

Christian Medical & Dental Society, P.O. Box 830689, Richardson, TX 75083-0689 214-783-8384. Encourages Christian students and doctors to apply a Christian mindset in the fields of medicine and dentistry.

Christian Military Fellowship, P.O. Box 1207, Englewood, CO 80150 303-761-1959. Works within the military society with emphasis toward the enlisted ranks.

Christian Ministries Management Association, P.O. Box 4638, Diamond Bar, CA 91765 714-861-8861. Association of Christians involved in management of Christian organizations.

Christian Mission for the United Nations Community, 99 Lafayette Ave., White Plains, NY 10603 914-948-5700. Ministry based at the United Nations and from there to leaders throughout the world.

Christian Missionary Fellowship, P.O. Box 26306, Indianapolis, IN 46226 317-542-9256. Assists the local church in world evangelism. Recruits, equips, and sends missionaries to unreached peoples.

Christian Research Institute, Inc., P.O. Box 500, San Juan Capistrano, CA 92693 714-855-9926. Studies cults, the world of the occult, and Christian apologetics. Expertise spans 300 areas of biblical research and data.

Christian Service Brigade, P.O. Box 150, Wheaton, IL 60189 708-665-0630. Provides programs, training, and counsel in leadership of children.

Christian Service Foundation, Inc., P.O. Box 41, Wichita Falls, TX 76307 817-767-3303. Ministers to military personnel in the Wichita Falls area.

Christian Solidarity International, Inc., 12600 Billington Rd., Silver Spring, MD 20904 301-984-0298. Works in Communist, Islamic, Hindu, and totalitarian-ruled

ECFA MEMBERS cont.

countries where Christians are persecuted for their faith.

Christian Stewardship Association, 917 Beville Rd., Suite #C, S. Daytona, FL 32119 904-760-3170. An association of evangelical IRS Section 501 (c) (3) organizations. Promotes Christian stewardship.

Christian Television Network, P.O. Box 6922, Clearwater, FL 34618 813-535-5622. A nationwide 24-hour Christian network.

Christian Television of Ohio, Inc., P.O. Box 770, Thornville, OH 43076 614-833-0771. 24-hour Christian programming in 145 counties in Central Ohio.

Christian Witness Support Team, P.O. Box 1226, Reedley, CA 93654 209-591-0667. Serves national ministries in the third world.

Christianity Today, Inc., 465 Gundersen Drive, Carol Stream, IL 60188 708-260-6200. Promotes the fundamental truths of the Scriptures through the publication of *Christianity Today, Leadership, Partnership, Today's Christian Woman, Campus Life,* and *Christian History.*

Christians in Action, Inc., P.O. Box 728, Woodlake, CA 93286 209-564-3762. Specializes in personal evangelism and indigenous church planting.

Church Extension Plan, P.O. Box 12629, Salem, OR 97309-0629 503-399-0552. Provides capital loans to churches across the country for new construction, building purchases, remodeling, refinancing, etc.

Church of the Saviour, 651 N. Wayne Ave., Wayne, PA 19087 215-688-6302. Exists to exalt the living God, equip God's people, and evangelize the nations.

Church Resource Ministries, P.O. Box 5189, Fullerton, CA 92635 714-879-5540. Trains church leaders with the focus on church growth, renewal, and the establishment of new churches.

Churches Alive International, P.O. Box 3800, San Bernadino, CA 92413 714-886-5361. Helps local churches establish and multiply discipling ministries.

Cincinnati Bible College & Seminary, P.O. Box 043200, Cincinnati, OH 45204-3200 513-244-8100. Special-purpose institution to prepare people for Christian service.

Circle Urban Ministries, 118 N. Central Ave., Chicago, IL 60644 312-921-1446. Aids disadvantaged residents in the Austin neighborhood of Chicago.

The City Mission of Schenectady, Inc., P.O. Box 760, Schenectady, NY 12301 518-346-2275. Mission work to those not reached by regular church organizations.

City Mission Society, Inc., P.O. Box 496, Buffalo, NY 14205 716-854-8181. Full-service gospel rescue mission in western New York. Open 24 hours a day. Serves over 300 meals daily. Chapel services and Bible studies.

City Union Mission, Inc., 1108 East 10th Street, Kansas City, MO 64106 816-474-9380. Provides material relief: food, clothing, shelter. Counseling. Transition to housing stability and useful job skills.

CityTeam Ministries, P.O. Box 143, San Jose, CA 95103 408-998-4770. Serves disadvantaged people of cities through Rescue Missions. Family outreach, youth outreach, cross-cultural ministries.

CMJ/U.S.A. (A Christian Ministry Among Jewish People), 10523 Main Street, #38, Fairfax, VA 22030 703-273-0711. Ministers to Jewish people. Educates Christians, especially Episcopalians, as to the Jewish origins of the Church, their continuing obligations to the Jewish people.

Coalition for Christian Outreach, 6740 Fifth Ave., Pittsburgh, PA 15208 412-363-3303. Works with tomorrow's leaders on college and university campuses in western Pennsylvania, eastern Ohio, northern West Virginia.

Colorado Christian University, 180 S. Garrison Street, Lakewood, CO 80226 303-238-5386. Equips for Christian ministry.

Columbia Bible College and Seminary, P.O. Box 3122, Columbia, SC 29230 803-754-4100. Nondenominational Bible college with a seminary, extension school, secondary boarding school (Ben Lippen School), and an FM radio station (WMHK).

Community Chaplain Service, Inc., P.O. Box E-734, New Bedford, MA 02742 508-997-3174. Career missionary chaplains minister in nursing homes.

Compassion International, Inc., P.O. Box 7000, Colorado Springs, CO 80933 719-594-9900. Increases awareness and builds understanding concerning the problems facing needy children.

Coral Ridge Ministries, Inc., 5555 N. Federal Highway, Fort Lauderdale, FL 33308 305-771-8840. Coral Ridge Presbyterian Church. Westminster Academy, a K–12 school with 950 students. TV and Radio broadcasts.

Cornerstone Church, 6930 Wood Haven Rd., Roanoke, VA 24019 703-362-2187. Family-oriented, charismatic church.

Covenant Fellowship of Presbyterians, P.O. Box 22409, Louisville, KY 40222-0409 502-339-0204. Strives for renewal in the Presbyterian Church (U.S.A.).

Covenant Theological Seminary, 12330 Conway Rd., St. Louis, MO 63141 314-434-4044. Trains ministers, particularly for the Presbyterian Church in America.

Crichton College, P.O. Box 12144, Memphis, TN 38182-0144 901-458-7526. Four- year college offering eight programs of study: Bible and theology, natural sciences, music, psychology, elementary education, church ministries, and secondary education.

Crisis Pregnancy Center of the Lehigh Valley, P.O. Box 1716, Allentown, PA 18105 215-821-0943.. Outreach to women in the Greater Lehigh Valley Community with crisis pregnancies. Offers alternatives to abortion.

Crisis Pregnancy Support Center 1915 1/2 Church Street, Nashville, TN 37203 615-321-0005. Network of support for women facing unexpected pregnancy.

CRISTA Ministries, 19303 Fremont Ave. North, Seattle, WA 98133 206-546-7200. Seven distinct ministries: CRISTA schools, World Concern, CRISTA Senior Community, Intercristo, CRISTA Broadcasting, CRISTA Camps, and CRISTA Counseling Service.

Crown Ministries, Inc., 530 Crown Oak Centre Drive, Longwood, FL 32750 407-331-6000. Trains people to be financially faithful. Scriptural financial principles are taught in a small group study.

Dallas Theological Seminary, 3909 Swiss Ave., Dallas, TX 75204 214-824-3094. An institutional organization of higher education. Consists of seven programs of study, five master level programs, and two doctoral programs.

Dave Roever Evangelistic Association, Inc., P.O. Box 136130, Ft. Worth, TX 76136 817-237-8491. Supports the ministry of evangelist Dave Roever as he conducts assemblies in public high schools and speaks in crusades, churches, youth rallies, men's retreats, etc. Distributes audio and video tapes, books, newsletters. Weekly television program.

Dayspring Enterprises International, P.O. Box 3309, Virginia Beach, VA 23454 804-428-1092. Innovative use of media in the two-thirds world by means of the publication, production, distribution, broadcast, and exhibition of educational and dramatic programs on motion picture films, slides, video and audio tapes, records, and by printed materials.

Daystar Communications, P.O. Box 3027, Arcadia, CA 91006 818-358-5338. U.S.-based support organization of Daystar University College in Nairobi, Kenya.

Denver Area Youth for Christ, Inc., 1400 S. Emerson Street, Denver, CO 80210 303-744-2715. Campus Life. High school and junior high campuses, youth guidance, incarcerated kids, and urban ministries reaching youth through the probation and court system.

Denver Conservative Baptist Seminary, P.O. Box 10,000, Denver, CO 80210 303-761-2482. Graduate theological school.

Detroit Metro Youth for Christ, 24331 West Eight Mile Rd., Detroit, MI 48219

ECFA MEMBERS cont.

313-533-3900. Four major ministry divisions: Campus Life, Youth Guidance, Urban, and Quizzing and Music.

Detroit Rescue Mission Ministries, P.O. Box 2087, Detroit, MI 48231 313-993-4700. Provides emergency shelter, food, substance abuse counseling, and work training in the Detroit metropolitan area.

Discipleship Counseling Services, P.O. Box 802045, Dallas, TX 75380 214-960-8501. Radio and teaching ministry that concentrates on effectiveness in biblical counseling and discipleship.

Don Anderson Ministries, Inc., P.O. Box 6611, Tyler, TX 75711 214-597-3018. Communication, camping, and counseling.

Eastern European Bible Mission, P.O. Box 110, Colorado Springs, CO 80901-0110 719-577-4450. Strengthens the church in Eastern Europe.

Eastern European Seminary, Inc., 6730 LBJ Freeway, #2195, Dallas, TX 75240 214-404-8077. Seminary-level curriculum in six Eastern Bloc languages.

Echoing Hills Village, Inc., Route 2, Warsaw, OH 43844 614-327-2311. Services developmentally disabled.

ECL/Door of Hope International, P.O. Box 303, Glendale, CA 91209 818-956-7500. Prints and distributes Bibles and Christian literature, supports national Christian workers and pastors in the Soviet Union.

Ed Robb Evangelistic Association, P.O. Box 1945, Marshall, TX 75671 214-938-8305. Evangelism, reform and renewal. Publishes *The Challenge*.

Edgewood Children's Ranch, Inc., 1451 Edgewood Ranch Rd., Orlando, FL 32811 407-295-2464. Christian boarding school; children are accepted on the basis of need.

Elim Bible Institute, 7245 College Street, Lima, NY 14485 716-582-1230. Preparation for ministry.

Elim Fellowship, Inc., 7245 College Street, Lima, NY 14485 716-582-2790. Establishes and maintains churches and missions in the U.S. and abroad; licenses and ordains Christian ministries; buys, handles, and sells property; establishes and maintains orphanages, schools (parochial and Bible), and maintains homes for the aged.

Emmanuel International Mission, P.O. Box 10082, Port Huron, MI 48301-0082 313-985-8730. Recruits, trains, and prepares Christian personnel for disaster relief, emergency relief, and community development programs.

Emmaus Bible College, 2570 Asbury Rd., Dubuque, IA 52001-3096 319-588-8000. Associated with Plymouth or Christian Brethren; undergraduate and graduate programs; correspondence school.

Encounter Ministries, Inc., P.O. Box 757800, Memphis, TN 38175 901-757-7977. Radio ministry, distribution of tapes and literature; Institute for Biblical Preaching.

English Language Institute/China, P.O. Box 265, San Dimas, CA 91773 714-599-6773. Recruits, selects, trains, and helps place qualified teachers in Chinese universities.

Eternal Truth Ministries, Inc., P.O. Box 1853, Huntington Beach, CA 92647 714-847-1710. Teaching and writing ministry; conferences and retreats. Support for the preparation of Bible study material.

EuroVision, Inc., P.O. Box 1136, Claremont, CA 91711-1136 714-621-1070. Evangelism, discipling, and leadership training. Provides Bible, Christian literature, relief, and other resources to the church in eastern Europe and the Soviet Union.

Evangelical Assoc. for the Promotion of Education, P.O. Box 238, St. Davids, PA 19087 215-341-1722. Christian development organization in inner-city neighborhoods.

Evangelical Child and Family Agency, 1530 N. Main Street, Wheaton, IL 60187 708-653-6400. Adoption, foster family care, services to unmarried parents, and family counseling.

Evangelical Ministries, Inc., 1716 Spruce Street, Philadelphia, PA 19103 215-546-3696. "The Bible Study Hour," a weekly radio broadcast on 189 stations in the U.S., Canada, the Caribbean, and China. James M. Boice is speaker; *Bible Study Magazine*, Bible study seminars, and study books.

Evangelical Presbyterian Church, 26049 Five Mile Rd., Detroit, MI 48239 313-532-9555. Denomination of Reformed tradition. Nine presbyteries and 135 churches with membership of over 40,000 nationwide and in Argentina.

Evangelism Explosion III International, Inc., P.O. Box 23820, Fort Lauderdale, FL 33307 305-491-6100. Lay evangelism.

Evangelistic Association of New England, 279 Cambridge Street, Burlington, MA 01803 617-229-1990. Resource agency to help churches reach and serve their communities.

Evansville Rescue Mission, Inc., 300 S.E. Seventh Street, Evansville, IN 47713 812-423-5244. Ministers to the homeless and needy.

EvanTell, Inc., 9212 Markville Drive, Dallas, TX 75243 214-690-3624. Evangelistic crusades, evangelism seminars, and development of materials to equip Christians to evangelize.

Every Child Ministries, Inc., P.O. Box 715, Crown Point, IN 46307 219-996-4201. Equips African churches in evangelistic, missionary, and church planting programs.

Every Home for Christ/World Literature Crusade, P.O. Box 7139, Canoga Park, CA 91604 818-341-7870. Mobilizes and trains the church to participate in the systematic personal presentation of the gospel to every home.

Faith Haven CFLYO, 7824 West Hollow Rd., Naples, NY 14512 716-374-5659. Provides temporary Christian environment for young unmarried women going through a crisis pregnancy.

Faith Venture Visuals, Inc., P.O. Box 423, Lititz, PA 17543 717-626-8503. Conducts seminars on making and using overhead transparencies. Distribution, consultation, and custom transparency making/designing.

Family Hope Services, Inc., 4203 Boone Ave. North, New Hope, MN 55428 612-533-3734. Supports youth and their families during difficult times.

Family Life Broadcasting System, P.O. Box 35300, Tucson, AZ 85740 602-742-6976. Radio ministry.

Far East Broadcasting Co., Inc., P.O. Box 1, La Mirada, CA 90637 213-947-4651. Operates 32 broadcasting stations in the Philippines, South Korea, Seychelles, Saipan, and San Francisco in over 100 languages.

Fellowship Bible Church, 12601 Hinson Rd., Little Rock, AR 72212 501-224-7171. Independent evangelical church.

Fellowship of Christian Athletes, 8701 Leeds Rd., Kansas City, MO 64129 816-921-0909. Ministers to athletes and coaches.

Fellowship of Christians in Univ. and Schools, 139 East Putnam Ave., Greenwich, CT 06830 203-622-0430. Nondenominational organization of alumni, teachers, administrators, parents, and friends of independent secondary schools for the purpose of conveying the traditional Christian message to students.

Fellowship of Companies for Christ, 2920 Brandywine Rd., #150, Atlanta, GA 30341 404-457-9700. Equips and encourages Christian chief executive officers to operate their businesses and conduct their personal lives according to biblical principles.

Fellowship of Independent Missions, Inc., P.O. Box 72, Fairless Hills, PA 19030 215-752-1170. FIM meets the need of each missionary or mission to serve with the full influence of his individuality and creativity, while providing the adhesive quality and discipline of an effective organization. Missionaries are responsible to the FIM Board.

Fellowship Urban Outreach, 200 Plymouth Ave., San Francisco, CA 94112 415-585-6002. Fellowship Academy, Fellowship Bible Institute, and community projects such as a preschool, prison visits, and food and clothing distribution to needy families.

ECFA MEMBERS cont.

First Assembly of God of Fremont, 4760 Thornton Ave., Fremont, CA 94536 415-793-8687. Exists for the purpose of knowing God and properly responding to him in such a way that others will come to know him and properly respond to him.

The First Baptist Church of Modesto, California, P.O. Box 4309, Modesto, CA 95352 209-521-0181. Unaffiliated local Baptist church with a regional and world outreach.

First Evangelical Free Church, 2801 N. Brea Blvd., Fullerton, CA 92635 714-529-5544. Worship, instruction, fellowship, and expression.

Focus on the Family, 801 Corporate Center Drive, Pomona, CA 91768 714-620-8500. Dedicated to preserving Christian values for the home. Daily radio broadcast.

Food for the Hungry, Inc., P.O. Box E, Scottsdale, AZ 85252 602-998-3100. Provides food and material aid for disaster relief, conducts ongoing relief and rehabilitation programs. Initiates integrated community development projects. Hunger Corps, Child Sponsorship Program.

Ford Philpot Evangelistic Association, Inc., P.O. Box 3000, Lexington, KY 40533 606-276-1479. TV program that includes interviews, music, and a Christian message. Citywide and areawide evangelistic crusades.

Forest Home, Inc., 40000 Valley of the Falls Drive, Forest Falls, CA 92339 714-794-1127. Conferences for all ages.

The Forum for Scriptural Christianity, Inc., P.O. Box 150, Wilmore, KY 40390 606-858-4661. Committed to renewal within the United Methodist Church. Bimonthly *Good News* magazine, renewal groups, political strategy.

Free Methodist Church of North America, 901 College Ave., Winona Lake, IN 46590 219-267-7656. Denomination with support ministries for local churches, missions, and child support programs in other countries; coordination of denominational higher education institutions.

The Free Methodist Foundation, P.O. Box 580, Spring Arbor, MI 49283 517-750-2727. Provides support to the people and ministries of the Free Methodist church through giving assistance, investments in pension and trust funds, loan assistance, trustee for charitable trusts and counsel in fund-raising endeavors.

French Camp Academy, School Street, French Camp, MS 39745 601-547-6482. Provides Christian school and home for young people with family problems.

Fresno Christian Schools, Inc., 7280 N. Cedar, Fresno, CA 93710 209-299-1695. Christian day school sponsored by eight evangelical churches in Fresno.

Fresno Pacific College, 1717 S. Chestnut Ave., Fresno, CA 93702 209-453-2000. Christian higher education.

The Friends of Israel Gospel Ministry, P.O. Box 908, Bellmawr, NJ 08031 609-853-5590. Evangelical faith mission to Jewish people and their Gentile neighbors. A staff of 97 serve in seven countries on four continents.

Friendship Crisis Pregnancy Center, Inc., P.O. Box 1491, Morristown, NJ 07962 201-538-0967. Provides information and support to women facing unplanned or crisis pregnancies.

Friendship Village of Schaumburg, 350 W. Schaumburg Rd., Schaumburg, IL 60194 708-884-5000. Provides quality living arrangements and services to persons of retirement age.

Frontiers-MIO, Inc., P.O. Box 40159, Pasadena, CA 91104 818-798-0807. Plants churches among the Muslim people.

Fuller Theological Seminary, 135 N. Oakland Ave., Pasadena, CA 91182 818-584-5200. Schools of Theology, Psychology, and World Mission.

Gary Case Evangelistic Ministries, Inc., P.O. Box 70-114, Louisville, KY 40270 812-969-2888. Local church revivals, camp meetings, area crusades, evangelism on the foreign fields, mission conferences, and youth conferences.

Gateway Rescue Mission, Inc., P.O. Box 3763, Jackson, MS 39207-9987 601-353-5864. Provides bathing facilities, lodging, hot meals, clothing, and a daily evangelistic service for homeless street people.

The Gathering/U.S.A, Inc., 106 E. Church Street, Orlando, FL 32801 407-422-9200. Citywide outreach breakfasts or lunch gatherings, Bible study groups, and individual discipleship. Also sponsors social and mission outreach projects.

General Baptist Foreign Mission Society, Inc., 100 Stinson Drive, Poplar Bluff, MO 63901 314-785-7746. Evangelism, church planting, child care, schools, health care, support of national ministries in the Philippines and Jamaica, a camping ministry in Jamaica, and missions education to U.S. constituency.

General Synod, Assoc. Reformed Presbyterian Church, One Cleveland Street, Greenville, SC 29601 803-232-8297. 180 churches located in 16 states and the District of Columbia; missionaries in three countries. Erskine College and Erskine Theological Seminary, Bonclarken Conference Center.

Generation Ministries, Inc., 3320 Shea Blvd. #150, Phoenix, AZ 85028 602-996-9922. Research, speaking, and writing ministry focusing on teenagers, parents, and youth workers.

Globe Missionary Evangelism, P.O. Box 3138, Pensacola, FL 32516-9987 904-453-4318. Charismatic sending agency; more than 200 missionaries in over 19 countries.

God's Bible School, 1810 Young Street, Cincinnati, OH 45210 513-721-7944. Bible College, Christian high school, and noncollegiate correspondence course. Publishes *God's Revivalist* and *Bible Advocate*. Maintains six inner-city missions.

God's World Publications, Inc., P.O. Box 2330, Asheville, NC 28802 704-253-8063. Publishes *World Magazine* to provide current news and practical commentary on issues.

Good News Mission, 1036 S. Highland Street, Arlington, VA 22204 703-979-2200. Largest supplier of civil jail and prison chaplains in the U.S. Ministers to prisoners, ex-offenders, correctional staff, and their families.

Gordon College, 255 Grapevine Rd., Wenham, MA 01984 508-927-2300. College education in the liberal arts and sciences; Bible.

Gordon-Conwell Theological Seminary, 130 Essex Street, South Hamilton, MA 01982 508-468-7111. Graduate school offering: Doctor of Ministry, Master of Divinity, Master of Religious Education, and Master of Arts in Theological Studies.

Gospel Films, Inc., P.O. Box 455, Muskegon, MI 49443 616-773-3361. Produces and/or distributes, without profit, religious and educational films.

Gospel for Asia, Inc., 1932 Walnut Plaza, Carrollton, TX 75006 214-416-0340. Educates Christians and enlists prayer and financial support for native missions.

Gospel Literature International, P.O. Box 488, Rosemead, CA 91770 818-288-2812. Provides copyrighted English Christian education curriculum materials and books for translation and adaptation into other languages. Provides support to Christian publishers in more than 60 nations.

Gospel Missions of India, P.O. Box 1043, Warren, MI 48090 313-577-8298. Assists the work of the gospel within the nation of India.

Gospel Volunteers, Inc., CAMP-of-the-WOODS, Speculator, NY 12164 518-548-4311.Operates CAMP-of-the-WOODS, Woodlands Conference Center, Tapawingo Island Camp for girls.

Gospel-Rescue Mission, P.O. Box 1371, Grants Pass, OR 97526 503-479-8869. Ministers to men, women, and children, helping them to help themselves.

Grace College of the Bible, Inc., 1515 S. 10th Street, Omaha, NE 68108 402-449-2800. Curriculum consists of Biblical/Theological Studies, as well as co-curricular experiences; provides education for non-vocational Christian ministries.

Grace Community Church, 13248 Roscoe Blvd., Sun Valley, CA 91352 818-909-5505.

ECFA MEMBERS cont.

Independent, evangelical, Protestant church.

Grace Community Church of the Valley, P.O. Box 26967, Tempe, AZ 85285-6967 602-894-2201. 4,100 members, average Sunday school attendance is 3,200. Operates a preschool and grade school.

Grace Schools, Inc., 200 Seminary Drive, Winona Lake, IN 46590 219-372-5100. Grace College and Grace Theological Seminary is affiliated with the fellowship of Grace Brethren Churches.

The Greater Baltimore Crisis Pregnancy Center, P.O. Box 11372, Baltimore, MD 21239 301-625-0102. Provides emotional support, practical assistance to women with crisis pregnancies.

Greater Europe Mission, P.O. Box 668, Wheaton, IL 60189 708-462-8050. Ministers to the people of greater Europe.

Greater Minneapolis Association of Evangelicals, 3361 Republic Ave., Minneapolis, MN 55426 612-920-8147. Social concerns outreach extension of over 150 member churches and Christian organizations in the Minneapolis area.

H.O.P.E. Bible Mission Inc., P.O. Box 161M, Morristown, NJ 07963-0161 201-543-4492. Works in New York City from a center called the Voyager. Summer camp in Brookside, NJ.

Haluwasa, Inc., R.D. 5, Ehrke Rd., Hammonton, NJ 08037 609-561-3081. Bible camp and church activity center.

Harvest Evangelism, Inc., P.O. Box 20310, San Jose, CA 95160-0310 408-248-5855. Motivates, trains, and mobilizes national leaders in evangelism and church planting.

Harvesting In Spanish (HIS), 245 S. Benton Street, Denver, CO 80226 303-232-3030. Distributes Spanish Bibles and Christian literature. Child care. Ministers to Indians as well as prostitutes and derelicts.

Hasten International, Inc., 1611 West First Street, Winston-Salem, NC 27104-4397 919-721-1075. Provides physical relief, whenever possible. Trains the national to help his own people.

Haven of Rest Ministries, 2410 Hyperion Ave., Los Angeles, CA 90027 213-664-2103. Daily half-hour radio program on more than 350 radio stations. Publishes *Anchor* and *The Log*.

Haven of Rest Ministries, Inc., P.O. Box 1758, Akron, OH 44309-1758 216-535-1563. Provides emergency and residential care to disadvantaged people.

Help for Christian Nationals, Inc., P.O. Box 381006, Duncanville, TX 75138 214-780-5909. Serves Christian national workers throughout the world.

High Adventure Ministries Inc., P.O. Box 7466, Van Nuys, CA 91409 818-701-5133. International radio broadcasting. Owns and operates facilities in the Middle East and North America.

Highland Christian Mission Foundation, P.O. Box 16528, Rochester, NY 14616 716-865-7210. Provides Bible instruction, general academic education, and vocational training to the people of the Highlands area of Papua New Guinea. Operates high school and five elementary schools.

His Branches, Inc., 344 Arnett Blvd., Rochester, NY 14619 716-235-9000. Coordinates and facilitates the work of groups serving the inner-city areas of Rochester.

His Mansion Ministries, P.O. Box 40, Hillsboro, NH 03244 603-464-5555 and **His Mansion Midwest**, P.O. Box 186, Prospect Hts., IL 60070 708-870-1576. Residential care facilities for emotionally and behaviorally hurting young people; special program for pregnant women.

Hobe Sound Bible College, Inc., P.O. Box 1065, Hobe Sound, FL 33475 407-546-5534. Four-year Bible college providing degrees in ministry, missions, music, and education.

Holt International Children's Services, Inc., P.O. Box 2880, Eugene, OR 97402 503-687-2202. International adoption and child care agency serving homeless children in Asia and Latin America.

Home Sweet Home Mission, Inc., 300 Mission Drive, Bloomington, IL 61701 309-828-7356. Provides food, clothing, shelter, counseling, spiritual nurture to people in need in McLean and contiguous counties of Illinois.

Honey Creek Christian Homes, P.O. Box 208, Lowell, MI 49331-9241 616-897-8461. Child care and family service organizations; works with pregnant teens and multi-handicapped young adults.

HoneyWord Foundation, P.O. Box 18035, Tampa, FL 33679-8035 813-832-1234. Produces Bible curriculum and study materials.

Hope for the Hungry, P.O. Box 786, Belton, TX 76513 817-939-0124. Shares the Bread of Life with a starving world.

Hospitality House, Inc., 1220 Logan Ave. North, Minneapolis, MN 55411 612-522-4485. Seeks to repair the family unit through a network of referrals, counseling, and relationship building.

Houghton College, P.O. Box 128, Houghton, NY 14744 716-567-2211. Liberal arts institution with a rural main campus and a suburban campus near Buffalo, NY. Owned and operated by the Wesleyan Church.

House of Ichthus, Turning Point, P.O. Box 10357, Pompano Beach, FL 33061 305-781-1400. Rehabilitation center for men 18 years or older.

House of Samuel, Inc., 2430 N. Sycamore Blvd., Tucson, AZ 85712 602-325-2662. Foster placement and adoption agency throughout Arizona. Also provides services for children in Central and South America.

Hume Lake Christian Camps, Inc., 256 N. Maple, Fresno, CA 93702 209-251-6043. Camping center divided into four major areas: Ponderosa Camp for high schoolers, Meadow Ranch Camp for junior highs, Wagon Train Camp for juniors, and the Lakeview adult program.

Huntington College, 2303 College Ave., Huntington, IN 46750 219-356-6000. Liberal arts college affiliated with the Church of the United Brethren in Christ.

In Touch Ministries, 777 West Peachtree Street, NE, Atlanta, GA 30308 404-347-8500. A television and radio broadcast ministry that presents the teaching ministry of Dr. Charles F. Stanley. Supported by a discipling follow-up program.

In Touch Mission International, Inc., P.O. Box 28240, Tempe, AZ 85281 602-968-4100. Ministry of evangelism and support to Christians living in communist countries.

India Gospel Outreach, P.O. Box 381, Alta Loma, CA 91701 714-988-7165.. Plans to plant dynamic churches in each of India's castes and tribes by the year 2000.

India National Inland Mission, P.O. Box 42584, Los Angeles, CA 90050 818-241-4010. Headquartered in New Delhi, India, with outreach concentrated in the northern states of India. Includes Grace Bible College, children's home for orphans, and evangelistic services.

India Rural Evangelical Fellowship, Inc., 8915 A Robin Drive, Des Plaines, IL 60016 708-297-6414. An independent evangelistic ministry in South India with national evangelists, orphanage, school, and medical work.

Indiana Wesleyan University, 4201 S. Washington Street, Marion, IN 46953 317-674-6901. Liberal arts coeducational college related to The Wesleyan Church.

Inner City Impact, 2704 West North Ave., Chicago, IL 60647 312-384-4200. Works with young people in multi-ethnic, inner-city communities.

Insight for Living, 211 East Imperial Highway, #100, Fullerton, CA 92635 714-870-9161. Daily "Insight for Living" broadcast heard on five continents; cassette tapes, Bible study guides, seminars.

Institute for Advanced Christian Studies, TEDS 2065 Half Day Rd., Deerfield, IL 60015 708-945-8800. Fosters the development and articulation of Christian perspectives through conferences, research, and writing by evangelical scholars. Provides grants for scholars with an earned doctorate in the forefront of their fields of study.

Institute for Creation Research, P.O. Box 2667, El Cajon, CA 92021 619-448-0900.

ECFA MEMBERS cont.

Research, education, and speaking in the areas of biblical and scientific creationism.

Institute in Basic Life Principles, Inc., Box One, Oak Brook, IL 60522-3001 708-323-9800. Seminars to define biblical principles and train others to implement these principles.

Inter-Varsity Christian Fellowship, P.O. Box 7895, Madison, WI 53707 608-274-9001. Establishes and assists Christian groups on college and university campuses, nursing schools, and seminaries.

INTERDEV, P.O. Box 30945, Seattle, WA 98103 206-789-8330. Identifies major language groups where there is little or no church. Brings resource agencies together for development of long-term strategy evangelism and development of the church.

Interest Ministries, 218 W. Willow, Wheaton, IL 60187 708-653-6573. Serves approximately 1,200 congregations with a Christian Brethren identity.

International Aid Inc., 17011 West Hickory, Spring Lake, MI 49456 616-846-7490. Relief and mission service organization. Provides health and medical supplies, home care products. Receives donations of hospital equipment, drugs, and medical supplies.

International Bible Society, P.O. Box 62970, Colorado Springs, CO 80962-2970 719-488-9200. Translates, publishes, and distributes God's Word. Sponsor of New International Version of the Bible. Outreach includes below-cost Scripture sales and worldwide granting of Scripture.

International Chaplain's Ministry, P.O. Box 476, Edmonds, WA 98020 206-774-9544. Provides a holistic Christian ministry to officers, personnel, and families of emergency service organizations and to victims and families these organizations serve during moments of crisis.

International Child Care (U.S.A.), Inc., P.O. Box 2645, Toledo, OH 43606 419-472-7470. Program objective is to enable Haitian health service personnel to control tuberculosis in Haiti.

International Christian Media Commission, P.O. Box 70632, Seattle, WA 98107 206-781-0461. Facilitates ongoing flow of ideas, information, news, and continued dialogue among Christian media people and church leaders.

International Christian Outreach and Relief Group, P.O. Box 68187, Seattle, WA 98168 206-321-6673. Helps Filopino people meet their spiritual, physical, material and emotional needs. Focuses on children.

International Friendship Ministries, Inc., P.O. Box 12504, Columbia, SC 29211 803-799-3452. Shares the gospel of Jesus Christ with international students studying in U.S. colleges and universities through friendship and hospitality.

International Institute for Christian Studies, 1121 Old Concord Rd., Salisbury, NC 28144 704-638-0840. Assists people of the Third World as they lead their countries in education, economic, political, and spiritual development. Assists Third World universities in establishing departments of Christian studies.

International Lifeline, Inc., P.O. Box 32714, Oklahoma City, OK 73123 405-728-2828. Provides medical assistance, volunteer personnel, food, and education to underdeveloped countries.

International Ministries to Israel, 3323 N. Ridge Ave., Arlington Heights, IL 60004 708-394-4405. Ministers the gospel to the Jewish people.

International Missions, Inc., P.O. Box 14866, Reading, PA 19612-4866 215-375-0300. Establishes local, indigenous churches among Chinese, Hindus, Muslims, and Oriental people.

International Needs, Inc., P.O. Box 889, Scranton, PA 18501 717-346-0455. Helps nationals serve God by building prayer partnership teams, leadership training, short-term mission teams, and financial assistance.

International Service Fellowship, P.O. Box 418, Upper Darby, PA 19082 215-352-0581. Ministers in South Asia and the

Middle East. Provides medical, educational, professional, and technical personnel.

International Society of Christian Endeavor, P.O. Box 1110, Columbus, OH 43216 614-258-9545. Promotes Christianity among young people.

International Students Incorporated, P.O. Box C, Colorado Springs, CO 80901 719-576-2700. A cross-cultural outreach program to befriend, evangelize, and disciple international students.

International Teams, P.O. Box 203, Prospect Heights, IL 60070 708-870-3800. Trains and sends summer, two-year, and career missionaries to Europe and Asia for evangelism, discipling, and church planting. Promotes community development among the urban poor, assists refugees from Eastern Europe.

International Union of Gospel Missions, P.O. Box 10780, Kansas City, MO 64118 816-436-6334. An association of rescue ministries. Provides services to members, promotes and establishes new rescue ministries.

Iranian Christians International, Inc., P.O. Box 2415, Ann Arbor, MI 48106 313-769-5529. Reaches and disciples Iranians for Jesus Christ. Trains Iranian believers to return to Iran as church leaders and as cross-cultural missionaries to other unreached peoples.

Issachar, P.O. Box 6788, Lynwood, WA 98036 206-744-0400. Provides consulting, planning, educational materials, and services to local churches, denominations, parachurch groups, and lay leaders who desire to take advantage of the resources God has given them for world evangelization. Particular attention is paid to nations where innovative and non-traditional methods are essential for success.

JAARS, Inc., (Jungle Aviation and Radio Service) Box 248, Waxhaw, NC 28173 704-843-6000. Training and support center for Wycliffe Bible translators.

Jack Shaw Ministries, Inc., P.O. Box 3778, Johnstown, PA 15904 814-269-3377. Christian hospital in Kenya, East Africa.

Jews for Jesus, 60 Haight Street, San Francisco, CA 94102 415-864-2600. An outreach by Jewish Christian evangelists. Personal visitation, tract distribution, media ads in secular newspapers and magazines.

John Abraham Memorial Christian Relief Fund, P.O. Box 30007, Amarillo, TX 79120 806-383-7631. Funds and manages Christian children's homes in India and Honduras and the Dominican Republic. Family feeding project in Honduras and the Dominican, medical clinic in India, schools for underprivileged children in Africa and the Dominican Republic.

John Brown University, 1957 West University, Siloam Springs, AR 72761 501-524-3131. Bachelor degree programs including distinctive programs in broadcasting, journalism, business administration, education, and construction.

John Guest Evangelistic Team, 3366 Burton Street, SE, Grand Rapids, MI 49546 616-942-5600. Organizes citywide, evangelistic–renewal crusades; provides materials and training for pastors.

John M. Perkins Foundation, P.O. Box 40125, Pasadena, CA 91104 818-791-7439. Supports churches and other Christian organizations; grants aid to the needy; assists minorities in bettering their lives. Attempts to lessen racial tensions in a spirit of Christian harmony.

Joni and Friends, P.O. Box 3333, Agoura Hills, CA 91301 818-707-5664. Brings together the church and disabled people through evangelism, encouragement, inspiration, and practical services. Assists persons with disabilities toward independence and fulfillment.

Joy of Jesus, Inc., 12255 Camden, Detroit, MI 48213 313-839-4747. Summer camp with community follow-up provides Christian growth and fellowship opportunities to the total family on a year-round basis.

Joy Ranch, Inc., P.O. Box 727, Hillsville, VA 24343 703-236-5578. Residential facility providing care to dependent, neglected children. Operates Christian school.

ECFA MEMBERS cont.

Kenmore New Covenant Tabernacle, 1 World Ministry Center, Tonawanda, NY 14223 716-877-9882. One of the fastest growing and most progressive churches in the Northeastern United States. A Jewish-Christian fellowship with more than 50 departments of ministry.

Key Life Network, Inc., 160 Harbor Drive, Key Biscayne, FL 33149 305-854-8444. 15-minute daily radio broadcasts by Rev. Stephen Brown. "Key Life Tapes" available free of charge.

Kids Alive International, 2507 Cumberland Drive, Valparaiso, IN 46383 219-464-9035. Dedicated to meeting the spiritual, physical, and emotional needs of children in Beirut, Lebanon, Ramallah (West Bank), Jordan, Hong Kong, and Taiwan.

The King's College, Lodge Rd., Briarcliff Manor, NY 10510 914-944-5659. Christian liberal arts college. Bachelor of arts or bachelor of science degree in over 20 areas of concentration. Maintains a daily radio program, "The King's Hour," hosted by College Chancellor Dr. Robert A. Cook.

Knoxville Union Rescue Mission, Inc., P.O. Box 3352, Knoxville, TN 37927 615-673-6540. Provides food, clothing, and shelter for the homeless.

Lamb & Lion Ministries, P.O. Box K, McKinney, TX 75069 214-736-3567. Daily radio program, cassettes, books, seminars, and monthly prophetic newsletter.

Lamb's Players, Inc., P.O. Box 26, National City, CA 92105 619-474-3385. Presents the historic Christian worldview through a varied use of the dramatic arts. International touring company performs on campuses, in theaters, churches, prisons, and military installations.

The Langham Foundation, 2336 Lawndale Ave., Evanston, IL 60201 708-864-0490. Supports the worldwide ministry of John Stott—author and Rector Emeritus of All Souls Church, London—in evangelism, preaching, and seminary teaching. Provides scholarships to Third World students, helps laymen integrate biblical faith and contemporary issues. Supplies significant Christian books to Third World pastors, scholars, and students.

Latin America Mission, Inc., P.O. Box 52-7900, Miami, FL 33152-7900 305-884-8400. Works with and under the direction of Latin organizations to train and further the outreach of national churches and ministries. Emphasis on large cities in Latin America.

Lausanne Committee for World Evangelization—U.S., 5970 Fairview Rd., #202, Charlotte, NC 28210 704-554-6803. Brings Christian leaders together to develop vision, leadership, and strategies for world evangelization.

Lay Renewal Ministries, Inc., 3101 Bartold, St. Louis, MO 63143 314-647-0717. Conducts renewal events, leadership development, and church consultation. Researches trends and resources.

Lebanon Rescue Mission, Inc., P.O. Box 5, Lebanon, PA 17042 717-273-2301. Gives board and lodging to transients, distributes clothing and food to the needy; temporary shelter to families in need.

Leighton Ford Ministries, 6230 Fairview Rd., #300, Charlotte, NC 28210 704-366-8020. A fellowship of associates committed to world evangelism.

LeTourneau Ministries International, P.O. Box 489, Rockwall, TX 75087 214-771-8325. Assists organizations and national churches with a unique strategy of concentrated evangelism and church planting techniques; assists with necessary resources to construct the kind of church facility needed to carry on this kind of work.

LeTourneau University, P.O. Box 7001, Longview, TX 75607-7001 214-753-0231. Four-year programs in the liberal arts and sciences, engineering and technology, and business administration.

Liberty Christian College, P.O. Box 3138, Pensacola, FL 32516 904-453-3451. Offers associate, bachelor's, and master's degrees.

Liebenzell Mission of USA, Inc., P.O. Box 66, Schooley's Mountain, NJ 07870 201-852-3044. Camp and guest house for conferences and retreats. Recruits and sends missionaries to the Micronesian Islands, Japan, Africa, New Guinea.

Life Action Ministries, 2000 Morris Drive, Niles, MI 49120 616-695-2751. Revival crusades, multi-media musical productions, high school assemblies, revival publications, camp program.

Life Challenge of Tennessee, Inc., P.O. Box 60362, Nashville, TN 37206 615-226-6857. Outreach and educational programs; counseling; residential training in Christian discipleship for young adults (17–36) with life-controlling problems (primarily chemical dependency).

LIFE Ministries, P.O. Box 200, San Dimas, CA 91773 714-599-8491. Missionary organization in Japan involved in church planting, national leadership training, and student evangelism through teaching conversational English. Career missionaries, short-termers, and summer workers.

Lifewater International, P.O. Box 1126, Arcadia, CA 91077 818-962-8985. Consortium of water resource specialists. Combines training, experience, and faith in assisting relief/development organizations to plan, implement, and maintain water projects.

Light of Life Rescue Mission, Inc., 10 East N. Ave., Pittsburgh, PA 15212 412-321-4716. Rescue mission in inner-city Pittsburgh; gospel services, counseling, meals, lodgings, and rehabilitation program.

Lighthouse Mission, 520 E. Market, Indianapolis, IN 46204 317-636-0209. Assists and cares for needy persons. Assists in obtaining employment and rehabilitation.

Ligonier Ministries, Inc., P.O. Box 7500, Orlando, FL 32854 407-834-1633. Teaching fellowship of Dr. R.C. Sproul. Video and audio cassette tapes, curriculum, and regional conferences.

Lincoln Christian College and Seminary, P.O. Box 178, Lincoln, IL 62656 217-732-3168. Undergraduate and graduate educational ministry.

Link Care Foundation, Inc., 1734 West Shaw Ave., Fresno, CA 93711 209-439-5920. Counseling and mental health services to missionaries, Christian workers, and the community of Fresno. Provides housing for senior citizens and missionaries in program.

Little Galilee Christian Assembly, Inc., R.R. 2, Box 266, Clinton, IL 61727 217-935-3809. Conducts camps, conferences, and rallies.

Living Bibles International, U.S., 351 Main Place, Carol Stream, IL 60188 708-369-0100. Worldwide Scripture translation and distribution.

Lloyd Ogilvie Ministries, Inc., 6037 Hollywood Blvd., Hollywood, CA 90028 213-464-7690. "Let God Love You" television and radio ministry. The television program is a 30-minute format airing on Sundays. The radio program is a 25-minute daily broadcast. Programs are comprised of messages by Dr. Lloyd Ogilvie.

LOGOI, Inc., 4100 West Flagler Street, #B-3, Miami, FL 33134 305-446-8297. Provides biblical, theological, and ministerial training to Spanish-speaking Christians. Target audiences are those already in service living in outlying areas with no access to theological training.

Long Beach Rescue Mission, P.O. Box 1969, Long Beach, CA 90801 213-591-1292. Provides gospel services, emergency and long-term shelter, meals, counseling, and rehabilitation to the needy.

Los Angeles Mission, P.O. Box 5749, Los Angeles, CA 90055 213-629-1227. Relief and rehabilitation agency that provides food, shelter, clothing, shaves and showers, counseling, and rehabilitation programs for destitute and homeless people.

Lost and Found, Inc., 9189 S. Turkey Creek Rd., Morrison, CO 80465 303-697-5049. Treats people caught in an addictive process. Offers primary and secondary residential care, outpatient counseling, wilderness experiences, DUI/DWAI classes, cult/occult interventions, community education, etc.

ECFA MEMBERS cont.

Love Basket, Inc., 4472 Goldman Rd., Hillsboro, MO 63050 314-789-4100. An international adoption ministry placing destitute children in foreign countries with Christian families. Also has domestic adoptive placement program.

Loving Grace Ministries, Inc., P.O. Box 500, Lafayette, NJ 07848 603-788-4782. Live syndicated one-hour call-in radio program, "Let's Talk About Jesus," crusades, seminars, retreats, Holy Land pilgrimages, home-study Bible courses.

Luis Palau Evangelistic Association, P.O. Box 1173, Portland, OR 97207 503-643-0777. Desires to stimulate, revive, and mobilize the church to effective evangelism.

Luke Ministries, 1310 West Country Rd. B-2, Roseville, MN 55113 612-631-1180. Develops followers of Jesus Christ in the business community through evangelistic Bible studies.

The Luke Society, Inc., P.O. Box 871, Vicksburg, MS 39180 601-638-1629. Christian physicians and dentists helping the poor in the United States and Third World countries through community health and the gospel.

Lutheran Bible Institute in California, 641 S. Western Ave., Anaheim, CA 92804 714-827-1940. Two-year college of biblical studies, serves the Lutheran Church as a movement which fosters renewal and promotes evangelism and missions.

Lutheran Bible Institute of Seattle, Providence Heights, Issaquah, WA 98027 206-392-0400. College-level school offering in-depth biblical and related courses preparing for lay ministries and church-related vocations.

Lutheran Bible Translators, P.O. Box 2050, Aurora, IL 60507 708-897-0660. Analyzes unwritten languages and translates the Bible into the vernacular.

Macedonian Ministry of Missions, P.O. Box 210304, Bedford, TX 76095 817-540-2770. Provides practical ministry training; primary focus overseas is in Third World countries assisting native evangelists, pastors, and their congregations through intensive Bible training seminars. Committed to the local church at home as well.

Malcolm Smith Ministries, Inc., Box 29747, San Antonio, TX 78229-0747 512-558-3838. Audio and video teaching tapes, books, a daily radio program "Covenant Love", bimonthly teaching journal *Living Word*, and seminars.

Manna Bible Institute, Inc., 700 East Church Lane, Philadelphia, PA 19144-1496 215-843-3600. College-level day program in Philadelphia, adult education evening program. Sponsors a federally funded head-start program, Excelsior Christian Academy, and Camp Discovery Summer Program.

Manna International Relief and Development, P.O. Box 3507, Redwood City, CA 94064 415-365-3663. International relief and development organization. Short-term disaster relief and long-term projects designed to promote self-sufficiency and self-direction. Existing programs stress public health, agricultural development, water development.

MAP International, P.O. Box 50, Brunswick, GA 31521-0050 912-265-6010. Global health organization that provides donated medicines and supplies to Africa, Asia, and Latin America. Works in community health development, coordinating projects to improve water supplies, food production, and health education.

Market Street Mission, Inc., 9 Market Street, Morristown, NJ 07960 201-538-0431. Provides for the needs of homeless, indigent, troubled, and alcoholic and/or drug addicted people.

Mars Hill Broadcasting Co., Inc., 4044 Makyes Rd., Syracuse, NY 13215 315-469-5051. Operates radio stations WMHR-FM 102.9 Syracuse, NY, and WMHN-FM 89.3 Webster, NY. Delivers service to 13 translator stations and WJSL-FM, Houghton College, Houghton, NY.

Mastermedia International, Inc., 2102 Palm Ave., Highland, CA 92346 714-864-5250. Evangelism and discipleship to leaders in the film and television industries by one-on-one appointments and small-group meetings and retreats. Seeks to create an awareness of the impact of media on society through publications, radio, TV, and speaking events.

Match-Two (M-2) Prisoner Outreach, P.O. Box 447, San Quentin, CA 94964 415-457-8701. Prison visitation ministry.

Media Associates International, Inc., P.O. Box 218, Bloomingdale, IL 60108 708-893-1141. Assists Third World Christian nationals in becoming effective creators, producers, distributors, and users of the media.

Medical Teams International, Inc., P.O. Box 231177, Portland, OR 97223 503-624-0229. Relief and development agency.

Menconi Ministries, P.O. Box 969, Cardiff by the Sea, CA 92007-0969 619-436-8676. Challenges Christians to evaluate the effect of entertainment on their spiritual lives.

The Mendenhall Ministries, P.O. Box 368, Mendenhall, MS 39114 601-847-3421. Ministers to the poor, rural areas of Mississippi; develops models that can be replicated in other communities and countries.

Mercy Corps International, 3030 S.W. First Ave., Portland, OR 97201 503-242-1032. Emergency relief, self-help development projects, and development education.

Mercy Medical Airlift, P.O. Box 1628, Arlington, VA 22210 703-471-1112. Provides medical air transportation for patients who cannot afford commercial air ambulance, and cost-effective air transportation for staff and volunteers of churches and nonprofit Christian organizations.

Messiah Village, P.O. Box 2015, Mechanicsburg, PA 17055-2015 717-697-4666. Brethren in Christ retirement village. Independent living, health care and related services.

The Messianic Vision, 9057 B Gaither Rd., Gaithersburg, MD 20877 301-963-4400. Dedicated to reaching Jewish people through radio, seminars, and evangelistic meetings.

Mexican Medical Inc., 13910 Lyons Valley Rd., #C, Jamul, CA 92035 619-669-1410. Medical outreach, cross-cultural ministries, evangelism, and relief assistance.

Miami Rescue Mission, Inc., P.O. Box 420620, Miami, FL 33175 305-573-4390. Ministry to the homeless. Offers a six-month Christian Regeneration Program for those who choose a new way of life.

Miami Valley Christian Television, Inc., P.O. Box 26, Dayton, OH 45401 513-323-0026. Produces and distributes programs, materials, and helps through its television stations to encourage Christian faith; coordinates projects to assist the needy.

Mid-America Teen Challenge Training Center, Inc., P.O. Box 1089, Cape Girardeau, MO 63701 314-335-6508. Residential care program for men with life-controlling problems.

Middle East Media, P.O. Box 359, Lynnwood, WA 98046 206-778-0752. Uses the mass media to communicate the gospel to Muslims of the Middle East, North Africa, and elsewhere.

Midwest Challenge, Inc., P.O. Box 7364, Minneapolis, MN 55407 612-825-6871. Counsels people to apply biblical principles to overcome life-dominating problems, particularly substance abuse and prostitution.

Minnesota Bible College, 920 Mayowood Rd. S.W., Rochester, MN 55902 507-288-4563. Provides Christian education characterized by the ideals of the Restoration Movement heritage, as expressed in Scripture.

Mission Aviation Fellowship, P.O. Box 3202, Redlands, CA 92373-0998 714-794-1151. Aviation and related ministries.

Mission Safety International, Inc., P.O. Box 1632, Elizabethton, TN 37644 615-543-3534. Assists missionary/Christian oriented aviation organizations in aviation safety.

The Mission Society for United Methodists, Inc., P.O. Box 1103, Decatur, GA

ECFA MEMBERS cont.

30331 404-378-8746. Voluntary association of United Methodist and other Wesleyan related groups, congregations, pastors, and laypersons seeking to expand missionary outreach.

Mission to the World, P.O. Box 29765, Atlanta, GA 30359-0765 404-320-3373. Affiliated with The Presbyterian Church in America. Places and supervises personnel on the foreign mission field.

Mission to Unreached Peoples, 22014 7th Ave. S., #101, Seattle, WA 98198 206-824-7550. Plants churches among unreached people groups. Recruits and sends teams of committed Christian lay people, including tentmakers.

Missionary Athletes International, Inc., P.O. Box 945, La Habra, CA 90633 213-690-4934. Soccer sports evangelism ministry; soccer camps, tours, and local teams.

Missionary Internship, Inc., P.O. Box 457, Farmington, MI 48332 313-474-9110. Cross-cultural orientation and training organization serving IFMA & EFMA mission agencies.

Missionary World Service and Evangelism, P.O. Box 123, Wilmore, KY 40390 606-858-3171. Assists mission organizations with volunteer work and witness crusades; also local congregations in evangelism, missions, and discipleship with crusades, missionary conferences, seminars, and discipleship training.

The Montrose Broadcasting Corporation, P.O. Box 248, Montrose, PA 18801 717-278-2811. Owns and operates non-commercial radio stations WPEL-AM-FM in Montrose and WPGM-AM-FM Danville, PA.

The Moody Bible Institute of Chicago, 820 N. LaSalle Street, Chicago, IL 60610 312-329-4123. Bible institute, correspondence school, missionary aviation; radio stations; publication and distribution of books; films.

Mount Hermon Association, Inc., P.O. Box 413, Mount Hermon, CA 95041 408-335-4466. Christian camp and conference programming.

Mount Vernon Christian Academy, 4449 Northside Drive, N.W., Atlanta, GA 30327 404-256-4057. Christian college preparatory education.

Multimedia Ministries International, 18221 Torrence Ave., Lansing, IL 60438 708-895-7000. Assists Christian organizations in promoting their cause through mass media.

Multnomah School of the Bible, 8435 N.E. Glisan, Portland, OR 97220 503-255-0332. Education and literature (Multnomah Press and the Christian Supply Center stores).

Narramore Christian Foundation, P.O. Box 5000, Rosemead, CA 91770-0950 818-288-7000. Counseling ministry, monthly magazine, radio and TV programs, films, and personal enrichment groups.

Nashville Union Mission, Inc., P.O. Box 22157, Nashville, TN 37202 615-255-2475. Reaches out to those who need to rebuild their lives.

National Assoc. of Christian Physical Therapists, P.O. Box 100, Port Gibson, NY 14537-0100 315-331-4318. Christian physical therapy association. Sending agent for mission organizations who need a Christian physical therapist.

National Association of Evangelicals, 450 Gundersen Drive, Carol Stream, IL 60188 708-665-0500. Provides a united voice, fellowship, and services through national programs and the work of its commissions and affiliates.

National Christian Fellowship, P.O. Box 516, Carlsbad, CA 92008 619-431-9890. "Friendship evangelism" ministry to federal, state, and local public officials across America; Bible/prayer fellowship groups, governor's and mayor's prayer breakfasts. CERT International, a ministry of NCF, provides short-term lay missionary opportunities through medical assistance and humanitarian programs in response to emergency needs.

National Coalition Against Pornography, 800 Compton Rd., #9224, Cincinnati, OH

45231 513-521-6227. Denominations and organizations united to eliminate illegal, dangerous, hard-core pornography from our society.

The National Network of Youth Ministries, 17150 Via Del Campo, #102, San Diego, CA 92127 619-451-1111. Teaches and disciples high school students.

National Religious Broadcasters, Inc., P.O. Box 1926, Morristown, NJ 07962-1926 201-428-5400. An association of organizations engaged in religious programming for radio and television and the operation of religious radio and TV.

Navajo Gospel Mission, Inc., P.O. Box 3717, Flagstaff, AZ 86003 602-526-0875. Evangelization of North American Indian tribes.

Navajo Missions, Inc., P.O. Box 1230, Farmington, NM 87401 505-325-0255. Interdenominational mission outreach. Care of dependent Navajo children, Christian radio station, evangelism, printshop, and Christian bookstore.

The Navigators, P.O. Box 6000, Colorado Springs, CO 80934 719-598-1212. Teaches people to take the gospel to non-Christians and to disciple new believers in the faith.

Need, Inc., P.O. Box 54541, Phoenix, AZ 85078 602-992-1321. International Christian agency providing assistance to the displaced, disenfranchised, and needy people of the world.

Neues Leben International, 13832 N. 32nd Street, C-3, Phoenix, AZ 85032 602-482-2366. Biblical counseling and training ministry.

New Creation Ministries, P.O. Box 40 M-26, Atlantic Mine, MI 49905-0040 906-482-3611. Reaches out through educational activities to the chemically dependent and their family members; equips the Christian community to work with those who suffer because of addictions.

The New Directions Ministries, Inc., P.O. Box 2347, Burlington, NC 27216 919-227-1273. Interracial ministry committed to evangelism and discipleship. Particular orientation toward reconciliation in USA and cross-cultural ministry abroad. Catalyst between churches in America and the Third World.

New Horizons Youth Ministries, Inc., Roads 100 S. at 350 East, Marion, IN 46953 317-668-4009. Christian program for youth who are underachieving.

New Life Ranch, Inc., Rt. 1 Box 274, Colcord, OK 74338 918-422-5506. Summer camps and short retreats during the school year.

New Life, Inc., 10901 Lake Ridge Rd., Knoxville, TN 37922 615-675-4420. Adult friendship evangelism, discipling, leadership training.

New Mexico Boys Ranch, Inc., Boys Ranch, NM 87002 505-864-2177. New Mexico Boys Ranch, New Mexico Girls Ranch, and Hart Youth Ranch are residential child-care centers for children from troubled backgrounds. Families for Children is an adoption and foster care agency.

Niños de Mexico, P.O. Box 309, Union, MO 63084 314-583-2000. Missionary project of the Christian Churches and Churches of Christ. Engaged in the evangelism of Mexico, care of homeless children.

Northern Christian Radio, Inc., P.O. Box 695, Gaylord, MI 49735 517-732-6274. Radio ministry operating two noncommercial educational FM radio stations in northern Michigan; an affiliate of the Moody Broadcasting Network.

Northern Pines of Minnesota, Inc., 6701 Penn Ave. South, Richfield, MN 55423 612-861-5100. Operates week-long family conferences at Lake Geneva, WI.

Northwest Conservative Baptist Association, Inc., P.O. Box 30029, Portland, OR 97230-0029 503-669-1515. Missions agency established in Idaho, Oregon, and Washington to establish new churches and provide services for existing churches.

Northwestern College, 3003 N. Snelling Ave., St. Paul, MN 55113 612-631-5100. Educational programs from one-year certificates to bachelor degree programs. Noncommercial, Christian satellite network of radio stations. Seminars and conferences.

ECFA MEMBERS cont.

O.C. Ministries, Inc., 25 Corning Ave., Milpitas, CA 95035-5336 408-263-1101. Overseas Crusades equips national Christians to reach their nation for Christ.

Oak Hills Fellowship, 1600 Oak Hills Rd. S.W., Bemidji, MN 56601 218-751-8670. Home mission organization with several divisions: Oak Hills Bible College, International Messengers, Camp Oak Hills, Oak Hills Bible Conference, and Oak Hills Church Ministries.

Officers' Christian Fellowship of the U.S.A., P.O. Box 1177, Englewood, CO 80150-1177 303-761-1984. Ministry to cadets and midshipmen at service academies and ROTC schools and to officers located at bases throughout the world; Bible studies, newsletter, *Command* magazine, and retreats.

Okinawa Christian School, P.O. Box 90031, Gainesville, FL 32607 904-371-6012. Ministers to Asian, Asian-American, American missionary dependents and American military dependents from its mission school facility in Okinawa, Japan.

Olive Branch Mission, 1047 West Madison St., Chicago, IL 60607 312-243-3373. Provides a soup kitchen, day shelter, and emergency housing. The Wesleyan Urban Coalition provides learning and service experiences for college and seminary students.

Olive Crest Treatment Centers, Inc., 1300 No. Kellogg Drive, #D, Anaheim, CA 92807 714-777-4999. Provides an alternative to institutional care of abused/neglected/abandoned children: a small surrogate family setting that is structured, safe, and nurturing. Also offers a foster family program for children.

OMS International, Inc., P.O. Box A, Greenwood, IN 46142 317-881-6751. Establishes and maintains schools for the training of missionaries, pastors, evangelists, and their children. Publications, radio, social welfare, and relief work.

Open Air Campaigners, P.O. Box 2440, Plainfield, NJ 07060 201-757-8427. Open air outreach.

Open Doors With Brother Andrew, Inc., P.O. Box 27001, Santa Ana, CA 92799 714-531-6000. Delivery of Bibles and other aids to the church in the restricted countries of the world. Mobilizes and trains the church in the free world to identify with and become involved in assisting the suffering church.

Operation Mobilization, P.O. Box 2277, Peachtree City, GA 30269 404-631-0432. Biblical teaching and life-style, cross-cultural discipleship training teams and long-term workers. Widely known for the international outreach of the ships *Doulos* and *Logos*.

The Orange County Rescue Mission, P.O. Box 1833, Santa Ana, CA 92703 714-835-0499. Provides temporary shelter, live-in, rehabilitation program, job search assistance.

Outreach, Incorporated, P.O. Box 1000, Grand Rapids, MI 49501 616-363-7817. Evangelism and Christian education through radio, television, and distribution of biblical literature. Scholarships for Christian leaders within their own countries; theological training.

Overseas Christian Servicemen's Centers, P.O. Box 1268, Englewood, CO 80150 303-762-1400. Ministry to the U.S. military community. A special division, Malachi Ministries, ministers to youth.

Overseas Council, Theological Education & Missions, P.O. Box 751, Greenwood, IN 46142 317-882-4174. Assists evangelical theological institutions in developing churches of the Third World.

Ozark Christian College, P.O. Box 1866, Joplin, MO 64801 417-624-2518. Coeducational Christian college.

Ozark Conference Center, 1300 West Park Drive, #5A, Little Rock, AR 72204 501-666-3266. Bible conferences for adults, pastors, lay leaders, and families.

P.R.O. Missions, Inc., P.O. Box 11448, Memphis, TN 38111 901-458-0325. Supports missionary activities, projects, and establishments.

Pacific Island Ministries, 701 Welch Rd., A-2215, Palo Alto, CA 94304 415-328-

8203. Development of indigenous Christian leadership for church growth in the Pacific Ocean area, particularly Papua New Guinea. Pioneers in remote areas.

Pacific Missionary Aviation, P.O. Box 3209, Agana, GU 96910 671-646-6464. Evangelism, discipleship, leadership, training, church planting, and support.

Paraclete Social Outreach, Inc., P.O. Box 2596, Toledo, OH 43606 419-472-4800. Networks Christian homes for foster care to troubled, dependent, and neglected youth. Helps older teens to become independent and coordinates counseling services to troubled families and youth.

Partners in Christ International, P.O. Box 1715, Chandler, AZ 85244-1715 602-821-9321. Trains indigenous pastors and leaders; operates a children's home in Mexico. Provides opportunities for U.S. churches to participate in cross-cultural ministry/projects in Mexico.

Partners International, P.O. Box 15025, San Jose, CA 95112 408-453-3800. Works in partnership with nationals in over 40 countries. All ministries are under national boards which set their goals, design their policies, and implement their programs.

People of Destiny International, 7881-B Beechcraft Ave., Gaithersburg, MD 20879 301-948-4890. Church planting, leadership development, conferences.

Persecuted Church Commission, Inc., P.O. Box 1340, Kingston, NY 12401 914-382-1275. Ministers to Christians in the USSR through prayer and letters of encouragement. Supports Christian activities among all denominations in the USSR.

Personal Ministries, P.O. Box 413, New Lenox, IL 60451-0413 815-485-4900. Bible study conferences in North America, Latin America, and Asia.

Pine Cove, Inc., P.O. Box 9055, Tyler, TX 75711 214-561-0231. Interdenominational camp and conference center.

Pioneer Bible Translators, P.O. Box 381030, Duncanville, TX 75138-1030 214-296-4843. Translates God's Word into languages in which there is no written language or Bible. Team includes not only translators and literacy specialists, but also teachers, evangelists, buyer-shippers, builders, mechanics, accountants, and computer specialists.

Pioneer Clubs, P.O. Box 788, Wheaton, IL 60189 708-293-1600. Helps children and youth put Christ in every phase of life, to nurture healthy relationships, and to develop a positive self-image. Assists adults in understanding children and their development.

Pioneers, P.O. Box 527, Sterling, VA 22170 703-478-0004. Sends missionaries to the five blocks of unreached people groups in the world: Chinese, Hindu, Buddhist, Muslim, Tribal. Tentmaking missionaries as well as national workers are used to penetrate "closed" restricted access countries.

The Pocket Testament League, P.O. Box 800, Lititz, PA 17543-7026 717-626-1919. Combines Scripture distribution with worldwide evangelism. Encourages daily reading of the Bible by Christians; correspondence courses designed to lead people to Christ.

Portland Rescue Mission, P.O. Box 3713, Portland, OR 97208-3713 503-227-0421. Provides food, lodging, clothing, and a drug and alcohol recovery program; family and individual counseling.

Prakash Association, U.S.A., 99 Airport Blvd., Freedom, CA 95019 408-722-2244. Develops self-supporting, educational institutes and churches in India. Trains nationals to become Christian businessmen and spiritual leaders in their local areas.

Precept Ministries of Reach Out, Inc., P.O. Box 182218, Chattanooga, TN 37422 615-892-6814. Bible study and conference center.

Presbyterian Evangelistic Fellowship, Inc., P.O. Box 1890, Decatur, GA 30034 404-244-0740. Trains and assists biblical evangelism as an extended arm of the local church.

Priority Living, Inc., 18002 Irvine Blvd., #102, Tustin, CA 92680 714-544-8903. Evangelical ministry serving business and

ECFA MEMBERS cont.

professional men and women. Directs the unchurched to local, Bible-teaching churches. Emphasizes biblical principles for practical living.

Prison Fellowship Ministries, P.O. Box 17500, Washington, DC 20041 703-478-0100. Assists prisoners, ex-prisoners, and their families through outreach programs. Involved in national criminal justice reform. Seeks to mobilize churches and volunteers for involvement in prison ministry.

Probe Ministries International, 1900 Firman Drive, #100, Richardson, TX 75081 214-480-0240. Bible study and conference center.

Project Partner With Christ, Inc., P.O. Box 1054, Middletown, OH 45042 513-425-0938. Supports the national church in the Third World to evangelize, disciple, and plant churches.

Racerunners, Inc., P.O. Box 59230, Birmingham, AL 35259 205-870-1188. Big brother, big sister program where young adults act as role models to high school students.

Radio Bible Class, Inc., P.O. Box 22, Grand Rapids, MI 49555 616-942-6770. Teaches the Word of God through audio, video, and correspondence media.

Radio Voice of Christ, Inc., P.O. Box 7145, Beaverton, OR 97007 503-649-0717. Farsi-language broadcast outreach to Iran and to Iranians in some Persian Gulf countries.

Rainbow Acres, Inc., P.O. Box 1326, Camp Verde, AZ 86322 602-567-5231. Residential/vocational ranch communities for mentally handicapped adults.

The Raleigh Rescue Mission, Inc., P.O. Box 27391, Raleigh, NC 27611 919-828-2003. Work therapy, counseling, and job training.

Ravi Zacharias International Ministries, Inc., 4725 Peachtree Corners Circle, #250, Norcross, GA 30092 404-449-6766. Resource centers, seminars, open forums in churches and the "hotbeds of intellectualism."

Reap International, Inc., 972 West Ninth Street, Upland, CA 91786 714-981-5777. Serves medical missions by providing rebuilt medical equipment; on-site technical service; training and maintenance of medical equipment.

Reformed Theological Seminary, 5422 Clinton Blvd., Jackson, MS 39209 601-922-4988. An institute of theological studies committed to the Reformed faith.

Regent College Foundation, P.O. Box 274, Mercer Island, WA 98040 206-236-1471. Conducts and promotes seminars, lectures, and extension classes on issues of theological education; participates in fund raising for specific programs and provides some scholarship funds for students who want to obtain theological education.

Regent University, CBN, Virginia Beach, VA 23464-9800 804-523-7400. Includes five colleges: education and human services, communication and the arts, law and government, administration and management, and theology and ministry.

Reign Ministries, Inc., 5517 Warwick Pl., Minneapolis, MN 55436 612-925-3519. Supplements the efforts of churches and organizations in becoming more effective centers and more aggressive witnesses to God's redeeming power.

Rescue Ministries, P.O. Box 298, Youngstown, OH 44501 216-744-5485. Provides emergency shelter, clothing, furniture, referrals, and counseling. Residential facility for crisis pregnancy.

Rescue Mission Alliance of Syracuse, New York, 120 Gifford Street, Fayetteville, NY 13202 315-472-6251. Serves people whose needs go unfulfilled. Seeks to develop the whole person in physical, mental, and spiritual areas.

Richmond Rescue Mission, P.O. Box 1112, Richmond, CA 94802 415-233-5333. Provides emergency shelter and meals, food boxes for needy families, and clothing and furniture as available.

Rio Grande Bible Institute, Inc., 4300 S. Business 281, Edinburg, TX 78539 512-380-8100. Prepares Spanish-speaking Christian leaders to minister. Provides Spanish language program for those interested in missionary service in Spanish areas; Spanish broadcasts.

Riverside Christian Ministries, Inc., 968 N.W. 2nd Street, Miami, FL 33128 305-545-0926. Reentry and support programs for prisoners and their families.

Riverwoods Christian Center, 35 W 701 Riverwoods Lane, St. Charles, IL 60174 708-584-2222. Ministers to the economically disadvantaged people of the Fox River Valley through camp and community ministries.

Rochester Youth for Christ, Inc., P.O. Box 69, Rochester, NY 14601 716-436-8944. Seeks to aid in the moral and mental improvement of teenagers through social gatherings and entertainments that are instructive and inspirational, helping them to realize the importance of balance in mental, spiritual, social, and physical development.

Romanian Missionary Society, P.O. Box 527, Wheaton, IL 60187 708-665-6503. Translation of biblical literature into the Romanian language; radio broadcasts; other humanitarian aid to Romanian refugees.

Rural Home Missionary Association, P.O. Box 300, Morton, IL 61550 309-263-2350. Plants and establishes independent Bible churches in rural America.

Samaritan's Purse, Inc., P.O. Box 3000, Boone, NC 28607 704-262-1980. Responds to emergency needs in crisis areas of the world through missionaries and national churches. World Medical Mission, its medical arm, recruits Christian physicians for voluntary short-term service in evangelical mission hospitals overseas.

San Diego Rescue Mission, Inc., 1150 J Street, P.O. Box 80427, San Diego, CA 92101 619-234-2109. Provides shelter, medical services and spiritual advice to homeless men. These men perform the day-to-day tasks needed to maintain the facility—a unique program wherein the "homeless" care for the homeless.

Scripture Press Ministries, P.O. Box 650, Glen Ellyn, IL 60138 708-668-6000. Provides leadership training programs, support materials and literature programs to foster spiritual growth. These programs are carried out in U.S. churches, correctional institutions, hospitals, mission organizations, overseas Christian schools, seminars, and translation of Sunday school curriculum and Bible reference books.

Scripture Union, Inc., 7000 Ludlow Street, Upper Darby, PA 19082 215-352-5400. Seeks to open God's Word creatively with people, using programs like "Operation Quiet Time," a congregation-wide daily Bible study and prayer effort.

Search Ministries, Inc., P.O. Box 521, Lutherville, MD 21093 301-252-1246. Life-style evangelism helps Christians provide friends with a comfortable, natural opportunity to think through their beliefs.

Seattle Pacific University, 3307 3rd Ave. West, Seattle, WA 98119 206-281-2222. An evangelical Christian university; undergraduate and graduate disciplines.

SEND International, P.O. Box 513, Farmington, MI 48332 313-477-4210. Missionary agency serving the Philippines, Hong Kong, Taiwan, Japan, Spain, Alaska, and Northwest Canada.

Serve International, 120 Interstate N. Parkway East, #404, Atlanta, GA 30339 404-952-3434. Interdenominational relational evangelism equipping ministry. Serve's Friendly Witness Building Process helps believers grow from profession of faith to responsible evangelistic reproduction.

Shalom International Outreach, Inc., P.O. Box 4400, Costa Mesa, CA 92628 714-966-1377. Challenges the church to confront anti-semitism and other racial bigotry.

The Sheepfold, Inc., P.O. Box 992, Tustin, CA 92681 714-669-9569. Shelter for homeless women with children.

Shepherd's Gate, P.O. Box 894, Livermore, CA 94550 415-449-0163. Emergency shelter for homeless women and children.

SIM USA, Inc., P.O. Box 7900, Charlotte, NC 28241 704-529-5100. Interdenominational mission agency working primarily

ECFA MEMBERS cont.

in South America, Africa, and Southern Asia.

Sky Ranches, Inc., 9330 LBJ Freeway, #850, Dallas, TX 75243 214-437-9505. Christian camping and related activities.

Slavic Gospel Association, Inc., P.O. Box 1122, Wheaton, IL 60189 708-690-8900. Russian radio broadcasts; Bible and Christian literature translation, production, and distribution; and personal evangelism to Russian- and other Slavic-speaking people.

Songtime Inc., P.O. Box 350, Boston, MA 02101 617-848-7787. National radio ministry.

SonScape Re-Creation Ministries, Inc., P.O. Box 7777, Pagosa Springs, CO 81147 303-264-4777. Retreat center for pastors, professional staff, missionaries, and their families.

Sound Words Communications, Inc., 1000 S. 84th Street, Lincoln, NE 68505 402-483-4541. Provides systematic study of the Bible using various media.

South America Mission, Inc., P.O. Box 6560, Lake Worth, FL 33466 407-965-1833. Establishes self-supporting, self-governing, and self-propagating churches in Bolivia, Brazil, Colombia, and Peru.

South Evangelical Presbyterian Fellowship, 3780 S. Broadway, Englewood, CO 80110 303-761-8780. Ministers to those in need, supplying both physical and spiritual aid.

South Hills Community Church, 6601 Camden Ave., San Jose, CA 95120 408-268-1676. Non-denominational evangelical church in San Jose's Silicon Valley.

South Side Mission of Peoria, Inc., P.O. Box 5579, Peoria, IL 61602 309-676-4604. To evangelize and disciple the youth of the Peoria inner city. New Promise Center (a women's and children's shelter), King's Kids Nursery School, Camp Kearney, Break Out, Youth Ministries, and Second Touch Clothing store.

Southeastern Bible College, 3001 Highway 280 East, Birmingham, AL 35243-4181 205-269-0880. Offers Christian higher education.

Spanish Evangelical Enterprises, P.O. Box 452424, Miami, FL 33245 305-754-5301. Promotes and establishes the Christian faith throughout Spanish-speaking countries.

Spiritual Counterfeits Project, Inc., P.O. Box 4308, Berkeley, CA 94704 415-540-0300. Researches various religious groups from a Christian perspective; publishes and distributes literature and maintains research files and a library; educates Christians about current religious trends in Western society.

Spiritual Overseers Service International, 4362 Vale St., Irvine, CA 92714 714-852-1002. Sends experienced men and women overseas for two to three weeks to teach and train national Christian ministers and leaders.

Sports World Ministries, Inc., P.O. Box 500, New Tazewell, TN 37825 615-626-8291. Trains and sends the professional football player to reach young America with a call to "Say no to drugs forever and yes to God."

Spring Arbor College, P.O. Box 219, Spring Arbor, MI 49283 517-750-1200. In addition to a strong liberal arts program, the college provides nontraditional delivery of degree completion programs for adult learners.

Spring Hill Camps, P.O. Box 100, Evart, MI 49631 616-734-2616. Youth camps, family camps, retreats, conferences.

STEER, Inc., P.O. Box 1236, Bismarck, ND 58502 701-258-4911. Evangelical, agricultural, fund-raising organization for missions worldwide. A farmer/rancher buys livestock or plants a crop. The profit is sent to missions.

Steve Wingfield Ministries, Inc., P.O. Box 1464, Harrisonburg, VA 22801 703-828-4747. Supports the local church in evangelism and discipleship.

Student Mobilization, P.O. Box 24805, Little Rock, AR 72221-4805 501-225-4488. Evangelizes and equips college students for lifelong ministry. Works on small college campuses in the South Central U.S. Ministries include Campus Outreach,

The Kaleo Summer Project, The Graduate Training Center and Pioneer Missions.

Summit Chaplain Services, P.O. Box 728, Akron, OH 44309 216-376-7388. Evangelizes and disciples those in prisons, their families, and staff serving in correctional facilities.

Summit Christian College, 1025 West Rudisill Blvd., Fort Wayne, IN 46807 219-456-2111. Coeducational institution of higher education in the Bible college tradition.

Summit Ministries, P.O. Box 207, Manitou Springs, CO 80829 719-685-9103. Training ministry for young adults, helping high school and college age students develop a Christian philosophy of life. Arms them with facts about what Christians are to stand for and why, as well as what we stand against.

Sunday Breakfast Association, Inc., P.O. Box 296, Philadelphia, PA 19105 215-922-6400. Shelters and counsels needy men, women, and children; distributes Bibles and other Christian literature; conducts a Sunday school and a summer camp for children.

Taylor University, Reade Ave., Upland, IN 46989 317-998-5198. Offers liberal arts and professional training.

TCM International, Inc., P.O. Box 24560, Indianapolis, IN 46224 317-299-0333. Missionaries, short-term workers, and specialized volunteers minister in Eastern Europe.

Teen Challenge of Arizona, Inc., P.O. Box 5966, Tucson, AZ 85703 602-322-0981. Drug and alcohol rehabilitation program.

Teen Challenge of Chattanooga, Inc., P.O. Box 2280, Chattanooga, TN 37409-0280 615-756-5558. Ministers to people who have drug, alcohol, and other life-controlling problems.

Teen Challenge of New Mexico, Inc., P.O. Box 20610, Albuquerque, NM 87154 505-281-8467. Ministers to people who have life-controlling problems.

Teen Challenge of Southern California, Inc., P.O. Box 5039, Riverside, CA 92517 714-682-8990. Ministers to people who have life-controlling problems.

Teen Challenge Training Center, Inc., P.O. Box 98, Rehrersburg, PA 19550 717-933-4181. Center for men who have life-controlling problems with drugs, alcohol, and crime.

Teen Challenge, Inc., 444 Clinton Ave., Brooklyn, NY 11238-1602 718-789-1414. Ministers to people with life-controlling problems.

Teen Ranch, Inc., 2861 Main, Marlette, MI 48453 517-635-7511. Works with troubled boys, 11–17 years of age, helping them to build a respect for self, others, academic achievement, the home, and to return to society as productive, confident young men.

Tele-Missions International, Inc., P.O. Box 563, Valley Cottage, NY 10989 914-268-9222. Mass-media, crusades, literature, counseling, seminars, and scholarships to aid students preparing for Christian service.

Texas Bible College, 2918 Vance Jackson, San Antonio, TX 78213 512-366-1611. Preparation for a ministry or to enhance a current ministry.

Timber-lee Christian Center, 2381 Scout Rd., East Troy, WI 53120 414-642-7345. Year-round facility for seminars and retreats, recreation activities, and educational opportunities.

TITUS International Institute, P.O. Box 3074, Chattanooga, TN 37404 615-629-5514. Assists in upgrading the quality of instruction in Bible Institutes worldwide. Produces video-based educational materials that can supplement the curricular program for training nationals as well as U.S. students.

Toccoa Falls College, P.O. Box 800068, Toccoa Falls, GA 30598 404-886-6831. Prepares men and women for service.

Today's Family, P.O. Box 22111, Phoenix, AZ 85028 602-867-2999. Conferences, film series, audio cassettes, radio and television programs.

Town and Country Manor, 555 East Memory Lane, Santa Ana, CA 92806 714-547-

ECFA MEMBERS cont.

7581. Retirement center with skilled and intermediate care. Affiliated with The Christian and Missionary Alliance.

Trans World Missions, P.O. Box 10, Glendale, CA 91209 213-663-1176. Focuses on indigenous church planting and training national leaders in Mexico, Central America, South America, and the Caribbean.

Trans World Radio, 700 Shunpike Rd., Chatham, NJ 07928 201-966-2700. Radio evangelistic ministry to more than 80% of the world's population.

Transformation International Enterprises, 1050 17th Street NW, #820, Washington, DC 20036 202-223-4909. Enables the unemployed and underemployed poor in developing countries to become productive, self-supporting citizens. Provides micro-economic development training and capital access.

Tri-City Union Gospel Mission, P.O. Box 1443, Pasco, WA 99301 509-547-2112. Provides food, shelter, clothing, spiritual guidance to unwed mothers, homeless families, and runaways.

Trinity Bible College, 700 Main Street, Ellendale, ND 58436 701-349-3621. Provides Bible-centered courses of training to prepare for ministry at home and abroad.

Trinity Christian Academy, 17001 Addison Rd., Addison, TX 75248 214-931-8325. Provides quality alternative to secular school education for children from families who want their own biblical values, corresponding moral emphases, and Christian worldview reinforced by the school. Kindergarten through grade twelve.

Trinity Christian Community, 1619 Prytania Street, New Orleans, LA 70130 504-581-6541. Ministers to the urban poor in New Orleans and other urban areas.

Trinity Episcopal School for Ministry, 311 Eleventh Street, Ambridge, PA 15003 412-266-3838. Trains men and women called to lay and ordained ministry in the Episcopal Church, in the wider Anglican Communion, and in the church of Christ throughout the world.

Trinity School of Cape Cod, 10 Carter Rd., S. Yarmouth, MA 02664 508-394-4118. Christian day school, pre-kindergarten through ninth grade.

Union Gospel Mission Association of Seattle, P.O. Box 202, Seattle, WA 98111 206-723-0767. Rescue ministry of Seattle area churches involved in emergency services, rehabilitation, youth programs, senior services, jail and prison ministry.

Union Gospel Mission of St. Paul, 435 E. University Ave., St. Paul, MN 55101-4495 612-292-1721. Provides services to the community. Free and low-income housing; medical clinics, secondhand store.

Union Mission Settlement, Inc., P.O. Box 112, Charleston, WV 25321 304-925-0366. Rescue mission with a transient hostel, adult personal care home with nursing services, recovery program for men.

Union Rescue Mission, P.O. Box 629, Los Angeles, CA 90053 213-628-6103. A community-designed mission to communicate principles of Christian living and relieve suffering. Specialized help for jobs, education and recreation, alcoholics.

United World Mission Incorporated, P.O. Box 250, Union Mills, NC 28167 704-287-8996. Evangelism and church planting. Major strategies are urban evangelism, training nationals to work among unreached peoples groups.

Utah Institute for Biblical Studies, P.O. Box 2096, Salt Lake City, UT 84110 801-359-9572. College level courses for people interested in pursuing biblical studies.

Vennard College, Vennard College, University Park, IA 52595 515-673-8391. Bible college with a Wesleyan-Arminian theological tradition.

Vietnam Ministries, Inc., P.O. Box 4568, Anaheim, CA 92803 714-758-8767. Publishes and distributes Christian literature, provides leadership and training to Vietnamese-speaking individuals and churches.

Voice of Calvary Ministries, P.O. Box 10562, Jackson, MS 39209 601-353-1635. Black-led ministry of Christians seeking to express the love of Christ in the poor communities of Jackson, Mississippi.

The Voice of Salvation, Inc., P.O. Box 890, Springville, CA 93265 209-539-3959. Missionary society ministering to Slavic people in communist lands and in the West.

Walk Thru the Bible Ministries, Inc., P.O. Box 80587, Atlanta, GA 30366 404-458-9300. Seminars; devotional guides (*The Daily Walk, Closer Walk, Youth Walk,* and *Family Walk);* study tours.

The Walter Hoving Home, Inc., P.O. Box 194, Garrison, NY 10524 914-424-3674. Drug and alcohol rehabilitation center focusing on women aged 17 to 50.

Washington Bible College, 6511 Princess Garden Parkway, Lanham, MD 20706 301-552-1400. Undergraduate and graduate biblical and professional education; resource center for Christian laymen and the continuing education of pastors, missionaries, and other Christian workers.

Water Street Rescue Mission, 210 S. Prince Street, Lancaster, PA 17603 717-393-7709. Emergency services, rehabilitation, prevention programs.

Waterfront Rescue Mission, Inc., P.O. Box 854, Pensacola, FL 32594 904-438-4027. Transient facilities, Bargain Center Store, rehabilitation and discipleship programs, youth Bible clubs.

Wears Valley Bible Conference Center Inc., Route 7, Box 291, Sevierville, TN 37862 615-453-2382. Retreats, conferences, and camping for the Christian family.

WEGO, Inc. (World Encounter Gospel Organization), P.O. Box 763187, Dallas, TX 75376-3187 214-943-6365. Servicing agency for missionaries.

Wesley Biblical Seminary, P.O. Box 9938, Jackson, MS 39286 601-957-1314. Graduate school of theology.

The Wesleyan Church Corporation, P.O. Box 50434, Indianapolis, IN 46250 317-842-0444. Receives, holds, and manages assets of the Wesleyan Church.

Western Conservative Baptist Seminary, 5511 Southeast Hawthorne Blvd., Portland, OR 97215 503-233-8561. Trains men and women for Christian leadership.

Western Indian Ministries, P.O. Drawer F, Window Rock, AZ 86515 505-371-5749. Trains Navajo leadership. Ministry includes church growth, radio, crisis ministries, counseling, day school for Navajo children.

Westminster Theological Seminary, P.O. Box 27009, Philadelphia, PA 19118 215-887-5511. Trains men for the gospel ministry as pastors, evangelists, and teachers as set forth in the Westminster Confession of Faith and Catechisms and the fundamental principles of Presbyterian church government.

Westmont College, 955 La Paz Rd., Santa Barbara, CA 93108 805-969-5051. Undergraduate liberal arts program.

Wheaton College, 501 East Seminary, Wheaton, IL 60187 708-260-5000. Independent, liberal arts college.

Wheeler Rescue Mission, Inc., 245 N. Delaware Street, Indianapolis, IN 46204 317-635-3575. Housing for men, clothing, counseling.

William Taylor Foundation, Taylor University, Reade Ave., Upland, IN 46989 317-998-5239. Support organization for Taylor University. Works with alumni and friends on estate plans and deferred gifts.

Wilson Family Living, P.O. Box 3400, Orange, CA 92665 714-637-7900. Facilitates good family relationships through seminars, radio.

Windsent, Inc., P.O. Box 101, Ortonville, MN 56256 605-432-9571. Supports the proclamation of the gospel through the media; encourages Christian believers to stand for the truths and moral principles of historic Christianity.

Winebrenner Theological Seminary, P.O. Box 478, Findlay, OH 45839 419-422-4824. Provides theological education for

ECFA MEMBERS cont.

ministerial candidates in the Churches of God, General Conference.

WLBF-FM, Montgomery Educational Radio, Inc., P.O. Box 17140, Montgomery, AL 36117 205-271-8900. Listener-supported FM station, affiliated with the Moody Broadcasting Network of Chicago.

Women for Christ, P.O. Box 517, Winnetka, IL 60093 708-446-9295. Non-affiliated women's ministry. Seminars and conferences with special emphasis on strengthening family relationships, supporting working women and ministering to women in leadership positions.

Word of Grace Communications, P.O. Box 4000, Panorama City, CA 91412 818-764-5904. Communication branch of John MacArthur's ministry which includes "Grace To You" daily radio program, tapes, and books.

Words of Hope, Inc., P.O. Box 1706, Grand Rapids, MI 49503 616-459-6181. Worldwide radio and media ministry of the Reformed Church in America.

World Emergency Relief, P.O. Box 977, Glendale, CA 91209 714-593-7140. Short- and long-term relief assistance to victims of natural disasters. Assists in long-term development projects such as orphanages, schools, hospitals and vocational programs internationally and in the U.S. Also sponsors several feeding programs.

World Evangelical Fellowship, P.O. Box WEF, Wheaton, IL 60189 708-668-0440. Provides the structure and forum for evangelicals worldwide to identify together, defend the faith together, and cooperate forcefully in advancing the gospel.

World Evangelistic Enterprise Corporation, 2348 Troy Rd., Springfield, OH 45504 513-399-7837. Principal ministry is non-commercial radio station WEEC; supports two radio missionary families in Brazil and Korea.

World Gospel Crusades, Inc., P.O. Box 3, Upland, CA 91785 714-982-1564. Trains nationals in South and Central America to reach every home with a witness, a Gospel of John, Bible correspondence courses, and follow-up.

World Gospel Mission, P.O. Box WGM, Marion, IN 46952 317-664-7331. Cross-cultural ministries such as church planting, biblical training centers, education, medical, literature, radio, agricultural.

World Home Bible League, 16801 S. Van Dam Rd., South Holland, IL 60473 708-331-2094. Scripture placement agency through local churches in Third World countries.

World Impact, Inc., 2001 S. Vermont Ave., Los Angeles, CA 90007 213-735-1137. Bible studies, worship services, schools, medical/dental clinic, housing in inner-city communities.

World Medical Mission, Inc., P.O. Box 3000, Boone, NC 28607 704-262-1980. Recruits physicians for short-term service in mission hospitals.

World Messianic Fellowships, Inc., P.O. Box 449, Lynbrook, NY 11563 516-593-1724. Outreach to Jews; trains missionaries for Jewish work.

World Mission Prayer League, Inc., 232 Clifton Ave., Minneapolis, MN 55403 612-871-6843. Independent Lutheran mission society.

World Missionary Press, Inc., P.O. Box 120, New Paris, IN 46553 219-831-2111. Produces and mails millions of free Scripture-by-subject booklets in over 235 languages.

World Opportunities International, 1415 Cahuenga Blvd., Hollywood, CA 90028 213-466-7187. Missions outreach to some 51 countries, relief distribution including food, clothing, and medical supplies.

World Radio Missionary Fellowship, Inc., P.O. Box 553000, Opa Locka, FL 33055-0401 305-624-4252. In South America, HCJB broadcasts from Ecuador in key languages to major world areas by shortwave radio; local radio in Latin America. In Panama, WRMF assists in operating HOXO's Spanish/English station. In Europe, it assists local groups in developing radio ministries. In the USA, WRMF assists World Radio Network, Inc. to operate five stations along the Mexican border.

World Relief Corporation, P.O. Box WRC, Wheaton, IL 60189 708-665-0235. Aids victims of war and natural disaster—specializing in helping people to help themselves.

World Servants, 8233 Gator Lane, #6, West Palm Beach, FL 33411 407-790-0800. Seeks to expand the mission vision of the church through training seminars and short-term missions familiarization trips.

World Thrust, Inc., P.O. Box 450105, Tucker, GA 30345-0105 404-939-5215. Serves as a mobilizing force for world evangelization. It is a catalytic and multiplication ministry focusing primarily on the senior pastor and key church leaders. Provides seminars, consultation, foreign mission exposure trips and overseas work projects.

World Vision, Inc., 919 West Huntington Drive, Monrovia, CA 91016 818-357-7979. Relief and development organizations in more than 80 countries.

World Wide Pictures, Inc., 1201 Hennepin Ave., Minneapolis, MN 55403 612-338-3335. Producer and distributor of Billy Graham evangelistic films.

World Witness, One Cleveland Street, Greenville, SC 29601 803-233-5226. Board of Foreign Missions of the Associate Reformed Presbyterian Church.

World-Wide Missions, P.O. Box 7125, Pasadena, CA 91109-7125 818-355-9495. Ministers to needy peoples in 32 underdeveloped countries.

Worldteam USA, P.O. Box 143038, Coral Gables, FL 33114 305-446-0861. Church-planting teams in unreached cities and people groups.

Worldwide Discipleship Association, Inc., 110 Carnegie Pl., #100, Fayetteville, GA 30214 404-460-1337. Works with college students and pastors in training laymen in the churches.

Worldwide Friendship, Inc., P.O. Box 8809, Minneapolis, MN 55408 612-827-5197. Seeks to reach internationals for Christ who have come to the Twin City area to study. Provides free services, programs, and activities; outreach ministry in Egypt.

WRVM, Inc., P.O. Box 212, Suring, WI 54174 414-842-2839. Christian radio station broadcast 24 hours a day to northeast Wisconsin and south central Upper Michigan.

Wycliffe Associates, Inc., P.O. Box 2000, Orange, CA 92669 714-639-9950. Service ministry for lay participation in Wycliffe Bible Translators. Encourages and allows lay people to become directly involved in projects for Bible translation. Projects include building and/or funding of translation centers, missionary housing, equipment, new country start-ups, vehicles, and other needs.

Wycliffe Bible Translators, Inc., P.O. Box 2727, Huntington Beach, CA 92647 714-536-9346. Provides translation of the Scriptures for the 3,000 languages that do not have them.

Young Life, P.O. Box 520, Colorado Springs, CO 80901 719-473-4262. Ministry with adolescents. Ministry starts when trained staff and volunteers befriend teenagers. Nationwide camps offer young people an opportunity to learn about themselves and their Creator.

Youth Challenge International Bible Institute, R.D.#2, Box 33, Sunbury, PA 17801 717-286-6442. A three-year, college-level educational community that provides specialized training for the Youth Challenge conceptual approach in rehabilitating troubled youth.

Youth for Christ/Southern Minnesota, P.O. Box 172, Mankato, MN 56001 507-345-4334. Outreach ministry to junior and senior high school students.

Youth for Christ/USA, Inc., P.O. Box 419, Wheaton, IL 60189 708-668-6600. Youth evangelism and the discipleship of young people into the church: Campus Life Clubs, Youth Guidance for delinquent teens, Minority/Urban for the unique needs of urban centers, World Outreach in 53 countries.

ECFA MEMBERS cont.

Youth Guidance, Inc., R.D. #2, Duff Rd., Sewickley, PA 15143 412-741-8550. Brings troubled young people together with Christian adults in a long-term one-to-one friendship. Trains the volunteer to be a friend and spiritual guide.

Youth Haven, Inc., P.O. Box 97, Rives Junction, MI 49277 517-569-3328. Year round ministry to underprivileged children.

Youth Investment Foundation, 15306 Minnetonka Industrial Rd., Minnetonka, MN 55343 612-938-6123. Works with alienated suburban and small-town youth.

YUGO Ministries, P.O. Box 25, San Dimas, CA 91773 714-592-6621. Missionary outreach to the border areas of Mexico. Short-term ministry program.

Zwemer Institute of Muslim Studies, 1401 S. Shamrock, Monrovia, CA 91016 818-303-3058. Brings opportunities for ministry to Muslims into focus. Weekend Muslim Awareness Seminars and publications, research, church-planting strategies. Field teams coordinate Muslim evangelism in strategic urban centers.

Source: Evangelical Council for Financial Accountability May 1990 Member Profile Directory.

CHRISTIAN FOUNDATIONS WITH NATIONAL INTERESTS

Artevel Foundation, Well's Fargo Center, 333 South Grand Avenue, Suite 4150, Los Angeles, CA 90071-3164 213-680-9212

Recipient Types: Aged, Bible societies, Bible translation, child welfare, colleges & universities, community services, counseling, emergency relief, family services, food distribution, homeless, hospitals, inner-city populations, international relief, missionaries, missions, nursing homes, pastoral counseling, religious education, right-to-life issues, seminaries, shelters, stewardship, substance abuse, women's affairs, and youth ministry.

Believers Foundation, 1570 Dutch Hollow Road, P.O. Box 3175, Elida, OH 45807 419-339-4441

Recipient Types: Bible societies, churches, missions, and religious education.

Ash Family Foundation, 84 Lake Padgett Drive, Land O'Lakes, FL 33539 813-996-4313

Recipient Types: Athletics, campus crusades, churches, colleges and universities, prison work, religious broadcasting, religious centers, religious organizations, religious welfare, youth ministry, and youth organizations.

Atkinson, Myrtle L., Foundation, P.O. Box 688, LaCanada, CA 91011 818-790-7019

Recipient Types: Athletics, Bible societies, Bible study, Bible translation, campus crusades, churches, colleges and universities, distribution of religious materials, disabled, divinity schools, emergency relief, ministries, minority education, missionaries, missions, prison work, refugee services, religious broadcasting, religious education, religious organizations, seminaries, youth ministries, and youth organizations.

Christian Workers Foundation, 3038 Bankhead Avenue, Montgomery, AL 36106 205-263-5571

Recipient Types: Bible study, campus crusades, colleges and universities, parochial education—secondary, religious education, youth ministry, youth organizations, and youth welfare.

Aurora Foundation, P.O. Box 1848, Bradenton, FL 34206 813-748-4100

Recipient Types: Bible societies, Bible study, Bible translation, campus ministries, child welfare, churches, colleges and universities, distribution of religious materials, ministries, missionaries, missions, religious broadcasting, religious education, religious organizations, religious welfare, youth ministries, and youth organizations.

Berry, Lowell, Foundation, One Kaiser Plaza, Suite 995, Oakland, CA 94612 415-452-0433

Recipient Types: Campus crusades, churches, colleges and universities, community services, missions, prison work, religious education, religious higher education, religious organizations, religious welfare, seminaries, and youth organizations.

Caddock Foundation, Inc., 1717 Chicago Avenue, Riverside, CA 92507 714-788-1700 Recipient Types: Aged, Bible societies, Bible study, Bible translation, campus crusades, campus ministries, child welfare, Christian centers, churches, colleges and universities, counseling, distribution of religious materials, family services, ministries, missionaries, missions, nursing homes, prison work, religious broadcasting, religious centers, religious organizations, religious welfare, and youth organizations.

Chatlos Foundation, Inc, 122 East 42nd Street, New York, NY 10168 212-867-9630

Recipient Types: Aged, Bible study, Bible translation, campus crusades, campus ministries, colleges & universities, community centers, disabled, emergency relief, international relief, ministries, missions, prison work, religious centers, religious education, religious broadcasting, religious organizations, seminaries, shelters, youth ministry, and youth organizations.

C.I.O.S., 4515 Lake Shore Street, Waco, TX 76710 817-757-0174

Recipient Types: Bible societies, Bible study, Bible translation, campus crusades, child welfare, churches, colleges and universities, distribution of religious materials, divinity schools, family services, international relief, ministries, missionaries, minority education, missions, parochial education-secondary, prison work, religious broadcasting, religious education, religious organizations, seminaries, youth ministry, and youth organizations.

Crowell, Henry P. and Susan C., Trust, Lock Box 442, Chicago, IL 60690 312-372-5202

Recipient Types: Aged, Bible societies, Bible study, churches, colleges and universities, disabled, family services, inner-city populations, international relief, ministries, missions, parochial education-secondary, prison work, religious broadcasting, religious education, religious higher education, religious organizations, religious welfare, seminaries, youth ministry, youth organizations, and youth welfare.

DeMoss, Arthur S., Foundation, St. Davids Center, Suite A-300, St. Davids, PA 19087 215-254-5500

Recipient Types: Campus crusades, child welfare, churches, colleges and universities, community services, distribution of religious materials, disabled, ministries, missions, prison work, religious broadcasting, religious centers, religious education, religious higher education, religious organizations, religious welfare, right-to-life issues, seminaries, and youth welfare.

Firestone, Harvey S., Trust No. 1 Fund, c/o Bank One Akron, 50 South Main Street, Akron, OH 44308 216-375-1865

Recipient Types: Bible societies, churches, homeless, international relief, and ministries.

First Fruit, Inc., 7400 West 20th Avenue, Lakewood, CO 80215 303-232-4084 Recipient Types: Bible societies, Bible study, Bible translation, child welfare, clinics, community development, community services, counseling, distribution of religious materials, emergency relief, family services, food distribution, health care in-home, hospitals, international development, international health care, international relief, medical assistance, ministries, missionaries, missions, prison work, refugee services, religious broadcasting, religious welfare, rural populations, and substance abuse.

Helms Foundation, Inc., 25765 Quilla Road, P.O. Box 55827, Valencia, CA 91355 805-253-3485

CHRISTIAN FOUNDATIONS . . . cont.

Recipient Types: Churches, colleges and universities, hospitals, ministries, prison work, religious education, religious higher education, religious organizations, religious welfare, seminaries, youth ministry, and youth welfare.

Huston Foundation, P.O. Box 139, Gladwyne, PA 19035 215-527-4371

Recipient Types: Athletics, Bible study, Bible translation, campus crusades, campus ministries, child welfare, churches, colleges and universities, family services, medical assistance, ministries, missions, parochial education-secondary, religious broadcasting, religious education, religious organizations, religious welfare, youth ministries, and youth organizations.

Johnson Foundation, 225 Merrill Street, Birmingham, MI 48011 313-646-7500

Recipient Types: Athletics, Bible study, campus crusades, Christian centers, churches, clothes distribution, colleges and universities, counseling, emergency relief, food distribution, homeless, inner-city populations, medical assistance, minority education, missionaries, missions, religious broadcasting, religious organizations, right-to-life issues, seminaries, substance abuse, youth ministry, and youth organizations.

Jubilee Foundation, 175 West Jackson, Suite 800, Chicago, IL 60604 312-922-2494

Recipient Types: Campus crusades, campus ministries, Christian centers, churches, clothes distribution, colleges and universities, counseling, distribution of religious materials, emergency relief, family services, food distribution, inner-city populations, medical assistance, ministries, minority education, missionaries, missions, religious broadcasting, religious education, religious higher education, religious organizations, youth ministry, and youth organizations.

Kejr Foundation, Inc., 6500 Xerxes Avenue, South, Minneapolis, MN 55423 612-920-0574

Recipient Types: Bible societies, campus ministries, churches, distribution of religious materials, ministries, missions, religious education, religious higher education, religious organizations, and youth ministries.

Kresge Foundation, P.O. Box 3151, Troy, MI 48007 313-643-9630

Recipient Types: Colleges and universities, hospitals, nursing homes, religious centers, religious higher education, religious organizations, and religious welfare.

Lamb, Kirkland S. and Rena B., Foundation, 1312 Eckles Drive, Tampa, FL 33612

Recipient Types: Churches, international relief, missionaries, missions, religious broadcasting, religious organizations, seminaries, and youth ministry.

Luce, Henry, Foundation, 111 West 50th Street, New York, NY 10020 212-489-7700

Recipient Types: Colleges and universities, divinity schools, religious education, and seminaries.

Maclellan Foundation, Provident Building, Suite 501, Chattanooga, TN 37402 615-755-1366

Recipient Types: Missions, prison work, religious broadcasting, religious education, religious higher education, religious organizations, seminaries, youth ministries, youth organizations, and youth welfare.

Mostyn Foundation, Inc., c/o James C. Edwards and Company, Inc., 805 Third Avenue, New York, NY 10022 212-319-8490

Recipient Types: Churches, ministries, religious education, and religious organizations.

Oldham Little Church Foundation, 5177 Richmond Avenue, Suite 1068, Houston, TX 77056 713-621-4190

Recipient Types: Churches and missions.

Rainbow Fund, P.O. Box 937, Fort Valley, GA 31030 912-825-2021

Recipient Types: Athletics, campus crusades, churches, colleges and universities, ministries, missions, parochial education-secondary, religious broadcasting, religious education, religious higher education, religious organizations, religious welfare, seminaries, and youth organizations.

Stewardship Foundation, P.O. Box 1278, Tacoma, WA 98401 206-272-8336

Recipient Types: Aged, athletics, Bible societies, Bible study, Bible translation, campus crusades, child welfare, Christian centers, churches, civil rights, clinics, clothes distribution, colleges and universities, community development, community services, counseling, disabled, distribution of religious materials, emergency relief, employment, family services, food distribution, health care in-home, homeless, hospitals, human rights, inner-city populations, international development, medical assistance, ministries, minority education, missionaries, missions, parochial education-elementary, parochial education-secondary, pastoral counseling, prison work, religious broadcasting, religious centers, religious education, religious higher education, religious organizations, right-to-life issues, rural populations, seminaries, substance abuse, youth ministry, youth organizations, and youth welfare.

Storehouse Foundation, P.O. Box 1532, Camden, SC 29020 803-432-8677

Recipient Types: Bible study, Bible translation, campus crusades, campus ministries, churches, ministries, distribution of religious materials, missionaries, missions, religious broadcasting, and religious welfare.

Tell Foundation, 4010 North 38th Avenue, Phoenix, AZ 85019 602-278-6209

Recipient Types: Bible study, campus crusades, campus ministries, churches, colleges and universities, community services, distribution of religious materials, family services, hospitals, international relief, medical assistance, ministries, missions, parochial education-elementary, parochial education-secondary, prison work, religious broadcasting, religious education, religious organizations, religious welfare, youth ministries, and youth welfare.

Tell, Paul P., Foundation, Inc., 1105 Trans Ohio Building, 7 West Bowery Street, Akron, OH 44308 216-434-8355

Recipient Types: Bible societies, Bible study, Bible translation, campus crusades, child welfare, churches, colleges and universities, disabled, distribution of religious materials, emergency relief, international relief, ministries, missionaries, missions, parochial education-secondary, prison work, religious broadcasting, religious communities, seminaries, youth ministry, and youth organizations.

Vermeer Foundation, c/o Vermeer Manufacturing Company, Box 200, Pella, IA 50219 515-628-3141

Recipient Types: Athletics, Bible societies, Bible study, Bible translation, child welfare, Christian centers, churches, colleges and universities, counseling, distribution of religious materials, family services, medical assistance, ministries, missionaries, missions, parochial education-elementary, parochial education-secondary, pastoral counseling, prison work, religious broadcasting, religious higher education, right-to-life issues, stewardship, youth ministry, and youth organizations.

Ware Foundation, 147 Alhambra Cir., #215, Coral Gables, FL 33134 305-443-8728

Recipient Types: Bible societies, campus crusades, churches, colleges and universities, distribution of religious materials, hospices, medical assistance, ministries, missions, religious broadcasting, religious education, religious organizations, religious welfare, youth ministries, and youth organizations.

Source: *Fund Raiser's Guide to Religious Philanthropy.* Copyright © 1990. The Taft Group, 12300 Twinbrook Parkway, Suite 450, Rockville, MD 20852. Used by permission.

CHRISTIAN MANAGEMENT AWARDS

Awarded by Christian Ministries Management Association to an individual or an organization who has made a significant contribution to the development and advancement of Christian management and practice.

Year	*Recipient*	*Affiliation*	*Location*
1981	Richard Schmidt	Foursquare Missions International	Los Angeles, CA
1982	George Martinez	Good Shepherd Church	Deming, NM
1983	Arthur C. Borden	Evangl. Cncl for Financial Accountability	Washington, DC
1984	No award given		
1985	Richard Capin	OMS International	Greenwood, IN
1986	Ted Engstrom	World Vision	Monrovia, CA
1987	Lorne Sanny	The Navigators	Colorado Springs, CO
1988	George Wilson	Billy Graham Evangelistic Association	Minneapolis, MN
	Harold Beaty	Wycliffe Bible Translators	Huntington Beach, CA
1989	Eugene Habecker	Huntington College	Huntington, IN
1990	Peter Drucker	Claremont College	Claremont, CA

Social and Political Concerns

ONE DAY IN THE LIVES OF AMERICA'S CHILDREN

Every day in the USA:

- 2,795 teens get pregnant
- 372 teens miscarry
- 1,106 teens have abortions
- 1,295 teens give birth
- 689 babies are born to women who have had inadequate prenatal care
- 719 babies are born at low birthweight (less than 5 lbs., 8 oz.)
- 129 babies are born at very low birthweight (less than 3 lbs., 5 oz.)
- 67 babies die before one month of life
- 105 babies die before their first birthday
- 27 children die from poverty
- 10 children are killed by guns
- 30 children are wounded by guns
- 6 teenagers commit suicide
- 135,000 children bring a gun to school
- 7,742 teenagers become sexually active
- 623 teenagers get syphilis or gonorrhea
- 211 children are arrested for drug abuse
- 437 children are arrested for drinking or drunken driving
- 1,512 teenagers drop out of school
- 1,849 children are abused or neglected
- 3,288 children run away from home
- 1,629 children are in adult jails
- 2,556 children are born out of wedlock
- 2,989 children see their parents divorced
- 34,285 people lose jobs

Source: Children's Defense Fund

"" FOCUS QUOTE **American culture is no longer a paradigm of Christian values. Isn't it a fascinating paradox that while Russian children are studying Bibles in their classrooms, American kids are being sequestered from them? . . . Perhaps someday America will become a target. Not for missiles, but for Russian missionaries.** —Rolf Zettersten, senior vice president, *Focus on the Family* magazine, March 1990 issue.

MOST IMPORTANT PROBLEM FACING THE NATION

What Adults Think

	1989 %	*1987* %	*1985* %	*1983* %
Drugs, drug abuse	27	11	2	—
Poverty, homeless, hunger	8	5	6	—
Economy in general	7	10	6	8
Federal budget deficit	6	11	18	5
Environment, pollution	6	—	—	—
Fear of war, international tensions	4	23	27	2
High cost of living, inflation	3	5	11	18

	1989 %	*1987* %	*1985* %	*1983* %
Ethics, moral decline	3	5	2	4
Crime	3	3	4	2
Unemployment	2	13	20	53
Trade deficit	2	3	—	—
Dissatisfaction with government	2	5	—	2
Abortion	2	—	—	—
Quality of education	1	—	—	—
Interest rates	*	—	—	2
Recession/depression	*	—	—	—
Other economic problems	12	21	16	6
None, don't know	8	4	3	—

* Less than one-half of one percent. Source: The Gallup Organization, Inc., poll. July 1989. Used by permission.

FOCUS QUOTE

If I straighten the pictures on the walls of your home, I am committing no sin, am I? But suppose that your house were afire, and I still went calmly about straightening pictures, what would you say? Would you think me merely stupid or very wicked? . . . The world today is on fire. What are you doing to extinguish the fire? —Corrie ten Boom in *Amazing Love.*

MOST IMPORTANT PROBLEM FACING THE NATION

What Teenagers Think

	1989 %	*1987* %	*1985* %	*1983* %
Drug abuse	32	10	3	2
Fear of war, military issues	14	26	43	38
Economic issues	13	9	16	26
Environment, pollution	7	*	1	1
Political issues	6	6	10	2
AIDS	5	11	1	—
Crime	3	2	1	1
Abortion	2	*	1	—
Alcohol abuse	1	2	*	—
Miscellaneous	9	12	7	5
Don't know	9	11	18	12

* Less than one-half of one percent. Source: The Gallup Organization, Inc., poll. July 1989. Used by permission.

FOCUS FACT

More than 10,000 babies were aborted in the USA during the 58 hours it took to rescue Jessica McClure from an abandoned well in Midland, TX, October 14–16, 1987.

The Who, When and Where of Abortion

Each year three out of every 100 American women age 15 to 44 choose to end unwanted pregnancies—1.5 million abortions in all. Only .01 percent of abortions occur after 24 weeks, and most of those are for urgent therapeutic reasons.

Age	Estimated rate per 1,000 women in category
15-17 years	32.2
18-19 years	62.4
20-24 years	54.6
25-29 years	33.0
30-34 years	17.9
35-39 years	9.8
40 and over	3.4

Race	
White	23.0
Nonwhite	52.6

Family Income	
Under $11,000	62.2
$11,000-$24,999	32.5
$25,000 and over	16.5

Figures above based on 1987 data

Length of Pregnancy*	1983	1973
8 weeks and under	50.3%	38.2%
9-10 weeks	26.9%	29.8%
11-12 weeks	13.3%	17.5%
13-15 weeks	5.3%	6.0%
16-20 weeks	3.4%	7.2%
21 weeks and over	0.8%	1.4%

*Time since last menstrual period

Locations*	
Hospitals	13%
Abortion clinics	60%
Other clinics	23%
M.D.'s offices	4%

*1985 figures

Source: The Alan Guttmacher Institute and *Newsweek*, July 17, 1989 issue.

Should Abortion Be Legal in This Case?

Majority wants it legal if:	Should be legal	Should be illegal
Pregnancy results from rape	86%	8%
Pregnancy results from incest	83%	11%
Potential genetic deformity	52%	31%
Definite genetic deformity	65%	23%
Woman's physical health in danger	81%	11%
Saving the life of a woman	86%	7%

Majority wants it illegal if:	Should be legal	Should be illegal
A woman is a minor	35%	50%
Wrong time in life to have a child	12%	82%
Not desired gender	3%	93%
Woman cannot afford a child	16%	75%
As a means of birth control	6%	89%
Pregnancy would cause too much emotional strain	23%	64%
Father unwilling to help raise the child	10%	83%
Father absent	11%	81%
Mother wants abortion—father wants baby	14%	72%
Father wants abortion—mother wants baby	11%	75%

Source: *Boston Globe*/WBZ-TV poll, March 27-29, 1989.

PRO-LIFE ORGANIZATIONS

Arizona
Crisis Pregnancy Center, Inc.
1124 N. 3rd Avenue
Tucson, AZ 85705
602-622-5774

California
Women Exploited By Abortion (WEBA)
3553B North Paris Blvd. #4
Paris, CA 92370
714-657-0334

Washington, D.C.
Ad Hoc Committee in Defense of Life, Inc.
1187 National Press Bldg.
Washington, DC 20045
202-347-8686

National Right to Life Committee, Inc.
419 7th Street NW, Suite 500
Washington, DC 20004
202-626-8800

Florida
Legal Action for Women
1145 Candlewood Circle
Pensacola, FL 32514
904-474-1091

Illinois
Americans United for Life
343 S. Dearborn Street, Suite 1804
Chicago, IL 60604
312-786-9494

Pro-Life Action League
6160 North Cicero Avenue
Chicago, IL 60646
312-777-2900

Indiana
Open Arms
6919 E. 10th Street, Bldg. F
Indianapolis, IN 46219
317-359-9950

Minnesota
New Beginnings
40 25th Avenue North
St. Cloud, MN 56303
612-255-1252

Missouri
Pro-Life Direct Action League
P.O. Box 11881
St. Louis, MO 63105
314-863-1022

New Hampshire
His Mansion
P.O. Box G
Hillsboro, NH 03244
603-464-5555

New York
Operation Rescue
P.O. Box 1180
Binghamton, NY 13902
607-723-4012

Pennsylvania
Loving and Caring Inc.
1817 Olde Homestead Lane
Lancaster, PA 17601
717-293-3230

Tennessee
American Rights Coalition
P.O. Box 487
Chattanooga, TN 37405
1-800-634-2224

Texas
Americans Against Abortion
Box 70
Lindale, TX 75771
214-963-8671

Virginia
American Life League Inc.
P.O. Box 1350
Stafford, VA 22554
703-659-4171

Christian Action Council
701 West Broad Street, Suite 405
Falls Church, VA 22046
703-237-2100

Liberty Godparent Ministries
P.O. Box 27000
Lynchburg, VA 24506
1-800-368-3336 (hotline)
804-384-3043 (office)

National Pro Life Political Action Committee
2525 Wilson Blvd.
Arlington, VA 22201
703-528-1515

Women of Ramah
701 W. Broad St., Suite 405
Falls Church, VA 22046

FOCUS FACT

At least 45 members (out of 435 total in the House) changed their pro-life position to pro-abortion in 1989. —November 1989 issue of *Washington Watch*

“ ” FOCUS QUOTE **The 1990s will be much worse than the 1980s.**—The National Commission on AIDS

DEATHS FROM AIDS

Year	*Number of Deaths*
1993	53,000-76,000
1992	49,000-64,000
1991	43,000-52,000
1990	37,000-42,000
1989	20,422
1988	18,488
1987	14,796
1986	11,108
1985	6,505

National AIDS Information Clearinghouse and the U.S. Centers for Disease Control

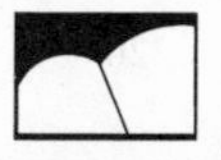

FOCUS BOOKS

The Least of These: What Everyone Should Know About Abortion **by Curt Young. Moody Press.**

Who Broke the Baby? **by Jean Garton. Bethany House Publishers.**

Abortion: Questions and Answers **by Dr. and Mrs. J.C. Wilke. Haynes and Associates Publishing Inc.**

Mom, I'm Pregnant **by Bev O'Brien. Tyndale House Publishers.**

Should I Keep My Baby? **by Martha Zimmerman. Bethany House Publishers.**

PEOPLE SPEAK OUT ABOUT AIDS

Do you think it is likely or is not likely that AIDS will eventually become an epidemic for the population at large?

Date	*Likely* %	*Not likely* %	*No opinion* %
11/89	68	26	6
10/88	69	23	8
10/87	51	42	7

Do you personally know anyone who has contracted AIDS?

	11/89 %	*11/86* %	*8/85* %
Yes	13	6	4
No	87	94	96
	100	100	100

How concerned are you that you will get AIDS?

	Nov 1989 %	*Oct 1988* %	*Oct 1987* %
Very concerned	15	19	20
A little concerned	21	19	22
Not very concerned	21	26	21
Not at all concerned	42	36	37
No opinion	1		
	100	100	100

How concerned are you that a member of your family will get AIDS?

	%
Very concerned	27
A little concerned	30
Not very concerned	19
Not at all concerned	22
No opinion	2
	100

Source: The Gallup Poll. October 12-15, 1989.

“ ” FOCUS QUOTE **Many churches who thought they would never have to deal with AIDS—especially urban churches—will have to, and sooner than they think. All our experiences have told us that if there isn't a policy in place, when a problem surfaces it can quickly get out of hand and be very detrimental to the congregation.**—Shepherd Smith, president, Americans for a Sound AIDS policy, on his concern that only a handful of churches have AIDS policies in place. *Christianity Today* magazine, June 18, 1990 issue.

AIDS ORGANIZATIONS

National AIDS Prevention Institute,
P.O. Box 2500, Culpeper, VA 22701
703-825-4040

Walter Reed Army Institute of Research,
Department of Virus Diseases,
Washington, DC 20307
301-427-5176

Americans for a Sound AIDS Policy,
P.O. Box 17433,
Washington, DC 20041
703-471-7350

Love and Action, 3 Church Circle,
Annapolis, MD 21401
301-268-3442

The Bridge: Living with AIDS,
1759 Oak Street, San Francisco, CA
94117
415-552-AIDS

FOCUS BOOKS

AIDS and Young People **by Robert Redfield and Wanda Franz. Regnery Gateway, Inc.**

Gays, AIDS and You **by Enrique Rueda and Michael Schwartz. Devin Adair Company**

Number of Drug Users

12–17 years of age (pop. 20,250,000)

Marijuana & Hashish	17%
Cocaine	3%
Alcohol	50%

18–25 years of age (pop. 29,688,000)

Marijuana & Hashish	56%
Cocaine	20%
Alcohol	90%

These estimates were developed from the 1988 National Household Survey on Drug Abuse

Source: *USA Today* telephone poll by Gordon S. Black Associates. October, 1989.

What People Say about Drugs (Part 1)

A USA TODAY poll on illegal drugs reveals widespread concern.

Fear of drug violence tops list of concerns

Those who say they are concerned "a great deal" about:

Large majority thinks drug problems are worse than most people think...

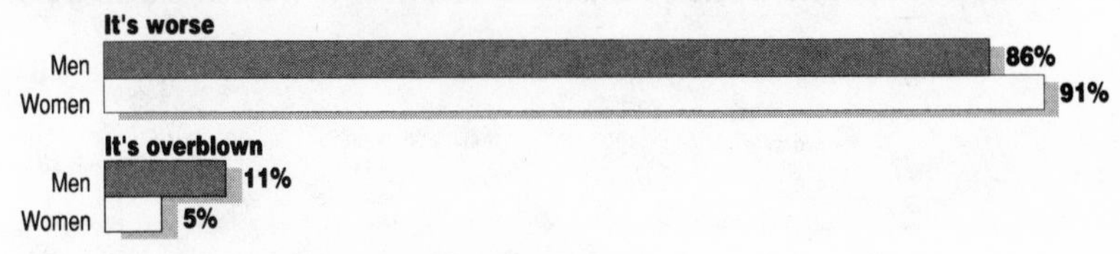

...But half think the battle can be won

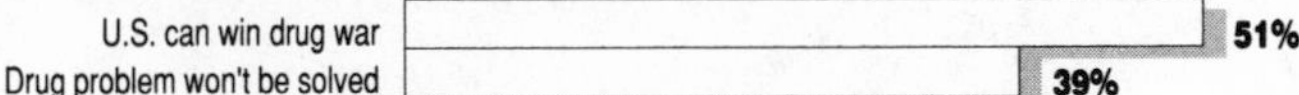

What we see as key to drug war victory

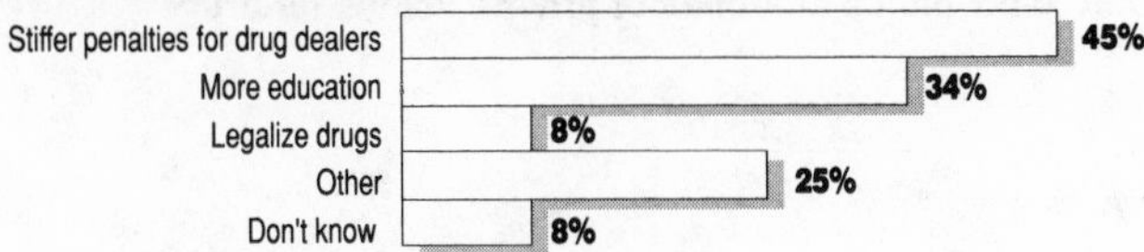

Percentage who view drug addicts as

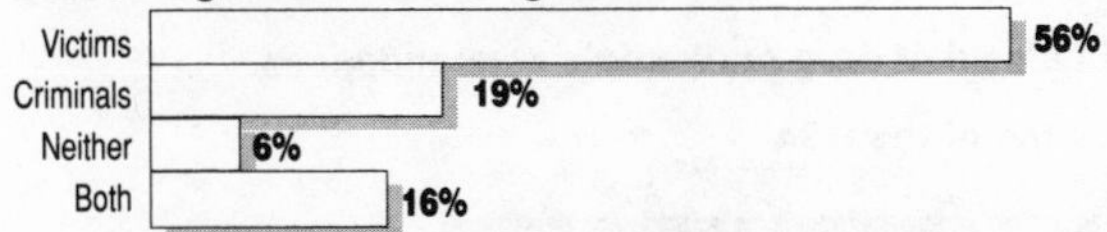

More women than men favor higher taxes for drug war

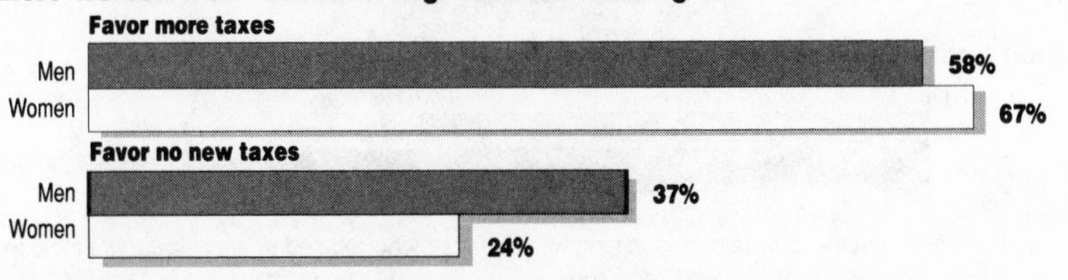

Source: An Oct. 15-16, 1989 USA TODAY telephone poll of 814 people by Gordon S. Black Associates. Sampling error is plus or minus 3.5 percent.

What People Say about Drugs (Part 2)

How much people would pay in new anti-drug taxes

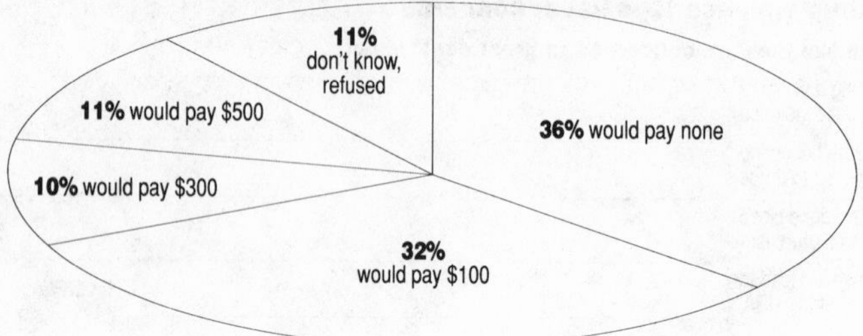

Hours per week people would be willing to volunteer to work in the drug war

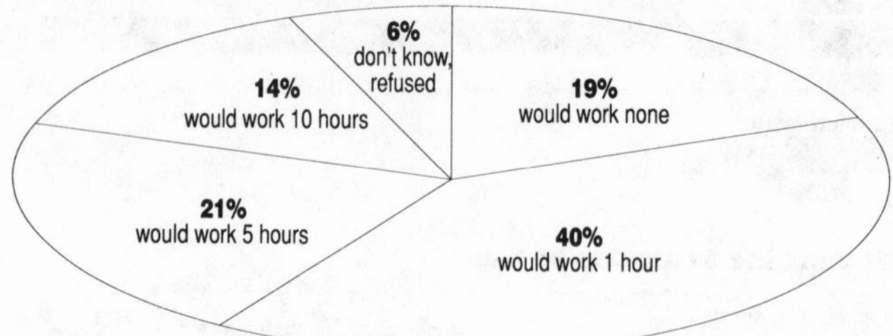

Six in 10 would not allow police searches of private homes for drugs without a warrant

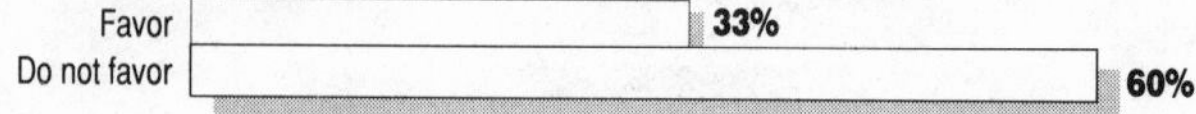

More older respondents afraid of drug epidemic's consequences

Drug use will lead to decline of the USA

That bribes and threats will corrupt the government

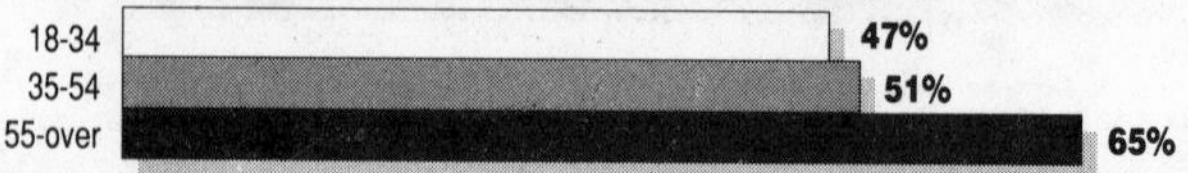

Note: In most questions, answers of "don't know" and those who refused to answer are not included.

Source: An Oct. 15–16, 1989 USA TODAY telephone poll of 814 people by Gordon S. Black Associates. Sampling error is plus or minus 3.5 percent.

FOCUS FACT

60% of young people, age 25 and under, have tried drugs. Alcohol and drug abuse cost America over $175 billion in 1983 in reduced productivity, treatment, crime, and related costs.

WHO DOES, DOESN'T DO DRUGS

Drug abuse is more common among the affluent and the poor than in middle-income groups, according to a survey conducted by the Media-Advertising Partnership for a Drug-free America. Other findings of the survey of 4,737 adults:

- 20% consider cocaine use a status symbol
- 11% feel that occasional use of cocaine is not risky
- 29% think cigarettes are worse than marijuana
- 26% think it's OK to smoke marijuana in private
- Women today are nearly identical to men in their use of marijuana and cocaine
- Blacks and Hispanics are more likely to be drug abusers than the general public
- About 30% of those 18 to 35 have used cocaine at least once
- Regular church attendance is strongly related to much lower levels of drug abuse among all populations

Source: *USA Today,* December 6, 1989.

FOCUS FACT

The United States has the highest rate of teen alcohol and drug use of any industrialized nation. The drug problem in this country is 10 times greater than in Japan.

TEENAGERS SAY SUBSTANCE ABUSE IS THEIR BIGGEST PROBLEM

Teenagers were asked: What do you feel is the biggest problem facing people your age?

	1989 %	*1987* %	*1985* %	*1983* %	*1977* %
Drug abuse	60	54	40	35	27
Peer pressures	13	10	8	8	5
Alcohol abuse	11	12	14	10	7
Teenage pregnancy	8	11	3	-	-
School problems	3	1	4	5	3
Teenage gangs	3	-	-	-	-
Problems in growing up	2	2	5	1	6
Unemployment	1	2	8	16	6
Teenage suicide	1	2	3	-	-
Getting along with parents	1	2	2	5	20
Career uncertainties	1	-	-	3	3
AIDS	*	5	-	-	-
Economic problems	*	1	3	2	3
Financing college	1	3	1	-	-
Fear of war	*	1	2	4	-
Miscellaneous	7	5	7	5	12
Don't know	6	8	13	18	14

*Less than one-half of one percent. Source: The Gallup Organization, Inc., poll. July 1989. Used by permission.

FOCUS FACT

How can you know whom to contact about your social and political concerns, what to say, and when to say it? Keep in touch with an organization providing "inside Washington" information. The Family Research Council's publication, *Washington Watch,* will keep you on target with the latest reports from the nation's capitol—free of charge. To receive *Washington Watch,* telephone or write: The Family Research Council, 601 Pennsylvania Ave. NW, Suite 901, Washington, DC 20004. 202-393-2100. Request it by name.

FOCUS QUOTE

We're seeing a lot of 9 and 10 year olds—they're not all getting caught (for drugs) but they tell us they are dealing.

—Melinda Mills, supervising probation officer, San Francisco Juvenile Court

EFFECTIVE ANTI-DRUG CAMPAIGNERS: TEENS TELL WHOM THEY WOULD LISTEN TO

	Teens %
Former drug addicts	71
Sports figures	55
Rock stars	47
Physicians	33
Policemen	32
Ministers, priests, or rabbis	24
Scientists	22
Teachers	16
Congressmen	16

Source: The Gallup Organization, Inc., poll. July 1989. Used by permission.

TOP SEVEN PROBLEMS IN PUBLIC SCHOOLS—THEN AND NOW

1940	*1988*
1. Talking	1. Drug abuse
2. Chewing gum	2. Alcohol abuse
3. Making noise	3. Pregnancy
4. Running in the halls	4. Suicide
5. Getting out of line	5. Rape
6. Wearing improper clothes	6. Robbery
7. Not putting paper in the wastebasket	7. Assault

FOCUS FACT

A survey of youngsters in Minnesota's public schools indicates young people who abuse alcohol and other drugs often do so to escape personal problems. Peer pressure—often cited as the cause of adolescent drinking and drug use—is not the most common factor in drug and alcohol abuse, based on replies from 91,175 youngsters in the sixth, ninth, and twelfth grades.

Source: *USA Today,* July 21, 1989.

Source: Updated information provided by Department of Commerce.

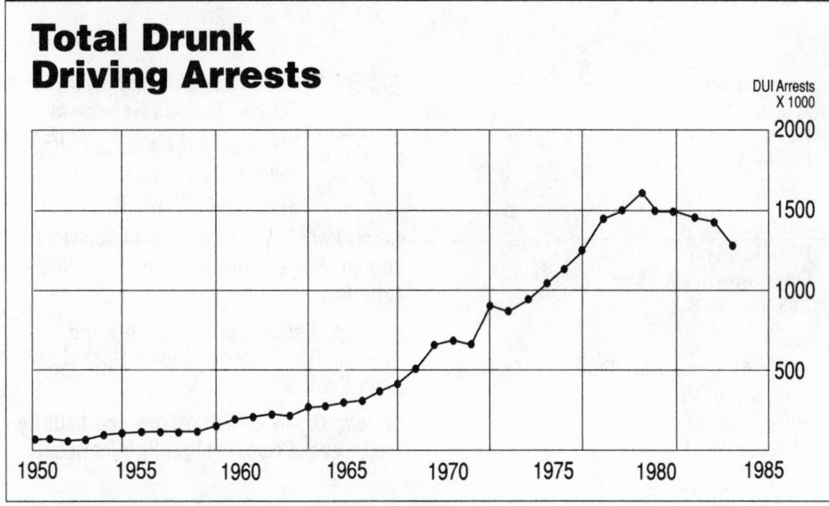

Source: Updated information provided by Logos Research Institute.

ANTI-DRUG ORGANIZATIONS

Nat'l Fed. of Parents for Drug-Free Youth
800-554-KIDS

National Referral Hotline
800-COCAINE

Parents Resource for Drug Education
(PRIDE)
800-241-9746

Arizona
Calvary Rehabilitation Center
329 N. Third Avenue
Phoenix, AZ 85003
602-254-7092

California
New Life Treatment Centers
570 Glenneyre, Suite 107
Laguna Beach, CA 92651
1-800-227-LIFE

Overcomers Outreach, Inc.
2290 W. Whittier Blvd., Suite D
La Habra, CA 90631
213-697-3994

Victory Outreach
454 Cobera Avenue
LaPuente, CA 91746
818-961-4910

Kentucky
Possibilities Unlimited, Inc
4514 Briar Hill Road
Lexington, KY 40516
606-229-0445

Michigan
Alcoholics for Christ
1316 North Campbell Road
Royal Oak, MI 48067
1-800-441-7877

New Mexico
Support
3812 Central SE
Albuquerque, NM 87108
505-265-6417

New Jersey
Salvation Army
799 Bloomfield Avenue
Verona, NJ 07044
201-239-0606

New York
Walter Hoving Home for Women
P.O. Box 194
Garrison, NY 10524
914-424-3674

Pennsylvania

New Life for Girls
RD 3, Box D700
Dover, PA 17315
717-266-5414

Toughlove
P.O. Box 1069
Doylestown, PA 18901
215-348-7090

Texas

Mothers Against Drunk Driving (MADD)
669 Airport Freeway, Suite 3
Hurst, TX 76053
817-268-MADD

FOCUS BOOKS

Drugs and Drinking **by Jay Strack. Thomas Nelson, Inc.**

Dying for a Drink **by Anderson Spickard and Barbara R. Thompson. Word, Inc.**

Smart Kids, Stupid Choices **by Kevin Leman. Regal Books/Gospel Light Publications.**

A Secret Hell **by Claire Costales and Priscilla Barak. Regal Books/ Gospel Light Publications.**

Staying Dry **by Claire Costales and Jo Berry. Regal Books/Gospel Light Publications.**

Divorce Rates
per 1000 Population 1950–1990

Rate per 1000

6
5
4
3
2
1
0

1950–1953
1954–1956
1957–1959
1960–1962
1963–1965
1966–1968
1969–1971
1972–1974
1975–1977
1978–1980
1981–1983
1984–1986
1987–1990

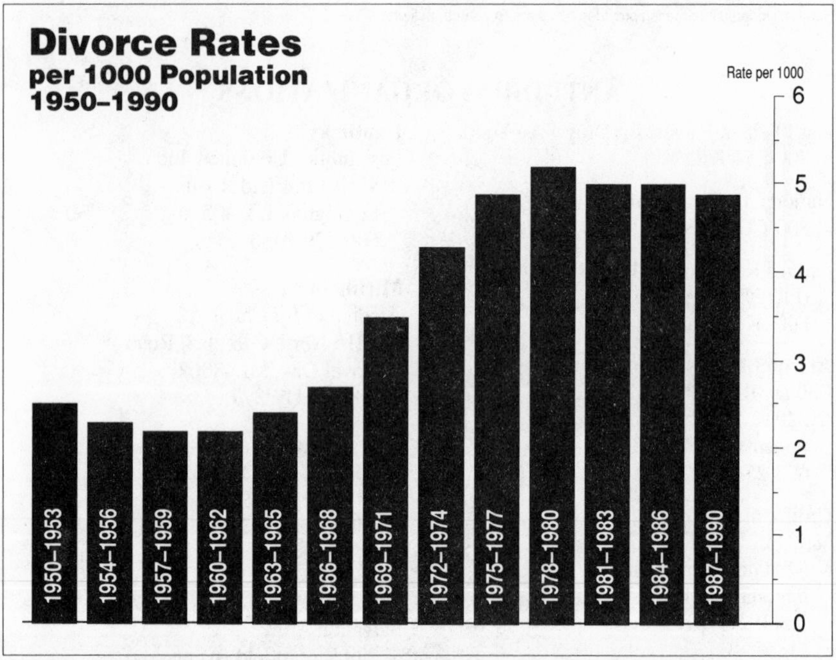

Source: *The American Family under Siege.* Published by Family Research Council, Washington, D.C.

FOCUS FACT

Fatal accidents related to drinking drivers resulted in 20,659 deaths in 1986—more than one-third of all fatal accidents on the highways.
—U.S. Bureau of the Census

FOCUS FACT

Divorce reform was supposed to be a panacea for women trapped in bad marriages. Instead it has trapped many of them in poverty.

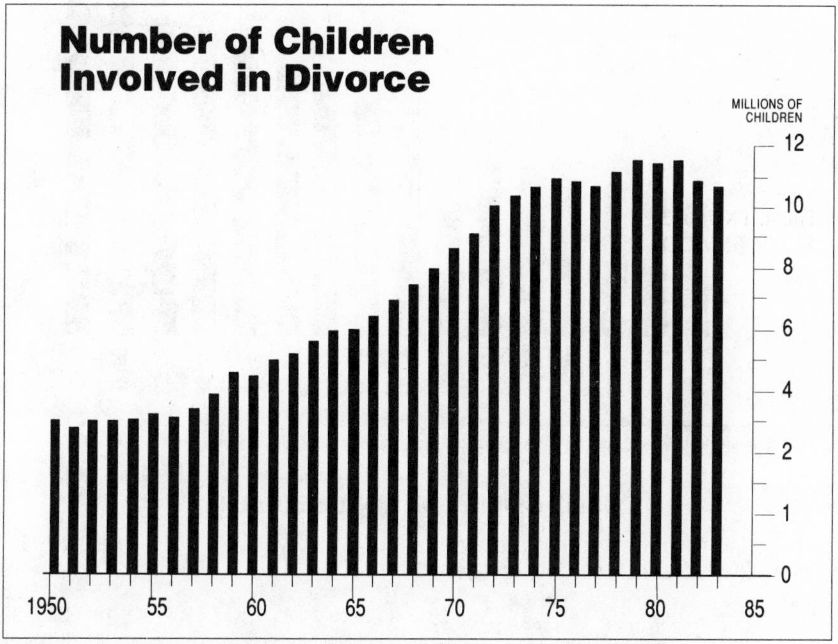

Number of Children Involved in Divorce

MILLIONS OF CHILDREN

12
10
8
6
4
2
1
0

1950 55 60 65 70 75 80 85

Source: *The American Family under Siege.* Published by Family Research Council, Washington, D.C.

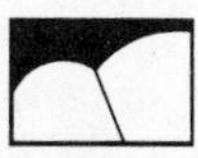

FOCUS BOOKS

The Divorce Decision **by Gary Richmond. Word, Inc.**

Reconcilable Differences **by Jim Talley. Thomas Nelson, Inc.**

Children and Divorce: What to Expect and How to Help **by Archibald D. Hart. Word, Inc.**

Growing Through Divorce **by Jim Smoke. Harvest House Publishers.**

Single Parenting: A Wilderness Journey **by Robert Barnes. Tyndale House Publishers.**

FOCUS FACT

Children of divorce are absent from school more frequently and are more likely to repeat a grade, to be placed in remedial reading classes, and to be referred to a school psychologist.

Source: *Education Daily,* September 7, 1983

FOCUS FACT

In the 1950s most single-parent households were composed of widows. Today they are composed primarily of divorcees and unwed mothers.

Source: *The American Family Under Siege.* Published by Family Research Council, Washington, DC.

Female Single Parent Households

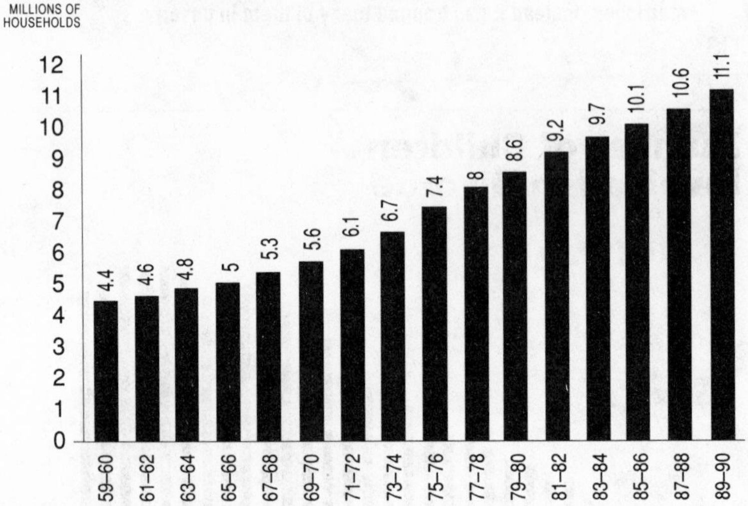

MILLIONS OF HOUSEHOLDS

Years	Millions of households
59–60	4.4
61–62	4.6
63–64	4.8
65–66	5
67–68	5.3
69–70	5.6
71–72	6.1
73–74	6.7
75–76	7.4
77–78	8
79–80	8.6
81–82	9.2
83–84	9.7
85–86	10.1
87–88	10.6
89–90	11.1

Source: *The American Family under Siege.* Published by Family Research Council, Washington, D.C.

PUBLIC OPINION ON HOMOSEXUALITY

Do you think homosexual relations between consenting adults should or should not be legal?

	1989 %	*1987* %	*1986* %	*1985* %	*1982* %	*1977* %
Legal	47	33	33	44	45	43
Not legal	36	55	54	47	39	43
Don't know/ No opinion	17	12	13	9	16	14
	100	100	100	100	100	100

There has been considerable discussion in the news regarding the rights of homosexual men and women. In general, do you think homosexuals should or should not have equal rights in terms of job opportunities?

	1989 %	*1982* %	*1977* %
Yes, should	71	59	56
No, should not	18	28	33
No opinion	11	13	11
	100	100	100

Percent saying homosexuals should be hired for each occupation.

	1989 %	*1987* %	*1985* %	*1982* %	*1977* %
Salespersons	79	72	71	70	68
Armed forces	60	55	55	52	51
Doctors	56	49	52	50	44
Clergy	44	42	41	38	36
Elementary school teachers	42	33	36	32	27

Source: The Gallup Poll, October 12-15, 1989.

FOCUS FACT

Efforts to organize homosexuals on the local level have resulted in some 3,000 organizations. San Francisco has a homosexual telephone directory listing some 600 businesses owned or managed by homosexuals, largely catering to a homosexual clientele.

MINISTRIES AND ORGANIZATIONS THAT OFFER HELP TO THE HOMOSEXUAL

California

Desert Stream
1415 Santa Monica Mall, Suite 201
Santa Monica, CA 90401 / 213-395-9137

Exodus International
P.O. Box 2121
San Rafael, CA 94912 / 415-454-1017

New Life Treatment Center Inc.
570 Glenneyre Avenue, Suite 107
Laguna Beach, CA 92651 / 1-800-227-LIFE

Spatula Ministries
P.O. Box 444
LaHabra, CA 90631 / 213-691-7369

Florida

Victory House
719 SW 4th Court
Fort Lauderdale, FL 33312 /
305-463-0848

Illinois

Homosexuals Anonymous
P.O. Box 732
Hillside, IL 60162 / 708-449-3321

Minnesota

Outpost
1821 University Avenue South
St. Paul, MN 55104 / 612-645-2530

Pennsylvania

Homosexuals Anonymous Fellowship Services
Box 78821
Reading, PA 19603 / 1-800-253-3000

“” FOCUS QUOTE

AIDS patients are afraid to talk. Their image of God is what they receive from the church as a whole, and so often, because the church has rejected them for being homosexuals or drug users or prostitutes, they think God hates them too. —Jeff Collins, director of Love & Action, about AIDS patients he works with, in *Christianity Today.*

RESPONSE TO THE PORNOGRAPHY ARGUMENTS

1. **Pornography is harmless. A 1970 Presidential Commission Report said so.** The Majority Report of the 1970 Presidential Commission on Obscenity and Pornography was called a "scientific scandal" by many in the scientific community. It was rejected by the U.S. Senate by a vote of 60 to 5. The Hill-Link Minority Report of that Commission was read into the record in both Houses of Congress as a "responsible position on the issues." The Hill-Link Report cited numerous instances where evidence was suppressed when it went counter to the pre-determined "findings" of the majority report. The Hill-Link Report and the chapters by Dr. Victor B. Cline in *Where do you Draw the Line?* expose the majority report for what it was. In addition, studies in the Hill-Link Report show linkages between exposure to obscene material and sexual deviancy, promiscuity, affiliation with criminal groups, and more. However, extremists who want obscenity laws repealed as the majority report recommended began a campaign in early 1977 to have the report resurrected and considered a reputable document.

The Supreme Court in Paris Theatre v. Slaton (June, 1973) said: "The sum of experience, including that of the past two decades, affords an ample basis for legislatures to conclude

RESPONSE TO THE PORNOGRAPHY ARGUMENTS cont.

that a sensitive, key relationship of human existence, central to family life, community welfare and the development of human personality, can be debased and distorted by crass commercial exploitation of sex."

2. **You can't legislate morality.** On its face this cliche is absurd because every law legislates morality. Every law sets some standard for its citizens, and every citizen must ultimately make the moral decision to obey and disobey.

Private morals are private. Public morals are the business of the entire community and the officers empowered by the community to defend the welfare of the community against the willful minority. Commercial obscenity is public business. It is public morality that obscenity laws are designed to safeguard, not private morality.

FOCUS FACT

According to the Gay Teachers Association of New York City, there are up to 10,000 homosexual teachers in New York City.

3. **Obscenity is in the eye of the beholder. What is obscene to you may not be obscene to me.** This implies that obscenity is subjective. It is not. It is the description or depiction of specific sexual activity, the description or depiction of which is prohibited by law, to protect the common good. It is as objective as stealing or murder. This statement also denies the existence of evil.

4. **I'd rather see people make love than make violence.** There is no love in pornography. It is totally loveless, debasing women, children, and humanity generally. In addition, violence is inherent in pornography.

5. **War, poverty, hunger, violence are the real obscenities. Sex is not obscene.** The extension of the word *obscenity* to cover all kinds of social evils is a recent development in our language. It is a well-known technique to confuse and blunt the force of obscenity law.

Of course sex is not obscene. It is the design and creation of God. It is the debasing abuse of sex that is obscene. And, as in the past, so now all over the country, legislatures and the judiciary definitely specify certain abuses of sex as obscene.

6. **If you don't like porn films and books, you don't have to see them or buy them, but don't interfere with my rights to see or buy them.** I don't see or buy pornography, but it is there polluting the environment in which I am trying to raise my children. Society says it does not want it there, and has enacted laws against it.

The United States Supreme Court has said that what you do in the privacy of your home is your own business, but your privacy right does not extend to the marketplace. It is against the law for anyone to sell or exhibit obscenity to you.

7. **Well, the Supreme Court has said a lot of things, but it still can't define obscenity.** This statement is incorrect. The Supreme Court defined obscenity in June of 1973 to the satisfaction of the majority of the American people.

8. **Freedom of expression is protected by the First Amendment.** It most certainly is. But the Supreme Court has said, and has always held, that obscenity is not protected by the First Amendment. It is not protected expression, any more than libel or slander are. Obscenity is not a First Amendment issue. It is a crime, and 90 percent of the traffic in hard-core pornography in the country is controlled by organized crime.

9. **Who are you to tell me what I can see or read? You are imposing your morality on me.** Nobody can tell you what to see or to read, but the community can tell you what commercial spectacles and literature cannot be sold or distributed to you—if you choose to live in that community. The community sets up standards for itself, and has a right to legislate to protect those standards.

Nobody is imposing his morality on anybody. It is only the consensus of the community that determines the standards of public decency. When that consensus is properly manifested in public law, that is community or public morality, not "ours."

This implies there should be no law regulating the traffic in pornography.

10. **Obscenity is a victimless crime.** There is no such thing as a victimless crime. In every crime there is a seller or seducer, and the person who purchases, or the seduced. That person is the immediate victim, and society is the ultimate victim, for with each seduction the moral fabric of society is diminished. The victimless crimes theory is an active and insidious attack on almost all laws dealing with public morality, maintaining there is no victim when consenting adults indulge in drugs, prostitution, obscenity, homosexuality, adultery, incest, gambling, etc.

A glaring instance of victimization in obscenity are the children used in child pornography.

For centuries civil communities have maintained laws against such behavior as detrimental to the public health, morals and welfare.

Denmark and the Boston Combat Zone have recently and vividly proved that increase in commercial pornography causes concentration of violent prostitution and organized crime.

11. **When "consenting adults" go to see a dirty movie, no one is being harmed.** Regarding so-called "consenting adults." The United States Supreme Court said in Paris Theatre in June of 1973: "We categorically disapprove the theory that obscene films acquire constitutional immunity from state regulation simply because they are exhibited for consenting adults only. Rights and interests other than those of the advocates are involved. These include the interest of the public in the quality of life, the total community environment, the tone of commerce, and, possibly, the public safety itself."

FOCUS BOOKS

***Growing Up Straight: What Every Family Should Know About Homosexuality* by George A. Rekers. Moody Press.**

***How Will I Tell My Mother?* by Jerry Arteburn. Oliver Nelson Books.**

***Where Does a Mother Go to Resign?* by Barbara Johnson. Bethany House Publishers.**

***The Broken Image* by Leanne Payne. Crossway Books/Good News Publishers.**

***The Return of Love* by Alex Davidson. InterVarsity Press.**

---

12. **If you'd let pornography flow freely, people would get bored and the problem would take care of itself.** This boredom or satiation theory is invalid. (See *Where Do You Draw the Line?* by Dr. Victor B. Cline). Heavy users of pornography do not get bored. They go deeper and deeper into more and more bizarre forms of it.

Professor Irving Kristol said in the same volume, "I would like to go along with this theory (boredom) but I cannot. I think it is false. The sexual pleasure one gets from pornography is autoerotic and infantile; put bluntly, it is a masturbatory exercise of the imagination when it is not masturbation pure and simple. Now, people who masturbate do not get tired of masturbation, just as sadists don't get bored with voyeurism. In other words, infantile

RESPONSE TO THE PORNOGRAPHY ARGUMENTS cont.

sexuality is not only a permanent temptation—it can easily become a self-reinforcing neurosis."

Denmark is often brought up when the boredom theory is espoused. Denmark legalized pornography, the argument goes, and porn profits dropped because people got bored. Denmark's porn profits are falling, but not because of boredom. Underworld infiltration of the porn industry, gangland violence, and tie-ins with traffic in narcotics forced the Copenhagen police to close down dozens of smut dens, and all live sex shows have been outlawed. (Associated Press Reports, 1972-76).

Remember, every day children are seeing pornography for the first time. Pornography strikes at children in the mail, at newsstands, etc.

13. **How do you define obscenity?** How I define obscenity is not the issue. The Supreme Court has defined obscenity to the satisfaction of most. The test for obscenity is: materials which "taken as a whole appeal to the prurient interest in sex, which portray sexual conduct in a patently offensive way, and which, taken as a whole, do not have serious literary, artistic, political or scientific value."

14. **But the Supreme Court left it to communities to decide what is obscene.** This is an oversimplification and a misleading one. Community Standards is not the test for obscenity, but a part of the test for obscenity, and has been part of the test for obscenity since 1957. In 1973 the Court said: "The basic guidelines for the trier of the fact must be: a) whether the average person, applying contemporary community standards, would find that the work taken as a whole appeals to the prurient interest, b) whether the work depicts or describes, in a patently offensive way, sexual conduct specifically defined by the applicable state law, etc." It is the "trier of the fact," a jury or a judge who decides what is obscene under the guidelines.

15. **How is a producer or publisher to know his material is obscene when the court can't even decide what is obscene?** The court has decided what is obscene, and it is up to a person who traffics in pornography to be alert to, and know what the Supreme Court decisions are. The Court said in its landmark Miller decision when it defined obscenity. "We are satisfied that these prerequisites (the three-part test) will provide fair notice to a dealer in such materials that his public and commercial activities may bring prosecution."

16. **Why be concerned about obscenity when there is so much violent crime?** They're related. Pornography outlets breed and attract violent crime.

17. **The porno industry is flourishing and growing, so the American people must want it or simply don't care.** Certainly there are some who want it. That's what makes it so profitable. And obviously there are some who don't care. But all surveys show that the majority of Americans are vehemently opposed to the traffic in pornography and want it stopped. The majority do care, but they are confused and discouraged in the face of a highly organized industry and the loud prophets of false freedom. One of the major factors in the growth of the pornography traffic is the lack of vigorous enforcement of obscenity laws, particularly at the federal level.

18. **Why bother enforcing the law? The "adult" book stores and porno movie houses keep operating while their owners are in the courts.** Continuous, vigorous enforcement of the law is the answer. When arrests and prosecutions begin, the sex industry is put on warning. Prison sentences, fines, legal fees will put the pornographers out of business. Atlanta, Jacksonville, and Cincinnati are clean cities because of vigorous, continuous enforcement of the law. And experts say that with aggressive enforcement of federal law, the back of the porno industry would be broken in 18 months.

TEN THINGS YOU CAN DO TO COMBAT PORNOGRAPHY

1. **Become knowledgeable** about the issues concerning pornography. This can be accomplished by reading and reviewing current literature and tapes on the subject.

A number of excellent video and audio tapes may be purchased from the National Coalition Against Pornography, 800 Compton Road, Suite 9224, Cincinnati, OH 45231. Contact them for recommendations about which tapes will meet your specific needs. Become familiar with the findings and recommendations in the Report by the Attorney General's Commission on Pornography or National Coalition Against Pornography's summary of the lengthy report. You may get information about obtaining copies of these documents from National Coalition Against Pornography at the above address. (Note: the full report contains extremely offensive material and profanity, while the summary has omitted this material.)

Two books recommended by the National Coalition Against Pornography are *The Mind Polluters,* by Dr. Jerry Kirk, and *The Seduction of Society,* by William A. Stanmeyer. These may be purchased from National Coalition Against Pornography for $7.95 each, which includes the book price of $6.95, plus $1 for postage and handling.

2. **Call and write those who are responsible for enforcing laws** against crime. Included in this group of people are sheriffs, police chiefs, prosecutors and your state's attorney general. Tell those and any other officials that you oppose pornography and want anti-obscenity laws to be vigorously enforced as recommended by the Attorney General's Commission on Pornography. Talk to your friends, relatives, co-workers, fellow church members, etc., and ask them to convey similar views to these officials.

3. **Call and write those who hold elected positions** in city or county government, such as your mayor and the members of your city and county councils. Express your views against pornography and ask them to seek vigorous enforcement of laws and ordinances against obscenity. If existing laws or ordinances are weak, ask those officials to pass stronger ones. Get friends and acquaintances to make similar requests.

4. **Write your Governor and state legislators** and ask them to seek revision of state anti-obscenity laws so that they are as strong as allowed by the state and federal constitutions. Refer specifically to the recommendations by the Attorney General's Commission on Pornography in this regard. Ask them to contact appropriate law enforcement officials and demand vigorous enforcement of laws against obscenity. Ask others to write as well.

5. **Write the President, Attorney General, your Congressman, and U.S. Senators**. Ask them to strengthen federal laws against pornography. Also ask them to contact such enforcement agencies as the Department of Justice, Customs Bureau, and the Post Office

FOCUS FACT

Porn is an $8-billion-a-year business in the United States, which includes:

- **more than 450 different pornographic magazines**
- **nearly 20,000 adult bookstores**
- **800 adult movie theaters**
- **two million pornographic video casettes**
- **more than 165,000 purveyors of pornography including producers, publishers, distributors, retailers, writers, and photographers.**

Source: Jerry R. Kirk in *The Winnable War.*

Department and demand intensified efforts to enforce federal laws against obscenity as recommended by the Commission on Pornography.

6. **Write representatives of the news media** and "letters to the editor" about your views against pornography. Include the truth that obscenity is not protected by the First Amendment to the United States Constitution any more than libel or slander are forms of protected speech.

7. **Initiate a petition to public officials**, stating your concern and disapproval of the public display and sale of pornography—films, video cassettes, books and magazines. Solicit the support for petitions among your friends, neighbors, church members, civic and school groups.

FOCUS BOOKS

Pornography: The Human Tragedy **edited by Tom Minnery. Tyndale House Publishers.**

The Mind Polluters **by Jerry R. Kirk. Thomas Nelson, Inc.**

Out of the Shadows **by Patrick Carnes. CompCare Publications.**

The Case Against Pornography **by Donald Wildmon. Victor Books.**

The Seduction of Society **by William Stanmeyer. Servant Books.**

8. **Use this step-by-step procedure and strategy in contacting neighborhood stores** which display and sell pornographic materials:

a. Courteously speak to the store manager and tell him that his display and sale of pornographic magazines and materials is offensive to you. Ask him to: (1) put these out of sight, and (2) seek a change in business policy which will discontinue the sale of this material.

b. After a short time, if he still continues to display and sell these products, again speak to the store manager and tell him of your concern. Ask whether he has communicated your concerns to his headquarters and sought a change in corporate policy so as to discontinue selling the material; if he has not, repeat your request that he do so. Leave him a copy of a courteous letter stating your concerns, requests, and prior conversations with him on this issue. Tell him you will stop patronizing his store if he does not comply.

c. If the merchant persists in openly promoting and selling these materials, write a letter to the headquarters office of the store telling them of your concern; send a copy of your letter to the store manager. Enlist other friends to focus a stream of "Friendly Complaint" letters at the local store, with copies to the corporate headquarters.

d. If there is no change in store practices, stop buying at this store. Write the local store and headquarters office and tell them you will no longer patronize their business. Get others to write similar letters.

9. **Contact National Coalition Against Pornography** for the names and addresses of organizations that may be able to help you. There are a number of ways that those under the National Coalition Against Pornography umbrella can be of assistance, and will gladly help you determine who and where they are.

10. **Join with others** in all of your efforts. Be persistent—changing months or years of business practices takes time. So keep a positive attitude and don't become discouraged. Others have fought similar battles and won, and so can you.

Source: National Coalition Against Pornography.

ORGANIZATIONS THAT FIGHT THE SPREAD OF PORNOGRAPHY

Arizona
Children's Legal Foundation
2845 E. Camelback Road, Suite 740
Phoenix, AR 85016
602-381-1322

Mississippi
American Family Association
P.O. Drawer 2440
Tupelo, MS 38803
601-844-5036

New York
Morality in Media, Inc.
475 Riverside Drive
New York, NY 10115
212-870-3222

Ohio
National Coalition Against Pornography
800 Compton Road, Suite 9224
Cincinnati, OH 45231
513-521-6227

National Consultation on Pornography, Inc.
5742 Hamilton Avenue
Cincinnati, OH 45224

FOCUS FACT

—Rape rates are highest in states which have high sales of sexually explicit materials and lax restrictions and enforcement of pornography.
—Rapists are 15 times as likely as non-offenders to have had exposure to hard-core pornography before the age of 10.
—A crackdown on adult bookstores, X-rated movie theaters, and massage parlors in Cincinnati resulted in a 42 percent decrease in assaults, prostitution, and drug trafficking, and an 83 percent drop in rapes, robberies, and aggravated assaults.
—A study of Michigan State Police Department Lieutenant Darrell Pope showed that 41 percent of the 38,000 sexual assault cases on file in Michigan involved some use of pornographic materials during or just prior to the act.
—Adult bookstores outnumber McDonald's restaurants in the United States by a margin of at least three to one.

Source: Leigh Ann Metzger in *Understanding the Problem of Pornography*. Published by Family Research Council.

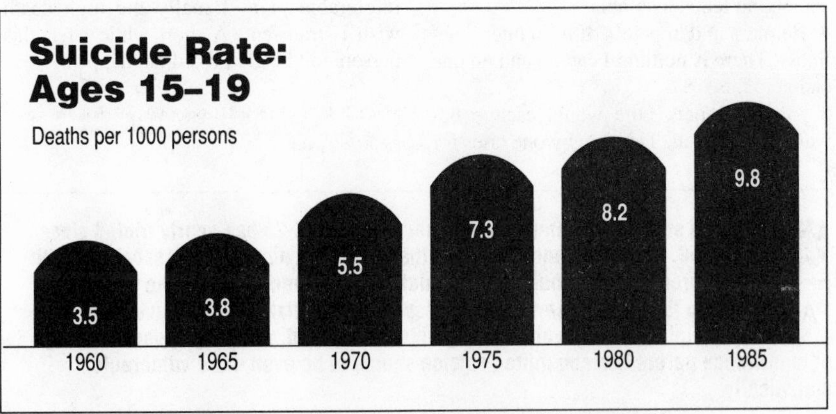

Source: *The American Family Under Siege* published by Family Research Council, Washington, DC.

SIX TYPES OF SUICIDE

1. Rational (figured out a way to escape further pain)
2. Reaction (following loss)
3. Vengeful (to punish someone)
4. Manipulative (to thwart someone's plan)
5. Psychotic (to fulfill a delusion)
6. Accidental (spontaneous decision reconsidered too late)

Source: Edwin Shneidman in *Definition of Suicide*. Published by John Wiley & Sons, New York, NY.

FOCUS FACT

Suicide is the second leading cause of death for adolescents following accidents (of which many are suspected as suicide related). Factors most commonly identified with teen suicide are:

- **Changing moral climate**
- **High divorce rate**
- **High mobility of American society**
- **Frequent abuse of alcohol and other drugs**
- **Glorification of violence in the mass media**
- **Easy availability of guns.**

—Bill Blackburn in *What You Should Know About Suicide*

COMMON CHARACTERISTICS IN SUICIDE

1. Unendurable psychic pain. It builds until at last one says, "Too far. No farther."
2. Unmet needs accumulate with growing frustration. Every suicide is logical to the one who decides. It is faulty logic, to be sure, but it constricts finally to only one opinion.
3. A solution is sought to stop consciousness. Getting very upset even over trivia is critical at this point, especially if there is something lethal available.
4. Helpless and hopeless. It is an utter loneliness. There is nothing I can do and no one can help me.
5. Ambivalence. One wants escape but wants life as well. That is why one cries for help. 80 percent of suicide victims communicate their intention.
6. Constriction. A tunnel-visioning narrows until the focus can no longer even include loved ones who nurture. It is not simply that they are disregarded, they are not even within the range of what is in the mind.
7. Egression is the point where one takes leave from the mind which mediates the intolerable pain. Usually the high death wish is transient. A short while later, this person will be glad it did not happen.

Source: B. D. Garfinkel and H. Golombek, editors in *The Adolescent and Mood Disturbances*. Published by International Press, New York, NY.

FOCUS FACT

The suicide rate among young people ages 15-23 has nearly tripled since 1950. Some evidence suggests that suicide is not so often associated with depression in teenagers as in adults. Many young people who take their own lives have been noted as displaying impulsive, aggressive, and anti-social behavior, which is frequently associated with drug abuse. A young person whose parent has committed suicide seems to be even more vulnerable statistically.

MAJOR 19TH-CENTURY EVANGELICAL SOCIAL REFORM MOVEMENTS

Reform Movement	*Key Evangelical Leaders*	*Reform Organizations*	*Results Achieved*
Abolition of Slavery	Samuel Hopkins (1721–1803) Lyman Beecher (1775–1863) Charles G. Finney (1792–1875) John Brown (1800–1859) Theodore Weld (1803–1895) Jonathan Blanchard (1811–1892) Harriet Beecher Stowe (1811–1896)	1807—Friends of Humanity Association 1817—Colonization Society 1818—American Conventions for Promoting the Abolition of Slavery and Improving the Condition of the African Race 1833— American Anti-Slavery Society 1840—Liberty Party 1848—Free Soil Party	1861–1865—Civil War 1863—Emancipation Proclamation 1865—Thirteenth Amendment 1866—Fourteenth Amendment
Prohibition of Alcoholic Beverages	Lyman Beecher (1775–1863) Frances Willard (1839–1898) Billy Sunday (1862–1935)	1813—Massachusetts Society for the Suppression of Intemperance 1826—American Society for the Promotion of Temperance 1836—American Temperance Union 1840—Washingtonians 1869—National Prohibition Party 1874—Women's Christian Temperance Union 1893—Anti-Saloon League	1846—Maine passed Prohibition Ordinance 1847–1855—Thirteen other states followed 1919–1932—Prohibition Amendment in force
Women's Rights	Emma Willard (1787–1870) Matthew Vassar (1792–1868) Angelina Grimke (1792–1873) Mary Lyon (1797–1849)	1848—Women's Rights Convention 1869—National Woman Suffrage Association 1869—American Woman Suffrage Association 1892—Federal Woman Suffrage Association	1821— "Female Seminary" founded in Troy, New York 1836—Mt. Holyoke College founded 1861—Vassar College founded 1917—Suffrage to women granted by New York 1918—Fourteen other states followed 1920—Woman Suffrage Amendment

WHAT TO WATCH FOR ON CAPITOL HILL IN 1991

Gary L. Bauer, president, Family Research Council

The 102nd Congress begins January 1991. What can we expect to see in Washington in 1991? What will be the major moral battles fought on Capitol Hill?

Things unlooked for have a way of stealing into the most innocuous pieces of legislation, and planned political advances never materialize. Yet I can say with confidence that the battles of the 102nd Congress will be determined by the unfinished business of the 101st and by the outcome of the November 1990 elections. By reviewing the significant battles of the 101st Congress, we can get a sense of the direction that Congress is heading. Several issues of great import to the family are yet unresolved.

Child Care

One of the major social issue debates of the 101st Congress was child care. Should the federal government offer financial assistance to working parents only, to the exclusion of "stay at home moms," or should relief also be provided to families that care for their own children? The question of religion figured prominently as well, as legislators argued over subsidizing church-based day care.

Liberals galvanized support for the notorious ABC bill (the Act for Better Child Care). It created a new federal day care bureaucracy, putting Uncle Sam in the babysitting business in a big way. It provided day-care subsidies for working mothers, but no relief whatsoever for those families making the sacrifices necessary to raise their children at home. The ABC bill would have made it nearly impossible for religious day-care centers to survive, unless they forsook religious elements and became essentially secular centers in order to receive federal subsidies. It was, in every respect, a bill unfavorable to traditional family values.

Pro-family forces rallied behind a measure which would have provided tax relief to middle-to-low income families with young children, whether or not both parents worked. The bill addressed church and state concerns, because no money flowed directly to the religious day-care centers. Dollars went to families without discrimination, and parents were then free to choose the care that best fit their priorities.

But the ABC bill was passed in both houses, and as of June 30, 1990, the President was holding firm in his pledge to veto any child care bill that discriminated against mothers at home or religious day care providers—like the ABC bill.

If the president follows through on his promise, and the Congress fails to override his veto, I don't think we'll see the issue again in '91. If the liberals somehow prevail, they will be back to ask for an *increase* in child care subsidies, new regulations and increased bureaucracy. Either way, the child care issue needs to be watched.

Parental Leave

A phenomena occurs in Washington, DC, every two years. I call it the "bi-annual family migration." Our nation goes through an election cycle, and politicians become champions of "family policy" overnight. Like swallows returning to San Juan Capistrano, politicians return to the family. Child care was one attempt. The other was parental leave.

Both houses passed the Parental Leave Act in 1990. It was a Congressional directive to American businesses, requiring them to give new mothers up to twelve weeks leave after the birth of a child, with the assurance that they could return to their jobs. It sounded like the answer to a mother's prayers. But this kind of Parental Leave is about as pro-family as the ABC child care bill. The Parental Leave act prods new moms to get back to work, and child care a la ABC will mother their children for them.

There's nothing wrong with a woman choosing to return to work. But public opinion polls show that an overwhelming majority of women want to be mothers for more than three months. Parental leave of this nature offers them nothing. It mandates a benefit, passes the tab on to the business community, but forsakes family integrity and the true needs of mothers and children.

President Bush vetoed the bill. So unless the liberals override, we will see another attempt at parental leave legislation in '91. Here's an alternative: encourage businesses to allow women the *option* of short-term leave, or an extended leave period with a promise of preferential treatment when they want to come back to work. Mothers could stay home while their children are in their tender years, and return to the marketplace without having to start from the bottom rung of the ladder.

Health Care

With the growing size of the federal deficit and the accompanying budgetary restraints, tax-and-spend politicians have to find new ways to fund their pork barrel politics. Mandating benefits through federal law, and then passing the cost on to the states or to the private sector is becoming the procedure of choice. Parental leave and day care are two examples. Health care may well be next.

There is a growing philosophical consensus that health care is a fundamental right. Although the founding fathers would find the notion ludicrous, many well-meaning people read into the democratic principles of our nation a guarantee of health coverage. Coupled with the severe pressures being placed upon the community of the insured by the growing community of the uninsured, the time is ripe for a real federal health care boondoggle.

In 1990, a proposal was floated in the Senate that would have required businesses to provide health coverage for their employees. Any prudent financial analyst will tell you this would cripple American competitiveness and very likely hurt many more people than it would help. The loss of jobs, a reduction in other benefits, and the destruction of many small businesses would have its greatest detrimental effect on lower-echelon employees—the very people whom proponents of such ideas want to assist. A number of powerful lobby groups—like the National Education Association—have joined hands with liberal legislators to push for some sort of national health care system.

Abortion

As a result of the Supreme Court decision in *Webster v. Reproductive Health Services* in the summer of 1989, the abortion issue has largely been returned to the state legislatures. This is in keeping with a trend affecting many "family issues." Nevertheless, there will be attempts in Congress to increase federal funding of abortion services, both in the United States and overseas.

Also, pro-abortion congressmen will try to push a bill known as the Freedom of Choice Act. It would codify in federal statute what *Roe v. Wade* did through judicial decree—legalize abortion on demand at any time for any reason throughout all nine months of pregnancy. The Act would preclude any state action to regulate abortion on demand. Barring a total pro-life defeat at the polls in November 1990, I don't believe the liberals have a chance at getting this through into law. But there may well be a fight.

The current environmental enthusiasm is creating momentum for family-planning activities in underdeveloped countries. Population alarmists advocate that reproduction is out of control (this has been statistically debunked). Consequently, there will be pressure to expand U.S. involvement in international family-planning organizations. Two of the biggest operations—International Planned Parenthood and the United Nations (UNFPA)—are deeply involved in abortion, including *forced* abortion and sterilization programs in the People's Republic of China. Currently, our nation does not fund these groups because of such activity, thanks to a policy enacted by the Reagan administration in 1985 known as the "Mexico City" policy.

A major drive will be to overturn the Mexico City policy, and start U.S. dollars flowing to abortion programs overseas. An attempt to do such was squelched in 1990. We will see continued attempts to increase Medicaid funding of abortion in the U.S. as well.

Perhaps the biggest push for abortion

WHAT TO WATCH FOR ON CAPITOL HILL IN 1991 cont.

services will be focused upon the French abortion pill RU486. Currently, there are no plans in the federal government to allow the abortifacient into the U.S. But pressure from the private and political sector will be intense. The American Medical Association came out in favor of allowing RU486 into the U.S. late in '90, and feminists favor it as well. With increasing state regulations on abortion following the *Webster* decision, RU486 will be seen as the easiest way around the laws. The push will be on, both in Congress and on the Administration, to let RU486 into the country.

Pornography and Censorship

The winnable war against pornography has moved largely into the courts and out of the legislatures. We have the necessary laws to close down the pornographers. Now we need to support federal, state, and local attorneys as they bring charges against the purveyors of smut.

But one aspect of this particular debate which more than likely will carry over into 1991 is the controversy over federal subsidy of pornographic "art."

The National Endowment for the Arts more than lost its bearings when it subsidized the work of Robert Mapplethorpe and Andre Serrano in 1989. One of these so-called artists produced a display of homoerotic photographs too perverse to describe. The other toured an exhibit featuring a photo of a crucifix submerged in urine. And to the shock of the artistic highbrows, the public didn't like it. Our friends in Congress felt that the government had better things to do with our hard-earned money, so they pressed for bans on the funding of art which is "obscene or pornographic, including the depiction of sadomasochism, homoeroticism or the exploitation of children." Now the artists are howling censorship.

The issue at hand seems pretty straightforward: why should taxpayers pay for some pervert to shock and offend them? The artist is free to create what he will, but the public doesn't have to subsidize mockery and denigration of its most cherished values.

The fireworks over the NEA shed some light on a greater problem. We've got a federal agency spending taxpayer funds to erode and destroy traditional Judeo-Christian values through Western culture. The war will not end on the issue of pornography, but will extend into the total vision of the National Endowment.

Homosexuality

Our culture is developing a strange and distorted view of "civil rights." Homosexuality, once considered a perversion, is now viewed as alternative life-style, merely one option in the smorgasbord of sexuality. Worse yet, the homosexuals in turn claim that they are a "minority," deserving of all the special protections we grant to the handicapped or racial minorities. As a result, the gay lobby has become one of the most powerful, intimidating forces in politics. Whether under the guise of helping the handicapped, AIDS, or "Hate Crimes" legislation, the gay lobby is advancing its agenda.

On a Sunday morning in New York last year, 4,500 protestors converged on St. Patrick's Cathedral. The demonstrators were mostly angry gays and pro-abortion activists. Their goal was to try to stop the Mass offered by Cardinal John O'Connor. Their hatred for Cardinal O'Connor stems from his refusal to back down over the church's position on homosexuality and abortion. When the Cardinal rose to deliver his homily, the protestors began shouting and throwing condoms, drowning out the sermon. Many chained themselves to the pews, and lay in the aisles to block the priests serving communion. One angry activist broke the eucharist and threw it to the ground. Police arrested thirty-seven people inside the Cathedral.

Later in the year, President Bush invited gay activists to the White House for the signing of a "Hate Crimes" bill. For the first time, "sexual orientation" was codified as a class in a federal statute. The bill itself seems harmless enough. It merely tells the Attorney General to compile statistics on hate crimes in the U.S.—including those against gays. But the homosexuals know this was a major advance toward their ultimate goal of a federal "gay rights" law.

In 1991, homosexuals will press even harder for special inclusion in otherwise neutral legislation. The events at St. Patrick's should remove any lingering doubts that this is a debate among honorable men. The people behind the gay rights movement have used violence and intimidation to silence their political opponents, and they will not stop at the door of your church, either.

Economics

Now that the president has signaled a cave-in on taxes, we could be entering a new tax-and-spend cycle. Over the past four decades, the tax burden in America has shifted to families. In 1950, a median-income family of four paid 2 percent of its annual income to the federal government in income and payroll taxes. Today, a median-income family of four sends 24 percent of its earnings to the Federal Treasury. Furthermore, if the dependant deduction had been indexed to keep pace with the rate of inflation, it would be at $6,000 today.

We hear talk of a "peace dividend," an economic kickback from the end of the Cold War. If there is any truth to the matter—which is up for debate—then families ought to be first in line. But voters will need to be vigilant. We offered Congress an opportunity in 1990 to erase just one of the inequities in the tax code's bias against families with children, and they voted it down. In a tax-and-spend feeding frenzy, it will take serious determination to ensure that Congress doesn't raid the family pocketbook more than it already does. Reversing the bias altogether will take herculean efforts.

Supreme Court

We can't predict with certainty when a vacancy on the United States Supreme Court will occur, but three of the justices are over eighty, and a fourth is reported to be seriously ill. [Ed. note: At the time of publication, Supreme Court Justice William J Brennan had resigned his seat, and a new justice had yet to be confirmed by the Senate.] The balance of the High Court is of utmost significance to pro-family citizens.

The most important rulings of the court in recent terms have been decided by very narrow margins—usually 5-4. Abortion, religious liberty, the rights of parents, pornography, and many more crucial issues will be impacted by future court rulings. A wrong appointment could set the pro-family movement back for many years. If President Bush picks a justice in the tradition of the more liberal members of the court, he or she will support decisions that undermine family values.

The President will need to hear from you when a vacancy is imminent. He'll need to be reminded that only a solid pro-life, pro-family justice is acceptable as a Supreme Court nominee. If the President does select someone with good credentials, we can expect a real firefight on Capitol Hill (nominees must be confirmed by the Senate). Our opponents know how significant the next appointment will be, and they are prepared to fight. We must be prepared as well.

Crime

One of the most underrated family issues is crime. Increasingly, Americans are becoming fearful just to walk their own neighborhood streets at night—and not just in the inner cities. The homicide rate for young men is skyrocketing. Other violent crimes are on the rise. And all the while, groups like the ACLU are working to set criminals free.

A major crime bill was pushed through the Senate in the summer of 1990, but troubled waters lay ahead in the House as fall approached. It may be that an omnibus crime bill will be part of the action in 1991. This has pro-family ramifications on many fronts. For example, Congress wants to address the issue of violence against women and children. At the same time, they are unwilling to examine the evidence that pornography significantly contributes to acts of violence against women and children. Pressure from constituents can sensitize legislators to these issues.

At the heart of the debate will be the balance we give to securing the safety of

American families versus the rights of accused criminals. The balance needs to fall in favor of the families.

What You Can Do

The most effective grass-roots pressure is to be informed, accurate, and timely. I encourage Christian citizens to keep up on the issues. Find a way to stay up-to-the-minute on information.

Second, the target of your letter or phone call must be precise. If your congressman has already voted on an bill, and it is now on the president's desk, the White House is the proper point of contact. Sometimes it is a federal agency that needs to hear from you, and not your representatives on Capitol Hill.

Third, the timing of your action is crucial to its success. Congress and the White House visit thousands of issues each year, and this week's crisis is next week's forgotten business. The most important thing to know is *when* to call or write.

GUIDE TO POLITICAL ACTION

The following step-by-step instructions for sending persuasive messages to congressmen and other leaders has been prepared by Richard Cizik, policy analyst for the National Association of Evangelicals. He gives some basic rules for composing effective letters that will get a representative's attention, and tells how even a phone call can be successful.

A complete congressional directory with Senate and House committee assignments and a list of Cabinet members follows for your convenience in knowing who and where to write.

The Letter

One of the most frequently asked questions is "Do contacts with legislators make a difference?" A government official, a veteran of about 20 years on Capitol Hill, once said: "If the average member of Congress received as many as half a dozen letters scrawled in pencil on brown wrapping paper, it would be enough to change his vote on most issues." Perhaps he has exaggerated, but his remarks indicate that members of Congress want to know what their constituents are thinking.

A 1983 survey of 219 top congressional staffers conducted by *The Washingtonian Magazine* confirms this. According to the survey, the most influential factors in the decision-making process of members of Congress were (in order of priority): (1) a member's political philosophy, (2) constituent opinion, (3) office mail, (4) the White House position, (5) party leaders, (6) press back home, (7) Washington lobbies, (8) the national media.

These results reveal the importance placed on constituent thinking. Aside from a member's political philosophy, constituent opinion and office mail are more likely to determine his position on issues than even the position held by the White House or party leaders—proof that constituents are thus some of the most important people in a legislator's life.

The most important influence upon a congressman's voting behavior remains his ideological predisposition. His convictions will determine how he votes on a host of issues. Like anyone else, members of Congress indulge in selective perception and recall of what they hear. Most messages that a congressman hears or reads raise the prominence of a particular issue as much as they change attitudes on a subject. Letters force a member to think more about an issue and to become more prone to express whatever bias he has regarding it.

Messages from constituents serve more as triggers than as persuaders, unless the member's opinion is not yet formed. In that case, letters and phone calls from constituents become more influential in making the decision. Most congressional staffers agree that even one well-written letter on a subject can start the staff thinking about that issue. These aides see each letter as representing the opinions of many people who do not write. A number of letters on the same topic may prompt the assignment of a staff member to draft a position-paper for the congressman. In some cases, a letter may actually change a legislator's mind, particularly when a member is wavering on an issue.

But whether or not a communication from a constituent is the determining factor in a member's voting behavior, it is not ignored. Members of Congress and administration officials—at least those who want to remain in Washington—are sensitive to the feelings and opinions of their constituents. The pros and cons are counted and the administrative assistant to a member of Congress regularly reports on the mail received. Telegrams sometimes go directly to the legislator's desk. Phone calls are also tallied and reported.

Communication with elected officials, therefore, should be regarded not only as a privilege of citizenship but also as a responsibility. Members of Congress respect and appreciate that communication. Even a letter disagreeing with an elected official's stated position is worthwhile, because it can help your representative to understand the other side of that issue. Do not become discouraged, however, if, following your literary effort, the member's vote is still unfavorable to your position. It is important to remember that other persuasive people have also contacted the member, and the next time the vote may go your way.

It is critical, though, that your message be presented as effectively as possible. On the first occasion, writing a letter to your congressman may seem difficult. But it can be done and done well. You do not need to be an expert on an issue to get attention. Neither do you need to be a literary wizard. Here are some basic rules to follow:

1. Concentrate on your own delegation. Your two senators and your representative have an obligation to consider your view. Generally, as a courtesy, letters from outside a congressman's district are forwarded to the congressman from whose district it was sent. Of course, if a staffer doesn't have the time to do this, the letter will end up in the wastebasket.

2. Confine your letter to one specific legislative subject. This ensures that it will be seen by the right staff member. To do otherwise is to decrease the force of your argument and complicate any response to it. Also, tell the legislator exactly what you want done.

3. Ask the legislator to tell you his position on the matter. Will he support or oppose this legislation? He has a responsibility to inform you as to where he stands.

4. Write in your own words. Mass-produced letters that are part of a mail campaign or petition drive are of little influence. Form letters usually receive form replies. In other words, your congressman or his staff assistants will measure your interest in an issue by the amount of time you take to inform him of your beliefs. If you are willing to take only 30 seconds (the time it takes to sign a petition, postcard or form letter) to protest your representative's action or inaction, he will conclude that you are really not serious about your concern. A two- or three-sentence personal letter has more impact that a preprinted postcard. This kind of seriousness is a measurement of your capacity to elect another representative.

5. Be brief. Letters that are more than one page are saved for another day. Completeness and clarity are both possible on one page. It will take more effort to condense your ideas into a single page, but it's worth it if you want to be read. Letters need not be typed, but they must be legible.

6. Give your reasons for taking a stand. But avoid emotional arguments or language that is demanding or threatening. While the subject may be emotion-laden, use facts and illustrations to make your point. Statements like "Vote against HR 100, I'm bitterly opposed" do not help much. But a letter which says, "I'm a small hardware dealer, and HR 100 will put me out of business for the following reasons . . ." says much more. If you disagree with your legislator, say so but do not berate him. Try to keep the dialogue open. Your attitude will inevitably come through and it should be polite and positive. Displaying anger or resentment in a letter only makes it easier to ignore. Your legislator will only assume that you wouldn't vote for him even if he did what you ask, and you want him to think of you as a potential supporter.

GUIDE TO POLITICAL ACTION cont.

7. *Do not assume that your member is well-informed about a given issue.* A member can't stay on top of everything. Treat him with respect, but do explain the situation.

8. *Be constructive.* Indicate how a bill is counter-productive. Letters should, whenever possible, include the bill number or the popular title since there can be many bills concerning any given topic.

9. *Ask for a response.* Request an answer to a specific question. A well-formulated question will often get a more personal response. Write a letter that cannot be answered by a computer.

10. *Be timely.* Read the newspaper or institutional newsletters for dates of scheduled floor votes or committee action. Obviously, your letter should come as early as possible before decisions are made. By doing so it's possible to encourage the legislator to take the right position before the opposition gets to him. The best time to write is when you first learn that Congress is going to consider the issue.

11. *Be accurate and courteous.* Be certain that your name and address are on both the envelope and letter. Write legibly and spell names accurately. Use proper etiquette. Any legislator is called "Honorable" on the envelope and inside address. The salutation, however, treats senators and representatives differently. Representatives are addressed as "Mr.," "Ms." or "Mrs.," while senators are called "Senator."

12. *Point out the moral issues involved.* Explain why you are for a particular position. Since legislators get so much mail from special interest groups, they need to hear from citizens who are primarily concerned with what seems right to them on moral grounds.

13. *If you have expert knowledge, share it.* Of all letters pouring into a congressman's office, perhaps one in a hundred comes from a constituent who is a real expert in that subject. All opinions expressed are important, but those from someone with real experience are a gold mine to conscientious members.

14. *Say "well done" when deserved.* Your members of Congress are human, too, and appreciate a word of thanks from people who believe they have done the right thing. Thank your legislator if he voted for your position on an issue. Very few constituents bother to do this. It will be appreciated! Also, do this while the vote is still fresh in the congressman's mind. If possible, phone after a vote and leave a message of thanks.

15. *Avoid becoming a constant "pen pal."* Quality, not quantity, is what counts. Write when you feel like it, but don't try to instruct your congressman on every issue that comes up. Writing only once a month is a good rule. One of the pet peeves on Capitol Hill is the "pen pal" who weighs down the mail every few days with long tomes on every conceivable subject.

16. *Always keep copies of correspondence.* Retain and file a copy of your letter and the reply from your representative. They are especially useful should you arrange an interview to discuss your concerns.

17. *Try to get together with others.* Join with others, if possible, and write your own individual letters in a group. There is motivation and support in numbers. If you've never written a letter to a legislator, hearing of someone else's experience can encourage you to try your own hand at it. If you receive a negative response, it helps to have others with whom to talk it over.

Correct Forms of Address, Salutation, and Closing

Note: Except for the president, the following items are closed with "Sincerely Yours."

President
The President
The White House
Washington, DC 20500

Dear Mr. President:
Very Respectfully Yours,

Vice President
The Vice President
The White House
Washington, DC 20500
Dear Mr. Vice President:

Members of the Cabinet
The Honorable James A. Baker III
The Secretary of State
Washington, DC 20301
Dear Mr. Baker:

Senators
The Honorable Robert Dole
United States Senate
Washington, DC 20510
Dear Senator Dole:

Representative
The Honorable Nancy Pelosi
House of Representatives
Washington, DC 20515
Dear Ms. Pelosi:

Judiciary
The Honorable Sandra Day O'Connor
Associate Justice
(or Chief Justice, as appropriate)
United States Supreme Court
Washington, DC 20543
My dear Justice O'Connor:
or
My dear Mr. (Miss or Mrs.) Chief Justice:
(when addressing this officer)

The Follow-Up Letter

Whatever the response, write a follow-up letter. If your congressman cannot comply with your request for legislative support, he may send back a letter agreeing with you on some other area of interest. Ignore this kind of flattery.

But if your legislator does disagree with you, write back promptly, refuting his arguments and once more asking him to take the position you favor. If you fail to follow up, the legislator and his staff will have little reason to reconsider his position. They will get the impression that either his letter persuaded you or that you didn't care strongly enough about the issue to pursue it further.

When follow-up letters arrive in a congressional office, the picture can change. These letters will communicate that the legislator's position is raising serious objections from constituents. Make these letters thoughtful and courteous, but insistent. This will require the staff to draft answers to your points.

Cover at least three elements in follow-up letters:

1. *Express thanks* for the legislator's candidness in stating his position.

2. *Tell him you disagree* and proceed to refute his arguments. Make new points, if you can.

3. *Ask a question or two,* so the staff will have to think about the issue and respond. Some suggested questions include: Have you consulted . . .? Did you know . . .?

Above all, do not get discouraged. Remember, your legislator needs your help in casting votes. The "ballot box" is not far away. It's painted red, white and blue, and it reads "U.S. Mail."

Telegrams

There is only one use for a telegram or mailgram and that is when it is too late for a letter. They are especially helpful to reemphasize your position just before the vote on a critical issue.

Telegrams are fast, but costly. Western Union will deliver a telegram of 10 words or less within two to five hours for $13.95; delivery by a messenger costs $25.90. Mailgrams have almost made telegrams obsolete. They provide next-day service by mail for a message of 50 words or less for about $13.95. Western Union also has available the "opinion gram." It provides same-day service to members of Congress using a telex system. A message of 20 words or less costs approximately $8.95.

GUIDE TO POLITICAL ACTION cont.

Telephone Calls

You can also register your opinion by telephone call, although this is usually only effective if the issue you are calling about is well known to your legislator. If you've not written a letter, a phone call will at least get you on the record. Many constituents incorrectly assume that they must call the legislator's Washington office to register a viewpoint or talk about an issue. A call to the congressional district office is just as effective, especially if you can generate a large volume of calls. When you call the local office, indicate that you want to register a citizen opinion or talk briefly with a staff member who is handling a particular issue. Briefly state your position and ask for a reply from the congressman.

When calls come into the local office, the Washington office is informed. Since most people are too apathetic to make a call, a dozen or more calls to the local offices can really make a difference. Staff in the district office are usually more politically oriented, and very sensitive to what constituents are thinking.

A number of cautions about phone usage are in order. If you do use the phone to talk to staffers about an issue, avoid overdoing it. The constituent who calls once or twice a week to chat about issues can become annoying to staffers who are trying to handle their normally heavy work load.

Naturally, not every letter you send to an elected official will have the desired effect. Don't be discouraged. Many other people are clamoring for your congressman's attention, including some very persuasive lobbyists. He may also have received thousands of letters with an opposing perspective. But your views are important, too. They're just as worthy of your congressman's consideration as anyone's. Don't forget: *Your communication counts!*

Cabinet Directory

Vice President: Dan Quayle, 20501
Agriculture: Clayton K. Yeutter, 20250
Attorney General: Richard Thornburgh, 20530
CIA Director: William Webster, 20505
Commerce: Robert A. Mosbacher, 20230
Defense: Dick Cheney, 20301
Education: Lauro F. Cavazos, 20202
Energy: James D. Watkins, 20585
Health and Human Services: Dr. Louis W. Sullivan, 20201
Housing and Urban Development: Jack Kemp, 20410
Interior: Manual Luman Jr., 20240
Labor: Elizabeth Dole, 20210
**National Drug Policy Director*: William J. Bennett, 20500
State: James A. Baker III, 20520
Transportation: Samuel K. Skinner, 20590
UN Ambassador: Thomas R. Pickering, 799 United Nations Plaza, New York, NY 10017
Veterans' Affairs: Edward J. Derwinski
* Not official cabinet status

Supreme Court Justices

Chief Justice: William H. Rehnquist
Associate Justices:
Byron R. White
Thurgood Marshall
Harry A. Blackmun
Antonin Scalia
Sandra Day O'Connor
Anthony Kennedy
John Paul Stevens
One justice to be appointed (formerly William J. Brennan Jr.'s seat)

A Note About Addresses

Most agencies and departments of the government have their own zip codes. In order to write to them you need only the name of the person and the department, Washington, DC, plus zip code.

Phone Numbers in Washington

Federal Information Center: (Operators can direct you to the agency or department you wish to call.) 202-655-4000

Capitol: (Call this number for all House and Senate offices.) 202-224-3121
White House: 202-456-1414 (switchboard), or 202-456-7639 (public opinion expressions).

Congressional Directory, 101st Congress

Numbers in the left-hand column indicate the congressional district; numbers following the name indicate committees. Committee code numbers correspond to the numbers given the committees in the list following. Senate committees are numbered 1–16. House committees are numbered 17–38.

Alabama

Senators:
- Howell Heflin (D) - 1, 12
- Richard C. Shelby (D) - 3, 4

Representatives:
- 1 Sonny Callahan (R) - 24
- 2 William L. Dickinson (R) - 19, 27
- 3 Glen Browder (D) - 19, 34
- 4 Tom Bevill (D) - 18
- 5 Ronnie G. Flippo (D) - 38
- 6 Ben Erdreich (D) - 20, 26
- 7 Claude Harris (D) - 17, 37

Alaska

Senators:
- Frank H. Murkowski (R) - 7, 10, 16
- Ted Stevens (R) - 2, 6, 11, 14

Representative:
- Don Young (R) - 28, 30, 31

Arizona

Senators:
- Dennis DeConcini (D) - 2, 12, 16
- John McCain (R) - 3, 6

Representatives:
- 1 John J. Rhodes III (R) - 28, 35
- 2 Morris K. Udall (D) - 25, 28, 31
- 3 Bob Stump (R) - 19, 37
- 4 John Kyl (R) - 19, 26
- 5 Jim Kolbe (R) - 18

Arkansas

Senators:
- Dale Bumpers (D) - 2, 7, 15
- David Pryor (D) - 1, 9, 11

Representatives:
- 1 Bill Alexander (D) - 18
- 2 Tommy F. Robinson (D) - 19, 23, 37
- 3 John Paul Hammerschmidt (R) - 32, 37
- 4 Beryl F. Anthony Jr. (D) - 38

California

Senators:
- Alan Cranston (D) - 4, 10, 16
- Pete Wilson (R) - 1, 3, 6

Representatives:
- 1 Douglas H. Bosco (D) - 30, 32
- 2 Wally Herger (R) - 17, 30
- 3 Robert T. Matsui (D) - 38
- 4 Vic Fazio (D) - 18, 21, 36
- 5 Nancy Pelosi (D) - 20, 26
- 6 Barbara Boxer (D) - 19, 21
- 7 George Miller (D) - 21, 28
- 8 Ronald V. Dellums (D) - 19, 22
- 9 Pete Stark (D) - 22, 38
- 10 Don Edwards (D) - 29, 37
- 11 Tom Lantos (D) - 25, 26
- 12 Tom Campbell (R) - 34, 35
- 13 Norman Y. Mineta (D) - 32, 34
- 14 Norman D. Shumway (R) - 20, 30
- 15 Gary Condit (D) - 17, 26
- 16 Leon E. Panetta (D) 17, 27
- 17 Charles Pashayan Jr. (R) - 28, 31, 36
- 18 Richard H. Lehman (D) - 20, 28
- 19 Robert J. Lagomarsino (R) - 25, 28
- 20 William Thomas (R) - 21, 27, 38
- 21 Elton Gallegly (R) - 28, 35
- 22 Carlos J. Moorhead (R) - 24, 29
- 23 Anthony C. Beilenson (D) - 33
- 24 Henry A. Waxman (D) - 24, 26
- 25 Edward R. Roybal (D) - 18
- 26 Howard L. Berman (D) - 25, 29
- 27 Mel E. Levine (D) - 25, 28
- 28 Julian C. Dixon (D) - 18, 36
- 29 Augustus F. Hawkins (D) - 23
- 30 Matthew G. Martinez (D) - 23, 26, 35
- 31 Mervyn M. Dymally (D) - 22, 25, 31
- 32 Glenn M. Anderson (D) - 30, 32
- 33 David Dreier (R) - 20, 35
- 34 Esteban Torres (D) - 20, 35
- 35 Jerry Lewis (R) - 18
- 36 George E. Brown Jr. (D) - 17, 34

GUIDE TO POLITICAL ACTION cont.

37 Al McCandless (R) - 26, 20
38 Robert Dornan (R) - 25, 37
39 William E. Dannemeyer (R) - 24, 29
40 C. Christopher Cox (R) - 26, 32
41 Bill Lowery (R) - 18
42 Dana Rohrabacher (R) - 22, 34
43 Ronald C. Packard (R) - 32, 34
44 Jim Bates (D) - 24, 27
45 Duncan L. Hunter (R) - 19

Colorado
Senators:
Timothy E. Wirth (D) - 3, 4, 5, 7
William L. Armstrong (R) - 4, 5, 9
Representatives:
1 Patricia Schroeder (D) - 19, 29, 31
2 David Skaggs (D) - 32, 34
3 Ben N. Campbell (D) - 17, 28
4 Hank Brown (R) - 38
5 Joel Hefley (R) - 34, 35
6 Dan Schaefer (R) - 24

Connecticut
Senators:
Christopher J. Dodd (D) - 4, 5, 10, 13, 14
J. I. Lieberman (D) - 8, 11, 15
Representatives:
1 Barbara B. Kennelly (D) - 38
2 Samuel Gejdenson (D) - 25, 27, 28
3 Bruce A. Morrison (D) - 20, 22, 29
4 Christopher Shays (R) - 26, 34
5 John G. Rowland (R) - 19, 37
6 Nancy L. Johnson (R) - 21, 32

Delaware
Senators:
Joseph R. Biden Jr. (D) - 10, 12
William V. Roth Jr. (R) - 9, 11
Representative:
Thomas R. Carper (D) - 20, 30

Florida
Senators:
Connie Mack III (R) - 4, 10
Bob Graham (D) - 4, 8, 16
Representatives:
1 Earl Hutto (D) - 19, 30
2 Bill Grant (D) - 26, 32
3 Charles E. Bennett (D) - 19, 30
4 Craig T. James (R) - 29, 37
5 Bill McCollum (R) - 20, 29
6 Clifford B. Stearns (R) - 20, 37
7 Sam M. Gibbons (D) - 38
8 C. W. (Bill) Young (R) - 18
9 Michael Bilirakis (R) - 24, 37
10 Andy Ireland (R) - 19, 35
11 Bill Nelson (D) - 20, 34
12 Tom Lewis (R) - 17, 34
13 Porter J. Goss (R) - 25, 30
14 Harry A. Johnston II (D) - 25, 34
15 E. Clay Shaw Jr. (R) - 29, 32
16 Lawrence J. Smith (D) - 25, 29
17 William Lehman (D) - 18
18 Ileana Ros-Lehtinen (R) - 25, 26
19 Dante B. Fascell (D) - 25

Georgia
Senators:
Sam Nunn (D) - 3, 11, 15
Wyche Fowler Jr. (D) - 1, 5, 7
Representatives:
1 Lindsay Thomas (D) - 18
2 Charles F. Hatcher (D) - 17, 35
3 Richard Ray (D) - 19, 35
4 Ben Jones (D) - 32, 37
5 John Lewis (D) - 28, 32
6 Newt Gingrich (R) - 27, 32
7 George Darden (D) - 19, 28
8 J. Roy Rowland (D) - 32, 37
9 Ed Jenkins (D) - 21, 38
10 Doug Barnard Jr. (D) - 20, 26

Hawaii
Senators:
Daniel K. Inouye (D) - 2, 6, 14
Spark M. Matsunaga (D) - 9, 13, 16
Representatives:
1 Patricia Saiki (R) - 20, 30
2 Daniel K. Akaka (D) - 18

Idaho
Senators:
James A. McClure (R) - 2, 7, 14
Steven D. Symms (R) - 3, 5, 8
Representatives:
1 Larry Craig (R) - 26, 28, 36
2 Richard H. Stallings (D) - 17, 34

Illinois
Senators:
Alan J. Dixon (D) - 3, 4, 15

Paul Simon (D) - 5, 10, 12, 13
Representatives:
1 Charles A. Hayes (D) - 23, 35
2 Gus Savage (D) - 32, 35
3 Marty Russo (D) - 21, 38
4 George Sangmeister (D) - 29, 37
5 William O. Lipinski (D) - 30, 32
6 Henry J. Hyde (R) - 25, 29
7 Cardiss Collins (D) - 24, 26
8 Dan Rostenkowski (D) - 38
9 Sidney R. Yates (D) - 18
10 John E. Porter (R) - 18
11 Frank Annunzio (D) - 20, 27
12 Phillip M. Crane (R) - 38
13 Harris Fawell (R) - 23, 34
14 Dennis Hastert (R) - 26, 32
15 Edward R. Madigan (R) - 17, 24
16 Lynn M. Martin (R) - 19, 22
17 Lane Evans (D) - 17, 37
18 Robert H. Michel (R)
19 Terry Bruce (D) - 24, 34
20 Richard J. Durbin (D) - 18, 21
21 Jerry Costello (D)
22 Glenn Poshard (D) - 23, 35

Indiana
Senators:
Richard G. Lugar (R) - 1, 10
Daniel R. Coats (R) - 3, 13
Representatives:
1 Peter Visclosky (D) - 23, 28, 32
2 Philip R. Sharp (D) - 24, 28
3 John Hiler (R) - 20, 35
4 Jill Long (D) - 17, 37
5 James Jontz (D) - 17, 23, 37
6 Danny L. Burton (R) - 25, 31, 37
7 John T. Myers (R) - 18, 31, 36
8 Frank McCloskey (D) - 19, 31
9 Lee H. Hamilton (D) - 25, 34
10 Andy Jacobs Jr. (D) - 38

Iowa
Senators:
Charles E. Grassley (R) - 2, 5, 12
Tom Harkin (D) - 1, 2, 13, 15
Representatives:
1 Jim Leach (R) - 20, 25
2 Tom J. Tauke (R) - 23, 24
3 David R. Nagle (D) - 17, 34
4 Neal Smith (D) - 18, 35
5 Jim Ross Lightfoot (R) - 26, 32
6 Fred Grandy (R) - 17, 23

Kansas
Senators:
Robert Dole (R) - 1, 9, 14
Nancy Landon Kassebaum (D) - 5, 6, 10
Representatives:
1 Pat Roberts (R) - 17, 27
2 Jim Slattery (D) - 21, 24
3 Jan Meyers (R) - 25, 35
4 Dan Glickman (D) - 17, 29, 34
5 Robert Whittaker (R) - 24

Kentucky
Senators:
Wendell H. Ford (D) - 6, 7, 14
Mitch McConnell (R) - 1, 10
Representatives:
1 Carroll Hubbard Jr. (D) - 20, 30
2 William H. Natcher (D) - 18
3 Romano L. Mazzoli (D) - 22, 29, 35
4 Jim Bunning (R) - 20, 30
5 Harold Rogers (R) - 18, 21
6 Larry J. Hopkins (R) - 17, 19
7 Carl C. Perkins (D) - 23, 32, 34

Louisiana
Senators:
J. Bennett Johnston Jr. (D) - 2, 5, 7
John B. Breaux (D) - 1, 6, 8
Representatives:
1 Robert L. Livingston (R) - 18
2 Lindy Boggs (D) - 18
3 W. J. Tauzin (D) - 24, 30
4 Jim McCrery (R)
5 Jerry Huckaby (D) - 17, 28
6 Richard H. Baker (R) - 28, 35
7 Jimmy Hayes (D) - 32, 34
8 Clyde C. Holloway (R) - 17, 35

Maine
Senators:
William S. Cohen (R) - 3, 11
George J. Mitchell (D) - 8, 9, 11, 16
Representatives:
1 Joseph E. Brennen (D) - 19, 30
2 Olympia J. Snowe (R) - 25

Maryland
Senators:
Barbara A. Mikulski (D) - 2, 8, 13, 15
Paul S. Sarbanes (D) - 4, 10

GUIDE TO POLITICAL ACTION cont.

Representatives:
- 1 Roy P. Dyson (D) - 19, 30
- 2 Helen Bentley (R) - 30, 32
- 3 Benjamin L. Cardin (D) - 29, 32
- 4 Thomas McMillen (D) - 20, 34
- 5 Steny H. Hoyer (D) - 18
- 6 Beverly B. Byron (D) - 19, 28
- 7 Kweisi Mfume (D) - 20, 35
- 8 Constance A. Morella (R) - 31, 34

Massachusetts

Senators:
- Edward M. Kennedy (D) - 3, 12, 13
- John F. Kerry (D) - 6, 10, 15

Representatives:
- 1 Silvioi O. Conte (R) - 18, 35
- 2 Richard E. Neal (D) - 20, 35
- 3 Joseph D. Early (D) - 18
- 4 Barney Frank (D) - 20, 26, 29
- 5 Chester G. Atkins (D) - 21, 23, 25, 36
- 6 Nicholas Mavroules (D) - 19, 35
- 7 Edward J. Markey (D) - 24, 28
- 8 Joseph P. Kennedy II (D) - 20, 37
- 9 Joe Moakley (D) - 33
- 10 Gerry E. Studds (D) - 25, 30
- 11 Brian J. Donnelly (D) - 38

Michigan

Senators:
- Carl Levin (D) - 3, 11, 15
- Donald W. Riegle Jr. (D) - 4, 5, 6, 9

Representatives:
- 1 John Conyers Jr. (D) - 26, 29, 35
- 2 Carl D. Pursell (R) - 18
- 3 Howard Wolpe (D) - 21, 25
- 4 Fred Upton (R) - 32, 35
- 5 Paul B. Henry (R) - 23, 34
- 6 Bob Carr (D) - 18
- 7 Dale E. Kildee (D) - 23, 28
- 8 Bob Traxler (D) - 18
- 9 Guy Vander Jagt (R) - 38
- 10 Bill Schuette (R) - 17
- 11 Robert W. Davis (R) - 19, 30
- 12 David E. Bonior (D) - 33
- 13 George W. Crockett Jr. (D) - 25, 29
- 14 Dennis M. Hertel (D) - 19, 30
- 15 William D. Ford (D) - 23, 31
- 16 John D. Dingell (D) - 24
- 17 Sander M. Levin (D) - 38
- 18 William S. Broomfield (R) - 25, 35

Minnesota

Senators:
- Rudy Boschwitz (R) - 1, 5, 10, 15
- David Durenberger (R) - 8, 9

Representatives:
- 1 Timothy J. Penny (D) - 17, 23, 37
- 2 Vin Weber (R) - 18
- 3 Bill Frenzel (R) - 27, 38
- 4 Bruce F. Vento (D) - 20, 28
- 5 Martin Olav Sabo (D) - 18
- 6 Gerry Sikorski (D) - 24, 31
- 7 Arlan Strangeland (R) - 17, 32
- 9 James L. Oberstar (D) - 21, 32

Mississippi

Senators:
- Trent Lott (R) - 3, 6, 15
- Thad Cochran (R) - 1, 2, 13

Representatives:
- 1 Jamie L. Whitten (D) - 18
- 2 Mike Espy (D) - 17, 21
- 3 G. V. (Sonny) Montgomery (D) - 19, 37
- 4 Mike Parker (D) - 32, 37
- 5 Gene Taylor (D) - 18, 30

Missouri

Senators:
- John C. Danforth (R) - 5, 6, 9
- Christopher (Kit) Bond (R) - 1, 4, 15

Representatives:
- 1 William (Bill) Clay (D) - 23, 27, 31
- 2 Jack Buechner (R) - 21, 34
- 3 Richard A. Gephardt (D) - 38
- 4 Ike Skelton (D) - 19, 35
- 5 Alan Wheat (D) - 22, 33
- 6 E. Thomas Coleman (R) - 17, 23
- 7 Mel Hancock (R) - 32, 35
- 8 Bill Emerson (R) - 17, 28
- 9 Harold L. Volkmer (D) - 17, 34

Montana

Senators:
- Max Baucus (D) - 8, 9, 15
- Conrad Burns (R) - 6, 7, 15

Representatives:
- 1 Pat Williams (D) - 21, 23
- 2 Ron Marlenee (R) - 17, 28

Nebraska

Senators:
- J. James Exon (D) - 3, 5, 6

Robert Kerrey (D) - 1, 2
Representatives:
1 Douglas K. Bereuter (R) - 20, 25
2 Peter Hoagland (D) - 20, 35
3 Virginia Smith (R) - 18

Nevada
Senators:
Richard H. Bryan (D) - 4, 6
Harry Reid (D) - 2, 8
Representatives:
1 James A. Bilbray (D) - 25, 35
2 Barbara Vucanovich (R) - 27, 28

New Hampshire
Senators:
Gordon J. Humphrey (R) - 3, 12, 13
Warren Rudman (R) - 2, 5, 11, 15
Representatives:
1 Robert C. Smith (R) - 34
2 Charles Douglas (R) - 26, 29

New Jersey
Senators:
Bill Bradley (D) - 7, 9
Frank R. Lautenberg (D) - 2, 5, 8
Representatives:
1 James J. Florio (D) - 24, 37
2 William J. Hughes (D) - 29, 30
3 Frank Pallone Jr. (D) - 30, 32
4 Christopher H. Smith (R) - 25, 37
5 Marge Roukema (R) - 20, 23
6 Bernard J. Dwyer (D) - 18, 36
7 Matthew J. Rinaldo (R) - 24
8 Robert A. Roe (D) - 32, 34
9 Robert G. Torricelli (D) - 25, 34
10 Donald Payne (D) - 23, 26
11 Dean A. Gallo (R) - 32, 35
12 Jim Courter (R) - 19
13 James Saxton (R) - 20, 30
14 Frank J. Guarini (D) - 21, 38

New Mexico
Senators:
Pete V. Domenici (R) - 2, 5, 7
Jeff Bingaman (D) - 3, 7, 11
Representatives:
1 Steven H. Schiff (R) - 26, 34
2 Joe Skeen (R) - 18
3 William B. Richardson (D) - 23, 24, 28

New York
Senators:
Daniel P. Moynihan (D) - 8, 9, 10, 14
Alfonse M. D'Amato (R) - 2, 4, 15
Representatives:
1 George J. Hochbrueckner (D) - 19, 30, 34
2 Thomas J. Downey (D) - 38
3 Robert J. Mrazek (D) - 18
4 Norman F. Lent (R) - 24, 30
5 Raymond J. McGrath (R) - 38
6 Floyd H. Flake (D) - 20, 35
7 Gary L. Ackerman (D) - 25, 31
8 James J. Scheuer (D) - 24, 34
9 Thomas J. Manton (D) - 20, 30
10 Charles E. Schumer (D) - 20, 21, 29
11 Edolphus Towns (D) - 26, 32
12 Major R. Owens (D) - 23, 26
13 Stephen J. Solarz (D) - 23, 25, 31
14 Guy V. Molinari (R) - 32
15 S. William Green (R) - 18
16 Charles B. Rangel (D) - 38
17 Ted Weiss (D) - 25, 26
18 Robert Garcia (D) - 20, 31
19 Eliot L. Engel (D) - 25
20 Nita M. Lowey (D) - 23, 30
21 Hamilton Fish Jr. (R) - 29
22 Benjamin A. Gilman (R) - 25, 31
23 Michael R. McNulty (D) - 19, 35
24 Gerald B. Solomon (R) - 25, 37
25 Sherwood L. Boehlert (R) - 32, 34
26 David O'Brian Martin (R) - 19
27 James T. Walsh (R) - 17
28 Matthew F. McHugh (D) - 18
29 Frank Horton (R) - 26, 31
30 Louise M. Slaughter (D) - 26, 32
31 William Paxon (R) - 20
32 John J. LaFalce (D) - 20, 35
33 Henry J. Nowak (D) - 32, 34
34 Amo Houghton Jr. (R) - 21, 26

North Carolina
Senators:
Terry Sanford (D) - 4, 5, 10
Jesse Helms (R) - 1, 10, 14
Representatives:
1 Walter B. Jones (D) - 17, 30
2 I. T. Valentine Jr. (D) - 32, 34
3 Martin Lancaster (D) - 17, 32, 35
4 David E. Price (D) - 20, 34
5 Stephen L. Neal (D) - 20, 26
6 Howard Coble (R) - 29, 30

GUIDE TO POLITICAL ACTION cont.

7 Charles Rose (D) - 17, 27
8 W. G. (Bill) Hefner (D) - 18
9 J. Alex McMillan (R) - 20, 35
10 Cass Ballenger (R) - 23, 32
11 James McClure Clarke (D) - 25, 28

North Dakota
Senators:
Kent Conrad (D) - 1, 5, 7
Quentin N. Burdick (D) - 2, 8
Representative:
Bryon L. Dorgan (D) - 38

Ohio
Senators:
John H. Glenn Jr. (D) - 3, 11
Howard M. Metzenbaum (D) - 7, 12, 13
Representatives:
1 Thomas A. Luken (D) - 24, 35
2 Willis D. (Bill) Gradison Jr. (R) - 21, 38
3 Tony P. Hall (D) - 33
4 Michael G. Oxley (R) - 24
5 Paul E. Gillmor (R) - 20, 27
6 Bob McEwen (R) - 32, 37
7 Michael De Wine (R) - 25, 29
8 Donald E. Lukens (R) - 25, 26
9 Marcy Kaptur (D) - 20, 37
10 Clarence E. Miller (R) - 18
11 Dennis E. Eckart (D) - 24, 35
12 John R. Kasich (R) - 19
13 Don J. Pease (D) - 38
14 Thomas C. Sawyer (D) - 23, 26
15 Chalmers P. Wylie (R) - 20, 37
16 Ralph S. Regula (R) - 18
17 James Traficant Jr. (D) - 32, 34
18 Douglas Applegate (D) - 32, 37
19 Edward F. Feighan (D) - 25, 29
20 Mary Rose Oakar (D) - 20, 27, 31
21 Louis Stokes (D) - 18

Oklahoma
Senators:
David L. Boren (D) - 1, 9, 15
Don Nickles (R) - 2, 5, 7
Representatives:
1 James M. Inhofe (R) - 26, 32
2 Mike Synar (D) - 24, 26, 29
3 Wes Watkins (D) - 18
4 Dave McCurdy (D) - 19, 34
5 Mickey Edwards (R) - 18, 21
6 Glenn English (D) - 17, 26

Oregon
Senators:
Mark O Hatfield (R) - 2, 7, 14
Robert W. Packwood (R) - 6, 9
Representatives:
1 Les AuCoin (D) - 18
2 Robert F. (Bob) Smith (R) - 17
3 Ron Wyden (D) - 24, 35
4 Peter A. DeFazio (D) - 28, 32, 35
5 Denny Smith (R)

Pennsylvania
Senators:
H. John Heinz III (R) - 4, 9, 11
Arlen Specter (R) - 2, 12, 16
Representatives:
1 Thomas M. Foglietta (D) - 19, 30
2 William H. Gray III (D) - 18, 21, 22
3 Robert A. Borski (D) - 30, 32
4 Joseph P. Kolter (D) - 26, 27, 32
5 Richard T. Schulze (R) - 38
6 Gus Yatron (D) - 25, 31
7 Curt Weldon (R) - 19, 30
8 Peter Kostmayer (D) - 25, 28
9 Bud Shuster (R) - 32
10 Joseph M. McDade (R) - 18, 35
11 Paul E. Kanjorski (D) - 20, 34, 37
12 John P. Murtha (D) - 18
13 Lawrence Coughlin (R) - 18
14 William J. Coyne (D) - 38
15 Donald L. Ritter (R) - 24, 34
16 Robert S. Walker (R) - 26, 34
17 George W. Gekas (R) - 29
18 Doug Walgren (D) - 24, 34
19 William F. Goodling (R) - 21, 23
20 Joseph M. Gaydos (D) - 23, 27, 36
21 Thomas J. Ridge (R) - 20, 37
22 Austin J. Murphy (D) - 23, 28
23 William F. Clinger Jr. (R) - 26, 32

Rhode Island
Senators:
John H. Chafee (R) - 4, 8, 9
Claiborne Pell (D) - 10, 13, 14
Representatives:
1 Ronald K. Machtley (R) - 19
2 Claudine Schneider (R) - 30, 34

South Carolina
Senators:
Ernest F. Hollings (D) - 2, 5, 6
Strom Thurmond (R) - 3, 12, 13, 16
Representatives:
1 Arthur Ravenel Jr. (R) - 19
2 Floyd Spence (R) - 19, 36
3 Butler Derrick (D) - 21, 33
4 Liz J. Patterson (D) - 20, 37
5 John M. Spratt Jr. (D) - 19, 26
6 Robin Tallon Jr. (D) - 17, 30

South Dakota
Senators:
Thomas A. Daschle (D) - 1, 9
Larry Pressler (R) - 6, 8, 10, 15
Representative:
Tim Johnson (D) - 17, 37

Tennessee
Senators:
Albert Gore Jr. (D) - 3, 6, 14
James R. Sasser (D) - 2, 4, 5, 11, 15
Representatives:
1 James H. Quillen (R) - 33
2 John J. Duncan (R) - 32
3 Marilyn Lloyd (D) - 19, 34
4 James H. Cooper (D) - 24, 35
5 Bob Clement (D)
6 Bart Gordon (D) - 33
7 Don K. Sundquist (R) - 32, 37
8 John S. Tanner (D) - 19, 34
9 Harold E. Ford (D) - 38

Texas
Senators:
Lloyd Bentsen (D) - 6, 9
Phil Gramm (R) - 3, 4
Representatives:
1 Jim Chapman (D) - 32, 34
2 Charles Wilson (D) - 18
3 Steve Bartlett (R) - 20, 23
4 Ralph M. Hall (D) - 24, 34
5 John Bryant (D) - 24, 29, 37
6 Joe L. Barton (R) - 24
7 Bill Archer (R) - 38
8 Jack Fields (R) - 24, 30
9 Jack Brooks (D) - 26, 29
10 J. J. Pickle (D) - 38
11 Marvin Leath (D) - 19, 21
12 Peter Geren (D) - 32, 37
13 Bill Sarpalius (D) - 17, 35
14 Greg Laughlin (D) - 30, 32
15 E. (Kika) de la Garza (D) - 17
16 Ronald D. Coleman (D) - 18
17 Charles W. Stenholm (D) - 17, 37
18 Craig Washington (D)
19 Larry Combest (R) - 17, 22
20 Henry B. Gonzalez (D) - 20, 35
21 Lamar Smith (R) - 29, 34
22 Tom DeLay (R) - 18
23 Albert G. Bustamante (D) - 19, 26
24 Martin Frost (D) - 21, 33
25 Mike A. Andrews (D) - 38
26 Richard K. Armey (R) - 21, 23
27 Solomon P. Ortiz (D) - 19, 30

Utah
Senators:
Jake Garn (R) - 2, 4, 14
Orrin G. Hatch (R) - 12, 13
Representatives:
1 James V. Hansen (R) - 19, 28, 36
2 Wayne Owens (D) - 25, 28
3 Howard C. Nielson (R) - 24, 26

Vermont
Senators:
Patrick J. Leahy (D) - 1, 2, 12
James M. Jeffords (R) - 8, 13, 16
Representative:
Peter P. Smith (R) - 23, 26

Virginia
Senators:
Charles S. Robb (D) - 5, 6, 10
John W. Warner (R) - 3, 8, 14
Representatives:
1 Herbert S. Bateman (R) - 19, 30
2 Owen B. Pickett (D) - 19, 30
3 Thomas J. Bliley Jr. (R) - 22, 24
4 Norman Sisisky (D) - 19, 35
5 Lewis F. Payne Jr. (D)
6 James R. Olin (D) - 17, 35
7 D. French Slaughter (R) - 29, 34, 35
8 Stan Parris (R) - 20, 22
9 Frederick C. Boucher (D) - 24, 29, 34
10 Frank R. Wolf (R) - 18

Washington
Senators:
Slade Gorton (R) - 1, 3, 6
Brock Adams (D) - 6, 10, 13, 14

GUIDE TO POLITICAL ACTION cont.

Representatives:
1 John Miller (R) - 25, 30
2 Allan Swift (D) - 24, 27
3 Jolene Unsoeld (D) - 23, 30
4 Sid Morrison (R) - 17, 34
5 Thomas S. Foley (D) - 21
6 Norman D. Dicks (D) - 18
7 Jim McDermott (D) - 20, 28
8 Rodney Chandler (R) - 38

West Virginia
Senators:
Robert C. Byrd (D) - 2, 12, 14
John D. (Jay) Rockefeller IV (D) - 6, 9, 16
Representatives:
1 Alan B. Mollohan (D) - 18, 36
2 Harley O. Staggers Jr. (D) - 17, 29, 37
3 Robert E. Wise Jr. (D) - 23, 26, 32
4 Nick (Joe) Rahall II (D) - 28, 32

Wisconsin
Senators:
Robert W. Kasten Jr. (R) - 2, 5, 6, 15
Herbert Kohl (D) - 11, 12
Representatives:
1 Les Aspin (D) - 19
2 Robert W. Kastenmeier (D) - 29
3 Steve Gunderson (R) - 17, 23
4 Gerald Kleczka (D) - 20, 26
5 Jim Moody (D) - 38
6 Thomas E. Petri (R) - 23, 32, 36
7 David R. Obey (D) - 18
8 Toby Roth (R) - 20, 25
9 F. James Sensenbrenner Jr. (R) - 29, 34

Wyoming
Senators:
Alan K. Simpson (R) - 8, 12, 16
Malcolm Wallop (R) - 7, 9, 15
Representative:
Craig Thomas - 26, 28

District of Columbia
Delegate:
Walter E. Fauntroy (D) - 20, 22

American Samoa
Delegate:
Eni F. H. Faleomavaega (D) - 25, 28

Puerto Rico
Resident Commissioner:
Jaime B. Fuster (D) - 25, 28

Virgin Islands
Delegate:
Ron de Lugo (D) - 28, 31, 32

Guam
Delegate:
Ben Blaz (R) - 19, 25, 28

Senate Committees
1. Agriculture, Nutrition & Forestry 202-224-2035
2. Appropriations 202-224-3471
3. Armed Services 202-224-3871
4. Banking, Housing & Urban Affairs 202-224-7391
5. Budget 202-224-0642
6. Commerce, Science & Transportation 202-224-5115
7. Energy & Natural Resources 202-224-4971
8. Environment & Public Works 202-224-6176
9. Finance 202-224-4515
10. Foreign Relations 202-224-4651
11. Governmental Affairs 202-224-4751
12. Judiciary 202-224-5225
13. Labor & Human Resources 202-224-5375
14. Rules and Administration 202-224-6352
15. Small Business 202-224-5175
16. Veterans' Affairs 202-224-9126

House Committees
17. Agriculture 202-225-2171
18. Appropriations 202-225-2771
19. Armed Services 202-225-4151
20. Banking, Finance & Urban Affairs 202-225-4247
21. Budget 202-226-7200
22. District of Columbia 202-225-4457
23. Education & Labor 202-225-4527
24. Energy & Commerce 202-225-2927
25. Foreign Affairs 202-225-5021
26. Government Operations 202-225-5051

27. House Administration 202-225-2061
28. Interior & Insular Affairs 202-225-2761
29. Judiciary 202-225-3951
30. Merchant Marine & Fisheries 202-225-4047
31. Post Office & Civil Service 202-225-4054
32. Public Works & Transportation 202-225-4472
33. Rules 202-225-9486
34. Science, Space & Technology 202-225-6371
35. Small Business 202-225-5821
36. Standards of Official Conduct 202-225-7103
37. Veterans' Affairs 202-225-3527
38. Ways & Means 202-225-3625

Powers and Composition of the Congress
The legislative powers and organization of Congress are defined in Article I of the Constitution. A Senate and a House of Representatives are chosen by direct election.

There are two senators from each state. One-third of them are elected every two years for six-year terms.

The federal census determines each state's portion of 435 representative seats. State legislatures determine Congressional district boundaries. Every state has at least one representative. Representatives are elected for two-year terms.

Requirements A senator must be at least 30 years old, a U.S. citizen for at least nine years, and a resident of the state in which he/she is elected.

Responsibilities In addition to writing federal laws, the Congress has the power to conduct investigations, monitor federal agencies, impeach federal officials including the president, declare war, approve treaties, raise or lower taxes, appropriate money, approve top federal agency and judicial appointments and all armed forces officer appointments.

A two-thirds majority in each chamber will override a presidential veto.

Benefits The annual salary of a member of Congress in 1990 is $96,600. A retirement system offers liberal pension benefits.

In addition, a member of Congress receives free office space, complete with furnishings, machines and supplies. Funds are provided for staff salaries, phone bills, trips home and operation of home offices.

Printing and radio-television broadcast taping facilities are provided. Banking facilities are available in the Capitol and free parking is provided. Office complexes have gymnasium facilities, dining facilities and post offices. An attending physician is in the Capitol, and congresspersons can take advantage of a complete laboratory, x-rays, pharmacy, physiotherapy and electro-cardiographic service. Along with a health insurance plan, medical care is available at Walter Reed Army and Bethesda Naval Hospitals.

Committee Membership Members usually try to get membership on committees related to their personal interests and background and to economic interests of their district and state. However, if given the opportunity early in their careers, many members will seek membership in the powerful appropriations committees that control the flow of money to programs authorized by other committees.

Other powerful committees to which many members seek to obtain membership are the Senate Finance Committee and the House Ways and Means Committee; these committees consider tax legislation. The House and Senate budget committees, which now allow Congress to compete with the White House in establishing national priorities through a national budget, also are desirable assignments.

Committee assignments in the House and Senate are determined by special committes of Democrats and Republicans in each chamber. A party caucus in each chamber makes the final approval of assignments.

GUIDE TO POLITICAL ACTION cont.

Congressional Party Leaders

SENATE

President of the Senate: Dan Quayle
President Pro-Tempore: Robert C. Byrd (D-WV)
Majority Leader: George J. Mitchell (D-ME)
Majority Whip: Alan Cranston (D-CA)
Minority Leader: Robert Dole (R-KS)
Minority Whip: Alan Simpson (R-WY)

HOUSE

Speaker: Thomas S. Foley (D-WA)
Majority Leader: Richard A. Gephardt (D-MO)
Majority Whip: William Gray (D-PA)
Minority Leader: Robert H. Michel (R-IL)
Minority Whip: Newt Gingrich (R-GA)

Sports

SPOTLIGHT ON:

SPOTLIGHT ON CHRISTIAN ATHLETES

Dave Dravecky
Pitcher
San Francisco Giants

The pressure was relentless from the crowd, from the manager, even from the expectations of your friends and family back home. The pressure could be relentless from inside yourself. But God was concerned only that you did your best. And he was bigger than all the rest combined. . . . When I reached the mound I took a deep breath, looked around, and thought of Jesus as my only audience. I couldn't fail, really.

I was certainly scared while I waited for the results of my biopsy. The possibility of losing my life seemed very real. I might lose Janice, Tiffany, Jonathan. They might lose me. But we could never lose the love of God. He was watching over me and my family. I was conscious of his eyes on me, his loving eyes. He was my audience.

You always wonder how it will be to go through a difficult time. You talk about the love of God, yet you can't help wondering: When tough times come will you really be able to live it? We found that we could. We found that faith carried us through our troubles, day by day.

Desmoid tumors can come back after second surgeries, third surgeries, any number of surgeries. My doctors have continued to emphasize that my life is not at risk, but they've been frank to tell me that I may be in treatment for a long time. The ultimate decision, if nothing else succeeds, would be to amputate my arm. We're far, far away from that as of yet, but if it comes to it, I'll be ready.

I've learned to put my life in God's hands. The hardest part of the last two years has been the uncertainty. I had to learn to do what was within my grasp, one day at a time, and leave control of the rest trustingly to God. Such are the lessons that come when a man faces adversity. I don't think I could have gained them in any other way.

—Selected from: *Comeback* by Dave Dravecky with Tim Stafford. Published by Zondervan Publishing House and Harper & Row, Publishers.

Dave Dravecky's emotional comeback August 10, 1989, after cancer surgery brought 34,810 fans at Candlestick Park to their feet to cheer him on with 8 standing ovations. Said Giants manager Roger Craig about the event, "I've seen a lot in baseball . . . but I've never seen such drama as this one." Doctors had told Dave he would never pitch again. Dravecky's seven-inning, one-hit performance that day earned a 4-3 win over the Cincinnati Reds. *USA Today*'s Rod Beaton said Dravecky's miracle comeback "could rank among the comeback stories of the decade." Dave Dravecky announced his retirement from baseball November 13, 1989, after learning the cancer had reappeared and he would need to undergo more surgery.

Nickname: Neck
Born: February 14, 1956 in Youngstown, OH. Grew up in Boardman, OH.
Personal status: 6′, 215 lbs. Wife, Janice; two children, Tiffany Marie and Jonathan David.
Home: Boardman, OH.
Church affiliation: Word of Grace (Non-denominational).
Career highlights/awards: Played for San Diego Padres 1982-1987 and San Francisco Giants 1987-1989. Pitched two shutout innings in 1983 All-Star Game; had five strikeouts in 4 2/3 innings in 1984 World Series. Lowest ERA was 1.99. Was Giant's Opening Day starter, hurling a three-hitter at Los Angeles April 4, 1989, to win 5-1 over Fernando Valenzuela. Received American Cancer Society Courage Award from President George Bush on March 22, 1990.
Likes: Spending time with my wife and family.
Dislikes: Lima beans.
Hobbies/leisure time activities: Reading, golf, swimming.
Favorite Bible verse: We do not lose heart. Though outwardly we are wasting away, yet inwardly we are being renewed day by day. For our light and momentary troubles are achieving for us an eternal glory that far outweighs them all. So we fix our eyes not on what is seen, but on what is unseen. For what is seen is temporary, but what is unseen is eternal (2 Corinthians 4:16-18, NIV).
The best thing about baseball is: The challenge as a pitcher being one on one against the batter.
The best thing about life is: Serving God and being with my wife and kids.
What I want my children to learn from me: That Jesus Christ is the most important thing in my life and in their lives. My whole purpose here on earth is to do all I can to see them on the other side, in heaven.

A.C. Green
Forward
Los Angeles Lakers

A. C. Green was selected by the Lakers in the first round of the 1985 college draft (23rd overall). During the 1988-1989 season A.C. averaged career highs in points (13.3) and rebounds (9.0) as he has every season he's been in the league. The initials A.C., like his father's, do not stand for full names—his name is simply A.C. Green, Jr.

Born: October 4, 1963. Grew up in Portland, OR.
Personal status: 6′ 9″, 224 lbs. Wears size 15 shoes. Single. Two older brothers.
Home: Portland, OR.
Church affiliation: Non-denominational.
Career highlights/awards: During the 1988-1989 season led Lakers in rebounds for the third year in a row averaging 9.0, the most by a Laker since Earvin Johnson took 9.6 in

1981-1982. Selected by NBA coaches to the league's All-Defensive second team, the only Laker so honored. Career high 33 points at Seattle April 4. Was selected as Pac-10 Player of the Year as a junior.

Likes: Tennis, bowling, baseball, golf and eating frozen yogurt.

Dislikes: Gossip, disloyalty, compromise, pro-choice rulings.

Hobbies/leisure time activities: Frequently speak to youth groups, bowling, sampling new yogurt flavors.

Favorite book: This Present Darkness and *Piercing the Darkness* by Frank E. Peretti. Published by Crossway Books.

Favorite Bible verse: Seek first his kingdom and his righteousness, and all these things will be given to you as well (Matthew 6:33 NIV). I am the way and the truth and the life. No one comes to the Father except through me (John 14:6 NIV).

The best thing about basketball is: The friendships you make and having a job you enjoy.

The best thing about life is: Knowing that my best relationship is with Jesus Christ.

Orel Hershiser IV

Pitcher
Los Angeles Dodgers

The average fan, unless he played at a fairly high level, would not be able to catch—let alone hit—a major league pitch.

It's my faith that lifts me up when I've failed. It's my faith that reminds me of my true insignificance when the world has been laid at my feet because of my success throwing a ball.

Our marriage had, and has, the usual rough spots that most couples endure, but a truly Christian marriage is different. The marriage with Christ at its head consists of a man and a woman who are unwaveringly committed to each other, regardless what might be said or done in anger or a weak moment. While we might express ourselves bluntly in frustration, separation or divorce is not even part of our vocabulary. That's a bedrock security that both of us know and enjoy. It allows us to be honest with each other, working through our problems without fear of losing each other.

My faith has been a balancing agent in my life. Christ thrills me with who I am in him, and reminds me gently who I am not.

Selected from: *Out of the Blue* by Orel Hershiser with Jerry B. Jenkins. Published by Wolgemuth & Hyatt, Publishers. Copyright © 1989 by Orel Leonard Hershiser, IV. *Out of the Blue* reached the *New York Times* best-seller list for nine weeks in 1989.

April 27, 1990 Orel Hershiser underwent rotator cuff surgery bringing an early end to his 1990 season, the second year of a three-year, $7.9 million contract. He had not missed a start since 1984 when he joined the Dodgers rotation.

Nickname: Bulldog. My manager, Tommy Lasorda, gave me the nickname because he thought I needed it. I never thought I needed it, so I don't personally use it, but he sure does. My teammates and a lot of my friends call me "O."

Born: September 16, 1958, in Buffalo, NY. Grew up in Southfield, MI and Cherry Hill, NJ.
Personal status: 6′ 3″, 190 lbs. Wife, Jamie; two sons, Orel Leonard V born November 24, 1984, whom we call Quinton, and Jordan Douglas born September 15, 1988.
Home: Pasadena, CA during the baseball season; Vero Beach, FL during the off-season and spring training.
Church affiliation: Lake Avenue Congregational Church, Pasadena, CA.
Career highlights/awards: In 1988, set major league record for most consecutive scoreless innings pitched—59. Named Most Valuable Player of the 1988 National League Championship series; Most Valuable Player of the 1988 World Series. National League Cy Young Award winner (best pitcher) for 1988. *Sports Illustrated* Sportsman of the Year, 1988. *The Sporting News* Major League Player of the Year, 1988. Associated Press Professional Athlete of the Year, 1988.
Likes: Competition, golf, lots of family time.
Dislikes: Being away from Jamie and the boys so much during the season.
Hobbies/leisure time activities: Golf, tennis, playing with the kids.
Favorite Bible verse: God so loved the world that he gave his one and only Son, that whoever believes in him shall not perish but have eternal life (John 3:16, NIV).
The best thing about baseball is: Its combination of complexity and simplicity. It is easy to understand and easy to play, but at the major league level, the competition is incredible, the strategy complicated, and the level of ability staggering. I love going against the percentages, having to think all the time, and competing at such an intense level.
The best thing about life is: Knowing Jesus Christ, getting your priorities in order, and sharing your faith and your abundance with others.
What I want my children to learn from me: Priorities—God, your wife, your children, others, and then your job.

Steve Jones
PGA Tour

When asked to what he attributed his phenomenal start in 1989: To my faith in Jesus Christ. It's my number-one goal in life to do his will. He's given me patience so I can play golf and be comfortable out on the course. Even when I get a little nervous, I can still have fun out there.

. . . I told myself I could apply [Philippians 3:13, 14] to my golf as well as to my life in general. I would forget "those things which are behind"—missed putts, poorly played shots—and reach forward to "those things which are before," keeping my eyes on Christ.

Selected from: "A New Breed on the Pro Tour" by Jim Adair in *Power for Living*, January 7, 1990. Published by Scripture Press Publications, Inc.

Steve Jones won 1989 honors as the player with the best putting average on the PGA Tour. He was the only PGA player besides Player of the Year Tom Kite to capture three titles: the Tournament of Champions, Bob Hope Chrysler Classic, and the Canadian Open. Career earnings: $1,239,997.

Born: December 17, 1958, in Artesia, NM.
Personal status: 6′ 4″, 200 lbs. Wife, Bonnie.
Home: Phoenix, AZ.
Church affiliation: Scottsdale Bible Church, Phoenix, AZ.
Career highlights/awards: Four tour victories: 1988 AT&T Pebble Beach Pro-Am, 1989 MONY Tournament of Champions, 1989 Bob Hope Chrysler Classic, 1989 Canadian Open.
Likes: Knowledge of the Word of God, sharing my faith with neighbors around the dinner table, concerts, Bible studies.
Dislikes: Misuse of the Word of God. Biggest dislike in golf is slow play during tournament.
Hobbies/leisure time activities: Snow skiing, reading, bicycling.
Favorite book: Heir to a Dream by "Pistol Pete" Maravich.
Favorite Bible verse: God . . . wants all men to be saved and to come to a knowledge of the truth (1 Timothy 2:3-4, NIV).
The best thing about golf is: To play outdoors and travel to different places. The individuality of the sport is a special challenge.
The best thing about life is: Knowing that Jesus has saved me from my sins, the knowledge of eternal security.
What I want people to learn from me: To love God and trust him.

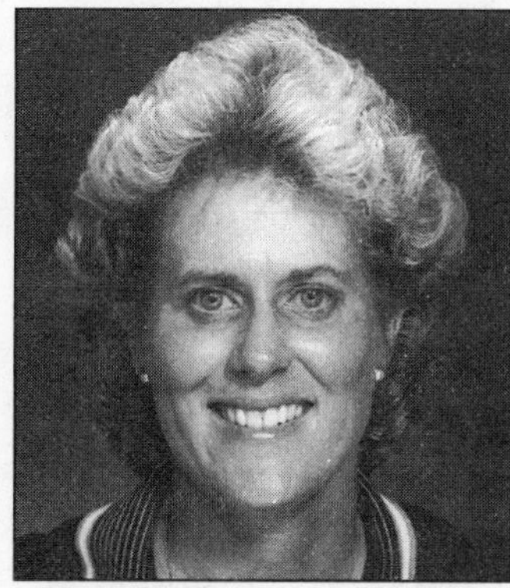

Betsy King
LPGA Tour

It's nice to be named 1989 Player of the Year. But I'd rather have respect as a person than as a player.

In my pre-Christian days I didn't feel any special commitment to charity and to the church. The use of my time and money to help others has been a big change. My commitment of a week each fall to work with other LPGA golfers to help build houses for poor families in Appalachia is an outgrowth of my Christian commitment.

I learned an important principle: I could be 100% committed to Christ and at the same time fully committed to my occupation. It had a great releasing power on me and gave me a new perspective for my career. The principle is found in Colossians 3:23: "Whatever you do, work at it with all your heart, as working for the Lord, not for men" (NIV).

Selected from: "What Betsy King has said about . . . " by Jim Adair in *The Christian Reader,* July/August 1990. Published by Tyndale House Publishers.

In 1989 Betsy King shattered many LPGA all-time records. She won the LPGA's 1989 Rolex Player of the Year for the second time in her career. King earned 76 points in Rolex Player of the Year competition, 10 points more than runners-up Nancy Lopez and Beth Daniel. She won six tournaments, including the Women's U.S. Open and the LPGA World Championship titles. Since 1984 she has won 20 victories, more than any other LPGA contestant during the six-year span. Her $654,132 winnings set a new LPGA record. She ranks third in total career earnings: $2,469,694.

Born: August 13, 1955, in Reading, PA.
Personal Status: 5′ 6″, blue eyes, blonde hair. Single. One brother, Lee.

Home: Limekiln, PA.
Church affiliation: Praise Cathedral, Phoenix, AZ.
Career highlights/awards: 1984 and 1989 Rolex Player of the Year. Received *Golf Digest*'s Most Improved Player Award in 1984. Named South Carolina's 1985 Professional Athlete of the Year. Received LPGA Good Samaritan Award in 1987 that acknowledges humanitarian, charitable efforts to improve health or alleviate physical suffering. Received *Golf Magazine*'s and *Golf Illustrated*'s Player of the Year Awards in 1987. 1989 awards included *Golf Digest*'s Mickey Wright Award, Founder's Cup, *Golf World*'s Player of the Year, Golf Writer's Association of America's Female Player of the Year.
Likes: The friendships made with the people of the LPGA Tour. Theatre, concerts, and all sports.
Dislikes: Living out of a suitcase 40 weeks a year.

FOCUS FACT

The average professional football squad outweighs the average college squad by 2500 lbs. The average college squad outweighs the average high school squad by 2000 lbs.—*Boyd's Book of Odd Facts*

Hobbies/leisure time activities: Enjoy working out, reading, relaxing, watching TV. I spend a week each year with other LPGA players in the Tennessee mountains helping to build homes with Appalachia Habitat for Humanity.
Favorite book: Loving God by Charles Colson. Published by Zondervan Publishing House.
Favorite Bible verse: He who began a good work in you will carry it on to completion until the day of Christ Jesus (Philippians 1:6 NIV).
The best thing about golf is: The opportunity to compete and strive to be better.
The best thing about life is: My relationships with family, friends, God.

Tom Landry
Retired Coach
Dallas Cowboys

Even though I'd gone to church all my life, I had never understood Christianity. I had been a spectator all my life when God wanted me to be a participant. If I really believed what the Bible said, I needed to be practicing it in my life.

The primary challenge of coaching in the National Football League can be boiled down to a one-sentence job description: To get people to do what they don't want to do in order to achieve what they want to achieve.

We often resent rules because they limit what we can do. Yet without the rules that define a football game, you can't play the game, let alone enjoy it. The same thing is true in life. To live and enjoy the freedom we have in America, we have to live by the rules of society. To live life to its fullest and truly enjoy it, we need to understand and abide by the rules God spells out in the Bible. God isn't out to spoil our fun; he knows

that life without limits results in anarchy and misery.

If winning is the only thing that matters, then you'd do anything to win. You'd cheat. You'd sacrifice your marriage or your family to win. Relationships wouldn't matter. People wouldn't matter. Winning would be worth any price you had to pay. I don't believe that.

I've seen the difference character makes in individual football players. Give me a choice between an outstanding athlete with poor character and a lesser athlete of good character, and I'll choose the latter every time. The athlete with good character will often perform to his fullest potential and be a successful football player while the outstanding athlete with poor character will usually fail to play up to his potential and often won't even achieve average performance.

Faith, more than anything else, enabled me to last twenty-nine years on the sidelines of the Dallas Cowboys. It's that faith that has allowed me to keep my perspective and not feel devastated or bitter about being fired. And it's that faith that gives me hope for whatever the future holds for me outside of professional football.

Selected from: *Tom Landry: An Autobiography: The Man Under the Hat* by Tom Landry with Gregg Lewis. Published by Zondervan Publishing House and Harper & Row, Publishers.

Tom Landry Day in Dallas, TX, in April 1989 was a fitting tribute to a remarkable 29-year career as coach of the Dallas Cowboys. More than 100,000 people turned out to the "Hats Off to Tom Landry Day Parade." After the parade Tom Landry said, "The cheers, the applause, the waving banners and the constant calls of 'Tom! Tom! We love you!' made me feel that never in my life had I been so affirmed, so loved." In January 1990 Landry was elected to the Pro Football Hall of Fame in his first year of eligibility.

Born: September 11, 1924 in Mission, TX.

Personal status: 6′ 1″, 200 lbs. Wife, Alicia; three children, Tom, Jr., Kitty and Lisa.

Home: Dallas, TX.

Church affiliation: Highland Park United Methodist Church, Dallas, TX.

Career highlights/awards: Defensive HB with the New York Yankees Football team in 1949, New York Giants Football team from 1950 to 1955. 1954 All Pro team. Elected to the Pro Football Hall of Fame in January 1990 in first year of eligibility. Baylor University Medical Center named a $16 million sports medicine and research center in my honor.

Likes: Being with family. Favorite color is blue. Hero is Winston Churchill.

Dislikes: Traveling excessively.

Hobbies/leisure time activities: Golf, vacation with family.

Favorite book: Centennial by James Michener. Westerns by Louis L'Armour.

Favorite Bible verse: It was not through law that Abraham and his offspring received the promise that he would be heir of the world, but through the righteousness that comes by faith (Romans 4:13, NIV).

The best thing about football is: Competition!

The best thing about life is: Knowing Jesus Christ as Lord and Savior.

What I want my children to learn from me: Success in life is a matter of priority. If God is number one, all other things will fall in place.

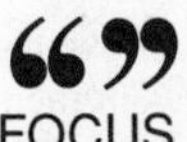

FOCUS QUOTE

No one knows more about how a kid played a game than his mother. A father watches the whole game but a mother watches only her son.—John Madden, CBS sports analyst

Allen Rice
Running Back
Minnesota Vikings

I enjoy preaching and speaking for the Lord, so when the Vikings get a request for a religious function, I get the bulk of those requests.
If you don't have football, you don't have football. But if you don't have Jesus, you don't have eternal life.

Selected from: *Into the End Zone* by Robert Darden. Published by Thomas Nelson Publishers.

Allen Rice played in every game in 1988 and enjoyed his most productive statistical season. Finished second on the team in rushing attempts, yards and TDs and ranked fourth in receiving and receiving yards. In 1989 Allen was injured in the fourth game and missed the rest of the season.

Nickname: Most people call me by my middle name, Troy.
Born: April 5, 1962 in Houston, TX.
Personal status: 5′ 10″, 206 lbs. Wife, Cheryl; two daughters, Fallon, born August 24, 1987, and Alyncia, born March 2, 1990. Ordained minister.
Home: Eden Prairie, MN.
Church affiliation: Emmanuel Tabernacle Church of God in Christ, Minneapolis, MN; Rock of Salvation Church of God in Christ, Houston, TX.
Career highlights/awards: Named Outstanding Team Player at Baylor University.
Likes: Southern catfish, clothes, practical jokes.
Dislikes: Cats.
Hobbies/leisure time activities: Dominos, racquetball, basketball. I conduct a football camp once a year in Minnesota. Frequently speak to youth groups with my wife, Cheryl, who is a singer.
Favorite book: A Testament of Hope: The Essential Writings of Martin Luther King, Jr. Edited by James M. Washington. Published by Harper & Row.
Favorite Bible verse: We are more than conquerors through him who loved us (Romans 8:37, NIV). If anyone is thirsty, let him come to me and drink (John 7:37, NIV).
The best thing about football is: Because of the media attention and fan adulation, the world of sports provides an extraordinary platform to proclaim the Gospel of Jesus Christ.
The best thing about life is: To know God through a personal relationship with Jesus Christ. This takes us to the highest level of living that exists. In this relationship, there is true love, joy, peace, contentment, self-fulfillment and, most importantly, eternal life.
What I want my children to learn from me: That God loves them. I want them to know that if Daddy can't be with them, as long as they have Jesus, they can make it. I want them to know that they are precious and created in God's image for his glory. I want them to know and to see through my life that life can be beautiful. I want them to learn to be giving. But I also want them to learn to have fun and enjoy life to the utmost.

Ted Schulz
PGA Tour

Ted Schulz represents one of the better success stories on the 1989 PGA Tour. He went from winning only $17,838 in 1987, to being off the Tour in 1988, to an impressive $391,855 in 1989.

Born: October 29, 1959, in Louisville, KY.
Personal status: 6′ 2″, 195 lbs. Wife, Diane.
Home: Louisville, KY.
Church affiliation: Southeast Christian Church, Louisville, KY.
Career highlights/awards: Won 1983 Kentucky State Amateur, 1984 and 1988 Kentucky State Open, 1989 Southern Open. Named Rookie of the Year.
Likes: All sports, games.
Dislikes: Traffic jams, travel, sin.
Hobbies/leisure time activities: Bible study, games.
Favorite book: The Man In the Mirror by Patrick Morley. Published by Wolgemuth and Hyatt.
Favorite Bible verse: Ask and it will be given to you; seek and you will find; knock and the door will be opened to you (Matthew 7:7 NIV).
The best thing about golf is: I can make a living and enjoy it at the same time.
The best thing about life is: Knowing someday I'll be with God. This gives me peace.
What I want people to learn from me: I want people to learn biblical principles and to love the Lord.

Mike Singletary
Linebacker
Chicago Bears

I spent almost all of my life until the age of seven in and out of the hospital. Pneumonia, high blood pressure, oxygen tents, emergency visits to the hospital. The house, the hospital, and the church were my life; playgrounds, a dream. Sometimes I was so sick my mom would just look at me and start crying.

My wife has had the greatest influence on my Christian walk and is the most important person in my life.

God said, "If you want answers, you have to be honest with yourself, first of all; then with the people around you." That's the hardest thing I ever had to do. To be honest with everyone meant doing the toughest thing of all: getting off that white horse, showing everyone that Mike Singletary wasn't the perfect guy he was saying he was.

Sources: *Into the End Zone* by Robert Darden, published by Thomas Nelson Publishers, Copyright © 1989 by Thomas Nelson and *Calling the Shots* by Mike Singletary with Armen Keteyian. Published by Contemporary Books. © 1986 by Mike Singletary and Armen Keteyian.

Mike Singletary capped off a brilliant 1988 season by earning his 6th consecutive trip to the Pro Bowl as one of two unanimous selections. Led the Bears with a career-high 170 tackles, including 89 solo tackles, also a team best. Has finished as team's first or second leading tackler each of the last seven seasons. Singletary is active in community services, speaking to youth groups in Chicago and Houston. He donates time to the Better Hearing Institute, Hemophilia Foundation of Illinois, Drug and Substance Abuse.

Nickname: Samurai. I scream when I hit someone—loud, karate-like yells. When I get excited I scream and throw my arms around the way the late John Belushi did on "Saturday Night Live" a few years ago.

Born: October 9, 1958, in Houston, TX.

Personal status: 6′, 228 lbs. Wife, Kim; three children, Kristen, Matthew and Jill.

Home: Lake Forest, IL.

Church affiliation: Willow Creek Community Church, South Barrington, IL.

Career highlights/awards: Named 1988 NFL Defensive Player of the Year by Associated Press and *Pro Football Weekly*. Named NFC Defensive Player of Year by UPI and *Football News*. Named to virtually every All Pro team. Conference "Player of the Year" final two seasons at Baylor University.

Likes: To be at home with my family. Southern meal with smothered chicken, red beans, rice and corn bread. Music.

Dislikes: To see young kids drop out of school without a purpose or goal. Eating in a place that is not clean.

Hobbies/leisure time activities: Reading.

Favorite book: The Amazing Results of Positive Thinking by Norman Vincent Peale.

Favorite Bible verse: Blessed is the man who perseveres under trail, because when he has stood the test, he will receive the crown of life that God has promised to those who love him (James 1:12, NIV).

The best thing about football is: When I step onto the field I'm playing for the glory of God, and I won't settle for second best. I won't leave one ounce of energy in the locker room.

My bottom-line philosophy about life is: Whatever you have, take it, multiply it as much as you can, and then give, whether it's on the field, the office, or at home.

Henry Soles, Jr.
Senior Chaplain
Chicago Bulls

Sometimes all you have to do is listen because that's what they want. They don't know who to trust. Even though you're surrounded by a whole lot of people, it can be very lonely.

They're pro athletes, they're on the road a lot. Their families are hurting sometimes. We've prayed for families and have done family counseling and marital counseling because that's a problem in professional sports. The wife sometimes feels like she's left out of the whole picture. For instance, her husband goes away for a long period of time, he comes home, he wants some home cooking. Well, she wants to go out because she's been

home all the time. The children might feel sometimes that Daddy is a stranger because they haven't seen him.

How does one deal with sudden fame without getting a big head? It's very difficult. That's where religious values come into play. It puts things into perspective. We let them know that sports is just a slice of life, not all of life.

Henry Soles wears many hats. He is a pastor, executive, award-winning editor, musician and community activist. He is president of Intersports Associates, Inc., a ministry to professional athletes and their families and sponsor of Bible studies for the Chicago Cubs, Chicago White Sox and Chicago Bulls. He serves on nine local community boards as well as the Pro Basketball Fellowship board. Both Henry and his wife, Effie, are ordained ministers with the African Methodist Episcopal Church.

Nickname: Hank or Junior.

Born: August 17, 1935, in Anniston, AL. Grew up in Plainfield, NJ.

Personal status: 6′ 4″, 195 lbs. Wife, Effie.

Home: Wheaton, IL.

Church affiliation: Senior pastor of City Church of Chicago. Wife, Effie, is associate pastor.

Career highlights/awards: Trip to Kenya for missionary work and basketball clinics. Meeting and conversing with a member of the British Royal Family. Leading a group of ministers and their wives on a tour of Israel. Being nominated for a television Emmy award. Compiling *Soul Food New Testament*, published by Tyndale House Publishers.

FOCUS FACT

The origin of football dates back almost 2500 years. There was a ball-kicking game played by Athenians, Spartans, and Corinthians which Greeks called Episkuros. The Romans had a similar game called Harpastum. The game as played in the United States dates back to the British game of rugby.

Likes: My wife's infectious smile and hearty laugh. Sharing the Good News of the Gospel. Travelling.

Dislikes: Injustices against the poor and disadvantaged.

Hobbies/leisure time activities: Playing the piano, singing, volunteer activities, sports, writing.

Favorite book: The Great Classics, books on Christian topics, social issues and business.

Favorite Bible verse: Trust in the Lord will all your heart and lean not on your own understanding; in all your ways acknowledge him and he will make your paths straight (Proverbs 3: 5-6, NIV).

The best thing about sports is: It promotes teamwork, discipline, setting goals, physical and mental conditioning.

The best thing about life is: Jesus Christ.

What I want people to learn from me: That God loves them. And that when they allow him to control their lives, they'll experience abundant life.

Bob Wieland

Weightlifter, Marathon Runner

After being denied the National Power Lifting Championships' bantamweight title: I'm not bitter. Who would ever have anticipated someone with no legs breaking the world record?

. . . God was mapping out in my mind a bigger project. I remembered Canadian Terry Fox's walk, and the Lord was giving me a new twist. I said to Harry, "I want to walk all the way across the country and share my testimony. We could use it as a fund-raising event, encouraging corporations and individuals to pledge money to charity and relief organizations—you know, so many dollars for each mile walked. While in Vietnam, I had wanted to feed hungry kids who were begging for food. Now since I've been back home, I've seen that people here are starving spiritually. I want to introduce them to Jesus. I want to do anything I can to stop both physical and spiritual hunger."

The Lord Jesus Christ . . . is my power source. And whether the finish line is at the end of a cinder track or at the gates of heaven, the race is only run one step at a time.

Selected from: *One Step At a Time* by Bob Wieland as told to Sarah Nichols. Published by Zondervan Publishing House. *One Step At a Time* received *Campus Life* Magazine's 1990 Award of Merit/Biography.

Bob Wieland has been credited with "the greatest physical accomplishment ever in the history of sports." A star athlete in college, he was close to signing a contract to pitch for the Philadelphia Phillies when he went to Vietnam to serve his country as a combat medic. June 14, 1969, while on a search and destroy mission with his platoon, Wieland stepped on a 82-millimeter mortar round powerful enough to put a tank out of commission. He went flying one way, his legs went flying another. He went to Vietnam a 6′ 3″, 200-pound athlete and returned home a 3′ 5″, 87-pound double amputee.

Eight years later he broke the official world record in the bench press, lifting 303 pounds at the Senior National Power Lifting Championships in competition against able-bodied opponents in the bantamweight division only to be refused the world record-holder because of a technical rule that shoes must be worn during competition.

Born: February 19, 1946

Personal status: Wife, Jackey, a former fashion designer and interior decorator. Family includes three dogs.

Home: Arcadia, CA.

Church affiliation: Crenshaw Christian Center, Los Angeles, CA.

Career highlights/awards: Former 4-time world record holder in the bench press competition against able-bodied individuals. Walked 4,900,016 miles across America on my hands in 3 years, 8 months and 6 days. Competed in the 1986 and 1987 New York City Marathon; the 1987 and 1988 Los Angeles Marathon and 1989 Marine Corp Marathon. The only amputee to complete the grueling Iron Man Tri Athalon course in Kona, HI—2.4 mile swim, 112 mile bike ride, 26 mile marathon. In 1988 named the USA Track Athlete of the Year. In 1989 set a world record 35 day, 5 minute bike race across America using arm power. Appointed to the President's Council on Physical Fitness and Sports.

Likes: All sports, dining out, travel.

Hobbies/leisure time activities: Weightlifting.
Favorite Bible verse: Nothing is impossible with God (Luke 1:37, NIV).
The best thing about sports is: Crossing the finish line.
The best thing about life is: Living.

CHRISTIAN ATHLETIC ORGANIZATIONS

Athletes for Kids
P.O. Box 40945, Washington, DC 20016
Trains athletes to speak to the issues of drugs and pornography.

Athletes in Action
7899 Lexington Drive #220, Colorado Springs, CO 80920
To proclaim the gospel to the four billion people that are influenced by sports.

Athletes International Ministries
13613 N. Cave Creek Road, Phoenix, AZ 85022
Ministers to athletes from every sport.

Athletic Ministries Intl., Inc.
P.O. Box 241076, Memphis, TN 38124
Basketball ministry, primarily through half time events and other speaking opportunities.

Baseball Chapel, Inc.
P.O. Box 300, Bloomingdale, NJ 07403
Chapel services for professional ball players—all major league teams and most minor league cities. Newsletter available at no cost.

Champions for Christ
P.O. 1799, Gainesville, FL 32602
Champions for Christ chapters on major university campuses and professional teams.

Christian College Sports News Network
P.O. Box 2656, Montreat, NC 28757
Radio coverage of Christian college sports.

Christian Sports Outreach, Intl.
12480 Wayzata Blvd., Minnetonka, MN 55343
Sports evangelism worldwide.

Christian Team Ministries, Inc.
1025 Grange Road, Meadow Vista, CA 95722
Ministers to the running and fitness population. Newsletter. Christian Runner's Association (CRA) chapters.

Christian Youth Athletics
1607 Cromwell Bridge Road, P.O. Box 10294, Baltimore, MD 21234
Ministers to youth by instruction in sports: baseball, T-ball, soccer and basketball.

Christlike Living Ministries
P.O. Box 627, Branson, MO 65616
Produces materials and conducts seminars that help Christian athletes and coaches represent Christ in athletic competition.

Fellowship of Christian Anglers Society
P.O. Box 434, Moraga, CA 94556
Helps develop sense of balance and Christian leisure ethic in today's stress filled world through teaching fishing skills. Newsletter. Conferences.

Fellowship of Christian Athletes
8701 Leeds Road, Kansas City, MO 64129
Strives to strengthen moral, mental and spiritual fiber of the athletes and coaches of America. Fellowship evangelism.

Four Winds Christian Athletics
P.O. Box 29331, Minneapolis, MN 55429
Evangelistic outreach at major world competitions and U.S. meets. Predominately track and field.

Friendship Sports International
P.O. Box 221, Upland, IN 46989
Sends collegiate and college athletes and coaches overseas for short term coaching clinic ministry.

Golf Fellowship
P.O. Box 1911, Maitland, FL 32751
Network of Christian golfers throughout the world. Training videos. Manual for sponsoring a fund raising golf tournament. Conducts "Kids 'N Dads Golf Days." Family golf clinics.

Hockey Ministries International
P.O. Box 36, Beaconsfield, PQ H9W 5T6
Hockey camps and evangelism

Lay Witnesses for Christ, Int.
P.O. Box 127, Hurst, TX 76053
Chapel services for athletes. Olympic outreach. "Evening With the Stars" evangelistic meeting with testimonies of athletes. Offers sports evangelism training.

Lightrider, Inc.
P.O. Box 178, Upland, IN 46989
Provides opportunity to travel and experience God's creation. Physical involvement is limited to skiing, swimming, hiking, climbing, rubber rafting. Takes groups of 30 adults or teenagers from any location within a five-hour driving radius of Upland, IN to any destination on the North American Continent north of the Rio Grande.

Lo Debar Race Track Ministry
P.O. Box 4822, Hollywood, FL 33083
Ministers to personnel within the race track industry.

Ministry to Golfers
1904 North Adams Street, Arlington, VA 22201
Fellowship and Bible study among Tour Pros. Publishes Links Letter. Conducts Executive Golf Seminars.

Missionary Athletes International, Inc.
P.O. Box 945, LaHabra, CA 90633
Soccer evangelism.

Morning Star Christian Fellowship
P.O. Box 2022, Napa, CA 94558
Works with local churches in developing a sports fellowship.

Motorsports Ministries
4760 Thornton Avenue, Fremont, CA 94536
Motorsports chapel ministry at the professional racing level, including I.M.S.A. Camel GT, C.A.R.T. Indy cars, and Trans-Am, Pikes Peak, Sports Cam Club of America. Has monthly newsletter.

N.B.C. Camps
N. 21808 Panorama Road, Colbert, WA 99005
Sports evangelism through basketball, volleyball, track and soccer camps. Sends tour teams overseas. Staff available to speak at functions throughout the Northwest.

News Release Basketball
1949 Lake Whatcom Blvd., Bellingham, WA 98226
Basketball sports evangelism tours to Europe.

Pass Ministry
9 Meadowrue Drive, Mt. Laurel, NJ 08054
PASS (Pro Athletes Spiritual Service) is a division of the Association of Baptists for World Evangelism (ABWE). Offers assistance and services to pro athletes and to those who minister to them. Informs and encourages those associated with ABWE on how to use a sports ministry.

Pro Athletes for Christ
P.O. Box 271073, Tampa, FL 33688
Offers counsel to those called to serve in an athletic ministry. Pro Athlete Speakers Bureau. Organizes outreach opportunities.

Pro Athletes Outreach
P.O. Box 1044, Issaquah, WA 98027
Leadership training ministry for pro athletes and their spouses. Publishes "Sportspage" tabloid quarterly. Conducts tennis, baseball and football conferences.

Pro Basketball Fellowship
106 E. Church Street, Orlando, FL 32801
Provides regular chapel services for NBA teams and mission opportunities for Christian ball players.

Professional Skiers Fellowship
401 Ute Lane, Gunnison, CO 81230
Fellowship groups and Bible studies at ski areas. Evangelistic outreach to ski racers. Ski instructor conferences.

Sports Ambassadors
25 Corning Avenue, Milpitas, CA 95035
Establishes indigenous sports ministries overseas as an ongoing missionary effort.

Sports Outreach Institute
P.O. Box 119, Monroe, VA 24574
Develops models of sports outreach that can be used by churches. Provides research and training.

Sports World Ministries, Inc.
P.O. Box 500, New Tazewell, TN 27825

Sports evangelism by ex-pro football athletes to collegiate and college campuses.

The Tennis Ministry
135 Fir Hill, Akron, OH 44304
Fellowship and evangelistic outreach on the pro tour. Puts together tennis mission trips to other countries.

Unlimited Potential, Inc.
P.O. Box 1355, Warsaw, IN 46580
Baseball clinics worldwide, taught by professional baseball athletes and collegiate coaches.

Victory Ministry
7420 Stone Creek Avenue, Anaheim, CA 92808
Chapel services and Bible studies for the California Major League football and baseball clubs.

Women's Tennis Ministry
3417 Worth Hills Drive, Fort Worth, TX 76109
Offers fellowship and outreach opportunities to the women on the international professional tennis circuit.

World Sports
160 Harbor Drive, Key Biscayne, FL 33149
Encourages worldwide sharing of information and working relationships between athletes, churches, denominations and mission agencies. Offers educational and sports skill evangelism videos, conferences, and development of new sports ministries.

Writers Guide

1991 CHRISTIAN WRITERS CONFERENCES AND WORKSHOPS

Arizona

Arizona Christian Writers Seminar. Place to be announced, March 1991. Contact: Donna Goodrich, 648 S. Pima St., Mesa AZ 85210. 602-962-6694.

Arizona Christian Writers Seminar. Phoenix, usually held in November. Contact: Reg A. Forder, Box 5168, Phoenix AZ 85010. 602-838-4919. Attendance: 300.

Christian Writers Conference. Living Water Worship and Teaching Center, Cornville; usually held in October. Contact: Jamie Buckingham/David Manuel, Box 443, Cornville AZ 86325. 602-634-4421. Attendance: 40–60.

Prescott Christian Writers Seminar. Prescott, September. Contact: Barbara Spangler, Box 26449, Prescott Valley AZ 86312. 602-772-6263. Or Pauline Dunn, 1840 Iron Springs Rd. #A2F, Prescott AZ 86301. 601-778-7342.

California

Biola University Writers Institute. La Mirada, July 28–31, 1991. Contact: Susan Titus, 13800 Biola Ave., La Mirada CA 90639. 213-944-0351, ext. 3441. Attendance: 350–400.

Christian Writers Fellowship of Orange County. Huntington Beach, March and October 1991. contact: Larry Clark, 2222 S. Maddock, Santa Ana CA 92704. 714-549-3440. Attendance: 60.

Christian Writers Guild Writers Conference. Clovis area, Spring. Contact: Dorothy Smith, Box 1677, Clovis CA 93613-1677. 209-226-3433.

Evergreen Inspirational Writers/Speakers Conference. March 1991. Contact: Mary Beckwith, Evergreen Communications, 2085-A Sperry Ave, Ventura CA 93003. 805-650-9248. Attendance: 35.

Lodi All-Day Christian Writers Workshop. San Joaquin Delta College, 1992 (biennial). Contact: Dee Porter, 103 Koni Court, Lodi CA 95290. 209-334-0603.

Mount Hermon Christian Writers Conference. Mount Hermon (near Santa Cruz), March 22–26, 1991. Contact: David R. Talbott, Box 413, Mount Hermon CA 95041. 408-335-4466. Attendance: 150–300.

Narramore Christian Writers Conference. Narramore Christian Foundation/Rosemead, May 1991. Contact: Dr. Clyde M. Narramore, Box 5000, Rosemead CA 91770. 818-288-7000.

San Diego School of Christian Writing. Point Loma College/San Diego, June 19–22, 1991. Contact: Candace Walters, Box 1171, La Mesa CA 92022. 619-444-3600. Attendance: 150.

Santa Clara Valley Christian Writers. San Jose, usually held in October. Contact: Pamela Erickson, 71 Park Village Ave., San Jose CA 95136. 408-281-8926. Attendance: 100+.

The Christian Writers Guild Workshops. Held in various locations. Contact: Norman B. Rohrer, 260 Fern Ln., Hume CA 93628. 209-335-2333.

Writing for the Religious Marketplace. San Diego State University, usually held in October. Contact: Jan Wahl, SDSU, 5630 Hardy St., San Diego CA 92182.

Writing for the Religious Market. University of California Ext., September. Contact: Susan Parkhill, program assistant, University of California Extension, Riverside CA 92521-0112.

1991 CHRISTIAN WRITERS CONFERENCES AND WORKSHOPS cont.

Colorado

Christian Writers Conference–Pikes Peak Area. Colorado Springs, Fall 1991. Contact: Lynn Dyatt, 3506 Brady Blvd., Colorado Springs CO 80909. 719-574-2164.

Colorado Christian Communicators Writers Conference. Colorado Springs, usually held in September. Contact: Madalene Harris, Box 8118, Colorado Springs CO 80933. 719-685-9432. Attendance: 125.

Colorado Christian Writers Conference. Denver, March 1–2, 1991. Contact: Debbie Barker, Box 3303, Lyons CO 80540. 303-823-5718. Attendance: 110.

Connecticut

Wesleyan Writers Conference. Middletown, June 1991. Contact: Anne Greene, c/o Wesleyan University, Middletown CT 06457. 203-347-9411, ext. 2448.

Florida

Writers in Touch. Park Avenue Retreat Center/Titusville, February 1991. Contact: Billie Wilson, Park Avenue Baptist Church, 2600 Park Avenue, Titusville FL 32780. 305-269-6702. Attendance: 200.

Georgia

Northeast Georgia Writers Conference. October 1992 (biennial). Contact: Elouise Whitten, 660 Crestview Terrace, Gainesville GA 30501. 404-532-03007.

Idaho

Absolute Beginners in Christian Writing. Hayden, Various dates 1991. Contact: Linda Hutton, Box 1870, Hayden ID 83835. 208-772-6184.

North Idaho Christian Writers Assn. Seminars. Quarterly full-day seminars; dates open. Contact: Sheri Stone, Box 97, Post Falls ID 83854. 208-772-3936.

Illinois

Christian Writers Institute Conference. Wheaton, June 1991. Contact: June Eaton, Christian Writers Institute, 388 E. Gundersen Dr., Wheaton IL 60188. 708-653-4200. Attendance: 250.

Evangelical Press Association Convention. St. Charles, May 6–8, 1991. Contact: Gary Warner, Box 4550, Overland Park KS 66204. 913-381-2017. Attendance: 350.

Mississippi Valley Writers Conference. Augustana College/Rock Island, June 1991. Contact: David R. Collins, 3403 45th St., Moline IL 61265. 309-762-8985. Attendance: 90.

Moody Write-To-Publish Conference. Chicago, June 1991. Contact: Les Keylock, Moody Bible Institute, 820 N. LaSalle, Chicago IL 60610. 312-329-4030. Attendance: 200.

Indiana

Indiana Wesleyan University Christian Writers Conference. Marion, May 1991. Contact: R. Duane Thompson, 4201 S. Washington, Marion IN 46953. 317-674-6901. Attendance: 100.

Iowa

Humor in Writing Workshop. Sioux City (tentative), October 1991. Contact: Rev. Marvin Ceynar, Box B, Moville IA 51039. 712-873-3678. Attendance: 25–50. Some financial help available for registrants.

Midwest Writers Association. Location and date not established. Contact: Midwest Writers Association, R.R. 2 Box 164, Algona IA 50511.

Kansas

BCCC Creative Writing Workshop. Butler County Community College, El Dorado; usually held in October. Contact: Lois Friesen, 901 S. Haverhill Rd., El Dorado KS 67042. 316-321-5083, ext. 233. Attendance: 250.

Lamplighters Christian Writers Conference. Bethel College/North Newton, usually held in July. Contact: Sharon Stanhope, Box 415, Benton KS 67017. 316-778-1043. Attendance: 100–250.

Catholic Press Association Annual Convention. Usually held in May (location varies). Contact: Regina Salzmann, 119 N. Park Ave., Rockville Centre NY 11570. 516-766-3400. Attendance: 375.

Mid-Atlantic Christian Writers Conference. Chesapeake Lodge at Sandy Cove. Usually held in October. Contact: Gordon Ressler, Sandy Cove, Box B, North East MD 21901. Attendance: 200.

Review and Herald Writers Week. Review &

Herald Publishing Assn., Hagerstown; usually held in August. Contact: Penny E. Wheeler, Review and Herald, 55 W. Oak Ridge Dr., Hagerstown MD 21740. 301-791-7000. Attendance: 50.

Massachusetts

Cape Cod Writers Conference. Craigville Conference Center; usually held in August. Contact: Marion Vuilleumier, c/o Cape Cod Conservatory, Rt. 132. West Barnstable MA 02668. 508-775-4811. Attendance: 150. Also offers Cape Arts Workshops (week long) in July and early August (script writing, children's book illustration and poetry—perhaps others).

Hephzibah Christian Writers Conference. Monterey, usually held in August. Contact: Lois Ewald, Hephzibah House, 51 W. 75th St., New York NY 10023. 413-528-0814. Attendance: 80.

Michigan

Andrews University Christian Writers Workshop. Berrien Springs, June 1991. Contact: R. Lynn Sauls, Andrews University, Berrien Springs MI 49104. 616-471-3286/3125/3040. Attendance: 70.

Christian Writing Seminar. Clawson, June 1991. contact: Mae Hoover, 23720 Lahser, Southfield MI 48034. 313-356-0906.

Maranatha Christian Writers Seminar. Muskegon, usually held in August. Contact: Leona Hertel, 4759 Lake Harbor Rd., Muskegon MI 49441. 616-0798-2161. Attendance: limited to 50. Three $110 tuition scholarships available.

Michigan Christian Writers Workshop. Grandville, May 1991. Contact: LeRoy Koopman, 3000 Ivanrest SW, Grandville, MI 49418. 616-538-3470.

Michigan Northwoods Writers Conference. Glen Arbor, usually held in July. Contact: Robert Karner, 1 Old Homestead Rd., Glen Arbor MI 49636. 616-334-3072.

Spring Arbor Summer Institute For Christian Writers. Spring Arbor, June 1991. Contact: Wally Metts, 112 Main St., Spring Arbor MI 49283. 517-750-1200, ext. 368. Attendance: Limited to 30.

Minnesota

Minnesota Guild Freelance Writing Seminar. Minneapolis area, spring and/or fall 1991. Contact: Joyce Ellis, 17372 Evener Way, Eden Prairie MN 55436. 612-934-7042.

Missouri

Greater St. Louis Inspirational Writers Workshop. St. Louis metro area; write for dates. Contact: Lila Wold Shelburne, 23 Blackberry, St. Charles MO 63301. 314-946-8533.

Mark Twain Writers Conference. Hannibal-LaGrange College, June 1991. Contact: Dr. James C. Hefley, 31 Holiday Dr., Hannibal MO 63401. 314-221-2462. Attendance: 60–75.

Nazarene Writers Conferences. Held regionally across country at Nazarene Colleges; various dates. Contact: Dr. Cecil Paul, Box 419527, Kansas City MO 64141. 816-931-1900.

Nevada

Heavenly Hope Christian Writers Conference. Las Vegas; date open. Contact: Cheryl L. Williams, 5275 Plainview Ave., Las Vegas NV 89122. 702-454-5729.

New Mexico

Southwest Christian Writers Seminar. Farmington, usually held in August. Contact: Margaret Cheasebro, Box 2635, Farmington NM 87499. 505-334-2869. Attendance: 35.

New York

Artsfest '91 Writers Workshop. New York, May 1991. Contact: Lisa Ledlow, 123 W 57th St., New York NY 10019. 212-975-0170, ext. 53. Attendance: 50–100.

New York Writers Guild Seminars. Western New York, spring and/or fall 1991. Contact: Janice Wise, Slusson Rd., West Monroe NY 13167. 315-668-2874.

Syracuse Christian Writers Guild. Liverpool, date open. Contact: Jeri Doner, RR Box 471, Whiting Rd., Jordan NY 13080. 315-689-6389.

North Carolina

Blue Ridge Writers Conference. Black Mountain, June 1991. Contact: Yvonne Lehman, Box 188, Black Mountain NC 28711. 704-669-8421. Attendance: 80–100.

Decision School of Christian Writing. The Cove near Ashville NC, August 1992 (tentative). Contact: Ann Tatlock, Decision School of Christian Writing, Box

1991 CHRISTIAN WRITERS CONFERENCES AND WORKSHOPS cont.

779, Minneapolis MN 55440.

Star Books Writers Workshop. Acqueduct near Chapel Hill, usually held in October. Contact: Becky McLeod, 300 Pleasant St., Angier NC 27501.

Ohio

Cincinnati Bible College Christian Writers Workshop. Cincinnati, usually held in September. Contact: Dana Eynon, 2700 Gateway Ave., Cincinnati OH 45204. 513-244-8181.

Mid-America Christian Writers Conference. Bergamo Center near Dayton, September 1991 (held every 2–3 years). Contact: Elaine Wright Colvin and Mark Plunkett, Box 11337, Bainbridge Island WA 98110. 206-842-9103. Attendance: 200.

Ohio Fellowship Christian Writers Seminar. Marion, April 1991. Contact: John G. Hoffman, 233 W. Church St., Marion OH 43302. 614-387-6683.

Writers World Conference. Akron, May 1991. Contact: Tom Raber, Box 966, Cuyahoga Falls OH 44223. Attendance: 100–200.

Oklahoma

Professionalism in Writing School. Tulsa, March 15–16, 1991. Contact: Myrna Marshall, 1320 N. 157th E. Ave., Tulsa OK 74116. 918-437-2886. Attendance: 125.

Pennsylvania

Christian Writers Workshop. Northeastern Christian Junior College, Villanova; usually held mid-October. Contact: Eva Walker Myer, 1860 Montgomery Ave., Villanova PA 19085. 215-525-6780. Attendance: 100.

Greater Philadelphia Christian Writers Fellowship Spring Conference. Havertown, May 1991. Contact: Marlene Bagnull, 316 Blanchard Rd., Drexel Hill PA 19026. 215-626-6833. Attendance: 175.

Pittsburgh Theological Seminary Writers Workshop. Pittsburgh, April 1991. Speaker: Dr. Roland W. Tapp. Contact: Jeanette Rapp, Director of Continuing Education, PTS, 616 N. Highland Ave., Pittsburg PA 15206. 412-362-5610. Attendance: limited to 25.

St. Davids Christian Writers Conference. St. Davids, June 1991. Contact: Samuel Whyte, 1775 Eden Rd., Lancaster PA 17601. 717-394-6758. Attendance: 150–180.

Tennessee

Christian Writers Grand Ole Workshop. Nashville, June 1991. Contact: Dr. John Warren Steen, 6511 Currywood Dr., Nashville TN 37205.

Randall House Publications Writers Conference. Nashville, May 1991. Contact: Dr. Malcolm C. Fry, Box 17306, 114 Bush Rd., Nashville TN 37217. 615-361-1221. Attendance: 50–75.

Southern Baptist Writers Workshop. Nashville, usually held in July. Contact Bob Dean, 127 Ninth Ave. N., Nashville TN 37234. 615-251-2939. Attendance: 70.

Texas

Christian Writers League of America Writers Conference. Harlingen, February 1991. Contact: Dr. Noel W. Dudley, 2101 Treasure Hills #344, Harlingen TX 78550. 512-425-7415. Attendance: 50.

The Art of Writing, the Act of Writing. Longview, March 1991. Contact: Ernestine Finigan, Box 8513, Marshall TX 75670. 214-935-3047 or 938-0756 (days). Attendance: 50+.

Frontiers in Writing. Amarillo College, usually held in August. Contact: Doris R. Meredith, Box 19303, Amarillo TX 79114. 806-352-3889. Attendance: 150.

Washington

Adventists Writers Association Class. Auburn, June 1991. Contact: Marion Forschler, 18115 - 116th Ave. SE, Renton WA 98058. 206-235-1435. Attendance: 50–75.

Christian Artists International Music Conference. Lynnwood, usually held in September. Contact: Nathan Csakany, Box 2134, Lynnwood WA 98036. 206-775-4833. Attendance: 200.

Seattle Pacific Christian Writers Conference. Seattle, June 24–26, 1991. Contact: Linda Wagner, Humanities Dept., Seattle Pacific University, Seattle WA 98119. 206-281-2036. Attendance: 200.

Wisconsin

Green Lake Christian Writers Conference. Green Lake, usually held in July. Contact: Arlo R. Reichter, American Baptist

Assembly, Green Lake WI 54941. 800-558-8898 (outside WI), 414-748-2357 (inside WI), or 414-294-3323. Attendance: 100.

The Salvation Army Christian Writers Conference. Camp Lake, April 1992 (held every 2 years). Contact: Mrs. Major Charles Moffitt, 860 N. Dearborn St., Chicago IL 60610. 312-440-4653. Attendance: 65–70.

Timber-Lee Christian Writers Conference. Timber-Lee Christian Center/East Troy, Spring 1991. Contact: Gene Schroeppel, Timber-Lee Christian Center, 2381 Scout Rd., East Troy WI 53120. 414-642-7345. Attendance: 40–45.

Word & Pen Writers Seminar. Oshkosh, usually held in October. Contact: Beth A. Ziarnik, 1865 Indian Point Rd., Oshkosh WI 54901. 414-235-0664.

The Writing Academy Seminar. Yahara Center/Madison, August 11–16, 1991. Keynote speaker: Sally Stuart. Contact: Mary K. Kasting, 5129 Marble Ct., Indianapolis IN 46237. 317-784-0314.

Canada

Ontario Bible College Writers Conference/God Uses Ink. Willowdale, Ontario; usually held in November. Contact: Dr. John Unger, Ontario Bible College, 25 Ballyconnor Court, Willowdale, Ontario M2M 4B3 Canada. 416-226-6380, ext. 29. Attendance: 175–200.

Source: Sally E. Stuart, free-lance writer, consultant, and publisher of *The Christian Writers' Market Guide*. For more information about these publications write to 17768 SW Point Forest Ct., Aloha, OR 97006 or phone 503-642-9844.

1990 NEW WORD LIST

James Lowe, New Words Editor, Merriam-Webster, Inc., reads voraciously, looking for new words. When a word begins to appear over and over, it becomes a candidate for acceptance into Webster dictionaries and thus an established word in our language. Only 20 to 25 new words are selected for the *Collegiate Dictionary* each year.

bully pulpit n : a prominent public position (as a political office) that provides an opportunity for expounding one's views

bunker mentality n : a state of mind especially among members of a group that is characterized by chauvinistic defensiveness and self-righteous intolerance of criticism

chimichanga n : a tortilla wrapped around a filling (as of meat) and deep-fried

chocoholic n : a person who craves or compulsively consumes chocolate

couch potato n : a person who spends a great deal of time watching television

deep pocket n 1 : a person or an organization having substantial financial resources 2 pl : substantial financial resources

fajita n : marinated beef or chicken or sometimes shrimp grilled or broiled and served usually with a flour tortilla and various spicy sauces

faux adj : imitation, ersatz

ibuprofen n : an anti-inflammatory drug used to relieve pain and fever

loose cannon n : a dangerously uncontrollable person or thing

microwavable or **microwaveable** adj : capable of being heated or cooked in a microwave oven

nuclear winter n: the chilling of climate that is hypothesized to be a consequence of nuclear war and to result from the prolonged blockage of sunlight by high-altitude dust clouds produced by nuclear explosions

poison pill n : a financial tactic (as increasing indebtedness) used by a company to deter an unwanted takeover by another company

rust belt n : the northeastern and midwestern states of the U.S. in which heavy industry has declined

shiitake n : a large dark Oriental mushroom widely cultivated on woods of the beech family for its edible flavorful cap

sound bite n : a brief videotaped statement (as by a public official) that is telecast on a news program

telemarketing n : the marketing of goods or services by telephone

televangelist n : an evangelist who conducts regularly televised religious services

wish list n : a list of desired but often realistically unobtainable items

zidovudine n : an antiviral drug used to treat AIDS—called also **azidothymidine** or **AZT**

Source: From *Webster's Ninth New Collegiate Dictionary.* Copyright © 1990 by Merriam-Webster Inc., publisher of the Merriam-Webster ® dictionaries. Used by permission.

EVANGELICAL CLICHES

Christians have developed a vocabulary that may or may not be understandable to non-Christians. While many of these words and phrases are essential to clear writing, writers should be wary of Christian jargon. Unconsciously, some authors have allowed the rhetorical language of sermons, hymns, and devotional literature to shape their prose, resulting in indefiniteness, lack or originality, and at worst, insincerity. Here are a few cliches to avoid:

abundant life
after God's own heart
believe on (the name of the Lord)
born again
burden on my heart
carnal desires
Christian walk
daily walk
den of iniquity
depths of depravity
depths of despair
desires of the flesh
devout Catholic
epitome of evil
eternal refuge
eternal resting place
eternal reward
fervent prayer
forever and ever
from on high
get into the Word
giant of the faith
God-fearing man (or woman)
God made known to me
God revealed to me
God-shaped vacuum
good Christian
groanings of the spirit
grounded in the faith
grounded in the Word
heart of the gospel
heavenly angels
heavenly anthems
hellfire and damnation
hopeless sinner
inspired Word of God
just pray (just ask)
laid upon my heart
let go and let God
life-changing experience
life everlasting
life of sin
lift up the Lord
lift (someone) up in prayer
lusts of the flesh
meet his (or her) Maker
moved by the Spirit
of old (as in "Abraham of old")
passions of the flesh
pearly gates
prayer warrior
precious blood of Jesus
prepare our hearts
primrose path
realms of glory
rooted in the faith
rooted in the Word
saving knowledge of Christ
seventh heaven
share a verse (of Scripture)
sins of the fathers
snares of the Devil
sorely tempted
soul of humility
soul-stirring message
spiritual high
spiritual state
spoke to my heart
stand before the judgment seat
stars in one's crown
storms (tempests) of life
straight and narrow
take it to the Lord
throughout eternity
time immemorial
traveling mercies
trials and tribulations
trophies of grace
trust and obey
unto eternity
unspoken needs
uphold in prayer
urgings of the spirit
vale of tears
victorious living
walk with God
watch and pray
wicked ways
wiles of the Devil
wondrous ways of God
word of prayer

Taken from the *Christian Writer's Manual of Style* by Bob Hudson and Shelley Townsend. Copyright © 1988 by The Zondervan Corporation. Used by permission.

BOOKLIST: A WRITER'S REFERENCE LIBRARY

Standard References

The Chicago Manual of Style. 13th ed. Chicago: University of Chicago Press, 1982.

The NIV Study Bible. Grand Rapids: Zondervan, 1985.

12,000 Words: A Supplement to Webster's Third New International Dictionary. Springfield, Mass.: Merriam-Webster, 1986.

Webster's Ninth New Collegiate Dictionary. Springfield, Mass.: Merriam-Webster, 1985.

English Usage, Style, and Grammar

Bernstein, Theodore M. *The Careful Writer: A Modern Guide to English Usage*. New York: Atheneum, 1965.

Dos, Don'ts & Maybes of English Usage. New York: Times Books, 1977.

Miss Thistlebottom's Hobgoblins: The Careful Writer's Guide to the Taboos, Bugbears and Outmoded Rules of English Usage. New York: Simon and Schuster, 1984.

Copperud, Roy H. *American Usage and Style: The Consensus*. New York: Van Nostrand Reinhold, 1979.

Curme, George O. *English Grammar.* New York: Barnes & Noble, 1967.

Fernald, James C. *English Grammar Simplified*. New York: Barnes & Noble, 1979.

Follet, Wilson. *Modern American Usage: A Guide*. Edited and completed by Jacques Barzun and others. New York: Hill and Wang, 1966.

Fowler, H. W. *A Dictionary of Modern English Usage*. 2d ed. London: Oxford University Press, 1983.

Gordon, Karen Elizabeth. *The Transitive Vampire: A Handbook of Grammar for the Innocent, the Eager, and the Doomed.* New York: Times Books, 1984.

———. *The Well-Tempered Sentence: A Punctuation Handbook for the Innocent, the Eager, and the Doomed.* New Haven: Ticknor and Fields, 1983.

Johnson, Edward D. *The Handbook of Good English*. New York: Facts on File, 1982.

Morris, William, and Mary Morris. *Harper Dictionary of Contemporary Usage*. 2d ed. New York: Harper & Row, 1985.

Opdycke, John B. *Harper's English Grammar.* New York: Warner Books, 1983.

Paxson, William C. *The Mentor Guide to Punctuation*. New York: Mentor Books/ New American Library, 1986.

Shaw, Harry. *Punctuate It Right!* New York: Harper & Row, 1963.

———. *Errors in English and Ways to Correct Them*. 3d ed. New York: Harper & Row, 1986.

Shertzer, Margaret. *The Elements of Grammar.* New York: Macmillan, 1986.

Strunk, William, Jr., and E. B. White. *The Elements of Style*. 3d ed. New York: Macmillan, 1979.

Success with Words: A Guide to the American Language. Pleasantville, N.Y.: Reader's Digest Association, 1983.

Words into Type. 3d ed. Englewood Cliffs, NJ: Prentice-Hall, 1974.

Writing, Revising, and Editing

1. General

Appelbaum, Judith, and Nancy Evans. *How to Get Happily Published*. New York: Harper & Row, 1978.

Atchity, Kenneth. *A Writer's Time: A Guide to the Creative Process, From Vision Through Revision*. New York: W. W. Norton, 1986.

Barzun, Jacques. *On Writing, Editing and Publishing*. 2d ed. Chicago: University of Chicago Press, 1986.

Simple and Direct: A Rhetoric for Writers. Rev. ed. New York: Harper & Row, 1984.

Boston, Bruce O., ed. *STET! Tricks of the Trade for Writers and Editors*. Alexandria, VA.: Editorial Experts, 1986.

Boswell, John. *The Awful Truth about Publishing: Why They Always Reject Your Manuscript . . . and What You Can Do about It*. New York: Warner Books, 1986.

Cheney, Theodore A. Rees. *Getting the Words Right: How to Revise, Edit and Rewrite.* Cincinnati: Writer's Digest Books, 1983.

Flesch, Rudolf. *The Art of Readable Writing.* Rev. ed. New York: Harper & Row, 1974.

Graves, Robert, and Alan Hodge. *The Reader Over Your Shoulder: A Handbook for Writers of English Prose.* 2d ed. New York: Random House, 1979.

Gunning, Robert. *The Technique of Clear Writing.* Rev. ed. New York: McGraw-Hill, 1968.

Plotnik, Arthur. *The Elements of Editing: A Modern Guide for Editors and Journalists.* New York: Macmillan, 1982.

Read, Herbert. *English Prose Style.* New York: Pantheon Books, 1952.

Stainton, Elsie Myers. *Author and Editor at Work: Making a Better Book.* Toronto: University of Toronto Press, 1982.

Zinsser, William. *On Writing Well: An Informal Guide to Writing Nonfiction.* 3d ed. New York: Harper & Row, 1985.

2. Religious

Anderson, Margaret J. *The Christian Writers Handbook.* Rev. ed. New York: Harper & Row, 1983.

Aycock, Don M., and Leonard George Goss. *Writing Religiously: A Guide to Writing Nonfiction Religious Books.* Grand Rapids: Baker, 1984.

———. *Inside Religious Publishing.* Grand Rapids: Zondervan, 1989.

Gentz, William H. *The Religious Writer's Marketplace: The Definitive Sourcebook.* Rev. ed. Philadelphia: Running Press, 1985.

Gentz, William, et al. *Writing to Inspire: A Guide to Writing and Publishing for the Expanding Religious Market.* Cincinnati: Writers Digest Books, 1982.

Herr, Ethel. *An Introduction to Christian Writing.* Wheaton, IL: Tyndale House, 1983.

McCarthy, David S. *Practical Guide for the Christian Writer.* Valley Forge, PA: Judson Press, 1983.

Schell, Mildred. *Wanted: Writers for the Christian Market.* Valley Forge, PA: Judson Press, 1975.

Spencer, Sue Nichols. *Words on Target: For Better Christian Communication.* Richmond: John Knox Press, 1964.

Wirt, Sherwood E. *Getting into Print.* Nashville: Nelson, 1977.

The Making of a Writer: A Christian Writers Guide. Minneapolis: Augsburg, 1987.

Special Aspects of Writing and Editing

1. Copyediting and proofreading

Butcher, Judith. *Copy-editing: The Cambridge Handbook.* New York: Cambridge University Press, 1975.

Judd, Karen. *Copyediting: A Practical Guide.* Los Altos, CA: William Kaufmann, 1982.

McNaughton, Harry H. *Proofreading and Copyediting.* New York: Hastings House, 1973.

Smith, Peggy. *Mark My Words: Instruction and Practice in Proofreading.* Alexandria, VA: Editorial Experts, 1987.

Simplified Proofreading. Alexandria, VA: Editorial Experts, 1984.

2. Gender-specific language

Equality in Print: A Guide for Editors and Publishers. Chicago: Chicago Women in Publishing, 1978.

Guidelines for Creating Positive Sexual and Racial Images in Educational Materials. New York: Macmillan, 1975.

Maggio, Rosalie. *The Nonsexist Word Finder: A Dictionary of Gender-Free Usage.* Phoenix: Oryx, 1987.

Miller, Casey, and Kate Swift. *The Handbook of Nonsexist Writing.* New York: Lippincott and Crowell, 1980.

Supplement to the Publication Manual of the American Psychological Association. 2d ed. Washington, DC: APA, 1974.

Wiley Guidelines on Sexism in Language. New York: John Wiley and Sons, 1977.

3. Indexing

Collison, Robert L. *Indexing Books.* Rev. ed. Tuckahoe, NY: John de Graff, 1967.

Spiker, Sina. *Indexing Your Book: A Practical Guide for Authors.* Madison: University of Wisconsin Press, 1954.

4. Writing and word processing

An Author's Primer to Word Processing. New York: Association of American Publishers, 1983.

Chicago Guide to Preparing Electronic Manuscripts. Chicago: University of Chicago Press, 1987.

McWilliams, Peter A. *The Word Processing Book: A Short Course in Computer Literacy*. New York: Ballantine/Prelude Press, 1982.

Zinsser, William. *Writing With a Word Processor*. New York: Harper & Row, 1983.

5. Copyright

Johnston, Donald F. *Copyright Handbook*. New York: R.R. Bowker, 1978.

Nimmer, Melville B. *Nimmer on Copyright: Literary, Musical, Artistic Property*. 4 vols. New York: Matthew Bender. Continually updated.

Strong, William S. *The Copyright Book: A Practical Guide*. Cambridge: MIT Press, 1984.

The Publishing Business

Adler, Bill. *Inside Publishing*. Indianapolis: Bobbs-Merrill, 1982.

Bailey, Herbert S., Jr. *The Art and Science of Book Publishing*. Austin: University of Texas Press, 1970.

Balkin, Richard. *A Writer's Guide to Book Publishing*. Revised and expanded edition. New York: Hawthorn/Dutton, 1981.

Brownstone, David M., and Irene M. Franck. *The Dictionary of Publishing*. New York: Van Nostrand Reinhold, 1982.

Current Christian Books. Colorado Springs: Christian Booksellers Association Service Corporation. Published annually.

Dessauer, John P. *Book Publishing: What It Is, What It Does*. 2d ed. New York: R.R. Bowker, 1981.

Duke, Judith S. *Religious Publishing and Communications*. White Plains, NY: Knowledge and Industry Publications, 1981.

Lee, Marshall. *Bookmaking: The Illustrated Guide to Design, Production, Editing*. Rev. ed. New York: R.R. Bowker, 1980.

Literary Market Place (LMP). New York: R.R. Bowker. Published annually.

Polking, Kirk, ed. *Writer's Encyclopedia*. Cincinnati: Writer's Digest Books, 1983.

Shatzkin, Leonard. *In Cold Type: Overcoming the Book Crisis*. Boston: Houghton Mifflin, 1982.

Journals for Writers and Editors

1. General trade magazines

The Editorial Eye. Newsletter on style, usage, and professional standards published by Editorial Experts, Inc., 85 S. Bragg St., Alexandria, VA 22312.

Publishers Weekly: The International News Magazine of Book Publishing. Published by the Cahners Publishing Company, 249 W. 17th St., New York, NY 10011.

Righting Words: The Journal of Language and Editing. Published by the Righting Words Corporation, 425 E. 65th St., New York, NY 10021.

Scholarly Publishing. Journal published quarterly by the University of Toronto Press, Toronto, Canada M52 1A6.

Small Press: The Magazine for Independent/In-House/Desktop Publishing. Published by the Meckler Corporation, P.O. Box 3000, Denville, NJ 07834.

2. For writers and editors of religious books

Books & Religion: A Quarterly Review. Trinity Church, 74 Trinity Place, New York, NY 10006.

Bookstore Journal. The official publication of the Christian Booksellers Association, 2620 Venetucci Blvd., P.O. Box 200, Colorado Springs, CO 80901.

The Inspirational Writer. Writer's Digest, 1507 Dana Ave., Cincinnati, OH 45207.

Christianity and Literature. Calvin College, Grand Rapids, MI 49506.

Suppliers of Books on Writing, Editing, and Publishing

Editorial Experts, Inc., 85 Bragg St., Alexandria, VA 22312. Supplies their own newsletter, *The Editorial Eye*, and their own publications for editors and proofreaders.

Mehitabels, P.O. Box 60357, Palo Alto, CA 94306. General books for writers and editors.

Ross Book Service, 3718 Seminary Rd., Seminary PO, Alexandria, VA 22304. General books for writers and editors.

WRITER'S MAGAZINES

The Apple Blossom Connection, Box 325, Stacyville IA 50476. Monthly. Secular.

Aspiring Writer's Report, Box 2218, 5306 Gunpowder, Gillette WY 82716. Monthly newsletter. Secular.

Byline Magazine, Box 130596, Edmond OK 73013. 405-348-3325. General publication for free lance writers and poets. Marcia Preston, executive editor/publisher; submit to Kathryn Fanning, managing editor. To inform, instruct and encourage beginning free-lance writers. Publishes new and professional writers. Monthly magazine; circ. 2,000. 80–90% free lance. Query (preferred) or complete ms. Pays $50, on acceptance, for first rights. Articles 1,500–2,000 words (buys 72/year); short stories 1,000–3,000 words (send complete ms). Reports in 1 month. Holiday/seasonal 4 months ahead. Writer's guidelines; sample copy $3.

Poetry: Free verse, traditional (any style); 4–36 lines. Pays $3–5. Writing themes.

Fillers: Cartoons, prose. Pays $15.

Tips: "All our material, except fiction, must have a writing theme with the new free lancer in mind. We have a Student Page for writers under 18."

Canadian Writer's Journal, 58 Madsen Ave., Beaconsfield, Quebec H9W 4T7 Canada. 514-630-4413. Ronald J. Cooke, editor; submit to Alice M. Daly, associate editor. How-to articles for writers only. Bimonthly journal; circ. 3,000. 50% free lance. Query. Pays up to $15 on publication, for one-time rights. Articles 500–1,000 words (buys 30–35/year). Reports in 2 weeks on query, 1 month on ms. No guidelines; sample copy for $3 and a 5x7 SASE/$1 Canadian postage or IRC.

Channels—Magazine of Creative Christian Writing, Box 3262, Harlingen TX 78551. Nondenominational. Submit to editor. To glorify God with the literary art—the creative word. Preserve the best of contemporary Christian creative efforts in literature from across the country. Triannual magazine; circ. 500. Accepts 100% of material from members only. Complete ms. Pays in copies and tear sheets (hopes to start paying soon), for one-time and reprint rights. Articles and short stories 1,000–1,500 words; book reviews 50–150 words. Reports in 4–8 weeks. Holiday/seasonal 6 months ahead. Accepts simultaneous submissions. Writers' guidelines; sample copy $3.75.

Poetry: Free verse, traditional; 20–24 lines. Submit maximum 6 poems.

Fillers: Prose; 50–250 words.

Tips: "Channels in a showcase for members' work—thus not open to non-members. Membership is $10/year and includes many benefits, including free help with rewrites."

Chips Off the Writer's Block, Box 83371, Los Angeles CA 90083. Secular. Wanda Windham, editor. For writers. Newsletter published 6 times/year; circ. 300. 100% free lance. Query or complete ms. Pays in copies, for one-time rights. Articles 500–1,200 words; short stories 1,000–1,200 (uses little fiction); book reviews 500 words. Reports in 3–4 weeks. Holiday/seasonal 10 months ahead. Accepts simultaneous submissions. Writers' guidelines; sample copy $1.

Fillers: Prose; 100–200 words.

Tips: "Editor will work with beginning and unpublished writers and encourages participation from readers/writers."

The Christian Communicator, Joy Publishing, 26131 Avenida Aeropuerto, San Juan Capistrano CA 92675. Interdenominational. Submit to The Editor. Deals with the craft of writing and marketing for the free-lance, inspirational writer. Monthly newsletter; circ. 1,500. Established 1988, 50% free lance. Query or complete ms. Pays 6–10 cents/word, on acceptance, for first rights and some reprints. Articles 1,200 words; book reviews 500 words. Reports in 4–6 weeks. Holiday/seasonal 6 months ahead. Writers' guidelines; sample copy for a 9x12 SASE/45 cents postage.

Poetry: Buys 12–36/year. Free verse, light verse, traditional; 4–24 lines. Submit maximum 6 poems.

Fillers: Cartoons, prose; 250 words.

Columns/Departments: Tips for (or from) Beginners; 600–800 words.

Tips: "We are mainly looking for how-to articles on specifics in the craft of free lance writing and marketing. We're brand new and still developing an editorial focus."

Christian Writers Newsletter, Box 8220, Knoxville TN 37996-4800. 615-522-3026. Nondenominational. David E. Sumner, editor. Instruction, information, and inspiration for Christian writers. Bimonthly newsletter; circ. 400. 75% free lance. Query or complete ms. Pays $10–50 for assigned articles, $5–20 for unsolicited; on acceptance; for first, one-time or reprint rights. Articles 50–500 words (buys 25/year). Reports in 2 weeks on query, 4–6 weeks on ms. Writers' guidelines; sample copy for No. 10 SASE/25 cents postage.

Fillers: Anecdotes, cartoons, newsbreaks, short humor; to 100 words. Pays $5–10.

Tips: "We don't publish articles unless they teach, inform, inspire, motivate or help in some way. I prefer articles written in 3rd person rather than 1st. Aim for providing original and useful information."

Connections, Box 18803, Alexandria VA 22323. Secular. Beth Kessler, publisher. Deals with the creative process. Published 5 times/year. Query. Pays 10 cents/word, on acceptance, for first rights. Articles, essays, and personal accounts 300–1,000 words (informal style).

The Cosmet Newsletter (The COSMET Newsletter), Box 703, San Francisco CA 94101. Secular. Richard Morris, editor. Solid how-to information on publishing topics. Query. Pays $60, on acceptance, for first NA Serial Rights. Articles 1,500–2,000 words.

The Creative Urge, M. Talarico & Daughter Publications, Drawer 417, Oceanside CA 92054. 619-722-8829. Secular. Marjorie Talarico, editor. Publishes the results of beginner and professional writer's creative urge. Monthly; circ. 300. Query or complete ms. Pays in copies for first rights or reprints. Articles and short stories 1,500 average, 600–800 words minimum, 4,000 words maximum. Reports in 2–8 weeks. Accepts simultaneous submissions. Not in topical listings. Writers' guidelines; sample copy $2.50 and a 9x12 SASE/85 cents postage.

Experiences, A Newsletter For Writers, 1529 Wolfe St., Norfolk VA 23502. Mary Joyce Porcelli, editor. Pays in copies.

Fiction Writers Monthly, 163 Joralemon St., Brooklyn Heights NY 11202 718-237-1097. Kathryn Falk, editor. How-to-get-published magazine. Monthly. Book reviews and author interviews. Send $3 for sample kit.

The Final Draft, The Writers Refinery, Box 47786, Phoenix AZ 85068-7786. 602-944-5268. Libbi Goodman, editorial director. How-to and publication opportunity for writers. Monthly newsletter: circ. 800. Complete ms. Pays $5–20 for articles ($4–15 for fiction), on publication, for first or reprint rights. Makes work-for-hire assignments. Articles 500–3,000 words (buys 100/year); short stories 500–1,500 words (buys 3–12/year). Reports in 1 month. Holiday/seasonal 6 months ahead. Writers' guidelines; sample copy for $1 and No. 10 SASE/25 cents postage.

Poetry: Buys 20/yr. All forms; no religious; 4–25 lines. Pays $2–5. Submit maximum 5 poems.

WRITER'S MAGAZINES cont.

Fillers: Anecdotes, facts, short humor; 225–375 words. Pays $2–5.

Tips: "Articles, fiction, fillers and poetry all must be slanted toward writers."

Good News: Christians in Journalism, Crown Creations Associates, Box 11626, St. Paul MN 55111. Steven M. Deyo, editor. For Christians who are journalists, for journalists interested in the issues of media ethics, and for students considering a career in journalism. No information on payment.

Housewife-Writer's Forum, Drawer 1518, Lafayette CA 94549. 415-932-1143. Secular. Deborah Haeseler, editor. Publishes the writings of housewife-writers. Bimonthly newsletter/literary magazine; circ. 200. Estab. 1988. 100% free lance. Query or complete ms. Pays $1–10, on publication, for one-time rights. Articles (buys 6–12/year) and short stories (buys 6/year) to 2,000 words. Reports in 2 weeks on query, 1 month on ms. Holiday/seasonal 6 months ahead. Accepts simultaneous submissions and reprints. Writers' guidelines/contest information; sample copy $3.

Poetry: Buys 15–20/year. Avant-garde, free verse, haiku, humorous, light verse, traditional. Pays $1. Submit maximum 10 poems.

Fillers: Anecdotes, facts, short humor, hints (on writing or running a home); 25–300 words. Pays $1.

Tips: Send complete ms. on fiction.

The Inspirer, Box 354, Henderson KY 42420. 502-826-5720. Billy Edwards, editor. To encourage other believers in their Christian life. (Especially open to writers who are physically disabled.) Magazine. Short inspirational articles, 400–450 words.

The Intelligent MAC, Box 11626, St. Paul MN 55111. 612-644-0709. Steven Deyo, editor. "We are a resource for writers and publishers who use the Macintosh computer for word processing or desktop publishing." Bimonthly newsletter; circ. 100. 20% free lance. Query or complete ms. Pays free software (review or public domain), on acceptance, for one-time rights. Articles 500–800 words; book reviews 200–400 words. Reports in 1–3 weeks. Holiday/seasonal 2 months ahead. prefers to get Macintosh format disks. Sample copy for $2/No. 10 SASE/45 cents postage.

Fillers: Cartoons and prose (any length).

Tips: "This is a publication of the Smartmac users group. We use articles on any subject that has to do with the Macintosh computer."

Literary Markets, Drawer 1310, Point Roberts WA 98281-1310. 604-277-4829. Secular. Bill Marles, editor. Opportunities for poets and literary writers. Newsletter published 6 times/year; circ. 1,200. 16% free lance. Complete ms. Pays in subscription for one-time rights. Articles 250 words. Reports in 2 months. Accepts simultaneous submissions; serials. No guidelines; sample copy $1.

Poetry: Buys 6/year. Free verse, traditional; 30 lines.

Living Streams, Box 1321, Vincennes IN 47591. Interdenominational. Kevin Hrebik, editor. Inspirational and Christian literature revolving around (but not limited to) the natural seasons. Quarterly journal. Estab. 1988. 100% free lance. Complete ms. Pays in copies only for now, for one-time rights. Articles and short stories to 1,200 words (uses 10–12 pieces/issue). Writers' guidelines; sample copy for $3.75.

Poetry: Uses 30–40 poems/issue. Free verse, traditional, special forms; 6–24 lines. Submit maximum 6–10 poems.

Tips: Only publishes subscribers.

Merlyn's Pen. The National Magazine of Student Writing, Box 1058, East Greenwich RI 02818. Secular, R. James Stahl, editor. Written by students in grades 7–10 only. Magazine. Short stories to 2,500 words; reviews and travel pieces to 1,000 words. Pays in copies. Students send for guidelines.

Poetry: To 100 lines.

Midwest Writer's Association Newsletter, R.R. 2 Box 164, Algona IA 50511. 515-295-5002. Regional/secular. Joanne Walker, president. Writing information. Bimonthly newsletter for writers and poets; circ. 100. 100% free lance. Complete ms. Pays in copies for one-time use. Articles 500 words; book reviews 300 words. Reports in 30 days. Holiday/seasonal 4 months ahead. Accepts simultaneous submissions.

Writers' guidelines; sample copy $2.

Poetry: Free verse, traditional; to 1 page.

Fillers: Cartoons, prose; 300 words.

The National Writer, Box 24614, Chicago, IL 60624. 312-521-5550. Secular/black audience. Gregory L. Campbell, editor. Dedicated to the awareness and encouragement of the writer and reader. Quarterly newsletter. 99% free lance. Query. Pays in copies or small sum. Articles 200–2,000 words. Reports at least 3 months before publication. Holiday/seasonal 6 months ahead. Accepts simultaneous submissions. Writers' guidelines and theme list; sample copy for No. 10 SASE/45 cents postage.

Poetry: Free verse, traditional; to 30 lines.

Fillers: Cartoons, prose, quizzes.

Prose & Writers (formerly Coda: Poets & Writers Newsletter). 201 W. 54th St., New York NY 10019. Secular. Lisa Merrill, managing editor. Bimonthly. No religious material.

Senior Scribes, 1200 S. Courthouse Rd., Arlington VA 22204. Secular. Pauline W. Reiher, editor. For senior adult writers. Pays in copies. Articles, essays, and nostalgia 250–300 words. No guidelines; sample copy 50 cents.

Poetry: For writers.

Tips: No religious material.

Teachers & Writers, 5 Union Square W, New York NY 10003. 212-691-6590. Ron Padgett, editor. On teaching creative and imaginative writing. Magazine published 5 times/year; circ. 1,500–2,000. Query. Pays in copies. Articles 3,000–6,000 words. Sample copy $2.50.

Poetry: Uses.

Working Writer, Box 2545, Elton Hills MI 48018-0545. 313-731-3737. Barbara K. Johnson, editor/publisher. Query or complete ms. Published 10 times/year. Pays in copies for first rights. Articles 600–1,000 (shorter better); columns up to 350 words. Reports in 6–8 weeks. Writers' guidelines; sample copy for 39 cents postage.

The Writer, 120 Boylston St., Boston MA 02116. Secular. Sylvia K. Burack, editor-in-chief/publisher; submit to Elizabeth Preston, managing editor. How-to for writers. Monthly magazine. 20–25% free lance. Pays on acceptance, for first rights. Articles about 2,000 words. Reports promptly. Sample copy $2.50.

Writers Anchor, 100 Greenwood Rd., York PA 17404. 717-792-0228. York Christian Writers/nondenominational. Rita Atwell Holler, editor. For Christian writers. Quarterly newsletter; circ. 30. 100% free lance. Complete ms. Pays in copies. Not copyrighted. Articles 50–150 words (uses 16/year). Reports in 2–4 weeks. Holiday/seasonal 6 months ahead. Deadlines are the 15th of March, June, September, and December. Writers'

WRITER'S MAGAZINES cont.

guidelines; sample copy for No. 10 SASE/25 cents postage.

Poetry: Uses 4/year. Avant-garde, free verse, haiku, light verse, traditional; to 22 lines. Submit maximum 4 poems.

Fillers: Anecdotes, facts, newsbreaks, quizzes, word puzzles to 150 words. Columns/Departments: Uses 6/year. Book reviews (writing books); 150 words.

Questions/Answers (writing only); 35 words. Games (writing only); 150 words.

Tips: "Be willing to rework the ms to fit our newsletter."

Writers Connection, 1601 Saratoga-Sunnyvale Rd., Ste. 180, Cupertino CA 95014. 408-973-0227. General newsletter with nuts and bolts information on writing and publishing in all fields. Meera Lester, editor. Monthly; circ. 3,500. 60% free lance. Query or complete ms. Pays in copies, subscription, memberships or seminars. Articles 1,800–2,000 words. Reports in 3 weeks. Holiday/seasonal 2 months ahead. Accepts simultaneous submissions and reprints; serials. Not in topical listings. Free writer's guidelines and sample copy.

Writer's Digest, 1507 Dana Ave., Cincinnati OH 45207. 513-531-2222. Secular. Bill Brohaugh, editor. Information on writing and publishing. Monthly magazine; circ. 225,000. 90% free lance. Pays 10 cents/word & up, on acceptance, for one-time or reprint rights. Articles 500–3,000 words (buys 90–100/year). Reports in 2 weeks. Holiday/seasonal 8 months ahead. Kill fee 20%. Writers' guidelines; sample copy $2.75.

Poetry: Buys 24/year. Light verse on writing; 2–20 lines. Pays $10–50. Submit maximum 8 poems.

Fillers: Buys 24/year. Anecdotes and short humor on writing; 50–200 words. Pays 10 cents/word.

The Writer's Exchange, Box 394, Society Hill SC 29593. Gene Boone, editor. Uses poetry of all types, including religious material. Quarterly newsletter; circ. about 100. 90% free lance. Pays in copies for first rights. Holiday/seasonal 6 months ahead. Accepts simultaneous submissions. Writers' guidelines; sample copy $1.

Poetry: Free verse, traditional; 20 lines.

Fillers: Cartoons, prose, quizzes, 350 words.

Writer's Gazette, Rt. 2 Box 290, Eclectic AL 36024. Trouvere Company/secular. Brenda Williamson, editor. Information for writers and to further their careers by publishing short stories and poetry that is usually not about writing, but uses that theme also. Quarterly magazine; circ. 1,800. 99% free lance. Complete ms. Pays $1–10, on acceptance, for one-time rights. Articles to 2,500 words (buys 20/year); short stories to 2,500 words (buys 12/year). Reports in 5–8 weeks. Holiday/seasonal 6 months ahead. Accepts simultaneous submissions and reprints. Writers' guidelines and theme list; sample copy $4 and 9x12 SASE/85 cents postage.

Poetry: Buys 150/year. Avant-garde, free verse, haiku, light verse, traditional; any length. Pays $5. No limit on submissions.

Fillers: Buys 10/year. Anecdotes, cartoons, facts, jokes, newsbreaks, quizzes, short humor, word puzzles; to 100 words. Pays $3.

Tips: "Stick with what you know. Seek unique concepts to the theme you do write about. Short is always better than long. Most open to poetry."

Writer's Guidelines, RD 1, Ward Rd., Box 71, Mohawk NY 13407, Secular. Carol Ann Vercz, editor. Informational, educational, and entertaining. Monthly magazine; circ. 1,000. 100% free lance. Query. Pays 2 cents/word; on publication; for one-time rights, 1 cent/word for reprints. Articles 500–1,200 words (buys 200/year); short stories 1,500 words. Reports in 6 weeks. Holiday/seasonal 6 months ahead. Accepts simultaneous submissions. Writers' guidelines; sample copy $3.

Poetry: Buys 100/year. Traditional; 6–25 lines. Pays 25 cents/line. Submit maximum 6 poems.

Fillers: Buys 15/year. Anecdotes, cartoons, facts, prose. Pays $1–5.

Tips: "Looking for ideas for new columns."

Writer's Info, Box 1870, Hayden ID 83835. 208-772-6184. Hutton Publications. Linda Hutton, editor. Tips for free-lancers writing for religious markets. Monthly newsletter; circ. 150. 90% free lance. Complete ms. Pays $1–10, on acceptance, for first, one-time and reprint rights. Articles 100–300 words (buys 100/year). Reports in one month. Holiday/seasonal 9 months ahead. Accepts simultaneous submissions. Writer's guidelines; sample copy for No. 10 SASE/45 cents postage.

Poetry: Buys 50/year. Free verse, light verse, traditional (no shaped poetry); 2–16 lines. Pays $1–10. Submit maximum 3 poems.

Fillers: Buys 10/year. Anecdotes, cartoons, short humor; 10–100 words. Pays $1–10.

Tips: "No erotica or how to write erotica. Join a writers' critique group or take a creative writing class for some professional perspective."

Writers' Journal, Box 65798, St. Paul MN 55165. 612-221-0326. Secular. John Hall, publisher; submit to Marilyn Bailey, editor. Monthly journal; circ. 5,500. 30% free lance. Complete ms. Pays $15–50, on publication, for first rights. Articles 500–1,500 words (buys 30–40/year). Reports in 1 month on query, 6 weeks on ms. Holiday/seasonal 4 months ahead. Writers' guidelines; sample copy $2.

Poetry: Buys 10–15/year. Avant-garde, free verse, haiku, light verse, traditional; to 25 lines. Pays $4–15. Submit maximum 3 poems.

Contest: Runs one poetry contest each spring. Cash prizes for winner and runner-up; 2 honorable mentions.

Writer's Lifeline, Box 1641, Cornwall, Ontario K6H 5V6 Canada. 613-932-2135. Stephen Gill, managing editor. For professional free-lancers and beginning writers. Needs articles of interest to writers, news items of national and international interest, letters to the editor, poetry, interviews. Needs book reviewers; pays in book reviewed and copies. Bimonthly magazine; circ. 1,500.

The Writer's Nook News, 10957 Chardon Rd., Chardon OH 44024. 216-285-0942. Secular. Eugene Ortiz, editor/publisher. Dedicated to giving free-lance writers specific information for their immediate practical use in getting published and staying published. Quarterly newsletter; circ. 5,000. 100% free lance. Complete ms. Pays $6–24, on acceptance, for first rights. Not copyrighted. Articles 100–400 words (buys 100/year). Reports in 2 weeks. Holiday/seasonal 5 months ahead. Writers' guidelines; sample copy for $2 and 9x12 SASE/45 cents postage.

Fillers: Buys 20/year. Facts, newsbreaks; 20–100 words. Pays $1.20–6.00.

Tips: "Articles must be specific, terse, and contain information my readers can put to immediate practical use. I want light, newsy pieces; absolutely no fluff!"

Source: *The Christian Writers' Market Guide* by Sally E. Stuart. For more information about these publications write to 17768 SW Point Forest Ct., Aloha, OR 97006 or phone 503-642-9844.

Index

Page numbers in italics refer to charts or graphs.

N

O

P